The Cambridge Biography

D. H. LAWRENCE

1885–1930

◆

DAVID ELLIS

MARK KINKEAD-WEEKES

JOHN WORTHEN

From reviews of Volume 1 of the Cambridge Biography

'it is hard to imagine that this biography will soon be superseded'.

Sir Frank Kermode, *The Guardian*

'[This is] a work of impeccable scholarship, and comes provided with an impressive apparatus of notes, appendices, chronological tables, family trees, an exemplary index, and complete lists of Lawrence's prose and verse writings in the relevant period, making it an invaluable resource for serious students of Lawrence; but it is also written in a lucid, unpretentious style which lay readers will find accessible and enjoyable.'

David Lodge, *The New York Review of Books*

'This is a superb biography. Apart from the compelling narrative there are judicious excursions into the mix of rurality and the mining industry that formed the background to Lawrence's life. There are portraits of the family members and ... insights into Lawrence's admiring bluestockings and into the less well-known early works that led up to *Sons and Lovers* ... Cambridge have already given us ... a decent edition of Lawrence's fiction; now they are embarked on what should be the definitive life.'

Anthony Curtis, *The Financial Times*

'[Worthen] has researched deeply, reading everything even remotely relevant, and is able to be authoritative where others have conjectured. [This] is a warm as well as a serious book, for he clearly loves his subject, and makes us share his feeling. The theme of the development of the miner's son and sickly scholarship boy with warring parents is a wonderful one, and he grasps all its possibilities in the 500 pages of his narrative.'

Claire Tomalin, *The Independent on Sunday*

'One of this biography's great merits is that Worthen understands the dangers of creating a life from a work of fiction. He uses Lawrence's fiction intelligently. He never forgets that even the most apparently autobiographical novels rearrange real events in order to make an artistic point. They cannot be trusted, as too many biographers trust them, to do the biographer's work for him. The other great merit, apart from the wonderfully detailed and engrossing reconstruction of a period and a society, is its attitude to Lawrence himself. Worthen is unfailingly sympathetic, as a biographer should be, yet he never falls into the trap of supposing his hero to be perfect ... This definitive book will be a hard act ... to follow.'

Allan Massie, *Weekend Telegraph*

'Worthen's depiction of Eastwood is on something of a scholarly par with Lawrence's evocation of it in *Sons and Lovers*.'

Janet Byrne, *The New York Times Book Review*

'Literary scholars who thought they knew Lawrence and his circle well will be surprised by the subtlety, aptness, and psychological nuance of Worthen's presentation and interpretation. It is as if for the first time we see Lawrence whole ... this persuasive biogrpahy is compulsive reading from cover to cover. A major event in modern literary studies.'

Keith Cushman, *Library Journal*

'Worthen sets the record straight in a thousand little ways, and there emerges a complex genius, ruthless, sensitive and fully alive.'

Publishers' Weekly

'... extremely thorough and careful ...'

Jeffrey Meyers, *English Literature in Transition*

D. H. LAWRENCE

TRIUMPH TO EXILE

1912–1922

◆

MARK KINKEAD-WEEKES

CAMBRIDGE
UNIVERSITY PRESS

Published by the Press Syndicate of the University of Cambridge
The Pitt Building, Trumpington Street, Cambridge CB2 1RP
40 West 20th Street, New York, NY 10011–4211, USA
10 Stamford Road, Oakleigh, Melbourne 3166, Australia

First published 1996

Printed in Great Britain at the University Press, Cambridge

A catalogue record for this book is available from the British Library

Library of Congress cataloguing in publication data

Kinkead-Weekes, Mark.
D. H. Lawrence: triumph to exile, 1912–1922/Mark Kinkead-Weekes.
p.   cm. – (The Cambridge biography: D. H. Lawrence, 1885–1930)
Includes bibliographical references (p.) and index.
1. Lawrence, D. H. (David Herbert), 1885–1930 – Biography. 2. Authors, English – 20th century
– Biography. I. Title. II. Series: Cambridge biography.
PR6023.A93Z6379   1996
823'.912–dc20

[B]   95–36102
                                                                                                          CIP

ISBN 0 521 25420 5 hardback

CE

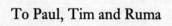
To Paul, Tim and Ruma

CONTENTS

CONTENTS

CONTENTS

PART THREE: *Cornwall*

PART FOUR: *A Kind of Wintering*

CONTENTS

xiii

◆

AUTHORS' PREFACE

The need for a new Biography of a writer about whose life – to put it mildly – much has been written, arises from the mass of new information in the Cambridge collected *Letters* and *Works*, which makes all existing biographies out of date. This can be said without insult or injury to previous biographers, whose work we gratefully acknowledge. But it would be strange indeed if over two thousand unpublished letters and postcards, the editing and annotation of the thousands previously known, and the researches of an international team into how and when each of the writings came into existence, did not substantially alter and correct the existing picture of Lawrence's life. We are deeply indebted to all the Cambridge editors who have allowed us access to their work, published and unpublished.

No amount of new material, however, can make any biographical overview the final word, and we express this conviction in the form of one work by three authors: not only a new 'Life' but also, we believe, a new kind of biography. Each author has taken responsibility for a different period of Lawrence's life, the first volume ending with the completion of *Sons and Lovers*, the second with Lawrence's departure from Europe in 1922. From the beginning, we have collaborated very closely, and subjected one another's work to intensive scrutiny and comment. We have acted as research assistants to one another, have challenged the half-conscious tendency of every biographer to turn a blind eye to inconvenient items of evidence and have argued out fundamental positions. Nevertheless, though the whole will be joint work – in that sense – from first to last, each author is finally responsible for the Lawrence who emerges from his particular period. Three Lawrences, striking the reader as both the same and different, will (we believe) answer all the more to ordinary experience of other people.

There might seem, however, to be danger here of dissonant or even contra-dictory answers to the question of who Lawrence was and what he was really like. Can three people, however closely they work together, be sufficiently in harmony to capture Lawrence's identity? It seems to us that the assumptions which prompt such questions are dubious. Our culture does often appear bound by the idea of a personal core or centre, an 'essential self', out of which character grows in a process of development. Yet in Lawrence's own writings, though there is plenty of support for the notion of an essential self, there is also a characteristic and no less powerful emphasis on fluidity and change. It was Lawrence who denounced 'the old stable ego of the character' in the kinds of novel he no longer wanted to write, and whose preferred way of imagining his progress through life was in terms of rebirth, again and again, into new states of being. To have three people write his life is an explicit (even dramatic) acknowledgement that, however important the continuities, the Lawrence of the last years (for example) is so different from the 19-year-old who visited the Haggs Farm, that it sometimes seems only by accident that they share the same name. There is a hardly less striking and significant difference between the writer who sent off *Sons and Lovers* to its publisher in November 1912, and the author of *Women in Love* expelled from Cornwall, by order of the military authorities, less than five years later.

There are of course important continuities in Lawrence's life, because certain elements in his nature remained constant: he himself felt, at the age of 43, that 'I am somewhere still the same Bert who rushed with such joy to the Haggs.' We are confident that we agree enough about these not to produce a contradictory effect upon readers of all three volumes. Our biography overall, and our individual volumes themselves, will not however show Lawrence's life evolving with steady emotional logic from initial premises. Of all the dangers biographers have to fear, the so-called 'genetic fallacy' – explanation in terms of origins – should be less in evidence here. We have learned to distrust hindsight, because reading the later man back into the earlier always implies determinism. We believe that our one work by three writers, each allowing his particular material rather than any overview to dictate his form, will produce the necessary tension between a continuous and a continuously changing Lawrence, in a way that no synoptic view could achieve. In biographies which succeed in rising above the conscientious enumeration of one thing after another, a pattern of interpretation is established early, and later events are then selected and arranged with a predictability which plays false to the actualities and unexpectedness of life – especially life as our subject himself saw it.

Avoiding this predictability, through three points of view, has seemed to us very important – and we hope our procedure has an additional advantage. Because our biography is based on more documentary evidence than any previous one, and because (unlike some biographers) we have always acknowledged Lawrence to be a writer, each volume has to be detailed, and long – and for the reader to find the same manner in three lengthy books might be more than flesh and blood could bear. Variety of approach will at least mean variety of style: three different voices to tell Lawrence's story – but at the same time give the lie, by their very difference, to the idea that any single view, however detailed and comprehensive, could ever be 'definitive'; any pattern of interpretation *the* pattern.

David Ellis – Mark Kinkead-Weekes – John Worthen
Canterbury – Ramsgate – Swansea
March 1990

ILLUSTRATIONS

CHRONOLOGY

(May 1912–February 1922)

(The chronology of Lawrence's writing, and of the first publication of individual poems, stories, essays and sketches will be found in Appendices I and II.)

3 May 1912	London; leaves England with Frieda, travels (via Dover and Ostend) to Metz
4–8 May 1912	With Frieda in Metz
7 May 1912	Trouble with military guard
8–11 May 1912	DHL goes to Trier
11 May 1912	To Waldbröl (via Koblenz, Niederlahnstein, Troisdorf, Hennef)
19 May 1912	To Bonn and Drachenfels
23 May 1912	*The Trespasser*
24 May 1912	DHL leaves Waldbröl for Munich, meets Frieda
25 May–1 June 1912	Beuerberg
1 June–5 August 1912	Icking
5 August 1912	DHL and Frieda leave Icking for Tyrol and Italy, reach Bad Tölz
6–8 August 1912	To Röhrlmoos; Hubertus/Glashütte and Achensee; Jenbach and Kufstein
9 August 1912	Jenbach to Mayrhofen
10–26 August 1912	At Mayrhofen, joined by David Garnett 18 August, and Harold Hobson later
26–27 August 1912	With Garnett and Hobson to hay-hut beyond Ginzling; next day to Dominicus-Hütte
28 August 1912	Over Pfitscherjoch to ?Gasthof Elefant near Afens
29 August 1912	To Sterzing (Garnett and Hobson to Munich)
29 August–1 September 1912	DHL and Frieda in Sterzing

1–2 September 1912	To Jaufenhaus; wrong turning back to Sterzing, then Bozen by train
3–4 September 1912	To Trento; then Riva, Lago di Garda
5–18 September 1912	At Riva
18 September 1912–2? April 1913	At Villa Igéa, Villa di Gargnano, Lago di Garda
11 December 1912–2 January 1913	Harold Hobson visits over Christmas
February 1913	*Love Poems and Others*
16 February 1913	Visit to Campione
27 February 1913	Antonia (Cyriax) Almgrem visits
2?–11 April 1913	At San Gaudenzio, Lago di Garda
11 April 1913	To Verona
14 April 1913	From Verona to Munich (via Innsbruck)
19 April–17 June 1913	At Irschenhausen
29 May 1913	*Sons and Lovers* published
17 June 1913	Leave for England (arrive early morning 19 June)
19 June–9 July 1913	At The Cearne, Edenbridge (home of Edward Garnett); several visits to London; meet Katherine Mansfield and John Middleton Murry
30 June–1 July 1913	Frieda meets clandestinely with her children, this soon discovered by Maude Weekley
9 July 1913	Overnight in Hampstead en route for Kingsgate; see Katherine Mansfield, and meet Norman Douglas
10–29 July 1913	At Kingsgate, Broadstairs, Kent
16 July 1913	Visited by Henry Savage
20 July 1913	Introduced to Herbert and Cynthia Asquith by Edward Marsh
28 July 1913	Weekley granted injunction against Frieda
29–31 July 1913	Stay with Gordon Campbell, 9 Selwood Terrace, South Kensington.
31 July 1913	Frieda to Germany
31 July–2 August 1913	DHL at The Cearne
2–6 August 1913	At Eastwood (staying with Hopkins) for his sister Ada's wedding on 4 August
6 August 1913	At Downshire Hill (London flat of Edward Garnett)

7 August 1913	To Irschenhausen overnight
8? August–17 September 1913	With Frieda in Irschenhausen
17 September 1913	DHL leaves Irschenhausen for Überlingen, Switzerland; Frieda for Baden-Baden
18–26 September 1913	Lake Constance, down the Rhine to Schaffhausen, to Zürich, Lucerne, over the Gotthard to Airolo, Bellinzona, Lugano, Como
26 September 1913	Joins Frieda in Milan
28 September–4 October 1913	Albergo delle Palme, Lerici
4 October–8 June 1914	Villino Ettore Gambrosier in Fiascherino, Gulf of Spezia
18 October 1913	Frieda's divorce hearing in London
29 November 1913	Visited by Wilfrid Gibson, Lascelles and Catherine Abercrombie, R. C. Trevelyan and Aubrey Waterfield
13–15 December 1913	Weekend at Aubrey Waterfield's castle in Aulla
c. 26 December 1913	Ezra Pound proposes DHL for the Polignac Prize in poetry
19 January 1914	Visited by Edward Marsh and James Strachey Barnes
25 January–25 February 1914	Visited by Constance Garnett and Vera Volkhovsky (who stays longer)
8? March 1914	Levanto, at the home of Amfiteatrov
1 April 1914	*The Widowing of Mrs. Holroyd* published in New York by Mitchell Kennerley
27 April 1914	Decree absolute pronounced in Frieda's divorce case
?30 April–?27 May 1914	Visited by Ivy Low
5 May 1914	Herbert Trench visits
16–17 May 1914	Weekend in Spezia with the Consul Thomas Dunlop and Madge Dunlop
28 May–1? June 1914	Aulla, with the Waterfields
8 June 1914	Leave Fiascherino
9 June 1914	In Turin; Frieda to Baden-Baden
10–17? June 1914	To Switzerland (with A. P. Lewis): Aosta, Grand St Bernard, Martigny, Visp, Interlaken, Bern

18–22 June 1914	Heidelberg (at Alfred Weber's) and rejoins Frieda
24 June 1914	Arrive in England
24 June–15 August 1914	9 Selwood Terrace, South Kensington
27 June 1914	Introduced to Rupert Brooke by Marsh
c. 28 June 1914	Meet Catherine Jackson (later to marry Donald Carswell)
30 June 1914	Accepts J. B. Pinker as agent, and contract from Methuen for 'The Wedding Ring' (*The Rainbow*)
1 July 1914	Meets Wyndham Lewis
4–7 July 1914	At The Cearne
13 July 1914	DHL and Frieda married at the Kensington Registry Office
18–23 July 1914	Visits Ada at Ripley, Derbyshire; Frieda identifies and enters Weekley's house in Chiswick
30 July 1914	Meets Amy Lowell, Richard and Hilda Aldington ('H.D.')
31 July–8 August 1914	Walking tour in Westmorland with A. P. Lewis, S. S. Koteliansky and W. K. Horne; Frieda in S. Kensington
5 August 1914	Barrow-in-Furness; having learned that war has been declared on 4 August
10 August 1914	Methuen returns manuscript of 'The Wedding Ring' (*Rainbow*)
c. 13 August 1914	Meet Lady Ottoline Morrell
15? August 1914–21 January 1915	The Triangle, Bellingdon Lane, Chesham, Buckinghamshire, near Gilbert and Mary Cannan
24 August 1914	Meet Compton Mackenzie
19–20 September 1914	London, visits British Museum
10–11 October 1914	Visited by the Murrys, and (on 11th) Koteliansky
16–26 October 1914	Murry and Katherine Mansfield stay, then move into cottage nearby
16 October 1914	Receives £50 from the Royal Literary Fund
29–30 October 1914	London (at Catherine Jackson's)
c. 5 November 1914	Helen Dudley 'for a couple of days'

8 November 1914	Visited by W. K. and Maisie Horne, and A. P. Lewis
21–23 November 1914	London; sees Horne, Koteliansky and ?Mark Gertler's studio
26 November 1914	*The Prussian Officer and Other Stories*
7?–10 December 1914	Visits Ada at Ripley, Derbyshire; Frieda sees Ernest Weekley in Nottingham
10–12? December 1914	Stays with Edward Garnett in London
25 December 1915	Christmas dinner at the Cannans'
3 January 1915	First mention of Rananim
21 January 1915	To London (staying with Dr David and Edith Eder); meet E. M. Forster at Lady Ottoline's
22 January 1915	Visit Duncan Grant's studio with Forster and David Garnett
23 January–30 July 1915	Greatham, Pulborough, Sussex (Viola Meynell's cottage)
1 February 1915	Lady Ottoline visits
8 February 1915	Lady Ottoline brings Bertrand Russell to Greatham
10–12 February 1915	Visited by Forster
15–16 February 1915	London: a meeting at Koteliansky's house
16 February 1915	Visited by Lady Cynthia
17–24 February 1915	Visited by Murry
23 February 1915	Visited by Lady Ottoline
6–8 March 1915	Weekend at Cambridge with Russell; meets Maynard Keynes, G. E. Moore, G. H. Hardy (F. M. Hueffer and Violet Hunt call at Greatham)
8 March 1915	Meets G. Lowes Dickinson at Lady Ottoline's
13–14 March 1915	Koteliansky and Katherine Mansfield visit
20–21 March 1915	London with Frieda (at Barbara Low's)
24 March 1915	Visited by Gilbert and Mary Cannan
27–28 March 1915	Visited by Murry
1–3 April 1915	Visited by Russell
3–5 April 1915	Koteliansky and Barbara Low invited for Easter; she stays till 8 April

17–18 April 1915	Visited by David Garnett and Francis Birrell
29 April 1915	Worthing by bus
6 May 1915	Chichester with Eleanor Farjeon
7–10 May 1915	In London (at Basil Proctor's)
10 May 1915	Examined for bankruptcy by the Probate and Admiralty Division of the High Court, London
11–12 May 1915	Brighton with Lady Cynthia
c. 19 May 1915	To Bognor with Monica Saleeby
27 May–4? June 1915	Frieda in London (at Barbara Low's)
5 and 19 June 1915	Lady Cynthia and Harold Baker visit
12–16 June 1915	At Garsington, Oxford (Lady Ottoline's)
19 June 1915	Visited by Lady Cynthia and Herbert Asquith
19–20 June 1915	Visited by Russell
21 June 1915	At Littlehampton with Lady Cynthia and Herbert Asquith
c. 7–20 July 1915	Frieda in London
10–11 July 1915	Joins Frieda in London (staying with Dollie Radford in Hampstead)
20 July 1915	Visited by Lady Cynthia and Katharine Asquith
25 July 1915	Leave Greatham; Littlehampton with Viola Meynell to visit Lady Cynthia
30 July–4 August 1915	At 12 Bayford Road, Littlehampton
2 August 1915	To Chichester with Dollie Radford
4 August–21 December 1915	1 Byron Villas, Vale of Health, Hampstead, London
6 August 1915	Formal permission for Frieda to see children in lawyer's office
5 September 1915	First mention of the The Signature
30 September 1915	The Rainbow (30 November in New York)
4 and 18 October, and 1 November 1915	'The Crown' I–III in Signature, Nos. 1–3.
3 November 1915	Magistrate's warrant issued for suppression of The Rainbow
3 and 5 November 1915	Police call at Methuen to confiscate copies and sheets

5 November 1915	Obtain passports for the USA; hear about *The Rainbow*; party in the studio of Dorothy Brett
8–11 November 1915	DHL at Garsington
13 November 1915	*The Rainbow* on trial and ordered to be destroyed, Bow Street Magistrates Court, London
16 November 1915	Meets Philip Heseltine
17 November 1915	Lady Cynthia visits, takes DHL to House of Commons to consult with Philip Morrell M.P.; DHL calls on Robert Nichols in hospital
18 November 1915	Morrell asks question in the Commons about the suppression of *The Rainbow*
19 November 1915	Russell visits
29 November–2 December 1915	Visit Garsington with Heseltine and Hasan Suhrawardy
1 December 1915	Morrell asks second question in the Commons about the suppression of *The Rainbow*
6 December 1915	Elected a member of the Incorporated Society of Authors, Playwrights and Composers
10 December 1915	Aldous Huxley to tea; Murry unexpectedly arrives from France
11 December 1915	DHL to Battersea recruiting office to attest, does not do so
21–24 December 1915	At 2 Hurst Close, Garden Suburb, London (Vere Collins)
24–29 December 1915	Visits Ada at Ripley
29 December 1915	To London (at the Eders')
30 December 1915–29 February 1916	At Porthcothan, St Merryn, Padstow, Cornwall (J. D. Beresford's holiday house)
1 January–21? February 1916	Heseltine stays (joined by Minnie Lucie Channing 26 January–21? February)
c. 7 January–*c.* 1 February 1916	Catches cold and grows seriously ill (examined by Dr Maitland Radford by 24 January)
10–22 January 1916	Visited by Dikran Kouyoumdjian (Michael Arlen)

xxix

11 February 1916	First mention of the 'Rainbow Books and Music' publishing scheme
22 February 1916	House-hunting in Zennor
29 February–17 March 1916	Tinner's Arms, Zennor, St Ives, Cornwall
17 March 1916–October 1917	Higher Tregerthen, Zennor, St Ives, Cornwall
?5 April 1916	Murry and Katherine Mansfield come to live at Higher Tregerthen
ante 22 April 1916	Relationship with Heseltine broken off
25 May 1916	Military Service Bill becomes law
c. 13–16 June 1916	Murry and Katherine Mansfield leave for Mylor, South Cornwall
c. 15 June 1916	*Twilight in Italy*
24 June 1916	General Conscription goes into effect
28–29 June 1916	Bodmin; medical examination for military service; granted complete exemption
July 1916	*Amores* published in England (in USA on 25 September 1916)
c. 16 July 1916	Move into cottage at Higher Tregerthen formerly occupied by the Murrys
22–23? July 1916	To Mylor, visiting the Murrys
31 July–6? August 1916	Visited by Dollie Radford
c. 10–15 August 1916	Visited by Barbara Low
16 September 1916	Frieda to London to see children (stays with Dollie Radford)
?September 1916	Murry visits with Frederick Goodyear
28 September–c. 3 October 1916	Catherine Carswell visits
c. 7 November 1916	Visited by Robert Mountsier and Esther Andrews
22 November 1916	In St Ives
Christmas 1916	Visited by Mountsier (till 31 December) and Esther Andrews (till c. 12 January 1917)
31 December 1916–1 January 1917	Mountsier under arrest at Scotland Yard
12 February 1917	Refused fresh passports for USA
?28–31 March 1917	Frieda to London (at Dollie Radford's) to see children
6 April 1917	USA declares war on Germany

?after 11 April–11 May 1917	Esther Andrews at Higher Tregerthen
14–18 April 1917	Visits Ada at Ripley
19 April 1917	At Nottingham
19–25 April 1917	London (at Koteliansky's, 5 Acacia Road, St John's Wood)
25–27 April 1917	Chapel Farm Cottage, Hermitage, Berkshire
27 April 1917	Returns to Higher Tregerthen
4 May 1917	In Penzance
30 May 1917	In St Ives
8 June 1917	In Penzance
c. 16–19 June 1917	London to see specialist (stays at Dollie Radford's)
23 June 1917	Bodmin (for Army medical re-examination)
by August 1917	Mail under surveillance
?3 September (or 29 August) 1917	Visit Cecil Gray at Bosigran
?29–30 September 1917	Visit Cecil Gray at Bosigran
11 October 1917	To Penzance with Hockings; Frieda to Bosigran
12 October 1917	Police raid Higher Tregerthen; DHL and Frieda ordered out of Cornwall by 15 October under DORA
15 October 1917	London (at Dollie Radford's)
c. 20 October–30 November 1917	44 Mecklenburgh Square (Hilda Aldington's flat) and meet Dorothy (Arabella) Yorke
31 October 1917	To the opera with Ada
2 November 1917	Seeks permission from War Office to return to Cornwall (refused c. 15 November)
13 and 20 November 1920	To the opera with Cynthia Asquith
16 November 1917	Meets John Galsworthy
26 November 1917	*Look! We Have Come Through!* (in USA by Huebsch in 1918)
30 November–18 December 1917	13B Earls Court Square (Mrs Gray's flat)
11 December 1917	Visited by CID; asks Lady Cynthia Asquith to intervene
18 December 1917–2 May 1918	Chapel Farm Cottage, Hermitage, Newbury, Berkshire

28 December 1917–11 January 1918	Ripley (at Ada's)
4? January 1918	London (at Koteliansky's)
12 January 1918	Hermitage
26 February 1918	Temporarily lodge with Bessie Lowe in Hermitage; introduce themselves to Cecily Lambert and Violet Monk
5–6 March 1918	DHL to London (at Koteliansky's)
6 March 1918	Hermitage
5–12 April 1918	Ripley
before 18 April 1918	Frieda to London to see the children
19 April 1918	Decides to keep lease of smaller cottage at Higher Tregerthen (relinquished 28 December)
2 May 1918–24 April 1919	Mountain Cottage, Middleton-by-Wirksworth, Derbyshire
18–20 May 1918	Visited by Ada and Emily with their children, and Arthur Lawrence
21 May 1918	Visited by Sallie Hopkin (joined by Willie 23 May)
13?–26 June 1918	Dorothy Yorke visits
14 June 1918	Visits Eastwood; applies for assistance from Royal Literary Fund
22–24 June 1918	Willie, Sallie and Enid Hopkin, and Kitty Allcock visit
27 June 1918	Nancy Henry visits
30 June 1918	Eastwood and Ripley
12 July 1918	Receives £50 from Royal Literary Fund
3?–9 August 1918	Fritz and Ada Krenkow visit
12–16 August 1918	London (at Kot's)
17–20 August 1918	Mersea, Essex (staying with Barbara Low and Edith Eder)
20–22 August 1918	London (at Kot's)
22–26 August 1918	Hermitage (with Margaret Radford)
26–31 August 1918	Ross-on-Wye, Herefordshire (with Carswells)
31 August 1918	Return to Middleton-by-Wirksworth
11 September 1918	Called for Army medical re-examination at Derby; graded 'for secondary work' by military authorities (26 September)

October 1918	*New Poems* (in USA by Huebsch on 11 June 1920)
7 October 1918	London (at Dollie Radford's); visits the Murrys
c. 14 October 1918	Visits G. S. Freeman, editor of *The Times Educational Supplement*, who requests articles
22 October–19? November 1918	Hermitage
11 November 1918	Armistice
12 November 1918	London for Armistice party (at Montague Shearman's)
19? November 1918	London (at Kot's?); visit Catherine Carswell, Katherine Mansfield, Richard Aldington
28 November 1918	Returns to Middleton-by-Wirksworth (Frieda, at Hermitage, returns to Middleton 14 December)
30 November–1 December 1918	At Ripley (and visits Eastwood)
19 December 1918	Matlock
25–27 December 1918	Ripley
29 January 1919	Matlock
8–9 February 1919	Emily and Peggy King visit
c. 15 February–17 March 1919	Ripley; DHL collapsed with influenza
6 March 1919	Murry asks for contributions to *Athenæum*
17 March 1919	Return to Mountain Cottage with Ada and Jackie Clarke
24 April 1919	Leave Middleton; in Birmingham
25 April–28 July 1919	Return to Hermitage (staying with Margaret Radford)
3–4 July 1919	London to obtain passports (at Barbara Low's and then Kot's)
5–6 July 1919	To the Forge House, Otford, Kent (Helen Thomas's), with Vere Collins
7 July 1919	London
8 July 1919	Returns to Hermitage
?23–27 July 1919	London (at Kot's); sees Edward Marsh, meets Thomas Moult
28 July–29 August 1919	Myrtle Cottage, Pangbourne, Berkshire (at Rosalind Baynes's)

August 1919	Second edition of *New Poems*
3–?20 August 1919	Visited by Ada and Jack, and Emily and Peggy
20 August 1919	Visit Margaret Radford at Hermitage; visit Cecily Lambert and Violet Monk
22 August 1919	Joined by Rosalind Baynes, and by Godwin Baynes on ?24 August
26 August 1919	Mapledurham on the river
29 August–12 September 1919	Grimsbury Farm, Long Lane, Newbury, Berkshire (staying with Cecily Lambert and Violet Monk)
12 September–4 November 1919	Hermitage
14 October 1919	London (at Catherine Carswell's in Hampstead)
15 October 1919	Frieda departs for Germany
16 October 1919	Visits Douglas Goldring
17 October 1919	Returns to Hermitage
c. 20–25 October 1919	Ripley
4–14 November 1919	London (at Kot's); visits Goldring, Thomas Dunlop, Richard Adington; meets Max Plowman
14 November 1919	Paris, en route for Italy
15–17 November 1919	Modane; Val Salice, Turin (staying with Sir Walter and Lady Becker)
17–19 November 1919	Genoa; Lerici
19 November–10 December 1919	Florence; sees Norman Douglas; meets Maurice Magnus
20 November 1919	*Bay* published in England by Cyril Beaumont
3 December 1919	Frieda arrives from Baden-Baden
10–13 December 1919	Rome
13–22 December 1919	Picinisco (staying with Orazio Cervi)
22 December 1919	Naples, via Atina and Cassino
23 December 1919	To Capri
25 December 1919–26 February 1920	Palazzo Ferraro, Capri; friendship with Compton Mackenzie and Francis and Jessica Brett Young
27 December 1919	Breaks with Pinker
20 January 1920	Gilbert Cannan's 'A Defense of Lawrence' in *New York Tribune*

27–29 January 1920	Amalfi
early February 1920	Ill with 'flu'
7 February 1920	Breaks with Murry, and with Katherine Mansfield
16 February 1920	Asks Mountsier to act as his American agent (accepted on 26 March)
19–21? February 1920	Visits Magnus at Montecassino
26 February–2 March 1920	To Sicily (Agrigento, Syracuse, Catania) with Brett Youngs
3 March 1920	Giardini and Taormina
6 March 1920	Frieda arrives with Mary Cannan
8 March–2 August 1920	Fontana Vecchia, Taormina, Sicily
9 March 1920	Confirms Seltzer as American publisher
10–13 March 1920	*The Widowing of Mrs. Holroyd* produced by Altrincham Stage Society, Cheshire
April 1920	Shestov's *All Things are Possible* (tr. Kot and DHL)
8 April 1920	Visited by Gilbert Cannan
ante 18 April 1920	Charcoal sketch by Jan Juta
ante 18 April 1920	Catania
24–29 April 1920	Randazzo with Jan Juta, Réné Hansard and Alan Insole; Maniace (visits the Duca di Bronte, 25 April); Syracuse
26 April–*c.*10 May 1920	Magnus arrives and appeals for help
May 1920	*Touch and Go* (in USA by Seltzer on 5 June)
17–28 May 1920	Malta with Mary Cannan; visits Magnus, meets Borg and Salomone
c. 7 July 1920	Curtis Brown approaches DHL to act as agent
2–?3 August 1920	To Montecassino
?4–6 August 1920	In Rome with Juta and Insole
7–12 August 1920	San Filippo, Anticoli-Corrado, near Rome (with Juta and Insole); Juta does a second charcoal sketch
12–15 August 1920	Florence
16–18 August 1920	Milan; Frieda to Baden-Baden; DHL meets up with Percy and Irene Whittley
18 August–1 September 1920	With Whittleys to Lake Como and Venice

2 September 1920	Florence
3–28 September 1920	Villa Canovaia, San Gervasio (borrowed from Rosalind Baynes); sees Reginald Turner and Anna di Chiara
8 September 1920	Picnic at Settignano
16 September 1920	Anton Kippenberg granted German translation rights for one year (later extended till 1924)
ante 24 September 1920	Meets Carlota Thrasher
28 September–14 October 1920	Venice; sees Juta and Insole; joined by Frieda 7 October
14–17 October 1920	Florence, Rome, Naples, Taormina
18 October 1920–9 April 1921	Fontana Vecchia
9 November 1920	*Women in Love* published in USA by Seltzer (in England by Secker, June 1921)
25 November 1920	*The Lost Girl* published in England by Secker (in USA by Seltzer, January 1921)
29 November 1920	Cattle fair at Letojanni
4–6 January 1921	To Messina and Palermo
6–13 January 1921	Via Trapani to Sardinia; visits Cagliari, Mandas, Sorgono, Nuoro, Terranova (Olbia); returns to Sicily (Fontana Vecchia) via Civitavecchia, Rome and Naples
c. 27 January 1921	Visited by Juta and Insole; Juta paints DHL's portrait in oils
February 1921	*Movements in European History*; *The Widowing of Mrs. Holroyd* reissued in USA
11–14 March 1921	Palermo; sees Frieda off to Baden-Baden
by 16 March 1921	Portrait by Millicent Beveridge
c. 16 March 1921	Asks Barbara Low to act as his English agent
4 April 1921	Asks Curtis Brown to be his English agent
9 April 1921	Palermo
15–19 April 1921	Capri; meets Earl and Achsah Brewster, and Faith Mackenzie
19–20 April 1921	Rome

?21–23 April 1921	Florence; sees Rebecca West and Norman Douglas
23 April 1921	Leaves for Baden-Baden
26 April 1921	Baden-Baden
27 April–10 July 1921	Hotel Krône, Ebersteinburg, Baden-Baden
10 May 1921	*Psychoanalysis and the Unconscious* published in USA (in England, July 1923)
5–*c*. 27 July 1921	Mountsier visits
10–18 July 1921	To Zell-am-See via Constance and Bregenz, Austria
20 July–25 August 1921	At Villa Alpensee, Thumersbach, Zell-am-See
13–16 August 1921	Mountsier visits; then leaves for Paris
25 August 1921	To 32 Via dei Bardi, Florence
30 August 1921	Mary Cannan visits
2 September 1921	Heseltine threatens libel action over *Women in Love* (settled 15 November)
10–17 September 1921	Catherine and Donald Carswell visit
12 September 1921	Percy and Irene Whittley visit
19 September 1921	First batch of proofs for German translation of *The Rainbow* from Dr Anton Kippenberg
20–22 September 1921	To Siena (21st) and Rome (22nd) with Whittleys
c. 23–27 September 1921	Visit Earl and Achsah Brewster in Capri
28 September 1921–20 February 1922	At Fontana Vecchia
5 November 1921	Begins correspondence with Mabel Dodge Sterne
2 December 1921	*Sea and Sardinia* published in USA
9 December 1921	*Tortoises* published in USA; acknowledges James Tait Black Memorial Prize for *The Lost Girl*
20–26 February 1922	To Naples, via Palermo
26 February 1922	Leave Naples for Ceylon aboard *R.M.S. Osterley*

Metz, Trier and Waldbröl

Over the Alps from Icking to Lake Garda

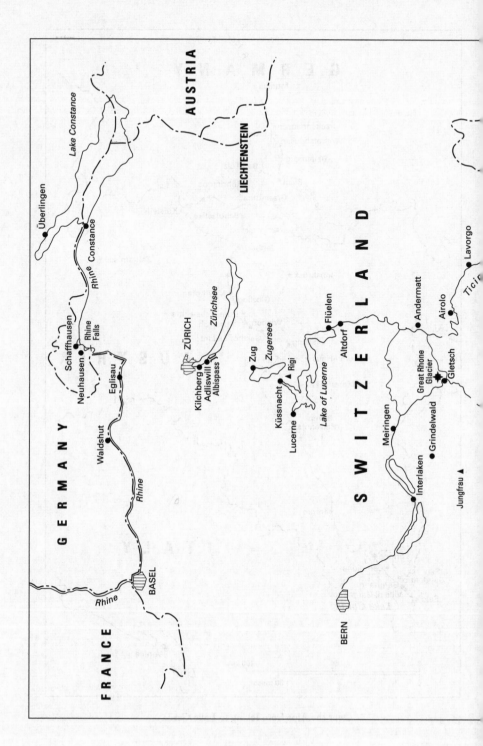

xl

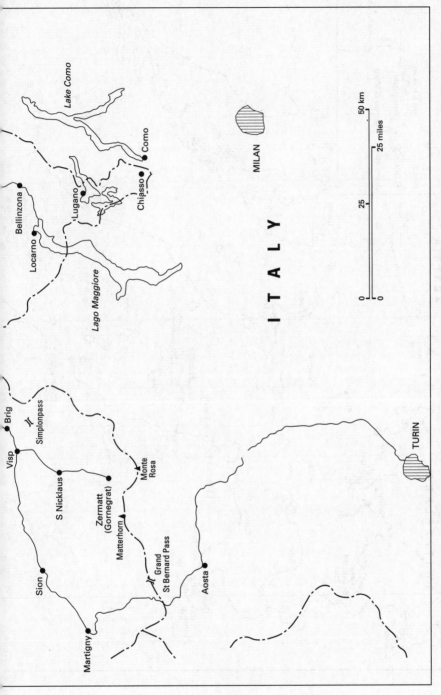

The return journeys: Baden–Baden to Milan, September 1913; and back through Switzerland with A. P. Lewis, Turin to Baden–Baden, June 1914

xli

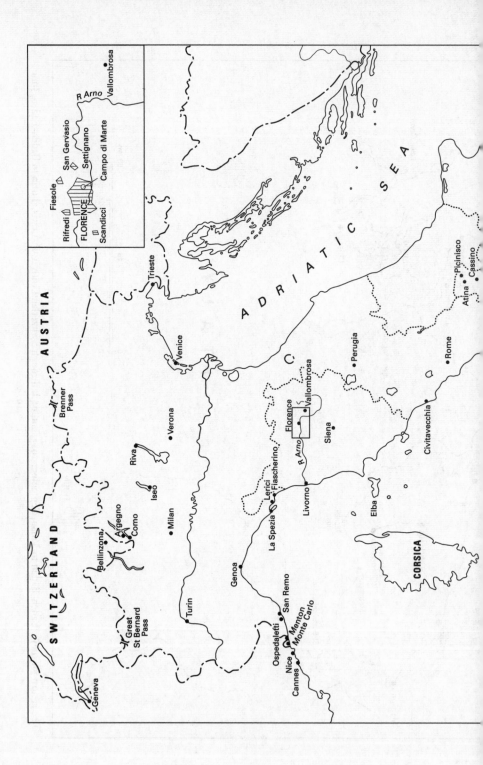

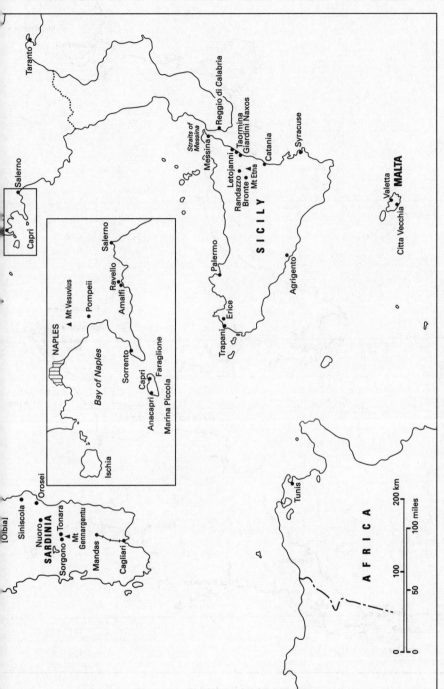

Lawrence in Italy, 1912–22

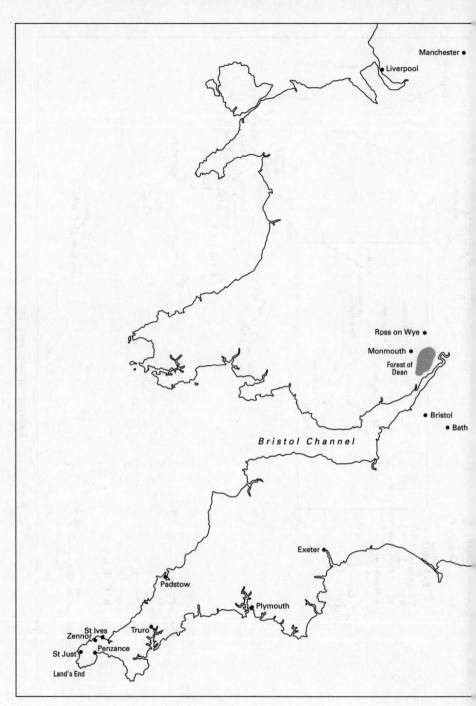

Manchester •

• Liverpool

Ross on Wye •

Monmouth •

Forest of
Dean

• Bristol

• Bath

Bristol Channel

Exeter •

Padstow

Plymouth

St Ives
Zennor
Truro
St Just
Penzance
Land's End

Lawrence in England, 1913–19

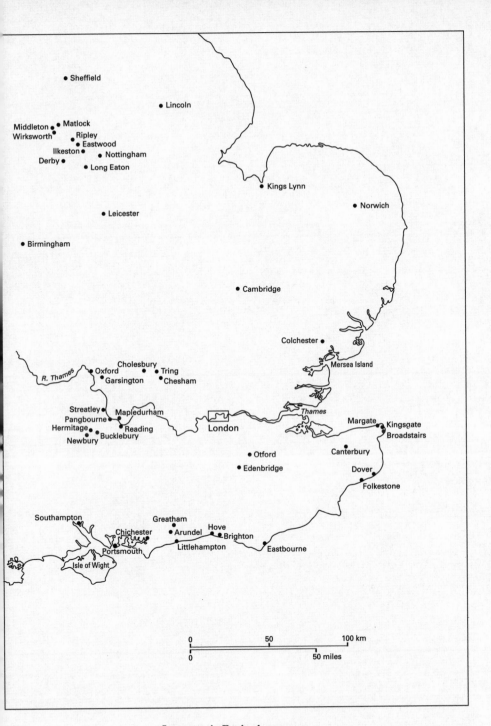

Lawrence in England, 1913–19

xlv

D. H. LAWRENCE

1912–1922

PART ONE

◆

*A World
of
Promise*

◆

CHAPTER ONE

May–November 1912

NEW LIFE

'Let us go forward, shall we?' said Birkin. He wanted to be at the tip of their
projection. So they left off looking at the faint sparks that glimmered out of
nowhere, in the far distance, called England, and turned their faces to the
unfathomed night in front.

They went right to the bows of the softly plunging vessel. In the complete
obscurity, Birkin found a comparatively sheltered nook, where a great rope
was coiled up. It was quite near the very point of the ship, near the black,
unpierced space ahead. Here they sat down, folded together, folded round
with the same rug, creeping in nearer and ever nearer to one another, till it
seemed they had crept right in to each other, and become one substance. It
was very cold, and the darkness was palpable.

(*Women in Love*, 387: 21–32)

I The Fight for Frieda

Lovers moving into unfathomed darkness, in transit from the dead nowhere of
the past to a yet unborn but already tangible future: this experience is at the
heart of Lawrence's great wartime fictions.

In fact, it is also reminiscent of Friday 3 May 1912 on the ferry from Dover to
Ostend. Frieda Weekley had kissed her husband and her schoolboy son in
Nottingham; had taken her two small girls to stay with her husband's parents in
London; and had met her new young lover at 2.00 p.m. outside the 1st-Class
Ladies' room at Charing Cross Station.[1] Yet there were painful differences
between life and fiction: Ursula in *Women in Love* is wholly committed to Birkin,
but Frieda was not committed to Lawrence. Her tickets were returns, booked by
her professor husband. She was going to join her family in the garrison town of
Metz, where her father the Baron von Richthofen was about to celebrate the
fiftieth anniversary of his joining the Army – and she had no intention of leaving
her children or her husband, as she later confessed.[2]

She was nevertheless in love. From the moment the previous March when a
'long thin figure' with 'light, sure movements' strode into her drawing-room in
Nottingham, on a spring morning with the curtains blowing at open french
windows and the children playing in the garden, she had been fascinated by a

strange new force in her life. She was amused by the young man's fierce denunciation of women; intrigued by his views on Oedipus; and disconcerted later when he remarked how little she noticed her husband, and mocked her for having no idea how to light the gas in the absence of her maid. 'Such a direct critic! It was something my High and Mightiness was very little accustomed to.' Yet his fervent admiration – 'You are the most wonderful woman in all England' – restored her self-belief and lifted her depression. On an outing to the Holbrooks' farm at Moorgreen near Eastwood, as she watched Lawrence wholly absorbed in floating paper boats and daisies for her little girls in the brook, she suddenly knew that she loved him. It was a straightforward matter for her to suggest that he stay the night one Sunday when Ernest Weekley was away.[3]

Freud's disciple Otto Gross, whose mistress both Frieda and her elder sister Else had been, had persuaded her that sex should be completely free, and that she herself was the Woman of the Future, with a rich creative gift of womanhood it was her mission to express and share, especially for the salvation of others.[4] The combination now of a 'new tenderness', desire and something a little maternal (in an experienced 32-year-old towards a young man of 26, who had known only frustration in his sexual relations with younger women) was irresistible. Yet he refused to sleep with her under her husband's roof, and once they had done so elsewhere, he wanted her to tell Weekley, and come away with him openly. (She did not know until later that she had eclipsed a relationship with another married woman, Alice Dax,[5] whose consummation in *her* husband's house may have troubled Lawrence's conscience.) They spent a precious weekend at The Cearne, the home of Edward Garnett, Lawrence's literary mentor, who had no respect for the conventions,[6] but love stolen at intervals was not enough. The prospect of 'at least one week together' (i. 386), using the von Richthofen celebrations in Germany, must have seemed a godsend.

Lawrence had come to Weekley's house that day in March to ask advice about securing a Lektorship in English at a German university. After his dangerous illness at the end of 1911 he had given up his teaching post in Croydon on doctor's orders; but planned to visit his uncle Fritz Krenkow's relations in the Rhineland,[7] and perhaps become fluent enough in German to add to his qualifications for re-employment if he failed to make a living as a writer. So now they arranged to travel and to have at least their week (or more) together during (and perhaps after) the anniversary celebrations. Then Lawrence must go on to the Krenkows, and Frieda remain with her family – having minimised the risk of scandal.

She was keeping her options open, or perhaps simply reacting to unresolved impulses. Though smitten by Lawrence, she had successfully managed three previous affairs,[8] and she had no intention of giving up her marriage for her new

new lover, let alone deserting her children. Lawrence was sure of no more than a week, though both before they left and after arriving in Metz he kept pressuring her to commit herself and to free them both from disguise and subterfuge. He could not tell his own family or friends (except Garnett, and George Neville his boyhood companion, who would keep the secret); but he insisted that Frieda should tell Weekley, and shortly before they left, she tried. She may have had her own reasons too. Her marriage was obviously unsatisfying, Nottingham was tedious and there may have been at the back of her mind an envy of her two sisters and of her namesake the wife of Otto Gross, who all had open and 'civilised' arrangements with their husbands which permitted them to live separate lives in sexual freedom. So – perhaps testing the ground as well as meeting Lawrence's demand for honesty – she did get as far as confessing her affairs with Gross and with the anarchist Ernst Frick – but she said nothing of the Nottingham businessman William Dowson, or her new lover, or of travelling to Germany with him. The reception of what she did say might have been enough to scare her. She had told Lawrence that her husband was a gentleman in whom the brute could 'leap up' (i. 388); she knew also how Weekley idolised her, and what pain and shock the truth would cause. Her daughters, playing on the stairs outside the study, would remember their mother hurrying out in tears. However, perhaps after an initial outburst, Frieda was able to write to her namesake Frieda Gross that Weekley had been 'very good'.[9] When she kissed her son Monty on his way to school and Elsa and Barby on Hampstead Heath, she may have been too overwrought to think at all clearly. It was perhaps a more intense parting than usual since she could not know what would come of it; but she had certainly not decided anything – and was intending to consult her mother and sisters in Metz.

Moreover, as the ferry plunged into the dark on 3 May, the couple in the bow had baggage, as couples tend not to do in fiction. In hers were the fashionable dresses she would need in Metz; and the letters from Gross with their fervent sexual theories and their image of herself and her mission. In Lawrence's were some new clothes too, after which expense he had only £11 in cash (i. 390); but also the manuscript of his third novel 'Paul Morel', which would later become *Sons and Lovers* and had already been rewritten, as his young-love Jessie Chambers had suggested, to bring it closer to life.[10] She had hoped he would be able to diagnose his emotional dependency on his mother, and return to what Jessie thought the true love of his life – for her. That would now never happen; but there were many old hurts and complexes (only partly embodied in those manuscript pages) of which Frieda could have had no more than glimpses from a world utterly remote: the destructive tensions of the coal-miner's home; the death of the mother; failures and betrayals with Jessie, Helen Corke, Louie Burrows and Alice Dax; and the painful mess of Lawrence's emotional life at the end of 1911. If Frieda had felt herself suffocating or sleepwalking in bourgeois Nottingham, Lawrence's serious collapse in 1911 had been more than merely physical illness. Now each had seen and responded to a vision of new vitality in and through the other: for her, the thin young figure with his extraordinary quickening life, perceptive and direct, who 'saw through' her and revealed her to herself;[11] for him, a marvellous tawny vitality, a Juno-like physique, an odd mixture of sophistication and naïveté, a spontaneous acting on impulse, a free strange being trapped in conventional middle-class suburbia. Yet the baggage would have to be carried ashore into the new life and opened. Ursula and Birkin in the later fiction of *Women in Love* are almost free of their past. Frieda and Lawrence were not, and not at all sure of each other or themselves.

In Metz, precious time frittered away as Frieda became involved with the anniversary, and also in much earnest talk with her mother and her sisters, especially Else the eldest – while Lawrence spent long hours over the weekend wandering through the streets, looking into the Cathedral, sitting in cafés over beers or gazing down from his hotel bedroom on the animated scenes below. It became clear that he was to be hidden from Frieda's father. Though the Baron had a mistress and an illegitimate son, he had stern (and double) standards concerning public morals and the outward preservation of marital respectability, and drew a line between mistresses and other men's wives.[12] Frieda's mother and sisters, in contrast, did not seem shocked to be told that she had a new lover in tow and when they met him were even (in varying degrees) sympathetic; but they were also strongly opposed to Lawrence's idea of a clear and clean break with Weekley. They had seen no need to break from their husbands. All were accustomed to situations of marital infidelity, sustained with sophistication and outward *politesse*.

Frieda's mother had much to bear from her husband's gambling as well as his extramarital relationship, but she took no moral line. Lawrence described her to Garnett a few weeks later as 'utterly non-moral, very kind' (i. 409), though his dramatisings of her, later, catch a note of lamentation.[13] She feared the public reaction of which her husband's anger would be only the start. She was naturally concerned lest her daughter separate from Weekley before she had come to some advantageous arrangement with him; let alone forfeit her reputation, and the comfort and status of an upper-middle-class home, by running off with a penniless nobody. Worst of all, Frieda risked losing her children were she to be divorced as the guilty party; and if in her naïveté and distraction she had not yet realised this, she must do so now. There was a clear alternative scenario in the eldest daughter's situation. Beautiful and brilliant, Else Jaffe was a feminine path finder who had not only taken a doctorate but become a factory inspector in the world of men. She too was married to a professor, of the University of Munich;

but had been mistress to Gross and borne his son, whom she brought up with her two other children by Edgar Jaffe; and was now the mistress of Professor Alfred Weber, having finally chosen him rather than his more famous elder brother Max who had also been in love with her. Despite all this, she remained on friendly terms with her husband who lived his own life, and was building a little place in the country to improve it. Else had a house in Wolfratshausen, Edgar a flat in Munich, Weber a flat near Else as well as his own home in Heidelberg. It was all very civilised. Meanwhile Frieda's youngest sister Johanna von Schreibershofen (nicknamed 'Nusch'), rich and fashionable, seems to have regarded Frieda's affair with amusement. Lawrence described her as 'very beautiful, married to a brute of a swanky officer in Berlin' (in fact aide-de-camp to the Crown Prince) 'and, in a large, splendid way – cocotte' (i. 395).[14]

So they were not shocked. Nor were they unsympathetic to Lawrence. Else teased him with gentle irony, yet liked him well enough. She was perhaps intellectually more ready than the others to be interested in him as a promising writer; and though she may not have thought him good enough for Frieda at first, she was prepared to help in her own way. The Baroness pitied his youth and inexperience. She would later give him a thorough scolding, but she was also impressed by the way he took it. After an unexpected and embarrassed meeting at the May fair when Lawrence narrowly escaped being noticed by the Baron, Nusch, instead of reacting against the odd figure in cap and raincoat, suddenly told Frieda she could trust him.[15] Yet all agreed that Frieda must not risk a scandal that might lose her the children. She should return to England, and seek the kind of accommodation with Weekley that Else had achieved with Edgar Jaffe. Lawrence should be patient, and wait discreetly in the background to see how things worked out.

However he became more determined as Frieda apparently weakened. On the Monday, the day of the celebrations, he wrote to complain that she had not come to him early in the morning as she had promised; that he didn't even know where to find her;[16] and that their precious time was slipping by. For, 'if you put up your fingers, and count your days in Germany, and compare them with the days to follow in Nottingham, then you will see, you – I don't mean it – are selling sovereigns at a penny each. No, *you* are not doing it – but it's being done' (i. 391).

Stress and unhappiness mounted as all initiative was taken from him in endless talk among the von Richthofen women. He felt humiliated at being hidden so furtively away when he wanted everything in the open. He was 'not cross' with Else he said, though he could hardly help resenting her influence, but 'I wish I had the management of our affairs.' He was 'not keen' to lunch at the Baron's house under false pretences. He wanted to get Frieda out of Metz and away from family pressure; though he still thought she would have to go

9

back to England afterwards. He had his hair cut, and walked out into the country towards the village of Scy, as he would describe in 'French Sons of Germany'[17] – finding his growing antipathy to Metz, so dominated by German soldiers, reinforced by growing sympathy for its Frenchmen, also under the control of foreigners. By the next day, after having sat for two hours in his room without moving a muscle, he could stand it no longer and took things into his own hands. 'No more dishonour, no more lies', he insisted (i. 392–3) – and wrote to Ernest Weekley.

He left it to Frieda whether to post the letter or write herself in similar terms. She posted it, a decisive move, since it could (and would) figure in a divorce – but though she had acquiesced, he had taken it upon himself to force her hand, and to rebel against her family's attempt to direct *his* affairs in directing Frieda's future, keeping him out of sight. He told Weekley that his own position was 'torture', though there was no comparing their sufferings.

I love your wife and she loves me. I am not frivolous or impertinent. Mrs. Weekley is afraid of being stunted and not allowed to grow, and so she must live her own life ... largely and abundantly. It is her nature. To me it means the future. I feel as if my effort of life was all for her. (i. 392)

The play he later based on the situation, *The Fight for Barbara*, insisted that for both their sakes 'he' had to decide for 'her'.

No sooner were the days of concealment from her husband numbered moreover, than fate took a hand to prevent further concealment from her father. Having at long last the chance of a few hours together, Lawrence and Frieda wandered out over the river – and strayed into a prohibited military area. As they sat talking, a guard appeared and threatened Lawrence with arrest as an English spy, letting him go only on condition he was vouched for by Baron von Richthofen. A meeting had to be arranged between the 'fierce' German aristocrat, and the coal-miner's son. Social rituals were icily gone through. A cigarette was offered – and Lawrence fumbled in lighting it. There followed a polite enquiry in French – to which Lawrence made a grammatical error in reply. The Baron coldly corrected him. Then total silence ... and Frieda's father concluded that he was dealing with an unmannerly lout.[18] It seemed best that Lawrence should leave Metz, and Else persuaded him to go eighty miles away along the Moselle to Trier, on condition that Frieda would join him the following weekend. By the afternoon of Wednesday 8 May he was there – after only four days in Metz, and very little time alone together.

Meanwhile, as soon as Frieda had gone and before Lawrence's letter arrived, Weekley had begun to brood over what she had told him, and to suspect a more recent lover than the two she had confessed were all in the past. He wrote, demanding reassurance: a telegram to say either *'nicht wahr'* according to *Mr*

Noon (not true), or '*ganz recent*' (quite recently). 'My child, what are you doing?' her father asked. 'I always thought you had so much sense. I know the world.' Frieda answered: 'Yes, that may be, but you never knew the best.'[19]

II Separation

Lawrence was happier in Trier, sitting under apple-blossom among vineyards above the town writing letters, the postcards those in England would expect, and one or more of his 'German Impressions', [20] while waiting (he hoped) for Frieda to arrive on Saturday and share his room as 'my wife' (i. 393). She came on Friday 10 May instead, but chaperoned by her mother and Nusch (who soon opted out of the embassy);[21] and under strict orders from the Baron to return the same evening. Appearances were still being kept up, in the hope that Weekley might yet be persuaded to overlook everything short of open betrayal; but after another argument Lawrence insisted on taking Frieda to the post office to send the '*ganz recent*' telegram (i. 409), since his letter had already disposed of the alternative. The lovers were allowed a walk into the countryside (and made love in a dry ditch under a beech tree),[22] before the von Richthofens caught their train, presumably not knowing what had been done, but still anxious that Lawrence and Frieda should keep apart.

Since he had in any case to go to the Krenkows soon, Lawrence had to agree perforce. He had probably already written the first version of a ballad about a 'Wayward Woman' who cannot make up her mind between her husband and her lovers.[23] The next day, he left for Waldbröl in the Rhineland, his hopes for time alone with Frieda punctured.

However, his letter had already burned some boats, as Weekley's response to Frieda would show:

I bear him no ill-will and hope you will be happy with him. But have some pity on me … Let me know at once that you agree to a divorce. The thing can be managed very quietly, but unless you help by an admission, this will be difficult … You loved me once – help me now – but quickly.[24]

Was it still possible after this to patch up just enough reconciliation – her 'guilt' not having gone too far – to permit *judicial* separation in a civilised manner, with joint custody of the children, or would it have to be divorce? The day after Lawrence left, a telegram arrived in Metz: 'kein moeglichkeit' – no possibility of reconciliation or 'arrangement' (i. 409).

Nearing the end of a nine-hour train journey on the Saturday, and waiting for his third change at Hennef beside the water-meadows and the river, Lawrence wrote to Frieda for the second time that day: 'my detachment leaves me, and I know I only love you. The rest is nothing at all. And the promise of life with you is all richness' (i. 398). His 'detachment' implies its opposite. When under extreme stress, his psychological defence was to go right outside himself, to insulate himself against all feeling, to be silent, utterly withdrawn.[25] The family opposition, and Frieda's wavering, had fastened his will all the more firmly. He had had to fight all the way to be open with Weekley, detesting the lies and subterfuge which made him feel unclean. His letter had shown his belief that love had its own laws, and self-fulfilment its own imperatives; but if their relationship was 'right' for Frieda's sake, and his own, it could not be right to go on deceiving her husband or pretending to her father. It had been a young man's letter, written with little imagination of what it would be like for Weekley to read it (as Lawrence later recognised),[26] but it was honest, and Weekley responded to that. Moreover the conspiracy had meant constant humiliation, and isolation all the more tense for one who had never been abroad and had only a smattering of German. He had been unable to work on 'Paul Morel'. He resented the aggressiveness of the German military occupiers of what had been a French town. This went into all three of the sketches about Metz which he completed within the next week (i. 405), including one about his arrest. (On the journey to Waldbröl he may have suffered yet another humiliation, bawled out for having the wrong kind of ticket by an inspector he could not understand.)[27] Frieda had her family phalanx around her, he had nobody but her – and must have felt that their relationship too was being occupied and overruled, albeit with civility. It had all been an immense strain – but suddenly 'Bei Hennef', it lifted, his underlying certainty came through, intense feeling returned unthreateningly, to be caught in a fine poem. (Yet part of its fineness is the half-heard commentary of the little river at Hennef, whose 'twittering' in the twilit background might suggest that certainties, too, are only moments, in a flow.[28])

Now at Waldbröl it was his turn to relax a little, and Frieda's to suffer alone. 'Here, I am so respectable, and so good', he wrote, 'it is quite a rest' (i. 399). Karl Krenkow was a 'good' if not very interesting man married to his cousin Hannah, and the family were kind and welcoming. Hannah restored his bruised ego by finding him quite attractive and flirting a little, but respectably, though she did not love her husband. (Moreover the letters and 'Hail in the Rhineland', written in Waldbröl, conceal the fact that she was 14 years older than Lawrence.) He also grew fond of the old man who had brought her up, Opa Stülchen, with whom he got on famously. Here his German was a source of amusement rather than embarrassing, and he began to practise. On the first day there was another fair, but this one held no humiliation, only pleasure in the unfamiliar: 'a Herz – a great heart of cake, covered with sugar, and sugar grapes, and sugar roses, and a bird, a dove – and three pieces of poetry' (i. 399). The little village 'miles from everywhere', with its slow buff oxen plodding in front of wagons and its dog-drawn milk cart (i. 410); and the countryside where ruddy-gold broom was in flower, and every peasant greeted Hannah as she walked with the young Englishman before the big hailstorm; these were havens of restoration.[29] By now he had begun to work every morning, and by 16 May four German sketches were sent away to the *Westminster Gazette*.[30] He needed the money.

Then he got down to revising the third version of 'Paul Morel', and before he left Waldbröl just over a week later he had finished all but ten pages. The revision of the first part, the Morels' marriage and Paul's childhood, seems to have been mostly pruning and tidying with a view to publication, though some social detail about pedlars was added and an active little Paul looking after his baby brother no longer counterpointed his fits of weeping. But when Lawrence had told Walter de la Mare on 11 April, before leaving for Germany, that 'There are parts I want to change' (i. 383), he was thinking of more serious matters than these. He had gone, ten days earlier, to get Jessie Chambers's reactions to what he had done to reshape the novel closer to life, following her advice. It must have been a fraught occasion, and since he had latterly taken to sending her the manuscript by post rather than delivering it himself, he was clearly apprehensive. The 'defeat' of Miriam in the novel will have killed any hope of Jessie's that reliving the past might have changed Lawrence's feelings about *her*. There may also, already, have been something even worse in the chapter now called 'The Test on Miriam', but since that was substantially rewritten in Waldbröl and later, we have no way of knowing.[31] Jessie would eventually see in the final version of the 'Test' the most intimate, private and risky episode in her life, when she agreed to sleep with Lawrence, not only about to be published to the world, but also treated as a sexual test which she had failed; but we cannot be certain what she read in April 1912. It may have been milder.

Nevertheless, she had strong objections to make to the novel. The weekend before he saw her, Lawrence talked about it to George Neville, and was left in no doubt that there would be trouble over 'the bedroom scene' – but had remained 'adamant'.[32] There was, however, no outburst of recrimination. In her memoir twenty years later Jessie recalled how 'Between pride and anguish I found it impossible to tell him that the account he had given of our friendship amounted to a travesty of the real thing.' She simply said she had 'put some notes in with the manuscript'.[33] These, the so-called 'Miriam Papers', have survived because Lawrence took them to Germany with him to think about when he revised the novel and left them there. They consist of the latter part of version III's chapter ix (which would be revised into 'Lad and Girl Love' for *Sons and Lovers*), with Jessie's marginal remarks; her commentary on that chapter; and three scenes in her hand: Miriam with her sister Agatha as Paul arrives, Paul pinning flowers into Miriam's dress and the crisis scene on Easter Monday (1906, in real life). An additional description of Miriam at eighteen may be Jessie's response to the second rather than the third version of 'Paul Morel'.[34] Together these are Jessie's final attempt to change the portrayal of Paul and Miriam before the crisis on Easter Monday, which (in her view) had damaged a relationship that had been 'pure' in them both and wholly unconscious of sexuality, but had then been forced into consciousness, before they were ready, by the interference of Lawrence's family. She insisted that he had back-dated tensions and motives which came only after and because of those family pressures. Having thought again however, Lawrence held on the whole to what he had done. He accepted many of Jessie's criticisms in detail; and her belief that Easter Monday marked a watershed;[35] but though he allowed Miriam in her spirituality to be largely unconscious of sex, Paul is troubled before the end of the chapter and the sexual tensions and jealousies are clearly there, whether conscious or not, a fictive decision whatever 'the truth' may have been – perhaps different for each.

No 'Miriam Papers' survive for whatever was replaced by the 'Test'. If anything like it was there, Jessie may not have been able to write about that, even to him in private. (She could not write of the final version in her public memoir, after twenty years. Only in private letters later still, to a scholar of whose sympathy she felt assured, could she say something of how she had felt when 'an association that we each regarded as binding and sacred' was treated as a 'test' which had failed; and how 'his attitude to me as a human being, struck me as brutal and false'.[36]) What seems most likely however, is that it was in Waldbröl that Lawrence first deliberately decided to make his treatment of the *later* relationship of Paul and Miriam much more explicitly sexual – and more so still, when he revised again in Italy that autumn.[37] He was becoming ruthless. Whatever had been the case in the real-life sexual relationship, and however the reasons for its failure might have appeared to each, he now claimed the right to treat the failure in his novel, and to shape it within the total structure and pattern of the *fiction*, regardless of other considerations.

The use of real people by writers is always a vexed problem, and *Sons and Lovers* is a particularly challenging case. It had been clear even earlier that Lawrence would acknowledge no limit to an artist's freedom to use, and reshape imaginatively, the people he knew. He had been quite unmoved when Alice Hall and her family objected to what they saw as a portrait in *The White Peacock*. He had only half-apologised over an apparent slight to a Croydon colleague in *The Trespasser*, insisting that it had been for an artistic reason.[38] Quite apart from the difference between truth-to-fact and the art of fiction however, the unfairness of *Sons and Lovers* was not only that 'Miriam' was so recognisable, but also that Jessie had no way of answering that would not increase the damage. Nevertheless, justice to Jessie Chambers and justice to Miriam are questions of a different order, one of biography, the other of literary criticism, which should not be confused. They intersect, but the nature of that intersection can only be established when each has been treated in its own proper terms.

The question of *why* it seemed necessary to Lawrence, for his fictive purposes, to treat Miriam as he did, had better wait for the last revision in Gargnano when the form of his novel finally became clear to him, 'like life, but always my theme' (i. 477). About *how* he could do so, however, something can be said at once. In Waldbröl, he looked back at his former self and all his former relationships as over a ravine. The past might still be painful to recall, but must have seemed increasingly another country. He did not feel at ease about Jessie; but the twinges were minor compared with the urge to explore the new understanding of the nature of past failure, that had come from his relationship with Frieda. The relative weight of feeling became clear when he wrote to Jessie from the Rhineland, combining some concern for her with much more ruthlessness about the novel: 'I'm sorry it turned out as it has. You'll have to go on forgiving me' (i. 408). He also now corrected the proofs of 'Snapdragon', the best of his poems about his ex-fiancée Louie Burrows, for the *English Review* – but his immediate thought was that he would never have to write to Frieda in such sexual frustration.[39] The gulf that now divided him from Eastwood made it easier to care less about injustice to the women in that distanced life.

Meanwhile Frieda, after Else returned to Munich and Nusch to Berlin, was left alone with her parents in Metz, and under ever increasing pressure from them and from Weekley. The family view was consistently opposed to Lawrence's, but Frieda and her husband began to vacillate, and so to increase each other's suffering. Weekley had spoken of divorce under the first influence of Lawrence's letter, but soon found he could not face the disgrace – in those days considerable. He feared it might damage or even (in his wilder moments) end his university career, and ruin the prospects of the children. (Indeed he believed all his life that the divorce, which came two years later, prevented him from gaining a post in Cambridge or Oxford.) He determined to close the Nottingham house and make a new home for the children with his parents and sister in London, to protect them from local gossip; but he could not make up his mind whether to divorce or judicially separate from Frieda, and ended by doing nothing with increasing hysteria, stoked by her changing responses to his changing moods. He wrote to the Baroness:

Today two letters came from Frieda; in one she speaks of a compromise, in the second she says she will come to help me with the moving. Dear Mama, please make her understand what a state I am in: I cannot see her handwriting without trembling like an old cripple – to see her again would be my death. I would kill myself and the children too ... Today I had to lecture for four hours and take part in a long session of the Senate. I have desperately to stretch every nerve in order not to cry out hysterically, and then I am weak as a child and can only lie there and think – if only for a quarter of an hour I could not think![40]

Letters came to Frieda from his sister Maude and from a friend in Nottingham, begging her to reconsider before it was too late, and to pity the broken-hearted man and the children who would grow up motherless. These were torture, and made the threat of losing the children real, if it had not been so before. Frieda's letters to Lawrence, which we can only guess at from his replies, seem to have insisted that she must go to England to try to talk to Weekley, and soon belied any optimism that 'The tragedy' was going to 'slacken off' (i. 399). Indeed the pressures became so unbearable that she decided to flee from Metz to Else's (where she took to her bed for two days),[41] and begged Lawrence to come to her.

Yet he would not come at once. He did not think she should or could face an English judicial separation, with the still-likely consequence of disgrace. He did not want to be left stranded in Munich if she went to England; and would much rather stay in Waldbröl if need be, till she came back. He was upset and worried by her stress and suffering – but he himself needed the restoration of 'decent sanity' that Waldbröl was providing (i. 402), and the chance to make some money, which they would also need. (He was always practical about money, as his mother had brought him up to be. He sent the journalistic pieces to de la Mare, and it was very important to finish revising 'Paul Morel'.) Most of all, if and when he came to Munich it must be on different terms. There was to be no more of her vacillating between one life and another which he had embodied in 'The Wayward Woman'. He had originally settled for a week together, and left the rest to the future. Now, in the relative peace of Waldbröl and after the new certainty of 'Bei Hennef', he had made up his mind. Whatever the legal situation, which was up to Weekley, he was thinking very seriously now about marriage in the sense of permanent commitment.

Frieda had had no idea of breaking one commitment only to create another. She had probably hoped to make the most of her affair with Lawrence for as long as it lasted, without having to forgo her children or a comfortable income. Now there seemed less hope of that, but even if it came to divorce she doubted that she would want to be married again – whereas Lawrence insisted that coming to join her in Munich would be his marriage, the start so far as he was concerned of a permanent commitment to their life together.[42] He wanted time to prepare himself, 'even a bit religiously'. It had become for him 'a great thing – not a thing to be snatched and clumsily handled. I will not come to you unless it is safely, and firmly. When I have come, things shall not put us apart again' (i. 401). Now he positively wanted children by her, which he had never thought before. (She had momentarily worried that she might be pregnant.) He wanted 'a sort of vigil with myself' like a knight of old. He no longer wanted passion; his 'sex desire' had become 'calm, a steady sort of force, instead of a storm . . . I shall love you all my life. That also is a new idea to me. But I believe it' (i. 403).

Frieda had let herself in for something far more serious than she had originally intended; but her feelings had also deepened. She wrote to Garnett that she now loved Lawrence 'with a 1000 different loves ... we want the same thing and our fighting will be against other people *never* with each other' (i. 400). Yet Lawrence had once more gone beyond what she wanted, which was not this talk of marriage – and he was disregarding, it must have seemed, what she most needed in her stress just then: simply to have him with her. Her letters to Waldbröl were emotional (where he wanted a quiet and decisive commitment); and reproachful (he denied that he was frightened or reluctant, or did not love her enough, or was unnatural, a tyrant, or like all her men, a rat forsaking a sinking ship). She began to try, though how seriously remains unclear, to make him jealous about Udo von Henning, an officer and another of the sexually unfulfilled men she felt a mission to save (who showed her his soulful poetry, and may also have had embarrassingly to meet and vouch for Lawrence after the arrest.)[43] Lawrence riposted with Hannah's growing attraction to him, 'So there!' (i. 406); and (unfortunately) put an arch note of sexual risk into 'Hail in the Rhineland'. He not only refused to be jealous – if Frieda wanted Henning she should have him, though it wouldn't be much more than a dose of pain-killer – but also reacted against the maternal element in her sexuality and her sense of mission. He compared her with the wet-nurse in Maupassant's story, who satisfied a young man's hunger and relieved her own pain by suckling him (i. 406–7). The further charge that such 'love' babyfied rather than restored its object, and his desire to straighten himself out before coming to her, were connected with 'Paul Morel' – which he also wanted (and needed) to finish revising before setting off for Munich.

Even their dreams seemed to support Lawrence's claim that he could wait because he was now certain; whereas 'it is *you* who would hurry who are undecided' (i. 403). He dreamed outwards, in guilt: that Ernest was wild with fury but broke down, so that his injurer 'had to comfort him' (i. 396). Frieda had a nightmare about an airman falling through the sky (perhaps fusing her lover with her distant cousin Manfred); but Lawrence was probably right to see this as distrust of his high-flying feeling and aspiration: 'I was only a weak spot in your soul. Round the thought of *me* – all your fear' (i. 404). By contrast, on a Sunday trip along the Rhine from Bonn, the last treat of his stay with the Krenkows, he looked up from writing postcards in a cafe on top of the Drachenfels, to watch two butterflies mating: 'If they can spin and kiss at this height, there in mid-air – then why should I bother about myself' (i. 408).[44]

As the revision of his novel neared the end however, he became impatient to be with Frieda: 'The soles of my feet burn' (i. 409). Despite insisting (in German) that she must marry him, he was still unsure of her. She had originally planned to return home at the beginning of August and was looking no further ahead; he thought he might go back to the Krenkows then (i. 406–7). At last, however, what *he* thought of as his marriage began on 24 May, after a fifteen-hour train journey. Late at night, Frieda (and Edgar Jaffe) met him at Munich station (but Edgar soon vanished), and they went to a hotel. Sometime the next day they took the train to Else's Jaffe's house at Wolfratshausen, and that night went a few stations further on to Beuerberg (where they arrived in pitch dark and pouring rain). It might not have seemed the most auspicious beginning, as they contemplated the large bare bedroom in the Gasthaus (with its oleograph of Mary with seven swords in her heart); or as they ate among the peasants and their beerpots in the big public room. That night may indeed have been 'a failure', as in the poem 'First Morning', but they awoke to a beauty whose every detail remained vivid eight years later.[45]

III   Beuerberg and Icking

Morning after honeymoon morning they breakfasted under red and white chestnut trees in the garden, on its ledge above a weir in the river Loisach, where manned rafts floated down the pale jade glacier water. Across the little village green, with its great trees, were a white convent and a white-necked church with a black onion-dome, and two white and black farmhouses with enormous sweeping roofs. The water-meadows by the river were vivid with multicoloured Alpine flowers; the mountains in the distance sparkled blue with snow; the air was crystalline. And ('First Morning' would affirm, then or later) it seemed that all this beauty centred in their love. One day they watched a passion play, for this was Oberammergau country. Another, they went into the mountains, and sat on a little pier by the Kochelsee with their feet dangling, putting Frieda's rings on their toes to see how they looked under water (i. 413). A sudden storm made them run in different directions and lose each other[46] – only to realise their need the more.

Yet this little allegory soon began to be tested more harshly. They visited Else at Wolfratshausen; and it was from there that Lawrence would 'date' the poems which – then or later – began to explore the cruel paradox that shadowed their happiness and caused dissension for a long time to come. Another letter seems to have arrived from Weekley: he would not now divorce her (i. 415). In one way this bound her to Lawrence; but in another it split them, because of her agonising, now, about the children (which Weekley had begun to talk about as *his*), and Lawrence's reaction to that. Neither could help the division within as well as between them: the tension between what they wanted to and did feel for each other at moments when the suffering was greatest, and what was bound to well up more hurtfully from the subconscious. We cannot of course use the poems in *Look! We Have Come Through!* (1917), let alone *Mr Noon* (1920), as reliable biographical evidence. We do not know how many of the poems were written in 1912, and most of those we do know about were significantly rewritten in 1917.[47] The even later comic novel also bears a suspiciously close relation to the poem-sequence which had already dramatised and rearranged experience. Moreover the quick of Lawrence's use of imagination to explore his problems lay precisely in the freedom to select, isolate and heighten certain elements, and to create literary circumstances in which their significance could be explored. Nonetheless he himself associated with Wolfratshausen his first realisation of what could surge through, and in spite of, his longing to comfort her, and hers to cling to him: corrosive resentment against him as the cause of her suffering – he had after all forced matters – and a black nihilism in him if she withdrew, a bitter sense of being betrayed and denied. Even if contemporary, the poems are no evidence of the proportion of these feelings to the love and confidence that came from sexual happiness, but they do adumbrate the first psychological shadows.

Immediate good, however, also came from Wolfratshausen. Alfred Weber was there, 'such a jolly fellow' (i. 413); and since he was about to return to the university in Heidelberg he offered them his flat in Icking, rent-free – which was important since they had been paying Whitsun holiday prices at Beuerberg, and were running short again. In Icking they set up their first 'home' above Frau Leitner's shop, in four rooms with a kitchen and a balcony. There Lawrence could write, looking out over the little white hamlet, the milky green river Isar, 'and a plain of dark woods – all in shadow. Then there's the great blue wall of mountains, only their tops, all snowy, glittering in far-off sunshine against a pale blue sky' (i. 415). Here they stayed for all of June and July, and into early August – when Frieda had originally meant to go back to Nottingham.

In Icking, both elements of the paradox intensified. He now felt confident enough to tell a few more people about Frieda: his sister Ada; Sallie Hopkin (the older woman he had always trusted most); and his closest fellow-teacher and friend at Croydon, Arthur McLeod. To these few, whose sympathy was assured, he felt he could now talk about his happiness: 'I never knew what love was before ... The world is wonderful and beautiful and good beyond one's wildest imagination', he told Sallie (i. 414). On the basis of his new experience he could be earnest with McLeod about the source of the latter's melancholy: his lack of the trust to open himself to others (i. 418). For many months however it was only to these very few, and Garnett, that Lawrence himself would be able to confide in letters. There was Jessie Chambers also, but not for long. Enclosed with a newsy letter to her family (now lost) there came, she told Emile Delavenay many years later, an 'almost hysterical message' for her ears only: 'I daren't think of Weekley ... I only know I love Frieda ... I can think of nothing but Anna Karenina' (i. 412). It must have been painful to imagine Jessie receiving the news and he certainly continued to feel agonised about Weekley, yet no hysteria appears anywhere in the letters we have, nor indeed detectably here. The word may be Jessie's reaction to emotions that were most unwelcome, to her. We know what Lawrence thought later of Anna Karenina: that her tragedy came from foolishly allowing the opinions of others to split her from Vronsky. He would certainly have thought the same now; and if he wanted nobody else to know about him and Frieda yet – not even Louie Burrows, Helen Corke or May Holbrook, to whom only postcards went – it was to make sure that Frieda stayed with him in spite of the disapproval he might expect. The more they were committed to each other, the more they would have to sacrifice relationships they had cared for.

Friends were one thing, however; Monty, Elsa and Barbie quite another. Even though, like most children of a well-to-do middle class, their closest relationships were with their nurse (the beloved Ida Wilhelmy), Frieda had been a loving and playful mother.[48] She may have exaggerated to herself what the loss of her would mean to them; but had every excuse if so, since the letters which begged her to return made this their most powerful argument. Images of the children's grief and her own aching sense of loss must have magnified any tiff with Lawrence, in bitter resentment of what the liaison with him was costing – as she had never intended. She would naturally seize on the slightest hope that Weekley might come to an arrangement that would give her access, at least. She would be plunged into black desolation every time he told her that she no longer had any rights. And when Frieda was miserable, she gave herself up to her emotions, collapsed on the floor, making uncontrollable sounds of agony.[49] The more she felt she had no alternative but to stay with Lawrence, the fiercer her subconscious resentment might become.

This would have caused tension enough had Lawrence been a well-adjusted and confident young man, with a happy home behind him to make him sympathise with the loss of hers. Instead he had been struggling, before he met her, to diagnose in 'Paul Morel' the source of his own psychic malaise. Though it was not yet *Sons and Lovers*, the central insight was becoming clear: that mother-love, however life-giving, can also be destructive. This had already barbed his teasing when Frieda tried to make him jealous of von Henning, calling into question the nature of her sexuality and her idea of herself. The poem 'She Looks Back', whenever written, defines the battle grounds: in her, the 'wife' (to Lawrence) in danger of murder by the 'mother'; in him, her tears poignant to his loving sympathy, but in their salt also (like Lot's wife, turning back to the land of death) corroding, denying the new life. The Magna Mater, the Mater Dolorosa with swords in her heart, became his enemy, not only because Frieda's maternal longings might take her away from him, but also because they got into her feeling *for* him, and his, about his growing dependence on her.

Of the two occasions when Frieda did leave him while they were at Icking, taking herself off to Else's for three or four days at a time, one seems to have been a quarrel over 'Lot's wife', Frieda's mother-feelings; but the other may have come about because she found in a notebook a poem of 1910 about *his* mother-feeling, which seemed evidence to her that mother-fixation had made him incapable of real love for another woman, to her outrage and contempt. The conclusion reads:

> You sweet love, my mother
> Twice you have blooded me,
> Once with your blood at birth-time
> Once with your misery.
> And twice you have washed me clean,
> Twice-wonderful things to see.
>
> And so, my love, Oh mother
> I shall always be true to thee.
> Twice I am born, my mother
> As Christ said it should be,
> And who can bear me a third time?
> —None love—I am true to thee.

Frieda scribbled words of hate against each stanza; and wrote after the whole poem:

Yes, worse luck – what a poem to write! yes, you are free, poor devil, from the heart's homelife free, [a complete misreading of the point of stanza 2] *lonely you shall be, you have chosen it, you chose freely, now go your way. – Misery, <an> a sad, old woman's misery you have chosen, you poor man, and you cling to it with all your power. I have tried I have fought, I have nearly killed myself in the battle to get you into connection with myself and other people, sadly I proved to my self that I can love, but never you – Now I will leave you for some days and I will see if being alone will help you to see me as I am, I will heal again by myself, you cannot help me, you are a sad thing, I know your secret and your despair, I have seen you are ashamed – I have made you better, that is my reward –*[50]

These deeper issues tended to escalate the clashes of temperament which beset all lovers in their first adjustments at close quarters. Frieda and Lawrence were very different in character and class. Her splendid carelessness was an effect of her upbringing, and having always been waited on by servants: she couldn't cook, or launder, or look after her clothes, and simply threw away her shoes when a heel came off. Lawrence hardly knew whether to be more impressed, or shocked from his mother's tradition of prudence and thrift. But Frieda's spontaneity, her carelessness of convention, her abandon to the moment and its emotions, were also part of her very being – and were in the strongest contrast with his 'English' hatred of showing his feelings, and his physical guardedness, which occasionally broke out into wild temper, or gaiety, or mimicry, but was usually kept under tight control. These differences in background and temperament were part of their attraction for each other, but could also seem symptomatic of the bigger divisions which threatened their life together. Were his control (or inhibition), his unwillingness to say 'I love you', and his glooms and tempers, perhaps the signs of an inability to love, which would mean she had abandoned her sunshine self to something dark and cold and underground? Beneath what she called her 'hard bright shell'[51] she was not as confident as she seemed – which is why Gross's theories and his idea of her had been so important. Her defence when she felt herself under threat was to counter-attack with no holds barred, blind to the complex man in front of her, and trying with devastating intuition to mock and destroy his manhood. For his part Lawrence could suspect her emotional nature, that so attracted him, of being a mode of possessiveness, or of turbulent waters running shallow. At Waldbröl he had contrasted his deep, steady and lifelong feeling with what seemed more passionate but was hasty and unsure. Not until they left Icking did he feel any confidence in her commitment to him – and then he was soon proved wrong. His new novel was also sharpening its realisation of the possessiveness, often quasi-maternal, that could lie under effusive feminine feeling.

Both were assertive and stubborn in argument; both had short fuses. Little wonder then that the honeymoon at Beuerberg was followed, in Icking, by the first of a long (and subsequently notorious) sequence of rows; and even by the first separations, though never for long. At the end of a month in their earliest 'home' Lawrence was telling Garnett of the 'great war ... waged in this little flat on the Isarthal', and how 'real tragedy' lay in 'the inner war which is waged between people who love each other' – despite their happiness and their 'fearfully good times together' (i. 419). The merest trifle, in a context of joyousness, could prove explosive. 'Folk down here are very nice, and the country is lovely. F. raves over glow-worms, I over fire-flies, and we nearly murder each other' (i. 420). It is a joke and not a joke, because the rows were over nothing, *and* over something important or they would not have happened. Years later in *Mr Noon*, Lawrence misremembered the details but probably located the detonator accurately enough, in Gilbert's reaction to Johanna's gush of feeling. For Lawrence this would be another 'Miriam' scene: the quasi-maternal possessiveness revealed in yearning over the dear little things one could hold in one's hand, as opposed to his feeling for the other free, quick, uncatchable sparks of life. But for Frieda, it would be the dark man coming between her and the sun, destroying – for no reason – her innocent and spontaneous joy.[52]

More important, however, it was at Icking that Lawrence began to experience what was to become the essence of new life to him, and the central insight of his new writing after the backward look of *Sons and Lovers*: that the 'war' between lovers might go *through* 'tragedy' to become liberation and enrichment. Frieda's greatest gift to him was to refuse to let him dominate, and to fight him into self-exposure and self-knowledge.

At the beginning of July, Weekley seemed 'half crazed' again. New 'storms of letters' implored her to renounce her ideas of love and come back to give her life to her children.

Weekley would have her back, on those conditions. The children are miserable, missing her so much. She lies on the floor in misery – and then is fearfully angry with me because I won't say 'stay for my sake'. I say 'decide what you want most, to live with me and share my rotten chances, or go back to security, and your children – decide for *yourself* – Choose for yourself.' And then she almost hates me, because I won't say 'I love you – stay with me whatever happens.' I *do* love her. If she left me, I do not think I should be alive six months hence. And she won't leave me, I think.

She had however gone just then to Wolfratshausen for four nights, to look after Else's children while she was away – and to get away from him, or why was he not with her? 'God, how I love her –' (he goes on) 'and the agony of it. She is a woman who also makes a man suffer, by being blind to him when her anger or resentment is roused' (i. 420–1).

Yet five days later they had come through 'avenues of tragedy'. Frieda had written 'definitely she could never come back'. Weekley replied, 'then she must forego the children. There was a cyclone of letters. I wrote also. Now things are beginning to calm down.' Though Weekley had become ever more desperate, Lawrence had come to think him 'rather fine – never, for one moment, denies his love for F, and never says anything against her herself, only against the previous lover ... who put these "ideas" into her head' (i. 424). For his part, Weekley said Lawrence had been 'ehrlich' (honest, as indeed he had), and that he had a great future. There would however be no divorce; Frieda was condemned to 'live in sin', having given up her last chance now of ever going back to Nottingham as a respectable woman. But if there was to be no more pretence of being merely on holiday with her family, this also removed the main reason for staying in Germany – especially since Weber would want his flat for the summer vacation. Both of them may have begun to react against the role and influence in their affairs of Frieda's oldest sister, for all Else's kindness. The same letter announced a new plan to walk through the Tyrol into Italy.

This was not merely because Italy would be cheaper, though they now had only £23 between them (i. 424, 430), even after a cheque for Lawrence's 'Schoolmaster' poems in the *Westminster Gazette* and some help from Frieda's sisters, not for the first or the last time. It was also because they had won through to a new 'Hinterland der Seele' (i. 425), in Frieda's phrase. Their battles had so changed their inner soul-scape, they felt, that the need to adventure further beyond the boundaries of the known seemed to follow naturally. Indeed Frieda would have preferred 'to clear out of Europe, and get to somewhere uncivilised', but Lawrence, more prudent as usual, thought he might have to find some opportunity to earn, back in Germany, the following winter. Nevertheless he too felt that love had made him 'barbaric', with new insight into the 'wild scope' of his nature, which the English habitually fence off. Now 'all my little pathetic sadness and softness goes, and I am often frightened at the thing I find myself' (i. 424–5). Though Frieda continued to dread his lapses into cold self-containment, their sexual happiness had sprung not so much from any prowess as from what she later called a generosity – which must for him also have been a courage – of giving himself altogether. In other ways, too, he shed inhibitions with her. She drifted naked round the flat, and got up when she felt like it. They bathed nude in the river, though he could not share her ecstasy, 'fearfully voluptuous, rolling in the pale green water' (i. 425). She made him dance,[53] recapturing something of his father's gift, though not with his or Frieda's flamy physicality – there was always some irony in the performance. He loosed his vein of mimicry which left her helpless with laughter, as he acted out a revival meeting, or some comic situation with himself cast as clown.[54] But it was also good for him to fight. Instead of closing up, he learned to 'fight tooth and claw' not only to keep his mate but also against her. 'She says I'm reverting' (to savagery), 'but I'm not – I'm only coming out wholesome and myself. Say I'm right, and I ought to be always common. I *loathe* Paul Morel' (i. 427). Here too the growth was away from his mother towards his father, and from middle-class to working-class behaviour; but putting it in merely class terms falsifies. He was learning a Blakean kind of wisdom: that one may become wholesome by the exposure of unwholesomeness, and whole by being broken apart and at peace through passionate antagonism. She fought his detachment, his passivity, his assertiveness, his dependency. If she made him loathe the Paul Morel in himself, he would have looked back with all the greater scorn at previous surrogates like Cyril and Siegmund in his first two novels. All alone with Frieda 'in this tiny savage little place' (i. 427); through the flaming rows as well as the sexual fulfilment; and the 'nights in the little bed where we sleep together' (i. 430) at peace against the world; he was developing not only a happier but a stronger self.

The same was true of Frieda. Otto Gross had idolised her in one way, and Weekley in another. Both made her think highly of herself, though both also left her miserably insecure on her pedestal, knowing that she could not live up to their images. She had never however been criticised, contradicted, fought with as Lawrence did from the first. She had believed, after Gross, 'that if only sex were "free" the world would straightaway turn into a paradise'. He had presented her to herself as a 'golden child', 'the woman of the future', full of love, laughter, and greatness of soul, whose gift of herself could be profoundly liberating, as it had been to him, and who must above all be free.[55] Weekley had seen her much more conventionally, as the snow-pure wife and loving mother, in whom could be invested, with absolute trust, a man's highest and most civilised domestic ideals, and who would be always at the back of him while he did his work – though he waxed sarcastic about her efforts to improve her mind.[56] Came Lawrence, who not only attacked each idealisation with an element of the other, but also, by hammering at her faults and loving her in spite of them, freed her to be and to value just herself. He believed with Gross that she had the right to fulfil her life, but saw her 'free-love' affairs as shallow and indulgent. He insisted that there would be no fulfilment without an absolute commitment of the self, a marriage, that would secure the self and its expression in the world, though not in Weekley's terms, and deeply distrusting his ideal of motherhood. On the other hand, though he saw in Frieda what Gross had seen – the youth and newness, the vitality, the largeness of soul – he was much more down to earth, and saw also the spoilt and inefficient woman, the gushing and possessive female, and the insecurity behind the bright and sometimes arrogant mask. He would not let her dominate, either. He fought *her* as well as for her, but in forcing her also to fight him, she was made to show herself just as she was, and find that he loved her nevertheless, as she had not been loved before. Above all, where she had been established as the life-giver, and was so again, this time she was overcome by *his* gift of life: 'Everything he met had the newness of a creation just that moment come into being. I didn't want people, I didn't want anything,' – except of course the children – 'I only wanted to revel in this new world Lawrence had given me ... "You have a genius for living," he told me. "Maybe, but you brought it out in me." '[57]

IV   Lawrence at Work

She was also fascinated by watching him at work, for on the balcony at Icking he had begun to write again. He soon finished the revision of 'Paul Morel' that had been almost complete at Waldbröl, and sent the manuscript to Heinemann on 9 June. Writing to Walter de la Mare the next day, he was confident, but also a little anxious for the professional reader's support with the publisher, since he needed the novel to come out and get him 'onto my feet'. He anticipated possible criticisms: that it might seem 'loose' to Flaubertians (like his earlier 'patron' Ford Madox Hueffer); that 'the childhood part' might be too long (if so, he would cut); and that 'perhaps you'll want me to spoil some of the good stuff' (presumably the sexual scenes). 'But', he went on 'it is rather great. Some

Germans who really know a good thing when they see it speak in high praise' (i. 417). Else and Edgar Jaffe may have read it, and perhaps Weber too. On 23 May, his last day at Waldbröl, his second novel *The Trespasser* had been published; and by the beginning of July Garnett had sent him the reviews which were mostly favourable – though a Nottingham one, to Frieda's delight, labelled it 'A Reprehensible Jaunt'.[58]

He had been working on stories in the meantime: the early version of 'The Christening' (having its origin perhaps in the birth of Neville's illegitimate child, but still untransformed by the speech which now concludes it); 'Once—!' (starting from complex feelings about Nusch, the 'cocotte', as well as Frieda); and rewrites of 'Delilah and Mr. Bircumshaw' (seeing a failing marriage in other terms than those of the Morels), and of 'The Fly in the Ointment' (written as 'The Blot' in Croydon, about a teacher surprising a burglar).[59] 'But, under the influence of Frieda,' he wrote to Garnett on 29 June, referring particularly to the first two, 'I am afraid their moral tone would not agree with my countrymen' (i. 420). More to the point, though all have their interest for his development, none was yet as imaginatively probing as Lawrence was about to be. There was also a surge of poems, though we cannot tell how many since only ten have survived in original versions.[60] One or two of them, also, might have shocked contemporary readers. Lawrence was quite unprepared however for the shock he himself received at the beginning of July: Heinemann rejected 'Paul Morel' outright.

He thought it lacked unity, and 'its want of reticence' made it unfit for publication in England, where the 'tyranny of the Libraries' damned any outspoken book. He proclaimed himself still 'a great admirer', and thought parts of the novel 'as good as anything I have ever read of yours'. But as a whole:

> it seems to me painfully mistaken, if for no other reason than that one has no sympathy for any character in the book. A writer must create interest in his characters. Even, after a while, one's interest in Paul flags, – while, in the early part, the degradation of his mother, supposed to be of gentler birth, is almost inconceivable. (i. 421 n. 4)

De la Mare also wrote, and though his letter to Lawrence is lost we can see from two letters to Garnett how he too was critical, though not of its indecency: 'I read it in MS., and thought – apart from the fineness of individual passages – that it was badly put together and a bit too violent here and there' (i. 423 n.1). It needed 'pulling together', for 'the real theme of the story is not arrived at till half way through' (i. 424 n.1).

These letters came at the height of the crisis over Weekley at the start of July, and were as heavy a blow to Lawrence's hopes of being able to support Frieda financially, as to his pride in what he rightly thought was his best work yet. He blew off his rage to Garnett, in a storm of cursing at the publisher and his spineless bloodless spunkless countrymen – which calmed him enough to concede in a postscript that Heinemann might be quite right in business terms (i. 422). (Less forgiveable was a reference to him a few days later, i.424, as a 'rotten little Jew'; a first anti-Semitism perhaps picked up in Germany.)[61] Fortunately the letter crossed with a proposal from Garnett, told of the rejection by de la Mare, that Duckworth might take the book instead – and he himself would help as he had done for *The Trespasser*, with any licking into shape that might be necessary.

Duckworth had no reason to regret having taken over *The Trespasser* from Heinemann; and Garnett may have read part of 'Paul Morel' when Frieda and Lawrence spent a weekend at The Cearne before they left for Germany, and left the early chapters of the manuscript behind. As a friend, the lanky, ungainly, eccentric, sardonically kind intellectual, with his impatience of convention and his cynical view of the 'establishment', had been the chief support to Lawrence since October 1911.[62] He had not been shocked but rather affectionately and hospitably amused by Frieda and their dilemma. (He lived largely apart from but on friendly terms with his wife Constance, the translator mainly responsible for the new vogue of Russian fiction.) So both Lawrence and Frieda thought of him as the only man in England who would give them refuge if they needed it. As literary mentor he had taken the place of Hueffer, and had proved even more invaluable. He was less bound by ideas of what 'the novel' *should* be, and helped a number of very different writers to find themselves – and their market, for though he had a more adventurous sense of what the English public would buy than most other publisher's readers, his record of success showed that he was also very astute. He looked for individuality first (of any kind, whether in Conrad, Hudson, Galsworthy, Henry Lawson or E. Nesbit) and next for the conviction that the author really knew the kind of 'life', be it outer or inner, that he or she was writing about. Then he would give manuscripts a detailed criticism of language and image that was sensitive to the writer's peculiar sensibility, but merciless to indulgence. It was a remarkable achievement to help writers as different as Conrad and Lawrence. Most important of all for Lawrence was his fidelity. He had come to the rescue of *The Trespasser*, and now he was doing so again at a far more serious crisis, both with overall faith, and with detailed criticism. When Lawrence's circle had narrowed extraordinarily because of the 'elopement', leaving him only four people with whom he could share any of his deepest concerns, he could write to Garnett about both his life and his work as to an ideal father-figure who was yet, thank heaven, rather more like a much older brother, both in age and in outlook.[63]

The manuscript was posted to England again on 4 July for Garnett to go through, and the move to Italy put off until the parcel could come back. Garnett's first notes arrived on the 18th, and the manuscript itself with more notes on the 22nd. 'What a Trojan of energy and conscientiousness you are!' wrote Lawrence in gratitude. 'I'm going to slave like a Turk at the novel – see if I won't do you credit. I begin in earnest tomorrow – having spent the day in thought (?)' (i. 427). In their remaining two weeks in Icking the first 79 pages of *Sons and Lovers* took shape.

Fortunately, six discarded fragments of the third version of 'Paul Morel' survive – left behind with Else – and by comparing these with the final manuscript of *Sons and Lovers* it is possible to see how Lawrence began to reshape the book, interleaving rewritten sections with bits of 'Paul Morel' that still, with some revision, seemed satisfactory.[64] The most telling criticism had been the lack of clear connection between the first part of the book (the marriage of the Morels and Paul's childhood) and the story of his love affairs. So Lawrence condensed or cut 'documentary' material, less concerned now with background, and struck a new early keynote, to make the story of Paul's elder brother clearly anticipate an overall theme. Now the brilliant little scene at the Wakes brings home, in a reader's first experience of Mrs Morel, the intensity of her relationship with her first born, William, and how absolutely centred upon her the little boy's life has already become. In chapter III the title is changed from 'Morel Reaps the Whirlwind' to 'The Casting off of Morel, the Taking on of William'. Moreover, instead of the first fragment's picture of Mrs Morel in her doorway, contrasting the beautiful sunset and the free flight of the swifts with the drunken miners and the disgrace of her husband, Lawrence created a cheerful Walter for the reader's first glimpse of him: by no means drunk, though well-pleased with himself after his day of helping in the bar, and with the coconut he has got for the children. The dramatically contrasted voices show that the final version will try for a more complex balance than before:

"Nay, tha niver said thankyer for nowt i' thy life, did ter?" ...

"A man will part with anything so long as he's drunk, and you're drunk along with him," said Mrs Morel.

"Eh tha mucky little 'ussy, who's drunk, I sh'd like ter know?"[65]

A number of changes in these first 79 pages confirm that Lawrence's months with Frieda, and the clear break with his previous life, had made it possible for him to see Mrs Morel more critically, and to make Walter somewhat more sympathetic at first, in the important early stages of a reader's response. Lawrence expands the miner's cheerful making-and-mending in the house (cf. Fragment 2) and the picture of him alone in the early morning (cf. Fragment 3); makes it clearer that Morel was more ill than drunk in the first 'battle' (cf. Fragment 2); and cuts (cf. Fragment 5) the comic scene with Jerry and the bottle of beer in the sick-room (which had survived from the second version) since the amused contempt of the narrative was indistinguishable from Mrs Morel's.

However he also underlines Morel's deterioration under his wife's now sharpened contempt: he is made meaner to the children, more dangerously violent in the second big quarrel and (in a new episode not in Fragment 4) undeniably more contemptible now, in his humiliating show of leaving home. Lawrence is not shifting sympathy so much as hardening contrast and underlining theme: the humiliation becomes the 'turn' in the casting off of the husband and the taking on of the eldest son. 'Delilah and Mr. Bircumshaw' had shown a new grasp of how a woman can destroy a man; and there had been several signs of new sharpness about the destructiveness of mother-love. The final rewriting of 'Paul Morel' into *Sons and Lovers* would hatch both insights into the existing texture, creating more complexity, though it could not alter the main lines of the earlier drawing.

V Visitors

Two visitors interrupted the work of revision at Icking. The first was Garnett's son David, 'Bunny', who had just completed his first year studying botany at the Royal College of Science and was holidaying in Munich, attending also some lectures at the university. He was twenty, impulsive, good-looking, energetic; and (what was most charming) warmly attracted to them as a pair, because of their happiness. 'Lawrence and Frieda were more than twice as attractive to me together than they would have been separately. I was completely charmed by each of them and at once worshipped them.' When nobody else (with the exception of Bunny's father) seemed convinced that they belonged together, the hero-worship of this delightful lad must have been particularly healing. His autobiography paints vivid portraits of them at Icking.[66] On the platform, Lawrence looked 'fearfully English' – though also very working class – with 'a scrubby little moustache' and 'the most beautiful lively, blue eyes'. He was

slight in build, with a weak, narrow chest and shoulders, but he was a fair height [5 feet 9 inches] and very light in his movements. This lightness gave him a sort of grace. His hair was of a colour, and grew in a particular way, which I have never seen except in English working men. It was bright mud-colour, with a streak of red in it, a thick mat, parted on one side ... His forehead was broad, but not high, his nose too short and lumpy, his face colourless, like a red-haired man's, his chin (he had not then grown a beard) altogether too large, and round like a hairpin – rather a Philip IV sort of chin – and the lower lip, rather red and moist, under the scrubby toothbrush moustache ... [O]nce you looked into his eyes you were completely charmed, they were so beautiful and alive, dancing with gaiety. His smile lit up all his face as he looked at you, asking you silently: 'Come on ... let's have some fun', and the invitation of this look was irresistible, at least to me.

At first Frieda seemed 'the handsome sister of the sweating German mother' who had romped with her children in the train:

she had the same sturdy body, as strong as a horse, the same magnificent shoulders, but her head and the expression of her eyes were very different. Her head and the whole carriage of her body were noble. Her eyes were green, with a lot of tawny yellow in them, the nose straight. She looked one dead in the eyes, fearlessly judging one and, at that moment, she was extraordinarily like a lioness: eyes and colouring, and the swift power of her lazy leap up from the hammock where she had been lying.

The attraction was mutual. 'We are awfully fond of him', Lawrence wrote to Edward. Swimming in the Isar, 'He simply smashes his way through the water, while F. sits on the bank bursting with admiration, and I am green with envy.' He imitated Mordkin, Pavlova's partner in Diaghilev's Russian Ballet, dancing:

with great orange and yellow and red and dark green scarves of F's, and his legs and arms bare; while I sit on the sofa and do the music, and burst with laughter, and F. stands out on the balcony in the dark, scared. Such a prancing whirl of legs and arms and raving colours you never saw: And F. shrieks when he brandishes the murderous knife in my music-making face; and somebody calls in German from below: 'Go and trample somewhere else,' and at last he falls panting. Oh the delightful Bunny! (i. 429)

They made him promise to come and join them part of the way (at Mayrhofen) in their walk towards Italy, with his friend Harold Hobson, whom Bunny was expecting to meet in Munich.

The second visitation was much more problematic. Frieda's mother, on a visit to Else, descended on them also unannounced, to make one final plea. The move to Italy, shedding the last pretence of being with her family, was bound to seem a crowning defiance of Weekley, irretrievable, as Lawrence thought too. Up to now, Frieda might have left at any time, but now 'I have at last nailed F.'s nose to my wagon', he told Garnett, in the same letter of 4 August that described how Frieda's mother had 'schimpfed' or scolded him. 'At last, I think, she can't leave me – at least for the present: despite the loss of her children.' But the Baroness had done her best. She stayed an hour, and spent it 'abusing' him 'like a washerwoman' – in German:

I sat and gasped. 'Who was I, did I think, that a Baronesse should clean my boots and empty my slops: she, the daughter of a high-born and highly-cultured gentleman ... No decent man, no man with common sense of decency, could expect to have a woman, the wife of a clever professor, living with him like a barmaid,[67] and he not even able to keep her in shoes.' – So she went on. – Then, in München, to Else, her eldest daughter, says I am a lovable and trustworthy person. – You see I saw her off gracefully from the station.

(i. 429–30)

Later they would become firm friends. But the patience and courtesy which impressed the mother, enraged the daughter. His letter claims not to know why she should accuse him, along with all the world, of being 'a rotter at the present moment'. (It seems odd that he hadn't heard already!) But even without the later 'evidence' of *The Fight for Barbara* (the first idea of which he had probably been sketching out on 18 July before the visit), and years later of *Mr Noon*,[68] the letter itself reveals the reason. He thought of retorting 'I don't think!' to the Baroness's description of her husband, but said not a word. Both the later comic dramatisations present him as having withdrawn, again, sitting utterly silent and shrunk into himself, so that the only defence had come from Frieda. This may exaggerate but is convincing; as is Frieda's response to what she may well have thought pusillanimous. In both fictions 'she' proceeds to attack 'his' lack of manliness. If Lawrence truly had not learned yet why Frieda was angry, the dramatic fictions are indeed fictitious – the later one merely deriving from and heightening the earlier. Yet the night before they left for Italy may not have been among their most peaceful, and Lawrence was right to be not quite sure, even now, that Frieda was firmly committed to him.

VI   Over the Alps[69]

On Monday morning 5 August they set out, and walked along the Isar to Wolfratshausen, where they avoided Else, but bought a spirit-stove (nicknamed the kitchenino) on which they could cook by the roadside or in a bedroom, to save money. It was about to rain as they reached a station on the light railway, so they took it to Bichl, to join the high road to Austria at the foot of the mountains, and then walked about 12 kilometres in the rain (passing several peasant-looking roadside Christs) to Bad Tölz. Having found a cheap room, they cheered themselves up by an evening in the little summer theatre.

Next day was sunny. They went up through Lengries ($8\frac{1}{2}$km.) into the high rocky valley of the young Isar, where woodmen were building rafts, before taking what looked like a short-cut over the ridge to join the road to Mayrhofen. However in late afternoon the path petered out and they had to scramble over to the one to Röhrlmoos, by which time it was almost dark, and Frieda was dragging her feet. In search of somewhere to sleep, they found beside the path a tiny chapel, where Lawrence lit the altar candles and was fascinated by the ex-voto pictures covering the walls. He wanted to stay there, but Frieda had set her heart on the romance of sleeping in a hay-hut, and there was one close by. Alas, it proved cold and uncomfortable in the hay, and they woke to an icy grey dawn. Frieda went for water, barefoot over the frozen grass; Lawrence coaxed a fire of sticks since they had used all the fuel for the cooker. They shivered over tea and the last of their bread, and set off again. A bit further on they saw a light and asked the way from a spectral couple in an isolated Alpine cabin – but about an hour down the gorge lay a hamlet, Hubertus, and coffee in the wooden house of a forester who had hunted with the Crown Prince! They were now on the right road, not far from the border, but much in need of rest and it was raining, so they hired a room in Glashütte and slept till afternoon. At four it was raining again, so they took the post-bus into Austria, to Achensee with its Hotel Scholastika by the 'dark, deep lake'. They found lodging in a farmhouse, where Frieda dived under the blue-and-white duvet, and Lawrence foraged for a meal to cook snugly in the bedroom with its painted Tyrolean furniture – happy to be out of Germany, among kind people in easygoing Austria.

On Thursday they started off along the lake, and walked the 20 kilometres to Jenbach, the junction where the old Imperial Road and the railway ran to Innsbruck and over the Brenner Pass to Italy. First, however, they had to see to their luggage, which meant the train in the other direction to the border town of Kufstein, 'under its dark castle',[70] where they duly unpacked some new clothes, saw their bags through the customs and sent them on to Mayrhofen, before taking the train back to Jenbach the next day. The silence of *Mr Noon* about their journey down the Zillertal suggests they may have taken the light-gauge railway. At Mayrhofen, 'in a farmhouse at the foot of the mountains, just by a lovely stream that tears along and is as bright as glass' (i. 433), they settled down to wait for Bunny.

There the world caught up with them. More agonising letters from Weekley made Frieda, as miserable as a cat wanting only to 'crawl under the bed' (i. 438), begin to think again that she had better go to England soon. Yet this seemed less likely now, for their relation had grown firmer, and the earliest Weekley would allow her to see the children was at Easter (i. 440). Lawrence told Sallie Hopkin that they had 'struggled through some bad times into a wonderful naked intimacy, all kindled with warmth, that I know at last is love' (i. 440); though he also told Garnett they wanted 'free breathing-space' between them as well as intimacy (i. 439), a tension by no means yet resolved. Frieda confessed that he had cured her of theorising and taught her a new mode of understanding, 'that is morality, I think' (i. 439). They wandered happily among wild flowers up the three valleys which met near the house; drinking sometimes with mountain peasants in a Gasthaus where they also 'dance[d] a little' (i. 441). Sometimes Frieda could take her clothes off and lie in the sun. Lawrence had become interested in the roadside crucifixes which were everywhere, particularly a fine one in the Dornauberg-Klamm, a steep valley between pine-clad hills, where the mule-road skirted the left bank of the river. There (or in Tuxtal) his guilt suddenly made him see Weekley's face in a muleteer's who turned to look at him – from which came a powerful poem about knowing himself hated.[71]

There was time to think about work again. There was a letter from Hueffer, to say that the English publisher Martin Secker was keen to 'run' Lawrence permanently; and in a moment of lessened confidence he wondered whether to give Secker 'Paul Morel' (i. 433–4). For Heinemann had now refused his poems also; and since Garnett had not written for some time, the silence may have begun to suggest that *he* did not care for the novel all that much. They needed money, quickly. Soon however a letter came from Garnett, and confidence returned. In reply he sent the first version of a narrative poem set in Wolfratshausen, 'The Young Soldier with Bloody Spurs'; and wondered whether Duckworth might not do his poems too. Though the *Westminster Gazette* had refused two of the sketches ('The English and the Germans' and 'A Spy is Arrested') as too anti-German, he not only asked Garnett where else to send them, but set to work finishing another two at Mayrhofen which couldn't be faulted on those grounds: 'A Chapel Among the Mountains' and 'A Hay-hut Among the Mountains'. He wanted to get on with recasting 'Paul Morel', but needed a run at it, and began to think of settling somewhere on Lake Garda.[72]

On Sunday 18th Bunny arrived and took a room in the house opposite. He describes how Lawrence already knew the affairs of everyone in the village; how he could write regardless of what was going on around him and 'scribbled away at odd moments in the corner, jumping up continually to look after the cooking'; while Frieda kept 'bubbling over with some new thing she had seen from the window'. The bad moments when the post came from England were met, he says, with courage, high spirits and self-mockery. He thought Lawrence the only great mimic he ever knew, with a genius for bringing Yeats, or Pound, instantly before one. But

the person whom Lawrence most constantly made fun of was himself ... of a shy and gawky Lawrence being patronised by literary lions, of a winsome Lawrence charming his landlady, a sentimental Lawrence being put in his place by his landlady's daughter, of a bad-tempered whining Lawrence picking a quarrel with Frieda over nothing. There was more than a little of Charlie Chaplin in his acting: but bitterer, less sentimental. Frieda and I laughed at him until laughing was an agony.

In the evenings they acted charades, Bunny coaching them in another uproarious 'Diaghilev' scene of Judith and Holofernes.[73]

Soon his friend Harold Hobson arrived from Russia, where he had gone in pursuit of a girl he met at The Cearne in 1904. Harold was the son of the economist J. A. Hobson, and was studying engineering in London at King's College: a tall, thin, handsome and cynical young man, whose dislike of the social pretensions of his American mother had led him to see 'the whole social structure, with its pretences and proprieties' as 'the work of parasitic women intent on thwarting the natural instincts of men'. He told indecent stories on principle (anti-woman, and their hypocrisies); and had a good line of lamentation about being unloved. Not surprisingly, Frieda was immediately attracted to him, and an amused Lawrence thought him 'a ripping fellow', and swapped bawdy stories, if Bunny is to be believed.[74]

On Monday 26 August the four of them set out together over the covered bridge across the river, planning to follow the Zemm valley into the mountains and over the Pfitscherjoch pass to Sterzing, where Bunny and Hobson could catch a train back to Munich, while Lawrence and Frieda would go on to Italy having sent their baggage ahead again. They went past the 'large, pale Christ' once more and up through the wet forests (Bunny, with pressing book in his rucksack, botanising on the way), beyond Ginzling and the last village on the road, into the open rocky uplands. There they spent the night in a double-decker hay-hut, burrowing deep into the hay as the practised camper Bunny directed, and hence more warmly than before, though it snowed in the night. The next day they went on upwards in hot sunshine. The younger men swam in mountain streams, Lawrence and Bunny botanised, Harold and Frieda talked of her feelings about the children, and his love-affairs. In the late afternoon they reached the Dominicus-Hütte, the last accommodation before the pass, 'a wonderful place—the last upland cradle', a mile beyond which was 'a vast precipice, like a wall, and beyond that a cluster of mountain peaks, in heaven alone, snow and sky-rock. That was the end.' Having secured their rooms, Lawrence and Bunny went for a last bit of botanising before nightfall, and Frieda and Harold for a walk, towards another hay-hut.

On Wednesday they crossed the Pfitscherjoch. At the top of the pass came a view over blunter peaks of a 'single great sky-living blade of rock' which Gilbert in *Mr Noon* thinks one of the great moments in his life.[75] Now it was downhill to St Jakob, and along the valley through Wieden, where they saw the brutalised Christus Lawrence later described with a kind of horror. Somehow the companionship had got edgier, and Harold and Bunny seemed suddenly anxious to get back to Munich. As the afternoon drew on towards dusk, Frieda began to drag her feet again, and Lawrence to nag about getting on, if they were to reach Sterzing and the railway that night. Bunny sprang to her defence and there was nearly a quarrel. At nightfall they found an inn near Afens still seven miles short, said farewells before going to bed, and before dawn on Thursday Harold and Bunny were on their way. Frieda and Lawrence followed more leisurely, arriving in the picturesque mediaeval high street by afternoon. They stayed two nights in Sterzing, though (*Mr Noon* says) not very happily, whether because they missed the young men, or because of the primitive shaft-toilet, or because Frieda seemed tired and disinclined to move while Lawrence felt cooped up.[76]

On Sunday 1 September however, they started confidently up the Jaufental on the last stage to Italy by way of Meran, though not by the obvious high road. Instead, Lawrence picked another path that looked shorter, up the long valley of the Jaufenbach, crossing the stream several times as they went, past the last hamlet and 'across the desolate, end-of-the-world valley-head, towards the cliffs and the shutting-in slopes'. Up these, as night was falling, they had a fearful scramble, with Frieda eventually in tears, crying that she could go no further, and Lawrence going on without her. Angry and humiliated, she hit back. She forced him to stop, and then told him that Hobson had 'had' her, in the hay-hut near the Dominicus-Hütte.

If *Mr Noon* is accurate, the statement was vengeful rather than confessional; a declaration, too, that she still felt herself free, and would do just as she chose. Her battle instinct was always to hurt him where he felt most vulnerable. Moreover, unlike similar stories about von Henning in Metz and a wood-cutter at Icking, which may be true but may also have been stories by Frieda to put Lawrence in his place, this one came to Bunny direct from Hobson. Ironically, Frieda would have been attracted to Hobson in exactly the same ways as to Lawrence when they first met: piqued by his attacks on woman, moved (to some degree maternally) by his young man's 'compleynte of love', amused and attracted by his vitality and humour, and seeing no reason why the mutual attraction should not be consummated. This was the free spirit; but it would have been further justified in her mind by the belief – fostered by Gross – that she could do the young man good, and repair the damage his mother and his girls had done. ('*I have made you better, that is my reward*' she had written on Lawrence's mother-poem.) *Mr Noon* has Johanna say (not in excuse, since she feels no need to apologise) 'he told me he wanted me so badly—'. [77] For Frieda, such a plea would be all the more potent, as meaning more than just desire.

It must have been a painful blow to Lawrence, who had so recently come to believe that she was committed to him at last. He had claimed that they both wanted freedom as well as naked intimacy, but he meant 'free breathing-space' *between* them and she, clearly now, meant something quite different. Humiliation, jealousy, a sense of betrayal, and resentment of the privileged youth who had so casually come into their life and made such haste out of it, must have twisted his feelings. There will have been the greatest temptation to withdraw coldly into himself. But he had liked Hobson, and when Frieda was hesitating over going back to Weekley, had said that she must choose for herself. He remained true now to what he had said and felt, and showed how final his love for her had become, by forgiving her in a rush of feeling, and insisting (again *Mr Noon* convinces) that she hadn't really meant what she had done, and that it didn't therefore signify. Like Johanna, Frieda would not have been too pleased by this.[78]

It was nine o'clock before they wearily reached the Sterzinger Jaufenhaus – and next morning, perhaps still in stress, they took the wrong turning. The wooden building stood in a loop of the highway to Meran. Imagining that the way south must lie directly opposite the track they had come down in the darkness, they turned to the right, and walked nearly all day along the twisting road. In mid-afternoon they began to recognise things. They had walked all the way back to Sterzing.

They could not bear to sleep there again, so decided to miss out Meran altogether and take the Rome express straight to Bozen (Bolzano) that same evening, in spite of the expense. At the station he wrote to Bunny and McLeod, hiding his feelings. On the train Frieda insisted on a dining-car meal they could ill afford, and they then had some difficulty finding a cheap room in Bozen. But the next day, having had enough of walking, they took the train again to Trento, and found at last that though the station still felt Austrian and the streets were full of Austrian troops, the town spoke Italian – of which they knew almost nothing.[79] They slept in a room above a restaurant, but the privy was unspeakable, and there was a cockroach in the bedroom to match the stained walls and sheets. In the Piazza di Dante Frieda, faced with more room hunting in the slack southern town that she found alien, and feeling unbearably frumpish in a wrinkled dress and Burberry and a battered panama hat, onto which the dye from the ribbon had run, slumped down and burst into tears. They had always intended to go to Lake Garda, and a poster of Riva decided them to go at once. A train was about to depart, but it was held up for them – and so to Riva 'and there the lake-head glittering in the sun'.[80]

They found a beautiful room with a painted ceiling. Though Frieda felt shabbier than ever in the resort town, and Lawrence looked like a tramp in frayed trousers and a shapeless straw hat he had bought for 3/6 in Munich (i. 455), they found Riva delightful. Still under Austrian rule (the border was a few miles down the lake), and full of 'Chocolate Soldiers' in fancy uniforms promenading with elegant ladies (i. 452), it gave them nevertheless their first full sense of 'Italy'.[81] Grapes, figs, peaches were abundant (though Frieda overdid them and got colic). There were 'miles of vineyards and olive woods. The lake is dark blue, purple, and clear as a jewel, with swarms of fishes. And the boats have lemon-coloured sails' (i. 456). Then to Frieda's joy a parcel of dresses and fashionable hats arrived from Nusch – and they retrieved their baggage. The only trouble now was that they had almost no money left. Lodging with two little old ladies in their Villa Leonardi was relatively expensive, so they were forced still to brave the maid's displeasure and cook meals in their bedroom, to get by (i. 451).

Lawrence asked Garnett whether Duckworth could pay him at once for *The Trespasser*; and after some fruitless house hunting in Riva, they went off by steamer down the lake to Villa di Gargnano where they had been recommended to Pietro di Pauli, who owned houses there. He offered them 'the bottom flat' of the Villa Igéa (in fact the first floor above a semi-basement, with steps down to the garden): a large dining-room with three windows, kitchen, two bedrooms, furnished – 'big pretty rooms' looking over the garden and across the road to the lake, and 'clean as a flower' (i. 453) – for 80 lire a month (about 66/-) with everything supplied. When Duckworth sent £50, in notes as requested (i. 453), they were at last set up comfortably in a place of their own where Lawrence could work, for the winter at least. Whether they might go to England in the spring, for Frieda to see her children and Lawrence to attend his sister Ada's wedding, was a decision that could wait. They moved in on 18 September.[82]

In the first weeks 'Italy', seen with the eye (however sharp) of a tourist just beginning to learn the language, was essentially three things: a fresh and liberating beauty of nature as Beuerberg had been, but here seen behind a tumbledown world of man; a contrasting poverty that made Lawrence with his £50 seem 'a howling gentleman and swell' (i. 466), but was nevertheless compatible with vitality and pride, if also, inevitably, with cheating and smuggling across the lake; and a peasant community dramatically different from the class ethos of his mother. 'Italy' seemed synonymous with 'decrepit': Trento 'a pure Italian ancient decrepit town' (i. 450); Riva, under its Austrian veneer, 'as Italian as an ice-cream man. Now I speak in signs' (i. 455); Gargnano, where everything is 'Italian and weird and tumble-down, and seems to belong to the past' (i. 458). The peasants seemed desperately poor, and the currency trashy. Yet (he wrote) the men were healthy and muscular, walked proud and sang; the women had straight shapely backs; the soldiers were good-looking and animal; the fishermen lounged around the little harbour like kings – and the landscape surrounding them was breathtakingly beautiful, even at its darkest. In contrast and retrospect, his 'England' of the Midlands and London seemed grubby, unliving, full of despair; and his new conception of the essence of life was becoming the antithesis of what his mother had stood for.

I can't bear to be in England when I am in Italy. It makes me feel so soiled ... I don't believe England need be so grubby. What does it matter if one is poor, and risks ones livelihood, and reputation. One *can* have the necessary things, life, and love, and clean warmth ... The Italians here sing. They are very poor ... But they are healthy ... And they go by the window proudly ... I think they haven't many ideas, but they look well, and they have strong blood.

I go in a little place to drink wine near Bogliaco. It is the living room of the house ... The family is having supper. [The father] brings me red wine to another table, then sits down again, and the mother ladles him soup from the bowl ... Then he nods and 'click-clicks' to the small baby, that the mother, young and proud, is feeding with soup from a big spoon. The grandfather, white moustached, sits a bit effaced by the father. A little girl eats soup. The grandmother by the big, open fire sits and quietly scolds another little girl. It reminds me so of home when I was a boy. They are all so warm with life. The father reaches his thick brown hand to play with the baby ... (i. 460)

'It reminds me so of home when I was a boy' ... Was Lawrence altogether aware of the bearing of what he was seeing, on his father's house and his father's world? He would have needed only to sharpen such a focus, and Part I of *Sons and Lovers* would have been transformed. It might have made a significant difference had the reshaping of the novel begun at Gargnano, instead of continuing from a point where – though Walter had been made a little more sympathetic at first – the married life of the Morels and the degradation of the father had already been established. As Lawrence's understanding of Italian peasant life and its sense of family and community developed, he might have become not only more critical of Mrs Morel, as indeed did happen, but also better able to imagine, and contrast with her, a sense of the working-class vitality and community of Nottinghamshire miners, which he had never been allowed to experience, so that the novel as we have it can give only occasional glimpses.

The equivalents of Mrs Morel in Gargnano were the two ladies whose visits made up the Lawrences' social life, along with their landlord Signor di Pauli. In the letters, these become comic figures: Pietro with his quaint French, 'grand manners and a jaw like a dog' (i. 453), a gentleman sadly out of his time, with a wife too young for him; the schoolmistress Signorina Feltrinelli, gloved, and with a squint, who gave them Italian lessons; and Signora Samuelli the proprietress of the Cervo inn, a German, whose housewifely eye Frieda feared so much that Lawrence had to scrub the flat from end to end every time she was coming for coffee.[83]

In these first weeks in Italy, too, the strain between them seemed to lessen. Lawrence could feel it wonderful again 'how one can keep going further in love' (i. 458), and joke once more about Frieda's free-and-easiness, whether carelessly emptying her slops out of the window onto some old lady (i. 462), or staying in bed all morning and insisting that he talk to her when (puritanical soul and working man that he was) he knew he should not be loafing (i. 466).[84] And Frieda could see his 'great points' clearly again:

the absolute freshness of things, nothing is ever stale or old and in spite of his lots of unrealities he is simple and real underneath. Life *is* good with him, je ne demande pas mieux, yes and it is *love*, but thank the Lord *passion* as well – It has *really* been a success, in spite of the misery left behind, in spite of the always missing the children ... (i. 449)

However, reams of letters from England were still forwarded by the Baroness; and were still liable to plunge Frieda into bottomless misery, and to set her and Lawrence against each other in fierce battles of love and hate. Weekley's display of suffering went on being 'bowel-twisting' (i. 457).[85] He sent a photograph of the little girls looking 'adorable but sad' which seemed to tear pieces from Frieda's soul (i. 467). Continuing to believe that she would realise her mistake, he advanced the date when he would allow her to see the children from Easter to Christmas and then, growing more desperate in October, even offered to let her have a flat in London with the children if she would give Lawrence up. It was too late. Once she 'would have loved it', but now she knew that whether at any one moment she loved or hated Lawrence, she 'would rather die than do without him and his life along of mine' (i. 467). Lawrence left the decision about Christmas to her, and she decided against.

VII   New Meanings of Pain

Moreover she could feel that he too was making the break with his past and its tragedy, and that she was helping him to do so in his work as well as in his life. He had no sooner got to Riva than he began to write again: the last of his German impressions which might have become his first travel-book, had the *Westminster Gazette* returned the two manuscripts they rejected. He sent 'Christs in the Tyrol' to de la Mare, along with the 'Chapel' and 'Hay-Hut' sketches, on 5 September, the day after he wrote it. A slighter and more travel-sketchy piece than its later version in *Twilight in Italy*, its Christs are described as he happened upon them, whereas 'The Crucifix Across the Mountains' reordered the experience into post-*Rainbow* oppositions. Yet the original essay has a significant theme for the Lawrence of September 1912. It is about pain; but setting its surprising tone and context early: 'I, who see a tragedy in every cow, began by suffering from the Secession pictures in Munich.'[86]

Lawrence says so little about his first encounter with the intellectual and cultural life of Germany that it seems worth pausing over this. He must have talked to Edgar Jaffe, with whom he stayed in Munich on one of the occasions when Frieda left him, and who was a far more interesting person and intellect than the comic little professor of *Mr Noon*. Jaffe owned a Secessionist, or more strictly a *Blaue Reiter*, picture by Franz Marc. He could have had much to tell Lawrence about the bohemians of Schwabing, and the intellectual ferment of their 'decadent' attack on the German equivalent of Victorianism, of which the successive phases of Secessionist painting were only one example. Lawrence would later name a character after the Countess zu Reventlow, artist and bohemian, whom Frieda too had met at the Cafe Stephanie, though the Countess had left Munich by 1912. There must have been much talk with Frieda of Gross's ideas of 'psycho-sexual' liberation and his break with Freud – about whom Lawrence had also begun to hear from Frieda at their first meeting, though at third hand. It was there that Frieda had met Ernst Frick, who, she said, looked 'as though he would not hurt a fly'.[87] Conversely, Lawrence could have heard much from talk with Else and Alfred Weber about the opposite culture of Heidelberg and its new rational and social-scientific enlightenment, centred now on the Webers and particularly Max. There may even have been, as *Mr Noon* suggests, some argument about Goethe, that arch-exemplar of eight-eenth-century Enlightenment – though the 1920 comic novel is no safe guide to Lawrence's ideas in 1912. Whether or not he did indulge in 'ignorant' denigration of Goethe however, allusions in the letters suggest that he may have been reading him, or about him.[88]

What is certain is that 'Christs in the Tyrol', in its preliminary and not too serious way, begins a process of imaginative exploration opposed both to emotional Expressionism and to rational Enlightenment, as merely different modes of self-importance and irreverence. The Christs did not interest Lawrence in Christianity. He had renounced that – as he had explained to the Eastwood Congregational minister the Rev. Robert Reid – precisely over what theologians call the Problem of Pain, which made it impossible for him to believe in a loving God.[89] But the crucifixes, and indeed the ex-voto pictures of the chapel among the mountains, did move him deeply, and set him pondering the human significance of pain in ways that might be termed religious (as Expressionism and Rationalism were not) but did not require belief in the Christian God or the divinity of his Son. He sees the Christs in the Tyrol as 'carved by men ... to get at the meaning of their own soul's anguish' – whereas what bothered him about the sophisticated *Blaue Reiter* pictures was how they relished the sensation of self-expression for its own sake, becoming 'epicures in suffering'. (The same charge lies against the 'sensational' Christus he had seen at Wieden, which he supposed also 'fairly new', though it actually was not.[90]) Christianity may be as dead and broken as the last fallen Christus he came across, with only two arms left swinging from the nails; but the Crucifixion seems still to project some symbolic meaning at the heart of life, which is to be reverenced. These carvings, these 'human attempts at deciphering the riddle of pain' and overcoming the fear of death and suffering, are to be linked with 'all tragic art'. Lawrence cannot himself decipher the riddle of the man on the cross, and is left simply with a range of attitudes to suffering – but the essay has one further and deeper point to make. Whatever the 'meaning' may be, it must not be ultimately tragic. The 'I' who is self-mocked for seeing 'tragedy in every cow' is the Lawrence still suffering from being betrayed within the last two weeks by Frieda. He is the author of two tragic novels; and only waiting now for time in which to finish rewriting the next one, about the warping of Paul Morel, resulting from the painful life of his mother. Yet the Christs he respects in the essay are those with some 'kick' in them: the peasant 'struggling stubbornly against the fact of the nails'; or the great Christus of the Klamm which may express bitterness and waste, but was also the creation of a 'worker, who has whittled away in torment to see himself emerge out of the piece of timber, so that he can understand his own suffering, and see it take on the distinctness of an eternal thing, so that he can go on further, leaving it.'[91] That would serve very well as the aim for rewriting *Sons and Lovers*.

It is confirmed by his reaction, now, to the acceptance of suffering by contemporary writers: 'I hate Bennett's resignation. Tragedy ought really to be a great kick at misery. But *Anna of the Five Towns* seems like an acceptance – so does all the modern stuff since Flaubert. I hate it. I want to wash again quick, wash off England, the oldness and grubbiness and despair' (i. 459). He dislikes Strindberg, and Conrad makes him furious though his stories are '*so* good. But why this giving in before you start, that pervades all Conrad and such folks – the Writers among the Ruins. I can't forgive Conrad for being so sad and for giving in' (i. 465).

In the same letter (30 October) he says he will send Garnett *The Fight for Barbara*, written in the last three days, 'as a sort of interlude to Paul Morel. I've done all but the last hundred or so pages of that great work, and those I funk. But it'll be done easily in a fortnight ... This comedy will amuse you fearfully – much of it is word for word true –' (i. 466). What he was funking was the assisted death of Mrs Morel, and when he did write it, the tension made him ill. Yet the play was more than an interlude – unlike *The Merry-go-Round*, which had indeed been written to distract him while his mother was actually dying. The new play was a first dramatising of the major Lawrencian theme of coming *through* battle, fear and the tragic. Frieda complained half jokingly, since she thought it good, that Lawrence had made himself 'the "strong, silent man", the *wretch*, he *did* hang on to me, but not quite so unflinchingly and I did *not* wobble so ...' (i. 476). What is more important however than unmeasurable truth-to-life, is the significance of the fight. Behind the surface struggle of Barbara and Wesson against her parents' ideas of social and marital duty, and the emotional blackmail of her husband's display of suffering, lies the insistence that they have a right to warmth of life, a right to refuse to be limed by suffering whether in others or themselves. However, the fight 'for Barbara' is ultimately also the fight by Wesson against Barbara, and by Barbara against Wesson, to make each other stand up for and be true to their own deepest need, as opposed to their ideas. It is as important for Barbara to needle Wesson into barring the door (*not* leaving her free to condemn them both to suffer), as it is for him to insist that she commit herself to their relationship, as against superficial ideas of freedom, or putting her husband's suffering above her own and Wesson's right, and need, to be warm with life.

Duckworth had now accepted *Love Poems and Others*, and Lawrence corrected the proofs in October. Frieda did not have much respect for the collection: 'He has written heaps nicer poems than those "baby ones" some about his mother and lots since we have been together' (i. 449). Lawrence said her trouble was that there were 'too many heroines other than herself' (i. 462). But if this first collection amounted to a farewell to the past and its women – and as such should (he thought belatedly) have ended with the only poem in it addressed to Frieda, 'Bei Hennef' (i. 462) – then the completion of 'Paul Morel' would be even more so.

VIII 'Like life, but always my theme': *Sons and Lovers*

He had done half the rewriting of 'Paul Morel' by 3 October, and three-fifths by 15 October, when for the first time he announced the new title *Sons and Lovers* (i. 458, 462). By 18 November it was finished (i. 476).

The significance for a biographer of this final shaping of the novel is the paradox of its Janus faces – looking backwards and forwards at once, and lifelike, in being artwork. From one aspect it is a 'goodbye to all that', a retrospective coming to terms with the past. From another it is only possible because of the gulf which now separates a 'new' Lawrence from that past; and it anticipates both new growth in life and a new kind of art, though not yet fully grasped. It is both end and new beginning; an appropriate conclusion to one 'volume' of Lawrence's life (the first volume in this Cambridge Biography); and the threshold of another. As John Worthen's *The Early Years* reaches its end, the biographer's story and the fictive one stand side by side – related, yes, but demonstrably and significantly different. The fiction may be 'like life', and the product of Jessie Chambers's advice to make the third version more so than the second – yet her bitter complaint was precisely the freedom which Lawrence had taken, the degree he was prepared even to distort, in order to focus and clarify 'my theme' (i. 477). So though much of the density of its texture draws on memory, the biographer may also serve literary criticism by pointing out where the fiction departs from truth-to-life, freeing the critic to concentrate on imaginative and structural significance. 'Walter Morel' is not a 'true' portrait of Lawrence's father but (as the name privately registers) has been imaginatively heightened by much of the drunken violence of Lawrence's Uncle Walter. 'Mrs Morel' is of 'higher class' than her husband, but Mrs Lawrence was not, except in her own aspirations, accent and literacy. She was the daughter of an engine fitter who had lost his job through injury, and she had been rescued from poverty by her marriage. 'Miriam' recalls Jessie, but in a markedly selective and heightened fictiveness, demanded by the novel's theme and the system of comparison-and-contrast which explores it. 'Clara' draws on memories of three women, but is thus of course quite different from any.[92]

Frieda claimed the credit for a more sharply focused sense of theme. 'I think L. quite missed the point in "Paul Morel"', she wrote from Riva early in September. 'He really loved his mother more than any body, even with his other women, real love, sort of Oedipus, his mother must have been adorable – he is writing P.M. again, reads bits to me and we fight like blazes over it, he is so often beside the point ... ' (i. 449). Clearly the mother-poem she had reacted against so angrily had sharpened her eye, and ensured that she would determine to open Lawrence's, aided by what she had heard from Gross of Freud's ideas. Indeed, in *"Not I, But the Wind ..."* she turns around that poem's idea of being

42

twice born by his mother. 'I think a man is born twice: first his mother bears him, then he has to be reborn from the woman he loves' – but Lawrence had told her he could never have loved her in his mother's lifetime: 'she wouldn't have let me go'. Even now on Garda, his mother always seemed '*there* still to him', and he 'saw' her, vividly, in a little old woman on the lake steamer. At the end of the rewriting Frieda 'got fed up ... and wrote a skit called: "Paul Morel, or His Mother's Darling"', at which Lawrence was not amused.[93] The day after the manuscript was posted to Garnett she claimed: 'I feel quite responsible for "Paul". I wrote little female bits and lived it over in my own heart' (i. 479). *"Not I, But the Wind ..."* explains that Lawrence used to ask her how she thought both his mother and Miriam would have felt, so that she felt she too had 'lived and suffered that book'.

Yet Lawrence himself had already begun to stress the 'sons and lovers' theme in Icking, using the William story more clearly and fully to anticipate Paul's – and three versions of the novel lie behind his own growing insight, which he won slowly and cumulatively for himself.[94] Moreover, though he admitted Frieda's influence in making him more critical of Mrs Morel, he also cited her *example* to his own critical eye: 'She saves me, but can't save herself' (i. 462). Certainly his relationship with Frieda had made possible a much more critical view of Mrs Morel in *Sons and Lovers* than before; but it was also Frieda's own mother-feelings that helped him plot what Mrs Morel had in common with Miriam yearning over her little brother or the daffodils.

Nevertheless it was a new Lawrence, Frieda's Lawrence, who could say that he now loathed Paul Morel; who would finally bid a psychic farewell to his mother in two fine poems about the procession to the graves and their flickering candles on 1 November, the Day of the Dead;[95] and who steeled himself now to render the mercy killing of Mrs Morel and the near dereliction of Paul. It was clearly Frieda's Lawrence who wrote on 19 November – the day after he posted the manuscript – an extraordinary summary of the novel to Garnett, in defence of its '*form*', shaped 'patiently, out of sweat as well as blood':

It follows this idea: a woman of character and refinement goes into the lower class, and has no satisfaction in her own life. She has had a passion for her husband, so the children are born of passion, and have heaps of vitality. But as her sons grow up she selects them as lovers – first the eldest, then the second. These sons are *urged* into life by their reciprocal love of their mother – urged on and on. But when they come to manhood, they can't love, because their mother is the strongest power in their lives, and holds them ... As soon as the young men come into contact with women, there's a split. William gives his sex to a fribble, and his mother holds his soul. But the split kills him, because he doesn't know where he is. The next son gets a woman who fights for his soul – fights his mother. The son loves the mother – all the sons hate and are jealous of the father. The battle goes on between the mother and the girl, with the son as object. The mother gradually proves stronger, because of the tie of blood. The son decides to leave his soul in his mother's hands, and, like his elder brother, go for passion. He gets passion. Then the split begins to tell again. But, almost unconsciously, the mother realises what is the matter, and begins to die. The son casts off his mistress, attends to his mother dying. He is left in the end naked of everything, with the drift towards death. (i. 476–7)

It is no longer the tragedy of Paul – it is now both a family tragedy which keeps repeating itself, and the tragedy of 'thousands of young men in England' among whom Lawrence rather tactlessly includes Bunny, as well as Ruskin. 'Now tell me if I haven't worked out my theme, like life, but always my theme.'

No worthwhile fiction, of course, could be summarised so. Yet it was natural enough for Lawrence to insist on his structural 'form' – hoping to persuade Garnett (or de la Mare) that Part I had now been unified with Part II – in which the story of the Morel marriage, and the tragedy of William, and the failures in relationship of Paul, should all be seen as the same story. Yet this puts too much emphasis on 'my theme'. What makes Lawrence's novel 'like life' as well, is a kind of 'form' that is more like chiaroscuro than such heavy outlining and blocked-in structure could suggest, and that comes (as he went on to say) from a development that was 'slow like growth'. If the 'theme' shows how far Frieda's Lawrence has become able to understand his story by getting outside it, the 'lifelikeness' of the texture has much to do with the hatching of new insight into a fiction which has already grown through three previous stages, and with an authorial position still as much 'within' as 'outside' – the major differentiation from Joyce. Another of the Janus faces then is that the book is neither well-shaped artefact, now quite separate from its creator, nor disguised autobiography; because it is written by a Lawrence who is in the process of coming to terms as he writes, and as he shapes fiction out of life. Here literary criticism would go on to demonstrate how the point of view keeps shifting, sometimes almost sentence by sentence, now inside one character, now another, now authorial; how the sympathy of a reader keeps shifting too; and how much denser and more complex is the web of metaphor, and of comparisons and contrasts between the characters, than Lawrence's bald summary. But the point for the biographer must be to emphasise how in writing *Sons and Lovers* he was in fact writing a new self into existence, slowly, like growth, out of a past still embedded in the manuscript he was immersed in, but re-seeing now, month by month.

Though Jessie was wrong, then, to charge in her memoir that 'under the domination that had ruled his life' Lawrence had once more 'handed his mother the laurels of victory'; or when she testily contradicted any suggestion that Lawrence had meant to criticise his mother;[96] in another sense she was simply registering the continuing vitality and holding power of Mrs Morel within the

fiction. She had hoped that Lawrence's choice would alter as he relived the past
– but the self he was writing would not be built from denying what had been.
The essence of the new insight (and its tragedy) is that vitality itself may turn
destructive; that liveliness and deathliness are the obverse and reverse of each
other. Mrs Morel is attracted to Walter because his vitality is her opposite; but
by her seeking to change him according to her standards, he becomes degraded
and almost destroyed. When William falls in love, it is with a 'gypsy' quite
unlike and no rival to his mother, but that is also why he is always criticising her
and unable to come to terms with the split in himself; and why he works himself
into a breakdown, trying to cope with opposite responsibilities. Such judgement
however cannot deny or reject the qualities and energies in both William and his
mother which make them so vivid on the page, and make the strength of their
relationship life-giving, *and* destructive, and apparently inevitable. The writing
became a challenge to understanding not blame, still less rejection – but though
the understanding of the father had grown since 'Paul Morel', it had not yet
grown enough to suggest how such oppositions could be made creative.

   With Miriam and Clara, however, the splits are more obviously related to
divisions in Paul himself, and hence to self-diagnosis in Lawrence. It is this
which made him reject Jessie's objections to the 'pre-dating' of sexual consciousness. It seemed more important to show the oppositions as inevitably part of the
relationship, than to worry about when the characters first became conscious of
them. Moreover the structure of the probing of Paul, clearer in Gargnano than
in Eastwood, had requirements for 'Miriam', whether just to Jessie or not. The
decision not to make Paul a writer and intellectual – cutting out grammar school,
teacher training and university – also excised the very centre of Lawrence's
relationship with Jessie: their intellectual companionship, and what she called
her 'years of devotion to the development of his genius – devotion that had been
pure joy'.[97] This may have begun as a way of keeping the early versions of 'Paul
Morel' from getting too close to life, before Jessie herself changed that; but as
his vision slowly became clearer, it was helpful in other ways to keep Paul a
young worker who painted pictures. It concentrated attention on their relationship independent of his 'work'; and helped also to differentiate the pull of
Miriam from that of Mrs Morel, and hence to focus the split between different
sides of Paul. Lawrence could draw a sharper distinction than in life, where both
households loved books and the discussion of ideas, between the maternal life-
energy which urged Paul into achievement, and the spiritual and emotional
intensity of response to nature and art which makes Miriam unlike Mrs Morel,
and so draws Paul to her – without at all making her the nurse of his talent that
Jessie had been in life. This goes with a strong emphasis on Miriam's spirituality,
playing against Mrs Morel's much more secular and domestic view of things.
(Fiction may well have been essentially true to life here, but may also have

intensified for its own purposes.) So, once again, the novel will show the son strongly attracted by, but also strongly reacting against, what is unlike his mother. But in the story of the second son the pattern gets another twist, because the girl is also sufficiently *like* the mother to fight her for his 'soul'. Now the fiction underlines a string of ironies which Jessie was upset by, and which may have been unjust. Miriam is required to be as possessive, in a different register, as Mrs Morel; so that when the mother, or the son echoing her, accuses the girl of wanting to absorb, absorb, the ironies are reflexive. (The possessiveness in Jessie's memoir however, her jealousy and contemptuous dismissal of Louie Burrows, her certainty that her view of things was *the* truth about Lawrence, suggest that the fiction did have some truth to life. Yet some of Lawrence's feelings about *Frieda* will have got into the final portrait also, and the fiction required the emphasis.) Moreover, the reaction of Mrs Morel against the 'brutality' of Walter, which she had partly caused, is echoed in the reaction of Miriam and her mother against the brutality of their menfolk, which they have also partly caused. And this, in turn, has brought about in both Miriam and Paul an inhibiting 'purity' about sexuality, which means that she can only give herself as a sacrifice, and he can only take her by deliberately repressing part of himself. (Neville's evidence about Lawrence's squeamishness suggests that he may have foisted his own feelings onto Miriam, who was after all a farmer's daughter. Yet familiarity with farm-sex can easily go with a view of human sex as merely animal, which is the view of Lawrence's attraction to Louie that Jessie maintained.[98]) The 'love story' of Paul and Miriam then becomes a revelation of how the very things which attract him to the girl are also bound to repel him, as both treason to his mother, and reaction to how Miriam wants to hug his soul (but not his body) to herself.

The essential point, however, is that Paul and Miriam had become for Lawrence less a portrayal of Bert and Jessie than a means of analysing the split in himself, which his relationship with Frieda was helping him to see more clearly. The treatment of Clara's predecessor Frances Radford in 'Paul Morel' II suggests the rather crude terms of 'body' and 'spirit' in which this analysis began, before Frieda. It is already implicit that Paul will turn from a girl who is spiritual to an older, married woman, who will give him physical passion. (This probably meant that even *Sons and Lovers* would not explore, from the inside, what in fact its 'lifelike' art reveals without exploring, that there is a potential sexuality in Miriam despite her fear, and a courage despite her drawing back, which could have been encouraged into fulfilment by a less mixed-up and immature lover than Paul. Lawrence knew this perfectly well about Jessie, as his other stories about 'her' show. However, his use of Miriam to diagnose Paul's malaise could never have resulted in a choice of her against his mother; or in making a development of his love of Miriam the way to richer life for Paul.)

'Paul Morel' II stopped at an early stage of the relationship with the married woman; and unfortunately our knowledge of the third version stops at exactly the same point. Once again we cannot tell what Jessie read in April 1912. She wrote twenty years later that the character of 'Clara' was a composite of 'three people' (presumably Helen Corke, Alice Dax and Frieda); that the events 'had no foundation in fact' (an over-confidence, since we now know that Lawrence had slept with Alice, as well as Frieda); and that at the end of the affair 'Paul Morel calmly hands her back to her husband, and remains suspended over the abyss of his despair'.[99] It was almost certainly between early March and early April, while Lawrence was writing the last part of 'Paul Morel' IIIa, that he met Frieda (probably in early March),[100] told Alice Dax about her in a way that made clear their affair was over, and probably began to sleep with Frieda. However there is no way of telling how far he fictionalised from his experiences then; or whether the 'Passion' chapter (XII) we have now was created in Waldbröl as another of the changes he had in mind to make in revising. It may have been only in Italy with Frieda that he was able fully to grasp the essential distinction in *Sons and Lovers*: between the impersonal unity with the living universe discovered through sexual passion, and the personal relationship between individuals. Again, however, it is not the correspondence with life that matters most. One may be reminded now of Helen, now of Alice, now of Frieda, and may indeed think the fusion not quite perfect – but it is much more important to stress again how the relationship is structured in keeping with the diagnosis of Paul. ('I *loathe* Paul Morel.')

The very title 'Passion' was loaded, after Waldbröl, for it was there that Lawrence began to discover the difference between unstable passion and the total commitment of 'my marriage', a commitment Paul is incapable of making to Clara because of the split in him. The structure of *Sons and Lovers* makes it inevitable that the relation with Clara will fail for the reason opposite to the failure with Miriam. With Miriam, the personal relation feels like treason to his mother, and the split of 'body' and 'soul' (in them both) makes the impersonality and unconsciousness of passion feel like brutality. Yet without the dimension of 'soul' that comes from love between unique persons, the impersonal relation of sexual passion with Clara will satisfy less and less. Moreover Clara, who is as responsible for the brutalising of Dawes as Mrs Morel for Walter, values herself as person more than female, a point that could have been developed further, and might have unified the suffragist better with the suffering. Hence she belongs to the man who needs her as a person, her husband.

Paul's fight with Baxter Dawes may have grown out of a sense of guilt about both husbands, Henry Dax and Ernest Weekley – imagining also how, after a purgation of violent rage and hate, they might have become (gingerly) friends. The giving of Clara back to her husband is also a measure of Paul's malaise however, as *The Fight for Barbara* shows. Because of the split his mother's contempt for his father has produced in him, and because he is drawn to each woman by only half of himself, he cannot fight for either as Wesson fights for (and against) Barbara, and Lawrence for and against Frieda. His mother keeps her hold.

Here however Lawrence's summary for Garnett falsifies the most. So far from the mother 'almost unconsciously' realising 'what is the matter' and beginning to die, Mrs Morel, much truer to her character, holds on to life with so inflexible a will that her son has to help her out of it with an overdose of morphia. The act, however, secures a future. For though Paul is 'left in the end naked of everything, with the drift towards death' until the last sentence, that sentence sends him 'towards the faintly humming, glowing town, quickly'.[101] The last word retains its quick of life, though there is no knowing what he may find there.

Once again, we have no way of knowing how 'Paul Morel' III ended, and cannot assume that it was as now. We do know that Lawrence 'funked' tackling the death of Mrs Morel in Gargnano (i. 466), and that when he did so, he became ill. This suggests that the previous account was less harrowing, since there was no such distress in Eastwood or Walbröl, though Jessie did remember seeing him on Easter Monday at the station looking miserable.[102] It is unlikely, too, that 'Paul Morel' was as revealing of the secret knowledge of the nature of their relationship, that comes to mother and son at the end. It seems likely, and most distressing of all, that Lawrence only now decided to show the killing of the mother by the son – Oresteian rather than 'sort of Oedipus' (i. 449) – especially since it had its source in life. Beside this, the justification within the book of allowing a sliver of hope to Paul Morel (and the writing, whenever, of the two Days of the Dead poems), falls into place. Frieda seems to confirm that this was new – though her memory was not always trustworthy – by relating Lawrence's illness to 'all this "house of Atreus" feeling'. The otherwise inexplicable ignoring, in his summary, of the final sentence he had just written, might come from extreme reluctance to talk of how it connected with the final 'killing' of the mother – both in fiction and (it would appear from his admission a year later) in fact.[103]

The final 'kick against tragedy' had however also been prefigured by the shape of his own life, by 'Christs in the Tyrol', and by the rejection of the 'Writers among the Ruins' (such as Bennett and Conrad). He had done as much as he could to 'understand his own suffering, and see it take on itself the distinctness of an eternal thing', so that he could 'go on further, leaving it'.[104] *His* 'faintly humming, glowing town' had had Frieda in it – and through her, though always embattled, a new life, which helped him see and thereby begin to shed the sickness of the old.

In another more pervasive way, *Sons and Lovers* looks forward rather than back. What is strangest and most haunting is a new kind of utterance, behind the drama and the consciousness of the characters, suggesting a whole new perspective against which the human action has to be seen. When at the end of an ugly battle Mrs Morel is thrust out into her moonlit garden; when in a moment of guilt she tries to give her baby back to the sun; when Paul and Miriam stand before the rose-bush; when the scents of madonna lilies and iris precipitate Paul's decision against Miriam; and when in the field where the peewits cry Paul and Clara feel at one with the thrust of the grass stems and the wheel of the stars, the book begins to move decisively beyond 'character' and individual 'psychology'. Lawrence is becoming dissatisfied with an art confined to the 'personal', and has begun to feel his way imaginatively towards an art which can render impersonal forces (both unitary and 'singling out') below the level of consciousness, and help to diagnose more deeply the 'splits' which turn what ought to be creative into destruction. In such passages, the shape of potential integration begins to appear shadowily behind the experience of failure. It is still 'in the background'. Lawrence has not yet learned fully to articulate what he senses – but it is there, and is yet another reason why *Sons and Lovers* holds more than a tragic sense of life.

CHAPTER TWO

◆

November 1912–December 1913

NEW UTTERANCE

We are always just us two and we live so hard on each other ...
(i. 521)
And think, there will something come forth from us,
We two, folded so small together,
There will something come forth from us.
Children, acts, utterance ...
('Wedlock', V, 1–4)

I Unhappy Christmas

As Lawrence put his novel in the post on 18 November 1912, it must have felt like freedom. The next day he at last told Louie Burrows that he was living with someone he loved and hoped to marry,[1] and managed to say – though apology never came easily – that 'the wrong' of their broken engagement 'was all on my side. I think of you with respect and gratitude, for you were good to me' (i. 480). His battles would begin again soon enough. One of them was now to find a way beyond *Sons and Lovers*.

At first he was content to collect himself a little. He painted four pictures as Christmas presents;[2] he wandered into mountain villages above Gargnano; he gathered armfuls of Christmas roses; the Italian lessons continued. McLeod had sent 'a treasureful' of books which kept Frieda happy (i. 481), and re-introduced Lawrence to the fiction of Mark Rutherford.[3]

Then things began to go wrong. At the end of November Garnett wrote to say that *Sons and Lovers* was too long; though he also proposed to cut it himself. 'I sit in sadness and grief', Lawrence replied. 'I daren't say anything. All right, take out what you think necessary ... but don't scold me too hard, it makes me wither up ... I'm so afraid you'll repress me' (i. 481–2). He was upset enough to have said a great deal more, had it not been so important to get the novel accepted quickly and collect a much-needed advance; and had he not been so dependent on Garnett's support, advice, agency and friendship. Even so, pique shows a little with the news that he has been approached by an agent (probably Curtis Brown)[4] for an 'enterprising' publisher; a comfort 'after your wigging'.

Weekley was still being histrionic. Now he sent back Frieda's Christmas

50

postal order for the children, threatening death for the insult since 'that filthy hound' had signed it (i. 484). Early in December the von Richthofens made a 'grand onslaught' through Else (i. 485), to pressure Frieda into accepting a separate establishment with the children, provided she would break with Lawrence. Else urged him to sacrifice himself; but he denied the value of that. If Frieda could live happily alone with the children he would agree, 'But if she would only be sacrificing her life, I would not let her go if I could keep her.' For such sacrifice would prove 'a curse' to the children, and 'sap their strength because they would have to support her life as they grew up', always feeling they had 'to live *for her*, to pay back' (i. 486) – as his novel had forcefully disclosed.[5] Frieda stayed. Then Weekley countered with another ultimatum. He would divorce her only if she agreed to a complete severance from the children as well as from him; but that she could never accept. Nor however if there were a divorce, would she consider marrying Lawrence: 'She says a woman can only have one husband – only belong to one man' (i. 489); and worse, the idea of remarriage gave her 'creeps' (i. 498). Her angst over the children and her not valuing him enough to commit herself seemed again two sides of the same coin, undoing much of the good of her decision to stay.

Into a state of stress, then, arrived Harold Hobson, taking up an invitation to come for Christmas made in very different circumstances. He also arrived unexpectedly, ahead of his letter, as they sat at breakfast on 11 December (i. 488–9). It was brave, or very egotistic, or both. The elder Garnetts had noted his thick-skinned assurance,[6] but even so he must have felt some misgiving. Yet Lawrence and Frieda prided themselves on being unconventional; Lawrence had liked him; and all three felt they were to be congratulated on trying to put the past behind them – though Lawrence found it a greater strain than he would publicly admit. Hobson's cynicism and comic lamentations were still amusing, and Lawrence bravely proclaimed that he could 'trust H. as my friend now' (i. 489) – but there was tension. He stayed till New Year; and though he put up in the Hotel Cervo rather than the Villa Igéa where they had room but no bedding, and though company was welcome after three months alone together, the strain began to show.[7] Lawrence is rueful about Frieda pulling hairs from his tail instead of lionising him (i. 493–4), and must have resented being put down in front of Hobson. He writes a little sadly to McLeod that to have company is 'very jolly. But I'd rather you had come. I need one of my own friends rather badly just now' (i. 488). To make things worse, about 20 December he caught a 'venomous' cold and retired to bed with the blues (i. 490, 491), while Frieda and Hobson entertained each other.

Indeed the more his letters proclaim 'we've been awfully jolly together, the three of us' (i. 494), the clearer it becomes that Christmas itself was a disaster. To Bunny on the 29 December he is determinedly cheerful; yet when Frieda adds her postscript his customary interjections have none of their usual humour but are scrawled irritably across the paper (i. 494–5). He would not have liked her calling him, as much as Hobson who made a performance of it, a 'sad and tragic' figure; especially since Hobson's 'tragedy' is put down to his 'strong virility' having no outlet; while she claims to have discovered in Lawrence 'abysses of elusive, destructive, spiritual tragedy' – 'balls!' he scribbled; and '*Shit!*' when she went on to say that her tragedy over the children was 'child's play' compared to his. 'I had a hell of a time' – the truth comes out – 'L torturing me, H being that 'umpy, but now we have had some jolly days, peace and goodwill all round'. 'I dont fink' is Lawrence's comment. To a typical Frieda-whimsy about the sexy ex-sailor postman – 'Lawrence is jealous of him. I *do* love him, the sailor' – he rejoins 'balls-aching rot'. When she finally asks Bunny not to 'think nasty things about me ... I am really quite good and weep no more!', Lawrence scribbles 'Bitch!'; and when she finishes 'I appreciate your letters, though they dont appreciate me' – 'Arse-licking'.

The trouble went deeper than tension over Hobson, or Lawrence's jealous insecurity, or Frieda's urge to stick pins in him rather than admit his claims on her. To the elder Garnett she confesses: 'The tragedy was in its zenith just at Xmas; in spite of heroic efforts and loftiest sentiments [presumably Else's language and Lawrence's reply] one feels more like mincepies and parcels *almost* Xmas cards at that time and of course I was ignored by all my friends, the outcast' (i. 497). To tell herself (or be told by Lawrence) that she had chosen her lot, had not made it feel any better. Ghosts of Christmases past had clearly haunted this one. Christmas at the Weekleys' had the full German/English family and child-centred emphasis; and nothing could have brought home more devastatingly Frieda's childless and outcast state than the absence of cards, and the gap where Monty, Elsa and Barby ought to have been. As had happened in Germany, Lawrence's suffering over her suffering made it worse. In February, when things had improved again, she was able to see the double-sided effect of her grief: 'Lawrence is in a state of utter misery then and I can't help it much – Rejoicing on the one hand like *anything* that he cares so much[,] on the other the children and the misery of it' (i. 521). Her main feeling at Christmas however was how his constant enquiries tortured her: 'he chases my poor emotions, till they drop like panting hares' (i. 498). Ironically, the more tender and concerned he was, the more irritating his questions about the state of her feelings – especially if tinged with implication that her grief was somehow treachery to him. At the same time she confesses the ambivalence in herself which made him probe at her with such barbed tenderness: 'there are 2 sides to human love, one that wants to be faithful, the other wants to run, my running one was uppermost, but it's going to be faithful now. I used to think I should never have enough love, now I think I have got as much as I can swallow' (i. 498).

It is in this letter however that the mere idea of marriage gives her 'creeps'. Yet by 29 December things were on the mend. Weekley finally agreed to divorce her, and the legal requirement to have no direct communication meant at least that his hysterical letters would cease. *Look! We Have Come Through!* makes the New Year a turning point into new life for them both, out of conflict.[8] The divorce papers would be served on 4 March – when 'Signor Lavrenchy' saw himself described as one who had ' "*habitually* committed adultery." – What a nasty habit!' (i. 524). Hoping that Frieda might yet be awarded access, he approached a lawyer, Edward Garnett's brother Robert.[9] There was still 'haffling and caffling' about seeing the children in the Easter holidays (i. 523), but they expected that Frieda's 'sort of blind, stupid trust' would be rewarded, and that they would go to England then (i. 497). (Easter would be early, on 23 March.)

At the end of February, however, came another unexpected guest. They had never met Antonia Almgrem – known as 'Tony' Cyriax (her maiden name) – but had almost certainly heard of her, probably even that she had helped Bunny lose his virginity. She had married a fellow art-student in Sweden but had recently left him, and was now in great fear that he was pursuing her. This may have been paranoid; yet Constance Garnett thought him mentally disturbed,[10] and felt it so urgent to get Tony out of England fast that she was packed off to Gargnano, without waiting for a reply to the letter asking if she could come. A telegram arrived on 27 February (while they were discussing the letter), by which time it was already too late to get to Desenzano, the junction from Verona (i. 520). So Lawrence set out to meet her and her young daughter Gisela at Salò (i. 522).

The visit was not unwelcome. There was the problem of what would happen when Lawrence and Frieda went to England for Easter; but Frieda was glad of the company because, new start or no, 'We are always just us two and we live so hard on each other[;] one day like the lions that ate each other, there will be nothing but two tails left' (i. 521). Lawrence thought at least Tony could share the housework; 'I feel I've cooked cart-loads of food and scrubbed acres of dirty board' – but as he wrote this, Tony was 'prodding the cauliflower with a fountain pen', 'It explains the whole situation' (i. 523). Bunny describes her as 'cool and brown' with 'huge dark eyes which seemed to grow bigger as she responded to my father's teasing'; but she was also 'full of spirit' and would not be crushed. She had lived in Lapland; and Lawrence found her 'very interesting' – enough to make Frieda the jealous one this time, though not for long. 'I had a pang of jealousy because of her, but the bubble's pricked. L. approaches all people (women specially) as if they were Gothic cathedrals, then he finds that they are little houses and hates them for it!' (i. 533). Frieda admired Tony's independence, although 'she is chasing greatness as if it were a rabbit and she wants to put salt on its tail!' But (tartly) she thought the husband a fool to pursue someone so cold, especially since 'She is a sensationalist, [who] loves all this chasing game' (i. 534). Constance Garnett, who had not yet met Frieda, thought these comments acute.[11]

Soon they were able to settle mother and daughter in San Gaudenzio, a farmhouse up behind Gargnano on the way to Muslone, 'perched on the brim of the mountains over the lake, in a farm-stead of olives and vines, a situation beautiful as a dream'. It cost only 30 lire a month (about 24/-) as against 1.50 lire a night at the Cervo, 'and the folk *are* nice' (i. 526, 520). About 13 March they themselves were finding the lakeside getting too hot, and planned to leave for England 'in about a week' (i. 528).

This is from a letter to Jessie after eight months' silence, telling her to expect his spare set of proofs of *Sons and Lovers*.[12] She had written 'a damned affected letter' (i. 526) after receiving her copy of *Love Poems and Others*; but Lawrence too could show that 'it isn't so easy to write naturally to a quondam lover'. It was not a good idea to tell Jessie that 'Frieda and I discuss you endlessly' (i. 528) – and far worse was to come.

Though Easter was very close now, they did not leave as planned. For the end of the week brought Else Jaffe, on her way to Rome, with the news that Frieda would *not* be allowed to see the children in the Easter holidays after all. The idea of going to England was promptly abandoned, a truly bitter blow (i. 530). Frieda 'had looked on it as a dead certainty' (i. 531). Once again she was plunged into misery, with the usual effect on Lawrence who was already feeling seedy with another cold, caught during a sudden spell of rain. For a moment, by herself at the lakeside, Frieda was so 'flayed' by 'her misery' that she undressed, waded in and felt an impulse to slip under.[13] Things were made worse when Else, in rich-elder-sister mood, pressed them to join her in Rome instead. 'As she is a person who arranges other folk's affairs,' wrote Lawrence morosely, 'I suppose we shall go' (i. 530).

Moreover when Jessie looked into the proofs she decided to break with him altogether. In 1935 she claimed that she had only to glance at them to see that what had hurt her most remained unaltered. Yet her letter to Helen Corke on [16 March] describes a physical distress far worse than her response to the previous version in Spring 1912: 'I sit in front of the fire and shiver as if I had ague fits.'[14] In fact the novel she had read in 1912 had been very considerably altered – only, from her point of view, infinitely for the worse. Every page of what was now 'The Test on Miriam' had been rewritten; yet she would not have had to read far (beginning with the hurt of the title itself) to produce the reaction she described to Helen Corke. She quickly sent the proofs on to Ada, as she had been asked to do. Then she sent back the letter Lawrence had enclosed with them. Though at first he could not believe she had meant it, the breach was absolute.[15]

All this gave Lawrence 'the humpiest hump, O Gawd!', said Frieda, 'I am a heroic person, to stand him day for day, I tell you! ... I think I'll put him on a little stool in the garden like his mother, "now cry there, misery"' (i. 531).[16] However she later admitted that she had also given him 'a hell of a time, that's to say he took it over the children, I was so *very* sure to see them at Easter, it was a fixture in my head'. As the rain poured down; and Frieda went on and on about the children; and Lawrence got humpier and humpier but kept asking 'a dozen times a day in all keys, are you miserable' (i. 534); it must have been the Christmas misery all over again.

However at the end of March they decided to join Tony at San Gaudenzio instead of Else in Rome, and perhaps go to England later.

II How to Get Beyond *Sons and Lovers?*

(a) False Starts

We should remember however that Lawrence's was also a writing life, lived perhaps as vividly on paper as with people. Writing, he could both distance and focus the other life of relationship. Between 19 November and the end of March he was struggling not only to 'come through' with Frieda, but also to find a way beyond, around, an unrepeatable achievement. Each different attempt moreover reveals something he thought *Sons and Lovers* lacked – something (then) that needed to be added to the writing self which was also the man's mode of perceiving.

Even at Icking in August 1912 he had thought of doing a novel 'purely of the common people' (i. 431), and on 30 October, nearing the end of *Sons and Lovers*, he named his idea 'Scargill Street' – which ran across the hill, just below his birthplace in Eastwood, 'between the squares' of miners' houses.[17] As scholarship boy, Lawrence was an early example of a growing phenomenon: those working-class children whose 'higher' education cut them off from the world of their fathers. As long as his mother was alive, his writing showed little interest in the communal life and values of miners like Arthur Lawrence; though after her death the colliery sketches of Spring 1912 began to suggest what he might do in rendering the life of 'the common people', helped by focusing without reference to his own home, and despite his limited experience. As he grew more critical of his mother in writing *Sons and Lovers*, the sense may have grown of how much in his father's world had only been glimpsed in its pages, though by the time he saw the peasant family in Bogliaco the first part of the novel was already set. Yet his remark then how that family in its vitality and tenderness 'reminds me so of home when I was a boy' (i. 460), suggests the possibility of a very different view of a working-class home, perhaps, in Scargill Street.

After he finished *Sons and Lovers*, his father and his vivid language often came to mind. He sent him 5/- for Christmas and a letter which has not survived (i. 484). In January, Weekley's vacillation 'would wear the heart out of a wheel-barrow trundle, as my father would say' (i. 506). He may have the hump, but when Frieda sits on top 'it's as big as the "doom of St Paul's", as my father always says' (i. 534); and he uses his father's 'pottery' for 'poetry' when the critics do not seem to value his *Love Poems* (i. 536). Above all, a letter to the artist Ernest Collings[18] on 17 January forges another link between the Italian peasant and Walter Morel:

My great religion is a belief in the blood, the flesh, as being wiser than the intellect. We can go wrong in our minds. But what our blood feels and believes and says, is always true. The intellect is only a bit and a bridle. What do I care about knowledge. All I want is to answer to my blood, direct, without fribbling intervention of mind, or moral, or what not. I conceive a man's body as a kind of flame, like a candle flame forever upright and yet flowing: and the intellect is just the light that is shed onto the things around. And I am not so much concerned with the things around; – which is really mind: – but with the mystery of the flame forever flowing, coming God knows how from out of practically nowhere, and being *itself* ... That is why I like to live in Italy. The people are so unconscious.

It is *being*, being oneself, that is all-important; and one must (as Blake thought) act on one's desires, for the 'living of [one's] full flame' (i. 503–4).[19]

This immediately recalls the early contrast between Paul's mother and father – and suggests that Lawrence had been thinking again about how Mrs Morel destroyed the flame which attracted her

She was a puritan, who considered everything one did should be useful, either towards improving this world, or increasing one's chances in the next. Therefore the dusky, golden softness of his man's sensuous flame of life, that flowed from off his flesh like the flame off a candle, not baffled and gripped into incandescence by thought and spirit as her life was, seemed to her something wonderful, beyond her.[20]

Living in Italy had also made him more impatient with English class-consciousness. 'Scargill Street' would have had to avoid the fault he saw in Stephen Reynolds when he read *Alongshore* (1910) in December, that 'he swanks his acquaintance with the longshoremen so hugely. He writes *de haut en bas* like any old salt talking to a clerk from London – except that he's the clerk himself, carefully got up as the salt' (i. 488). He himself could 'get along with anybody', being 'common', but 'Frieda is a lady, and I hate her when she talks to the common people. She is not a bit stuck-up, really more humble than I am, but she makes the *de haut en bas* of class distinction felt – even with my sister. It is as she was bred and fed, and can't be otherwise' (i. 502).

However, even after laying his mother to rest in his novel it was too soon to be able to write an antithetical novel about a mining community. It would have come too close to home once more. There is no evidence that 'Scargill Street' was ever begun. Yet reading *The Revolution in Tanner's Lane*, just now, may have given him an idea of how to create more distance; for Rutherford's 'revolution' in the souls of a jobbing printer and the chapel folk of Cowfold began in 1814, and ended in 1840 nearly half a century before he wrote.

So when on 17 December Lawrence began to think seriously about writing again, it was an historical novel he now had in mind. It had to be fiction rather than poetry because he was '*resisting* too hard to write poetry – *resisting* the strain of Weekley, and the tragedy there is in keeping Frieda. To write poetry one has to let oneself fuse in the current – but I daren't' (i. 488). The new idea was 'a sort of life of Robert Burns', transporting him to the Midlands and feeling free to alter circumstances, but remaining true to the man. 'I have always been fond of him, as of a sort of brother' (i. 489). The novel was still to be 'of the common people', but a different kind. Though in the surviving fragments[21] the girl's father is a collier, come to work the gin pits described at the beginning of *Sons and Lovers*, the main concern is with country people working land hired from landlords, not unlike the Italian peasants. Indeed, while the first episode has to do with gathering wood in Sherwood forest, the scene soon shifts to an 'inn' very like the drinking places – mere rooms in peasant houses – which Lawrence had visited in Bogliaco and villages like Muslone, though also and quite naturally recalling 'Rollivers' in Hardy's *Tess*.

Yet if historical distancing might solve some of the difficulties of 'Scargill Street', the affinity between Burns and himself would create others. The danger was there from the start in the immediate move from 'He seems a good deal like myself – nicer in most ways', to 'I think I can do him almost like an autobiography' (i. 487). He might imagine similar but also refreshingly different experience: the struggle of a common man for education; the discussion groups of intelligent young working men; the friendship of brothers; the growth away from the father (ironically over the son's passion for dancing, but with no 'class' loading and within a context of respect); the sexual affairs and the clash with puritan morality; the short spell learning a trade; the development of the poet (though in *dialect* and convivial folksong); the feeling for nature and animals; the local success followed by the much greater one in the metropolis, but the consequent loathing of class-pretension and patronage – and the taking to drink, as seen now in a man he admired and loved as a sort of brother, and 'a man for a' that'. All this, together with the challenge of imagining conditions on the Notts/ Derby border in the second half of the eighteenth century, might well seem attractive. Yet how (with the temptation of autobiography) to avoid repeating oneself – even though several of the above themes had not figured in *Sons and Lovers*? Lawrence placed his singing-lad at the Haggs Farm, just beginning a love-affair with a girl called Mary Renshaw – the Midlands equivalent of

'Highland Mary' in whom Lawrence had declared his interest in the letter which first announced the idea of the novel.[22] He gives her a Scot's red hair and pink complexion, yet there cannot but be some *déjà vu* in lad-and-lass love in that familiar landscape. Yet there are also new things, if crude as yet: the sense of a *mysterious* life, both in the snared rabbit which the lad releases, made newly sensitive by the first encounter with the girl, and in the wonder of her face under his lips in moonlight: 'it was the darkness he was kissing, discovering. It was the night he had his mouth upon.'[23]

As Lawrence sat in bed on Christmas eve however, nursing his cold, chewing Italian nougat and 'writing a bit' at his new novel, he himself judged it 'so far more clever than good' (i. 491). (He also thought Collings quite right to prefer the contemporary realism of his *English Review* 'Odour of Chrysanthemums' to the historical romance of 'A Fragment of Stained Glass'.) Five days later he had decided to set the 'Burns novel' aside for something very different, and seems never to have touched it again.

His new idea shows what he thought had been wrong with it: historical fiction did not have distance enough, nor the life of Burns enough shape. Its successor, by contrast, would have 'a bit of a plot, and I don't think it'll be unwieldy, because it'll be further off from me and won't come down on my head so often' (i. 496–7). If this (as seems certain) was the fragment 'Elsa Culverwell',[24] he would get further from himself not only by having a heroine, but by writing in her first-person female. In 'Paul Morel' II[25] (before Jessie's advice) Lawrence had placed 'Miriam' not at Haggs Farm but in a family based on the Cullens of Eastwood: George Henry, the shopkeeper of 'London House' on the Nottingham Road, notorious for his unsuccessful schemes (clothing factory, private colliery, brickworks, cinema); his semi-invalid wife; their respected governess Miss Wright who taught Emily and Ada Lawrence music and young Bert French; and Miss Pidsley who managed what remained of the business. Miriam takes the place filled in life by Florence ('Flossie') Cullen, who trained as a nurse, then played the piano in the cinema, and who makes a brief appearance in the novel as the elder sister Lucy. When Jessie advised bringing 'Paul Morel' closer to real life, Miriam was restored to Jessie's background, and all the Cullen material was removed – to become now the setting for Elsa Culverwell.

She begins on a very firm note: 'My mother made a failure of her life. I am making a success of mine.'[26] The twenty surviving pages establish, as crisply, Elsa's memory of her home: that ineffectual enthusiast frittering his fortune away; the higher born mother who brought to her loveless marriage some money but not enough, and who so despised trade that she withdrew at last entirely into her dark bedroom with its huge mahogany furniture; the white-haired governess who became the invalid's prop and Elsa's surrogate mother; and the soft-spoken manageress of the clothing factory, which only made enough barely to support them because it was left in her capable hands. The situation is created with brio, not only because Lawrence had done it before, but also because his heroine is already so sure of the difference between her mother's failure and her own success. We hear casually that she has a husband now – and as the fragment ends she has just recalled meeting a working-class lad, son of a stonemason, who has 'the straightest stare in his blue eyes that has ever been seen since the Vikings'.[27] He is clumsy, but has a mind of his own, and his humorous defiance of his father makes her laugh. The contrast would seem, then, to be between a deathly marriage in terms of money and class, without sexual love; and a mésalliance in socio-economic terms, but founded on sexual fulfilment between very different people. The 'bit of a plot' seems likely to build from Elsa's determination to be independent – she has already begun to give piano lessons (as both Flossie and Miss Wright did) – and to make a life with the man of her choice, this one, or another, in spite of everyone's disapproval. The basic contrast is reminiscent also of 'Two Marriages', the early and (in 1913) still unpublished version of 'Daughters of the Vicar'.[28]

Lawrence now felt more strongly about 'class' however, and more emancipated from his mother's world, and this probably led to the abandonment of 'Elsa Culverwell', as we see from what took its place. Though 'Scargill Street' and the 'Burns novel' had proved unworkable, the newly imaginative sympathy with 'the common people' had by no means lessened. It was merely coming out now in anti-bourgeois form. To have conceived a heroine who must escape the deathly enclosure of class and money implies a strongly satirical purpose; but the first-person voice of a daughter was not perhaps ideal for excoriating the world of her parents. The sharper she became, the less attractive she might sound – and if Lawrence wanted to hit harder, third-person narrative might be more suitable as well as easier to handle. Moreover, having said he wanted greater distance, he had already succumbed to temptation again in giving the stonemason's son a Nottingham High School education, like his. He could only get himself out of the fiction – it would seem – by having a cast made up entirely of 'the common people', or by making the heroine rebel to still greater effect in third-person satire. In fact he chose both ways, one after the other.

(b) Non-autobiographical Eastwood

On 12 January 1913, apparently out of nowhere, Lawrence suddenly sent Garnett 'a new play ... neither a comedy nor a tragedy – just ordinary. It is quite objective ... laid out properly, planned and progressive' (i. 500–1). It was not of course out of nowhere. He had recently been watching, from Pietro di Pauli's box in the converted church that served Gargnano as a theatre, a travelling company perform 'Ghosts' and 'Hamlet' in Italian, and a play by

D'Annunzio[29] – vivid experiences that set him thinking in more ways than one. Though it had come quickly, *The Daughter-in-Law* is not only well-made but (arguably) Lawrence's best, and his most original play. For the letter to Garnett misses out the most important feature: it is in Nottinghamshire dialect. As Hamlet became revealingly 'other' when speaking in Italian, the 'sons and lovers' theme sounds quite different in the dialect of Arthur Lawrence. The play succeeds in being the work about 'the common people' he had wanted to write; and drama in dialect precludes the authorial condescension he had disliked in Reynolds. As an exploration of the miners' world moreover, there is implicit criticism of *Sons and Lovers*. The case against the dominating mother who has sapped the manhood of her sons can be more powerfully made, since dialect prevents Luther and the sharp-tongued Mrs Gascoyne from slipping into Lawrence-and-his-mother, or arousing partisan or guilty feelings attached to his own past. Each character has a fine part, a vital language, a fully imagined point-of-view, with no authorial thumb in the scale. No class-feeling clouds the vision. It is there however as subject, in damaging interplay with archetypal family tensions. The attitude to women of the sons of dominating mothers; the struggle for possession of a man between his mother and his wife; the instinctive alliance between brothers or mothers or wives; the relation between the working man, his woman and his money; the mores of work people regarding extramarital love and illegitimate babies; are all finely explored and dramatised – but also interestingly complicated because Minnie, the daughter-in-law who has taken Luther from his mother, seems to have moved into the grey area between classes. She has some education, has been a governess and has absorbed ideas and values very different from those of working-class wives. These both sharpen her conflicts with others and bring her into conflict with herself; for she is not really bourgeois. She has learned an English which differentiates her, but it is always accented, and slips occasionally and tellingly into a dialect still native to her. Moreover, the problem of how to achieve better man–woman relationship, despite the inhibiting and distorting forces in 'class' and 'family', gets yet another dimension from the analogy between power relations in the home and those in the coal-mines – about which miners and their women tend to have very different views. It is a good play, in which the characters release the problems rather than the problems and 'ideas' dictating the characters. This may be what Lawrence meant by hoping for an audience who wanted something different from 'the rather bony, bloodless drama we get nowadays – it is time for a reaction against Shaw and Galsworthy and Barker and Irishy (except Synge) people' (i. 509). Unfortunately, with the significant exception of Synge, Lawrence as dialect dramatist was far ahead of his time.

The play is indeed neither comedy nor tragedy. It reflects again the new opposition to tragedy of late 1912–13, and his faith that human beings have it in themselves and their relationships to transcend circumstance. Much is finely comic: the verbal duels between Mrs Gascoyne and Mrs Purdy, or Joe and his mother, and the funny and touching scene when Luther discovers that he is illegitimately a father. Yet the ending is by no means optimistic. As Luther weeps in the arms of Minnie, after they have apparently sent bourgeois aspiration up the chimney and seen off blacklegging, there is still a crucial ambiguity in Minnie's 'Oh, my love!', coming just after 'trust me—trust yourself to me. Let me have you now for my own.'[30] The words and tears can mean such different things – liberation, or new dominance? It is characteristic of Lawrence to end with a question rather than a conclusion, though he risks leaving the audience unsure.

In the same letter of 12 January, he announced the superseding of 'Elsa Culverwell' by a fiction whose satire would not be inhibited by having her narrate: 'I'm simmering a new work that I shall not tell you about, because it may not come off. But the thought of it fills me with a curious pleasure – venomous, almost. I want to get it off my chest' (i. 501). This is also the letter which comments on Frieda's inbred class-feeling.

Yet five days later, he tells Collings not only about his religion of the blood rather than the conscious intellect, but also about the religious importance of Frieda to him: 'It is hopeless for me to try to do anything without I have a woman at the back of me ... a woman I love sort of keeps me in direct communication with the unknown, in which otherwise I am a bit lost' (i. 503). How would these feelings consort with satire?

By 17 January he had already written 80 pages of the new venomous novel, 'a most curious work, which gives me great joy to write, but which, I am afraid, will give most folk extreme annoyance to read; if it doesn't bore them' (i. 505). One sees why venom about Eastwood might annoy those of Lawrence's folk who might read it; but why did he fear readers might be bored? Was it perhaps as reaction to what is harder to understand than social satire, because it seeks to explore the unknown? By mid-January he was being driven not only to satirise what he now thought deathly in his background; but also to clarify his 'religious' understanding of the sources of new life, as he had not done since (as a 22-year-old) he had voiced his rejection of Christianity to the Rev. Robert Reid.[31] Indeed it became necessary to explore this second impulse before going back to the new novel. But how best do it?

(c) Behind the Human Action

His first idea was to confront the problem directly, by reconceiving what he had rejected. On 17 January, 'Frieda is reading the bible, and suddenly announces "I rather like Christ". It seems funny' (i. 506). She read anything that came to hand, and had decided opinions which they would then argue about, but it is not clear why she was reading the Bible just then. Maybe she had finished everything else in the house – but Christmas in a Catholic country may also have interested her again in the Christianity of her youth; perhaps particularly in one of the Bible's greatest passages, the Gospel reading for the Eucharist on Christmas Day, the opening of the Gospel according to St John.

If *The Daughter-in-Law* widens the social vision of *Sons and Lovers*; the so-called 'Foreword to *Sons and Lovers*',[32] sent to Garnett on 20 January (i. 507), seeks to go behind the novel's characters and relationships, behind even the psychological dimension, to its religious significance: what *Sons and Lovers* had implicitly revealed about the nature of the universal creativity men call God, or the Gods. 'One has to be so terribly religious, ' he told Collings, 'to be an artist' (i. 519) – and for the first time he thought it necessary also to be a theologian, that is, to find language for the ideology embedded in the revelation of his own text. However he hastened to reassure Garnett, confronted by this strange document, that he had not the least intention of publishing it. He had written it in order to understand his own writing more deeply. What for instance had he meant, not only by the record of human failure in his best novel, but also by his belief in the blood as wiser than the intellect; and his feeling that he could only do his best work with a woman behind him to put him in direct communication with the *unknown*?

The 'Foreword' begins by asserting that St John got everything the wrong way round. Far from the Word having been made Flesh, it is the Flesh that is infinite, 'the Father' (or more properly the Mother) of all that is finite, i.e.'the Son', from Adam to Christ to ourselves. So, 'Out of the Flesh cometh the Word, which blossoms for a moment and is no more.' This bodily life-energy which brings every living thing into being, remains unutterable and unknowable in itself, but continues to animate everything, and be partially and temporally uttered by each thing, so long as it remains true to its own mysterious inborn being. However the command to love one's neighbour as one's self can become dangerous, and deny or desecrate the 'God the Father' in us, if we fail to understand the meaning of 'as one's self'. For the primary life-principle of everything is to be true to the God-in-it, the mysterious individuality which is aware, in the body and the blood, of what it needs and must do. If the 'Son' our *conscious* self, in its ideas of itself and of the other, either seeks to sacrifice itself to another, or to use another for itself, this makes the Son usurp the Father and will always produce ruin, as life-energy withdraws. (This is a deeper view of the sons-and-lovers theme, and bears also on Else's and Weekley's call for sacrifice.) Moreover the Word of conscious choice and obligation, cannot bind flesh to flesh. If a man and a woman are not one in the Flesh (in this religious but still bodily meaning) no Word (e.g.'marriage') can make them so or flower in them.

But if they are, the Word will confirm what is of the Father, and will therefore live and produce Him, through the finite Son (e.g. Lawrence with Frieda behind him) in utterance:

the flutter of petals, the rose, the Father through the Son wasting himself in a moment of consciousness, consciousness of His own infinitude and gloriousness, a Rose, a Clapping of the Hands, a Spark of Joy thrown off from the Fire to die ruddy in mid-darkness, a Snip of Flame, the Holy Ghost, the Revelation. And so, the eternal Trinity.

Conversely, to blaspheme against the Father in oneself *or* another is certainly to perish or become destructive (as his mother and father had).

Moreover, being with Frieda had taught him that it is also the wrong way round to think of Woman as born of Man; for as the Flesh was made Word to dwell among us, so

Woman lay in travail, and gave birth to Man, who in his hour uttered his word ... And God the Father, the Inscrutable, the Unknowable, we know in the Flesh, in Woman. She is the door for our in-going and our out-coming. In her we go back to the Father: but like the witnesses of the Transfiguration, blind and unconscious.

Rather, as the bee moves continuously between the hive and the flower, so man must move in a continuous creative rhythm between the source of his renewal in his woman, *and* his utterance, 'the glad cry "This is I—I am I!"', which is his life's work. 'And this glad cry when we know, is the Holy Ghost the Comforter.' But if the man does not come home to and 'utter' his woman in this way, if he 'deny, or be too weak' (his father, Weekley) she will inevitably expel him; and if she does not find another stronger man, or he another woman, they will both become destructive. He will consume his own flesh and destroy himself and his flame of life ('either with wine, or other kindling'); and she will wear herself out in sickness, or in fighting her man, or she will turn to her son and say 'Be you my Go-Between.' Then, since he can never be received as his mother's lover in the Flesh, the son will waste himself away, or tear himself in two, 'and his wife in her despair shall hope for sons, that she may have her lover in her hour'[33] – except, presumably, in the case of the author of the 'Foreword', who believes he has now found the ultimate and universal gospel which *Sons and Lovers* showed only in its negation, as did the Weekley and the Cullen 'marriages'.

Frieda says that they 'fought over' this 'Foreword' (i. 510); and though that may be only her way of claiming credit for helping to shape the argument, its final state may not altogether have pleased her. She would have approved the vision of woman as primary life-giver and creative source, which so corresponded to the picture of herself which Gross had given her. She might not, however, have liked the evidence that even now Lawrence could still slip into seeing his family tragedy through his mother's eyes, as the result of his father's weakness rather than primarily her denial of the 'flame'. And she might have queried the gender-specification which seemed (as yet) not to allow power of utterance to Woman – or, for that matter, being a source of renewal to Man.

But what is most significant for both the writer and the man is the new sense of human fulfilment as coming through a systole and diastole between *differently* creative life-forces, far beyond questions of character and motivation – each force 'divine', but requiring the other in order to be fully creative, so that only from their full interrelationship would come the fruition which had escaped all the people of *Sons and Lovers*. In that sense it *is* a Foreword, not to *Sons and Lovers* but to a deeper fiction, still to be written, about both marriage and self-integration.

Shortly after 26 January Lawrence tried another experiment, a less conceptual way of understanding the conditions for vital relationship, by exploring the aridity that must result when a woman and a man deny god-life to each other and in themselves. One of the editors of *Rhythm*,[34] Katherine Mansfield, had written to ask whether he had a story for the magazine. Lawrence suggested they might like to print 'The Soiled Rose' at the same time as *Forum*, which had bought it for America; and also that they might offer him something for review. He added, 'I shall be writing a short tale before many days are out, and I'll send it to you' (i. 507). What he seems to have written, but never sent, was a symbolic fable – perhaps remembering E. M. Forster's Pan-fable 'Other Kingdom', which he could have read in the *English Review*.[35] In this fictive form, he could start from a realistic situation, then build behind it a psychological dimension in the reverie of husband and wife, and finally suggest a kind of theological under-standing in the symbolic rhapsody of a young girl, reacting against their dryness with her youth and instinctive wisdom-of-the-flesh. So 'The Overtone' finally sees failed marriage in the light of a necessary relating of Pan to Christ.

Just before Christmas a letter had arrived from Sallie Hopkin, one of the few people he had told about Frieda.[36] He wrote two letters in reply, the second because he thought he had lost the first, which had in fact been posted. In both he says how odd it seemed that her letter had come just when he and Frieda had been talking about her 'for two hours' (i. 492). He speaks of the hard time they have had, but is confident that they are succeeding. Moreover, 'Once you've known what love *can* be, there's no disappointment any more, and no despair.' If people mostly fail, still 'they needn't doubt *love*. It's their own fault. I'll do my life work, sticking up for the love between man and woman ... I shall always be a priest of love, and now a glad one' (i. 492–3). Similarly in the first letter he had promised 'I shall do a novel about Love Triumphant one day. I shall do my work for women, better than the suffrage' (i. 490) – somewhat cheekily, given Sallie's suffragism.

'The Overtone' is not about Love Triumphant, but perhaps it was another necessary step. It begins with a married couple in their fifties, in a cottage on the river Soar one 'lustrous' summer night; he on the sofa, pretending to read; she talking to another quiet woman about the suffrage and the need for 'State-endowment of mothers'; while the young girl Elsa pays no attention to the words, but only accepts 'the feeling of the woman's heart as she spoke', which 'drifted also to the girl's heart, like a sort of inarticulate music'. It is the 'overtones' in this 'music' which the story (like the dreamy girl) picks up. Will Renshaw is handsome, blue-eyed and sandy-fair like a Dane, surprisingly youthful; Edith is beautiful and apparently harmonious both in her dress and her nature – they look rather like Sallie and Willie heightened – but *their* marriage is childless and will never ripen.

Responding to the moonlight now, Will is carried back to a crisis, six months after their marriage. Overcome by the beauty of the moon, the sense of life everywhere 'at a flash with itself', he had persuaded Edith to come with him up the hill to a ledge on the cliff above the river. There he begged her, as she stood back shadowy, to strip naked and make love in the moonlight without shame or stain. But she refused, and thereafter their love became mixed with hate and sterile. She thinks a man's body ugly, he gradually ceases to come to her.

Yet the girl, sifting a bowl of potpourri, feels 'the nights behind like a purple bowl into which the woman's heart-beats were shed, like rose leaves fallen and left to wither and go brown'. For Mrs Renshaw had waited for him, as a garden waits for sunshine and rain, till eventually it goes parched and hard. Now the music the girl picks up is a 'bitter psalm', the woman-garden's prose poem of complaint, like an inversion of the Song of Solomon. The girl, 'hearing' the despair, goes out into the night and weeps, 'For what should she do for herself.'

Renshaw calls out mockingly 'Come on, don't be alarmed—Pan is dead.' There is no need for a nymph to fear satyrs now. As Edith joins them, they recall how that cry is supposed to have gone up at the birth of Christ – and they stab at each other (and themselves) for the link between that death and the death of their love. The girl however bursts into a rhapsody, intuiting that Pan *and* Christ are as necessary, in their opposition and relationship, as night and day. She is a nymph of Dionysos, who must look at night in every man's eyes for the faun who will harvest and fulfil her. In the daytime of man and woman however, out of the wood, nymph and faun must touch the cross in conscious promise to 'deal fairly'.[37] So her rhapsody hymns both opposites, Christ and Pan, and the absolute need to participate in both though they differ as light from dark.

It no longer matters who was to blame for the drying up of the marriage, the woman who denied or the man who failed; and the gender-language of the 'Foreword' is turning into a sense of how, if love is to grow and triumph – as

Lawrence believed his and Frieda's would – women and men must fulfil themselves and each other in *both opposite modes*, without fear or inhibition, but also responsibly and with commitment. 'Pan' and 'Christ' are gods who must vitalise each lover with opposite yet complementary life-forces, for if either dies, so will love. 'The Overtone' is not much of a story, and perhaps over-lyricised – but it marks yet another step behind mere stories of character, motive and blame.

III   The Last of Gargnano

By 1 February Lawrence had gone back to his still untitled novel – it would become 'The Insurrection of Miss Houghton' – and had written another 26 pages, 106 in all. Significantly, his view of it seems to have changed, and the emphasis is no longer on its venom. He thought Garnett would hate it, but 'when it is re-written, it might find a good public among the Meredithy public' – presumably those interested in the difference between the true and the false ways of modern love: 'It is quite different in manner from my other stuff – far less visualised ... And it is good too. I think, do you know, I have inside me a sort of answer to the *want* of today: to the real, deep want of the English people, not to just what they fancy they want' (i. 511).

Between 5 and 18 February he also worked on the first batch of proofs of *Sons and Lovers*. Now that the full text is available one can see that insofar as it had been necessary to cut, Garnett had done so expertly, but also how much the cutting damaged the web of comparison and contrast, especially by truncating the vivid portrayal of William.[38] Lawrence tried to look on the bright side: 'It goes well, in print ... Don't you think I get people into my grip? You did the pruning jolly well, and I am grateful. I hope you'll live a long long time, to barber up my novels for me before they're published. I wish I weren't so profuse – or prolix, or whatever it is. But I shall get better' (i. 517).

By the 18th he had returned to the novel which was now 'going quite fast. It is awfully exciting, thrilling, to my mind – a bit outspoken, perhaps. I shall write it as long as I like to start with, then write it smaller' (i. 517). The emphasis seems to have shifted from the satirical to the serious, from the heroine's rejection of her bourgeois background, to the exploration of her relationship with her lover. For the rest of the month he moved between the new work and the proofs as they came – growing, however, increasingly anxious about money.

Indeed his willingness to accept Garnett's barbering had everything to do with the urgent need to get the novel published and earning. He was upset by the reviews of his *Love Poems*[39] – which meant even fewer sales. He still harboured the suspicion (after Heinemann's letter) that Garnett was under orders to expurgate the sexual scenes, but however annoying – 'I've got the pip horribly at present' – he was prepared to let Duckworth cut 'a hundred shady pages', for 'It's got to sell, I've got to live' (i. 526). Could Duckworth advance him £50, which would 'take me on five months or so' (i. 527)? (The previous £50 had lasted since 16 September.)

By 5 March the new novel – 'a weird thing' (i. 525) – was half done, but financial anxiety also began to affect it now, since the more serious it became about love, the more (for Lawrence) it had to deal outspokenly with sexuality, and the more danger there would be of non-acceptance by the circulating libraries which could make a huge difference in the sales of fiction.[40] Six days later he was telling Garnett:

I am a damned curse unto myself. I've written rather more than half of a most fascinating (to me) novel. But nobody will ever dare to publish it. I feel I could knock my head against the wall. Yet I love and adore this new book. It's all crude as yet ... most cumbersome and floundering – but I think it's great – so new, so really a stratum deeper than I think anybody has ever gone, in a novel ... It is all analytical – quite unlike *Sons and Lovers*, not a bit visualised. But nobody will publish it. I wish I had never been born. But I'm going to stick at it, get it done, and then write another, shorter, absolutely impeccable – as far as morals go – novel ... I'll do it – or else what am I going to live on, and keep Frieda on withal. (i. 526)

For three months he had been experimenting with forms new to him: an historical novel, a first-person narrative by the central character, a dialect play, a symbolic fable, and the first of his philosophical writings. Now imagination seemed to be taking him into territory uncharted by anyone, where a new kind of vision would need a new kind of art. The only hints of what he was attempting (since 'The Insurrection of Miss Houghton' has not survived) are what seem explicit criticisms of *Sons and Lovers* by an author trying to go 'a stratum deeper', however crudely as yet. He has become uneasily aware that the struggle to unify *Sons and Lovers* had given the characters more definition than he is happy with now, 'putting a thick black line round the figures to throw out [i. e, emphasise] the composition' (i. 522). The absence of the 'visual' implies less interest in external description and drama, as emphasis shifts from character-in-action to exploration of what could be felt only in the blood. (This had begun in *Sons and Lovers*, though still often starting from the visual: Mrs Morel's garden or Miriam's rose bush.) '[A]ll analytical' implies the psychologist's attempt to understand movements of consciousness that the characters themselves cannot. Yet how reconcile this struggle for a new art with the fear that it may not be publishable?

In the upset and depression that came with Else's visit, and resulted at the end of March in the move from Villa di Gargnano up to San Gaudenzio high above the lake. Lawrence finally decided to set 'Miss Houghton' on one side and get on instead with the 'impeccable' novel that would sell. By 22 March he had begun 'The Sisters' and written 46 pages – but though he tried to cheer himself that 'Miss Houghton' would 'be none the worse for waiting a while' (i. 530), it remained the one he cared about.

The need to earn some money also produced, before Lawrence and Frieda left Gargnano, an appropriate farewell: the three sketches of 'By the Lago di Garda', sent first for family reading to Ada, but then to the *English Review* which published them in September. Though the *Westminster* had only taken three of his German travel sketches,[41] they had paid quite well, and must have given him confidence in his talent for such things and in the market, especially since he now had sunnier and non-political subjects readily to hand. The performances of 'The Theatre' took place between 28 December and 16 January. 'The Spinner and the Monks' is set on a Saturday in early February. The weather took a marked turn for the better then, after the bad spell of gales and snow in the second half of January, and on Monday 10 February a letter (i. 514) describes the profusion of flowers mentioned in the sketch, though weather-boards would still enclose the lemon garden of Pietro di Pauli. The same day Lawrence told Else the *English Review* had asked him for an article on German women poets, and suggested she should do it instead.[42] He may have begun to think of his alternative then, though he probably finished between setting 'Miss Houghton' aside and starting the new novel – and for the same reason.

The Italian sketches are vivacious and often humorous, observant, evocative – without the 'philosophical' significance they would acquire when rewritten into *Twilight in Italy* two and a half years later. The old woman on the terrace of San Tommaso spins in the present while the monks below move only between past and future: the pale murdered body of their Lord and the white light of the spirit to come. In the Casa di P., Lawrence reflects on Italian man, wife, child; and in the 'Lemon Gardens', on the economic facts which are changing the landscape. In the theatre the performances of Enrico Marconi ('Enrico Perse-valli') and his company bear on the truth of the blood as against the intellect and, therefore, confirm Lawrence's dislike of Ibsen and of Hamlet. At their most serious, the comments are those of an intelligent man on what happens to be before him, without philosophical pattern; while at its lightest the vivacity can thin into whimsy or cuteness. The predominant impression, however, in this first extended and light-hearted tribute to Italy, is of Lawrence's sheer enjoyment and awakening, the fact (as he wrote to May Holbrook) that 'shifting about breaks down a lot of barriers' (i. 499). He had made a home in Villa di Gargnano, under no obligation to anyone, and though there had been hard times with Frieda 'the stress of my own life would have been a hundred times harder, if it hadn't been for this lake' (i. 499).

IV   At San Gaudenzio, and Irschenhausen

They were only to be a fortnight in San Gaudenzio with Tony Cyriax (though she stayed on, and wrote a book about it); but it was a happy time, and significant, since from it dates the beginning of Lawrence's greatest work. There too he became 'Lorenzo', named by Tony's daughter (i. 538). It was a 'lovely place', with vines and olives stretching to the cliff's edge above the lake; and a sunny lemon garden where he sat to write.

The mountains are covered with snow opposite. – Then the Capelli – the people – are *fearfully* nice. The place is almost like an inn – illegal, there is no licence – so that people are always coming – handsome young men who are conscripts and just about to flee to America, and so on. One need never be alone ... Last Sunday there was a band – cello, mandoline and two weird guitars – playing all evening while we danced. Nay, even there was a wild and handsome one-legged man with a deltoid like a boss of brass, who danced Frieda, and then Tony, like a wooden-legged angel. (i. 535–6)[43]

It will be seen from this that Lawrence might have gone on here to write early versions of the other essays which would eventually make up 'On the Lago di Garda' in *Twilight in Italy* – but he almost certainly did not.[44] There is no evidence of such early versions, and a great deal which suggests that Lawrence's 'memories' were reshaped under the influence of *The Rainbow* and to serve the thematic and artistic purposes of *Twilight in Italy*. (Sometimes they seem invented.)[45]

What he *was* writing in the high and sunny lemon garden, looking out across the lake, was the fiction that had replaced 'Miss Houghton' and would eventually turn into his greatest work. 'I did 200 pages of a novel', he told Bunny on 5 April, 'a novel I love – then I put it aside to do a pot-boiler – it was *too* improper. The pot-boiler is at page 110, and has developed into an earnest and painful work – God help it and me' (i. 536). What had made 'Miss Houghton' improper had also transformed the 'pot-boiler': his serious concern with sexual relationship.

At the same time he was bidding a last farewell to *Sons and Lovers*, 'so sick of the last lot of proofs ... that I have scarcely patience to correct them'. He asked Collings to do a sketch of a coal-mine for the cover; and just before they left to meet Else in Verona on 11 April (i. 538) he sent off the last proofs – a symbolic act. It was 'the end of my youthful period' (i. 551).

Else was on her way back from Rome to Germany, but Lawrence and Frieda's plans had got no further yet than Munich. They might stay with Edgar, or go on with Else to Heidelberg to see Weber; or house-sit for her in Wolfratshausen before going on to England (i. 539). (Though Duckworth had advanced the £50 Lawrence had asked for, they still had to watch expenses.) After two days in

Verona they caught the overnight train to Munich on 14 April, but then disagreement surfaced. After the renewed onslaught by Frieda's family at Christmas, Lawrence felt uneasy about living in their pockets; and wanted to go to England quickly, even if he had to go alone. Naturally, Frieda wanted to spend some time near Else. Lawrence's health settled the argument; he caught another 'frightful cold' coming from 'warm Garda' and finding Bavaria under snow. Moreover, he had 'a horror' of Frieda's new notion that she would see the children 'by hook or crook – chiefly by crook' (i. 542), by lying in wait as they came from school. It seemed best to stay a while, and let the Baroness see whether the children might be allowed to come to her at Baden-Baden, where the von Richthofens had now retired, and Frieda could visit also. Moreover, Edgar offered the use of his new chalet at Irschenhausen – where they could be alone together, close to Else, but not too close.

Lawrence was not pleased to be back. Germany seemed 'narrow and cruel' after Italy; and he felt – especially reading *The New Machiavelli*, though he admired Wells – that England would be as depressing (i. 543). That was partly owing to his illness; but he felt moral disapproval coming, as soon as they turned their faces north. Italy 'is so non-moral' and 'leaves the soul so free'; whereas over Germany and England 'like the grey skies, lies the gloom of the dark moral judgment and condemnation and reservation of the people. Italy does not judge. I shall want to go back there' (i. 544). Though the Jaffes probably made no such judgement – given their own situation – they may have warned him about exposing Frieda to the condemnation of conventional people. They were being hidden away again. 'We feel awfully at present', wrote Frieda, 'as if nobody would have anything to do with us, quite outcasts we feel!';[46] and Lawrence noted how 'Heaps of folk love me alone – if I were alone – and of course all the world adores Frieda – when I'm not there. But together we seem to be a pest' (i. 546).

He was further upset by hearing more from Edward Garnett now about Jessie Chambers's reply to *Sons and Lovers*: her novel 'The Rathe Primrose',[47] which he now asked Garnett to send. Her returning his letter had hurt; so, now, did news of her judgement of him:

It's all very well for Miss Chambers to be spiritual – perhaps she can bring it off – I can't. She bottled me up till I was going to burst. – But as long as the cork sat tight (herself the cork) there was spiritual calm. When the cork was blown out, and Mr Lawrence foamed, Miriam said 'This yeastiness I disown: it was not so in my day.' God bless her, she always looked down on me – spiritually ... And look, she is bitterly ashamed of having had me – as if I had dragged her spiritual plumage in the mud. Call that love! Ah well. (i. 545)

Frieda was even less fair, as she leaped to his defence.

Miriam's letter [presumably to Garnett] hurt me; that she should only think with bitterness of all the good things they had together, seems hardly credible! L. *had* loved her, and when she sent his letter back, he *wouldn't* believe; the generosity lies on his side, seems to me! She says: my aim has been to preserve the integrity of the spiritual values! Oh, those spiritual values! People must be mean and pigs to want spiritual values as if they weren't there! He never did her the wrong of spiritualizing her altogether, but she idealized him, the worst of crimes in love! Don't you think one wants to be loved with one's littleness, one's everything of shame and all; but after all he left her; and her world is nothing now, quite empty, after he had made it full for her! He left her behind in her old world of 'spiritual values'.[48]

She has learned something about Weekley and herself, but is unimaginative about Jessie's situation, if acute about her spiritualising. She was reacting against her reading too: the Polish dramatist Wyspianski seemed: 'All guilt and bad conscience, conscience mad.'[49]

Lawrence however liked the little wooden house in its hilly meadow at the edge of a fir-wood, looking out at the Alps.[50] 'It is lonely. The deer feed sometimes in the corner among the flowers. But they fly with great bounds when I go out. And when I whistle to a hare among the grass, he dances round in wild bewilderment' (i. 543). If they were to stay for 'a month or two' until the school summer holidays, he would try to finish the new book which was growing strangely. 'I am doing a novel which I have never grasped. Damn its eyes, there I am at page 145,' – on 23 April – 'and I've no notion what it's about. I hate it. F. says it is good. But it's like a novel in a foreign language I don't know very well – I can only just make out what it is about' (i. 544). At the beginning of May he tells Garnett, who had been away, about the abandonment of 'Miss Houghton' – still 'next my heart' – and the new novel which 'seems to have come by itself', now 180 pages.

It will only have 300 pages. It was meant to be for the 'jeunes filles', but already it has fallen from grace. I can only write what I feel pretty strongly about: and that, at present, is the relations between men and women. After all it is *the* problem of today, the establishment of a new relation, or the re-adjustment of the old one, between men and women. (i. 546)

He expected to finish 'The Sisters' in a month. The pressure to complete a novel that the libraries would be sure to take was stronger than ever. Sure enough, *Love Poems* had sold only 100 copies owing to the reviews. Even friends (he thought) had been afraid to praise 'for fear of the folk coming down on them for immorality' (i. 548). This made an ironic contrast with his own praise of the first *Georgian Poetry* – including his 'Snapdragon', omitted from *Love Poems* – when the editors of *Rhythm* took up his offer to review for them. From Gargnano he had hailed the anthology as a burst of non-Christian but religious joy in natural life, starting from joy in being 'ourselves': 'It is the return of the blood, that has been held back, as when the heart's action is arrested by fear. Now the warmth of blood is in everything, quick, healthy, passionate blood ... To love passionately, but completely, is our one desire.'[51] (The other Georgian poets may have been a little surprised!) Moreover the fate of *Love Poems* seemed a bad omen for *Sons and Lovers*; for if that 'does not go, I shan't have enough money to return to the South. It's touch and go with me now' (i. 548).

Yet he never hesitated to follow where his exploratory imagination and his deepest concerns were taking him, as they began strangely to transform the pot-boiler. By 13 May it was two-thirds done; by the 17th he had written 256 pages 'but still can't see the end very clear' (i. 548, 550); by 1 June he was on p. 283; and he finished a few days later (ii.20). Only the ending has survived, but this, though novelettish compared to what it would become, reveals that 'The Sisters' was the precursor of *Women in Love* (as the story of Anna Houghton, his answer to the 'acceptance' of Bennett's Anna, of the Five Towns, was of *The Lost Girl*).

As 'Miss Houghton' had begun from satire on bourgeois Eastwood before going on to deal seriously with the sexual insurrection of her marriage; so 'The Sisters' began at the expense of Frieda, or at least one side of her. Garnett was sent the first half in May and seems to have responded sardonically. 'We roared over the "remarkable females"', wrote Frieda, 'you just hit them! The worst, it's like his impudence, they are *me*, these beastly, superior arrogant females!' (One of them may in fact have been drawn from Else, with Lawrence's mixed feelings.)

Lawrence *hated* me just over the children, I daresay *I* was'nt all I might have been, so he wrote this! I know now why Göthe wrote *Iphigenie* ... so superb she is, but I ll be hanged if any man wants to love her, as well be married to the tablets of the ten commandments, though mind you a man looks for that in a woman too! The book will be all right in the end, you trust me for my own sake, they will have to be women and not superior flounders – (i. 549)

Lawrence for his part says he knew all along what ailed the book, and promises to make it right. 'I shall put it in the third person ... But it did me good to theorise myself out, and to depict Friedas God Almightiness in all its glory. That was the first crude fermenting of the book. I'll make it into art now' (i. 550). Until Garnett's letter Frieda had rather liked 'her portrait in straight pleats and Athena sort of pose', but he had been teasing. One von Richthofen sister was a bluestocking and a manager of other people's affairs, and though Lawrence liked her he did not enjoy being managed. The other had decided opinions also – in the same letter she speaks of her tendency to lay down the law as 'Ellaing' (i. 550), like her fictional counterpart. But if, as had happened with the satire of 'Miss Houghton', the teasing had turned serious and 'theorising', it will have been about the blood versus the intellect in the sisters, and whether such modern women, 'superior flounders', superb Athenas in pleats, could love and be loved. Unfortunately the Ella story has completely disappeared; but it is likely that the same question was being asked there, and the novel grew 'painful' too about the men.

This was certainly the case with Gerald, in the ending (pp. 291–6) that has survived.[52] Gudrun, pregnant with his child, confronts him and Loerke ('a decent fellow, really'). Gerald now wants to marry her, and though she suspects it may be only because of the baby, she takes him back. Loerke however accuses him of trusting to his position to play with women, and his strength to threaten men; and he is forced to see the German's face 'broken into lines of real agony'. Gerald keeps saying he didn't '*know*' whether he could love Gudrun; but in this scene he is like 'a creature that follows its instinct blindly'. Now he can accept humiliation before Loerke, and find tears of tenderness. 'He was something he had feared he never could be: he had got something he had pretended to disbelieve in. And, breathing hard, he knew that this was his life's fulfilment, and a wave of faith, warm, strong, religious faith went over him.' Only, he is forced to measure the damage his inability to love has caused; and 'his forehead' is 'hard with pain' as Gudrun draws him to her at the end.[53]

We know nothing of Ella's man, but since the book had been 'flippant' (ii. 68, 165) and 'often vulgar and jeering' (ii. 165) at the sisters' expense, and since Lawrence had tried first-person narrative again, the mockery probably came from Ella's lover as narrator. This might connect the fiction with the mood of the last 'Gargnano' poems in the 1917 sequence *Look! We Have Come Through!* – though (again) we cannot be certain of the date of these. In 'Lady Wife' he refuses to be grateful for her condescension – like the angels to Abraham – in staying with him:

> 'Rise up and go, I have no use for you
> And your blithe, glad mien.
> No angels here, for me no goddesses,
> Nor any Queen.'

'Loggerheads' mocks her

> ... stock-taking
> Of my manly breast;
> [to] Find out if I'm sound or bankrupt,
> Or a poor thing at best.

'Both Sides of the Medal' refers to Hobson's visit and explores the hatred *in* sexual love.[54] In the poems 'dated' from New Year to St Valentine's Day however, cleansed by desire and hate, man and woman are reborn of each other and into spring, 'placed' in San Gaudenzio.[55] We do not know how much later hindsight went into these poems as we read them now. Yet it may be that Ella's lover in the new fiction too, like the tale he narrated, might have had to grow out of jeering into an earnest and painful learning to love; in which case even this 'first crude fermenting' may have anticipated the central story-line of Ursula and Birkin, in the great novel that eventually grew out of it.

Yet no sooner was 'The Sisters' finished than Lawrence realised that both the first-person narration and the flippancy had to go – the one perhaps the cause of the other – especially if his fiction were to do his work for women and for 'Love Triumphant'. (There was already a formal difficulty in that much of the Gerald/Gudrun story, taking place in private, had to be in the third person anyway – like the fragment that we have.)[56]

Nor did the springtime with Frieda outlast the move back to Bavaria, and the disagreement about what to do, and his illness. Once again (in June) 'the trouble about the children has knocked us both a bit loose at the joints' (ii. 21). Indeed Frieda had run away again to Else's at Wolfratshausen for two days – having, this time, broken a plate over his head while washing the dishes.

> I was astonished I thought I was mild and good! My small nephew *was* shocked at my departure, he loves L, he said: Tante Frieda, now you will get tired of this man and 3 uncles from one aunt are too much! He was distressed! However we are L and I such friends, I will wear a fragment of that plate in a locket round my neck ... No, no, love is no crucifixion, or if it is, then it will rise from the grave on the third day (after a broken plate or two!). (ii. 23–4)

Thus the first violence recorded in the marriage came from her (however deserved); but she signed herself jauntily by his new name for her, 'The one and only ... Phoenix' – and the next day they left for England, at last.

The stay in Irschenhausen had also produced three stories of disturbing new psychological probing. Lawrence once referred to 'New Eve and Old Adam' as autobiographical (ii. 21), but his title finally proclaimed his sense of its generality. What is newest moreover, is the concentrated attempt to render undercurrents of feeling and spasms of behaviour which remain largely mysterious to both wife and husband; which they do not intend; which indeed run counter to their sense of themselves and the strong physical attraction that draws them to each other. Under the surface of their year-long love there goes on 'almost continuously that battle between them which so many married people fight, without knowing why' and which renders them 'elemental, like impersonal forces'. It happens almost unconsciously. When the woman is fascinated by the telegraph-workman suspended free in space above the houses; when she rebels against Brahms's tempo as she plays; when she uses the telegram from a mysterious 'Richard' to assert her right to seek from other men the simple warmth and rest her husband Peter (she says) never gives her; we seem to be looking not only at *this* character, but at an intense female longing for 'independence' which must inevitably (almost generically) rebel against the commitment of love and marriage. The response of the 'old Adam' in Peter Moest seems a no less inevitable gut reaction: to the undertone of triumph as she fondles him; to the infinitesimal 'twist' in her apparently tender look 'that could not come loose to him' and so easily turns to hate; and to 'that curious little strain in her eyes, which was waiting for him to submit to her, and then would spurn him again'.[57]

Lawrence gives to Paula what sound like Frieda's charges at her angriest: that the man is afraid to trust himself to love her; that his loving seems (still like Paul's of Clara) an impersonal instinct that has no sense of *her*; that his very closeness wears her out; that he seems to use her up and give nothing back.[58] 'Sometimes' (and here the story *is* 'autobiographical', since the husband is a businessman not a writer) 'she thought he was a big fountain pen which was always sucking at her blood for ink' – and all this despite sexual satisfaction.

What they can *say* to each other, moreover, doesn't make sense. What does she mean by saying she '*must* have rest', when she does not do anything? Or that he 'uses [her] soul up'?

"... *I* don't know what you do, but it is something ghastly." ...

"It is very vague, " ...

"I know ... I can't put it into words—but there it is—You—you don't love. I pour myself out to you, and then—there's nothing there—You simply aren't there." ...

"We have come to the incomprehensible ... "

Only when she has gone off ostensibly to meet the other man, while her husband lies sleeplessly in the dark, does he begin to listen to 'that dark, unknown being, which lived below all his consciousness in the eternal gloom of his blood'; on top of which thought merely spins like 'the iridescence of oil on a dark stream'. In that medium he can begin to sense how her inner being recoils from the very intimacy she had desired, but (deep within) cannot bear, because she wants her life for herself – and how his own blood, 'moved to its depths by her revulsion', nevertheless 'heaved and swung towards its own rest, surging blindly to its own re-settling' – though he suffers more than ever before.

The rest of the story switches between mental and blood-consciousness. The telegram is soon explained: it was meant for a namesake, and only used by Paula to hit at her husband. There is however new cause for anger as she becomes excited by a mission to 'save' the young sender – another von Henning, or Hobson – which seems to confirm to her husband that there is 'no core to the woman. She was full of generosity and bigness and kindness, but there was no heart in her, no security, no place for one single man.' When he tries to do her justice, and think about her charges against him, he cannot understand and feels only resentment. Only when his blood strikes 'like flame across his consciousness' as she comes to him does he feel 'the deadness going out of him; the real life, released, flowing into his body again.'[59] Tension is suddenly gone. But will she ever really give herself to him as a wife, rather than as a mistress? Will he ever be able to trust himself to her? At the end they have separated again, and are denouncing their ideas of each other in terms of their mental consciousness once more. The story has no resolution; but the terms of its questioning seem clear, and coming as a kind of epilogue to 'The Sisters' it suggests the kind of exploration the new fiction was aiming for, at its most 'earnest and painful'. It is moving beyond the conception of character which largely governed *Sons and Lovers*, to some sense of more hidden and archetypal blood-impulses within the tensions of marriage – though their ultimate nature and cause, let alone the way through them, seem no clearer yet than (probably) in life.

The two German soldier stories, 'Honour and Arms' (later renamed 'The Prussian Officer') and 'Vin Ordinaire' (later re-named 'The Thorn in the Flesh'), are not autobiographical at all – but they push to extremes this new sense of how powerful but subconscious impulses may drive people to unwilled and 'abnormal' behaviour, apparently counter to their conception of themselves; and here wholly destructively. ('I was astonished', cried Frieda, 'I thought I was mild and good.') Both probably derived from Frieda's anecdotes about her father. He 'appears' in one; and an incident with his orderly may lie at a distance behind the other,[60] though the brutality of its officer is heightened beyond all portraiture. Both push to extremes Lawrence's antipathy to German militarism in the sketches of 1912; and his sense of cruelty in the air of Bavaria in 1913. However, both stories also have deeper concerns than the brutality that can be involved in soldiering and its power structures – though that is where they start.

'Vin Ordinaire' was the last of the three to be written, but is perhaps worth discussing first, since it shows an Eve and an Adam who lack courage to act on new knowledge. This is the story of the soldier who wets himself, in his horror of height, when he is forced to climb a rampart. As the sergeant's face thrusts at him in rage, Bachmann throws an arm up defensively, knocking his tormentor over the edge – and walks away, a deserter. His actions are all reflex; to *walk* away proves he has no idea what he is doing. Equally on impulse he seeks refuge with a maid-servant, who works in a big house nearby. She shelters him; but in this first version neither is able to carry through the moment of passion they experience in their stress. He spends the night alone in her room, passively waiting; while she shares the room of the governess, in frustration and some hate. 'It was for him to finish what he had begun. Every fibre of her hurt with a kind of painful sensibility of him! Why could he not set her free to be herself again?'[61] The next day he is arrested, and at the end she faces her employer, unable to understand the Baron's tone, which oddly blends raillery with anger. Ideas of themselves have been ruptured by revelations of the blood: Bachmann is not the handsome soldier, a bit of a daredevil, that he seemed; the girl is not the puritan virgin proclaimed by her room. But because neither of them acts on their new knowledge, the tragedy is unrelieved by anything but the Baron's anger (unconscious, and amoral) at a life wasted, a road not taken – which reveals something also about the Baron's life. It is not a story of the wisdom of the blood, but of vin ordinaire, thin and sour.

It was however 'Honour and Arms'[62] that Lawrence was most proud of as he was leaving Irschenhausen: 'the best short story I have ever done' (ii. 21). In its extremity it is indeed a turning point in his view of character, and (unlike 'Vin Ordinaire') it achieved virtually its final shape at first writing. The previous November, Lawrence had been reading Garnett's play about Joan of Arc and a pamphlet about atrocities in Persia, and concluded that 'Cruelty is a form of perverted sex', to which celibate priests and soldiers with only casual women were particularly liable. 'It is sex lust fermented makes atrocity' (i. 469). So 'Honour and Arms' – the title an irony on ideas of respect and rank – deepens military bullying into something more sinister. An officer, unsatisfied by casual affairs with women, is attracted to his orderly but will not admit what he feels. Repression turns into sadistic cruelty, and eventually produces in its victim an instinctive and absolute moment of revolt, not the 'accident' of 'Vin Ordinaire' but murder, followed by the disintegration of the man who has killed.

Yet to treat the story as essentially about repressed homosexuality and sadism – the extreme exploration of the gap in all three stories between ideas of the self and blood-being – is to oversimplify. For one thing, it has still a third of its length to go *after* the murder. For another, homosexuality seems no more adequate an account of what it is that is repressed, than reaction against sadism explains why the orderly so disintegrates after the killing. If the licence which military life gives to bullying and cruelty is the top layer of the story, and the 'abnormal' psychology the underlying exploration – what is it, at the story's heart, against which the 'abnormal' is measured, and seen as so destructive?

It begins with a series of oppositions: the hot valley set against the pale blue, snowy mountains; the dark sweaty horse against the pale blue rider; one man fair, the other dark; one face marked by a consciousness at war with life, the other seeming 'never to have thought, only to have received life direct through his senses'. The captain is attracted to something free and (unconsciously) physically sure, a kind of spontaneity he lacks – yet in the very attraction lies a deeper irritant than repressed homosexuality. For the opposite kind of life calls his kind radically in question, so that the very attraction seems to lessen and imperil the self – as in 'New Eve and Old Adam', as much as between men here. And this is as true of the orderly when he meets the officer's eyes, 'bluey, like fire' and feels 'something sink deeper, deeper into his soul, where nothing had ever gone before ... Some of his natural completeness in himself was gone'. But the officer 'did not choose to be touched into life by his servant' – *there* is the idea of rank, and the repression of homosexuality, and more. The orderly too learns (as the powerless tend to do when confronted by the powerful) to look past the other, not eye-to-eye. It is not the attraction, but the repression of response that is 'perverted'. From that comes the obsessive physical cruelty of the captain, and the increasing refusal of consciousness by the orderly, step by horribly convincing step, until the murder becomes inevitable.

Yet here is the heart of the story – for in killing his tormentor, it now becomes clear that the orderly has killed something in *himself*, which thirst and sunstroke merely accentuate and complete. (Similarly, in retrospect, the captain was deathly in repressing that part of himself which reached out to one who embodied it more fully.) The consequence to the orderly of killing the captain is the death in himself of kinds of living awareness, without which human life is impossible. He is imprisoned now in a deadly kind of consciousness, out of touch with the natural universe, any human being or even the needs of his own body – feeling only a now forever unfulfillable longing for the dimension furthest beyond himself, as he dies.

This story goes deeper than 'New Eve and Old Adam' in exploring how attraction and revulsion may be *connected* – and all three seem most interested now in what lies below conscious awareness. They also intensify a quality which Frieda now realised had been there in *Sons and Lovers*; while carrying much further a dimension to which she was initially hostile. When Garnett sent Jessie's manuscript to Irschenhausen, Frieda thought it 'very lovable', but because Jessie had 'never understood anything out of herself', only 'a faded photograph' of Lawrence's. By contrast, 'the amazing brutality' in *Sons and Lovers* brings home a truth about people that 'ought to develop into something finer, out of *itself*, not be suppressed, denied!' (i. 550). But how might something finer grow out of such subterranean and unacknowledged dualisms? On the other hand, just before *Sons and Lovers* was finished, she had thought Lawrence 'so stupid ... in *seeing* things, that cannot be seen with eyes, or touched, or smelt or heard' (i. 470). The more he sought to delve below personality and beyond the dimensions of conscious awareness (for she might have added 'or thought, or spoken' to her list), the more he would have to risk such criticism.

Lawrence himself was certain now that *Sons and Lovers* marked the end of a phase, and that he would not write in its style again (i. 551). The critical essay he wrote at Irschenhausen marked an equally definite rejection of the post-Flaubertian sense of 'form', which became the mark of modernism.

'German Books: Thomas Mann' was written for *Rhythm* (which turned into the *Blue Review* before printing it in July). Mann is seen as the high point in

Germany of the Flaubertian craving for form-as-mastery, seeking to impose the will of the artist over the formlessness and corruption of life. Following a very dubious critical tactic that was to become habitual, Lawrence makes no distinction between author and protagonist; yet this was also part of a refusal to draw the sharp line between the artist who creates and the man who suffers, that modernism would postulate. So when Lawrence finds *Death in Venice* unwholesome, it is not merely a matter of the sickness inside the story, portrayed with such skill. It is also because Mann-as-artist is the latest 'sick sufferer from the complaint of Flaubert': 'Physical life is a disordered corruption, against which he can fight with only one weapon, his fine æsthetic sense, his feeling for beauty, for perfection, for a certain fitness which soothes him, and gives him an inner pleasure, however corrupt the stuff of life may be.' This radical disjunction between formed 'art' and corrupt 'life', however, makes art unliving; and prevents the artist from discovering in his work the source of new and better life. For that, art must have 'the rhythm of a living thing':

the rise of a poppy, then the after uplift of the bud, the shedding of the calyx and the spreading wide of the petals, the falling of the flower and the pride of the seed-head. There is an unexpectedness in this such as does not come from their carefully plotted and arranged developments. Even *Madame Bovary* seems to me dead in respect to the living rhythm of the whole work. While it is there in *Macbeth* like life itself.[63]

Even in stories about destructive marriages, brutal violence and murder, then, the pulse of life and growth should be discoverable. Each work will, however, have to find its own living form, though this may require repeated spontaneous reconceiving (as was Lawrence's way of development and revision) rather than filling in touch after touch to perfect a carefully conceived or preconceived design, as in Flaubert or Joyce. With this, Lawrence sets out on a different path than modernists such as Mann, Ford, Pound, Eliot or Joyce would take.

On Tuesday 17 June he and Frieda left Irschenhausen and arrived in England early on Thursday morning.

V In England Again

They came via Holland to Harwich, and went straight from London to Garnett's house The Cearne, near Edenbridge in Kent – the only house in England (Lawrence felt) where they were sure of a friendly reception. Though he and Frieda had been together for a year, he had still not told his family (except Ada). The Cearne was a household so broad-minded that both Louie Burrows and Helen Corke had harboured suspicions about it; yet even there he felt he had to tell the housekeeper Elizabeth ('Li') Whale that Frieda must pass as 'Mrs Lawrence' (ii. 22). Edward and Constance lived together or apart as

79

they pleased, at their flat in Hampstead or in the country, but remained on friendly and civilised terms. He had his office at Duckworth's in Henrietta Street; but as a publisher's reader much of his work could be done at home. She was engaged on her translations from the Russian which first made Turgenev, Tolstoy, Dostoevsky, Chekhov and Gogol widely available in English – seventy volumes in all. He had a relationship with the painter Nellie Heath, of which his wife was well aware, often sending Nellie regards when she wrote to him, as she did regularly whenever they were apart. When Lawrence first met him, Edward was spending only a few days in town and the rest in the country; while Constance was mostly in Hampstead with Bunny as he started at the Royal College of Science (so they had not been at The Cearne when Lawrence brought Frieda there in April 1912, before going to Germany). Constance was looking forward to meeting her now, despite the effect the shilly-shallying about dates had had on domestic arrangements! This time however Garnett was mostly in London, and Constance in the country with her younger sister Katherine Clayton, and Bunny who was preparing for an examination.[64]

The Cearne was set on a scarp (hence the name) 'on the last drop of the north downs, sheer overlooking the Weald of Kent', with woodland behind and a wide prospect in front. Though built only thirteen years earlier, Lawrence described it as 'exactly like the 15th century: brick floored hall, bare wood staircase, deep ingle nook with a great log fire, and two tiny windows one on either side of the chimney: and beautiful old furniture' (i. 314). He had loved being there, but was feeling apprehensive now, isolated and needing support. The first letter he wrote from The Cearne was to Frieda's little nephew Friedel who *had* stood up for him, and though it is written (in German) to interest a child, with descriptions of the 'rose-faces' at the window and how he has been helping to net the raspberries against the birds, there is a distinct touch of melancholy at being back in his 'native land' (ii. 25).

Through the eyes of Constance and Bunny we get the first outside impressions of Lawrence and Frieda after their year together. Predictably, now that they were so close to Frieda's children, previous arguments flared up, and they quarrelled fiercely as soon as politeness had worn off. Because they had been living in such isolation and had got used to behaving without social restraint, this may not have taken long. Immediately after the weekend Frieda consulted Robert Garnett in London. If, as seems likely, the lawyer counselled her to be cautious in the period before the divorce hearing, and not to try contacting the children without permission, she was in no mood to listen. The whole point of her coming to England was to see them and she was determined to do so, despite (also) Lawrence's moral objection to going behind Weekley's back. Bunny Garnett, who had so loved them as a couple the year before, seems now to have gone over entirely to Frieda's side – unless his later quarrel with Lawrence had taken over his memories by 1953.

Though Frieda (he says) had given up so much to live with Lawrence, so that any 'kind-hearted man would have felt an added tenderness and sympathy for her', his 'spiteful, ill-conditioned, ungenerous side' kept breaking out in jealousy of the children, and cruel anger with her for being unable to forget them. Lacking 'the instincts of a gentleman', Lawrence rationalised his feelings, 'attributed the whole trouble to faults in Frieda's character and never admitted the existence of imperfections in his own'. So, 'my sympathy was really all for Frieda and as she could get no support from Lawrence, I spent several afternoons in London with her, hanging round St Paul's School in the hope that she could intercept her son and see him for a moment or two.'[65] It was to be always thus. Those who took Frieda's side would accuse Lawrence of jealousy and spite; while his partisans would charge her with refusing to accept, in her self-centredness, the consequences of her own actions. What does ring true, however, is Bunny's contention that her unhappiness in being separated from her children was 'something simple and elemental' and 'as painful to watch as an animal in a trap'.

Constance, less partisan, saw differently, and we have her reactions at the time. She wrote on Saturday (probably 5 July) of a 'blessed calm' in the storms, apart from Frieda 'insisting on expecting Prof W. to come down here and shoot Lawrence' – for reasons that will soon become apparent. Constance didn't think their relation could survive such conflicts – and told him that 'as a sensible man' he should see this, 'and part before he makes things too hard for her'.

Well, he says I don't understand – that his love is of the permanent sort – and that it's all that F. only *half* loves him – but he'll *make* her love him altogether – (This apparently involves her forgetting the past!) I think the talk has had a good effect in making him behave a bit better – but F. is very tactless & her denseness in some directions makes him almost scream with anguish – & I'm afraid it's a bit beyond her to change effectually . . .[66]

Yet there was more behind the arguments now than either of the Garnetts could see. Lawrence was not being merely jealous and spiteful in objecting to Frieda's plan to see the children clandestinely. He had refused to sleep with her in Weekley's house, he had tried to get her to tell Weekley about him before they left England together, he was unwilling to dine with Frieda's father under false pretences and he had found the 'dishonour' and lies in Metz so intolerable that he had felt it essential to write to Weekley – a letter that would be used in the divorce proceedings. While believing that people had a right to act on their hearts' desires, in defiance if need be of conventional morality, he consistently believed in doing so *openly*, which is what had made Weekley in one of his quieter moments call him 'ehrlich'.

Moreover, against his better judgement (and Bunny's story), he did in fact give in to Frieda's feelings, and on 30 June went with her in a successful attempt to waylay Monty on his way home from Colet Court, the preparatory school for St Paul's, in West Kensington. Monty remembers catching 'a glimpse of Lawrence at some distance and realized that he had accompanied her but refrained from intruding on our meeting'. This must be why there had been the 'blessed calm'; and also why an exultant Frieda was talking about reprisals by Weekley against Lawrence, should he find out.[67]

And find out he did, through the detective efforts of his sister Maude, and with results disastrous to Frieda. Frieda had persuaded Monty to bring the girls to see her the next day (1 July). Maude, who felt responsible for the children when her brother was about his duties in Nottingham, soon sensed that something was up, examined the children and discovered a letter from Frieda, probably by searching Monty's room.[68] (There had been another clandestine meeting with Frieda – and Katherine Mansfield – early in July.)[69] The response of the Weekleys was not immediate, but it was decisive. Weekley first wrote a furious letter for Frieda via her mother – with divorce proceedings under way he could not write direct. Then he applied for a court order against her. Maude, in a sworn statement before a Commissioner of Oaths on 24 July, testified that on 1 July she had 'observed the agitation of the said children and questioned the eldest', discovering how 'the Respondent' had met him, and then his sisters on 1 July. On 4 July (she went on) 'I found on the staircase ... a document in the handwriting of the Respondent which had apparently been dropped by the said [Montague Weekley]'; and handed it to her brother. After hearing counsel, and affidavits by Weekley (dated 14 July) and Maude, the Registrar of the High Court signed an Order on Summons on 28 July awarding Weekley legal custody until further notice (i.e. *before* the divorce), and restraining Frieda 'from interfering or attempting to interfere with the said children'.[70]

Frieda would have done better to have listened to Lawrence's scruples, and to have made a fresh appeal to Weekley on the grounds that she was back in England and nearby. Now there could be no question of that, and she would be breaking the law if she tried to see the children in secret again. After they moved to the Kent coast (unaware of what was brewing), Monty remembers that 'Katherine Mansfield delivered messages from my mother'; and Lawrence meant to send a half sovereign (10 shillings) on 21 July for her to give them, but forgot to put it into his letter of instructions about how to get hold of Monty.[71]

After the court order, there could be no more of that. On 28 July, the day of the court hearing, the writing was already on the wall, though its meaning was still hidden:

Frieda is very sad because Mrs Murry went to St Pauls to see Monty, and he sent word by another boy 'that he was not to talk to people who came to the school to see him'. So she – Frieda – thinks they have brought all kinds of pressure to bear, and have instilled all kinds of horror into the lad. God knows. But Weekley is an unutterable fool. He wrote the most hideous letter to the Frau Baronin [altered from 'Frieda'] – is altogether acting the maniacal part of the 'mari trompé'. (ii. 51)

Monty had just turned thirteen; the girls were two years and four years younger.

There was more to the quarrels of late June, then, than jealousy and spite from Lawrence. Indeed, Constance Garnett's sympathy had turned his way. Two days before they were due to leave, she wrote of the 'peaceful time' they had had, netting the strawberries together: 'Lawrence very sweet – he is a nice person in the house – & F rather trying – She won't let things drop.' She warned Edward however (who would see them in town) not to talk of their relationship, 'or they'll be at hammer & tongs again'.[72] On Wednesday 9 July they went to London, on their way to Kingsgate on the Kent coast, between Margate and Broadstairs, where they had taken a flat. (Frieda and Weekley had holidayed in Margate once, with the children.)[73]

This was a day given to the literary contacts Lawrence needed in order to go on living and writing abroad. They called on Garnett and saw Duckworth too. They met, and liked, Norman Douglas who had become assistant editor of the *English Review*. They called at the 'office' in Chancery Lane of that 'daft paper' run by 'nice' folk (i. 519), for which Lawrence had written two reviews now, and saw Katherine Mansfield again – having already had the first sunny meeting recalled by John Middleton Murry so vividly in 1935:

Frieda's lovely fair hair glowed under her panama. We rode in a bus to have lunch together in Soho, and Frieda was surprised and delighted to catch Katherine and me making faces at one another. For Lawrence and she had formed the curious idea that we were wealthy and important people: the kind of people, I suppose, who finance daft magazines. We liked one another, and when it emerged, as it quickly did, that Katherine and I were not married, and that Katherine like Frieda was waiting to be divorced, it began to appear ... that we were made for one another.

This works up the original account of 'Straw hats, and sunshine, and gaiety' in *Reminiscences* (1933) and is not altogether reliable.[74] Nevertheless, the sense of two couples delighted with each other is clear in the accounts of both – though Lawrence's, based on what Katherine told him, had its inaccuracies too.

Murry was 23. He was not in fact 'of the common people' (ii. 31) – his father had a clerkship in the Registry in Somerset House and a lower-middle-class home in Peckham – but he, too, had been a scholarship boy, to Christ's Hospital School, and then to Oxford. (There was no rich but fickle benefactor – ii.32; that was an invention of Katherine's.) He then boldly decided to live in Paris and edit *Rhythm*, with a well-off fellow undergraduate, rather than work for Greats; though he did take his Finals and achieved a second class after little preparation.

He had been living with Katherine for six months. However *Rhythm* collapsed when its publisher decamped, leaving Murry liable for a large debt, which meant selling up their first real home together. They started again with the *Blue Review*, helped by Edward Marsh – but the July number (with Lawrence's essay on Thomas Mann) would prove to be the last. Murry had to support himself by reviewing for the *Westminster Gazette* and selling the books afterwards. Katherine had an allowance of £120 a year at this time from her father, the Governor of the Bank of New Zealand, though she had pledged this to pay off the debt.[75]

Katherine (née Kathleen Beauchamp), at 24, had published a book of stories and worked on A. R. Orage's periodical *New Age*. A rebel against her respectable colonial background, she had married the gentlemanly George Bowden to conceal her pregnancy by someone else, but ran away on the marriage night. He had never reproached or pursued her; and though they had recently talked about divorce (at her invitation) she let the matter drop. Though Murry did not know this, she had lost the baby – and she herself did not know she had caught gonorrhoea from its father. She was a complex character, a chameleon, but the combination of laughter and sadness she had projected at these first meetings made a deep impression on Lawrence; and Frieda was clearly touched by her sympathy over the children and her readiness to help: 'She went to see them, talked to them and took them letters from me. I loved her like a younger sister.'[76] (Katherine would have enjoyed the subversion of the bourgeois.) Though by throwing in her lot with Murry she had quarrelled with *New Age* – whose editor, she said, had taught her to think – she retained the bohemian iconoclasm that had drawn her to its writers. She was striking-looking, small, dark, with bobbed hair and a Japanese fringe, witty, enigmatic, formidable, funny and deliberately unconventional. They had found her in the flat-cum-office in Chancery Lane, sitting on a floor cushion beside a bowl of goldfish, with her legs showing.[77]

Murry was also on the short side, with a scholarly stoop that made him look smaller than he was. He had a little-boy-lost look which could be very attractive; an earnest enthusiasm which had won over artists and writers to *Rhythm* when he was still a clever undergraduate. His face oddly blended sensitivity with a nose broken at school; he had what Katherine called a 'lovely frightening mouth'; and fine hazel eyes that never quite focused on you as he talked.

Lawrence found 28 Percy Avenue, Kingsgate 'a most jolly little flat. The big bedroom has a balcony that looks across the fields at the sea. Then the house has a tent, [i.e. to change in, at the beach] and the way-down to the sea is just near, so one can bathe' (ii. 32). Soon he was describing the little bay where 'great waves come and pitch one high up, so I feel like Horace, about to smite my cranium on the sky', though he could 'only swim a little bit and am a clown in the water' (ii. 46). (Kent bathers will smile at an account which sounds like Bondi Beach.) Yet he felt alien among the holiday-makers; and the note of unthinking anti-Semitism, first heard in Bavaria, sounds again: 'What have I to do with fat fatherly Jews and their motor cars and their bathing tents' (ii. 37); 'I feel horribly out of place among these Jews' villas, and the babies and papas' (ii. 39). Their stay was transformed however, by happy accident.

Out of the blue came a cheque for £3 from Edward Marsh, being a seventeenth share of the profits of *Georgian Poetry*. Lawrence thanked him delightedly, adding 'I should like to see you very much. I suppose you won't be Margate way? (Dont be insulted, at any rate)' (ii. 36). He had not grasped the social difference between the people's Margate and Dickens's Broadstairs to which Kingsgate belongs. Far from being insulted, Winston Churchill's private secretary was already engaged to pay a visit there the following Sunday, to Herbert ('Beb') Asquith the second son of the Prime Minister, and his wife the Hon. Cynthia Asquith, daughter of Lord Elcho, who had taken a holiday house at the bottom of Percy Avenue, nearest the sea. Lawrence immediately invited Marsh to tea, but on the Sunday morning (20 July) Marsh called to say that the Asquiths would like 'the Lawrences' to come to them instead. (Later, Lawrence apologised for the deception, ii. 93.)

After their year of isolation, this must have been 'society' indeed. Lawrence was always conscious of rank; vain of Frieda's and very pleased (while pretending not to be) at any social contact of which his mother would have been proud. But these were interesting and attractive people anyway. Eddie Marsh was dapper, clever, amusing and kind, and knew just about 'everybody'. An 'Apostle' at Cambridge with G. E. Moore, Bertrand Russell and Oswald Sickert; a friend of Max Beerbohm and Raymond Asquith at Oxford; moving with equal ease in the literary salon of Edmund Gosse or the balls of the season; inveterate theatre-goer; he was also a scholar who produced a fine translation of Horace, and a civil servant efficient and astute enough to be chosen by Churchill as his right-hand man. He was to all appearance an Edwardian man-about-town with eyeglass; finicky about good form in dress and speech; and with an oddly high voice from a child's disease that arrested his sexual development and made him a lifelong bachelor on easy terms with both sexes. He was intelligent, witty and open to the new. Without being exactly rich, he was already becoming a Maecenas to the poets and artists of a younger generation, using a share of a state grant to the family of his great-grandfather, the assassinated Prime Minister Spencer Perceval, to help young artists like Duncan Grant, Mark Gertler, Gaudier-Brzeska and Stanley Spencer. His anthology *Georgian Poetry* proved an influential boost to its fifteen British poets, and the careful apportioning of the profits was typical. He was a personal friend of most of them, particularly Rupert

Brooke (whose London base was the spare bedroom in Marsh's home in Raymond Buildings Chancery Lane, when E. M. Forster or someone else was not using it), and the more needy J. E. Flecker and W. H. Davies, whom he helped with friendship as much as patronage. He had enabled the Murrys to start again with the *Blue Review*.[78]

Cynthia Asquith (soon to be Lady Cynthia when her father inherited as Earl of Wemyss) was not only an aristocrat but also one of the most beautiful society women in London, with an extraordinary head of reddish-gold hair ('the colour of the best marmalade', said the leading actress Mrs Patrick Campbell, describing it to Sargent), a wide rather sensitive mouth and wide-apart, slanting green eyes. She was very conscious of her beauty, and proud of the number of painters who wished to immortalise it (Burne-Jones, Sargent and von Glehn already; Augustus John and others to come). She had grown up in not one but three great houses: Clouds near Stourhead, her birthplace, built by her Wyndham parents; Stanway, the Elcho home in the Cotswolds, which she loved 'as I have loved very few human beings'; and Gosford near Edinburgh, seat of the Earls of Wemyss. She made the rounds of a number of others and the engagements of the season in London, the life of a high-society lady of her time. Her father however was not at all impressed by the marriage which often seated her also at the Prime Minister's dining-table. For Beb's grandfather had worked in the wool trade; he was a younger son; the P.M. was a Liberal (and Lord Elcho an arch-Conservative); and negotiations about the engagement took place in the midst of the constitutional crisis of 1910 over the House of Lords, which inflamed political feelings. The marriage settlement was consequently much smaller than might have been expected. The young couple would have £900 a year (though ten times what Lawrence had earned as a teacher) – enough for Beb not to have to practise at the Bar or work otherwise for a living, but not enough for their tastes and expectations.[79]

However Cynthia and Beb, while never rebellious, were somewhat different from their sort. Her mother belonged to the cultivated circle who became known as the Souls – and Cynthia had a soul-searching and self-doubting side in odd contrast with her social assurance. Sudden withdrawal and remoteness complicated her attractiveness to men. Intelligent, imaginative, often ironic, she might have been an actress if not such a lady – indeed in 1910 she rejected a role in a Herbert Trench production that ran for 192 performances. And though Beb was by no means charismatic (unlike his brilliant elder brother Raymond, centre of the Balliol circle to which Cynthia had been drawn) but rather silent and reserved, he shared her interest in literature and wrote publishable poetry. Both were somewhat at odds with their social roles. To Lawrence she seemed the kind of 'dreaming woman', unfulfilled despite her poise, who always fascinated his imagination.

They were at Kingsgate recovering. She had been suspected of tuberculosis and had just spent three months in a sanatorium, though she was now pronounced well. Her son John was just over a year old, but even before the sanatorium she had been away on visits much of the time, leaving him in the nursery, so she had seen very little of him in that crucial phase of babyhood. A photograph at Kingsgate shows a chortling infant (Lawrence's 'fat and smiling John'; ii. 63) with a pretty mother in a fashionable summer hat: see Illustration 17. No shadow falls – yet.

Kingsgate must have been instantly transformed for 'the Lawrences', who spent much of their time with these new friends; and no less for the Asquiths. She was struck at once by his difference from other people, not in degree but kind:

he was preternaturally alive ... half faun half prophet, and very young ... He wasted no time – he never did – on small talk ... Words welled out of him ... at times colloquially, almost challengingly so, but often with a startling beauty of utterance. His voice was now harsh, now soft. One moment he was lyrically, contagiously joyous; the next sardonic, gibing ... From first to last I very much liked Frieda. Exuberant, warm, burgeoning, she radiated health, strength, and generosity of nature ...

One sees why Frieda was never jealous, though Lawrence's attraction to Cynthia proved enduring. Frieda thought her 'lovely as Botticelli's Venus', but recognised her remoteness as well as Lawrence's caution; and Cynthia never took sides.[80] Her 'Soul' quality, moreover, would call from Lawrence – though not just yet – letters of a kind he wrote to few others, many of them amongst his most significant.

Lawrence had hoped that 'the Murrys' – a convenient term, despite their unmarried state – would also come down that Sunday, but they did not, and Lawrence was surprised to learn from Marsh that they probably had not been able to afford the rail-fare. He immediately wrote to scold Murry for not borrowing from him, and enclosed a guinea – half for the fare, and half for Monty via Katherine – insisting that they come down the following weekend (ii. 45–6). They did, bringing their friend Gordon Campbell, a lean Irish barrister who loved 'philosophical discussion. They bathed 'naked in the half-light', Lawrence cooked a tasty meal and on the way home in the train the Murrys read *Sons and Lovers* with such admiration that Katherine started an autobiographical novel, though she soon abandoned it. Friendships were confirmed, and when the Lawrences had two nights in town after leaving Kingsgate, it was with Campbell and his wife Beatrice – an artist from Dublin – that they stayed, at Selwood Terrace in Kensington. Beatrice would remember Frieda drenched and weeping, after waiting in vain to see the children on their way from school.[81] This must have been immediately after the granting of the injunction, though it could not yet have been served.

Lawrence's affairs went better. He and Frieda dined with W. L. George, the novelist, who was to do an article on Lawrence in the *Bookman*; and lunched at Raymond Buildings with Marsh, W. H. Davies and Wilfrid Gibson. Collings, whom Lawrence had not yet met, came to tea at the Murrys', and Lawrence visited the Poetry Bookshop to meet Harold Monro who ran it, with Gibson. Though he had failed to see de la Mare or Hueffer, or his Croydon friend McLeod, he had dramatically increased his circle.

One more friendship had been forged at Kingsgate when the poet and reviewer Henry Savage came for the day. He had praised *The White Peacock*, as had his friend the poet Richard Middleton. Now Middleton was dead, a suicide; and Lawrence found Savage rather a 'sad dog' too, worried about his wife and their coming child (ii. 43). He always had the gift of making people talk immediately of their most intimate and deep concerns, and did the same himself. Lying 'sprawled on the cliffs', he 'suddenly struck his chest violently. "I've something here, Savage, " he said, "that is harder than concrete. If I don't get it out it will kill me."' He did not mean, Savage thought, anything physical, but rather 'the dark, strange forces' he expressed in his work. It was no gloomy day however; they had an 'exciting debauch' of a meal (ii. 43) and remembered each other with pleasure.[82]

After two nights in London Lawrence and Frieda went in different directions. He had to be at his sister Ada's wedding on 4 August, but he could not spring Frieda on his family then. In any case, she was anxious to get back to Bavaria before her mother left Else's for Baden-Baden. Her whole reason for being in England had vanished, leaving her with the image of 'little white faces' forbidden to speak to her and looking 'at me as if I were an evil ghost'.[83] She told Else that it was like having 'living pieces of flesh ... torn from one, luckily I think the children do not feel it *so* much' (ii. 50). She could only hope that Ernest would calm down once the divorce was complete. She was glad that Lawrence had had 'Much to-do' made over him; glad too that she had been a success with their new friends; but she saw no reason to stay any longer. Lawrence saw her off on 31 July, went to The Cearne for two nights, and then to Nottingham on 2 August.

In Eastwood he stayed with Willie and Sallie Hopkin (whom he had asked not to tell Alice Dax he was coming; ii. 42). He wanted only to see his family, but it must have been an awkward time for him with them too. The wedding itself 'went off all right' (ii. 55); but he missed Frieda, and after stopping briefly in Garnett's flat, he left for Irschenhausen on the 7th.

VI   Stories for a Living

His main affair in England had been to recover all the unpublished manuscripts of sketches and stories he had left with or sent to Garnett and Ada, and to prepare them for publication in magazines. *Sons and Lovers* had been generally well received by the critics[84] but it had not sold well, largely because of the reluctance of the libraries to take it at first. He knew 'Miss Houghton' was 'improper'; and 'The Sisters' too, having been intended as a seller, had already fallen from grace in that respect. So, having had £50 of his royalties of *Sons and Lovers* in advance, leaving only £50 on publication, he had now to earn enough to finance a return to Italy for another winter. The publication of single stories and sketches in magazines or weekly papers like the *Saturday Westminster* would be more profitable than a volume. So as soon as he reached The Cearne in June he began to collect and revise.

Garnett had arranged for the one story so far sent to America to be professionally typed by Douglas Clayton, a printer in Croydon, whose mother Katherine (Constance Garnett's sister) Lawrence had met and liked at The Cearne. He worked on the manuscripts whenever he had a chance, both there and in Kingsgate; sent them to Douglas via his mother; and had the new typescripts back to send to magazines, while the manuscripts went to The Cearne or were kept by the Claytons. Constance also acted as his banker for what remained of the Duckworth advance royalties. After Robert Garnett's fee, and the payments to Douglas Clayton, about £38 remained on 18 July (ii. 42).

The unpublished sketches about the chapel and the hay-hut in the mountains could not be found. ('Christs in the Tyrol' had appeared in the *Westminster Gazette* in March.) The story 'Intimacy' (soon to be renamed 'Witch à la Mode') was also feared lost but turned up among Frieda's intimate underwear. Clayton typed thirteen pieces in July and one in August; and Lawrence promised to keep a list. It would have read as follows (with the eventual success rate up to August 1914): 'The Fly in the Ointment' and 'A Sick Collier' (taken by the *New Statesman*); 'Strike-Pay I, Her Turn' and 'Strike-Pay II, Ephraim's Half-Sovereign' (taken by the *Saturday Westminster Gazette*); 'The Christening', 'The Shadow in the Rose Garden'[85] and 'The White Stocking' (all taken by the *Smart Set*); 'Honour and Arms' and 'Vin Ordinaire' (taken by the *English Review*, but damagingly cut by Norman Douglas); 'Once—!' (rejected by the *Smart Set* as 'too hot' (ii. 67) and also by the *English Review*); 'Two Marriages' (retitled 'Daughters of the Vicar') and 'Love among the Haystacks' (both too long for anything but serialisation, and though revised now, rejected again for the same reason); 'The Witch à la Mode' (unplaced); and the only new one, finished during their stay in England, 'The Primrose Path' (also unplaced).[86]

When Katherine Clayton remarked that 'New Eve and Old Adam' was 'unworthy' of him (ii. 38), he took her word for it and did not even have it typed. (He may also have thought it gave away too much.) It is not clear what had happened to 'Delilah and Mr Bircumshaw', rewritten in Germany in 1912; or to 'The Old Adam' which he had revised in 1911. Heinemann still had the Croydon sketches 'A Lesson on a Tortoise' and 'Lessford's Rabbits', probably through the agency of de la Mare.[87] Lawrence seems to have forgotten 'A Prelude', 'A Modern Lover' and 'The Overtone' altogether. But he had clearly made a sustained effort to capitalise on his early writings as much as he possibly could; 'drudging away' and 'swotting away' at them – 'How glad I shall be when I have cleared that mess up!' (ii. 39, 41). He also decided it was time to have a professional agent, perhaps at Garnett's suggestion. Garnett had declined to hand him over to James Pinker – agent to Conrad, James, Wells and Bennett – when Pinker first offered his services in 1912,[88] and was still ready to continue as mentor to the novelist – indeed as go-between for the couple of stories that were to be entrusted to Pinker now. However placing shorter works was not Garnett's business, and he had not been good at what looked like becoming an expanding responsibility. It would be sensible now to see whether Pinker could do better.

Some stories, such as 'The White Stocking', had been transformed from earlier versions, but were yet to reach their final form. In this case one of his very earliest pieces – entered in 1907 for the *Nottinghamshire Guardian* competition under the category 'Amusing' – had now become a story of how sexual jealousy could lead to violence; but was still undeveloped in comparison with its rewriting in 1914, where it is best treated. (See below p. xxx.) Others such as 'Love among the Haystacks' were to disappear again after magazine rejection, despite their 1913 revision. Here, in the story of the first sexual experience of two brothers in the hayfields, is both a reversal of 'Vin Ordinaire', and a still-crude anticipation of Tom and Lydia in *The Rainbow*. Tender sexuality (as opposed to the 'passionate' egotism of the younger brother and the foreign governess) leads a clumsy young man and a displaced woman to new life and self-respect. The only new story 'The Primrose Path' had its beginning in family gossip, perhaps brought to mind by thinking in Kingsgate about his own return as prodigal son for Ada's wedding. The story of his mother's favourite (though black sheep) brother, who deserted his wife, went to Australia with one woman, and returned to live with yet another and much younger one, as his wife lay dying, would have been a pleasantly sardonic contrast to his own more primrosy and much better destined path.[89]

VII Back to Irschenhausen

Invigorated by being with Frieda again, he found Bavaria 'so living: so quick' (ii. 58) with room to breathe, and was eager to get to work. His visit to Eastwood had given him the idea of doing some hometown sketches, and on his fourth day in Irschenhausen he told Willie Hopkin that he had written one, and proposed to do others on 'Artists of Eastwood' and the' Primitive Methodist Chapel' (ii. 57). His last messages to Garnett were about recovering his Eastwood play

The Widowing of Mrs. Holroyd, which Garnett had interested Mitchell Kennerley, the American publisher of *Sons and Lovers* in bringing out, but which
Lawrence had not seen for nearly two years. There may now have been an
attempt to get the Eastwood sketch(es) into the *Daily Mail* – but nothing was
published, or has survived, and the idea of a series or column, with Hopkin's
help, was abandoned.[90] In retrospect, England seemed 'dark and woolly', as
though in seven weeks he had never 'really wakened up' (ii. 58).

He was struck again by the beauty of Irschenhausen: the pine-woods behind
the little wooden house, the sweeping clarity of the Alps in front, the autumn
crocuses, the deer jumping up and down to shake off the rain and the squirrels
(he joked) hanging themselves out to dry (ii. 63, 65). There was also less
isolation. 11 August was Frieda's birthday. In procession came her niece
'crowned with flowers', and her nephews carrying fruits and sweets and
perfume, to be received by Frieda in new and colourful Bavarian costume (see
Illustration 8), the gift of Else, and 'gorgious' [sic] new sandals from Edgar.
Peter (aged 7) recited birthday verses and Friedel blew the mouth-organ.
Lawrence thought it comic and a bit embarrassing – Englishman that he was –
but his description is affectionate (ii. 57–8, 60). Children rushed about wildly,
having an 'air bath' in their striped bathing costumes (ii. 57). (When it rained,
Lawrence took a shower running round the house in his.) Edgar came to stay
and talked about economics and capitalism – not greatly to Lawrence's pleasure
(ii. 63). One evening there was a candle-lit dinner in the wood behind the house;
and (wrote Frieda) 'we see a great many more people than we used to last year'
(ii. 60), or for that matter a few months before, when she had felt an outcast. To
Lawrence also, 'Her people are very friendly again' (ii. 67), presumably now that
there could be no preventing the divorce. There was much to do and to see;
from the Sunday market at Wolfratshausen, to the big Munich art exhibition
which occupied fifty rooms at the Glaspalast, with pictures and sculptures from
eleven European countries.[91]

He and Frieda were 'friends' again, and, she told Bunny: the Lord has been
good to me in letting me not be so miserable any more about the children. I *do*
enjoy things again – I am sorry you saw me so much steeped in misery and I
think you helped me over it a bit, I don't understand how, but you did'
(ii. 60).[92] Lawrence, too, wrote to the Murrys that he and Frieda had stopped
trying to strangle each other! Instead 'I have assumed the forbearance of a
Christian martyr, and manage to hug it round me for an odd ten minutes'.[93] He
was much happier in himself. When a letter from Marsh asked him 'as a personal
favour' to pay more attention to the rhythms of his poetry, he was at first rather
snide about 'Eddie-dear', to Cynthia Asquith (ii. 62). When he replied to Marsh
himself however, the criticism brought his clearest statement so far about the
aim of his maturing and now 'freer' poetry:

I think you will find my verse smoother – not because I consciously attend to rhythms, but because I am no longer so criss-crossy in myself. I think, don't you know, that my rhythms fit my mood pretty well, in the verse. And if the mood is out of joint, the rhythm often is. I have always tried to get an emotion out in its own course, without altering it. It needs the finest instinct imaginable, much finer than the skill of the craftsmen … Remember, skilled verse is dead in fifty years – I am thinking of your admiration of Flecker. (ii. 61)

He mentions Yone Noguchi (who 'doesn't quite bring it off')[94] and Whitman ('Sometimes … perfect') as examples of what he means.

The effort to earn enough to be able to winter again in Italy seemed to be prospering, as the first colliery sketches came out in the *Westminster* and the three Lake Garda ones in the *English Review*, in September. For the latter he would get £25, though the *English Review* was a notoriously slow payer. Austin Harrison, its editor, had also accepted 'Honour and Arms' from Pinker, and liked it so much that he thought of doing 'Vin Ordinaire', and two more, at £15 apiece. A cheque for $35 came from the *Smart Set*, for two poems, and Ezra Pound paid for another that would come out in November. If the magazine would pay such sums for poetry, stories might be even more lucrative in America.[95] On such hopes, and Edgar's praise of the Leghorn coast where he was about to take a holiday at Lerici (famous also for its connections with Shelley and Byron), they decided to try for a new home thereabouts. They were still very short of cash right now, and the *Westminster* cheque never arrived at Irschenhausen – Lawrence had eventually to ask from Lerici for £10 from his dwindling balance with the Garnetts (iii. 79) – but the expense of getting to Italy could at least be minimised. Since Frieda insisted on going to see her parents at Baden-Baden[96] before moving south, Lawrence would walk again, across Switzerland, and she would join him later. She wanted no more walking it seems, though her family probably offered to pay her train-fare. There are traces of the arguments that always flared when they were changing places. Lawrence told Savage on 8 September that though he believed as strongly as ever that 'stable happiness' is only to be found in union with a woman: 'I wish to add that my state of bliss is by no means perfect' (ii. 71).

He had fulfilled his promise to work however. Having recovered *The Widowing of Mrs. Holroyd* from Garnett he immediately wanted to revise it, and when he had finished by 24 August, with (he thought) the play 'pretty much altered and much improved', he sent it off to Kennerley via Duckworth (ii. 65). It was an unpleasant surprise then to hear in early September that Kennerley already had the play in proof from the unrevised ribbon copy sent by Garnett. Lawrence hastened to apologise for the trouble his late revision would cause – but he wanted the alterations made all the same: 'I hated it in the last act, where the man and the woman wrangled rather shallowly across the dead body of the husband. And it seemed nasty that they should make love where he lay drunk' (ii. 71). He needed his revised typescript back, to make the necessary changes in the proofs – but when the latter came in October to Fiascherino on the Gulf of Spezia, where he and Frieda had settled, they came without it. At first, sitting on the rocks, he tried to recreate his August revisions on the proofs from memory (ii. 80), but he had to abandon the attempt – and eventually, after misunderstandings and vicissitudes (and extra expense to Kennerley), the alterations were made in New York by Edward Björkman, editor of the series in which the play was to appear.[97] Though only the printed text survives, there is a last important clue to Lawrence's revision. He had told Kennerley that there was one speech in it which he could not create again: 'the keystone of the play, and I *will* have it in' (ii. 78). This must be Elizabeth's monologue as she sponges the dead body in the final act – important because of the play's relation to the earlier story 'Odour of Chrysanthemums'. Holroyd had behaved even worse than the husband in the story (or than Walter Morel), making more acceptable the temptation Blackmore represents to his wife. Yet as against the story, where the wife was regarded as wholly justified in having fought the 'recreant', the play has the dead body bring home to the widow *her* failure, to love him enough – and the pity of it.[98] It is another step beyond *Sons and Lovers*, in a process of re-imagining. (A last step was yet to come, the following summer.) Garnett had warned that Lawrence might have to pay for excessive correction in proof, but Kennerley made no charge, and Lawrence professed himself delighted by 'all the beautiful and laudatory things' in Björkman's preface (ii. 80) – though he was less so in private.[99] This was the first of his plays to be printed.

It was 'The Sisters' however that he most wanted to get on with; but in trying to lose the mocking element in the first version he made two false starts. Once again he felt that he did not quite know what he was doing; telling Murry that it was: 'like working in a dream, rather uncomfortable – as if you can't get solid hold of yourself. "Hello my lad, are you there!" I say to myself, when I see the sentences stalking by.'[100] On 4 September however he could tell Garnett that there was 'quite a new beginning – a new basis altogether ... It is much more interesting in its new form – not so damned flippant' (ii. 67–8). This involved much more than a change of tone, however, or even of narrative point-of-view into a more serious third-person. Though the evidence does not appear for some time, the book now set off on a path so different that it would eventually turn into a separate novel: *The Rainbow*. The mockery vanished when he decided to go *behind* the previous story, to discover in the upbringing of his heroines what had made them what they were. More crucially still, his recent revisiting of the country of his heart seems to have influenced him to place the young sisters in a setting that was not Frieda's and Else's, or Jessie's, but another family he knew very well. This in turn meant the story would concentrate on the sister he had loved. He decided to base the young Ella on Louie Burrows, the one woman in his earlier love life about whom (impossible though it had proved to marry and live with her) he felt no rancour.[101]

It is not clear how far back this new 'Sisters' went into Ella's childhood, since only the last bit he wrote has survived; but the further back it started, the more it would also keep *him* out – that problem that had beset several of his attempts since *Sons and Lovers*. He had not met Louie until they were both at the Ilkeston Pupil-Teacher Centre; so he could begin and go a good way, using memories of the Burrows family, without being personally involved. There would of course be the problem of whether the heroine should have a love-affair before meeting her lover of the original 'Sisters'; and if so, what kind of affair and how 'autobiographical' it should be. There would also be the problem of how to meld the young Ella with the older one based on Frieda. Yet (if he thought of these at all) they could wait until a later stage while he got on with what was essentially a new story at first, and would remain so for some time.

He promised to forget about short stories now, and by 15 September, four days after turning 28, and two days before he was due to set out on his walk through Switzerland to Italy, he had written 100 pages of 'The Sisters II': 'It is queer. It is rather fine, I think. I am in it now, deep ... I shan't do anything but the Sisters now. I hope to have it done in a month. I *do* wonder what you will think of it' (ii. 74–5). Moreover the new basis solved another problem, all the more vital since it had become clear how damaging the initial reluctance of the libraries to take *Sons and Lovers* had been. 'It's a weird novel you'll get from me this time: but *perfectly* proper. The libraries will put it on their Sunday School prize list.' He said he would take it with him in his rucksack, and even claimed to have written a little at Constance (ii. 76), though when the walking began it must soon have left him too tired to do more.

VIII Across Switzerland[102]

Lawrence started from Munich to Überlingen by rail on Wednesday 17 September, then by steamer to Constance the next day. In misty weather the lake was depressing but he loved the 'old towns with roofs sticking up so high, and tiles all colours – sometimes peacock blue and green' (ii. 76). On Friday he took a steamer down the Rhine to Schaffhausen. It was misty again, but the early morning sun behind bluish haze made it seem like the beginning of the world, and he much preferred the mediaeval riverside villages to Schaffhausen and even its falls, caught between a bygone past and modern industry. In the afternoon he set out over flatlands, twelve miles to where the river rushed again between high banks, and after nightfall reached Eglisau with its lights shining on the water.

There was a fine covered bridge, and a Gasthaus nearby where he put up for the night – along with a group of vagrants on relief vouchers.[103]

Over the covered bridge in the morning thundered a troop of Swiss cavalry. These local citizen-soldiers with their baggy uniforms and their discussions with their officer were very different from the German military he had so disliked in Metz and Bavaria. Having walked thirteen miles to Oerlikon and taken a tram to look at Zürich, however, he was overcome by the 'soulless ordinariness' of this Switzerland. After a meal, a stroll through the market and a rest by the lake side, he wanted only to get away, and took a steamer up the lake in thin rain, to Kilchberg. It was getting dark, but he walked on another three miles to (probably) Adliswil. In the Gasthaus, whose landlord seemed about to have delirium tremens, he met a group of Italian exiles who allowed him to watch them getting up a play. They had found work in a silk-spinning mill, but could not go home because they had evaded military service. (In transition between the Italy of Lake Garda and the industrial north, they would become the central concern of the penultimate essay in *Twilight in Italy*.)

On Sunday morning (21 September) he climbed two miles up the Albispass which commanded fine views like a relief map: back over Lake Zürich, and south to the lake of Zug ten miles away where he was headed. Then, through 'fat agricultural land' he walked on, feeling very hostile to the respectable church-goers in black broadcloth going home for Sunday dinner, reminding him of the 'null "propriety"' of childhood Sundays in Eastwood. Though he had already done a good day's walk, and it rained, he pressed on for some hours on sore feet beside the 'steamy, reedy lake', stopping for tea in a lakeside tearoom kept by two little old ladies. He would have spent the night there (he says), but he had impulsively pretended to be the son of a doctor from Graz; and 'had developed my Austrian character too far'.[104] (The doctor from Graz he knew of, 'who was always wandering about' was Otto Gross who had wandered into Frieda's bed. Now headed in the direction of Ascona and Frieda Gross, Lawrence had clearly been thinking about and imagining *his* Frieda's past.) So he had to go on still further, into Zug and 'a detestable brutal inn', the penalty for pretence. This day he had walked twenty-five miles and climbed 2,600 feet.

Monday he liked even less. It must have taken him some three and a half hours to climb the Rigi pass (6,000 feet), two hours or so down the other side, and another three and a half hours to Lucerne. He had driven himself so hard that he had got there two days earlier than expected; but he did not like Lucerne either, and would not even spend the night there. At about 6.30 he took an express steamer 22 miles to Fluelen at the other end of the lake, arriving after nine o'clock. There he found a good German inn and was happy. In the dining-room was an English clerk who had set out, speaking no German, on a circular hike which had taken him over a hundred mountain miles in the last four days and left him exhausted – to Lawrence's wonder and pity first, and then some irritation at a doggedly foolish exercise of will without pleasure. (Yet, as *Twilight* does not clarify, he might have been thinking of his own dogged pressing-on too, and the little pleasure of his last two days.)

The morning of Tuesday was sunny, the lake was blue and by nightfall he knew he would be at the crest of his journey, the St Gotthard Pass. He set out up the valley between snow-capped mountains towards Altdorf ($2\frac{1}{2}$ miles), passing droves of cows being herded home from a cattle fair, and quiet villages seemingly forgotten. For most of the day he climbed slowly, sometimes above and sometimes below the twisting railway, where villages were now ledged precariously beside 'green, hanging meadows, with pine trees behind, and the valley bottom far below'. Sometimes the path led through isolated farmyards, and once through the garden of a village priest busy garlanding an archway. Then however came the factory area of Erstfeld, and the touristy clutter at the mouth of the St Gotthard railway tunnel; so he swerved aside up the pass itself, over Devil's Bridge and along high moorland to the resort and barrack-town of Andermatt. It was twilight, but in its snowless state the ski-town felt merely touristy; and once again he could not bring himself to stay. On he went in gathering darkness, a naked hill on one side, the high moorland on the other, with the sound of icy streams in his ears, the two miles to Hospenthal: 'the little village with the broken castle that stands for ever frozen at the point where the track parts', one way to the Furka Pass, the other over the top of the Gotthard. Here he found a room and a good meal in a silent wooden house, kept by a nervous woman who turned out to be deaf; but Lawrence felt happy 'free, in this heavy, ice-cold air, this upper world, alone'. He must also have been very tired – this day he had walked thirty miles, climbing to 4, 700 feet.

In the morning he paid his bill – rather more than the three shillings a day he had been trying to keep to – and set off, as the morning mist cleared to a perfect day, on the three hours' climb to the top of the pass at 7,000 feet. On the way he met a young Swiss, and they went along together. Like the English clerk, this lad was on a circular holiday walk (and would be going back through the railway tunnel); but he was an athlete, striding along in great boots with manifest pleasure. At the top of the pass the citizens' army was on military exercise, firing across the snow-slopes, and they were whistled at to hurry over a bridge before it closed. Lawrence characteristically refused to run and was yelled at; but his companion longed for his time of National Service to come. At the head of the pass were reedy lakes and a hotel, where a haughty French maid served them glasses of milk. At midday, in hot sun, they started the descent through a 'great cleft' in the mountains, much steeper than the way up. A little river fell headlong in cascades. Rather than take the road, the young Swiss led the way on narrow tracks, and they cascaded down like the water 'leaping from level to level, leaping, running, leaping, descending headlong' into the tree line. It was very swift but also very tiring. Gradually the gully opened out into a valley, and they saw Airolo below, with 'the railway emerging from its hole' and 'the whole valley like a cornucopia full of sunshine' – along which they went more slowly, passing more barracks and more military manoeuvres. At Airolo the young German Swiss suddenly looked a foreigner in the little Italianate town. They had a late lunch at the railway station, happily sharing Lawrence's, since the other had only been able to afford some beer and bread and sausage, before he caught his train back through the tunnel. Lawrence decided to take 1.20 francs' worth of rail journey too; the fifteen miles to Lavorgo. He must have felt recovered from the scramble, for he proceeded to go on a further twenty-five miles to Bellinzona along the modern highway down the Ticino valley. He could hardly have walked it all, however – and in *Twilight* could only remember the 'sordid' road,[105] and its strip-development, not the valley it ran through.

On Thursday he walked thirteen miles from Bellinzona over the plain to Locarno, which he reached about noon. By evening he was at Lugano, twenty-five miles on. He clearly walked some of this, remembering later a girl with handsome bare legs the colour of brass who called out mockingly to him, but the zest had gone out of the journey now, and he probably rode the last part. On Friday he took first a steamer to Capolago, then the cog-wheel and narrow-gauge railway to Monte Generoso, then over the border at Chiasso, and finally the train to Como. That evening he met Frieda in Milan, 'with its imitation hedge-hog of a cathedral and its hateful town Italians' (ii. 88). Switzerland, though beautiful, was 'too touristy ... spoilt' (ii. 79).

The significance of this journey for biography is the bearing of the distances he walked on the state of his health. Bunny Garnett later claimed that his anger over Lawrence's behaviour to Frieda at the Cearne was tempered by forgiveness once he 'caught sight of one of Frieda's handkerchiefs, marked with a coronet in the corner, crumpled in Lawrence's hand, after a fit of coughing and spotted with bright arterial blood'. The account is circumstantial – Frieda had bought those handkerchiefs in Munich the previous spring[106] – but the inference that Lawrence already had consumption is probably misleading. After a sputum test he had been certified free of the disease at the beginning of 1912; and though he had caught colds in the winter on Lake Garda, and in the spring on arriving in Germany which may well have left him coughing badly, possibly even coughing spots of blood – since it is possible to have lesions which heal – he could hardly have been seriously coughing arterial blood in July but able to walk twenty-five miles a day uphill on consecutive days in September. Moreover the problem of when exactly Lawrence 'had' the disease that killed him is continually complicated by the tendency of his friends to backdate it by hindsight, in memoirs written some time after his death.[107]

Lawrence himself was unusually forthcoming (and ironically confident) about his health at just this time, when Savage asked him. He replied on 15 September, just before setting out on his walk, that he had been 'pretty ill' with pneumonia for 'the third time' in late 1911, so 'my lungs are crocky, but I'm not consumptive', even if 'the type, as they say. I am not really afraid of consumption, I don't know why – I don't think I shall ever die of *that*.' As he always would do, he attributed his illnesses to 'sheer distress and nerve strain' which (being English) he had bottled up, to play havoc inside. 'I am so damnably violent, really, and self destructive. One sits so tight on the crater of one's passions and emotions. I am just learning – thanks to Frieda – to let go a bit' (ii. 72–3).

This was of course what he wanted to believe, but there was some empiric evidence also. His most dangerous attacks of pneumonia since the one in babyhood: another after the death of his elder brother, and the third at the end of 1911, had indeed come at times when 'sheer distress and nerve strain' had run him down. It is interesting that he should so justify physically, as well as psychologically, the newly uninhibited behaviour which developed in his isolation with Frieda; and credit her with teaching him, through their constant battles, to understand and cope better with his violent feelings by getting them outside himself, rather than bottling them up. However, supposing he did carry the tubercle (as thousands did at the time) and even have occasional lesions, worsened by his tendency to catch colds and coughs, he was far tougher than many, and his active habits may have helped to hold back the development of the disease – if he had it.

Now they were back in Italy where winter would be warmer.

IX   Fiascherino

They arrived in the Albergo delle Palme in Lerici on Sunday night, 28 September, to join Edgar Jaffe who had been house hunting for them. On the 30th Lawrence joyously announced that the perfect place had been found at Fiascherino, along the coast:

There is a little tiny bay half shut in by rocks, and smothered by olive woods that slope down swiftly. Then there is one pink, flat, fisherman's house. Then there is the villino of Ettore Gambrosier, a four-roomed pink cottage among a vine garden, just over the water, and under the olive woods. There, D.V., is my next home. It is exquisite. (ii. 78)

It would be 60 lire a month, plus another 25 'for the woman who does all the work and washing'. At once Lawrence wrote to the Murrys, inviting them to come and promising to find them something similar.[108] They moved in on 4 October, and Fiascherino proved to be one of their happiest homes.

They found they could manage on about 130 lire a month (about £5 10/-), which included the devoted service not only of Felice Fiori but also her daughter Ellide who often came to help. The place at first was very dirty – the owner only camped there in the olive-cropping season – so it took some cleaning (by Lawrence!) before they could see 'the dark floor flushing crimson, the dawn of deep red bricks arise from out this night of filth' (ii. 88). (Ellide, said he, had never seen a scrubbing-brush!) At first they were also plagued by fleas. But Felice, sixty, wizened, barefoot, kissed Frieda's hand feudally and served them faithfully; something Frieda may have missed more than she admitted. It was amazing to see Felice walking with half a hundredweight of charcoal on her head (for fornello cooking, again) and to hear her whistle in consent to any request. Figs and oranges grew in the garden and olive groves shimmered above – Lawrence said he always expected to see Christ and his disciples walking there. Boats passed continually along the gulf of Spezia, including warships from the naval base, and there were spectacular sunsets. He could run from his gate right into the sea and, being a poor swimmer, he revelled in having a sheltered bay of clear buoyant water. Lerici was easiest reached by boat around the headlands, and soon they could borrow one from the peasants in the other cottage – though Frieda was suspicious of his rowing, and there were ructions when they tried to row together!

They mostly loved their isolation, despite its drawbacks. For the post and groceries there was a scramble over the rocky path to 'our village' (or conversely, that 'sea-robbers nest') Tellaro, perched on a rocky ledge with the church so overhanging the sea that the surge echoes in its nave, and the bell-rope allegedly once fell over the parapet into the arms of an octopus, who tolled the bell. It was very irritating, after a half-hour trudge and a hunt for the postmaster, to be met with 'a wave of the hand that implies a vacuum in space, and a "niente, signore, niente oggi, niente, niente"' (ii. 22, 86). Since there was no road, everything that came from Lerici had to come by row-boat round the headland – including the piano that Frieda insisted on hiring from Spezia, whose arrival was a minor epic. For the dentist, or the bank, or the picture-framer, they went across from Lerici by the workmen's steamer to Spezia.[109]

In so isolated a place however, the locals were friendlier than in the relatively tourist area of Lake Garda, where Lawrence had drunk wine with the peasants in Bogliaco, but Frieda had only socialised with the hostess of the Hotel Cervo and her German visitors, or the schoolmistress and the Signor di P. It would have been the same in Lerici, associated after Shelley and Byron with a tradition of British visitors; but here they soon became friendly with the *contadini* in the other cottage who turned out to be cousins of Ellide.[110] They had meals in each other's houses, and Luigi and Gentile would sometimes come over with a guitar to play and sing. This in turn got the Lawrences invited as guests of honour to a peasant wedding on 29 November (ii. 109), a most elaborate affair, for which Lawrence donned his best black suit and patent-leather boots.[111] The church service, not very religious, as he describes it (ii. 126), was in Tellaro at 7.30 a.m. Then after 'a wedding breakfast that nearly killed us' at the bride's house, 'we set off in a troup, bride in white silk, with bridegroom, leading, and climbed and climbed up slippery goat roads' an hour and a half to Ameglia, where the civic ceremony had to be performed at 10 by the Mayor, while the village children swarmed 'like wolves yelling ... Evviva i Sposi' and demanding sweets from the bride, who traditionally carried a white bagful for the purpose. Then all the way back to Fiascherino for the lunch for twenty-five people in the upper room of the 'other' house: nine fowls, followed by the octopuses with arms half a yard long that Lawrence had watched Ezechiele the bridegroom haul from the sea (ii. 118).

In mid-meal when red wine was flowing Lawrence was called out, and there were their first visitors: three Georgian poets, Lascelles Abercrombie (with his wife Catherine), Wilfrid Gibson and R. C. Trevelyan, with his friend Aubrey Waterfield who was a painter. He had heard much of Abercrombie (who had reviewed *Sons and Lovers*) and something of Trevelyan from Marsh, who had put them all in his anthology. (It had been his suggestion that they look Lawrence up, so they sent him a joint postcard to show they had met.) Waterfield describes how a sailor showed them the way:

You never saw such an enchanting winter place – a bay facing right into the afternoon sun until the last ray of daylight; a peasant house on the beach built in a high wall that sheltered the podere; the other side of the wall a *pergola*, a little stream ending in a crystal clear pool by the beach and another *contadino* house with a garden gate on the beach. In the second house Lawrence was living; it is reached through the gate on the beach close beside the stream, in fact stepping stones lead up to it through a small garden, a child's garden of little paths and beds on its own promontory; and the house is called *Bijou*.

Lawrence never confessed to *that*! Waterfield had been told that he was consumptive and his verse 'decadent' (probably by Bob Trevelyan who did not admire it), so he saw what he expected; and interpreted accordingly the pallor of a man who had just been walking for three hours up and down steep goat-paths:

I have never seen a man look so ill as Lawrence; he was quite colourless with fine eyes full of restlessness. He ran here and there to make us all comfortable and then returned to his feast of chickens. 'A table full of chickens,' he said, 'with their legs wild in the air, you know how they look.'

They lay on the rocks to wait (rocks, thought Waterfield, like a Turner painting in the setting sun); then had tea with the Lawrences before walking to Sarzana.[112]

Lawrence and Frieda liked them all, but he found it strange to leave his Italian feast 'and descend into the thin atmosphere of a little group of cultured Englishman' [sic] (ii. 118). They seemed 'so shadowy and funny, after the crude, strong, rather passionate men at the wedding' (ii. 116); but their manners made him suddenly and unusually a bit ashamed of his own.

The Waterfields then 'let us in for society' (ii. 120) – that is, the society of well-to-do British expatriates living nearby. Waterfield and his wife Lina had rented (on an income of £600 a year) the castle at Aulla about twelve miles away, 'on a bluff of rock, with all the jagged Apennines prowling round, two rivers creeping out of the fastness to meet at the foot of the fortress, where is a tiny town' (ii. 127). The Lawrences went for a weekend in December and Lawrence told Lina how, as he looked at the mountains from the roof-garden, it seemed 'as though wild beasts were circling round a fire and he was filled with a feeling of apprehension' (ii. 122).[113] He politely admired his host's paintings, but privately told Cynthia Asquith they were by an 'artist gentleman ... in the manner of various defunct gentleman artists – their ghosts haunted his canvases like the ghosts of old dead soldiers his castle hall' (ii. 128–9). The Waterfields were kind, introducing them to the Huntingdons and the Pearses who lived near Lerici, and taking them to picnic 'in castles of the Malaspina family', but Lawrence was sensitive to patronage, and the Waterfields did not care for Frieda:

we both felt sorry for the poor woman, because I do not think she is really intellectually his companion, and it will soon bore him to hear her tell how she is really as responsible for his writing as he is himself. It seems she only does it to blind herself for deserting the children. She suffers a great deal at times on this account, and I do not think he would have any hesitation in deserting her if he thought for a moment she interfered with the full flight of his 'temperament'.

They thought that it 'would be the best in the end for all parties' if Weekley would take her back, but that her living with Lawrence was bound to end in disaster. Waterfield, though drawn to Lawrence, also thought him 'very egotistical and unbalanced'. Both he and Lina were greatly shocked when he told them that Paul's overdosing of Mrs Morel in *Sons and Lovers* was true. Nonetheless the relationship more than survived these and other surprises, though Lina must have struggled to contain hers when Frieda arrived for their first visit in full Bavarian costume; and Lawrence his, when he cooked a big lunch for them in Fiascherino and they turned up at half-past two.[114] The new acquaintances certainly enriched their second stay in Italy and made it quite different from the first. Lawrence specially liked Mrs Pearse, who had 'a beautiful house where the Empress Frederick of Germany spent a winter with them' (ii. 133); and who dined the Lawrences there with a Count Seckendorf – but who also came to Fiascherino and allowed herself to be rowed back by her host in the peasants' boat. He was flattered by the attention of these people, all a great deal older as well as richer than himself, but he liked them, as well as Luigi, Severino and Gentile, as people. He knew it might make a difference when 'all our dark history comes out' (ii. 133), though both couples had lived in Italy for forty years and he hoped they would not be too shocked.

For on 13 October the decree nisi of the divorce proceedings had been pronounced on grounds of Frieda's adultery – attested to by Weekley and other (unnamed) witnesses, together with a formal deposition by Signora Samuelli of Gargnano.[115] Lawrence was cited as co-respondent, and his letter to Weekley was cited in the *News of the World* and quoted more extensively in the *Nottinghamshire Guardian*. Weekley was awarded custody of the children. There was only the wait now for the decree absolute, six months later – but at long last he had to tell his family now, and there was much indignation (ii. 109). Fortunately, England seemed a long way away again, and his past could be viewed dispassionately across the gap, though he continued to need old friends like McLeod to 'believe in one rather generously'. He had been worried that 'you had gone off from me a bit, because of *Sons and Lovers*. But one sheds ones sicknesses in books – repeats and presents again ones emotions, to be master of them' (ii. 90).

It was however to new friends that his most interesting thoughts were addressed in these first few months back in Italy. Marsh had made him think more deeply about his poetry than before, and – still under pressure about rhythm – he was able now to formulate a quite different kind of scansion from the conventional one; a way of reading whereby rhythm came about less by stresses than by the natural movement, pause and '*lingering* of the voice according to the feeling – it is the hidden *emotional* pattern that makes poetry, not the obvious form' (ii. 104). Though he had been irritated by Marsh's criticism at first, he was grateful now: 'I always thank God when a man will say straight out to me, what he has to say. But it's rare when one will' (ii. 106).

To Savage, he pondered what lay behind the suicide of his friend Middleton: the relation between the personal and the creative life of an artist. Going behind Middleton's poems to his essays, particularly those on women, Lawrence sees evidence of failure to satisfy or be satisfied sexually-and-psychically (for he would admit no separation). It is no good going to woman with poetry, idealism, or worship of beauty; she must be satisfied or she will inevitably cast the man aside. The artist, too, cannot deceive or be deceived, but must be satisfied as much in his sexuality as in his creativity, body and soul.[116] Yet Middleton (thought Lawrence), like so many puritanical Northern Europeans, despised the life of the body as a 'lower self' and secretly 'hated his flesh and blood' (ii. 95). The argument joins that of the essay on Thomas Mann: from Flaubert onward most modern art, in seeking 'purity' in the mastery of style over the corruption of life, 'is the art of self-hate and self-murder' (ii. 101). It was not surprising that a literally suicidal tendency has spread across Europe – Middleton taking chloroform at 29 is only another instance. But could anything have saved him?

Lawrence insists that by 'sex' he does not simply mean the forms of sexual intercourse. 'Sex is the fountain head, where life bubbles up into the person from the unknown' (ii. 102) and becomes activity, expression, thought, spirit-and-flesh as one. So sexual activity without creative relationship is simply debauch, which increases self-disgust. In the most interesting of the letters Lawrence speculates that, if solipsism is the greatest danger to the writer, heterosexual relationship may not be the only cure. The lyric poet combusts his moods into poetry and burns himself out. Middleton however had 'exhausted most of his moods: his one-man show was over: it needed to become a two person show'. If he could have found a woman he could love and who could love him, that would have been best; but, Lawrence broods:

most women don't leave scope to the man's imagination ... I should like to know why nearly every man that approaches greatness tends to homosexuality, whether he admits it or not: so that he loves the *body* of a man better than the body of a woman – as I believe the Greeks did, sculptors and all, by far. I believe a man projects his own image on another man, like on a mirror. But from a woman he wants himself re-born, re-constructed. So he can always get satisfaction from a man, but it is the hardest thing in life to get ones soul and body satisfied from a woman, so that one is free from oneself. And one is kept by all tradition and instinct from loving men, or a man – for it means just extinction of all the purposive influences. And one doesn't believe in one's power to find and to form the woman in whom one can be free – and one shoots oneself, if one is vital and feels powerfully and down to the core. (ii. 115)

He is not sure he knows what he is talking about, but it seems simple-minded to read this as a confession of his own homosexuality.[117] The use of 'one' shows that Lawrence is trying to imagine himself into what he thinks Middleton's predicament may have been; the discussion is rather theoretical (and not at all nervous), and the letter is written in the confidence that *he* had finally found a woman he could love and be loved by; who demonstrably liberated his imagination; and through whom he felt he had been 're-born' into new selfhood – albeit of course with all the inevitable difficulty involved in the breaking of self-enclosure by relationship with the 'other'. He had written a 'theological' account of this in the 'Foreword to *Sons and Lovers*'; and had recently found in Jane Harrison's *Ancient Art and Ritual* (1913) a confirmation of his belief that art essentially came 'out of religious yearning' (ii. 90), the desire to transform oneself. He always took *that* to be the significance of sex, rather than the physical pleasure; and the letter to Savage clearly implies that the greater otherness in heterosexuality makes it *more* transforming, though (failing that) a homosexual relationship might have saved Middleton from fatal solipsism.

However, that said, what does seem interesting is his willingness to consider himself not homosexual but *bisexual*, and to confess (if that be the right word for something so unashamed) to being attracted even more to the male body (as more like oneself) than to the female. George Neville tells of Lawrence's horror when told that women had pubic hair (though in a context of fascination with the female body). *The White Peacock* created a physical attraction and tenderness between young men,[118] but it would be a mistake to read too much into that, either, since his relationships with Jessie, Louie, Helen and Alice would seem to suggest that (even supposing his own sexuality till then indeterminate) he had found it rather too easy than otherwise to be attracted to female bodies also! It is a defect of our culture that we adopt such crudely binary language for sexual feeling, whereas other cultures recognise a much wider spectrum in which, for example, it is quite natural for young men to express mutual attraction physically, and to lust after women too. Lawrence's lack of shame about his range of feeling may be salutary – though his thoughts about it are still (he says) naïve. Most of all, however, he is thinking of Middleton in *contrast* with his good fortune in finding Frieda.

Moreover, he tells Murry in November what he had learned by committing himself to her. After being reproached by both Lawrence and Frieda for not answering their invitation to come to Fiascherino,[119] Murry had written of financial difficulties after the collapse of the *Blue Review*, the uncreative wear and tear of making a living by reviewing and his fear that these were affecting his relationship with Katherine. In keeping with what he had written to Else about self-sacrifice, and to Savage about the need for fulfilment if one were to be truly creative, Lawrence had no doubt about what Murry should do. He and Katherine should 'consult your own hearts, honestly'. Were they prepared to commit themselves exclusively to each other? 'It means forfeiting something. But the only principle I can see in this life, is that one *must* forfeit the less for the greater' (ii. 110). If they were, a number of consequences followed. Murry would have to become man enough to satisfy her, and he could only do so by fulfilling his own potential which (Lawrence saw clearly) would be as a critic. That, and not that he should slave at hackwork to give her luxuries, is what she would really want from him; and, to achieve it, he ought to respect her love enough to live on her money if necessary: 'You insult her. A woman unsatisfied must have luxuries. But a woman who loves a man would sleep on a board' (ii. 111). Yet if they came to Italy they could live in comfort on 185 lire a month – fifty more than the Lawrences needed, and the translation into lire of the £7 Katherine had told him Murry earned from the *Westminster* a week. On the other hand, if he hadn't the courage to trust either himself, or her love, it would be no wonder if she became dissatisfied with him.

He did not realise that Murry's work for the *Westminster* could not be done abroad (though he urged him to give it up, anyway), nor that Katherine had mortgaged her allowance to their creditors. Nevertheless he had put his finger unerringly on the essential lack of commitment to each other of Jack and Katherine; and the soundness of his advice would be shown when they came to follow it at Bandol two years later, where they had their happiest and most creative months together, and found their true voices for the first time. Lawrence's letter, however, is really about Frieda and himself: a testament of faith in the fundamental health of their relationship and his new selfhood now, because of the gamble they had taken. (His two latest stories, 'The Primrose Path' and 'The Mortal Coil' – the latter finished only a few weeks before the letter to Murry – were both markings of the opposite: tales of men who were unable to commit themselves, and so turned their women deathly, poisonous, dissatisfied; or if they gambled, gambled for the wrong things and destroyed themselves and those they 'loved'.) The question he wanted Katherine to answer: 'Could I live in a little place in Italy with Jack, and be lonely, have rather a bare life, but be happy'? (ii. 110), was one that could be answered triumphantly in his own case and (he clearly believed) in Frieda's, now.

One unfortunate result of the new happiness and sociability in Fiascherino, however, was that 'The Sisters' slowed to a halt. In early October, Lawrence had tried to recreate his earlier alterations onto the proofs of *Mrs. Holroyd*. Then, being down to his last 50 lire after paying the advance on the villino, and still waiting for the cheques from the *Westminster* and the *English Review* and the £10 he had asked for from Garnett, he jumped at Austin Harrison's offer to print in the *Review* not only his two existing German soldier stories, but two more as a sort of series, only at £15 each which was less than Pinker was asking. He had to ask Pinker to agree – not the best start – and it turned out to be a bad move, since having got them cut-rate, the *English Review* only published the first two anyway.[120] At the time however it seemed sensible; he thought 'Once—!' would do as the third if Harrison would risk it, and sat down to write as the fourth 'one I have had in mind for a long time' (ii. 82), which he was 'just finishing' on 31 October (ii. 99). This was 'The Mortal Coil', based on an anecdote told to Frieda by her father from his gambling days, about a young officer who ruins himself at the tables and is forced also to confront the additional disgrace of the discovery, in his room, of the body of the mistress he had treated with utter selfishness.

Lawrence also sent copies of a number of poems to Marsh (including 'Grief', inscribed by 'David Herbert/Son of Arthur John Lawrence', in memory of his mother), and some to Harrison.[121] Yet the novel that in Germany had seemed all-important made almost no progress. He tried to start again when he had done *Mrs. Holroyd*. On 6 October he told Garnett he was 'working away', and that it was '*so* different, so different from anything I have yet written, that I do nothing but wonder what it is like. When I get to page 200 I shall send you the MS. for your opinion' (ii. 82) – but it would be 6 January before the promise was redeemed (ii. 134). As money for his harvest of stories and sketches began to come in he could afford twenty-five litres of wine, and (for once) to loaf – since the sense of urgency was removed. He rationalised his unwillingness to get on: he had had a bad cold, was tired in his soul, or just lazy and enjoying himself;[122] but perhaps the main reason was the simplest: 'I was a fool to move in the midst of a flow' (ii. 99).

At the beginning of November he did start again; though it was still going slowly in mid-December, for 'it is so beautiful, one can't work' (ii. 119). On 21 December he promised to send the first half in a 'few days' (ii. 127); but on Boxing Day (26 December) – writing to Ezra Pound, who wanted to put him up for the Polignac Prize for poetry[123] – he was still in a mood when he would rather go rowing than 'grinding my nose off on the mill-stone of a novel' (ii. 132). By the end of the month however he had thought of a new title, 'The Wedding Ring', and was telling Garnett to expect a novel written almost in a different language from his last: 'I shan't write in the same manner as *Sons and Lovers* again, I think: in that hard, violent style full of sensation and presentation' (ii. 132).

So by Christmas everything had come together: happiness with Frieda, the novel getting going again, nomination for a poetry prize and perhaps a new volume of poems in America,[124] a range of new friendships – in marked contrast to the miserable Christmas in Gargnano. Sixteen peasants came in on Christmas Eve, and they sang the Pastorella at midnight. On Christmas Day Lawrence and Frieda went 'to English service in the Cochranes private chapel – lambs we looked I can tell you' (ii. 133). (A very wealthy man, Cochrane had entertained them to dinner with a butler and footman to wait on the four of them. He had also paid for an Anglican parson John Wood to come out, for six months.) They went on to a Christmas meal with the Huntingdons, and lunched with the Pearses on Boxing Day. Time, when happy, seemed to pass so quickly that 'One ought to live to be 1000, at the rate of these days' (ii. 131).

◆

CHAPTER THREE

January–November 1914
THE WEDDING RING

> You know that the perfect statue is in the marble, the kernel of it. But the
> thing is the getting it out clean.
>
> (ii. 146)

> I began a novel seven times. I have written quite a thousand pages that I
> shall burn. But now, thank God, Frieda and I are together, and the work is
> of me and her, and it is beautiful, I think.
>
> (ii. 161)

I 'It just missed being itself'

On 6 January 1914, at last, Lawrence sent off the first half of the new 'Sisters',
telling Garnett that 'the whole scheme of the book is changed – widened and
deepened' (ii. 134). Now he hoped to finish in six or eight weeks.

Distractions continued, however. He helped the peasant women harvest
olives; and went with his new friend John Wood, the Cochranes' clergyman, to
visit English sailors in Spezia harbour. Frieda, as ever, lazed happily in her
hammock;[1] but they were also 'always having visits or visiting' (ii. 135). On 19
January he took the steamer to Spezia to meet Eddie Marsh and his friend Jim
Barnes, and bring them back through the olive groves in the moonlight. After
supper outside, looking over the bay, they talked – and a scrap of remembered
conversation shows how happiness at Fiascherino had quietened grief and
conflict. 'Isn't "Farfalla" a beautiful word?' said Frieda. 'If I have a daughter I
will call her Farfalla' (Italian for 'butterfly'). 'They'd only call her Fanny', said
Marsh, and Lawrence laughed. Though as 'always' he looked to Marsh 'as
white as an apple dumpling ... he seemed extremely well for him, came for a
long walk without seeming the least tired – in good spirits'.[2] On 25 January
Constance Garnett arrived with her young friend Vera Volkhovsky, to spend a
month at the Albergo delle Palme, and another social round began.[3]

By then, however, he had almost finished the novel. When Marsh arrived he
had done 340 pages and was defining the difference from *Sons and Lovers* in new
terms, sensing how, behind contrasts in form and style, he was developing a new
way of looking at human beings. He thought that the 'Laocoon writhing and

shrieking' had gone,[4] and there was now 'a bit of stillness, like the wide, still, unseeing eyes of a Venus of Melos':

There is something in the Greek sculpture that my soul is hungry for – something of the eternal stillness that lies under all movement, under all life, like a source, incorruptible and inexhaustible. It is deeper than change, and struggling. So long I have acknowledged only the struggle, the stream, the change. And now I begin to feel something of the source, the great impersonal which never changes and out of which all change comes.

He began to feel this also in himself: 'so much one has fought and struggled, and shed so much blood and made so many scars and disfigured oneself'; but all the time in him, and in others, 'there is the unscarred and beautiful . . . a glimpse of the eternal and unchangeable that they are' – albeit some remain 'strange forms half-uttered' (ii. 137–8).

This was not of course wholly new. In *Sons and Lovers*, after the impersonality of sexual passion, Paul and Clara momentarily feel something of that stillness, in touch with life 'at the source'; though almost immediately they are caught up again in the change and struggle of the personal life in which their relationship founders. In the 'Foreword' Lawrence had begun to apply religious language to that 'source . . . out of which all change comes', and to the deeper *impersonal* modes of being in men and women which (he sensed) lay behind all personal conflicts.[5] What was new was the attempt to make that deeper dimension the ground (now) of the novel's exploration. The classical statue, perhaps focused by Jane Harrison's contention that art comes 'out of religious yearning', infuses the body with mysterious insight, stilled, because attuned to an incorruptible 'source' of being. Presumably, to look at the Hellenistic 'Laocoon' is to want to know about the characters and the causes of the hectic external battle; whereas the 'unseeing' eyes are directed inward, to the source of harmony – or discord.[6]

Yet to try to tap that kind of being in the young girl growing up in a large family, and experiencing her first scarring failure in sexual relationship, was to risk alienating all the admirers of *Sons and Lovers*, with Edward Garnett at their head. The more the new work determined to explore the inward and hidden; grown impatient with the firmly outlined personalities of *Sons and Lovers*; the more undefined and unsatisfying the characterisation might seem. Above all, the new 'stillness' would involve turning away from drama, which had been one of the great strengths in *Sons and Lovers*. Garnett was warned that 'You may not find it as exciting as you expected', and McLeod that it was 'weird' (ii. 134, 136).

So Lawrence was 'not very much surprised, nor even very much hurt' to find Garnett highly critical of the first half. He even agreed with two major charges: that Ella's first love-affair (with Ben Templeman) was 'wrong' – though she had to have 'some experience before she meets her Mr Birkin' – and that her character was 'incoherent', which had come from 'trying to graft on to the character of Louie the character, more or less, of Frieda'. He was troubled however about 'the artistic side being in the background' (ii. 142). It is not clear whose phrase this is or what it means: probably 'you have pushed the novelist's art to the rear'? Or just possibly 'all your art has gone into creating background (rather than characters and action)'? Anyway, what is interesting about Lawrence's refusal to accept *this* criticism is that he now draws a clear connection between his new way of writing, and a change in himself because of his marriage: 'I have no longer the joy in creating vivid scenes, that I had in *Sons and Lovers*. I don't care much more about accumulating objects in the powerful light of emotion, and making a scene of them. I have to write differently ... I am going through a transition stage myself.' So the novel is transitional and he will put it in the fire if need be, but 'it must produce its flowers'. Even if these be 'frail or shadowy, they will be all right if they are true to their hour. – It is not so easy for one to be married. In marriage one must become something else. And I am changing, one way or the other.' He is no longer interested in 'manners and circumstance and scenes' (ii. 142–3). Without being able to say clearly where he is headed, it is plain that it is away from the traditional English novel.

He proposes to send Garnett 150 pages of the second half; hoping he will agree that Ella, as shown now, had to have had 'a love episode, a significant one' though 'it must not be a Templeman episode'. He feels this second half 'very beautiful', though perhaps not 'sufficiently incorporated to please you. I do not try to incorporate it very much – I prefer the permeating beauty.' If Garnett still dislikes what he has done, however, he will abandon it and its 'exhaustive method', and write 'pure object and story' (ii. 142–3); presumably for the money.

Garnett disliked the second batch even more. Indeed this time he went beyond charges of failed execution, to reject (Lawrence felt) all he was trying to do, and hence his new *self*. For several months he did not reveal how much this second letter upset him; but the effect of even the first one on the new work was dramatic – for no sooner had he come back from Spezia, having posted the second batch, than he decided to abandon the book unfinished (ii. 144). He did not however return to more traditional fiction, character and plot. He had to live by his writing – but he still had £50 in the bank at Spezia which could be made to last till May. By 31 January he had decided to try for what he still believed in, by beginning all over again.

On 7 February he wrote (but to Mitchell Kennerley, rather than Garnett) to say he had started afresh, and would get the new version typed though he did not know how he would pay for it. He had regained confidence about publication; and was now beginning to think of Kennerley (who had offered to publish a volume of poems as well as the new novel, and to place stories in America) as a possible alternative patron and adviser (ii. 144). He spent two afternoons in the boat, happily prodding for shellfish under the rocks – then told McLeod what had happened, in another memorable sculptural image.

I have begun my novel again – for about the seventh time ... I had nearly finished it. It was full of beautiful things, but it missed – I knew that it just missed being itself. So here I am, must sit down and write it out again. I know it is quite a lovely novel really – you know that the perfect statue is in the marble, the kernel of it. But the thing is the getting it out clean. (ii. 146)

Already spring was coming; it was a good time to start anew.

Fortunately a few pages (373–80) of 'The Sisters II' have survived – probably the last he wrote but never sent to Garnett when he abandoned the book. From these one can see what he was after, but also how much he was prepared to risk seeming 'vague' (ii. 143) and 'shadowy' and not 'incorporated' enough, in going for impersonal source rather than personal character, and preferring to explore what lay half-hidden in the background rather than action front-of-stage.

Ella is about to leave Walmsley Mill after a tiff with Birkin. Her family being away on holiday, she has spent much of her time alone: 'She felt her life was going on inside her, she could not concern herself with outside things ... her soul was so busy'. When with Birkin however, underlying (but impersonal) tensions break through. She suddenly sees him as threatening, and flinches; and then throws her arms around him asking 'in a muffled, tortured voice' if he loves her.

She clung to him. But his breast was strange to her. His arms were around her tight, hard, compressing her, he was quivering, rigid, holding her against him. But he was strange to her. He was strange to her, and it was almost agony. He was cold to her, however he held her hard in his power and quivered. She felt he was cold to her. And the quivering man stiffened with desire was strange and horrible to her. She got free again, and, with her hands to her temples, she slid away to the floor at his feet, unable to stand, unable to hold her body erect. She must double up, for she could not bear it. But she got up to go away. And before she reached the door, she was crouching on the floor again, holding her temples in agony. Her womb, her belly, her heart were all in agony. She crouched together on the floor, crying like some wild animal in pain, with a kind of mooing noise, very dreadful to hear, a sound she was unaware of, that came from her unproduced, out of the depths of her body in torture.

Birkin's response is dealt with similarly 'exhaustively':

He stood white to the gills, with wide, dark eyes staring blankly. His heart inside him felt red-hot, so that he panted as he breathed. His mind was blank. He knew she did not feel him any more. He knew he had no part in her, that he was out of place. And he had nothing to say—But gradually he grew a little calmer, his eyes lost their wide, dark, hollow look. He was coming to himself.

"What did I do?" he asked.

It has little to do with Birkin personally, and everything with the coming to the surface of the deep bruise inflicted on Ella's inner being by her earlier love affair. She will explain that she is 'really not hysterical ... it is working the old strain off that makes one so upset'. At the same time she knows 'that something was taking place, implicating her with him, which she could never revoke or escape. And blindly, almost shrinking, she lapsed forward.' Birkin, too, is afraid. 'It seems', he writes, 'that everything has come toppling down ... and here I am entangled in the ruins and fragments of my old life, and struggling to get out. You seem to me some land beyond—'[7]

The fiction is not autobiographical, but it has used life, and one can glimpse the connection with how Lawrence felt his marriage was changing him, and therefore changing what, and how, he wanted to write. What seems most overdone about the scene is in fact directly adapted from life: he has transferred to Ella's trauma over a failed love-affair, Frieda's trauma over her lost children – and also used his own experience of feeling utterly excluded and helpless in the presence of such abandonment to grief (i. 421). Moreover a glimpse of Templeman at the end of the fragment confirms that what Birkin must overcome is once again the charge that (like Paul Morel, or Gerald in the first 'Sisters', or Moest in 'New Eve and Old Adam') he cannot give *himself* in love – hence the woman's fear of sexual passion that seems combined with self-absorption. Though there can be no guessing the story of Ella's earlier affair, or what Garnett thought was 'wrong' about it, that glimpse of Templeman suggests the nature of the hurt he inflicted, and also why it should bring such a powerful response from the recesses of her being, when she feels it may be happening again with Birkin. Templeman's 'peculiar, straying walk, the odd, separate look', and his short-sightedness, all seem to point to a man absorbed in himself, impervious to all that is 'other' – and hence destructive of the inner being of any woman unfortunate enough to be in love with him.[8] Conversely, Birkin's 'wide, dark eyes staring blankly' because of intense feeling – followed by a collapse of his old life and the longing for Ella as a 'land beyond' – are an indication that he has been touched to the quick of his being, the 'source' of new unsolipsistic life. Lawrence's new art seems determined to deal – at whatever cost in normal novelistic terms – with what lies behind Ella's collapsed mooing cry, Birkin's 'red-hot' heart, and suddenly 'unseeing' eyes; that is, with movements of inner being which now seem to him much more important than all the forms of outer behaviour, speech or character. It seems clear that the novel was to end, not merely with a wedding ring, but with Ella and Birkin beginning to find their true selves, 'the eternal and unchangeable that they are', and ceasing to be 'strange forms half-uttered'.

However, Garnett's response convinced Lawrence that the novel had 'missed being itself'. Though he remained sure that a perfect statue was there still, *in* the marble of the fiction, he had yet to find the way to get it out clean.

II Starting Again

Indeed he had trouble getting going again. On 9 February he spoke of beginning for the seventh time; by 7 March this had become the eleventh, though at last it was on its way (ii. 153).

Part of the trouble was social: 'we are eternally going out to lunch or dinner when we don't want to, and amusing rather elderly, but very nice people whom we don't want to amuse' (ii. 153). The main reason was the arrival of Constance Garnett, with her young friend Vera Volkhovsky, to spend a month at the Albergo delle Palme. (Vera stayed on longer.) Lawrence went over to Spezia to meet them on 25 January, and as well as visits to them in Lerici and from them to Fiascherino, and walks and expeditions, they were introduced to all the new expatriate acquaintances and were duly entertained by all.

The place and its people suddenly look different through the eyes of a rather sharp English lady. She thought her room by the sea delightful enough, but her first impression of Lerici was practical and class-conscious. 'This is a working class place' she told Edward, so there are few tourists and even fewer middle class – hence the cheapness – only peasants, factory hands and sailors, and 'a large sprinkling of very uninviting-looking young women. Lawrence says the sailors bring a lot of shady characters in their train.' He sounds suddenly rather defensive! These had not been matters of first interest to him. To Bunny a week later she again speaks of the 'squalid working class population' and the tall houses and passages like ravines 'very dark & chilly. Nowhere a trace of care or of decoration', everywhere filth and smells. Yet the beauty of the countryside into which Lawrence walked with her, and the views from the hills, won her over.[9]

She was also tart about his new friends. She thought he and Frieda seemed more settled, and his cough had gone, though 'he looks holloweyed & thin, of course ... Frieda blooms like a rose. They see a great deal of all the respectable English people here', and 'are very popular' – though that might be because English expatriate communities are so dull; and they might not be so welcome were it known that they were unmarried. (She was wrong about that, as it happened.) Moreover, 'I should have thought they'd have found all these English residents rather a bore – I mean they strike me as having nothing in common with them ... But you know what a social creature he is & besides I believe it flatters him to feel that even with these people he can be a success.'[10] That seems acute. Significantly, too, she lets us glimpse the cost to Lawrence of her husband's criticism – which his letters conceal. He had a row with Frieda within a week of Constance's arrival; the first we have heard of for some time. Often the quarrels that visitors reported were the result of the pressures or temptations *they* introduced. We have Frieda's own word for it now (writing to Edward), that it was 'jolly to have Mrs Garnett here' because 'I go to her and pour out my Lawrence woes to her and she listens patiently and feelingly, so I never feel I am disloyal to L' (ii. 151). That might have looked different to Lawrence. However he seemed to have taken Garnett's criticisms well – at first. On 31 January, only two days after Lawrence's reply to the first letter, and six since her own arrival, Constance reports that he had already begun writing again 'with great spirit. He told me of your letter & said you were quite right. He didn't seem downcast, at all, but I fancy full of confidence that he could get it right.' She admired his pluck and industry, though she feared he would soon exhaust material from his previous life and find little in his new one. But on 5 February there is a different story; signs of trouble in Lawrence, and with Frieda:

Lawrence has put a good face on the blow about his novel, but he has looked very white & pinched the last two days. He says he agrees with you entirely. Frieda & he seem to have been having a set-to yesterday & the day before – & both looked as though they had been crying – but today they are both happier again. Lawrence is a queer little changeling – there's a sort of little demon of perversity in him, & yet he is so full of bonhomie & genuine friendliness & kindness. Frieda shows to much greater advantage in her own house.[11]

Constance also knew her better, after the confidings. However (as she prepared to leave) we find that the row may have been about a deeper problem of loyalty than Frieda's imparting of 'Lawrence woes'.

About 21 February, Frieda wrote to Garnett in terms that show his second letter had been critical of her, too.

I have been so cross with you! You attacked me in your letter and I was cross but I am afraid you were right and made me realise my wrongs in a way – I had'nt cared twopence about L's novel; Over the children I thought he was beastly, he hated me for being miserable, not a moment of misery did he put up with; he denied all the suffering and suffered all the more – like his mother before him; how we fought over this! In revenge I did not care about his writing. If he denies my life and suffering I deny his art, so you see he wrote without me at the back of him. (ii. 150–1)

Though the second 'Sisters' might be a failure, she thought there was something deeper trying to struggle out in it than there had been in *Sons and Lovers*, which she felt had had no 'Hinterland der Seele': 'I who am a believer though I dont know in what, to me it seems an irreligious book'. Writers tend to concentrate on externals – the 'pretty curl in the neck', rather than 'the living, striving *she*' within. Now she will throw herself into the novel, knowing that 'you men cant do things alone – Just as little as we can *live* alone', and feeling that she has got over the worst 'with E. and the children' now (ii. 151).

Her view of *Sons and Lovers* is mostly hindsight. At the time she had been impatient with Lawrence's first attempts to capture a hinterland that could not be seen or touched, or thought or spoken by the characters; and her sense of what he was up to is belated – yet this letter is significant. She had indeed been fighting to make him bring his feelings into the open and live them through; and to force him to pay attention and imagination to hers, instead of closing himself off from his own suffering and the other person's as he used to do. She had broken him open, again and again – and in both 'New Eve and Old Adam' and 'The Sisters', he had begun to imagine sensitively from her point of view. Since Christmas 1912, not only had the 'religious' sense been becoming more and more articulate in them both, but Lawrence had also specifically acknowledged Frieda's part in this, and generalised it into the theology of the 'Foreword'. We have his word, not only that he did need a woman at the back of him to be truly creative, but that this was because she put him in touch with 'the unknown' – not through any ideas or beliefs, but through the encounter with the entirely 'other', stranger and opposite, in sexual relationship. Though Frieda's language of '*she*' and the 'curl' is crude, compared with the letter Lawrence had already written to Garnett, it is clear that the row about her denial of his art had now brought her into unison with his deepest purpose, in the novel he had been struggling to write.

She had not deeply cared about his writing. She had boasted to Dowson that she knew someone who would be 'better than Galsworthy', had been fascinated by watching Lawrence at work in Icking; and felt pleased and proud of contributing feminine insight to the creation of Miriam and Mrs Morel; but Lawrence had been amused by her tendency to judge the worth of his poems by whether or not she was the heroine. It was important in her relationship with Else that Lawrence should be recognised, so she was happy to report the 'to-do' that had been made of him that summer in England – a bad summer for *her* – but there is in the word itself a tinge of surprise. Moreover, the new work had begun by mocking a 'Godalmightiness' recognisably hers; and though the book had grown to be more and more seriously about a woman finding herself, Lawrence's promised work for woman more valuable than the suffrage, Frieda had much preferred the discarded 'The Insurrection of Miss Houghton'; and the second 'Sisters' had based the development of the girl Ella not on her, but Louie Burrows. So her letter to Garnett marks a significant change of attitude.[12]

It would be a new start in several ways. To feel Frieda solidly behind his writing for the first time, especially in its deeper religious as well as feminist purpose, would help rebuild the confidence that Garnett's disapproval had undermined. He could rely on her to be critical; but more constructively perhaps than before, since she now felt she had a personal stake. It would be more likely that, in the effort to fuse the young with the older Ella in rewriting, Frieda would contribute memories from her own childhood. But above all, the change of title to 'The Wedding Ring' implied that the new book would be not merely about Ella but about marriage, so the insights that came from his relationship with Frieda might transfuse the whole imaginative journey, not just the ending.

Most significantly of all, given his association of the new way of writing with *his* 'marriage', the inverted commas were now to be removed. On 22 February Lawrence quietly announced to May Holbrook that they had decided to marry in June (ii. 149). The very idea of marrying the author of *Sons and Lovers* had given Frieda the creeps; but she had committed herself now to marry the author of the rewritten 'Wedding Ring'. At the end of February, however, still trying to find a new beginning, he had to take one more criticism of the second 'Sisters'; though it may have been easier because he had so firmly abandoned it, and because of what had happened with Frieda. Before she left, Constance spoke her mind about the book':

He said he had begun it again because it was so 'boshy, don't you know' & suggested I should read it. Well, having now read most of it, I agree with him that it *is* awfully poor stuff. The characters aren't living at all, one doesn't believe in them, or take them at the author's apparent valuation. They seem simply invented to hang the pages of description of sexual experiences and emotions on to, & the theories about these emotions. And I felt all the time that all the love part is ladled out so disproportionately that it isn't effective. It palls really because there's no light & shade – it all seems cheap intensity and violence at the same hysterical pitch all through. It seems to me much below The White Peacock and The Trespasser & I'm glad he realises it isn't up to much. Of course there are very good bits in it – & the underlying notion is good & strong – but it's so incredibly shapeless & inartistic – so sloppy in its presentation. I feel uneasy about his future if he can go off like that. But the new beginning he has made is very promising (though of course he sets off at the top note of intensity with the father of the heroines & one doesn't see how the interest can rise after that quite).[13]

Perhaps it is as well that a fragment has survived to be judged against this slashing critique. Lawrence was obviously still learning his new way of writing, but the scene between Ella and Birkin hardly seems that bad – though Constance may not have read so far, and the affair with Templeman may have been 'boshier', particularly if Lawrence had tried to invent something quite different from his own experience with Louie. The force of Constance's reaction, however, holds some threat even for a development beyond the relative crudity of the second 'Sisters'. The complaint of unvaried pitch and lack of light and shade may well have been just – but the charges of excessive sex, violence, hysteria, anticipate the reactions of readers who would object to the whole vision of the human being which Lawrence's later form and style try to articulate.

However, Constance also provides a valuable clue to the latest set of false starts. The second 'Sisters' had gone behind the first one, to discover how and why Ella had become what she was and behaved as she did, which meant going into her girlhood and first love-affair, perhaps even her childhood (though that is not certain). What does seem clear now, is that for 'The Wedding Ring', concerned not merely with Ella but with marriage – Lawrence had decided to go even further back, before the birth of his heroine, and to begin the seventh time with the 'intensity' of her father, and (presumably) his courtship of her mother. Constance implies that this was quite different from the start of 'Sisters II'. But four more attempts, before the fiction finally took off, suggest that he was still dissatisfied. Another lucky survival reveals that 'The Wedding Ring' finally began – though probably not in much detail – with Ella's grandparents.[14]

On February 25 Constance left for home. On 7 March Lawrence told Savage that he had started 'for about the eleventh time', but that at last 'It is on its legs and is going strong' (ii. 153).

III The Social Round

Yet social distractions continued. Vera Volkhovsky stayed on for a while. In early March Lawrence and Frieda were invited to an extraordinary cosmopolitan lunch for twenty-six guests in Levanto. The host was the popular and prolific Russian writer Aleksander Amfiteatrov, 'a great fat laughing man'; and among the guests was one Peshkov who claimed to be (but actually was not) 'an adopted son of Maxim Gorky, little, dark, agile, full of life, and a great wild Cossack wife whom he had married for passion and had come to hate'.[15] The odd assortment at table made Lawrence feel suddenly 'English and stable and solid in comparison' though he loved their 'absolute carelessness about everything but just what interested them' (ii. 155). They would see more of these Russians. On a lovely spring day they went picknicking 'high up' in the hills, probably with the Waterfields, looking over at the Carrara mountains, the valley of the Magra and the sea coast sweeping round (ii. 156). Else came on a visit in April.

There were new friends among the locals too. A 24-year-old seminarian from Sarzana got tipsy visiting in Tellaro, and lost his way back, requiring strong coffee and redirection; after which he began to bring Frieda music. (The fragment of 'Sisters II' describes Ella singing, alone at her piano: 'Her idea of time was sketchy, but she had a strong, rather beautiful voice'.[16]) The Tellaro schoolmistress Eva Rainusso would come by, partly to help Lawrence with his Italian, but also because she was in love with the handsome guitar-playing Luigi, though he alas less so with her. On Holy Thursday night (by custom here, the crucifixion was on Thursday) they watched the procession in Tellaro carrying Jesus to the tomb. A new Italian acquaintance, Gamba – a friend of the Futurists Boccioni and Marinetti – maintained that the Renaissance had seen a resurgence of the Roman spirit (mathematic, rational, material, individualist) overthrowing the German mysticism of the Middle Ages[17] – but Lawrence remained puzzled by the mixture of rational materialism with superstition in the religion of Tellaro. Yet the procession through the dark stair-like streets, the flickering candles on the sills, the noise of clappers in front ('the grinding of the bones of Judas'), the hoarse sound of the sea mingled with the mournful chanting, made 'a fearful impression' on him. 'It is the *mystery* that does it – it is Death itself, robbed of its horrors, and only Fear and Wonder going humbly behind' (ii. 164). At Easter a priest arrived to bless their house (ii. 163).

Though the decree absolute of Frieda's divorce was published in *The Times* law report on 27 April, the English expatriates remained friendly. On 5 May the poet and playwright Herbert Trench came to see them, and invited them to Florence. The Baronessa di Rescis, a friend of Mrs Pearse, invited them to the Abruzzi. They had become such friends now with the British Consul at Spezia, Thomas Dunlop, that his wife Madge offered to type 'The Wedding Ring'. (They also took the news of the divorce 'very nicely'; ii. 168.) The Lawrences spent a weekend with them in mid May (ii. 174).[18]

They had themselves acquired a house guest in May. Ivy Low had written Lawrence a fan-letter, hailing him, after *Sons and Lovers*, as the most important new novelist for her generation, and telling him that admiration for his work had become a touchstone to literary friends such as Viola Meynell and Catherine Jackson. He replied (on the Baronial notepaper they had been using up) and after a brief correspondence invited her to visit. She came, 'rigged out' in her friend Catherine Jackson's 'only "tailor made"' outfit,[19] and an embroidered Rumanian blouse.

She was a sprightly 25-year-old, niece to Barbara Low (a pioneer of Freudian psychoanalysis in Britain) and already the author of two novels, the second of which the libraries had refused to take. Though her memory cannot always be relied upon she gives a lively account of the villino and its inhabitants. Only from her do we learn of the little building at the gate, covered with vines and with pink and blue flowers waving from its roof – and over its door 'in charmingly spaced capitals' the word 'latrina', new to her, but clearly for strangers who came to help Ettore with his harvest. With her too we can enter the house, and see where they had their meals outside.

The villa itself was divided in the middle by a stone staircase – on one side was the sitting room, and a bedroom over it; on the other, the kitchen, and a bedroom over that. They had a table and a cottage-piano and a bookshelf and a sofa and a chair or two in the sitting room, and a bed and a washstand in each of the bedrooms. In front of the villa was a vegetable garden and to the left a little path leading up to a rustic summerhouse with a mushroom-like stone table in the middle.

She could not recall her first impression of Lawrence in Spezia, but she thought Frieda very pretty, though 'a bit sloppy and arty' and with 'the limpest hand I had ever taken in mine; it simply fell out of my clasp'. Lawrence asked whether he struck her as working class, and then complained when she said yes (albeit in a quiet, tired, skilled-workman sort of way, not one of a factory mob), whereas he had had much more complimentary thoughts about her in the boat. She probably took him altogether too seriously – for what she wanted to say was 'I loved you the moment I saw you', and to change places with her hostess.

The visit, unsurprisingly, ran into difficulties. Lawrence thought her 'rather a nice girl' (ii. 169), and enjoyed walks with her to get the groceries, talking endlessly. Frieda, Ivy remembered, 'used to say that the last thing she saw of us as we went down the garden path was our wagging heads inclined toward one another, and that when we returned, the first thing she saw was our jaws opening and shutting'. The first week, for Ivy, 'was the happiest I had ever known'; but then – inexplicably to her – she began to be found fault with, for having no sense of rhythm (when she kept bumping into Lawrence as they walked), for not helping in the house and kitchen (though Frieda seldom did), for her musical taste, for not understanding people, for being fidgety and garrulous. What never seems to have occurred to her was that she was simply outstaying her welcome. Lawrence had thought she was only coming for 'a short time' (ii. 168), 'a few days' (ii. 169). She says she stayed six weeks, and though this is almost certainly misremembered, and Catherine Carswell's 'month' more likely,[20] it was still far too long for a man who was trying to finish a book – and whose wife was getting restive about the hero-worship. Each would get irritated when the other paid much attention to or got much from some new acquaintance. Ivy records a visit by the 'Peshkovs' when Frieda, 'who always loved a new man, contributed honey to the atmosphere' but Lawrence, having carefully discussed a story of the man's, then pulled him to pieces as soon as they had gone, perhaps 'unconsciously' (says Ivy) 'irritated by Frieda's enthusiasms'. (She saw some jealousies more clearly than others.) When finally they took her to Sarzana – one of the peasants was driving his cart to the station – she and Lawrence were gloomy (she says), but 'Frieda chatted pleasantly at first and then relapsed into one of her luxurious catlike trances, in which she could enjoy God's sunshine and scenery without bothering herself about the complicated people He had put into them.' There were tears at the tiny dusty station, and Ivy says she felt her self-confidence in ruins for some time afterwards, but the friendship held and was to be renewed in the summer.

Lawrence's sociability was dealt another blow. There had been silence from Murry since Lawrence had urged them to come to Italy on Katherine's allowance. In fact they had gone to Paris to escape creditors and write; but Murry could not live on reviews of French books for *The Times Literary Supplement*; and when he was offered the post of art critic to the *Westminster* he decided to return, at the cost of selling everything they had, and going through bankruptcy proceedings on 27 March. The same day, Katherine's constant acolyte Ida Baker had left for Rhodesia to look after her ailing father.[21] So Murry was keeping his courage up when he wrote now that they were all right – but Lawrence was relieved to have a letter at last. He had feared they thought him 'an interfering Sunday-school Superintendent sort of person who went too far in his superintending and became impossible: – stepped the just too far, which is the crime of crimes' (ii. 160). He felt guilty. He was 'always going in headlong and crawling out ignominious and furious, mostly with myself'. Behind the self-reproach however lay another hurt. For Murry seems to have reported Marsh and Campbell as saying that Lawrence tried to be all things to all men.

'It is so horribly difficult', writes an obviously hurt Lawrence, 'not to betray oneself, somehow, with all the different people ... But really, one *can* only be towards each person that which corresponds to him, more or less.' The charge was only half true of his friendships across classes, from peasants to rich English expatriates, and intellectuals, but Constance Garnett had also perceived how he wanted to be a social success – and there was enough truth to make him angry: 'Oh, I think to myself, if only one could have a few real friends, who will understand a bit along with one. They are all against one. I feel Marsh against me with the whole of his being: and Campbell would like to be, for he is a perverse devil' (ii. 160–1). Whatever Marsh may actually have said about peasants, poets and plutocrats in Fiascherino he was well-disposed to Lawrence (and had befriended Murry even more). Campbell was about to invite them to stay in Selwood Terrace when they came to England. Lawrence's anger perhaps betrays an atom of truth in the charge, though it was hardly kind of Murry to pass it on.

IV 'The Wedding Ring'

The week after the Amfiteatrov lunch his novel was going 'slowly' (ii. 156), but by 3 April he could tell Murry that, despite the false starts and 'quite a thousand pages that I shall burn ... Frieda and I are together, and the work is of me and her ... I have done two-thirds' (ii. 161). On 22 April he posted Garnett what had been typed, expecting there would only be 80 pages to write now, which he thought might take three more weeks. He could guess the length, and go quickly, because he was near the end of 'The Sisters II' (Ella having met her school inspector) and was revising from the last of 'The Sisters I': 'I am sure of this now, this novel. It is a big and beautiful work. Before, I could not get my soul into it. That was because of the struggle and the resistance between Frieda and me. Now you will find her and me in the novel, I think, and the work is of both of us' (ii. 164).

Though he had restrained his feelings about Garnett's criticism, the more he thought about that second letter the sharper the distinction he wanted to draw now, between criticism of failures in execution, and refusal to accept the whole purpose of the author. He had proved himself willing to accept critical advice – but he was 'not after all a child working erratically. All the time, underneath, there is something deep evolving itself out in me. And it is *hard* to express a new thing, in sincerity' (ii. 165) He wanted perceptive help – not to be told the new work was '*common*' and sent back to the first 'Sisters', which may have held 'the germ of this novel: woman becoming individual, self-responsible, taking her own initiative', but which he now thought immaturely flippant and jeering. For 'primarily I am a passionately religious man, and my novels must be written from the depth of my religious experience.' It was when his 'deep feeling doesn't find its way out' that 'a sort of jeer comes instead, and sentimentality, and purplism. But you should see the religious, earnest, suffering man in me'. Constance had told him he had 'no true nobility – with all my cleverness and charm. But that is not true' (ii. 165).

A letter to Pinker the same day shows him beginning to wonder whether, if Garnett proved lukewarm about 'The Wedding Ring' too, it might be better to take it to another publisher, as Garnett had said he was free to do. He still felt he ought to give Duckworth first option; but now as a matter 'of gratitude, or perhaps of moral obligation, that is all' (ii. 167). Both Pinker and Curtis Brown implied – as they naturally would – that *Sons and Lovers* ought to have done better. He had received only £25 from Kennerley so far,[22] and £100 in advances from Duckworth, who had sent an account showing the book still £15 short of repaying his advance. There was only a little left in the bank. He did not think Garnett believed in his work commercially, and did not want to involve his friend in Duckworth losing money;[23] yet he was now being told that he could earn £300 for the new book from the publisher Methuen, more than all three of his novels had made together. On the other hand, if he broke with Duckworth he could hardly expect Garnett to go on reading and advising on everything he wrote. He owed him a great deal – but more was riding on his response to 'The Wedding Ring' than had ever been the case before.

For the past fortnight, Lawrence told Savage on 7 May, he had felt 'seedy', often a sign of stress. Ivy was with them, he was struggling to finish the book, and he feared it might be rejected because 'it is what they call improper'

(ii. 169). However he urged Murry the next day not to 'give up feeling that people *do* want to hear what you say':

Four days, and I shall have finished my novel, pray God ... Can you understand how cruelly I feel the want of friends who will believe in me a bit. People think I'm a sort of queer fish that can write: that is all. And how I loathe it. There isn't a soul cares a damn for me, except Frieda – and it's rough to have all the burden put on her. (ii. 171)

The following day with about 3,000 words to go, he told Garnett that Frieda wanted the novel called '*The Rainbow*' (ii 173). By the 16th it was finished and typed, and he was checking the last of the typescript at the Dunlops' house in La Spezia (ii. 174).

Remembering the cutting of *Sons and Lovers*, Lawrence expected Garnett to 'swear when you see the length. It's a magnum opus with a vengeance' (ii. 173).[24] Another survival, the report on it by Kennerley's reader Alfred Kuttner, confirms that it had not only fused 'Sisters I' with 'Sisters II' but now dealt with three generations of Brangwens. (Kuttner complained because he thought the 'real story' had to do with Ella and Gudrun, and it was not 'until we are almost half way through' that 'we deal with them'.) So 'The Wedding Ring' had grown towards *The Rainbow*, but with many differences still – and the action went well on into what is now *Women in Love*. The Ella and Birkin story must have ended with their marriage; and a remark of Kuttner's about Gerald 'raping Gudrun in the boathouse' – perhaps his way of describing an early version of the scene in chapter twenty-four of *Women in Love* – might suggest that the denouement of their story may have stayed broadly as it was in 'The Sisters I': an illegitimate child, but a hopeful ending also. Kuttner, who had written a Freudian review of *Sons and Lovers*, thought Lawrence had repeated himself, was too obsessed by sex and ought perhaps to get himself psycho-analysed, though he also expressed some admiration.[25] As Lawrence posted duplicate typescripts to Garnett and to Kennerley however, he was confident of the future.

In his last three weeks in Fiascherino he felt lazy again. He had an idea for his next novel which would require reading in the British Museum (no hint as to what and why) – and he also thought he 'ought to do some Ligurian sketches' though not just yet (ii. 175). What he did do was some reading in the Futurists. He had initially come across them in translation, in the first issue of Harold Monro's *Poetry and Drama* in 1913. (In August that year he chose poems to send Monro that he hoped he 'might find futuristic'; ii. 53 – though how much knowledge that implies is a question.[26]) Now on 2 June 1914 he told McLeod, always the correspondent he thought most interested in discussing new ideas, that he has been reading 'a fat book' of Futurist poetry, and a 'book of pictures – and I read Marinetti's and Paolo Buzzi's manifestations and essays – and Sofficis essays on cubism and futurism' (ii. 180). All were in Italian, and the last only recently published. The books (and impetus) must have come from his new acquaintance Gamba, who may also have discussed them with him.[27]

Lawrence's reactions were decidedly mixed. He liked their determination to be 'honest and stick by what is in us' (even if that tended to mean what is 'horrid'); and to purge 'old forms and sentimentalities' – though it was silly and like college students 'to deny every scrap of tradition and experience', and he did not agree with their alternative idea of progress 'down the purely male or intellectual or scientific line'.

They will even use their intuition for intellectual and scientific purpose. The one thing about their art is that it *isn't* art, but ultra scientific attempts to make diagrams of certain physic or mental states. It is ultra–ultra intellectual, going beyond Maeterlinck and the Symbolistes ... the most self conscious, intentional, pseudo scientific stuff on the face of the earth. Marinetti begins 'Italy is like a great Dreadnought surrounded by her torpedo boats'. That is it exactly – a great mechanism. Italy has got to go through the most mechanical and dead stage of all – everything is appraised according to its mechanic value – everything is subject to the laws of physics. (ii. 180–1)

Since the seeds of a good deal of Lawrence's later thinking lie here, it is as well to be careful about what is being said. It is not (yet) an attack on science nor on the intellect, though he did now think there was another and greater wisdom in the body and the blood. Maths had been his best subject at school; botany the study and 'Botany' Smith the professor he had most cared for and learned from at university, and the teaching of botany as well as art and literature what he liked and did best at Croydon.[28] He knew something of science, and took his knowledge seriously. Marinetti and the Futurists were not scientists, but painters and poets, and Lawrence is speaking, as artist, not against the Futurist enthusiasm for movement, power, speed and the beauty of machines, but against trying to turn art into pseudo-science. Art for him cannot be 'ultra-ultra intellectual', intentional, conscious. Nor can the artist's portrayal of the *whole* human being aspire (or be reduced) to intellectual abstraction like geometry, or the functionalism of a machine working wholly by the laws of physics. Science may be required to 'progress' along 'purely' intellectual lines (though its progress surely depends on intuition, too?); but to require 'everything', and especially art, to do so is deadening. Lawrence is not necessarily attacking science in arguing that there is more to human and national life than scientific intellect.

The 'Foreword to *Sons and Lovers*', in calling woman the embodiment of the creative being of 'God the Father', and man the embodiment of the knowing of the 'Son', had prepared for naming the intellect 'male' here. Lawrence's gender specification raises all sorts of problems, but also hints at what the nature of his answer to the Futurists will be, ensuring another kind of 'progress', in different, less exclusive, and less conscious terms:

I think the only re-sourcing of art, re-vivifying it, is to make it more the joint work of man and woman. I think *the* one thing to do, is for men to have courage to draw nearer to women, expose themselves to them, and be altered by them: and for women to accept and admit men. That is the only way for art and civilisation to get a new life, a new start – by bringing themselves together, men and women – revealing themselves each to the other, gaining great blind knowledge and suffering and joy, which it will take a big further lapse of civilisation to exploit and work out. Because the source of all life and knowledge is in man and woman, and the source of all living is in the interchange and the meeting and mingling of these two: man-life and woman-life, man knowledge and woman-knowledge, man-being and woman-being. (ii. 181)

The last sentence points towards a greater and welcome doubleness, beyond the earlier simpler gender division.

As always, he is generalising from his own experience of how his marriage had resourced and revivified his art – and hinting (by hindsight) how and why the focus of his novel had shifted from woman finding herself, to a series of men and women 'bringing themselves together' in marriage. His emphasis falls wholly on the experience out of which (he thinks) new artistic vision comes, and not on technique or form – which seem to be secondary and consequent modes of articulating what has been gained by revelation, through 'great blind knowledge and suffering and joy'. His sense – too simple perhaps – of the gap which separated him from the aspiration to formal and linguistic mastery which he saw linking Flaubert and the Symbolistes with Maeterlinck and Mann, is growing stronger.

Three days later came Garnett's intensely disappointing response to 'The Wedding Ring'. He found it still 'shaky', objected to its 'psychology', and thought that only Lawrence's cleverness might 'pull the thing through' (ii. 183, 182). (He also seemed to accept that it was not settled who should publish the book, and that Lawrence should see Pinker as soon as he got to London.) The letter of 5 June in which Lawrence expressed his disagreement with Garnett, is probably the most widely quoted of all the letters in which he discussed his art, but it is so important that it must bear repeating. He has also been thinking again about the possible usefulness of Marinetti's pseudo-science.

I don't think the psychology is wrong: it is only that I have a different attitude to my characters, and that necessitates a different attitude in you, which you are not as yet prepared to give ... I think the book is a bit futuristic – quite unconsciously so. But when I read Marinetti – 'the profound intuitions of life added one to the other, word by word, according to their illogical conception, will give us the general lines of an intuitive physiology of matter' I see something of what I am after. (ii. 182)

Here Marinetti paradoxically seems to fuse an artistic process of language with his scientific materialism. Lawrence thought the Italian 'obfuscated',[29] and it was not the physiology of matter he cared about, but he struggled to explain why Marinetti has an important point in refusing to separate human beings from the rest of the physical universe – though he is also 'stupid' in reducing humanity to what can be dealt with in the languages of the material sciences. Might the artist not find a language which could trace in human beings the operation of forces or 'wills' not merely human, but affecting humans and nature alike? That interests Lawrence much more 'than the old-fashioned human element – which causes one to conceive a character in a certain moral scheme and make him consistent'. Even in the great Russians, Turgenev, Tolstoy, Dostoevsky, 'the moral scheme into which all the characters fit – and it is nearly the same scheme – is, whatever the extraordinariness of the characters themselves, dull, old, dead' (ii. 182–3). (Constance Garnett's husband would not like that!) To go on defining humanity as sapiens, hence distinct from the rest of the world, and to be characterised in terms of thought, choice and moral value, has become (for Lawrence) deadening now. So, even if Marinetti is silly to say that the heat of metal or wood is 'more passionate, for us, than the laughter or tears of a woman',[30] Lawrence too wants to get beyond what the woman '*feels*' – which 'presumes an *ego* to feel with' – to what she '*is*', as a result of forces as world-wide and phenomenal as those studied in scientific languages. However, humanity must not be reduced to the merely material, either: 'That is where the futurists are stupid. Instead of looking for the new human phenomenon, they will only look for the phenomena of the science of physics to be found in human being. They are crassly stupid. But if anyone would give them eyes, they would pull the right apples off the tree ...' (ii. 82–3).

He is struggling now for a subtler way of looking at the relation between science and art than the simple opposition of his previous letter. Art must find – by Marinetti's 'profound intuitions of life added one to the other, word by word' – a language as universal and therefore both human and preterhuman (Lawrence's perhaps misleading word is 'inhuman') as those which study all matter and energy in physics or all living things in physiology. There is already a hint that the new language may be in some sort of continuity with a very old one: Adam and Eve in the garden, God the Father (or Mother) and the Son, and an apple, of knowledge of good-and-evil deeper than the 'certain moral scheme' of the nineteenth century. Therefore:

You mustn't look in my novel for the old stable ego of the character. There is another ego, according to whose action the individual is unrecognisable, and passes through, as it were, allotropic states which it needs a deeper sense than any we've been used to exercise, to discover are states of the same single radically-unchanged element. (Like as diamond and coal are the same pure single element of carbon. The ordinary novel would trace the history of the diamond – but I say 'diamond, what! This is carbon.' And my diamond might be coal or soot, and my theme is carbon.)

You must not say my novel is shaky – It is not perfect, because I am not expert in what I want to do. But it is the real thing, say what you like. And I shall get my reception, if not now, then before long. Again I say, don't look for the development of the novel to follow the lines of certain [i.e. consistently defined] characters: the characters fall into the form of some other rhythmic form, like when one draws a fiddle-bow across a fine tray delicately sanded, the sand takes lines unknown. (ii. 182–4)

The idea of the human being that lay behind characterisation in the nineteenth-century novel is attacked on two fronts. On the one hand the fiction of the Future must subvert the old stable *ego* (the idea of the human being as self-determining by will and choice) by going deeper than ever before, under the surface of conscious motivation, revealing what lies hidden in the depths of the psyche where the human being is moved by preter-human forces; the seven-eighths of the iceberg hidden from ordinary view. On the other hand, it must also subvert the idea of the old *stable* ego – an assumption behind every character-reference – and show human beings as continually fluctuating and changeful, definable only in their response to different pressures and tempera-tures (in each new situation) of forces within and relationships without. As carbon remains elementally the same when pressured and heated into apparently quite different forms – or water whether solid, liquid or gas – the unique elemental human being will always be there. Yet the theme of the new fiction will not be the dramatically different appearances for their own sake, but the revelation *in* these of the forces which are determining them. Hidden patterns and rhythms will appear in each situation (as they do in the Chladni acoustic experiments,[31] a different pattern produced by each different note); but revealing the previously unknown operation of 'forces' as universal as those in the physics of sound.

It does not of course follow that 'The Wedding Ring' had achieved the task of revealing the deepest forces at work in Ella, and showing her as infinitely fluctuating and changeful yet always recognisably herself. Indeed, Lawrence admits that he is 'not expert in what I want to do'. Yet in responding to the Futurists he had gone a long step towards clarifying what it was that he wanted. (He had told Collings in March, having received a book of drawings dedicated to him,[32] 'I think, unless one is so pure by instinct that one does the right thing without knowing, then one *must* know what one is after'; ii. 159.) He now realised he was 'after' no less than a revolutionary break with the classical European novel; and that this meant inevitable difficulty, even for the most intelligent and sympathetic of readers whose sensibilities had been developed within nineteenth-century concepts of character and of form. There is also, now, a definite change in his relationship with Garnett. Confident that the future is ultimately on his side, he no longer speaks as to a mentor.

This was the last letter he wrote from Fiascherino.

V Off for the Summer

As the end of waiting for the decree absolute drew near, Frieda's thoughts fixed again on the possibility of a new start in getting access to her children. Lawrence was not hopeful. He thought Weekley acted a series of stock roles but was not humanely 'flexible' (ii. 162). He remembered only too well how, 'gone mad on his injuries and his rights, [he] raves about shooting the miserable me and himself and other vague people, if there is any mention of Frieda's even seeing the children' (ii. 163). But in mid-April they began to wonder whether the divorce and their marriage might make a difference; especially since they had been told that a boy had the right to elect his own guardian at the age of 14. Monty would be 14 in July, which might give them some 'pull' over his father. By 6 May their plans were becoming more definite: 'leaving here about June 14th – coming to London – staying three weeks to get married ... then Frieda will try to see the children ... Weekley is still raving, but slightly abated. I have hopes' (ii. 167–8). After that, they might 'go into the country for a month', or to Germany, but would be in Italy again by the end of September (ii. 170), perhaps taking in Florence and the Abruzzi on the way back. Frieda even had a letter direct from Weekley after the divorce, 'much milder. He will come round in the end. The divorce is a load off him, I suppose' (ii. 174).

Lawrence toyed with the idea of going to England by ship, first with Frieda, and then, when she decided to go by way of Baden-Baden, by tramp steamer on his own (ii. 175). Finally he decided to walk through Switzerland once more, but by a different route and with a new friend. A. P. Lewis was a skilled engineer with Vickers-Maxim in Spezia (ii. 184), but we know virtually nothing else about him.[33] Since Lawrence told Garnett on 5 June he was not going by sea 'because of the filthy weather' (ii. 184), though three days earlier he had still intended to sail, the decision seems to have been made very late. It was not financial necessity this time. Since 22 April £30 had come in. And of course there would be a big down payment in London for 'The Wedding Ring' if, as seemed likely, he were to accept Pinker's offer. There had been farewell entertainments by the Huntingdons, the Pearses and the Cochranes. On 8 June they left, fully intending to return 'to this beloved, beautiful little cottage' (ii. 149), at the end of the summer.

Unlike his two previous Alpine expeditions, Lawrence never described this one. We have only four postcards written during the journey, and a brief note from

Heidelberg afterwards, from which to establish his route and its timing; though there are also a few clues from the later fiction.

On Tuesday 9 June he and Frieda were in Turin, where (he told Ada) there was 'a great strike commotion' (ii. 184 and n. 4). A general strike had been called for the following day but there was violence beforehand. *The Times* reported that 'rioting on Tuesday led to three deaths and to the wounding of some forty persons ... the city yesterday looked, as our Correspondent tells us, like a "city of the dead"'. On the 10th, however, when the strike began, Frieda was on her train and Lawrence en route to Aosta (where he spent the night) and the Great St Bernard Pass.

On the Wednesday evening he wrote Ada a second postcard, with a picture of St Bernard's famous eleventh-century hospice and monastery. They had struggled up through snow, for the last part more than a yard deep. 'You have no idea how beautiful it is. Tonight I sleep in the monastery – such a lovely little panelled room – and tomorrow on again. I love it dearly.' Two days later he told Bunny how 'hospitable and courteous' the monks had been (ii. 185).

He posted two picture-postcards (of Zermatt and the Matterhorn) at Visp on the 13th. The one to Bunny tells of having 'walked from Aosta over the Gd St Bernard to Martigny' – so it was probably at Martigny that he had spent the night of the 11th, having come 45 kilometres downhill from the monastery. From Martigny his route swung east along the valley of the Rhône, following the poplar-bordered road built by Napoleon's engineers towards Brigue; and then through the upland Val de Conches to Gletsch, close by the great Rhône Glacier. From there he could either follow the Furka pass, to touch his previous route into Italy at Andermatt before turning towards Meiringen (94km.); or, more probably, take a shorter but steeper route closer to the Jungfrau, following the river Aar towards Meiringen (37km.); from which Interlaken was another 29 km. He had told Ada to write to him *poste restante* at Interlaken, and that he expected to be in Switzerland 'a week or so' (ii. 184; i.e. till about 16–17 June); but there is no way of knowing where he stopped or stayed. Even the Visp postmark is dubious evidence. Though he often wrote his postcards at the end of the day and posted them the next morning, Visp is too far (66km.) for a day's walk from Martigny. If he and Lewis did spend a night there, they may have gone much of the way by bus. On the other hand, there had been little snow on Lawrence's two previous walks, so it is also possible that his description of the Alpine resort in the final chapters of *Women in Love* may have been based on a visit to one of the famous ones en route. (He had never experienced any such snowscape, and would have no other opportunity before he wrote that novel, whose original 'Prologue' describes two friends in the mountains.[34]) Visp was the junction for Zermatt, so the postcards may have come from side-tracking there. From Zermatt, on a highly-recommended 1½ hour expedition by rail to see the fabulous panorama from Gornegrat – a pull-out in Baedeker[35] – he could have seen, amongst a flowering of peaks on all sides, the twin peaks (Zwillingen and Jumeaux) above the Gorner glacier, looking very like the woman-shape that Gudrun worshipped. All we know, however, is that he and Lewis 'wandered over Switzerland – mid snow and ice like Excelsior – finishing up with Exhibitions in Bern' (ii. 186).

From there he could have joined Frieda in Baden-Baden, but by Thursday the 18th he was staying in Heidelberg with Alfred Weber (Else's lover, who had loaned them his apartment in Icking in 1912). The Baron was ill – Frieda said 'ill and broken' – and Frieda herself was 'not quite well, so she will stay on in Baden until Monday or Tuesday', when they would go to England together. Meanwhile 'I am with Prof Weber ... hearing the latest things in German philosophy and political economy. I am like a little half fledged bird opening my beak *Very* wide to gulp down the fat phrases. But it is all very interesting' (ii. 185–6).[36]

They arrived in London on Wednesday 24 June.

VI The London Whirl

The previous spring Lawrence had felt that The Cearne was the only house in England that would have them. Now from the Campbells' in Selwood Terrace – Beatrice being in Ireland for the birth of her second baby (ii. 187) – he set out to meet last year's friends again, and made many new contacts. He was soon in touch with Georgians, Imagists, Vorticists,[37] Bloomsbury; being entertained by Marsh and by Bunny Garnett, by Lady St Helier,[38] by H. G. Wells, by Lady Ottoline Morrell. There was a new group of friends and contacts in Hampstead, among them the first English Freudians. Before mid-July he had accepted a fat contract (£300) for his novel with Methuen; had agreed to compensate Duckworth and Edward Garnett by putting together a volume of short stories; and had taken on a new contract from another publisher, Nisbet, for 'a little book on Hardy's people' (ii. 198). He opened a London bank account. And he got married.

The most immediately necessary business was, of course, the decision about who should publish his novel. (Though Lawrence definitely preferred the new title now, we had better continue to use 'The Wedding Ring', since it was still very different from the – as yet unwritten – work we know as *The Rainbow*.) He rushed round 'busy and breathless' (ii. 187) to see Duckworth on the 26th, when the idea of the compensatory book of stories was mooted, and on Tuesday 30 June he made up his mind. Garnett was not in his office; Lawrence hung around on the pavement wondering whether to go to Pinker; 'And there was very little time, because we had to lunch with Lady St. Helier. And Frieda was so disappointed she couldn't have any money.' Most of all he remembered Duckworth's rather 'peremptory' tone when he refused to match Methuen's offer – 'So I went to Pinker, and signed his agreement, and took his cheque, and opened an acc. with the London County and Westminster Bank – et me voilà. I am sorry' (ii. 189). Though he would be spending the next weekend at The Cearne, and would be working with Garnett on the book of stories, their ways were parting.

'Me voilà' indeed – this was prosperity, with more to come. Pinker probably gave him a personal cheque for £100, in advance of Methuen's for £150, with another £150 to come on publication, less of course Pinker's 10% commission. Yet there was also cause for regret. Garnett had failed to respond to his new work. Yet Lawrence was breaking with his most sympathetic critic, a mentor who knew what the market would accept, and who was a close enough friend to have his advice taken seriously. For good or ill, Lawrence would have only his own judgement to rely on, now. Pinker was a successful agent to a number of important writers, but he was no critic, and would remain an agent on commission rather than a friend.

Waiting for them at Selwood Terrace, was an invitation from Lawrence's 'poetic adviser' (ii. 154) Marsh, to lunch at the Moulin d'Or with Rupert Brooke, who had been in America when they were last in England. Lawrence knew of Brooke through both Marsh and Bunny Garnett, and poetically through *Georgian Poetry* and *New Numbers*, and wanted to meet him. Brooke had (mostly) admired *Sons and Lovers*. 'It's so extraordinarily vivid in conception of scenes. He's always *hectic*, isn't he, a little? But I must proceed. He's a big man.' Brooke struck everybody as glamorous, with blue eyes and brown-gold hair 'just a shade longer than it need have been'; suntanned from his stay in Tahiti, but so fair (Frieda recalled) that he blushed easily.[39] Here sat on one side of the table the erstwhile Eastwood 'pagan', scholarship-boy and pupil-teacher, one of the young progressives who gathered in Willie Hopkin's provincial sitting-room; and on the other the golden Rugbean, Cambridge Apostle, and 'neo-pagan', as Virginia Woolf called those lovers of the countryside and outdoor-life, camping, boating, nude bathing, informal relations between the sexes, who centred on him and the Olivier girls. (The Lawrences were about to meet them too.) He and Frieda would probably not have known much – though Bunny knew something – of the mess Brooke had made of his emotional life: his flirtations with homosexuality, his hopeless love for Noel Olivier and his messy affair with Ka Cox, followed by the near-suicidal depression from which he had fled to America and the south Pacific. Yet Frieda did remember that 'He wasn't a bit happy or fulfilled', and that 'the beauty of him was strangely sad', though that might have been with hindsight.[40] There was contrast, but also similarity, especially with the Lawrence of early 1912 when he was Brooke's age now, and before he met Frieda; and there were grave ironies for the future. But they got on well, and promised to meet again.

Lawrence had now met the most important Georgians (except Edward Thomas and Robert Frost, who had not been in the first anthology but would last the best of all). He had hailed Marsh's collection as matching his own optimism and access of joy in 1913, and had liked Abercrombie, Gibson and Trevelyan when they met (and De la Mare whom he already knew) – but his differences from them were already far greater than the similarities.

To be fair to the Georgians we should contrast them with the predecessors they rebelled against, rather than with the greater and later poetic revolution of Modernism. In that perspective one can see how Lawrence could seem Georgian at first. If *Howards End* be the archetypal Georgian novel, the author of *The White Peacock* and *The Trespasser* might seem something of a Georgian as well as an aesthete; and it is easy to see why Georgians would admire *Sons and Lovers*, while finding it somewhat hectic and ill-formed. Lawrence, too, set the natural world as an enduring value against modern social and individual failure; though his evocation is already more powerful and complex than Forster's rather weekend lyricism. Georgian too are Lawrence's complaints against the pessimism of the Edwardians: Conrad's gloom; Bennett's acceptance; the sense, for all his admiration of Wells, of a deprived little boy with his nose pressed against a cold shop-window.[41] Nevertheless he had no sooner written his enthusiastic review of the 'joy' in the Georgians, than he became increasingly critical of both their poetics and their underlying attitudes.

His arguments with Marsh over rhythm clarified the difference between his 'ear' and the one which had selected the anthology. Lawrence's maturing verse now aimed to find its rhythm through integrity of feeling exactly expressed in the free movement and lingering of the poet's voice – in the line of Whitman, rather than the patterns of stressed and unstressed syllables in conventional English scansion. He criticised in Hodgson the banality of feeling which existed only in the author and the stock response of the reader, but was not created in the poem; and he connected the 'habituated ear' in Marsh's admiration of Flecker with 'feeling' that 'crouches subservient' to the metre (ii. 102–5). However much Lawrence shared the Georgian reaction against Edwardian poetic rhetoric, and their counter aim of a poetry of direct speech and genuine experience, 'just looking at things as themselves – neither as useful nor moral nor ugly, nor anything else', and free from moralising, posing or Ideas;[42] nevertheless his passionately intimate exploration of the inner self was bound to seem 'hectic' when opposed to Georgian lyricism and restraint, his lines undisciplined, and his leaps of feeling obscure. He for his part denounced the bucolics of Abercrombie's 'The End of the World' (set in a village pub); and detected behind its irony a suppressed hatred and 'gloating over the coming destruction' (ii. 176–7). He might have found similar dark spots in the plangent lyricism of Brooke; a sense of things going wrong in the psyche below the surface. Brooke knew this himself. He had recently written, in terms Lawrence would have greatly approved, of the contrast between England and the civilisation – his word – he had found in Tahiti:

... while they are not so foolish as to 'think', their intelligence is incredibly lively and subtle, their sense of humour and their intuitions of other people's feelings are very keen and living ... A white man living with them ... soon learns to *be* his body (and so his true mind), instead of using it as a stupid convenience for his personality, a moment's umbrella against the world.[43]

If Brooke said that kind of thing at lunch, no wonder they got on well. By contrast, the enlistment of the great god Pan by such as James Stephens seemed merely absurd to Lawrence. He would continue to be represented in the Georgian anthologies, but when he had hailed, as Georgian, an 'exceeding keen relish and appreciation of life' with the 'return' of 'quick, healthy, passionate blood' he had spoken mostly for himself.[44]

Bunny Garnett linked the Georgian with the neo-pagan and with Bloomsbury (where his grandfather had been the British Museum's Librarian, and a web of contacts remained through his literary parents). Bunny, too, put on a dinner for the Lawrences to meet more of his friends than had been possible the previous year. In the back room of Gustave's in Soho there were 'about eighteen' guests: Frankie Birrell, Daphne and Noel Olivier, Adrian Stephen and his future wife Karen Costello, Katherine Mansfield and Murry, Gilbert and Mary Cannan (she had been married to J. M. Barrie) and (less certainly) James Strachey and Arthur Waley.[45] Through the Cannans, Lawrence would soon meet Lady Ottoline Morrell and Compton Mackenzie. In 1914 Cannan and Mackenzie, together with Forster, Walpole and sometimes, and less certainly, Lawrence, were regarded as the pick of the new generation of novelists. So W. L. George had written in the *Bookman*; and Henry James in *The Times Literary Supplement*, though he placed Lawrence 'in the dusty rear' (and Mackenzie in the lead).[46] (A survey in the *Athenaeum* in Spring 1914, however, omitted him entirely.) Bunny remembered that 'Lawrence and Frieda were extremely sociable and agreeable'.[47] The web of literary contacts was growing wider again.

Through Ivy Low came another circle of new friendships, which we may think of as 'Hampstead'. Very soon after their arrival he met her again with Catherine Jackson, who lived almost next door in Holly Bush Road, and whose suit she had worn to Fiascherino. Also present was Viola Meynell, daughter of the poetess Alice Meynell, though we do not hear much of her yet. Ivy had come to Fiascherino as ambassadress for all three, but it would have been

Catherine's admiration which counted most when he met them. For she was no young fan, but an experienced reviewer for the *Glasgow Herald* and nearly five years older than Lawrence. She had been brought up in Glasgow, had studied at the Art School and had also been allowed to follow the degree course in English Literature at Glasgow University by Sir Walter Raleigh, who later moved to Oxford (and had enjoyed meeting Lawrence and Frieda at Kingsgate). The head of the Life department at the Art School had been Maurice Greiffenhagen, whose *Idyll* had so obsessed Lawrence's imagination. After the tragic collapse of Catherine's marriage – which ended in a violent attack on her, the confinement of her husband in a mental hospital suffering from progressive paranoia and a pioneering struggle to have the marriage annulled – she became involved in 'a long and hopeless affair' with Greiffenhagen, though when she met Lawrence that was all over. She would soon agree to marry Donald Carswell, a journalist and (later) lawyer who had been devoted to her since student days.[48] She too had written a novel.

Characteristically, Lawrence at once offered to read it, and spent four hours discussing it in detail in his first week in London, amongst all his other affairs. As she remembered when she came to write his biography, he was not 'critical' as that is usually understood.

He read that he might find out what the writer would be at, and, having found out, that he might expound it to the writer who, as often as not, is only half conscious of the character of the impulses underlying all literary effort.

It was this, with his astonishing patience, his delighted recognition of any sign of vitality and his infectious insistence upon the hardest work, that made him unique among critics.[49]

He saw real potential in her novel, despite its '*beastly* style' (ii. 188); and she found him 'swift and flamelike', wonderfully lively, helpful and unpretentious. As they walked to the bus after their first meeting, past the churchyard where her child lay buried, she found herself 'talking to him as if I had known him all my life'. It was not, she immediately adds with the Scots quality he liked in her, that he encouraged confidences or offered intimacies; but 'he gave an immediate sense of freedom, and his responses were so perfectly fresh, while they were puzzling, that it seemed a waste of time to talk about anything with him except one's real concerns'. Frieda struck her, at first, as 'a typical German *Frau* of the blonde, gushing type'.

She wore a tight coat and skirt of horse-cloth check that positively obscured her finely cut, rather angry Prussian features. To discover how magnificent she could look, I had to see her marching about a cottage hatless and in an overall or, still better, in peasant costume. After that her handsomeness never escaped me, and I admired her greatly.[50]

Though good-looking, Catherine was no beauty, and her friendship was given to them both (if at different levels), representing no threat to Frieda. It would last.

Through Ivy, also, came friendship with a radical and Jewish Hampstead: her aunt Barbara Low, and another pioneering English Freudian Dr. David Eder (also socialist reformer and Zionist) who was married to Barbara's sister Edith. Lawrence had read Eder in *New Age* and had alluded to his pamphlet on 'The State Endowment of Motherhood' in *The White Peacock* and 'The Overtone'. Soon he would meet the psychoanalyst Ernest Jones too, and his first wife. This was rather more challenging than Frieda's memories of conversations with Gross. It would bring Lawrence to denounce Freudian readings of *Sons and Lovers*, and gradually to formulate what he thought a radical disagreement with Freudianism (though he seems never to have read much if any Freud himself);[51] but there were hours of lively and highly intelligent discussion with Barbara and the Eders, and again the friendships lasted.

Lawrence always wanted his friends to like one another, and though the Murrys were not enthusiastic, a picnic was arranged on Hampstead Heath. Lawrences, Murrys and Campbell emerged from the underground station, to walk up the hill. Murry recalls how they

hung back a little, so that the Lawrences were well ahead. Suddenly, there was a piercing cry of 'Lawrence!' and we had a hasty glimpse of a young lady, clad it seemed in a kimono, rushing with enthusiastic arms outspread down the hill. 'Good God!' said Campbell, 'I won't have *that*!' said Katherine. With one accord we sped down the hill, round the corner, and fled.

When Lawrence turned to introduce them nobody was there; he felt a fool and was furious. Katherine explained later that she couldn't bear effusiveness – 'Like her own Kezia,' said Murry, 'she could not bear things that rushed at her.' He sounds rather proud of their stand-offishness.[52] In mid-August they were all invited by H. G. Wells to a party in Church Row, and since he and Katherine admired Wells (says Murry) they accepted, but still without pleasure in such occasions – especially since Lawrence insisted on going in evening dress.

Now Lawrence, who looked his lithe and limber self in many kinds of attire, did not resemble himself at all when locked into a dress-suit ... But something warned me ... that this initiation into the dress-suit world was for him a serious and ritual affair ... So I held my peace, and tried to make his bow-tie a little more dashing – in vain, for Lawrence had bought the kind of bow-tie which I associated with nonconformist parsons ...[53]

Then Murry 'began to be annoyed with Lawrence, for allowing himself to be turned into this unnatural exhibition', and with Frieda 'for being totally unaware that her husband looked silly. She had the blissful habit of being completely preoccupied with her own appearance.' They made 'a forlorn and somewhat irritable procession', and Katherine only made things worse by trying to make a joke of it. Unsurprisingly, they had a miserable time, and, 'as we returned, Lawrence was apocalyptic in his denunciation of H. G. Wells, who had nevertheless been very decent, and genuinely pleased to meet him'.[54] Katherine teased that the effusiveness of the ladies there had been lavished on Wells, not him, and this 'discreet insinuation that he had been letting himself down touched Lawrence on the raw'. (She also felt 'indignant with him for making himself cheap' when they first went to Lady Ottoline Morrell's in August, and so behaved 'icily' herself.)[55] The episode is full of ironies. Wells, given his own background, could easily have imagined what made Lawrence behave as he did, where the rich banker's daughter, and the clerk's son who had made it to Christ's Hospital and Oxford, saw only foolish hobbledehoydom and conceit. Yet there was also a clash of temperament which had not had time to show itself in their brief meetings the previous year.

Before the end of August Lawrence was also in touch with, and differentiating himself from, the other new movements in the London scene: Imagism and Vorticism – both connected with Ezra Pound.

He and Pound had met through Hueffer in 1909; and since then Pound had been instrumental (with characteristic energy and generosity) in helping him to get published in magazines over which he had influence: the *Smart Set*, the *Egoist* and Harriet Monroe's *Poetry* in Chicago. However, though he could '*recognize*' Lawrence's qualities, and grant his prose 'first place among the younger men' (in 1913), and even concede that his poems in the *English* had 'learned the proper treatment of modern subjects before I did'; in fact he got little pleasure from them and thought Lawrence himself a 'Detestable person', though he 'needs watching'. Lawrence in turn thought the young Pound somewhat of 'a mountebank' – and made him one of his special mimic turns. Moreover he was very much aware (by 1914) of Pound the publicist by faction, and though willing to benefit, never inclined to be a camp-follower.[56] Indeed from the very first evening they spent together in Pound's comfortable attic studio in Church Walk, Lawrence had his finger on the essential difference between them, though the form it took in November 1909 was temporary. 'He is a well-known American poet – a good one. He is 24, like me – but his god is beauty, mine, life' (i. 145). This was the ninetyish and Provençal Pound. Had Lawrence said 'art' instead of 'beauty', the contrast would have done for the later Imagist and Vorticist too.

In April 1912, Pound, Richard Aldington and Hilda Doolittle ('H.D.') had proclaimed three principles of good writing: 'Direct treatment of the "thing" whether subjective or objective', 'To use absolutely no word that does not contribute to the presentation' and 'As regarding rhythm: to compose in the sequence of the musical phrase not in sequence of a metronome'.[57] These are rather vague. Both Brooke and Lawrence could tick the first, though not necessarily in the same sense as the Imagists. Lawrence had written to Marsh in terms very close to the third, though he would have preferred 'vocal phrasing' to 'musical phrase'. The second means little without defining the nature of the 'presentation'. Shortly afterwards however, Pound coined the term Imagiste, and went on to define the Image as 'that which presents an intellectual and emotional complex in an instant of time'.[58] This is more helpful, though whether the presence of images (so defined) *in* a poem would suffice to make the poem and the poet Imagist, would become a disruptive question. There were such images in Lawrence's poems in the *English Review*, but he was not featured in *Des Imagistes* (planned by mid-1913 though not published until 1914). When Pound came to review *Love Poems*, it was only the dialect 'narrative' poems he was able to admire, though in that case highly. By 1914 however Pound was tiring of Imagism, and the others were getting 'fed-up with Ezra' and his dictatorship. They welcomed into their midst another American poet, Amy Lowell – rich, Bostonian, more than amply proportioned, patrician, yet amiable – but at a dinner she gave to celebrate the anthology Pound treated her 'with ill-bred, impertinent levity', and there was a rift which led to his cutting himself off from the group. Imagism became (in Pound's view) 'Amygism', a dilution into *vers libre* with striking images, which could of course include Lawrence – as Pound specifically objected.[59] On 30 July 1914 Amy invited Lawrence to dinner in her suite at the Berkeley, where he met Aldington and H.D.:

As guest of honour Lawrence sat next to Amy, and they made a curious contrast if only because one was so lean and the other so plump ...

Amy came out well that evening. There was not a trace of condescension in her and she did a difficult thing well – she expressed her warm admiration for Lawrence's work without flattery or insincerity and without embarrassing him.[60]

In the new Imagist anthologies which were to appear under her editorship, Lawrence would be regularly included – making him the only poet who appeared as both Georgian and Imagist, which were meant to be opposed. That of course might be a way of saying that he really belonged to neither group.

Indeed, between the stricter kind of Imagism, and the Lawrence of 1914, there were major differences – though their full extent only became apparent later when Pound joined forces with T. S. Eliot (who arrived in England in August 1914), and began also to admire Joyce as much as, and then more than, Lawrence. For Imagism (though H.D. was its only important poet besides Pound) was a forerunner of the Modernism of Pound, Eliot and Joyce. Lawrence was profoundly anti-Modernist in their sense, wanting art to elicit the unconsciously creative rhythms of living rather than aim at deliberate selection and discipline, Flaubertian 'form', let alone a separate and self-sufficient art world in which the creative artist could be quite distinct from the man who suffered. Moreover Imagism derived also from the classicism of T. E. Hulme, who attacked the Romantic idea 'that man, the individual, is an infinite reservoir of possibilities' – which Lawrence religiously believed – and who called for 'dry, hard, classical verse', distilled into achieved form by banishing the discursive, the confessional and the descriptive, all very Lawrencian.[61] (In the pure Imagist poem the experience had to be evoked entirely through sharply focused visual perceptions, created 'out there', not described or told.) Only thus could poetic art become self-contained, self-existent, no longer attached to its author. Lawrence's insistence that he wrote in order to change people was old-fashioned – the Imagists were contemptuous of the public, and saw themselves as appealing only to a tiny discriminating elite. Moreover the *instant* in which the Image presented its intellectual and emotional complex meant insistence on spatial rather than temporal form,[62] hence tended to stasis, rather than narrative or dramatic development.

Indeed it may have been this, as much as clashes of personality, that made Pound break from Imagism in search of something more dynamic. Before the Berkeley dinner in 1914, he had joined Percy Wyndham Lewis in Vorticism, and its short-lived periodical *Blast* (subtitled 'Review of the Great English Vortex'), whose first issue was published on 20 June. On 1 July Lawrence met Lewis, and there was such 'a heated and vivid discussion' (ii. 193) that he failed to get back to Selwood Terrace to keep a date with the faithful McLeod. *Blast* was primarily concerned to explode literary orthodoxy, shatter the 'enemies of culture' – among them the public library, the general reader, and the weekly press – and generally do the demolition-work to clear the way for a new dynamic poetry (Pound), painting (Lewis) and sculpture (Gaudier-Brzeska). It was wildly rhetorical, so there is a temptation to see it as one of Pound's publicity stunts – but all three were powerful artists, and though Vorticism never came to much as a movement the central image of the vortex is most suggestive, and appears in many guises in twentieth-century literature.

For Pound and Lewis in 1914, the accent fell on the energy of the vortex rather than the stillness at its centre; indeed the still centre is seen as the point at which the energy is at its radiant maximum;[63] and also the point at which the 'swirl' becomes shape and pattern. This has still some continuity with Imagism (only more dynamic now), because the artist must create the form which holds the energy in the achieved formal stability of the poem, or the Gaudier sculpture, or the Lewis painting.

Lawrence had already spoken of a 'stillness' at the 'source' of 'the struggle, the stream, the change', and so once again there were significant affinities. As with Futurism however, the differences were more important. For Pound (and

Eliot and Joyce) the central goal aspired to, through the whirlpool, was Flaubertian artistry – all the more as the swirl grew more violent – the formal mastery that Lawrence had attacked in his essay on Mann. As 'a passionately religious man' *he* thought the creative forces were in all living things and therefore available to all human beings, not the creation of the artist. The function of art was to reveal their nature to as wide an audience as possible. He refused to see art as essentially opposed to life. He wanted to communicate as widely as possible. But most of all, where Modernist emphasis fell on the artist-self as creator, Lawrence emphasised *transformation* of the self at the hands of the Other – hence the vital importance of sexual relationship. It would become ever clearer in the next few months how he saw the stillness at the centre of the vortex as incorruptible source not just of art, but of new life. A fortnight after meeting Wyndham Lewis, his rewriting of earlier stories into *The Prussian Officer* would show his new fiction pointing in a very different direction from Modernisms which he would have seen as dangerously enclosed – that deadly self-enclosure from which he had struggled to escape and which (he thought) had been the death of Middleton.

VII   Re-seeing the Stories

The astonishing transformation of these stories in less than three weeks of intense activity shows how Lawrence's art had achieved new vision and sureness, through the struggle to get hold of 'The Wedding Ring'. Since the latter has largely disappeared, the revision is our best pointer to the change since *Sons and Lovers*, and indeed 'The Sisters'.

When the idea of the volume of stories was mooted on 26 June, he asked McLeod to gather copies of everything that had appeared in magazines, since he didn't himself have a single copy and 'really don't know what stories I've published and what I haven't – God help me' (ii. 187). On 2 July, the day after he met Lewis, he wrote to Clayton to ask for manuscripts and typescripts of the unpublished ones (ii. 190). By 14 July, however, he had made up his mind. All those he finally chose had been published, except for 'Daughters of the Vicar' which was probably too long for the magazines. However he had also now 'gone over the stories very carefully' (ii. 197), all but 'Vin Ordinaire', which he sent three days later under a new title, 'The Thorn in the Flesh', wondering whether that might do also for the title of the book (ii. 198–9).

The revision was an astonishing burst of creativity. The difference his struggle for 'The Wedding Ring' had made can be seen in the virtual rewriting of even some of the best: 'Odour of Chrysanthemums', 'The White Stocking', 'Daughters of the Vicar'. This was more than stylistic improvement; it was a re-seeing, changing them into a wholly new *kind* of story. To be able to do this with such assurance so quickly was a clear sign that his vision was operating on a new plane, drawing on all he had discovered through his relationship with Frieda (and feeling her with him in his work). It was apt that the finishing of the revision should coincide with putting his wedding ring on Frieda's finger.

The shift of dimension is plain in 'Odour of Chrysanthemums' – the story about a failed marriage, ended by the husband's death in a mining accident – because the bulk of the tale is left largely as it was in the *English Review*, but the ending is totally re-seen and transforms the significance of the whole.[64] In 1911 (before *Sons and Lovers*), Elizabeth seemed entirely justified in her battle against the 'recreant' her husband, though with some rather ponderous authorial reflection on how society failed such men. Death has banished the drunk and 'disfigured coward, which gradually replaced her man'; but has restored to her again the 'clean young knight' she married, against whose degradation she had justly fought.[65] After *Sons and Lovers* however, Mrs. Holroyd's lament over the dead body in the closely related play had voiced an agonised sense of her own responsibility: for never having loved him, and hence for 'killing' his sense of the value of his life. Now however, in the new ending of the 1914 story, questions of personal feeling or blame are tellingly relegated to the self-indulgent lamentations of the old mother. Now, as Elizabeth embraces the dead body, she 'seemed to be listening, inquiring' – with an entirely new kind of question. Suddenly, as though she had never seen her husband before, he is revealed as utterly *strange*: a 'separate stranger with whom she had been living as one flesh'. In icy dread, questions multiply: 'Who am I? What have I been doing? I have been fighting a husband who did not exist. *He* existed all the time. What wrong have I done?' All the time, in sex, parenthood, personal relationship, blame, 'she had felt familiar with him',[66] but death reveals the utter otherness of the other, which in her self-enclosure she had denied – as responsible therefore as her husband for turning the relationship false and destructive. 'I' and 'he' are not merely personal pronouns; and the question of identity – no longer 'who', but 'what is he' – demands a kind of awe for the strangeness of another being. This is a new judgement, with far greater clarity than that of *Sons and Lovers*, on the marriage like that of Lawrence's parents, through the growth of his sense of the strangeness of Frieda. (Elizabeth's eyes, as she appears to listen, could be thought of as unseeing on one plane because seeing more deeply on another.)

The negative analysis of failure has a positive counterpart in the transforming of 'Vin Ordinaire' into 'The Thorn in the Flesh', which becomes a story of how the body, freeing itself from shame, can heal damage to the self. The crucial change is in the relation of Bachmann and the girl, also changing the import of the story as a whole.[67] She is no longer acquaintance but sweetheart, and he, made more sensitive than before, is all the more deeply ashamed of what the incident at the rampart has revealed to him about himself: 'Within his own flesh burned and smouldered the restless shame' seeming 'to displace his strength and his manhood'. In the rewriting however they do not spend the night apart, but overcome fear and shame in the union of their bodies, followed by the loss of themselves, in unconsciousness, out of which come a new gratitude, reverence and pride. At the end the power-situation remains as before, but whereas the arresting lieutenant sees Bachmann as object, the Baron sees 'the *man*', however helpless. The shell of him may be given over to military discipline as a prisoner standing to attention, but at a deeper level 'He remained true to himself'; and the girl hardly sees her employer because 'She was too much herself. The Baron saw the dark, naked soul of her body in her unseeing eyes.'[68] It is an extraordinary phrase, 'the soul of her body' – and will need *The Rainbow* to work out what it involves.

If the 'unseeing' inward gaze, in these two stories, begins to clarify what Lawrence meant by saying that he was concerned now with the incorruptible 'source' of truer selfhood rather than the scarring drama of battling egotisms, the nature of the source (or sources) remains obscure. In the rewriting of 'The White Stocking' the focus sharpens. He had already expanded it in 1913 from a slight anecdote of embarrassment, into a story of jealousy (not unconnected with his own experience), because the young wife feels still at liberty to flirt, and the husband demands commitment. Now it turns into something deeper, but also more frightening.[69] The temperature of the 1913 version was fairly low. Elsie's flirtatiousness was a relatively superficial and thoughtless expression of vitality. She can take risks because she feels sure of her husband; and is perversely defiant at the end since she knows she is in the wrong. Though Whiston becomes 'stiff with murderous rage', he manages to control himself for fear of hurting her, and the main effect of the episode is to jolt the marriage into awareness of new depths of feeling in them both. At the end she loves him 'down in the very kernel of her ... It had never gone so deep before'.[70] In 1914 however Lawrence not only increases her lively sexuality, but creates a more disturbing sense of the powerful attraction at the dance, not so much of her boss Sam Adams himself, though he is less vulgar now, but of what he offers Elsie that seems, later, to be missing from her marriage. Consequently her new display of defiance is more sexually taunting, and Whiston's response a far more dangerous rage – a blow – a bleeding mouth. The story now ends with a question rather than a resolution.

What the dance focuses, however, is not sexual satisfaction (as usually understood) or its lack, but a distinction between different dimensions in sexuality. In 1913 the dance had merely registered Adams, the man of the world, who knows what he wants, and whose savoir-faire contrasts with her rather clumsy and dull young suitor. In 1914 however, in three cumulative passages, Adams himself is lost to sight in the extraordinary impersonal experience she has through him. At first the emphasis is on flowing with him, united in one movement: 'carried in a kind of strong, warm flood, her feet moved of themselves, and only the music threw her away from him, threw her back to him'. The second time, however, 'she felt herself slipping away from herself' out of contact with the room which feels 'like under sea' (anticipating an important scene in *The Rainbow*). The man too is 'given up, oblivious, concentrated, into the dance. His eye was unseeing.' She feels she might give way any moment 'and sink molten: the fusion point was coming when she would fuse down into perfect unconsciousness'. But the third time (when she drops the white stocking which should have been a pocket handkerchief), she is torn not only by embarrassment but conflict, between loyalty to Whiston, and the lost 'peace' of her dance. Stronger still, however is the fear in which she agrees to marry Whiston, begging him to be good to her, the fear of losing herself. Just so, even after marriage, it is his 'yearning for surety' that makes him 'tense by not getting it'.

What is missing in their reasons for marrying, and in the marriage itself, is not then sex in the ordinary sense, but sex that involves and accepts complete surrender of the self. It becomes clear why Elsie's refusal of commitment – let alone her flaunting of herself in Sam's white stockings – should produce in this version a more ungovernable rage, and finally the ugly crashing blow across the mouth. This is something deeper than jealousy now, or betrayal, or even insecurity, though it is all these. (If we are to discover the bearing of the story on the Lawrence marriage, we need to see how much more deeply he is probing the *causes* of marital violence now, whatever the actual state of things.) The impulse of the self toward the other may seem to threaten the self, and produce powerful reactions. Fear of self-loss lies behind both Elsie's defiance and Whiston's violent rage. The greater the fear, the more vulnerable the self, the more intolerable the pressure of the other – especially if love seems replaced by contempt. Indeed, under enough pressure, the reaction of the self that feels its very being threatened, may become annihilating rage; as had been clarified in 'Honour and Arms'. The need to be, assert, defend oneself is a *force*, a 'source' as powerful, for good or ill, as the opposite desire to lose oneself in union with the other. Both 'sources' can heal, or destroy. (Medicines are poisonous; poisons can heal.) Here it is clearly for ill. Whiston stops himself 'in shame and nausea' at what he has done. There is no endorsement of violence. Orwell's jibe that the way to improve a woman's behaviour seems to be to sock her on the jaw is an uncharacteristic travesty. The blow has not solved or improved anything – unless by revealing what has been thoughtlessly risked, and clarifying what the choices for the young couple are. At the end, she sobs: '"I never meant——" "My love—my little love——" he cried, in anguish of spirit, holding her in his arms.'[71] But which way their marriage will go depends altogether on what they mean by 'love', since marriage increases the pressure of such opposite forces.

The story of the 'Two Marriages' of the daughters of the vicar was already there in 1911: the middle-class family stranded in genteel poverty in an uncaring mining district; the marriage of one daughter for purely material reasons (disguised as spiritual ones) to a clergyman who is hardly a physical being at all; the rebellion of the other, in a very different marriage to a young miner after the death of his dominating mother. These were already done with the realism and characterisation of 'Paul Morel' III, though also with some of its schematism. Then, into the 1913 revision, had gone the insights of *Sons and Lovers* and 'The Insurrection of Miss Houghton', sharpening the focus on both the mother-dependence from which Louisa rescues Alfred, and the deadening gentility and snobbery from which he helps her to escape. Some unease about the inequality of the match remained at the end of the 1911 story, but the 1913 version is already a powerful re-imagining of what the story of Walter and Mrs Morel might have been, if the vitality of physical love had overcome the spiritual and intellectual denial of the body, which reveals its full deathliness in the 'sacrifice' of Mary to Massy, who is all mind and will.[72]

In 1914, however, vision is transfigured again at two vital moments. As the middle-class girl washed coal-dust from the young miner's back, in 'Two Marriages', the physical surprise – 'His skin was beautifully white and unblemished, of an opaque, solid whiteness' – rapidly modulated into extreme embarrassment to them both, though blushes betray their sexual attraction. In 1914 Lawrence first makes Louisa *more* conscious of social difference and intrusion: she feels an 'almost repulsive intimacy being forced upon her. It was all so common, so like herding. She lost her own distinctness.' So conscious is she of difference 'from the common people' that, with his arms in the black water, she 'could scarcely conceive him as human'. But then comes revelation, in a quite different impersonal dimension. As the beautiful white skin appears:

Gradually Louisa saw it: this also was what he was. It fascinated her. Her feeling of separateness passed away: she ceased to draw back from contact with him and his mother. There was this living centre. Her heart ran hot. She had reached some goal in this beautiful, clear, male body. She loved him in a white, impersonal heat. But the sun-burnt, reddish neck and ears: they were more personal, more curious. A tenderness rose in her ... She put down the towel and went upstairs again, troubled in her heart.[73]

Similarly, the betrothal scene is no longer primarily concerned with physical passion arising out of her partly maternal response to his grief and despair after his mother's death. In the 1913 text they are unable to get near each other until, turning to go, she catches sight of his face 'all distorted with suffering' – and as she comforts him, his head pressed on her bosom, gradually 'the grief in him resolved into passion' and they kiss, 'with long, hurting kisses wherein death was transfused into desire'. In 1914 however, a crucial experience takes place *before* desire, and it no longer looks anything like maternal comforting. Now the emphasis falls on their being driven together by impersonal force, below the level of conscious feeling or choice; and then on an oblivion, 'a kind of death' in both, before the coming to new selfhood. They cease to be merely persons: 'She was to him something steady and immovable and eternal presented to him ... She saw his face all sombre and inscrutable, and he seemed eternal to her.' Louisa takes the initiative, against decorum, but it is because 'Something was carrying her' beyond herself, her words coming 'without her intervention'. Alfred is 'compelled' towards her, the expression on his face 'strange and inhuman':

Then, gradually, as he held her gripped, and his brain reeled round, and he felt himself falling, falling from himself, and whilst she, yielded up, swooned to a kind of death of herself, a moment of utter darkness came over him, and they began to wake up again as from a long sleep. He was himself ...

And at last she drew back her face and looked up at him, her eyes wet, and shining with light.[74]

This is more important than passion, though that will follow. Starting from awe at the strangeness of the other, this is Lawrence's account of the 'eternal' forces *in* people (strangely 'inhuman' only because shared in the unconscious with all living things); and of what happens at the still centre when the self does *not* fear to be given over to the other – so taking his art in a very different direction from Futurists, or Vorticists. What now matters most to him in sexual relationship, focused by his own marriage, is how the enclosed self has to '*die*' at the hands of the other for there to be new life. The last unease about the inequality of Louisa's marriage to a miner disappears, and the contrast between their life and the deathly snobbery and gentility of the Lindleys stands uncompromised. Moreover, as they are forced to break with a class-ridden England and make a life elsewhere (call it Canada), Lawrence seems newly ready to think of the life of a man and a woman apparently without reference to society at all – perhaps also the result of his last two years. In a novella, this allows an effective open ending; but might not such surgery raise as many problems as it solves?

On 13 July – the day before he sent all but the last story to Garnett, and proceeded to write 'The Thorn in the Flesh' – he and Frieda went to be married, in the Kensington Registry Office.

VIII 'Still' Photography – a Wedding

The witnesses were the Murrys and Gordon Campbell who took photographs afterwards in the backyard of 9 Selwood Terrace, including a towel on the washing-line. (Lawrence had asked Eddie Marsh, but he had been unable to come that mid-July day because of essential meetings and pressure of work at the Admiralty – some crisis seemed to be brewing ...) According to Frieda, the author of 'The Wedding Ring' had forgotten to buy one, so they had to stop the cab and dash into a goldsmith on the way. Frieda took off Weekley's ring and gave it to Katherine, who was buried with it on her finger. 'Heavens, how happy we all were!' Murry remembered. 'The time of being jolly together had really begun.'[75]

The friendships of the previous summer had been renewed in Selwood Terrace, bating the Murrys' dislike of the Lawrences' newer friends. Campbell's housekeeper sang 'Angels ever bright and fair' in the basement, while intense discussions took place in the little drawing-room, and Campbell alternately waxed gloomy over breakfast about 'Areland', or teased Frieda about 'the many new feminine admirers (one of them in especial good to look at) who were now attracted to Lawrence and his work'. That sounds like Hilda Doolittle. Even an awful trip to Richmond on a Thames steamer – with a man endlessly playing a harmonium, and urchins diving for sixpences in the vile river-bank mud – ended in laughter when the dignified Campbell trod on the bus-conductor's toe on the way home, and was greeted with 'Hallo, clumsy', to Frieda's and Katherine's delight.[76]

It seems worth pausing to look at *this* Lawrence and Frieda, in Campbell's wedding photographs (see Illustrations 1 and 2), two years and two months after they caught the Ostend ferry – and less than a month before they and their world began to be altered almost beyond recognition.

The photograph of the four looks uncomfortable, as such things do. Lawrence and Katherine, though self-conscious, are putting the best faces on it, handsome enough beside each other. He wears a snazzy straw boater, a wing collar and his best suit, and is quite good-looking with a moustache (no beard yet), though slim and a little stooped. Katherine looks neat and demure, her face in shadow under the slanting brim of a dark straw hat with a coloured scarf tied round it, to tone with the blouse under her dark suit. Frieda (it must be said) looks dumpy. She wears a plain straw hat uncompromisingly straight, an elaborate shawl-collared blouse with a big brooch, over a jacket which clearly will not button but is secured with a sash, through which is stuck what looks like a large rose straight from the bush. Murry, beside her, is in three-piece suit and watch chain, walking stick and book-under-arm, and a huge hat which hides how much shorter he actually is than Lawrence. That becomes clear from the second much less formal photo of just Lawrence, Murry and Frieda. The hats are gone, and Frieda is now in something altogether looser, and looks much prettier and happier as a result. Jack reveals surprisingly bandy legs. Lawrence (the sun shining on his bang of hair) is now the one who looks over-formal.

But it is not that kind of 'still' I have in mind. Rather, by freezing the biographical narrative at just this point, as it were at a crossroads, one becomes dramatically aware of a path blocked off. How *different* the lives and characters of Lawrence and Frieda might have become, if their world had allowed them to live as they planned – to have their August in Ireland, and then go back to beloved Fiascherino until next summer, when they could pick up all their contacts in London again . . .

This unbearded Lawrence is approaching (in his own view, as in most people's now) the peak of his powers. His finest work so far is with Methuen, he has a bank account into which another £150 will be paid when the novel is published, and in three days he will have finished his book of short stories which should complete the financing of another year abroad. His writing (as the last three weeks have demonstrated) has developed a new assurance. He has an agent who also works for Arnold Bennett and Joseph Conrad. His reputation seems certain to grow. As a poet, he is claimed by both Georgians and Imagists though he belongs to neither. He has affinities with Futurists and Vorticists, though he differs radically and creatively from both. Even his career as a playwright now looks promising. *The Widowing of Mrs. Holroyd*, has won golden reviews, and two theatre managers seem interested in producing it.[77] He is also newly in demand as a critic. Bertram Christian, of the publisher Nisbet's, had asked for 'a sort of interpretative essay on Thomas Hardy, of about 15,000 words' (ii. 193). It will not make much – £15 advance on royalties of $1\frac{1}{2}$d per copy and half profits in America – but he was paid nothing at all for the essay on Thomas Mann, and it is the commission itself that counts, especially since he is very interested in Hardy. (Marsh, whom he had asked to lend him the novels and Lascelles Abercrombie's book on Hardy, has sent him the works as a wedding present, to his huge delight; ii. 199 and n. 3.) He will begin as soon as the last of the stories is finished. It will be a marvellously creative and profitable summer.

Moreover he himself is sure that the new achievement is directly attributable to the success of his marriage; and that in an important though not simply autobiographical sense, his readers will find both him and Frieda *in* his new post-*Sons and Lovers* phase. Frieda had been really happy in Fiascherino, where there seemed (for her) just about the right blend and variety of social life and isolation. The marriage, now, has sealed the achievement of 'The Wedding Ring'. The trouble about the children remains, but (Lawrence has told Sallie Hopkin today) they intend to do something about it 'this week' – though he is expecting difficulty (ii. 196). At last he can feel that he has nailed Frieda's nose to his wagon (though the last time he said so he had been in for a nasty surprise), for at least she *is* Mrs Lawrence now, with no need to pretend any more.

Frieda too must feel content in almost every respect bar the pain over the children. It is far clearer than last year that she has chosen a man who is increasingly recognised, and that she can look forward both to greater comfort now, *and* to a continuance of the wandering and varied life that suits her well. Lawrence may be as difficult and as argumentative as she; their life may be stormy and occasionally violent; but it was she who taught him to express and live out his feelings as she does, she is not afraid of him and is sometimes violent herself and their life together is far more vital and interesting than anything she had known before.

They were sociable, but it must have seemed that society was something they could find when they wanted it, but do without much of the time, needing only each other. Since they required surprisingly little money and few possessions, they felt relatively unpressured by demands from outside. Sometimes the money ran short but something always seemed to turn up (or Else would help them), and Lawrence's work had grown more and more saleable. He was very English, and Frieda very German, but that clash, too, had proved creative, and under-lined the new (fought-for) wisdom about the escape from self-enclosure, through transformation at the hands of the other, the *stranger*. He was an intense arguer and denouncer, largely untroubled now by social niceties; but he liked people to stand up to him, and he had shown that he could accept and be grateful for intelligent criticism and argument. His only enemies were those his sexual relationships had hurt, and their families, and one or two who had resented being identifiable in his books – for he had little scruple about using people for artistic ends. This Lawrence was tempestuous (whereas two years before he had bottled up his feelings); but he was also fun to be with, and often very funny.

At this stage he was remarkably unpolitical. As a young man he had largely sympathised with Willie Hopkin's socialism, and broke with Christianity because he could not believe in any God who allowed suffering such as he had seen in the slums of Sneinton (i. 40). He had been a reader of the *New Age*. However his deepest thinking now had little socialist or even social content, being almost entirely concerned with the relation of man to woman, the self and the other. He thought Marsh's friend Barnes 'a rum chap, for I can't see how politics has got much to do with ... "letters" ' (ii. 91). Though sympathetic also with the ardent suffragism of Louie Burrows, Alice Dax and Sallie Hopkin, he hoped his work would do more for women seeking true selfhood than merely having the vote. On Garda he had heard Italians sing about Tripoli, but neither that nor the warships sailing to the base at Spezia, or Marinetti's image of the whole of Italy as a dreadnought, had drawn any political inference or comment. He had reacted strongly against the German military both at Metz and in Bavaria, and sensed something cruel and brutal in the air, but the reaction and the intuition were personal – the way they looked at him, and treated him, culminating in the arrest – rather than political. He had talked to Alfred Weber about what was new in

German philosophy and economics; but there was a glaring (if tactful) omission in 1914 – politics.

In addition to his other differences from Pound, Eliot and Joyce, he felt altogether comfortable with his nationality; and though he lived partly abroad by preference, for health and economy, he had no sense of exile or estrangement. He had broken with his working-class background, but had become increasingly anti-bourgeois, and thought of himself as classless (albeit 'common') – if with spasms of snobbery. He was no coterie writer. He felt increasingly confident indeed of an English audience out there waiting to hear from him; and only a month before he had told Garnett that even though his art was trying to change the orthodox way of looking at human beings, 'I shall get my reception, if not now, then before long' (ii. 184).

One looks at *this* Lawrence across a chasm, which was just about to open.

IX Disaster

Soon a disaster for Frieda was followed by a cataclysm for their world.

She claimed years later that she had not cared whether she was married or not, yet Lawrence was glad they were respectable. In fact, his letter to Sallie Hopkin on their wedding day gives a reason why respectability might have mattered rather more to Frieda than usual – for they were about to try to see the children that week, and test the hope that the divorce and remarriage would remove one ground for forbidding her access, as a disreputable woman.

Unfortunately, she damaged her chances almost beyond repair. Her first attempt was bad enough. Explaining why she would not be coming with him to Ripley on the 18th to see Ada, Lawrence wrote:

She is persisting in her efforts to get hold of the children. She has seen them – the little girls being escorted to school by a fattish white unwholesome maiden aunt who, when she saw their mother, shrieked to the children – 'Run, children, run' – and the poor little things were terrified and ran. Frieda has written to her mother to come. I *do* hope that old Baroness will turn up in a state of indignation. (ii. 199)

Worse was to come. Frieda was too impatient to wait for her mother; and Campbell had invited them to Ireland in August. The court order from the previous summer may never have been served because they kept changing their address – and Frieda seemed unable to grasp that she no longer had any legal right to see the children without Weekley's express consent. It was probably while Lawrence was in the Midlands for his long weekend that Frieda tried to locate the house in Chiswick to which Weekley had moved from Hampstead – and spotted her curtains from Nottingham. She was quite unable to resist bursting in to confront Maude (who hated her) and Weekley's mother. Barbie remembered vividly: 'She entered the nursery and found us at supper with Granny and Aunt Maude. She put her foot in it that evening; the law was invoked to restrain her. And while she stood at bay before our relations, we children gazed in horror at the strange woman she had then become.' They even joined in the vituperation.[78] Frieda had not realised either, how a year of persistent denigration could affect their attitude towards her. Though the Baroness did arrive – Catherine Carswell recalled meeting her[79] – and though, perhaps through her mediation, the threat of the law was not carried through, she was unable to mollify Weekley for the invasion of his family home and the frightening of the children and his womenfolk. It would be a long time before Frieda was allowed to see the children again.

On Friday 31 July, having just had from Pinker the last £50 of Methuen's advance, Lawrence took a holiday, a walking tour in the Lake District with three other men. Two he had not known before; but the third was A. P. Lewis, transferred by Vickers to their factory at Barrow-in-Furness where he now had a house. They had probably planned the reunion in Switzerland. Lewis's friend William K. Horne worked as a translator in the Russian Law Bureau in High Holborn; along with Samuel Solomonovitch Koteliansky. Of Horne we know little, but with 'Kot' Lawrence formed a firm and lasting friendship. Born in the Ukraine in 1880, he studied at the University of Kiev where his Jewishness and his habit of speaking his mind would not be to his advantage. Katherine's anecdote of how he came to London smells of polish: he was supposed to have called a political meeting of students, and when nobody was brave enough to turn up, began walking and never stopped until he got to London. There he dressed like the English (he thought) in tennis shoes, but when people stared he stayed indoors for weeks. In fact he had come to London on a scholarship in 1911, but he did think it unsafe to return – and for the rest, he was the sort of man people enjoyed telling such stories about because, set off against his somehow massive dignity and integrity, they seemed as delightfully incongruous as his party trick of howling like a dog, which (it was said) he had learned in order to discourage wolves when walking home in Russia at night. Leonard Woolf, who later published many of his literary translations from the Russian, said that if the prophet Jeremiah had been born in a ghetto village in the Ukraine in the eighties, that would have been Kot. Dorothy Brett describes him as:

so broad-shouldered that he looks short, his black hair brushed straight up 'en brosse,' his dark eyes set perhaps a trifle too close to his nose, the nose a delicate well-made arch, gold eye-glasses pinched onto it. He has an air of distinction, of power, and also a tremendous capacity for fun and enjoyment.

Lawrence must have been immediately attracted by Kot's passionate approval of what he thought good and hatred of what he thought bad, his vehement speech in its Russian accent, his inability to lie or disguise, his absolute acceptance of people he approved, of whom he would say 'That is a real person', his capacity for enjoyment – or denunciation. Kot in turn valued similar qualities in Lawrence.[80] Certainly they got on well from the start – even when they had to share a cottage bed (v. 355). Lawrence himself best describes what ended their tour:

I had been walking in Westmoreland, rather happy, with water-lilies twisted round my hat – big, heavy, white and gold water-lilies that we found in a pool high up – and girls who had come out on a spree and who were having tea in the upper room of an inn shrieked with laughter. And I remember also we crouched under the loose wall on the moors, and the rain flew by in streams, and the wind came rushing through the chinks in the wall behind one's head – and we shouted songs, and I imitated music hall turns, whilst the other men crouched under the wall and I pranked in the rain on the turf in the gorse, and Kotilianski groaned Hebrew music – Ranani Sadekim Badanoi.[81]

It seems like another life – we *were* happy – four men. Then we came down to Barrow in Furness, and saw that war was declared. (ii. 268)

Kot immediately went back to London, vanishing as though 'in a cloud' as soon as they had come down to 'Lewis' unattractive home' (v. 355). Lewis had to cry off too, as Vickers-Maxim called in all their men; though Lawrence went 'down the coast a few miles' for the rest of his week (ii 268).

Like millions of others he had not seriously imagined war would come, though on the 30th, the night before he left for Westmorland, Aldington remembered him coming into the Berkeley to Amy Lowell's dinner and saying at once, even before the introductions, that Marsh had just told him 'we shall be in the war'.[82] The company however didn't take this too seriously; and he could have had no idea how soon and disastrously he himself would be affected.

All too soon, anti-German hysteria began to threaten. David Garnett asked Lawrence and Frieda to supper in the Pond Place flat, to meet his college friend H. G. Newth. It was a pleasant evening, helped by the absent Edward's wine.[83] They liked Newth, Lawrence 'was in his sweetest and gentlest mood', and Frieda talked openly of her divided sympathies: her experience of the German court as a teenager, her dislike of the Kaiser and his culpability for what had happened, her admiration for her cousins who had joined the German air force and her worry for her family and Nusch, who was married to the Crown Prince's aide-de-camp. When they said goodbye about midnight, Newth (staying to help clear up) called down the staircase: ' "Auf Wiedersehen, Gnädige Baronin!" and Frieda called back gaily to us in German.' Such innocence ... Garnett's neighbours reported to the police, and within the following ten days or so three sets of detectives arrived to make enquiries. The last one told Bunny 'that Scotland Yard was getting hundreds of letters every day from people denouncing their neighbours and that they all had to be investigated'.[84]

On 10 August came a far more direct and heavy blow: Methuen returned the typescript of 'The Wedding Ring' to Pinker. 'Here is a state of affairs,' cried Lawrence, 'what is going to become of us?' (ii. 206). In a moment their whole situation had altered. Financial security had turned to embarrassment. In their confidence they had spent freely: all the first instalment advance (repaying debts, buying new clothes), and some of the last £50 as well – and now there would be no further £150. It was not clear whether Italy would enter the war; nor could they now afford to go back to Fiascherino. And how and where were they to live?

Methuen's representative would claim at the *Rainbow* trial in 1915 that they had returned the novel because it 'could not be published in its then form', implying a 'responsible' rejection on the grounds of obscenity; and this gets some backing from Pinker's letter to the Society of Authors after the trial. Yet it is difficult to square with Lawrence's previous and subsequent reactions to such experiences. His letters show not a trace of the rage (for example) with which he had greeted Heinemann's judgement that 'Paul Morel' was indecent. Not until October is there any mention of rewriting, and then, though there is clearly something to be done, his tone hardly suggests there had been any serious objection: 'I don't feel quite in the humour for tackling the novel just now. I suppose it will do just as well in a months time' (ii. 227–8). On the other hand there is evidence – explaining also why Lawrence felt no urgency despite his need for money – that the reaction of Methuen to the war was to suspend *all* new projects for six months, and therefore also the payment of royalties on them. If that was what they told Pinker, together with a request (perhaps conveyed by him more diplomatically to Lawrence) for some 'toning down' of the 'love passages' such as Kennerley had wanted for America (ii. 246), Methuen's statement at the trial and Lawrence's reactions at the time are reconcilable.[85] His only comment in his next note to Pinker six days later, is 'I wonder what is going to happen in the book trade' (ii. 208).

As soon as possible however, they had to find somewhere cheap to live, out of London. Gilbert Cannan came to the rescue.[86] Within a week he found them a farm cottage, not far from his own windmill-house near Chesham in Buckinghamshire: 'The Triangle' was 'tiny, but jolly – and 6/- a week in all. Unfortunately there is only one bedroom furnished. But I shall get a camp bed up.' There they would have to live an 'ultra-simple life' (ii. 208), 'sitting very tight on our last six pence, holding our breath' (ii. 211). When they had been on their beam-ends before, Frieda had got money from her family in Germany – but not now. Yet the Lawrences were always resilient: he whitewashed the cottage, she busied herself making blackberry jelly. They even liked the relative isolation (beside a farm off the road to Bellingham, $2\frac{1}{2}$ miles from Chesham station) especially since there were always new people to meet at the Cannans'. The letters put a brave face on things. Yet their position had changed beyond recognition since the end of July, and Lawrence worried (to Pinker) in early September that he could 'last out here only for another month' (ii. 212).

Help came – albeit in a form he found humiliating. Marsh had sent another little *Georgian Poetry* cheque, and posted another £10 as soon as he heard of their troubles (ii. 211, 213), with a warm letter accusing himself of having been a bad friend. Lawrence decided to keep that for absolute emergency. A further £10 came from the successful playwright Alfred Sutro, to whom (as to Maurice Hewlett, novelist and poet) Mary Cannan had written, asking whether the Royal Literary Fund could do anything to help. Lawrence was persuaded to make an application in September. He listed his actual resources, apart from royalties which he could not collect and a payment due from the *English Review*, as £3 – all that was left, now, of the £50 he had had in July. London and the Lake district had been expensive, and he probably had to pay a quarter's rent for the cottage in advance, perhaps even up to Christmas. Sutro and Hewlett organised letters of support from Marsh, Harold Monro and the novelist A. E. W. Mason, while Cannan wrote direct to the committee. About the same time Donald Carswell, who worked on *The Times* with F. S. Lowndes, appealed through him to his wife Mrs Belloc Lowndes, novelist and sister of Hilaire Belloc, who sat on the Council of the Society of Authors. They however were concerned lest 'the two Funds overlap', and since Sutro's payment had already been made as an emergency advance, pending the Royal Literary Fund Committee meeting, Lawrence's case was left to them.[87] He was awarded £50 in mid-October, by which time Pinker had produced £17 by selling 'Honour and Arms' to America.

They were not out of their difficulties, even so. He owed £20; and now Weekley's lawyers were claiming £145 costs for the divorce, though he vowed never to pay (ii. 226). On 21 October he had only 'about £70 in the world' (ii. 225), in effect £50, to last until the volume of stories appeared. (He was working on the proofs.) So the help was just enough to get him out of an emergency, but not enough to set him on his feet again – and he felt humiliated, which always brought out the worst in him. He almost wished Mary Cannan had not written; yet he knew it was his tale of woe that had prompted her and Marsh, as he must have hoped it would, and he felt ashamed of that, and of apparently not being able to manage for himself which he had always taken pride in doing. Resentment at having to appeal for help and owe gratitude afterwards went deep; and all the worse because he knew he should be grateful (and actually was, at heart). Concerning the Literary Fund however he could let his bile out, unattractively, in private: 'There is no joy in their tame thin-gutted charity. I would fillip it back at their old noses, the stodgy, stomachy authors, if I could afford it. But I can't' (ii. 223). Irritation about having to accept 'charity', and disappointment that it proved after all too little, weigh about equal with ingratitude. His real complaint was the one felt by all artists who know how hard they have worked, and what good work they have done: 'Have I not earned my whack – at least enough to live on –' (ii. 226). To Amy Lowell, who had thought carefully about how not to humiliate him and had hit on the bright idea of giving him a typewriter (ii. 222),[88] and to Marsh who had also been sensitive, he could respond with unalloyed thanks; but he was not one who could accept obligation easily.

Meanwhile, as autumn approached, his misery about the war deepened. Quite apart from Frieda's German origins and feelings, it was impossible for him to share the euphoria – like the girls on Barrow station telling their men to 'Let 'em 'ave it'. What he had seen in Bavaria had shown him there would be nothing heroic about the subjection of human beings to killing machinery. On 18 August the *Manchester Guardian* published an essay by 'H. D. Lawrence' called 'With the Guns' in which he described what he had seen: an artillery battery shelling an invisible target; men huddled in trenches; or vulnerably exposed at night, lit up by a star-shell. 'It is a war of artillery, a war of machines, and men no more than the subjective material of the machine. It is so unnatural as to be unthinkable. Yet we must think of it.'[89]

'The war is just hell for me', he wrote to Marsh in late August. 'I can't get away from it for a minute: live in a sort of coma, like one of those nightmares when you can't move ... I can't say we're happy, because we're not, Frieda and I' (ii. 211–12). Yet Marsh was secretary to the First Lord of the Admiralty, deeply involved – and when Frieda heard about his views on the war from the young painter Mark Gertler (perhaps the most interesting of the new friends they made through Cannan, and a protégé of Marsh),[90] she could not resist writing at once to Marsh in reproof. She was sceptical about stories of atrocities in Belgium, reminding him of those told in Germany about English atrocities in the Boer War (ii. 214–15). (Compton Mackenzie, whom Cannan took to meet them, portrays her coming down, resplendent in ringed stockings, from upstairs where she had been lying on her bed while Lawrence cleaned the cottage, and arguing similarly.)[91] She denounced the glorification of war, the growth of national chauvinisms, the waste and stupidity. If people could '*be* more individual then they could not have a war' (ii. 215); and all women should kick against it. Her points were good ones – but not perhaps altogether well-advised as a response to Marsh's generosity. Meanwhile Lawrence was growing angrier. 'What a miserable world. What colossal idiocy, this war. Out of sheer rage I've begun my book about Thomas Hardy', he wrote in early September (ii. 212). By mid-October Udo von Henning had been killed at Châlons, and also another of the von Richthofens' 'intimate officer-friends' (ii. 221). Lawrence had 'never come so near to hating mankind' for their folly, not only because of the death toll, but because of 'those who, being sensitive, will receive such a blow from the ghastliness ... that they will be crippled beings further burdening our sick society' (ii. 218).

X Taking the Strain

What with the misery of the war, Frieda's tensions (the children, Germany, her family, her father very ill now), money worries and the approach of an English winter Lawrence fell ill himself at the beginning of October. He had been claiming that they 'hardly quarrel any more' (ii. 221), and Frieda also felt 'more peaceful' (ii. 219), even after a glimpse of Ernest and the children – though 'not to speak to' – during a weekend in London in mid-September. (She seems to have been watching the house, but unable to risk going in again.) However, signs of depression and strain increase, and Lawrence's 'seediness' always made him 'disagreeable' (ii. 221). It was while he was ill this time that he grew his beard, and decided to keep it even after he got better. The beard was also, however, a sign of defiance, proclaiming oneself an outsider, when the enlisted and those intending-to-volunteer were going clean-shaven (or with moustaches to make them look older). He began to apologise, to Kot and to Catherine Carswell, when they spent a weekend with her in London, for 'tirades' (ii. 228, 233). He got angry about the war poems emerging from Harriet Monroe's competition in *Poetry* (Chicago) which he had refused to enter. In November, he wrote 'Ecce Homo', later revised as 'Eloi Eloi, Lama Sabachthani?' in response, about the desire to kill he now saw everywhere, and the desire to die – a poem very different from those of Brooke, or Julian Grenfell, or even Charles Sorley, all of whom seemed ready for death.

Into this situation arrived the Murrys to stay ten days in The Triangle, during which Lawrence, in a burst of energy and impatience with Murry's languid brushwork, drove them to paint and plaster 'Rose Tree Cottage', three miles away. They moved in on 26 October (ii. 226–7). Things had not gone well for them either, since the sunny days in July. In a fit of enthusiasm when war broke out, Murry and his Oxford friend Hugh Kingsmill enlisted in a bicycle battalion; but the next day Murry thought better of it and consulted a doctor, who gave him a certificate mentioning that he had suffered from pleurisy, and added 'Query T.B.' – which got him released. The doctor also said that Murry needed a holiday, so the novelist J. D. Beresford lent them his holiday house in Cornwall; but it did not go well. Katherine wrote in her diary on 30 August, the night before they travelled down: 'Tell me, is there a God? I do not trust Jack. I'm old tonight. Ah, I wish I had a lover to [?nurse] me, love me, hold me, comfort me, to stop me thinking.' They too were very short of money – though helped also by a cheque from Marsh.[92] Lawrence told Campbell (in Ireland, for the birth of his son) that he was worried about them after a gloomy letter from Murry, and it must have been he who persuaded them down to Chesham, and got Murry on his bicycle, to find a place where they too could live cheaply. He must have hoped the companionship would cheer them all.

For a while it did. The distance between the cottages kept their lives largely separate; and the three writers spent most of their time writing. Biographies of writers often falsify the proportion of their lives. However, the couples ate together twice a week – Lawrence doing most of the cooking – and sang as they washed up. They continued the animated discussions and arguments of Selwood Terrace. Katherine and Lawrence sided against Murry over Dostoevsky's advocacy of humility and love; Lawrence expounded the philosophy that was strangely expanding his little book on Hardy; they argued about tragedy. Whereas Murry's 1935 autobiography diffuses gloom, his first *Reminiscences* after Lawrence's death allow the initial enjoyment to come through. An entry in Katherine's diary for 3 November shows her 'deeply happy and free ... in my own self awake and stretching ... Can it be that one *can* renew oneself'.[93] They got to know one another better than before: the clever, complicated ex-colonial and the free-spirited daughter of the Baron, the vehement novelist with his new reddish beard, setting himself more and more against his society now, and the recessive intellectual, also grown away from his background, but still uncertain of, though much absorbed in, himself.

They gave hostages. With Katherine's closest female friend away in Rhodesia she became intimate with Frieda now, and dropped her defences: confiding her most guarded secret, the sexual passion for another woman in a seaside cottage on Wellington Bay, which had revealed her bisexuality to herself. Usually adept at presenting façades and sometimes economical with the truth, she was taking risks, for the Lawrences never had much idea of privacy. They, in turn, told the Murrys most intimate sexual details, as we shall see. (Another of Katherine's journal entries says 'L[awrence] was nice, very nice, sitting with a piece of string in his hand, on true sex'.) He talked of his childhood, his father coming home and banging about in his pit dirt, and how he had hated him. He became more angry about Murry's narrow-spirited and demanding father, and how he had damaged his son, than Murry was himself. Katherine reminisced about her trip into the 'back-blocks' of New Zealand, the Maori territories. And Frieda poured out her troubles over the children, about which Katherine had already been so sympathetic the summer before.[94]

Yet closer intimacy also exposed the differences which had been less obvious in sunnier and more casual days. The relation of Murry and Katherine was under strain, and by Christmas would be in deep trouble. Murry was always self-conscious, but the autobiographical novel he was working on every morning made him more self-absorbed than ever. (From tea to supper he was still trying to make a bare living doing journalism for the *Westminster Gazette*.) The most important moment – in his view – recorded in his private journal at this time, was a conversation with Katherine about the sudden realisation of the self 'as something apart and unattainable ... passed clear away from all its acts'[95] – but all Lawrence's emphasis was now on the mystery of the *Other*, with self-absorption identified as deathly. When Campbell came back from Ireland and began to visit them again, Katherine realised more strongly than ever that it was sharing a kind of high-souled intellectual discussion with *him*, with elements of mysticism and ecstasy, that Murry found truly exciting. (Lawrence also distrusted this, and warned Campbell that 'there is no real truth in ecstasy. All vital truth contains the memory of all that for which it is not true: Ecstasy achieves itself by virtue of *exclusion*' (ii. 247). She had been feeling Murry's inadequacy as lover and still more as cherisher. Part of her delighted in his little-boy-lost sexuality which (as his novel and his letters show) treasured most the safety of being held to a lover/mother's breast; and they both tended to see love as a childlike innocence and gaiety in the teeth of a hostile and tawdry world. She was however getting tired of being made to feel the older one, the one to do the cherishing. Still worse, her writing went badly in the cottage, which she began to dislike. When letters arrived from a bohemian writer-friend in Paris, Francis Carco, first to Jack, but then as love-letters to her which Jack refused to take seriously, she began to work herself up into a romantic excitement that her relationship with Murry lacked. The crunch would come when on 18 December she read, in his 'little red book', how he had told Campbell he didn't know whether she was 'more to me than a gratification'. She determined to leave.[96]

Moreover Lawrence felt more for Murry than Murry did for him. He was twenty-five to Lawrence's twenty-nine, and in all save intellect at this stage, his journal reveals him as young for his age. *Rhythm* had been a remarkable feat for an undergraduate, but he had projected greater authority as editor and reviewer than he actually had. He felt himself an 'artist', but knew he had done almost nothing worth the name, and had little of his own as yet to say to the world. He lived in his mind, where he was impressive, but in all else he was undeveloped as well as self-conscious; and it was this he was struggling to understand in the novel in which, he said later, he was 'analysing my own inward life to immobility'. (He called it *Still Life*.) Yet he was very attractive, most of all when he seemed wholly taken up with you. The book shows clearly and honestly, however, how an apparent emotionalism alternated with instinctive withdrawal from any commitment threatening the self. The boyish charm he so powerfully exerted was because he wanted to be loved, enjoyed the play of ideas and entered relationships enthusiastically – but he often failed to clarify the limits of his involvement, and would go on to the next with equal enthusiasm. (This would lead again and again to charges of betrayal, though it would also make the empathetic critic.) In fact, in 1914, he had very little sympathy for or under-standing of Lawrence's ideas or sense of mission or attitude to the war. When he describes Lawrence sitting 'in a chair by the stove, rocking himself to and fro and moaning', suddenly so overwhelmed by the horror of the war that he had made his way over to the Murrys' cottage in the dark, the picture is vivid: 'I can see him now, in his brown corduroy jacket, buttoned tight up to the neck, and his head bowed, radiating desolation'[97] – but the feeling itself must have been unimaginable to the young man who had so casually enlisted and de-enlisted, and whose main reaction to the war had been to feel that it belonged in another world from his. He made one intelligent comment on Lawrence's exposition of ideas from the 'Study of Thomas Hardy' he was working on, but never grasped how they might bear on conflict, sexuality or creativity. In fact he had no great opinion of Lawrence as a writer, confessing to the journal that both he and Gilbert Cannan 'always give me the feeling of absolute unreality in their books'. Indeed he thought little of his whole generation:

The clever and futile E. M. F[orster]., the clever and homunculous G. C[annan]., the crack-brained, sex-obsessed D.H.L. (tho' of him I hope) – are these really as negligible as they seem? And isn't it funny – a confession of incompetence – that I see in Gordon Campbell, the successful barrister who makes £1800 out of a single case, a finer than them all, not in their way, but on a different plane only to be attained to by me of known contemporaries?[98]

It was Campbell's mind that roused Murry to 'extraordinary mental excitement', and Campbell, not Lawrence, whom he adapted for his novel, as his protagon-ist's closest friend.

Murry also felt a growing antipathy towards Frieda, possibly fuelled by her relationship with Katherine. As early as 10 November a journal entry reads: 'Last night at the Lawrences. A great part of the time went in trimming a ridiculous kind of hat for Frieda. Why should she spend six guineas of D.H.L.'s money on clothes for her stupid self in London, when he's got hardly anything.' (The Literary Fund money had come.) He could not understand how Lawrence should claim to be 'conscious of F's participation in his work, to such an extent that it almost depended upon her active good-will', since he and Katherine 'work best in complete isolation, mental and physical'.[99] (His later claim to have felt something unmanly in Lawrence's 'subjection', however, was axe grinding by the author of Son of Woman, since there is no sign of this in the journal.) But in remarking how ill and greenish Lawrence looked now (as well as older with the beard), as compared to hobbledehoy vitality the year before, Murry was clear where the blame lay: 'Frieda just squanders his nervous energy.' He thought she played him traitor – though it is not clear why – and he could not understand what seemed idealistic self-deception about their marriage.

> There is no high degree of physical satisfaction for him. That is all wrong between them. F. accuses him of taking her 'as a dog does a bitch', and last night he explained his belief that even now we have to undergo a dual 'mortification' by saying that very often when he wants F. she does not want him at all, and that he has to recognise and fully allow for that. Sincerely I do not believe she loves *him* at all. She is in love with the idea of him as a famous and brilliant novelist – and that's all. And the idea that she should have been allowed to tyrannize over him with her damnably false 'love' for her children, is utterly repulsive to me.

He found her stupid, yet assertive, and could hardly forbear being openly rude to her. He was sure that Kot and Campbell hated her too, and (he says) Katherine felt that Frieda secretly loathed her,[100] though he often ventriloquised his feelings into Katherine's mouth.

As well as telling us a good deal about Murry, the diary entry certainly shows how Lawrence and Frieda were at odds again after having taken the strain quite well till mid-October, and it does seem likely that stress had affected their intimate life. Only, what kind of insight is Murry offering?

It seems not to have occurred to him that the tension had anything to do with him and Katherine, but it almost certainly did, without having been their fault. Having come for a weekend when Lawrence was feeling ill, they came again the next weekend (Lawrence still seedy), when they decided they would take the cottage, and then spent another ten days at the Lawrences' while it was made ready. Kot also came down to visit – only the second time he and Frieda had met. As with the Waterfields the year before, Frieda could never resist, on earliest acquaintance, appealing for sympathy over the children. Leonard Woolf retells Kot's story:

> At lunch Frieda began lamenting how much she missed her children ... Kot said: 'Frieda, you have left your children to marry Lawrence. You must choose either your children or Lawrence – and if you choose Lawrence, you must stop complaining about the children.' After lunch Frieda left them and Lawrence and Kot sat talking while outside the rain poured down in torrents. Suddenly the door opened and there stood a young woman with her skirts tucked up, in Wellington boots, soaking wet. She said: 'Lorenzo, Frieda has asked me to come and tell you that she will not come back.' 'Damn the woman,' shouted Lawrence in a fury, 'tell her I never want to see her again'. The young woman said nothing, but turned and went out into the rain.[101]

This was Kot's first glimpse of Katherine, whose lifelong friend he was to become.

Given Frieda's desire for sympathy, then, and Lawrence's irascible response to what he always saw as a public blaming of him for her loss, the presence of new acquaintances would always be likely to bring on a row. This would then escalate through the others taking sides ... this time, Katherine on Frieda's (*pace* Murry), and Murry and Kot decidedly on Lawrence's. Indeed Kot refused to come down again for some weeks, wrote what he called 'a long foolish letter' which he did not post (ii. 231), and when he did come, gave Frieda another talking to. Relations between them would never be easy. There was then another bigger crisis at the Cannans' near the beginning of November – either the same syndrome, or through Frieda flirting – and Murry's charge of treachery shows how partisanship intensified; as Lawrence's 'utter misery' shows what happened as soon as his anger wore off.

About 5 November yet another guest was wished into their spare bedroom, not much more than a week after the Murrys had moved out: a young American, Helen Dudley. Bertrand Russell had seduced her during a lecture tour, promising marriage, but then locked himself in his apartment when she followed him to London. Lady Ottoline Morrell, who had for some time been Russell's mistress, swallowed her feelings and tidied up after him,[102] persuading the Cannans to help – who asked the Lawrences to have Helen to stay. Since they owed their cottage to the Cannans, and also most of their social life in these months, they could hardly refuse. On 8 November, Horne, his wife Maisie, and Lewis came down (ii. 230). In the midst of all this Lawrence, still far from well, was trying to write his book on Hardy. About 17 November there was the worst row of all. After roast veal, and the washing the dishes (says Murry),

we were talking gaily enough when there was a mention of Frieda's children, and Frieda burst into tears. Lawrence went pale. In a moment, there was a fearful outburst. Ominously, there was no physical violence. Lawrence, though passionately angry, had kept control; and it was the more frightening. He had had enough, he said; she must go, she was draining the life out of him. She must go, she must go now. She knew what money he had; he would give her her share – more than her share. He went upstairs, and came down again, and counted out on the table to me sixteen sovereigns. Frieda was standing by the door, crying, with her hat and coat on, ready to go – but where?

The tactless mention of the children must have come from the Murrys, but he gave the Lawrences a talking to, and reconciled them – much to his surprise (and Katherine's) at what he described as his theatrical performance, which left him inwardly cold.[103] What is interesting however is that it was both a very serious crisis – where indeed could Frieda go? – and yet played to an audience by both Lawrences too, heightening drama and emotion more than if they had been alone.

To regard these anecdotes as simply indicative of what the marriage had become would however be misleading. They represent three occasions in over a month at a time of considerable stress. If only £32 remained from the £50, it was because between the first quarrel and the second Lawrence had asked Kot to get him a particular lapis lazuli necklace for Frieda (ii. 228), and because they had bought the new clothes in London which Murry so begrudged her. Immediately after the third rumpus, Lawrence agreed to go with her to Nottingham, to try a direct appeal to Weekley. The pattern is very reminiscent of what had happened the previous summer. As for the intimate sexual details – which both couples were unwise enough to confide – it is not very surprising that Frieda should respond to the quarrelling by refusing sex, whether simply because she was upset, or with intent. (She may also have used sexual humiliation as a weapon, as the heroines modelled on her do.) Lawrence's response might strike an unbiased onlooker as tolerant and understanding, of how such 'mortification' had to be accepted. There might however be a reaction, as the fiction shows, if the withdrawal went too far or became too deliberate. When a Lawrencian protagonist in his fiction takes his woman like an animal it tends to be because she has been deliberately withholding herself or running away; a counter-attack, in sex-war. On what did Murry base his remarks about physical satisfaction? Had Frieda complained of dissatisfaction?[104] Or (before one leaps to such conclusions, since it seems to be *his* pleasure that is in question in the passage) was it only that Lawrence had argued that 'true sex' was not a matter of pleasure, but of self-surrender to death and rebirth? (But what is true sex? How long is a piece of string?) There is no knowing, and it might be as well not to speculate with too much confidence, or generalise too easily from stressful circumstances.

Some proportion may be restored by realising what Lawrence was most concerned with at the time. Between early September and 18 November (when Murry confided to his journal his account of conflict between the Lawrences, and unsatisfactory sex) Lawrence had not spent most of his time quarrelling, nor with the Murrys. He had been writing his 'Study of Thomas Hardy', in which he worked out a conviction that conflict was the very ground of sexual relationship, and of creativity. Despite quarrels, even crises, it was a celebration of marriage – the marriage of opposites. On 18 November he was 'just finishing' (ii. 235).

XI A Confession of Faith

The 'little book on Hardy's people', commissioned by Bertram Christian back in July for Nisbet's 'Writers of the Day' series, expanded strangely, so much that it outgrew its commission, and remained unpublished in Lawrence's lifetime. Instead of 'a sort of interpretative essay' of only 15,000 words (ii. 193), it became also a complex exploration of Lawrence's deepest concerns.

For when he began in early September, it was the war even more than Hardy that occupied his mind: 'What a miserable world. What colossal idiocy, this war. Out of sheer rage I've begun my book about Thomas Hardy. It will be about anything but Thomas Hardy I am afraid – queer stuff – but not bad' (ii. 212). Thinking about Hardy impelled him to affirm his faith in human creativity despite the intensifying proof of man's destructiveness; despite also his personal worries: not having enough to live on now; the severe strain on his marriage; his increasing alienation from his society. He could neither join in war hysteria nor identify with pacifists. Yet the more he thought about these things, in turn, the deeper he saw into Hardy's achievement, and (he thought) his limitation. The problem was to weave it all together. He worked on a first draft through September. By early October (when he fell ill) he was both worried about the heterogeneity of what he had done – 'supposed to be about Thomas Hardy, but which seems to be about anything else in the world but that' (ii. 220) – and still confident that he could publish, for he asked Kot to type for him, and handed over the first fifty pages when his new friend came down on 11 October for that tense weekend. By then he had made three important decisions. If he was to define the essence of life and growth in a world apparently seeking to destroy itself, he had to begin at the beginning, with a living growing thing. He begins where his essay on Thomas Mann had left off, with a poppy – soon to become, indeed, the symbol of wartime tragedy and loss. But this was to be no tragic or pessimistic work; so despite its ostensible subject he decided against calling it the 'Study of Thomas Hardy', though this is the title by which it has been generally known. He called it 'Le Gai Savaire' (ii. 295), Nietzsche's 'Gay Science' of individual growth,[105] and earlier, the name given by the wandering mediaeval troubadours to their insouciant art (Lo gai saber), sung in a military world and in the face of their own homeless poverty. Yet Hardy remained in mind, even when the argument began apparently far off. A return to the Wessex novels would mark each deepening stage, and the destination.

Since gaiety was to be the keynote, the book begins light-heartedly about poppies and phoenixes and primitive men covering caves with paintings, in order to follow Christ's advice (often given in parable and symbol) to take no heed of material things, but consider the ruddy lily of the field, how it grows.[106] To his own anxiety about not having enough to live on, and to the competitive state-violence that had overcome Europe, the message of the poppy is the same: that self-preservation, whether in persons or nations, matters infinitely less than that every individual should seek to *be* and to flower, to the utmost in itself, before its end. 'The final aim of every living thing ... is the full achievement of itself.' If our concern is mainly with possession, and guarding it – or conversely, if we inhibit our own growth in pity for our neighbour – the life-force within us will go rotten. From here the argument spreads to the wrongs of society 'with some Fancyful Moralising'[107] about the suffrage and the poor; yet seriously too.

For if society suffers from money-sickness and sex-sickness, against which socialists and suffragists seek votes and laws, Lawrence believes that the real source of the ills, and therefore the only real solution, lies in the human heart and its power to heal its own greed and fear. If the youth of Europe are throwing themselves into war with glad cries it is either because they are sick of life in terms of self-preservation, or because they revel in destruction and death wish – yet the really vital firing line is where the leading shoot of individual being grows out into the unknown. It is for this, and not for work or wages that we must live – and our real material needs are smaller than we think.

What he finds extraordinary about Hardy's novels is how many of his people act not in self-preservation but by inner compulsion, bursting out of the 'walled city' that hems in their growth (though Hardy seems afraid of this, since the daring ones seem always to perish in the wilderness outside). In London, as well as buying clothes for Frieda, Lawrence had been to the British Museum where the Egyptian and Assyrian sculpture had spoken again to his sense of 'the tremendous *non-human* quality of life'. He wrote to Campbell of his belief in 'tremendous unknown forces of life, coming unseen and unperceived as out of the desert to the Egyptians, and driving us, forcing us, destroying us if we do not submit to be swept away' (ii. 218). And this too, he found in what he thought the first of Hardy's great novels, *The Return of the Native* and its imagining of Egdon Heath.

This is a constant revelation in Hardy's novels: that there exists a great background, vital and vivid, which matters more than the people who move upon it ... The vast, unexplored morality of life itself, what we call the immorality of nature, surrounds us in its eternal incomprehensibility, and in its midst goes on the little human morality play ...

The true 'moral' is that man 'must learn what it is to be at one, in his mind and will, with the primal impulses that rise in him' – even when these drive one out of society into the wilderness, and poverty – like himself and Frieda.

'Impulses', however – not, as before, the single impulse to maximum being. As he thinks, he experiences a quite different impulse, and so has to change his mind about work. For the real purpose and significance of work – for instance, writing, now – is not merely in order to eat and so preserve life. It is to *know* what one is *doing*; to make conscious the spontaneous processes of nature. He sees the impulse to know, and hence progressively to differentiate the self from the not-self through the growth of consciousness, as the other 'great aim and purpose in human life'.[108] (This will send him back to Hardy, to see which of his people are most individual, singled out – and pose all the more the question of why Hardy, who has an artist's predilection for such 'aristocrats', should always stand with the community against them, like Tolstoy and Anna Karenina?)

Now Lawrence opens his poppy to look more closely inside, and sees that at the heart of its life and growth there are indeed two life-forces, not one. They are 'male' and 'female', but in the delighted and far-reaching exploration which follows, the gender-specification gets complicated now in ways that undo much of the stereotyping of the 'Foreword to *Sons and Lovers*'. As Lawrence ranges through the history of art, it becomes clear that both opposites exist within everyone in differing proportions, their conflict being the source of creativity, and also defining its nature. (The weekend after Murry's diary entry, Lawrence took Frieda to London to the dentist, and went himself to the National Gallery. What might seem insupportable generalisations, about the psychological state of great artists, are actually precise responses to particular works there.[109]) Moreover, finding the two forces also in the Bible, which becomes indeed the great story of their opposition, they can equally (or better) be called 'God the Father' and 'God the Son' again – but not merely 'flesh' and mind-utterance now, but the impulse towards Oneness with All, and the opposite impulse to the other, the 'neighbour', which refines the self. Lawrence is also clear now that all the categories he uses are finally 'arbitrary, for the purpose of thought'.[110] So both 'male' and 'female' exist and conflict within every man and woman, as well as between them; and though the sexual act is a religious mystery 'for leaping off into the unknown, as from a cliff's edge' – more important than having children[111] – intercourse is not essential for laying hold of the 'beyond', and 'consummation' may take place in the spirit as well as the body.

'God the Father' is immutable, stable, all-embracing, one. Life according to this Law is a state of being in togetherness with all created things; an existence in the flesh, in sensation, linking us with the whole natural universe. But equally there operates throughout evolution the opposite force of 'God the Son'. This is the impulse to movement and change, from being to knowing, from undifferentiated oneness to perception of not-self, defining the self against the other. It is differentiation into the many: into separation, distinct self-awareness, thought and utterance, ever more complete individuation. The two impulses are always in conflict, but the conflict is the ground of all growth. From every successive clash is born a new dimension of personal life, or religion, or art. But beyond the Father and the Son is the Holy Spirit. Beyond sexual conflict is consummation, opening up a new world, as well as giving men and women to themselves more completely. Out of the dualism in the artist is created the work of art. There can however be no stasis, only a never-ending process. The whole inner history of mankind, visible in religion and art, is continual variation on an eternal dialectic which is never complete, since each new consummation leads to conflict on another level. Conflict is vital; if either force becomes too dominant the consummation may be partial or crippled. Battle is the condition of growth, but the aim is always to come through, ever beyond.

All this is not merely, for Lawrence, an idea-system in his mind. Part of his excitement, as he stands before Botticelli's *Mystic Nativity* or Raphael's *Madonna degli Ansidei*; or as he finally turns to the greatest of Hardy's novels *Tess of the d'Urbervilles* and *Jude the Obscure*, is to find his great opposites 'there' in interpretations that can be tested. There is of course much more to be said about that[112] – but what seems more immediately of concern to biography is how Lawrence believed himself to be making sense of his own life, sex and marriage. For as well as being a testament of creativity in a world apparently giving itself over to destruction; and a way of coming to terms with all that he felt about being broke, and unable to support Frieda, and at odds with nearly everyone in his 'city', the book was an important clarification of his attitude to society now; and a vindication of his marriage despite all the crises and furies that led others to suppose it could not possibly last.

For of course Murry was right (though perhaps in a deeper sense than he intended) that Lawrence idealised his marriage. Indeed Nietzsche had insisted that all philosophy was 'the confession of its originator, and a species of involuntary and unconscious auto-biography' – from which viewpoint Lawrence was being more conscious and honest than most, perhaps, in calling his attempt to realise his deepest beliefs (thinking in images, as befitted an imaginative man) 'a sort of Confessions of my Heart'[113] and a 'Confessio Fidei' (ii. 235, 243). If this was rationalisation, as in a sense it was, it was courageous rather than evasive or self-deceiving. For consider his acceptance of uncomfortable insights into unalterable conditions; and yet the gaiety with which a 'passionately religious man' contended that these were the source of growth, engendered by 'gods', forces that must not be denied, in himself or others. He knew that his conflict with Frieda would go on, and on – and yet it had demonstrably brought about a whole new dimension of his art. He knew that his work was separating him further from his society with each book – and for someone who, as Constance Garnett had seen, always wanted to be a social success, this was no small matter. His experience of the last two years had already made him perhaps a little too willing to see relationships almost apart from society, and this tendency would grow. (It is significant that he shows no interest in Hardy's *The Mayor of Casterbridge*.) He was whole-heartedly against this materialist and imperialist war, but how could a man who thought of conflict as he did, be a pacifist? He had become a markedly isolated figure. Bravest of all was the acceptance of bisexuality in himself, together with the insistence that this too was a universal and creative condition. Far from being a confession of 'homosexuality' as opposed to 'heterosexuality' however, this was a challenge to both these categorisations, and already contained the possibility of creative sexual relationships between people of the same gender.

When he finally comes to *Tess* and *Jude*, the oppositions are first seen as structural to the fictions – Tess torn apart between the opposite extremes of Alec and Angel, as Jude between Arabella and Sue – but then internalised within the characters. The analysis is penetrating, and generally accurate, albeit rather like an X-ray which pierces to the underlying structure, but leaves much of the body of the work shadowy, without the complex shifts of Hardy's narrative voice moving through its 'series of seemings', and his sense of history. Interestingly, the progression in the three chapters on Hardy, first setting people against 'the great background', then seeing them in terms of their individuality and then internalising the opposition, is also the development of his own fiction since *Sons and Lovers*. Indeed, as the next months would show, it was his rereading and thinking about Hardy that finally showed him how to turn 'The Wedding Ring' into *The Rainbow*.

In Abercrombie's book on Hardy (which Marsh had given him), it was the contention that 'The highest art must have a metaphysic'[114] that had most interested Lawrence, though he came to a very different account of what Hardy's was. Finally, however, his critique of his most admired predecessor focuses on Hardy's pessimism, which Abercrombie had refused to admit; and on the limitation (as it seemed to Lawrence) of Hardy's sense of tragedy. His own first novels had been tragic – he too had underlined passages in Schopenhauer. But, with Frieda in Italy, and increasingly hereafter, the young writer who had seen 'a tragedy in every cow' had come to see differently. *Sons and Lovers* may have been the tragedy of thousands of young men, but it had pointed in the direction of an integration that could not yet be achieved within it. As 'The Sisters' had turned into 'The Wedding Ring' the vision had clearly become more positive – and in the stories, the waste and horror came from nonrecognition or denial of what might have been liberating and creative. In the first part of the 'Study of Thomas Hardy', now, Lawrence was critical of Hardy (and Tolstoy) because the poppy-characters and aristocrats are defeated not by universal forces, as in the Greeks, but merely by society. But then he sees that in late Hardy, as in Shakespeare, people are destroyed by inner conflict too – yet Hardy, whose strength is that of God the Father, seems always prejudiced in favour of God the Son. Finally, Lawrence seeks a historical explanation, in terms of the history of the spirit. Between the 'Foreword' and the 'Hardy' he seems to have absorbed a Joachite way of looking at the evolution of human consciousness. Joachim de Fiore had seen human history as a sequence of epochs, culminating in a moment of reconciliation, which would inaugurate the Epoch of the Holy Spirit.[115] Lawrence, too, sees both Old and New Testament, and the inner history of mankind ever since, as a replacement of the rule of God the Father by the rule of God the Son – at the end of which stands Hardy, who cannot but see 'Love in conflict with the Law, and only Death the resultant, no Reconciliation'. Yet Lawrence believes, both about his marriage and his art, that he must strive for the Holy Ghost, the Comforter, true to his own being, but giving himself with suffering and joy to transformation by his opposite, knowing always they are two, yet two-in-one. Out of this he must strive for the 'supreme art', which is neither self-expression, nor the pitting of the self against the other to the submission of one, but 'which knows the struggle between the two conflicting laws, and knows the final reconciliation, where both are equal, two-in-one, complete. This is the supreme art, which yet remains to be done.'[116]

He would aim for it, in turning 'The Wedding Ring' into *The Rainbow*.

PART TWO

◆

Spear in the Side
(The Rainbow
and the War)

◆

CHAPTER FOUR

December 1914–May 1915

THE RAINBOW

I am working *frightfully* hard – rewriting my novel.
(ii. 239)

I A New Conception

No sooner had Lawrence finished 'Study of Thomas Hardy' towards the end of November 1914 than he took 'The Wedding Ring' from the drawer, not to tone down the love scenes but to start all over again, with a new focus on what it was about and the metaphysical shape it ought to have. By 3 December he was already 'working *frightfully* hard – rewriting' (ii. 239), and two days later, when he sent Kot – whom he had persuaded to type the 'Hardy' – the last of it, he also sent Pinker the first 100 pages of *The Rainbow* (ii. 239, 240).[1]

He had thought his novel complete, but sat down to it now in a ferment of new ideas. Thinking about Hardy had shown him a better way to begin: setting his characters against a 'great background', archetypal yet also precisely located in space and date on the Notts–Derby borderland he knew so well.[2] Then, like the later Hardy, he could go on to internalise the conflict of 'God the Father' and 'God the Son' within individuals and between them, in a more deeply comparative study of three generations of marriage.[3] The 'Hardy' would even suggest a new point at which (on second thoughts) to end. He had found in the Bible what would become the structure of his own book: 'Always the threefold utterance: the declaring of the God seen approaching, the rapture of contact, the anguished joy of remembrance, when the meeting has passed into separation.' He had cited the story of David as an example of the first phase, Solomon of the second and Job of the third; and explained how in Solomon's case rapture turned into rupture because the man was too weak and the woman conquered. Yet because there had been real contact 'the living thing was conserved, kept always alive and powerful, but restrained, restricted, partial'.[4] So as he took up again his three-generation story (which had in fact been written backwards, with the grandparents the least developed), he could see its shape more definitely now: a beautiful but partial 'Old Testament' dominated by 'God the Father'; a world of transition in which fulfilment is fused with failure and the promised land is seen but not entered; and a new world of separation almost unto death, but retaining in extremity the memory of an abiding covenant. (In the New Year, he decided to remove the Birkin material, and change what had been a happy ending to one of near tragedy, though with the promise of a new world.) He saw how to expand the first two marriages in the light of the conflict of opposites, before finally re-shaping the story of Ursula – as Ella was now renamed – and Skrebensky[5] in comparison and contrast. (Hence, even after cutting the material that became *Women in Love*, *The Rainbow* was still longer than 'The Wedding Ring'.)

The increasing self-consciousness in Hardy's characters (from the *Native* to *Tess* to *Jude*), would grow here too from generation to generation – demonstrating also (especially in Ursula) his new conception of character as 'allotropic' (ii. 183) and changeful under differing pressures. Yet, he felt, Hardy had not seen clearly where he was going, and had not gone far enough, the most liberating kind of affinity. Standing on Hardy's shoulders, he might see further.

His mind was more filled with the Bible than ever, with Christian theological language suddenly become meaningful in ordinary life; with the great stories (Genesis, the Flood, the journeying Israelites, the dance of David, the fiery furnace, Lot's wife, the sons of God and the daughters of men, the meanings of death and rebirth) to be retold again and again in his story, as reflected in human experience between 1840 and 1905. Powerful symbols had sprung to life in the 'Hardy', which the novelist's imagination might explore with much greater complexity in terms of human relationship. A whole new scene in Lincoln Cathedral would spring out of a remark about 'male' and 'female' in mediaeval cathedrals in chapter VII. The imagery of the axle and the wheel in chapters VI and VII could be put to sensitive use in the honeymoon of Anna and Will Brangwen. The polarities of light and darkness, which he had discussed in Rembrandt and Turner, could become, along with the phoenix in its crucible of flame, a major symbolic structuring for the whole novel. The column and ellipse in the mediaeval church, and in Raphael's *Madonna degli Ansidei*, fuse with the biblical pillars of fire and cloud to extend the significance of the rainbow-arch.

Here, in the struggle of criticism and fictive creation, rather than in the gossipy anecdotes retailed by friends and acquaintances and dutifully repeated by biographers ever since, was where the deepest life of Lawrence is to be found from early September to Christmas. Partly he could escape from a 'miserable world' into an imagined one. But there too he could learn more about the sources of the destructiveness, and the creativity, of the war in his cottage, and in the world at large.

II   The Last of the Year

Yet the outside world was nonetheless demanding and painful. Two days after sending Pinker the first 100 pages on 5 December – which imagine Lydia the foreigner marrying again, and Tom coming to terms with her child – he went with Frieda to Nottingham to try to rescue the situation about her children. She thought that if she could meet and talk to Weekley, she could change his attitude.

She only made things worse, once more. She hoped that taking him by surprise might jolt her ex-husband out of his set position and that, face to face, some of his old feeling for her might return. It was another bad miscalculation. His heart had hardened – and he bitterly resented being ambushed in Nottingham, where she might be recognised. He cannot be blamed too much. She had wronged him again and again before, then humiliated and disgraced him by running away with Lawrence, and he thought the scandal must damage his career. She had plotted to see the children behind his back, and he had been forced to go to law to stop her. She had even burst into his home and upset his elderly mother and his sister. Under his gentlemanly and cosmopolitan manner there were strong and sometimes hysterical feelings. He had 'morals' on his side. Yet he was (apparently) incapable of imagining, or caring about her suffering over the children, or of allowing her any rights at all, since the law gave him the power to refuse. Retelling Frieda's account, Lawrence tries to help her see it as 'music-hall' melodrama; but it must have hurt her intensely:

'You –' said the quondam husband, backing away – 'I hoped never to see you again.'

Frieda: 'Yes – I know.' ...

Quondam Husband: Aren't you ashamed to show your face where you are known? Isn't the commonest prostitute better than you?

Frieda: Oh no.

Quon. Husb.: Do you want to drive me off the face of the earth, Woman? Is there no place where I can have peace?

Frieda: You see I must speak to you about the children.

Quon. Husb.: You shall *not* have them – they don't want to see you ... Don't you know, my solicitors have instructions to arrest you, if you attempt to interfere with the children.

Frieda: I don't care.[6]

As Lawrence says, it might have been funny were it not altogether 'too painful, dragging out for three years, as it does' (ii. 244). Frieda adds in a postscript that they will try to go back to Italy 'soon' (ii. 245),[7] if Methuen will pay Lawrence for the new *Rainbow*. She has given up hope.

On 18 December – back at the Triangle, after visiting Ada in Ripley and

Garnett in London – he sent Pinker another 100 pages. (ii. 240, 245)[8] Two days later an important letter came out of the insight of 'Hardy'. He learned that Campbell too was writing a novel, which was going to end with a suicide. Lawrence begged him not to glorify that 'final act of egotism and vanity', but to think of the end of the Book of Job – where in the depths of suffering Job still recognises the creative power of God – and also of the great Christian message, which is not death on the cross but resurrection in the body. These are the perspectives against which tragedy should be set. Modern symbolism is all subjective self-expression, but 'The other way is to try to conceive the Whole, to build up a Whole by means of symbolism, because symbolism avoids the I and puts aside the egotist; and, in the Whole, to take our decent place' (ii. 247–8). He had been reading Mrs Jenner's *Christian Symbolism* in which, among other things, he found the graphic illustration of the phoenix which became his personal symbol, the sign of the continual death and renewal of the self.[9] Above all, he insists, the beings who are nearest God, the Cherubim, 'are absorbed forever in fiery praise'. Novels must be followed to their '*biggest* close – further than death, to the gladness' (ii. 250).

Now Lawrence and Frieda began to prepare for Christmas, to try to be glad – even though 'very disheartened by the war and everything' (ii. 251). The British Expeditionary Force, a professional army, had suffered heavy losses at Mons and the Marne and the first battle of Ypres, and now the entrenched positions ran all the way from the Vosges Mountains to the sea. Nobody could believe now that the war would be a short one. On 16 December Lawrence's prediction about the guns came home, as German battle-cruisers shelled Scarborough, where the Burrows family used to holiday, and where Lawrence had sent Ella and Gudrun in 'Sisters II'.

Kot was asked to bring down two flasks of Chianti to remind them of last Christmas in Italy; Lawrence made a rum punch; and Frieda some marzipan Murry thought 'problematic'. The Lawrences would have a party on Christmas Eve, followed by dinner at the Cannans' on Christmas Day. 'We made the cottage splendid with holly and mistletoe', Frieda remembered, 'we cooked and boiled, roasted and baked. Campbell and Koteliansky and the Murrys came, and Gertler and the Cannans.' Gilbert sang 'I feel, I feel like an eagle in the sky'; Koteliansky his Hebrew psalm; Katherine 'with a long, ridiculous face' a mock-mournful song about being an unlucky man, and '*Ton sirop est doux, Madeleine*' – which Lawrence wouldn't let Frieda sing afterwards, because (she says) it was 'too "fast" for him. This was the last time for years to come that we were really gay.' But a drunken Murry – who had been told by Frieda that Lawrence's novel was 'great', and 'had Marlowe and Fielding in an account of a genuine English wedding', reacted in sudden jealous belligerence. He noted next morning that when Lawrence said there was more to writing novels than creating characters, 'I have an already vague recollection of flinging up my arms and telling him that when he had created a character I would take off my hat to him – "several times a day".' But at the end they danced, Gertler vigorously while the others stamped and shouted – after which he talked 'a long Yiddish rigmarole' all the way home to his lodgings.[10]

Murry's relationship with Katherine was on the rocks. On the 18th she had found that wounding remark in his diary, and had written in her own:

That decides me – that frees me. I'll play this game no longer. I created the situation. ['Make me your mistress', she had said.] Very well, I'll do the other thing with *moderate* care, and before it is too late. That's all. He has made me feel like a girl. I've loved, loved just like any girl, – but I'm not a girl, and these feelings are not mine. For him I am hardly anything except a gratification and a comfort ... Jack, Jack, we are not going to stay together ... I am far away, and different from what you think.[11]

It was wonderful weather for Christmas – 'frosty clear and cold all day, the white frost pink in the bare hedges'. Murry went to the Lawrences' in the morning to get Chinese lanterns, and cut some newly yellow gorse with Katherine in the afternoon. But at the Cannans' party, despite the fine dining-table with its best linen and glass, things went awry. There was a gloomy beginning. Murry was conscious of hostility between him and Gertler (perhaps because Katherine seemed interested in him); the Lawrences were late; and nobody could carve the roast suckling-pig. Murry 'got up and sang stentorian French songs at the table', and drink loosed inhibition rather dangerously. The Cannans enjoyed acting in playlets as much as the Lawrences their charades. Gertler, Gilbert and Katherine did a music-hall sketch; after which Gertler, Katherine, Lawrence and Frieda did a playlet 'Driven from Home' – 'very badly', says Murry. Next, Murry, hurt at not having been picked and now 'very drunk', suggested one with himself, Gilbert and Mary: 'a cruel psychological murder', in which he played 'with an intense conviction'. Then Kot's talk about 'a play within a play', gave Murry the idea for yet another in which he could dramatise his and Katherine's private situation, casting Mark Gertler as the 'sentimental foreigner' – i.e. Carco – whom she had 'a sentimental desire to comfort', but scripting also her return to himself. But when it came to the point, Katherine refused to obey the script and continued making up to Gertler who, with his curly head and cherub face, was always excitable – even when not drunk and missing Dora Carrington, for whom he had an unrequited passion. He wrote her: 'Gilbert Cannan's party was most extraordinarily exciting. Katherine and myself – both very drunk – made passionate love to each other in front of everybody! And everybody was drunk too. No one knew whether to take it as a joke or scandal ...'[12] Lawrence was furious. He 'indignantly interrupted the drama' – says Murry – 'hustled me aside, and asked me with intense and passionate severity: "was I blind?". If not, how did I dare to expose myself? "It's not as though we didn't love you ... " But I was not blind at all.' Katherine moreover had got inside her role. When Lawrence took her to task about her behaviour with Gertler: 'You don't love him'; she would only say 'Yes I do, I do'; and Frieda cried 'I'll never speak to you again. You lead that young man on'. Gertler burst into tears of self-reproach. Frieda asked him to dance with her but he wouldn't. So she danced alone.[13]

It was a Dostoevskyan evening; a grotesque contrast with Christmas at Fiascherino.

In the trenches, soldiers from both sides had fraternised in no-man's-land ... for a little while.

Before the end of January the Lawrences were to leave the Triangle; in another three weeks Katherine was in France, and Murry alone.

III   A Man Writing

Meanwhile, Lawrence's creative life ran swift and newly sure of direction, as the pile of long typescript pages of 'The Wedding Ring' were steadily replaced by the smaller handwritten pages of *The Rainbow*.

If we look over his shoulder, we can see ways in which the fictive world might relate to the man imagining – without playing his creative imagination false by crude ideas about 'sources', or simple extrapolations of literature to life. (Literary criticism is something else again.) Lawrence often wrote best when his imagination took off from real people and settings; though in growing backwards, this novel had steadily moved away from *him*. Perhaps we should ask how both the typescript on one side of the table (most of which we cannot alas make out) and the growing pile of manuscript on the other, came to be imagined in ways relatively free of personal pressures – so enabling him all the better to use, clarify, and deepen now, the insights of his 'Hardy'.

We do not know how much there was about Ella's grandparents in 'The Wedding Ring', but the timeless prelude of the Brangwen men and women with which the novel now opens could not have been written before Lawrence had grasped his Opposites, and the importance of setting characters against a great background.[14] As we then imagine him day after day at Chesham, refocusing and expanding the story of Tom and Lydia Brangwen, and her little daughter Anna, it must have been with a much clearer and deeper sense now of the nature of their conflicts, and their marriage. At the same time he was also *testing* his new theoretical metaphysic against the concretely imagined life of this man, this woman, this child. He wrote steadily and fast, at an average rate of seven pages a day – much more sometimes, given the preparations for Christmas.

We must remember however, in guessing at origins and development, the testimony of all creative writers: how the imagination transforms whatever its starting-point may have been, how scenes take shape and characters pull with their own life, how one goes to bed and wakes up with a whole episode in mind that seems to have come from nowhere, or how one suddenly *sees* – for the first time – what one had been driving at in those earlier pages, that can now be thrown away.

In 'The Wedding Ring', Lawrence had already given Tom a foreign wife, a Pole;[15] but the Brangwen farm was part of a landscape he knew very well. The mother of Louie Burrows – he would keep her name, Anna, in his story – had been brought up on a farm just outside the village of Cossall. When Lawrence began to visit Louie, her parents, Alfred and Anna Burrows, and their big family were living (as his 'Anna' and 'Will' would do) in a cottage between Cossall Church and the Parish Room. Every time he went to see Louie he passed the Marsh Farm, flanked by the Midland Railway, the Nottingham Canal and its viaduct, and watched over by the tower of Ilkeston church. To imagine a young Notts farmer, born just before 1840 to a family which had farmed there 'for over two hundred years', was to make possible a fusion of local history with biblical myth, in an actual landscape well known, loved and remembered. (When the story begins, The Marsh is still tucked away in a pre-industrial borderland, but canal, railway and colliery have already impinged on the consciousness of the Brangwens, and the entry into history will be one of the major themes of the book.)[16]

However, to make Ella's grandmother not merely a stranger, but a foreigner, a Pole, was to emphasise the importance of the transformation of the self at the hands of the strangely Other (or polar opposite), which Lawrence had come to see as the essence of marriage. He could then take advantage of useful elements in Frieda's background. Her mother was also named Anna. Her father's mother was a Polish Countess, and *her* mother had been a Skrebensky. The von Richthofen estates had been in 'Polish' Silesia. Frieda's father and grandfather had gambled ruinously, and the stories Lydia tells Tom have their source in von Richthofen family scandal. There is no telling how much of *The Rainbow*'s Lydia was already there in 'The Wedding Ring', but the imaginative potential seems clear. To imagine an 'elemental' ancestor was to be able to concentrate on certain things Lawrence valued in *his* foreign wife: her 'strangeness', her mysterious religious sense without a creed, her ruthless stripping of pretence (as when Lydia accuses Tom of denying her) and the liberating carelessness to be developed still further in her daughter. At the same time, by imagining a nineteenth-century refugee, these could be freed from all the other complexities and pressures on him of the very real modern woman, reading on the bed upstairs.

By calling Tom's wife Lydia, however – whenever he did so – Lawrence also privately signalled that her marriage was the latest and perhaps the most powerful re-imagining of the first part of *Sons and Lovers*. For Lydia was his mother's name, and the little figure in black whom Tom sees on the road outside Cossethay acts out an alternative scenario, brought now at last into fully diagnostic focus. Whereas Mrs Morel, having been attracted to her opposite, then destroyed him by trying to make him over in her terms, this is finally the story of a marriage in which each proves not only able to recognise and reverence the otherness of the other (*and* of the child); but even to 'die' themselves, into new life, through sexual relationship. In their betrothal – that elemental scene in which, though hardly anything can be said, a kiss can bring about a kind of death and a rebirth into a rich new life – Lawrence clarifies the essence of his marriage-of-opposites in realised human terms. The central insights of 'Odour of Chrysanthemums' and 'Daughters of the Vicar' – *The Prussian Officer* had been published on 29 November[17] – are re-embodied in a new context which (after 'Hardy') can explore both conflict and creativity, and understand more deeply the failure of his parents' marriage, and the conditions for success in his own. Here too is the 'Hardy' perspective on what is essential in human existence: man and woman meeting against the great background of universal forces; then journeying together across a vast landscape. They seem tiny figures in that aspect, yet (for Lawrence) they can lay hold on eternity through marriage, achievement enough to give value to any human life.

Tom Brangwen was probably first imagined as a combination of the young Alan Chambers – who had attracted Lawrence at first to The Haggs more strongly than Jessie – with an idealised version of his father or perhaps grandfather as a young man with an incipient drinking problem through frustration. (In another aspect, unlike *The White Peacock* this was to be a George Saxton who would find the woman through whom he could grow.) The new metaphysic required a character very different from himself: a Brangwen man who was mainly impelled by 'God the Father', only with an inarticulate longing in him, born of 'God the Son'. Thus liberated from autobiography, however, Lawrence was all the freer to explore a situation that came close to his, but was different enough not to be inhibiting. Tom and Lydia are the same ages as Lawrence and Frieda in 1913 when he began 'The Wedding Ring'. What is it like to be married to an older woman, who has been married before; who sometimes compares you with her first husband unflatteringly, though he never really satisfied her; and who sometimes wants you and sometimes does not? What *is* the effect on a woman of losing her children? Suppose she had custody of a daughter from the first marriage – how would one come to terms with that? (Perhaps she could be imagined as like Frieda when she was a little girl, with hair like a halo ...[18])

Above all, he could now continually clarify, deepen and expand the earlier work, page after page, because his 'Hardy' helped him to see, behind Tom's problems and conflicts with Lydia and her child, the fundamental conflict of 'God the Father' with 'God the Son': the impulse to togetherness with a lover and with all nature through the senses, in unity and stability; the opposing impulse to separate consciousness, defining itself against all that is not-self, in individuation and change. If Tom and Lydia were the last of the major characters to arrive, they became the first opportunity to clarify what made for a creative marriage of opposites. After revised stories, too, Lawrence could explore with greater complexity what it meant to reverence the mystery of the 'other' (contrast Elizabeth Bates)[19] before it was too late, and above all what was involved in 'dying' to the self and into new life (compare Alfred and Louisa) – which a treatise could not do. After 'Hardy', he could reshape this first marriage into an imaginative experience of an Old Testament world, containing the great mythic patterns: Genesis; the Journey towards the promised land behind the pillars of fire and cloud; Noah's Flood and the covenant of the rainbow. He could re-interpret the theological language of Christianity, so that baptism, confirmation, crucifixion, resurrection, transfiguration, could be seen to take place in everyday human life. In Tom, Lydia and little Anna he could bring out the full resonance of what he had seen in the Botticelli and Raphael holy families, and the 'sense of the Whole' of Fra Angelico; and explore the new imagery of phoenix, column, arch, threshold and doorway. The religious impulse of the 'passionately religious man' could find its first full expression, not always to the taste of irreligious modern readers, but unquestionably venturing into a 'Hinterland der Seele' or field of force (in its own language a 'beyond') which Frieda had felt lacking in *Sons and Lovers*, and for which Futurists and Vorticists had also felt the need, without (Lawrence thought) being able to conceive it in satisfactory terms.

There were some dangers also in the very excitement and force of Lawrence's newly worked out philosophy, and his new conception of character, subverting 'the old stable ego' with a sense of subconsciousness and flux. For ideas are of little significance in a novel unless they can be convincingly embodied. Because the characters cannot be articulately aware, themselves, of what is happening within them, the voicing of the deepest inner dimensions has to be authorial. Combine this with an urge to expound significant new ideas, and an upsurge of religious feeling – which had made the Bible and the language of Christianity seem newly relevant, so that he might almost feel he was rewriting the old sacred history into a new one for the twentieth century, a new prose for 'God' – and there comes a danger of religiosity and linguistic inflation. These can be effectively countered by dramatisation, into convincing experience of this man, this woman, this child; but Lawrence's success in doing so is for every reader to judge. In another direction, his increasing isolation from society in both life and philosophy, now, is having its effect. Occasionally one is aware of a village, a town, but the world is that of the Marsh Farm almost exclusively. Even there, rural unrest and Chartism are nowhere to be seen, though strong in Nottinghamshire in the 1840s. We never see Tom's labourers, though one or two are mentioned. (In the novel as we have it, even the experience of Tom working his land is lessened by cutting the manuscript's ploughing scene.)[20] All this heightens the sense of the archetypal, and is appropriate to the historical *development* of consciousness Lawrence wishes to show – but it also speaks of the Lawrence of 1914 rather more than of actual farming life on the Notts–Derby border in the second half of the nineteenth century.[21]

By 18 December he sent Pinker another 100 pages. The chapter then called 'Haste to the Wedding' begins on MS 199, and the 'genuine English wedding' was finished before 23 December. By 5 January, still in Chesham, he had done 300 pages, and it is clear that the novel had become very different from, and not merely an expansion of, 'The Wedding Ring'. 'It'll be a new sort of me for you to get used to ... I'm afraid, when Methuen gets the *Rainbow*, he'll wonder what changeling is foisted on him. For it *is* different from my other work. I am very glad with it. I am coming into my full feather at last, I think' (ii. 255).[22]

The imagining of Anna as a girl must have been fuelled, at least in its beginnings, both by memories of Ada (there is some resemblance to Lettie in *The White Peacock*) and by Frieda's memories of herself, for the episode of the rosary is slightly odd for Protestant Nottinghamshire but very suggestive of a convent-educated girl in Metz. Lawrence must also have heard Anna Burrows talk of her girlhood at The Marsh and at school in Nottingham – he was good at getting people to talk about themselves. What is certain (because of Louie's subsequent distress)[23] is that the young couple who set up house in the cottage beside the church were instantly recognisable as having sprung from Alfred and Anna Burrows of Church Cottage, Cossall. Lawrence recreated, in Will, Alfred's temperament and his peculiar 'clapping' laugh, his passion for architecture and art, his wood-carving and metalwork, his devotion to the little church of which he was organist and how his evening classes in woodwork led to an appointment as Handcraft Instructor for the new County Education Department in Leicestershire, where the family moved and where Lawrence visited them in Quorn.[24]

Yet the significance of all this is not its 'sources' in life, but its imaginative liberation. Here, even more than with Tom and Lydia, the creation of a couple who are *not* Lawrence and Frieda allowed his imagination freely to explore some of their own deepest problems. He could use episodes from his life, like the argument with Louie and her parents about how much money is needed to get engaged – and could also put some of himself into the young Will and then look at it: the hobbledehoyness and enthusiastic talk, the interest in art, the hot temper he shared with Alfred Burrows, the obsessiveness, above all the deep uncertainty of self (behind surface egotism) which produces both Will's readiness to abandon himself, but also his fastening onto Anna, and his difficulty in standing alone. Here Lawrence was able to look at what humiliated and infuriated him most about himself and his marriage, and bring out something of the misery he felt when the woman he needed at the back of him withdrew. For there is also much of Frieda in Anna's self-sufficient egotism, her unwillingness to commit herself, her splendid carelessness, her aggression, her ruthless attack on her husband's ideas from the stance of common sense, her obsession with her children and her motherhood – though it was Anna Burrows who had had all those children. However, Lawrence was also freed to imagine, now, the satisfactions as well as the dangers of preferring motherhood and domesticity to the onward voyage of the soul.

Yet, one repeats, this is merely to suggest starting-points for the creative writer, and hence something of the complex excitement of that writing life at Chesham which, day by day, proceeded to fill those outlines, and pursue those characters wherever they pulled. In the courting scene in the moonlit cornfield (which could not have been shaped before 1914) the opposites came rhythmically and dramatically to life in human action – embodying now what Lawrence had tried to explain to Garnett, how human beings respond below the level of 'the old stable ego' to universal 'forces', that yet remain profoundly non-mechanical, unlike the conceptions of the Futurists. In imagining the honeymoon, details from life (Anna staying in bed, careless about spilt tea on the pillow)[25] could fuse with an extraordinary imaginative experience of security and peace at the still centre of the vortex, the hub of the wheel, the heart of a world in flux (as at Beuerberg). Lawrence must have felt everything coming together, with great conviction. Yet the conviction for a reader has once again to lie also in the realisation of the difficulty of marriage: the clash of temperaments; the dramatic battles of will which pit 'his' overdependent pressure against 'her' self-guarding resistance; 'her' compulsive motherhood against 'his' shaming need of her in order to prop and stay himself. Here again is the importance of Lawrence the *novelist*. For the theory of the marriage of opposites was surely too simply optimistic as it appeared in 'Le Gai Savaire'? Though it acknowledged that some selves could inhibit their own growth and go rotten or play touch-and-go with death, it had not shown how the marriage of opposites could lead to *mutual* damage, or even destruction, as well as to creativity. That discovery in *The Rainbow* is made through constant comparison and contrast between the generations, so that the reader can set the betrothal scene of Tom and Lydia, and the subsequent readiness of each to die to the other, against the partial frustration at the end of the corn-stacking scene, and what it turns into when the pregnant Anna dances herself to her Lord against the shadowy importunate man in the doorway.[26] But these, too, only gain their effect through the realistic sequence of tensions, quarrels and reconciliations the young couple experience, to which the experience of Lawrence with Frieda has contributed and is contributing – but in which he is required to imagine Anna's view as powerfully as Will's.

So, between 18 December and 5 January, Lawrence reshaped the middle generation of 'The Wedding Ring' into a full comparison and contrast with the world of Tom and Lydia, summing up the contrast (under the sign of the rainbow) at the end of the chapter called 'Anna Victrix'. Then, however, he produced a whole new leap of imagination: the scene in Lincoln cathedral. He clearly wanted to stand back, and – having explored the complex and fluctuating story of the two individuals – to set it once more against the perspective of 'the Whole', as he had insisted true art had to do. This meant imagining a kind of echo chamber in which 'God the Son' could once again confront 'God the Father' essentially, but in an encompassing vision of God the Holy Spirit, fairly allowing each its measure and its kind of truth. So, building on an aside about cathedrals in 'Hardy', he gives imaginative expression to the unitary vision, the ecstatic self-abandonment to an inclusive whole in Will, and the drive to multiplicity, distinction and freedom of the separate and conscious self in Anna, as the opposite responses to Lincoln cathedral conflict with each other. (In Lawrence's religious vision the deepest drive in Anna is also 'godly'.)[27] He also wanted to recognise the opening up of new horizons in the second generation, as well as their partial failure and destructiveness as compared with the first. As Will and Anna argue about art and religion, they have become aware of dimensions that were closed to their parents in their 'Old Testament' world. The young couple are moving into nineteenth-century history and consciousness: products of the industrial revolution and the start of the revolution in education, and of the decline of Christianity in the face of science and rational scepticism.[28] Yet the greater dimensions of consciousness seem not only to heighten the conflict within and between the lovers, but also threaten to change creativity into destruction. What began in the moonlit cornfield opens up its dangers: the over-assertiveness of Will now meets active antagonism in Anna, and the conflict is permanently damaging, as she begins not just to withhold herself, now, but to weaken something in him. There is more to marry than in the earlier generation, but marriage seems therefore to have become more difficult. Lawrence is posing the challenge to himself and Frieda, with new clarity. (The whole nature and extent of his development since *Sons and Lovers* might be encapsulated in the difference between this chapter and the visit of Paul and Mrs Morel to the same cathedral.)

Between 5 and 20 January, still at Chesham, he finished three more short chapters: 'The Child' (though without the second half we have now), 'The

Marsh and the Flood', and 'The Widening Circle'. But first, on 7 January, sending the third hundred pages to Pinker, he announced a major decision: to split the work in two, removing the whole of Ella/Ursula's relationship with Birkin and Gudrun's with Gerald and Loerke, and saving these for a continuation which would become *Women in Love*. This shows how much he had added to 'The Wedding Ring'.[29] '[I]t was so unwieldy. It needs to be in two volumes' (ii. 256). Moreover, its ending had been optimistic for Ella, and even for Gudrun, after disaster and failure in their earlier relationships. But the 'threefold' shape which 'Hardy' had seen in the Bible had ended in tragic severance, though retaining 'the anguished joy of remembrance, when the meeting has passed into separation'. In its contrast of the second generation with the first the cathedral chapter, just written, implies that the third pair of lovers, with even greater consciousness, might find it harder still to marry their oppositions. Although the Whole might still point towards fulfilment, removing Ursula's relationship with Birkin meant that *The Rainbow* itself would have the curve of tragedy – but for the covenant symbolised in its title and central image.

Now 'The Child' reverses the gender of the sons-and-lovers theme: to show how the partial failure of a marriage makes a father so turn to his daughter that he both stirs her into consciousness too early, and exploits her as a substitute 'lover' in dangerous ways. Lawrence could bring together – the more powerfully and clearly because impersonally now – his understanding of what had happened to himself, and of Louie's difficult relation with her father, and perhaps also Frieda's with the Baron, since the episode of the gardening began from a childhood memory of hers. Lawrence liked and was very good with children; and he must have wondered (since a scare in Waldbröl) about being a father himself; though there had been less than a month, so far, in which a child of theirs could have been both legitimate and affordable. He had thought a good deal about how children should be treated.[30] Whereas Tom respects the child-being of little Anna, holding back from burdening her with his needs, there is something very damaging in the ways that Will makes his child a substitute for his withdrawn wife. (What Lawrence said to Murry about having to accept the 'mortification' of a wife's occasional withdrawal, as Tom did with Lydia, gains new point.)

'The Marsh and the Flood' allows an imaginative fusion of local history with biblical myth. The flood actually happened, remembered by Louie's mother with fear,[31] and made real by Lawrence's imagination; but in the novel it also, as in the Bible, separates an 'old' world finally from a new one. Only, the world which is drowned was not wicked. Indeed, it contained the essence of 'the Whole' of life and eternity, though limited and undeveloped. And Noah the Just dies in the Flood, though not without having prophesied (at the wedding) in a drunkenness that was no disgrace, but rather the gayest wisdom he could achieve. Dead, he can be seen by wife and daughter to embody something eternal.

'The Widening Circle' begins to explore in the girlhood of Ursula new dimensions of education and emancipation, and also the internalisation within the girl of the conflicts of her grandparents and parents – the move in Hardy's fiction from the *Native* through *Tess*, to *Jude*. The feelings of the romantic and aspiring eldest daughter in a welter of smaller siblings re-imagine Louie. The experience of separation from the village children, in her move from the village school to the High School for Girls in Nottingham, fuses her alienation with Lawrence's. Yet Ursula's feeling for the ancient rhythms of the year, and the legend of the sons of God and the daughters of men, speaks of her grandparents still there within her; while the intensity with which she is drawn to her father's world of art and religion, yet reacts away with her mother's (God the Daughter's) defiance and scepticism, shows a new extremity of feeling, and of awareness. Indeed, Ursula's feelings get so close to her creator's that the apostrophe which ends the chapter breaks fiction into sermon, from Lawrence, on his quarrel with a Christianity that (he thinks) does not understand its own theology. The insistence that it is resurrection in the flesh that is the central meaning, not crucifixion, had been the theme of a letter to Gordon Campbell on 20 December, and would fill his thoughts again as he wrote to Cynthia Asquith at the end of January, about his state of mind since the outbreak of war.

On 20 January, just before leaving the Triangle, he sent Pinker 'what pages of the novel I have' and wondered 'when Methuen would want to publish the book – have you any idea?' (ii. 260).[32]

IV Another Country

By the New Year, Lawrence had grown restless at Chesham. It had been a refuge; yet they had never much cared for the place, even if the people had been kind. The Cannans had helped when help was badly needed. They had found the cottage, they had approached committee members of the Literary Fund, and their Mill House had provided the kind of society the Lawrences liked – there at intervals when they wanted it. Down to Cholesbury at weekends came interesting people: Elliott Seabrooke the painter whom Lawrence liked very much, Compton Mackenzie, the historian G. M. Trevelyan, the playwright John Leslie Palmer. The young were also welcome: Frankie Birrell, son of the Irish Secretary in Asquith's Cabinet came to the Cannans with Bunny Garnett, and Carrington with Gertler. Gilbert liked to keep in touch with the young-of-promise, and indeed to help those not yet as successful as himself. (Like Marsh, he had helped the Murrys as well as Gertler.) There may well have been other visitors whom the letters do not happen to mention. The Cannans might be 'scandalous' after Mary's divorce, but they still had many friendships among intellectuals and artists, including Lady Ottoline Morrell (to whom they had introduced Lawrence), Bertrand Russell, Granville-Barker, Hugh Walpole, Maurice Hewlett and so on. Mary was not an intellectual – since leaving the stage her main interests were interior decoration, gardening and her dogs – but she was a gracious hostess. Since she was almost old enough to be Gilbert's mother, she dressed, made-up and dyed her hair very carefully, to preserve the beauty which had drawn Barrie first to cast and then to marry her. She might talk rather too much – but she was warm and outgoing and the Lawrences liked her. Gilbert was more remote. This was largely defensive: an unhappy upbringing had left him less self-confident than he appeared; and the need to prove his worth (and also vindicate Mary's choice) made him drive himself to write too much and too fast in his circular study in the Mill beside the house. Tall, with a mop of corn-coloured hair and an aquiline beak of a nose, his withdrawn persona concealed a romantic and idealistic temperament – expressing itself, alas, with too great facility, though in 1914 he seemed much more successful than Lawrence in every way.[33]

The major effect of Chesham, however, was to increase Lawrence's alienation from English society. July 1914 had seen him happily in touch with new movements in London, and conforming with social respectability at Kensington Registry Office. Then the war opened a chasm between the Lawrences and the vast majority of English people. At first Chesham must have seemed a refuge in that sense too. Though Gilbert (to please Mary) became a Special Constable for a while, he was becoming more and more opposed to the war, and ended up working against conscription with Bertrand Russell and Lowes Dickinson. Gertler voiced a young artist's denunciation of a war fought for materialist reasons, and felt this strongly enough to break with Eddie Marsh and lose his greatly needed patronage. Much of the talk in the Mill House was anti-war, and many of the people who came there would soon declare for pacifism.

'Study of Thomas Hardy' proclaimed that the full achievement of the self, which is the aim of all living things, *must* drive the living soul away from the walled city into the wilderness. At first this merely opposed self-fulfilment to self-preservation (for which walls and cities were invented); but soon Lawrence was denouncing war fever in the fortified city as the product of a death wish. Yet he was so far from being pacifist that he founded his whole metaphysic of creativity on conflict. So his position became doubly isolated, able neither to join the patriotic fervour inside the walls, nor to feel at home in the country house where pacifist intellectuals and artists gathered.

His growing sense of isolation needed a stronger symbolism. Early in the New Year it appears in a letter to Kot: the idea of Rananim, a small community or colony of like-minded souls who would make a clean break from a sick society.

Katherine's journal makes it clear that the original dream was of sailing away to an island (though it had 'come too late' for her).[34] It was only a dream of course, something to talk about in the dark days; but for Lawrence, who thought in images, it was more than just an expression of discontent. It was a psychological language to focus distress at alienation, and redefine what sense of 'community' was still possible for him to imagine.

The name came from the first line of Psalm 33 in Hebrew – Rannani Zadikim l'Adonoi, Rejoice in the Lord O ye Righteous – which Kot had sung in the Lake District, and again at the Lawrences' Christmas party. This also echoed Lawrence's sermon to Campbell about the Cherubim and the end (rather than the middle) of the book of Job: whether in adversity or heaven, the central activity must be to praise the Lord. If Lawrence asked Kot about the Hebrew, he would have learned that the word Ra'annanim, meaning 'green, fresh or flourishing', qualified 'the righteous' (zadikim), in Psalm xcii. 14, so that righteousness was associated with growing, like the poppy. On 3 January he wrote to Kot:

> What about Rananim? Oh, but, we are going. We are going to found an Order of the Knights of Rananim. The motto is 'Fier' – or the Latin equivalent. The badge is So:
> [Sketch]
> an eagle, or phoenix argent, rising from a flaming nest of scarlet, on a black background. And our flag, the blazing, ten-pointed star, scarlet on a black background.
> [Sketch]
>
> (ii. 252–3, and cf. n. 2)

(See Illustration 32.) He went on to ask Kot to buy him Chapman's Homer. There is nothing pacifist about any of this, but it calls for a very different kind of militancy than that of the trenches. He had just made Skrebensky's father a Knight of Malta in his novel, so he had in mind also the origins of that great order and its dedication to St John. On the same day he thanked Lady Ottoline Morrell, who had written to praise *The Prussian Officer*: 'One wants the appreciation of the few', for life is 'an affair of aristocrats'. Though a democrat in politics, he thinks the state 'a vulgar institution', and Liberty and Equality only necessary as 'an arrangement for myriads of peoples' living together' – but as for Fraternity, 'one doesn't have brothers by arrangement'.

> In so far as I am myself, Fierté, Inégalité, Hostilité.
> It doesn't sound very French, but never mind. I think the time has come to wave the oriflamme and rally against humanity and Ho, Ho, St John and the New Jerusalem. (ii. 253–4)

Associations proliferate: oriflamme (the ancient royal banner of France), tongues of fire, ten-pointed star, phoenix-flame, Holy Ghost, cherubim-blaze, poppy-scarlet asserted against black; the Christmas star of new birth, and the phoenix-symbol of continual rebirth through death (which Will Brangwen carved on the butter stamper). Ho Ho for a new order of Knighthood and Revelation on the island of Rananim, following its star (every order has one), and founding not a walled city but a New Jerusalem. And hey for a new 'aristocracy' of troubadours and 'gai savaire', separating itself in pride of self-being from the materialist state, which has gone to war to preserve its possessions against Germany, and because of a death wish with no longing for resurrection.

There is game here, and cheering oneself up, particularly since he had caught another cold. The cottage was damp, and the countryside flooded, 'the duckpond is right across the lane, so to get to the high-road one must wade' (ii. 255). But there is also an exploring of new feelings of alienation: the beginnings of a new 'aristocratic' politics which would soon issue in the hostile diagnosis of Skrebensky the soldier and collective-man; and a wholly new sense – only partly owing to the failure of his work to sell, since *The Prussian Officer* 'struggles along, like all my books' (ii. 255) – of writing for the few now, rather than having an answer to the secret need of the many. As his cold lingered on miserably into mid-January, and he heard that Boots libraries were refusing to stock the new stories, [35] Lawrence grew to dislike more and more the 'meagre' country and 'this miserable little cottage' (ii. 259, 257). Also, the thermometer of his wealth was once again 'nearly at zero' (ii. 254), though in the nick of time Pinker sent £5 (possibly an extra payment from the *Metropolitan* for 'Honour and Arms' but maybe from Pinker himself, who often quietly helped his writers from his own pocket; ii. 256 and n. 3)). Also, what with seediness and depression, and perhaps Frieda being edgy with Kot who came to talk of Rananim but may have said something to offend her again, there was another spat between the Lawrences, and another seeking by Frieda of consolation from Katherine, whose thoughts were now elsewhere, and whom Frieda tired 'to death'.[36]

Then Viola Meynell offered them her cottage at Greatham in Sussex, rent-free. Her father Wilfrid, writer and publisher, had bought an eighty-acre estate with a big old house, 'Humphreys', as a country home for Alice his poet wife; and had fitted up farm buildings and cottages for each of his daughters. Viola must have heard from Catherine Jackson that The Triangle was not ideal. (She had been down to Chesham sometime before her wedding to Donald Carswell in early January, and had found Lawrence 'holding on to himself against depression'.[37]) Viola spent much of her time in London, and there were spare bedrooms both in her 'Shed Hall' and in the big house, for her to come down to at weekends, but her offer was nonetheless very generous and opportune. Lawrence was wary at first, since 'the whole formidable and poetic' (he might have added Catholic) 'Meynell family is down there in the Meynell settlement'

(ii. 255). But, he blamed The Triangle and its dampness for making him ill, so he decided to accept, and began at once to feel 'happy in the prospect of being on the move again' (ii. 258).

They left The Triangle on 21 January, had lunch with Lady Ottoline Morrell at 44 Bedford Square,[38] tea with Edward Garnett and then dinner with Lady Ottoline again before going to stay with the Eders in Hampstead. The Eders must have heard about Rananim too, probably in the more 'left-wing' terms (since Eder was a socialist) in which Lawrence had developed his idea in a letter to Willie Hopkin just before leaving Chesham:

I want to gather together about twenty souls and sail away from this world of war and squalor and found a little colony where there shall be no money but a sort of communism as far as necessaries of life go, and some real decency. It is to be a colony built up on the real decency which is in each member of the Community – a community which is established upon the assumption of goodness in the members, instead of the assumption of badness. (ii. 259)

(This is not incompatible with what 'Le Gai Savaire' meant by 'aristocracy', though the dream's naïveté is showing.)

Bunny was also at Lady Ottoline's dinner, as was E. M. Forster who sat next to Lawrence. After dinner the painter Duncan Grant joined the party for dancing as did Gertler and Carrington. The Lawrences had to go off to Hampstead, but the next day, 22 January, Grant invited them, Forster and Bunny to tea in his studio, since Ottoline had talked of his pictures and Lawrence had expressed an interest in seeing them. Grant was the leading painter of the Bloomsbury group and would soon be at the centre of Bunny's life. He lived and worked with Vanessa Bell (sister of Virginia Woolf and wife of Clive Bell), but was predominantly homosexual and would later take Bunny to live with them.[39] Bloomsbury art looked (with Roger Fry) forward from Cézanne to Modernist Paris, whereas the Slade School of Art produced the very different work of Augustus John, Stanley Spencer and Gertler. Unfortunately, the more Lawrence saw of Grant's painting, the more he disliked it, and said so. Very soon (says Bunny) Forster 'made some gentle remark about catching a train to Weybridge and faded out of the studio' while Lawrence went on, and on. As he talked, 'he held his head on one side, as though in pain, and looked more at the floor than at the pictures'. Frieda kept trying to rescue the situation. 'Each time that Duncan rose in silence and brought out another picture, she exclaimed: "Ah, Lorenzo! I like this one so much better! It is beautiful!" Her interventions were ignored by both sides.' Even when Kot arrived to collect them, this failed to stop the diatribe. 'Duncan himself appeared to have developed toothache and sat with his hands on his knees, rocking himself gently in his chair, not attempting a word in defence of his works. Everything, however, has an end', and at last the visitors disappeared into the foggy night, leaving Bunny with Grant, in silence.[40]

Why was Lawrence so distressed and embarrassed? – More so than seems likely from mere artistic disagreement. The avoidance of others' eyes, and the inability to stop, are like his behaviour when he first read his poems in public as a gauche young teacher,[41] but at this stage of his life – and talk – they suggest a degree of inner disturbance that must be significant, and an inability, as yet, to put his finger on its cause. (Bunny's 1955 account, which mocks Lawrence's attempt to explain in artistic terms, is understandably partisan. Grant himself, in his only published comment, remained remarkably polite and dignified.)[42]

On the evening of 23 January 'after a wonderful long drive in the [Meynell] motor car through deep snow, and between narrow hedges, and pale winter darkness' (ii. 261), they arrived at their new home: another world. 'The cottage is rather splendid – something monastic about it – severe white walls and oaken furniture – beautiful. And there is bathroom and all. And the country is very fine ...' Partly they were delighted by a new comfort, and easement of money worries – no more damp, a bathroom and hot water, even a maid-servant Hilda whom they were not allowed to pay, so that they only had to find the cost of their food – but it was also a place and a country which exactly matched Lawrence's mood and his inner need just then.

It was not an island, but might just as well have been, since they mostly had the estate to themselves. Having brought them down, the Meynells went back to London after the weekend (except for Viola's sister Monica who was separated from her husband Dr Saleeby) and that was to be the pattern. Moreover all Lawrence's descriptions stress the monastic: what had been a long cattle shed and still showed its beams, now felt 'like a monks refectory' (ii. 262). Frieda was 'a bit frightened of the cloistral severity' (ii. 261); but it was just what Lawrence wanted: a sense of quasi-monastic isolation matching, as The Triangle had never done, the religious seriousness in which *The Rainbow* had been conceived. Better still there were no other monks. Best of all, it had two spare beds so that candidates for Rananim could be invited to come – and go. Much of the estate was beautiful woodland and beyond it rose the great shoulder of the South Downs, whence a walker could command a magnificent view all the way to Arundel in one direction, and the sea in another, and back down to the Sussex villages, the woods and farms below. There could be no better place to finish *The Rainbow*.

As well as leaving its mark on his fiction, this new place helped him explore his apparent over-reaction to Bloomsbury as encountered in Grant and Forster. Lady Ottoline Morrell wrote in defence of Grant, but Lawrence replied that he had burnt her letter. He insisted that he '*really* liked' Grant himself, but his work was not only too Futuristically intellectual, but also defective from the new perspective of 'Le Gai Savaire' and what he had done so far of *The Rainbow*. 'Tell him not to make silly experiments in the futuristic line ... But to seek out the terms in which he shall state his whole.' All art, he now thought, had to be like Will Brangwen's favourite picture, Fra Angelico's *Last Judgement*:

a whole conception of the existence of Man – creation, good, evil, life, death, resurrection, the separating of the stream of good and evil, and its return to the eternal source. It is an Absolute we are all after, a statement of the whole scheme – the issue, the progress through Time – and the return – making unchangeable eternity. (ii. 263)

Grant might of course have retorted that no such 'Absolute' was now conceivable, and that art had to do with the artist's achievement of significant form – in his case in the space of the canvas, or perhaps, experimentally, on a moving roll – having no necessary relationship with objects in life at all. But while Lawrence did not reject abstract art as such, he insisted that abstraction, to be meaningful, must abstract from life, and must still serve a vision of the whole of it. No such vision, he thought, could be built up *out* of geometric figures already wholly abstract, or by pictorial architecture in itself.[43] What was needed was the equivalent of what he had tried to do in the 'Study of Thomas Hardy' and its art criticism, to 'abstract' a new kind of inclusive vision from the 'instances' provided by the great artists of the past: 'Rembrandt, Corot, Goya, Monet have been preparing us our instances – now for the great hand which can collect all the instances into an absolute statement of the whole' (ii. 263).[44]

On 28 January he begged Forster to come down to Greatham, in a letter which fuses with Rananim the need for a vision of the Whole, and his sense that Forster must get beyond his concern with merely personal and class relations and personal fulfilment. Lawrence feels himself of no class, he who used to gossip with an under-servant from Welbeck, and now talks with Lady Ottoline. He wants vision no longer limited to man, but the metaphysical equivalent of the view from the Downs:

It is time for us now to look all round, round the whole ring of the horizon – not just out of a room with a view; it is time to gather again a conception of the Whole ... of the beginning and the end, of heaven and hell, of good and evil flowing from God through humanity as through a filter, and returning back to god as angels and demons ...

In my Island, I wanted people to come without class or money ... each coming with all his desires, yet knowing that his life is but a tiny section of a Whole: so that he shall fulfil his life in relation to the Whole. I wanted a real community, not built out of abstinence or equality, but out of many fulfilled individualities seeking greater fulfilment. (ii. 265–6)

His friends however seem bent on private fulfilment, though he knows how difficult it is to get to one's metamorphosis and crucifixion, and beyond that to a resurrection which can take part in the fulfilment of the Whole. (Frieda characteristically and refreshingly cut this down to size. It's a 'very angelic letter', said her postscript, but she knows that Forster, who listens so carefully 'with the whole of you', won't 'overlook the little twisted horns and the hoof'; ii. 267.)

The atmosphere of the 'little monastery' (ii. 264; especially after the story of Tom and Lydia in which there *had* been a kind of death and resurrection and a vision beyond the merely human), seemed to encourage a religious perspective on his own life too. When a letter arrived from Lady Cynthia Asquith asking what had happened to them – they had not contacted her in the early summer when she was having her second baby, nor thereafter because they did not want to argue about the war with the daughter-in-law of the Prime Minister – it was again in terms of crucifixion and resurrection that Lawrence replied. He described how he had heard the news of war, and how it:

finished me: it was the spear through the side of all sorrows and hopes ...

And since then, since I came back, things have not existed for me ... All the while, I swear, my soul lay in the tomb – not dead, but with the flat stone over it, a corpse, become corpse cold ... And all the time I knew I should have to rise again.

... But now I don't feel so dead. I feel hopeful. I couldn't tell you how fragile and tender the hope is – the new shoot of life. But I feel hopeful now about the war.

... I know we shall all come through, rise again and walk healed and whole and new ...

It sounds preachy, but I don't quite know how to say it. (ii. 268–9)

In a way this is nonsense. To have written 'Le Gai Savaire' and over half of *The Rainbow* in those five months was hardly corpse-like. Yet it was because he felt so much better at Greatham that, looking back, his time at Chesham seemed all bodily illness and 'black in spirit' (ii. 271), and his writing achieved in spite of that. The preachy language, daring to apply to himself the imagery of Golgotha and Easter, must have seemed the most graphic way to proclaim a truth experienced but only recently understood. His letter to Savage had placed the vital importance of sexual relation not in pleasure, but in the escape from deadly self-enclosure through the encounter with an Other. Since then, re-imagining the stories and the novel had shown him how and why the crucial experience within sexual relationship was dying, to be born again. It was his *writing*, in grasping this truth from his life, that had enabled him to overcome the deathliness of the war in his own spirit, and to feel now the ripple of new life in the blood.

V   Candidates for Rananim?

A few days later the hope was greatly strengthened, when Lady Ottoline came to Greatham. Here was a great lady he had known about since boyhood, sister to the grandest Duke from his own shire, who had sought him out because she admired his work.[45] Not only could they talk Nottingham from their utterly different backgrounds; she was in a state to respond most enthusiastically to his present vision, and so intensify his confidence in it.

In 1911 she had begun an affair with Bertrand Russell, and carried it on with the acquiescence of her husband, Philip Morrell, provided it remained discreet. In return, she refused to leave him and her daughter Julian, and was content (as Russell could never be) with occasional meetings and rather mild and snatched love-making. She felt no strong sexual attraction to Russell; indeed found him rather crude and brutal as a lover; but she was endlessly fascinated by the power of his intellect. He made her more confident of her intelligence; she opened him up to worlds he had not dreamed of. They wrote to each other at least once a day and often more, about all they were thinking and feeling, and influenced each other profoundly.

Russell came from an even more distinguished family.[46] (His grandfather Lord John Russell had helped to draft the Reform Act of 1832 and resigned as Prime Minister on the defeat of the second parliamentary reform bill.) Russell and G. E. Moore were Cambridge's most notable philosophers, but his private life was much less successful. By 1902 he had fallen entirely out of love with his wife Alys and they separated, to her lasting distress. His affair with Ottoline modified his excessive intellectualism, and made him more aware of worlds of feeling, imagination, art and spirituality than he had ever been, though he could never come very far to meet her deeply religious temperament and belief, which remained a bone of contention. He also remained arrogant and remarkably self-centred, yet attractive to women in spite of his looks. Above all he had a mind like a knife, though that also could seem hard and impervious.

By the end of 1914 – when Russell was 42 and Ottoline a year younger – their relationship was in difficulties. He wanted three things she could not give him: constant companionship, sexual satisfaction without reserve, and children. (She had had an operation after the birth of Julian.) Early in 1914 came the first signs that he might look elsewhere, a brief flirtation with a German lady. In March he set out for three months teaching in America, and on a final visit to Chicago he slept with Helen Dudley, with whose parents he was staying. Though Ottoline was hurt by an amazingly insensitive letter in which he argued that this would make no difference to them, the rift was patched up; and as we have seen Ottoline helped to protect him when the young woman arrived in pursuit.[47] Almost immediately Russell was considering another affair, with his new research assistant Irene Cooper-Willis, and consulting Ottoline about it. (He decided against – though reluctant to lose her help with his work!) The trouble clearly lay with his loneliness and desire for constant companionship, as well as with a randiness that Ottoline could not satisfy. She knew and felt responsible about this, without hope of remedy, though they continued to have 'times' (her word) of great closeness. Nor was Russell able truly to meet her on the spiritual level where she felt her deepest life lay.

This was the lady, now Bloomsbury's chief hostess, nervy yet rather over-whelming, who arrived at Greatham on 1 February. She was strikingly tall, auburn-haired, long nosed and strong chinned, with a sing-song voice. She often wore extraordinary clothes, though she was in plain purple velvet and pearls on this occasion. She had planned that Russell should be with her, so had more than one motive for the expedition; and had been in two minds whether or not to go herself when he could not;[48] but she and Lawrence probably affected each other all the more strongly at first in Russell's absence. That same evening Lawrence wrote her an ecstatic letter, outlining the new community – of which she was now to be the centre. The argument is as before: individuals must fulfil their 'deep desires' but also complete them within a greater whole, must aim 'to live by the *best* they know' instead of merely trying to guard against the worst and with 'the flesh and the spirit in league together'. He called for a 'communism based, not on poverty, but on riches, not on humility, but on pride' (ii. 271–3). Writing to her, the religious impulse is reinforced: he is calling not for a new religion but rather:

to fulfil what religion we have ... To be or not to be is no longer the question. The question now, is how shall we fulfil our declaration 'God is' ... And a man shall not come to save his own soul ... He shall come because he knows that his own soul is not the be-all and the end-all, but that all souls of all things do but compose the body of God, and that God indeed Shall *Be* ... We will be Sons of God ... (ii. 272–3)

She was greatly impressed; promised to try to bring Russell down at the weekend; and in fact did so the Monday following (8 February). Lawrence was nervous about meeting him – 'I feel as if I should stutter' (ii. 274) – but again the meeting went very well.

(Meanwhile Frieda was confident enough to ask Lady Ottoline to write to Weekley (ii. 281); imagining he would feel so honoured at the thought of the children having her for a friend that he would let them see Frieda at Bedford Square. Ottoline thought this 'Rather a difficult Task but I will do my best'.[49] However, Weekley was either less snobbish than the Lawrence who told her 'I really do honour your birth ... I would give a great deal to have been born an aristocrat' (ii. 281), or too antipathetic to Frieda now, for such inducements to have any effect.)

With equal confidence after their meeting that Russell shared his enthusiasm for a revolution of heart and mind, if not his wholesale rejection of modern society, Lawrence insisted that life must no longer be measured by money and that 'Economic Life' must be made 'the means to actual life', at once.

There must be a revolution in the state. It shall begin by the nationalising of all industries and means of communication, and of the land – in one fell blow. Then a man shall have his wages whether he is sick or well or old – if anything prevents his working, he shall have his wages just the same. So we shall not live in fear of the wolf ...

Which practically resolves the whole economic question for the present. All dispossessed owners shall receive a proportionate income – no capital recompense – for the space of, say, fifty years.

Something like this must be done. It is no use saying a man's soul should be free, if his boots hurt him so much he can't walk. All our ideals are cant and hypocrisy till we have burst the fetters of this money. (ii. 282–3)

Naïveté is showing again, though this does no more than politicise 'Le Gai Savaire's central and cogent argument about the proper proportion between self-preservation and being oneself to the utmost – and there is an uncomfortable truth in the last paragraph. Russell had a private income and great expectations, though he lived frugally; Ottoline and Philip had just bought Garsington Manor. Yet the fate of Russia, which was to try to do 'something like this' two years later, shows (to us, at least, looking back) the simple-mindedness of so generalising from the individual to the state, as Lawrence was to make a habit of doing, paying no heed to the dimensions between: the nature of political and economic institutions and the power of groups, or the kind of power that might be necessary to bring such radical change about. The state is not just the individual writ large. Russell commented sadly on his new friend: 'thinking (as the young do) that because *he* sees the desirability of Socialism it can be got in a few years' strenuous work. I feel his optimism difficult to cope with – I can't share it & don't want to discourage it. He is extraordinarily young ...' (He was 29.) But Russell was also impressed by a very different kind of mind. In his own way Lawrence 'is amazing; he sees through and through one ... He is infallible. He is like Ezekiel or some other Old Testament prophet ... '[50] He immediately invited Lawrence to come to meet the best minds in Cambridge, to be found of course in Trinity, Russell's college, and King's, the college of Forster and of Keynes.

The rest of Lawrence's letter to him, however, was about Forster, who had also come down to Greatham, on the 10th.[51]

Just before Forster's visit Lawrence read his 'Story of a Panic',[52] and criticised his tendency to associate a return to Pan with universal love. For Lawrence, this is to confuse the Father with the Son. 'Pan' is what the poppy grows from, 'the undifferentiated root and stem drawing out of unfathomable darkness, and my Angels and Devils' (as in Fra Angelico) 'are old-fashioned symbols of the flower into which we strive to burst'.[53] It is no good crying 'back to Pan'; no plant can grow backwards towards its root:

One must live from the source, through all the racings and heats of Pan, and on to my beloved angels and devils, with their aureoles and their feet upon the flowers of light, and with their red-mouthed despairs and destructions ... Don't be alarmed – I seem to 'stunt' because I use old terms for my feeling, because I am not inventive or creative enough. (ii. 276)

(This would issue in a meditation on inner evolution in the manuscript of *The Rainbow*, as Ursula looks at a cell through her microscope.[54])

Lawrence had read *Howards End* in June 1911 and immediately pressed it on Louie Burrows as 'exceedingly good and very discussable' (i. 278).[55] Forster's 'only connect' and his 'rainbow bridge' had very probably stayed in his mind ever since and were now reaching Lawrencian expression. At Lady Ottoline's Forster had been greatly taken by Lawrence, though he had not been given much opportunity to answer him back. Though characteristically detaching himself from the scene in Grant's studio, Forster had actually not been frightened off either by Lawrence's criticism of Grant, or by the comments on his own work – since he too had been seeking, in his own way, for a sense of the Whole. He also reacted robustly to Frieda's postscripts by refusing 'to have dealings with a firm'.[56] The first day at Greatham was enchanting: a long walk over the Downs with Lawrence talking of childhood and birds, beasts and flowers; and in the evening a new Lawrence hobby of painting bee-boxes. But after tea on the second day, as Forster must have known would happen, Lawrence launched himself on the requirements for Rananim, and a consequent critique of Forster's books and his whole attitude to life – including his homosexuality. For all his rather spinsterly persona, Forster was a great deal more robust than he seemed. He probably realised that the harangue was a mark of the value Lawrence put on him as a writer and an influence, though the lack of reticence must have been disconcerting. Yet after his first visit to India and the writing of *Maurice*, his unpublishable novel of homosexual love, Forster was more at home with himself, and his (as yet) celibate homosexuality, than he had ever been before. However, as the hour at Greatham grew later and later, he began to get irritated. At first he tried to pass it off. To an insistence that he change his life, he asked apparently 'ruefully, "How do you know I'm not dead?"' But he must have been angered, both by Lawrence's seeming assumption that heterosexual relationship was the prime necessity for growth, and at his ignorance about homosexuality (Forster thought), both in others and as a possibility in himself. Finally he took up his candlestick, muttering that the Lawrences were 'just playing round his knees' (ii. 282), and took himself off to bed without saying good-night. Lawrence however rather liked that; he liked people to stand up to him. And though Forster wrote him a tough and outspoken letter afterwards,[57] and some coolness resulted for a while, they continued to respect each other – from a safer distance.

Yet, even while Forster was still with them, Lawrence got 'a feeling of acute misery' from him, and was miserable himself that all his haranguing seemed so fruitless: 'We have talked so hard – about a revolution – at least I have talked – it is my fate, God help me – and now I wonder, are my words gone like seed spilt on a hard floor, only reckoned an untidiness there' (ii. 280). As his letter to Savage had shown, he was in fact neither hostile to homosexuality in the artist, nor unaware of homosexual feeling in himself. Moreover 'Le Gai Savaire' had proclaimed bisexuality in everybody, and recognised that the 'marriage of opposites', in consequence, need not be excusively between a man and a woman, or require sexual intercourse. However – as the unmarried, and homosexuals of both sexes, are likely to feel – the Lawrence of 1914 could sometimes sound (as Forster's letter put it) like a 'deaf impercipient fanatic who has nosed over his own little sexual round until he believes that there is no other path for others to take'. Yet Forster's anger, his defence of his sexuality and perhaps a barb or two about his host's, were enough to set Lawrence thinking again about what he had said to Savage.

So he used his letter to Russell to try to clarify the combination of scepticism, homosexuality and inertia he detected in Forster. This seems an odd letter to write to one man about another when he had only just met both of them; yet Lawrence at this time was so absorbed in his own thought processes that they often came pouring out, as though from pent-up pressure, with little sense of how they might seem to their recipient. However, Russell was a member of the Cambridge Apostles – an elite society which had been taken over by the homosexual leadership of Keynes and Strachey – and may have said something about Forster (also an Apostle) at Greatham, two days before Forster came.

To Savage, Lawrence had argued that same-sex love was attractive because it allowed one to project oneself upon another like oneself, whereas heterosexual sex was more difficult and challenging because of the otherness of the other, but therefore also more creative.[58] Yet how then explain an unashamed homosexual, who chooses not to engage in sexual activity? The new Lawrence of Rananim explains it as a lack of faith that the creative forces in sexuality can change the world, a faithlessness particularly worrying in a creative artist. Forster (he argues) *does not believe that any beauty or any divine utterance is any good any more* – Lawrence's italics – and therefore, neither his manhood nor his social passion ('the desire to work for humanity') can be satisfied. To take a woman (or even, Lawrence should have said, a man) would help Forster 'fight clear to his own basic, primal being', as the letter to Savage had argued; but to Lawrence now, and he thinks to Forster too, that is not enough unless the 'venture in upon the coasts of the unknown' is also to 'open my discovery to all humanity'. What however if one's society cannot hear (as Gilbert Cannan had warned), or move, or come along? Then one goes on simply repeating one's discovery; and the 'repeating of a known reaction upon myself is sensationalism', a kind of 'masterbation' (sic), whether it be done with a woman, or still more with a man in sodomy.[59] But a man without faith may yet be a strong soul with 'too much honour for the other body' to be willing 'to use it as a means of masterbation. So he remains neutral, inactive. That is Forster' (ii. 283–5).

There were perhaps more straightforward explanations for Forster's failure to publish between *Howards End* and *A Passage to India*, and for his reluctance to embark upon Keynesian or Stracheyan homosexual adventures. What seems more significant is the implication of Lawrence's argument for his own marriage. From an escapist dream, Rananim had developed into the idea of a revolutionary movement to change the world. Without such a social purpose, might one's own sexual relationship become the repetition of a known reaction?

Nor was Forster the only candidate for Rananim who disappointed. Lawrence took the chance of another lift in the Meynell motor on 15 February, and went up to London to talk to a gathering including Ottoline, Kot, Campbell and John Hope-Johnstone, who had been tutor to the children of Augustus John. Unfortunately there was an argument with Campbell over religion, which Campbell thought a matter of private emotion and mysticism, and Lawrence a matter of bringing 'God' into new communal existence in the world – after which both sides were left rather scornful. Nonetheless, Lawrence assured Ottoline, 'in spite of everything, I am confident we will have our revolution' (ii. 288). If the Irishmen were too concerned with 'ecstasies' however, Lady Cynthia, when she came down the next day, proved too cool a personality to qualify. Frieda thought her 'quite nice, but – I feel sorry for her – She is poor in feeling' (ii. 288); and in his new mood Lawrence had to confess 'she wearies me a bit' (ii. 289).

Now Murry arrived, ill, and miserable, across the flooded fields, requiring to be comforted, rubbed with camphorated oil[60] and put to bed. He had suffered a double blow of rejection by the two people he cared for most, Katherine and Gordon Campbell, had caught a severe fluey cold and could bear his loneliness no longer.

Since discovering in Murry's diary what he had told Campbell about her, Katherine had worked up her romantic fantasy about Francis Carco, to which Carco readily responded. Hiring a cleaning lady had made no difference to her dislike of Rose Tree Cottage and indeed of wintry England. The exchange of letters with Carco grew warmer, and when he asked her to come to France she decided to go. Her beloved younger brother Leslie had arrived in England to enlist. Meeting him at the bank when she went to draw her allowance,[61] she spun him a story that she wanted to go to France, with Jack, to do a series of war sketches for which one of the monthlies had offered a contract. Leslie duly reported this to New Zealand, and moreover gave her the £10 she needed 'for a week' in Paris. Her feelings swirled one way and another. The Lawrences left. She went to London several times (Kot now always on hand); but when Carco received the photo she had had taken for him, and urged her to come immediately (even though he had enlisted, and was now stationed near Besançon, technically in the Zone des Armées), she went, regardless, on 19 February. The next day she wrote in her journal a letter to 'darling' Frieda from Gray in France, about her adventure and 'le petit soldat joyeux et jeune', though it is not clear whether she ever sent it.[62]

At the beginning of February, moreover, Murry had written Campbell an extraordinary letter: so upset, because Campbell had not come down for the weekend, that the letter reads for all the world like one from a jilted lover. Indeed, provided that one does not think in too sexual terms, that is what it is. Murry's physical feelings were not strong, but he had attached himself emotionally and intellectually to Campbell, sharing his friend's tendency to be excited to a kind of ecstasy by semi-mystical ideas, and greatly admiring Campbell's mind and forensic ability. He was scornful about the domesticity of Campbell's wife; and what he told him about his feeling for Katherine may have been meant to suggest that Campbell was more important to him – which was how Katherine took it. Now, even though at the back of his mind he knew that to make so much of Campbell having 'failed' him was extraordinary, he could not stop himself from writing – though he did not show Campbell the letter until 1952 (or quote it either in his *Reminiscences* or *Between Two Worlds*).

Why in God's name should it have been important that I was waiting for you to come here on Saturday week, that I rode into Chesham miserable after your telegram came, that I made myself cheerful again coming back with the thought that you would come after all, that I tried to work in the evening, and when I heard a cart stop outside, my heart stopped too, stopped so that I could hardly breathe for a long while – it all seems silly as I write it – were it not that I went through it ... now I can see that I must have loved you as one man seldom loves another. I look back at myself and find that I would have given you anything ... We might have pulled off some great thing together; but you were divided – perhaps I was divided too. Perhaps we came together too late ... I can hear Lawrence say that it would only have been possible between a man and a woman. I don't think so. It was possible for us, had you been other than you are ... I seem to have served up too much of my naked soul to the world – it has always been trodden on, but this was the most unkindest cut of all.[63]

In his journal he wrote of how 'appallingly sensitive' he had become in isolation; 'My nervous apprehensions of contact with people have become a nightmare now – a curious mixture of hate, envy, contempt, the idea that I am failed, and that I am not valued ... ' It was in this mood that, unable to bear the thought of another day alone, he took himself to Greatham on 17 February. Though he could think of nothing 'except my unutterable miseries, my solitude and my mucous membranes' he recognised that 'The Lawrences were very good to me today – may I requite them.' On the 18th he was able to go walking, and on the

19th to talk to Lawrence about Campbell. Lawrence told him what Campbell had said when they met in London, that 'what there was between M and me was the most regrettable part of each of us.' Murry was now sure that neither had understood the other, and began to suspect that Campbell 'used me merely as a means for some intellectual sensationalism'.

On the 21st he walked to the top of the Downs and was obviously better, but the next day Frieda went down with his cold and took to her bed, while Lawrence laid linoleum. (He would soon get the fluey cold as well, unable to get rid of it until well into March.) In the evening they talked 'about the revolution'. Lawrence insisted, as to Forster, that it was no good just writing novels, 'we had first to change the conditions, without which people either wd. not hear or our novels be only a tale'. He told Murry about *The Rainbow*, but went on, sadly, that he would only write one more novel (its continuation), for he felt that he was doomed to be 'a fore-runner, like John the Baptist'. But when Murry said that in his novel, too, the characters would end up right outside society and its mores, Lawrence said 'What novels we could write, if we wrote of the whole good we knew.' And soon they were planning 'a scheme for publishing weekly pamphlets in which the Revolution shd. be expounded by us individually'. Lawrence clearly thought they were at one.

Murry did not mean to deceive. It was a dangerous time for them both, emotionally. Murry needed a prop after the double desertion and it was easy to exaggerate, a little, what Lawrence had meant to him and meant now:

I said how much calmness and happiness I had gained from him during the last six months – since the war began that he was the only man I had met whom I felt definitely to be older than me, that we made a real combination, from which something I felt must come. He said that when we four were together he felt that the new conditions, the new vitality really *were*, and that if we had not met down in Bucks, he would never have believed that it might be. I said I looked forward to the fight ...[64]

Lawrence, hungry for man-to-man friendship and support from Murry – who seemed at his most attractive as he listened – was only too ready to believe in him and his work. He immediately wrote off to Ottoline:

He is one of the men of the future – you will see. He is with me for the Revolution. He is just finishing his novel – his first – *very* good. At present he is my partner – the only man who quite simply is with me – One day he'll be ahead of me. Because he'll build up the temple if I carve out the way ... (ii. 291)

But he had not read the novel, which Murry jealously guarded, and when in 1916 he did, he saw that Murry was never going to be a novelist. However, his own uneasiness about the cost to his personality of the prophetic mantle he was donning, seems to have issued in a sense of how much 'purer' Murry's 'effort' was, even in its inertia.[65] The silent listener can often be credited in this way by the talker who fears he talks too much. Yet the young Murry in his journal had a more scrupulous conscience than the older Murry in his reminiscences. At the time he was at least partly aware of seeming to feel more than he actually did: 'At first, though I agreed, I felt an uneasiness, whether I were playing the hypocrite in agreeing; I wondered whether I were merely trying to cling on to his skirts because I knew that he was a proven writer with a tried audience.' Then he thought he *was* perhaps on the same track, though again, faced with Lawrence's apprehension about the struggle, 'though agreeing, I did not feel it badly'. When Lawrence went on about nationalisation, Murry knew it was not thought out, but 'Part of the time I was thinking of the remainder of my novel, wh. is to be finished, in first writing, before I write pamphlets with him.' It was understandable enough, given the emotional needs of both at the time, and given Murry's chameleon quality, which under the influence of Lawrence's excitement took on some of its colouring, for a while.

When Lady Ottoline came down again on 23 February, however, Murry confided rather different feelings to his journal. Because 'L. was the centre of attraction', he felt fiercely jealous, and 'unreal and self-conscious even during the walk to the top of the Downs ... I resented O.M.'s admiration of him, even though I felt it was deserved.' So he began to talk, about his past in Paris, and his acquaintance with the lesbian painter 'George Banks':

strangely exaggerated – and then having told resented L's laughter at it and Banks. I felt I may laugh not he. Somehow I am hurt and sad about it, hungry for Tig [Katherine], and want to go away. I want Tig to comfort me. Is it weakness – the oyster without the shell. Why in God's name should I be anxious to impress O.M. because L. was there. Comparatively I feel empty. Am I really empty or filled with future things?[66]

The next day he had two letters from Tig and a wire to say she would be back the following day, whereupon he left Greatham at once to meet her. (Her fantasy about Carco had collapsed, but though she and Murry managed a reconciliation, she was convinced that she could only work abroad, and soon set out for Paris again, to occupy Carco's empty flat, leaving Murry in rooms in London.)

At least, Lawrence wrote to Mary Cannan on 24 February, Murry seemed 'much better in spirit, in being and in belief'. He himself was also clear now about the nature of the change in Rananim that had come about in Greatham because of his new relationship with Ottoline and Russell. The 'island scheme' had been 'a sort of running away from the problem'. Now Rananim had indeed to be, not an escape from society, but a revolutionary group aiming to change society in *this* island, from within: 'We must form a revolutionary party. I have talked about it with various people – also Bertrand Russell. I am going to stay with him in Cambridge ... The book I wrote – mostly philosophicalish, slightly about Hardy – I want to re-write and publish in pamphlets' (ii. 292–3). He did not, however, want the revolution to depend on him, and did not want to be regarded as a *Wunderkind*; 'It is not *I* who matter – it is what is said through me' (ii. 280). Moreover the essence of his vision was that individuals should sink their small personal aims into communal and 'social passion' – by which he meant the passion of every person 'to be within himself the whole of mankind' (ii. 294) and to feel himself charged with its fate (ii. 302), so that the forming of a real if small community would be already the nucleus of a greater change. As he told Campbell, 'in me, and in you, is the living organic English nation' (ii. 301). He knew well enough what tolerance a logical (he called it 'abstract') thinker like Russell had to have, when confronted with his sort of language: 'I wish you'd tell me when I am foolish and over-insistent ... I don't want you to put up with my talk, when it is foolish, because you think perhaps it is passionate' (ii. 294–5). But at the same time he insisted, 'My world is real, it is a true world, and it is a world I have in my measure understood' – and it was easier for Russell to enter his, than for him to enter Russell's for which training was required. He knew he could be 'stupid' and 'impertinent' (ii. 298), and 'vain' (ii. 303); and how hard it was 'for us each one to be his intrinsic self' (ii. 298): 'Not *me* – the little, vain, personal D. H. Lawrence – but that unnameable me which is not vain nor personal, but strong, and glad, and ultimately sure, but so blind, so groping, so tongue-tied, so staggering' (ii. 302). As he prepared to go to Cambridge to be introduced to influential people by Russell, he felt 'a real hastening of love' for him; and told Ottoline that he thought of her as 'a special type' like Cassandra or the 'great women saints', who were 'the great *media* of truth' coming through them (as in Delphi) 'from the depths ... below the consciousness, and below the range of the will' (ii. 297–8). He thought Murry had at last stopped worrying about his private soul, and that he and Campbell, and perhaps Forster, 'and our women – and any one who will be added on to us' could form a league, 'carried on one impulse' (ii. 302).

He and Frieda were still suffering from the fluey cold – but he set off for Cambridge in high hopes.

VI Lawrence's 'woman'?

And what of Frieda, amid all this? Lawrence's excited letters from Greatham give a partly false impression, because he has free rein in them. Where Frieda adds postscripts, these show what must have been continually the case during their daily life in Greatham, that she kept bringing him back to earth, partly through a common sense that distrusted his higher flights, and partly because she felt she was regarded as an unequal partner in many of these new relationships, and resented that, very much.

Moreover she had a private grief. On 21 February she heard her father had died – but of course could not attend the funeral and had to mourn alone.

Since these new friends who came to Greatham were strongly anti-war, there was less need for her to feel defensive about her nationality, or aggressive about anti-German propaganda and hysteria, than she had done in the first months of the war. What she did feel affronted by was the attitude towards 'Lawrence's wife'. She had been used to think of herself as no less distinguished in her way than her younger husband, if not more so. Gross had made her feel her value as a woman. She was an aristocrat, and Lawrence was not a gentleman (as Weekley had kept telling her). In Germany she was the senior partner, and his equal among Italians or even English expatriates who did not know his work. But in London that July, still more than the previous year, she had to come to terms with intimations that the world might not only come to think him 'a *great* man', as she had retorted to Weekley (ii. 244), but might write her off as that ignominious creature the great man's woman.

She continued a spirited correspondence with Kot about his criticisms of her, making a distinction she felt important:

So you wish me to write my 'Xanthippe' lectures down instead of delivering them orally to poor Lawrence. But you see I am also his wife on this earth, the wife to the *man* as distinguished from the *artist*; to that latter I would always submit but, you see, some things I just *know* and he doesn't. Don't talk as if I were such a bad wife and he a blooming angel.[67]

She tells him about Forster's refusal to deal with 'a firm', and goes on: 'I believe everybody feels like that, I feel everybody against me, but then I can stand up to it thank God. And you will be my friend too, soon.' However, a fortnight later:

your attitude to me is not really and truly a good one – I can feel it – You think I do not count besides Lawrence, but I take myself, my ideals and life quite as seriously as he does his – This you will not allow, and it is our quarrel, you think I am conceited, I cant help that – but it hurts me very much when you think I do not count as a human being – But you do not think much of women, they are not human beings in your eyes ... (ii. 290)

She refused to be in awe of Russell either, and wrote to assure him his visit had been 'very stimulating'. What Lawrence had reported him as saying of her – we do not know what it was, but he did not have a high opinion of the intelligence of women – was 'rather true, but you have left out the impersonal me (I don't know what to call it), the impersonal that is in everybody'. She thought he had been 'a little cross' because she 'did not respect enough your work, which I could never understand; that particular manmade thing, you call it intellect, is a mystery, rather a thrilling one to me ... it's your form of *Wille zur Macht*'.[68] She felt it was really against women too, as Kot's was. (The feeling of Kot for

Katherine and of Russell for Ottoline might seem to disprove this, but those women were 'intellectuals' as she was quite happy not to be.) For Ottoline she had only gratitude at this point because of her readiness to try to help about the children,[69] but the warning signs were out for all the new friends who could read them. She would not bear condescension.

It was important to her therefore to insist on writing, even after Forster's objection, to tell him *her* opinion of *Howards End*: 'a beautiful book' – though she had no great hopes for the happy ending, 'broken Henry's remain Henry's as I know to my cost'. However, she went on: 'As to the firm you *did* hit a little sore point with me – Poor author's wife, who does her little best and everybody wishes her to Jericho – Poor second fiddle, the surprise at her existence! She goes on playing her little accompaniment so bravely! Tut-Tut, tra la-la!' (ii. 277–8). After Forster's visit and his non-thank-you letter, she wrote to defend Lawrence – who was in London at the time – in terms startlingly honest in their wifely view, yet no less genuinely four-square beside, though not behind, her husband.

Your letter was not very nice – Of course you like us, even if you don't admit it. Neither L nor I are tout le monde, and what he preaches to you is just exactly what you say yourself in your books ... God knows he is a fool, and undeveloped, but he is so genuine, a genuine force, inhuman like one also – and such a strain; but you ought to help him, he is really very inarticulate and *unformed* ... You are *not* to mind L's 'customs beastly, manners none'; think, *I* have to put up with them, and they have improved ...[70]

In fact, it was she who had taught him to be uninhibited – and she was certainly so with him. Thus she constantly pointed to the personal horns and cloven hoof behind the angelic talk; accused him of vanity when he got on his high horse; yet continued to support the genuineness underneath – 'I think at the *bottom* he is pure, but on top not always' (ii. 303). Murry's journal records a moment of friction not for once concerned with the children. She accused Lawrence of 'inhumanity' as she did to Forster. Lawrence countered: 'She will slither and slip from my point of view to Ernst's and from Ernst's to mine' – between true 'aristocracy' and the bourgeois. 'Commonsense', said Frieda.[71]

VII Ursula

On 1 February, after a week at Greatham, Lawrence reported progress on *The Rainbow*. He had 'done 450 pages out of 600 or so'. Pinker could tell Methuen 'that the whole will be sent in by the end of the month, and that there shall be no very flagrant love-passages in it (at least, to my thinking)' (ii. 270). He thought 150 more pages would do to adapt the story of the failed affair with 'Charles' Skrebensky (which had replaced, in 'The Wedding Ring', the one with Ben

Templeman which Garnett thought 'wrong') – but it would take over a hundred pages more. He had now persuaded Viola Meynell to type the novel for him. She may not have known quite how big a job she was taking on! The next day he wrote to Campbell, who had served as a Territorial, for useful detail about a 21-year-old subaltern in the Royal Engineers. 'What would he be? What would he earn? What would he do? Where would he live?' (ii. 274). Anton Skrebensky is to be not only a soldier but a man of machinery.[72]

The story of the maiden Ella had begun in the second 'Sisters' with a re-imagining of Louie. She is still vivid in the young Ursula of 'First Love' (ch. XI): the dark hair and tawny colouring, the blossoming into beauty, the mix-up between the weekday world and the Sunday one of her devout Anglican upbringing, the growing tension between awakening sexuality and abiding spirituality, the increasingly strained relation with her parents. The main rewriting into *The Rainbow* must have been to emphasise how Ursula internalises all the contradictions of her grandparents and her parents, with a new degree of conscious awareness appropriate to the third generation (as Lawrence was now conceiving the historical 'progress'), and thus the increased difficulty confronting the 'slim, smouldering girl'. The vivid evocation of girlhood however is not from memory of 1905–6 but is pushed back several years in imagination, and heightened to intensity by new understanding of the opposites, behind the Louie he met at the Ilkeston Pupil-Teacher Centre, and later loved and left.

Skrebensky, by contrast, is the most invented of all the main characters – and it shows. We know no more than his name in 'The Wedding Ring', where he had clearly been made different from Ben Templeman by giving him Polish ancestry. His father Baron Skrebensky could then be modelled on the local Vicar of Greasley, Baron von Hube, a refugee from the Polish Insurrection of 1863, which also showed how a Polish woman could come to Cossethay. Young Skrebensky may already have been a soldier also, if Lawrence's search for something different, together with Frieda's new readiness to interest herself in the creation of the fiction, had led him to begin from her first beau. Anton Skrebensky's appearance (in *The Rainbow*), the hair 'brushed up in the German fashion straight from his brow';[73] the impression of a horseman rather than a sapper; and his tales of goings-on between young officers and shop-girls in the cathedral (which appear in Frieda's memoirs) would tend to suggest such beginnings – whether in 'The Wedding Ring', or now. But the determination to make him an engineer in *The Rainbow* speaks also of 1915, and of Lawrence's attitude to a war of machinery which would subject the living body to the machine, and the individual to the regiment. So, even though the novel's history ends in 1905, it is being rewritten in 1915 to cast a long shadow ahead. Skrebensky is vivid enough as an attractive young man, whose apparent self-assurance may however prove as deceptive as Will's. The early courtship scenes create the excitement of sexual awakening, and of first self-definition against one's opposite, without running the risk of offending Methuen again – as Lawrence assured Pinker after writing them. At the same time, the lines of comparison and contrast with the first and second generation are clearly drawn as the young lovers walk under the trees where her parents and grandparents had walked, or sit or kiss in churches no longer holy, or swing above the crowd at the fair. But thereafter, the strength of Lawrence's feelings about the war, and the mass-men who threw themselves into it, produce a temptation to write Skrebensky down in the act of creating him, and to overwrite the potential destructiveness in the young girl of the third generation.

Again, this can be countered by drama and vividly imagined scene – or by a reader's sense of an opening out now, albeit to dangerous excess, of what was already potential in earlier generations, below the level of awareness. Test cases might be the young lovers' canal-bank argument about the nation and the individual, followed by their encounter with the bargeman; or the leap of imagination when Ursula is first carried away (like Elsie in 'The White Stocking') dancing in the dark before the bonfires; and then turns on her lover like a maenad under the influence of the moon. In showing how a female violence may be subconsciously aroused by the male threat to the self, even in a young girl, this is disturbing, and it will become more so (and more underlined) in revision. Moreover Lawrence then becomes so pressurised by his feelings against the soldier, seen as mass-man who disguises as patriotism or service his lack of individuality, that he cannot resist also preaching at Skrebensky in the narrative voice, so that an authorial thumb weighs heavy in the scale. The young officer is in danger of becoming a character wholly determined by his function in the novel's thematic pattern rather than a complexly imagined human being, capable of change.

Now, however, came a new imagining that would prove crucial to the fate of the novel – and its author. Though at the beginning of February he had been confident that there would be 'no very flagrant love-passages', within a fortnight he had become uneasy about Methuen again, and with reason. He had heard that Boots circulating library had refused his new stories – headed by the one apparently about homosexuality. Now Forster brought 'a ghastly rumour of the *Prussian Officer*'s being withdrawn from circulation, by order of the police' (ii. 280). This turned out not to be true, but he had extra cause to worry that *The Rainbow* might be thought 'impossible to print ... as it stands' (ii. 280); for there had been a crucial change since the beginning of the month. He had embarked on the chapter called 'Shame', about a lesbian love affair of Ursula with her schoolmistress Winifred Inger.[74]

What made him risk it?

There were both 'literary' and 'life' reasons. The Ursula story is strongly

structured, enacting his new 'allotropic' sense of character shaped (after 'Hardy')
by opposite 'forces'. Since he now saw Ursula as containing all the contradictions
of earlier generations, made worse by her own awareness of them, he went on to
imagine – writing new sections where necessary – how she would continually
respond to attractions which maximised one side of her, but would afterwards
react with the full force of the opposite side, ending in a wasteland rather than a
promised land, never finding a Whole fulfilment. So there would be a relation
purely of the senses offered by Anthony Schofield (drawing on the Pan-like vine
grafter Lawrence had met in San Gaudenzio); set against the promise of a life of
pure mind at Nottingham University; from which again she reacts to a purely
'dark', sensually sexual relation with the Skrebensky who returns from Africa;
and then inevitably, more intensely still, reacts against *that* with the full force of
her moon-bright, aspiring side, destroying something in her lover once and for
all. So what was implicit in the wedding dance followed by the maenad under
the moon is finally brought out to the full. One can therefore see why, without
any other reason at all, there would have to be a purely 'female' world to set
against the 'male world' of Brinsley Street School which was already there in
'The Wedding Ring' (as the chief means to independence available to young
women, a theme from the start).

However, life pressures pointed in the same direction. After his visit, Forster
wrote to E. J. Dent of how Lawrence ignored his own homosexual side, visible –
Forster thought quite unconsciously – in the bathing scene in *The White
Peacock*.[75] As I have suggested, it may be a cultural poverty to require such
scenes to be seen as repressed homosexuality – but by 1915, in any case,
Lawrence was by no means unconscious of potential homosexuality in himself.
He had admitted it without embarrassment to Savage in 1913, had universalised
it in 'Hardy' in 1914, and had pondered the nature (and limitation) of sexual
attraction to someone of one's own gender, both to Savage and, (now) brooding
about Forster, masturbation and sodomy, to Russell. If some lingering worry or
repression about his own sexuality remained – hinted perhaps in the sudden and
significantly inconsistent idea that in intercourse the man and woman may
become momentarily 'pure' male or female, by interchange of elements presumably 'impure'[76] – nevertheless the main argument of 'Hardy' must have
seemed to its author a satisfactory coming-to-terms. There is not the slightest
derogation of Michelangelo's homosexual art, though it is consistent with the
whole argument to see him as – in fine excess – an extreme, of which the
opposites are Raphael in one way and Turner in another, equally excessively.
Sappho is to be admired as much as Dido, and for the same reason. A change of
attitude to Sue, whom he had originally blamed as Jude's destroyer, is also
significant – why should not *every* 'abnormal' but highly developed kind of
person be respected?[77]

All this, however, was theoretical. Now actual instances had disturbed his imagination again. He had learned from Frieda, who kept no secrets, that Katherine had experienced intensely lesbian feelings for an older girl in a week-end cottage in Wellington Bay.[78] Then he had seen Bunny Garnett obviously atttracted to Douglas Grant – and found himself much more disturbed than could be explained by his dislike of Grant's pictures on artistic grounds. The full implications of that juxtaposition of Bloomsbury art and homosexuality would remain obscure as yet; but awareness of actual homosexuality in people he liked – for he liked Grant too[79] – and at the same time the recognition that it was disturbing to him, clearly demanded (from a writer with imaginative courage) further exploration. On top of this had come Forster; and the revelation of Murry's feeling for Campbell – and perhaps also an awareness of his own feeling for Murry, of a similarly non-physical kind (on the evidence), but nevertheless a kind of love.

So what *did* he think were the creativities and the deformations of homosexual relationship, for people he cared about, now? And behind that, for him, since he had recognised bisexuality in himself? Apparently incidentally, he put homosexual nuances into the seemingly minor character and career of Tom Brangwen the younger, who goes like Bunny to Imperial College, and has a relationship with an older scientist which hints at sexual dimensions and eventual falling out.

So also, in February, Lawrence wrote 'Shame' – in which imaginative exploration was easier because it would be a relation between females, not implicating him. The 'shame' is Ursula's, for whom her lesbian affair always remains a disturbing secret. Lawrence's treatment of its beginning and fulfil-ment, however, is wholly sympathetic. He brings out an excitement both physical and intellectual, a sense of beauty, an enlargement of the whole being, that are in no way qualitatively different from a heterosexual love-affair. This of course would make it even more shocking at a time when the very existence of 'sapphism' was hardly recognised except for scientific writers on 'perversions', or the avant-garde. Winifred *is* an 'opposite' in her Greek statuesque beauty, her apparently firm sense of herself, her scientific intellect, her calm rationalism, her feminist rebelliousness against men. And Lawrence's intensive neologism, 'enrichening', sums up what the sexual relationship with Winifred does for Ursula in opening new dimensions in her life. (The bathing scenes are unabashedly sexual.)

Why, then, does Ursula come to think her teenage affair shameful? And what does her author think, as he imagines the relationship through to its end? Why, especially, is Winifred associated with and indeed palmed off on Uncle Tom Brangwen and the horrible new colliery at Wiggiston? Is this just a smear? Or are there hidden connections, in Lawrence's imagination, between homosexuality, scientific intellectualism, industry and cynicism?

The letter to Savage argued that homosexual relations were easier because the partners were more alike – but might they therefore, being more self-reflexive than transforming, come to stultify someone whose many-sidedness and longing for total fulfilment are as intense as Ursula's? The critique of Michelangelo in 'Hardy' had suggested how homosexual delight in one's own kind of flesh could cry out for firmness of outline. Can that only come from greater opposition? Hence Ursula's feeling that the body she loved has come to seem clayey, insufficiently formed?

The outcome should not however be mistaken as a simple judgement against homosexuality. For though Winifred can no more fulfil the whole of Ursula than her other partial relationships, it is not Winifred's being but her compromise of it that finally seems shameful. Like the other feminists in the book, and understandably in relation to the times, she is a half-hearted Diana, a covert rebel rather than a real revolutionary – but when she compromises with a marriage within a system she despises, it is *mauvaise foi*, a cynicism about the power of sexuality to transform, at the hands of one's opposite. Winifred and Tom are *alike*, despite their genders; indeed more alike than Winifred and Ursula. Both have overdeveloped scientific intellects (the defect of the Futurists, and of Grant combining homosexuality with mathematical abstraction). That in turn connects with the industrialism that has produced the great modern colliery (which, revising, Lawrence will call 'mathematical'); and 'the hideous abstraction of the town',[80] the ugly lines and squares without communal centre; and the people who see themselves only as functions within a machine-system while their marriages become a side-show. And *that* shows the cynicism which has lost faith in transformation and all 'social passion'. It seems there are also hetero-sexual Cities of the Plain, Gomorrah perhaps as well as Sodom. *It is not gender but the nature of relationship that is finally important.* The subconscious connec-tions which had begun to disturb in Grant's studio are not yet fully worked out in 'Shame'; but they had demanded an exploration which made February a fateful month for *The Rainbow*.

'The Male World', about Ursula's struggles as schoolteacher, was drawn (in 'The Wedding Ring') from his own experience in Eastwood (as pupil-teacher) and Croydon, and from Jessie Chambers's trouble with her class, and Louie Burrows's with her Head. It was because schoolteaching was much the most immediate avenue to female independence that Louie, Jessie and Helen Corke had taken it. Now Ursula learns how the price that may have to be paid for success is a damaging division between the public and the private personality, involving a suppression of part of the self. She discovers that schools are systems of power, and (*pace* Nietzsche) that relations of power damage as well as strengthen the self. The rewriting here suggests what generally happened when Lawrence was revising material already in 'The Wedding Ring'. The inner dimensions (of power, and its cost in violence and self-violation in this case) were implicit before, but the rewriting continually brings them out with greater emphasis and intensity.[81]

Ursula's experience of university is the most directly autobiographical section of all, mirroring Lawrence's own disillusion[82] – with the major difference that Ursula is not a novelist who can spend much of her time there writing a first novel. It is also however sharply thematised within the new structure, bringing out both the sterility and pretension of (supposedly) 'pure mind' – especially to someone who has turned down Antony Schofield's offer of a world of pure sense-experience, which she respects – and also how the university is really like a factory, selling qualifications for commerce. As Ursula looks through her microscope, she has not (yet) quite grasped what it is for the cell to 'be itself',[83] which will come only in proof revision; but she has become aware of a darkness in which wild things prowl outside the narrow circle of the mind's light (an image which occurred in *Sons and Lovers* and recurred on the battlements at Aulla), and of a life-mystery the intellect cannot grasp. Hence the pretension of the Biology Lecturer who thinks that all life-processes will eventually be reducible to scientific laws. What follows is the Lawrencian 'sense of the Whole' – though in a rhapsody in which the narrator's 'I' again takes over from the consciousness of the character, perhaps a reason for cutting it later. All stages of evolution from the primeval marsh where great lizards wallow, to ape and tiger, to 'me'; and all future potentialities, reaching even to the gates of paradise; are simultaneously present. The whole potency is inside everyone; bestial and angelic; touching the origin and the ultimate; regressive and progressive at once.

So when Skrebensky comes back from Africa, Ursula reacts against the world of the mind with her 'darker' sexual self, achieving with him a consummation of that side of her, and now wholly rejecting the 'light' of separate consciousness and civilisation. Then she reacts again, even more extremely with the full force of her bright aspiring self, in fierce moonlight, where like a harpy she destroys part of Skrebensky for ever. All this is almost certainly new, as it involves the pushing of opposites to extremes which had become the structure of *The Rainbow*, teasing out the full implications of the wedding dance and its aftermath, itself new after the revision of 'The White Stocking' and the dialectic of 'Hardy'.

Lawrence was driven further and further from what he was supposed to be doing, that is, toning down the love scenes of 'The Wedding Ring'. Though by his own standards he was moderately careful,[84] scene after scene became risky by the standards of the time.

In the disintegration of Skrebensky, he explored what he most feared in himself – a dependency on Frieda grown so great that if she left him he might go to pieces. Ironically, the need for (relative) discretion brought with it a different kind of risk in his development of the danger of too-ready self-abandon, from Tom, to Will, to Skrebensky. Because he dared not be too explicit in rendering Skrebensky's purely sexual consummation with Ursula when she is at university, he risks misreading of why Skrebensky cannot, later, open up for her the 'beyond' she longs for. This has nothing to do with sexual potency as such, which is not at all Skrebensky's problem. Sex for Lawrence, and for his heroine now, has become far more than physical satisfaction – it is the way to resurrection after a death of the self. However, the archway-threshold to a whole new life beyond, which sexual lovers can open for each other, depends upon the individuality of each, standing firmly based in their own opposite strengths. But Skrebensky has no sense of himself other than as part of some collective: a nation, a regiment, a couple. In him, Lawrence explores not a worry about impotence so much as a fear – common to writers and actors – that the eagerness to sink the self in others betrays an insufficiency of self. And in the leap of imagination which also captures both the intensity of Ursula's longing for a 'beyond', and the destructiveness which her frustration releases, Lawrence has been able to tap into, and understand for the first time, his own 'inexplicable' experiences in moonlight, which Jessie describes at Mablethorpe, Robin Hood's Bay and Flamborough between 1906 and 1908,[85] beginning at Ursula's age, though she is sexually experienced as he was not.

As the novel neared its close, its use of space and season at Greatham shows how Lawrence has entirely reconceived whatever had been in 'The Wedding Ring'. As Ursula runs naked to the dew-pond on the Downs, and still more as she gazes down on the brave little train far below which Lawrence described to Ottoline on 11 February,[86] the fiction draws on a new geography – and maybe also an ironic allusion to *Howards End*. Moreover the removal of the Birkin material required a new ending: one that could complete the tragic curve of the generations, yet also hold a promise of redemption. Each couple has more to marry than the last, but the widening circles of awareness and emancipation have made marriage ever more difficult, and have revealed ever greater potential for destruction in what had seemed the sources of creativity. Yet the Lawrence of February 1915 was absolutely convinced that it was resurrection and not death (despite the war) that was the central meaning both of history and of his own bible-for-our-time; and he was filled by new religious hope at Greatham.

The climactic scene he imagined – the great shire horses – confronts an Ursula too ready now to deny the elemental forces in herself, in reaction to what she has done, with the powerful presence of those forces and their eternal challenge to marry opposites and go through, beyond. The sophisticated, highly educated, self-conscious Brangwen woman of the twentieth century City, must be faced again with the great background of her grandfather's world: the big wind through which he walked to propose, the earth with its looming trees, the teeming rain, the power of the animal world he so confidently mastered, the fire from their nostrils. The elemental world reveals, again, the clash of opposites in all created things, which she must meet, and pass through as (in her terror) a kind of death. But aware as the modern woman is, she cannot. She runs away, collapses into inertia like a stone beneath the Flood, miscarries Skrebensky's baby, nearly dies quite literally. Only, in her illness she realises what has been wrong: that she has tried to be the creator of herself and her relationships, falsely. She must learn to trust herself instead to the creative forces in the cosmos, as a nut does when it is shed naked into a new world, of Genesis. Reborn after a kind of death, she must wait for the coming of a Son of God, her opposite. Out of her window she sees a rainbow, a covenant as in the Bible, promising that the apparent destruction and corruption of the world are not the end, and that a new world can follow.

Again it seems impertinent to talk of 'sources' – the only justification being to keep imagining Lawrence the writer, writing. He had been reading Van Gogh's letters, and thinking about the tragedy of a man who so desperately wanted unified experience and relationship, but burnt himself out alone; and who wrote of himself as an old cab-horse, longing to live and procreate 'with other horses, also free'.[87] If only, Lawrence thought, Van Gogh could have *been* either the animal or the angel of himself, or better, could have married both, he need not have mutilated himself and gone mad. As Lawrence walked through farmland at ploughing time, the great horses, the animal-of-oneself, and the looming Post-Impressionist horses he had seen in *Blaue Reiter* pictures in Munich, began to fuse in his imagination.[88] The closing pages are very much end-of-February, the border of storm and spring, winter death and new life, 'the vivid reality of acorns in February lying on the floor of a wood with their shells burst and discarded and the kernel issued naked, to put itself forth'.[89] He had already written to Russell of how 'There comes a point when the shell, the form of life, is a prison to the life' (ii. 285), which has to be broken if new life is to come. So the end of his novel imagines an internal process in Ursula, which gives her the faith to see, externally too, that however much the landscape covered by ugly new houses, and its inhabitants, seem enclosed in hard yet brittle casing, this might yet be like nuts in February and burst open to new growth. It is true that the hope is not warranted by the history in the book, though it comes from his faith that the creative forces always remain available. If he had written 'could' instead of 'would' in his affirmations of the future,[90] the final vision might not have seemed so much an assertion of his own optimism, rather than a conclusion which holds the whole past of the book and yet opens to the future as he intended. Yet, as in the Bible, the covenant of renewal has a price – no less than the death of the old self and the old form of society.

He knew now that he might have put publication at risk again, and he desperately needed the money. 'Do you think Methuen is ready to back up this novel of mine?' he asked Pinker, a week before he finished – wondering at the same time whether he was too late for the Spring list. 'He must make some fight for it. It is worth it, and he must do it. It will never be popular. But he can make it known what it is, and prevent the mean little fry from pulling it down' (ii. 294). Yet when he actually finished he was exultant. On 2 March he wrote to Viola Meynell – now sharing the typing with Eleanor Farjeon – 'I have finished my *Rainbow*, bended it and set it firm. Now off and away to find the pots of gold at its feet' (ii. 299).

But rainbows recede, and a postscript follows: 'Tell me which parts you think the publisher will decidedly object to.'

VIII Cambridge – and After

It was with great expectations that Lawrence then set out for Cambridge on Saturday 6 March, having nervously written to ask whether he would need black tie to dine at Trinity.

I feel frightfully important coming to Cambridge – quite momentous the occasion is to me. I don't want to be horribly impressed and intimidated, but am afraid I may be ... Don't make me see too many people at once, or I lose my wits. I am afraid of concourses and clans and societies and cliques – not so much of individuals. Truly I am rather afraid. (ii. 300)

He was of course meeting an Apostolic clique, and the Trinity clan of philosophers, classicists and mathematicians, within the privileged concourse of Cambridge, in a class-ridden English society. He had reason, given his background, accent and provincial education, to feel intimidated, even though he had confronted foreign countries and foreign manners before. He was unfortunately rather unwell again, after a recurrence of the fluey cold. He gave up the idea of visiting Ottoline on the way, and on the 4th was uncertain whether he would go at all (ii. 303). Yet at first the visit, at its most intimidating, went not too badly. At dinner on the Saturday evening he sat between Russell and G. E. Moore, who was a benign but also a shy man who spoke a different kind of language, so that communication was difficult. After dinner however there was talk in the combination room, and Lawrence began to relax and speak out. Russell wrote afterwards to Ottoline that G. H. Hardy, the mathematician, whom he greatly respected, 'was *immensely* impressed by him – after seeing him he went round to Winstanley to tell him everybody here was utterly trivial & at last he had met a real man'. However the next day, for Lawrence, was 'one of the crises in my life' (ii. 321).

This was because of his encounters with John Maynard Keynes. Ottoline had told Russell that Keynes would be in Cambridge, and thought Lawrence should get to know him.[91] Russell duly invited Keynes to a private dinner on the Sunday evening; but they also walked round to his rooms in King's late on Sunday morning – and Lawrence's dislike of 'Cambridge' crystallised.

Lawrence had rather liked him before [Keynes must, then, also have been a guest on Saturday evening] – but seeing him this morning at 11, in pyjamas, just awake, he felt him corrupt & unclean. Lawrence has quick sensitive impressions which I don't understand, tho' they would seem quite natural to you. They are marvellous. I love him more & more. I wouldn't dream of discouraging his socialist revolution ... He talks so well about it that he *almost* makes me believe in it. I am afraid he is not happy here, & will heave a great sigh of relief when he gets away.[92]

Earlier in the letter he had said that Lawrence 'hates everybody here'. If Russell was so impressed with Lawrence's powers of intuition he cannot have told him that Keynes was an active and promiscuous sodomite – though Keynes made no secret of his predilections among his Apostle and Bloomsbury intimates; and he and Lytton Strachey had greatly increased the number of homosexuals elected to the society and hence its homosexual tone. But whatever in Keynes's appearance or behaviour set imagination working that morning, Lawrence was in no doubt of what he intuited, or his response. 'I never knew what it meant', he would tell Bunny:

till I saw K., till I saw him at Cambridge. We went into his rooms at midday, and it was very sunny. He was not there, so Russell was writing a note. Then suddenly a door opened and K. was there, blinking from sleep, standing in his pyjamas. And as he stood there gradually a knowledge passed into me, which has been like a little madness to me ever since. And it was carried along with the most dreadful sense of repulsiveness – something like carrion – a vulture gives me the same feeling ... (ii. 320)

It was hardly surprising that the dinner that evening in Russell's rooms in Nevile's Court was not a success. The next day, Russell told Ottoline that it had been 'interesting but rather dreadful' and that Lawrence had left in the morning 'disgusted with Camb., but not with me I think. I felt that we got on *very* well with each other, & made real progress towards intimacy. His intuitive perceptiveness is *wonderful* – it leaves me gasping in admiration.' At dinner, said Russell:

Keynes was hard, intellectual, insincere – using intellect to hide the torment & discord in his soul. [A Lawrencian verdict?] We pressed him hard about his purpose in life – he spoke as tho' he only wanted a succession of agreeable moments, which of course is not really true. Lawrence likes him but can't get on with him; I get on with him, but dislike him. Lawrence has the same feeling against sodomy as I have; you had nearly made me believe there is no great harm in it, but I have reverted, & all the examples I know confirm me in thinking it sterilizing.[93]

Keynes's memories (in 1938) were uncertain, but he recalled that Lawrence 'was morose from the outset and said very little, apart from indefinite expressions of irritable dissent'. They sat round the fireplace, Lawrence 'in rather a crouching position with his head down' – just as at Grant's – while they took turns standing at the fireplace and talked '*at*' him, trying to get 'him to participate'. Keynes partly imagined how his 'Bloomsbury' and 'Cambridge' might have seemed to Lawrence:

If, therefore, I altogether ignore our merits – our charm, our intelligence, our unworldliness, our affection – I can see us as water-spiders, gracefully skimming, as light and reasonable as air, the surface of the stream without any contact at all with the eddies and currents underneath. And if I imagine us as coming under the observation of Lawrence's ignorant, jealous, irritable, hostile eyes, what a combination of qualities we offered to arouse his passionate distaste; this thin rationalism skipping on the crust of the lava, ignoring both the reality and the value of the vulgar passions, joined to libertinism and comprehensive irreverence, too clever by half ... All this was very unfair to poor, silly, well-meaning us.[94]

But though Keynes may have given and Lawrence taken a less than fair impression, what Lawrence had seen went much deeper than this admits and was more disturbing to himself. Russell was more perceptive when, at the end of his letter, he connected the vehemence of Lawrence's hate with his passionate belief in love; yet saw also the inexperience: 'he imagines men more like him than they are. I think his thinking is quite honest, but there are painful things it hasn't realized.'Yet Cambridge was a crisis precisely because it began a whole process of painful realisation – first of all within himself – which would radically change his writing, and his thought about 'corruption'. He had *theorised* about homosexuality. Now he had been disturbed with intimations of something he thought predatory, unwholesome, irreverent, corruptly clever.

He went home via Bedford Square where he spent Monday evening, and met 'Goldie' Lowes Dickinson whom Ottoline had specially invited, but about whom he says nothing. The next weekend Katherine Mansfield and Kot came down, and took his mind off what had happened. (Katherine had been suffering badly from her 'rheumatism' – in fact a gonorrheal infection she had contracted in Germany some years before.[95] Her relationship with Murry was now on again, though he did not come with her, probably because he was looking for new rooms in London. They had decided to give up their cottage and live in town; though, soon after, Katherine felt unable to work there, and went back to Paris.) Though Lawrence was still unwell, and Katherine could not walk as far as the Downs, it seems to have been harmonious all round. But as soon as his friends had gone, Lawrence fell into black depression. He tried to begin rewriting his philosophy as he had said he would, but, he told Russell:

all the time I am struggling in the dark – very deep in the dark – and cut off from everybody and everything. Sometimes I seem to stumble into the light, for a day, or even two days – then in I plunge again, god knows where and into what utter darkness of chaos. I don't mind very much. But sometimes I am afraid of the terrible things that are real, in the darkness, and of the entire unreality of these things I see. It becomes like a madness at last, to know one is all the time walking in a pale assembly of an unreal world ... whilst oneself is all the while a piece of darkness pulsating in shocks, and the shocks and the darkness are real.

... I wanted to write this to ask you please to be with me – in the underworld – or at any rate to wait for me. Don't let me go, that is all ... I feel there is something to go through – something very important. It may be it is only in my own soul – but it seems to grow more and more looming ... (ii. 307)[96]

Cambridge had made him 'very black and down. I cannot bear its smell of rottenness, marsh-stagnancy. I get a melancholic malaria. How can so sick people rise up? They must die first' (ii. 309). Yet it was characteristic of Lawrence to see that the sickness was also in him; and no less characteristic to feel that what was in him was everywhere. Nietzsche had written of insight *Beyond Good and Evil*, but Lawrence now insists that evil is real and ubiquitous. Having once threatened to push Kot off a bus to punish his melancholy, he confessed he was so 'depressed by the sense of evil in the world' it would soon be Kot's turn to shove (ii. 310). With sure instinct, he immersed himself in reading Dostoevsky: *The Idiot*, then *The Brothers Karamazov* and then the letters. He was back in bed, still with the fluey cold – also now partly gastric, 'a sore throat in the middle of one's belly' (ii. 315) – which he had never shaken off. His old liberal optimism and tolerance, he now saw, were naïve:

It is no good now, thinking that to understand a man from his own point of view is to be happy about him. I can imagine the mind of a rat, as it slithers along in the dark, pointing its sharp nose. But I can never feel happy about it, I must always want to kill it. It contains a principle of evil. There *is* a principle of evil. Let us acknowledge it once and for all. I saw it so plainly in Keynes at Cambridge, it made me sick. I am sick with the knowledge of the prevalence of evil, as if it were some insidious disease.

I have been reading Dostoievsky's *Idiot*. I don't like Dostoievsky. He is again like the rat, slithering along in hate, in the shadows, and, in order to belong to the light, professing love, all love. But his nose is sharp with hate, his running is shadowy and rat-like, he is a will fixed and gripped like a trap. He is not nice. (ii. 311)

Dostoevsky's letters seemed to Lawrence to confirm that he was a genius, but one of hate and disintegration, his Christianity a disguise.

What an amazing person he was – a pure introvert, a purely disintegrating will – there was not a grain of the passion of love within him – all the passion of hate, of evil. Yet a great man. It has become, I think, now, a supreme wickedness to set up a Christ-worship as Dostoevsky did: it is the outcome of an evil will, disguising itself in terms of love. (ii. 314)

By 8 April, a month after the Cambridge visit, he felt he was coming through the struggle with the 'Powers of Darkness' in himself (ii. 315) – and was therefore able to diagnose in others what he had discovered in D. H. Lawrence. The simple temptation is to see his depression and misery, perhaps even the renewed illness, as psychosomatic reaction against his own latent homosexuality: horrified to think he might 'really' be *like* Keynes (who looked somewhat rattish with his sharp intelligent face,[97] and whom Lawrence had 'liked' on one level); and therefore desperate to dissociate himself from a sharp-nosed foraging sewer-bestiality – yet capable at his most honest of admitting subterranean attraction to what in another part of himself he wanted to kill.

There is some truth in this. Yet it greatly oversimplifies the nature and scope of the Evil that he now thought he saw everywhere underneath pretensions to humanitarianism or love. He was on the way to a crucial modification of his idea of character and belief in the creativity of conflict. Did Russell (certainly no homosexual) talk at the Union of Democratic Control, 'of the nations kissing each other, when your soul prowls the frontier all the time most jealously, to defend what it has and to seize what it can' – the real motive for the war against which Russell and Lowes Dickinson were working in the U.D.C. 'It makes me laugh when you admit it. But we are all like that' (ii. 309–10). On 8 April he told Ottoline:

Shelley believed in the principle of Evil, coeval with the Principle of Good. That is right.
... Do not tell me there is no Devil. There is a Prince of Darkness. Sometimes I wish I could let go, and be really wicked – kill and murder – but kill chiefly. I do want to kill. But I want to select whom I shall kill. Then I shall enjoy it. The war is no good. It is this black desire I have become conscious of. We cant so much about goodness – it is canting. Tell Russell he does the same – let him recognise the powerful malignant will in him. This is the very worst wickedness, that we refuse to recognise the passionate evil that is in us. This makes us secret and rotten. (ii. 315)

He knew that repression only increased the rottenness, the capacity for deadly hate and malignancy. (Indeed he wrote to consult David Eder about his symptoms and ailments; ii. 317 – Eder who was both physician and psychiatrist.) Everything had to be let out. 'Those who know how to love must know how to slay. If we are not to be given up to love, then let us be given up to the contest with the dragon' (ii. 316). Rottenness must be cut away; 'surgery is pure hate of the defect in the loved thing. And it is surgery we want, Cambridge wants, England wants, I want' (ii. 318). The war might have done it, but England is 'unaware of the mortification in its own body' and won't have it touched or acknowledged. The only hope is to 'look to the young'. But there was one more recognition to come, as two of 'the young' arrived at Greatham.

On the weekend of 17–18 April Bunny Garnett came with Frankie Birrell, and what had disturbed Lawrence when he had seen Bunny with Grant, now came to full consciousness in belated realisation that Birrell was homosexual, and in love with Bunny – who looked 'so wretched ... and your hand shaky – and everything wrong' (ii. 320). The two young men had come to Chesham together without raising any vibrations, and Lawrence did not dislike Birrell then, or when he first arrived now, 'tired and a bit lost and wondering':

I love him. But my God, to hear him talk sends me mad. To hear these young people talking really fills me with black fury: they talk endlessly, but endlessly – and never, never a good or a real thing said. Their attitude is so irreverent and blatant. They are cased each in a hard little shell of his own, and out of this they talk words. There is never for one second any outgoing of feeling, and no reverence – not a crumb or grain of reverence. I cannot stand it. I *will not* have people like this – I had rather be alone. They made me dream in the night of a beetle that bites like a scorpion. But I killed it – a very large beetle. I scotched it – and it ran off – but I came upon it again and killed it. It is this horror of little swarming selves that I can't stand: Birrells, D. Grants, and Keynses ...

I like David Garnett – but there is something wrong with him. Is he also like Keynes and Grant. It is enough to drive one frantic. It makes me long for my Italy. Sometimes I think I can't stand this England any more: it is too wicked and perverse. (ii. 319)

Homosexuality seemed now (to him) indelibly associated with brittle intellectualism, self-enclosure, *irreverence*; connecting the four men as much and as hatefully as their sexuality. (Indeed, three of them were not averse to heterosexual satisfaction, Bunny by no means so.) Instinctively, nightmarishly, Lawrence intuited something poisonous to all he had come to hold most vital. Such people were not morally wrong, but *corrupt*. His letters to Savage and Russell had feared lest homosexual relationships be merely sensational and confirm self-enclosure. Now he had met for the first time what he had theorised about – and thought he saw something darker, actively subversive of all he reverenced.

He tried to talk to Bunny about all this; but on Monday was still upset enough to write the letter which would damage their friendship beyond repair. (Since Bunny quoted from it so selectively as to make his treatment of the breach in later reminiscences disingenuous, and since the letter itself became public only in 1981, it had better be quoted extensively.)

I can't bear to think of you, David, so wretched as you are – and your hand shaky – and everything wrong. It is foolish of you to say that it doesn't matter either way – the men loving men. It doesn't matter in the public way. But it matters so much, David, to the man himself – at any rate to us northern nations – that it is like a blow of triumphant decay, when I meet Birrell or the others. I simply can't bear it. It is so wrong, it is unbearable. It makes a form of inward corruption which truly makes me scarce able to live. Why is there this horrible sense of frowstiness, so repulsive, as if it came from deep inward dirt – a sort of sewer – deep in men like K and B and D. G. It is something almost unbearable to me. And not from any moral disapprobation. I myself never considered Plato very wrong, or Oscar Wilde. I never knew what it meant till I saw K., till I saw him at Cambridge. [There follows the description quoted above p. 209] . . .

Never bring B. to see me any more. There is something nasty about him, like black-beetles. He is horrible and unclean. I feel as if I should go mad, if I think of your set, D.G. and K. and B. It makes me dream of beetles. In Cambridge I had a similar dream. Somehow, I can't bear it. It is wrong beyond all bounds of wrongness. I had felt it slightly before, in the Stracheys. But it came full upon me in K., and in D.G. And yesterday I knew it again, in B.

David, my dear, I love your father and I love your mother . . . you must leave these 'friends', these beetles. You must wrench away and start a new life. B. and D.G. are done for, I think – done for for ever. K. I am not sure. But you, my dear, you can be all right. You can come away, and grow whole, and love a woman, and marry her, and make life good, and be happy. Now David, in the name of everything that is called love, leave this set and stop this blasphemy against love. It isn't that I speak from a moral code. Truly I didn't know it was wrong, till I saw K. that morning in Cambridge. It was one of the crises in my life. It sent me mad with misery and hostility and rage. Go away, David, and try to love a woman. My God, I could kiss Eleanor Farjeon[98] with my body and soul, when I think how good she is, in comparison. But the Oliviers, and such girls, are wrong.

I could sit and howl in a corner like a child, I feel so bad about it all. (ii. 320–1)

Frieda was more tactful. She too feared that Bunny's 'vital interest is in men' and that he tended to 'loose and forget *yourself* in other men' though he had it in him 'to stand for yourself and by yourself'.[99] However, she said nothing about homosexuality, assumed that he would marry, and that his 'unbelief' was only owing to an affair (with Anna Hepburn) which had 'something hopeless in it from the beginning'. But Lawrence in a final postscript urged him not to marry anybody. 'Go right away and be alone and work, and come to your real self. But do leave this group of "friends". You have always known the wrong people – Harolds, and Olivier girls. Do go away, right away, and be by yourself' (ii. 322).

Later, in 1955, Bunny told a melodramatic story about how Lawrence's malignant will had then caused Frankie's tongue to swell so much on the Saturday night that he could not talk – but he carefully obscured what had upset Lawrence so much.[100] When he finally released the letter he annotated it copiously, but disingenuously, since Lawrence never doubted the affection Bunny felt for Grant, Keynes and Lytton Strachey, which indeed was lifelong, nor urged him to marry Eleanor Farjeon, nor indeed rested his case on any certainty that he was actually then having an affair with Birrell, though Lawrence undoubtedly feared so.[101] His intuition was accurate, though he mistook the circumstances. Bunny had been sleeping with Grant since January – to Birrell's distress. Moreover Lawrence's charge was against the whole Cambridge and Bloomsbury set to which Bunny seemed so devoted, because of the confirmation (when Birrell and he were together) of how homosexuality seemed to go with brittle and irreverent talk, self-enclosure, sensationalism, promiscuity. *That* – no simple homophobia – was what Lawrence felt was 'a form of inward corruption', an ethos in which Bunny would lose himself. The dream insects invert the *Rainbow* imagery. Against the nut breaking clear of its rind to create new growth, is set now the self-encased beetle that only oozes nastiness when its casing is ruptured. What he feared was that David would become, and remain, one of 'the sordid people who crept hard-scaled and foul on the face of the earth's corruption',[102] setting himself against the whole 'sacred' meaning of the rainbow, and the new life that could only fully come (Lawrence believed) from the marriage of the sons of god with the daughters of men. In 1912 he had seen Bunny as a mother's boy, another Paul Morel. Now Bunny was turning wilfully aside from the path which (Lawrence thought) had led to his own salvation.

Yet it is easy to sympathise with Bunny. The Lawrences had no respect for privacy, no idea that there need be limits to their interest in and discussion of other people's intimate affairs and relations. Though Bunny himself loved gossiping about other people all his life, he was certainly not used to being spoken to so bluntly. He had an edgy relation with his father, but Edward would never have told him off like that. He deeply resented such intrusion and interference. Lawrence had worried that he had 'trampled in forbidden places' when writing to the Murrys about their relationship – but this was far worse. He may also not have managed to convey, to an angry young man, all the implications he now saw in Bloomsbuggery. The young Bunny was idealistic, enthusiastic, impulsive, flattered by the attention and kindness (as he saw it) of ex-Cambridge men, whom he viewed with an outsider's admiration, and so resented Lawrence's imputations the more. Lawrence's view of homosexuality will have seemed narrowly puritanical, as against the tolerance and sophistication of free spirits – though Bunny's concealments (even as late as 1981) show deep unease, as does indeed the lasting intensity of his resentment.[103] Finally, though he had little idea of the hinterland of Lawrence's reaction, he did understand that a choice was being demanded between the Lawrences and the whole Cambridge-Bloomsbury set; between serious commitment in heterosexual marriage, and the hedonism, promiscuity and variety of sexual relationships in the circle Lawrence was objecting to. (The inclusion of Harold Hobson and the Olivier girls in the 'wrongness' shows Lawrence's objection to heterosexual as well as homosexual promiscuity. Harold's he knew of personally. The Olivier girls were not promiscuous, but their neo-paganism led others beside Lawrence to think that they might be.)[104] Egotist and hedonist, bisexual and promiscuous womaniser, but also affectionate friend and enthusiastic Bloomsburian that Bunny was, there was never any doubt which way the verdict would go. The sad thing, however, was that he never acknowledged the pain and tenderness in Lawrence's letter or the genuine concern that underlay the interference, but in showing it to Keynes, encouraged him to see its basic motivation as jealousy, over himself.[105] He never forgave Lawrence, and most of his reminiscences contain an element of putting-down. Only for Frieda, whose hedonism was much closer to his own, did the old affection survive. They did not meet again until 1918.

Lawrence's beetle dreams were instinctive revulsion, not merely against his own homosexual side, but all that now went with it. Yet this was surely to question the optimistic basis of 'Le Gai Savaire': the belief that conflict of the male and female within is creative, and thus, since everyone is bisexual, relations of all kinds can be creative too, even if homosexual ones are liable to be too self-reflexive or to satisfy only part of a complex personality. When Lawrence wrote to Forster about 'devils' there had been no revulsion. His tone was rather that of Blake or Nietzsche: the Blake of *The Marriage of Heaven and Hell*, where devils and angels are equally part of the Whole, and can easily change places in different conditions, since everything that lives is holy and all Seven Sins are aspects of God; or the Nietzsche of *Beyond Good and Evil*, where antithesis is denied, and what has been called 'evil' may be a 'virtue' if it aids the Will to Power. But now? In the letter that exulted over the finishing of *The Rainbow* he had told Viola Meynell that he was 'going to begin a book about Life – more rainbows, but in different skies', to be published in pamphlets (since Nisbet had rejected the 'Study of Thomas Hardy'), 'my initiation of the great and happy revolution' (ii. 299). It would surely have to be a different, less happy philosophy now?

And what of *The Rainbow*?

IX   Re-Visions

In his black depression after Cambridge he was no longer sure of 'The Signal', and not feeling like 'The Phoenix' (projected titles for the rewriting of the philosophy; ii. 300, 303). Viola had however begun typing *The Rainbow*, and by about 19 March he had got the first chapter (ii. 308), and began to revise. The story of Tom and Lydia, now the starkest contrast with his new sense of evil, seems to have reassured him about the basis of his thinking: 'It really puts a new thing in the world, almost a new vision of life' (ii. 308). Russell came down for a weekend at the end of the month, and the sense of their 'kinship' held (ii. 312).

By 8 April he had begun the new philosophy, which would not tell people now that they are 'angels in disguise' but rather 'dogs and swine, bloodsuckers' (ii. 313); though he was at last coming out of his 'cursed blackness', albeit still in bed, and harbouring some murderous thoughts. By then he had revised about a third of the novel (ii 314), and until the end of May the two processes of revision went on, intertwined.

Now he thought of calling the philosophy 'Morgenrot' (ii 315), after Nietzsche again.[106] Though this is the letter that urges recognition of 'the passionate evil that is in us', and the next day he wrote the one saying 'Those who know how to love must know how to slay,' the title shows resurgent faith: that to recognise the prevalence of evil makes it possible to overcome it, and find new light and life. Other than that, we can tell little about this phase of rethinking. By 20 April he had written 40 pages (ii. 325). On 8 June he sent Forster and Russell copies of what had been typed, first by Kot again but then by himself 're-composing as I go' (ii. 352), amounting to about a quarter of what he planned (ii. 355). 'Re-composing' suggests that he was working on the early non-Hardy material of 'Le Gai Savaire', probably cutting all the literary and art criticism, and etching a far darker sense of the destructive potential in human beings, individually and collectively, in the war. By 9 July however this attempt had broken down 'in the middle', and ten days later he realised that he would need to begin again on a different basis (ii. 362, 367).

Since the typescript is gone, the only hints at its content must come from the letters. Lawrence's realisation of inner evil had not only to do with the poisonous corruption of beetle and scorpion that threatened him, but also significantly related the opponents of war to those who carried it on. In both Russell the pacifist, and himself the nay-sayer, he discovered a coiling violence, possessive, aggressive, which 'prowls the frontiers', not only guards what it has but 'seize[s] what it can' (ii. 310); issuing in a murderous rage at what threatens or prevents the self, a fierce desire to kill. These were the real and undeclared 'war aims', all the more certainly since even those who opposed the war ought to admit that they felt them too – but they led in terrible directions. There had been carnage in the battle of Neuve Chapelle in March, but on 22 April at Ypres war took on a new dimension of horror: the Germans used poison gas. In the battle which continued to the third week in May, the British lost 60,000 men. On the afternoon of 7 May the *Lusitania* was torpedoed by a U-boat, and four days later anti-German rioting began in London, with frenzied attacks on shops and individuals. Typically, Lawrence was both horrified at the 'madness ... this frenzy of hatred', but also confessed that he understood it only too well: 'I am mad with rage myself. I would like to kill a million Germans – two million' (ii. 340).

Moreover, in insisting that such things were indeed *evil* the Nietzschean title began to signal a growing difference from, as well as a lasting affinity with, the

German philosopher. Lawrence not only saw that Power might be that of a lethal and mad Darkness, but began also to worry about the Will.

In both the aristocratic ladies to whom he had written in such religious terms, he detected something dangerous. By 23 April he heard that the 17-year-old Belgian refugee Maria Nys, to whom Ottoline had given a home, had attempted suicide. He expressed his horror, but insisted that Ottoline must acknowledge the cause in herself: the 'strong, old-developed *will*' which had 'enveloped' the girl so that she lived under its dominance:

and then you want to put her away from you, eject her from your will. So that when she says it was because she couldn't bear being left,[107] that she took the poison, it is a good deal true ...

Why must you always use your *will* so much, why can't you let things be, without always grasping and trying to know and to dominate [his final charge against his own Ursula]. I'm too like this myself.

... *why* will you use power instead of love ... (ii. 326)

Moreover, when Lady Cynthia pressed him in May for advice about her son – the 'fat and smiling John' of Kingsgate – who had begun to show symptoms that would eventually be recognised as autism, he at first resented but then took on the task. Again, Cynthia herself (he thought) was the cause, in her lack of faith. The new morning depends on 'belief': not only that there is a Great Will, essentially creative rather than Schopenhauerian (or Hardy-esque), but also that each individual soul has a significant role to play, affining itself to that. To feel bound by circumstances, disbelieving 'that all things rest within the scope of a Great Will ... a belief in God, or belief in Love – what you like', is to be a dead soul. To believe in such a great Will, yet think that 'the agency of the particular soul is insignificant' is 'unbelief: *much more insidious* than atheism' (his italics). John at Kingsgate had seemed a happy soul 'intrinsically'. If he is recalcitrant now, rejecting his mother, it must be because he knows that, whatever she says, she does not act as though she believes in a world governed by love and joy. Instead, she tries to make him love and obey *her*. 'Your own soul is deficient, so it fights for the love of the child. And the child's soul, born in the womb of your unbelief, laughs at you and defies you, almost jeers at you, almost hates you.' She must not try to make him love or obey her, must not exert authority; only, when necessary, appeal to the sense of love and justice, the 'believing soul' of the child, not to give trouble to other people: 'Put yourself aside ... You have no right to his love. Care only for his good and well-being: make *no* demands on him. But for yourself, you must learn to believe in God ... It is not our wickedness which kills us, but our unbelief' (ii. 336–7). These would be hard words to swallow, but (spoken to a fashionable woman whose nurse brought up her children) they have a wisdom. There is both Nietzsche and anti-Nietzsche in the argument that the individual will-to-be-oneself-to-the-maximum, must also be able to put itself aside in order to give the maximum new life, secure in belief that the universe is governed by a great creative power. (Yet *could* anyone now believe 'that we in England shall unite in our knowledge of God to live to the best of our knowledge – Prime Ministers [like her father-in-law] and capitalists and artizans all working in pure effort towards God – here, tomorrow, in this England'?)

At Worthing on the Sussex coast with Frieda a fortnight earlier at the end of April, Lawrence had just heard of the death of Rupert Brooke: 'the fatuity of it all', the sunny man killed by sunstroke (it was first rumoured), the cruel irony so 'in keeping ... the real climax of his pose'. The beach front had been crowded with soldiers.

Can I ever tell you how ugly they were: 'to insects – sensual lust.' I like sensual lust – but insectwise, no – it is obscene. I like men to be beasts – but insects – one insect mounted on another – oh God! The soldiers at Worthing are like that – they remind me of lice or bugs: – 'to insects – sensual lust'. They will murder their officers one day. They are teeming insects. What massive creeping hell is not let loose nowadays.

It isn't my disordered imagination. There is a wagtail sitting on the gatepost. I see how sweet and swift heaven is. But hell is slow and creeping and viscous, and insect-teeming: as is this Europe now – this England. (ii. 330–1)

Everything seemed to come nightmarishly together, Dmitri Karamazov, Cambridge and Bloomsbury homosexuality, the 'horror of little swarming selves', beetles, teeming regimented mass-men secretly filled with bloodlust. How was 'Morgenrot' to explain the abyss between the heaven of the natural world in its annual renewal, and this vision of man-made hell and corruption? London in early May looked ashy to him as to Skrebensky, only worse: 'like some hoary massive underworld ... The traffic flows through the rigid grey streets like the rivers of Hell through their banks of dry, rocky ash' (ii. 339). How account for the awful paradox of *this* spring, 'very beautiful – very brilliant, upon a black undertone of the war horror' (ii. 347)? As he finished revising *The Rainbow* at the end of May his faith in resurrection was still strong – 'Our sense of the Absolute is the only sense left to us' (ii. 348) – but there was also 'death and more death' first, 'till we are black and swollen with death' (ii. 352). It is not even clear how much more he wrote of 'Morgenrot' after the section he sent to Forster and to Russell.

However, by and perhaps before 9 July, when he told Ottoline his philosophy had broken down, he was hard at work on the proofs of *The Rainbow*, and feeling, again, that 'Whatever else it is, it is the voyage of discovery toward the real and eternal and unknown land' (ii. 362). Yet the new darker vision was bound to have affected *The Rainbow* too.

Viola Meynell, discovering the size of the opus she had undertaken to type, handed over half to her friend Eleanor Farjeon who had visited Greatham and met Lawrence, propped up in bed against pillows in early March. From mid-March, when Viola finished the first 71 pages (ii. 308), till 31 May, Lawrence revised the novel extensively as batches of typescript arrived. He made no attempt to check them against the manuscript, but as well as revision in the usual sense it was another re-seeing. For after Cambridge he was no longer the Lawrence of the manuscript.

This made no difference to the story of Tom and Lydia, because theirs was the Old World, limited, relatively unaware, but unspoilt – helping indeed to restore his faith against the powers of darkness. The changes sharpen the focus, but do not change the vision.

With Anna and Will however, because they were closer to himself and Frieda, and also the fulcrum of the novel's analysis of how creative conflict might turn into destruction, the newly darker vision was bound to make a difference. In two places, Lawrence wrote lengthy new sections into the typescript. He reconceived the cathedral scene which now seemed too one-sided, by underlining a destructiveness in Anna's response to Will's ecstasy. She had seemed to know more and better than her husband; and there had been a similar tendency at the end of 'Anna Victrix' to lay the stress too exclusively on the failure and limitation of Will. Lawrence now corrects that, and shows the opposite responses to the cathedral as equally reductive. In Will's, he merely intensifies the ecstasy of abandonment he distrusted in Campbell; but Anna's response is transformed. She is made more resentful of being momentarily overcome: resisting the pull to the altar by seizing on the little carved mediaeval faces in far more anti-religious and mocking a fashion. They become not merely human but wicked; and she is jeering and malicious (as Frieda could be), exulting not just in multiplicity, but in destroying something in Will. Her desire for wider freedom and space becomes more than self-protection: becomes an urge to destroy whatever threatens her self; as Will's desire for unity had already revealed too easy self-abandon, turning ugly if thwarted. Lawrence had already been heightening Will's darkly violent potential, to evil. Now, in the cathedral, each is shown to have a half-truth, but the conflict becomes more clearly destructive, more ironic in exposing what has happened to the rich potential of the corn-stacking.[108]

The other new autograph section was a leap of imagination. At the end of 'The Child' he had written only briefly and generally of 'some months' in which Anna

let herself go, she gave him also his full measure, she considered nothing. Children and everything she let go, and gave way to her last desires, till he and she had gone all the devious and never-to-be-recorded ways of desire and satisfaction, to the very end, till they had had everything, and knew no more

Lawrence now replaced this by a new half chapter: Will's escapade with a factory girl in Nottingham, followed by a new relation with his wife, issuing in 'a sensuality violent and extreme as death', but also an 'Absolute Beauty' and a kind of liberation. Here he began to explore his new awareness of the darkness of the human heart, predatory, capable of savage violence and lust; and an anal sexuality without tenderness. Yet simultaneously, he began to rediscover faith that even in *that* 'dark' dimension, true opposition, accepted and gone through, could become creative again. The couple whose love had turned into victory for the wife and defeat of the husband, to the cost of both, prove able to discover new life through lust. Will becomes a new man with a new public role.

When he comes home roused and dangerous, because his attempt to seduce the girl he picked up has been frustrated, Anna is not merely unafraid of this husband grown suddenly strange; she sees him as excitingly *other* again; and is at long last willing to abandon herself to him, neither defensive nor dominating. 'It was as if he were a perfect stranger, as if she were infinitely and essentially strange to him'.[109] They become discoverers together, and what they discover is an 'Absolute Beauty'. Pure sensuality (it seems) is absolute, not relative, because it is a beauty purely of the body divorced from the person, so having nothing to do with relationship between persons or the tenderness that results. It is also absolute because entirely at one extreme of the dialectic of opposites, a marriage purely of the sensual sides of the self and the other. The Lawrence who had imagined the 'dark' relation of Ursula and Skrebensky has now pushed his analysis of sexuality one stage further. In February, as he wrote his sermon on evolution while Ursula looked through her microscope, he had insisted that all the stages of human evolution were co-present in the human being, who is still tiger and ape as well as reaching in spiritual aspiration to the gates of paradise. At the end of 'The Child', there had been the idea that married sex should be able to include all possibilities, even the 'never-to-be-recorded' ones. Now however, imagining what he had merely hinted at before, he does more than merely include. He recovers Blake's faith that even the predatory cruelty of the 'Tyger' can be an agent of the Great Creator – so even anal lust can be creative too, always provided (still) that it is not like that of his nightmare insects, the self mounted on the other in a mode wholly self-enclosed, whether dominating or passive, and hence essentially masturbatory. Will now fiercely wishes that he had the rough tongue of a tiger, to lick till the blood comes; and other beauties they discover are 'sinister, tropical', a 'heavy, fundamental gratification' – the language being as explicit as it dares.[110] Yet because there is once again a full sense of otherness, with no victory or defeat, no imposing or abasing of the self, but, rather, mutual self-abandon to discovery and liberation, it would seem that even this coming together in pure darkness, this marriage only of the dark sides of themselves, can have some of the effects which their relation as lovers had failed to achieve. Anna is recalled from her trance of motherhood to live more in herself; Will is not only more founded in himself but becomes a man with a role in society.

This is not advocacy. The dark relation is partial, less than the full marriage of opposites that Anna and Will failed to achieve. Indeed Lawrence still sees it as dangerous: 'a sensuality violent and extreme as death. They had no conscious intimacy, no tenderness of love. It was all the lust and the infinite, maddening intoxication of the senses, a passion of death.'[111] In reducing the fullness of the self and the full possibilities of relationship, this new relation is potentially deadly. Human life indeed cannot *occupy* the Absolute at either extreme of Lawrence's dialectic. Those are the domain of the 'Gods' – and the nearer the approach to either, the more deadly. Yet (it seems) being willing to die to the self by touching the Absolute at moments, in and through the Other, even at only one extreme and in only one kind, can still bring about a kind of rebirth – albeit on a more limited level than the full marriage of opposites.

Lawrence's imagination had kept on searching, through his own dark night of the soul in March and April, for a way back to the belief that every kind of living *can* be holy, if only it can find the way to marry the not-self, in some mode of death and resurrection. This implies no less horror at the sort of homosexuality he thought either used the other to masturbate the self, or cared so little for the self as to find gratification in being used for others' purposes (like the soldiers in Worthing). But it does suggest a question which 'Shame' does not settle, and which would sometime have to be taken up again. Did he still believe, after Cambridge, what he had thought in 1913, that some people, less complex than Ursula, might be saved by homosexual relationship, if heterosexual relationship had failed? Could same-sex relationship escape 'insect lust' – i.e. mutual masturbation or buggering domination or abuse – as Anna's and Will's, though partly anal, seemed to do? On the other hand (though one must be very careful about this) Lawrence's imagination had also managed to confront something very private, and potentially 'shameful'. What had so shocked Murry, that Lawrence sometimes took Frieda 'like a dog', might have to do with no more than her withdrawal and his sense of humiliating dependence. Yet if this went too far into sex war or superiority, might something impersonal and fierce, called forth from the male animal-self, be not only justifiable but liberating, to both? Excuse and rationalisation? Or anal sex confronted, and understood?

Certainly Lawrence's imagination had proved very courageous, or very foolhardy, in its willingness to explore the darkness of which he had become so conscious, heedless of risk. Perhaps he felt he had been oblique enough to get away with it – but he soon began to worry again. He had promised Ottoline that she could read the revised typescript, and on 8 April he sent her pages 1–263. By 23 April however, when he sent the next batch, he had revised as far as page

388, well past the Nottingham episode. It was hardly surprising that he should write anxiously to Pinker that day:

I hope you are willing to fight for this novel. It is nearly three years of hard work, and I am proud of it, and it must be stood up for. I'm afraid there are parts of it Methuen wont want to publish. He must. I will take out sentences and phrases, but I won't take out paragraphs or pages. So you must tell me in detail if there are real objections to printing any parts ...

Oh God, I hope I'm not going to have a miserable time over this book, now I've at last got it pretty much to its real being. (ii. 327)

A week later he asked Pinker whether Ottoline was sending the typescript on to him, as she had promised, and thanked him for 'assurances' of support (ii. 331).

As he turned to revise the story of Ursula and Skrebensky, however, he was not concerned to tone down anything, but rather to make more explicit the 'dark' and the destructive aspects. When he pruned, it was what he thought redundant.[112] In keeping with his new sense of violence, however, and the urge to kill he had found in himself, he intensified Ursula's destructiveness under the moon at the wedding dance, and heavily underlined the imagery to emphasise how what should have been harvest in the promised land had become the sterility and corruption of the Cities of the Plain. Conversely he insisted even more on the 'fecundity' of the dark sexual relationship when Skrebensky returns from South Africa – much to Ottoline's dislike of his reiteration, in which she anticipated other readers. More successfully, he gave to Skrebensky an intensification of his own horror of London as an ashy Wasteland – a passage which would influence both T. S. Eliot and Scott Fitzgerald. But since the story of Ursula and Skrebensky had already been stamped with the imprint of the war, it was largely a matter of sharpening the focus.

Though the historical action ended in 1905, the novel had much to say now about 1915. The primary imaginative drive had been the exploration of how conflict was the source of creativity when opposites married, and the self was ready to die into new life through another. Each generation however, more conscious of self than the last, found it harder to marry fully – and in failure came ever greater and more destructive violence. The men seem to lose individuality as the women increase in self-awareness, and in both, atrophy of one 'force' brings dangerous hypertrophy of its opposite. Loss of individuality is dangerous in two ways: Will's inchoate lack of self turns evil when the need to merge or absorb is thwarted; Skrebensky can only conceive of himself as part of a collective, an army, a state seeking Lebensraum. Other people, insufficiently differentiated, marshy or clayey, identify with what they really despise. Yet overdeveloped individuals, assertive, domineering, are no less dangerous. Newly aggressive self-awareness and self-preservation resist challenge from the 'other' with increasing violence and destructiveness from Anna to Ursula. All these phenomena – and the imagery of clay and marsh – are not without point in a novel which reached its final state between November 1914 and mid-1915. Yet the episode of the horses, and Ursula's recovery and final vision, continue to insist that the great opposites are always there with their promise of renewal – to souls prepared to break free from their old selves and forms of life, and trust to the creative forces in the world instead of trying to will themselves and their relationships

Years of work might also be at risk from another direction. The end of April had brought a nasty shock. In the divorce, Weekley was awarded costs, but though an order had been issued on 5 December 1913, for £144/12/10, Lawrence had not paid. Now, on 23 February 1915 he was warned he would have to attend before one of the Registrars of the Probate, Divorce and Admiralty Division of the High Court, to be examined as to his means (ii. 327 n. 2). On 29 April he told Russell he had been served with an order to appear on 10 May; but that he would not pay even if he were able to, and thought he would be declared bankrupt (as Murry had been). 'I cannot tell you', he wrote, 'how this reinforces in me my utter hatred of the whole establishment ... But softly – softly. I will do my best to lay a mine under their foundations' (ii. 328). It was bad enough to have to go and answer questions about his means of subsistence and the debts owing to him, but far worse was the prospect of losing the final payment from Methuen which was all he had to live on. He was afraid to hand in the typescript in case 'the detestable Goldbergs' – i.e. Messrs Goldberg, Newall, Braun and Co., Weekley's solicitors – might serve a summons on him and on Methuen, ordering the payment to be made to *them*, as soon as it became due. He wrote to ask Robert Garnett to act for him again and to make 'some arrangement' (ii. 348), 'to pay over a term of years' (ii. 354) – but it is not clear what happened at the examination,[113] except that no bankruptcy order was made. In mid-June he got Pinker to give him £90 for *The Rainbow* before publication, and another £42/10/0 which was probably for poems published in *Poetry* and the *Egoist* and perhaps also for the republication of *The White Peacock* in 1915, for which Pinker may have negotiated a lump sum (ii. 358). On Robert Garnett's advice, he had submitted the typescript to Pinker on 31 May:

I hope you will like the book: also that it is not very improper. It did not seem to me very improper, as I went through it. But then I feel very incompetent to judge, on that point.

My beloved book, I am sorry to give it to you to be printed. I could weep tears in my heart, when I read these pages. (ii. 349)[114]

CHAPTER FIVE

◆

May–November 1915

RAINBOW'S END

> ... Now off and away to find the pots of gold at its feet.
> (ii. 299)

I 'This world on top'

As spring 1915 warmed into summer the Meynells came down more often, and the outer life became steadily more crowded and demanding as *The Rainbow* drew towards its end. In March and April Lawrence fell ill again, and began to think this cottage, also, might be damp. At Easter and Whitsun the Meynells arrived in force, so that the danger of 'invasion' grew too great (ii. 323), and Frieda, too, grew resentful.[1] By then, in a pattern now familiar, they were quarrelling, and thinking of moving again.

While Lawrence was away in Cambridge, Frieda had a surprise visit from Ford Madox Hueffer on behalf of the Ministry of Information (he said), to see whether he could do anything to stop Lawrence being persecuted for being 'pro-German'. Ford's stories are notoriously unreliable – he says Lawrence was there, though his companion Violet Hunt confirms that Frieda was alone – but in his new work with C. F. G. Masterman he could have been asked to investigate his former protégé who had married a German. If so, what happened was unfortunate. Frieda gave them tea, but they got involved in a flaming row about the Belgian refugees, the subject of Ford's recent poem *Antwerp*. ('Dirty Belgians!' Violet reports 'Brynhild' as saying, 'Who cares for them!') As they left, Frieda hoped they might meet again, but Violet could not reciprocate.[2]

Lawrence was still unwell when Kot and Katherine came for the weekend of 13 March. The next weekend the Lawrences were in London, staying with Barbara Low in Golders Green; seeing Kot, Horne and Murry. Lawrence's friendship with Barbara Low had been warming since the previous summer. In February he thanked her for sending paints to his little niece Peggy in Glasgow for him, and invited her to Greatham (ii. 289). In March he joked about unconscious association, and called Dostoevsky an 'introvert' à la Jung (ii. 314). (But the jokes, about cattishness and waspishness, also suggest some asperity between Barbara and Frieda, who began to refer to Barbara behind her back as 'the princess of Judea'.[3])

About 24 March the Cannans came. Lawrence felt again a power for good in Gilbert, and Mary '*is* rather a dear', if 'shallow' (ii. 311). It was reassuring to have faith in his friends renewed, when his sense of evil was becoming so powerful. Moreover Ottoline – planning her move to Garsington as soon as the tenants' lease was up – thought of converting some old monastic buildings for the use of guests, and offered to make part of them a home for the Lawrences, to his delight. He asked for plans and discussed them eagerly, though late in March he was still 'not very well' and, after Cambridge, depressed.

Murry came for the last weekend in March – and was ticked off for having accepted Katherine's departure so fatalistically. Lawrence talked about them 'an awful lot' (Murry told her), nine-tenths of it wrong and the rest Murry couldn't understand; but he had not troubled to correct Lawrence, for there was 'good feeling' between them and 'nothing else matters'. Yet he didn't see how his sense of his physical relation with Katherine could 'shock' or seem 'crude'.[4] Though Lawrence had expounded the ideas of 'Hardy' to him, Murry had never grasped them, still less the linking of sex with the need to die to the self – an idea he certainly did not share. Lawrence was more cross and disappointed now than Murry realised. (He had probably forgotten how they were supposed to be agreed.) A week later however, Lawrence felt 'all right again towards him. My spleen has worked itself off' (ii. 313).

For first Russell and then Barbara and Kot had come down and heartened him. Russell arrived on Thursday April 1 and stayed till the Easter weekend. Both felt their relationship had strengthened. 'We have had a good time', Lawrence told Ottoline, 'really been people living together ... I am sad now, and want to weep in my corner, but it is largely with relief. I know Russell is with me, really, now' (ii. 312). Russell was more cautious, though he felt 'exalted' and taken 'out of myself', and had found Lawrence's view of human nature 'very congenial'. Given the man's 'pugnacity' however, Russell foresaw 'awful fights' over his generalisations from himself. Russell felt no desire for conflict with Ottoline, did not ever want to bang her about and did not think everybody a 'Tyger'. They argued about what she would be like if she lost control. Lawrence thought fierce; Russell thought still gentle, and that Lawrence too, beneath all his fierceness, had 'a fund of gentleness & universal love' of a kind 'just as deep as the tiger'. His sense of 'evil' was excessive, but nonetheless 'I feel he helps one to understand many things'.[5]

No sooner had Russell left on the Saturday than Barbara and Kot arrived bearing bottles of Chianti, as at Christmas, for a dinner on Sunday evening – 'all the hosts of Midian present' (ii. 312). (Were these the Meynells and their guests in the big house, or did Lawrence see his Easter dinner as a little circle of the faithful while the hosts of evil prowled and prowled around, as in the hymn

'Christian, dost thou see them'?) Eleanor Farjeon's description is of later occasions, but this must have been similar (minus a rumpus for once):

When we supped at Shed hall it was Lawrence, not Frieda, who dished up the meal in Viola's little kitchen, where he had painted all the common pots and jars with bright designs in stripes and spots. He made the simplicities of cottage life delightful, basting the mutton and stirring the onion sauce with the happy concentration of a child who is doing something it likes. Boiled onions did not contradict him, or baked lamb let fall the remarks that excited his nerves to the pitch that sent Frieda weeping, but unsubdued, out of the room.[6]

His irritability seems to have been well under control at Easter, except a little at Barbara's Hampstead rationality: 'I like her, but she gets on my nerves with her eternal: "but *do* you think" – "but, look here, *isn't* it rather that – – – – – – ." I want to say: "For Gods sake woman, stop haggling". And she is so deprecating, and so persistent. O God!' (ii. 313). He would rather be opposed than moderated. Conversely, he worried about Kot's massive inertia. 'You are getting simply a monolith. You *must* rouse yourself. You *must* do something – anything. Really it is a disgrace to be as inert as you are' (ii. 313). But it was a happy weekend – indeed, Barbara stayed on till the Thursday – and he liked Kot more than ever. The powers of darkness had not gone away (and he was reading Dostoevsky), but he felt that he was coming through.

Only he could not get well. He was in bed again the second week in April with the cold that felt like a sore throat in the belly, 'very horrid and tiring and irritating. I am afraid this house is damp. Frieda has had a very bad raw cold for the last two weeks again. I think soon we shall move from here – because of the dampness' (ii. 315). Might the 'monastic buildings' at Garsington be dryer (ii. 325), and (as he began 'Morgenrot') quieter?

For Viola's sister Madeline had let her cottage to Dollie Radford,[7] a 50–year-old poet and playwright (and friend of Constance Garnett) who had come down as a guest of the Meynells before Easter. She could only stay for short spells, since her husband the poet and Fabian Ernest Radford had become mentally unstable, and needed her care, but she invited Eleanor Farjeon to stay with her daughter Margaret in 'Rackham', remotest of the Meynell cottages – which one came to through the woods, and discovered 'like a secret' in a dip crowded with flowers, with a lawn and a little stream beyond. For the rest of April (once Lawrence was on his feet again) and most of May, there was 'a constant coming and going' between the cottages, meals in one or the other, and walks and conversations.[8]

Dollie described her first impressions to her son Maitland (the friend Bunny had gone walking with in Germany in 1912, now serving as a doctor in France).

[Lawrence] is a sweet man – so simple & kind, touchingly childlike, & brim full of sensibility & perception. I should think he understands most human matters at a first glance – just a genius & a very delicate & subtle nature. I find none of the roughness spoken of by Connie [Garnett].[9]

First impressions often tell one most about their recorder. Lawrence had clearly responded to her warmth and kindliness, and they became firm friends.

He also liked Eleanor very much, as his letter to Bunny shows. She was plain, and a late-developer (she admitted) at the age of thirty-four, but full of vitality and enthusiasm, and just beginning to publish poetry and fiction like her friend Viola. She had fallen in love with Edward Thomas, and also (fortunately) with his wife Helen and their children, and was moreover devoted to their friends the Robert Frosts, so she was in no danger of idolising Lawrence. She did not like his refusal to rein himself in, careless of creating embarrassment; but she accepted it along with all the things she did like about him and his work. Above all she was unafraid, which was always the way to win his respect. '[A]lthough he had the fiercest personality I had yet encountered, I was not shy or self-conscious with him; he braced me even when he damned my enthusiasms', in a voice of 'startling variety and range; in fury and excitement it ran the gamut from a bass growl to a shrill snarl'.[10] Through them would come more new friendships, with Maitland Radford, Eleanor's brother Bertie and his wife Joan. But the weekday quiet of Greatham was no more.

Moreover weekends became very crowded. 17–18 April, when Bunny and Birrell came, was a case in point:

To escape from visitors, I must go to Italy again. Madame Sowerby [Olivia Meynell] has been down – and McQueen [also a friend of Ottoline's, recently wounded at Ypres] – and God knows who.

... I am beginning to get unstuck from this place. There is too great a danger from invasion from the other houses. I cannot stand the perpetual wash of forced visitors, under the door. (ii. 323)

The Garsington scheme had come to nothing because the Morrells had received a swingeing estimate for the cost of conversion – not perhaps helped by Lawrence's (otherwise practical) suggestions that a bathroom would be invaluable, as would a partition of the big room to save heating so large a space and to give him somewhere to write (ii. 317). Though he now said that he could not have borne to be tied anyway, he was disappointed; and denounced the 'vile contractors' with characteristic extravagance. Perhaps they could have a couple of rooms in the gardener's cottage to tide them over? For he was definitely thinking of leaving Greatham now. He had got to page 40 of 'Morgenrot' – 'very good and rather terrible, and nobody will ever publish it' (ii. 325) – and a few days later he had revised up to page 388 of *The Rainbow*; but it was becoming harder to work. That same weekend Bertie and Joan Farjeon had also been down, and the seldom-seen Francis Meynell as well as all the rest of the family, and the folk in Rackham Cottage. Bunny describes being taken to 'Humphreys' on Saturday evening to pay his respects, and then having Sunday breakfast with 'the Poetess and the Patriarch' and all the daughters and son: 'the big room, with its Italian bric-à-brac and Morris patterns ... filled with dark madonna-like girls and women'; the poetess 'stretched on the couch' (she had been unwell and had only recently been fetched down by Viola); and Francis who had run three miles to mass and was received with 'benign and holy joy ... like to a Blake engraving'.[11] Later on Sunday Eleanor describes 'a great gathering on the lawns behind "Humphreys" for cricket, croquet and other games. Lawrence came to watch. It was as hot as midsummer.' Afterwards there was chatter in the sun; and at supper in Shed Hall, says Bunny, 'Frankie talked, and I talked' – and Lawrence grew ominously silent ...

On another occasion the house-party all went to Rackham Cottage for charades and songs:

Bertie and I contributed some numbers from the nonsense repertoire which we had invented to amuse our friends; Lawrence sang the first Negro Spirituals we had heard, and set our brains jingling with an American ballad on the murder of President McKinley with words of brutal jocularity sung to an air of lilting sweetness.[12]

By the end of April however there was less and less to sing about. Frieda's letters show increasing irritation. 'The Meynellage' were getting on her nerves, Barbara was 'a nothing' and Russell had not replied to her letter. (Lawrence hurriedly asked Ottoline to tell him to do so, 'or else she feels he is trying to insult her'; ii. 325.) After Bunny and Birrell's visit, 'There are still more Meynells. I try to dodge out of the house, but I get caught, like a mouse in a trap.' She adds, ominously, that Lawrence 'has been seedy, so he will make me cross'. (She had been cross to have been so seedy at Greatham herself.)[13] So the evidence of renewed quarrelling dates probably from the second half of April.

Meanwhile Ottoline was displeased by Lawrence's explanation of Maria's suicide attempt. It seemed to her 'pure fandango!'; besides, will was often necessary, for instance 'when one thinks of Desmond' (MacCarthy). Russell had to reassure her that Lawrence's charge was 'absurd': 'Of course you have a terrific will, but you don't use it tyrannously. Lawrence dislikes any will except his own, & he doesn't realize the place of will in the world. He seems to think instinct alone sufficient. I think his meditation of Satan will cure him of this view.' Then came the summons to London, to attend the Registrar's hearing. Russell felt it 'very unfortunate that he should be driven to hate society more than he already did', even though this might 'distract him from sex'. Ottoline, who had been reading *The Rainbow* at Buxton, had found it 'too *entirely* sexual', and the psychology too influenced by Frieda, though she also thought the novel very good in parts.[14] At the end of the month came the expedition to Worthing by motor-bus, where Lawrence had his horrific vision of the soldiers, and of a hellish England, 'creeping and viscous, and insect-teeming'.

May therefore began badly. Sending the words of 'President McKinley' to Eleanor he told her he felt 'rude and cross' (ii. 333). Though Ottoline wrote him a letter he really appreciated, his philosophy kept 'getting stuck' (ii. 334), and he replied with a rather laconic note. On 6 May, the day before leaving for London and the hearing at Somerset House, he suddenly decided to accompany Eleanor on a walk she had planned, by way of the old Roman track over the Downs to Chichester. One suspects he needed to get away.

Having done so, however, he was at once 'in his angelic, child-like mood'. They got lost several times but did not care, sang 'scraps of songs,' 'seldom touched on the things that irked him unendurably', indeed talked only when they felt like it. 'We must be springlike!' he cried, and broke green branches to stick around their hats. The afternoon grew very hot, and he chanted – to a world pub-less for miles – 'I want my shandygaff'. When they got to the village of East Dean, past a tractor working in the fields, came the only discordant note of the day. Lawrence dropped his voice to say he *knew* the people who lived in such places, what they think and do, 'as I know my own skin'. His voice grew shrill 'I *hate* them!' But in the pub, as he ordered the shandies and addressed a few remarks to the locals his accent acquired 'a tang of dialect, whether deliberate or instinctive I don't know'. It is a sudden reminder of how far the author of *The Rainbow*, like its heroine, had travelled from Tom Brangwen's country. They were both tired (and Eleanor blistered) by the time they reached Chichester, had a meal, found her a lodging and waited on the station for his train back to Pulborough; but their talk grew more serious. What did she want most, he asked: 'A big personal experience? Or to take part in some great social upheaval?' She said the first, which he thought might be right for her. 'But why not both?' Why not indeed, except for the hint that the two things seemed at odds now for him.[15]

He and Frieda went up to London the next day (Friday the 7th) though the interview at Somerset House would not be until Monday; putting up this time at the flat of a young architect Basil Proctor whom they had met at Greatham. That night they dined with Murry and Kot at a restaurant and were disconcerted to discover that Katherine, who had been back for most of April, had gone off to Paris again – unable to write in Jack's two rooms, even after he had done them up. Murry was irritable at what he thought were their suspicions (especially Frieda's) that she had really gone to be with Carco again. The next evening his dislike of Frieda flared up. He had invited them to supper, he wrote Katherine, 'thinking that I ought to be nice to them', but they turned up very late, and with another man (presumably Proctor). For Murry, 'to find Frieda fatuously laughing on the doorstep, as though it were so very Bohemian to be an hour and a half late' was 'too much. After an hour of it, she decided that I was dull, and to prove to me what a party should be began to sing German sentimental songs in that idiotic voice of hers.' Lawrence kept on about the good times they had had in Buckinghamshire.

He must be blind to certain things ... But I do like Lawrence; though I *feel* that he is deteriorating – really getting feeble. Frieda is the Red Woman, the Whore of Babylon, the Abomination of Desolations that was to Fornicate in the High Places, and the Holy of Holies. I've just remembered that bit of Revelations – isn't it really Frieda, spiritually speaking?

Three days later he repaid Frieda's suspicions – and her greedy wolfing of most of the charcuterie before anyone else had a chance – with suspicions of his own. He found Lawrence alone, Frieda having gone off to the theatre, presumably with Proctor:

He was very sad. Poor devil he is so lonely, with that bitch of a Frieda, always playing traitor, and hurting him in every secret and intimate part of his soul. It's no good until he can get away from her – she's really wearing him out. No, it depressed me terribly to be with him last night. It was all so unreasonable & cruel ... But I think I shall ask him to come away with me for a fortnight's holiday during this summer to see if I can urge him to the point of leaving her.[16]

Again there is no telling what exactly Murry's accusation of treachery amounted to, and he is hardly an unbiased witness. (His idea of the marriage however: Frieda continually treacherous, Lawrence under her thumb and deteriorating as a result, would be fixed from now on.) Clearly however the Lawrences' relationship was under considerable strain once more, and she was defiant about having a good time in spite of him. He cannot have been good company while he was battling his powers of darkness, or when he was ill. She didn't like his new intellectual friends, adding Barbara to the list now of those she thought looked down on her. The rows at Greatham which Viola 'overlooked and underheard' and Eleanor ascribed to Frieda's contradictions,[17] would have been not only because of the Meynell invasions, but also because of Frieda's growing impatience with his pontificating and with those who found it impressive. Most of all, one suspects, she had got bored with Greatham, and when it began to liven up with flocks of young people in April this must have whetted her appetite for a jollier life. This probably explains why they had come to London earlier than necessary – and there may have been words on the Wednesday evening, making Lawrence suddenly decide to take his walk. Flirting and going out with one of Viola's young men would have been a natural one-in-the-eye for Lawrence.

Lawrence took her behaviour badly, though he kept up a front. After the examination at Somerset House, which he hated, they went home via Brighton, where they spent two days with Cynthia who had gone there with her children while Beb was in Flanders. Lawrence had written just before the Chichester walk, asking what had happened to her since their visit to Chichester together, in February. It was unusual for him to take the initiative, confirming that he felt in need of friendship; and she must immediately have suggested they come to see her. Apparently all went well – but he would later confess that as they lay talking on the cliffs the following day, he had felt suicidal. Cynthia was quite unaware of this, or indeed of any strain between the Lawrences. She thought them 'the most intoxicating company in the world. I never hoped to have such mental pleasure with anyone.' She was astonished at his 'X-ray' ability to make 'the most subtly true analyses of people, e.g. Papa and Mamma whom he has only seen for a few moments', and felt there was something significant in their lives that made hers suddenly seem superficial and blind. As at Kingsgate, she found herself fond of Frieda. 'She has spontaneousness and warm cleverness, and such adoration and understanding of him.' The Lawrences were clearly putting on a show, though not necessarily a false one, warmed by her obvious admiration for them *both*. They went to a cinema after dinner. After breakfast with the children next day they had a 'very interesting' philosophical discussion. About 11 a.m. they all three walked to the top of the cliff, lay there 'for about two hours and had one of the talks I shall always remember, though alas I could no more record it than a thrush's song!' Lawrence showed sympathetic interest in the 'wild, monkey mood' of little John, his impish defiance, and 'peculiar, indescribable detachment'.[18] But one gets a sudden glimpse of the abyss there could be between the 'inner' and the 'outer' Lawrence at this time, and of the need to proportion the one by the other in imagining him. For, he told her later: 'I did not take much notice of what I said, because my subconsciousness was occupied with the idea of how pleasant it would be to walk over the edge of the cliff. There seemed another, brighter sort of world away below, and this world on top is all torture and a flounder of stupidity' (ii. 335). The odd tone at the start of his letter, responding to her request to write down his advice about John, was partly his sense that he *had* put on a show; and partly because he was not sure how serious she was; and partly because he had lost confidence in himself – 'probably everything I say is pure bosh, a tangle of theory of my own' – though once he got going he talked himself into faith again, if with rather hollow hope. By the time they got back to Greatham it had been decided that Frieda would take rooms for herself in Hampstead, though they applied too late for the ones she wanted.

II Getting 'unstuck' from Greatham

The reason given out was so as to be near the children,[19] and this probably did figure largely in her conscious motivation. The quarrelling must also have been stoked by the claim for the costs of the divorce which had confirmed Weekley's right to forbid her access, and now seemed about to swallow their last hope of a bit more money – confirming her sense of being wronged, with everyone and everything against her including Lawrence. With Weekley, and with her family in Germany, she had been beloved and idolised and well-off. Whose fault was it, she may have felt, that she was now poor, childless and surrounded by people who were hostile to her as a German, and looked down on her as a person? By this time 'the children' had, while never ceasing to be a genuine distress, also become a language for more general discontent and irritation with her lot, and with him; and his with her. This is clear in the letters of both.

DHL: Friends are looking for another place for Frieda, also in Hampstead. Probably she will go and stay alone in them for some time, if she gets them. She spends her time thinking herself a wronged, injured and aggrieved person, because of the children, and because she is a German. I am angry and bored. I wish she would have her rooms in Hampstead, and leave me alone. (ii. 343)

Frieda: The hate of the Germans is getting so strong ... I am going to have a tiny flat in Hampstead, I think, I simply must be by myself sometimes, L is very wearing and also I will see the children on their way to school, that they do not get used to *not* seeing me ... But the deep rage I am in, when I think, that this is the law of man; and if I were a prostitute the children would be *mine* and a man would be obliged to pay me ... (ii. 344)

DHL: Isn't it a funny thing, if a woman has got her children, she doesn't care about them, and if she has a man, she doesn't care about him, she only wants her children. There is something in the talk about female perversity. Frieda only cares about her children now. It is as if women – or she – persisted in being unfortunate and hopelessly unsatisfied: if a man wants much, she becomes violently a mother and a man-hater, if her children want much, she becomes a violent disciple of 'love' as against domesticity or maternity. What a miserable creature! (ii. 345)

(An impartial observer might question the demandingness of both.) Lawrence even began to wonder aloud to Ottoline about his own monogamy. 'One tries hard to stick to ones ideal of one man-one woman, in love', but perhaps Ottoline was right, 'and one should go to different persons to get companionship for the different sides of ones nature' (ii. 345) – though that would risk trouble from Frieda's double standard about freedom, claiming wide latitude for herself, but fiercely jealous when other women showed interest in him.

In any case he could not leave Greatham just yet, even though Ottoline, wanting to help, invited them to Garsington where the Morrells had moved on 17 May. For Viola's sister Monica had had a nervous breakdown after the failure of her marriage to Dr Caleb Saleeby. Frieda, who disliked all illness, described this as merely 'hysterical ... she has no interest at all in anything, it's the spring, I suppose and nothing for her to do – and no man –' (ii. 344); but Lawrence was much more sympathetic. He went with Monica to Bognor about 19 May, in the car provided to take her out of herself: a windy day with an opalescent sea, misty, fit for legions of ghosts to come over from France. Women seemed fascinated by a soldier with an amputated leg – a portent to whose significance he would return. He had a pang of fear about the new Coalition Government, which was widely thought to herald conscription (ii. 342–3). Garsington would have to wait, since he felt he owed it to the Meynells to help Monica:

I won't move from here now until I leave for good. I look to escape during the next two or three weeks. I want to go away. The whole Meynellàge is down here – I like them – but they are so flusterous – and then Monica with her breakdown takes refuge in me, and is very heavy. It is altogether a crisis. And I must see this crisis through. (ii. 345)

An additional factor was 10-year-old Mary Saleeby, who had been allowed to run wild because her mother was so miserable and preoccupied. Described by Bunny as 'gnome-like', and by Eleanor (who knew her better, and was fond of her) as 'a rough-and-tumble ragamuffin little rebel ... undisciplined and beyond Monica's management, but ... full of strong and original qualities and gifts', she spent all her time on the nearby farm and was only interested in becoming a farmer. The clan grew worried, and decided that she should be sent to St Paul's School for Girls in London – only, she would need some preparation. She had taught herself to read and 'could *just* write', but she had never been to school. Lawrence stepped into the breach and agreed to give her $3\frac{1}{2}$ hours every morning for at least a month: 'for the child's sake, for nothing else', he insisted (ii. 340).[20] It is clear from Mary in person, and from one of her notebooks that survives, how careful Lawrence was to start from her, and her interests, rather than ideas of what she ought to know. Those who met Lawrence when they were children recall that he never talked down from a grown-up height, nor tried to lower himself to a child's level, but inclined courteously as to a smaller equal – and then, when properly acquainted, became great fun. (When Dollie and Eleanor spoke of him at this time as 'child-like' himself, they had in mind a spontaneity and unguardedness, without pretence or disguise – to which children instantly responded.) He clearly respected the 'otherness' of the child in practice as in theory;[21] and treated her as Tom treats little Anna, though his unhappiness with Frieda at the time had its analogies with Will's. He helped her put herself on paper with her own simple integrity. It was good teaching – and she remembered the tone and effect of it vividly more than seventy years later.

He had already made a herbaceous border for Viola; now he distracted himself from his troubles by gardening at Rackham Cottage, and 'only then' was he happy (ii. 344). Viola and Ivy Low had come to Shed Hall for Whitsun; and Rackham had become 'a seething pot' with six children and six grown-ups since the Lucases too were back for the holiday. Also, the Meynell parents came down. 'Monica gets better, but there are still great and wearying consultations. I wonder how long we shall stay now' (ii. 346). In fact, Frieda left for London the next day, 27 May, to put up with Barbara while looking for 'her' rooms in Hampstead. Wilfrid Meynell 'was pathetically grateful' that Lawrence was prepared to stay and help with Mary, and said so in front of Eleanor, but afterwards Lawrence 'exploded' that he did not want gratitude; 'somebody has got to'.[22]

There are glimpses of his unhappiness and loneliness, but also stubborn faith, in his response to the poetry he was sent by Eleanor (ii. 340–1) and by Margaret Radford. From both, he picked out poems about loneliness; though à propos of Margaret's, he distinguished a state 'where one lives in the presence of things blest, in the knowledge of the Infinite, the Eternal'; from loneliness, which 'is part of temporality and partiality'. It is we who confuse the two, and it is the knowledge of God, the 'Absolute', the 'Eternity', 'just this which is *not* loneliness, which avails against all loneliness' (ii. 350). Perhaps it did. On 29 May he wrote to Forster that 'there is a darkness between us all, separating us' (ii. 347). At the end of the month he heard about the termination of Russell's Fellowship at Trinity because he would not promise to spend his time on mathematics and philosophy rather than political work in opposition to the war. Lawrence urged him to see 'Entire separation' as a necessary stage before new life could start:

If they hound you out of Trinity, so much the better ... One must be entirely cast forth ... the darkness thrusts more and more between us all, like a sword, cutting us off entirely each from the other ... After this we shall know the change ... Only wait, and be ready ... When everything else is gone, and there is no touch nor sense of each other left, there is always the sense of God, of the Absolute. Our sense of the Absolute is the only sense left to us. (ii. 347–8)

Russell told Ottoline 'I *feel* he is right, that I should have 10 times the energy if I were done with respectability ... I like Lawrence's letter.'[23] On the last day of May, having made just two minor changes in the last four paragraphs of the *Rainbow* which clearly still represented his faith, he sent the typescript to Pinker.

As Frieda stayed away, Lawrence's tone about her grew more irritable, and his soul became 'filled with corrosive darkness, and cut off from everybody' (ii. 352). On 2 June he told Forster that Frieda was in town 'looking for her flat

– unless a bomb has dropped on her – killed by her own countrymen – it is the kind of fate she is cut out for' (ii. 351). The cross joke is however also anxious, for Zeppelins had attacked London the night before. And by 5 June Frieda was back, having found a flat for £36 a year, 'right on Hampstead Heath' in the Vale of Health, 'that we' – suddenly –'have almost taken. I feel that next winter I must be a good bit in London, for work' (ii. 354). When Cynthia Asquith motored over on the 5th with her friend Harold 'Bluetooth' Baker (Liberal M.P. and member of the Army Council), rather apprehensive about how he and the Lawrences would get on, all went well: 'Bluetooth did like him, to my satisfaction, and he didn't much mind the exuberant Hun.' They found Lawrence, walking with Wilfrid Meynell in the garden, 'looking – I'm afraid – very ill, but very picturesque and arresting in corduroy coat, with tawny beard and those curiously significant eyes'. She too was struck by the variability of his voice 'with its layers of harshness and softness ... every inch of his body talks with his tongue, and vividly, too'; and by his unusual ability to blend earnestness with whimsicality, humour with resentment. On his typewriter that day was 'a war story coming to life'. (He sent away 'England, My England' the next day, see pp. 252–4.) Cynthia did not, however, take to the Meynells. She thought Viola much the most human, but admitted bias, since Viola said *she* was 'the prettiest person she had ever seen'.[24]

On 8 June the 'first quarter' of 'Morgenrot' went to Russell and to Forster. Russell was not to 'think it bosh' or say 'there are beautiful things in it, or something like that. But help me, and tell me where I can say the thing better' (ii. 357–8). Having warned earlier, '*Never* expose yourself to the pack' (ii. 352), he was worried by Russell's attack on Lord Northcliffe in the *Labour Leader*. (The *Daily Mail* led the patriotic fervour for the war, and Northcliffe was to take charge of government propaganda in 1918.) Russell must not get into trouble now, but save himself for a bigger campaign to come.

Since Monica had taken Mary to the seaside for a fortnight, the Lawrences were now free to take up the invitation to Garsington, and disconcerted Ottoline by planning to arrive on Saturday the 12th and stay till her birthday on the 16th. 'What shall I do with them all that time?' she cried, begging Russell to come and help. He was also worried, because he could not 'make head or tail of Lawrence's philosophy. I dread talking to him about it. It is not sympathetic to me.' However in his next letter, though it still seemed 'rather uneducated stuff':

I believe there is a great deal in it – only the form is bad, & he doesn't know how to say only what is to the purpose. He will be angry & fight like a devil. I think the imagination out of which it springs is good – rather Blake-ish. But he lacks art, & loses intensity through lengthiness. However, I must read it again before I can feel sure about it.[25]

He agreed to help at Garsington. The Cannans, whom the Lawrences may have visited on the way, came along for the weekend, and Russell arrived as they left. The Morrells were doing up the old house; so guests were persuaded to help decorate the Red drawing-room, outlining the beams and the panels in gold paint. Lawrence, says Ottoline's journal, 'did his far quicker and straighter than any of us', and enjoyed it, but Frieda 'sat on the table in the middle of the room, swinging her legs and laughing and mocking at us ... She has a terrible irritant quality, and enjoys tormenting, and she liked to taunt me because I was taking trouble to make the house nice.' This was after the weekend, since Russell figures in the scene, up a ladder, nearly expiring from the heat. As soon became apparent, the real trouble had little to do with Ottoline's decoration, but had probably been building up for some time. As signs since February might have warned, Frieda grew aggressive whenever Lawrence got the attention and she felt undervalued.

She even said in a loud, challenging voice, 'I am just as remarkable and important as Lorenzo'. Indeed, in all our talks she was very aggressive and self-assertive. I began to fear she would make it difficult to be friends with him, she was already turning him against Bertie because Bertie didn't flatter her.

The significant phrase is 'all our talks', for it must have been then that Ottoline and Russell showed their admiration for Lawrence, and their low opinion of Frieda's intelligence – which she would especially resent from Ottoline. Otherwise the memories of the visit seem lively enough. Lawrence made a little wooden arbour to be covered with climbing roses; and there were the charades that both he and the Cannans loved. He read Swinburne aloud and told stories of his early life in Notts dialect. Little Julian (then 9) remembered his gentleness and his 'attentive smiling look when he talked to you'. None of these would irritate Frieda – but she did have a good opinion of her own very different kind of mind, and wanted it respected. Ottoline had been irritated by her letters because she 'thinks herself so clever'; but though calling her Nietzschean showed some sense of cultural difference, Ottoline still thought her 'a clever fool'. Frieda, for her part, had exempted Ottoline from her previous irritation with Kot, Forster and Russell, because she had been so ready to write to Weekley about the children – but was clearly turning against her now. Meanwhile Ottoline was unaware (she says) that there was tension between the Lawrences too, but:

apparently she became jealous and they had a miserable time together, fighting and quarrelling all night. He came down on the morning of their last day looking whipped, forlorn, and crestfallen, and she went off in a high temper to London. I shall always see that unhappy, distraught, pathetic figure standing in the hall hesitating whether he should remain here or whether he should follow her to London. Philip strongly urged him to assert himself and leave her. Of course he didn't ...

Russell, too, expressed disappointment that Lawrence would not stay. It had not been much of a birthday for Ottoline but, said Russell, 'In spite of Mrs Lawrence, it was really a *very* happy time for me', especially the evening when they had managed some time alone.[26]

Ottoline would be sure, now, that no matter how fierce the rows between the Lawrences or his abuse of Frieda to others, 'she will always win if she wants to', since 'however much he may rebel and complain', he seemed unable to leave her or face life alone. Ottoline expanded and rewrote her original journal entry to clarify the diagnosis which she formed later with Murry: a weak, gentle and sensitive Lawrence, whose nerves the constant battling with Frieda would wear out in time, and who would have to kill 'all his gentle tender side to go on with her', yet could never bring himself to go – but the outline must have formed that Wednesday. What she wrote to Russell at the time however, was that she 'didn't mind Mrs L except that it made me awfully miserable for poor Lawrence, who looked so unhappy and tired out by her. She is a mad Egotist. I wish she could die or go off with another man who would beat her!'[27] There must certainly have been a flaming row when Lawrence got back to Greatham.

On Saturday, however, Cynthia suddenly arrived in a car for tea, with not only John but a wounded Beb,[28] who had requisitioned one of the Downing Street motors. He had had a very lucky escape in Flanders: a splinter of shrapnel had grazed his lip and broken several teeth, but after a dental operation the previous Monday he was physically on the way to recovery. Lawrence, however, drew a contrast between his physical and his psychological state, for:

all his soul is left at the war. The war is the only reality to him. All this here is unreal, this England: only the trenches are Life to him. Cynthia is very unhappy – he is not even aware of her existence. He is spell-bound by the fighting line. He ought to die. It all seemed horrid, like hypnotism. (ii. 359–60)

It was a phenomenon to be repeated in every home where someone came back from the trenches, unable to share his appalling experience with those at home. 'He ought to die' is remarkably brutal – especially of a man he liked – but it is the remark of the author of 'England, My England', who had long ago maintained that the real tragedy would not be the dead, who were out of it, but the souls so maimed by violence that their inner life would be crippled forever.

That same evening Russell came again as he had promised – but naturally apprehensive now of what he might find. He had wanted to put the visit off, but lacked the courage because he was afraid it might hurt and 'make for a coolness, which I should mind dreadfully'. In fact, as far as his relationship with Lawrence was concerned, this meeting turned out to be the high-water mark, for it produced a plan to campaign in public together. Lawrence explained excitedly to Ottoline:

We think to have a lecture hall in London in the autumn, and give lectures: he on Ethics, I on Immortality: also to have meetings, to establish a little society or body around a *religious belief which leads to action*. We must centre in the Knowledge of the Infinite, of God. Then from this Centre each one of us must work to put the temporal things of our own natures and of our own circumstances in accord with the Eternal God we know. You must be president. You must preside over our meetings. You must be the centre-pin that holds us together ... (ii. 359)

The metaphor betrays his sense that they were likely to pull in different directions. Yet he hoped he was beginning to overcome the anti-religious worldliness of Russell who '*will* – apart from philosophical mathematics – be so temporal, so immediate'; but now (thought Lawrence) was coming to have a real 'belief in Eternity ... the absolute, an existence in the Infinite. It is very good and I am very glad' (ii. 358).

Russell saw the plan rather differently, and had America as well as London in his sights. 'I like the idea of analysing political institutions & beliefs – letting in the light of reason and liberty on cobwebbed caverns of superstition – Whether it is country air or America & Lawrence I don't know, but I feel full of happiness & hope and life.' They proposed to charge a guinea to cover the cost of the hall. There is just a glimpse of 'the infinite' – in secular terms – but it is still clear that the religious emphasis was almost all Lawrence's:

We talked of a plan for lecturing in the autumn on his religion, politics in the light of religion, & so on. I believe something might be made of it. I could make a splendid course on political ideas: morality, the State, property, marriage, war, taking them to their roots in human nature, & showing how each is a prison for the infinite in us. And leading on to the hope of a happier world.

He had also been reading 'Morgenrot' again, and changing his mind about it. 'Lawrence is *splendid*. I like his philosophy *very much* [underlined twice] now that I have read more. It is only the beginning that is poor.' By 24 June Ottoline was also finding its second chapter 'very wonderful' – and very like Russell. So, perhaps the idea of the three holding together in so public an enterprise did have some chance.

However, Russell that Sunday had a more threatening experience: his first sight of physical menace in the Lawrence marriage. (It is also our first evidence of this since Frieda struck Lawrence in Irschenhausen.) For, when Lawrence in his excitement sat down to write a long letter to Ottoline, Frieda

possessed herself of it & tore it up. Then he wrote another, which I hope will reach you [i.e. the letter quoted above]. He was *very* angry. She appeared on the little wall by the flower-bed, jeering. He said 'Come off that, lass, or I'll hit thee in the mouth. You've gone too far this time'.[29]

This gives rather a poignancy to the hopes of making Garsington the centre of Rananim which figure so hopefully in the rewritten letter:

That wonderful lawn, under the ilex trees, with the old house and its exquisite old front – it is *so* remote, so perfectly a small world to itself, where one *can* get away from the temporal things to consider the big things. We must draw together. Russell and I have really got somewhere. We must bring the Murrys in. Don't be doubtful of them. And Frieda will come round soon. It is the same thing with her as with all the Germans – all the world – she hates the Infinite, my immortality. But she will come round. (ii. 359)

That must have been more difficult to write a second time – but Lawrence knew his Frieda, and how their rows cleared the air; and come round she did before too long, though not completely.

On 21 June Cynthia sent a car to fetch them for the day to Littlehampton. She wanted Lawrence and Beb to have a talk, so she 'lingered behind with the Hun', and Frieda was able to unburden herself about 'her difficulties as the artist's wife' and how 'Lady Ottoline, etc., were horrid to her, treating her as an appendage and explaining her husband to her as being dropped straight from the sky.' Beb liked Lawrence, despite being told that ' "destruction" is the end, and not the means to an end, in the minds of soldiers', who suffer from 'subconscious "blood-lust"' – but unfortunately, like Russell, he found 'no room in his heart' for Frieda.[30] Shortly afterwards however, having spent a day away from all Meynells and unburdened herself to Cynthia, Frieda regained enough perspective to write to Ottoline.

Thank you for asking me to Garsington – I have been very cross and very miserable about you and L and me – When we came to you last time we were very antagonistic he and I and I was not at all happy. I thought you idealised him and you had a sort of unholy soulfulness between you that seems to me quite contrary to all good life – Say I was jealous, I may have been – but it was not only that – I know you are big and generous at the bottom and I want us to be friends – You see L. and I really love each other at the bottom, and he is so furious with me because of this very fact sometimes – You can help us a lot if you want to – But if you leave me out then there can be no good any-where it seems to me – But perhaps L. will come to you alone next time – We all want love and the good things to be, don't we? I know you don't mind my saying exactly what I think –

But Ottoline did mind. Sending the letter to Russell on 3 July she commented, 'rather crazy isn't she?'; and Russell replied that the letter was 'certainly rather mad'. He likened Frieda to a 'bouncing' German girl he knew who was 'healthy, animal, brutal, without a trace of humanity or any kind of moral feeling'.[31] They had cause to be offended. But so had Frieda.

By 8 July she was in London, arranging the flat; and Lawrence, left alone at Greatham again, had scribbled irritable comments all over the proposed outline of Russell's lectures. Though he would stay at Greatham another three weeks, and keep the idea of the lectures going for a while, in fact it was the beginning of the end of both.

III   More Radical Reconstruction?

His criticisms of Russell's idea of 'Philosophy of Social Reconstruction' open out the central difference, implicit already in their differing accounts of the original idea, between the rational and secular humanist and the 'passionately religious man'. Lawrence was mistaken (like Ottoline) in thinking that he could change Russell in this respect. Once formulated, moreover, the differences proved fatal to the enterprise. Each talked better in his own language than he listened to another kind — no infrequent characteristic of strong and independent minds; and once forcibly revealed, the gap became entrenched, unbridgeable.

Yet they agreed that the disease of modern life was (in Russell's words) the 'disintegration' brought about by 'subjectivism'. Lawrence wrote 'I think this is best' after the section on 'Subjectivism' and 'This too is good' after the section on 'War', both of which show his influence.[32] But these come *after* the outline of Russell's 'progressive' critique of social institutions. At the centre of Lawrence's criticism was a valid perception: that while they agreed about the disease, Russell saw the remedy in reforming social institutions, in the belief that greater freedom would lead to greater happiness; whereas Lawrence started from the need to reawaken those inner impulses in human beings which were most radically opposed to subjectivity, or there could be no reintegration of society. He begged Russell not to be 'angry that I have scribbled all over your work', but what Russell had written was

all social criticism; it isn't social reconstruction. You must take a plunge into another element if it is to be social reconstruction.

Primarily, you must allow and acknowledge and be prepared to proceed from the fundamental impulse in all of us towards The Truth, the fundamental passion also, the *most fundamental* passion in man, for Wholeness of Movement, Unanimity of Purpose, Oneness in Construction. *This is the principle of Construction*. The rest is all criticism, destruction. (ii. 361)

All Lawrence's criticisms originate in this: that if subjectivism *be* the evil, Russell is treating the symptoms rather than the disease in seeking to reform what he called 'The old cohesions: The State, Property, The Churches, Law and Morality, Marriage. All based on Power, not on Liberty and Love'. All do indeed 'want fundamental reconstruction', but what then is *fundamental?* It cannot be the desire for the liberty of the individual, since that, unchecked, *is* subjectivism. The check cannot be Russell's 'interest in others', because why should there be any interest in others in a subjective world? And if, as Russell seems to get round to believing in the end, there is an 'impulse of growth and creation' in human beings, an 'instinct' which needs 'spiritual freedom', 'love leading to children, and work which gives an outlet to their creative impulse' – Russell's final section 'Life made whole' – then what kind of impulse is it and how can it be awakened?[33] So while Lawrence urges '*Do, do* get these essays ready, for the love of God', they must go to the root of the disease, and above all 'you *must* put in the *positive idea*' (ii. 361). For Lawrence, it only becomes possible to lecture and convince others because there is in everybody (at whatever level) an impulse to truth, though 'the truth is a growing organism – or our conception of it is'. Moreover he thinks 'true' morality and law begin from a desire to create a better Whole, since all human beings have (he believes) 'the unanimous impulse, the impulse towards a unanimous movement. It isn't *the others* we are interested in, it *is The Whole*'.[34] How but by believing in and appealing to such an impulse, could people be persuaded to reconstruct society into new forms of integration, instead of the disintegrating subjectivity of the present? (In Lawrence's terms, where the individuation of the Son has run to excess, the impulse to unity, togetherness, of the Father must be reactivated.) He wants Russell to begin from and constantly appeal to these positive impulses, instead of merely negative criticism of the defective forms of social organisation we have now. Russell might not be too pleased to see his manuscript treated so, but there seems nothing fatally objectionable in this criticism.

He must have jibbed more, however, as Lawrence's 'religious' thinking opened out. Russell had conceded that 'Religion, in some form, seems necessary to a good society or a good individual life', meaning by religion 'devotion to an end outside the individual life, and even, in some sense, outside human life – like God or truth or art.' For Lawrence however, the religious sense was no mere ingredient of a good individual or social life, it was *the* condition for vital growth. For,

what is the principle of growth: is it not the conscience prescience of [sic] that which is to be; in the grown tissue is all the ungrown tissue of all time: this ungrown tissue *knows* its own relations: this knowledge in us I call the sense of truth. But it is as real, much realer, than all the tangible or obvious impulses we talk of.

One step more, and 'There is no living society possible but one which is held together by a great religious idea.' So 'The State *must* represent the deepest philosophical or religious belief.' Where Russell writes 'Some men can be happy through religion, but they are few', Lawrence counters: 'This is subjective religion. But unless the religious idea be living & extant, no one is happy.' Russell could attack the Christian creed or the Church with Lawrence's blessing; 'But one & all', he insisted, 'we must act from a profound religious belief – not individual.'[35]

From such a stance, too, particular disagreements might follow. Russell, progressively, wanted as little of the State as possible, with men belonging to all sorts of different groupings across geographic frontiers; Lawrence thought states should be founded on communal beliefs. Russell thought cruelty, envy, love of power 'almost always the result of a life in which some vital instinct is balked', so these could be 'cured by giving a free life to everyone'. Lawrence, with his newly focused sense of evil, thought they could only be combated by finding ways to 'educate the sense of truth & justice, & train us all to act from this supreme impulse'. Russell, predictably, noted: 'Mutual liberty now demanded, makes old form of marriage impossible', and opposed both monogamy and prostitution in favour of forms of common life which allowed 'some tolerance of light relations as experiments'. Lawrence, no less predictably, thought: 'The desire for monogamy is profound in us. But the most difficult thing in the world is to find a mate ... A man alone is only fragmentary – also a woman. *Completeness is in marriage*. But State-marriage is a lie.'[36]

Yet it might not have been disastrous that they set out from different ends of a problem on whose cause they were in complete agreement, or even that they came to different conclusions in some respects. Nor did Lawrence think it so, as his urging Russell to continue shows. But Russell was not used to being disagreed with so ferociously and radically. It had happened once before, with Wittgenstein, and he had been profoundly disturbed. (But Wittgenstein at least spoke a similar language.) He told Ottoline that Lawrence was 'disgusted' with his outline because 'it is not mystical & Blake-ish enough'. The 'impulse towards the truth' Lawrence insisted on, seemed to Russell:

merely an impulse to mistake his imaginations for the truth. He talks of a desire for one-ness with others which he believes to be the same as 'the impulse to truth'. I don't believe these things exist in most people. But I find those who have a strong imagination generally read their own natures into other people, instead of getting at other people by impartial observation. Lawrence is just as ferocious a critic as Wittgenstein, but I thought W. right & I think L. wrong. He is coming to see me Sat. I dread it. I don't know whether I shall still be able to feel any faith in my own ideas after arguing with him, although my reason is all against him ... I am depressed, partly by Lawrence's criticisms. I feel a worm, a useless creature ...

Yet if the impulse toward truth and the desire for oneness with others are subjective illusions, what *is* the point of lecturing, let alone trying to convince an audience that they are suffering from the disease of subjectivity and should espouse love and mutual liberty instead? Keynes, similarly, thought Russell absurd to believe the world irrational, yet think he could change it by reasoning. (Is *that* not to read the self into others? Or is there a desire for truth after all, that is not subjective?)[37]

Frieda had gone to London again to see to the new flat, staying with Dollie Radford. Lawrence went up for the weekend of 10–11 July, and took Russell to meet the (reunited) Murrys and Kot in the Law Bureau, 'all sitting together in a bare office high up, next door to the Holborn Restaurant, with the windows shut, smoking Russian cigarettes without a moment's intermission, idle & cynical. I thought Murry *beastly* & the whole atmosphere of the place dead and putrefying.' They also went to the zoo, before going to the Radfords. It was not a disastrous day for their personal relationship, but at the end of 'a terrific argument' Russell told Lawrence they should act independently.

His case was a good one – from a rationalist point of view. He understood, also, what was involved in bringing about political change, but Lawrence on politics seemed 'so wild that I could not formally work with him'. To someone of Russell's 'scientific temper' and 'respect for fact' Lawrence was 'undisciplined in thought, & mistakes wishes for facts. He is also muddle-headed. He says "facts" are quite unimportant, only "truths" matter.' He even said London was a fact not a truth and did not really exist, and that if people came to see this they would pull it down. (Yet T. S. Eliot with whom, and his new wife Vivien, Russell dined on the 13th, and who was so promising a student of Bradley, would also call London, in a poet's language, an 'Unreal city'.) Russell now thought Lawrence 'a little mad & not quite honest', needing to learn 'the lesson of individual impotence. And he regards all my attempts to make him acknowledge facts as mere timidity, lack of courage to think boldly, self-indulgence in pessimism.' The gap between their ideas of what needed to be done had widened; and now Russell had talked himself into simply disqualifying Lawrence's criticism that he lacked any radically positive vision. The would-be reformer could no longer work with the would-be revolutionary, and neither could adjust to the other's language. When Russell attacked Lawrence with his considerable forensic ability, neither came out well. He had complained that Lawrence took him too literally, and so misunderstood his irony, but he failed to see his own literalness when he challenged Lawrence to abolish London by preaching in Trafalgar Square, and Lawrence 'began to shuffle'. He had also accused Lawrence of lacking humour, but saw none himself when, having at last hammered 'a glimmer of the facts' into Lawrence's head 'he gets discouraged, & says he will go to the South Sea Islands & bask in the sun with 6 native wives. He is tough work. The trouble with him is a tendency to mad exaggeration.' And the trouble with Russell ...[38]

It is not too difficult to see from both sides now, but Lawrence was the juster when writing to Ottoline after getting back to Greatham – and infinitely juster than Russell's later accounts.[39] Indeed he still believed that they would work together.

He won't accept in his philosophy the Infinite, the Boundless, the Eternal, as the real starting point, and I think, whosoever will really set out on the journey towards Truth and the real end must do this, now. But I didn't quarrel with him. We have almost sworn Blutbruderschaft. We will set out together, he and I. We shall really be doing something, in the autumn.

He himself shrank from the idea of lecturing because he was 'very shy' and 'It will be horrible to stand up and say the things I feel most vitally, before an audience ... To have to speak in the body is a violation to me', whereas 'I am safe and remote, when I write' (ii. 363). But it had to be done.

Moreover, Lawrence proved able to learn from Russell's challenge to his religious attitude – not that he would change his basic view any more than Russell would, but he saw now that its Christian language was unnecessary and misleading. Russell had lent him John Burnet's *Early Greek Philosophy* (1892), and this had an immediate and profound effect upon him. For he discovered philosophical forebears who reassured him at this critical time that his way of thinking had an even longer tradition than Russell's; but he also became convinced that their 'elemental' terms might be a better language to communicate his thought than the Christian ones he had been using. In these pre-Socratic thinkers, who sought behind the face of things to identify the fundamental, elemental forces which shaped the cosmos, he found his own kind of thinking anticipated. Anaximander had believed in one universal existent or substance from which opposite elements separated out and warred, and into which they returned; Anaxagoras, that each of the 'opposites' had a portion of the other in it. Heracleitus thought the Opposites were actually one, opposite faces of the fiery energy which is the 'thought' that rules the world. Life for him was an ever-flowing stream in which all things were in constant change through constant opposition, but keeping measure, so that when any became predominant the balance would restore itself by reaction. Empedocles thought the world was built out of the four elements of earth, air, fire and water, put in motion by a force of strife, but bound together by a force to unity which he called love. All would have understood better than Russell why Lawrence thought that the remedy for too great subjectivity and separation was not to start from existing and corrupt facts and institutions, but from the opposite impulse which is always there in all of us, to unity. To Heracleitus, you must couple 'things whole and things not whole, what is drawn together and what is drawn asunder, the harmonious and the discordant. The one is made up of all things and all things issue from the one.' It was Heracleitus with whom Lawrence recognised the greatest affinity, delighting not merely in what he said, but in the teasing aphorisms in which his oppositions – like Blake's, and often Nietzsche's – were cast. (For Russell, Blake suggested 'mysticism'; for Lawrence the habit of 'contrary' thinking Blake shared with Nietzsche, though behind that also the religous attitude which finally took Lawrence in Blakean rather than Nietzschean directions.) The merest selection of Heracleitan maxims will suggest both the sense of affinity and the joy with which Lawrence must have read him.

The sun is new every day.
  God is day and night, winter and summer, war and peace, surfeit and hunger.
  Cold things become warm, and what is warm cools; what is wet dries, and the parched is moistened.
  It is the opposite that is good for us.
  You cannot step twice into the same river, for fresh waters are ever flowing in upon you.
  Men would not have known the name of justice if these things (i.e .injustice) were not.
  The way up and the way down is one and the same.
  It rests by changing.[40]

Russell's outline proclaimed there was 'No need of hate or conflict: only the failure of inward joy brings them about.' Lawrence countered (like Blake's 'without contraries is no progression'):

There will always be hate & conflict. It is a principle of growth: every bud must burst its cover, & the cover doesn't want to be burst. But let our hatred & conflict be *really* part of our vital growth, the outcome of our *growing*, not of our desire for sensation.

Now here was Heracleitus scorning Homer for saying ' "Would that strife might perish from among gods and men!". He did not see that he was praying for the destruction of the universe; for, if his prayer were heard, all things would pass away'.[41] Before long, Heracleitus would help Lawrence pick up his own philosophy which he had abandoned, and find the way out of the impasse it had reached as he struggled to accommodate his terrible new sense of evil and corruption, with his belief that the clash of oppositions was ultimately the ground of growth.

Immediately however, another aspect of Heracleitus seems to have brought to a head Lawrence's progressive disillusion with democracy. 'Study of Thomas Hardy' had been 'aristocratic' in insisting that each person should seek maximum self-development, and nobody should be held down in order that the backward should catch up. But he had still believed in liberty and equality of citizens in relation to the state; and – with some naïveté – had thought that socialist nationalisation and redistribution of income would solve the whole economic question, so that all could be free for the really important task of developing their maximum selves. But Russell was a convinced democrat both in politics and economics, where his solution lay (as *New Age* had also argued) in syndicalism. The aims of socialism would be achieved not by nationalisation and state ownership, but by having all economic units owned and run by the workers in them (Russell thought) through democratic election of management. Lawrence scribbled against the heading '*THE STATE*': 'What State? ... There are 2 conceptions of the State now: 1. Monarchy 2. Democracy. Democracy is the falser.' This was no mere spasm of irritation, for now, stirred up by Heracleitus as well as Russell, he found he did not believe in a democratic state at all any longer. On 14 July he wrote to Russell:

Are you doing the lectures. I have dropped writing my philosophy, but I go on working very hard in my soul. I shall lift up my voice in the autumn, and in connection with you, not apart. I have been wrong, much too Christian, in my philosophy. These early Greeks have clarified my soul. I must drop all about God.

You must drop all your democracy. You must not believe in 'the people'. One class is no better than another. It must be a case of Wisdom, or Truth. Let the working classes *be* working classes. That is the truth.

There must be an aristocracy of people who have wisdom, and there must be a Ruler: a Kaiser: no Presidents and democracies. I shall write out Herakleitos, on tablets of bronze.

'And it is law, too, to obey the counsel of one.'

'For what thought or wisdom have they? They follow the poets and take the crowd as their teacher, knowing not that there are many bad and few good ...' (ii. 364–5)

(Heracleitus had written scornfully of the spirit of egalitarianism in the men of his native Ephesus, who had thrown out their greatest man, Hermodorus, saying 'we will have none who is best among us'.)[42]

However, as so often with Lawrence, the thought turns out to be less up in the air than it looks. He is responding to the Welsh miners' strike which had just broken out and which, in a nation at war, suggested that 'the whole state is collapsing', and that the War would 'develop into the last great war between labour and capital' (ii. 366). He didn't want one in power any more than the other (ii. 368); he thought a victory for labour would cause chaos like the French revolution (ii. 366), and instead of Liberty, Equality and Fraternity now, he wanted 'a government based on good, better and best'. Russell was too old-fashioned:

A new constructive idea of a new state is needed *immediately*. Criticism is *unnecessary*. It is behind the times. You *must* [underlined fifteen times] work out the idea of a new state, not go on criticising this old one ... And the idea is, that every man shall vote according to his understanding, and that the highest understanding must dictate for the lower understandings ... the highest aim of the government is the highest good of the *soul* of the individual ... (ii. 366)

As he develops this idea in his next few letters, it becomes clear that he is not simply anti-working class, though he does not think the 'working man' (such as the miners he knew in Eastwood) 'fit to elect the ultimate government of the country' (ii. 367).[43] Instead, he picked up Russell's economic idea that the workers should have a vote in the areas that concern them most, and that they know most about, and politicised it in all respects, and for *all* classes and both sexes. Instead of a mass electorate (which read the *Daily Mail* and *John Bull* and produced the parliament which pursued the war) there should be a hierarchy of elections, so that:

The electors for the highest places should be the governors of the bigger districts – the whole thing should work upwards, every man voting for that which he more or less understands through contact – no canvassing of mass votes.

And women shall vote equally with the men, but for different things ... And if a system works up to a Dictator who controls the greater industrial side of the national life, it must work up to a Dictatrix who controls the things relating to private life. And the women shall have absolutely equal voice with regard to marriage, custody of children etc. (ii. 368)

His political naïveté shows again in the attempt to separate policy making by area and sex – is not every level or division of society vitally affected by the others? – and still more so in the combination of 'Dictator' and 'Dictatrix' with election. Lawrence should perhaps have read his Heracleitus more closely and seen a warning against poets (as well as crowds) trying to provide political leadership. On the other hand, those who have accused him of fascism on this evidence ought to have read more closely – and less anachronistically also.

Russell was plunged in such gloom now that Lawrence thought him 'vitally, emotionally, much too inexperienced in personal contact and conflict, for a man of his age and calibre'. (He had noted, 'It isn't that life has been too much for him, but too little.') Ottoline should tell Russell 'not to write lachrymose letters to me of disillusion and disappointment and age: that sounds like 19, almost like David Garnett' (ii. 366–7). He still hoped for a meeting of true minds at Garsington; but by the end of the month it was clear that the issue of democracy was another serious division, not surprisingly, given Russell's work for the Union of Democratic Control. Lawrence had made it clear that he did not want tyranny but strong government by the most capable, an 'elected aristocracy' (ii. 371), and that both his supreme rulers were to be elected; but Russell remained sure that they should lecture independently, and that was not enough for Lawrence.

We must have the same general ideas if we are going to be or to do anything. I will listen gladly to all your ideas: but we must *put our ideas together*. This is a united effort, or it is nothing – a mere tiresome playing about, lecturing and so on. It is no mere personal voice that must be raised: but a sound, living idea round which we all rally. (ii. 371)

Russell no longer thought that possible, and felt 'tired and disgusted with myself'. Ottoline, too, was depressed, and unwell – and she had not liked Russell's outline much, either.[44]

IV   A Last Look at *The Rainbow*

It was also in these last three weeks of July when Frieda was mostly in London and Lawrence stayed on alone at Shed Hall, teaching the child in the mornings once more, that he put the last touches to *The Rainbow* – not all of them voluntarily. The proofs had arrived by the 9th, before he went to London for the weekend to argue with Russell. And as he began to carry through a final clarification, he thought well of what he had done. 'Whatever else it is, it is the voyage of discovery towards the real and eternal and unknown land. We are like Columbus, we have our back upon Europe, till we come to the new world' (ii. 362).

It was typical of him that he should make the proof stage not a correction but another recension. In fact Methuen's printers had done well, and the amount of actual proof-correction would have been small; but Lawrence made so many changes that Methuen eventually exercised their contractual right to charge him for exceeding the printer's free corrections allowance of six shillings per sixteen pages, and reduced his final cheque by £9/3/9 – much to his annoyance (ii. 406 and n. 3). For Lawrence, no work was ever finished. If Truth was a continual process of discovery, so *a fortiori* was fiction, and the process would go on until an external hand intervened and removed the last opportunity to change and grow.

It must have been some consolation to him in his loneliness without Frieda, and with his Rananim revolution collapsing, to reoccupy his finest imagined world so far. He was broadly satisfied with its vision. This time there would be no new episodes, or different conceptions of existing ones – only a last process of sharpening, clarifying, intensifying – page by page through the 463 that the printed text had become.

Occasionally one can detect a particular pointedness in a change. When he finally called the great colliery at Wiggiston 'mathematical' he was merely sharpening the link between the scientific temper, industrialisation and dehumanisation, which had been there before – but he may have written the word with a little extra zest because of the argument he had just had with Russell on the 10th. Now, too, he was clearer about Ursula's insight when she saw the cell move under her microscope. After cutting the sermon about all stages of evolution from the marsh to the gates of paradise being co-present in the human being, the typescript revision had substituted:

[Suddenly in her mind the] world gleamed strangely, with an intense light, like the nucleus of the creature under the microscope. Suddenly she had passed away into an intensely-gleaming light of knowledge.

In the typescript revision he went on to describe her sense of being transfigured and 'pushed with the growing tip onto the verge of Paradise', seeing its light in the nucleus of the cambium on her slide. In proof, however, he changed the emphasis from Ursula's inner and subjective experience to what the life that she sees *is* – with all his insistence against Russell that the Infinite is here and now and must be the starting-point, in the laboratory as much as anywhere else, for a truer vision.

She could not understand what it all was. She only knew it was not limited mechanical energy, nor mere purpose of self-preservation and self-assertion. It was a consummation, a being infinite. Self was a oneness with the infinite. To be oneself was a supreme, gleaming triumph of infinity.[45]

That was what he had been trying to say to Russell about the impulse to oneness and to the infinite, which were indeed the same truth, the Heracleitan fire visible in the smallest unit of life, and the necessary dynamic of growth.

He had changed almost nothing in the ending when he revised the typescript, but now, far from wanting to modify its optimism, Russell's pessimism called out an even stronger organ note about Truth, and one or two changes that may have had Russell in mind. The rainbow stands on 'the earth' now, not merely Ursula's subjective 'heart'. Instead of 'self-care and self-conceit' there is Russell's word 'disintegration' for the contemporary malaise. And instead of the last words being about the corruption to be transcended, Lawrence now prunes, and adds a final vision of transcendence, in the 'clean rain of heaven':

She saw in the rainbow the earth's new architecture, the old, brittle corruption of houses and factories swept away, the world built up in a living fabric of Truth, fitting to the over-arching heaven.

He still used 'would' where it might have been wiser to write 'could' – but he was again writing against Russell in this final assertion that there would always be, in everyone, the impulse to Truth and over-arching unity.[46]

Yet these changes would not stand out as different in kind from the hundreds of others that he made in proof, as the last stage in the process of clarification and sharper focusing that had been going on since *The Rainbow* took shape in manuscript. Not every change was an improvement of course; occasionally he failed to get back inside what he had written; but generally the novel gained a great deal from its final retouching – though £9/3/9 was more than a quarter's rent of the new flat.

On 13 July, however, he had to deal with a demand for changes of a different sort, for Pinker began to pass on, from Methuen, requests for self-censorship

(ii. 364) that Lawrence had been half-expecting ever since he asked Viola to tell him which places might offend. More were demanded a week later; and on 26 July he sent back 'slips and pages' separately from the main series in which he was 'now at p. 192 of the revised proofs, the final form':

I have cut out, as I said I would, all the *phrases* objected to. The passages and paragraphs marked I cannot alter. There is nothing offensive in them, beyond the very substance they contain, and that is no more offensive than that of all the rest of the novel. The libraries won't object to the book any less, or approve of it any more, if these passages are cut out. And I cant cut them out, because they are living parts of an organic whole. Those who object, will object to the book altogether. These bits won't affect them particularly. (ii. 369–70)

It was a brave stand, especially since he knew perfectly well after *Sons and Lovers* and *The Prussian Officer* that a refusal to stock the book by lending libraries such as Mudies, Boots and Smiths would make a big difference, as much as 2,000 copies, to the sales. It was all very well to 'Tell Methuen, he need not be afraid. If the novel doesn't pay him back this year, it will before very long. Does he expect me to be popular? I shan't be that. But I am a safe speculation'. Publishers cannot take too long a view.

Because Pinker's files have partly disappeared and Lawrence never kept letters, it is impossible to be sure exactly what was objected to; and it is not as easy as one might think to guess what alterations would be demanded by a respectable publisher, with his eye on library sales in 1915. The thirteen expurgations that the American publisher was to make, without Lawrence's consent, are the most likely passages that Lawrence might have *refused* to cut; and suggest that the episode of the Nottingham girl and its aftermath (though not the anal suggestion); the relationship with Winifred Inger; and the going away together of Ursula and Skrebensky were among the main areas of sensitivity.[47] There seem to have been no objections, since there are no significant changes, to the treatment of Ursula's loss of virginity under the oak-tree, or her destruction of Skrebensky on the beach. That the American publisher was also not bothered by Tom's affair with the girl at Matlock, or by Anna's dancing in the nude, may on the other hand have been because Lawrence did make changes there – though it is not possible to be sure that these were simply the result of outside interference. For, in the vast majority of what seem the likeliest cases of self-censorship, there could have been other good reasons for the alteration. Or, to put it the other way round, if Lawrence did bowdlerise himself, as his letter to Pinker suggests he did in certain 'phrases', he nearly always did more than that, and rewrote with some fresh imaginative emphasis.[48]

At least Pinker seemed satisfied, since Lawrence thanked him on 29 July for his 'assurance concerning Methuen' (ii. 372). The order to begin printing was placed by Methuen on 16 August,[49] aiming for publication in the autumn. Whatever the frustrations with Russell, and the publisher's pussyfooting, two and a half years' work, now, seemed at long last coming to fruition, as Lawrence prepared to leave Greatham at the end of July.

V   Farewell to Greatham, 'this England'

In the same letter, he thanked Pinker for selling 'England, My England' to the *English Review*. He had finished it by 6 June, to meet Pinker's request for something for the *Strand*; but already he suspected that 'England will not publish' (ii. 354) – though America might – because it was so deeply anti-war.[50]

It would later become one of the most hurtful examples of his ruthlessness in using scenes and people 'from life' – but in judging this, we need to distinguish the 1915 story from the very different, rewritten and much longer version of late 1921, by a Lawrence who had by then put England decisively behind him.[51]

Though the setting in the 1915 version is recognisably Rackham Cottage to those who knew the place, it is not named. Apart from one or two little-known details – and in sharp contrast with 1921 – there is nothing to identify 'Humphreys' or its owners.[52] Above all, apart from 'Evelyn's small private income, love of gardening and decision to enlist, which must have applied to many many thousands of Englishmen, there is nothing to point specifically to Percy Lucas, Madeline's husband. (Beb Asquith, also, did not work for a living; Cynthia Asquith, too, found it hard to make ends meet on their private incomes; and Beb joined the artillery as Evelyn does, but Percy Lucas did not.) There is nothing about the interest in folk music, and especially Morris dancing, which in the 1921 version pointed identifiably to a man who by then *had* been killed in action (in 1916), though he was very much alive when the story was first written. Evelyn was never meant to portray Percy Lucas.[53] Indeed Lawrence had barely met him, if at all. The Lucases were mostly in London while the Lawrences were at Greatham. Madeline and her daughters came down for Easter (after which their cottage was lent to the Radfords) and again in May when Rackham became 'a seething pot' at Whitsun (ii. 346), but it is not clear whether Percy was there on either occasion. He *may* have come down on leave from Epsom, where he was stationed, and worked a while in his garden which Lawrence had been helping to keep up; but the only date we can be certain of was 23 June, weeks after the story was written and posted.[54]

The ruthlessness of the 1915 story was to use the accident that had left little Sylvia Lucas in a leg brace, after she had cut her knee on a rusty sickle abandoned in long grass – though there is no hint in 1915, unlike 1921 again, that her father might be in any way to blame. (It was Maitland Radford, visiting Viola in September 1913, who recognised that the injury was more serious than the local doctor supposed, and persuaded a leading surgeon in the London hospital where he worked that the child was in mortal danger from blood-poisoning and should be operated on at once.[55]) This was the one detail in 1915 that pointed to the Lucases and would seem bound to distress them, so that a more scrupulous writer might have hesitated to use it. Judges ought to postpone condemnation, however, until they have asked what Lawrence used it *for*.

It was not for a critical portrayal of the Lucases; nor are the characters and the tension between them as complex as they would become. It is essentially a *war* story, as Cynthia Asquith called it (probably echoing Lawrence's own description), when she saw it taking shape on his typewriter – and to concentrate on 'the Lucases' is to defuse its impact and miss its point.

The title sardonically echoes the patriotic refrain from Henley's 'England' (1900): 'What have I done for you, England, my England?/ What is there I would not do,/ England, my own?' The old house and the garden Evelyn has made are not seen (as they would be, later) in the perspective of ancient Britain. Rather they are a 'dream', a 'mirage' of peace and beauty which have 'no context, no relation with the world' any longer. And the love between the couple, though still capable of filling 'the old, silent hollow where the cottage stood, with flowers and magnificence of the whole universe', has turned to battle, as with weapons of iron.[56] From this opening, the story builds a series of purely destructive oppositions. Winifred becomes authoritarian, Evelyn hardens in resistance. She worries about money, and about her husband amounting to nothing, and being supported by her father. So the passion she has for him hardens into duty and conscience; and he, deprived of the physical life that is all-in-all to him, becomes first stoically indifferent, then null, then nihilist. There is no mention of 'England' in all this.

Now the accident to the child is, precisely, the turning-point, turning readers *away* from matters of individual character and responsibility. The 'sharp old iron in the garden' which cuts and poisons the little girl – a curiously non-specific phrasing – recalls the 'iron' weapons in the 'silent fight ... as if fated' between husband and wife, for which there 'was no apparent reason'. What cripples the child and has poisoned the marriage is nobody's fault, but seems something destructively latent *in* the modern world, which is why the peace, beauty and love of the old-world house and garden are no longer safe, or real. To Evelyn there is something 'malignant, a triumph of evil and of nothingness' against which he feels paralysed; to Winifred it is his passivity that is evil, hateful.[57]

Then comes the war, and its clarification: for both husband and wife become instantly attuned to what had been latent within them and their whole world. 'As he worked in the garden he felt the seethe of the war was with him. His consciousness had now a field of activity. The reaction in his soul could cease from being neutral; it had a positive form to take.' When he enlists, encouraged by his wife and her father, Winifred may feel he is at last 'doing what was right' and amounting to something, and even be thrilled by 'his new arrogance and callousness as a soldier' – but 'Somewhere at the back was the death he was going to meet ... He was really a soldier. His soul had accepted the significance. He was a potential destructive force, ready to be destroyed ... What had he to do with love and the creative side of life? ... He was a destructive spirit entering into destruction.'

He doesn't believe in patriotism, and is irritated when leave-taking momentarily calls on 'his loving constructive self ... He hated his wife for her little fit of passion at the last' – for she too 'had wanted it, this condition of affairs'. Lawrence would tell the wounded Beb a fortnight later that destruction had become an end in itself, and not a means to anything else.

Most markedly, indeed rather melodramatically, the ending differs from the later one, illustrating also what Lawrence meant by his 1915 talk about 'blood-lust' being intrinsic to the soldier. Up to the last moments the two versions coincide, including the mistake about what a 'machine gun' is.[58] (Lawrence made Evelyn join the artillery, not merely thinking of Beb, but also in order to use the experience recorded in 'With the Guns' – complete with the officer spotting from the top of an iron platform – but unfortunately he lacked a technical vocabulary.) At the very end however, the two versions differ utterly. In 1915, a fatally wounded Evelyn kills three Germans with his revolver before he is bayoneted to death, and the iron finally enters his vitals and mutilates his face. That answers Henley's question of what men and women were prepared to do – but it is not 'for England'. Shortly before the story appeared in the *English Review* in October, Lawrence told Cynthia that it was 'about the Lucases', but immediately qualified this: 'The story is the story of most men and women who are married today – of most men at the war, and wives at home' (ii. 386) – all with the seethe of the war in them.

So there was also a symbolism in turning his back on the beauty and peace of the Greatham where he had finished his *Rainbow*, but which had come to seem an escape from the real world. There his marriage, also, had come under stress, and it had been a question (as he worked in the garden of Rackham) whether he too could ever *do* anything in the world. Having left Greatham on 30 July, he wrote a thank-you letter to Viola from Littlehampton on the 31st:

I am *very glad* you lent it to us. It has a special atmosphere, and I feel as if I had been born afresh there, got a new, sure, separate soul: as a monk in a monastery, or St John in the wilderness. Now we must go back into the world to fight. I don't want to, they are so many and they have so many roots. But we must set about cleaning the face of the earth a bit, or everything will perish. (ii. 374)

To fight – but not Evelyn's way.

In the outer life, too, the coil of personalities gave way to the sense of an 'England' coming to an end.

On 20 July Cynthia had brought her sister-in-law Katharine Asquith (wife of Raymond, the Prime Minister's eldest son), with Harold Baker again, to meet Lawrence. Still alone, he talked 'enthrallingly'. Katharine 'loved him and was most anxious to know what effect she was producing', but it was not as much as she might have hoped (though Lawrence liked her too), for his next letter was mainly an exposition of his new 'politics'. That at least proved, said Cynthia, that Lawrence was not in love with *her*, and was indeed impatient of talk about her beauty. What he admired in Cynthia was a hard stoicism and realism, facing the truth.

She then invited the Lawrences to her little Michael's first birthday tea at Littlehampton on Sunday 25 July, and they brought Viola, who (said Cynthia tartly) 'never moves without a copybook in which she enters notes for her novels'. Cynthia felt ill and depressed and it was 'the least successful of all my Lawrence meetings'. There had been some question of the Lawrences going to Garsington again, but Ottoline had written to say she had no room for Frieda, 'and Frieda is furious with her. Slight semi-facetious, but distinct, friction between the Lawrences. First time I have ever seen it.'[59] Lawrence subsequently wrote to Ottoline to say he would love to come if they were 'going to be a little group filled with one spirit and striving for one end', but he was not interested in being one of 'a little set of individuals each one concerned with himself and his own personal fling at the world' (ii. 372).

They would go instead to Littlehampton for the Bank Holiday weekend after leaving Greatham. 'I feel I want to be blown and washed, and to forget' (ii. 372). From there he wrote his good-bye to Greatham in language very reminiscent of the end of *The Rainbow*.

It is very healing, I think, to have all the land behind one, all this England with its weight of myriad amorphous houses, put back, and only the variegated pebbles, and the little waves, and the great far-off dividing line of sea and sky ... If one could only sweep clear this England, of all its houses and pavements, so that we could all begin again!

He watched a little family looking out to sea and thought 'how nice they are, clean and isolated' – but England and the English made him sad: 'They are all like prisoners born in prison' (ii. 373–4).

On Monday he told Ottoline that they would make a new start when they had got their own souls ready (ii. 374). The next day he wrote to Cynthia (who had gone to Dublin) about the untouched silvery world that lay over the river beyond the ferry, with no houses and no people: 'the flat unfinished world running with foam and noise and silvery light, and a few gulls swinging like a

half-born thought. It is a great thing to realise that the original world is still there
– perfectly clean and pure . . . ' But looking back at Littlehampton, he felt sick at
the uncleanness 'we have super-imposed on the clean world', the 'amorphous
houses like an eruption'; all full of a diseased spirit of ownership and money,
desire to possess. 'England, My England' was also, it seems, 'about' and for the
Asquiths:

Of course your husband will go to the war and love it much better than you, if you want
him to make money . . . the fact that you would ask him to work, put his soul into getting
it, makes him love better war and pure destruction . . . If he is in antagonism, he is in
antagonism. And he will escape, with joy, from the necessity for money and the
production of money, into war, which is its pure destruction. (ii. 375–6)

One must destroy the blind desire for money and possession: 'The only
permanent thing is *consummation* in love or hate'.

Wind-blown, wave-washed, feeling clearer and cleaner after four days on the
beach with Frieda, and expeditions with the Radfords, it was time to make a new
beginning, in London.

VI Apocalypse, Now

In Hampstead 'the infinite' was 'swallowed up in chairs and scrubbing
brushes and waste paper baskets' (ii. 377), for a while. Moving made him feel
'dislocated' and he did not care for London, but he threw himself as always into
the cleaning and fixing up, and could sing 'all day long' at that, often 'the
evangelical hymns of his youth'. (Hampstead may not have been too familiar
with 'Sun of my soul, thou Saviour dear'.) A London flat had always been
Frieda's idea for herself – though it had come, she complained, when she was
too old to make the best use of it. Given her increasing dislike of the
'Meynellàge', the move had not come a moment too soon; but now she was
happy again, setting up their first real home with furniture of their own. Friends
gave housewarming presents: Catherine Carswell an 'old-fashioned gilt mirror',
and somebody £10 (perhaps the Radfords clubbing together), for a 'beautiful
blue Persian rug' that would henceforward go with them everywhere.[60] The
man who distrusted possessions was acquiring some, including (through Ada)
his mother's brass candlesticks which were the nearest he ever got to household
gods. Tables, chairs and a writing-desk were bought second-hand. Catherine
remembered one exhausting expedition to Camden Town; another, to the
Caledonian Market, would provide a single chair, and details for a chapter in
Women in Love. There were new pots and pans which Lawrence vowed to keep
spotless within and without; and he set to work on a loose-cover for a second-
hand settee. Frieda was bought a Chinese coat, perhaps to confirm the peace.

On 6 August came a surprise: she heard from Ernest's solicitor that she could at last see the children – only for half an hour, and in his office, but she was 'in *bliss*. It's a beginning, the relief of it makes one quite giddy – I do not know what made E. do it, perhaps the children themselves – I shall see them on the *11th* which is my birthday' (ii. 377). It was no plea by the children, as the upshot would show, but she had been standing on the pavement again, so that the children should at least be reminded of her existence, and Ernest must have realised that her coming to live in London would mean that this would go on, and on, unless he came to some compromise.

Unfortunately, she had never imagined the effect of three years' absence on the children, especially the youngest – who has left the only record of the meeting. When Weekley, who never spoke of Frieda, suddenly asked, 'Would you like to see Mama?' Barbie answered, 'Not very much', apprehensively. Her mother 'had become rather an unreal figure by then'. When the day came, 'We were all nervous ... Monty took charge. Frieda came in looking excited, but in tears, with an open box of sweets in her hand. Monty talked quite cheerfully with her, but we were all relieved when the lawyer's clerk diffidently entered to say that the half hour was over.'[61] Children cannot disguise, and it would be hard to guess what will have hurt more, Monty's overt diplomacy, or the relief on three faces when their ordeal was over. Frieda's disappointment will have been all the more cruel because it was something she had longed for so much, and so long – and Lawrence (as the 'cause') will have paid much of the price again. By early September, when she had caught cold to annoy her all the more, he told Cynthia ruefully 'She hates me for the present', but unlike Evelyn, he joked, 'I shall not go to the war' (ii. 386).

Cynthia was out of town still, but coming to London meant for the Lawrences that other friends were now close by. They renewed acquaintance with Richard and Hilda Aldington (who, to her deep distress, had lost their baby in the spring).[62] The Radfords were very near at Well Walk, the Carswells and Ivy not far away, Barbara Low and the Eders also in easy reach. With Kot there was a temporary coolness. When Katherine came back from Paris she found a Murry who had become rather more secure because he had established himself as the regular reviewer of French books for *The Times Literary Supplement*, as well as contributing still to the *Westminster*. Moreover Katherine's own allowance was now £120 a year. So in June they had moved from the rooms in Elgin Crescent she had found so inadequate, to a house at 5 Acacia Road in St John's Wood with a garden and a servant, for £52 p.a. compared with £36 for 1 Byron Villas. There Kot, who had become increasingly devoted to Katherine, was a frequent visitor, closer to them at this stage than to Lawrence. (Katherine's brother Leslie, in uniform, and in training, came to stay at Acacia Road too that August.) It may have been because Murry's antipathy to Frieda strengthened Kot's own view of the Lawrence marriage that Kot wrote a letter in late July about the conditions for further relationship between them. Lawrence at that time had not known how to answer: 'My feelings are confused and suffering under various sorts of shocks in one direction and another. I hope you will not mind if we leave it for a while, this question of a relationship between us, until I am settled and dependable' (ii. 369). Hence Kot did not come to Byron Villas until 26 August – Lawrence having put off a date some days earlier because of Frieda's cold. He would countenance no relation that excluded Frieda – but the friendship was restored.

It was ironic that the move to the metropolis, where one's friends were so much more easily accessible, should have accentuated matters of personality. Renewed contact with Russell and Murry made Lawrence angrily (because finally) aware of the failure of the kind of Rananim he had hoped could be founded on a community of belief and purpose, rather than mere personal relationship. For it was not ultimately a disagreement about ideas which drove Russell further and further away; nor – it became clear – was there any agreement in outlook and purpose with Murry to build upon.

Russell was soon invited to Hampstead, but the gap between his secular and humanist reformism and Lawrence's intensity about spiritual revolution deepened now into a chasm. Lawrence saw that Russell's 'vanity' was 'piqued' by being told that the lectures '*must* be different'; though he was less aware of the egotism in his own anger, in his letter to Cynthia. Behind that, however, was something deeper:

I am so sick of people: they preserve an evil, bad, separating spirit under the warm cloak of good words ... They all want the same thing: a continuing in this state of disintegration wherein each separate little ego is an independent little principality by itself. What does Russell really want? He wants to keep his own little established ego, his finite and ready-defined self intact, free from contact and connection. He wants to be ultimately a free agent. That's what they all want, ultimately – (ii. 378)

The ultimate split came about because of the intensity with which Lawrence, egotist though he was – like everybody, perhaps more than most, though not more than Russell – did *not* want that. It was because he so hated and feared self-enclosure in himself, that he so insisted on the force in human beings that resisted it. In a sense he *had* to believe, intensely, that a longing for 'unanimity in truth' lay deeper in people than their egos (ii. 380); though it remained egotistic to conceive unanimity so much in his own terms. Whereas Russell, agreeing that subjectivity was the central problem, was armoured enough in his own rationality to believe with Swift's Houyhnhnms, that reason was a sufficient guide for a rational creature, and that by applying it to social problems subjectivity could be overcome.

The sadness of the collapsing relationship was that they might have supplied each other's defects. Lawrence had much to learn from Russell – had he depended less on assurance that they were of the same mind, as opposed to unanimous in wanting to develop common ground. Russell might have been able, had he not been so piqued by the criticism of himself, and hence so impatient and unimaginative about Lawrence's idiom, to make him see what was wrong in extrapolating a politics from far too narrow a base. There was, surely, nothing reprehensible in the basic premise which underlay both Lawrence's 'socialism' and his only apparently contradictory belief in hierarchy: the insistence that souls were born different, and should in a healthy society develop differently, though each as fully as possible.[63] The idea that the necessary conditions could simply be established by wholesale nationalisation and an equal wage for everyone had been tossed out with an air of getting less important things out of the way in order to get down to more important ones. But hardened into intransigence rather than questioning by the clash with Russell, it was very unworldly (at least) of Lawrence to tell Cynthia now that 'If we have a right spirit, then our Lords and our Ladies will appear, as the flowers come forth from nowhere in the spring' (ii. 380), let alone to imagine they would then be immediately recognised and elected to hierarchical power by plebeians ready and willing to serve. It might seem as daft to imagine that London could then be pulled down, and rebuilt beautifully, and the whole idea of money be abolished – that is, if one took this seriously as political thinking, rather than frustration and intransigence because nobody would take seriously his wholly serious demand that social thinking *begin* from the determination of human value, no matter how subversive of the way things are. On Russell's ground Lawrence could never compete, and the more obvious this got, the sillier he became – from Russell's point of view. Yet it was not silly – though it might seem impractical – to insist that politics had to be determined by human value rather than immediate practicability, if it were seriously hoped to change society for the better. If he had been more willing to listen to Russell's criticism and Russell to listen to his, he might have got Russell to think more deeply about premises, and more imaginatively about the modes of being in which he was most deficient. Each was in his way a genius, among the highest of their kind. That they should have been so drawn to each other, and yet prove incapable of working together, was a twentieth-century portent and not an encouraging one.

With Murry, personality obtruded in a very different but no less infuriating way – and Frieda, happier in London, refused to take her husband's radicalism seriously. Murry

says he believes in what I say, because he believes in me ... He says the whole thing is personal: that between him and me it is a case of Lawrence and Murry, not of any union in an *idea*. He thinks the introduction of any idea, particularly of any political idea, highly dangerous and deplorable. The thing should be left personal, each man just expressing himself. – Frieda says things are not so bad as I pretend, that people are good, that life is also good, that London is also good and that this civilisation is great and wonderful. She thinks if the war were over things would be pretty well all right.

But they are all wrong. (ii. 380)

Lawrence felt himself ground between an upper and a nether millstone. With Russell, what should have been a constructive relation of ideas (for they did have a great deal in common) was contaminated by clashes of personality; with Murry the personalities seemed harmonious now, yet what a slender and vulnerable basis on which to try to change other people, when any quarrel would ruin the whole work! In both ways, as well as by his wife, he was being told that his ideas were unimportant. The temperature of his anger, then, at the realisation that people only valued him *personally*, proves that he was not, as Russell was to claim, driven by personal megalomania. Yet the very excess in pouring all this out to Cynthia shows it came from the depths. In 'real bitterness', he felt 'as if Russell and Lady Ottoline were traitors':

They betray the real truth. They come to me, and they make me talk, and they enjoy it, it gives them a profoundly gratifying sensation. And that is all. As if what I say were meant only to give them gratification, because of the flavour of personality: as if I were a cake or a wine or a pudding. They then say, I – D.H.L. am wonderful, I am an exceedingly valuable personality, but that the things I say are extravaganzas, illusions. They say I cannot think.

... they filch my life for a sensation unto themselves, all my effort, which is my life, they betray, they are like Judas: they turn it all to their own static selves, convert it into the static nullity. The result is for them a gratifying sensation, a tickling, and for me a real bleeding.

But I know them now ... (ii. 380–1)

The 'Foreword to *Sons and Lovers*' and the 'Study of Thomas Hardy' declared that a man's work is his life made articulate: there was no personal Lawrence distinct from the life-blood in his words. The letter marked another turning point: the conception of Rananim that had grown at Greatham had to be discarded. There would be no lectures with Russell, or shared ideas with Murry, or like-minded community. 'I do believe there are people who wait for the spirit of truth. But I think one can't find them personally. I had hoped and tried to get a little nucleus of living people together. But I think it is no good. One must start direct with the open public, without associates. But how to begin, and when, I don't yet know' (ii. 381).

In fact he did know one possibility; and another would revive at the beginning of

September. He had already thought of reworking his German and Italian sketches into a book, and had finished a revised version of 'Christs in the Tyrol' before leaving Greatham. On 20 August, four days after the bitter letter to Cynthia, he sent off a rewritten 'The Spinner and the Monks' (ii. 381 and n. 5) – and the creation of what would become *Twilight in Italy* then progressed steadily into October. Here was his best way of touching 'living people', instead of in socio-political terms where he was at his weakest. His next letter to Cynthia on 5 September announced another idea: a variant of that earlier scheme of publishing his philosophy in pamphlet form. There might be associates after all in creating a little magazine to be called *The Signature*, where he could do 'the preaching', outlining 'the beliefs by which one can resurrect the world'; Murry his 'ideas on freedom for the individual soul'; Katherine 'her little satirical sketches'; and 'perhaps' Russell and Cannan would join in (ii. 386).

But the 'perhaps', and the fact that the three principals would be free to do very different kinds of thing, show that Rananim had been painfully laid by. And though in August there had been signs that others might value his words rather than his personality – Esmé Percy wanting to produce *The Widowing of Mrs. Holroyd*, and Marsh (despite their disagreement about the war), wanting poetry for the second Georgian anthology[64] – Lawrence's 'soul' was 'still fizzling savagely'. His quarrel with Russell was soul-deep, he looked at people in London with 'dumb fury', and 'the persistent nothingness of the war makes me feel like a paralytic convulsed with rage' (ii. 385–6). But now the rage sounds a little rhetorical. In fact he was embarked on another intensely creative period – but its final catalyst was the most apocalyptic vision yet of the end of his world, giving a Last Judgement on those ruled by personality.

He tried to be patient. He told Ottoline that the silences between them were only temporary, and that he always wanted them to be friends 'in the deep, honorable, permanent sense'. Though he found it difficult to be 'true to my deepest self' – that complaint of the mercurial man – and though allowances had to be made for 'extreme lapses' between friends, he did 'believe in our permanent friendship' and hoped he and Russell had only 'parted for a little while' (ii. 388–9). In fact Ottoline's relationship with Russell was also on the wane. Her growing love of Garsington found no echo in a man who had no feeling for the countryside. Though he spent much of the summer in the flat she and Morrell had made for him in the bailiff's house, she wrote in her diary in mid-July after a walk with him that she found him 'so stiff, so self-absorbed, so harsh and unbending in mind or body, that I can hardly look at him'. Meanwhile he was taking increasing interest not only in his protégé T. S. Eliot but also in Eliot's flirtatious and highly strung new wife.[65] Lawrence may nevertheless have thought his own relationship with Garsington was imperilled by his quarrel with Russell as well as by Frieda's with Ottoline. However, 'Our coming to see you depends on us all three, you and me and Frieda. When we all want it, to make the new thing, the new world that is to be, then we will come' (ii. 389). He invited her to visit them in Hampstead, where Forster had just come – another friendship that had, he thought, survived despite lapses.[66] So, 'let us all have patience with each other: though I'm the worst for patience' (ii. 390).

Indeed he was, and he soon ran out of it with Russell. He had written on 5 September to tell him about the new plan for *The Signature*, and that it included 'you and Cannan if you care to join'. But he hoped Russell would do 'something serious', and he only wanted 'people who really care, and who really want a new world, to subscribe' (ii. 387). However, a note on the back of the letter says 'Ans. *Yes* as to writing, *no* as to money' (ii. 387 n. 1). When he sent an answer in those terms, enclosing an article called 'The Danger to Civilisation' but refusing to subscribe to the venture (ii. 392), Lawrence broke off the relationship altogether. It was not so much Russell's arguments themselves as his tone and assumptions, coupled with the deliberate refusal of even 2/6-worth of support, that made Lawrence sure that a deliberate double blow was intended. In the article, Russell argues reasons physical, moral, economic and mental, to show that prolonging the war will damage all the nations concerned, and hence European civilisation as a whole. Indeed, 'The collective life of Europe, which has been carried on in the most wonderful upward movement known to history, will have received a wound which may well prove mortal.'[67] The writer (who adopts the lofty tone of one of the flowers of that civilisation) quite clearly believes in Progress, and wishes the war ended quickly so that its march may continue. To Lawrence, who believed that the war had come about because of a rottenness within supposedly civilised people and who was looking for a radical revolt against the past and a new kind of world, such complacency, and such lofty dismissal of all he had so passionately argued, was the final evidence that Russell would neither look inside himself as Lawrence had done, nor work for a new world with him – and was moreover (as in his forensic fierceness) concealing the desire to slap him in the face, behind a mask of superior reason and pacifism.

Yet it was also something far more serious. On 8 September a Zeppelin raid on London killed twenty people. Lawrence saw the airship: 'high up, like a bright golden finger, quite small, among a fragile incandescence of clouds. And underneath it were splashes of fire as the shells fired from earth burst. Then there were flashes near the ground – and the shaking noise.'

For him it was a vision of the end of the world they knew.

It seemed as if the cosmic order were gone, as if there had come a new order, a new heavens above us: and as if the world in anger were trying to revoke it . . .

So it seems our cosmos is burst, burst at last . . . our world is gone, and we are like dust in the air.

But there must be a new heaven and a new earth, a clearer, eternal moon above, and a clean world below. (ii. 390)

This reinforcement of his sense of crisis made it the worst time for Russell's article, and its tone, to strike upon an eye and ear more attuned to prophecy than to superior reason. For against *that* perspective – the end of a world; the moment of truth between Evil and Good; a Day of Judgement between the civilisation of which Russell cast himself as spokesman, and the longing for a wholly different order which he denied – Lawrence saw between the lines, and beyond the reasoning in the article, to a psychological reaction *against* radical change. That linked Russell with the gunfire. Russell's civilisation concealed the 'anger' of the guns attempting to 'revoke' the apocalyptic crisis (ii. 390). Russell might preach peace and liberty, but in fact he was violently resistant to real change – just as within Lawrence's fictive Winifred and Evelyn had lurked not so much concern for the future of England, but first ego, personality, and then the seethe of destruction.

Lawrence could see now how Evelyn and Russell were linked:

The fact is that you, in the essay, are all the time a lie.

Your basic desire is the maximum of desire of war, you are really the super-war-spirit. What you want is to jab and strike, like the soldier with the bayonet, only you are sublimated into words. And you are like a soldier who might jab man after man with his bayonet, saying 'this is for ultimate peace' ... You are satisfying in an indirect, false way your lust to jab and strike. Either satisfy it in a direct and honorable way, saying 'I hate you all, liars and swine, and am out to set upon you', or stick to mathematics, where you can be true ...

You are simply *full* of repressed desires, which have become savage and anti-social. And they come out in this sheep's clothing of peace propaganda. As a woman said to me, who had been to one of your meetings: 'It seemed so strange, with his face looking so evil, to be talking about peace and love. He can't have *meant* what he said'.

I believe in your inherent power for realising the truth. But I don't believe in your will, not for a second. Your will is false and cruel. You are too full of devilish repressions to be anything but lustful and cruel ... It is a perverted, mental blood-lust. Why don't you own it.

Let us become strangers again, I think it is better. (ii. 392)

This may have been angrily exaggerated, even hateful and cruel; a frustrated ego striking at someone who refused to accept him at his own valuation. Unfortunately it was also partly true, though not the whole truth; and it was not as though Lawrence failed to see in himself the evil he saw in Russell, for he had done so long before. The difference was that he admitted it, as the necessary step before it could be transcended. Could Russell? Lawrence was used, as Russell was not, to accepting the grains of truth in radical denunciations (such as Frieda's) and, after the thunderstorm had cleared the air, holding again to the truth of relationship. Would Russell? The moment he had sent the letter, Lawrence had a spasm of grief and felt 'like going into a corner to cry, as I used to do when I was a child' (ii. 393). Would Russell care as much?

The difference is revealing; for Russell first over-reacted, and then dismissed the challenge altogether, before finally, years later, proving by the jabbing and striking of his public statements that Lawrence had seen what was indeed there.[68] Initially, as he had done several times before when a personal crisis occurred, he contemplated suicide – a psychological habit not of confrontation, but evasion. For within twenty-four hours of thinking Lawrence must be right, 'a healthier reaction set in, and I decided to have done with such morbidness' (ii. 392–3 n. 5). He seems never to have seriously weighed what *portion* of truth there might be in what Lawrence had said.

It may be, also, that it was good for Lawrence to stop brooding over their disagreement, and free his mind for writing his own kind of philosophy. The challenge would be, then, to find *impersonal* terms in which to explain the nature of the apocalypse of 1915, and how it could lead to a new world for those who gave themselves to it, rather than attempting to revoke or frustrate its process.

VII Thought-travelling

He attempted this in two ways: a 'philosophical' travel-book, and a book of philosophy that was also a journey of the mind. The two were interlinked: the letter of 5 September announcing the plan for the *Signature* also said that 'Meanwhile' he was putting together 'a book of sketches, about the nations, Italian[,] German and English, full of philosophising and struggling to show things real' (ii. 386). By then he had already rewritten three that had been in print – the first before leaving Greatham – and he finished 'The Theatre' (probably the last he had written in 1913) the following day, 6 September (ii. 387). Some options had already closed: he was not going to recreate his journey with Frieda, since he was excluding the chapel and hay-hut in the mountains; nor could it really be a book about three nations, since he had not recast any of his other sketches about Germany. By 11 September when he sent off 'San Gaudenzio' (ii. 390 and n. 4), it was clear that Italy would be the centre. There was then a pause, while the six essays of 'The Crown' for *Signature* occupied his full attention. When the sketches began to flow again in October the book had clearly become 'Italian Studies', as he named it on 26 October when he sent the full typescript to Pinker (ii. 417).[69] Was the first one, about crucifixes in Germany, then an odd appendage, and the whole an anthology rather than a book? That depends rather on what one thinks a travel-book is or should be.

(a) Perspective from Travels Past

The new aim of impersonality shows itself as the personal 'I' largely disappears from the first essay; as does the 1913 idea of the Christs as the work of men who strove 'to get at the meaning of their own soul's anguish', like the writer struggling with *Sons and Lovers* at the time. Now he rearranges the Christs, careless of the order in which he had encountered them, to embody a history of developing consciousness as in *The Rainbow*: the peasant (Brangwen man) Christ; then the little one in red flannel who broods on being and non-being; then the great Christus of the Klamm, carved by a disillusioned artist who has consciously realised his people's dread of death; and then the opposite modes in which faithless modern consciousness asserts itself against the fact and pain of dissolution. The spirited but self-flattering posture of the 'D'Annunzio' Christ is set against the 'sensational' one (at Wieden) who *will* not die, but continues to experience and express in his bloodshot gaze the violation of man-crucified-by-death. Finally, above the snowline, a broken image confirms that the old religion is meaningless now; but what sense of purpose in life and death can follow, 'in the stark, sterile place of rock and cold'?[70] The travelling is only partly geographical; but mostly through the interior of human development in time. It is also (for Lawrence) an impersonal journey through memory whose significance is only now perceived; yet the new insight stands or falls by the evocation of the carvings themselves. Struggling to show things real, and philosophising, seem united – so far.

Indeed, the first essay becomes a prologue to the whole: revealed now as less a matter of going from Germany to Italy or comparing them, than a voyage to discover the bearing of the inner past of humankind on the apocalyptic crisis of the present. (None of the other German sketches could contribute to this.) Meanwhile the biographer watches an earlier self being made over as well as recreated, bringing home how the writing of the 'Hardy' and *The Rainbow* had so altered his vision that he was bound to reconceive what he had 'seen' before. So, what did the Lawrence of 1915 see now, as he reread his three sketches of Gargnano in 1913?

Once again he clears the personal Lawrence from the rendering of 'The Spinner and the Monks'; and whereas the only link between the essays had been that they shared the same 'I', they are now significantly related. What had been there on the sunny terrace of San Tommaso but could not be understood yet, is focused with new zest by eyes fresh from the Christs, because it is their opposite. The journey into self-consciousness contrasts with its complete absence. The same physical details, remaining concrete and pretending to no more than they embody, become more resonant as they manifest 'Hardy's 'God the Father' and the novel's 'Brangwen men'. The old woman is experienced now as wholly unified with her world of sun, stone and caper-bush; but by the same token she is not conscious of her spinning, her eyes have 'no looking in them', and to her, he is only 'a piece of the environment'.[71] The 'I' is only there to render his *difference* – without which, however, there could be no rendering. And what of the other Italy, of dark alleys and smelly underways, and the shadowy ravine where he hunts for flowers? Indeed, the lakeside is a world split in three: mountain snow, earth and underworld. So the 'I' (in 1915) has another impersonal function: to move through these dimensions, conscious of each in turn, and trying to marry them (as he selects a daisy and periwinkles to go with the wintry and shadow flowers); rather than walk, as the monks do among their wintry vines, a borderline of transition which is neither the one thing nor the other.

So the earlier sketches become related – but 'The Lemon Gardens' sounds a harsher note (now) about transition and the marrying of opposites. Here, instead of re-seeing throughout, two long passages get rather obviously inserted into the experience of 1913, to establish what was really at issue in its key moments of comedy and tragedy: the comedy of the recalcitrant door spring, where the 'I' finds himself cast as a representative of all industrialised England-and-America, and the tragedy of the suddenly perceived impotence of Signor di P. and his lemon gardens to engender a future. Where 'Hardy' had seen a Joachite progress from the era of the Father to that of the Son, and the dawn now of the Age of the Reconciler; the much darker vision of 1915 sees, behind the Englishman and the Italian in the doorway, two ways in which Europeans have become destructive and nihilistic. After the balanced high point of the Renaissance (Botticelli, still), came a split. Michelangelo heralded an 'Italian' regression into the body – but the advance of consciousness nevertheless proceeds until the Flesh and the senses become self-conscious, knowing their aim, which is 'supreme sensation'. Sexuality becomes destructive; and in seeking the maximum of conscious sensation the flesh begins not only to consume the 'other' but even to react upon and destroy itself: the impulse of the Tiger, flatheaded and predatory, becomes the soldier desiring consummation in an ecstasy of destruction and self-destruction. Conversely, the Northern races deny the supreme-self-in-the-body and seek to know the not-self, from which concern with the 'other' came both democracy and above all the rise of science and industry. Again, however, the growth of consciousness has turned destructive in a scientific war of machines, 'an unthinkable hell' – which yet hypocritically claims to be in the service of mankind, trying to be both Tiger and Lamb in one, 'Which is just ghastly nothingness ... nil, nihil, nought.'[72] And what of the Future? The Signora di P., playing in the sunny patio with a child not hers, reveals the tragedy of the civilised Signor di P., and prepares the visitor for the passing of his lemon gardens.[73] The Italian sees godhead in the phallus and procreation – but how if the Flesh has become impotent to project itself into the future? And what if the lemon gardens (growing sun-fruit despite subalpine cold) have no future either because of new industrial-age transport from sunnier places? Moreover the Lawrence of 1915 is losing faith in the possibility of marrying opposites, as he broods on the Italian wanting to be more Northern, and the Northerner more Italian. There is no going back to the old bodily and unconscious 'Italy' of the spinner; and Lawrence cannot see his padrone's longing to go the way of prosperous industrial England without bitter irony, as he thinks of England's 'teeming swarms of disintegrated human beings'.[74]

One trouble is that the two incidents can hardly bear the weight of such generalisation, so that showing things real and the philosophising which had fused in the earlier essays, now pull damagingly apart. Another is that this must be the impasse that 'Morgenrot' had reached: for if each 'opposite' has deteriorated, and their marriage no longer seems possible in 1915, what *is* the way forward? When he first revised the sketch, Lawrence had no idea. He originally ended his second digression with a rhetorical plea to move beyond both kinds of limitation:

We know that in Eternity exists a great world of truth ... And it is our business to set the whole living world into relation to the eternal truth.

When we have done that, we shall have re-created paradise, there will be complete Heaven. We can at any rate begin the job.

But what does this mean, and how do we start? Luckily Lawrence himself felt the emptiness of his rhetoric, for on 5 September he asked Clayton to substitute an entirely negative passage beginning (then): 'It is time to leave off, to cease entirely from what we are doing, and from what we have been doing for hundreds of years.'[75] He has only two certainties now: that there is no way forward by 'seeking one Infinite, ignoring, trying to eliminate the other';[76] and that even though we must acknowledge and know both, it is fatal to confuse them or seek to make one lie down with the other, for they must always *be* separate and opposite. Yet how, at this appalling time of breakdown and transition, they can actually be related in the lives of modern people, there is no telling, yet.

The revised 'The Theatre' continues to explore the ironies of transition, and (like the Spinner) the 1913 centres of interest, Ibsen's *Ghosts* and *Hamlet*, come ideally on cue, and can be refocused without violence to the original experience. In the account of '*I Spettri*' (*Ghosts*) Lawrence sees deeper into the performance of the Italian actor who acts his own transitional state, still driven by the flesh which his spirit no longer wants, yet frustrated by his inability to gain the life of 'the spirit that fulfils in the world the new germ of an idea'. In this way he is far more moving than Ibsen performed perfectly in Munich – where the drama of the North seemed 'to be fingering with the mind the secret places and sources of the blood, impertinent, irreverent, nasty'.[77] After the light relief of two performances of melodrama and sentimentality comes '*Amleto*', perfectly fitting the previous analysis in his Northern revolt from the flesh and his spirit of self-conscious disintegration. Now however both Italian actor and English spectator are in transition. The Italian has only just reached the 'Hamlet' stage, but (Lawrence insists) he will never progress by compromise: 'He is neither one nor the other. He has neither being nor not-being. He is as equivocal as the monks ... He has still to let go, to know what not-being is, before he can *be*.'[78] In that 'letting go' may lie the first hint of a way forward. But in the meantime the divisions in the audience have also become a spectrum of 'Italian' transition: the 'Joseph' guarding his little family, still in the world of the spinner, the Bersaglieri huddling against a world beyond, the new corrupt freethinkers, the hostility between Italian and German. In the darkness of a new ending, searchlights swing across the lake. It is 1913, peacetime, but a premonition of 1915's apocalypse.

'San Gaudenzio' – almost certainly a new essay – then tackles the question posed by this new sense that the Opposites must remain separate nowadays: what then of the belief in marriage? The story of Paolo and Maria, the couple in whose farmhouse the Lawrences had stayed, is conceived in terms of *The Rainbow* but proceeds – a sombre postscript – to show how a marriage of opposites, having flowered through conflict, can in time become less and less capable of flowering fully again. A comparison of Lawrence's account of the couple with Tony Cyriax's shows much in common. Both see the man's courtesy, his thoughtfulness (albeit uneducated and slow) and how he is so wrapped up in his land that he was untouched by his four years in America. Both see the woman as overfond of money, unscrupulous, tempestuous, but also with wider horizons than others in the village, anxious to get on. Both see the children in descending order of attractiveness.[79] But Lawrence sees far more in these facts. He heightens the opposition in *Rainbow* terms; and shows the couple also as a contrast between an older Italy, attractive but static (like the spinner), almost feudal, and the new commercial Italy (taking off from the end of 'The Lemon Gardens'). Above all else, he shows the children as the outcome of a process which first issues in a flower uniting the best of both, the eldest boy 'Giovanni', but then turns towards withdrawal and hatred, 'terrible disintegrated opposition and otherness'; for 'Marco', the second boy, has 'some discrepancy in him. He was not unified'. (This is supported by Tony's account.) And the ironically named 'Felicina', the product of a phase of greater disintegration when the parents have learned to withdraw from each other almost completely, is 'self-conscious', and also 'affected, cold, selfish'. (Tony agrees that it was perhaps 'difficult to love her'.) The flowering of the marriage of opposites now seems subject to *season*. Suddenly it becomes clear why Lawrence opened the essay with an account of the wild flowers of Garda-side, season by season. Now also, remembering, there seems poignant inevitability in the 'passing away' of things. 'San Gaudenzio is already becoming a thing of the past',[80] Paolo's old order is almost gone. With this, another plank was in place to bridge Lawrence's impasse, and make it possible to reconcile his previous philosophy with a new sense of direction beyond apocalypse.

(b) 'The Crown' – Travel in the Mind

He sent off 'San Gaudenzio' on 11 September – the fourth essay in what had become an integrated exploration of how the past might illuminate the problem of the present, and show the way to a better future. But instead of going on with any further 'journey into the interior' via Italy, he must have realised with some excitement how to take his direct philosophising past the impasse which had made him abandon it. He turned straightaway to his contribution to *Signature*: the six essays called 'The Crown'. Nine days later he sent the opening essay to the 'little Jew in the Mile End Rd' whom they had found to print the paper (ii. 397);[81] and by 2 October he had done all six (ii. 405). Two days later the first issue appeared.

We can now watch the author of *The Rainbow* visibly turning into the man who would write *Women in Love*. The first two essays restate the central dialectic of 'Hardy', confirmed by Heracleitus, purged of its Christian terminology, and also of its literary and art criticism, and rendered now (hopefully) in more popular terms for a wider audience. Instead of the Persons of the Christian Trinity, the Opposites are imaged in the two beasts of the royal coat of arms and the nursery rhyme about the lion and the unicorn fighting for the crown, or rather, fighting under it, producing it out of the clash of their opposition; as from the crashing waves, the clashing cymbals, the interfusing elements, are born the foam, the music, the iridescent rainbow – absolute, while time swirls the Opposites away. But there can be no victory, defeat or cessation – or everything would perish. The Crown is the *raison d'être* of existence. It is what the opposites are for. Already the gay wisdom has a more sombre side: a sharper realisation, focused by the war, that sometimes there is chaos in which no creation takes place, and sometimes indeed the lion and unicorn go mad, turn in on themselves, seek to triumph in their own partiality and become destructive. Yet the manifest horror of the world of 1915 has not dampened Lawrence's faith that an underlying creativity is at work in the universe – through conflict.

Only how could this be reconciled with the facts of experience in 1915, and his darker perception that this seemed a time when the Opposites had deteriorated to a point where they could no longer be married?

Out of the writing of the new Italian essays came a double answer: that the only way forward must be to let go, let go of the past completely, and that the marriage of opposites is bound to be seasonal. In the third essay for *Signature*, now, Lawrence begins to analyse 'the flux of corruption', the process of disintegration that – he now sees – *must* follow consummation, at least for a season, cyclically:

This is the terror and wonder of dark returning to dark, and of light returning to light, the two departing back to their Sources. This we cannot bear to think of. It is the temporal flux of corruption, as the flux together was the temporal flux of creation. The flux is temporal. It is only the perfect meeting, the perfect utter interpenetration into oneness, the kiss, the blow, the two-in-one, that is timeless and absolute.[82]

Corruption seems terrible to us, caught as we are in the perspective of time. It is not however evil, but necessary. Yet evil begins 'when that which is temporal and relative asserts itself [as] consummate and complete'. The rest of the essay and the three which follow explore the difference between a 'corruption' which is part of a divine process, and a vile and evil hardening into death that can know no rebirth. The word itself carries no judgement: both disintegrative going-apart and creative coming-together are necessary life-processes, and there are times when life may 'even, for a while be purely in one, or purely in the other'. For life is 'really in the two', in necessary succession. But 'corruption, like creation, is only divine when all is given up to it'.[83]

There are two ways in which the human *will* can distort 'pure' corruption into vileness. Consummation attains to timelessness, but on earth everything is, and must be, carried past the moment of fulfilment by the swirl of time – and the process can even have a kind of beauty, as of the lotus or swan standing in mud, or the salt-corroding sea. If however the human will tries to arrest this process, to assert the old attainment past the stage of its necessary coming apart, rottenness inevitably follows – and the attempt to hold on to, possess, what is past its time, also thwarts new growth. For only when the previous consummation has completely disintegrated back to its original elements, can the creative process begin again. When people determine to preserve old forms of society or relationship or value, these inevitably go horribly rotten. A second form of vileness comes when people enclose themselves within the process of corruption, believing this to be the only life; and seek their satisfaction from increasing consciousness of it. The soul can form a shell around itself within which the 'going apart' is *enjoyed* in 'sensational gratification', or 'reduction ' either in the flesh or in the mind. Human relationship can become a friction of ego upon ego by which men and women use each other to disintegrate themselves and each other, no union is possible, and excitement comes from mutually destructive sex war. (Or perhaps sophisticated souls at a time of decadence seek similarly to 'reduce' themselves with less developed individuals of the same sex – in pederasty, or homosexual affairs with social inferiors.)[84] At last the only sensation left to be explored, is the frisson of risking death, and eventually the experience of killing or being killed. The war has come about for both reasons. To arrest a divine process is to become carrion-foul, like a vulture that used to be an eagle and could have been again; or it is to live in a sepulchre that could have been a womb. England and Germany, fighting to preserve old forms, are the lion become dog and the eagle become vulture – both forms of deadly decay. On the other hand, there is 'the desire to deal death and to take death' – the war comes from the death wish of a generation.

Yet the 'God' which is still present in corruption can be liberated, if the barren egoism of the will can be overcome. If people will only give themselves up to the forces which are going on within them, there can be no evil. (Russell should have hit back, openly – it would have been far less damaging.) 'God' is in destruction *and* in creation; 'in the flowing together and the flowing apart'. 'Only perpetuation is a sin.'[85] We must let go of the old; when corruption is necessary, all must be given up to it; for then the creative process can and will begin again, a new dawn, a new world.

(c) In the Half-light

The final essays of the travel-book, which began to flow again in October as soon as 'The Crown' was finished, are all about states of transition, the half-light between worlds. After the seasonal decline of the marriage of opposites traced in 'San Gaudenzio', a season has come when there can be no more than a reaching out of one opposite to another. 'The Dance' and 'Il Duro', a matched pair, explore how the 'Northern' and the 'Italian' are attracted, but recoil – and 'John' rounds off the exploration, touched on in 'San Gaudenzio' and 'Il Duro', of how Italians are drawn to an America they cannot join.[86] 'Italians in Exile' and 'The Return Journey' form another matched pair, in which expatriates of one kind and another are in transit between 'Italy' and 'the North', or walk the line between.

In 'The Dance', the faces of the Northern women show a 'transported wonder' as they are swept by their peasant partners into a different rhythm, 'drifting and palpitating as if their souls shook and resounded to a breeze that was subtly rushing upon them, through them' – till at each climax, swung from earth, 'the woman's body seemed like a boat lifted over the powerful, exquisite wave of the man's body, perfect, for a moment'. For a moment, there becomes possible the two-in-one of the wedding dance in *The Rainbow* – but it can lead nowhere now. When the one-legged wood-cutter beckons from the doorway, gesturing towards the darkness – he is in Cyriax too, the biographical irony (see p. 769 note 77) a gift, and private joke – the blonde Northern woman becomes angry. He is 'stupid, absurd'.[87] Then as the men sing in obscene dialect it is aimed against the foreigners, until Maria puts a stop to it. Soon the foreigners have had enough – though Maria has her profit.

'Il Duro', on the other hand, is even more a creature of the senses than Antony Schofield, the gardener of *The Rainbow* partly drawn from him, with the same touches of the goat and the satyr, at once 'beautiful' and 'sinister', and with his 'clear golden skin, and perfectly turned face, something godlike', if also 'slightly malignant'. Indeed, Pan walks San Gaudenzio in the shape of 'Il Duro'. He has been to America like Paolo, without being touched by the experience, for, more than Paolo and much more than Signor di P., he is at one with his earth. To watch him mixing dung and lime for grafting the vines is like watching a divine force (in Lawrence's sense) in action, so 'amazingly swift and sure, like a god' that it fills the Northern Lawrence 'with a sort of panic' – because it is an 'animal god ... without thought', cutting, cutting at new shoot and stock, to engender, heedlessly. But his inscrutable opposition to the very idea of marrying, and the way that, though a womaniser, he seems to feel a magnetic attraction, almost love, towards the Englishman, give Lawrence 'a feeling of vivid sadness, a sadness that gleamed like phosphorescence' – an image increasingly used to suggest decay after completion. For Il Duro 'has achieved [his] final shape and has nothing more to achieve'. The attraction he feels is not for D. H. Lawrence personally. It cannot, moreover, and will not come to anything. Il Duro seems to have no further power to reach out in the spirit, so Lawrence, though fascinated by the other's 'static perfection', is also 'repelled'.[88]

But the young Italian 'John', in the 'down-at-heel, sordid respectability' of his shabby American clothes, will be inevitably drawn back to the America which has insulted, bullied and despised him, for though he loves his father and is fond of his wife and child, Italy has become a 'past' that can no longer satisfy. In Northern terms he is half-baked, half-educated, a hanger-on to the fringes of American life, but 'He had gone out and faced the world, and he had kept his place, stranger and Dago though he was.' Now he is compelled to do so again, to choose as 'future' what lies there, seeming 'scarcely like a person with individual choice', but rather 'a creature under the influence of fate which was disintegrating the old life and precipitating him, a fragment inconclusive, into the new chaos'. There is something heroic about him as his face is 'set outwards, away from it all—whither, neither he nor anybody knew, but he called it America'.[89] Yet for this he leaves father (whom he may not see again), wife and child, and all that 'Italy' has come to mean to Lawrence. There are painful question marks over both the fragmentariness of his potential, and the chaos he is going into. So the heroic fuses with the pathetic in tremulous balance. The only thing that is certain is disintegration.

We have been watching the travel through memory become a coherent book and no mere collection of sketches, though it has yet to find an appropriate title. It may be 'Italian Studies' in terms of its material – yet as in 'John', the process in *time*, that compels human souls impersonally throughout, is neither confined to Italy, nor indeed are Italians all of a kind that could be described in terms of national characteristics. Appropriately, then, the final two chapters juxtapose several sorts of people moving in different ways and directions through the borderland between 'Italy' and 'the North', as though drawn by magnetic force.

'Italians in Exile' is about Lawrence's meeting on the German–Swiss border, on his walk to Italy in 1913, with the group of Italian expatriate millworkers (see p. 95). 'The North', too, is not homogeneous. The chapter has already contrasted the picturesque past of the Rhineland with the modern present of factories in both Germany and Switzerland, and with the deadening bourgeois ordinariness of the Swiss. (The drunken landlord and his delirium tremens gain symbolic resonance within the book as a whole; a sign of disintegration below the surface of material prosperity.) These Italian factory-workers are amusing themselves in the evenings by reading through a play – so à propos, that if it were not so it would have had to be invented, to pick up 'Enrico Persevalli' in 'The Theatre'. The leading spirit Giuseppino – a most appropriate name for one who leads the way in exile into foreign territory, whither his brothers will have to follow – is intelligent, has learnt good German and speaks with contempt of the peasants on Lake Garda, which the Lawrence who had been so drawn to them resents. This modern Italian is 'Quick, vivid, and sharp', intellectual, remembered as a luminous face – but Lawrence can hardly remember the thin body, 'evanescent, like a shadow'. The others form a spectrum, but even the one who seems still part of 'the old tradition' is, unlike Il Duro, 'curiously subject to a new purpose, as if there were some greater new will that included him, sensuous, mindless as he was'. They love Italy passionately and miss the sun, their blood and senses are still 'Italian', the minds of most (save Joseph) are 'not developed', yet they will not go back, for 'a new tiny flower was struggling to open in them'. Lawrence, the 'I' who is there less as personality than to represent 'the North', has very ambiguous feelings again about the paradox: that just when the North is trying to turn its back on Christianity and become 'Dionysiac', the South is trying to break free in the other direction. He cannot but admire the flame that burns in Giuseppino the anarchist, yet he knows what suffering lies ahead, and after his Northern experience can feel no rosy illusion about the goals of this rebel against the Father, and new-fledged disciple of the Son. Moreover, afterwards, by a kind of 'negative magnetism', he could not bear to see or even think of them again, or look at the anarchist paper they gave him. Indeed, 'the moment my memory touched them, my whole soul stopped and was null ... I shrink involuntarily away, I do not know why this is.' (Perhaps, in 1915, it might be because of people like Russell who think that all can be remedied by some freedom and social reconstruction? And also the knowledge, now, that the path so alluring to Giuseppino has led, in the North, to the Zeppelin in the sky?)[90] But mostly it is because the 'I' is on a border, too, in transit in the opposite direction. Realisation is dawning, though it is not quite clear yet, that now is a time of reverse magnetism, when opposites go apart, instinctively repelled rather than attracted by each other.

So 'The Return Journey' sees, first, an ironic glimpse of two Northerners walking the borderland in some attraction to 'the South', but unable in different ways to *cross* the frontier in any meaningful sense; while Lawrence has crossed back again for the second time, only to know beyond question that what he is crossing for will be less and less to be found. The young Englishman he meets, on a walking tour holiday, has driven himself so hard that he is 'sick with fatigue and over-exhaustion'; but the life of the body and the blood is not to be had by driving the body to its limits by will power. The machine man, trying to become physical, only reveals himself more clearly by treating his body as though it were a machine. And, 'only to walk along the ridge and to descend on the same side! My God, it was killing to the soul.' On the other hand the young Swiss with his great boots, his membership of the Sportverein, and his naïve looking forward to citizens' military service, though physical enough in an earnest sort of way, is also only on holiday. He crosses only a little way, before making the return journey, quickly, into German Switzerland again, ultimately as neutral and circular as the holidaying Englishman, and the monks.

Whereas Lawrence, going on from the borderland down the new highway to Milan, finds more and more evidence of disintegration into a new Italy which fills him with horror 'as if the whole social form were breaking down, and the human element swarmed within the disintegration, like maggots in cheese'. However, when he gets to Milan and sits in the cathedral square, drinking bitter Campari and watching the swarm of the new 'Italian city-men drink and talk vivaciously', he is forced to realise, at last, that *life*, at certain times and seasons of which this is one, may consist *in* disintegration, terrible though that seems – and however the balance of his final sentences may still tremble towards the horror of it.[91]

For only after disintegration and darkness are complete, he now believed, could there come that other half-light, of dawn.

VIII Disaster

He was about to test this, himself. At the end of September he seemed on the crest of a wave: *The Rainbow* out on the 30th, his travel-book and his essays for *Signature* finished – but what followed was a double disaster.

The printing bill for *Signature* would be £30 for six issues, and because he had regained his hope of finding 'associates' and making some public impact, he determined to hold meetings at which his ideas could be discussed after each publication day. So he hired a room in Fisher Street, off Red Lion Square between Holborn and Bloomsbury, and spent about £3/5/0 on a second-hand carpet, a long table and some chairs.[92] Upwards of 250 subscribers at half-a-crown would be required if the venture was to break even. Moreover the idea of the meetings was optimistic to say the least, though it shows how strongly Lawrence longed not to be so isolated. He had made a real effort to make his thought more transparent. Nevertheless he was defining the significance of 1915 in imagistic and theoretic terms not easy to grasp at once, let alone become immediately activated by. Also, the kind of people he wanted to reach were not necessarily the kind who would turn out at 8 p.m. of an October night to a little room in Fisher Street. Neither Murry nor Katherine, nor Kot who had agreed to handle the financial side, involved themselves with the meetings.

By 22 September, despite leaflets and letters to friends old and new, urging them to approach their friends also, there were only 30 subscribers. By 2 October, two days before publication day, the subscription list had reached 'about £7', i.e. 56.[93] But perhaps the first issue might bring more, and the first review of *The Rainbow* in the *Evening Standard* the day after publication on 30 September, was favourable. Unknown to Lawrence, however, the prospects of the novel were darkening. Methuen's were apprehensive, having had only 240 advance orders, and fearing – as it turned out with good reason – that the circulating libraries would refuse it. On 5 October with *Signature* about to appear, Lawrence complained to Pinker about the charges for his alterations, and asked what the libraries were doing (ii. 406).[94]

Then disasters came thick and fast. The first *Signature* made little if any impression on autumnal London. The next day Robert Lynd in the *Daily News* called *The Rainbow* 'a monotonous wilderness of phallicism' and its characters 'as lacking in the inhibitions of ordinary civilised life as savages'. Lawrence was upset, and went off to Acacia Road to find comfort, but got none. As Murry's autobiography would explain, 'We neither of us liked *The Rainbow* and Katherine quite definitely hated parts of it', especially Anna dancing naked, which she called ' "female" – her most damning adjective'. (She had a more private reason for hating Ursula's affair with Winfred Inger.) Murry, for his part 'disliked it on instinct. There was a warm, close, heavy promiscuity of flesh about it which repelled me.' In fact, his only difference from Lynd was that he 'happened to be friends with Lawrence, and Robert Lynd didn't'.[95] Nor did their contributions to *The Signature* seem likely to increase its impact. The first of Katherine's (writing as 'Matilda Berry') were rather slight though charming evocations of childhood, the product of reminiscing under the pear tree in Acacia Road with her beloved brother Leslie before he left for the trenches on the 4th. (Her third contribution, 'The Little Governess', was however a very different matter, and with 'The Crown', all that has lasted of the venture.) Murry's ongoing 'There Was a Little Man', on his feelings about the war and personal freedom, was almost wholly self-enclosed and of little interest to anyone but himself. Three days later Katherine's brother, teaching his men how to throw a hand-grenade, had one blow up in his hand and was killed. Katherine was absolutely devastated when she had the telegram on the 11th – not only incapable now of taking any interest in anything else, but soon to feel that she could not bear London and England any longer, and must leave.

Lawrence's misery would rapidly increase to that point too – though for the moment he took imaginative refuge in the world of his Italian sketches (finishing 'Il Duro' on the 8th and 'Italians in Exile' on the 12th). In ironic contrast to that animated meeting with the Italians in 1913, the *Signature* meeting in Fisher Street on the 11th was a flop – though the faithful Kot had brought coal for a fire and Frieda even helped prepare the room. Some more subscriptions trickled in, but by the time the second issue came out on the 18th, it was clear that the break-even target would never be reached.[96] They decided to cut their losses: there would be only one more issue on 1 November (so the fourth, fifth and sixth essays of 'The Crown' would remain unpublished); and one more meeting at Fisher Street on the 24th, though only because he had not given notice in time to cancel. So, in fiasco, ended his hopes of finding soul-allies for his revolution, through 'preaching' his ideas directly.

He took his failure very hard indeed. Announcing the cancellations to Kot, he declared: 'My soul is torn out of me now: I can't stop here any longer and acquiesce in this which is the spirit now: I would rather die' (ii. 413). He began to think about going to America. He had invested more than anybody around him realized in the twin belief that there *was*, in the souls of a sizable number of English people, a subterranean longing for a new world, and that his words could provide the impetus to release powerful hidden energies for change. It was a devastating blow to discover that his preachments had proved so apparently irrelevant to people's concerns in 1915. Having been immersed in an isolated world of imaginative struggle at Greatham had kept him to some extent unaware how ill-aligned he was with the spirit of that year: the mesmerising bad news from the front, the mounting casualties affecting family after family, the wounded pouring in through the London terminals, the Zeppelin raids, the sense (for those at home) of being subject to forces over which one had no control, taking away one's loved ones and (if one was lucky) returning them at intervals taciturn and changed, the awareness not of the psychological corruption Lawrence talked about (true though that might be deep down), but of mounting and very concrete national crisis. Cynthia Asquith, for example, one of his greatest admirers, had little room for sympathy for him just now, though she knew he was 'sore' about *Signature*. Her beloved brother Yvo Charteris was killed at Loos on the 19th, after only three weeks in France. Writing in sympathy two days later, Lawrence could yet not stop himself from insisting that 'the whole spirit which we now maintain ... is *wrong*, so awfully wrong, that it is like a great consuming fire' (ii. 414), so he had to get away, rather than acquiesce, though 'Englishness is my very vision' (ii. 414). But her diary has no space for this letter, wholly taken up as it is with how Yvo's death has 'emptied the future', and with Katharine Asquith's agony over Raymond leaving for the front.[97]

By 18 October, moreover, Methuen knew that *The Rainbow* was 'a dangerous fiasco' since none of the big libraries or bookstalls 'would touch it' because of 'the author's obstinate refusal to make the necessary alterations'.[98] They would refuse his next book if it were so outspoken. But from the 22nd the pace of disaster quickened beyond all foreseeing. James Douglas not only denounced the novel in the *Star* – 'These people are not human beings. They are creatures who are immeasurably lower than the lowest animal in the Zoo' – but called for prosecution. When art, Douglas fumed, refuses to 'conform to the ordered laws that govern human society ... it must pay the penalty. The sanitary inspector of literature must notify it and call for its isolation. The wind of war is sweeping over our life ... A thing like *The Rainbow* has no right to exist in the wind of war.' The next day, Clement Shorter in the *Sphere* conceded that the book had been written 'from artistic impulses', and he had reservations about literary censorship, but he too judged that 'There is no form of viciousness, of suggestiveness, that is not reflected in these pages.' His suggestion that, after this, no writer who was also an artist need fear prosecution, would also have rung alarms in official ears. He found 'no justification whatever for the perpetration of such a book'.[99] On 26 October, if Lawrence felt any elation about sending the complete manuscript of his travel-book to Pinker, it must have been dampened by also having to write to Else about the death of little Peter, her son by Otto Gross (ii. 415–16). Around the 28th, Methuen quietly removed *The Rainbow* from their advertisements, which W. L. George spotted, and telephoned Methuen to find out what was going on (ii. 440). By 5 November the police were making their second visit to Methuen, to complete a confiscation of all unsold copies and unbound sheets under the Obscene Publications Act of 1857 – with the publisher's full co-operation. (Only then did Lawrence hear the full extent of the trouble.) Methuen also began voluntarily to recall copies that had already gone out to bookshops. They seem to have thought that the hearing before a magistrate, which was scheduled for 13 November, to determine whether the book should be destroyed, would be a formality not heard in public court, and did not instruct counsel – but they were mistaken. The law did not require the author to be informed, or represented in any way – and Methuen made no attempt at any time to communicate with Lawrence. Pinker later testified that they had not only taken 'no steps whatever to defend the book or to protect the author's interest' but had also tried to discourage anyone else from doing so.[100]

Lawrence thought, afterwards, that the prosecution was 'instigated by the National Purity League, Dr Horton and Co, nonconformity' (ii. 477), presumably by complaint to the police and the Home Office, but there is no confirmation of this. It has also been suggested that there might have been a political motive, after the police enquiries in 1914, Ford's visit to Greatham and perhaps Lawrence's association with Russell who was rapidly becoming a nuisance in Government eyes. A Home Office minute of 1930 states that the proceedings were initiated by the Director of Public Prosecutions himself, and the chosen prosecutor, Herbert Muskett, often handled important cases, so the personnel might seem rather powerful for a case of mere literary obscenity. Moreover a note on the Home Office memorandum prepared after the trial for the Home Secretary (to help him answer a written parliamentary question by Philip Morrell) has a note of a file number 'As to a Mrs Weekley, living at address of D. H. Lawrence' which has been taken to refer to an Intelligence file.[101]

However the evidence is somewhat shaky, quite apart from Ford's unreliability. The note about the file – which is in red ink, and may be much later than the memorandum – also makes it likely that it originated before Frieda's marriage to Lawrence, and hence *before* the war, and may have had to do with a passport. It is true that some quite well-known people had been approached about *Signature*, and Cynthia admits to having been teased about *The Rainbow* within the Prime Minister's family, so there may have been talk about both at his dinner table. The German name in the novel's dedication, together with the signs of hostility to soldierly patriotism and imperialism in Ursula's denunciations of Skrebensky, might have given offence in those dark days of the war. On the other hand, the prosecution needs no more explanation than the reviews, which were cited in court; and indeed the Home Office considered prosecuting the novel *again*, after Lawrence's death, when only its 'obscenity' could have been at issue.[102] It remains possible that the journalistic demands for prosecution were seen as an opportunity to discredit an author whose opposition to the war might become a nuisance – but the evidence is far from conclusive, and the fate of *Signature* soon demonstrated how little of a threat he was.

Meanwhile at the end of October, suffering from the reviews but still in ignorance of what was brewing, Lawrence applied for passports for America, though there too *The Rainbow* was causing concern. George H. Doran, who had accepted the book on Pinker's recommendation, took fright when he received it. He thought about alterations, but then telegraphed his decision not to go ahead, though he softened the blow by finding another, smaller publisher, Benjamin Huebsch, who was prepared to risk it (ii. 419 n. 2; 420 n. 2). Lawrence wondered whether to publish in America at all, and suspected Huebsch's motives: 'Is he somebody disreputable, or what?' (ii. 426). It was terrible enough that the work of religious imagination which had cost two and a half years of struggle should be accused of obscenity; but it would be worse to have that become the reason for publishing. Fortunately Huebsch would turn out to be liberal, courageous and also creatively devious. (Admiring reports from the two quite formidable 'readers' he chose to advise him suggest that *The Rainbow* might get a hearing in America that was being denied it in England, though alas no word of this reached Lawrence now.)[103]

He took refuge in imagination. On 28 October he lunched with Cynthia and Beb and despite his troubles 'was in excellent form, really delightful' – so that she found it difficult to believe that he was the man who had written *The Rainbow*, that 'strange, bewildering, disturbing book'.[104] Two days later he sent her a story containing a 'word-sketch' of her (ii. 420, 418). In 'The Thimble' a 27-year-old wife awaits the homecoming of a husband whose face has been mutilated by shrapnel. For all her fashionable beauty and high-bred stoicism she is terribly nervous: she has realised that the man she married, in love with his glamour as a soldier, does not exist, and that she has no idea of what the unknown 'he' she is waiting for is like, especially after what has happened. Nervously feeling down the sides of a sofa bought in a great-house sale, her fingers bring up a heavy jewelled thimble, belonging to some dead aristocrat. When her husband arrives, and she sees how he has hovered between life and death, both come to realise that they have already died to their old selves and are as helpless as the new-born to face their future – and yet that they must try to love. Is 'resurrection' possible? The first step is to throw the thimble out of the window, symbol of the dead past. Cynthia did not understand the symbolism, and insisted that 'large feet' had been 'gratuitously put in'; but thought 'some of his character hints are damnably good'.[105] (Indeed Beb would have flinched at one or two sentences which again align the husband with Evelyn in 'England, My England'.) But several of the circumstances are quite different from the Asquiths', and once again Lawrence's concern was not with portraiture but, as he told Cynthia, with resurrection: 'The fact of resurrection is everything, now: whether we dead can rise from the dead, and love, and live, in a new life, here' (ii. 420). (He had also written his poem 'Resurrection' in October.) Three days later, 2 November, he sent her a copy of the poem 'The Turning Back', filled with the sense of the innumerable ghosts of the slain that he had pictured in the mist that day in Bognor. The slaughter has gone too far – the things fought for, 'goods, and homes and land', even survival, no longer matter. What supremely matters is that the living should 'take our ghosts into our hearts', 'let the weapons slip from out our hands' and seek to love again.

> For we have gone too far, oh much too far
> Towards the darkness and the shadow of death;
> Let us turn back, lest we should all be lost
>   . . .
> Let us go back, the only way is love. (ii. 423)[106]

When Cynthia objected that this seemed an unpatriotic call to 'down tools' at a time of national crisis, and insisted that it was possible still to love and be complete on the personal level even in the midst of war, he insisted the reverse was true. War comes from a spirit of disintegration which will inevitably atomise people into single entities – whereas love is a spirit of creation 'making an integral unity out of many disintegrated factors'. He would have to leave England because he was for love and anti-war; so 'I can never agree to the complete disintegration, never stand witness to it, never.' Better anything, even a German victory, than that the 'quick' of the living organism of Europe perish, for 'There are unrevealed buds which can come forward into another epoch of civilisation, if only we can shed this dead form and be strong in the spirit of love and creation' (ii. 424–5).

On 5 November he heard that *The Rainbow* was being suppressed. 'I am not very much moved', he told Pinker (the next day), 'am beyond that by now. I only curse them all, body and soul, root, branch and leaf, to eternal damnation' (ii. 429). It was, apart from embarking on the Ostend ferry with Frieda, the most determining moment of his life so far – and as sometimes happens when everything becomes very clear, he may have been calmer than might have been expected – though the sickening impact of the news is unimaginable. Their passports had arrived. He would go to America, in 'about a fortnight'.

The evening he heard the news – of all evenings – they had accepted an invitation to the studio of a young painter, a friend of Gertler's from the Slade, the Hon. Dorothy Brett, whom Gertler had introduced to Byron Villas not long before. She gave Gertler and Carrington, the Lawrences, the Murrys and Kot supper, and they were busy playing charades when a whole party of gate-crashers burst in. Among them was Lytton Strachey with his dinner hosts the St John Hutchinsons, Clive Bell (whose mistress Mary Hutchinson was) and Iris Tree. The whole atmosphere of the party changed, and as Brett doggedly played the pianola for dancing, became steadily more drunken – ending with Murry quite incapable. Across the room, Strachey watched as Frieda danced with Clive:

I was surprised to find that I liked her looks very much – she actually seemed (there's no other word for it) a lady: as for him I've rarely seen anyone so pathetic, miserable, ill, and obviously devoured by internal distresses. He behaved to everyone with the greatest cordiality, but I noticed for a second a look of intense disgust and hatred flash into his face ... caused by – ah! – whom.[107]

Neither Brett nor Strachey were aware that he had just heard about the police at Methuen. Meanwhile Ottoline offered refuge in Garsington, where (without Frieda) he found a precious interval of peace from 8 to 11 November. She may have expected rage, but he only wanted quiet. He helped plant irises by the ponds, and drove with her into Oxford to look at the colleges and the Ashmolean. He thought briefly about rallying support, but mostly he wanted to emigrate – for he could hardly bear, in these lovely old places, the thought of England and the 2,000 years of civilisation behind it that was 'now collapsing ... So much beauty and pathos of old things passing away and no new things coming ... my God, it breaks my soul –' (ii. 431). He told Eddie Marsh that he felt 'so sick, in body and soul, that if I don't go away I shall die', and asked for a loan to help him get to Florida, where he thought he could borrow somewhere to live from a friend of Dollie Radford (ii. 429). Marsh sent £20, to add to the £40 which was all that remained of the Methuen advance; and Ottoline would add another £30 before long.[108]

On 13 November in the Bow Street Court, the Prosecutor and the Magistrate held the floor unopposed, and Methuen had their reward for co-operating. Muskett called them 'a publishing house of old standing and the highest repute' who had behaved 'with the strictest propriety' – though it was difficult to see how they had lent their 'great name' to such a work. The Magistrate, Sir John Dickinson, followed suit almost exactly. Methuen took their cue and apologised; their representative claiming that they had twice acted decisively to get the author to change certain passages, when they first received the manuscript and when they got it back, but admitting that they had perhaps been unwise in not scrutinising the final version more closely. Though it was quite clear that the prosecution would be unopposed, both Sir John and Muskett (who said he had consulted the Director of Public Prosecutions) went out of their way to execrate the novel, which might suggest a determination to discredit the absent author, known to be opposed to the war. (Sir John had lost his only son at the front six weeks before.) The two most hostile reviews were read out in court. Muskett called the novel 'a mass of obscenity of thought, idea, and action throughout, wrapped up in language which he supposed would be regarded in some quarters as an artistic and intellectual effort'. Sir John, having tartly called attention to the chapter 'Shame' – to the discomfiture of Methuen's man who had said that though he found it 'disgraceful' now, two colleagues had not seen anything wrong – went on to declare that 'he had never read anything more disgusting than this book ... It was appalling to think of the harm that such a book might have done. It was utter filth, nothing else would describe it.' He imposed no fine, but made the order for the destruction of all the copies and sheets that had been confiscated, and awarded costs (10 guineas) against the publishers.[109]

Such was England's official verdict on one of the great novels of the language. It would not be available in Britain again for another eleven years.

It is impossible to exaggerate the effect of this on Lawrence. He had been made to feel a contemptible alien in his homeland. He had lost his audience. 'It is the end of my writing for England', he told Pinker when the police raided Methuen, 'I will try to change my public' (ii. 429). The reports of the trial can only have strengthened these feelings, a thousandfold.

He prepared now to sail to America from Liverpool on 24 November on the White Star liner *Adriatic*. 1 Byron Villas was put up to let. On the 15th he wrote to beg Russell to come and see him before they left, despite their quarrel (ii. 436), and urged Cynthia in a 'parting letter' the next day to get to know Lady Ottoline, and to try to 'get the *intrinsic* reality clear' within her own soul (ii. 437). She was to remember that he and Frieda would always stand by her, as she should stand by them. Maybe she and Beb would come to America eventually, too.

Perhaps, over there, was some hope for the future.

PART THREE

◆

Cornwall

◆

CHAPTER SIX

November 1915–December 1916

MID-WINTER LIFE

Our lives have been all autumnal and wintry. Now it is mid-winter. But we
are strong enough to give way, to pass away, and to be born again.
(ii. 481–2)

I Internal Exile

By 16 November 1915, Lawrence was firmly planning to leave London within a
week, to say good-bye to his sisters at Ripley. From there, he and Frieda would
go to Liverpool and board a liner on the 24th for New York (ii. 435). This was a
turning-point which might have made his life very different, if he had gone –
but he did not, and the reasons were very characteristic.

Though he longed above all now to get away – if also dreading it, knowing
that emigration would mean 'changing the land of my soul as well as my mere
domicile' (ii. 428) – there was also a stubborn impulse not to go before putting
up a fight. W. L. George had asked the Incorporated Society of Authors,
Playwrights and Composers to take up the case of *The Rainbow*, and on
11 November Lawrence had replied to their enquiry and asked for membership.
Two days later, the day of the trial, it seemed possible that Pinker might
persuade a number of writers, de la Mare, Forster, Murry, J. D. Beresford,
Hugh Walpole and Gilbert Cannan, to write a letter to the papers in his support
(ii. 435). Pinker may also have told him that Clive Bell had wanted to do
something. Bell and Lytton Strachey, probably unbeknown to Lawrence, had
tried to persuade J. C. Squire, literary editor of the *New Statesman*: that some
protest should be made at an obvious injustice, irrespective of whether they
personally admired the book or not. (Instead, Squire wrote a hostile review.)[1]
Lawrence had met Bell, and 'rather' liked him (ii. 435).

In fact, not a single well-known writer stood up for *The Rainbow* and its
author in public – with the honourable exception of Arnold Bennett, some
weeks later. Lesser figures who tried to do so were punished or silenced by
newspaper editors anxious not to be seen breaking ranks on such an issue, or at
such a time. Catherine Carswell, who had written a largely admiring but by no
means uncritical review for the *Glasgow Herald* on 4 November, was sacked for
it. A perceptive notice by Herbert Watson for the *Daily Telegraph* was first held

over, to await the result of the court case, and then suppressed – and has only recently come to light.[2] Not only had official England made up its mind and carried out its 'justice', but there would be no protest in its press. Moreover the Murrys, who Lawrence thought of as (with Kot) his closest friends, were coping with Katherine's own tragedy and understandably had little sympathy to spare. They had decided to leave for the south of France, and by 18 November were in Marseilles. (Kot took over the lease of 5 Acacia Road, with his friends the Farbmans.)

Lawrence's 'horrible feeling of hopelessness' (ii. 433) was justified, yet it would have been most unlike him to give in to it altogether, and his feelings began to change. On 16 November he seemed determined to shake the dust of England from his shoes as soon as possible. The next day he began to think that after all he ought perhaps to stay awhile and put up a fight first, though he did not really want to (e.g. ii. 439). Something had given him fresh hope. By the end of the month, though he still felt heartbroken and still intended to go to Florida before long, he was trying hard to fight back first. Then most ironically, a fortnight later, he found he could not bring himself to comply with new official requirements for leaving the country, and would have to stay in England anyway – an exile and alien in his own land, rather than abroad.

The change of mind by the 17th had several causes. He heard from Pinker that day that the Committee of the Authors' Society had agreed to consider his case, and had asked for full information on the actions of the publisher and 'whether the author had the opportunity of being heard'.[3] If nobody would support the book itself, perhaps a case could be made against the injustice that had condemned it without giving its author a chance to defend himself. Moreover Philip Morrell now proposed to raise precisely that question in the House of Commons. On the 17th, by happenstance, the Prime Minister's wife had lent Cynthia a car in which she went off to visit the Lawrences in Hampstead. A telegram arrived from Morrell asking Lawrence to come to see him in the House as soon as possible, so Cynthia took him to Westminster. The next day the Liberal M.P. asked the Home Secretary at question time

whether his attention has been called to the proceedings recently instituted by the Commissioner of Police for the suppression of a book by Mr. D. H. Lawrence, entitled 'The Rainbow'; whether the police were acting with the knowledge and authority of the Home Office; and whether the author of the book had any opportunity of replying to the charge made against him?

To which Sir John Simon replied that the action had been 'taken by the police in pursuance of their ordinary duty' for which 'Home Office authorisation is not required'. 'The publishers, and not the author, were the defendants' and had been given 'the customary opportunity to produce such evidence as they considered necessary in their defence'.[4] Morrell then gave notice of a written question, concentrating on the injustice to the author, to which the Home Secretary would have to reply on 1 December.

Though he still wished to leave, Lawrence now felt he ought to stay to see the outcome, both in the Authors' Society and in the Commons. Supportive letters began to arrive in the aftermath of the trial. Unfortunately he never kept correspondence so there is no knowing the extent of this private support, but letters came not only from old friends like Constance Garnett (ii. 441; Edward was away), but also from strangers such as Oliver Lodge, eminent scientist and Principal of the University of Birmingham (ii. 440). The novelist May Sinclair seems also to have written. He began to wonder whether H. G. Wells, Henry James and Arnold Bennett might be willing to speak for him.[5]

He had also got to know more people in London than happen to be mentioned in his letters, and many new or newish friends may have been quite strongly supportive. It is only by chance, for example, that we know about Herbert Watson, over whose death in the trenches, later, Lawrence would express hitherto inexplicable grief (iii. 101);[6] and though the letters show that in late September he recommended to Marsh and Harriet Monroe the poems of 'Anna Wickham' (ii. 400–1), this hardly suggests the degree of friendship revealed in a little-known essay by Anna Hepburn (her real name), written after his death. He probably met her in 1914 through Bunny Garnett who had an affair with her – but she must have been quite often in Byron Villas, where she felt their 'communion was profound and exceedingly serious', and by no means one-sided, since he 'not only let me talk but appeared interested in what I said'. She drew a distinction between the man and his ideas, particularly about women, who (she charged) he confined to their sexuality; and she was amused by the 'burlesque' of his attempts to subdue Frieda. She felt for the 'caritas' rather than the Board School teacher in him; but he clearly had become a warm friend of this handsome, big, dark, gypsyish woman and passionate feminist, so much so that 'My nerves remember him, and, perhaps as he would have it, also my blood. After sixteen years it is as if he had just gone out of the room.' So strong a libertarian would have left him in no doubt of her support over what had been done to him and his novel.[7] He had also been sought out (and amused) by Hugh Meredith, one of Forster's greatest friends, Professor of Economics at Queen's University Belfast and a poet who nevertheless denounced all language, and who claimed to be going mad but took it remarkably humorously. The letter that first mentions Meredith, also mentions Lawrence's liking for H. J. Massingham, an acquaintanceship of which we know almost nothing,[8] and that he is about to meet Bernard Shaw and A. J. Balfour (now First Lord of the Admiralty), though of such a meeting there is no record. Though we know so much of Lawrence's daily life, there are many gaps. He knew Zinaida Vengerova (Russian feminist, and friend of Constance Garnett and of Kot) well enough to entrust her with his own set of the proofs of *The Rainbow*, in the hope that she could organise a Russian translation; but of their acquaintance we know nothing.[9] Vere Bischoff-Collins of the Educational Division of Oxford University Press wrote in support and offered refuge not only then but (valuably) later as well.[10] When Lawrence speaks of 'letters from a lot of people' (ii. 440) about *The Rainbow*, therefore, there may have been a degree of private support in welcome contrast with the lack of any in public, other than Philip Morrell's.

These were people of an age with Lawrence or older, but the most heartening phenomenon of all, in mid-November, was the rallying to him of a number of young people in their early twenties. On 16 November he met Philip Heseltine,[11] a 21-year-old ex-Etonian who had developed, while still at school, a promising musical talent and a precocious devotion to the work of the composer Frederick Delius. After a year at Christ Church, Oxford, Heseltine had persuaded his mother (who gave him a small private income) to allow him to leave and study at the University of London instead, but he was uncertain of his direction and sure only of his interest in music – as against the more worldly kind of career that would please his mother and stepfather. He had a flat in Rossetti Mansions, Chelsea, and had begun to frequent the Café Royal and mingle with its arty and bohemian regulars. (It may have been either through his anthropologist friend Boris de Croustchoff or the sculptor Jacob Epstein that he acquired an African carving, which proclaimed, in another way, his belonging to an avant-garde.) His Oxford friend Robert Nichols had introduced him to Lawrence's work in 1914, and for it he developed another of his intense enthusiasms. In October 1914 he wrote Delius that the first three novels were 'simply unrivaled [sic], in depth of insight and beauty of language, by any other contemporary writer'; and he told Nichols 'no modern prose style' was 'so perfect' as Lawrence's in *Sons and Lovers*. It is unclear how he came to meet Lawrence now, but it was probably through writing to denounce the suppression of what he assured Delius was 'a perfectly magnificent book'.[12] Into the meeting would have gone not only the young man's enthusiasm for the work, but also his rebellious feelings about the hypocrisy and injustice of the older generation, confronted with manifest genius.

As it happened, the 22-year-old Nichols[13] was then in the Lord Knutsford Hospital for Officers, suffering from what was not yet recognised as shell-shock. He too must have written to Lawrence who visited him there and, discovering that Nichols wrote poetry, asked to read some. Delighted to find he could admire it, he promised to help with publication. 'You are a poet, my dear fellow: I am *so glad*: the first I have found: the future' (ii. 444). With such ardent young adherents, Lawrence rapidly recovered the faith in the future that he could never quite lose. He wanted very much to believe that there was a life-force in people which his words could liberate; and though his elders and most contemporaries had proved too hardened in 'corruption' to listen, and had felt so threatened by his work that they had banded together to destroy it, here seemed proof that Rananim was still possible with a younger group. Immediately the dream revived.

Moreover the idea of going to Florida (at the end of the year, now) suddenly seemed quite practical. For though there turned out to be no house on the estate of Dollie's friend, his description of the landscape around Fort Myers sounded attractive, and he offered Lawrence letters of introduction. Also, Delius had tried orange planting in Florida for two years, near Jacksonville, and still owned the property. At once Philip wrote to ask whether Lawrence could live there, and announced his intention of going too. Delius wrote back discouragingly. The climate of California would be much better for someone Philip had described as consumptive; the place would be tropically overgrown and the house probably derelict; and they would be so isolated that they would have to live on canned food – but up to mid-December the dream was still alive. By then, Philip had a doctor's certificate to prove his incapacity for military service and was sure that 'some half-dozen' young people would join Lawrence.[14]

So, though no help was forthcoming from older writers like James or Wells, the support of these young people kept Lawrence optimistic, and persuaded him not to leave for America just yet. Soon he was at Garsington again, with Frieda this time, having persuaded Ottoline also to invite Heseltine and one of his Oxford friends, a Muslim Indian Shahid Hasan Suhrawardy, who claimed direct descent from the Prophet. (Another friend of Heseltine's, Dikran Kouyoumdjian, who would later achieve wealth and fame as the popular novelist 'Michael Arlen', would visit Garsington with Philip a fortnight later. A third friend, Boris de Croustchoff, a young Russian anthropologist and bibliophile, didn't go on either occasion but was also a 'possible' for the new Rananim.)[15] Perhaps, wrote Lawrence to Cynthia on the 28th – when he might have been nearing New York – they would get away by Christmas, and sail straight to Florida by cargo boat, without risking the wintry climate of New York. This letter was not only full of the language of resurrection again – though he had another spasm of doubt over writing such things to Cynthia – but he also enclosed an extract from his October poem of that title:

> Now like a crocus in the autumn time
> My soul comes naked from the falling night
> Of death, a cyclamen, a crocus flower
> Of windy autumn when the winds all sweep
> The hosts away to death, where heap on heap
> The leaves are smouldering in a funeral wind. (ii. 455)[16]

Making another new start, he bought himself a suit and Frieda a coat, skirt and overcoat; he trimmed a toque hat for her with fur; and off they went to Garsington on Monday 29th (ii. 454), to see a disastrous November out.

Moreover Russell had come to Byron Villas (on the 19th) and they made up the worst of their quarrel. Once again Lawrence 'liked Bertie very much', indeed had found him 'more simple and real' than ever before – though he thought it less than 'manly' to be reproached for his letter as though he had set out 'wantonly' to hurt him (ii. 450). In fact, drawing from his own experience with Frieda, he thought the new quiet simplicity might be the product of his outburst, like the calm clarity after a thunderstorm. They would see Russell, too, at Garsington where he still had rooms.

Lawrence was struck again by the sheer beauty of the old house in its countryside; and thanked Ottoline afterwards with a prose poem about it, as the epitome of all that was best in the past (ii. 459–60). In mid-week there were no hordes of guests. Before Philip Morrell went to hear the Home Secretary's response to his written question on 1 December, there was animated and hopeful discussion about the possibility of republishing *The Rainbow* privately, by subscription. Letters immediately went off to Catherine Carswell for Donald's legal opinion on whether reprinting would infringe Methuen's rights (ii. 456), and to Pinker asking him to find out whether Methuen had any objection, and would sell the plates (ii. 457). From the Rumanian diplomat Prince Antoine Bibesco came the suggestion of a Paris publisher, Conard, whom Pinker also knew (ii. 453, 458).[17] Moreover an unexpected suggestion came from the Home Secretary in reply to Morrell in the Commons the next day. Sir John Simon confirmed that the author had no rights at all in the matter, and that the police and magistrate had acted perfectly legally. Pressed however, by Morrell and a Labour politician, to admit the gap between law and natural justice, Sir John replied: 'I imagine it will be possible, if the author thinks he has been wrongly treated, for another copy to be seized by arrangement, in order that he might defend the book.'[18] The fight suddenly seemed less hopeless.

At Garsington they passionately discussed not only *The Rainbow* but also politics, and (with Suhrawardy) India. Lawrence noted ruefully 'I always shout too loud' (ii. 466). But there was escapist fun too. Ottoline's famous trunk of dressing-up materials was opened in the hall – she had 'heaps of coloured cloths and things, like an Eastern bazaar. One can dress up splendidly' (ii. 465), and Lawrence always loved acting in charades. (It may have been on this occasion that he did Othello.) Heseltine probably played his host's pianola – he had one of his own – and he became strongly attracted to 'Mademoiselle', Julian's young governess Juliette Baillot. With her fair hair in tight buns on either side of her pretty and self-possessed head, the Swiss girl was a striking contrast to the dark-haired artist's model Minnie Channing, nicknamed 'Puma', with whom Philip had become involved.[19] Juliette agreed to write to Philip; but Ottoline could not share Lawrence's enthusiasm for his new friends. With an eye perhaps sharpened by noticing the flirtation, she thought the tall, blonde young musician 'soft and so degenerate that he seems somehow corrupt'. He cultivated a cynicism which Lawrence warned him was leaving traces on his face; and though Ottoline was broad-minded, his manners and conversation were distinctly un-Bloomsbury. Neither undergraduatish beer-drinking and motor-bikes, nor Café Royal wine-and-womanising would have appealed to her. She was even harsher about the others. She describes Kouyoumdjian as 'a fat dark-blooded tight-skinned Armenian Jew' with 'a certain vulgar sexual force, but ... very coarse-grained and conceited'; and she was disturbed by the anti-colonial attitude of Suhrawardy, 'extremely anti-English, but like all Indians quite foreign and remote'. Her antipathy to Frieda had grown stronger: she thought of her now as 'devilish ... a wild beast, quite uncontrolled, cruel to Lawrence, and madly jealous if she thinks anyone esteems Lawrence more than her'. Conversely the young men made the mistake, had they wanted to make an impression on their hostess, of constantly flattering Frieda; and Ottoline tired of their boastfulness. These might be Frieda's kind of people, but they were not Garsington's – though they did come once more without Lawrence, a fortnight later.[20]

Nonetheless Lawrence wrote that there had been 'some fine hours', and he was touched by the gift of a tapestry she had embroidered for him. He knew now that though he had a real bond with Ottoline, neither could escape 'the inevitable friction' with his wife: 'Frieda hates me because she says I am a *favorite*, which is ignominious (she says), also she says I am a traitor to her. But let it be – it is a bore' (ii. 462).

At first, back in London, he continued optimistic, both about moving to Florida at the end of the year and doing something about *The Rainbow* now. Pinker had sent him £40 in response to his appeal to make up Marsh and Ottoline's money to the £100 he thought he would need to get to Florida, and then subsist long enough to start earning (ii. 450, 458).[21] A cargo boat (the *Crown [?Corona] de Leon*) would leave from Glasgow on 20 December for the West Indies (ii. 462); and a tenant was found to take over the lease of 1 Byron Villas from that date (ii. 472). Donald Carswell believed there would be a good case for libel against James Douglas and Clement Shorter; and wanted to discuss this and the Home Secretary's suggestion of staging a second prosecution, with Philip Morrell (ii. 462–3). Methuen replied nastily to Pinker that the plates of the novel had been destroyed; that after the police action 'no copyright can exist in the book'; and that indeed, since Lawrence had failed to provide the copyright work he had been paid for, he should refund the £300 advance – but this at least implied that he could go ahead with private or foreign republication if he could find a publisher to risk it. Prince Bibesco came to Hampstead and promised, genially, to help with Conard and drum up subscribers; and Vere Collins also came to give advice about private publication.[22]

However all these possibilities melted into thin air. Though the Georgian poet John Drinkwater and Edward Garnett were willing to protest (ii. 447, 464 n. 2), and Bernard Shaw, having sent £5 (ii. 449), would clearly have done so too, the proposed letter seems never to have been organised. Perhaps Pinker felt it would compromise his agency. Perhaps he was discouraged by the response of Wells, Galsworthy, James (if he made one) and even Bennett (see p. 815 note 5). Maybe people who had seemed ready to sign a protest got cold feet. Perhaps it seemed more practical to collect money – and Pinker may, as Lawrence suspected, have made up much of the £40 himself (ii. 458). After the Home Secretary's clarification of the Obscene Publications Act, Philip Morrell concluded, probably rightly, that there was no hope of succeeding in a lawsuit – and Lawrence himself felt that, after all, his 'spirit will not rise to it ... I am not going to pay any more out of my soul, even for the sake of beating them' (ii. 462). He and Frieda had both caught heavy colds and, living on his nerves, he was becoming run-down. On 8 December came the not unexpected news that the committee of the Society of Authors had taken legal advice and come 'to the conclusion that in the present circumstances they could not take any useful action on the general principles involved' (ii. 469 n. 3).

Once more he longed to get away – and yet another candidate for Florida appeared: a shy, heavily bespectacled, highly intelligent young man from Balliol who had just made his first visit to Garsington. Ottoline wanted him to get to know Lawrence, so Aldous Huxley came to Hampstead for tea on 10 December. Before tea was over, he was invited to Florida, 'and though I was an intellectually cautious young man, not at all inclined to enthusiasms, though Lawrence had startled and embarrassed me with sincerities of a kind to which my upbringing had not accustomed me, I answered yes'.[23] Lawrence and Frieda were always likely to embarrass, whether by intimate revelations about themselves or by their curiosity about the private lives of their friends. Already Lawrence had begun to offer advice about Heseltine's love-life generally and his relations with the two young women in particular. He was also highly taken with Ottoline's niece, Dorothy Warren whom he thought 'beautiful' (ii. 516), and he and Frieda seem to have engaged in some match-making (according to Nichols) by trying to pair her off with one of them – a possibility which dissolved in laughter when they discovered the plot. She too was to come to Florida – hence Heseltine's 'some half-dozen'.[24]

At a deeper level, letters to Ottoline and to Russell now suggest an urgent need to escape inwardly also; to let go of all this frenzied activity of mind and will and resistance, and withdraw into darkness and unconsciousness within. In advising Ottoline how to get beyond her unhappiness about her life – the worsening war, the split in the Liberal party and the Cabinet over conscription, and the love-affair with Russell so clearly ending as he became more and more involved with the Eliots – Lawrence was also advising himself:

We must all submit to be helpless and obliterated, quite obliterated, destroyed, cast away into nothingness ... Do not struggle with your will, to dominate your conscious life – do not do it. Only drift, and let go – let go, entirely, and become dark, quite dark ... Forget, utterly forget ...

I tell this to you, I tell it to myself – to let go, to release from my will everything that my will would hold, to lapse back into darkness and unknowing. There must be deep winter before there can be spring. (ii. 468–9)

He was reading Sir James Frazer's *Golden Bough* and *Totem and Exogamy* just now, and in Frazer's accounts of earlier cultures and beliefs he found a new confirmation of the view he had expounded to Collings in 1913, 'that there is another seat of consciousness than the brain and the nerve system', the blood (ii. 470; cf. i. 503–4). While apparently diagnosing an imbalance in Russell he knew it was also a danger for himself, since:

the tragedy of this our life, and of your life, is that the mental and nerve consciousness exerts a tyranny over the blood-consciousness, and that your will has gone completely over to the mental consciousness, and is engaged in the destruction of your blood-being ... Now it is necessary for us to realise that there is this other great half of our life active in the darkness ...

Do you know what science says about these things? It is *very* important: the whole of our future life depends on it. (ii. 470–1)

It was to be an impulse of 'blood-consciousness' rather than any thoughtful decision or willed act that would determine his next four years, making him a writer alienated from his nation, an exile within before he became an exile in fact.

Though they had passports, he discovered that these were no longer enough to be allowed to leave. Conscription was in the air, since Kitchener's recruitment campaign – Your country needs YOU – had not produced the numbers that were needed to stanch the ever-increasing losses in France and the disaster in the Dardanelles. Lloyd George was manoeuvring for power, but was still being resisted by Asquith and Liberals of an older stamp. A scheme devised by Lord Derby provided a compromise between volunteering and compulsion. All males of military age had to 'attest' their willingness to serve King and Country if required, but it was hoped that there would be so many of these 'volunteers' that acceptance could be selective, and there would be no need for the compulsion which England had always avoided – so far.

So to a recruiting station Lawrence went, on 11 December, 'to be attested and to get a military exemption' (ii. 474). He would certainly have been rejected, but though he waited two hours in the queue winding into Battersea Town Hall, he simply could not bring himself to go through with what for him would have been utter hypocrisy. He was *not* willing to serve in this war, and would not deceive. He was struck by the decency of the men in the queue and even the officials, and felt as always that there was a power in them waiting to break through the 'strange, patient spirit' that seemed to possess them all 'as under a doom, a bad fate'. His blood rebelled, and on a sudden impulse he broke away, 'in face of the table where one's name was to be written, and went out, across the hall away from all the underworld of this spectral submission, and climbed a bus, and in a while saw the fugitive sunshine across the river on the spectral, sunlit towers at Westminster' (ii. 474). With an odd sense of triumph, his mind was full of that dark hero of the Romantics, the arch-refuser to serve. Like Milton's Satan ('flying over the world and knowing he had won at last') he felt not only subversive, alienated from the beauty of a world in which he now had no part save antagonist, but also victorious in defiance. Yet that image was too negative to last. The mid-winter sunshine generated the thought of hidden growth; and the letter concludes with the need to 'nourish in the darkness the unuttered buds of the new life that shall be', with 'patience, only patience, and endless courage to reject false, dead things and false, killing processes' (ii. 474–5).

He could not leave Britain now, and to that extent had simplified his choices. He may even have been relieved not to have to face all the problems that 'Florida' would have presented. He was ill again; and a solution would have to be found quickly since 1 Byron Villas had to be vacated and its furniture distributed to new owners in nine days' time. There was talk of the Radfords' new holiday home in Berkshire, or of possibly having Bertie's rooms in Garsington for a little (ii. 476), but the solution arrived with the sudden reappearance of Murry. In the south of France the mistral had raged, and he had felt so excluded by Katherine's grief over her brother that he had burst out at her in anger.[25] It was decided that she would take lodgings in Bandol and try to overcome her grief by writing about her childhood (as in 'Autumns', for *Signature*), and Murry would come back to London for a while to give her space. He appeared in Hampstead the evening of the 10th (ii. 471), and Lawrence was struck by how he could be both miserable and somehow pleased about his own sensitivity, even chirpy in retailing what a dreadful time he had had, which took the edge off sympathy. He brought along an ex-Brasenose friend, Frederick Goodyear, whom Lawrence liked despite his being 'on the same Oxford introspective line', concerned with his own 'inner life' (ii. 472); whereas, he told Katherine, he himself was weary of personality and only interested now in 'relations based upon some unanimous accord in truth or belief, and a harmony of *purpose*'. Murry, forever fingering his soul, 'irritates me and falsifies me, and I must tell him so. He makes *me* false. If that must always be so, then there is no relation between us' (ii. 472–3). They must try again more impersonally, but danger had been signalled.

The Murrys had borrowed the novelist J. D. Beresford's holiday house in Cornwall in 1914; and Jack went to ask whether the Lawrences might have it now, until the holiday season. Beresford had been willing to protest about *The Rainbow*, and when Murry saw him on the 19th,[26] he readily agreed. So to North Cornwall they would go. At least it was about as near to America as it was possible to get, now. The thought of Florida had not been entirely given up, but meanwhile Rananim would be c/o Porthcothan, St Merryn, Padstow.

In the last week in London Lawrence was ill in bed again (ii. 478), though there were two brighter moments, each somewhat spoilt. A copy of the American *Rainbow* arrived; but he found that it had been expurgated without permission in a number of places.[27] He also heard now about Arnold Bennett's compliment to *The Rainbow* in the *Daily News* – but also that he had told Pinker that its construction was faulty. Lawrence retorted: 'Tell Arnold Bennett that all rules of construction hold good only for novels which are copies of other novels. A book which is not a copy of other books has its own construction' (ii. 479). Still, he thought Bennett 'generous', whether for the support in the *Daily News*, or perhaps for contributing to Pinker's £40, or both.[28]

Now it only remained to empty 1 Byron Villas and go, almost free of possessions again, for which Lawrence gave thanks. From 21 to 24 December they stayed with Vere Collins in Hampstead Garden Suburb. He was struck by Lawrence's versatility. 'While with us he cooked an omelette; furbished a hat of his wife; examined a Dutch cupboard my wife had recently bought, and said what its period was; came out into the garden and gave me hints on transplanting cabbages' – and was also inclined to monopolise the conversation.[29] From there the Lawrences went north to spend Christmas with his sisters and their children in Ripley.

Being with his family seemed to plunge him painfully back into the past when he so longed for a future. He had a violent argument with his brother George, a Baptist preacher – probably over religion. Moreover this visit to the Midlands began to confirm feelings about the miners that had already found their way into *The Rainbow* but now deepened his reaction against democracy. To Russell he might make the claims of blood-consciousness as against mental-consciousness, but he was now 'sad beyond words' that the miners 'can't *think*' in any but industrial terms, 'only wages and money and machinery'. The combination of their 'strange, dark, sensual life, so violent, and hopeless at the bottom ... with this horrible paucity and materialism of mental consciousness' made him want to scream. Guild Socialism must come, giving unions authority in industrial matters, but if there is no reaching '*towards the highest*', the miners' political advancement will be levelling down, or even 'a reduction to the lowest'. But this is less thought than powerful emotion, with its sources in his childhood:

God, how all my boyhood comes back – so violent, so dark, the mind always dark and without understanding, the senses violently active ... These men, whom I love so much – and the life has such a power over me ...

... They are still so living, so vulnerable, so darkly passionate. I love them like brothers – but my God, I hate them too: I don't intend to own them as masters ... One must conquer them also – think beyond them, know beyond them, act beyond them. (ii. 489–90)

Though he had been steadily growing away from his mother's world towards his father's, his feelings are still deeply ambivalent, his politics less social than psychological.

On 29 December they were back in London, spending the night with the Eders. The next day they left for Cornwall.

II   Rananim at Porthcothan

On the journey, between what now seemed a dead or darkly disturbing past and a future incapable of being born, Cornwall seemed only a temporary refuge until they could get out of England altogether. Yet at least, in the big clear rooms of the old house there was a lovely silence (but for the wind in the chimneys), a deep peace – and a housekeeper, Emma Pollard. As Lawrence looked down the lane at the cove with its wild winter breakers, he began to focus a landscape that became ever more meaningful.

I love being here: such a calm, old, slightly deserted house – a farm-house; and the country remote and desolate and unconnected: it belongs still to the days before Christianity, the days of Druids, or of desolate Celtic magic and conjuring; and the sea is so grey and shaggy, and the wind so restless, as if it had never found a home since the days of Iseult. Here I think my life begins again – one is free. Here the autumn is gone by, it is pure winter of forgetfulness. (ii. 493)

Very soon it ceases to reflect feelings of desolation and disconnection, and Iseult changes to Tristan, coming back to where, tragedy or no, his affinity lies.

I like Cornwall very much. It is not England. It is bare and dark and elemental, Tristan's land. I lie looking down at a cove where the waves come white under a low, black headland, which slopes up in bare green-brown, bare and sad under a level sky. It is old, Celtic, pre-christian – Tristan and his boat, and his horn. (ii. 503)

Not England, *pre*-Christian, *elemental* – it may be bare and sad, this wintry landscape, but it is no wasteland, rather a place of regeneration by going back to the beginnings; behind where the deathliness began, behind the so-called

Christian civilisation that had led England to the trenches and destroyed *The Rainbow*, behind Plato and Socrates and Jesus, to rediscover roots and elements from which new life could grow. He would be free again to love and to write. Within two days he conceived the germ of a 'mid-winter story of oblivion' (ii. 493) – about a man who has turned his back on misdirected years in entire forgetfulness, and returns now to live and win back love, where he belongs.[30]

Heseltine quickly came down to join them, arriving on New Year's Day 1916. The house was spacious enough to allow some privacy and they continued to get on well (he stayed till the last week of February). He shared expenses[31] – and since he too was escaping from a life that had gone wrong, they both needed companionship and support. In London, he had already confided his relationship with Puma, and Lawrence had seen for himself the beginning of the counter-attraction to Juliette. Since then, however, Philip's problems had greatly increased – for Puma was pregnant. He told Delius that he had found his 'Vrenchen' (appropriately the Juliet-figure in Delius's 'Village-opera') in Juliette, who wrote him 'long, wonderful letters'; but on the other hand he was 'still worried to death by the little model I took away in the summer in sheer desperation of loneliness'. She had stayed with him 'a good deal' in the winter too, since 'she had no home and little money', but he 'never really liked her'. Now she was pregnant. He could luckily draw on a recent legacy of £100 for her immediate needs; but he had 'no idea what is to become of the child' which she can't afford to keep, and he had 'far too little liking for her to want to help her afterwards. As it is, I reproach myself for having been too Christian, too weakly compassionate towards her.'[32]

Lawrence thought him Hamletty. Soon after their meeting, and before this extra reason for Philip to be wrapped up in his troubles, Lawrence had urged him to resist in his love-life and his music the 'reducing, analytic, introspective process, which has gone on pure and uninterrupted since the Renaissance'. These days, he wrote, introspection 'has reached the point when it has practically no more to reveal to us, and can only produce sensationalism'. Perhaps because the memory of Bunny was still raw, and he saw some resemblance in the young blonde Oxonian, he immediately went on to make the connection with what he had seen in Cambridge and Bloomsbury: the links between self-centredness, intellectualism and homosexuality. Whereas the love between man and woman is a mode of synthesis, homosexual love reduces complexity, and where it increases consciousness, does so in disintegrative modes whether analytic or sensational. Philip must not lose, through introspection, 'the power to love really and profoundly, from the bottom of your soul', a woman, not men. Music too, and all other art, 'must become now synthetic, metaphysical, giving a musical utterance to the sense of the Whole' (ii. 447–8), not reduced to the expression of the private and personal self.

Though Lawrence had said he was 'not going to urge and constrain any more' (ii. 499), he could not help being assertive in argument – and Philip, at 21, saw his music in self-expressive terms. Yet he was able to stick to his own view without losing his admiration for Lawrence as artist and man.

I don't want to identify myself with him in anything beyond his broad desire for an ampler and fuller life ... He is a very great artist, but hard and autocratic in his views and outlook, and his artistic canons I find utterly and entirely unsympathetic to my nature. He seems to be too metaphysical, too anxious to be comprehensive in a detached way and to care too little for purely personal, analytical, and introspective art. His views are somewhat at variance with his own achievements. But he is, nevertheless, an arresting figure, a great and atttractive personality, and his passion for a new, clean untrammelled life is very splendid.

Heseltine was also no mere admiring acolyte, but had something to contribute to Lawrence's new concerns. His African and Tibetan carvings, his knowledge of Celtic mythology, his interest in the occult (begun at Oxford),[33] would all have been a further stimulus to the reading in non-English and pre-Christian civilisations which Lawrence began in Cornwall. Heseltine was also strongly anti-Christian, and though his parade of amoral sensuality and readiness to *épater le bourgeois* was a rather obvious reaction against his own Eton-and-Christ-Church background and his mother, his enthusiastic support against the moral outrage which had destroyed *The Rainbow* must have been very welcome, despite the immaturity which sometimes made Lawrence see him as still 'empty, uncreated' (ii. 501), except for 'echoes from the past, and reactions against the past' – though he would 'perhaps come to being soon' (ii. 501–2).

Lawrence was very ready to make the best of things just now, and seemed to be recovering his spirits – but the stress of the past three months was not to be denied. He caught cold again about 7 January (ii. 501), not surprising in mid-winter. (Frieda joked about having 'to hang on to L. on the rocks or he would be blown away like a little bit of foam'.[34]) Unfortunately for Rananim, no sooner had he begun to sicken than Kouyoumdjian arrived, on the 10th, 'and brought the atmosphere of London with him' (ii. 504), all the friction of personality on which Lawrence had been trying to turn his back, and the last thing a sick man wanted.

Suddenly there was tension all round. The two young men became 'most antagonistic' to each other, which was 'trying'; and Heseltine was like a weather vane about Puma: 'He says he despises her and can't stand her, that she's vicious and a prostitute, but he [will] be running back to her in a little while, I know. She's not so bad, really. I'm not sure whether her touch of licentious profligacy in sex isn't better than his deep-seated conscious, mental licentiousness.'

Kouyoumdjian was in love with Dorothy Warren and gloomy about his chances, so 'more self-assertive than ever, and tiresome'.

It is such a bore, about these young people, that they must be so insistently self-sufficient, always either tacitly or noisily asserting themselves. Heseltine silently and obstinately asserts himself, Kouyoumdjian noisily and offensively. But why should they want to assert themselves, nobody wants to obliterate them or mitigate them ... They spend their time in automatic reaction from everything, even from that which is most sympathetic with them. (ii. 504)

It would seem that Lawrencian counsels had not gone down well.

On the other hand, from his thoughts about self-centredness, overdeveloped intellect and homosexuality, and (now) about young people veering from extreme to extreme in pure reaction, came the germ of a new focus on modern disintegration. He had made only a start on the new story and could not see how to go on, but before 13 January (still thinking he had only a bad cold) he left it and 'suddenly launched off into my philosophy again' (ii. 505). Only, he felt worse and worse. Soon he decided he could put up with Kouyoumdjian no longer and must ask him to leave. The parting was not amicable. Heseltine reported that the Armenian had virtually to be expelled, 'he proved so intolerable to all of us and so impervious to our hints of displeasure at his presence'. Kouyoumdjian threatened to write a skit for *New Age* about an author, whose works were 'too good to be published', being overcome by his subconsciousness at night.[35] Nothing came of this, but the tranquillity had been broken.

Lawrence's 'winter sickness and inflammation' rapidly grew worse than anything since 1911 (ii. 507). Mid-winter was always a dangerous time for his health, but after the stresses of 1915 a collapse was probably inevitable as soon as he relaxed the tight hold he had been keeping on himself through months of tension. Soon his condition grew serious enough for Frieda, who hated illness and was not the most sympathetic of nurses, actually to appeal to Russell for help.

I am so worried about Lawrence. He isn't at all well. I really don't know what to do ... I feel it such a responsibility, it's too much for me. He might just die because everything is too much for him ... Do come, it might do you good and I would be very glad. There are so few people Lawrence can bear the sight of.[36]

Since she knew that Russell disliked her and that his relations with Lawrence were fragile still, the appeal was a sign of desperation; and there was little chance that Russell would come (though he had gone down to Torquay in December to look after Mrs Eliot) – since he was about to start the course of lectures at Caxton Hall he and Lawrence had planned to share.[37]

Lawrence continued to write letters and, as always, to make light of the illness itself, but when Murry and Kot hinted at the impracticality of Florida – which Lawrence probably knew well enough at the back of his mind – there came a spasm of gloom:

I feel absolutely run to earth, like a fox they have chased till it can't go any further, and doesn't know what to do. I don't know what to do nor how to go on ... What good is it all. There is nothing but betrayal and denial ...

... There is no Florida, there's only this, this England, which nauseates my soul, nauseates my spirit and my body – this England. One might as well be blown over the cliffs here in the strong wind ... I must own to you, that I am beaten, knocked out entirely. (ii. 500)

To Kot he wrote bleakly: 'I don't care about any people, none, so long as they won't try to claim attention from me' (ii. 498). He was happy for the Murrys in Bandol – but his situation was in sharp contrast. He continued to believe in 'miracle' (ii. 501) and would not accept *this* kind of life; but at the height of his fever now he thought he might actually be dying, experiencing (for the third time) 'the sense of dissolution, that horrible feeling one has when one is really ill' (ii. 512) – a crisis almost as bad as those of 1901 and 1911. When he did recover it left him, for a while, with a numbness 'like a tiny bit of paralysis' all down the right side.

Frieda must have appealed to Dollie too, for help more useful than Russell's arrived. Maitland Radford, who had been commissioned into the Royal Army Medical Corps but was now at St Mary's Hospital in Carshalton, came down specially to examine Lawrence. He diagnosed bronchitis, aggravated and perhaps brought on by nervous prostration. 'Maitland Radford says that the pain and inflammation is *referred* from the nerves, there is no organic illness at all, except the mucous [presumably the mucous membranes] in the bronchi etc are weak' (ii. 512). Lawrence believed that illness came when one's life went wrong; and as always was anxious to minimise any possibility of 'organic illness'. So he told the Hopkins, when he had begun to improve, that it had been 'soul-sickness after London and the state of things' (ii. 514). Nevertheless, there had clearly been high fever, respiratory inflammation, pain and that slight muscular numbness, perhaps brought on by prolonged coughing.

Was this the onset of the tuberculosis that had been threatened before, and which the intensity of Lawrence's denials shows he always feared? (The question is of some importance because of speculation that he had not only developed consumption by then but was infectious enough to give it to Katherine in the coming months.)[38] Radford's diagnosis and his decision not to call for a sputum test appear to rule this out. It is true that doctors were often unwilling to certify tuberculosis unless they were sure – though in that case they were legally bound to do so. It was, however difficult to be sure, at that date, since four of the five main symptoms – fever, sweating, loss of weight, coughing – also applied to related diseases such as pneumonia, pleurisy and bronchitis, whereas the fifth, the haemorrhaging of blood, meant that the disease had already reached an advanced state. Though Lawrence had clearly been coughing a good deal of mucus, Radford would not have ignored blood, nor have talked (if blood were present) of bronchitis aggravated by nervous prostration. Moreover a sputum test, though not mandatory as in Lawrence's previous dangerous illness when he was a teacher, would have settled the matter as it did then. Doctors might sometimes collude with their patient's fear of the disease and its social opprobrium by softening their diagnosis – and Lawrence could not afford a sanatorium even if he could have been persuaded to try one. Yet a doctor who was also a personal friend would probably have had a test done if he had thought it at all advisable, lest the condition worsen and prove fatal through failure to treat it in time. What Radford prescribed was rest, peace and quiet, and special nourishing foods which the generosity of Ottoline provided (ii. 517). By 25 January Lawrence was feeling better (ii. 514), though still confined indoors. 'If I get up and go out I get worse again at once', he wrote two days later, 'But I can sit in bed and read or do my poems' (ii. 516).

For he had decided to put together, from notebooks he had asked Thomas Dunlop to recover from Fiascherino, a second volume of poems which might earn a little money. By the beginning of February what was to be *Amores* was ready, 'a sort of inner history of my life, from 20 to 26' (ii. 521, i.e. before he met Frieda) – mostly a recension of previous work, though some poems like 'The Wild Common' were substantially rewritten.[39] Also, the proofs of his 'Italian Studies' had arrived. He was 'not unhappy' – but the metaphor of mid-winter death and rebirth had proved almost literal in its first part. Indeed, the collapse may have left its mark on his nervous system, increasing both his tendency to nervous irritation and rage, and the degree to which this made him ill.

When Heseltine brought Puma down to stay at the end of the month, however, she was welcome. Despite her nickname, Lawrence thought her 'a quiet, quite nice little thing really, unobtrusive and affectionate. He is fond of her, as a matter of fact, in spite of what he says' (ii. 517). Ironically, it was because he liked them both and found it no strain to have them at close quarters as he got better, that he grew more and more interested in their affairs, and the split he saw in Heseltine. There seemed such a contradiction between his wild, drunken and licentious side, and the intellectual, poetic, aspiring sensibility that came uppermost in his letters to Delius; a seesawing between slightly manic gaiety and black depression; or fierce satire and gentleness. At this stage of his life his personality was probably unformed rather than unstable as it would become; but he was nervy and highly strung, he already suffered badly enough from 'nervous stricture' to be certified unfit for military service, and Lawrence was being perceptive rather than critical when he thought of his young friend as 'uncreated' or 'disintegrated'.

The coming of Puma began to clarify Lawrence's perception (as thinker, and later as novelist) of what that split might involve, and he was clearly working it out for himself when he wrote to Ottoline about the pair. Before Puma arrived Philip had been very ready to discuss his mixed feelings, and the contrast between her and Juliette. Indeed, with Kouyoumdjian, the evening amusement had been the creation of a play about the situation. So it was not too surprising that Lawrence, uninhibited anyway, should feel no apparent scruple about discussing his insights with Ottoline, who would obviously be interested.

About H. and Mlle. – I tell him he ought to tell her [i.e. about Puma]. I suppose he will. It is queer. He declares he does not like this one, the Puma, but he does really. He declares he wants her to go. But he is really attached to her in the senses, in the unconsciousness, in the blood. He is always fighting away from this. But in so doing he is a fool. She is very nice and very real and simple, we like her. His affection for Mlle. is a desire for the light because he is in the dark. If he were in the light he would want the dark. He wants Mlle. for *companionship*, not for the blood connection, the dark, sensuous relation. With Puma he has this second, dark relation, but not the first. She is quite intelligent, in her way, but no mental consciousness; no white consciousness, if you understand, all intuition, in the dark, the consciousness of the senses. But she is quite fine and subtle in that way, quite, and I esteem her there *quite* as much as I esteem him.

Perhaps he is very split, and would always have the two things separate ... (ii. 539)

He goes on to argue how for such people 'I really believe in two wives'; and to thank God that by contrast he feels himself 'more and more unified ... And Frieda and I become more and more truly married'. (That of course would please Ottoline not one whit, since Frieda to her was the 'devil' who was ruining Lawrence's life, and who had now written her another denunciation – of which more later.) Lawrence seems unaware that Ottoline might see a threat to a young woman for whom she was responsible, from a young man she thought degenerate, and who had become involved with another young woman he himself had spoken of as a prostitute – though Lawrence had wondered whether her touch of licentiousness was not preferable to Heseltine's mental kind. Since he clearly liked them both, moreover, and had liked Juliette too, his letter is one of affectionate interest and analysis, not moral judgement – but Ottoline might read it differently. (At least he did not disclose the pregnancy.)

Most of all perhaps, his naïveté about possible reactions to his diagnosis of 'split' and 'disintegration' in these young people may have been because his attention was so taken up with the light this threw on his philosophy – which he proceeded to recast when he recovered. By 15 February he had 'nearly done the first, the destructive, half of my philosophy. At last it can stand' (ii. 538). As

'The Crown' had been a rewriting of 'Study of Thomas Hardy' to take account of a more destructive and violent world, and distinguish what was deathly from the 'corruption' that was necessary before regeneration could begin; so this new version clearly began with new insight into disintegration, intending to go on to the characteristic Lawrencian cry for renewal. He posted this first half to Garsington on 27 February (ii. 558), two days before he and Frieda left Porthcothan.

It was called 'Goats and Compasses' and it is lost now, possibly destroyed by the young man who had partly inspired it. The only descriptions we have are from hostile witnesses. According to Heseltine's friend Cecil Gray (whom Lawrence became friendly with in Cornwall, see below, but who had broken with Lawrence when he wrote), it was 'Lawrence at his very worst: a bombastic, pseudo-mystical, psycho-philosophical treatise dealing largely with homosexuality – a subject, by the way, in which Lawrence displayed a suspiciously lively interest at that time.' Ottoline, too, thought it 'dreadful stuff, bad in *every* way, matter and form ... It is rubbish, a child of Frieda's.' By then, she had taken new offence at Frieda, so could not help being biased and joining the line of Lawrence's friends who were unable to grasp what he was saying.[40] (In his splendid self-parody, however, in the 'Pompadour' chapter of *Women in Love*, he showed himself able to see how easy it was to react against his rhetoric rather than attend to its import.) Fortunately, it is possible now to infer the outlines of the argument of the new work, and to judge for ourselves.

To understand the concern with homosexuality we need to recall the whole process of self-examination which began in 1913 by acknowledging homoerotic feelings, unworried, because his relation with Frieda had saved *him* from Middleton's tragic solipsism. He knew himself to be bisexual, but was convinced that a greater degree of 'otherness' made heterosexual relationship the more creative and transforming, if more difficult. In 'Hardy' he proceeded to argue that *every* human being was bisexual, and that the conflict between 'male' and 'female' in the self and in relationships was only one aspect of the universal opposition between impulses to unity and to individuation, whose marriage was the ground of growth. *The Rainbow* set out to explore how that opposition could transform lovers through marriage, or become increasingly destructive as increasing selfhood made it more difficult to abandon the self to the other.[41] In February 1915, after meeting Forster, he extended his view of homosexuality as narcissistic, explaining to Russell the contrast he saw between love, the breaking of the bounds of the self in encountering the opposite and unknown, and the use of a body *like* the self as a form of masturbation, of which sodomy is the extreme – something Forster was too honourable to do, though he could not believe in marriage with the other. When, however, Lawrence met practising homosexuals (Grant, Keynes, Birrell, even Bunny

Garnett) he was horrified and disgusted, and realised that for all his theory of sodomy he had never known 'what it meant'. This, bringing nightmares of beetles, was however more than a repression of his own homosexual tendencies – since he characteristically set out at once to discover why he had been so upset, what the beetles meant, and what the connection was with the over-powering sense of evil he had begun to feel even before he went to Cam-bridge.[42] In revising *The Rainbow* he imagined a lesbian relationship that was enriching, though it could not satisfy the whole of Ursula; and an anal sexuality between Will and Anna that could liberate (because newly fascinated by the otherness of the other), though it too only satisfied part of the self. At the end of the novel two contrasting images explored how enclosure could become either growth, or corruption: the nut which bursts its shell and submits to the creative forces in the cosmos (as Ursula must learn to do), as against 'hard-scaled' self-enclosure that goes rotten inside.[43]

By late 1915 his broodings on 'Cambridge' and 'Bloomsbury' had traced close links between hard brittleness of intellect, egotistic will, irreverence, self-enclosure and homosexuality. Moreover, even though all the homosexuals he met were pacifists, he saw direct connections with the evil of war, coiling within proponents and opponents alike, including himself. As he explained to Cynthia Asquith, the spirit of war was essentially disintegrative in more than the obvious sense, because it resolved all relation with the other into either enmity or self-preservation. And although in 'The Crown' he was able to see 'corruption' as part of the cycle of growth, since (at times) disintegration was necessary before life could renew itself; nevertheless he drew a sharp contrast between that and a deathly hardening into wilful self-enclosure, finding its gratification in narcis-sistic analysis or sensation. Homosexuality is again seen as rejecting transforma-tion by the truly other, and preferring instead self-gratification or self-reduction by that which either reflects or is less than the self. On meeting Heseltine, he warned of the dangers of Hamlettish introspection as a process of enclosing the self and unfitting it for heterosexual love, that is, the power to abandon oneself wholly to the wholly other in order to be transformed, as against homosexuality which is finally reductive.[44]

Set against this, Gray's feline insinuation that Lawrence was simply letting his own homosexuality out of the bag seems impertinent. Lawrence always saw sex in terms less of pleasure or self-satisfaction, than of change and growth – so when he tries to understand homosexuality it is always what it *means* that concerns him. Though, of course, the connections he was plotting in answer to that question were to be found (and resisted) in himself, they were also much more obvious in the homosexual intellectuals and artists he had met. His responses were not simply homophobic – as *The Rainbow* had bravely proved, and got itself destroyed as a result. The phobia was against all he thought most disintegrative in modern life, strikingly embodied in the *kind* of homosexual he encountered at the heart of English civilisation.

'Goats and Compasses' must then have recast 'The Crown' – of which only the first three essays had been published – by putting the 'destructive' half of the argument first this time. The title – a common inn sign held to be a corruption of 'God encompasseth us' – would be an ironic ikon of how the encompassing, omnipresent, creative forces in their eternal opposition, requiring to be married, had degenerated into goatish lust and sensation on one side, and on the other the reductive intellectual compasses which Blake (always important to Lawrence) had pictured in the hands of Newton and The Ancient of Days – each extreme as disintegrative as the other. Moreover he now saw the young as escalating this destructive process in continual reaction from one extreme to the other: hence youthful idealism issuing in bloodlust and death wish in world war. Hence also the seesawing between introspective intellect and licentiousness in his young friends – at each extreme, moreover, wilfully self-enclosed and assertive, antagonistic to the other. Hence the prevalence of homosexuality, making love into self-projection or self-reduction. Hence supposedly Christian civilisations in destructive and sterile death-throes, seeking to preserve their own worn-out forms of life. When Ottoline described the work as 'A gospel of hate and of violent individualism' attacking 'the will, love and sympathy',[45] she was probably mistaking 'the destructive' half (which was all she had been sent) for the whole. He had certainly criticised both her and Russell, early in their friendship, as worshippers of will who believed that they could control their own inner being; and had warned them that despite their apparent civilisation, there was inside them a violence and hatred they refused to recognise, and so could not expose and heal. His was not, however, a gospel advocating hate and denying love. Rather, his attack was on people who professed love and peace while actually betraying inner venom and violence. Love itself would become destructive if the lovers' inner evil were not exposed and overcome. And though he continued to believe that (in the words of 'Hardy') 'The final aim of every living thing ... is the full achievement of itself',[46] this could not be 'violent individualism' while he also continued to believe, as Ottoline inconsistently recognised, that the essential mode of regeneration lay (still) in 'love between men and women'. As he sent it to her, the emphasis of his letter was all on renewal (ii. 556–7).

III Witherings

As he was writing, however, relationships both old and new began to wither on the vine, and soon the last hope of Rananim would rest in the absent Murrys.

The friendship with Russell, still fragile after their partial reconciliation, was the first to go. They had combined to give Ottoline, for Christmas, a portfolio of reproductions of the Ajanta frescoes[47] – which Lawrence found deeply moving because of the 'complete, almost perfect relations between the men and the women' (ii. 489). He had sent Russell (as of old) his thoughts about blood-being (ii. 470–1), which Russell hated. He even asked him to come to Florida 'and be president of us' (ii. 490), but this lacked conviction; and though there was a friendly letter in January from Cornwall (ii. 505), the basic divisions had only been papered over. The nearness of Russell's first Caxton Hall lecture gave him an excuse not to come to Cornwall in answer to Frieda's plea – only for the apparent success of the lectures[48] then to reawaken Lawrence's old hostility to their approach, and some jealousy too, by the contrast with his own failure. When Russell's next letter wondered more pessimistically whether the lectures would have any lasting effect, Lawrence was sorry, but 'my heart doesn't soften to him just yet' because he 'is obstinate in going his own way' (ii. 538). On 19 February the basic opposition broke out again, irritably: 'I didn't like your letter. What's the good of living as you do, any way. I don't believe your lectures *are* good ... What's the good of sticking in the damned ship and haranguing the merchant-pilgrims in their own language. Why don't you drop overboard? ... One must be an outlaw these days' (ii. 546). Since Russell had lost his fellowship of Trinity because of his opposition to the war, and was before long to go to prison for principled actions, here it was Lawrence who was impertinent. At a deeper level however his point was still that Russell's social and political focus was merely reformist, treating the symptom rather than the disease. Moreover,

You said in your lecture on education that you didn't set much count by the unconscious. That is sheer perversity. The whole of the consciousness and the conscious content is old hat – the mill-stone round your neck.

Do cut it – cut your will and leave your old self behind. Even your mathematics are only *dead* truth: and no matter how fine you grind the dead meal, you'll not bring it to life again.

Do stop working and writing altogether and become a creature instead of a mechanical instrument ... be a baby, and not a savant any more. [The allusion is to Nietzsche.[49]] Don't *do* anything any more – but for heavens sake begin to *be* ...

Oh, and I want to ask you, when you make your will, do leave me enough to live on. I want you to live for ever. But I want you to make me in some part your heir.

... You had better come and live near us ... (ii. 546–7)

Neither invitation was likely to be accepted; given the letter's contradictory desires to condemn and to keep a filament of friendship unbroken. A letter from Frieda just before leaving for Zennor was similarly ambivalent (ii. 553). She reproaches Russell for not really caring for Lawrence despite his protestations, or respecting her though she respects him. Nevertheless she invites him down, backed by a friendly postscript from her husband. Lawrence himself wrote again

1 and 2 The wedding photographs, 9 Selwood Terrace, South Kensington, London, 13 July 1914
1 Lawrence, Katherine Mansfield, Frieda, John Middleton Murry (cf. pp. 142–3)

2 Murry, Frieda, Lawrence

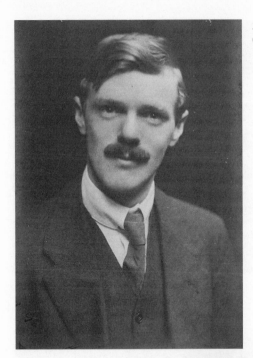

3 D. H. Lawrence, 26 June 1913
(by W. G. Parker)

4 D. H. Lawrence, *c.* 1915
(by Bassano and Vandyke)

5 D. H. Lawrence at Mountain Cottage, Middleton-by-Wirksworth, Derbyshire, 1918

6 D. H. Lawrence, October 1919

7 D. H. Lawrence, *c.* 19 September 1921

8 Frieda at Irschenhausen on her birthday, 11 August 1913, wearing the
Bavarian costume given to her by the Jaffes (cf. (ii.57–60) and p. 91)

9 Frieda and Lawrence at Grimsbury Farm, Hermitage, near Newbury, Berkshire, probably September 1919

10 Frieda, October 1919

11 Frieda, *c.* 19 September 1921

12 Baroness von Richthofen, c. 192[

13 Else Jaffe, 1916

14 Edgar Jaffe, c. 1915–16

15 Edward Garnett, *c.* 1908

16 David ('Bunny') Garnett, *c.* 1922

17 The Hon. Cynthia Asquith with John,
Kingsgate, Broadstairs, Summer 1913

18 Lady Cynthia Asquith

19 Edward Marsh, 1912
(by Eliott Seabrooke)

20 Katherine Mansfield and John Middleton Murry, *c.* 1914

21 S. S. Koteliansky

22 Mark Gertler

23 Mary Cannan, *c.* 1910

24 Gilbert Cannan, *c.* 1910

25 Dr David Eder

26 Viola Meynell

27 Catherine Carswell, *c.* 1914

28 Icking bei München, the Leitners downstairs, Alfred Weber's flat upstairs

29 Villa di Gargnano, Lago di Garda: the Villa di Paoli (left) and Villa Igéa (rear)

30 The Villa Igéa

31 The Meynell estate in Greatham, Sussex: Shed Hall (left) and Humphreys (right), with Monica Saleeby's house in the background

32 The heraldry of Rananim, 3 January 1915 (misdated by Lawrence)

in March, repeating the invitation, and clearly hoping not to have given lasting offence by his hectoring and his politics: 'Are you still cross with me for being a schoolmaster and for not respecting the rights of man? Don't be, it isn't worth it' (ii. 574). He and Frieda always thought that if one blew off one's oppositions and irritations openly (even the one about being so poor and unheeded, when others were successful and well-off), it would clear the air and allow one to pick up the relationship all the better. This friendship however, did not recover from what must have seemed straightforwardly offensive – though Ottoline tried to excuse Lawrence as both ill and unbalanced by worry about conscription, which was imminent now.[50]

The friendship with Ottoline was also damaged at Porthcothan. The Morrells' support over *The Rainbow* (despite her mixed response) had been very important to Lawrence, and in their isolation in Cornwall her kindness was even more valuable. She worried about how he would take the winter there, and sent him a bright red-orange sweater which made him feel like a robin (ii. 503), and a counterpane to keep him warm (ii. 538). He depended on her for books, mostly from the London Library, for a new course of reading when he was confined to his bed;[51] and he wrote her long letters about them at a time when the circle of his correspondents had become smaller than at any point since 1912. It was her generosity, too, that supplied the special foods (concentrated meat extract, soluble milk casein, etc.) which Maitland had prescribed but which the Lawrences, income-less and eking out the money that had been collected for them to go to America, could ill afford (ii. 517, 522). It was in recognition of her generosity and sympathy that Lawrence dedicated *Amores* to her. There were even two friendly letters from Frieda in January, seconding Lawrence's invitation to make them a visit. Ottoline was apprehensive, remembering the fierce argument over Nietzsche at their last meeting – but Frieda was obviously making an effort, though she may also have chafed under Ottoline's patronage. Then, when Ottoline was supposed to be coming in the last week of January but asked to postpone because she was unwell, Frieda suddenly fired off another letter which effectively put an end to any idea of venturing into her lair. 'Isn't Fri[e]da a madwoman!!' wrote Ottoline to Russell, 'She would drive me mad too. I wonder why she makes this attack on me ... I have written her an answer as soothing as I could – but she puts my back up so.'[52] She sent the letter not only to Russell, but afterwards and significantly to Murry and Katherine who had been making overtures since Murry's Christmas at Garsington, which Lawrence had arranged. Her visit was never paid – so, as it happened, she never saw Lawrence again.

She was not innocent of offence. The Bloomsbury vice of gossip behind people's backs had backfired, confirming Frieda's suspicion of the real attitudes beneath Ottoline's ladylike manners. Heseltine and Kouyoumdjian had told

Frieda what had been said at Garsington about her and her marriage. Frieda's reproach was neither mad nor unjustified, nor indeed a breach in relations, and showed perhaps more imagination about Ottoline's experience than she had shown about Frieda's.

> ... I know in your heart, you have been my enemy. You thought that Lawrence ought to leave me, that I am bad for him, that he does not care for me ... both his behaviour and mine stupidly give this impression to other people – But you don't know what we have been to each other in these trying years, how he has grown and so have I and our fights have been the lesser unreal thing – You have been very unfair to me, I think, you have tried to put me down as of no account – I could understand that as you must have had to put up with some terrible artist's wives ... But you are good and understanding and I do think it's our real desire to be friends! We ought to be in spite of differences in temperament.[53]

Lawrence tried to repair the damage. On 24 January he diplomatically assumed that Ottoline's visit had merely been postponed – perhaps wisely, since she was none too well and he was still convalescent – and he offered an apology on Frieda's behalf which she might not have done herself.

> Frieda was sorry she sent you a disagreeable letter when you were ill. But Heseltine and Kouyoumdjian had been telling her the things you said about her – and her and me – so she was cross. But she is not really cross. Perhaps the way we behave to one another she and I makes everybody believe that there is real incompatibility between us. But you know that really we are married to each other – I know you know it. (ii. 512)

There is apology, but also a statement of the condition on which future relationship would depend. Three days later (just after Puma arrived) he argued in Blakean terms that opposition could become truer friendship: 'Let the trouble between you and F. be forgotten now. Your natures are different and opposite. But why shouldn't opposites exist in a state of peace, like day and night. You will always speak different languages, and stand on different shores of the sea. But why not? Why should life be a homogeneity?' (ii. 517). On 15 February, his diagnosis of the split in Heseltine, and how it might require polygamous kinds of fulfilment, goes on:

> For myself, thank God, I feel myself becoming more and more unified, more and more a oneness. And Frieda and I become more and more truly married – for which I thank heaven. It has been such a fight. But it is coming right. And then we can all three be real friends. Then we shall be really happy, all of us, in our relation. (ii. 539)

He implied that Frieda's attacks on Ottoline arose out of marital strain caused by a split in *him*, which made him (in Frieda's eyes) too drawn to Ottoline's soulfulness;[54] but conversely, that his becoming more unified would strengthen the marriage and temper his relation with Ottoline into a calmer friendship which Frieda could accept, and join. This was however, also a statement of his priorities, and an insistence that his wife and his marriage be respected.

Having heard that it was Heseltine who had landed her in trouble, Ottoline wrote to reproach him, and got a counterblast in reply which will not have made her more sympathetic to his pursuit of Juliette. He quoted from the *Iliad* (xi. 312–3): 'Him do I hate even as I hate Hell Fire,/ Who says one thing and hides another in his heart'. He admitted that he was tactless, but it was 'because I am convinced that tact, so far from providing a cure for misunderstandings, merely suppresses them for a while, after which they break out with renewed virulence'. Frieda had been 'most unjustly maligned behind her back'. He had helped bring things into the open. He was not at all repentant.[55]

Though Ottoline was not likely to be convinced now by Lawrence constantly sending Frieda's love along with his, Frieda did write a reconciling letter just before they left Porthcothan.[56] It remained to be seen whether Ottoline would understand or accept what Lawrence had told her. Though she still cared about him, the relationship was being steadily eroded by hostility between the women.

Unfortunately the newer friendships fared no better; for the breach with Kouyoumdjian was followed, at the end of their stay at Porthcothan, by a breach with Heseltine too.

In February, with characteristic slightly manic enthusiasm, Heseltine took up the idea of publishing new work by subscription which had been floated both by Murry and by Clive Bell before Christmas, and which Lawrence had presumably mentioned in one of their discussions of the philistine British public which would not support or tolerate serious works of art. The classic case was *The Rainbow*, so the new scheme was to be called 'The Rainbow Books and Music', and the republication of the suppressed novel at 7/6 would be the first bait for subscribers. Heseltine ordered at his own expense – he had '£150 a year of his own' and an allowance from his mother (ii. 549) – 1,000 copies of a circular, the proof of which arrived on 17 February (ii. 542). Ottoline reacted strongly to its arrogance; for example:

It is monstrous that the herd should lord it over the uttered word. The swine has only to grunt disapprobation, and the very angels of heaven will be compelled to silence.

It is time that enough people of courage and passionate soul should rise up to form a nucleus of the living truth; since there must be those among us who care more for the truth than for any advantage.[57]

This was Heseltine's writing, though with distinct Lawrencian echoes. In the last week of February Philip left for London with Puma to see to the sending out of the circular, intending also to visit some of Lawrence's friends and drum up support. The friendship was still intact. After their own move to Zennor on the

29th, indeed, Lawrence would even suggest to the Murrys on 8 March – as a remarkably ill-conceived part of his plan to set up Rananim anew – that Heseltine might have a room in the larger cottage at Higher Tregerthen which he wanted Katherine and Murry to take (ii. 564).

Yet on that same day Heseltine was declaring in a letter to Nichols that he was not going back to Lawrence. For 'he has no real sympathy. All he likes in one is the potential convert to his own reactionary creed. I believe firmly that he is a fine thinker and a consummate artist, but personal relation with him is almost impossible. At least so it appears at present.'[58] In Lawrence's letter to Ottoline on 25 February there are traces of an argument before Heseltine left Porthcothan, which reveal what Lawrence had seemed unsympathetic and dictatorial about, though in the self-same letter he assures her that Philip 'is really very good and I depend on him and believe in him' (ii. 557). Lawrence must have told him, in his lecturing way, what he now tells Ottoline: that Philip was unfair to Puma, was idealising Juliette and would react against her just as surely if he stayed with her 'exclusively'. He has faith in Heseltine, 'But he is exasperating, because he is always in such a state of mad reaction against things, all mad reactions.' The chiming of the word is no accident. The 'reactionary creed' Heseltine objected to was not the politics we mean by the word, but the demand that Philip accept, as applying to him, the diagnosis of destructive 'reaction' from one extreme to another that Lawrence had been formulating in 'Goats and Compasses'.

Though smarting under this personal application of the new philosophical work, Philip still believed Lawrence to be a 'fine thinker' and was recommending it in the circular for 'The Rainbow Books and Music'. Worse was however to come, and sometime before 22 April when Heseltine wrote to Delius about it, the relationship was broken – as was the publishing scheme, for there had been only 30 replies from 600 circulars. Heseltine even now maintained that Lawrence was 'a fine artist and a hard, though horribly distorted, thinker': 'But personal relationship with him is impossible – he acts as a subtle and deadly poison. The affair by which I found him out is far too long to enter upon here ... The man really must be a bit mad, though his behaviour nearly landed me in a fearful fix – indeed, it was calculated to do so.'[59] Though we cannot know for certain what had happened, the strong likelihood is that Heseltine thought Lawrence had torpedoed his chances with Juliette. Before Puma came to Cornwall, he had wanted to be rid of her. He certainly did not want the blonde and pure girl to know about the dark and sensual one, still less that he had so recently taken up with Puma again – but Lawrence insisted he ought to tell Juliette (ii. 539), probably about the pregnancy too, though we do not know for sure. (He had detested lies and subterfuge with Weekley.) So, if Philip now blamed Juliette's rejection of him on her finding out about Puma through Lawrence's indiscretion to Ottoline, and still more if Ottoline had confronted him with a recognisably Lawrencian diagnosis of his unreliability, or even (as she had a habit of doing) actually showed him Lawrence's letter, both the remark about poison and the 'fix' would be clear enough.[60] He had done no more than tell Ottoline what he had told Heseltine himself, on a subject which the young man discussed quite openly; but it was nonetheless a betrayal of confidence. (An irony however appears in Heseltine's defence to Ottoline of his own tactlessness, and of bringing things into the open.)

The result of Lawrence's 'interference' with Bunny Garnett had not persuaded him to be more careful. He was to see the other side of Heseltine now. Instead of sending back 'Goats and Compasses' which Ottoline entrusted to him, he not only used it for toilet paper (according to Gray) but threatened to write a critical exposure. He imagined how reviewers would 'gloat' over a revelation of the 'distorted soul' of this 'monster of obscenity'. He himself gloated to Delius (with more callowness than imagination) about how 'comically perturbed' Lawrence became, and how he had 'practically no friends left'.[61] Heseltine's revenge may have sorted ill with the line he had taken about the bourgeois and *The Rainbow*, but he knew where the jugular was. Lawrence gathered what shreds of dignity he could: 'It has become ludicrous and rather shameful. I only wish that you and Puma should not talk about us, for decency's sake. I assure you I shall have nothing to say of you and her. The whole business is so shamefully fit for a Kouyoumdjian sketch' (ii. 598). It would of course come to more than that; for Heseltine would not be quiet – nor, within the year, would Lawrence.

So, within three months of the move to Cornwall, his hopes of Rananim among the young, too, had dissolved.

IV   Rananim at Zennor

The Beresfords wanted their house at the beginning of March. Lawrence appears never to have considered leaving Cornwall, though he did not much care for the Cornish. In fact, because of his illness, he had met very few, and it is to these that his generalisations should be traced.[62] In a fit of irritation at the end of his stay he rants that the Cornish 'have got the souls of insects' (ii. 552), he has never in his life come across such innerly selfish and greedy people, they are only tolerable as servants (though even Emma is grasping, now) – and he wishes they could be exterminated. Four days later he confesses ashamedly to Beatrice Beresford, who had taken him up sharply on this, that he had been exasperated 'past bearing' because he had found the people from whom he had tried to hire houses 'so *greedy*'; asking three, four, even five guineas a week, which meant that even now (on their last day) they had nowhere definite to live. He liked Emma and hated having been unjust to her (ii. 559). Worry had lain behind his anger – and his illness had left him more irritable than ever, though the episode also shows, once again, how he would respond when someone stood up to him.

Vile individuals notwithstanding, Cornwall was where he wanted to stay. Maitland Radford had holidayed in Zennor, so they went for the day to look, and found it 'wild and remote and beautiful' (ii. 554). Nearer still to Land's End was psychologically right for a man who had wanted to cut loose from England altogether. On Leap Year's day they moved into the Tinner's Arms at Zennor, with high hopes of finding a house that would be cheap enough for them, that is, no more than £1 a week.[63] On 5 March he wrote excitedly to the Murrys:

It is a most beautiful place: a tiny granite village nestling under high, shaggy moor-hills, and a big sweep of lovely sea beyond, such a lovely sea, lovelier even than the Mediterranean. It is 5 miles from St. Ives, and 7 miles from Penzance ... It is all gorse now, flickering with flower ... It is the best place I have been in, I think. (ii. 563)

At Higher Tregerthen they had found two cottages for rent unfurnished, standing at right angles to each other, only a few strides apart. The smaller had just two rooms, but would be only £5 a year! – and that would be theirs. The larger had 'a funny little tower at one end' with a tower room for a study, and was to be had for £16 p.a (ii. 564–5). This the Murrys must take. He had been urging them to come for months now – and in fact they had already written (on the 4th) that they would.

Their decision had not come easily, for after their miseries at the end of 1915 they had been very happy and productive together at Bandol. After Murry had left her in December Katherine wrote Lawrence an ill and despairing letter. Murry happened to be at Byron Villas when it came, and was told roundly that her misery was his fault because he never offered her a new life, would not break with his past and was 'always whining & never making a decision'. He should never have left her alone.[64] Shocked out of self-absorption, Murry decided to rejoin her after Christmas. Since Katherine had also rediscovered her dependence on him, they wrote themselves into love again. At Christmas at Garsington indeed, Murry won Ottoline's sympathy by talking constantly of Katherine. Strachey and Clive Bell (he told Katherine) also liked him because they thought 'that between me and you there is actually happening that incredible thing called a *grande passion* ... And I imagine that something of the glamour of it hangs about me nowadays'. This was partly self-dramatisation and myth-making to win friends and influence people, like his manipulation of Katherine's image after her death; but it also persuaded *him* and cured his indecisions. Ottoline told Russell about Murry's 'wonderful devotion' to Katherine and how he had rushed off back to her in France. He made sure of a welcome at Garsington when they returned.

You have made me feel that there is at least one place in England which is a haven for us both, and I know that Katherine will be as happy in that knowledge as I.

I went to you in terror ... I came away feeling that we – I can never regard myself alone – had found a friend – pour toujours, to use our magic word.[65]

At Bandol moreover self-image and reality began to coincide for a while. Their three months at the Villa Pauline were their happiest and most productive ever. Each found, as a writer, a newly authentic voice, Katherine in 'The Aloe' (later condensed into 'Prelude') and Murry in his book on Dostoevsky.

So they were not anxious to leave. Moreover, though Lawrence wrote that he saw his other friendships 'as across the grave', and urged them to come and live with them 'in unanimity' (ii. 482), he wanted a relationship that did not depend on personal affinity or intellectual agreement, which were the Murrys' currency. (It did not matter, therefore, what the new young friends he had such hopes for were, personally.) With the Murrys too he wanted 'no *personal* obligation, no personal idea. Let it be a union in the unconsciousness, not in the consciousness.' As he urged Katherine to get better and come back so they could 'all try to be happy *together*', there was an implied proviso.

In any case however, the proposal left Katherine 'cold'. They were not the joining kind, 'not made to do that kind of thing ever'. In fact they had their eyes on Garsington. On Murry's way to Bandol a second letter told Ottoline how precious the new friendship was, especially since he and Katherine never seemed to take root in places, 'or in the hearts of those who call themselves our friends. I am not whining at all – tho' Lorenzo says I do – for it is a fair price to pay for our own secret and transcendent happiness together. But there are times when we suffer terribly.' Both wrote from Bandol in late January. Katherine had only met Ottoline once, briefly, when Lawrence had taken them to Bedford Square, but tells her now that 'ever since the day when Murry came and said: "There's a perfectly wonderful woman in England"', she had wanted to write – which she does with unction, begging Ottoline to 'remember that you are real and lovely to us both and that we are ever grateful to you because you are'. Murry brackets Ottoline with Lawrence as one of the few who 'understand'; though in Lawrence's 'mood of shaking his English dust from his shoes, he made me yet more miserable. I love him so much that I cannot bear the thought of more suffering for him'. At Garsington he knew 'that Katherine and I and Lawrence really had a resting place in England'.[66] One name however is pointedly missing.

No wonder then that Ottoline should turn to these new friends for support against Frieda – or that they should rejoice together as first Kouyoumdjian, and later and especially Heseltine departed. Having got back Frieda's late January denunciation from Russell, Ottoline sent it to Bandol with the news that

Heseltine had betrayed her confidence – but they also heard from Lawrence, just recovering from his illness, that Heseltine was still at Porthcothan and beginning to be included in the plans to live together with them. Worse still, though Lawrence might write 'I feel you are my only real friends in the world' (ii. 533), Heseltine appeared to be muscling in on the scheme for private publication which Murry claimed as his – though Clive Bell had also been proposing something similar. Moreover Frieda had written to Katherine, perhaps picking up some hint of their new relation with Ottoline, in terms she thought 'censorious', though Lawrence denied this. On 4 March Katherine drafted a peace-making reply in her journal: 'Thank you for your letter, dear, but you really haven't been right in judging us first the kind of traitors that you did. Jack *never* would hear a word against Lawrence'. He would however against Frieda, and her suspicion of some collusion between Ottoline and the Murrys was not so easily laid to rest. So when she wrote a welcoming letter on 8 March, to put an end to 'any more soulharrassing, we are *friends* and we wont bother anymore about the *deep* things, they are all right, just let's live like the lilies in the field' (ii. 571); she could not resist asking also whether 'the old Ott.' had said '*horrid* things' about her, and hoping that Jack 'didn't swallow them all'. (Indeed it seems she had gone on brooding about this, since she had sent another angry letter to Ottoline soon after arriving in Zennor.)[67]

The Murrys had also talked of treachery, being jealous and upset about the friendship with Heseltine.[68] Lawrence wrote back reassuringly. 'Now don't get in a state, you two, about nothing. The Publishing scheme has not yet become at all real or important, to me.' He explained, rather disingenuously, that the enthusiasm was Heseltine's, and that they were not to 'think his friendship hurts ours. It doesn't touch it ... We must treasure and value very much any one who will *really* be added on to us.' Yet his illness had made him newly vulnerable.

I begin to tremble and feel sick at the slightest upset: your letter for instance. Do be mild with me for a bit. Don't get silly notions. I've waited for you for two years now,[69] and am far more constant to you than ever you are to me – or ever will be. Which you know. So don't use foolish language. I believe in you, and there's the end of it. (ii. 548–9)

That kind of belief, and not a relation built upon the ups and downs of personal feeling, is what he wanted.

The Murrys were not to be mollified about Heseltine, however, and with some justification, since 'The Rainbow Books and Music' had gone as far as a circular without them (though the need to get *The Rainbow* back in print, for Lawrence's sake, might have seemed an important consideration). On 26 February Katherine thanked Ottoline for showing them Frieda's letter: She was pleased that 'the Armenian is gone but I wish he had taken Haseltine [sic] with him ... What a pity it is that dear Lorenzo sees rainbows around so many dull

people and pots of gold in so many mean hearts. But he will never change –'
Murry added a postscript: 'We are going to stay with the Lawrences for ever
and ever as perhaps you know; I daresay eternity will last the whole of the
summer.'[70] He did not relish a letter from Lawrence with a very different
opinion of Dostoevsky from his own, or the suggestion that if he had not finished
his book, they might do it together![71]

Moreover the Lawrence whom they were joining was much changed from the
Lawrence they had left. Their lack of sympathy with *The Rainbow* and their
absence as he absorbed the blow may have prevented them from imagining what
its destruction had meant to him. At a distance they may not have realised,
either, how ill he had been in Porthcothan. Most of all, caught up in their own
exciting progress as writers and their happiness together, it was perhaps only
natural that they paid little attention to the signs of an important change in
Lawrence's way of thinking. While he had been ill he had been engaged on a
significant course of reading. The landscape round Porthcothan spoke to him of
worlds wholly other than the corrupt present: of what was un-English, pre-
Christian and 'primitive' if one defined 'civilisation' as post-Socratic and rational.
It was the supposed peak of Christian civilisation that had created the trenches
and the hordes of enthusiastic young men rushing into them, their names filling
the newspaper columns of casualties every day, and even more so in 1916. It was
in the name of that civilisation that the attempt of a 'passionately religious man'
to create a new prose for 'God' had been declared obscene and destroyed. The
great evolution of rational science was just about to reach its apotheosis in late
February in the bombardments of Verdun, but had already showed clearly
enough what feats could be engineered by mass-men like Skrebensky. So in
January and February Lawrence began to ask Ottoline for books that would take
him back *behind* the whole Graeco-Roman–Christian civilisation that was now so
visibly coming apart. He read Hesiod's *Homeric Hymns*, and responded immediately to the frontispiece of Dionysos crossing the sea – now that Apollo's reign
must end.[72]

He read a history of the East and loved it. 'Babylon, Nineveh, Ashburnipal,
how one somehow, suddenly understands it.' The long stretch of pre-Greek
history gave a comforting perspective to the convulsion and mass-killing of the
present.

I cannot tell you the joy of ranging far back there seeing the hordes surge out of Arabia,
or over the edge of the Iranian plateau. It is like looking at the morning star. The world is
very big, and the course of mankind is stupendous. What does a crashing down of nations
and empires matter, here and there! What is death, in the individual! I don't care if sixty
million individuals die: the seed is not in the masses, it is elsewhere. (ii. 528–9)

It is of course because he *did* care that he had to search for lost secrets of better living. He read Maspéro's *Egypte* (with profit for the future *Women in Love*), but found it too academic and asked for another 'not too big', because I like to fill it in myself' (ii. 529).[73] (Like most imaginative writers he was an inspired extracter rather than a student of learned works.) He also enjoyed Coulton's translation (*From St. Francis to Dante*) of the *Chronicle* of the Franciscan Salimbene, because he liked to see people 'as they were when the Christian idea was still only a graft upon their lives, had not entered in their blood ... One has to recover the original self, now' (ii. 538). His interests had also turned to ethnology and 'primitive religion'. He had been reading Frazer's *Golden Bough* and *Totem and Exogamy* the previous December, and had written that important letter to Russell about 'blood-consciousness'. He had been interested also in the West African carving he had seen in Heseltine's London flat; as well as by the Indian Ajanta frescoes which seemed 'the most perfect things I have ever seen – Botticelli is vulgar beside them'. In the perfection of their relation of man and woman they marked 'the zenith of a very lovely civilisation, the crest of a very perfect wave of human developement' (ii. 489).[74] There were, then, civilisations quite as worthy and far less destructive than the European one. Tylor's *Primitive Culture*, despite its arrogant talk of 'lower' and 'higher' cultures, impressed upon him the idea that all over the world men shared similar ways of thinking, in the so-called primitive cultures that preceded so-called civilisation. He also read Gilbert Murray on the development of Greek religion, disliking the style, 'But the stuff of the book interests me *enormously*' (ii. 559). He would have been interested in anything Heseltine had to tell him about his reading in the occult (though this was probably an early stage in Philip's study) since that too might seam back into pre-Socratic and pre-Christian modes of thought and religious experience.[75] In Cornwall he could try to go back to 'the primeval world that is strong and completely unsaddened' (ii. 512), before what had gone wrong began.

The Murrys had no idea of all this, as they agreed to come to Zennor. By mid-February however they had realised that if they wanted to retain their special friendship they needed to respond positively to Lawrence's urging – and Katherine cabled accordingly as early as the 17th (ii. 545), which hardly suggests that they were as 'non-committal' as Murry later claimed.[76] Moreover Lawrence was whole-hearted and his enthusiasm was infectious. 'Good,' he cried, 'all is well between us all. No more quarrels and quibbles. Let it be agreed for ever. I am Blutbruder: a Blutbruderschaft between us all. Tell K. *not* to be so queasy' (ii. 570).

They would arrive in April, when it would be warm enough for Katherine. In the meantime Lawrence busied himself (and his London friends) to get what remained of their own possessions from the Hampstead house gathered together and sent down – for now they were to have a home again. With a clear realisation that it was Katherine's sensitivities that would be important, he asked their new landlord Captain Short, a retired seaman, 'soft like a child, with a mania for fussing' but 'a perfect dear' (ii. 576–7, 581), to move the privy from where it dominated the view from the Murrys' cottage, and to get some colour-washing done before their arrival. They went to St Ives to buy coconut-matting, and furniture from Benney's auction. Lawrence made a rough dresser and shelves, and planned to cover the spring on the hillside from which their water had to be fetched – a little point he had omitted to mention to the Murrys, along with the outside privy, and a damp patch in the dining-room which boded none too well for the stone cottages as a whole. He was busy and happy; feeling the spring coming, watching the lambs frisk round the big boulders in the grass. 'Never mind that you don't like my philosophy', he wrote to Ottoline, 'it doesn't matter' (ii. 580). Perhaps he might go on with 'Miss Houghton' again if he could get the manuscript back from Germany where he had left it in 1913, but he was in no hurry to write. His mind was set on the Murrys' arrival; the realisation of Rananim like a 'little monastery' (once again), such as those in the dark ages which had kept the hope of a better life alive.

V Wuthering

At last they came, in the first week of April. Murry recalled nearly twenty years later that no sooner were they alone in the Tinner's Arms than Katherine, who had not wanted to leave Bandol and had not cared for Cornwall in 1914, cried out 'I shall *never* like this place'; and although he enjoyed the expeditions to St Ives and Benney's, he so shared her foreboding that he painted his chairs black, as against Lawrence's cheerful colour-scheme of pink and white and royal blue. Murry's memory tended to be selective, and he wanted later to present the episode as doomed from the start. Yet he remembered also what fun it had been to be with Lawrence again, experiencing 'the warm and irresistible intimacy with which he surrounded one, an atmosphere established as it were by a kindly gardener who had, very precisely, decided that you were to grow, and who, by that act, awakened in you the feeling that there was something in you which could grow'.[77] Moreover Katherine – despite all the grey boulders, and the occasional adder which Lawrence liked in its slim elegance, like 'a dainty and superb princess' (ii. 599) – soon found the landscape and its spring flowers 'very lovely just now', and even lovelier in memory. She would later tell Virginia Woolf that for all the imperfection of the cottage,

there is a – – – something – – which makes one long for it. Immediately you get there – you are *free* free as air ... It is a place where you sit on the stairs & watch the lovely light inhabiting the room below. After nightfall the house has three voices – If you are in the tower & someone comes from the far cottage – he comes from far away – You go by the edge of the fields to Katie Berryman's for the bread. You walk home along the rim of the Atlantic with the big fresh loaf – & when you arrive the house is like a ship. I mustn't talk about it – It bewitched me –

Near the end of her life she told Brett she 'had a whole spring full of blue-bells one year with Lawrence. I shall never forget it. And it was warm, not very sunny, the shadows raced over the silky grass and the cuckoos sang.' Frieda remembered 'days of complete harmony': how they went out in a boat and sang '*Row, row, row your boat ... Merrily, merrily ... Life is but a dream*'; how they enjoyed getting the Murrys' cottage ready in a 'frenzy' of painting and polishing; and how she loved walking with Katherine to Zennor and watching her stamp her foot against the wind, or sitting in the sun under the foxgloves and talking 'like two Indian braves, as she said ... She told me many things from her life ... Since then whenever I see foxgloves I must think of Katherine.'[78]

Yet, between the lines of their letters at the time, there soon appear the signs of strain. It was ten days before the Murrys got into their house, and neither the damp in the dining-room nor the leaking roof of the tower had been cured. There were days of mist and lashing rain which were bad for both health and spirits. Katherine, alone with the little maid she had hired and called 'the Cornish Pasty', felt sometimes that they 'had drifted out to sea – and would never be seen again'.[79] Lawrence thought that neither of the Murrys were 'very well in health' nor 'acclimatised here yet' (ii. 599); and though on warm days he felt he was getting really well, he was 'seedy' again at the beginning of May (ii. 603). There was increasing stress and anxiety about the rapidly nearing threat of conscription. (The Derby scheme had failed to produce men in sufficient numbers to replace the casualties; the power of Lloyd George had increased in the Cabinet; the Military Service Act had been passed in January, and would bring in conscription from May.) The battle of Verdun had started at the end of February, and as the carnage steadily increased, there was increasing pressure on the British to do something on the Somme; while the Easter rebellion in Dublin was yet another sign of things coming apart. When a policeman arrived, 'to arrest Murry' wrote Katherine, but in fact to check his status as (officially) a single man, the menace of the outside world could not be avoided by their isolation. It came home to Lawrence, too, that this time he could not simply refuse, and there were more outbursts of anger rooted in anxiety. His letters fiercely denounce England's blood-sucking allies; and anticipate Yeats's view that the Irish rebel leaders were 'mostly ... nothings who happen to have become tragically significant in death' (ii. 611); but above all they voice another spasm of loathing and shame over what had happened to liberal and democratic England and to Englishmen. Seediness and anxiety inflamed again the irritable nerves his illness had left behind.

There were explosions – and barely a month after they arrived Katherine and Murry were secretly preparing to leave. On 11 May Katherine described to Kot the worst instance of marital violence by Lawrence of which we have evidence; hence worth quoting in full.

You may laugh as much as you like at this letter, darling, all about the COMMUNITY. It *is* rather funny.

Frieda and I do not even speak to each other at present. Lawrence is about one million miles away, although he lives next door. He and I still speak but his very voice is faint like a voice coming over a telephone wire. It is all because I cannot stand the situation between these two, for one thing. It is degrading – it offends one's soul beyond words. I don't know which disgusts one worse – when they are very loving and playing with each other or when they are roaring at each other and he is pulling out Frieda's hair and saying 'I'll cut your bloody throat, you bitch' and Frieda is running up and down the road screaming for 'Jack' to save her!! This is only a half of what literally happened last Friday night. You know, Catalina, Lawrence isn't healthy any more; he has gone a little bit out of his mind. If he is contradicted about *anything* he gets into a frenzy, quite beside himself and it goes on until he is so exhausted that he cannot stand and has to go to bed and stay there until he has recovered. And whatever your disagreement is about he says it is because you have gone wrong in your sex and belong to an obscene spirit. These rages occur whenever I see him for more than a casual moment for if ever I say anything that isn't quite 'safe' off he goes! It is like sitting on a railway station with Lawrence's temper like a big black engine puffing and snorting. I can think of nothing, I am blind to everything, waiting for the moment when with a final shriek – off it will go! When he is in a rage with Frieda he says it is she who has done this to him and that she is 'a bug who has fed on my life'. I think that is true. I think he is suffering from quite genuine monomania at present, through having endured so much from her. Let me tell you what happened on Friday. I went across to them for tea. Frieda said Shelleys Ode to a Skylark was false. Lawrence said: 'You are showing off; you don't know anything about it.' Then she began '*Now* I have had enough. Out of my house – you little God Almighty you. Ive had enough of you. Are you going to keep your mouth shut or aren't you.' Said Lawrence: 'I'll give you a dab on the cheek to quiet you, you dirty hussy'. Etc. Etc. So I left the house. At dinner time Frieda appeared. 'I have finally done with him. It is all over for ever.' She then went out of the kitchen & began to walk round and round the house in the dark. Suddenly Lawrence appeared and made a kind of horrible blind rush at her and they began to scream and scuffle. He beat her – he beat her to death – her head and face and breast and pulled out her hair. All the while she screamed for Murry to help her. Finally they dashed into the kitchen and round and round the table. I shall never forget how L. looked. He was so white – almost green and he just hit – thumped the big soft woman. Then he fell into one chair and she into another. No one said a word. A silence fell except for Frieda's sobs and sniffs. In a way I felt almost glad that the tension between them was over for ever – and that they had made an end of their 'intimacy'. L. sat staring at the floor, biting his nails. Frieda sobbed. Suddenly, after a long time – about a quarter of an hour – L. looked up and asked Murry a question about French literature. Murry replied. Little by little, the three drew up to the table. Then F. poured herself out some coffee. Then she and L. glided into talk, began to discuss some 'very rich but very good macaroni cheese'. And next day, whipped himself, and far more thoroughly than he had ever beaten Frieda, he was running about taking her up her breakfast to her bed and trimming her a hat.

Am I wrong in not being able to accept these people just as they are – laughing when they laugh and going away from them when they fight? *Tell me*. For I cannot. It seems to me so *degraded* – so horrible to see I cant stand it. And I feel so furiously angry: I *hate* them for it. F. is such a liar, too. To my face she is all sweetness. She used to bring me in flowers, tell me how 'exquisite' I was – how my clothes suited me – that I had never been so 'really beautiful'. Ugh! how humiliating! Thank Heaven it is over. I must be the real enemy of such a person. And what is hardest of all to bear is Lawrence's 'hang doggedness'. He is so completely in her power and yet I am sure that in his heart he loathes his slavery. She is not even a good natured person really; she is evil hearted and her mind is simply riddled with what she calls 'sexual symbols'. Its an ugly position for Lawrence but I cant be sorry for him just now. The sight of his humiliating dependence makes me too furious . . .

I am very much alone here. It is not a really nice place. It is so full of huge stones, but now that I am writing I do not care for the time. It is so very temporary. It may all be over next month; in fact it will be. I don't belong to anybody here. In fact I have no being, but I am making preparations for changing everything. Write to me when you can and scold me.

Goodbye for now. Dont forget me.

I am always   Kissienka.[80]

Only, how are we to understand episodes like this on a level deeper than gossipy anecdote? We certainly need to see though very different points of view, and remember that three of those involved were writers. Katherine's letter is a story, which we can watch her honing to Ottoline a little later; and a deeper sense of what was at stake for all of them depends also on understanding its bearing on their writing, which *was* living to them, at its most intense.

Frieda's point of view has to be discovered between the lines and is not best served by seeing her simply as a victim. If Katherine and she were not on speaking terms now, this was because of an earlier explosion, not by Lawrence, and caused by the Murrys. Jack (like Heseltine) relayed what Ottoline had said about Frieda at Garsington and in letters afterwards, as Frieda had suspected. She was predictably enraged. Off went the last and fiercest of her denunciations of Ottoline, within a few days of the Murrys' arrival at Zennor:

Now for over a year I was ready to be your friend – but steadily and persistently you have treated me with arrogance and insolence! . . . You have told lies about me, you have tried to separate Lawrence and me because you wanted some sort of unwholesome relation with him – All the time you felt good and holy! This love that was between Lawrence and me was something that passed your understanding ... But I have had enough! Either you treat me with ordinary courtesy and respect or I wish neither to hear from you or see you again ...[81]

A row with the Murrys followed; for Ottoline, true to form, sent this letter to them as she had sent the earlier one, only for Frieda (who had no respect for privacy) to recognise the handwriting and open the envelope. She had done her best to be welcoming, especially to Katherine with whom she had shared intimate confidences, and whom she continued to think of as 'exquisite' all her life. The suspicion that Katherine and Jack were lining up with the Ott, and hence with her kind of intellectual and spiritual contempt for the 'fleshly' woman Lawrence had married, and who was supposedly spoiling his life, would be intensely irritating to Frieda.

On 12 April Murry wrote a weasel letter to tell Ottoline what had happened and borrow £10 – perhaps as a safety measure in case of a rapid getaway.

Frieda's letter is outrageous. But more outrageous still is the fact that she knows that you sent it to us ... Lawrence is at present completely on F's side in this quarrel (which isn't a quarrel but an indecent attack), and he spent a long while trying to convince us that for us to remain friendly with you was black treachery to him. It is hopelessly ludicrous, and perhaps we have managed to convince him that there is not the least reason why we should turn and rend you. At all events he has forgotten about it for the moment. F., however, is not likely to forget. I'm afraid, terribly afraid, that we may drift into a final rumpus with her: but we shall try our hardest not to for L's sake ... In many ways L. seems to me to be much happier, much younger than I have known him for the last two years. On the other hand he has bought this at a price. I feel he has quite definitely lost something ... his present carelessness seems to me due to a despair instead of to a superfluity of life, as it used to be. I feel he will not create anything very much in the future. [In a fortnight, he would begin *Women in Love*.]

F. is *monstrum, horrendum, informe, ingens*. Really we are frightened of her. She is sure to break out against us sooner or later, if only because she feels that we imperil her present triumph over L. We have tried to like her for three years now and we haven't got any further towards the end. There is in her an ultimate vulgarity which does appal us both. And that is the reason why she so turned against you, I think. Because she is no longer married to a man who can afford to keep 3 servants, she really does feel herself *déclassé*. Nothing that you could have done would have saved you from her, simply because of this. She despises herself for having thrown up Professor W. for L.; and when a woman like that despises herself ... You know how much we love you ...[82]

Certainly this letter says everything Ottoline (though not Lawrence) would want to hear – but such an atmosphere, barely a week after the Murrys' arrival, would not have improved Lawrence's temper, though he had clearly tried to forget it. He also wrote to Ottoline, saying it was best that Frieda should have said what she felt, since 'the only thing to try for is a free, natural, unstrained relationship, without exclusions or enclosures' (ii. 592) – but this was not Ottoline's way, and though he went on writing at intervals, the silences on both sides got longer.

So Katherine, writing to Gordon Campbell's wife Beatrice the day before the big rumpus she describes above, is already being tart about Lawrence's irritability, and Frieda 'looking at the childrens photographs, I suppose', and the new talk of blood-affinity with animals, and sexual symbols everywhere. She suggested that their cottage be named 'The Phallus', which Frieda thought a very good idea! But embedded in the sarcasm is a vivid picture of Frieda contentedly doing the laundry – the only kind of housework she enjoyed. 'She says this place suits her', says Katherine, 'I am sure it does.'[83] The two women are alone, and separate, but Frieda seems centred in her own world as Katherine in her complexity could never be. Stresses remained: the children only occasionally accessible and now an expensive journey away, being a German woman in an England at war, Lawrence's complete worldly failure and poverty when he had seemed on the point of high success, the collapse of his health. Embattled or not however, Frieda was happiest when she had Lawrence to herself. She was always possessive, and explosively jealous of any threat to her pre-eminence with him, and beside him, which was what had first soured her relations with Ottoline and also lay behind her resentment of the Murrys' attitude and rivalry now.

Despite some distance and dislike however, the day before the battle seemed peaceful enough; though we may glimpse through the eyes of the seemingly contented woman, alone at her wash-tub, a cloud already bigger than a man's hand, in Lawrence being away all day with Murry. The battle itself clarifies what Frieda thought the danger was, and why she broke out at *Lawrence*. For she was the aggressor. Nobody has ever asked why she should, so suddenly, have denounced Shelley when Katherine mentioned him; but she knew what she was doing and what effect it might have. For she, to whom Lawrence read all his work, must have known how Shelley, and specifically that poem 'To a Skylark' (1820), occupied a crucial role in his dialectic thought.[84] It represented for him – 'Hail to thee, blithe spirit, bird thou never wert' – the extreme of mental and spiritual consciousness as opposed to the life of the body and the blood. It was the intellectualism of Ottoline, and Jack, and Katherine, and their claims to soulful sensitivity and spirituality, that seemed most 'false' to Frieda, like the 'soul-mush' she accused Lawrence of wanting with Ottoline. Behind her onslaught, then, is her rage that Lawrence was betraying himself, and her, by being so drawn to them. Moreover his fury is a sure sign that there was something hatefully accurate in the charge.

Katherine, as she describes the row to Kot, is less personally guarded (to the friend whose support she could most rely on) than when she hones her story for

Ottoline later. Her letter creates a splendidly vivid scene, a little masterpiece of *writing*, but it gives a good deal away too, especially as it moves from sardonic comedy, to disgust, and finally to real personal bleakness. Murry, in his myth-making, claimed 'She was a woman simple and lovely in all her ways' – but all her biographers dismiss that as travesty. She kept inventing herself (having started as neither Katherine nor Mansfield) and constantly made up names and personae for everyone close to her. She hid herself behind masks; she constantly played roles and told whoppers; she could be very funny and rather formidable; she was promiscuous and bisexual; ribald and sophisticated, complex and contradictory, a colonial chameleon taking on metropolitan colourings – but behind all her manipulations of herself and of others, there was an overriding need to be in *control* of her life, that came from uncertain identity, and hence fear of commitment, lest one be taken over. She would both long, and fear, to 'belong'. When she had been with the Lawrences before she had had her own base – but now she was on their ground. She could not stand being rushed at, but Lawrence and Frieda did just that. She had hated being a fat little girl (and had tried to make herself 'exquisite'); now she clearly found Frieda grown physically unbounded, an 'immense german christmas pudding' as her letter to Ottoline put it. However, Frieda's being so assuredly herself must also have shown Katherine her own uncertainties, which she would resent.

Above all, we can perhaps see through her eyes how the Lawrences' lack of control would horrify. Two years later she confessed in her journal: 'My own fits of temper are really terrifying ... Lawrence and Frieda over again. I am more like L. than anybody, we are unthinkably alike, in fact.'[85] The vivid metaphor of Lawrence's temper as a great steam-engine shows her fear of the boiler within. Yet it was not only violence she recoiled from, but even more significantly the open tenderness, the 'intimacy', the (to Katherine) indecent exposure which hid nothing. Moreover it would seem not only 'degrading' but dangerous, to herself – for the Lawrences were equally open and probing of their friends, which kept getting them into trouble. They valued individuality but not privacy – and Katherine had bared her most private self to Frieda, only to have Lawrence use the confidence in *The Rainbow*. Katherine had not minded his views on sex at Chesham when she thought him 'nice, very nice, sitting with a piece of string in his hand, on true sex'.[86] But it would be very different if, having just begun his new novel (as we shall see) by exploring homoerotic feeling between men, he were now arguing with *her* about sexuality, including hers. The tart remarks about phallicism, and how one could not contradict Lawrence 'about *anything*' without being told that 'you have gone wrong in your sex and belong to an obscene spirit', make new sense, as does the charge that Frieda was 'a liar', so puzzling in the letter.

Katherine, too, felt deserted and jealous when Murry kept going off with

Lawrence. The Murrys' sexual relation, which was often boy-and-girl-like rather than passionate, may have seemed frail when threatened not only by Lawrence's irritable dogma, but also by his influence on Murry. She joked about Jack losing his horn-rimmed spectacles at every stile when out with Lawrence; but the bleakness at her letter's end – this bare stony place where she has no being, and belongs to nobody – becomes powerfully suggestive. Worst of all, only when *writing* could she fully live, but sardonic letters were all she could and did write here. The contrast with Bandol must have been unbearable. For there she had at last truly found herself, in 'The Aloe'. When she condensed it into 'Prelude', later,[87] revision confirmed that success had come from keeping her satiric and cynical side at bay, so that childlike sensitivity, at one with what it sees, could well through a coolly objective adult medium. In harmony with lost child-brother and intelligent critic-husband-cum-boyish-lover at Bandol, she had written her best so far. But neither the childlike nor the objectively adult vision could flourish in the disturbance at Higher Tregerthen; where self-defence and loneliness brought out her tartest self. She would have to go, and try to 'chang[e] everything'; including, once more, her relationship with Jack.

Murry's feeling for Lawrence in 1914–15 was simply personal affection. It was Gordon Campbell whose mind had fascinated him to ardour and hero-worship, and whose rejection, coming almost simultaneously with Katherine's at Chesham, affected him most. Though he and Lawrence had co-operated on *Signature*, this meant to Murry each man contributing his own handwriting, and 'There Was a Little Man' was remarkably self-absorbed. He did not share (or understand) Lawrence's ideas, or his attitude to the war, and as he himself said his only difference from Robert Lynd who helped destroy *The Rainbow* was his friendship with the author. Lawrence must often have mistaken silence for support, his deep need encouraging belief in their commitment to each other. He saw in Murry the image of the beloved man-friend he longed for – but though Murry wanted to be loved, and entered relationships with enthusiasm, he often persuaded others, and himself, that he felt more than he actually did. The word 'love' came easily to him but he was actually elusive; alternating fervour with instinctive withdrawal from any commitment threatening the self. He lived in his intelligence, obsessively introspective; and in his first novel he had exemplified Lawrence's fear of the hegemony of intellect by analysing himself (as he confessed) 'to immobility'. He also had a streak of mysticism, a sense of himself as above all a spiritual being. It is clear from his novel how little the life of the body then meant to him. At this stage his sexuality treasured most the security of being held to a lover/mother's breast; indeed he and Katherine conceived love as essentially a childlike innocence and gaiety, in the teeth of a hostile and tawdry world[88] – hence the pet names, the anthropomorphic dolls and cats. Above all, though what Lawrence wanted was community based on impersonal commitment, Murry could not conceive any other than personal relations. In Katherine's story of the rumpus, it is his *silence* one notices.

On 14 May however he prepared their way back to Garsington by offering his friend's head on a platter. He now thought Lawrence 'seriously, perhaps even dangerously ill ... all to pieces ... If we go – and we shall, very soon, for good – then I think he will probably develop some mania (in the exact & medical sense)'. He 'expects something of Katherine & me that we can't give – a certain intimacy ... which being *demanded*, is utterly impossible to give'.

There have been scenes between him & Frieda which were simply nervous mad, which, having once happened, should have made it inconceivable that they should still live together. But they do live together: and they pretend to be in love – there's something strangely *indecent* about it ... I'm still deeply fond of him: but I respect him much less ... one always hates a sick man. I neither agree with his ideas, nor am I stimulated by my opposition to them. In almost everything he consciously & deliberately says or does, I detect a taint of illness or hysteria, so that I am compelled to keep silence.

The letter ends, rather greasily, 'I hope for our sakes that you love us as much as we do you ... Katherine sends "her dear love" – those were her very words.' (She had still only seen Ottoline once.) The intention was clear enough.

One should nevertheless try to do justice to Murry's bewilderment, and his sense of danger to himself under pressure from Lawrence's assertiveness, which had not grown less in isolation. The days together, of which Katherine and Frieda were jealous, may have felt like bombardment to Murry. His resentment shows in a scrap of writing that has survived: 'I am tired with the effort to suck life from the words of another man, to kindle with my own breath the dead embers of his thought. They will not live, they will not flame, to me they are dead. Is it I who am dead, or they?'[89] Yet he would not openly oppose.

Most of all, what Murry had been writing at Bandol had been *his* first real finding of himself: his book on Dostoevsky in which for the first time he felt he had something truly significant to say. However, Dostoevsky had also been important in Lawrence's darkening vision since *The Rainbow* – and their views were diametrically opposed. Could mere affection meet the stress, not only of some new bees in his friend's bonnet, but also of Lawrencian attacks on Murry's new-found confidence? Jack's reportage, like Katherine's, was coloured by feeling that not only their decencies, their innermost personalities, and their relationship were at risk – Katherine's withdrawal into herself threatening to leave him paralysed with his old self-consciousness – but also their newly-achieved writing selves.

What then of Lawrence's rage and violence, the irritable assertion, the lack of control? It ought to be possible to see, fairly, where gossip is blind, an opposition so radical that neither side could tell the truth about the other. Charitably, we might follow Lawrence's only direct comment, on the Murrys' departure: 'They should have a soft valley, with leaves and the ring-dove cooing' (ii. 610); which chimes well with Murry's complaint to Ottoline, that 'Here the heights are always wuthering'! Perhaps what we are watching is a real-life version of Emily Brontë's opposition of Heights people with Grange people; the Murrys' stories no more (and no less) able to tell the whole truth, than those of Nellie or Lockwood? Yet that, though helpful, evades what Dostoevsky had helped to bring home to Lawrence, when read in a world at war. Murry, the intellectual, saw a thought-adventurer confronting the death of God: first by asserting individual will to the uttermost, Stavrogin; and then by exploring how absence of self-will, in the goodness of Prince Myshkin, makes him seem an 'idiot'. Finally, in *The Brothers Karamazov*, the sensualist and the nihilist confront the imitation of Christ *as man*, in Alyosha, who for Murry was Dostoevsky's message to a world in which there could be no God. (The terrible irony is that, challenged to *be* Alyosha in a Dostoevskyan situation, Murry fled.)

Lawrence, however, admired Dostoevsky as wizard rat, as underworld explorer of the darkness, the hate, the violence, the evil in people, such as he was discovering everywhere, including himself. To him therefore, Dostoevsky's apparent assertion of loving goodness is sham, and it is especially wicked to proffer Christianity now, when the war has unmistakably exposed the destructiveness within so-called Christian civilisation. He remained religious but his faith was based on creative conflict through which even violence and disintegration could become conditions of renewal, but only by facing them in oneself and going *through*. To go on pretending to be civilised, and trying to preserve outworn social forms, was to become still more deathly.

He was not the Lawrence they had left in 1915 and whom, even then, they were unable to understand. Convinced now that Christianity was played out, it made perfect sense to him to seek hints of lost wisdom in pre-Christian cultures, Celtic, early Greek, Egyptian; to read Frazer on totem, and Tylor on primitive culture – but we saw Katherine's reaction to talk of blood-affinity with animals, and Murry's to the idea of blood-brothership. Above all, they simply could not conceive his new conviction that the most important relationships were *not* personal likings or intellectual agreements, but blood-commitments of faith and loyalty by which man could transcend the conscious ego, and recover truer kinds of relation than those of the modern wasteland. Murry and Katherine reserved the right to come and go according to the ups and downs of personal feeling or intellectual affinity; they recognised a code of behaviour that tried to regulate and lubricate the friction of one personality on another, and they both flinched from any commitment that would compromise the freedom of the self. The relation Lawrence wanted was the opposite: that one could voice one's feelings openly; might freely hate as well as love; might fight or be tender; but all the time be finally committed, once and for all, in a 'blood' relation by no means merely personal. It was because they had never understood Lawrence's conviction that conflict was part of and necessary for growth, that they thought he insisted on agreement, discipleship. What he wanted was a spontaneous opposition-and-relation of contraries who nevertheless remained committed to each other; even the sort of violence, if it came to that, which could blow the sky clean of friction, and let comradeship and tenderness revive; whereas repression bred malice and treachery – did it not? So it was that the Murrys found 'degrading', 'disgusting' and 'indecent', not merely the absence of the gentleness and restraint they prized but, even more, that for the Lawrences violence did *not* imply severance; and that tenderness, intimacy, service could follow the most radical denunciation. (We do not know what Frieda said between tea and dinner, but may be sure that she not only attacked the hypocrisy of preaching as Lawrence did and yet messing on with the Murrys' intellectualism and spirituality, but probably also impugned his manhood – as his heroines tend to do when angry with their men.) She too, of course, could be physically as well as verbally violent. A few months later she again struck him on the head, with a stoneware plate this time, and when his back was turned – but *that* was his only complaint.

It was inherent in the Murrys' mode of behaviour that they should write to other people about the Lawrences as they did, but at the same time determine not to have 'a great quarrel. What's the good? We shall manage it so that our parting will seem necessary for quite other reasons.' There were some last 'peaceful and happy interludes': the excitement when a Spanish coal-ship ran aground nearby and the crew came ashore; and a drive over the moors to Penzance and the beach near Marazion where they 'played with heaps of tiny white shells'. However this experience of the gentler coast, says Murry, 'brought Katherine's determination to a head', so he set off to look for somewhere for them to live on that side, and succeeded in finding a cottage (called 'Sunnyside') at Mylor. They moved in mid-June.[90] Though Murry in his autobiography tried to set his happiness with Katherine off against the Lawrencian storms, in fact their relationship was severely strained also. She wrote from Mylor that she was 'numb' with misery; and before the end of the month she was making an assignation with Gertler (which she didn't keep) and arranging to be at Garsington without Murry.[91] On 7 July Lawrence told Kot that the Murrys had made 'a contract whereby each of them is free ... I think she and Jack have worn out anything that was between them. – I like her better than him. He was rather horrid when he was here' (ii. 623). He knew now that 'Murry and I are not really associates. How I deceive myself. I am a liar to myself, about people' (ii. 617).

If we want to understand Lawrence's point-of-view at its deepest, however, we have to look to the new novel he had been writing since late April.

VI 'The second half of *The Rainbow*'

On 26 April he told Cynthia Asquith it was under way: 'The world crackles and busts, but that is another matter, external, in chaos. One has a certain order inviolable in one's soul' (ii. 601). From the start, then, the new fiction was apocalyptic – conceived as it was in the exploding world of Verdun, the Somme and the Easter Rising – but also a struggle for an order beneath his overwhelming sense of violence and personal disturbance. His inability to conceive an audience after what had happened to *The Rainbow* is immediately apparent. He told Barbara Low on 1 May he had begun 'the second half of the *Rainbow*. But already it is beyond all hope of ever being published, because of the things it says' (ii. 602). He had led off, defiantly, by exploring homosexual feeling between men.

And more than that, it is beyond all possibility even to offer it to a world, a putrescent mankind like ours. I feel I cannot *touch* humanity, even in thought, it is abhorrent to me.

But a work of art is an act of faith, as Michael Angelo says, and one goes on writing, to the unseen witnesses.

He was taking up what had been the original 'Sisters' in 1913, transformed into the second half of 'The Wedding Ring' in 1914 and put aside in early January 1915 when he realised that what was becoming *The Rainbow* would be far too long if it were to include Ursula's relationship with Birkin and Gudrun's with Gerald. Yet the rewriting now, by a different Lawrence in a different world, brought once again the sense of exploring the unknown; the new novel 'a stranger to me even as I write it. I don't know what the end will be' (ii. 604).

By 19 May he told Pinker that he was 'half way through ... a sequel to the *Rainbow*, though quite unlike it' (ii. 606) – and to mention this to his agent suggests he now thought of publication after all. If so, he had already decided to drop the original defiant start. On 24 May (by when it was clear that the Murrys would leave) he told Ottoline he had got 'a long way ... It comes rapidly, and is very good. When one is shaken to the very depths, one finds reality in the unreal world. At present my real world is the world of my inner soul, which reflects on to the novel I write. The outer world is there to be endured, it is not real ...' (ii. 610). At the end of the month he told Forster (after a long gap between letters) that 'in this book I am free at last, thank God' and feels 'rather triumphant', even though 'Nearly everybody has dropped off from me' (ii. 612). He had 'married Ursula ... Two thirds of the novel are written. It goes on pretty fast, and very easy. I have not travailed over it. It is the book of my free soul' (ii. 614). By 19 June it was 'nearly done' (ii. 617), and ten days later Pinker was told that only an epilogue chapter remained to be written (ii. 619, 669), and he was definitely thinking of publication (ii. 619, 627). He would try typing himself, and re-writing at the same time.

Of this first version in its two phases, only the cancelled opening chapters and four final notebooks (beginning with Gudrun running through the snow and ending with Gerald's death) survive. What have these bits of a new 'The Sisters' to tell biographers?

Despite the eagerness of some to see the cancelled 'Prologue' in confessional terms, its exploration of homoerotic feeling between men has at least as much structural as personal significance, even if (as in everything else) the novelist may draw on himself. His starting from a relationship between two men who find each other more attractive than women, *and equally*, from two women who find the idea of marriage with a man unthinkable, probably sprang from the diagnosis of a modern condition in 'Goats and Compasses', as did the split and reactionary vacillation between the goatlike and the overly spiritual in the 'Prologue' affair between Birkin and Hermione (who looks like Ottoline, but is strongly reminiscent of Jessie Chambers). After Lawrence's years of thinking on the subject, to interpret his 'Prologue' as merely revealing that he was 'a homosexual' is extraordinarily reductive – quite apart from his own rejection in 'Hardy' of exclusive categories of gender and sexuality. He had long acknowledged homoerotic feelings, but that is the beginning of a complex question, and no categoric conclusion. Moreover – significantly – reductive biography has combined with careless reading in the failure to notice that there are two *kinds* of homoerotic feeling in the 'Prologue', announcing a distinction that will be the major theme in the novel. This will so apply to *all* being 'in love', that the nature of the loving has clearly become much more important than the gender of the lovers, transcending homophobia.

Between Birkin and Gerald, contrasted in temperament and physique, there is a 'trembling nearness' and a nascent 'tenderness', which they repress. Climbing in the mountains away from the everyday world, they become aware of how their 'transcendent intimacy' can transfigure them and make each feel 'another life' in himself 'like an essential flame'. Yet though they knew, for a moment, that 'they loved each other', when they get back down to the social world 'they would have none of it'. The language is that of *The Rainbow*'s marriage of opposites and mutual transformation; but unpublishable after the reaction to Ursula's affair with Winifred. Here, re-transposed to men, is 'the hot, flushing, roused attraction'[92] which one sex is supposed to feel for the other, but which Birkin, despite his intimacies with women, has so far only felt for men, though he has always rejected it.

At this point however a double opposition begins. Birkin is the intellectual and spiritual pole of the contraries, physically frail; whereas the men who attract him are all physical creatures and men of action, uninteresting intellectually. By contrast what attracts him to women is intelligence and 'soul'. The apotheosis of this is his relationship with Hermione, a year younger than himself, and known since they were students. (Indeed, Jessie thought even the final published version another variation of Miriam.)[93] She is jealous and contemptuous of his relation with the 'coarse, unsusceptible ... Gerald Criches of this world', as also of the fleshly women with whom Birkin occasionally tries to 'prostitute' himself. When however he either reduces himself with her to pure consciousness and spirit, or worse, tries without true desire to take her physically while she sacrifices herself (like Miriam), it is for him to run 'from death to death', becoming hollowed out and spectral.

Moreover within the attraction of men for Birkin there are two distinct desires. With his opposites ('white-skinned, keen-limbed men with eyes like blue-flashing ice ... the northmen ... distinct') he is drawn to what is not-him, a kind of physical 'light' which might transfigure both. To a 'strange Cornish type of man' however, with 'dark eyes that one can enter and plunge into ... night-smelling men ... the living substance of the viscous, universal, heavy darkness', he is drawn in a very different way: 'to know ... to have him, as it were to eat him, to take the very substance of him'. This, and the 'rabbit-like way in which the strong, softly-built man ate' looks forward to what, after several revisions, will be identified as sado-masochism; and already it is obviously a sexuality which asserts the self at the expense, and ultimately the annihilation, of the other. The whole point here is less to distinguish 'homosexual' from 'heterosexual' relationships, than to begin exploring the difference in *both alike* between relationships that can transfigure, and those that are deathly because they disintegrate the self and destroy the other. Are there, even now, relationships (of whatever gender) which can integrate the conflicts within the self and with others to create new life? Or must, at the end of a life-cycle, 'Decay and decomposition ... take their own way' as Birkin seems to suspect: 'How to get away from this process of reduction, how escape this phosphorescent passage into the tomb ... this was the unconscious problem which tortured Birkin day and night.'[94]

It is highly unlikely that this had anything to do with a homosexual attraction to Murry. Murry was neither of his 'types'. He was intellectual and soulful, and it was *that* which made him lovable to Lawrence and drew Frieda's wrath. Gerald and Gudrun had of course been conceived in the first 'Sisters' before Lawrence ever met the Murrys; and it is not at all surprising that Murry never recognised himself in the final version, since Lawrence put nothing into the character that resembles him – unlike the features in Gudrun which would develop through thinking about Katherine. The possible real-life 'sources' of Gerald – given all that misleads in the phrase – lie outwardly in Philip Barber of

Lambclose and the coal-owning firm of Barber, Walker & Co.; and inwardly in Lawrence's admiration for his dead brother, for Alan Chambers, for the muscular lady-killer George Neville and the good-looking athletic Bunny Garnett – all transformed well beyond 'life' by the power of Lawrence's imagination. 'Little' Murry had the dark eyes of the other type, but certainly not the physical aura; and, as we have seen and will see again, the last thing Lawrence wanted was to 'eat' him. Moreover, though Lawrence would develop in 1917 a close friendship with William Henry Hocking, his young Cornish neighbour at Higher Tregerthen Farm (see below), and may indeed have felt attracted to him at first sight, he can have had only a passing acquaintance as yet, when he was altogether taken up with the Murrys. (He never mentions him before August.) What Lawrence *would* take from the failure of his friendship with Murry at Higher Tregerthen, and explore, was the offer of blood-brotherhood which he had made to both Katherine and Jack. It was this that led Murry long afterwards (with typical knowingness, but little understanding) to claim that *Women in Love* was essentially a contrast between Lawrence's relation with Frieda and his with Katherine, misrepresented; but Murry did not suppose blood-brotherhood involved homosexual relationship, though he could never see what it did involve.[95]

That however was a question the novel set out to answer; in a fashion sharply distinguished from those kinds of homosexual feeling and practice Lawrence thought destructive, but clearly of the *same* nature as his violent but creative relationship with Frieda. The evidence is in the revision of the first version between July and November, where it becomes plain that the question of relationship between men was soon subsumed in – and had probably always been subordinate to – the much more important questions which had shaken Lawrence to the depths in the contretemps with the Murrys: the laying bare of the split in himself between intellect/spirit and the life of the body, which he had diagnosed to Ottoline as a major source of difficulty in his marriage; and, deeper still, of the violence, hate and urge to destroy which the rumpuses at Higher Tregerthen had brought into the open in the Lawrences – and more covertly, in the Murrys too – an exploration of two very different kinds of violence, in two very different kinds of love, irrespective of gender.

The final notebooks moreover, even without the epilogue, make it clear that one of these is quite literally deathly – very unlike the hopeful ending of the original 'Sisters'.

VII 'The Sisters' III (July–November)

Lawrence's decision to type the novel confirmed that he *was* now aiming for publication. He had to – he had been living all this time in Cornwall on the money that had been collected for the abortive move to America; and though he had a roof over his head for the rest of the year, by 12 July he had only £6 left (ii.630). Another £50 came from Pinker (ii. 630), but Lawrence was increasingly unhappy about being unable to support himself.[96]

Before he could begin however, he had to go to Bodmin at the end of June to be examined for military service – but returned triumphantly with a total exemption. It was not as bad as he had feared. He hated being marched from the station 'like a criminal' (ii. 618); the humiliation of thirty men being examined in their shirts; the spurious atmosphere, keyed-up, but with (he thought) a sense of wrongness underneath. The pillow he slept on was 'like an old withered vegetable marrow tied up in a bag';[97] but the men all seemed *decent* (ii. 625). He admired their readiness to suffer for what they thought their duty to their fellow men; but why hadn't they the courage to reject suffering in defence of their own integrity? He felt the glamour of 'camaradérie' – Whitman's word – but at once rejected it in association with militarism (ii. 618). He told his Board that 'the doctors said I had had consumption' but 'didn't produce any certificate. I didn't think it fair to Jones' (ii. 623). The leading English Freudian had subscribed to *Signature*, and had probably given him a letter to take to the Battersea Town Hall the previous December, when he was intending to emigrate. The notion that it would have been unfair to Jones to produce it, however, suggests he thought that Jones had stretched the facts, which was acceptable when only attestation was at issue, but might be embarrassing if not confirmed by full professional examination now.[98] Lawrence spoke crisply, and was believed without a certificate – indeed to the naked eye he was unfit to be a soldier, even a clerkly one.

The experience left its mark on the novel: his reflections on 'the nation', property and one's duty to one's neighbour, voiced to Catherine Carswell and Thomas Dunlop soon afterwards, became matters of debate among the wedding party at 'Shortlands'.

We first hear of the typing in mid-July, after Lawrence had helped the Hockings with haymaking on the farm, (which will have reminded him of The Haggs and Alan Chambers) and had decided to take over two rooms in what had been the Murrys' house. We can now imagine him typing in the tower where Katherine had written to Kot. It was to become 'one of the labours of Hercules' that went on for month after month (ii. 665). At the end of August there was a deluge and he caught cold again, with neuralgia (ii. 648). Throughout September the weather continued wet and stormy, and he spent much of the time in bed. Frieda became worried once more when she returned from a visit to London in mid month[99] to find him ill and deeply depressed; and by mid-October the revision of the novel was still only two-thirds done. At that stage he decided that enough was enough (ii. 666); the typing was bad for his nerves and was making him ill; so he persuaded Pinker to have it completed in his office instead (ii. 668), while he finished the rest of the draft in pencil in another set of notebooks. (Lawrence's typing stops just before what is now 'Excurse'.) Though he was in bed once more, the revision then fairly slipped along until the last notebook went off to Pinker on 31 October (ii. 669). Still an epilogue remained to be written – but when the typescript came back he (typically) began another major revision instead.

So what does this version reveal of Lawrence's struggle to come to terms with what had happened to his world and to himself since *The Rainbow*, and with the violence of 1916, both within and at large? The novel's apocalyptic vision made Frieda want it called 'Dies Irae' (ii. 669) – but Lawrence wanted the emphasis to fall on love (as he understood it), and the later notebooks are already titled 'Women in Love' though the novel we know in print had not yet fully found itself. For a biographer, the main issues in this draft (the first we can read in full, ignoring the revisions on the typescript) are its use of 'real' people; the exploration of violence; and the question whether the novel exposes a sick author and marriage, or shows sickness beginning to be shed.

Though feelings about Ottoline, Puma and Katherine went into Lawrence's developing creation, his motives were more than personal. He had liked and at some level still did like all three, despite the tensions that had arisen. Of course he was by no means devoid of malice or vindictiveness, but these were not what the characters of Hermione, the Pussum and Gudrun were *for*. The Pussum and Hermione developed as necessary extremes in the imaginative spectrum of 'women in love', between which the capacity of Gudrun and Ursula to reduce themselves or be transformed through conflict with their lovers can be gauged. If there had been no Lady Ottoline, Lawrence would have had to invent a Lady Compasses. It was *necessary* for this imagined world to have at one extreme a woman whose essential life was all mental consciousness, including the remains of her sensuality, who believed she could control her self and all others through her will and who was intensely spiritual. Coming at the end of a great cycle, she should be a *Kulturträger*, an apotheosis of civilisation; but because her civilisation is in decay, she must also be a withered priestess, beset by neurotic uncertainty that makes her batten on the 'other' to prop her against the loss of self, which she sees as an abyss. Should that abyss open, she will betray a destructive, even murderous violence, all the more shocking because of her cultured spirituality. Having known Ottoline undoubtedly helped Lawrence to this conception, gave him remarkable physical features and an ambience to work with, put a glint in his eye and also helped him sharpen his understanding of the 'Compasses' tendency of Bloomsbury, Cambridge and the fin-de-siècle in England generally. However, the character Hermione not only over-intensifies some and omits many other features of Ottoline Morrell;[100] it also draws from quite other sources: Jessie Chambers, Helen Corke and probably others, it hardly matters now. Hermione's physical violence came from Frieda, but, Lawrence was sure, was a potential in every woman as in every man, though Ottoline and Katherine repressed it. It was equally necessary to have in the Pussum an opposite creature, of almost total sensuality – even to her kind of intelligence – who offers herself as an odalisque or slave and acquires power through doing so, and who lives in and through the disintegration of the self in the world of artistic nihilism and bohemia.[101] If there had been no Miss Channing to select from and intensify, he would have had to invent Miss Goat. Even with Halliday, veering between 'broken ... Christ' and depraved sensualist,[102] Lawrence was motivated by more than personal revenge, for he was not only re-imagining (albeit more intensely and, yes, with a glint now) the diagnosis he had already openly made in the time of his friendship with Philip Heseltine, but also using it to diagnose something in Birkin, who is a reflection of himself. As his alienation and isolation grew, he clearly cared less and less about the feelings of people he used for his fictive purposes; yet those purposes were much more creative and structural than vindictive. The overriding impulse was to explore to extremes the impulses which war within and between the two sisters and the men with whom they fall in love; and (in this art of 'articulate extremity') to follow the opposite violences of those conflicts to their final resolution. In the heat of such imagination, ties with real life soon melted away.

Even in its penultimate state, the novel was an extraordinarily brave and disturbing exploration of violence; a 'war novel' no less for being set in a world apparently at peace.[103] For wherever we look, violence breaks out: Gerald spurring his mare at the railway-crossing, Gudrun dancing herself against the Highland bullocks then striking her lover in the face, the death scream of a rabbit in Gerald's grasp, the blow that fells Loerke, the near murder of Gudrun. All these were already present in this version. So were Birkin hurling rocks at the reflection of the moon, Gerald and Birkin wrestling in the library, Ursula flinging Birkin's engagement rings in his face with fierce abuse – but whereas one sequence leads progressively to death, the other results (as the Murrys could not accept) in tenderness, reverence, truth-telling, new life. Given also the murderous blow Hermione strikes Birkin, as well as the Pussum stabbing a knife into a man's hand in the Pompadour, it is clear that Lawrence saw the world of 1916 as one in which violent hatred, and the impulse to strike at anything that threatened the self, lurked everywhere and only a little below the surface, whether cultured or bohemian. The major challenge of the novel, then, is whether there can be a violence that is creative as well as a violence that destroys.

For any love it would seem, any deep relation between the self and another, produces both inner and outer war, opening splits within the self and conflict with its opposite. What seems to make the difference, again, is whether the self can give itself over, accept oblivion and transformation at the other's hands, or whether it seeks to dominate, or absorb, or use the other to gratify its sense of power, of which the final extreme is killing. In 'The Sisters' III now, in the months of Verdun and the Somme, the characters are far more disintegrated than in *The Rainbow*, and react at first with even greater violence to the war of the sexes that lies within being in love. Yet at the same water party in which Gudrun strikes the first blow, a wholly different way of loving is revealed. Poised in a fragile canoe, Gudrun is overcome by the beauty of the male opposite, no longer seen as a threat, while Gerald for the first time is able to lapse out of himself into his surroundings, instead of his usual urge to dominate. Will they be able, 'in love', to integrate the upper- and the sub-conscious, the dark and the light selves, as the rosy and deep blue lanterns are constellated in the dark water? Which way will they, and Ursula and Birkin, go?

At the novel's centre, three leaps of imagination show directions toward new life, or death, in this apocalyptic fiction of Last Things and Judgements – though the novel has some way to go yet, in clarifying what imagination brings to the surface.

Birkin stones the moon in the pond, in destructive misogyny, resentment, repudiation – but afterwards there is peace. It would seem that the disintegration of consciousness has nowadays to be almost complete before life can be renewed; only this is no mere symbolism, but a powerful experience of rocking, crashing, destructive force, as Birkin seeks to obliterate the fiercely bright light from the black water, yet watches it re-form, looking quite different, whole and composed, at peace. The violence makes Birkin and the watching Ursula oblivious of self, the mind spilled out, but afterwards there is a new tenderness and a new sense of how love may get beyond personality. It is hard to put into words, though, and as soon as talk begins, misunderstanding grows. Indeed, in this version, Lawrence himself has not fully grasped what it is that Birkin (and he himself) wants from love, or how it relates to or differs from a male chauvinism that Birkin slips into, and Ursula resents. Yet there does seem to be a violence that leads through disintegration to harmony, tenderness, renewal.

In stark contrast, the violence when the great buck rabbit Bismarck is hauled out by the ears, to be sketched, exposes much that is hidden, not only in Gerald and Gudrun but (by extension) in other characters as well. The frenzied kicking and scratching animal shows the instinctive fight in all living creatures against what threatens them; but his life-force, far from winning respect or wonder, brings welling up instead a savage and destructive cruelty in the apparently civilised man and woman, exerting their will and power almost to the death. Though the full implications of what Lawrence has imagined have yet to emerge, disturbing potentialities are revealed in the lovers and their 'love', through the power struggle with the animal. The desire to dominate and control may drive men, and women, to destroy. Even art, and seeking to *know*, may be modes of domination or possession. Victims may exert strange provocation and power. Hermione and the Pussum come into new focus too.

The wrestling of Gerald and Birkin explores the question whether there could be a love between men as potentially transforming as the creative love between men and women – and suggests what Lawrence meant by the Blutbrüderschaft Murry had rejected. Here too is the attraction and challenge of opposites. Here too what begins as release of frustration and resentment intensifies into violence, as the underworld creature on the Chinese lantern which Gudrun rejected, and which reappeared in the moon writhing on the pond, becomes visible once more in the struggling naked limbs of the wrestlers in the library. This is no symbolic substitute for homosexual intercourse however, since it contains *itself* the experience Lawrence thought central to every creative marriage of opposites: the momentary oblivion of the self, followed by an access of new life – which could occur in a kiss (in *The Rainbow*) or a touch of fingers in wonder in the Saracen's Head in this novel, and now, clearly, does not depend on gender any more than on intercourse. What looks at first like a struggle to dominate, becomes through the loss of self a moment of oblivion and renewal, issuing in new tenderness and truth as with Birkin and Ursula by the pond; markedly different from the cruelty with the rabbit and the secret satisfaction in violence itself. It would seem that what Lawrence wanted from Murry was not discipleship or personal intimacy, but creative and impersonal conflict within a committed friendship;[104] but Gerald flinches away as Murry had done. (But see also below, p. 397.)

From these central scenes, the paths of the two pairs begin to diverge. Of most interest to the biographer is the decisive chapter in which Lawrence explores a 'rumpus' not unlike the one Katherine described, and related also to Frieda's rows with Ottoline. (Frieda said later that it, too, had 'happened'.)[105] Though the lovers do not quite come to blows, an ugly violence does erupt, first in Ursula's jealousy of Birkin's relationship with Hermione, then in her deeper denunciation of the split in him between goat and compasses, 'dirty' sex and soul-mush, climaxed by flinging his engagement rings in his face. What is really important, however, is not any question of the truth of the accusation but rather the lashing out of her psyche in pure rejection of commitment. It is equally important that Birkin does not summon ego and intellect to defend himself but just the opposite: his mind spills out, he lapses into the oblivion that abandons self, and once again (as by the pond), after the storm of violence the tension is suddenly gone, the air is clear, words of truth and tenderness can be spoken, and the rings that pledge the marriage of opposites can be given and accepted. Conflicts and splits remain, but afterwards, out of reverence for the mystery of the other, can come complete sexual fulfilment – though once again much needs to be clarified. Though this may be disturbing to us, Lawrence thought violence by both men and women could heal as well as destroy.

Meanwhile the contrast with the other couple becomes clearer too, as Gudrun and Gerald kiss below the bridge and as he goes from his father's grave to her bed. There is much at first to remind one of the wonder and beauty in the canoe, but more that is different: for in kissing her Gerald seems to absorb her into himself; while Gudrun first thrills to his mastery, and then turns wonder into desire to know him, hold him in hand, a possession like her carvings. When he takes her it is to fill a void in himself, which leaves her not oblivious but horribly conscious. As they tread a more and more dangerous path towards tragedy, their way of being in love steadily intensifies sex war in which one always dominates or uses the other; a war of will and power, and finally of survival, as love turns to hate or the frisson of defiance. As characters they are splendidly dramatic and interesting. Lawrence put into Gerald all his fascination with power: handsome physical strength (very different from his own scrawny body), the power of mind over matter, the power of technology which revolutionised the coal industry in his lifetime. He put into the Gudrun of 1916 much of his fascination with Katherine: her stylish dress and sardonic wit, her art of the miniature and her liking to pin people in a phrase, her bohemianism, her unwillingness to commit herself, her inhibitions and secrecies, her ambiguous admiration and resentment of male power – though he also left much out. Indeed Gerald and Gudrun, the destructive ones, may seem the more interesting couple.

If so, the reason lies in Birkin. The Lawrence of 1916 was a deeply disturbed man (though with good cause), and in 'The Sisters' III Birkin often seems a mere mouthpiece for his author's bile. Lawrence conceived him as a sick man, hoping presumably to find a way to shed the sickness – but too often he used the character at this stage simply to voice his own alienation, misanthropy and despair; or to preach sermons drawn from his philosophic writings. There also got into Birkin's arguments with Ursula not only Lawrence's reaction against the dominating and demanding side of Frieda, but the charge that had underlain all the rows ostensibly over the children: that she was never really committed to him and never really respected him, in her heart – yet this was only too easily confused with ideas of the headship of the male. Too often Birkin sounds unpleasantly chauvinist; though he also seems to be struggling to formulate a view of 'love' (a word he hates) that has nothing to do with dominance or subservience on the one hand, or sensuality on the other, of which Birkin seems oddly afraid at times.

Before the end, however, Lawrence had become aware of something laughable in Birkin's rhetoric, through a last contribution from Katherine. While drinking in the Café Royal with Kot and Gertler in September 1916, she heard two Indians with Oxford accents – one was Suhrawardy – accompanied by a red-haired woman, reading out and mocking Lawrence's *Amores* which had been published in July. She went over, asked to see the book, then walked out with it.[106] Her refusal to have Lawrence belittled, even though they were estranged, showed an instinctive blood-sistership that the Murry of 1916 never matched. When he heard about it Lawrence was horrified, wanted to hide, and gave vent to another paroxysm of misanthropy (ii. 649–50). Yet when he decided to imagine it in his novel he turned it into self-criticism, a fine parody of the worst faults of his writing: his tendencies to fruity preaching, overwriting and salvationism – perceiving, too, how these could prevent attention to what he was trying to communicate. It would seem that by *dramatising* criticism of Birkin, sickness might be shed – and this, along with the need to clarify what he had imagined, would be much in his mind when he began to rewrite. Even at this stage few novels have been as searching in self-exposure and as ready to confront uncomfortable discoveries.

VIII   The Narrowing Circle

Even if it were not important for the biographer to gauge Lawrence's effort at self-knowledge in 1916, writing the novel virtually *was* his life from the Murrys' departure till November. His circle had shrunk again, as in the first months with Frieda, to a few acquaintances in a new place, and a handful of older London friends. To juxtapose three Lawrences in July 1912, July 1914 and July 1916, shows very graphically how his fortunes had curved from isolation to high promise, and right back to isolation again, rather worse than before.

The young Lawrence who began at Icking to turn 'Paul Morel' into *Sons and Lovers* had broken with his world. However, after their first battles he thought he had nailed Frieda's nose to his wagon, and a new adventure of Italy and liberating fiction lay just ahead. The Lawrence who married Frieda in London two years later was achieving his promise. 'The Wedding Ring' was with the publisher, the stories of *The Prussian Officer* had taken a new shape that showed how his art had deepened, he had love, reputation, many friends, and influence that would soon extend to Bloomsbury and Cambridge, the centres (he thought) of English life. The Lawrence who sat in what had been Katherine's tower to type and revise 'The Sisters' III, while slaughter mounted on the Somme and continued at Verdun, was a more lonely and alienated figure than ever before. From July to late November, it was imagination that seemed most real.

Yet if Rananim had failed yet again, his feeling for Cornwall remained, as foxgloves blossomed and hay-harvest came. The Lawrences liked Katie Berryman in the little Zennor store, and her brother Tom who would drive them by pony trap to Penzance or St Ives, and Captain Short and his daughter and son-in-law, Irene and Percy Whittley. After the great relief of Bodmin, and before beginning on 'The Sisters' III again, Lawrence took time off. He helped with the hay-harvest on the Hocking farm at Higher Tregerthen; demonstrating how sheaves were tied in the Midlands but not impressing the locals, and probably in his state of health a 'helper' more tolerated than really useful.[107] It must have been now that the Lawrences got to know the Hocking family better, especially the eldest son William Henry, though at this stage Lawrence had mixed feelings about him. He was attracted to the young farmer, but he was also impatient with him in these first months of acquaintance; and very much feared that he might become 'a burden' (ii. 647). He would not invite William Henry into the house, or encourage him to get to know Dollie Radford or Barbara Low when they came to stay; though he later appealed to them to look after him if he should come to London as he longed to do. Yet he was moved by the young farmer's sense of a further life from which he was debarred, and to which he thought Lawrence might open the door. 'He is *really* interested in things', wrote Lawrence:

but he hasn't enough mental development, mental continuity. That is the terrible fate of those who have a high *sensuous* development, and very little mental: centuries of sensuous culture, and then sprung into mental life, in one generation ... he suffers *badly*, and his people hate him – because he *will* take the intellectual attitude ... (ii. 642–3)

He gave a gesture of William Henry's to Gerald:

'Yes, there's something one wants ... But shall I ever get it? – I want it –' he puts his hand to his chest with a queer, grasping movement – 'I can feel the want of it here – but shall I ever get it? – That's what I begin to doubt ...' (ii. 664)[108]

Frieda also liked the young farmer and thought him interesting, though she characteristically said that what he needed was a woman (ii. 642) – obviously unaware that he was courting. It is unlikely however, once Lawrence began to write in earnest, that he would have found much time for a new friendship at this stage, even if he had not been laid up in bed so continually.

He had not yet broken decisively with the old friends. Towards the end of July there was a not very successful visit to the Murrys at Mylor, to which Katherine had returned for a while. They picnicked up the creek and had some difficulty rowing back against a choppy tide, which was apt, since little would be done 'merrily' among them now. Katherine described wryly to Ottoline how they watched Lawrence leave, 'in a little open boat pulled by an old old man. Lawrence wore a broad white linen hat and he carried a ruck sack on his back. He looked rather as though the people of Falmouth had cried to him as the Macedonians did to Paul and he was on his way over to help them.' (There is, significantly again, no mention of Frieda, though she was there.)[109] At the end of August Murry's *Fyodor Dostoevsky: A Critical Study* came out, and he sent

Lawrence a copy – but Lawrence's letter of acknowledgement underscored once more their fundamental disagreement (ii. 646). By this time Murry had solved both conscription and financial problems by going to work for the War Office, having first appealed to Eddie Marsh and then met J. T. Sheppard at Garsington who got him taken on, as a translator at first, compiling intelligence from foreign newspapers. Within six months he became editor of a 'Daily Review of the Foreign Press' circulated to all Heads of Government Departments; in a year he doubled his salary; and by 1918 he was Chief Censor. The co-editor of *Signature* had joined the establishment.[110]

Early in September, having heard of Katherine's gesture at the Café Royal, Lawrence repented a little of saying he wanted to be left alone, and wrote letters to them both which have not survived. Katherine felt he had been insulting in the one to her, probably by repeating his view that she needed to 'die' to her old self and learn to be alone, so he had to write again pacifically. When Frederick Goodyear came to Mylor on leave from the front and wanted to see Lawrence again, Murry took him over to Higher Tregerthen. Lawrence showed them his vegetable garden, 'squatting like a pitman ... uncovering with delicate hands his beetroots from the pea-haulm that straggled over them. Goodyear watched him with a quizzical admiration'.[111] Lawrence was quizzical too, about Goodyear's combination of great good-humour with a kind of nihilism: he had come from India and insisted on getting to the front because he was 'bored'. He was killed soon afterwards, so the encounter by the garden seems almost symbolic; but though Lawrence and Goodyear got on well, there would be no renewed friendship with Murry yet awhile.

Katherine and Murry had continued to work their way, often separately, into Ottoline's good graces – Jack even telling her in September that he thought he was falling in love with her. Since Kot kept in touch with all four, and was no diplomat, what was said on both sides did not stay hidden. Near the end of September Lawrence told Ottoline, after a silence of months, 'I can see you and Katharine talking together, and can overhear at least a few things you say' (ii. 656).[112] In October he told Kot he wanted nothing to do with the 'toad' in Murry but thought he might still respond (since people are 'dual and opposite') if 'a bit of what to me is true and real' came out, though 'all the rest of himself he can take elsewhere' (ii. 666–7). He had written to Jack, on 11 October, that when he said he was done with him he meant with the *old* him, in the hope that new young selves were taking place however painfully in them both (ii. 662), but Murry had never replied. Four days later Frieda told Kot she had had enough:

As Katherine does not write to me, I believe you must have told Jack what I said – I am *glad* if you have – I should have had to have it out with them sometimes – It is time that Jack stopped the lies he tells about people to satisfy his own meanness – They are as mean as they can be to everybody, *then* they turn round and say: are'nt people *vile*. And Katherine never opposes Jack's vileness, but rather enjoys it – To me they have been so mean – especially Jack, wherever they have been, they have turned people against me, tried to regard me as a 'quantité négligable'. Well, from my point I am not going to put up with it a minute longer ... You know I love Katherine, but I blame her when she believes Jack, when she knows better herself – But enough – I always *knew* it all – And I am no angel myself, but they have done me infinitely more harm than ever I did to them, so let there be some kind of justice. (ii. 667–8)

By early November, Lawrence too had done with the Murrys 'for ever' (iii. 23). Ottoline had gathered she was the 'villainess' of his new novel (iii. 41), and it was obvious who had told her. In December, Murry '*not being an artist*, but only a little ego, is a little muckspout ... I have liked him and I don't like him any more. Basta!' (iii. 53). He emits 'the same kind of stink' as Dostoevsky, because he too can 'ooze with such loving words' while filled with hate underneath. 'As for his novel' (which had now appeared), 'It is the kind of wriggling self-abuse which I can't make head or tail of. But then, as Murry says, I am not clever enough.' There is some pique again (as with Russell). With a critical book and a novel out, and his new secure position in the War Office, Murry was a very different figure from the lad who had staggered across the fields to Greatham in the rain, to be cared for by the author of *Sons and Lovers* and *The Rainbow*. Even then, as Lawrence told Campbell, Murry had secretly thought himself 'the equal of the highest' (iii. 63); but now he had something to show for that self-belief, and it revealed itself in a new condescending attitude to Lawrence and his work.

That work inevitably led now to a final breach with Ottoline, though Lawrence took surprisingly long to realise this. In late May he had written her the letter which described how, when shaken to the depths, his inner soul had become the only real world (ii. 608–10). In his novel, already, the Hermione of the 'Prologue' must have taken more from Ottoline, though without the manuscript we cannot tell just how. Yet there was no personal animus, as the letter shows. However, Ottoline was '*very cool*' (ii. 612) after the last outburst from Frieda, and there was silence during all the months in which the manuscript was first completed and then revised. Lawrence, as isolated as a monk in his tower, clearly felt free to let imagination take its course – and at the end of September he actually wondered whether he could come and finish the novel at Garsington. On 3 October however there are signs of unease as he wrote again, sorry to hear she had been ill once more:

As for my novel, I don't know if I hate it or not. I think everybody else will hate it. But this cannot be helped. I know it is true, the book. And it is another world, in which I can live apart from this foul world which I will not accept or acknowledge or even enter. The world of my novel is big and fearless – yes, I love it, and love it passionately. It only seems

341

to me horrible to have to publish it.

... I will send it you when it is done – and if you are well. (ii. 659)

It was an honourable, but a doomed course. He had heard in July of the death of Percy Lucas and in a sudden spasm of guilt had wished 'England, My England' had never been written – but there, too, the sense of an *imaginative* truth kept the last word. 'If it was a true story, it shouldn't really damage ... It should do good, at the long run' (ii. 635–6) – which of course is fine so long as you are not the one to feel identifiable, or whose kindness seems to have been met with black ingratitude. Lawrence hoped that Ottoline would not ask for the manuscript, but he must have known she would – and it must now have been dawning on him (very belatedly) how it would look from her point of view. He *knew*, of course, how his fiction had demanded a woman with a certain greatness of extremity, only some of whose characteristics were inspired by Ottoline. Indeed, when in late November he asked Donald Carswell to look carefully through the revised typescript with a lawyer's eye for anything that might cause trouble, he still was not thinking of Ottoline but of Heseltine and the Puma, who 'are taken from life – nobody else at all lifelike' (iii. 36). In December however, sure now that he would have to give Ottoline the novel to read, he asked Catherine Carswell, anxiously: 'Do you think it would really hurt her – the Hermione? Would you be hurt, if there was some of you in Hermione? You see it isn't really her at all – only suggested by her. It is probable she will think Hermione has nothing to do with her' (iii. 44). There was little hope of *that*. When a typescript eventually reached Ottoline, she found it utterly unforgivable.

Just a few older friends remained. After the Lawrences returned from Mylor, Dollie Radford had come down for a visit; and it was with her that Frieda stayed when she went up to see the children. Barbara Low came in August, and they liked her better than before because of how she stood up for herself. 'There is something fierce and courageous in her', said Lawrence ('wild and untamable' said Frieda; ii. 642), 'which wins one's respect' (ii. 647). After she left he told Cynthia he felt like St Anthony in the wilderness, or one of the desert monks of Nitria (ii. 648–9).[113] His and Cynthia's feelings about the war were now so widely sundered – she had lost a second brother – that they could only gesture across space. Moreover for nine weeks from the end of August to the end of October Lawrence was indoors; isolated in his ill health, though hardly Saharan since it rained most of the time. (It was not until the bad weather finally broke in late November that they could go to St Ives again.)

It was raining when Catherine Carswell came down at the end of September, but she got on with them both as well as ever. She was no threat to Frieda; indeed her appearance in her long petticoat and woollen vest, when she came across to get a book, merely brought from Lawrence a mild if puritanical rebuke for appearing in underclothes. Again it was her Scottish independence of mind that they liked; and though she witnessed many of their rows – indeed it was she who was told now of the biff with the stoneware plate – she saw more deeply into these than the Murrys had, and never underestimated Frieda or her value to Lawrence. She only stayed for a long weekend because Donald got lonely and wired her to come back, which despite teasing she did;[114] but the visit reinforced their relationship. When on 21 November, soon after finishing, Lawrence sent one typescript of 'The Sisters' III to the Carswells as well as the other to Pinker, it was not only for Don's legal advice about whether Halliday and the Pussum might be libellous (iii. 36). He respected Catherine's critical judgement.

In October came another reinforcement of affinity. Mark Gertler too had seen one of his closest friendships end in bitterness (when Gilbert Cannan made his novel *Mendel* out of what Gertler had told him about his life).[115] Gertler too had been faithful in opposition to the war, even at the cost of losing the patronage of Marsh which had been his main means of support. But when he sent a photograph of his new painting *The Merry-Go-Round* it was a revelation. Here was a great work of art which was remarkably congruous with what Lawrence had been doing – and his admiration for Gertler's 'terrible and dreadful picture ... the best *modern* picture I have seen', sprang from immediate understanding and affinity. (He would proceed to alter the whole nature of Loerke's frieze in *Women in Love* and in so doing add to his sense of that character's stature.) The picture shows sailors and their women being pleasured by a machine, a carousel, in 'violent mechanical rotation and complex involution, and ghastly, utterly mindless human intensity of sensational extremity'. He saw in it a 'soul-tearing obscenity', a very modern kind of perversion; and was overcome by what sense of 'destruction and horror' must lie behind the picture. Yet the corruption it painted was also a life-process:

the same thing that makes leaves go scarlet and copper-green at this time of year. It is a terrifying coloured flame of decomposition, your inner flame. – But dear God, it is a real flame enough, undeniable in heaven and earth. – It would take a Jew to paint this picture. It would need your national history to get you here, without disintegrating you first. You are of an older race than I, and in these ultimate processes you are beyond me, older than I am. But I think I am sufficiently the same, to be able to understand. (ii. 660)[116]

His letter 'reads awkward' – the very phrase enacts his sense of clumsiness. He knows he must not translate the picture into 'ideas' and that 'language is no medium between us'; but 'I must say, I have, for you, in your work, reverence, the reverence for the great articulate extremity of art.' That phrase would exactly describe his new novel also. In saluting Gertler: 'You are twenty-five, and have painted this picture – I tell you, it takes three thousand years to get where your picture is', he must have felt he was vindicating his own endeavour, too; though he was 'upset' because the picture was such a 'maelström of destruction', without his own sense of how decomposition could lead to Spring. It was also a war picture, as his was a war novel; because both indicted a world in which man's violent urge to exert his will to power, by means of machinery, had led to his deadly subjection to the machine and to the terrible machine-deaths that filled each daily newspaper in the year of the Somme. There was a last irony too. In postscript, Lawrence added 'Get somebody to suggest that the picture be bought *by the nation* – it ought to be' – but the picture was unsaleable and spent Gertler's lifetime in his studio. The nation no more wanted it, then, than Lawrence's two great novels. It hangs in the Tate . . . now.

There remained also Lawrence's irrepressible hope in the 'new'; and over from Penzance in November, friends of Hilda and Richard Aldington, came two American journalists and admirers, Robert Mountsier and Esther Andrews. Esther was about the same age as Lawrence, Mountsier three years younger. He was tall and gentlemanly, with a high forehead, brown eyes and light brown hair; and though quiet, 'a very exacting person, frugal, well-mannered, well spoken, well read . . . sure of himself and his capabilities. Forthright and upright and of strong opinions'. Esther was glamorous, dressed in vivid colours, slim and fairly tall (about 5'7"). She had a husky voice and an 'international accent', perhaps the result of her time on the stage. She was witty, funny and 'a wonderful mimic'.[117]

Lawrence had already been thinking about America again when Kot had asked about books for boys that might be translated into Russian. Lawrence had suggested Fenimore Cooper, Dana and Melville (ii. 615); and began to reread the leading American writers, and to rediscover just how good he thought they were. He told Amy Lowell he was coming to see American writing as more advanced in decadence than the English – a good thing, since it meant they were nearer to the final going apart from which new life would come. He was particularly struck by how American authors dealt with 'the primary elemental forces, kinetic, dynamic' with 'the *human* unit almost lost' (iii. 30). Perhaps he himself might be an 'American' writer? His new friends reawakened the idea of emigrating.

Amy Lowell had proved more than a loyal editor who regularly took his poems for her Imagist anthologies; for after 'conspiring' with Hilda Aldington about how to help Lawrence financially, she sent him £60 in November – enough to see him through the winter, at the simple level they had maintained.[118] This was an act of great kindness, and of faith in him at a time when he needed *that* even more than money. Moreover Pinker sent a second £50 (as an advance on the novel and the new stories) which, with Amy's gift, made up the £150 Lawrence had thought in July would get him through another year (ii. 619).

However, as Christmas approached, he grew gloomy. He had thought of going to London, but couldn't face it. In an effort to earn money he had reworked 'The Mortal Coil', finished 'Samson and Delilah' and made a small collection of 'war' poems which he thought of dedicating to Cynthia,[119] – but no sooner had he sent his novel away, than he began to feel pessimistic about its prospects. Then came what he saw as political disaster. On Monday 11 December he sensed 'a terrible wave of depression' in Cornwall (iii. 49), with people in Penzance market saying England was beaten, as the news came of the fall of Asquith and his replacement by Lloyd George. For Lawrence this was the death-blow to the liberal and decent England he had cared about. First had come the attempt to force conscience in the Derby Scheme – Lord Derby was now to be Secretary of State for War – next the deadly blow of conscription. Now finally the old England was gone, replaced by the 'patriotism' of Horatio Bottomley and the demagoguery of Lloyd George. To celebrate Christmas now would be an 'ugly farce' (iii. 57).

Nevertheless he invited Esther and Mountsier down again, and the actual festival with them and the Hocking family was 'jolly' – but on Boxing Day reaction set in: 'my heart never felt so down in the dirt, as it does now' (iii. 64).

◆

CHAPTER SEVEN

January–October 1917
ORPHEUS DESCENDING

When we have become very still, when there is an inner silence as complete
as death, then, as in the grave, we hear the rare, superfine whispering of
the new direction; the intelligence comes.
('The Reality of Peace')

I Nightmare Begins

The isolation of 1916 had deepened the gap between the interior world of the
novelist and the external one; harmfully, since 'there *is* a gnawing craving in
oneself, to move and live not only as a single, satisfied individual, but as a real
representative of the whole race' (iii. 63). Yet he felt '*no connection* with the rest
of people' now, except in antagonism, a Laocoon writhing in the folds of the
serpents (iii. 64) – the very image he had contrasted in 1913 with the inner core
of quietness out of which *The Rainbow* had begun to develop. From the outset,
1917 seemed intent on melodramatising that.

On Christmas Eve, wet and stormy outside, came a knocking at the door. The
American couple had come earlier with gifts of fresh fruit and American goodies,
and Esther Andrews was crouching at the fire making maple-syrup fudge when
the knocking came. It was the burly sergeant of police from St Ives, his black
cape-mackintosh streaming wet from the long cycle-ride – come to inspect
Mountsier's papers. Mountsier took it coolly however; the policeman apologised
for troubling them; and left.[1]

It seemed a formality; no different from the inspection of Murry's papers
earlier. It was inevitable that a stranger of military age coming to a remote area
would be questioned. Even in London, John Cournos had to appear at a London
recruiting office, and was asked (American or no) whether he did not owe it to
Britain to enlist. American neutrality did not make Americans popular. Moreover the German declaration of unrestricted submarine warfare had made coastal
areas especially sensitive to the presence of strangers. When Cournos wished to
join Richard and Hilda Aldington in their move to Devon in March 1916, it was
with some difficulty that he 'managed to obtain an identity book required for
aliens, without which I could not make the journey'.[2] Recently, Lawrence and
Frieda had been stopped on their way back from Zennor along the cliff path by

the sea, to have their shopping bag examined by two uniformed men who seemed to suspect them of concealing a camera, much to their indignation. But though there must have been some grumbling in the cottage on Christmas Eve after the sergeant had left, the incident probably seemed mere officiousness, perhaps a result of Mountsier having been stopped once before by a policeman in St Ives, to whom he had responded less coolly than now.[3]

If so, there was a nasty surprise to come. On his return to London at the year's end, Mountsier was arrested, taken to Scotland Yard, interrogated, strip searched, kept in a cell overnight and not set free until the following evening. Lawrence was first shocked, and then angry about the 'insolent pawing' to which his friend had been subjected (iii. 68). Esther, still in Cornwall, was horrified that her flat (where Mountsier had been staying) had been searched.[4]

Biographers have always assumed that Mountsier was a victim of suspicions which the Lawrences had aroused. It has even been maintained that they had been under surveillance since 1914. This, however, is most unlikely – they would never have been permitted to go on living in Cornwall for the whole of 1916 if there had been any real suspicion of them in official quarters.[5] True, Lawrence made no secret of his views about the war. He had denounced Lloyd George's first speech as Prime Minister to people he met in Penzance market, and may have talked similarly in St Ives when he went to buy Christmas presents in the Cornish Stone Shop. Zennor would know his views through Katie Berryman's shop; and more to the point, letters and German newspapers came to Zennor from Frieda's family via Frieda Gross in Switzerland, and Frieda was never inhibited about expressing *her* opinions. Though it would be known locally that he had been interviewed at Bodmin and had been rejected, there may have been envious murmurs from those whose loved ones had been conscripted. His beard proclaimed nonconformity, his German wife would always create suspicion and the new horror of submarines had indeed begun to recreate some of the hysteria about spies that had affected them in 1914. It was not surprising that uniformed men who didn't know them should stop them on the cliff path. Two merchant ships, one a neutral Norwegian, would be torpedoed in clear sight of those cliffs in February with the loss of all hands. Stanley Hocking saw one crew drown and Lawrence shared his horror, even though (secure in his own Englishness) he seemed not to realise that such things were bound to have consequences for himself and Frieda. Nor is it surprising that there was anti-American feeling as pressure on the United States to declare war was whipped up by the press day by day; and if Mountsier, with American ideas about civil liberties, had been dismissive to a policeman enquiring about his identity book in St Ives, it may well have been resented.

However, new research[6] has shown that so far from Mountsier being suspected because of the Lawrences, the growth of official suspicion of the

Lawrences in 1917 was owing to their friendship with Mountsier. For there were plausible reasons for his detention. The Germans had recruited a spy ring of American journalists, among whom George Vaux Bacon was a central figure. By the autumn of 1916 an informer had identified Bacon and a spymaster called 'Sanders' (actually A. A. Sander), who had instructed agents to find out about English defences, munitions and morale, and to determine 'the possibilities of further trouble' in Ireland, where the Germans had helped finance the Easter Rebellion. As soon as Bacon reached England via Amsterdam, he was under surveillance by Scotland Yard and his correspondence was scrutinised. He was carefully watched when he went to Ireland, and on his return to England early in December he was arrested, and confessed, after which two others were arrested in the United States. According to the indictment (to which these eventually pleaded guilty) the main aim of the ring was to provide sailing dates and destinations of shipping, and to assess the effect of submarine sinkings on the food supply. Now here was Mountsier, who had been literary editor on the New York *Sun*, but who had come back to England a second time in the autumn, the period of the conspiracy. Why? He claimed to be interested in literary figures and socialites; but he interviewed experts on food supplies in relation to the submarine campaign, made two trips to Cornwall within two months and (most suspicious of all) crossed to Ireland just as the spies were instructed to do, and less than four weeks after Bacon had been there.[7] Moreover (as the authorities would know if they read Mountsier's mail after they let him go), Lawrence suggested he talk to Russell who was '*very* anti-war' and could put him in touch with 'all the Union of Democratic Control people' (iii. 71); and Mountsier had already encouraged Esther to write articles on Woolwich (i.e. the Arsenal munitions factory) and the employment of women to replace conscripted men.[8] He even tried to get an article out of Lawrence, who however replied that he couldn't 'write about women and the war, and labour' (iii. 78).

Scotland Yard could find no hard evidence to connect Mountsier with the spy ring however, and indeed the subjects he was interested in were those that any journalist would think likely to interest American readers. He had to be released; but he had not been cleared and may have been questioned again before he was allowed to leave the country.[9]

Plausible the detention may have been but it was probably a mistake – and ironic, since Mountsier was anglophile (iii. 70) and supported the United States' entry into the war, though he volunteered for the Red Cross rather than American forces. Be that as it may, by August 1917 Lawrence's mail was certainly being read, and this may have begun from January. (There had been no sign of it before.)[10] In hindsight, that visit by a not unfriendly sergeant on Christmas eve casts a long dark shadow ahead.

II Voices of Rejection

Dramatically confirmed in his belief that the England he cared about had gone for ever, Lawrence determined again to leave – even more so as his new novel was rejected by publisher after publisher. Under the contract for *The Rainbow* Methuen had an option on his next three novels but had cancelled it by 20 December (iii. 58). By mid-January Duckworth had also refused (iii. 80); as did Martin Secker who explained that he could not increase his commitments until the war was over. On 23 January Constable told Pinker that on the advice of two readers they too must reject the book. Was it ready for publication when there was so much alteration, not always consistent, in the typescript? (It had been revised quite heavily since November.) This was not the time for 'expressions of antipathy to England and the forms of English civilisation'. Also, 'when people are sacrificing all that is dearest to them for their country' the book seemed 'bound to rouse the resentment both of the reviewers and the public', who were unlikely to welcome its 'destructive philosophy' either.[11] Although understandable – and not unsympathetic, for Constable offered to reconsider if the book were altered and compressed – this spelled disaster. By the end of January it was obvious that the 'masterpiece' (he was sure) on which he had worked for most of 1916 was unlikely to find an audience in England, and indeed that 'it is no good writing for England any more ... Therefore I have got to get out some way or other' (iii. 67). He began to say he did not even want the novel published now (iii. 72, 76) and it was no good trying (iii. 78); though his belief in it never wavered. However he clutched at Kot's idea of a translation into Russian, if only as a means of persuading Pinker to have the whole thing retyped. Kot paid him £10 in advance; which Catherine Carswell thought a tactful way of helping a proud man in need.[12]

A further barrier to publication had arisen, out of the death-blow to a friendship. While one typescript had been making the rounds of publishers and was now being retyped, the duplicate had gone from the Carswells to Esther Andrews, Barbara Low and Hilda Aldington and then, as promised, to Garsington. Ottoline, inevitably, was deeply upset and furious at what she took to be her portrait in Hermione; made yet more painful by her conflation of his characters with Lawrence himself.[13]

I was called every name from an 'old hag', obsessed by sex-mania, to a corrupt Sapphist. He described me as his own discarded Mistress, who, in my sitting-room, which was minutely described, had tried to bash him over the head with a paper weight ... In another scene I had attempted to make indecent advances to the Heroine, who was a glorified Frieda. My dresses were dirty; I was rude and insolent to my guests ... The only assuagement to the shock was that all the worst parts were written in Frieda's handwriting.

(Apart from her misreadings, what she mistook for Frieda's handiwork was actually transcription of Lawrence's revisions. Had Ottoline read the other typescript, Frieda's handwriting would have appeared in quite different – and fewer – places.)[14]

She was not merely upset. Philip went to Pinker to threaten action for libel, and even (according to Cynthia Asquith) to invite him to Garsington to meet for himself the lady whose vicious caricature he was trying to get published. Frieda poured scorn: telling Kot that Ottoline had tried to play 'Salome to L's John the Baptist!!', and Campbell that she had written like 'a vulgar cook who writes to her young man' to ask 'for an opal pin back she had given him!! Lawrence wrote and said that he had given it to me, I keep it, be more careful another time to whom you give your friendship so freely!'[15] She ended by saying how happy she and Lawrence now were. To her, the final breach with Ottoline was not unpleasing – but the Morrells' threats would hardly help the novel's prospects in England.

Ottoline was wrong to think he had set out deliberately to wound her; yet there are twinges of conscience in his letter of early December when it became clear that she had been told she was the novel's 'villainess' and that she wanted to see what he had written. He replied then placatingly; but when in February Ottoline began to try to stop publication, a salving anger grew.

Really, the world has gone completely dotty! Hermione is not much more like Ottoline Morrell than Queen Victoria, the house they claim as theirs is a Georgian house in Derbyshire I know very well – etc. Ottoline flatters herself. – There *is* a hint of her in the character of Hermione: but so there is a hint of a million women, if it comes to that.[16]

Anyway, they could make libel cases for ever, they haven't half a leg to stand on.

But it doesn't matter. It is no use trying to publish the novel in England in this state of affairs. There must come a change first. So it can all lie by ... And poor vindictive old Ottoline can be left to her vanity of identifying herself with Hermione. (iii. 95)

Yet it nagged away at him. In March he begged Gertler to say 'how much likeness you can see between Hermione and the Ott', who was 'really too disgusting, with her threats of legal proceedings ... We have flattered her above all bounds, in attending to her at all' (iii. 109). In April he told Cynthia that Hermione was not merely *not* Ottoline but 'infinitely superior';[17] and Kot that Ottoline 'would go any length' to damage him now, and all her 'crowd' were 'full of malice' (iii. 112). Yet he was impatient at the time the retyping was taking, for 'I would like to look at Ottoline Morrells imaginary portrait again' (iii. 104). There is conscience in the wish and the ambiguous terminology – and Ottoline was certainly damaged. 'The hurt that he had done me', she said many years later, 'made a very great mark in my life.' She had opened her heart and mind to Lawrence as to nobody but Philip (of whose infidelities she was shortly to learn) and Russell (now infatuated with Colette Malleson).[18] Other writers would caricature her with more malicious intent; but none would hurt her so much – partly by being so perceptive about the facets of her nature he *had* used.

By mid-February, then, it seemed increasingly unlikely that he could sell his best work in England. He was back where he had been after the destruction of *The Rainbow*, but even more isolated now. The need to leave intensified. Towards the end of 1916 he had thought of going back to Italy (e.g. iii. 33); but after getting to know Mountsier and Esther his mind became fixed on America again. Surely his exemption from military service had removed the only obstacle? Even before he began to despair of publishing *Women in Love* he wrote for advice and help in getting passports to Marsh, Campbell (as a prominent lawyer) and Cynthia – though he worried about appealing to her after the fall of her father-in-law, and a recent scandal about the improper use of influence by a society lady (iii. 67, 80, 69). (She did not in fact reply for some time, though this may have been because she was in Brighton to be near Beb.) He gave assurances that 'we are not spies, and I will neither write nor talk about the war to the Americans' (iii. 70). Marsh sent an application form for the endorsement of the 1915 passports, and advised him to give work and business reasons, so Pinker was asked to be ready with confirmation (iii. 84, 75–6). A book on American literature would obviously be best done in America (iii. 73); but might Pinker also say he had to be in New York for the publishing of *Twilight in Italy*, *The Rainbow* and *Women in Love?*[19] Asking permission to use Marsh as a reference, Lawrence gives his word 'that I won't do anything at all, or say anything, to injure the cause of England in the war. I don't want even to think of the war' (iii. 81). Though he still felt *this* war was 'utterly wrong' he was no pacifist, let alone engaged in 'public pacifist activity' (iii. 84). He had even been convinced by Cynthia (who had lost two brothers and a brother-in-law) that he was wrong to generalise about the war from his own feelings, which might be 'falsities to another man, and almost insults' (iii. 33). At the end of January he sent off the forms, pleading ill health, failure to make any money in England, and the consequent need to place his writings in America; but he knew Frieda's birthplace could be a problem and it was in considerable anxiety that he waited. 'It is time for me to pray for the help of the unseen, for I don't know how much longer I can keep my head up' (iii. 89).

In fact more was emotionally at stake than worries over money or even the fate of his novel, upset though he was by the rejections. (He now had the £110 from Amy and Pinker; and his new stories, to which 'The Horse-Dealer's Daughter'[20] had been added in January, were proving inoffensive enough to be acceptable.) The real pressures were psychological, and intense.

Everything that had happened personally and publicly since the fall of Asquith in early December had combined to make the very atmosphere of

England seem inimical. He could no longer feel any part of the England of Lloyd George, and Horatio Bottomley's *John Bull*, and the Special Branch and military who pawed at him and Mountsier as spies. He felt more horror than ever at the war world: the submarines nosing like killer-rats in the darkness; the neutral seamen drowning in sight of the Cornish coast on a 'wonderfully beautiful' day; and English submariners perishing in the depths of the Clyde. All this seemed 'the maximum of evil' (iii. 88) – so much so that his 'old great belief in the oneness and wholeness of humanity is torn clean across, for ever' (iii. 84). He felt distanced from most of his remaining friends. He had not seen Kot and Gertler since 1915; Kot sometimes 'wearies me to extinction' (iii. 83), and communication with Gertler had been infrequent. Gilbert Cannan's life had collapsed into scandal and mess, in which Lawrence felt unable to reach him now.[21] For Murry he felt mostly 'loathing', though perhaps 'still, somewhere, I am fond of him' (iii. 83); but really, 'they are gone, like the leaves of last autumn. The Ott., the Murries – they are gone into the ground. Only for poor Katharine and her lies I feel rather sorry' (iii. 90). Eddie Marsh and Cynthia Asquith were kindly still, but the worse the war became, the more distanced he felt from them. Campbell's words of witty comfort, that one could go on thinking even in prison and jest on the blasted heath (iii. 80), seemed superficial to one who knew that neither bitter laughter nor tragic railing would help against the evil he felt all around. It had become imperative, even for the breath of life, to get *away*.

For 'psychic health is more important than the physical' (iii. 75) – though physically, too, he was at 'low-water mark' in late January (iii. 83), in bed again after a sudden fall of snow. Worse, he now felt psychically trapped and suffocated, unable to breathe, and the metaphors are the more powerful coming from a man who knew only too literally what it was like to have difficulty drawing breath. 'All the oxygen seems gone out of the vital atmosphere here, and one gutters like a suffocated candle' (iii. 76). 'I can't live in England any more. It oppresses one's lungs, one cannot breathe' (iii. 78). He felt 'up to the chin in the flood of things ... the foul world of mud is rising and trying to envelope us' (iii. 89); or like a winged creature caught in a 'vinegary fly-trap' (iii. 83), because the 'atmosphere of the country is poisonous to an incredible degree ... I shall die in the fumes' (iii. 92). He had 'cared deeply and bitterly' about England (iii. 91); but the more he felt its earth too old, and its skies about to fall, the more his longing for somewhere 'where the air one breathes nourishes the new things in one's soul, and the soil is good and vivid' (iii. 80) became identified with the Pacific and the West coast of the United States (e.g. iii. 70).

The difference from the idea of Florida in 1915 was that the new friends and candidates for Rananim were American now. He told Catherine Carswell – exempted as a Scot from his feelings about the English – that the only other people he really wanted to see in London were Esther and Mountsier, and Hilda

Aldington through whom he had met them. He thought H.D. much the best of the Imagists since Pound had gone his own way; and she had replaced Marsh as the critic of his own poetry that he most respected (iii. 84). He had sent her several of his newer poems (iii. 94), and not merely for publication as to Harriet Monroe and Amy Lowell. And whereas in 1915 it had been young English artists like Heseltine and Nichols who gave him hope after the debacle of *The Rainbow*; now it was 'Montague' and 'Hadaffah' (by association with the biblical Esther, called also Hadassah) who made him feel that America could really be a New World for him. He liked Esther 'very much' from the start (iii. 25), and thought Mountsier 'very nice and gentle and decent in every way, a man one likes to know' (iii. 27). Though 'living together' (which in any case would endear them to the Lawrences) they made a queer, gentle couple, so old-old, that they are more innocent than children' (iii. 25).[22] In a very ungentle world, these might seem almost from another planet, and their combination of New World innocence with 'old-old' metropolitan 'decadence' was to shape his whole idea of and attraction to America.

He always generalised widely (or wildly) from particular experience, and the habit had grown in the isolation of Cornwall. It was in the immediate context of the American pair's first visit from Penzance that he announced what would be the leading idea in his aim to 'transfer all my life to America', for there:

the *skies* are not so old, the air is newer, the earth is not tired. Don't think I have any illusions about the people, the life. The people and the life are monstrous. I want, at length, to get a place in the far west mountains, from which one can see the distant Pacific Ocean, and there live facing the bright west. – But I also think that America, being so much *worse*, falser, further gone than England, is nearer to freedom. England has a long and awful process of corruption and death to go through. America has dry-rotted to a point where the final *seed* of the new is almost left ready to sprout. (iii. 25)

As they talked of the advanced industrialism of America, the seamier side of fashion and the clothes trade and the motor industry; or about respectable society and its views on marriage to which Esther was vehemently opposed (and perhaps Mountsier too since he never married) they must have sounded sharply modern. Yet she was warm-hearted and affectionate, and he shy-seeming if anything: 'a queer, gentle couple'.

So the corruption that *The Crown* and *Women in Love* had seen as vitally necessary for new growth, might seem to have gone even faster in the New World than in the Old; making all the more encouraging the combination of so much unspoilt earth and sky with a disintegration so far advanced in the cities as to be nearly ready for new growth. In Amy's latest book – especially since the Lowells were among the foremost American families – he found more evidence in support of his idea, which seemed to apply to H.D.'s poetry also. (The artist would always be a sensitive indicator.)

I have come to understand you Americans a little, to realise how much older you are than us, how much further you and your art are really, developed, outstripping us by far in decadence and non-emotional aestheticism, how much beyond us you are in the last stages of human apprehension of the physico-sensational world, apprehension of things non-human, not conceptual. (iii. 30)

This made new sense of the apparent impersonality and aestheticism of the American Imagists, their cool classicism and distrust of the emotive, their commitment to 'no ideas but in things' (as William Carlos Williams would later put it), their creation of complex correlatives in images drawn from sea, earth, sky – rather than the machine-imagery of the Futurists. Yet with those too there was a link, for Amy and H.D. have also come to the last futuristic stage of 'physical apprehension, the *human* unit almost lost, the primary elemental forces, kinetic, dynamic ... that hard universe of Matter and Force where life is not yet known, come to pass again' (iii. 30).

It was almost certainly talk with Esther and Mountsier about American literature that suddenly enthused him with a whole new project, though it had been germinating for some time. He had told Kot in June 1916 how good he thought *Moby Dick*, and the Leatherstocking novels, and Dana's *Two Years Before the Mast* which he had just been reading (ii. 615, 614). In late November, after the first visit of Esther and Mountsier, he asked Kot to get him Fenimore Cooper's *Pathfinder* and *The Last of the Mohicans*, and Melville's *Omoo* or *Typee* (iii. 40), and is soon telling Catherine that *The Deerslayer* is a 'lovely mature and sensitive art' beside which – as with Hardy – the modern Russians and the French are '*obvious* and coarse' (iii. 41). Discussion with the two Americans will have gone on again at Christmas; and it is easy to see how in Cooper and Melville the juxtaposition of unspoilt nature and natural man, with the results of American individualism and progress, would have confirmed his idea of how fast American 'corruption' had proceeded and been diagnosed. In the same letter in which he commiserates with Mountsier over his arrest, he orders a list of ten American authors (iii. 65–6)[23] – and the idea of a book on American literature is announced soon afterwards.

So the 1915 idea of Rananim in Florida wasn't wrong, only the people and the particular place. The old dream was re-charged by the new débâcle, but it is also clear why it had now to be relocated. When escape, new earth and new air were in the ascendant, it was *Typee* and *Omoo* that fired the imagination, and the Marquesas Islands and the Pacific that embodied the dream of 'a sort of Garden of Eden of blameless but fulfilled souls, in some sufficiently remote spot' (iii. 65), where, away from the world, there could 'be a little community, a monastery, a school – a little Hesperides of the soul and body' (iii. 70). The Rananim-game provided conscious escapism and emotional comfort as always. Yet once the passport applications were made it had a serious point too. If Esther and Mountsier represented well-read young America; and if American writers had taught readers to accept work which was 'true and unlying' as he felt his own to be (iii. 73), then surely there would be a public in America which he could no longer hope to find in England. He would have to go to New York to make contact with publishers, but need not stay in the citified and industrialised East, the heart of American corruption. No, after making the necessary contacts, the 'living direction' was 'west and southwards' (iii. 78) for someone anxious to turn his back on the whole of Europe *and* on industrialised and corrupt Yankeedom. A psychic need for the Pacific remained, but in California there were mountains from which one could face 'the bright west' (iii. 25), and forests, and wilderness – and nevertheless reach readers on the other coast. The worst fear was that America might give in to pressure and go to war; but he could not bear to believe that would happen.

Came another blow: the authorities refused to endorse their passports. By 12 February there was no hope of sailing with their new American friends as they had planned. He did not give up all hope; perhaps he could try again after an interval, since the refusal was not by the Foreign Office but 'in the interests of National Service' (iii. 92),[24] and his rejection at Bodmin on medical grounds gave him hope that the authorities might change their minds about his suitability for National Service too.

The refusal was 'a bitter blow' all the same (iii. 92). 'One cannot stand any greater pressure of foulness. Cry aloud to the good spirit now, for we are in a bad way' (iii. 93).

III   Orpheus (with Eurydice) Replies

In the same letter however, he promised to send Catherine his deepest response to his troubles. On 29 January he had told Pinker that he had been 'doing out' a book of poems, perhaps the last 'for years to come' but also 'my chief poems, and best', which he thought of calling 'Poems of a Married Man' (iii. 86). Less than a week later, he told Catherine it was '*very nearly* ready'. It would be 'a sort of final conclusion of the old life in me', but though it might have as motto the last words of Eurydice in Virgil's *Georgics* (iv. 497) – 'And now farewell' – the farewell would be to Hades, not her. Yet he did not 'much want to submit the MS. for publication. It is very intimate and vital to me' (iii. 87). On 18 February he finished: 'And I feel more inclined to burst into tears than any thing. I can't send this MS. to Pinker yet … I loathe it to go to a publisher. I feel for the moment most passionately and bitterly tender about it. I wonder what it will seem to you' (iii. 94). He asked Catherine to send the manuscript on to Hilda Aldington. Years later, Catherine wrote:

I shall never forget reading those poems in the author's neat handwriting in the tiny room over a garage to which we had moved upon Donald's being called up ...

By the light of a candle I read the poems through. I confess that no other poet except Hardy (and Shakespeare in his sonnets) has so deeply conveyed to me the wistfulness of humanity as distilled in a noble heart – a heart the nobler for its perfect admission of imperfections.[25]

If England in early 1917 had come to seem a kind of hell, the volume which was eventually called *Look! We have Come Through!* was a tribute to his Eurydice (*not* to be left behind!), and also a farewell to a whole phase of his life with her. At the end of 1912, *Sons and Lovers* had dramatically reshaped autobiographical material, drawing a line under the time before he left England with Frieda. Now they were trying to leave again, and though they had not gone yet, the break had been made within. In early 1917 he had again the sense of an ending, and the need for another imaginative exploration coming out of life, but no less significantly *dramatised* in the light of later understanding, hard-won through writing *The Rainbow* and *Women in Love*. By reshaping personal and intimate poems about himself and Frieda, and building them (along with new ones) into a new structure, he could hope fittingly to end and to comprehend their life in Europe, before they left for America. *Women in Love*, also implicitly a vindication of Frieda and of the violence of their marriage, had taken the full liberties of fiction. These poems would be more true-to-life – underlined by including an actual love-letter, which Catherine later persuaded him to drop – yet they would nonetheless be shaped and dramatised into a thematic sequence, unfolding the central meaning of marriage as Lawrence saw it now. Indeed, its ending would be no tragedy, but a Persephone story of resurrection into new spring, albeit tentative and painful.

So, finding the England of 1917 increasingly stifling, he took himself imaginatively back to Bavaria, and Lake Garda, and pre-war London, and the world of *The Rainbow*. This time however he was by no means merely improving and arranging another collection of pre-existing poems, as he had done with *Love Poems* and *Amores*.

The most important biographical point to be made about *Look!* is that we cannot assume the poems were written when and where they purport to have been. Sixty of the sequence we now read appear to date before Zennor but only twenty, or perhaps twenty-one, of these exist in versions earlier than 1917, and all but three of those have been substantially reconceived and in many cases transformed in the light of a later vision. Even 'Green' and 'On the Balcony' – and 'Bei Hennef' which was only included in 1928 – read differently in a new context and new relation to other poems in the sequence.[26] True, there were probably more in the 'brown Tagebuch of Frieda's' left behind in Fiascherino in 1914 and recovered by Dunlop in late 1916, but since it has disappeared there is no telling which, or how many. One might have a subjective feeling that some poems seem close to experience, vividly recalled, but a feeling is all it can be – and that could just as well be a sign of successful dramatic imagination. No poem, for example, could seem more rawly of its moment than 'Mutilation', which dramatises the lover's state of mind when his beloved seems to have deserted him – as when Frieda ran off to her sister's, hence the label 'Wolfratshausen'. But what are the 'Tuatha de Danaan' doing in Bavaria in 1912? The suspicion that the old Celtic gods may be being invoked in Cornwall in January 1917 is reinforced by Lawrence's memory, in the 'Nightmare' chapter of *Kangaroo*, of having called on them after the fall of Asquith.[27] (To read drama rather than lyric autobiography is of course also to read by quite different literary criteria of style and form, not expecting a dramatic character in agony to speak in lyric perfection or sublimation.) Moreover it seems highly probable that whole poems which are labelled with earlier places were written in Zennor, in order to fill out and point up the design and meaning Lawrence now wanted for the whole. We have to be even more careful than usual about using imaginative work as biographical evidence for an earlier period. And so far from *Mr Noon* being any corroboration, it seems likely that the comic novel was based three years later very much *on* the dramatic sequence, especially when that conflicts with the evidence of the letters which were of course no longer available to him. What *Look!* does however tell us, and tell us very powerfully, is what Orpheus on his way out of Hades (with Eurydice) *now* wished to sing, in dramatic re-imagination, about marriage – based on his own.

The Rose poems for example, labelled 'Icking' and hence purporting to date between 1 June and 5 August 1912, might serve as a miniature of the whole process. Frieda lovingly preserved an original set of four which would have been among the poems, 'heaps nicer' than those about other women, of which she boasted to Garnett in September 1912. They must also have been in the Tagebuch from which Lawrence chose them (with five others) to be the first to 'blossom forth', when he sent them on 7 August 1913 to be typed by Douglas Clayton. In 1917 for *Look!* however, he dropped the fourth poem altogether and so transformed the other three that in themselves, and still more by their placing in the sequence, they became essentially different. It is not merely that sentimentalities are banished. The confidence of young love becomes transfused with intimations of transience and mortality; yet these also heighten a newly warm and tender apprehension of beauty affirmed in the face of time.[28] 'River Roses' keeps its first vital and happy stanza, but in the second there are new darker notes, as the rose scent becomes icy and fear replaces the original rosy kisses. As twilight darkens, the snake and the marsh of 'The Crown' and *Women in Love* speak now of having to come to terms with Birkin's dark river of corruption, as well as green water and rosiness. The new 'experience' has only initially and superficially to do with an experience of 1912. 'Gloire de Dijon' is even more tellingly transformed in the light of later vision. The first stanza is poetically and rhythmically much improved as its rhythm enacts the painterly movement of light down the woman's body, warmed by her skin and swaying breasts into glow and then fuller glow, as the 'gloire' rose warms from pink through pale yellow to yellow-gold. As the woman washes herself in the second stanza, however, something much deeper than the interplay of light and crumpling shoulders now catches the attention, for whereas originally the water merely shook and freshened, soon outshone by the vitality of the body, now the metaphoric emphasis is on roses *falling*, rain-dishevelled by the seasonal change that will soon destroy their beauty. A fanciful conceit of rivalry between woman-beauty and rose-beauty is replaced by a moving sense of richness-in-transience. 'Mellow' and 'golden shadow' are deepened as their paradox opens out. It becomes a love poem about a woman already passing her best, and a body seen as all the more beautiful because on the point of change from ripeness to overripeness and decay. It has become a poem of 1917 as *opposed* to 1912.[29]

Nor is this merely a change brought about in personal feeling by time: for it furthers a major theme of the sequence as a whole. 'Roses on the Breakfast Table' is freed from sentimental fancy too, as the poem re-sees playfulness and youth; but now the fallen petals (originally little boats waiting for a fairy wind and laden with kisses) become harbingers of the fall of the roses that have not fallen yet; and focus a new perception, as sharp as tender, of the transience of 'her' sense of 'his' beauty also. Yet this is fused with acceptance as he looks at the 'rumpled young roses' whose transient 'day' he shares.[30]

In 1917, two poems take the place of the rejected original. None of the possible reasons for not risking early versions could possibly apply to these.[31] Had they existed in 1913 they would certainly have been sent with the others. 'I am like a rose' is a poem of dramatised joy:

> I am myself at last; now I achieve
> My very self. I, with the wonder mellow,
> Full of fine warmth, I issue forth in clear
> And single me, perfected from my fellow...

'Rose of all the World' explains the consonance of this selving with the natural force in 'Rose-leaves that whirl in colour round a core/ Of seed-specks'; but goes on to an argument strongly reminiscent of 'Hardy'.[32] 'He' now maintains, against 'her' idea that it is the seed that is the purpose of the rose, that 'the seed is just left over/ From the red rose-flowers' fiery transience'; so she should blossom 'For rosiness only', more than justified in and by the instant of unclosing. The simpler 1912 poetry has been deepened and supplanted by later understanding, in the author of *The Rainbow* and 'The Crown' of the relation of beauty, individuation, transience, death and rebirth, for men and women and all living things. Of the rose poems we now read, three have become poems of 1917, and the other two were probably newly written then. If we could discover what was in the Tagebuch, we might find much the same proportion of transformation.

The biographer then should be asking what the sequence has to tell us about the Lawrence of 1917 rather than 1912; and to be seeing the poems as the creation of a dramatic *mythos* (in the Aristotelian sense) using himself and Frieda almost as ruthlessly as he used others, rather than as a too-intimate confession. It is a drama in several acts or, as Amy Lowell thought, a poetic novel.[33]

The first 'chapter' (from 'Moonrise' to 'Hymn to Priapus') is about states of the man's self after several failed love affairs and just before his meeting with the woman, and in the shaping Lawrence's double purpose becomes clear. He aims both to be faithful to an earlier self, and to stage it with later understanding, to foreshadow a later meaning. We can see this both in the splitting and adaptation of earlier poems to reveal immature states of mind, with an understanding not possible at the time;[34] and also in the way that poems change when we have read the whole sequence. 'Nonentity' for example seems to be just another expression of longing for non-being after the mother's death, but on rereading, it sounds thematic keynotes for the whole sequence. The longing for nonentity, dissolving the self into the cosmos, will turn out to anticipate not death but renewal. Conversely, Don Juan's callousness about his mistresses and pride in being beloved of 'Isis the mystery' will be destabilised later; yet priapic desire is indeed a liberation from the mother-complex and the cynicism which have left a young man 'worn and careful' or despairing.[35] The poems begin to read one another more complexly than each reads in itself. Lawrence has both represented and re-presented the young man he had been, using insight he did not have at the time, yet not falsifying the essence of what he then felt. If it be 'autobiographical' it is also dramatised, with a licence which makes it representative in yet another sense, like *Sons and Lovers*.

The next chapter however – 'Ballad of a Wilful Woman' to 'A Doe at Evening' – though set in Bavaria, continually re-sees the lovers of 1912 in the light of the vision of conflict, suffering, destructiveness and growth, in the fiction that succeeded *Sons and Lovers*.[36] The ceaseless flux announced in the 'Ballad' becomes a major theme of the whole sequence now. No poem *can* stand alone because the journey 'ends not anywhere',[37] so any resolution is temporary. (And whereas the original had been a coming to terms with a Wayward Woman's love-affairs and a final emphasis on her many-sided vitality; now the path ahead for a Wilful one, with the beggar as leader, grows darker and more painful.) Though the poetry seems 'true to life', from the first joyous confidence despite sexual failure (even if the first night was actually in Munich) to conflict, renewal and conflict again, the thematic relation of the poems to one another has become more significant than their relation to the actual experience of 1912, as the Rose poems show. Lawrence's sense of life, indeed, has become inseparable from the awareness of flux in the dance of opposites which he began to work out in 1914, and which grew deeper and more complex as the two major novels developed. So, as 1917 re-sees 1912, the moments of fulfilment, beauty and balance darken with awareness of their transience; but on the other hand, in continually looking backward and forward, the dark poems also get modified by their position in the sequence. Their humiliations, angers and Hamletty nihilism are placed within the rhythms of change and growth, through the conflict of love. The poems begin dancing between the dark and the light before the lovers do. What is mellow is poised between fulfilment and decay. 'She' learns to see 'The shadows that live in the sun';[38] but 'he', also, how the dark colours – up through green to gold. Indeed the chief reward, where we do have evidence of how Lawrence has re-worked poetry of 1912, is (with a few exceptions such as 'Green' and 'On the Balcony') to see precisely how his vision and understanding have grown, changed, deepened.

The next short chapter ('Song of a Man Who Is Not Loved' to 'Meeting Among the Mountains') shows however that there were limits to his ruthlessness about exposing Frieda and himself, since without biographical knowledge the sequence about the journey through the mountains to Italy remains somewhat opaque. Chatto and Windus – it turned out – would only publish if two poems were removed; and though Lawrence himself restored 'Song of a Man Who Is Loved' in 1928, it was left to the editors of the posthumous *Complete Poems* to restore 'Meeting Among the Mountains' – and they misplaced it.[39] Only when it is returned to its chronological position between 'Sinners' and 'Misery' does the ironic interplay of the poems reveal itself; and even then, the bitter contrast between the sense in which the man in this chapter's 'Song' is 'Not Loved' and the 'Misery' of the fourth poem is diminished if we do not know what happened in between. It was not until *Mr Noon* in 1920 that Lawrence was able to re-imagine Frieda telling him she had slept with Harold Hobson. However when Lawrence looked back in 1917, what he arranged was not a narrative story but four intense moments of emotion set against one another in powerfully ironic juxtaposition. Though labelled 'Glasshütte', 'Song of a Man Who is Not Loved' is not concerned with quarrelling over the path before they found the chapel and hay-hut, but with the horror of being alone in space, and 'driven' (Don Juan's word) by forces beyond the self. Against it is set 'Sinners', an ironically titled love poem of happiness alone together at Mayrhofen (where they waited for Bunny). However the inadequacy of that comes out before the big pale Christus where imagination, secretly aware of the injury the lover has done, realises the abandoned husband's despair and hate, and reads them into the muleteer's eyes. Then the tables are turned – a bitter irony – and direction and relationship are lost in such 'Misery' that a beautiful world becomes a pit-dungeon for the forgotten, with no way out.[40] Only in its apparent loss is love fully measured, in the pit of Hades.

In the fourth long chapter set on Lake Garda ('Sunday Afternoon in Italy' to 'Wedlock'), the relationship 'comes through', but only after two related battles to free the lovers from the past: the freedom from the mother dramatised in the two fine poems 'Giorno dei Morti' ('Service of All the Dead') and 'All Souls'; and the conversion of sex war into the Lawrencian mythos of death and rebirth. Here the sequence fills with hatred and violence. The green dog-star in a second *aubade* subverts the fulfilment of 'Green', and in yet another dawn the lover washes himself clean of hatred only to find he can feel nothing at all. Four poems[41] dramatise accusations we can imagine Lawrence making, and express the hate that was always liable to spring from the clash of his ego with Frieda's. Yet it is drama, not straightforward self-expression – and lest we too confidently take the poems as spontaneous outbursts of feeling that unhappy winter, we had better remember Lawrence saying in December that he couldn't write poetry then. Moreover we need to see the *structuring* which, with suggestions of a much later Lawrence, mimes the religious year of the soul from the day of the Dead to Candlemas, but at the same time rewrites Genesis and the visitations of the angels: until Eve is reborn, not from the rib but by exchange of blood with Adam, whose Noel that also is; the Virgin is purified in sex and sacrifice; and paradise is regained through 'death' and fiery purification. Indeed the fiercer rewriting of the original 'Purity'[42] suggests that where earlier versions do exist – as they do not often in this section – Lawrence may have deliberately heightened the ongoing storminess for dramatic and mythic purposes. For once again the Lawrence of 1917 is only too well aware that the battle is never over – which is why immediately after the tenderness of 'Birth Night' comes 'Rabbit Snared in the Night', that most horrific creation of sex-war violence, which bears the closest relation to the 'Rabbit' chapter in *Women in Love*, and to Birkin's belief that there are murderees as well as murderers.[43]

As the 'coming through' seems accomplished in the next short chapter ('History' to 'One Woman to All Women'), the hand of the Lawrence of 1917 keeps showing itself. He transforms poems such as the sentimental original of 'Song of a Man Who is Loved' (which are in fact the ones which show us the Lawrence of 1912–13), into maturer poems seen in the context of others in the sequence. He makes poems reread one another as the two 'Songs' now do (whenever the Unloved one was written); or as 'Wedlock' counterposes to the individual candle image of 'All Souls' a marriage of opposites, 'he' the flame to her candle, as 'she' the renewing source of his fire; or as 'Song of a Man Who Has Come Through' ends by transforming the tart biblical allusions in 'She Looks Back' and 'Lady Wife' into wonder, now. Neither of his previous collections had anything like this kind of continuous cross-reference. And in the title poem, the finest of all, he makes 'coming through' not at all conclusive, but a being spontaneously open to continuous transformation, by creative forces beyond the self – in poetry as in life. This is Lawrence's most powerful use of the Whitmanesque breath line, finding its own length and emphasis, a medium perfectly adapted to the theme of 'Not I, not I, but the wind that blows through me!'[44] I suspect that its close relation in thought and imagery with the poetic manifesto Lawrence wrote *after* the sequence had been published suggests that it is probably a poem of 1917.

Moreover, 'One Woman' speaking 'to All Women', turns into a comic irony about drawing conclusions, which is most unlikely at its ostensible date. It seems that what 'he' has experienced is true for 'her' too: 'How happy I am, how my heart in the wind rings true'. 'She' even captures, for the first time, what Birkin had been trying to say in the 1916 'Sisters' that he wanted from 'love', without ever quite managing to pin it down: something quite different from sexist domination. 'There's the beauty you cannot see, myself and him/ Balanced in glorious equilibrium,/ ... There's this other beauty, the way of the stars ... ' (So, though this poem is dated from Kensington at the time of their marriage in Summer 1914, it either is or has become a poem of 1917, whose central image will be written-in, over and over again, into *Women in Love* later that year.)[45] There is something ruthless, almost inhuman about 'him', yet 'his separate being liberates me/ And gives me peace!'; and what used to be feared has become beautiful, 'to be lifted and gone'. The sequence might have ended, triumphantly, just there.

But the next chapter will show ('People' to 'Craving for Spring') – the characteristic touch, now, of the author of 1917 – the instability of any such ending. It would have been false both to experience and to Lawrence's post-1914 dialectic art, where relationship cannot conclusively stabilise if it is not to die. New conflict not only will but must begin again if growth is to continue. The lovers may be triumphant, but they are cut off from their society – already implicit in the rejection of 'You other women' (in 'One Woman to All Women'). In 'People' and 'Street Lamps' we see the Unreal City of which Lawrence spoke to Russell (though they are made out of a poem of Croydon days before 1911, now split in two). People are a 'Ghost-flux of faces' drifting meaninglessly; London is a City of Dissolution, its lamps like burst suns or seed-pods drifting into the dark. So it becomes necessary to 'cross into another world', to find 'New Heaven and Earth'. However, both this poem and ' "She Said As Well To Me" ' show that the certainties of the previous chapter had come much too easily. Not only does conflict continue after marriage – and the whole world is now at war – but a reader must also realise now, if not before, that 'the author' of these poems is unreliable; himself a developing 'I' and imaginer, not at all omniscient. In fact the 'I' has been changing in a dynamic process throughout; and now the author of 'One Woman to All Women' can be seen to have been over-optimistic, to say the least, in so assimilating 'her' to 'his' vision. A wry comedy enters. What 'She' has *now* said 'As Well' seems at first only additional assurance and compliment, poking gentle fun at his physical shyness, and showing loving wonder at the clean straight body of a man that only God could have made; 'so that I began to wonder over myself, and what I was'. Yet Lawrence the dramatist had a fine ear for tone, and there is something in what 'She Said', which makes 'him' feel 'trammelled and hurt', not free, and which the poem goes on to pin down: how easy it is to 'love' without true respect. The man is not an 'instrument'[46] – her tone was Gudrun's, looking at the sleeping Gerald. He is not to be used, still less possessed. She would not dare to speak of or touch a wild creature so – weasel, adder, bull or Tyger (since the hint of Blake was ironic) or even a stag at evening. She does not see him as truly 'other'. The sense of him as strange and dangerous, put into her mouth in 'One Woman to All Women', was wishful thinking. 'She Said' is 'dated' to 'Greatham', i.e. 1915, but the adder and Gudrun's attitude suggest Zennor again.

Most of 'New Heaven and Earth' however (originally 'Terranova'), probably does date from Greatham. The sense of landing on a new shore might have been Ursula's at the end of *The Rainbow*; the old world looked back on with double horror for 'everything was tainted by myself' and hence *known*, Ursula's trouble. Moreover the world of 1915 has become a hell of death, mutilation and corruption in which 'he' is implicated, since he too is murderous and deathly. Yet 'it is good to have died and been trodden out ... absolutely to nothing', for with such 'death' comes resurrection of a self 'the same as before, yet unaccountably new'. More than ever, and turning the tables of the last poem, this depends on *his* truly experiencing the otherness of the other within what had seemed familiar, known, touching the 'flank' of the absolutely unknown he had lain beside for 'over a thousand nights',[47] without ever realising *her* true separateness and otherness. The 'she' he touched had been a projection of himself. (Here the Lawrence of *The Rainbow* turns into the Lawrence of *Women in Love*.) Only at the hands of the truly other can the self die to new life; but now he has been carried 'by the current of death' to a new shore, 'a new I'. Even now, however, when we are looking at post-*Rainbow* poetry and there is no longer any danger of distorting a pre-*Rainbow* Lawrence, we are not reading 'a poem of 1915'. For a new conclusion adds a descant on the greenness of the new world, like her eyes – linking back through 'Winter Dawn' to 'Green', each coming only now into its full reading – and like *Typee* (recently read), with fresh streams and 'White sands and fruits unknown and perfumes'. Yet the current will have to drown him again, holding him down to mysterious depths, that he may be kindled to life again in never-ending process. None the less Zennor, with which the sequence has caught up now, is an 'Elysium', if 'Lonelier than Lyonesse', where the woman has 'severed the connection' of his 'subjection/ To the All' and set him free – though 'Manifesto' is still unsatisfied, longing for 'her' to give herself away as completely as he does (and as he continually complained that Frieda did not), and 'perish on me, as I have perished on her'. Only then can they 'have each our separate being', free, fulfilled, distinct, yet in 'unutterable conjunction'. After that 'there will only remain' (a typical optimism, showing how much Lawrence wanted *not* to be isolated from his society), 'that all men detach themselves and become unique'.[48]

However – all life being cyclical, seasonal – at this terrible point in time and in the soul (late 1916), 'Autumn Rain' in the city falls like tears, on a world whose painful harvest is 'the sheaves of dead/men', on the Somme. In Winter the crowds of bright young women on the pavements seem 'Frost Flowers' whose beauty is scented with a wintry 'corruption', necessary (as 'The Crown' had explained), but repellent. The sequence ends with 'Craving for Spring' (1917), in a rhythm of longing whose intensity is both evocation (embodiment after embodiment of springing life), and invocation (since the intensity shows that what is longed for has not come, yet). 'He' speaks as for a world of longing: for those who have never flowered, for the 'winter-weary', for vindication 'against too much death'. Finally the voice is that of the prophet who represents the people, but whose greatest prayer is not to be like Moses, and 'die on the brink of such anticipation' – or worse, deceived.[49]

What a biographer needs is tact enough to hold onto both sides of a complex tension. If *Look!* is not an anthology of separate autobiographical lyrics, dated and placed between 1912 and 1917; neither is it purely a dramatic and mythic sequence, since the drama has grown out of and is still grounded in such personal experience, vividly recalled, that it has a brave (or embarrassing[50]) authenticity. It is a new genre, neither autobiographical anthology nor dramatic myth, because both. On the one hand it is Lawrence's apologia or vindication of his marriage as he saw it now. On the other, the 'We' of the title bear the same sort of relation to Frieda and Lawrence that 'Stephen Hero' had to Joyce, at once lifelike younger selves *and* developing 'characters' on a journey staged, restructured and often deliberately intensified from life for dramatic purposes. Yet if 'I' and 'She' are partly fictive, the *mythos* was no mere wish fulfilment either. Their behaviour explores what was for him a representative truth: that marriage (however turbulent) was, and had proved to be despite detractors in his case, the way out of Hades into new spring, new country, longed for in pain and promise.

IV   Waiting for Spring, in Fact

As it happened, spring came early in Cornwall that year. The day Lawrence sent the poems to Catherine, 18 February,[51] was 'overwhelmingly lovely' as he 'lay on the cliffs watching the gulls and hawks in the perfect sky. Already the pigeons were cooing, and it was as warm as summer' (iii. 94). In a few days new lambs were dancing. Despite the disappointment of his hopes for America, and having been seedy again, creative life and hope soon bubbled up once more as they always did in him. In fact, hardly had he posted the poems than he began writing seven 'little essays' called 'The Reality of Peace', and by 7 March he had finished (iii. 100). The world of man spun on its destructive way. There was upheaval in Russia; and distressing news of the death in Flanders of Herbert Watson. After a long silence Collings suddenly wrote, from a military hospital. Yet again came the old conviction that 'the living spirit' would always be greater than men's destructiveness (iii. 101), and he began to wonder – for the first time since *Signature* – whether he might not *do* something publicly to help it on. He had high hopes of 'The Reality of Peace', especially when Harrison of the *English Review* found the essays 'extraordinarily suggestive' (iii. 107). Hearing in late March of the peace demonstrations in Nottingham's Victoria Park, he felt 'like starting something somewhere: but hardly know yet where to begin' (iii. 106). (It was whistling against the wind however to imagine that the parliament which had just passed a new Military Service Act could be kicked out.) Moreover, and significantly, he simply could not face going to London.

Instead he determined, like Candide, to cultivate his garden. If he could earn very little in England and was not allowed to try America, he could at least become as self-supporting as possible. Even before their passports were refused he had declared that, if forced to stay, he would 'become a farmer' and help William Henry 'whom I like' (iii. 89). He had read Crèvecœur,[52] and imagination may have fused with practicality in aiming at something of the 'American Farmer's' sturdy independence. Soon he was asking Kot to get him a booklet from Suttons the seed specialists, on *Culture of Profitable Vegetables in Small Gardens* (iii. 103), and with some Hocking help and advice he made three gardens: the little one from the year before, 'a gem', with some vegetables as well as flowers; then half of 'the little field at the back of the red room' with 'many beautiful rows' of broad beans and spinach; and finally peas and beans in the field below that. 'I have worked hard', he wrote on 23 May. 'We *should* have mounds of vegetables' (iii. 127) – though by then it was rather dry, and soon he would be raging and finding fault with Christ for his ignorance of the real nature of lambs, those destructive and greedy little beasts, who had got at his broad beans (iii. 124). He sent back to Kot some Italian books of Monty Shearman's, saying he was awearied 'of passion and eroticism and sex perversion' (iii. 103), and soon he was saying that 'pure abstract thought' now interested him more than art's welter of emotions and sensation (iii. 110). Though the new typescript of his novel had at last arrived he left it aside. Fiction held no attraction now since he found human beings 'ultimately boring' and was 'happy in the thoughts only that transcend humanity' (iii. 127) – more interested now in the fate of his essays than the new book of poems. He was glad that Catherine and Esther liked those, but simply recorded H.D.'s verdict that 'they are not *eternal*, not sublimated' (iii. 102). She may indeed have influenced a curious spasm of classicism: he copied Piero de Cosimo's *Death of Procris* (iii. 103; who had the divine gift of a dart that always found its target, but had not been able to hide from pursuit),[53] and sent Margaret Radford a little plaque, probably of warriors from the Parthenon frieze (iii. 101 and n. 2). Sculpture too however now struck him as not 'abstracted' enough; its bulk frustrating 'the clarity of conception' (iii. 109) Finding peace, after the piercing disappointments of early 1917, seemed to depend for the moment on feeling abstracted and independent, *au dessus de la mêlée*.

At the end of March Frieda went to London for the first time since September 1916. (Weekley seems to have given permission for her to see the children twice a year now.) She was '*disgusted* to find that Ernst who poses as the tragic figure to the children, takes Gladys[54] (she is a handsome, coarse girl) out to dinner, flirts with her, but keeps of course the last respectability – Lord, I was so furious – but then he *is* both things, but the children are different, thank God!' (iii. 109). She had clearly not become indifferent. However, the problem of her relation to the children had settled somewhat, though she still had to be cautious with Lawrence. Before her trip, she asked Kot not to mention the matter when he next wrote. 'Lawrence feels much better about it but still he is sore and the less said the better, but it will all come right'[55] – though he would not go with her to London. Her relationship with Kot had also grown more friendly. She saw him, and Catherine, and Gertler in whom she found some change and recovery of peace after the double blow of the death of his father and Carrington's taking up with Lytton Strachey. These few, with Dolly, and Cynthia, now made up her total circle of friends outside Germany. (She always, though perhaps without meaning to, kept a little social distance from the farm folk in Cornwall.) Moreover they were really Lawrence's friends; she was not close to any; and all the other English people she had known since she came back to England had turned against her or lost touch. She was poor, isolated, an enemy alien. She was utterly dependent on Lawrence now. If she remained ebullient, as there is every reason to think she did – well, that was Frieda. She echoed his confidence that their spring would come again: 'Yes, I think our time will come – it will be fighting still and misery, but in the end we shall come through' (iii. 106), as his poems had said. She was glad to be back in Cornwall, and even (she says) helping in the garden.

By the middle of April, pressed to keep a promise to visit his sisters in Ripley, Lawrence felt calm enough to have a few days in London too. He sent a note to Murry (iii. 113) – somewhere, as he had said, still fond of him – and arranged to see Pinker and Harrison; then left for Derbyshire on 14 April. On the way back he saw Sallie Hopkin in Nottingham on Wednesday the 18th, and arrived in London the following afternoon to stay with Kot in Acacia Road. On Friday he seems to have rushed around, starting with Pinker at 11.30, then Harrison, then a visit to Cynthia Asquith in her new basement flat off Baker Street, then to Hampstead to see Catherine and Dollie. On Sunday he went with Cynthia and her baby son Michael to the zoo.[56] She had not seen him since 1915, and thought he looked 'better'. She still found 'great interest and vividness in his face and voice', as he repeated that the cause of John's psychological problems lay in her attitudes, and reproached her for 'subscribing to the war' by working in a hospital, though she was only doing genteel 'pantry-work'. Her liking was as strong as ever, and also her tolerance of his criticisms, though she still thought them merely 'theories'. Harrison was persuaded to take four of the 'Reality of Peace' essays instead of the three he had already accepted (iii. 138); and he also asked for poetry. Lawrence had now sent Pinker the manuscript of Look! and thought half a dozen of 'the more impersonal poems' might do (iii. 138). Suddenly his prospects seemed a little better. In March, 'The Thimble' had come out in Seven Arts in America and 'Samson and Delilah' in the English Review, while 'England, My England' was scheduled for America in the April Metropolitan. A small publisher, Eveleigh Nash, had even shown interest in Women in Love, though Lawrence felt uneasy at the idea of publishing it now, even if that were possible (iii. 111).

On Saturday in Acacia Road he met and was greatly taken by Fanny Stepniak, widow of the Russian revolutionary, who had become a close friend of Kot's.[57] Writing afterwards to Sallie, who had clearly not managed to conceal money worries and some dissatisfaction with her life, Lawrence cited the sixty-two-year-old widow as someone 'strong enough to have the just sense of values' and faith in them, rather than seeing as the world sees: 'I find in her a beauty infinitely lovelier than the beauty of the young women I know. She has lived, and suffered, and taken her place in the realities. Now, neither riches nor rank nor violence matter to her, she knows what life consists in, and she never fails her knowledge' (iii. 116). He thought the war might be over that summer because of strikes in Germany, strains among her allies and a Russia in turmoil needing peace; though he saw no 'real intention of peace' in the British government. After his trip to the Midlands he was again sure that there would be 'labour insurrections, purely selfish' and 'a smash-up' (iii. 116); but one had to stand aside, and wait.

The next day he was smitten by an attack of vomiting and diarrhœa. As usual, he sought a psychological explanation, 'the evil influence of aggregate London' (iii. 117), but an infection Emily King had suffered from in Ripley was more immediately to blame. He was ill for several days; but by Wednesday the 25th he had recovered enough to take up Dollie's invitation to spend a day or two at the Radfords' recently acquired country cottage in Berkshire.

At Hermitage the spring woods were 'so lovely, I shall never forget them' (iii. 120). Whitman-like he wrote Cynthia Asquith that the unfolding buds and the primroses were, really, 'stronger than all the armies and all the war. I feel as if the young grass growing would upset all the cannon on the face of the earth, and that man with his evil stupidity is after all nothing, the leaves just brush him aside. The principle of life is after all stronger than the principle of death ...' (iii. 118). Conversely, her 'desperation' came from 'submitting and acquiescing in things one *does not vitally believe in* ... One should stick by ones own soul and by nothing else.' It was enough for now, he told Kot (iii. 117), that it was spring; he would not bother about anything. Let Murry and Campbell, who had not replied to his notes, go their own way. Catherine, he thought, had looked 'very sad' when he saw her, but 'Things must work themselves out.' It was no good trying to *do* anything, and even to hate the war was in a sense to choose it and provoke more war in the soul. Far better to 'leave them to it, and to bring forth the flower of one's own happiness, single and apart'. Back in Cornwall, his seeds had come up and there was 'a strange joyfulness in the air. For those of us who can become single and alone, all will become perfectly right' (iii. 119).

However, unusually, he found a Frieda ill enough for him to send for the doctor, though Esther Andrews, whom she had invited to stay in the other cottage[58] seemed all right. Now it was a matter of planting white violets and crimson carnations brought from Berkshire; waiting for Frieda to recover and for 'The Reality of Peace' and the new book of poems to appear – but 'in the very middle of one's heart, one is happy' (iii. 120).

V 'The Reality of Peace'

Only five of the seven original essays have survived. The last four came out in the *English Review* from May to August 1917; the first, 'Whistling of Birds', would eventually be accepted by Murry for the *Athenæum* two years later.[59]

On 7 February Lawrence had been sitting in a nook of the cliffs, out of the biting wind. It was sunny, but everywhere lay birds killed by the worst frosts since February 1895. (In 1915 he had noted a similar contrast of lovely days with the thousands of human corpses in Flanders.) A fortnight later, spring had fully arrived, 'the lambs were dancing, and the birds whistled, the doves cooed all day' (iii. 97) – and he had posted *Look!* By 7 March his seven essays were finished and titled. He had told Cynthia Asquith the previous November that nations were 'external material facts. The reality of peace, the reality of war, lies in the hearts of the people: you, me, all the rest' (iii. 39).

By contrast with the interior drama of *Look!* the essays seem the product of his fit of abstraction, yet in context they are not without their revelation to the biographer.

The central perception of 'Whistling of Birds' is how swiftly and certainly, in nature, deathliness is transformed altogether into bird song. The birds are like 'little well-heads' from 'deep undersprings' which have only waited for the thaw. Suddenly, winter and death seem quite unreal: 'strange, the utter incompatibility of death with life'. The world, and we, are all one or all the other, 'never in our essence both at once'. What has the whistling bird to do with the torn and half-dismembered bodies all around? And by implication, in France. 'He did not cling to his death and his dead. There is no death, and the dead have buried their dead.' He 'lifted his wings ... and found himself carried on the impulse'. At the worst, the lowest point, despite 'the suffering, in spite of the myriads of torn dead' spring is not only certain, but all-embracing once its time has come.[60]

The second essay, opening 'The Reality of Peace' as we have it now, has a second point of faith for himself and for his world. In the depths, provided one is very still as in the grave, there will always be heard 'the rare, superfine whispering of the new direction'. Yet we cannot will where to go (for instance, to America), we can only choose whether or not to submit to and steer by that current out of the unknown, extinguishing our self-insistence and self-will. 'None of us know the way. The way is given on the way.' This demands life-courage like St Paul on the road to Damascus, something greater than the strength to die bravely. Who now dares to 'have done with himself, and with all the rest of the old-established world', and give himself over to the 'unresolved wonder', ceasing in a moment to be an agent of death and conformity – like us with our inventions of death-machinery and our desire to compel everyone to join in destruction. Inside one's own heart, is there a secret desire for more strife, that things should come apart? Or is there a 'quick, new desire to have new heaven and earth, and ... to make a beginning'? If so, the moment we accept that impulse 'as the treasure of our being', we are converted, 'transported' immediately 'across the unthinkable chasm, from the old dead way to the beginning of all that is to be'.[61]

In the depths both of his misfortune and the war, Lawrence the religious man is all the more passionately convinced that the impulse of renewal will always come, and moreover that it has only to be accepted, in full submission to the unknown, for change to be instantaneous and the way forward to reveal itself.

Yet there is a new sense of the price that some 'few' – like himself – have to pay. Most 'have only to know peace when it is given them'. But for the few 'there is the bitter necessity to understand the death that has been, so that we may pass quite clear of it'. Whereas 'The Crown' had approached corruption seasonally, as a stage which had to complete itself before new growth could start, Lawrence now speaks as one who, looking into *himself*, finds currents of both death and life within, and must win through to peace by understanding his own corruption and transcending it, beyond shame.

We are not only creatures of light and virtue. We are also alive in corruption and death. It is necessary to balance the dark against the light if we are ever going to be free ... From our bodies comes the issue of corruption as well as the issue of creation. We must have our being in both, our knowledge must consist in both.[62]

Yet it is not merely physically in body and blood, that man is a watershed from which a dark and a bright river flow to corruption or creation. We must also rip aside the veils of shame that hide from us our inner selves, for 'the tide of our own corruption is rising higher ... ' Instead of recoiling from 'some sickening issue of ourselves',

let us go down into ourselves, enter the hell of corruption and putrescence, and rise again, not fouled, but fulfilled and free. If there is a loathsome thought or suggestion,... let us admit it with simplicity, let us accept it, responsible for it. It is no good casting out devils. They belong to us, we must accept them and be at peace with them ... We are angels and we are devils, both ... But we are more even than this. We are whole beings, gifted with understanding. A full, undiminished being is complete beyond the angels and the devils.[63]

So the inner serpents in the marsh of the subconscious must come out into the light. They cannot in any case be killed; and what we try to exclude exerts over us the tyranny of repulsive fascination. 'Who am I that I should hold myself above my last or worst desire? My desires are me, they are the beginning of me, my stem and branch and root.' Nonetheless 'there is in me the great desire of creation' as well as 'the great desire of dissolution'; and it is creation that is 'primal and original'. So when Lawrence invites the snake in himself to 'lie down delicately in the sun of my mind' having (once admitted) its own beauty and righteousness, he also insists on 'just proportion'. 'I, who have the gift of understanding ... must keep most delicately and transcendingly the balance of creation within myself', the life impulse encompassing the deathly but free now of both horror and fascination. Yet understanding must always be *of* duality, of how death feeds life (for we must eat life to live), and life feeds death. 'We can never destroy death. We can only transcend it in pure understanding. We can envelop it and contain it. And then we are free.'[64]

(The biographer must needs wonder whether there was some particular snake in the marsh of Lawrence's mind, that so pressed for admission and transcendence – and in the context of Spring 1917 an answer becomes possible.)

The penultimate essay turns from the individual to the world. When it is an autumnal epoch the death wish begins to dominate and people want the sensation of violence, want to kill, break down, put asunder, perish. Yet even this (as in 'The Crown') can still be a necessary part of the life-cycle. Indeed there are 'heroes of passionate and beautiful death' (Tristan, Achilles, Napoleon) just as there are heroes of rebirth (Christ, St Paul, St Francis). But the real 'enemy and the abomination' are the hordes who are neither the one nor the other, lacking the courage or strength of either the life or the death impulse. They never burst into blossom, but vegetate in old forms and even grow fat on the dead body of the past. Such 'will never be flung into the transcendence' of death – though they rot slowly from within. At the thought of these multitudes Lawrence's gorge rises.

They are so many, their power is immense, and the negative power of their nullity bleeds us of life ...

There is an egoism far more ghastly than that of the tyrannous individual. It is the egoism of the flock ... the arrogant immitigable beings who have achieved a secure entity ... Nothing can be added to them, nor detracted. Enclosed and complete, they have their completion in the whole herd ... a multiplied nullity ... so strong that they can defy both life and death for a time ...[65]

Suddenly the pressure of feeling so unbalances him that the casualty lists seem actually desirable. *Let* death – in this case sweet and beautiful – 'Break in among the herd', 'make gaps' to purify the world and 'smash the complete will' of the hosts who 'thought to use death ... for their own base end of nullifaction'. Only let a few 'pure and single men' emerge who can 'give themselves to the unknown' and be fulfilled. For a passionate moment, rhetoric blurs realisation. Having abstracted death into an idea and men into images, he ceased momentarily to imagine real people dying and suffering. After blazing out however, the anger quietens into a more acceptable prayer: 'Let me find a few men who are distinct and at ease in themselves like stars. Let me derive no more from the body of mankind. Let me derive direct from life or direct from death, according to the impulse that is in me.'[66]

That finally is the choice for all men says the last essay, 'The Orbit'. There are always two ways and two goals (as in *Women in Love*) which can have a certain splendour of courage – and a no-road of negation. All human beings must choose for themselves: either to submit the will and so become 'a spark in a great tendency'; or to become self-enclosed, self-willed and null. All the great opposites (as in Blake and Heraclitus) ultimately work to balance and control each other. And man always has both in him: life and death, light and dark, tiger and lamb. Moreover, when 'we are both, and have the courage to be both, in our separate hour, therefore we transcend both, we pass into a beyond, we are roses': symbol of harmony and consummate peace. So we must never try to reduce ourselves to one polarity, for the life of each depends on resistance to and by the other. Neither can triumph without degenerating and destroying itself. Nor can they be reconciled, for that would be to neutralise each other and become null. Where peace lies is in *equilibrium*; when each impulse is allowed full force, balanced by its opposite, when 'suddenly, like a miracle, I find the peace of my orbit', rest in motion. 'It is not of love that we are fulfilled, but of love in such intimate equipoise with hate, that the transcendence takes place. It is not in pride that we are free, but in pride so perfectly matched by meekness that we are liberated as into blossom.' Man is 'a mixed handful of life' when he is born. He slowly singles himself out into manhood. Then he must meet the unknown of woman. He gives himself to 'love', that great force which unifies; he must also give himself to 'hate', which makes him passionately detach himself. (Marriage encompasses both love and hate, on philosophic as well as experiential grounds now.) Impelled to universal communion, made distinct by keen resistance and isolation – 'suddenly I lapse out of the duality into a sheer beauty of fulfilment, I am a rose of lovely peace'.[67]

VI Tensions with Eurydice

The last poem of *Look!*, craving for spring, cries out its confidence, but also at the very end the fear of Orpheus, lest he be mistaken. The last sentence of 'The Reality of Peace' proclaims, beyond love and hate, fusion and singling out, the harmony and peace of the moment of the rose.

Ironically, not much more than a month later, there began a greater distance from Frieda than ever before. It had always been she who had withdrawn, or threatened the relationship by getting involved with someone else. This time was different.

Throughout 1916, after the departure of the Murrys and the violence which their presence had detonated, the Lawrence household seems to have been about as peaceful as it could be. Lawrence was wholly involved with *Women in Love* in which Frieda could see her own vindication; so she had not been much upset to learn that the unpleasant woman in Cannan's *Mendel*, whose artist husband murders her and then kills himself, was supposedly modelled on her. In December she had told Kot: 'I never recognised myself! Except some of L's speeches I recognised – I was sorry that Gilbert made me quite so horrid – so vulgar – But there ... I want you to read L.s new novel – It is so *good* and to my satisfaction I am a nicer person there than Gilbert made me – ' (iii. 52). The autumn had been difficult – Lawrence had been ill for most of it, hardly venturing out of doors, the weather had been vile and she sometimes tired of their isolation – yet the usual tensions were muted. Lawrence could announce in October that 'Frieda and I have finished the long and bloody fight at last, and are at one' (ii. 662); and after she came back from seeing the children in London, even *that* tension seemed to have relaxed, if not altogether. At Christmas she enjoyed Mountsier and Esther as much as Lawrence did. When Mountsier left she wrote to him with real pleasure in describing Esther: 'Ester [sic] looks very well, in fact she *is* Hadaffah to-day with her hair done in a most bewitching outlandish way – She has also worked and done some clever stitches, now she is making a Russian blouse and cuts it about in an alarming manner – ' (iii. 66). Even though Frieda was ill after Christmas, and Esther was several times off to St Ives and to the sea with Lawrence, all was well while she was clearly 'Mountsy's girl – though there are glimpses of tension. Lawrence writes on 9 January: 'I don't think Hadaffah is in a particularly good humor: but that is as it is. I try my best to bring them both to reason – Frieda and Hadaf – but in vain. It is a duel without pistols for all of us' (iii. 72). This could be the first sign of jealousy on Frieda's part; yet Lawrence would hardly draw Mountsier's attention to that, and it seems more likely that the tension was between Esther and Mountsier, with Frieda taking the woman's side and Lawrence experiencing the fate of the peacemaker. When Esther returned to London she and Frieda were on good terms, since she was entrusted with buying two new coats (iii. 79), and Frieda wrote a cordial invitation to come again – whereas Esther's letters to Mountsier from Cornwall show some tension over his criticism of her work.[68] By mid-February their relationship was clearly in trouble.

Esther Andrews is very miserable about Mountsier. There is something very nice and lovable in him. But also underneath is the old worldly male, that is bent on this evil destructive process, and which battens on the ugliness of the war. There is a great ugliness and vultureness underneath, quite American. But I hope for the good to triumph in him also. (iii. 93)

Mountsier seems to have been more realistic about American entry into the war and much less opposed to it than Lawrence or Esther liked. By the time America did declare war on 6 April, Mountsier had gone home, but Esther's opposition was still making her irritable in June. (The declaration, of course, horrified Lawrence.)

At the same time, he may have tried to reason Esther out of putting pressure on her man while they were still together. Though he refused to do the article on women's war labour, he hinted that what he might have written would have lamented 'the tearing asunder of the sexes' in a situation which encouraged 'the assuming of the male activities by the female' (iii. 78) – in war work most obviously but perhaps psychologically too. He pointed Mountsier towards

Cannan's recent satirical fable on the subject in *Windmills* (dedicated to him); and even prophesied gloomily that 'woman will destroy man, intrinsically, in this country' (iii. 78–9). He had dramatised a husband's feelings about his wife's failure to respect him in ' "She Said As Well to Me" '; and even his deep sympathy for Catherine Carswell when her husband was called up did not stop him telling her to let him find his own man's way and stop trying to shelter him (iii. 97–8). Near three strong women, Lawrence's dread of man's subjection to 'managing' females surfaced again, despite their shared responses to the war.

Esther seems to have come down to Cornwall in his absence,[69] probably to seek consolation for her breach with Mountsier and America's entry into the war. Lawrence seems simply to have found her there, and Frieda sick in bed, when he got home on 27 April. Since Frieda always hated illness and was no better as a patient than as a nurse, it must have been a great relief to Esther when Lawrence arrived and at once summoned the doctor whom Frieda had refused to have. Frieda was in fact quite seriously ill with food poisoning which turned into the colitis which had troubled her before, and took some time to clear up. She was still drinking fermented milk on doctor's orders and feeling ill on 7 May (iii. 123), and was not reported as getting better until four days later, when Esther had gone back to London.

By then it seems certain that Frieda *was* jealous, and had made it clear that Esther had outstayed her welcome. It cannot have been pleasant to be ill upstairs while Lawrence was spending all day with a pretty, colourful, much younger and (by this time) more glamorous woman. Ironically, the situation reversed the case of Christmas 1912 – with the difference that Frieda had already slept with Hobson then. Yet Frieda's double standard never envisaged the freedom for Lawrence she claimed for herself, and storms blew up at any sign of attraction to another woman, in Fiascherino, and again at Garsington, though in neither case did the rival represent any sexual threat or Lawrence offer more than friendship. Nor does it seem very likely that much more actually happened now, though Mabel Dodge Luhan – not the most reliable of witnesses – claimed many years later that Frieda had told her this was the only time 'Lawrence was ever "unfaithful" to her! "But it was unsuccessful," she added, with a kind of bitter triumph!' Catherine Carswell, however, who knew Esther and had the story from both Frieda and Lawrence, suggests that the lack of success was Esther's: 'She was very unhappy, and in the strength of her unhappiness could not resist attaching herself to Lawrence and trying to match her strength against Frieda's – disastrously to herself. Yet she took away with her, when she left later that summer, an enduring admiration.'[70] This sounds rather more likely, given how Lawrence had come to stress commitment as against Frieda's ideas of free love. By contrast with his sexual relations and frustrations before he met her, he had become rather puritan than promiscuous in his view of marriage, upholding monogamy, though holding also (as he had to!) that strong and committed feeling for someone else could invalidate one marriage and create another. The main point however is that if he had felt strongly about Esther or (even) had played his marriage false by sleeping with her without much feeling (as Frieda did with Hobson), a mark would surely have been left on his writing, as in all his known sexual affairs. Though some might wish it otherwise, even Frieda's words to Mabel (with those inverted commas round 'unfaithful') may imply no more than her belief that she had quashed Lawrence's infatuation and seen her would-be rival off before their affair could come to anything; though Mabel clearly wanted to imply something more dramatic. In any case Lawrence went on sending good wishes through Catherine, though he did not bracket Frieda's name with his any more. He wrote Esther at least one (splendidly comic) letter; and arranged that she should rent Heseltine's flat when he came back to Cornwall. Esther, from Paris later, tried to help place a Lawrence story in an American magazine.[71] Catherine was certainly right about her 'enduring admiration' of which we have first-hand proof, in a text that has not the tone of a rejected or ejected mistress. For it was a letter of Esther's that helped influence Mabel to invite Lawrence to Taos.

It contains a vivid physical description of what he looked like in 1917: the tall figure, but 'so slightly built and so stooped' that he seems small and fragile; the head that seems too heavy for the body and hangs forward; the quick sure movements; the bleached-looking hair cut in a bang, contrasting with the soft silky red beard concealing a too-large chin, and the protruding underlip of an even more 'violent red'; the wide-apart eyes in the long slender face,[72] with – in the middle – 'a very podgy, almost vulgar, certainly undistinguished nose. There! Can you see him?' She described Frieda as 'a big, rosy German' brought up in luxury and wholly impractical, but with 'an expansive child-nature, very sunny and rich, living only in her emotions ... really all light and sun while Lawrence is dark', and seldom 'really gay'. She describes Lawrence's housekeeping and cooking on an open fire in the living-room. 'The little spotless sunny house in Cornwall had the most beautiful simplicity that I have ever seen.' She was certainly under Lawrence's spell: 'one of the most fascinating men I ever met ... He talks as brilliantly as he writes, and as frankly.' His philosophy 'pours out of him like an inspired message, and no matter how much you may differ when you are away from him, or how little able you are to follow his own particular mysticism, he makes you believe it when he is with you'. Although, 'at the slightest touch of adverse criticism or hostility' he becomes violent and vituperative, and 'has quarreled with everyone', 'the marvelously sweet side of his nature' is 'inarticulate. And yet he is the gentlest, kindest person in all human relations that anyone could be', and the locals 'adored him': 'When you are with him, you feel that there is not a corner of your mind or spirit or whatever you have that Lawrence doesn't see and be tolerant of. And he bares himself perfectly frankly ... there is no such thing as repression.' He is 'a Puritan, really', though 'his intellectual reaction against it is so violent that he hurls himself against it with all of himself, destroying himself as he does it.'[73]

It is more likely than not, however, that a green-eyed Frieda over-reacted, as she had done before, though Esther clearly bore no grudge. It would, in any case, be Lawrence who had to pay. This time, he seems to have reacted by withdrawing, spending more and more time in his garden and on the farm with William Henry. The pattern is very similar to his early relationship with Alan Chambers, when a male friendship out of doors became strongly preferable to the nagging and edginess at home – a friendship that deepened, but did not survive separation. At harvest time in 1916, after the departure of the Murrys, Lawrence had helped in the fields with the Hockings and had appreciated the difference between William Henry and the rest of his family, though he had feared he might become a nuisance. Moreover, as the weather worsened, and Lawrence grew both seedy and wholly preoccupied with the writing and rewriting of his novel, he would not have seen much of the Hockings. Once he had finished however, and felt better, there were shopping expeditions on William Henry's market-days at the end of November and in December. The whole family came to a Christmas party with the two Americans and the Lawrences in the tower. As the days grew sunny he began to go to Tregerthen farm again, and suddenly said on 9 February, 'If we have to stay here, I too shall become a farmer. I shall help the man just below, whom I like. But I still hope to go away' (iii. 89). When he decided to become more self-supporting and dug the three gardens he was probably helped by William Henry, and the friendship began to deepen. It was not surprising, then, that irritation with Frieda's jealousy over Esther, especially if it was unjustified, should have made male friendship more and more attractive, particularly after the failure of the hoped-for blood-brotherhood with Murry. He had always wanted a close male friend, but had never found a loyal one since Alan Chambers, and George Neville, whom he had had to leave behind. He had already explored the need, briefly in Tom's schoolboy David-and-Jonathan friendship in *The Rainbow*, and extensively in Birkin's relation with Gerald in the 1916 'Sisters' III (though the epilogue, with its question about why Birkin's love for Ursula was not enough, had not yet been conceived).[74]

There were also imaginative reasons, now, why a deepened attraction to William Henry, building on a new impatience with Frieda, should have reinforced that old longing for male friendship. We tend to forget how much the daily life of a writer may be coloured by the imaginative influence of what he has been reading and writing. His reading of Crèvecœur may well have lain behind the idea that at worst he could be a farmer, and his gardening for self-sufficiency

– and much of the new American reading was about friendships between males in the great outdoors. If his imagination had been captured by Dana, and Cooper, and Melville, and revived interest in Whitman, the active friendship with the Cornishman may well have had echoes for him of Leatherstocking and Chingachgook, Ishmael and Queequeg, Dana and Aikane, the camaraderie of Whitman.

He certainly did spend more and more time with William Henry, and away from Frieda, as spring moved into summer. And it is inevitable nowadays that, because he did so, there should be a question whether their relations might have become homosexual in the full sense. Frieda herself raised this possibility (though perhaps not intending so much) when she told Murry in 1953, in answer to his speculations and probably his terminology: 'I think the homosexuality in him was a short phase out of misery – I fought him and won – and that he wanted a deeper thing from you. I am aware so much as I am old of the elements in us, that we consist of. Do you know what I mean?'[75] Indeed if Lawrence ever showed himself to be 'a homosexual' it was now. Yet Frieda's reference to 'the elements in us' suggests she had come to share Lawrence's view of bisexuality, which requires rather more complex language.

There will never of course be any conclusive evidence – yet speculation ought surely to be disciplined by all the evidence we do have of what an experience of homosexual love-making would have meant to Lawrence. For Esther was right: he was against all repression, and had himself been engaged with the question of his bisexuality, in context after context, and with the greatest honesty and self-exposure since his letter to Savage in 1913. Moreover, he had striven to understand the instinctive outburst of shock and homophobia (and some self-recognition) which his first encounters with sodomites in 1915 had aroused. By 1916 he had come to see that the nature of sexual relationships was more important to him than the gender of the lovers. In the new novel, though he had discarded its original 'Prologue' with its distinction between two quite different kinds of homosexual feeling, he had clearly envisaged a male relationship which was essentially of the *same* kind as that between Birkin and Ursula and very unlike the destructive one between Gerald and Gudrun. He had come to re-imagine, at much greater depth than in *The White Peacock*, a kind of male love and tenderness that naturally (and at its best, unashamedly) expressed itself and was strengthened by physical contact, rivalry, even conflict, without necessarily implying urges to sodomy or mutual masturbation.

All this (in 1916) seems to have had as yet little to do with William Henry; or Murry, with whom Lawrence's relationship, though involving a kind of love and need that kept reviving after every disappointment, was essentially intellectual and spiritual.

What is the likelihood, then, that Lawrence's increasingly close attachment to

William Henry in 1917, at a time when he was rather fed up with Frieda, and attracted by the idea as well as the physical possibility of a male relationship like those he had been encountering in American writing, would have fulfilled itself in love-making?

The one photograph we have of William Henry, standing in a cornfield with a scythe, could have served as illustration to chapter v of *The White Peacock*, and suggests that he was indeed someone who would have attracted Lawrence physically (see Illustration 44). He was good-looking, dark-haired, square-jawed, with the muscular strength and white skin that Lawrence had admired in Chambers and Neville. The description of the 'strange Cornish type' in the 'Prologue', written not much more than a busy month after the Lawrences installed themselves at Higher Tregerthen, need not however relate particularly to William Henry whom Lawrence had barely met, though he may have contributed something. It was mainly and obviously conceived as opposite to the picturing of Gerald, though the very dark eyes and hair and the 'full, heavy, strongly-soft limbs' would fit. There might seem some particular physical awareness in the 'rather furtive, rabbit-like way in which the strong, softly-built man ate',[76] but this is connected thematically with the theme of domination that will reach a first crisis in 'Rabbit' – and it is very doubtful indeed that this was Lawrence's instantaneous reaction to William Henry. Indeed, the one direct contribution of the Cornishman to the book, the pressing of his hand on his chest in inarticulate longing for something he fears he will never get, which Lawrence gave to Gerald, squares with much other evidence to suggest an almost opposite basis for the beginning of the friendship. It was William Henry's longing to expand himself, to feel and understand things more fully and widely, that first attracted Lawrence. Theirs was a David-and-Jonathan relationship based on unlikeness – the relatively uneducated and physical countryman three years or so the older, with the writer and intellectual from the big city – but William Henry was a rather unusual Cornish farmer. He may have had to leave school early (as his brother Stanley did, at thirteen); but he read a good deal when he could, thought deeply, and had his own views and ways of doing things. He also had a rather mystical streak; and would have been as interesting to teach as Jessie (or Alan Chambers). It may indeed have been a sense of where that had led that made Lawrence keep the relationship at some distance in 1916, when he was preoccupied with *Women in Love*

In spring and summer 1917 came, however, the double joy of hard physical labour beside William Henry on the farm or in Lawrence's gardens, and the trips with him to market; along with the intense pleasure of intimate talk in which the young farmer's consciousness would open and expand. It must have felt like being back at the Haggs, becoming more and more *like* the working farm folk every day, and (he thought) accepted by them as he had been by the

378

Chambers family. In one realm, William Henry was the expert and the masterful one, though Lawrence probably also imagined himself more knowledgeable and helpful than he really was. In the other, the relationship was reversed, though the 'Nightmare' chapter of *Kangaroo* never confuses lack of education with yokeldom. Lawrence also gave young Stanley, then sixteen, French lessons in the farmhouse kitchen. Indeed the chapter convincingly suggests how Lawrence (insofar as Somers voices his author's memories) loved all the Hockings for 'the sensitiveness of their intelligence … they had an endless curiosity about the world, and an endless interest in what was *right*'. 'He' loved it when Mabel and Mary brought baskets of food into the field; but most of all 'he' loved working in the fields all day,

with the savage moors all round, and the hill with its pre-christian granite rocks rising like a great dark pyramid on the left, the sea in front … or resting, talking in the intervals with [William Henry], who loved a half-philosophical, mystical talking about the sun, and the moon, the mysterious powers of the moon at night, and the mysterious change in man with the change of seasons, and the mysterious effects of sex on a man.

There is evidence that one of the things they discussed, under the last heading, was Lawrence's theory of bisexuality, and probably even his feelings of attraction to men.[77]

Would it have gone any further? It seems, again, unlikely – despite the obvious desire of some biographers to produce a dramatic exposure – and despite Lawrence calling the young farmer John Thomas in 'The Nightmare'.[78] Though Esther's 'adored' sounds excessive, William Henry was obviously strongly drawn to and fascinated by Lawrence – but there is no evidence whatever of homosexual preference in him. (He was courting at the time and married soon afterwards.) And though Lawrence may have been feeling cool towards Frieda and neglectful of her, leaving her alone in the cottage day after day and even one stormy night, when she came running down to the farm kitchen in fear and found him there, it is a long step from that to homosexual actions. If it is rather doubtful that he had sex with Esther, he is no more likely to have done so with William Henry, though he probably did feel sexually attracted to them both. Moreover, he would have worried about the homosexual temptation on grounds other than fidelity (though he believed in that). Though *Women in Love* had imagined that relationship between men could be of the same essence as that between Birkin and Ursula, and hence creative and saving too, there is no reason to suppose that Lawrence felt different now about sodomy or mutual masturbation. Here 'The Reality of Peace' is doubly helpful: for it both suggests that he had made himself confront the question of whether he wanted sex with William Henry, which would indeed have been for him an adder in the marsh; but also suggests his answer: that once that dark anal fount of corruption had been openly confronted, the thought could lie down peacefully in the mind's sunshine, its taboo neutralised, but also no longer powerful through the fascination of the forbidden. For the converse would have meant going against everything he had been feeling, and hence thinking and writing, for the last four years. Even so, he might have done it, had his desire been strong enough – for his whole philosophy of life was based on flux, and on being true to one's changeful self no matter what it cost. But if he *had* so changed, after all that he had thought and said, he could not have gone on writing and saying the same sort of things. There would have had to be a major upheaval in his work and thought – and there is not. Those who wish to imagine him making furtive homosexual love in Cornwall must also posit continuous hypocrisy thereafter.

This is confirmed by a letter to Eunice Tietjens, advisory editor of *Poetry* (Chicago), that July. Perhaps stung by his criticisms of her poetry, she seems to have hit back by suggesting that the attitudes to sex in his work were extreme and abnormal. His answer had the same double import as his essay. He began by insisting there was 'all the difference in the world between *understanding* the extreme and awful workings of sex, or even fulfilling them, responsibly; and abnormal sex'; and went on to define 'abnormal' not in terms of categories of desire, but rather in a split between desire and will. 'Abnormal sex comes from the fulfilling of violent or extreme desires, *against the will.*' The abnormality lies however not in the desire but the will, 'the fixed will in ourselves, which asserts that these things *should not be*, that only a holy love should be'. For all desire comes from 'the unknown which is the Creator'; and is therefore holy, no matter what it is – the view of Blake. Therefore it is 'impious' to assert 'what *should be*, in face of what *is*'. Rather, 'It is our responsibility to know how to accept and live through that which *is*. It is the labouring under the burden of self-repudiation and shame which makes abnormality.' What is even worse, however, is to combine such condemnation with 'furtive fulfilment': *that* is not merely abnormal but splits the self even to 'madness' (iii. 140–1). If, then, he felt sexual attraction to the Cornish farmer – as seems quite probable – he would certainly have felt bound to admit it to himself without shame or repression, and would have examined what it was that he wanted responsibly – a word concerned with the nature of the desire and the relationship, and not with any doctrine. But if he had desired and sought homosexual fulfilment, it would not have been furtively – and it would certainly have had a marked effect on him and his work.

This is a question of character and integrity, not of morals or judgement of sexual preference. It is possible to charge the Lawrence of 1917 (should anyone so wish) with failing to imagine how fulfilled homosexuality might be fully as creative of rich new life as fulfilled heterosexuality. And it is possible to accuse him, contrariwise, of admitting and justifying homosexual impulses – and heterosexually anal ones – that (in someone's own view) he ought to have repressed altogether because they are disgusting. What ought to be impossible is to charge him with being 'a homosexual' who would not admit his true nature, or one who after furtive acts concealed himself in a lifelong hypocrisy.

It is moreover quite extraordinary how little those who propose a homosexual affair for Lawrence in Cornwall have considered the elementary question of how William Henry might have responded. There is not the slightest evidence of homosexual tendency in him. He was courting his future wife at the time, and married her in 1918. Moreover our only direct evidence, albeit second-hand, confirms not only that Lawrence did indeed talk to him about his own sexual nature, but also that the Cornishman, though continuing the friendship, was not at all likely to permit any change in its nature. He warned his younger brother to be careful – though there was no need for that.

In fact our culture is seriously at fault in having no language for the whole spectrum of possibility and satisfaction that lies between the admission of sexual attractiveness between men, and the fulfilment of sexual desire in acts of sodomy and mutual masturbation. The word 'homosexual' – especially if opposed to 'heterosexual' as though these were categorically exclusive – is of confusing span, and hence intolerable crudity. In many of the world's cultures male friendship is expressed physically, quite naturally. Men touch each other, put their arms around each other, kiss each other, admire and love each other, without either shame or necessary implication that they wish to go to bed; and without any sense that their behaviour is incongruous with their relations with women. Yet our culture apparently finds it necessary to label someone as '*a* homosexual' as *categorically opposed* to '*a* heterosexual', and to find in any sexual attraction between men the evidence of categoric 'homosexual' preference. Lawrence himself seems far wiser, more honest, and more humane, though he was so much a child of his Englishness as to have been probably rather physically inhibited than otherwise in his relations with other men. It is only after the wrestling match that Birkin can tell Gerald he is beautiful, or that their hands can clasp and stay clasped. One rather hopes that, after some bout of work in the fields, it got as close as that with William Henry.

VII   More New Friendships, New Horizons

It was not only the friendship at the Haggs that began to be re-enacted; for Philip Heseltine had reappeared at the Tinner's Arms in late March looking for somewhere to live nearby, and had settled in April in a wooden bungalow on a high ridge about two miles from Zennor, on the road to Penzance. Suddenly Murry wrote, too, explaining why he had not replied to the invitation to meet in London. (He and Katherine had decided to live apart, though they still saw each other daily, and Lawrence's letter had gone to an abandoned address.) Lawrence was still suspicious in both cases, after the débâcles of 1916. He does not mention Heseltine till May, when he told Murry he didn't 'like him any more, it can't come back, the liking' (iii. 122) – but gradually it did, since Heseltine showed himself as impulsive, susceptible, changeable and enthusiastic as ever. By contrast, the renewed contact with Murry was less successful. Now that he was working for the War Office, and very much part of Garsington, Murry had grown away too far, and Lawrence was rightly suspicious of his loving language. He did want to see him again, and wrote at the end of May to find out whether the Murrys would be coming down to Mylor that summer, but

You shouldn't say you love me. You disliked me intensely when you were here, and also at Mylor. – But why should we hate or love? We are two separate beings, representing what we represent separately. Yet even if we are opposites, even if at the root we are hostile – I don't say we are – there is no reason why we shouldn't meet somewhere. (iii. 127)

In August he wrote a long letter to Katherine 'quite in the old way', she told Ottoline, 'all about the leaves of the melon plant "speckled like a newt" and all about "the social egg which must collapse into nothingness, into *non-being*"' (iii. 149). But no meeting took place, and the correspondence fizzled out once more.

Through Heseltine, however, Lawrence made two new acquaintances. Philip's enthusiasm for Cornwall, the spectacular setting of his new home and its cheapness, soon brought down the young musician with whom he had shared his studio flat in 1916 after the break with Lawrence. A hurried visit in late May 1917 was enough to make Cecil Gray 'quite ecstatic' about Cornwall which he called 'the land of his dreams'; and he soon rented (for £10 a year) a big lonely house on the coast near Gurnard's Head, though he did not move into it till the end of June.[79] Lawrence, feeling friendly towards Heseltine again, met Gray on his brief visit and warmed to him too. Heseltine also introduced Lawrence to Meredith Starr, who had come with his new bride Lady Mary, daughter of the Earl of Stamford,[80] to live in a cottage at Treveal near St Ives. Starr was an odd fish, whom Lawrence did not like much and thought rather a joke, but his interest in the occult was to prove interesting – and indeed these three young men had rather more to offer Lawrence by way of fresh ideas and enthusiasms than the Murrys had done in 1916.

The major concern in June, however, was the arrival of fresh call-up papers summoning Lawrence to Bodmin on the 23rd. He was quite confident at first. He immediately asked the St Ives doctor who had attended Frieda, Dr John Rice, for a certificate of unfitness which he forwarded to the authorities, only to be told that they could not accept it (iii. 130–2). He then decided to go to London and see a specialist – and his tone darkened: 'It is a sickening wearying business'; 'somehow, I *can't* go to Bodmin again, after that last year's experience' (iii. 132). Even the weather seemed newly threatening; it began to rain 'in wild torrents', the air was charged with 'destructive electricity', and he felt 'as if bad things were on the wing' so that the doorposts ought to be smeared with hyssop and blood, like the Israelites in Egypt hoping it would all pass over (iii. 133). He went up to London for a long weekend in the middle of June, staying with Dollie Radford. He consulted David Eder, who probably referred him to a chest specialist since a certificate from himself would count no more than one from Dr Rice. And though Lawrence did not think he 'got much good out of the doctors' (confirming that he saw more than one) nevertheless something in the whole visit made him happier, freer, and now so confident that the examination at Bodmin 'will come out all right' as to be hardly troubled any more (iii. 134). This is the second careful examination (and possibly the most expert of all) since the severe illness of early 1916, and the third since the collapse of 1911 during which a sputum test proved negative. It would *not* have made him happier and freer, now, to have been told that he had consumption, even though this would have put a call-up out of the question. Moreover he would surely have been advised to do something about it (of which there is no sign), and the doctors would once again have had to be willing to avoid their legal duty to notify the authorities. What *would* have made him happier and freer, on the other hand, would be to have been told that his bronchial condition was bad enough to make rejection at Bodmin a near certainty; but not bad enough to be seriously worrying. And if he had been secretly torn two ways – by fear of the very diagnosis that would ensure rejection once and for all – the sense of 'new being' (iii. 134) would have been all the stronger and more specific. His hard work in his gardens, and perhaps already with William Henry on the farm, may have made him actually rather fitter than he had been for years, though the underlying tendency to illness was always there.

Once more a note to Murry, giving advance notice of his visit, failed to produce a meeting (iii. 132). Murry spent that weekend at Garsington. Cynthia Asquith was also away on a visit to the family home at Stanway. In any case the old contacts seemed to be drying up. From the whole of June only eight missives have survived. Two were the notes to Jack and Cynthia. Two notes went to Pinker and Eddie Marsh, the first hinting that he might need another advance because money was getting short, the second in gratitude for yet another £7/15 from *Georgian Poetry* out of the blue (iii. 135). Two were letters about second-hand furniture to the new friend Gray (iii. 129–30, 133–4), another an affectionate bread-and-butter letter to Dollie (iii. 134). The only letter for its own sake was to Catherine Carswell, the first for a month (iii. 130–2).

He came back to a wet and green Cornwall on 19 June, much happier than when he had left. Furthermore the examination went well, and also more quickly than on the previous occasion when he had had to stay overnight – though he still resented what he told Marsh had been a 'loathsome performance' (iii. 136). He left at seven in the morning to catch a train, was quickly examined, presumably presenting his London certificate, and was graded C3: unfit for military service but liable to call-up for light non-military service, since there were no rejections now. He seems to have got back to an anxious Frieda the same evening. *Kangaroo* recalls one of the farm daughters running up to the cottage to hear what had happened, and saying how glad she was.[81] There was little risk of a call to a light clerking job for the Zennor military.

As the summer ripened towards hay-harvest, so did his other new friendships, as well as the one with William Henry.

Heseltine had come back to Cornwall to escape the mess he had made of his life. Puma had had her baby on 13 July 1916, and though he had finally agreed to marry her (on 22 December) he had refused to cohabit, and sent her and their son into the country as Halliday had wanted to do in Lawrence's novel. She seems to have gone to live with or near his mother in Wales, who took responsibility for the child. Philip remained in emotional turmoil and (as he told his old girlfriend Viva Smith) 'on the verge of a complete collapse', but he had resisted 'blackmail', for 'really, one shouldn't have dealings with vampires'. To Phyl Crocker (whose family lived nearby in Cornwall) he bared his feelings about his marriage even more explicitly: 'The purely animal relation ... is not only disappointing and unsatisfactory in itself, but leaves behind it a long procession of phantoms, which one must destroy or be destroyed by', whether 'licensed' by marriage or not. Marriage indeed is a merely external social institution with '*nothing whatever* to do with human relationships of any kind'; and his own a 'supreme blasphemy'. He had been 'insane enough ... to make concession after concession' until,

> badgered by our mutual friend (with whom I had never had and could never have any but a purely bestial relation) to make her a final present of forty shillings worth of respectability in a 'certificate of marriage', I made no objection, seeing that the ceremonial meant no more to me than to make a mock of what was already a mockery. Voila tout!

He had come to Cornwall to get right away and recover, by himself.[82]

Though Lawrence had been none too pleased by his reappearance at first, by June he felt much more 'kindly' (iii. 134) – helped perhaps by not too close a proximity. Heseltine had found a situation on the highest point of the moors, facing two seas, so that he could watch the sun rise over one and set over the other without leaving the house. The gorse was ablaze, one could see foxes, and seals. This was a landscape healing enough in itself; but very soon Lawrence-like thoughts began also to appear in his letters, about the death of the self and its resurrection, about facing what one is, and has done, without shame and self-repudiation. He wrote two poems, one about the 'lost' Celtic golden land of 'Hy-Brasil' in the Western sea beyond the sunset; the other about ceasing to crucify himself with shame at having slain his 'purple' love. Before very long his whole attitude to Puma and the past underwent a complete revolution, in which Lawrence's influence played a part. On 17 June, from the London studio – Esther having gone to Paris – he wrote to Robert Nichols about a remarkable discovery. For years he had looked to love 'to give me the key of my own being, of reality', but had actually been pursuing 'a phantom of my own too-self-sufficient mind'. At last, however, he has 'found a direction and a peace'; 'Love has been with me all the while and it is I, and not Love that has been blind'. His idea of love had been illusion; reality was always in the one place he was certain it could not be:

I have found in Puma and my babe a greater and realer love than I have ever been able to imagine. In seeing them as they essentially are – as I can do now – instead of regarding them through the bleared spectacles of my own foulness, I can see at last, and clearly, the way, and the only way, to the fulfilment of my own being. All that I have hated and cursed in Puma has been myself – my foul old self – and that is dead, now, once and for all.

Within a few lines he is talking about Lawrence;[83] and it seems clear that Lawrence had been trying to heal the split in Heseltine and his view of sex that he had diagnosed in 1916, and to make him act responsibly according to 'what is' rather than some idea of 'what should be'. All Heseltine's admiration of the writer and thinker soon returned.

So it was that when Philip's enthusiasm about Cornwall brought Cecil Gray down to visit, he was immediately introduced to Lawrence. The 'big, lonely house on the wildest part of the coast' which Gray proceeded to take on a five-year lease was Bosigran Castle – in fact the name of the rocky headland on which it stood, with disused tin-workings at its side. It had seven rooms and a great view out to the Scilly Islands in front, but was only £10 a year, which Gray with his private income could well afford. Lawrence threw himself enthusiastically into getting furniture and liaising with workmen about colour schemes, just as for the Murrys the previous year; and went over himself to scrub and clean and get the house ready (e.g. iii. 128, 130). Gray moved down in the latter half of June.

He was a deceptively stolid-looking young man, fair-haired, pale, plumpish, myopically bespectacled – though with expressive grey eyes behind the lenses. He cultivated a world-weary air with 21-year-old cynicism; and drank a good deal to liven himself up (he said), so was often 'the better for drink', which he held well. He had a pawky wit, and made an amusing, lively and sometimes riotous companion when his enthusiasm was awakened. Yet he held back from revealing or committing himself at deeper levels; and beneath his douce Scots containment and canniness there was more than met the eye. He had shown as a child and at school that when threatened or challenged he could respond with astonishing violence.

In his autobiography, Gray states that he and the Lawrences 'used to meet virtually every day, either at his place or at mine, over a period of many months. We were, in fact, almost one household: when I was not visiting the Lawrences, they were visiting me.'[84] In this (and other things) he is unreliable. Bosigran was over four miles from Higher Tregerthen; accessible, but hardly for popping in and out. Invited to visit in the second week of July, Lawrence replied that he was busy with the Hockings' hay-harvest, but suggested that Gray and Croustchoff might come over to them instead (iii. 138). Gray also put them off at least once (iii. 151). The Lawrences probably went to Bosigran for the first time on 15 July. For almost the whole of August Frieda had an attack of neuritis in her leg which kept her in bed, only able to come downstairs towards the end of the month; and Lawrence was busy with a new book of philosophy. Only at the end of the month does he talk of another visit to Bosigran, offering to take blankets to spend the night (iii. 151) – in which case they must have gone by cart, as *Kangaroo* indeed suggests.[85] At the beginning of September Lawrence was helping with corn harvest, and in mid-month Frieda went to London for her six-monthly visit to see the children. In late September they spent a weekend at Gray's – a visit that was to have serious consequences. A ripening friendship there was, but less close, and with fewer visitings than Gray wished later to make out. Lawrence says in late September: 'He comes occasionally, occasionally we go to him. I like him' (iii. 163).

These new (or renewed) friendships did however have something to offer intellectually and imaginatively. Heseltine was always interested in non-Anglo-Saxon cultures, and will have stirred again Lawrence's own sense of the Celtic, and of Cornish mythology. Gray's passion for Hebridean music also struck an instant chord. Catherine Carswell tells sarcastically how they 'howled in what [was] ingenuously supposed to be the Gaelic, at the same time endeavouring to imitate the noise made by a seal' – but this music of the uttermost fringe of Europe, into which the sea and its wildlife seemed so to enter that the sounds were more than human, would go on echoing in Lawrence's imagination as late as *Mornings in Mexico*.[86] Most of all, however, it was probably Heseltine's interest in the occult, combining with and increased by the presence of a devoted occultist in the neighbourhood, that added a new dimension to Lawrence's imagination.

This was Starr – though Lawrence seems to have been interested in his bookshelf rather than the man himself or his magical and transcendental practices. Indeed the Starrs seemed a joke, if at times an expensive one:

They fast, or eat nettles: they descend naked into old mine-shafts, and there meditate for hours and hours, upon their own transcendent infinitude: they descend on us like a swarm of locusts, and devour all the food on shelf or board: they even gave a concert, and made most dreadful fools of themselves, in St Ives: violent correspondence in the *St. Ives Times*. (iii. 158)

In the course of the exchanges over what one correspondent called the 'buffoonery' of his 'concert play' *East and West*, Starr named Aleister Crowley as the only real modern genius, 'by far the greatest living artist in England'; and cited 'the celebrated Author' D. H. Lawrence, along with Epstein and Augustus John, as holding that 'ninety-nine percent of British art is worse than buffoonery'.[87] Nichols later blamed Heseltine's interest in 'black magic' on Starr, and (waspish as ever) recalled being introduced to 'some sort of impostor of that name ... a fellow with long hair, bulbous rings etc, & an infernal gas bag'. Indeed Heseltine, in another swing of feeling, later attributed the 'idiotic' emotionalism of his letter about his changed feelings for Puma 'to the reaction that inevitably overtakes those who tamper prematurely with the science vulgarly known as Black Magic'. Nevertheless his letters from Dublin, where he fled that September, fearing conscription, show the strength of his belief in a world permeated and influenced by spiritual beings. He recommended three books as keys to the lost Gnosis, but urged secrecy, for they are dangerous and must not fall into unfit hands. Though he had earlier shown an interest in psychical research, it was probably in Cornwall that he immersed himself in S. T. Klein's *Science and the Infinite*, J. M. Pryse's *The Apocalypse Unsealed* and the *History of Magic* by Eliphas Lévi – to which he later added the works of 'Hermes Trismegistus'.[88]

Lawrence's attitude differed both from Heseltine's enthusiasm and Nichols's contemptuous dismissal. Starr himself might be a joke, but his knowledge and his books opened up ideas and images that Lawrence could use. (As always, it is not clear how much he actually read, how much skilfully skimmed and how much gathered from talk – but what is certain is that, like Yeats, he took what was congenial and useful to him and simply ignored what was not.) There had been faint signs earlier that might suggest some awareness of Madame Blavatsky's theosophy – but no more than could have come entirely second-hand.[89] Now however some of Madame Blavatsky's ideas and images, and more especially Pryse's exposition of the *chakras* (the Hindu nervous system which could be activated and controlled by the initiate), become unmistakably visible and imaginatively influential – and there is evidence of his new knowledge and his attitude in his letters. In July, asking whether Waldo Frank (editor of *Seven Arts*) was a theosophist, he declared that he himself was not, though he liked the idea of 'a body of esoteric doctrine, defended from the herd', and thought the esoteric doctrines 'marvellously illuminating, historically'. He hated 'the esoteric forms' however, and though he was interested in magic, 'it is all part of the past, and part of a past self in us: and it is no good going back' (iii. 143). By late August he had discovered that David Eder had a similar interest, despite his commitment to Freud.

Have you read Blavatsky's *Secret Doctrine*? In many ways a bore, and not quite real. Yet one can glean a marvellous lot from it, enlarge the understanding immensely. Do you know the physical – physiological – interpretations of the esoteric doctrine? – the *chakras* and dualism in experience? The devils won't tell one anything, fully. Perhaps they don't understand themselves – the occultists – what they are talking about, or what their esotericism really means. But, probably, in the physiological interpretation, they do – and won't tell. Yet one can gather enough. Did you get Pryce's [sic] *Apocalypse Unsealed*? (iii. 150)[90]

In some ways the 'secret doctrine' was, for Lawrence, merely a new focusing of perceptions already implicit in his work. For example he particularly wanted to talk to Eder about 'the lunar myth' in Blavatsky, 'the lunar trinity – father – mother – son, with the son as consort of the mother, the *magna* Mater'; but this had been a concern of his since *Sons and Lovers*, and he wanted to discuss it because he knew that Freud's 'whole psycho-analysis rests on this myth' and it is 'the mill-stone of mill-stones round all our necks'. Yet here was a new world of images and conceptions that he could use (albeit with an esotericism that can baffle readers) to clarify, intensify and extend some elements of both his fiction and his thought.

He had been educated in the basics of science, and was knowledgeable about botany. He had used imagery of evolution freely in 'Hardy' and in *The Rainbow*, while insisting that all its stages were still present in modern man. But in late July he flatly denied that there is any evolution in man or nature – only unfolding of what was always there; or 'rotting back, through all the coloured phases of retrogression and corruption, back to nought' (iii. 139). In a sense this says no more than 'The Crown' had done; but its sudden vehemence – 'the truth of evolution is *not* true' – probably owes something to the continual attack on Western material science in Blavatsky and all theosophists, and their assertion, instead, of an ancient and *universal* wisdom now almost lost to sight but traceable back behind the Sanskrit scriptures. Far from evolving from primitive beginnings, modern humanity has degenerated from the great past which built civilisations in Egypt, Palenque (Mexico) and Mesopotamia – and may well have to vanish and grow again, like the races of the aeons that have been and are yet to be. We can probably date from now a new hostility in Lawrence to science in all its modern forms – which had, after all, produced the carnage of the war – and a more confident assertion of ancient kinds and ways of knowing, and symbolising, though this had already begun with his interest in the pre-Socratic, the Celtic and the so-called primitive. It would be founded, however, on no secret *doctrine*, but firmly on human experience, as the source and test of all symbolisms and symbolic meanings. When he wrote his essays on American literature, it would be with a nod in the direction of the occultist belief in a universal language of symbols, but also with an insistence that 'art-speech' was greater than any esoteric symbolism, because its symbols were not concepts but 'pure experience, emotional and passional, spiritual and perceptual, all at once'.[91] So when, in revising the new typescript of *Women in Love* into almost the novel we now have, he gave it an esoteric dimension using 'Starr's destructive electricity' (iii. 133), Pryse's *chakras*, and Blavatsky's ether, he was opening out (though not to everyone's satisfaction) what was already there in the experience of the previous version. Slowly, he would develop from these sources a new *physical* psychology, avowedly as a criticism of Freud; but it would be in very much his own dialectical form, based on his own experience – and radically opposed to the central theosophist idea of spirituality, and of spiritual development beyond the body. He took what he wanted and left the rest.

Blavatsky lost no opportunity to undermine the Jewish foundations of Christianity, and the Jewish idea of God. (She saw Jewish religion as derivative – and decadent – from Egypt and a far older, subtler and more complex universal religion.) After an argument with Kot in London, Lawrence (in a bad mood) wrote that the reason Jews have been hated was that they have always taken religion to minister to their own secret arrogance, while cringing before men. 'With them, the conscious ego is the absolute, and God is a name they flatter themselves with' (iii. 137). He called instead for 'pure reverence to the Holy Spirit', but felt that he could preach this to Kot because he was one of those 'near the mark'. He suddenly asked Waldo Frank if he was a Jew. 'The best of Jews is, that they *know* truth from untruth' (iii. 144); but the worst is that they betray their knowledge, fawn to the powers that be and cringe to Mammon and the material world. He said he was about to renounce his Jewish friends (of whom he now had several: Kot, the Lows, the Eders), though of course he did not. When he heard that Eder was thinking 'of going to Palestine with the Jewish contingent', i.e. the Palestine Commission (iii. 150) – a decision that would shape the rest of Eder's life and make him a greatly respected figure in the Zionist movement – Lawrence opined that Jewishness would be a millstone to him: 'Best cease to be a Jew, and let Jewry disappear' (iii. 150). It is true that it was the Jewish Idea to which Lawrence had become hostile, rather than Jews themselves with whom his friendship continued; but Blake on generalisation does come to mind.[92] The next sentence was the one asking whether Eder had read Blavatsky.

VIII   Lawrence's Harvest

(a) Philosophy

There was however a better harvest in his work. In April, having sent off 'The Reality of Peace' he had thought he might do some more short essays in philosophy, perhaps to fill the seven out into a book. He may have written 'Love', which seems to take off from the final paragraph of 'The Orbit': not only the faith in the fulfilment of the rose but also the emphasis on the duality of love, on which there is now as much stress, perhaps glancing at his own situation.[93] In early May he told Catherine he was only interested in his gardens and was not writing at all. He had begun typing out 'The Reality of Peace' in order to have another copy and, typically, had not been able to resist recasting the second (unpublished) essay, but 'suddenly I felt as if I was going dotty, straight out of my mind, so I left off. One can only wait and let the crisis come and go' (iii. 125). The necessity of waiting for the approach of the new, since man cannot create himself, is the whole theme of 'Life', which also has clear echoes of 'The Reality of Peace'[94] so it may have been after writing this that he decided to take its advice. (The sudden mental spasm shows the strain he was still under – as his ability to stand back and admit this in a letter, together with his instinctive knowledge of what best to do about it, show his underlying strength.) His gardens then took all his attention, so much so that he seems to have forgotten these two essays and to have come across them with some surprise five months later.

Soon however he began writing philosophy again, 'a slow job' (iii. 131), but by 27 July he had written 'a tiny book ... called philosophy because I don't know what else to call it. It might be called mysticism or metaphysic, though unjustly' (iii. 143). When the war ends 'and the gates are opened', he still wants to go to America. At the end of August he told Pinker that 'At the Gates' would 'make about 140 pp.' (iii. 152) and was almost ready to be sent for publication. It was based on the 'more superficial "Reality of Peace". But *this* is pure metaphysics, especially later on: and perfectly sound metaphysic, that will stand all the attacks of technical philosophers' – though he might leave out bits that 'might be very unpopular' (iii. 155). Later he told Kot that it was the fourth and final form of 'that philosophy which you once painfully and laboriously typed out' (iii. 163), that is, the 'Hardy', whose central 'metaphysic' had been recast into 'The Crown', and again into the lost 'Goats and Compasses'. We may guess, since 'At the Gates' too has been lost, that the work had been 'slow' because what he had been trying to forge was a concentration of his thought, melted down, hammered fine, the essential metal unalloyed. Our only witness to its quality is Heseltine writing from Dublin, now completely re-enthused and eager once more to get Lawrence published, in Ireland. He called the little book in one letter to Nichols 'the supreme utterance of all modern philosophy', but feared the partners of the Dublin firm Maunsel he has given it to will find it 'unintelligible' and 'shocking'. In another letter he called it 'a stupendous book' – so much so that he suspected Lawrence, like Yeats, had become the mouthpiece of some great spirit. It seems a pity that amid such enthusiasm he gave no descriptive account of it at all.[95]

(b) Women in Love

Lawrence's main concern in July, however, was to revise Pinker's new typescript, now firmly titled *Women in Love*. On 9 July Lawrence told the small publisher Cecil Palmer (who had expressed an interest) that he would just 'look it through once more' (iii. 137) and would send it in this week'; but the revision, as always, became so extensive that by the end of the month he wanted Huebsch told that the carbon copy was already out of date (iii. 144). The revised version came back from Palmer by 25 August (iii. 151), when Lawrence was occupied with *Look!* and the American essays (see below); but then in November he told Pinker that he was revising again. There would be one last look through in September 1919 – but the transformation of 'The Sisters' III of late 1916 into the *Women in Love* we have now was probably complete in all essentials by the end of 1917, so it seems appropriate to deal with it as a whole at this point.[96]

In June and still more in November 1917, enough time had passed for Lawrence to be able to see his work more clearly – aided by *Look!*, the latest clarifications of his metaphysic, and his new reading. More objectively now, he sharpened the dramatic interchanges and made cogent use of Ursula (and Gudrun and Gerald) to pin down Birkin's defects. Although nearly all the leaps of exploratory imagination opening up the subconscious were already there, he could see better now what they implied and where they led, and pull them together into a clearer analysis of the paths to new life or destruction, the apocalyptic parting of the 'ways' of love. The effect of comparing the two versions is a clicking into full focus – one had had the experience, but had not fully grasped the meaning – and also a continual enrichment and enlivening. It was a re-seeing of the whole imagined world, not merely a verbal improvement.

For the biographer, the critique of Birkin through Ursula is significant. From the start of their love-story in what would become 'An Island' Ursula is made much more critical as she responds to Birkin's misanthropic longing for a clean world emptied of people – though that is also visually animated in 'just uninterrupted grass, and a hare sitting up'. In 'The Sisters' III Ursula was 'frightened' but she also 'exulted' and felt 'liberated ... Yes, she hated humanity'. In 1917 she is still attracted and still exults, but now she hesitates as well, for 'she was dissatisfied with *him*'. She sees, and distrusts, how 'all the while, in spite of himself, he would have to be trying to save the world ... she hated the Salvator Mundi touch'. With 'a certain sharp contempt and hate of him' despite her attraction, his willingness to pour himself out to anybody seems 'a very insidious form of prostitution'. As the argument goes on about love the revision pins down 'a certain priggish Sunday-school stiffness over him, priggish and detestable. And yet, at the same time, the moulding of him was so quick and attractive ... something so alive, somewhere, in spite of the look of sickness.' This 'duality in feeling' will be carried through consistently now, in the presentation of his views as well as his character.[97]

Birkin also at last begins to grasp his idea of love in a way that will free it from chauvinism. In the original episode with the cats he saw Mino as properly insisting on 'male primacy' and 'a higher order of understanding'. Now, though chauvinism remains, it is easier to see something better beneath: a need to recognise 'a sort of fate', a 'superfine stability', in which (as the novel will establish) gender hierarchy will play no part. He *almost* grasps what he is after: 'Adam kept Eve in the indestructible paradise, when he kept her single with himself, like a star in its orbit.' Almost, but not quite, for Ursula at once seizes upon the implication, crying 'a satellite' – so Birkin goes on being criticised, and forced to free his thought from something that is distorting it. By partly misunderstanding, Ursula pushes Birkin to understand more clearly. At the 'Water-Party' his sermon on the marsh, while continuing to echo the central argument of 'The Crown', becomes part of a better dramatised situation and so again arouses a more interesting and ambivalent response. The deathly import of his vision is paradoxically enlivened (as with the hare earlier) when imagery of the dark river and its fauna and flora replaces the abstract language of the 'flux of corruption'; but whereas Gudrun's simple mockery originally left Birkin relatively untouched, now Ursula's opposition, springing from the flamy life in her, is a sharper criticism of his deathliness: 'You are a devil, you know, really ... You *want* us to be deathly.' Yet, in more than half persuading him, she brings out also a life potential despite his nihilism.[98]

Most of all, Lawrence is now able to dramatise the growth of the novel's central idea in Birkin's mind, because he had finally laid hold of it himself in *Look!* as 'the way of the stars', in 'One Woman to All Women'.[99] Though a star could image individual singleness in the novel of 1916, the idea of two stars in permanent orbit and equilibrium – symbolising how individual independence could be reconciled, in lovers, with absolute commitment and bonding – is newly and steadily written into *Women in Love*. As Gerald and Gudrun sit in the canoe the alternative 'way' open to them is given the crucial additions of 'space' between them and their being 'balanced in separation'. In the chapter that became 'Man to Man', Birkin in his illness, brooding on his hatred of the possessive female and Magna Mater and also on gender itself as a mark of imperfection, begins to ponder how that might be overcome by a kind of sexual relationship between 'two single beings, constellated together like two stars', yet each 'a single, separate being' with its own 'pure freedom', and without the 'horrible merging, mingling, self-abnegation of love'.[100] Sex war has not disappeared, but its remedy is coming into focus.

So, in 'Moony', Lawrence can both sharpen Ursula's attack on Birkin and then have him grasp the essential distinctions between different 'ways' of love, and of violence, that will clarify the central concerns of the novel as a whole. The previous version had already captured the stoning of the moon and the fleeting moment of truth and tenderness which followed, but also how as soon as they began to talk, conflict began again. Birkin insisted that Ursula accept him 'as a leader', she (very understandably) became annoyed, and the momentary peace broke up in rather childish rage. In 1917 however, Lawrence's new exploration has brought Birkin beyond the desire for leadership that had been blocking his and his author's understanding of something quite different. The desire (now) is for both lovers to be together in a dimension beyond their egos – though again, as soon as they argue, ego takes over. So Birkin's case is improved; but at the same time Lawrence has Ursula again denounce the 'Sunday school teacher' and 'preacher' in him, and charge that it is *he* who cannot let himself go. The conflict becomes more searchingly dramatic, with truth on both sides; and a better reorchestration of the process of violence and re-constellation that went before, since in this version conflict again ebbs, and peace again returns with humour and tenderness. Only, because Birkin is being investigated more searchingly now, he is made to realise an inconsistency: how he both longs for and *fears* dark sexual passion. Ursula is allowed to disturb and probe him (and perhaps his author) more deeply than before.[101]

Suddenly imagination responds with a new leap (a long new handwritten insertion): another West African carving, a woman with a face like a beetle. In grasping its significance, Birkin is able now to diagnose opposite kinds of disintegration in the 'fleurs du mal' people of this disintegrative time – and by contrast, the inclusive and recreative way of love that he wants with Ursula. To set an 'African' reduction of the self to sensuality, against an 'arctic' mode of dominating mind and will, helps discriminate different kinds of destructiveness in Gerald, Gudrun, Hermione, the Pussum, Halliday and Loerke. By contrast Birkin sees a 'way' in which sexual relationship can create 'a lovely state of free proud singleness, which accepts the obligation of the permanent connection with others, and with the other, submits to the yoke and leash of love, but never forfeits its own proud individual singleness, even while it loves and yields.'[102] Opinions may differ on how far this is attainable, but it is unquestionably what the Lawrence of 1917 wanted from his marriage, formulated with new clarity at a time when the marriage was under strain. It is also more firmly measured in the novel against the idea of 'free love' espoused by Gerald and Gudrun (and also Frieda, in life), while allowing them to sharpen their mockery of Birkin. In the earlier version's 'Threshold', Gudrun crudely caricatured Birkin's sex hierarchy; but now she understands what she rejects: the idea that 'if you accept the unison' there can be an 'equilibrium' that still leaves the self a different kind of freedom – but rejects it no less scornfully.[103]

This new understanding required a new imagining of the breakthrough in the love of Ursula and Birkin. The rumpus over the rings (reminiscent of the one in Cornwall)[104] was already in place; but its aftermath which completes the pattern of tenderness-through-violence announced in 'Moony' is altogether reconceived in a way that shows the influence of *Look!*, but also of Lawrence's new occult reading.

The scene in the Saracen's Head was originally done from Ursula's point of view. She can hardly believe that she is loved at last and is 'mortally frightened' that she will be let down again; but as his fingertips move 'delicately, finely over her face' she loses her fear in a 'dazzle of released, golden light'. Birkin too has been frightened, but her 'yielding up' creates in him 'a new star-like being' – one of the few uses of the image of a single star – and for the first time in his life he becomes heedlessly and serenely happy. Later however he begins to feel again the seething sexuality he fears. Wanting to hold onto the new gentleness, he forces Ursula into a false position of having to choose. She does not know what she wants, and despite the new certainty of their love, the chapter in 'The Sisters' ends with a dying fall. He asks whether their new 'peace of soul' isn't 'the greatest reality' – but 'her eyes were full of tears, and she did not answer'.

In 1917 he rewrote the scene largely from Ursula's point of view, making it centre on her perception, for the first time, of the full dimension of Birkin's 'otherness' – reversing 'She Said As Well To Me' in *Look!* The experience is about to be echoed as Birkin looks at Ursula in 'Flitting'; but since her war-cry has always been 'Do you love *me*?', while Birkin has struggled to explain how the deepest dimension of relationships is impersonal, Lawrence may have wanted her to make the discovery, as a moment of conversion. It is also, in its quality of wonder, a return to the 'religious' sense created in *The Rainbow* as (at last) she confronts a son of God, 'a strange creature from another world', from 'the beyond'. To give new force, however, to how much that strangeness depends on a mysterious strength of separate being, Lawrence wanted a new language of more-than-personal power. He found it (strangely enough!) in Pryse's *Apocalypse Unsealed* and in Blavatsky. Ursula and Birkin 'love' in the usual personal and sexual senses; but she discovers also 'More than that' now, as:

Unconsciously, with her sensitive finger-tips, she was tracing the back of his thighs, finding some mysterious life-flow there. She had discovered something, something more than wonderful, more wonderful than life itself. It was the strange mystery of his life-motion ... It was here she discovered him one of the Sons of God such as were in the beginning of the world, not a man, something other, something more.[105]

Pryse explains how, in the ancient Indian neurology, cosmic energy, *kundalini*, flowing through humans but coming from beyond them, can be generated from the ganglion or web of nerves (in the lower back, loins and thighs) whose centre is the base of the spine; and how, in its full circuit through all the other ganglia or *chakras* and the brain (a nervous system both sensual and spiritual), the whole being can be flooded with illumination. So what Ursula touches is described as 'a living fire', 'a dark flood of electric passion', 'a rich new circuit, a new current of passional electric energy': the psychic equivalent of the physical electricity which flows through but is not a property of the body which conducts it. Energy from beyond the lovers flows between them as between poles, and produces (with new intensity) that passing away into oblivion and reawakening into 'essential new being', that is the essence, for Lawrence, of true and creative sexual relationship – even though here it is only the touch of fingers in a public inn, waiting for tea. Once again it is a constellation of radiance and darkness after storm, and the discovery of new tenderness and peace. They touch now, will later take each other and marry; yet always retain their separate selves because each is a wholly unpossessable being, imbued with a life-force from beyond the self. To touch *that* is a mystical experience, but also intensely physical, and therefore 'mystically-physically satisfying' as no merely genital experience or pleasure (for Lawrence) could be.[106]

In a sense the esoteric language does no more than expand an experience of charisma in somebody unique – but it was probably the fusion of the spiritual with the physical in the ancient neurology that Lawrence found most suggestive. Yet by the same token his insistence (following Pryse) on giving the life-energy flowing through Birkin so precise a physical location in the lower back, loins and thighs has led to puzzle and misunderstanding – though attempts to read the scene in terms of covert homosexuality and anal obsession seem crass. The novel itself also holds a non-esoteric explanation of why it should be the back rather than the front of the body that speaks of singleness. Birkin muses on gender as imperfection, and the front of human bodies does seem to proclaim the need of a complementary half – whereas (as every dancer or athlete knows) the base of the spine is the fulcrum of individual and independent balance and movement.

Moreover, once the relationship is firmly founded in this kind of reverence and wonder – felt by Birkin for Ursula too, in 'Flitting' – it seems that it can include the whole being, all desires, all possibilities. The 'radiance' in the Saracen's Head is consummated in the pitch dark of Sherwood Forest;[107] and there is no longer anything to fear in sensuality of all kinds. The contrast with the disintegrative characters, and particularly with the way that the love of Gerald and Gudrun develops, becomes clearer – though again readers may be puzzled by some esoteric language. The other 'ways' of love are continually heightened now in imagery and dialogue: the 'arctic' glisten and gleam of the blonde Gerald, the darkness associated with the Pussum and the knowing as a means of power that links Gudrun with both Gerald and Hermione, and also sharpens their critique of Birkin. Lawrence's breach with Ottoline allows a heightening of Hermione well beyond any portraiture: indeed Birkin's new onslaught on Hermione's sensuality-in-the-head reaches such intensity that the handwritten insertion itself admits 'There was a sense of violation in the air'. Moreover Starr's 'destructive electricity' now becomes palpable in the novel in the scenes between Gerald and the Pussum and Gerald and Gudrun. In theosophy and magic, the latent powers in the cosmos can be generated in the self or directed to others both creatively and destructively. For Lawrence, no energy is evil in itself – but to reduce relationship to one dimension is sinister and may destroy. So when Gerald looks at the Pussum now, 'The electricity was turgid and voluptuously rich, in his limbs. He would be able to destroy her utterly'; and her gaze is a 'black flare'. That the relationship is from the start a sensuality of *power* is continually emphasised now in a language of 'black, electric flow'. Gerald feels its source in the base of his spine also – but the difference is that the relation here is all of one kind, felt in frissons of dominance and subjection. When the revision now makes Gudrun take Gerald's domination of the mare into her own sensuous consciousness, a similarity to the Pussum is clarified.[108]

Moreover the episode with the rabbit now points up a secret and dangerous 'obscenity', something more than the anger and violence in both man and woman towards what violently resisted and threatened them, which was already clear. Now, as well as the newly imaged 'whitish, electric gleam' of Gerald's 'arctic' will, and Gudrun's eyes 'black as night', there is a further esoteric language which explores sado-masochism, a fascination with power and pain, as an 'obscene' inversion of what Lawrence saw as the religious mystery of sex. As they gaze with fascination into the red gash the rabbit has scored in Gudrun's arm Gerald feels as though it were 'torn across his own brain ... letting through the forever unconscious, unthinkable red ether of the beyond, the obscene beyond'. However strained, the language is not unintelligible. 'Ether' is a metaphor for inner space analogous to the medium supposed to occupy outer space, and (in Blavatsky) also a potency within us out of which future forms of being and energy will evolve (hence a 'beyond'), which has been present in creation from the beginning; and a medium (as Eliphas Lévi wrote) through which 'all the nervous centres secretly communicate with one another'. What

Lawrence seems to be after is an obscene parody both of theosophist spiritual illumination in the initiate, and of the experience of dying into new radiant life, as Birkin and Ursula will do. The gash in the white flesh tears consciousness so that blood-fascination can come flooding through; a red oblivion followed by new awareness of self, parodying the Lawrencian 'death' and renewal through sex. Gerald and Gudrun become, for a horrible moment, 'new' creatures for whom sado-masochism could become the intensest way of life and sensual excitement. Their recognition of this at the end of the chapter has a 'nonchalance' which even eighty years later may still seem 'shocking'.[109]

The revision, then, takes the contrast between the two pairs of lovers and the different kinds of 'love' much further than before, as Lawrence sees deeper into the tendencies his novel had exposed. The other 'shocking' potential however – the homosexual feeling between the men – is rather toned down, as though, having made clear in 'Gladiatorial' what he wanted in male relationship, Lawrence was no longer as interested in exploring the homoerotic feelings that in the original 'Man to Man' scene he had given to an embarrassed Gerald. (This could have been novelist's transposition but might equally suggest, especially since the offer of 'Blutbrüderschaft' was a late and minor element, that there was no such *scene* in real life with Murry at all.) Now Gerald is made more secretive, the initiative comes from a Birkin suddenly aware that he must face 'the problem of love and eternal conjunction between two men', and the idea of a once-for-all commitment to blood-brotherhood is at the heart of the episode. There is no embarrassment in Birkin as he makes the offer, but Gerald wants to leave it 'till I understand it better', clearly not understanding that what Birkin is offering isn't homoerotic 'emotionalism' but an 'impersonal union that leaves one free' – a stage in fact towards understanding what he wants from Ursula.[110]

Finally, though, there was the challenge to realise in imagination the effect such a relationship would have on a wife; and to that extent Lawrence's friendship with William Henry, and Frieda's hostility to it, did make an impact on the novel. When in 1917 he finally got round to writing his epilogue, its concern is no longer with what would become of Gudrun. Now, too, the 'emotionalism' of Birkin's grief as he looks at his dead friend is purged by focusing on the bitter waste and denial of a love that might have made a difference. Birkin is clear that the kind of male relation he might have had with Gerald would not have threatened his relationship with Ursula. 'You are enough for me, as far as woman is concerned. You are all women to me. But I wanted a man friend, as eternal as you and I are eternal'. To Ursula however this is 'an obstinacy, a theory, a perversity':

"You can't have two kinds of love. Why should you!"
"It seems as if I can't," he said. "Yet I wanted it."

"You can't have it, because it's false, impossible," she said.

"I don't believe that," he answered.

And the question is left open ...[111]

(c) Look!, and American Literature

At the beginning of August came both the good news that Chatto and Windus had agreed to publish *Look!*; and the bad news that they wanted 'Song of a Man Who is Loved' and 'Meeting Among the Mountains' omitted, two poems renamed and other changes. They admired the book, and told Pinker it was not their desire:

to suggest an emasculated version of Mr. Lawrence's poems, but ... we feel that the number of passages referring to purely physical phenomena should be slightly reduced ... In addition we venture to question the good taste of the titles 'Candlemas' and 'Eve's Mass' as applied to poems of an amorous character. (iii. 145 n. 1)

(They also offered quite generous terms for poetry, twenty guineas in advance and a 15% royalty. Lawrence had begun to be anxious about money again – dropping a heavy hint about another advance, and privately abusive when Pinker failed to respond (iii. 135, 136) – but this, along with the £7/15/0 from *Georgian Poetry* in June and £13/10/0 which was owed from the *English Review*, might tide them over for a while – though there would be a cash-flow problem until the money actually came in.)

After *The Rainbow*, Lawrence could not have been too surprised by Chatto's objections, though he thought them absurd. The minor changes he made at once, though some spoiled 'the clarity and precision of the expression' (iii. 146); and he quickly altered the two titles to 'Valentine's Night' and 'New Year's Night' respectively. He pointed out that 'Meeting Among the Mountains' had already been published without offence in *Georgian Poetry*, and that without it the new volume would not be able to boast that cachet. But though prepared to concede all these, he fought hard to preserve 'Song of a Man Who is Loved', and only gave in, with an ill grace, when Chatto refused altogether to budge (iii. 148). One change from the manuscript he had made himself: the omission of the love-letter, as Catherine had advised.[112] The narrative 'Argument' which took its place kept the essential facts from life, but suggested something more impersonal and representative. On 14 August Lawrence posted the revised manuscript (iii. 148). A week later he sent Pinker copies of the deleted poems in the hope that they could eventually be included in the American edition (iii. 149) – or, perhaps with 'Rabbit Snared in the Night' and one or two others, be published separately in America (iii. 152). He completed the proofs for Chatto towards the end of September (iii. 164).

Palmer's return of the *Women in Love* typescript in late August did not upset him, partly because Palmer seemed 'rather nice' (iii. 152), making it clear that he liked the book and was only deterred by the risk; and partly because Lawrence thought he might do 'At the Gates' instead – though this too proved illusory. When he had been revising, however, he must have realised how the novel would strike Heseltine. Though they had not got as close as before he had a twinge of conscience, for as soon as the manuscript came back he offered it to Gray to read, which would mean that Heseltine (in Dublin) would be told about Halliday and the Pussum. As it happened, however, Gray was about to make a trip to London, the offer was not taken up, and Heseltine's enthusiasm for 'At the Gates' remained undimmed.

The same note to Gray on 25 August mentions that Lawrence had begun his book of essays on 'American Literature' (iii. 151). At first as always he had trouble hitting on a title – 'The Transcendental Element in American (Classic) Literature' (iii. 156); 'The Transcendental Element in Classic American Literature' (iii. 160), 'The Mystic Import of American Literature' (iii. 163) – but it soon becomes clear that ten essays were planned (iii. 154), and that the first 'classic' was to be Crêvecœur (iii. 160). An uneasily jocular letter to Amy Lowell, whose father was President of Harvard, offered her the dedication in the hope that she might influence the *Yale Review* or the *New Republic* (iii.156–7). He also mentioned the project to Waldo Frank (iii. 160), with an eye on *Seven Arts*. Coincidentally however, there arrived from the *Yale Review* early in October an invitation to write '40 or 50 MS. pages about contemporary English novelists'. He presumed this meant Wells, Bennett, Galsworthy, Compton Mackenzie and Gilbert Cannan, but did not 'care a rush for any of them, save Thomas Hardy, and he's not contemporary, and the *early* Conrad, which is also looming into distance' (iii. 166–7). However, he promised to consider and later did write the essay, but before he could do anything about it now, disaster struck.

IX Nightmare

On Thursday 11 October, market-day, Lawrence went to Penzance with William Henry, and his sister Mabel. Frieda made her way to Bosigran. At the day's end (according to *Kangaroo*) Lawrence grew angry at having to hang about until after seven waiting for William Henry to turn up, until theirs was almost the last trap to leave. He would never come to Penzance with him again, he said. When they got home it was to a badly frightened Frieda. The cottage had been searched in their absence, Lawrence's papers had been disturbed and the contents of her sewing basket were scattered all over the floor. She ran to the farm, to be told that men in uniform had come looking for them.[113]

The next morning, the men were back: a young military officer, the police sergeant from St Ives and two Criminal Investigation Department men in plain clothes. They presented a search-warrant, and read out a formal expulsion order signed by Major General W. G. B. Western, in command of Administration, Southern Command, Salisbury, giving them until Monday the 15th to pack up and leave. They would no longer be allowed to enter any area of military significance (including all coastal areas), and were required to report to the local police wherever they decided to go, within twenty-four hours of arrival. No reason was given, no appeal allowed. The subaltern put aside all questions and protests: he was acting under orders, did not himself know the reasons and would not tell them if he did. Meanwhile the CID men, with the cold professionalism of their kind, searched the cottage thoroughly from top to bottom, especially the books and papers. They queried some diagrams in a notebook, though Lawrence explained that they were botanical – many of his earlier poems had been written out in two old University notebooks, one of which contained botanical drawings – and also took away the letters that had come to Frieda from her family, and some papers, including the 'words' of the Hebridean seal song in case they might be in code. The Lawrences were obviously suspected of espionage. (He now had the distinction of having been under suspicion by both German and English soldiery.) Frieda was angry at first, about 'English liberty', and then tearful, protesting their innocence and sure that the persecution was racial, because of her German birth. She must above all have feared that she was going to be interned, despite her eighteen years of citizenship by marriage. Lawrence would indeed have withdrawn into himself, white and stony-faced, telling Frieda to be quiet, determined not to give his persecutors the slightest satisfaction, since they had the power and authority and he was helpless to resist. Stanley Hocking was working near the road as the men went past, and heard one of them say: 'That's a job I would rather not have to do.'[114]

Lawrence sent a note to ask Gray to come and give them moral support (iii. 167), hurriedly begged temporary refuge with Dollie Radford in London (iii. 168–9), and told Pinker and Cynthia Asquith the change of address and briefly what had happened (iii. 168). He probably hoped Cynthia had contacts who could help. Saturday and Sunday they packed – their Sunday dinners sent up from the farm – and Lawrence burned a whole pile of manuscripts and proofs.[115] On Monday they said good-bye to the Hocking family; Lawrence feeling rather upset that Uncle Henry had gone into the fields without waiting, though Stanley later explained that this was just because he was fond of them, and hated good-byes. William Henry drove them to Penzance in the trap while young Stanley followed with the heavy luggage in the cart. On the station an officer and a police sergeant were waiting to make sure that they got on the train, watching silently as the farewells took place. Lawrence was determined to come back, and may have said so. Then they were gone.[116]

To Cynthia, Lawrence said he could not 'conceive how I have incurred suspicion – have not the faintest notion. We are as innocent even of pacifist activities, let alone spying in any sort, as the rabbits of the field outside' (iii. 168). This was true; yet what had happened was not really beyond conceiving. The Mountsier arrest in January had been a danger signal, as had the search of Frieda's shopping bag on the cliff top. Lawrence himself, according to Frieda, had warned her not to wave her scarf about on the rocks, as she might seem to be signalling.[117] As the submarine sinkings mounted in the early part of the year, local hysteria and rumour mongering grew, and it is easy to see how the bearded outsider with the German wife might have become increasingly an object of suspicion; or why the local postman (who was a Wesleyan lay preacher, and beyond military age himself) might have delivered the buff-envelope call-up notices with a certain grim pleasure. The arrival of German newspapers and letters from Germany via Switzerland, would not have helped. If, when ships were sunk in sight of the locals, Frieda was overheard lamenting that the hunted submariners might also be young men like those she had known in childhood, the Cornish were not likely to see her point of view. And when Lawrence angrily denounced the 'lies' in the newspapers to the farmers in Penzance market, or William Henry perhaps talked about his friend's defiant opposition to call-up and war propaganda, these may well have been reported and chalked up against him. Gray even claims that Lawrence may have been overheard threatening to start 'a disruptive, pacifist, and nihilist campaign in the industrial north, with a view to bringing about a speedy end to the war', and though this is a typical exaggeration, Lawrence did express momentary interest in the reports of protest meetings in Nottingham's Victoria Park, and wonder whether he might involve himself; though (as Gray also says, though more rudely) the impulse was fugitive. Moreover the arrival of Heseltine, Gray and Starr – all young men suspiciously avoiding call-up, and holding subversive views about the war – might have fostered a conspiracy theory centring on their 'leader', the one with the German wife. Lawrence also appears to have been right that there was much local resentment over conscription, and there is evidence that there had been *no* volunteers for military service from Zennor, so that Lawrence might have been suspected of further fomenting local resistance to patriotic duty.[118]

Gray later claimed that he and the Lawrences were continually spied on by the locals who skulked in ditches and behind hedgerows to eavesdrop on private conversations – and his own paranoia reached a climax when he came to believe that his life had at one time been threatened.[119] At the centre of Lawrence's 'nightmare' too, as expressed in *Kangaroo*, was the feeling that he must have been surrounded by a miasma of malevolent suspicion and *personal* hatred, his privacy constantly violated by prying eyes, while he lived in blithe ignorance of any such thing.

It is of course impossible to know whether Cornishmen were constantly lurking in the hollow just below the windows of Higher Tregerthen to hear and report on what the Lawrences were saying. Nightmares are frightening precisely because they confound truth, fear and paranoia so that these become indistinguishable. The most dangerous suspicion however was no doing of the Cornish, but the assocation with Mountsier, registered with Scotland Yard and almost certainly also with the military command in Cornwall. By 13 August Lawrence remarked on the odd fact that a letter from Catherine posted on the 9th had taken four days to be delivered (iii. 147); and it seems likely that his mail had been read since January. If letters to him were being read, presumably letters from him would be thought even more significant – though as it happens his letters since April said very little about the war, because of his feeling of withdrawal from the 'unreal' world into the real one of the Cornish landscape and his work. He did however write, after returning from Bodmin in June, 'I should like to flourish a pistol under the nose of the fools who govern us. They make one spit with disgust' (iii. 136) – though of all people he chose Marsh to say it to! But it seems to have been the Lawrences' second weekend at Bosigran that brought matters to a head.

As they sat round the fire in Gray's music-room on the Saturday evening – the wind blowing a gale outside, the Lawrences as ever singing German songs – there came a banging at the door; and there stood a subaltern and three men, one with a lantern. (Lawrence, even in 'Nightmare', is probably more reliable than Gray who speaks of 'half a dozen or so men with loaded rifles' bursting in.)[120] A light had been seen coming from an upper window. This was a serious matter: every issue of the St Ives Times carried a notice of the exact time by which all black-out curtains had to be drawn. Gray denied the possibility, but the officer insisted on a search, and it seems that the curtain to a passage window upstairs had been secured by drawing pins, one of which had worked loose in the wind because the window had been left open. As the curtain flapped, an intermittent light could have shown, as it were in Morse, when Gray's housekeeper crossed with her candle on her way to bed. According to Gray: 'Finding nothing incriminating on the premises, the intruders withdrew, with operatic gestures like a Verdi chorus, and blood-curdling threats to the effect that I would hear more of the matter' – which tells one rather more about Gray than the situation. But hear more of the matter he certainly did, being summoned before the magistrates in St Ives to answer the charge of 'permitting an unobscured light in the house which was visible from the sea'. (Bosigran stood in a prominent position near Gurnard's Head.) Two things made it more serious than Gray had imagined. Though the magistrate accepted his account of the night in question, the deputy coast-watching officer Norman E. Cooke gave evidence that 'numerous complaints had been made of unobscured lights in defendant's house', suggesting more than the momentary passing of a candle on one occasion. 'The Bench took a serious view of the offence, the chairman (Mr David Howell) pointing out that the house was so situated that the light would be a guide to hostile submarines.' Although the same issue of the *St Ives Times* (5 October) remarks how its regular statistics reveal the success of the new defensive measures against submarines, since the number of sinkings had in fact declined markedly and steadily since the spring, a German submarine had recently been reported in the area. Gray was fined £20. It seems highly probable that his attitude towards the episode, and the Lawrences' association with him, may have encouraged the action against them less than a week later.

Yet Gray was not expelled, and the Army authorities in distant Salisbury would probably not have acted merely on local Cornish feeling either, though the Defence of the Realm Act had given them authoritarian powers to prohibit access to strategic areas.[121] What seems most likely is that ongoing suspicion about the journalist spy ring – since Mountsier had been released, but not cleared – coincided with local suspicion peaking in the Gray trial, and perhaps also with a specific denunciation from a source that a senior officer would have thought impeccable. Lawrence himself believed he had a specific enemy; and the Hocking family have suggested that it was the Vicar of Zennor and his daughter who denounced him. There is no other evidence of this, but many clergymen in the First World War led the way in patriotic fervour. Moreover Stanley Hocking, who sang in the choir, remembers being disconcerted when Lawrence challenged the idea of the physical resurrection of the dead, so a vicar – especially if he knew of Lawrence's marital history and the prosecution of his novel for obscenity – might have come to think him a danger to his flock.[122] This would have been increased by his association with the occultist Starr who had publicly praised the satanist Aleister Crowley in the *St Ives Times*. Political, patriotic and religious subversion might have come to seem connected in a subverter of morale. It seems far-fetched now, but the Germans appeared to be winning the war, and a degree of hysteria was understandable, though hardly forgivable in its results. The Major General, if there had been such a denunciation, might well have thought its coincidence with Scotland Yard suspicion merited action, to be on the safe side.

X And What of Frieda?

Lawrence had come to care deeply for his Cornish home, his isolation and the wild prehistoric landscape. The expulsion was a second major trauma from which in some ways he never recovered. He left vowing to find out what had happened, and to return. But it is by no means certain that Frieda felt the same.

The previous October she was already telling Kot that she was 'tired of being here alone',[123] and the coolness with Lawrence after the departure of Esther Andrews in the spring must have increased the loneliness a thousandfold. She was never really friendly with the family at the farm. Stanley Hocking recalled that she did not come and sit in their kitchen as Lawrence did. When she came for the milk it was because he was unwell; and the farm women, particularly, always felt that she was a lady and quite different from them. She was not unfriendly, nor was she disliked. And yet ... In the village too, she was an oddity with her accent and the multicoloured stockings that Katie Berryman – as close to a friend there as she had – would come round the counter to exclaim over; but when Cynthia Asquith sent her a hat she said she would not dare wear it outside the cottage because 'it would astonish the natives too much'. When Lawrence spent more and more time in the fields and with William Henry leaving her alone in the cottage even after dark, she must have become more and more discontented, worried and afraid – as well as angry and jealous. On at least one stormy night she came running down to the farm in fear, and must have been furious to find Lawrence contentedly sitting in the kitchen. The 'Night-mare' chapter seems wholly convincing when it makes 'Harriet' hear the young farmer's good-night to her husband outside the cottage door 'sound like a jeer'.[124] It was a bitter time to her, and she will have let Lawrence know it, with feeling.

Yet the fear must have been as strong as the irritation and the jealousy. For the first time she seemed to have lost some of her power over him; just when her own position had become utterly insecure. She had very few friends in England. On the two occasions when she bade him good-bye on his way to Bodmin to face the call-up, she must have been terrified of what might happen to her – for if he went, or was imprisoned for refusing, what on earth would she do? There was very little money – not even as much as had once been divided in the cottage at Chesham – and she was far more alone and helpless now, than when she had been friends with Katherine, the Cannans, the Garnetts, the Campbells. She must secretly have feared internment if Lawrence were taken. Once again, she may have reminded herself (and pointed out forcibly to him) all she had given up for his sake.

Moreover illness struck her down, unusually, in these last months. In April she had food poisoning followed by colitis and only got better in mid-May; then spent most of August unable to get about because of severe neuritis in her leg. Her hatred of being ill must have made time spent by Lawrence with Esther or William Henry all the harder to accept. Yet the more irritable jealous and forsaken she felt, and let Lawrence know she felt, the greater the attraction of the farm over the cottage must have become to him.

There are signs, however, that Lawrence did try to help, and that things had got better by September. As soon as Frieda recovered in mid-May he tried to persuade Sallie Hopkin to come down and stay (iii. 126); and it may also have been partly to get Frieda some diversion that he wondered at the end of the month whether the Murrys might be coming to Mylor again (iii. 127). In the first part of June there was a visitor, the first since Esther left. This was Mrs Tarry, their next-door neighbour from Byron Villas, and she had clearly been asked down for Frieda's sake (iii. 131). (Indeed he remarked on the 10th that another week of the visit was a week too long for him.) Moreover 'Nightmare' perhaps remembered truly how the Bodmin crisis may have brought him, too, a renewed sense of her importance to him, as 'Harriet' runs to meet 'Somers': 'her face very bright with fear and joy at seeing him back: very beautiful in his eyes. The only real thing, perhaps, left in his world.'[125] Then the coming of Heseltine (who had stood up for her to Ottoline), and the new friendship with Gray, and even the comedy of the Starrs, must also have helped to liven things up – she liked having young men around.

It is not clear, then, how significant it is that she was with Gray at Bosigran the day that the cottage was searched. The gimlet eyes of recent biographers have narrowed, in speculation that she may have been having another affair. Certainly Gray's arrival must have added much-needed interest to her life, though she would have been unable to take much advantage through August, or during the prolonged rains in early September after their first visit to Bosigran. The friendship may have intensified towards the end of the month when Lawrence was helping with the corn harvest, and in sympathy with the 'persecution' of Gray after their weekend in his house. Moreover Frieda was not monogamous, believed in free love, and was always convinced of her power to cure the problems of young men by giving herself to them. Certainly with Hobson (and perhaps in other cases) she was not at all averse to snapping her fingers in her husband's face in revenge for his shortcomings in attention or sympathy. Later, Gray would begin aggressively to take her side in arguments (as Bunny Garnett had done), and Frieda to hint at an affair. She may well have revenged herself for Lawrence's neglect by sleeping with Gray in Cornwall – though actual evidence there is none.

Still she may not have been too displeased to leave their isolation behind, and get back to town.

PART FOUR

◆

A Kind
of
Wintering

CHAPTER EIGHT

October 1917–September 1918

ON A LEDGE

I feel as if I were on a sort of ledge half way down a precipice, and didn't
know how to get up or down ...
(iii. 248)

I London Again

London felt closer to the war than Cornwall. Despite submarine sinkings off the
coast, Lawrence had immersed himself in a natural world for much of the
summer. In London however, as autumn gave way to winter, there was nightly
fear of air raids, and widespread awareness of how very badly the war was going:
the collapse of the Russian front, mutinies of French troops after the heavy
losses on the Aisne, appalling losses for the British in the mud and mustard-gas
of the third battle of Ypres (Passchendaele), and the débâcle of the Italian army
at Caporetto. Throughout 1916 and 1917 the main railway stations had been
crowded with wounded, and with uniformed men on precious but unreal
furlough from the hell of the trenches – incommunicable to civilians, even loving
ones. Since the first apocalyptic Zeppelin raids of 1915, Lawrence had few
contacts with those realities; whereas Richard Aldington, whom he saw within
days of arrival, had been in the trenches from January to July, and though
reasonably sympathetic about what had happened to the Lawrences could not
but see it in a larger perspective. Cynthia had lost not only two brothers and the
brilliant brother-in-law she had been strongly attracted to before they both
married, but also Lord Basil Blackwood whom she loved most of all; and Beb,
shell-shock or no, was back in the trenches. (Catherine was in Edinburgh where
Donald was in a military hospital.)

So when Lawrence wrote to Gray that London had 'gone mad ... thinks and
breathes and lives air-raids ... People are not people any more: they are factors,
really ghastly, like Lemures, evil spirits of the dead' (iii. 170), this was a first
shocked register of what he had been isolated from. When Cynthia suggested he
meet her (now widowed) sister-in-law again, whom he had liked in 1915, he was
'frightened of the misery of her' (iii. 177).

His own situation was precarious. Dollie, as always, had taken them in, but
they could not stay long. The 'Nightmare' chapter of *Kangaroo* pays tribute to

the staunch friendship of the little Fabian lady-poet 'with her cameo face, like a wise child, and her grey, bobbed hair. Such a frail little thing to have gone sailing these seas of ideas, and to suffer the awful breakdown of her husband', whom she still had constantly to nurse. She was far from well and understandably nervous about guests who had to report at police stations – though the Hampstead police took no interest when the Lawrences did so (iii. 170). The little Hampstead house, which David Garnett had described as like a chest of drawers always overflowing, had other calls on it from her grown-up children, and simply was not large enough for the Lawrences to stay, even had they wanted to.[1] Yet they were short of money for London living, and after losing the home they had paid for till next spring, could ill afford another rent.

Their first hope was to borrow her London flat from Gray's mother. Catherine was asked to visit her in the Caledonian Hotel in Edinburgh and did (iii. 169), but nothing came of this immediately. To the rescue with characteristic generosity came Hilda Aldington, described in 'Nightmare' as 'beautiful' and 'reckless'. Richard had been posted back in the summer for officer training and H.D. had been shuttling between London and visits to him at camp in Lichfield. Their close friend Cournos, who was strongly attracted to Hilda but loyally did nothing about it, had taken a smaller room upstairs when she first rented the big drawing-room at 44 Mecklenburgh Square. In August Hilda took in Dorothy ('Arabella') Yorke, Cournos's first love, who arrived unexpectedly from Paris, and he fell deeply in love with her again. When he left for St Petersburg in late 1917 to cover the stirring events in Russia, he begged H.D. to go on looking after her, so Arabella moved into his room.[2] Now Hilda took the Lawrences in, for a few days at first, but they stayed from 20 October till the end of November. They were lent the large room whenever Hilda went to Lichfield; but even when she was at home they managed, by dint of Lawrence taking the room upstairs while Frieda and Arabella shared the double bed and 'H.D.' slept on a camp-bed, all in the big first-floor room with its three great heavily-curtained windows.

At first, Lawrence was intent on getting the banning order undone. He wrote twice to the Major General in Salisbury, and tried to enlist the help of London friends and friends of friends. First was Cynthia, of course, though after the fall of her father-in-law the Asquith influence was lessened. Lawrence went to see her the day after he arrived in London, and she agreed to make enquiries, but without enthusiasm. His case came unfortunately just days after another appeal to the Asquiths, from the splendid Lady Angela Forbes, whom officialdom had at last succeeded (on a trumped-up charge) in ordering out of France where she had been running her famous soldiers' canteens. Here the Asquith influence *was* wheeled out, the ex-Prime Minister himself writing a 'scorcher' to Lord Derby and threatening to speak in the House, but Cynthia clearly found the prospect of taking on the Army distasteful, even in a rather more spectacular case than Lawrence's. She was nonetheless worried about him: he looked 'very gaunt', and she was well aware of the threat of London to his health, and his finances, since 'all the money he has in the world is the *prospect* of eighteen pounds for the publication of some poems all about bellies and breasts which he gave me to read'. But she had divided feelings about what had happened. 'People should either be left in peace *or* interned at the country's expense'; but 'after all, the woman *is* a German, and it doesn't seem unreasonable'.[3] She promised to do what she could, but doubted whether it would be much. If she did approach someone like Harold Baker, who served on the Army Council, had influence with the War Office and had met and liked Lawrence in 1915, he probably took a similar view. Certainly, when Frieda and Lawrence came to tea five days later on 21 October, and Eddie Marsh came in to see them – newly influential again since Lt. Col. Churchill had returned from the trenches to become Minister of Munitions under Lloyd George – 'We were not able to hold out any hopes of their being allowed to return to Cornwall. Their exclusion seems so very reasonable.' Lawrence was 'very sore and sulky' at first, but the old affections proved still to be there, though he said there were only eight people in the world now with whom he could spend more than two hours. He had been feeling cool towards Marsh since the débâcle over *The Rainbow*, but remarked after he left that there was a niceness in him after all; and Cynthia found as before that there was something 'hearty' and 'warming' about Frieda.[4] Yet the most promising sources of help could promise very little.

Campbell was now working in the Ministry of Munitions, and did try to help, though his contacts only produced talk of 'expediency'. Since nothing could be got out of the Major General, it seemed the only hope of discovering and disproving the reasons for their expulsion was from the Under-Secretary at the War Office. First however, on Campbell's advice, Lawrence wrote to Kot's friend Monty Shearman, the rich barrister from whom Kot had borrowed books for him and who was employed by the Foreign Ministry. Could he, perhaps through Jack Hutchinson, find out the reasons 'more directly', or at least discover who 'in the War Office Intelligence Department it would be possible or profitable to approach'? (iii. 175–6). They arranged to meet, but though this made Lawrence another acquaintance, it produced no explanations. Lawrence also asked Cynthia Asquith whether Frank Bigham, Assistant Commissioner of the Metropolitan Police, might know who 'the responsible man' was, whom it seemed impossible to identify or reach (iii. 177). The one significant omission in all this was Murry, who actually worked in the War Office. As it happened he fell seriously ill through overwork in the middle of November, threatened with tuberculosis it was thought, and it was arranged that he should spend the next two months at Garsington; but in late October and early November when

Lawrence did write to the War Office, Murry was presumably at his desk – yet there is no evidence of any effort to contact him. In mid-November the War Office formally replied: they would not be permitted to return to Cornwall (iii. 182). No reason was given.

He had however already begun to rally. At first he had been unable to go on with the American essays or 'do any work – none at all – only read and see people' (iii. 174); and both he and Frieda caught heavy colds; but by the end of October his old psychic resource had begun to operate again. Letters and excited conversation turned to Rananim once more, fostered this time by the Eders to cheer him up. The community was now to be on the lower slopes of the Andes. Relatives of Eder's owned a plantation in the Cauca Valley of Colombia (iii. 174), and Eder himself in his thirties had made an adventurous expedition there, over the Andes; followed (after a spell as a doctor in a mining village on the edge of the Lake District) by another journey 3,000 miles up the Amazon into Bolivia.[5] So now Lawrence day-dreamed excitedly to Catherine. He named his eight people: 'Eder and Mrs Eder, William Henry and Gray, and probably Hilda Aldington and maybe Kot and Dorothy Yorke' (iii. 173), and of course Catherine, though a hospitalised husband and a new baby admittedly created complications. He thought that Gray could find £1,000 – perhaps from something Gray had said about his finances in Cornwall. Since however Gray's allowance was only £200 a year – albeit, having rich parents, he had expectations of much more in time – he was somewhat surprised to discover this long afterwards, especially because Lawrence never mentioned it when he wrote in otherwise similar terms to Bosigran on 29 October (ii. 174). (Nor did Lawrence allow for tension between Hilda and Arabella which had already begun.) In wartime such an escape could only be a day-dream anyway, but as always it lifted his spirits, made him think of something other than his troubles and was a language for the confirmation of friendship – provided the friend would read between the lines. When however Lawrence wrote Gray that the scheme 'seems to occupy my heart', so he would be 'bitterly disappointed if it doesn't mean much to you' (iii. 175), back came practical Scottish doubts. Lawrence's next letter told him to annex the bottle of Hollands gin the next time he went past Tregerthen, and not to be a doubting Thomas (iii. 176); but perhaps Gray's reaction underlined what a paucity of letters had already suggested: 'You are so queer and evanescent, one feels one loses you a bit' (iii. 174). Gray was not one to commit himself (to Lawrence – or to Frieda), let alone to such a hare-brained idea. Besides, he hated mountains. Nevertheless the new Rananim made Lawrence more cheerful and no longer quite so anxious to get back to Cornwall at once: 'One seems to be, in some queer way, vitally active here. And then people, one or two, seem to give a strange new response' (iii. 174).

He was thinking mainly of the Eders as his next sentence shows, and also of

H.D.; for their support and stimulus had helped him get to work again. By 5 November he had done his piece for the *Yale Review* on 'The Limit to the British Novelist' (iii. 177). This probably contrasted his contemporaries with the qualities he had come to treasure in American writers, but unfortunately it has not survived. It came too late for the December number, the next after the article by a Mrs Gerould on which it was to comment, and Wilbur Cross thought it too direct a reply to be adaptable for some future issue.[6] (Lawrence must also have been annoyed by her airy admission that she had not bothered to read *him*, so he may also have been too fierce for Cross's taste; though his title shows he had been frying bigger fish.)

The Eders revived the idea of publication by subscription as the remedy for publishers' faint hearts about *Women in Love* (iii. 178). Edith not only persuaded him to put the idea to Pinker again, but determined to see Pinker herself (iii. 181). Soon came the notion of trying once more for the support of his most reputable authors; and Pinker arranged a lunch with Galsworthy on 16 November (iii. 183). Meanwhile Campbell and Kot suggested an approach to Joseph Hone, whom Lawrence had met at Selwood Terrace, to see whether Maunsel & Co. in Dublin for whom Hone worked as literary editor, and who had published translations by Kot and Murry, might be interested in publishing the novel (iii. 183 and n. 3). (Heseltine, in Dublin, had had the same idea, and drummed up supporting letters, of which one in high praise survives from Nichols.)[7] A feeler came from Fisher Unwin, who had been interested in publishing Lawrence for some time (iii. 184–5). By 28 November these new prospects had stimulated him to get out the typescript of the novel and do some more work on it (iii. 185). Hone had hinted that what *he* would most like to see would be 'At the Gates', which Secker had been looking at (iii. 185 n. 2). *Aaron's Rod* was also begun 'in the Mecklenburg Square days' (iii. 728) – though we do not know how much Lawrence had time to draft there before moving out at the end of November, how it began or whether the inhabitants of the big room were already in it.[8]

Unfortunately all these prospects (except, eventually, the novel) would come to nothing. Heseltine's fears of the conservatism of the partners in Maunsel proved accurate. They first turned down the novel, because 'they don't want to publish any English books during the war' (iii. 187); and then, having illogically asked to see the essays turned them down too, though Hone had been much impressed (iii. 196 n. 2). Nor would Fisher Unwin risk *Women in Love*; and he may also have declined 'At the Gates'. Somewhere in all this toing and froing – and through Heseltine's eventual revenge for Halliday and the Pussum, according to Hone – both typescripts of 'At the Gates' disappeared and have never come to light.[9] The lunch with Pinker and Galsworthy was a disaster. The two writers cordially disliked each other as Pinker must have feared, knowing them both. Lawrence thought Galsworthy a 'sawdust bore' (iii. 183) and knew at once he would loathe *Women in Love* (iii. 185). Galsworthy described 'that provincial genius' as 'Interesting, but a type I could not get on with. Obsessed with self. Dead eyes, and a red beard, long narrow pale face. A strange bird.'[10] Just before leaving London at the end of the year, Lawrence heard that George Moore admired his work (iii. 191). He asked Pinker to make enquiries and wrote to Moore himself in mid-January (iii. 196); but it turned out that what Moore admired was *Sons and Lovers* and to a lesser extent *The White Peacock*. He thought the later works abandoned human persons for 'vague animal abstractions', and advised Lawrence to keep the social classes separate, doubting it was wise to show miners' children or farm workers as having intellectual interests. It is not difficult to imagine Lawrence's reactions. (Frieda had been dismissive about Moore's *Salve* long before.)[11] So the last hope of an Irish salvation for *Women in Love*, or publication by subscription with the support of well-known authors, had to be dropped.

On 26 November, however, *Look! We have Come Through!* appeared. Lawrence was pleased with 'the get-up' (iii. 187) but the prospects were discouraging, since it was preceded by a review in *The Times Literary Supplement* which was kind enough to admit that Lawrence showed 'much of the art of writing and avoids banality', but complained of 'verbiage ... varied by orgies of extreme eroticism', and of 'excited morbid babble about one's own emotions which the Muse of poetry surely can only turn from with a pained distaste'. Though Chatto & Windus wrote reassuringly that Lawrence could dispense with such Muses 'so long as you have the appreciation of those who can recognise literature when they see it', they too were obviously disappointed by the result of sending an early review copy to an influential journal.[12] Serious discussion of the volume had to wait for an American review.

Moreover, a barb about the title had already come from Gray, who dared to question the truth of its claim about the Lawrence marriage. Frieda seems to have written him a satirical letter about Lawrence surrounding himself anew with female worship, Hilda having taken over Esther's role.[13] In reply, Gray followed the pattern of Bunny Garnett: having originally been attracted to the Lawrences as a pair, he began now aggressively to take Frieda's side. Indeed if Frieda had slept with him, it is not hard to see why he should deny Lawrence's claims for his marriage, without realising how relatively little her affairs meant to Frieda, or how Lawrence had tolerated them. But even if matters had not gone that far, enough had happened between the Lawrences in Cornwall since the poems were written to make the full confidence of the title seem more questionable now – especially to a recipient of Frieda's complaints. However, giving Lawrence the lie could hardly fail to bring a tart yet still friendly response.

I don't care what you accept or don't accept, either: it bores me a bit. But don't go throwing about accusations and calling me a liar gratuitously. Look, we have come through – whether you can see it or not. – Perhaps you are right to resent the impertinence of the 'Look!'. None the less, we have come through. – But enough of this – we can leave it alone henceforth, and abstain, me from underworlds etc, you from calling me a liar. (iii. 178)

(Since Gray seems also to have said he was broke, perhaps to explain why he had not yet come up to town, Lawrence sent £5 from money Eder had given him, £4 of it to repay Gray's help with their unexpected train fares up. Lawrence's letter shows once again how he would take criticism from those brave enough to make it to his face, even in personally wounding terms. He clearly did not *like* it; but the payment doesn't signal any break.)

The suggestion that he had been exploring 'underworlds' with Hilda must have come from a jibe of Frieda's at his poetic discussions with H.D., especially of her sequence 'Eurydice' in relation to his 'Resurrection'.[14] He turned the charge back on Gray and Frieda in a second letter the next day – a considered response to the jibe (according to Gray's later memory) that he allowed himself 'to become the object of a kind of esoteric female cult, an Adonis, Atthis, Dionysos religion of which he was the central figure, a Jesus Christ to a regiment of Mary Magdalenes', only too anxious to grease his feet.[15] Lawrence thought Gray only 'half right about the disciples and the alabaster box'. What was wrong lay less with the Magdalene than with 'the discipleship of the twelve'.

As for me and my 'women', I know what they are and aren't, and though there is a certain messiness, there is a further reality. Take away the subservience and feet-washing, and the pure understanding between the Magdalen and Jesus went deeper than the understanding between the disciples and Jesus, or Jesus and the Bethany women. But Jesus himself was frightened of the knowledge which subsisted between the Magdalen and him, a knowledge deeper than the knowledge of Christianity and 'good', deeper than love, anyhow.

He did not at all mind being told where he was wrong, 'not by you or anybody I respect' though he did not think Gray and Frieda were 'going for' him in anything serious. On the contrary, they both needed to go a 'world deeper in knowledge'.

It seems to me there is a whole world of knowledge to forsake, a new, deeper, lower one to *entamer*. And your hatred of me, like Frieda's hatred of me, is your cleavage to a world of knowledge and being which you ought to forsake, which, by organic law, you must depart from or die. And my 'women', Esther Andrews, Hilda Aldington etc, represent, in an impure and unproud, subservient, cringing, bad fashion I admit, – but represent none the less the threshold of a new world, or underworld, of knowledge and being. – And the Hebridean Songs, which represent you and Frieda in this, are songs of the damned: that is, songs of those who inhabit an underworld which is forever an underworld, never to be made open and whole. And you would like us all to inhabit a suggestive underworld which is never revealed or opened, only intimated, only *felt* between the initiated. – I won't have it. The old world must burst, the underworld must be open and whole, new world. – You want an emotional sensuous underworld, like Frieda and the Hebrideans: my 'women' want an ecstatic subtly-intellectual underworld, like the Greeks – Orphicism – like Magdalen at her feet-washing – and there you are. (iii. 179–80)

It is anybody's guess whether Lawrence's linking of Gray with Frieda here implies knowledge of an affair between them in Cornwall, or whether it merely perceives their affinity in the opposition the letter explores, and why Gray was taking Frieda's side against him. The passage in *Women in Love* where Birkin speaks to Gerald about hatred shows also that, for Lawrence, intense temporary hatreds were part of, and not the antithesis to, the development of creative friendship and love. Gray came to London a few days later on 12 November, and Lawrence met him at Paddington.

What happened at 44 Mecklenburgh Square would lead to the breakup of the Aldington marriage, and of relations between Cournos and Arabella, and to a long-lasting rupture between Cournos and Hilda, and to the end of Lawrence's relationships with both Hilda and Gray. It was more complex than dramatic, however – another of those episodes which require to be seen from all sides, especially since no less than five of the protagonists left books which deal with it to varying extents and in differing ways (in one case, moreover, very disingenuously).[16]

II The 'underworld' in 44 Mecklenburgh Square[17]

The Aldington marriage had been strained since the still birth of their child in 1915. Hilda felt that Richard had never understood what the loss of the baby meant to her – Lawrence alone, she thought, had instantly and intuitively known. Moreover the tragedy left her terrified of ever going through it again, so she became unwilling to have intercourse; having also been warned that it would be wiser not to conceive until after the war when she would be less nervy. Richard seems to have accepted this as part of their free marriage, not affecting their intense imaginative and intellectual life as poets together. He may also have resumed an earlier relationship with Brigit Patmore. He agonised about whether to enlist or not but in the end simply waited, till he was conscripted in 1916 after their time with Cournos in Devon. There they had made friends with Carl and Florence Fallas, and Richard became sexually involved with Flo to Hilda's distress. Free marriage or no, she thought her rival common, and feared the relationship would damage Richard the poet. She still tried to hold their marriage together however, and when Richard was called up as a private, training

at Corfe Castle, she went to be close to him there, writing Cournos some intense
and high-flown letters about her concern for the effect on her husband's poetic
spirit of a new existence he found degrading. As his regiment's embarkation for
France grew nearer, in November 1916, there was talk briefly of her going to
America, but she did not.

Instead she took the room in Mecklenburgh Square, with Cournos upstairs –
platonically, despite her having kissed him (after Richard was conscripted) in a
way which seemed to him a might-have-been were it not for their common
loyalty. In December 1916 Richard embarked for Flanders, where he served as
'runner' in a pioneer company engaged in trench digging, narrowly escaping
death more than once. He came back to be an officer cadet at the end of July
1917, Hilda took in Arabella in August, in late September Cournos left for
Russia and Arabella moved into his room. In October Richard came on leave and
kissed Arabella after a party, thereafter becoming increasingly obsessed with her,
though it is not clear when they first went to bed. The Lawrences moved in
when Richard had gone back to Lichfield. When he came on leave again in
December, he knew he would be going back to the trenches at the end of the
year. He openly spent most of his time with Arabella upstairs, and even slept
with her in Hilda's bed. Now the free marriage became intolerable to Hilda,
though she was torn by his belief that he was taking a doomed man's last
satisfaction which he could not get from his wife.[18]

At least so much detail is necessary, in order to understand something of
Hilda's state of mind in late 1917. She already had a special feeling for Lawrence
after 1915, though she had not seen him since his departure for Cornwall. He
also had a special feeling for her. He admired her poetry greatly, but also says
interestingly that he 'feared' it;[19] presumably because of its fusion of intense
feeling with cool impersonal 'Greek' and Imagist control, a contrast with his
own work that he could respect. They wrote letters and sent poems to each
other in 1916 and 1917 – partly because Hilda acted for Amy Lowell in
collecting poems for the successive Imagist anthologies, and was for a while the
literary editor of the *Egoist* after Richard was called-up (and until T. S. Eliot
took over); but also in mutual respect, though their poetic positions were very
different. In August 1916 she asked him why he did not write 'hymns to fire', or
love poems to a tree (ii. 645) – for she thought his poetry too insistently personal.
In March 1917 she thought the *Look!* poems 'too much body and emotions'
(iii. 102). She never did tell him what she thought of *Women in Love*, but *Bid
Me to Live* suggests that she found it long, confused and too sex-obsessed,
though she knew there was precious ore in it that she had been unable to
'dredge' out.[20]

These general criticisms are authenticated and explained by the contrast of
her own poetry; yet her 'novel' also shows how they conceal the depth of her

own response to Lawrence's poems, and especially his letters. One has to be careful how one uses *Bid Me to Live* as a source; but though (reaching its final form so long after the events it describes) its chronology is imprecise and sometimes confused, and its intensely brooding subjectivity a condition of its power, it strikes one as having been so refined by self-examination and exactitude of language – 'She brooded over each word, as if to hatch it' – as to seem remarkably authentic, from her point of view. It was in the rose poems of *Look!*, and especially the greatest of them, that she found the inner 'gloire' which for her linked Lawrence with Van Gogh as the archetypal artists who bid her to live and showed her what to live for: to capture the inner glory in all things. Long before the Lawrences came to Mecklenburgh Square she had read into two poems he sent her at Corfe Castle a personal message, a signal: 'You sent out a flare to me, that time in Dorset, before [Richard] went. Couldn't you have waited till he had gone?'[21] Here ironies begin. One of the two can be identified for certain: 'On That Day', to be published later in *New Poems*. In her unpublished 'Compassionate Friendship' she wrote: 'My heart contracted when I opened the book and found that poem he had sent me at Corfe Castle – was it in 1917 [it was summer 1916] ... There was that other poem "when you are dead I will bring roses and roses to cover your grave". It seems I had been dead, but the roses were to come later.'[22] 'On That Day' was in fact a revised version of a much earlier poem originally titled 'Her Birthday' and was an elegy to Lawrence's mother – but H.D. clearly took its strewing of roses, because 'you were brave' and 'a still queen' *personally*. The other poem (I think) was 'Resurrection', written at the end of 1915: an Orphic poem which shows the poet issuing forth like a frail flower from an 'embassy' into the underworld of death, emerging now like a cyclamen, a crocus, into an earth 'bitter ... amid the smoke/ From burning fires of many smouldering lives,/ All bitter and corroding to the grave'. Yet for all the frailty of the flower, 'I lift my inextinguishable flame/ Of immortality into the world,/ Of resurrection ...'[23] The imagery finds an inverted echo in H.D.'s 'Eurydice', which we know she began to write at Corfe Castle, and which figures in *Bid Me to Live*. The drafts remembered there, however, are about letting Orpheus go; while the final poem of May 1917 has become Eurydice's intense but controlled lament and reproach for Orpheus's backward look that has plunged her into hell again, when she might have lived once more. Yet 'hell is no worse than your earth' and 'At least I have the flowers of myself, / ... I have the fervour of myself for a presence/ and my own spirit for light.'[24]

So she seems to have seen Lawrence as, once again, *understanding* what she had gone through in having to 'give up' Richard (in more ways than one) in 1916, and as having sent her a personal message of tenderness and admiration for her courage and quietness under stress. His *Look!* and her 'Eurydice' must also have seemed to her ironically related. She was probably mistaken, however, to read a personal message into the sending of 'On That Day'. Lawrence had worked on it in Porthcothan, and it may simply have been among the recently finished poems that he sent with an eye on the Imagist anthology or the *Egoist*. There would be no doubt about his sympathy, however, and he certainly heard from her in August 1916 about Aldington's conscription (and perhaps her unhappiness). Unfortunately the whole correspondence has disappeared. Lawrence hardly ever kept letters; and Aldington, anxious in later years to minimise his ex-wife's relationship with Lawrence, burnt his to her, which she had kept in a red box with a miniature of her mother. Yet it was those letters which were for her the essence of Lawrence, 'just ordinary letters that you could chuck across a breakfast-tray to any husband, but that yet held the flame and the fire, the burning, the believing'.[25] There were only three or four of them, but she brooded over some of their sentences like talismans or runes, and one way of looking at *Bid Me to Live* is as an extended commentary and answer. Her 'Eurydice' was originally a dramatic dialogue, but Lawrence did not care for the Orpheus bit and told her to stick to the woman's point of view. This was not, as she imagined, because he thought of male and female as utterly distinct – if she had been able to read his novels she would have known that his view of sexuality was as 'mixed' as her own – but 'Go back to your frozen altars', though meant as advice about her poem, echoed in her mind also as a rune about herself and her frigidity. Later, she must have told Lawrence more about the state of her marriage, in letters which were primarily for other reasons. In October 1916 she asked for poems for the anthology, and told him she was not going to America but to Mecklenburgh Square. He sent her 'Terranova' (ii. 664 and n. 1; which became 'New Heaven and Earth' in *Look!*). In March 1917 she enclosed some of Amy's poems in a letter which was 'very sad and suppressed, everything is wrong' (iii. 105). It was probably now that he sent her a box of lettuces and carnations from his garden, and wrote a letter to cheer her up, and to counsel the courage to change. The sentences she broods over in the 'novel' sound like Lawrence made over into her own voice, but whatever he originally said, she turned into runes: 'Kick over your tiresome house of life, our languid lily of virtue nods perilously near the pit'. 'You are a living spirit in a living spirit city'. Significantly also, however, 'You are entangled in your own dreams.'[26]

So when he came to Mecklenburgh Square, just as her misery over Richard's new consignment of her to a kind of hell was intensifying, Lawrence was already firmly established in her mind as a source of sympathy and light. He on his part was also in the depths, but moved by her coming to the rescue. On the first evening (according to *Bid Me to Live*), 'Rico' [Lawrence] sat, sea-tanned and sun-tanned, still with the dust of Cornwall as it were on his corduroys and boots, with 'Elsa' [Frieda] on one side of him and 'Julia' [Hilda] on the other, and declared that they three were pledged once and for all: 'our love is written in blood, for all eternity'.[27] Lawrence's idea of Blutbrüderschaft went beyond the ups and downs of merely personal feeling; but Julia takes it as a personal declaration of love which, in her state of mind over Rafe/Richard and Arabella, is all the more life-giving.

If this happened – and it sounds convincing – it might well lie behind Frieda's sarcasms to Gray about a repeat of the episode with Esther, only worse. For the impassioned discussion between the two poets of Orpheus and Eurydice – hence Frieda's and Gray's jibes about 'underworlds' – coupled with Hilda's spiritual intensity and worship of Lawrence, would have seemed to Frieda to combine Ottoline's soul-mush with Katherine's intellect and attractiveness: just the ardent and bodiless intercourse that she most disliked, and that had caused the flaming row when the Murrys had been at Tregerthen. Hilda in full cry could be beautiful as a Greek statue sprung to impassioned life, her tall gawkiness become graceful, with an intensity of poetic speech that those who disliked her could caricature but which could also be charismatic. To have someone like that 'at Lawrence's feet', like the Magdalen wiping the ointment with her hair, would have been irritating to say the least.

There was, however, no rumpus this time, though there was some tension (such as 'You damn fool Frederico – I can tell you – ', followed by 'Shut-up, shut-up, shut-up, you damn Prussian, I don't want to hear anything you can tell me'). That, however, was not unusual; and nothing is more authentic in *Bid Me to Live* than the picture of Elsa 'placidly hemming the torn edge of an old jumper. Her work-bag spilled homely contents on the floor' or chainsmoking, with a cigarette hanging out of the corner of her mouth 'like an Uhlan'.[28] It must have helped that Hilda obviously liked Frieda, and was in no doubt of how centrally Lawrence's life and work were dependent on his marriage, though she was amused at Frieda's proprietary air. However Rico's rather theatrical pledge is countered in the novel by Elsa's 'This will leave me free for Vanio [Gray].' Authentic or not, joke or serious, warning or real intention, there is no means of telling; and Hilda who might have discovered the truth later from Gray, seems not to have done so. ('Elsa had or would have or had had a young friend [lover?], a musician.') At the time Julia interprets Elsa permissively, and so, if *Bid Me to Live* is accurate, did Arabella when told about this on a shopping expedition with Frieda.[29] So, left alone one afternoon with Lawrence, there occurred one of the crucial episodes in Hilda's life.

In *Bid Me to Live* she describes Rico sitting, scribbling absorbedly in a notebook, while Julia gazes out of the window at a branch of a plane-tree etched across the sky. Suddenly she senses him looking at her, a look (she feels) of deep communication. She pulls her chair close to him, and puts her hand upon his arm. He flinches away – though she never knew whether it was repulsion, a *noli me tangere* (Lawrence did in fact hate to be touched unexpectedly), or because he hears the voices of Elsa and Bella at the door. How does his flinching consort with the theatrical pledge written in blood for all eternity? Afterwards she wonders whether she should go up to him, in the little room upstairs.[30]

But she did not go – and for much of her life she went on wondering why, and whether it was the right decision, or where the other choice might have led. She subsequently connected it with two Blakean visions which did lead somehow to the centre of her psyche: one of a transfigured man with leaping dolphins behind him, partly someone she had just met, but looking with Lawrence's eyes; and another of a woman climbing steps into the sun, a vision of Nike, victory. When she had her analysis with Freud she propped a picture of Lawrence the life-giver on the mantelpiece of her hotel bedroom. It was because of Freud's advice to try to tell *her* truth of the whole episode and its aftermath that she struggled to write *Bid Me to Live*.[31]

Their relationship clearly meant more to her than to Lawrence, and she probably misunderstood his meaning on several occasions. Yet his letter answering Gray's attack on him (pp. 415–16 above) fails to do justice to the depth of his feelings. The distinction he draws may appear at first simply the old split between the sensual and the spiritual, but in fact is saying something more and different – though it does tend to confirm the basically non-carnal nature of his feelings for Hilda. The essential distinction he draws is between a mode of relation between the sexes which is merely sexual, and one which is sexual/religious in that its essence (whatever the nature of its expression) has to do with transforming the self through its 'death' and 'resurrection'. The first kind is secretive, sensual, remaining underground, between selves that will not change. The other sheds old selves in the 'underworld' of the unconscious in order to emerge in new and open life. The Magdalen understood this – hence the symbolism of the anointing as for a grave – as Christ's friends never did until after the crucifixion. (Hilda might also have described herself as 'passionately religious'.) The letter surprisingly links Frieda with Gudrun – so 'suggestive' with both Gerald and Loerke – rather than with Ursula – but that is a diagnosis of the nature of her relationship with Gray, however far it had gone, in contrast with her marriage to himself which was always out in the open, even to excess, and which he had no intention of betraying with Hilda (as probably with Esther). Yet in recognising that his relationship with Hilda was primarily 'ecstatic subtly-intellectual' in keeping with her nature, the letter does not perhaps acknowledge that the other side of the marriage of opposites was also a possibility. For though his marriage still held, it had quite definitely grown less close and more threatened in 1917. And if *Bid Me to Live* can be trusted, Lawrence too had a dream vision after the opportunity foregone. The next morning, Rico tells Julia, 'You were singing in a dream. I woke and found my face wet with tears.' (This suggests that we should look for his real rendering of Hilda in the future transformation of 'The Thimble' into 'The Ladybird', rather than in the portrait of a rather febrile neurotic which was all he needed for *Aaron's Rod*.)[32]

The effect on Hilda of this rejection – if that is what it was – was yet to come, after the Lawrences had left London. Meanwhile it is important to stress that they were living quite a lively social life outside Mecklenburgh Square, and were also subject to a stress of which *Bid Me to Live* says nothing.

III A Life on the Surface

They visited Cynthia Asquith several times, and entertained her also to an omelette lunch cooked by Lawrence on the primus in the Bloomsbury room. She persuaded him to come and watch Augustus John painting her portrait, and there was even talk of John doing a 'head' of him, though that came to nothing. The visit wasn't as disastrous as the one to Douglas Grant, but Lawrence's manner was again somewhat challenging. He was not impressed with the portrait, and though he liked John he thought him a spent force, a 'drowned corpse' (iii. 176) (presumably in alcohol), and kept muttering 'Mortuus est.'[33]

That season, Lady Cunard had lent Cynthia a box, one day a week, for the repertory of opera directed by Thomas Beecham at Drury Lane, and she took the Lawrences on several occasions. They saw *Madam Butterfly* (with Ada, on a flying visit), Moussorgsky's *Khovantchina*, and both *The Magic Flute* and *The Seraglio*. On the night of *Aida* Augustus John was of the party, together with a resplendent Guards Officer Yvo Grenfell, who was told by Frieda that her German brother-in-law's uniform was much grander than his. Lawrence asked whether he could bring Arabella to *The Seraglio*: 'American girl – elegant but poor – lives in this house – usually lives in Paris – like her very much' (iii. 183). Cynthia had also asked Yvo Grenfell again, and Robert Nichols whom Lawrence had not seen since 1915.[34] After Gray came up in mid-November he fulfilled an ambition to introduce Lawrence to the other neglected 'genius' he greatly admired, the composer Bernard Van Dieren. (With Heseltine, Gray had organised a recital of Van Dieren's music in the Wigmore Hall before they went down to Cornwall, and had come to blows with a critic over him in the Café Royal.) To his great disappointment now, his two lions had nothing to say, indeed found each other instantly antipathetic.[35]

Lawrence also of course saw Kot and Gertler, and through them got to know Monty Shearman. He saw something of Campbell, visited the Radfords in Hampstead, and probably the Eders too. When Aldington came down from Lichfield – the Lawrences having then to move to Mrs Gray's flat in Earls Court – there was a great poets' evening in the big room, 'four poets and three non-poets all fighting over poetry: a splendid time'. Nichols was probably the fourth poet since he certainly came to Mecklenburgh Square; though Lawrence also met the American John Gould Fletcher that December, and found him more 'hyper-sensitive' and less 'hearty' than he expected (iii. 190).[36] Cynthia introduced him to Charles Whibley, her literary mentor, the influential critic and editor who had known Whistler, Mallarmé and Valéry in Paris, and would influence T. S. Eliot. He thought Whibley perceptive, though across a generation gap (iii. 187). After the isolation in Cornwall, all this amounted to a fairly frenetic social existence.

They stayed in Mrs Gray's flat for the first fortnight in December. Though it tided them over, Lawrence loathed being there and looked to Cynthia altogether out of place. He thought it 'bourgeois' and 'with a retired Admiral downstairs' the epitome of 'the whitewashed devil of middleclass-dom' (iii. 186). However ungrateful this sounds, he had a new reason to see evil under the veneer of establishment respectability. (Fletcher had been surprised at his hatred for England, though he correctly ascribed it to underlying love, disillusioned.)[37] As if it were not enough that he had been thrown out of his home by the Army, and newly forbidden to return by the War Office, he was now being investigated by plain-clothes detectives from the CID. Gray, visiting on 11 December, came on one of these outside his mother's door, who subjected him 'to a mild form of third-degree examination concerning the Lawrences and my relations with them, which eventually reached such a pitch of impertinence and offensiveness that I told him to clear out or I would throw him out'. The man said there had been a letter from Cornwall, which implied to Lawrence that some particular enemy there was writing to one department after another (iii. 188). (It may, however, have come from the St Ives police, asking Scotland Yard where the subversives had got to. The Lawrences had reported themselves as instructed, both in Hampstead and at Bow Street – but a combination of poor communications and slow bureaucracy may have been responsible for this new persecution.) Aldington was visited and examined too, by a sleuth who also asked about Lawrence's books. (It may have helped that Aldington was now a commissioned officer.) So when Nichols supposed Lawrence's account of having been followed to Mecklenburgh Square by two men mere paranoia, he was very probably unjust.[38] 'Now this is *impossible*', wrote Lawrence to Shearman (iii. 189), asking for his help again, and he appealed also to Cynthia to contact her acquaintance the Assistant Commissioner of the Metropolitan Police (iii. 188). (She probably did not. She was being ardently courted by the war hero Brigadier Freyberg V.C. at the time.) On all sides were pressures to leave London. Mrs Gray needed her flat, Richard had still a fortnight of his last leave before the trenches again and (as Lawrence wrote to Amy), it felt 'hateful and humiliating and degrading' to be dogged by detectives, just 'because one has a beard and looks not quite the usual thing' (iii. 190). Fortunately, Margaret Radford was back in Hampstead now, and the cottage at the Hermitage was free. By 18 December they were there.

First, however, there was a farewell party at Mecklenburgh Square, at which everybody must have been very keyed up. The tensions generated by Richard's affair with Arabella were at their height. Arabella was as upset by Hilda's spiritual stranglehold on him – after apparently consenting to their relation as long as it was reasonably discreet – as Hilda was by their sexual obsession with each other and his brutal insensitivity to herself. Lawrence (according to *Bid Me to Live*) thought Arabella was suffering from suppressed hysteria, and this may well have been true. With her mother – whom he thought an '*entrepreneuse*' and Cournos portrayed as living vicariously through her daughter's amours – Arabella had been living on the edge in Paris, having an affair which may have ended in an abortion; and was deeply upset at having lost both the man and the child. Like Esther, she worked for a fashion magazine, and Cynthia thought her very chic. She dressed spectacularly 'like a drawing in *Vogue*'; she had up-slanting eyes, high cheek-bones and shiny black hair which could give her a touch of the Red Indian, or (drawn tight into a bun with hairpins) of the geisha (see Illustration 42); and she used elaborate make-up that could make her seem expressionless. She also had rather a toneless voice. But her feelings ran deep. She told Hilda that she had never come between a man and his wife before and had not intended to now[39] – but the attraction to Richard was no casual affair for her, as time would show. She would have been more and more on edge as the time for Richard's departure (and Cournos's return) grew nearer. Richard, for his part, was edging closer and closer to a nightmare that only those who had gone through it could possibly imagine. He very probably expected to die, for the casualty rate among subalterns was the highest of all. He must have been deeply fearful because he was imaginative and intelligent; and his feelings about the two women must have been in turmoil despite the egotism that told him he had a right to a last fling because of his wife's frigidity. Hilda was now upset about Lawrence as well as about Richard and Arabella; and Gray, whatever his relation to Frieda may have been, was showing signs of attraction to Hilda now, which will have pleased neither Frieda nor Lawrence. (Stirred into the mix was an Irish ex-Gordon Highlander, Captain J. R. White, who had served in the Boer War and had been active in Irish politics – but more of him later.)

Tensions would have been heightened by drink – and Lawrence, always sensitive to atmosphere, seems to have been wound up into the 'satyr' whom Hilda had seen once or twice in Mecklenburgh Square. She describes Rico imitating the landlady and how he had charmed her; and waxing malicious about Arabella's mother, his face a satyr mask red-bearded, teeth showing and eyes wrinkled with laughter, the voice going up into a high whinny in mimicry keenly observed and very funny – so long as you were not the butt.[40] Now, confronted as it were by the tragic, he made a satyr-play which embodied his sense of how the actors were pairing off, and drew some sardonic implications. It was the old Genesis story of sin in the garden that he made them play out.[41] Arabella and Richard were of course Adam and Eve, unable to resist their impulses. Splendidly, Frieda – pupil of Gross – was cast as the serpent-embodiment of sexual temptation, rebellion and stirring-up, and took her part with great good humour, wriggling on the floor and making growling noises until it was objected that serpents do not. Lawrence himself (as always) played God Almighty, her Opposite, doubtless very Puritan, dogmatic and fruitily biblical of speech, for he was good at taking himself off too. Gray, calm and fair-haired, with drawn umbrella, but far from angelic in fact, was none the less well cast as the angel at the gate who always ultimately fended you off – implying a sardonic comment on whatever the relation with Frieda may have been, and on the chances for Hilda of a compensatory pairing. (If Lawrence did say, as Rico does, that she and Gray were 'made for each other' it may have been a touch of spite and jeering as she suggests, or perhaps, given what would happen later, something more perceptive.)[42] Lawrence's genuine feeling for Hilda, however, came out in the role he gave her – for she was the Tree of Life, the helpless centre of the garden, whose real value was disregarded by Adam and Eve and known only to one of the players, albeit forbiddingly. If he now bade her to live, indeed dance, it was because of the life he saw in her.

All the same he may have been quite glad to get away from London and the nerve strain of the Aldingtons. He had liked Dollie's cottage on the edge of the woods when he had stayed there briefly earlier in the year – though when they arrived now on 18 December there was 'snow everywhere, and sharp frost: very cold but very pretty' (iii. 191). He was not in any case intending to stay much beyond Christmas, for he planned to go north with his sister Ada when she came back from a visit to Portsmouth. He asked Kot to meet her at Marylebone on her way down ('a tallish thin woman with dark furs, in a pale bluey-grey long coat'; iii. 192); and then to accompany her to Waterloo; but she was too independent for that, and made them laugh afterwards about Kot's 'pseudo-monocle [he seems to have broken one lens of his glasses], and your serious outgaze, and the relief you evidenced in fleeing' (iii. 193). Margaret Radford came to the cottage for a day or two, but they were then alone again, with 'a sort of buried-alive feeling which is very disagreeable' (iii. 192).

It must have been a very quiet Christmas; and by 28 December they were in the snowy Midlands. Ada now proposed to find a cottage for them in her neighbourhood, and necessarily at her expense. Lawrence did not like this, but tried to lessen his discomfort by telling Kot that the war would end soon, so he and the Lawrences could go to Russia and leave the cottage to his sister (iii. 193). Meanwhile they would come back to Hermitage in the New Year, temporarily. On 29 December he told Gertler that he was really 'better and happier in the country' and did not mind the cold, though this sounds like cheering himself up about a situation that gave him no choice. However he also confessed, while promising talks on what Gertler called 'deep subjects', that he found himself becoming more unsociable than ever: 'It is only at rare sympathetic moments that I feel like talking ... Yes, we will try to meet and talk. But my heart shuts up against people – practically everybody – nowadays. One has been so much insulted and let down' (iii. 194). While continuing to believe that they must all find new life or die, he thought it would have to be in themselves and not through Gertler's preoccupations, love or work – neither of which (it would appear) struck him as having been very successful in his own case as he looked back over 1917 – a gloomy verdict, though understandable.

IV Hermitage

They came back to Hermitage about 11 January 1918, Lawrence having caught 'just the wrong kind of chill' (iii. 195) in the Midlands. The cottage seemed cold and comfortless. For a week or more he sat in bed, not writing anything, but amusing himself learning twenty or thirty songs from *The Oxford Songbook*: among them 'The Camptown Races' (Frieda remembered), 'All Through the Night' and 'My Wife and I Live All Alone'.

They were not quite alone. They soon began to make friends with the Browns next door, the other half of Chapel Farm Cottage, and especially with little Hilda who formed a habit of dropping in after school. After a while she would stay for meals and singsongs, and Lawrence would help with her homework, waxing caustic over her teacher's failure to suggest short cuts in arithmetic. Later, when three soldiers were temporarily billeted next door, Hilda slept in the Lawrences' cottage. (The corporal stayed on until after the Armistice.)[43]

At first there were the inevitable enquiries by the police, discreetly after dark, but also once when Lawrence was working in the Browns' garden as he liked to do; but these stopped before long and life became very quiet.

He remained unwell for some time; the chill turning into a sore throat which was still bothering him in mid-February (iii. 208). He had however come to terms with the loss of Cornwall and felt no more longings to be back near the sea. Chapel Farm Cottage was at the very edge of Hermitage, across the track from the old farmhouse. The front bedroom window looked out over a field to the roofs and trees of the village. Behind was all woodland.

As the evening falls, and it is snowy, there is a clear yellow light, an evening star, and a moon. The trees get dark. Those without leaves seem to thrill their twigs above – the firs and pines slant heavy with snow – and I think of looking out of the Tregerthen window at the sea. And I no longer want the sea, the space, the abstraction. There is something living and rather splendid about trees. They stand up so proud, and are alive. (iii. 197)

It was a worry to know what to do about Higher Tregerthen, even so. He tried to sublet to Leonard and Virginia Woolf (iii. 198–9),[44] and later to first one and then another single lady, hoping that he could cling on to the lease of at least the smaller cottage. His correspondence with Captain Short, the owner, ran into difficulties, then eased into friendship once more. But though he was not quite ready to let go of his lease entirely, and still wanted to pay a farewell visit, he felt fairly sure that he would never live there again.[45]

This distancing was also true of his relationship with William Henry and indeed with all the Hockings, though he had news of them from Katie Berryman in January, and occasional letters, later, from Mary and Stanley. He had written to William Henry between October and Christmas but had no reply. The Cornish farmer was 'no correspondent' according to his brother, and though when they left he 'talked of coming to London soon' (iii. 181) it had never seemed very likely that he would get away.[46] In November Lawrence had told Gray, rather sourly, that he believed Mrs Hocking missed them most (iii. 179); and when his gloom deepened now towards the end of February, and the longing for Rananim, if only 'for a month or two', revived (iii. 214), William Henry's name was no longer on the list of candidates.

The generally anti-social mood before Christmas had deepened. He was momentarily touched when Heseltine sent from Dublin a reproduction from the Book of Kells (iii. 196); and pleased to hear that Ivy Low's new husband Litvinov had become the Plenipotentiary in London for the Russian revolutionary government. He even thought of offering help, though he did not suppose he would be 'much use at this point' (iii. 210). Yet these were gestures across a gap. More recent friendships were cooling too. Though he wrote to Gray still, his tone lacked warmth (iii. 197–9); and Aldington irritated him by seeing himself as Christ-like, about to be sacrificed in the trenches to atone for mankind (iii. 197). Some old friendships still held firm – Cynthia, Catherine, Kot, Gertler – but they were very few, and soon he would be telling Gertler that they all lived now in 'a state of tension against everything' (iii. 215), including each other. His state, in fact, was far worse than in early 1917, when the first thaw had worked its usual magic in him too. The end of January at Hermitage was warm, the snowdrops were out, but he thought of autumn rather than spring; and though birds sang loudly in the woods and 'One almost feels like a bird oneself, whistling out of the invisible' (iii. 201–2), the 'almost' marks the difference from the winter before. 'There's nae luck aboot the hoose', he wrote to Cynthia (iii. 202); and told Gray he was 'not very friendly lately. But ones self seems to contract more and more away from everything, and especially from people. It is a kind of wintering. The only thing to do is to let it *be* winter' (iii. 197). It did not help that his chill had become 'the very devil of a bad throat ... which gives me a queer feeling as if I was blind – why, I don't know. – and makes me talk in a senile fluty squeak very ignoble' (iii. 209). It helped still less that he was rapidly running out of money again, and more seriously than at any time since late 1914 – when at least he had had a novel in manuscript that a publisher thought commercially publishable after revision.

The hope that Maunsel might risk *Women in Love* having collapsed like all its predecessors, only private publication remained a last possibility to keep hope alive. When Michael Sadleir asked him to contribute to an anthology to be called *New Paths: Verse, Prose, Pictures 1917–1918*, Lawrence sent two poems, 'Labour Battalion' and 'No News';[47] and gratefully accepted Sadleir's offer to sound out his publisher Cyril Beaumont (who had also been a friend of Cynthia's brother Yvo) about doing the novel too. Might Beaumont be persuaded to publish if supplied with a list of subscribers? Might Cynthia approach Prince Bibesco again, and talk him into giving the scheme his patronage? Bibesco was involved with Cynthia's sister-in-law Elizabeth whom he eventually married that year, though at this particular moment the affair was on the rocks. Lawrence knew nothing of that – but at the back of his mind he must have suspected, by this time, that the chances of doing anything at all with the novel were slim.

In February he was 'coming to the last end of all my resources, as far as money goes' (iii. 205). He asked Pinker to approach Arnold Bennett yet again as a 'good-natured author' who was 'quite rich out of literature', for help to tide him over; but when Pinker passed on the letter, Bennett did not much care for its aggressive antagonism to the world and the public. Nevertheless he offered £1 a week for at least a year provided others would help too. He seems to have had Wells and Galsworthy in mind. (He also, secretly, gave Pinker £25 to help in a crisis.)[48] The proviso for regular help, however, predictably annoyed Lawrence when he heard of it; Pinker told Bennett, and that was that. In fact three such gifts would have solved Lawrence's difficulties, but Pinker already knew what Galsworthy's reaction would be, and obviously thought too little of the chances of finding other benefactors to take the matter any further. He also let a fortnight go by in silence, until in mid-February with 'exactly six pounds nineteen shillings in the world' (iii. 207), Lawrence was forced to write again and confess that 'in another fortnight I shall not have a penny to buy bread and margerine' (iii. 211). Pinker bestirred himself to extract a last (and, given its record, a surprisingly quick) payment for the recent appearance of 'Love' and 'Life' in the *English Review* (iii. 217). (He may however have advanced the nine guineas himself as he had done before, or have taken it out of Bennett's gift.)

Pinker also generously offered to let Lawrence's existing debt to him 'stand aside' (iii. 213). Meanwhile Gertler, asked to think of a possible patron (iii. 209), had not only approached Monty Shearman but told Kot as well, so that two cheques for £10 arrived (iii. 215). Shearman was rich; but Kot was not, and this was a worrying time for him because of the death of the proprietor of the Russian Bureau and the uncertainty of what might happen to it. Lawrence was greatly touched. When Cynthia sent another £5 (iii. 217), perhaps from Bibesco, the immediate crisis was over. Yet, as had happened in 1914, Lawrence so hated having to depend on charity that he lashed out with every appearance of ingratitude. Shearman managed to help without affronting his touchy pride, but that pride still needed a target to work rage off on – no matter how unfairly: 'It is damnable people like Pinker, my agent, who dangle a prospective fish on the end of a line, with grinning patronage, and just jerk it away every letter, that make me see red. I've got quite a lot of murder in my soul: heaven knows how I shall ever get it out' (iii. 216).

At the end of February Dollie Radford decided to bring her husband for a few days in the country, which meant of course that the Lawrences would have to move out temporarily. They found rooms with a Mrs Lowe in the village, but again the irritation spurted: 'Tomorrow Dollie Radford comes here with the madman ...' (iii. 218). Yet it was precisely her loyalty that he loved, respected and benefited from; and the irritation soon worked off. Hilda Brown remembered a 'really musical evening' around Bessie Lowe's piano; and it was now too that the Lawrences introduced themselves to two young women who were trying to run Grimsbury Farm, just outside the village. Not long before, Cecily Lambert had had her first glimpse[49] of Lawrence striding through the village, and Frieda 'hurrying along' behind, 'panting and rather dishevelled, trying vainly to catch up the man in front, who sped along on his toes almost as if he were being propelled by an invisible force and appearing as if he were trying to escape from the woman'. Actually he was hurrying to catch the post.

When they turned up at the farm, Cecily and her cousin Violet Monk were none too pleased to have visitors after an exhausting day, but they lit a fire in the parlour and produced all they had, bread and jam, and so began a friendship. (Before the Lawrences went north after Easter there would be a return visit to the cottage for dinner, cooked by an animated Lawrence whom Cecily remembered as 'very friendly and jolly', apart from a contretemps over the 'toffee-prunes' which Frieda had failed to soak before syruping and which were thus bullet-hard under the candy coating. Yet good-humour was recovered, Cecily had her first taste of gin, and they had 'a really enjoyable evening'.)

V A Trip to London

Early in March Lawrence went to London for a few days to try to change things for the better. They had not been able to afford the fares before, and these days there were also difficulties in staying with other people, for the German submarines had forced the introduction of food rationing. He would take food with him if Kot could put him up at Acacia Road. Frieda would stay behind. Her half-yearly visit to the children was due shortly, and though she missed London and wished they were nearer, she would wait her turn.

He wanted to meet Beaumont, and discover whether the private publication of *Women in Love* was practicable, but he went to see Cynthia first. She thought he looked 'well – not his gauntest – and he was in good talking form', indeed she had never known him 'nicer'. They talked over the idea – though Cynthia got the title wrong in her diary, muddling it with 'Goats and Compasses'. He had worked himself up into optimism now that 'Ottoline no longer minded about the book'. This was very wishful thinking. Asked by Kot a fortnight earlier how he felt about Ottoline, he had agreed that she was 'very nice, somewhere. I once was *very* fond of her – and I am still, in a way' (iii. 213), though the friendship was dead. He then characteristically projected his feelings onto her, and began to convince himself that she must feel the same. He embarrassed Gertler, who was spending a great deal of time at Garsington now, by asking him to sound her out about the book. Cynthia however had reason to be sceptical. Two days earlier she had lunched with Bibesco, hoping to discover whether he would help; but at table Desmond MacCarthy, who she thought might have been helpful, had spoken of Ottoline's pain at the 'obvious lampoon' and of the Morrells' threat of an action for libel. It was not Cynthia's way to be discouraging; but she had grave doubts about the whole project, though she had not read the novel yet. The next day after seeing Lawrence there was a family lunch at which Elizabeth confessed that Bibesco did not want to see her any more. Cynthia then went off to Regent's Park with a rather enamoured Whibley, and discussed Lawrence with him. Though he had liked Lawrence when she had introduced them, he was against publication of the novel; but said he could probably get Lawrence £100 from the Literary Fund which had helped him in 1914.[50]

Meanwhile, the same day (6 March), Lawrence went to see Beaumont – described by Cynthia as 'very fair, flaxen, fresh-complexioned, quite boyish-looking' – in his Charing Cross Road bookshop which specialised in 'the new poets', many of whom he had published. Beaumont was clear and businesslike about what the scheme would involve; but even clearer that his name was not to appear at all, nor a printer's, for fear of prosecution. It would have to be entirely Lawrence's responsibility. The book would cost about £375 to print. About £150 would be required before printing began; covering also the order forms which should then be sent out, saying the work was in hand and inviting subscriptions at a guinea. If an edition of 1,000 were sold out, Lawrence might make as much as £550. More realistically, Lawrence thought, it might make him '£200 or £300 – or more trouble' (iii. 220). This was much more professional than the earlier Heseltine plan (talk about which had probably caused Cynthia's muddle about 'Goats and Compasses'); and it anticipated what Lawrence would eventually succeed in doing, at a considerable profit, with *Lady Chatterley's Lover*. The big difficulty was to find the initial £150. Everything depended on what Bibesco 'would think fit to fob out. If he is a £20. touch, he is not much good. – But if he is more – why, he can have the book inscribed to him, if he likes' (iii. 220); but he would have to 'put the money right down – promises are no good ... If not, this thing can wait.' He was not to know that MacCarthy had already torpedoed his chances, although the Prince, as he began to transfer his amorous intentions from her sister-in-law to Cynthia herself, would not turn down her protégé at once. Perhaps on a hint of her scepticism about Ottoline however, Lawrence's irritation burst out again. Having told her that Ottoline 'no longer minded', he now asserted that 'she would like the thing to appear, for self-advertisement – and her sheep-faced fool of a husband would like to denounce it, for further self advertisement' (iii. 220). The following Saturday, despite finding Beaumont still 'full of amazement' after meeting Lawrence, and of the opinion that the plan might well succeed '*commercially*', Cynthia confided her doubts to her diary.

I'm not sure that I want even anonymously to godmother it in any way. I doubt whether its printing will do either Lawrence or the world any good ... We [Cynthia and Beaumont] agreed that the only course was to get the manuscript and let Bibesco read it for himself and make up his mind whether he wishes to proceed in the matter or not. Personally I don't feel very keen about it. Beaumont said that of course parts of it had merit – but it was worse than *The Rainbow*.

Two weeks later she had the typescript, and read it just as the new German offensive was starting, with Beb in the thick of it at St Quentin. Oppressed by the 'nightmare' of the battle she found Lawrence's novel 'nightmarish' too, though she did not see the causal connection in the book. She thought it 'interesting – painfully so, and full of extraordinary bits of stark writing, but what it is [sic] about and *why*? It seems a *mis*application of such a wealth of strenuous analysing and writing. Surely he is delirious ... or do I know nothing about human beings? ... morbid to a degree. I don't know *what* to think about it.[51] Nearly a year later Lawrence told Gertler that 'the buffoon-prince', having said that he would rather help him publish his work than give money direct, 'had the MS. of the novel, returned it without a word, and did nothing'

(iii. 315–16). It would be late 1919 before any hope of publishing *Women in Love* revived.

What sent Cynthia cycling to see Beaumont the Saturday after Lawrence's visit, however, was another plan, possibly conceived when he had returned the proofs of the poems for Sadleir's volume, just before coming to London (iii. 218). Beaumont always seemed more interested in poetry than in prose – and Lawrence suddenly remembered the 'book of tiny poems' ('All of Us') he had thought of dedicating to Cynthia, and had sent to Pinker in December 1916. As soon as he arrived in London he asked for the manuscript (iii. 218), and Beaumont showed a definite interest in something of that size, though he only offered £8 or £9. So Lawrence took the poems back to Hermitage and read them through again, before sending them to Cynthia on approval. He had held them back before, he said, 'because they are ironical and a bit wicked' (iii. 221). If she did not like them he might hold back still; but clearly the money would be useful, though he did not say so. Finding the poems sardonic – as they are, particularly those which deal with the attitudes to the war of Christians and women, and the weariness of men – but not erotic 'thank Heaven', the next day she duly got onto her new bicycle and took them to Charing Cross Road herself as Lawrence had suggested.

Before leaving London however he had one more visit to pay, though the only evidence is from *Bid Me to Live*. Hilda described how, after Julia's husband had gone back to embarkation-camp, Vane [Cecil Gray] came to see her in the middle of an air raid and took her to dinner and the cinema, and how she finally agreed to go down to Cornwall with him as he had been urging. ('He said, "I want two things, I want to finish my opera and I want a beautiful relationship with a woman."') Though she saw 'his detachment, his air of indifference, the feudal hallmarks', he seemed a refuge from the chaos of feeling after her husband and Rico had left her. Now, at the beginning of March, Rico came to Mecklenburgh Square and she told him what she had decided. This was only the third time they had been alone together, and the first since he had flinched from her hand on his sleeve. At the drunken party – jealous perhaps – he had jeered that she and Vane were meant for each other. Now he seemed puritanical in his 'city' suit; and he was shocked by her plan. He urged her to take *his* cottage instead, where she could see Vane often without compromising herself so openly. ' "Do you realise," he said, "what you are doing?"' He didn't ask whether she loved Vane, or he her; but another meaning seemed to murmur under his words: 'I am not happy about this', and 'It would make a difference ... don't you realise?'[52] Then Vane arrived.

Lawrence wrote two letters to Gray in March; but the first, though quite long, ended with a dying fall.

I don't know why you and I don't get on very well when we are together. But it seems we don't. It seems we are best apart. You seem to go winding on in some sort of process that just winds me in the other direction. You might just tell me when you think your process is ended, and we'll look at each other again. Meanwhile you dance on in some sort of sensuous dervish dance that winds my brain up like a ticking bomb. God save us, what a business it is even to be acquainted with another creature. But I suppose one day we might hit it off. Be quick and wind yourself to the end. The one thing I don't seem to be able to stand is the presence of anybody else – barring Frieda, sometimes. Perhaps I shall get over it. (iii. 224)

Gray would assert in his autobiography that the coolness and eventually the breach between them was because Lawrence wanted only disciples, which he could not be.[53] This is misleading in general, and untrue of the break between them in particular. Lawrence's next letter acknowledges a postcard which made them 'feel waves of Cornish malaise coming from the west'; but there was no breach (iii. 225–6). Gray was asked to fetch from the cottage and post to Hermitage two old notebooks of manuscript poems which had been left behind; and Lawrence wrote another quite friendly letter on 19 April (iii. 236–7) in which having decided to give up the bigger Tregerthen cottage, he asked Gray to pack up the belongings he wanted sent to him: his desk, the blue rug, the linen, his reference books and the manuscripts he had not burned, a chore having a certain symmetry with the start of their friendship. There would be two more letters in July (iii. 261–2, 265–6). If the friendship cooled, slowly, it was not because Lawrence wanted a discipleship which Gray was refusing; but because of another relationship altogether, to which Gray did not wish to draw attention.

VI   'A child of black fury'

Not long after the trip to London, in very spring-like weather, came an unexpected visitor: Captain James ('Jack') White, D.S.O., whom the Lawrences had met at Mecklenburgh Square. According to Hilda, Lawrence had cast him in the 'play' as the chorus of the damned. White's father was a Field Marshal who had commanded the British force besieged in Ladysmith and had then been governor of Gibraltar; but the son had proved a restless spirit and a great disappointment to his father, despite his commission and his Anglo-Boer War decoration. He had left the army and become involved in activities which led to him being banned from Ireland, and after the Easter rising had attempted to organise a strike of Welsh miners in the hope of saving Connolly, for which he went to prison. In 1918 he would have described himself as both Protestant-individualist and Irish nationalist; and as both a pro-Russian communist revolutionary and a Christian who believed in love as a life-force making for

433

unity in everything. Contradictions bothered him not at all, since he believed in acting on impulse which he felt always physically in the centre of his chest, before any rationalisation by the mind. He was a stormy petrel, a humorist, a misfit – as he titled his autobiography.[54]

The 'Punch in the Wind' chapter in *Aaron's Rod* which describes the visit of Jim Bricknell, and how he put an end to one of Lilly's diatribes by hitting him three times hard in the stomach, probably accords with an actual incident,[55] and (if so) is another extraordinary example, along with the Pompadour chapter in *Women in Love*, of Lawrence's ability to see and make a mockery of his own weaknesses. There is genuine comedy in Lilly's solemn preparation to meet the appeal to 'save' his visitor, despite having already told him to leave – only to suffer a very ironic outcome to an argument about Christ-like love – and also in his wife's satisfaction at seeing him paid out. (White had slapped *his* wife's face on their honeymoon, for insisting that Christ differed from other men in kind rather than degree.) The actual terms of the argument about Christ in *Aaron's Rod* sound like 1920 rather than 1918; and there is no telling whether the hollow man's voracious hunger in the novel is metaphor or memory; but the violence explodes when Lilly denounces Bricknell personally, and that rings true to life. It is easy to see why White was drawn to Lawrence; they shared some important points of view. But the casting of the charade in *Bid Me to Live* suggests that Lawrence may indeed have thought him a lost soul without direction once banished from Ireland, who sought to escape from his own emptiness through drink and womanising. It would have been all the more irritating, now, if Frieda seemed attracted and behaved accordingly. She had not had much company lately. It would be just like Lawrence to say what he thought without reckoning on an Irish reaction. However, both Lilly's intense and silent struggle to recover his breath, and his insistence that Bricknell had a perfect right to obey the impulse to hit him, are as Lawrencian as Birkin's reaction to being struck by Hermione.

There are other signs of strain with Frieda, probably exacerbated by growing uncertainty about where they were to live. Margaret Radford, a fey creature whom Lawrence had begun to think 'impossible' (iii. 226), was coming to Hermitage at Easter. He had finally decided to let the tower cottage at Higher Tregerthen go, though he arranged one more year's lease of the other cottage at £5 and would keep some belongings there. The choice now was either to go to Ada, or to find something nearby in Berkshire, and both seemed unattractive. He wrote to Willie Hopkin, asking him to enquire about a cottage he remembered visiting in Derbyshire; moreover

any little place, nice and separate, would do. I can't be jammed in among people any more. Frieda and I have lived so much alone, and in isolated places, that we suffer badly at being cooped up with other folk. Ada takes it very much amiss that we don't go and stay with her, to look round. But it is real purgatory to be in her little house, with everybody and everything whirling round. (iii. 223)

On the other hand, he 'quite shook with panic' at the thought of succumbing to the soporific charm of a cottage in a nearby village, 'fast asleep for ever'. They had found two possibilities in Hampstead Norris, one 'just under the hill, under the hazel-woods, with its little garden backing to the old church-yard, where the sunny, grey, square-towered church dozes on without rousing: the other on the hill touching the wood. Frieda of course is *dying* for one of these' (iii. 223). However, money was very short; and Lawrence felt 'a real panic' at the idea of taking another house – if only he could be a fox, or a bird, or a gypsy – let alone falling into a soft sort of sleep, 'writing pages that *seemed* beautifully important' (on American literature) 'and having visits from people who *seemed* all wrong' (iii. 224). He could not now stand anyone else around, except (he qualified) Frieda, 'sometimes'. One suspects she fancied being in the bosom of his family even less than he did, and it is easy to imagine the arguments. Nevertheless the decision was to go to the Midlands after Easter, to look for a cottage with which Ada might help financially.

Cynthia had told him of Whibley's readiness to support an application to the Royal Literary Fund, and though Lawrence objected to any proviso that he should promise to write something inoffensive, he would 'certainly go on writing' and was not 'married to the censor' (iii. 227),[56] so the application could go ahead. Yet he told Gertler – who maintained that painting was the centre of his life, especially after Carrington had taken up with Lytton Strachey – that he by no means felt the same about work: 'I go on working, because it is the one activity allowed to one, not because I care. I feel like a wild rat in a cage ... ' (iii. 226). He had hated applying for help in 1914 – a Freudian lapse of memory about the source of the grant, now, shows how much[57] – yet here he was in the same fix four years and two major novels later.

Despite his feelings about people, he invited Edith Eder down after David had set out for Palestine (iii. 226–7; though she did not come); and also Kot, who remained immovable as always. Barbara Low did visit for a few days before Easter. But on Easter Monday (1 April) he still felt 'horribly sick and surfeited of things'. Barbara had told him how tired Catherine Carswell had been of waiting, in the last weeks of her pregnancy. Lawrence thought he knew just how she felt.: 'I feel as if I had a child of black fury curled up inside my bowels. I'm sure I can feel exactly what it is to be pregnant, because of the weary bowel-burden of a kind of contained murder which I can't bring forth. We will both pray to be safely delivered' (iii. 231).

VII '... as if something important had died'

They left for the Midlands on 5 April, stayed a week in Ripley and found their
next home: 'a bungalow, on the brow of the steep valley at Via Gellia – near
Cromford' in Derbyshire (iii. 232). Ada, who negotiated the furnished rental at
£65 p.a., was also prepared to pay it and gave him another £20 to tide him over
the move. 'One rather hates taking money from ones hard-worked people', he
told Gertler, who knew from bitter experience just what this meant, and how
much was being understated. 'But this is a peculiar and crucial time, and one
must get through it somehow –' (iii. 240). He had been the adventurer into a
bigger world, and for a while had seemed about to become both famous and
prosperous. Now he had come almost full circle back to where he started but
with far gloomier prospects: a nearly unpublishable writer, dependent for the
roof over his head on the sister who stayed at home to run a business and on her
(now conscripted) shopkeeper husband. Yet there seemed little alternative. The
Radfords wanted the Hermitage cottage from the beginning of May.

Shortly after they got back to Hermitage, Frieda went to see her children at
the lawyer's office again. She was upset to learn that Monty was in the Officers
Training Corps, the public school cadets: 'it seemed terrible that he would have
to fight against his own relations, perhaps, and I said: "Let me hide you
somewhere in a cave or in a wood, I don't want you to go and fight, I don't want
you to be killed in this stupid war." But he was shocked.' An 18-year-old public-
schoolboy would be. (She had wondered to Cynthia in 1917 what was the good
of Beb being the Prime Minister's son if he could not be exempted from 'those
hellish trenches'.)[58] Otherwise, Lawrence reported, 'all went off quite pleasantly
and simply, apparently' (iii. 232).

He went on trying to make some money. Beaumont had shied at 'All of Us',
finding the ironic poems 'too doubtful little pills' (iii. 234); but had asked for
some more 'pretty-pretty' verse (iii. 230). Lawrence now tried a double strategy,
something old and something new. The new collection was a little book of
eighteen poems, 'all smallish, lyrical pieces ... it more or less refers to the war,
and is called *Bay*'; but when the old notebooks arrived from Cornwall he also
began to 'rake out' another collection which he told Gray (with an ironic side-
glance at his November attack) he would call '"Chorus of Women", or
something like that' (iii. 232–3). He also asked Ottoline, through Gertler, to
return the manuscripts he had left with her in 1915 (iii. 229), which she duly
did. 'Perhaps we shall meet in some sort of Afterwards,' Lawrence wrote in
acknowledgement, 'when the laugh is on a new side' (iii. 231). Beaumont's offer
for *Bay* was only £10 (iii. 233), hardly more than for 'All of Us'; though
Lawrence hoped (in vain, as it happened) that some of the poems might be
published separately in periodicals. At least *this* little book was 'Impeccable'

enough for the promised dedication to Cynthia (iii. 234). It was eventually illustrated by the Murrys' friend Ann Estelle Rice.[59] He supposed that 'Such a little book would not take long to come out' (iii. 234), but Beaumont was to take an unconscionable time – till November 1919. The other collection, of past work, would become part of the disingenuously titled *New Poems* in Autumn 1918.

He had done his best, but three weeks of it had proved exhausting, and the black mood came again. A sudden snowfall made the spring blossom look drab. The war news of a second German offensive (following their frighteningly successful onslaught on the Somme front) was terrible.

One seems to go through all the Ypres and Mount Kemmels and God knows what. In some blind and hypnotic fashion I do a few bits of poetry – beyond that, I am incapable of everything – except I dig and set potatoes, and go walks with Frieda – who is actually forbearing to demonstrate her impertinent happiness, and daring to know her monstrous angry unhappiness. I don't pretend to be 'happy' – and for the moment don't want to be. I am much too angry. My soul, or whatever it is, feels charged and surcharged with the blackest and most monstrous 'temper', a sort of hellish electricity . . . (iii. 239)

He started reading Gibbon's *Decline and Fall* and found it suited his mood. Those emperors who were 'indiscriminately bad' (iii. 239) and did what they liked until they were strangled, 'I can do with them' (iii. 233). He also read Frobenius on the great Yoruba civilisation which he claimed 'preceded Egypt and Carthage, and gave rise to the Atlantis myth'.[60] Although 'a tiresome writer' (iii. 233), Frobenius connected two of Lawrence's interests: the strange power of those West African sculptures which Heseltine, Gertler and Epstein owned, and which had so influenced the imaginative structure of *Women in Love*; and the theosophic contention that man had declined from great earlier civilisations, rather than progressing from primitivism. Sure enough, having got to the end of the first volume of Gibbon in the World's Classics which was all he had, he was soon reading 'another book on Occultism', particularly magic (iii. 239), which he doesn't name but which might have been Eliphas Lévi, also an interest of Heseltine's.[61] (He may have got hold of it through Edith Eder, with whom he had lately begun corresponding again; iii. 242.) He thought the subject 'very interesting, and important – though antipathetic to me . . . a reality – not by any means the nonsense Bertie Russell says it is' (iii. 239).

He was still feeling not a man so much as 'a walking phenomenon of suspended fury' (iii. 239). The trouble did not lie with Mountain Cottage itself, which was 'nice', commanding a wide view and with 'rather pretty little grounds' including a croquet lawn which he kept mentioning to cheer himself up (iii. 232, 240).[62] Yet his language betrays an undertone of enclosure, almost of unwilling re-entry to the womb: 'It is in the darkish Midlands, on the rim of a steep deep valley, looking over darkish, folded hills – exactly the navel of England, and feels exactly that' (iii. 240). This went with feeling 'hit right in the middle' himself, at a point of inner crisis and intense frustration. 'One keeps some sort of a superficial wits, but I think it would be wrong to assume that one is quite sane just now ... the storm is at its height – it will break soon' – presumably both in himself and in France, though what would come afterwards he did not know and did not care. A chance happening seemed not chance at all, but 'a sort of symbol of something – but I don't know of what.' Walking in the wood with Frieda, he found a dead owl: 'a lovely big warm-brown soft creature, lying in the grass at my feet, in the path, its throat eaten by weasels. It sticks in my mind curiously – as if something important had died this week-end – though what it can be I don't know.' Yet ends for him were always beginnings too, and he did not lose faith in that now despite what weasels had done to Minerva's bird. For – the other half-truth – 'we found some very lovely big cowslips, whose scent is really a communication direct from the source of creation – like the breath of God breathed into Adam. It breathes into the Adam in me' (iii. 240–1).

As he went north again, on 2 May, his life seemed poised in the balance. Something important had indeed died in him – though it would be another year before it became wholly clear what had changed in the author of *Look!* and of *Women in Love*. Yet a new Lawrence was indeed coming to be.

VIII Symbolic Meaning

The first clues to this come in his essays on 'classic' American literature. As always, under the troubled surface of his personal life a deeper writing life had been pursuing its own exploratory course. He had conceived the idea of the book in January 1917 and began writing in August and September; but the flow was broken by the expulsion from Cornwall. It was not till the end of January 1918 at Hermitage that he came back to it. There may have been 'nae luck aboot the hoose' in the next months, but it was not so in the book. By 19 February he had started his essay on Poe, sixth of the ten he planned – though he had lost his Everyman copy and had to replace it (iii. 212–13). By 12 March he thought he was nearing the 'final form' both of the essays and of his thinking, and might never need to write 'philosophy' again (iii. 224). He persuaded Kot (once more!) to type (iii. 217).

Again however came a break because of their move to Mountain Cottage; but by 7 May he told Edith Eder that as well as planting potatoes he had begun writing again. Yet now the book seemed 'never-to-be-finished' (iii. 242). He had its final title, *Studies in Classic American Literature*, but the idea had expanded and the end seemed much further away. The same letter suggests why. He asked Edith to 'lend or borrow for me anywhere a book which describes the human nervous system ... Ask Jones or somebody' (iii. 243). Unfortunately what arrived were pages from a 'medical book' which was 'repulsive with diagnoses' (iii. 244–5)! He needed physiology rather than medicine – but it had come home to him that what had started as literary criticism needed a new language to be worked out. The result was two general essays, and a revision of those he had already done – and just as his 'Hardy' had provided a metaphysic for the whole phase of writing that culminated in *The Rainbow*, *Women in Love* and *Look!*, these essays would form the basis for a new kind of psychology which would make him a different kind of novelist, and turn out to have educational and political implications.

Though he began writing the 'last' essay, on Whitman, in June 1918 (iii. 247) and hoped to send the whole to Pinker that month (iii. 255), the arrangements for typing collapsed, and it was not till 3 August that he sent what was now to be the opening essay 'The Spirit of Place', one of the new general ones, with a promise of 'six or seven more' in 'a week's time' (iii. 270).[63] The *English Review* accepted eight essays, publishing 'The Spirit of Place' in November 1918, followed by those on Franklin, Crèvecœur, Cooper (two essays), Poe, a much shortened essay on Hawthorne and the second general essay 'The Two Principles', which Harrison used (in June 1919) as a closing philosophical summary. Lawrence however had meant that essay to look forward as well as back, and to introduce a new theme of American man's encounter with the sea. Indeed by January 1919 the work consisted of twelve essays (iii. 324) – so four remained unpublished; the second part of the 'Hawthorne' which the *English Review* had not published, and which Lawrence would later expand, together with those on Dana, Melville[64] and Whitman.

These details make two important points. The sequence of composition differed in several respects from the final ordering. (Lawrence actually began not even with Franklin but with Crèvecœur; iii. 160.) This in turn shows that, as always, imaginative exploration came *before* ideas, though these then fed back into the texture and were placed as introduction and conclusion. It was terranova, unspoilt worlds of island, sea, forest and savages, 'America' at its most non-European and challenging to civilised consciousness, that was the imaginative generator, not any preconceived ideology. Moreover readers who know the book only from the much later 1922 rewriting will be surprised at how much more literary and exploratory the first versions are, how much closer to the texts and how different in tone, without the combative and dogmatic brio of a later Lawrence for whom 'America' had become a very different firsthand experience, and (by then) antagonist.

However the man who sat down to write in August 1917 had just finished a revision of *Women in Love* which showed him already thinking about Pryse's suggestion of a non-European neurology. When the whole idea of the work expanded in May 1918 he had seen how to turn Pryse into a new non-Freudian psychology, and been strengthened by Gibbon and Frobenius in his sense of European decadence – as opposed to civilisations that lay behind ancient Greece and Rome. There was great imaginative relief in turning away from the Europe which had been stifling him. His occult reading also reinforced his tendency to look for a metaphysic below the surface of literature, and sharpened his sense of how a symbolic meaning might run counter to a writer's conscious intention. More and more he began to see how the European malaise was shown up even more clearly in the Americans, but along with intimations of cure; so that the imaginative impact of the literature *and* intimations of a new way of looking at the psyche could work together, evolving a shape he discovered as he went. If the original manuscripts had survived – we have nothing earlier for the first eight than the version in the *English Review* – we would have been able to trace more exactly the growth of a delighted sense that this 'other' literature, covering about the same span as the English novel from Richardson to George Eliot but utterly different (and largely unappreciated by the English),[65] really did cohere into what seemed to him a deeply significant pattern and a whole. As it is, we must infer what we can from those eight essays and the unpublished ones which made up the 'work' completed by midsummer, and revised by September 1918.

(a) Franklin to Hawthorne

The argument began from two pairs of contrasts. What struck his critical eye about Crèvecœur was that the most lively and sensitive writing in the *Letters from an American Farmer* had little to do with the book's overt themes and attitudes. This would not surprise Lawrence, since his whole idea of creativity since 'Hardy' had been based on oppositions: especially that between consciousness through the senses which unite us with the external world, and ideas, which come from the process of individuation. What is new is his sense of how America so widened the gap between Crèvecœur's European ideas and his artist's openness to experience, that the phenomenon had to be seen psychologically, as happening within someone transplanted to a particular environment, rather than in religious terms of cosmic forces in universal conflict. Lawrence pays little or no attention to the features of the *Letters* which have interested literary historians or post-Jamesian critics: the definition of the new American, the advocacy of sturdy independence and freeholding, the account of how a new land and sea are made to bear fruit; or on the other hand the epistolary creation of the point of view of the farmer and his character-through-style, or the play between his apparent deference to his sophisticated European correspondent and its ironic intent. Instead, Lawrence goes for the most sensitively rendered *experience* of things as they are, as opposed to romantic idealism: how American king birds gorge on bees (but drive away the crows), the great hornets nesting inside the house, the irascible nature of the humming-bird, the fight between two big snakes, the quail whose feet would freeze to cleared ground if the farmer did not put out straw. At such moments the 'artist lives and sees and knows direct from the life-mystery itself' – though what he sees and knows is at odds with the conscious romanticism of this countryman of Rousseau, and his sentimentalism about nature and the natural man. How explain this? 'The artist is no longer European. Some little salt of the aboriginal America has entered into his blood'; and has brought out true artistry as opposed to egotistic idealism. His sensitivity towards the 'other' in the wild shows how the artist in him 'lives from the great sensual centres, his art is in terms of the great sensual understanding, dark and rich, and of that reserved, pagan tenderness to which we have almost lost the key'.[66]

The archetypal 'opposites' of *The Rainbow* are now located in the development of the human psyche from childhood (and from pagan prehistory). Pryse's Hindu neurology had spoken of two structures of the nervous system, the cerebro-spinal and the sympathetic; and four divisions of consciousness centred in the brain, the heart, the navel and the genitals. Discarding Pryse's hierarchy, Lawrence took what he wanted and used it differently to set up more complex dualisms than his original binary one in the 'Hardy' and *The Rainbow*. The first is between a primary kind of knowing, and 'mental understanding' which comes later. A baby's 'first-consciousness' comes not from the brain but from 'the great nerve centres of the breast and the bowels, the cardiac plexus and the solar plexus'. However these primary modes of consciousness hold a second contrast, between sensuous 'knowing' through the 'heart' and 'breast', as the baby (and we) reach out in wonder to be one with the world; and sensuous knowing through the 'bowels' or 'solar plexus' in which the baby (and we) umbilically draw all into ourselves.[67] America has stimulated Crèvecœur to tap back into primary knowing through the senses, bypassing his European and civilised mentality.

Whether Lawrence originally planned to write on him or not, Franklin made a striking contrast in both sets of terms. Like Crèvecœur he subordinated 'first-consciousness' to the mind, but thought he did so for the good of mankind, showing that any feeling he had came from the breast; whereas Crèvecœur's art, contradicting his conscious ideas, sprang from the 'dark' sensuous centre which took the outside world into the self. Moreover Franklin seemed a 'classic' case of how, in America, the civilised disease of trying to live according to an *idea* of human perfection, subordinating the passions and the senses to mind and will, had gone much further and faster than in Europe. This subverts the 'religious truth ... the same now as it ever has been: that preceding all our knowledge or will or effort is the central creative mystery, out of which issues the strange and for ever unaccountable emanation of creation'. Man cannot create but only fulfil or distort himself. Creativity springs within us, before and beyond our knowledge, and only after we *are* (in fullness of life) can we *know* or will creatively. But in America, 'The Pilgrim Fathers soon killed off in their people the spontaneous impulses and appetites of the self.' In Europe, idealists would go on seeking to unite all men in love or, like Rousseau, consciously to finger and know every impulse of feeling; but only 150 years after the Pilgrim Fathers landed, America had already produced Franklin who aimed to 'seize life within his own will, and control it by precept from his own consciousness'. His God was no creative mystery but the rational producer of a machine-like universe. In that image, Franklin sought to become productive by automatising himself, trying 'to subdue life so that it should work automatically to his will'. His list of virtues shows how he tried to govern or to break his spontaneous impulses – though 'he *could* not make himself tidy and neat in his business and in his surroundings, not even to the end of his days',[68] for nature will out. He succeeded materially as printer, philosopher, inventor, patriot, scientist, almanac moralist, virtuous and scrupulous always. But for Lawrence he was less than a man. Indeed in so *willing* to reduce the fullness of human being, in substituting utilitarian materialism for the mystery of creation, in wanting to be only a cog in a social wheel and seeking to influence everyone to be like him and cut down to his size, he was a kind of self-made monster.

Now a second contrast, within the work of a single writer, takes the diagnosis of disease (in Franklin) and the hint of remedy (in Crèvecœur) a long step further. The works of James Fenimore Cooper seemed to Lawrence to divide significantly into two quite different groups. The Anglo-American novels are 'thin and bloodless' heirs of Franklin. Cooper in his everyday persona, like his heroine Eve Effingham, is still culturally bound to Europe. Having finished her education there, Eve has become 'a real modern heroine; intrepid, calm, and self-collected ... clever and assured' (a forerunner of Henry James's Isabel Archer in *Portrait of a Lady*), and thereby 'a dreadful, self-determined thing'. Moreover, this false ideal of perfection is compounded by an even falser ideal of democratic equality. Because American Eve is committed to a theory that all persons are equal, she cannot obey her own finer instincts as a spontaneous individual and treat the parvenu and demagogue Septimus Dodge as he deserves. Yet since 'beauty' and 'wholeness' for Lawrence lie in fulfilling one's own true nature, the only need for democracy 'is to arrange the material world so that each man can be intrinsically himself, yielding service where he must instinctively yield respect or reverence, and taking command where instinctively he feels his own authority'. The American ideal is politically as well as psychologically false. People must learn to be themselves spontaneously, admitting the oppositions which define and concentrate life and on which creative living depends – 'Otherwise we shall wind ourselves up till the spring breaks.'

Suddenly there is a glimpse of Lawrence himself, still as haunted by the spectres of the dead in Flanders as he had been at the seaside in 1915. Psychological self-mutilation has led inevitably to destruction. Millions died because they obeyed ideas and fixed wills, against the promptings of 'the primal spontaneous self'. But what of their souls,

caught out of life unliberated and unappeased? ... They enter into us angrily and fill us with their destructive presence ... And if there is no peace for them, there is none for us ... unless we, by our active living, shall give them the life that they demand, the living motions that were frustrated in them now liberated and made free.[69]

That is the significance of Cooper's Leatherstocking novels, which in the next essay are seen as an imaginative act of atonement in an analogous situation. Cooper's America had decimated and expropriated the American Indians. But whereas in the Anglo-American novels Cooper had looked ahead to where 'the self-determined ego' of white America was heading; in the Leatherstocking books he not only looks *back*, but 'very beautifully gives the myth of the atonement, the communion between the soul of the white man and the soul of the Indian', gradually developed through imaginative journeying into the past. T. S. Eliot called this 'probably the most brilliant of critical essays' on these novels,[70] and the first brilliance is how Lawrence is able to explain the reverse chronology of the series, which begins in *The Pioneers* and *The Prairie* with the old age and death of Natty Bumppo, in a world which has no place for him (the world of Cooper's own childhood), and then moves steadily backwards to culminate in *Deerslayer*, when Natty and Chingachgook were young.

To see the sequence as essentially a mythic exploration within the psyche, is (as previously with Hardy) to X-ray through to an underlying structure, impatient with history and love story in the novels. So *The Last of the Mohicans* is 'the most imperfect of all the Leatherstocking books, the most broken, hesitating as it does between historical narrative ... and the true impulse of pure imaginative, creative revelation'. The Anglo-French war is mere catalyst; the real centre is the death of Uncas, leaving Natty and Chingachgook each 'concluded in himself ... from opposite ends of the earth, meeting now, beholding each other, and balanced in unspeakable conjunction—a love so profound, or so abstract, that it is unexpressed ... communicated by pure presence alone, without contact of word or touch'. (One cannot think of that as homosexual.) Cooper's imagination, in piercing through to what his race has destroyed, marks the inception in himself and the reader of a 'new race'. Moreover all the book's heterosexual relationships become, beneath the rather trashy surface, ways of talking about what has happened within the American psyche. Similarly, in *Pathfinder*, what interests Lawrence is not Natty's 'abortive love story', a mere temporary aberration. Rather, 'the splendour lies in the revelation of the spirit of place, the pristine beauty of the Great Lakes'; the aboriginal America both outside and within himself with which the white man has to come to terms. And so, finally, there is *Deerslayer*, for Lawrence 'the loveliest and best' of all. The 'pristine world' of Glimmerglass is 'perhaps, lovelier than any place created in language: lovelier than Hardy or Turgenev, lovelier than the lands in ancient poetry or Irish verse'; but its mythic spell lies 'in the luminous futurity which glimmers as a plasm in all the landscape' – a gleam of infinity, as in the 'life' under Ursula's microscope. How 'futurity'? Because Cooper, too, by the end,

sees beyond him, in face of him, that which he has been journeying away from ... the Red Man, the sensual being which for ages he has been destroying or fleeing from ...

This is the beauty of Deerslayer, that he knows at last that there are two ways, two mysteries—the Red Man's and his own ... now at last he acknowledges perfectly and in full the opposite mystery—the mystery of the other.

There is no future for Natty himself. Indeed, the whole series can be seen in retrospect as implying the need to dissolve his limited kind of whiteness away, though not as America and Europe have done, replacing it (between the 1823 novel and 1918) with something far deadlier and man-slaying. But Cooper's fiction is the birth of futurity: not 'our present factory-smoked futurity', but that of an unborn race.[71]

The critical book with its symbolic insights is also of course a Lawrencian mythos, of 1917–18. The American writers are helping him to a new psychological focus on what has to happen *within* people, before there can be new life. As with the 'Study of Thomas Hardy', the challenge to deal (however selectively) with the evidence of specific works of.art also makes his thought more concrete than in 'The Crown' or 'The Reality of Peace'. Most important of all, however, is the marked shift of emphasis.

In Spring 1917 he had suddenly become impatient with the swarming emotions of fiction, not unrelated to the tensions in his marriage after Easter. He felt abstract, wrote philosophy and worked in his garden and the hayfields with William Henry. As he began writing about the transcendental element in American literature in August and September, we can now see that (as well as the consolation of a vivid 'terranova' to live in, a Rananim of imagination) this literature offered another positive. It threw a psychological sidelight on his attraction to the 'sensual consciousness' of the young farmer; but it had little of significance to do with sexual relationship. After the swarming emotions in Mecklenburgh Square, that advantage would have increased. And whereas the whole phase from 'The Wedding Ring' to *Women in Love* had placed sexual relationship at the very centre of renewal, through the oblivion of the self at the hands of the other, in these new essays on the Americans the emphasis has shifted, markedly, to the need for a better balance within the self. Moreover, relationship with a woman is no longer the essential way to that. Or – perhaps a better way of putting the shift – relationship of any kind is becoming merely one modality of deeper and more transcendent crisis within the individual psyche. The Lawrence of 1917–18, while not denying his marriage and the value he put on it, no longer expects it to cure the disunity and malaise in himself, or in his world. The cure must be found within the self. It is no longer a question of better harmony between opposing impulses in two people, but a redressing (in each and everyone) of what has become a radical imbalance, by reasserting what has been almost lost (the spontaneous sensual nature) *against* what has become too dominant (the mind and will). This will have far-reaching implications not only for his view of relations between man and woman generally, and Frieda and himself in particular, but in many other directions too.

So, in a third pairing, Poe and Hawthorne only seem to be concerned with the sexual relationships of their characters, but Lawrence sees the deeper action as taking place within the psyche of the author. He makes hardly any distinction between author and protagonist in 'Ligeia' or even 'The Fall of the House of Usher'. The narrator in 'Ligeia', 'craving to analyse the being of the beloved', embodies Poe's own craving, 'the unspeakable craving of those whose souls are arrested, to gain mastery over the world through knowledge'. (This is why Poe's imagination strikes Lawrence as 'scientific', rather than 'artistic' like the best of Crèvecœur.) Narrator and beloved, one seeking to 'analyse and possess and know', to death, the other determined to fuse with him into one will and consciousness despite the death of the body, are both aspects of Poe's soul – 'arrested' because it is an advanced case of Franklin's crushing of the 'spontaneous self' by the 'self-determined ego'. In Cooper, the imagination reached out to the lost 'other'; in Poe there is no vital sense of an 'other' any longer, nor creative opposition within the self, only the consuming away of all that is not mind and will in a process enclosed in consciousness. The only vitality, indeed a sensational kind of satisfaction, lies in disintegrating the self (and others), anticipating the twentieth-century corruption that 'The Crown' and *Women in Love* had diagnosed. (This also explains Poe's addiction to alcohol and drugs, as well as his morbidly sensational imagination.) Similarly the 'incest' in the House of Usher is seen as the 'dissolution' of the soul through an unspeakable desire to possess or be possessed by what is most like itself. Once 'the self is broken, and the mystery of the recognition of *otherness* fails', the whole psyche becomes morbidly sensitive (aeolian harp-like), to every breath from outside, the overstrung nerves quivering 'on the edge of dissolution'. When polarity breaks, the whole 'house' comes crashing down.[72]

If Poe points forward to one kind of disintegration through consuming consciousness and will, Hawthorne shows the other, through the backlash of the sensual. His everyday persona labels Hester first a 'Scarlet Woman' and then an atoning penitent, but his 'serpent subtility' disguises what his 'symbology' is really doing. 'His pious blame is subtle commendation'. Hawthorne, too, reveals the 'collapse of the human psyche in the white race'. 'Openly he stands for the upper, spiritual, reasoned being' but secretly he wants to lame his spiritual self for ever. On Hester's scaffold there is no spiritual Mary of the Sacred Heart but a Scarlet Woman whose sign 'flashes with the great revenge of the serpent, as the primary or sensual psyche, which was perfectly subjected, humiliated, turns under the heel like the serpent of wrath, and bites back'. When Hester seduces Dimmesdale, the puritan 'saint' who has tried to become all spirit, 'the spiritual era' is at 'the beginning of the end'. And though 'in her upper mind' after his death she apparently holds to the 'old faith ... in love and self-sacrifice', in fact she continues to be a 'centre of mystic obstruction', secretly (and unconsciously) undermining the Puritanism of her neighbours – as her daughter does even more. Hester's adornment of the child shows what her own true nature remains; and Pearl, veering from extreme to extreme with 'recurrent mockery', each neutralising the other, is a little demon of disorder. Hawthorne 'did not choose to discover too much, openly. But he gives us all the data.'[73]

In the last $11\frac{1}{2}$ pages of the essay, not published by Harrison in the *English Review* and later expanded into a second essay, Chillingworth is seen as the male counterpart to Hester, an 'undoer'. In him 'the male sensual psyche subjected and turned back in recoil' must proceed malevolently with the undoing of the other half of the soul. So the torturing of Dimmesdale, as much as the 'sin' of Hester, becomes a 'dark necessity' stretching as far back as Christ, who started 'the triumph of the one half of the psyche, over the other half', and hence the inevitability of reaction. In *The Blithedale Romance*, the fictionalising of the Brook Farm experiment (heir to Crèvecœur 's romantic idealism) shows the failure of 'the attempt to work the sensual body from the spiritual centres' by another idealistic kind of suppression. What lay beneath the attempt at transcendence in all four characters reveals itself destructively. Hollingsworth, disguising sensuality in idealism, tries to dominate the narrator. Zenobia, the passionate sensual woman, is driven to drown herself. And both men, attracted to the 'spiritualistic medium', the utterly passive little sempstress Priscilla who no longer has any vital being of her own, actually want to use her for the last satisfaction of destroying their sensuality. The narrator/Hawthorne escapes but Hollingsworth becomes 'tottering and shaky' when he has married the white lily, all his vitality drawn out.[74]

With the Hawthorne essay the Lawrencian *mythos* of American literature formed itself into a remarkably coherent structure. Of course Lawrence was highly selective, very ready to slice through complexities and ambiguities; and of course what he came up with was a very Lawrencian story rather than a critical history in the writers' own terms. Moreover, three of the four American authors he cared most about and who had originally fuelled his enthusiasm for the whole enterprise – Dana, Melville and Whitman – had still to be fitted in. Yet when Lawrence added the two general essays it was probably the impression of a coherent argument, complete enough in eight, that struck Austin Harrison. For, with a general essay at beginning and end, that was what he published.

(b) General Perspectives

'The Spirit of Place' is however the kind of introduction one writes *after* one has discovered one's argument. Readers who began there were at once confronted by two apparently eccentric assertions: first, that there was formerly a universal mystic language, shared among the great civilisations from which ours has declined, and expressed in esoteric symbols which must be reinterpreted psychologically now; and second, that historical movements and migrations, the rise and fall of civilisations, are ultimately movements of the human psyche, in response to powerful 'magnetic' currents, set up in alternating circuits over centuries by unknown polarities. (Theosophy, cabbalistic magic and psychic 'electricity' have coloured Lawrence's recent reading of Frobenius and Gibbon.) However, to come at the essay in the order of composition is to see more clearly how it expresses Lawrence's deeper concerns *behind* the study of American writers and why, reacting to the Europe of 1917–18, he should have been so drawn to America and the 'Mystic Import' of its literature (iii. 163).

'It is time for us now to see that our great race experience is surpassed and exceeded. Our race *idea* may apparently hold good in the American mind'; but 'Life itself takes on a new reality, a new motion, even while the idea remains ostensibly the same'; and it is in white-American literature that both the decadence and the coming change can be detected most clearly. For, far from being a branch of English literature, American writing is strange and other. American ideas may relate to ours, but American 'art-speech' has already, responding to an 'alien quality' in the continent itself, begun symbolically to reveal the 'incipient newness within the old decadence'. Lawrence is not in fact interested in theosophic revival of old mysticisms; but in decoding (since art-speech reveals what 'plain speech almost deliberately conceals') the shape of the future as it once again takes a new direction away from the past. (He insists – against theosophy too – that 'art-speech' is a symbolism of *experience*, 'emotional and passional, spiritual and perceptual', expressing a state of being, not a mental concept as the occult symbol does.)

If the artist, reacting to experience but beyond his own awareness, is the sensitive feeler-out of what is to come, that might explain why the artist in Lawrence should have been so drawn to American literature, and why the man,

447

following behind, should so have wanted to go there without knowing why. It would seem that biographical reasons – personal reaction to the loss of his audience, to work destroyed and publication refused, to unjust expulsion and inability thereafter to earn a living – might not after all be the deepest ones. He had been insisting since 1914 that the deepest human feelings were impersonal. Now, in European crisis,

we must wake and sharpen in ourselves the subtle faculty for perceiving the greater inhuman forces that control us. It is our fatal limitation, at the present time, that we can only understand in terms of personal and conscious choice. We cannot see that great motions carry us and bring us to our place before we can even begin to know.

Moreover to have read Gibbon in May 1918 was to place such 'great motions' in a long and wide historical perspective; with an extraordinary sense of how processes of expansion and decay across centuries, leading to the collapse of Roman civilisation and its replacement by something new, might apply (inversely) to the expansion of Europe to America and the world-wide collapse of civilisation now. In fact, Lawrence's language of psychic polarity and magnetism is an 'art-speech' to embody his own *experience* of being drawn as if by magnetism before and beyond his understanding – an experience not unrelated to that of millions of Europeans since Columbus. Again he is not satisfied with conscious motivations such as the Pilgrim Fathers' search for religious freedom, or the Iberian and English colonisation in search of wealth. Behind those (he thought now) lay an obscurer urge, the counterpart of the movement that had sent the Romans north and east, to expansion of empire, and then to decay. The great movement which from the fifteenth century on the Atlantic seaboards impelled men west and south, was essentially an urge to satisfy more widely and intensely their civilisation's desire to control the inner life by the will, and then to exert power over nature. America became a field for inner and outer repression (over the sensual life and the native American), and then (after a Franklin-like mechanising of the self and its relations) for Yankee 'business' and industry – all happening faster and going further in the new conditions than in Europe. But after expansion comes decay and incipient change. In 'aboriginal' America, Europeans 'walked a new earth, were seized by a new electricity, and laid in line differently'. For there is a spirit of place which gets into bones, tissue and blood, transfusing people, and gradually transmuting their life stuff. Hence the ability of the most sensitive Americans, the writers, to capture the nature of the decadence, and the beginnings of recoil in the opposite direction. And hence the instinct of one D. H. Lawrence to long for America, to settle meanwhile for Cornwall, and to begin there his studies of the transcendental import of classical American literature, awaiting a breeze blowing from the future.[75]

'The Two Principles', which for Harrison made a conclusive summing up of the philosophy, was indeed partly so, and so need not delay us long. Behind an odd combination of the Bible's account of creation with pre-Socratic cosmology (the four elements of Empedocles) and with esoteric symbolism, is the desire for a language for growth and decay which could be simultaneously psychological *and* cosmic – unlike materialist science. Lawrence however (like Yeats) is after 'metaphors' and speaks happily of 'changing' them. He needs a language to insist on a paradox: that though life proceeds creatively by dividing itself, temporarily, it nevertheless remains primary, uncreatable, not finally divisible. Where the scientist defines 'life' biologically as arising out of matter and dying into it, Lawrence sees 'life' as creativity itself, continually throwing forth new products as material residue, but always going on to new creation, its essential oneness unbroken, without beginning or end. Both cosmically, and within the person, 'as life moves on in creative singleness, its substance divides and subdivides into multiplicity'; yet at each creative moment, all comes together with all, anew.

The first act of creation in the universe, as in the first human cell, is a division of singleness into duality; hence the 'two principles' of the title and its continuity with Lawrence's thinking since 'Hardy'. Then, however, the two immediately become four; and though this goes on to multiplicity, it is the one-to-two-then-two-to-four paradigm that is elemental, never forgetting that the process comes out of and constantly returns to oneness again. (Here is the advantage of combining Genesis with Empedocles for a cosmic explanation of the many coming out of and returning to the one.) In the human being, the psyche divides horizontally into 'upper' and 'lower' ganglia, and vertically into 'front' and 'back'; so that the make up of each of us depends on the way our 'first-consciousness' – preceding mental consciousness – *relates* the impulses of the great ganglia which control the face and the heart, the solar plexus and the loins and back. Moreover, in a second great dualism the for ever ongoing creativity of life depends also on the necessary alternation of coming-together, and of going-apart, as indeed 'The Crown' had insisted. So in one era souls may grow, internally and in relation with others, by harmonious marriage; whereas in other eras growth may be through a 'disintegrative soul ... active in the universe as a unit of sundering'. At all times however, consciousness in the mind is the product of this 'first' fourfold consciousness in the body, whether in balance and fulfilment, or in disharmony and destruction.[76]

Partly this is a theoretical summary of the psychology which Lawrence had developed in the critical essays from Crèvecœur to Hawthorne – though it is not quite clear, yet, why he needs the 'face' and the 'back' now, as well as the 'breast' and 'bowels'; nor why he needs a 'correspondence' between cosmic and elemental conflict and the conflict within the self. However this will soon become clear, since it is here that Lawrence meant the essay to look forward to that other extraordinary American achievement, 'the relation between the sea and the human psyche' in Dana and Melville, and the all-embracing stance of Whitman.[77] Fortunately, though the essays on these remained unpublished and were believed lost when Armin Arnold compiled *The Symbolic Meaning* using later and different ones, early versions have now come to light which allow us to see the 'book' as a whole.

(c) Dana and Melville

The two great American writers of the sea embody another way in which the psychic disintegration has proceeded through the attempt to conquer the 'lower' sensual centres of the self. Thus Dana, despite his wonderful plainness, is actually a kind of mystic, trying for the same sort of psychic conquest as the Johannine initiate (according to Pryse's interpretation of the Revelation of St John). On the surface, the young Harvard law student goes to sea because of his eye trouble, but at a deeper level he is drawn to go as an ordinary seaman 'before the mast', at one with sensual, unthinking, spontaneous humanity. Yet he wants this also in order to confront and ultimately overcome his own sensual self. The sea, the 'lower' element of the first division of creation but also the corrosive salt waters of dissolution, is the seething of the senses, inchoate or menacing. It is the sense of an *ending* which produces the melancholy of Dana's description of dawn at sea. The white albatross, at rest on the heaving waters, is an image of Dana's soul aspiration in ironic counterpoint to the great creative Spirit of the Beginning in the Book of Genesis. Yet the terrible physical struggles to round Cape Horn on the way to California, and back again, contain a kind of soul heroism. The sea 'tortures him, reduces his land flesh', finally makes him speechless with a swollen jaw and nearly kills other seamen with scurvy. Yet it also brings him out as 'a triumphant consciousness, a victorious spiritual being, victorious over his deep sensual self, by his victory over the sea'. He can now live 'deliberately' – and there is something epic about that.

However, Lawrence's response is deeply ambiguous. When the time for decreation has come, the pioneers – all the 'classic' Americans – are heroic, but heroes of *undoing*. 'If there is a great God, the perfect Creator, there is a corresponding great God, the Undoer, the Separator ... Zeus of the thunder-bolts, the earliest Ammon' (also the Yoruba God of Lightning, Shango, of whom he had learned from Frobenius); whose power is revealed to both Dana and Melville in the apparition of the corposant at the mast-head. But Dana 'Hamletises' by the Pacific; and in the episode of the floggings his liberal-minded horror is sentimental weakness to Lawrence.

The first version is much less aggressive about this than later versions were to become, and more critical of the captain who is originally seen as no less 'unformed' than the 'loose straggling character' he flogs; and just as implicated in the loss of unity that the 'disintegrative influence' of the sea has brought about. Sam embodies the crew at its most 'soft, vague, loose, shambling, inefficient, impudent'. The captain, who should be 'the positive or commanding nature, is becoming irritable, exacting, surcharged ... the unison is breaking'. This first version is, however, no more interested in the justice or brutality of the flogging of Sam (let alone of John, the sailor who dares to question it) than the later versions will be, and some may feel that Lawrence himself is allowing mental conception to override sensuous realisation. The *passion* of the act is its own excuse for him, as necessary as a thunderstorm to clear the air. For it is 'only the flash of lightning, the flash of anger and pain striking straight into the volitional centres [i.e. the back] of the negative physique, from the positive physique, that can re-adjust the two beings, make them clean and whole again. It is the electric catharsis. The flogging therefore is a purifying process to two drossy natures.' Man cannot live 'by spiritual love and reason alone'- that is, by the sympathetic 'breast' and the mind – and Dana's attempt to *overcome* the 'lower' self is re-focused. The sensual centres must (and will) have their due, as in Hawthorne, if necessary through 'the Thunderer, he who turns, and is wrathful'. The back, too, must be stung into life. At the end of the essay, however, the final emphasis is on the *son* of the Thunderer, Hermes the healer. The scurvy on the ship and Dana's own lock-jaw are healed by the *earthy* juices of onions and potatoes. After decreation, the 'latent creative principle' must work anew. It is very painful to come back to sensual life; the boy with scurvy shudders with anguish after drinking the juice. But the undoing must be followed by new creation: neither Dana's triumphant consciousness nor the salt sea, but creativity beginning again.[78]

Melville also turns to the great waters, but now like some Viking going 'home to the sea, encumbered with age and memories, and a sort of accomplished despair'. Once upon a time 'the blue-eyed race' rose like a flood to inundate 'the old, darkened' ones, but now 'it retreats in the ebb, back away from creation'.

At first, Melville instinctively turned to the Pacific, the first and oldest ocean, which bordered the earth and its great civilisations before the Flood and the sinking of Atlantis. (Once again theosophy helps Lawrence imagine a lost world whose universal language and symbols – 'The All-Father, the All-Mother, ... the Thunderer, the Tree' – are 'passional', springing from direct sensual contact with life at every point, rather than concepts or ideas.) But after its perfection came the Fall and the Flood: 'the Fall from pure sensual understanding, the birth of the upper spiritual understanding', and the wiping out of most of the old world. Ever since, and particularly after Christ, 'the new way of life, the spiritual-mental, struggled towards perfection', and, in its turn, to the inevitable decay and decreation of Melville's time (worsening to the end, the World War of 1914–18). In the South Sea island of Nukuheva however, Melville found a survival from the lost world. His descent down the gorge into the hidden valley of the Typee is both 'actual and pure dream-mystical: Down this narrow, steep, horrible dark gorge he slides and struggles as we struggle in a dream, or in the act of birth, to emerge in the green Eden of the first era, the valley of the timeless savages.'[79] They are however *not* 'savage', but retain the vestiges of 'some most perfect and beautiful sensual civilisation', in many ways more nuanced, refined and delicate than Melville's. Even their cannibalism (as Frobenius argued) is 'connected with a definite emotion':[80] not food but the survival of a form of communion, taking the 'other' into the self – the obverse of Christ's sacramental gift of himself in the Eucharist.

Yet, having found Typee, Melville could not stay. He *had* to get away; as even his flesh signalled by the mysterious wound that would not heal while he remained, but cleared up as soon as he left. Afterwards he yearns to be back. Yet however strong 'the passion to escape the white civilisation', and 'the nostalgic longing to sleep in the sleep of the bygone sensual mystery', the necessity to 'give his allegiance to the spiritual mystery of which he is the almost finished product' is even stronger. He *must* undergo the Dana experience and attempt the final victory of the spiritual over the sensual self – but he is one stage on from Dana, the last stage, ending not in triumph but in death by sea-water.

So *Moby Dick* becomes an apocalypse of undoing. The great white whale, warm-blooded like us, symbolises 'the last body of sensual being within the white race' in the salt depths. To try to annihilate *that*, in a final effort of the upper consciousness, is a doomed mania. Ahab embodies at its most intense the American effort to subject sensual being entirely to conscious will and self-direction. He has already been lamed and terribly warned. On his ivory leg he is like Hephaestos, product of a sundering quarrel between supreme powers. Lameness manifests the radical imbalance of the 'halves' of his psyche, and makes him active in undoing. Most lame gods are also associated with fire, and Ahab is indelibly marked in his flesh, additionally, by the lightning of the Thunderer, and served by a Zoroastrian crew of fire-worshippers. His three mates embody the reason (in Starbuck), the passional impulse (in Stubb, still 'fearless as fire' says Melville, but grown 'mechanical' now) and obstinate will without imagination (in Flask) – a 'fatal triangle of the disintegrate soul' when 'dominated by a mania'. Only Ishmael remains capable of reaching out to the lost world like the Melville of *Typee* (and like the Dana who felt a 'strong impulse of love' for the Kanaka whose name translated into 'Hope'). Indeed, the relationship with the savage Queequeg 'opens again in Ishmael's heart the floodgates of passional love', and overcomes his exclusive Presbyterian conscience in sharing the worship of Queequeg's god, as he would wish Queequeg to share his.

So begins the voyage, the hunt, as 'mythical, mystical' as any quest of Argonauts, yet 'all *actual*. This is the beauty—the identity of actual daily experience with profound metaphysical reality.' It is when Melville is fully the seaman, Lawrence thinks, 'moving and working with the waters, not self-consciously speculating' that he is at his best.[81] Eager to demonstrate this in a whole string of quotations, Lawrence originally went well beyond the length that the *English Review* could have tolerated. Moreover the urge to quote proved ultimately self-defeating and the essay peters out without making the major point: that it is the white whale and Ishmael who survive into a future, while the monomaniac undoers and would-be triumphalists are finally undone, dissolved away in the salt waters of the End, so that the new life-cycle can start. Since the Dana essay also ends rather oddly in food chemistry, it may have been the impression of two essays not quite worked out or properly rounded off that led Harrison not to publish them; though their existence in revised typescript suggests Lawrence's hope that they would be accepted too.

(d) Whitman

The Whitman essay could never have been published. It may not even have been sent to be typed in 1918. Indeed we can only infer the original from an autograph manuscript of September 1919, though it seems safe to assume that this does preserve the essential argument, since that is so with the Dana and Melville essays which survive in both forms.[82] The 1919 version was never printed either; indeed Lawrence himself expected Huebsch might find it 'politic not to publish' (iii. 400). For the essay, explicitly treating Whitman as homosexual, is the culmination of Lawrence's self-examination about homosexuality.

It is important however to see how a complex argument relates primarily to Whitman's place in the development which the essays have been tracing, such that he is both the heroic culmination and the propagator of a deadly half-truth – and thus to see how and why Lawrence is led to condemn Whitman's kind of homosexuality, while finally bringing himself to see how what had given him nightmares in 1915 could be a 'last mystery' rather than an abomination. (With this, however, he loses interest in homosexuality – though not in comradeship between men – until the final rejection in *Kangaroo*.)

Whitman is 'the last and greatest of the Americans' because he completes the American attempt to subordinate the 'lower' sensual centres to the 'upper' ones and both to a supreme consciousness. Where Dana sought to overcome his sensual self at sea; and Melville to kill the last 'quick' of sensual life; Whitman seeks to absorb his sensual self into his consciousness, and moreover to embrace All, identifying with everything, body and soul, so that nothing is excluded, and the Many become One in encompassing love and supreme enlightened consciousness. But this inevitably produces a reaction from those who 'find the highest reality in the single, separate distinctness of the soul' and who therefore are liable to regard Whitman as an 'arch-humbug'. The longing for unity is only one impulse in the continuous dialectic of human growth, and becomes fatal if it is regarded as an end. For 'this process of extreme physical sympathy, universal sympathy, *merging*, as Whitman rapturously calls it' so violates the single self as to become a process, if persisted in, of 'soul-death'. This is why some of Whitman's loveliest poetry is about death. It would seem that Whitman's quest, as much as Melville's, was deathly.

His merging is achieved by making himself the passive or negative pole, 'giving himself utterly' away to the other, in order to *know* everything. He also takes his own sexuality into consciousness in a process distinctly masturbatory. He sings of 'the mystery of the touch of the hands and fingers, those living tendrils of the upper spiritual centres, upon the lower body: the hands and fingers gathering and controlling the sheer sex motions'. Moreover all the organs of the upper centres which respond to the 'other' – not only fingers but mouth, tongue, nostrils, ears – work in Whitman to learn 'the dark, vital secrets of the lower self', to explore, subject and know it consciously. For Lawrence this is to become 'monstrous, a shattering half-truth, a devastating, thrilling half-lie'. Like some athletes, Whitman wants to be narcissistically aware of his body as he controls it. And though he gives himself away in order to know his own sensuality, he has no real sense of the otherness of the other. He regards woman as simply 'for merging, and for the state of consciousness, and self-conscious-ness, liberated during this merging' – a womb, a 'bath of birth' for his own dominant consciousness.[83]

The phrase recalls how Gerald used Gudrun in a way deadly for both – the reverse of the central Lawrencian idea of how solipsism can 'die' in oblivion through the 'other'. Indeed (Lawrence insists) man's rebirth from woman in either way cannot be without death of some kind; and if through 'merging' Whitman is born into dominant 'upper *consciousness*', then 'in the powerful, rich, dark sensual self, he is destroyed, reduced, annulled'. To persist in reducing part of the psyche results in disintegration. This is familiar enough – but now it brings a new understanding of violence. The 'violent reaction between man and woman, the inevitable hate in love' is a response to this necessity of death; for if man may love his bath of birth, he 'hates mystically that which is his death[:] "The womb, the tomb"' of his man's being – and presumably vice versa for the woman. Lawrence has thought further about the disunity in himself which he confessed to Ottoline, and about the rumpuses at Garsington and Zennor when Frieda denounced his 'soul-mush' with Ottoline and the Murrys, and he grew violent in response. It seems he is criticising in Whitman something he had been forced to recognise in himself; hence the blend of admiration for the honesty of Whitman's disclosure, and denunciation of what he disclosed. However Whitman also helped him to confront, fully now, the question about the sufficiency of marriage at the end of *Women in Love*.

For Whitman found he could not 'merge himself altogether into woman', partly because he was too proud to render up his free independence, and partly because complete merging is impossible between 'beings so categorically different'. This explains his homosexuality, for if he was not to 'yield himself to complete absorption and inglutination by the woman—a débâcle far too ignominious for a great man like Whitman' – he had to 'reconsider, and seek elsewhere his last mystic unification'. And though the context is the over-whelming desire to merge which Lawrence denounces; he is led to discuss 'the last circuit of vital polarisation' between man and man,[84] not only in homoerotic relationship but in sodomy.[85] Whitman is the first in modern life to dare to assert what the esoterics knew a thousand years before Plato; but in *Calamus* his vehemence is gone, and only hesitantly and cryptically can he speak of what may lie behind the 'love of comrades'. For there can indeed be a 'passional' circuit between the lower ganglia of man with man. Taking a step further than in *Women in Love*, in trying to understand how the energy at the base of the spine can be tapped, Lawrence revalues anal sex by contrasting in his strange new language a sexuality of the lower-front with that of the lower-back. The sexual passion of man for woman is usually polarised between the 'hypogastric' and 'sacral' ganglia which, when connected and switched on in the sex act through male entry to the vagina, refresh and re-establish the 'circuit of life, upon which both beings depend for their real, spontaneous living'.

But beyond all this is the cocygeal centre. There the deepest and most unknowable sensual reality breathes and sparkles darkly, in unspeakable power. Here, at the root of the spine, is the last clue to the lower body and being, as in the cerebellum is the last upper clue ... Here is our last and extremest reality. And the port, of egress and ingress, is the fundament, as the vagina is port to the other centre.

So that, in the last mystery of established polarity ... [t]he last perfect balance is between two men, in whom the deepest sensual centres, and also the extreme upper centres, vibrate in one circuit, and know their electric establishment and readjustment as does the circuit between man and woman. There is the same immediate connection, the same life-balance, the same perfection in fulfilled consciousness and being.

Lawrence is now acknowledging – as never before – that it *is* possible that both upper and lower centres could be polarised and fulfilled through sodomy, though differently from heterosexual fulfilment – whereas the Whitman kind of merging must break down the integrity of the soul. For 'true relation' depends crucially on both partners maintaining 'their sheer single, separate integrity, their inviolable singleness of being', equal in opposite duality, balanced against each other, finally (like Natty and Chingachgook) 'beyond emotion, beyond all merging, existing in the last extreme of mutual knowledge, almost beyond feeling, so deeply abstracted or concentrated ... balanced on the edge of death'. It is this essential kind of relation rather than the sexual act itself that seems even more important homosexually than heterosexually. So, Whitman the homosexual again 'mixed all up with emotion and merging' and 'believed in fusion, which is pure loss'. Lawrence is also as much against predatory homosexuality as ever. Any 'using one being for the gratification and increase of the other being' (such as the fusion in Greek pederasty where the older possessed and imposed his will on the younger) is deadly destructive. And that is why Whitman on the one hand hails 'manly love' ; but 'in the next breath it is death, death, all death'. Yet it takes a great soul so to bare itself – and it is for this fearless exposure that Lawrence most admires Whitman.

Moreover, in the closing paragraphs, he finds in Whitman's *poetry*, at its best, a spontaneity and wholeness that the half-truths of his ideas reduce, by their overbalance into mental consciousness. For there, in 'lovely blood-lapping' interplay of consonants and vowels, the 'primal soul utters itself in strange pulsations' and 'the whole soul speaks at once: sensual impulse instant with spiritual impulse, and the mind serving, giving pure attention' – as opposed to the senses serving the mind. It is for this (and its influence on his own poetry) that he finally salutes Whitman, 'because I owe the last strides into freedom to you. And in saluting you, I salute your great America.'

This essay is a crux for Lawrence's attitude towards practising homosexuality, whether by masturbation or sodomy, since it is the most explicit of all his musings, and the culmination of his long struggle to come to terms with potentialities in himself which he had first acknowledged in 1913. Yet the final endorsement is oddly theoretical; and while its whole point is to foster greater singleness than marriage can create alone, this seems to be still *in addition* to marriage, which remains 'the great life-circuit' on which 'the very life and being and equilibrium of man and woman depend'.[86] Moreover, if he has now brought himself to recognise that homosexual anal intercourse is capable of joining lowest with highest *chakras* in fulfilment, Whitman's kind of homosexuality remains unmistakably deathly in his view – all the more significantly because its source, an overbalance towards the 'upper centres' which tended to turn sensual experience into mental and spiritual consciousness, was present in himself, as were the independent man's resentment of dependence on woman, and the mystic hatred for the female bath of birth as also a lake of death for maleness. Indeed the whole current of the book not only makes Whitman the last deathly triumph of the American process of subjecting the sensual to the spiritual and mental, but values precisely what Whitman's kind of homosexuality is *not*, along with the signs in other writers of backlash and antidote, as pointing to new life. With Whitman's deathliness the American process of disintegration is almost complete – but the Americans are 'great' because they have accelerated the process of decadence, and because in the best of them the new has been made visible through the disintegration. It is there in Crèvecœur's sensuous art as opposed to his ideas; there in Cooper at the end though Deerslayer must die; there in what Hawthorne's secret self tells him in sensual recoil as opposed to his 'upper' consciousness; there when Dana confronts the Kanaka 'Hope' and drinks the earth-juice; there in Ishmael, Queequeg and the white whale; there in the possibility of a sensuous relation between males that fosters proud singleness (unlike Whitman's merging); and there in Whitman's poetry at its best when the whole psyche seems to speak at once. For Lawrence's goal remains the fulfilment of the whole – and it is because in modern decadence the 'upper' and unitary impulses of human being have grown so appallingly over-dominant that the 'lower' and singling-out ones must now be freed and activated to restore the balance. Indeed, for full psychic integration now, it may be necessary to go on beyond heterosexual relationship, as *Women in Love* had begun to imagine, in an additional relation between men – though not in Whitman's way. Perhaps he may have seen in his friendship with William Henry some reflection of the meanings he had discovered in Crèvecœur, Cooper and Melville.

Though his marriage remained intact after the strains of 1917 – Frieda's jealousy of his relations with Esther and William Henry, her relation with Gray and the tensions in Mecklenburgh Square, whatever the 'truth' of all these – the American essays announce that the sexual relationship of man and woman is no longer to occupy the centre of Lawrence's imagination. His relation with Frieda may have grown somewhat more distant. His impatience with heterosexual jealousies and intensities may have increased after Mecklenburgh Square – where *Aaron's Rod* began. We do not know whether from the start that book imagined a man putting his marriage behind him and setting out to look for something else – the quest was a classical form for American writers – nor whether it was her sense of having lost some of her power over him that made Frieda show angry unhappiness at Hermitage. Be that as it may, the American essays would certainly prove before long to have opened up a new field of imagination, and a new politics (opposed to Whitman's democracy) as well as a new psychology. The 'book' of 1918, though like 'Hardy' never published, was no less a source of work to come.

IX Life at Mountain Cottage

The original 'Whitman' was finished some time before 20 June (iii. 256), seven weeks after their arrival at Mountain Cottage.

How did they feel about the move? Frieda would have to cope with living for the first time on his family ground, though just distant enough from the

Nottingham where she was in disgrace. Even before they left she had lost some of her insouciance, showing her unhappiness instead of keeping her usual cheerful front. The move was not her choice. Lawrence himself had very mixed feelings about being back again so close to family and home territory. He might, much later and in another land, call it 'the country of my heart' (v. 592); but right now he felt 'queer and lost and exiled' (iii. 242).

Soon relatives and old friends began arriving. Ada probably came up almost at once to see them in. A family gathering was planned for the Whitsun weekend (iii. 242; 18–20 May), with Sallie Hopkin joining them the next Tuesday and Willie a couple of days later (iii. 243). Lawrence threatened (privately) to go walking in the hills, perhaps with Vere Collins, 'to escape the crowd' (iii. 242), but of course he could do no such thing. When the time came it was 'terribly hot' with 'violent thunder-storms', which made him feel 'limp and stupid' (iii. 244). His father came too; and Emily with her daughter Peggy aged 9 (both living with Ada now, Sam having been called-up); and Ada with her little son Jack aged 3, 'a very charming boy indeed' according to his uncle (iii. 245). It was 'queer – and a bit irritating, to be en famille again. I am no worshipper of family.' He thought it was like being in a swamp with meals for islands, whereas he had 'almost a passion for being alone ... Nevertheless, I feel it is good for me for some time to be with people, and en famille. It is a kind of drug, or soporific, a sort of fatness; it saves one' (iii. 245).

For however galling to be unsuccessful, poor and dependent, when surrounded by relatives again, there may have been some consolation in being simply accepted, and slipping back into being 'our Bert' again – for a while.

The family were all still there a week later, and though Ada and their father then went home, Emily and the two children stayed, and on 2 June Ada came back again briefly, with a hamper of goodies from Sallie (iii. 246). Indeed, Lawrence thought the children would stay for yet another fortnight if Ada sent her maid Lily up too. It is strange to think of him writing his essay on Whitman amid a houseful of respectable sisters and little children. Yet it was interesting to pick up old relationships, and see them in a new light. He wrote to Sallie with 'such regret' that the couple of days with them at Whitsuntide were so short, and seems to have meant it. The rhododendrons and peonies were out now, 'and rock-roses very lovely on the fields' (iii. 247). Moreover there was the opportunity for two kinds of practical psychological research. He was surprised, he told Cynthia:

how children are like barometers to their parents' feelings. There is some sort of queer, magnetic psychic connection – something a bit fatal, I believe. I feel I am all the time rescuing my nephew and my niece from their respective mothers, my two sisters: who have jaguars of wrath in their souls, however they purr to their offspring. The phenomenon of motherhood, in these days, is a strange and rather frightening phenomenon. (iii. 247)

He was always good with children, as small beings in their own right, and it is clear whose side he was on, here. He had done a great deal of thinking about mothers since he had been with his family last! There must have been a truce, too, in the old feelings of alienation from his father – now 72, and shrunken. But what did they talk about? (Growing vegetables and flowers, since his father was a keen gardener? Bossy women? The miners?)

He had often told Cynthia his dreams, and related a strange one now which suggests the turmoil and hurt still going on in his own psyche under the familial surface. He had been to 'some big, crowded fair somewhere' and coming back on the open road, he heard 'a strange crying overhead' from a bird being mauled by 'two pale spotted dogs', in mid-air. He clapped his hands, the dogs started away and the bird came falling to earth: 'a young peacock, blue all over like a peacock's neck, very lovely'. It kept crying, though not much hurt. 'A woman came running out of a cottage not far off, and took the bird, saying it would be all right. So I went my way' (iii. 247–8). He thought the dream connected with Cynthia's 'aura' in 'some oblique way'. It was the second vision in a month of a beautiful bird torn by beasts; and he always thought of Cynthia as someone who saw the brightness in him and would help when the world damaged it.

Indeed, he could confess to her how he felt helplessly stuck: 'I feel as if I were on a sort of ledge half way down a precipice, and didn't know how to get up or down' (iii. 248). His main hope just now was the application to the Royal Literary Fund, but that was humiliating. He had to ask Pinker to write again (iii. 249), as he had done in 1914. He had to put a figure to his own failure, replying to the secretary that whereas in the year to August 1914 he had earned '£400 or £500', since August 1917 he had made 'considerably less than £100' and it was 'with considerable chagrin that I fill in forms of application for help' (iii. 249–50). He also had to explain why he had not tried 'to obtain work in any Government department, because my health does not allow me to undertake any regular employment' (iii. 253) – without saying what he thought of the government. He filled in the forms and answered the questions with 'a black and angry heart', cursing 'the impertinent impudent questioners to hell and further' (iii. 251, 252). He even made himself appeal to Mary Cannan once more. In 1914 she had got several friends to help who had connections with the Fund. Now, however, the appeal was awkward because he and Frieda had never written to sympathise about her humiliating break up with Gilbert, though Lawrence was probably telling the truth when he assured Mary that he took her side. It was also humiliating for him to have once again to rehearse the story of persecution, his inability to make any money (even his grammar breaks down in the telling) and the pain of his nearly complete dependence on his sister now. At the end he retreats into memories of Cholesbury 'when we were happy with one another, really – even if we said spiteful things afterwards. I was happy, anyway' (iii 252). But the tone is uneasy. He liked Mary, but he could never have imagined having to appeal to her again. And now he could do nothing but wait, irritably, for the committee's verdict in July.

Moreover, as the war approached its final crisis, call-up papers came again from Cornwall, and though he sent them back, he knew he would have to be medically examined once more in Derby.

Yet he could go to Eastwood (to visit the Hopkins, and the Coopers who had been their next-door neighbours) and find that 'For the first time in my life I feel quite aimiably towards it' (iii. 250), his hatred gone, and no need to fight his beginnings any more. Indeed, he was laying them finally to rest. Though inside, life might be as 'wretched' as the outer world of war, 'such a ghastly stress, a horrid pressure on one, all the time – and gnawing anxiety' (iii. 254), he was able partly to distract himself by finishing the last gleaning from the old notebooks for a 'new' book of poems – albeit with some genuinely new ones 'made this spring'. He had dropped the idea of a division into two parts, 'In London' and 'A Choir of Women' (iii. 255); though he was prepared to revive it if Pinker so desired. Now he thought of calling it 'Coming Awake' (iii. 254), after a new poem[87] – but when Secker agreed to publish, he demanded that it be called *New Poems* and Lawrence gave in, though not happy to be so disingenuous (iii. 277, 291 and n. 3). The dedication this time was to Amy Lowell, who had recently delivered two lectures at the Brooklyn Institute in which she praised his poetry, though not unreservedly. Hilda Aldington had sent these on from Cornwall (iii. 253). He told Amy that he believed Hilda was 'happy' there, though with a diplomatic silence about the circumstances (iii. 254).

In any case Hilda would have been in his mind, for in an interval between family visits in June came the first visitor from the south, Arabella. She spent about a fortnight with them (iii. 256). From Mountain Cottage the intensities of Mecklenburgh Square must have fallen into distanced perspective for Lawrence, but Arabella's position was unenviable. Richard was gone and in constant danger in the trenches; Cournos was back from Russia very bitter at her betrayal in his absence, and wanting no more to do with her; Hilda was defiantly in Cornwall having shaken the dust of the ménage à trois from her sandals; and Arabella's own situation and finances were very unstable. All her supports had gone except her mother, determined still that she should be a success. Lawrence continued to think her 'very nice' in her brittle yet somehow gallant fashion (iii. 259), and she must have found being with them some comfort too (even the walks on the hills; iii. 261), since he recorded that she left 'in tears and grief. I hope she will come again soon – we became very fond of her' (iii. 257). But she never did.

Aaron's Rod would eventually show how she had caught his imagination,[88] but he had already abandoned it, since he said on 20 June he has finished everything he was writing and had 'a complete blank in front' (iii. 256).

While Arabella was still with them in the last week of June, the Hopkins came for another weekend, this time with Enid (now a young woman of 21) and her friend Kitty Allcock, a year younger. With the cottage so crowded the lasses had to sleep in an outhouse and walk 'bare-footed over the springy turf to the well at which we washed'. Kitty, who only saw Lawrence on one other occasion, remembered most the red beard, and 'his kindness and awareness'. They had meals outside on a trestle table: 'strange combinations of food' cooked by him with contributions brought by the Hopkins, partly because of rationing, but also because they were aware of his poverty. Kitty and Enid went walking on the hills to escape the charades and the folk-songs afterwards, for which she felt too shy.[89] It is a gentle glimpse of an irascible and unhappy man – but Lawrence was surprising himself to find how being with old friends and young people was helping him. For 'it is the human contact which means so much to one, really. Do you know, I quite suffered when they had gone away on Monday – and usually I am so glad to be alone.' He was finding 'change of scene' much less important than 'human warmth, when one can get it'; and that 'To be with people whose presence is an enrichment in the veins, is everything' (iii. 258). When he and Frieda were alone again for the first time for many weeks, he told Catherine (who had just given birth) how much better it was 'to have friends near one – and children – otherwise one thinks too much and is too much exposed' (iii. 259).[90]

It was now that he began to think of making his peace with Ottoline, but his tentative enquiry to Gertler about how she might take an overture (iii. 257) was met with such diplomatic conditions (since Gertler knew that Ottoline could not abide Frieda, and blamed the nastiest bits of *Women in Love* on her) that Lawrence flew into a rage again (iii. 260). Indeed, his sense that Gertler had become identified with Garsington was bound to cool their relationship too, though there was no breach. The friendship with Kot remained. He would not come to Derbyshire, but he sent another £10 cheque which Lawrence said he would try not to cash – and did not, since he was able to send it back later (iii. 256 and n. 2). (It is among the Koteliansky papers in the British Library.) But the man himself was immovable, and there was not much chance that he would ever travel north to see them.

Higher Tregerthen was fading rapidly into the distance. Lawrence was still corresponding with Gray, but there was a temporary contretemps with Captain Short about subletting the cottage in July to a friend of Mrs Yorke's (iii. 255–6), and things had changed markedly on the farm and in the village. William Henry had married, so his mother and sisters had to move elsewhere – another reason, probably, for the long courtship. Lawrence's sympathies were with Mrs Hocking in these 'ructions ... W.H. is rather a fool, and bores me ... If he had any decency he would go and live with Mary Quick in my cottage, and leave his mother on the farm' (iii. 261).[91] He threatened to tell him so if he ever wrote, but the Cornish farmer never did. Lawrence was equally sardonic about Gray's trouble with his housekeeper who was 'barking' about the living arrangements in Bosigran – something about which Lawrence too must have been none too happy, though not for moral reasons. And Katie Berryman was leaving her shop and the village – 'what will be left of Zennor?' (iii. 261). Very little, it seemed, for him.

There had also come out of the blue a letter from A. P. Lewis, now a wounded officer (iii. 260)[92] – but Spezia and the Alps and the Lake District before the war seemed (even more than Zennor) another world now. Lawrence never answered, perhaps because there seemed nothing to say. The 'ledge half way down a precipice', was determining what from the past could still seem real there.

One friendship from 1915, however, had suddenly borne new fruit. When first confronted with the prospect of his family en masse, Lawrence had toyed with the idea of escaping to walk in the hills with Vere Collins – the man from the Educational Books Division (in London) of Oxford University Press, who subscribed to *Signature* and had offered support over the suppression of *The Rainbow*. There had been a weekend with the Collinses before going down to Cornwall. Knowledge of Lawrence's friendships is shaped by the letters which survive, and this is a case where non-survival means ignorance. Lawrence must have kept in touch at intervals since 1915, and certainly made contact again before and during his visit to London in March 1918, for which Collins offered hospitality, though Lawrence chose to stay with Kot. The friendship was probably not close, but it now brought welcome help. For, well aware of Lawrence's desperate money worries and impressed (he said later) by his knowledge of history, Collins came up with the idea that he might write a little school-book on European history for children in the lower forms of secondary or the upper ones of primary school, where a lively style and imagination, which could interest young people, would be much more important than scholarly expertise. The Ministry of Education 'was urging schools to do more in teaching European history', but nothing had been done at junior level where what was wanted was not a 'formal, connected, text book, but a series of vivid sketches of movements and people'.[93] Perhaps this was why Lawrence suddenly began to read Gibbon, and as he did so, warmed to the idea. When Collins suggested that an assistant come to see him about it on her way back from a trip to Scotland in late June, he was persuaded; and from that visit of Nancy Henry, who would see the project through, a new friendship sprang.

She spent the night of 27 June in Mountain Cottage and soon convinced him that the idea was practicable with the help of some additional source-books. He was nearing the end of Gibbon now, and felt 'in a historical mood'. Gibbon's cynicism about human nature continued to appeal, and to strengthen his own belief that only aristocrats by nature could produce strong government – should that be possible at all. The 'chief feeling' he had got from Gibbon was 'that men were always alike, and always will be, and one must view the species with contempt'. History showed what was needed was a few individuals 'to *rule* the species. It is proper ruling they need, and always have needed. But it is impossible, because they can only be ruled as they are willing to be ruled: and that is swinishly or hypocritically' (iii. 262).

The book might be another way of taking him out of himself while earning something at last. At the month's end he visited Sallie in Eastwood and went on to Ada at Ripley, yet within a fortnight of Nancy's visit he had already finished a long first chapter (for which Gibbon was basis enough) on the Roman Empire and the founding of Constantinople. He had also taken a liking to Nancy, and an immediate interest in her circumstances. She seems not to have been on the permanent staff of the Press but a free-lance editor, supporting herself while her husband Leigh – poet, composer, and music critic, who before the war had been Gordon Craig's musical director in his famous Theatre School in Florence – was trapped in a German internment camp in Ruhleben. Just as on first meeting Catherine Carswell, years before, Lawrence immediately offered to help Nancy with a manuscript: a collection of poems which Leigh had sent from the camp. He selected forty-two that he thought would make 'a nice little book', tidied the presentation and asked Pinker to take it on; promising Nancy that if necessary he would 'send it round myself' (iii. 263). He was at work again.

All his other projects had seemed at a standstill. He had laid aside the new novel at only 150 manuscript pages; it had not found its stride or where it was going. Beaumont had evidently made no progress with *Bay* at all; nor was there any word yet from Pinker about publication of Secker's book of Lawrence poems. The typing of the American essays had stalled, so they too were unpublishable as yet. It must have seemed all the more important to get on with sample chapters of the little history book so as to earn a contract and a down payment – especially when the Literary Fund Committee, meeting on 10 June, awarded him only £50 again. His immediate response was abusive; and though the grant was 'something, anyhow' (iii. 265), it could make only a temporary difference while his basic situation remained as bad as ever. He could send Kot's cheque back (iii. 263), and he could afford now to promise Frieda a visit to London to see the children in August (iii. 267). He had told Gray ten days earlier that she was 'well' but 'about as happy and unhappy as you might expect' (iii. 261), so a trip to London would give her something to look forward to.

In the meantime, with only his three-year-old nephew to keep Frieda amused, he settled down to write his history and finished three specimen chapters by 26 July. He confessed that they were 'perhaps rather long'. Indeed the first would be divided later, so he had done what became the chapters on 'Rome', 'Constantinople', 'Christianity' and 'The Germans' – enough for OUP to decide whether to go on. He told Nancy that he wanted to write a 'serious' book, 'that would convey the true historic impression to children who are beginning to grasp realities. We should introduce the deep, philosophic note into education: deep philosophic reverence' (iii. 268–9). The chapters are nowhere near as solemn as this might suggest, but he believed the study of the past had to raise questions of value for young people – truth, fairness, freedom, order, tolerance, right and wrong; and ought to set them thinking also about how the ways of life of different peoples were derived from the differing values they prized most highly. Already 'North' and 'South', 'Eastern' and 'Western' are beginning to be contrasted in cultural as well as climatic ways; and already there are hints of a developing concern with the requirements of order, authority and peaceful growth. Historically, there is nothing original.The material comes from Gibbon, and now also from Tacitus, and there are mistakes as well as economical and lively assemblage and narrative. Where Lawrence is original however, reminding one again of what a good classroom teacher he may have been, is in his ability to imagine in ways that could not only bring the past vividly alive to children in mid-school, but also teach more than is apparent. To see the landscape through Constantine's eyes as he traces the boundaries of his new capital with his lance, not only makes it real, but also impresses a whole new geography on the imagination, where it will stick. One has taken in, painlessly, how 'Byzantium' would face 'East' in religion and politics as well. And the powerful imagining of the Hercynian forest, *before* the contrast of 'German' with 'Roman', ensures that the limits of the latter are vividly felt, so that both the great 'opposites' which, for Lawrence, go to the making of 'Europe', come home to imagination. At least, too, the chapters are not boring.[94]

Moreover, in arranging with Nancy for the typing, the rest of the American essays may have been included, and his hopes for them revived. He thought of going to London to see Pinker about them, and even of taking a little holiday afterwards, since the Carswells were spending some weeks in the Forest of Dean and invited them there. Catherine also offered the use of their London house, but once again Lawrence preferred to go to Kot (iii. 271). But first, his Aunt Ada and her husband Fritz Krenkow were coming to Mountain Cottage for the August bank holiday weekend (iii. 267). This must have seemed another plunge back into the past. It was at Aunt Ada's house in Leicester that his mother had fallen ill; they had been and still were very friendly with Louie Burrows; and it had been the Krenkows' idea that he should go to Germany after his own illness which had led to his meeting Frieda – but he had not seen them since 1912. He found his aunt a bit boring but Fritz more interesting. He was employed by a hosiery firm, but his real life's work was in Arabic studies in which he was to earn a considerable reputation. Yet as so often with the Lawrences, the visit proved a bit too long: 'We also', he told Catherine, 'are suffering badly from relatives – badly' (iii. 273). He and Frieda were impatient now for London. On Monday 12 August they went.

X   Town, and the Forest of Dean

Only two days later, town was already 'horribly boring and stultifying. It is like living in a sort of vacuum. – And we have to go out every evening – it is difficult to get things fitted in' (iii. 273). The crowded schedule may have been because he was wary, in his turn, of outstaying his welcome with Kot. Indeed Edith Eder and Barbara Low persuaded them, after Frieda's visit to the children, to spend a long weekend on Mersea Island near Colchester (iii. 274), before going back to Acacia Road very briefly. He saw Nancy Henry again, and heard that his specimen chapters were being considered by Herbert Ely who was responsible for OUP's Juvenile and Elementary Schools Department. If Ely approved, Lawrence promised to work hard at it when he got back to Derbyshire (iii. 276). He called on Pinker, and heard shortly afterwards that Secker would do the new book of poems. It may also have been now, galvanised by Lawrence and reassured about the typing (some more of which was collected), that Pinker began to negotiate with Harrison about publishing the American essays in the *English Review*, though the first would only appear in November. Lawrence saw Campbell, with whom he had been rather out of touch; and visited Enid Hopkin at the seed nursery where she now worked (iii. 273). Cynthia Asquith was visiting her father in Scotland, so he had no chance of a gossip about her new job as secretary to James Barrie (iii. 282); but he saw Dollie Radford (who at last had been persuaded that Ernest should be in a Home; iii. 274); and Arabella, who had news that Richard was out of the front line just now (iii. 280). He probably saw Gertler too. But there are signs of irritation with this social round, for which he was even less fitted after Mountain Cottage than before. Though he felt 'a curious nascent quality in the world' as though a change was coming at long last; he also confessed that there was 'some intangible counteraction ... between me and everybody' (iii. 276). He told Kot he had been 'a bit disgusted' with Campbell (iii. 285), whose job in the Ministry of Labour may perhaps have produced establishment attitudes. However relations between Frieda and Kot had improved somewhat, 'since open enmity is avowed' (iii. 277)!

He cut short their stay in London, preferring a long weekend at Hermitage (before he could leave for the Forest of Dean), even though he knew a 'very seedy' Margaret Radford would be in the cottage and he did not much care for her at the best of times (iii. 274). He felt he needed a break. Though he did indeed find a nervy Margaret 'horrible' (iii. 277), the place was as ever pleasant, peaceful and somnolent (iii. 276).

On 26 August they went to join Catherine, Donald and baby John, in the Vicarage in Upper Lydbrook near Ross-on-Wye which the Carswells were house sitting at next to no rent. (It says something both for their generosity and the steadiness of Lawrence's friendship with Catherine that he was able to accept the train fare from her without humiliation or resentment; iii. 274) At the station, he was like a schoolboy on holiday, and Frieda more 'ejaculatory' than ever.[95] He found the Carswells pleasant as always, if 'depressed' (iii. 277) – but they soon cheered one another up. The Vicarage sat behind a big brown church which looks out across the valley to an unspectacular village, straggling along the road against the hillside; but the country all around is beautiful. It must have reminded Lawrence of Nottinghamshire, for here was the same juxtaposition of forest and rich landscape with active coal-mines – though he was scornful of the small cages and winding gear by Notts standards – and also disused gin pits like the ones he had described at the beginning of *Sons and Lovers*. Yet – or therefore? – he felt a sudden 'malaise' on 'first tumbling into that forest of Lydbrook – which for some reason is curiously upsetting' (iii. 278). Catherine thought it might be because of 'the dark and ancient steepness of those woods'.[96] This was only a first impression however. He liked the walks carrying the baby (as if actually holding the future), especially the one to the spectacular ravine of the river Wye as it curves through Simmonds Yat. He enjoyed their expedition by train across the Welsh border to Monmouth: 'particularly the Church by the Monnow bridge – the bright, sunny town, and the tears in one's inside because there isn't *real* peace'; and the picnic on lard cakes, '*very nice* ... in the green riding' (iii. 278). They must have made an odd spectacle: Frieda's ample figure in the biggest and brightest of checks, Lawrence in a red-and-green striped blazer Aldington had given him, and his only pair of grey flannel trousers (both washed so often now that wrists and ankles stuck out), and sockless espadrilles to go with the beard – a combination likely to make heads turn in rural Here-fordshire. In the evenings they sang songs, the favourite being a duet with Donald in 'What Are the Wild Waves Saying'. They all disliked the formal vicarage drawing-room and much preferred sitting in the kitchen beside the walled garden, but Lawrence had brought a book of French songs with him and (says Catherine) 'even the hated china cabinets did not keep him away from the drawing-room piano', picking out tunes with one finger and an expression of 'intense and concentrated earnestness' as he learned French ballads off by heart. But Catherine preferred his odd voice in English folk-songs: 'A Cottage Well Thatched with Straw', she remembered, and 'Twanky-dillo' which he wrote out for her, and 'the prim absurd charm of Offenbach in English' which he 'rendered deliciously'.

It was at Lydbrook that he conceived his story 'The Blind Man', and in the vicarage kitchen that he first outlined the idea to Catherine and Letty, the old servant who came with the house. Catherine describes her as 'lovable, but almost half-witted', yet she too seemed (despite initial bewilderment) 'to breathe the dark air of the stable' in the story. After he had written it in November, friends would see traces of Catherine in Isabel Pervin.[97]

There was also intense talk, of course, and a chance of getting to know Donald much better than before. Interestingly it was to him that Lawrence wrote his thank-you letter, wanting him also to read the later American essays which had been left behind for Catherine. It had been for legal advice that he had asked Donald to read *Women in Love*, but now he had obviously come to respect his mind, though he also anticipated (having experienced) the kind of criticism that the trained lawyer would make. 'You will say I repeat myself – that I don't know the terms of real philosophy – and that my terms are empty – the empty Self – so don't *write* these things to me, I know them beforehand, and they make me cross' (iii. 278). Nevertheless Donald was to read the essays 'and see if you find anything in them'. Fortunately, he liked the one on Melville and *Moby Dick*.

On the last day of August the Lawrences were back at a Mountain Cottage 'strangely quiet, though the wind blusters and the rain beats on this little house' (iii. 278).

XI   Black September

It might have seemed that, despite storms outside, life was cheering up on the ledge. However a string of annoyances began, and got worse, till at the end of a black September Lawrence felt the chasm below even deeper than before. Donald and Catherine were to have visited, but the plans fell through.[98] Secker wanted the rather poor early poem 'Late in Life' left out of the new volume; and though Lawrence replied irritably that he did not care: 'I don't want to hear his literary criticisms' (iii. 278). Frieda's jealousy broke out again at what she saw as a new soul-friendship with Nancy, who seems to have written with some intensity about how she wanted to help Lawrence in his troubles. He felt he had to respond coolly, doubting 'if one person can help another, save by just *being*'. His troubles would 'have to resolve themselves somehow'. Nevertheless 'someone in the world whom one can really trust as a friend is a great blessing' – but, 'My wife gets angry when she reads your letter. – Why can *three* people never be proper friends? Nothing will be any good till they can.' Perhaps it might be managed nonetheless, 'so long as we adjust ourselves properly'; for he has his old 'great desire for permanency' (iii. 279) – but the warning is clear. There was no verdict yet on his specimen chapters.

Then came the post on 11 September, his thirty-third birthday – Christ's age when crucified, as he would point out. There was a letter from Nichols, that very minor poet, who had nevertheless been invited to lecture in America; and also the summons to another medical inspection at Derby (iii. 281). The combination was bound to enrage. Nichols proposed to include Lawrence in his lectures on poetry and wanted some biographical details, but the contrast of his circumstances with those of the Oxonian subaltern-poet was bound to be galling. Birthdays can become depressing surveys of one's life and progress, and as Lawrence prepared a potted autobiography now, his anger overflowed at being stranded like a fish out of water, and at the successful literary people like Bennett who refused to help (though this was far less true of Bennett than he thought).

Here am I, can't make a living to save my life, without caving in and accepting the filthy world at its own value. Which I won't do. – There remains the serious prospect of starving oneself out ... As for being a genius – the very word becomes an insult, at last ...

Yes, I like the free soul, that an artist is and must be, in you. How much you'll sail with, and how much against, the wind, that is your affair. But the wind is dead against a free spirit and a *real* art ... (iii. 281)

He tells Nichols about the call-up and how 'having been badgered about as I have, kicked out of Cornwall, and pushed about by the police, I'm damned if I will move one step at the bidding of such filthers'. Yet he knew perfectly well that he would have to obey the summons to Derby in the end – though he did actually send the papers back again, asking how they could expect anything of him 'if I am still a black-marked person' (iii. 283). The potted autobiography suggests a heritage (and alliance) of nonconforming fighters fallen on evil days, and ends with the nausea of a born outsider for the world in which he has to live.[99]

Another source of disturbance, however, can only be detected between the lines of a letter to Amy Lowell that same day. He thanked her for another cheque from the latest Imagist anthology. His volume of poems dedicated to her would be out in six weeks. He was glad to have the issue of *Poetry* with a piece on him by Fletcher.[100]

But in the middle of all this were two sentences whose restraint can only be gauged by outside evidence: 'Hilda has left Cornwall, and even had some idea of coming to America, I believe. But I don't expect she will' (iii. 280). He had to say something in reply to Amy's enquiries after Hilda and Richard, but he said as little as any man could. For he had recently heard that Hilda had become pregnant by Gray. It had happened in June. She warned her husband at the end of July, though she was not certain she was pregnant until she came to London about 21 August.[101] She probably wrote to Lawrence then. Perdita – well-chosen name – would be born on 31 March 1919, a birth involving some danger to both baby and mother.

Lawrence must have been deeply upset and angry. Though he had tried to dissuade Hilda from going to live with Gray – ostensibly to have peace to work on her *Iphigenia in Aulis* – he had gone on writing friendly letters, while acknowledging to Gray in March that their paths seemed to be diverging. As recently as 22 July he had told 'Grigio': 'When you feel like leaving Bosigran for a bit, you will come and stay here, will you, and we'll see where we are' (iii. 266). This is however the last letter to have survived – though maybe not the last to have been written. The cooling of the friendship was clearly *not* because Lawrence demanded unquestioning discipleship, or could not take criticism, as we have seen, and he had condoned Gray's relationship with Frieda, whatever that was. Gray's account allows no glimpse of the real reason for the breach. Disingenuously, he boasts of fluttering the dovecot on his visit to London, but says nothing at all of what happened in Cornwall afterwards.[102]

Lawrence's closeness to Hilda had begun in the aftermath of her miscarriage, aware of the terror of conceiving again which made her refuse to sleep with Aldington thereafter. Would he not have written to tell Gray what he thought of him now? This would not be a matter of social morality, since love had to be free, but he also demanded that it be responsible, not careless. (Gray however never accepted any responsibility or acknowledged paternity, even when he met Perdita as a young woman in Capri in 1947.) He would have been furious at Gray for putting Hilda so at risk psychologically and physically as well as socially – a rage fuelled also by his own refusal to take advantage of her, and by jealousy, heated still more if Gray had indeed slept with Frieda. With such powerful motivation, would Lawrence not have told Gray what he thought of him? It can only be speculation, but it does seem highly likely – and if so, given the ego visible everywhere in his writings, Gray's subsequent malice and determination to do Lawrence all the damage he could in 'reminiscences' after 1930, while concealing the real cause of the breach between them, would be more explicable.[103]

Lawrence certainly wrote to Hilda. Years later she quoted from his 'last letter': 'I hope never to see you again'.[104] His feelings must have been complicated. He cared deeply about her, and believed that they had pledged a lifelong kind of troth. For all we know, it may have been hard for him not to take advantage, and he too may have gone on wondering whether he had been too scrupulous. He continued to hear about her from Arabella and Richard, expressed concern for her, even wondered whether he might after all see her again. What he felt most however, was not merely disapproval or jealousy. He felt betrayed. 'Poor Hilda', he wrote to Arabella's mother on 16 December, 'Feeling sorry for her, one almost melts. But I *don't* trust her – ' (iii. 308).[105] It must have seemed that her giving herself to Gray devalued all she had claimed to feel for himself, by way of artistic affinity and companionship as well as love and loyalty. To sleep with Gray and risk bearing his child, moreover, also called in question all she had claimed to feel about sex and motherhood since 1915, and the whole of her behaviour to Aldington – and to Cournos, if Lawrence knew about that. (Cournos, for his part, could not understand how Lawrence could ever have preferred 'fat Frieda' to H.D.[106] Changing the names and seeing, behind the physical insult, Cournos's sense of Hilda's fineness, the incredulity might have done also for Lawrence's feeling about Hilda, himself and fattish Gray.) It probably made it even worse that, as time proved, she neither loved Gray nor wanted to stay with him. Lawrence had warned her that going to live at Bosigran was bound to make a difference. He could never have imagined it would be so great. Yet Hilda's sense of having been rejected by both her husband and Lawrence had had much to do with what happened.

It must have been this reaction that Richard had in mind when he replied to Hilda's letter of 26 August: 'I am sorry about the Lawrence business for your sake; but people are like that. I suspected the Gray business too. Artists! My God: *quel canaille*.'[107] It must have been unspeakable to get such news in the trenches, and know his wife to be without support. He tried hard to be noble and forgiving at first, though later he attempted to prevent the baby being registered in his name; and this in fact marked the final break up of his relationship with Hilda too. When he came back, it would be to Arabella.

The call-up and these other annoyances already made for a black September, but it would get still worse. For Lawrence could not avoid the medical examination, and his gesture of returning the papers merely elicited a curt instruction to attend at Derby on 26 instead of 21 September (iii. 286, 283). He blustered a bit more to relieve his feelings, but he had to go, or go to prison. He was fairly sure to be rejected. Yet conscription was such now – the German advance apparently halted and the counter-attack under way, but the cost in casualties enormous and the outcome still very much in balance – that there *was* a risk now of being made to do some menial task to release another man to the armed forces, unless he could show that he was doing something else of use. So he wrote to Cynthia asking if he too could become a secretary (iii. 282), since he could type. He had to do *something* or 'I shall burst or go cracked' (iii. 284). Veering in another direction, he thought of making contact with members of the Independent Labour Party, and becoming politically active: 'I had rather be hanged or put in prison than endure any more. So now I shall move actively, personally, do what I can. I am a desperado' (iii. 285). But he was not, nor a joiner in any direction – and it was late in the day for such public protest. He told Nancy just before he left for Derby that it would serve no purpose for him to defy the law as a mere individual, and that he had no taste for martyrdom (iii. 286).

So he went – and his description of the experience in the 'Nightmare' chapter of *Kangaroo* shows how its scarring remained with him for years to come. As against the relative courtesy and humanity with which he had been treated at Bodmin, this Board of elderly officers and the medical examiners who took their tone from them (all perfectly stay-at-home themselves), had become corrupted by their power, bullying and openly contemptuous of the specimens before them. These were all made to strip naked and wait on benches for long periods with only a jacket round their shoulders. One great streak of anger in Lawrence's account has less to do with himself than with horror at the way a big miner, his ugly body mercilessly exposed, was so harried and humiliated and confused as to *become* almost subhuman. Lawrence drew into himself in hatred, enough to endure being 'moved about like a block of meat, in the atmosphere of corrosive derision',[108] and made to do physical jerks in the nude in front of others. His information about his lungs was treated with sneering scepticism. At this moment he felt the hostility of his examiners crystallise; and it is conceivable that they were waiting for him because of the fuss he had already made about attending, though that may have been his paranoia. The last straw, however, was having to have his genitals felt in public, and then being made to bend over, further and further, while a young jackanapes cracking jokes peered up his anus ... a medical examination made into a public humiliation. He hated to be touched without his consent by anyone, and had written a poem about his wife's proprietary failure to respect his body. It was not however the medical inspection itself that rankled, so much as the insolent power of officials to expose and jest about men's 'privates' – the reverence for the body and the private self, so central to his thought, deliberately outraged.

He was placed in Grade 3, sedentary work only, but 'it kills me with speechless fury to be pawed by them. They shall *not* touch me again – such filth' (iii. 287). He was absolutely determined not to be drafted into anything by the military. Couldn't he be found work in the Ministry of Education, he asked Cynthia, given his teaching qualifications and experience? Could she not approach H. A. L. Fisher, the President of the Board of Education, whom she knew slightly? But, beyond that, the experience was a final watershed in his relation to his society. If he had persuaded himself in the past that it was as an *artist* that he served his people, he could do so no longer. 'I'm not going to squat in a cottage feeling their fine feelings for them, and flying for them a flag that only makes a fool of *me*. I'm out on a new track – let humanity go its own way – I go mine. But I *won't* be pawed and bullied by them – no' (iii 288).

It was the final step in the making of an alien.

◆

CHAPTER NINE

October 1918–November 1919

MARKING TIME

I *will* get out of Europe this year ...
(iii. 316)

I Interlude in the South

It seemed imperative now to find something to do that would prevent being drafted into war work, and for that he needed to go to London. He wrote to the Carswells and Gertler for ideas (iii. 288, 289); and angled with Pinker for a meeting with Bennett in the hope of work rather than money this time (iii. 289). Dollie Radford was away visiting her son but let them have 32 Well Walk, where they arrived on 7 October 1918.

Pinker had now negotiated for the first of the American essays to appear in the November *English Review*, and though Harrison offered only 5 guineas for it, Lawrence thought he would be willing to take more at that rate (iii. 286–7). This turned out to be so, producing £42 over eight months – little enough, but more than Lawrence had earned for a long time. *New Poems* was published in October while he was in London and made him another £10 or so.[1] There was still no word about the history; but the Carswells came up with an idea. If he wanted to do something in education, why not write for *The Times Educational Supplement*? Don knew the editor G. S. Freeman, and arranged an interview which went well enough for Lawrence – ever the optimist – to think he might be offered work for the *Literary Supplement* as well (iii. 291).[2] There was no more talk of getting a job – 'be damned to all jobs and jobbers' (iii. 292). As he had told the Royal Literary Fund Committee, his health would not allow regular employment, and his temperament still less. Yet now, with the hope that the American essays might come out serially, the European history-book be approved and some essays on education pave the way to regular work for the *Times* supplements, his future seemed more hopeful than at any moment since the expulsion from Cornwall. Those who knew him might doubt that he could ever adapt himself to the expectations of commissioning editors, but all he ever needed was some hope to keep him going. Moreover, as the Allied counter-attack in France gathered momentum, there seemed a real chance of an end to the war at last.

He made a personal peace with Katherine Mansfield (Mrs Murry since 3 May). He had not seen Jack on any of his London visits since the expulsion from Cornwall, though he had news of him from Kot and from Gertler (even more established at Garsington now than Murry). If 'a bit disgusted' at what Campbell had become, and at Gertler's 'Ottling' (iii. 270), Lawrence must have felt more so at the way Murry had worked himself into the War Office. He had become head of his Department of European news-gathering, and had indeed worked so hard that his health broke down in November 1917. He spent some months recuperating at Garsington from what was thought might be tuberculosis. When he came back he threw himself into his work as much as ever, as well as continuing to review French fiction for the *TLS* and political journalism for the *Nation*. (He would become Chief Censor in 1918, and be awarded the OBE in 1920.) Katherine's health however had broken down so seriously at the end of 1917 that her doctors ordered her to the south of France again. The diagnosis was 'dry pleurisy', but the doctors found a spot on a lung which made it imperative that she should never spend another winter in England. In January 1918 she left for Bandol, where she and Jack had been so happy and productive before they came to Cornwall – but in February she had her first haemorrhage, and in April a wearying journey back, with a long delay in Paris which was under bombardment. The wedding (in the same registry where they had been witnesses for Lawrence and Frieda) was a terrible let-down for her because of Jack's matter-of-fact behaviour; and it was thought advisable for her health that she should spend the rest of spring, alone again, in Cornwall. At the end of August however she and Jack had moved into a house in Hampstead – their first real home for several years – with servants, and the prospect of the regulated life she now had to lead. (A specialist told Murry that unless she went into a sanatorium she had only a few years to live, but the most she would do was to adopt a quieter and stricter regime.)[3]

She mended some bridges: with Kot, who had told Virginia Woolf in January that Katherine's 'lies & poses had proved too much for him' but who came at once when summoned; and with Ottoline, wounded by Jack's harsh review of the poems of Sassoon who had become her latest favourite. Katherine had been thinking about Lawrence too, noting in her journal how *like* him she was becoming, in the fits of temper she associated with her illness. When however she heard that the Lawrences were coming to London, and would be in Well Walk 'just round the corner', she was horrified:

I am sure they will turn up here, & though I have armed M. with every possible weapon & warned him against L. I have a terrible idea that they will fight – and it will be hideous and lacerating. L. has come up to look for work in an office – which of course he'll *never* do for more than three days. But altogether, I feel they are better as many miles away as

473

there *are* miles. Everytime the bell goes I hear Frieda's '*Well* Katherina – *here* we are!' and I turn cold with horror.[4]

However, a first meeting passed off well enough; and though Lawrence did not warm again to Murry he was genuinely concerned for Katherine. He saw in her what he perhaps secretly feared in himself, but also all the things that attracted him highlighted now, by the thought that she might die.

Moreover Frieda caught a bad cold, was ordered to bed by Maitland Radford and insisted on leaving London for the cottage in Hermitage as soon as she was well enough to move (iii. 292–3).

While Frieda was laid up, and later when he came up to town again by himself, Lawrence kept popping in to see Katherine and soon much of their old relation was re-established. It was obligatory to denigrate him to Ottoline of course, so Katherine records that he seemed to have 'quite forgotten' Frieda 'for the time', saying dismissively that she wanted him to be a German, 'and Im *not*'. He is still 'taken in by the most impossible charlatans' (such as Pryse, presumably, if he had been talking of his latest work); lacks a real sense of humour; and 'takes himself dreadfully seriously now-a-days' as a prophet crying woe in the wilderness – regarding Murry as 'a flipperty-gibbet' who would not take life seriously enough. But to Dorothy Brett she paints a very different picture.

I loved him: He was just his old merry, rich self, laughing, describing things, giving you pictures, full of enthusiasm and joy in a future where we were all 'vagabonds' – We simply did not talk about people. We kept to things like nuts and cowslips & fires in woods, and his black self *was* not. Oh, there is something so lovable in him – & his eagerness, his passionate eagerness for life – that is what one loves so.

Murry remembered coming home and finding them 'talking gaily together. I felt that I weighed on them like a lump of lead. It was the old gay talk of a new life in a new country', but he felt he could not participate because only he knew of the specialist's sentence on Katherine.[5] Yet both she and Lawrence knew well enough what an arterial haemorrhage meant – and their gaiety was precisely in the face of that. It was no accident that Lawrence did his best to keep his sunniest face turned; though this meant that they had not in fact got back to the full Blutbrüderschaft he had always wanted. In the next few months he would send her some of the most vital and vivid letters he ever wrote, seeking to lift her spirits. (But as it happened, after he returned to the Midlands they were never to meet again.)

Frieda was not seriously ill, though there was momentary fear of pleurisy, but as ever she hated being unwell at all and became depressed, perhaps also because of the way things were going for Germany. (Lawrence's odd remark to Katherine suggests that Frieda wanted him to feel more for her people.)

Certainly a flu-ridden London at the start of the terrible epidemic held no attraction for her; and Dollie also may have returned home, since Maitland was available to be consulted.[6] Lawrence thought merely of moving to Nancy's rooms in Adelaide Road, Chalk Farm, but that did not suit Frieda, and so it was to Hermitage they went as soon as she could travel. As well as the Murrys, there had been time to see Kot, of course, and Richard Aldington, home on leave, and Arabella, and to have news of Hilda. He probably did not see her, though he told Amy later that she had been in town, as was Gray whom he certainly did not meet (iii. 294). It was probably only through Richard that he knew Hilda was 'not so very well ... for her nerves are very shaken'; but he hoped the baby would 'soothe her and steady her' (iii. 314). In Hampstead he also called on Mrs Tarry and remarked wryly that she was the only happy person they had seen, for she had her son home, alive (iii. 294).

From 22 October till about 19 November they stayed in Chapel Cottage. In a few days Frieda was out with him gathering chestnuts in woods grown autumn-yellow. Soon she was quite well, and the cold he had caught too, was better (iii. 293) – while the flu epidemic raged on in London. Moreover peace in which to write, and a renewed friendship, inspired an unexpected creative outburst as opposed to the commissioned work he ought perhaps to have been getting on with. Lawrence had met, at Greatham in 1915, Bertie and Joan Farjeon, who had now recently acquired a holiday home at Bucklebury, just five miles from Hermitage. Since Lawrence had happy memories of them and Eleanor, he must have been pleased to renew acquaintance – probably in April before the Lawrences went north, and again in August. By late 1918 he knew their house well enough to know the exact location of a book he wanted to borrow.[7] Moreover Bertie was not only a singer of songs and a merry man; he was a playwright and dramatic critic, and it seems likely that it was animated conversation with him that inspired Lawrence to write another play himself, *Touch and Go* – his first since the revision of *The Widowing of Mrs. Holroyd* in 1913.

Having found no publisher for *Women in Love*, he used the employment of Gudrun at Shortlands as a starting-point – but the characters are different enough from those in the novel to make contrast more useful than comparison. It is a predominantly political play; the first product of Lawrence's return to the coal-mining Midlands. There must have been talk with his father and Willie Hopkin (especially), and in the newspapers, about the unrest in the coalfields as the war seemed about to end. What were the prospects of peace between capital and labour – or (to question more dramatically) between owners, miners and union leaders at local level? – Gibbon had set him thinking about government, reinforcing his own cynicism about both power-corrupted governors and the unwillingness of the people to be governed well. In the same letter in which he spoke of the permanence of Gibbon's insights, he mentioned an appalling explosion at a munitions factory in the Midlands in which 134 people were killed (iii. 262 and n. 1). His new play suggests the danger of explosion in the coalfields too. Moreover, seeing the Murrys again had given him an idea of how to connect his political main plot with a sub-plot about the malaise of the upper class. Annabel Wrath (the 'Gudrun' character) and Gerald Barlow do not at all portray the Murrys, but Lawrence had been struck by the idea of a woman forced to recognise a deathliness in herself and her relationships, and returning to find her lover even more corrupted by power within the system than when she left. Above all, the play differs from *Women in Love* in that it is not concerned with individual character. Instead (pre-Brecht) the protagonists perform representative attitudes, to bring out their full implications.

It begins in satire, as the street-orator Willie Houghton[8] mocks the supineness and materialism of the miners, and the manoeuvring of the union leaders who toady to both sides – but as Annabel points out, he can only show what the freedom he calls for is *not*. This middle-class socialism seems to favour a Labour government and the nationalisation of the mines in theory, but actually has no intrinsic belief in the miners or their leaders, or that the labour movement has any but materialist goals. (Nor does anyone else in the play, which is presumably why Lawrence's impulse to ally himself with the ILP was so short-lived.) The last scene will show that this kind of satirist finally lines up with the bosses. The union leader, Job Arthur Freer, has an emblematic name. He seems to stand primarily for patience (like Job's): for careful negotiation, compromise, gradual improvement, trying to strike a balance good for everyone – but this will not make him or the workers 'Freer'. For it would require the bosses to be Job's counterpart – whereas the first act shows Gerald the coal-owner becoming an embodiment of naked power, intransigence and aggression. A kind of analytical X-ray strips away the novel's character complexity in order to clarify where technological power allied to English class-contempt will go. The incompatibility of the benevolent Christianity of Gerald's father with industrial capitalism is shown even more crisply than before. Gerald becomes the 'son' of his fierce mother – who hates and despises the lower orders, is contemptuous of all civilised convention, and wants to beat the last 'softness' out of her son to give him the power to act alone. (Lawrence inspected the extreme of his own individualism.) There might have been another side to Gerald, as Annabel hoped and Job Arthur thought he was promised in the affair of the clerks' wage rise – but he goes on fighting with Annabel and hating her resistance; and at the end of Act III Scene i he exposes once and for all the violence and contempt at his bossy core, all civilised concealments ripped away. In a burst of temper he does what bosses really want to do. He brutally throws the trade unionist to the ground and kicks him, again, and again.

This precipitates out what is at the core of Job Arthur and his men: not merely money but something far deeper, the desire to get their 'own back': a nicely ambiguous phrase implying not merely revenge but also outrage at being treated as less than fully human. Yet the outcome is deeply ironic. As the argument about capital and labour turns from compromise into naked power-struggle and violence, 'Job' becomes 'Arthur', a war leader exercising tenuous control over class warriors. As their inner violence is liberated the miners lose their humour and become a baying mob, forcing the ladies and gentlemen to their knees and tumbling Gerald in the mud to be trampled and kicked in his turn. The agonised protests of the toffs at being bullied and treated as 'vermin', the pleas for a spark of decency since 'he's a man as you are', are wholly devalued since this dehumanisation parallels so exactly what Gerald has done. Should he complain that his face has been trodden on, they will 'easily answer that you've trodden on their souls'.[9] Nor however do good or evil alter with the numbers involved. There is no moral difference between the two acts of violence. The strength of the work is its determination to push potentialities to extremes on both sides, so that an audience may feel in the theatre that it really might be touch-and-go whether post-war England will come to violent class war – as in Russia.

Is there a way forward? This may be the wrong question, since the play is pre-Brechtian also in being more interested in exposure than solution. Moreover there are signs that it might be better (in Lawrence's eyes) that the compromises of wartime *should* break down into anarchy. The peacemakers do not seem to have the author's blessing. Not only does the play devalue Job Arthur's idea of triangular balance through just mediation, having a foot on each side of the see-saw of power; but Annabel also suspects that in private life triangular relation-ships may make things worse (as opposed to Birkin's view in *Women in Love*, perhaps altered by experience). Owing something to Arabella's sense of the deathliness of her free love in Paris, as well as to Katherine's situation, Lawrence makes his Annabel Wrath an angry young woman who has seen the error of her ways and does not want to be wrathful and destructive any longer. In the past that we do not see, she had been the female counterpart to Gerald's macho man in the sex war – but what we see now is a woman who wants to change and make a new start. She wants 'something more dignified, more religious if you like – anyhow, something *positive*'.[10] She criticises both Gerald and the bullying miners for their lack of these qualities. She even knows that real balance is not compromise but a quality of vital being with the courage (given opportunity) to live itself to the full. Yet she has no idea of *how* to be what she wants. Could it ever come about through becoming Mrs Barlow? What if livingness, these days, cannot be found in oneself or one's opposite – or one's world? Might it be only through experience of real chaos that people will activate the living spark in themselves and turn away from bullying on both sides? Whereas mediation and compromise merely postpone the necessary revolution? Only when he is kicked does Gerald discover that he is tired of his way of life and wants something better – but he is still in power, and still sneering at the lack of workers' leaders he can respect, when he leaves the stage.

Oliver (the ineffectual intellectual who has taken Birkin's place) has also tried to mediate, turning from side to side. He voices a kind of socialism resembling Lawrence's in 'Hardy'; but now its naïveté is exposed. To the angry workers he says:

You see, if you wanted to arrange things so that money flowed more naturally, so that it flowed naturally to every man, according to his needs, I think we could all agree. But you don't. What you want is to take it away from one set and give it to another – or keep it yourselves ... I want every man to be able to live and be free. But we shall never manage it by fighting over the money. If what you want is natural and good, I'm sure the owners would soon agree with you.

That is utopian nonsense, as Gerald immediately shows; and though Oliver calls for greater trust, he has no idea, in the context of power, how it could happen.

You want a better way, – but not his way: he wants a better way – but not your way. Why can't you both drop your buts, and simply say you want a better way, and believe yourselves and one another when you say it? Why can't you?[11]

That 'simply' is fatal evidence of Oliver's blindness to the realities of politics and political institutions. Perhaps Willie's quotation of Tiberius at the beginning (though he doesn't know it is from Gibbon), 'Oh, how eager these men are to be slaves'; and Gerald at the end shouting that he will only respect his men when they choose strong leaders, are nearer guides to the Lawrence of late 1918 – in which case the violence at the end is an improvement on the situation at the start. One of his September letters to Nancy had complained that there was 'no spirit of resistance' in the country (iii. 286), another to Kot welcomed what was happening in Lenin-led Russia, since 'Nothing but a real smelting down is any good for her: no matter how horrible it seems ... chaos is necessary for Russia. Russia will be all right – righter, in the end, than these old stiff senile nations of the West.' England, however, is probably too old for chaos. Her only hope is 'to be *wise*, and recover her decency' (iii. 284–5), but his play shows how tenuous (as he saw it) that hope must be. The play's force lies in its foreshadowing of post-war violence and power struggle in the coalfields, which duly came, though not as soon as he thought it would.

The trouble with having written again 'out of my deep and earnest self' firing up 'my last sparks of hope in the world', and crying out 'like a Balaams ass' (iii. 293) – i.e. turn back from this road! – was that he could not bring himself to do hack-work, particularly the Education essays (iii. 297), though he tried. Moreover his sense of having attempted something valuable brought his alienation from the public home to him even more strongly than before. If the play was to find an audience it would have to be anonymous, since 'my name is like red pepper in people's noses' (iii. 293). He sent it to Katherine who (sadly but predictably) disliked it from the first glance because it was '*black* with miners', though she might have had other reasons also. Catherine Carswell had reviewed plays for the *Glasgow Herald*, so he asked her to collect it from Katherine and show it to an influential friend of hers, but without much hope (iii. 297). When Amy Lowell accompanied her latest work *Can Grande's Castle* – Dante's refuge from the world – with some well-meant advice to cut down on his sexual explicitness if he wanted to be read,[12] he knew now that this would no longer help. 'Without the india-rubber I am damned along with the evil, with the india-rubber I am damned among the disappointing. You see what it is to have a reputation' (iii. 296). There was no sex in the new play, but that would merely upset expectations. Significantly, too, he had begun to wonder whether his agent had begun to give up on him, after *Women in Love* proved impossible to place. Pinker had shown little interest himself in the American essays or the poems; for it was novels which brought worthwhile percentages, and it was as a potentially selling novelist after *Sons and Lovers* that Pinker had taken him on. None of the latest initiatives had come about through his agency. Moreover Pinker had probably decided not to approach Bennett about finding Lawrence work,[13] feeling that by his secret £25 Bennett had done as much as could be expected; and this reluctance may have conveyed itself to Lawrence; fuelling resentment of Bennett unjustly, though in ignorance. Worse, Lawrence was still in debt to Pinker (or Pinker/Bennett) for advances to keep him going at all. Suddenly he felt a need to know where he stood:

I have an idea that you would rather not be bothered any longer with my work: which certainly must be no joy, nor profit, to you. Will you let me know if this is so. I remember you said when we made the agreement that it might be broken if either was dissatisfied. If you have any desire to break it just let me know.

Do I still owe you money. Will you tell me how much? (iii. 296)

A note on the letter, probably Pinker's, says '£15-14-3d' (iii. 296 n. 1) – and he must have written soothingly, since no more was said for the moment. Seeds of suspicion remained; but now, still unable to do hack-work, Lawrence did turn to fiction again, to write up the story whose idea he had first outlined to Catherine Carswell in the Forest of Dean.

'The Blind Man', in this first version, is rather different from the story we read now.[14] The intellectual Bertie Reid is not treated satirically, and only his name could suggest (but probably does not) any hint of Bertie Russell. (He is a

Scots barrister and man of letters, with little legs.) The ending is ironic in a different direction. In fact this 'Blind Man' gains the positive vision that *Touch and Go* may seem to lack. Lawrence had feared the psychic mutilation of those who would return from the trenches, but strangely, this story has the paradox of *Lear*, that a man may 'see' better by being blinded, and find 'the way' though he stumbled when he saw. The original idea, Catherine remembered, evoked the extraordinary power of the blind to seem quite at home in the utter darkness which frightens those who can see, so what she recalled as the centre was the war-blinded man 'delicately groping' about the stable.[15] But now Lawrence weaves in Birkin's sense of the insufficiency of a man and a woman alone, and the theme of male friendship from the American essays (quite distinct now from homosexuality); and pinpoints *touch* as the way of focusing most powerfully his long-held belief that the blood is wiser than the intellect.

Maurice had been a Tom Brangwen, feeling himself inferior because of the slowness of his brain – and hence jealous of Isabel's friendship with Bertie the intellectual and cultivated lawyer, and hostile to the man himself. But his blinding in the trenches not only intensifies his ability to live through his senses, but draws him closer to his wife so that they have a year in blissful isolation, all-in-all to each other, completed by the birth of a child. More significantly, the blindness brings home to Isabel not only the sadness of Maurice's limitation, but a sense that she is limited too: that there may be something he needs that she is quite unable to give. The end of the story shows what it is, and that the other man needs it as well. As the blind man feels Bertie's face and body, and persuades his 'opposite' to press his hands over the blind eyes and scars, and touch as he is touched, there comes about, through the blood-intimacy of touch, a new sense of being, a new kind of knowing and the blood-brotherhood, the total commitment to lasting relation, that Lawrence had always wanted with another man. For Wordsworth, the eye was 'the most despotic of our senses', so that it had to be laid asleep, along with the intellect it serves, before the full sense of the strangeness and mystery of the world could dawn on consciousness.[16] It is through touch (as always for Lawrence) that true relationship with the stranger, the other, can pulse along the blood, and bring that mysterious joy and tenderness in which Bertie is surprised into a kind of knowledge, and commitment he had not been capable of before. To call someone 'blind' proclaims deficiency, but Maurice has achieved truer vision, and must no longer be misnamed. When he tells Isabel this, and Bertie tells how the two men have pledged themselves 'for ever', Isabel bursts into tears. Her husband says it is because she is 'glad',[17] in the last words of the story, and on one level that is so. Yet on another there is also the grief of a woman at the revelation that her relationship with her man is not and never could have been enough for him, for all the strength of their marriage. That says something about Lawrence's sense of his own marriage and its isolation since Zennor; but it also voices a positive faith in the continuing possibility of private renewal through better relationships, man-woman *plus* man-man, despite the mutilations of the war (and Annabel's view in the play). This counterpoises *Touch and Go*'s political cynicism about England – though it may also suggest an ambiguity in its title, and the possibility that in public terms, too, something truer might come out of physical contact, in violence if nohow else.

II   Armistice – But Peace?

Meanwhile in the world outside peace seemed imminent at last, and after a disappointment on 9 November when the papers suggested it was very close and rejoicings started too soon (iii. 297), the Armistice came just two days later. The 'Nightmare' chapter of *Kangaroo* may well describe how Lawrence and Frieda spent the evening of the 11th (typically out of step with their society) singing German songs, and how Frieda was in tears.[18] Her feelings must certainly have been very complicated, and the melancholy songs she loved may have brought relief. Yet Lawrence and Frieda had also in fact gone up to London that extraordinary day, where Kot took them to an ongoing celebration in Monty Shearman's rooms in the Adelphi. At one time or another Osbert and Sacheverell Sitwell, Mary and Jack Hutchinson, Diaghilev, Massine, Lytton Strachey and Carrington, Henry and Lady Mond, Duncan Grant and Bunny Garnett were there and later many others. The streets were overflowing with singing and laughing crowds; with lorry-loads of munitions girls from the Arsenal, their faces stained yellow by picric acid fumes. Buses full of cheerful passengers explored new neighbourhoods. Everywhere was an air of mad rejoicing. Yet Bunny thought Lawrence 'looked ill and unhappy, with no trace of that gay sparkling love of life in his eyes which had been his most attractive feature six years before' – though Katherine's impression on seeing him again had been very different. Nor did he seem particularly pleased to see Bunny after their three-year-old estrangement, though Frieda was warmer. What struck Bunny most however was Lawrence's jeremiad, voiced with a kind of 'sombre joy', as people gathered round. There was no hope of true peace. The war was not over, since hate and evil had become stronger than ever; so it would soon break out once more. The Germans would rise again. Europe was done for, and England most of all. Even if fighting did not start again soon, the evil might be worse because the hate would be dammed up in men's hearts, and might break out eventually in forms worse than open war. Bunny never saw Lawrence again.[19] The Lawrences may not have stayed long, finding the celebrations accord so little with their mood.

Two days later the specimen chapters of the history came back from Nancy with Ely's approval, and Lawrence now planned to return to Mountain Cottage where he thought he could 'do it better' (iii. 298). He wanted another week in London first – might she put him up in Adelaide Road? – but after the weekend, because Austin Harrison was coming to discuss the publication of the rest of the American essays. (Urging Nancy to read Madame Blavatsky, he recommended the *Occult Review* and the occult bookshop kept by its publisher Rider; iii. 299.) Harrison duly came, with the news that an American had bought twenty copies of the issue with the first essay, which must have helped persuade him to do the series in the *English Review* (iii. 299). Lawrence quickly sent him the next two essays. He wanted Pinker to act on this evidence that there would be an American market, but the signs are clear now that he was no longer relying on his agent. He did not send Pinker the full manuscript, with the excuse that it was 'not typed' (iii. 299) – by which he may have meant not in duplicate, since the three original unpublished essays that have survived are in typescript,[20] or perhaps that he had decided not to have the Whitman typed at all. He had made nearly all the running with Harrison himself, and wanted in his indigence to keep the profits. Without the manuscript however, Pinker was unlikely to do anything about the essays in America, and as far as we know he never did. Lawrence also asked whether Pinker would let him defer paying the £15 he owed, 'and send me what little comes in'. He did however send him the new play, and announced that he had now 'written' *three* new stories – though this probably meant 'sketched out' or at most 'first drafted' in the case of two of these, which he would finish and send from Middleton.

When he wrote to Nancy he expected Frieda to come to London and back to Mountain Cottage with him – but there was clearly a battle over that. Frieda probably, and reasonably, feared the flu in London; and had no wish to return to the wintry bleakness of Mountain Cottage either. On the evidence of his remark to Katherine when he went up to London by himself, they had also been quarrelling about Germany. Frieda must have been very worried about her family, and may have expected him not only to share her feelings but to begin arranging for her to see them, perhaps even to live there again: 'She wants me to become a german, and Im *not*.' (She can have had little idea yet of what Germany would be like.) She had probably had enough, also, of being so near to his people in Derbyshire. Whereas Lawrence, knowing that Ada had paid for the year from May, must have felt it only right as well as practical that they should be there, instead of continuing to depend on Dollie's hospitality. At any rate, he not only went off to London by himself for just over a week, but then travelled straight back to Middleton without Frieda also – their first deliberate separation since she had demanded a London flat in 1915.

It is not clear where he put up in London. He wrote one letter from Kot's (iii. 299); but it was from Hampstead that he left for the north on 28 November, sharing a taxi with Catherine Carswell who was taking her baby to Edinburgh to get away from the flu (iii. 301, 306); so he must have spent part of the time at Well Walk. From there he saw Katherine for (as it happened) the last time. And it was to her that he would describe his journey north, his arrival at Cromford station in the dark rain and the drive to the cottage in the hackney-coachman's 'Vektawry' carriage (i.e. 'Victoria') with its hood up, 'away into the night, through a rustle of waters' (iii. 300). A neighbour had lit a blazing fire for him, but there was no bread till morning, so 'tea and sup on milk and potatoes, and look at the night – very dark, moving softly with misty rain – soft chink of water in the stable butts – wash myself before the fire – and so to bed, very snug'. It sounds just like his father. In the morning the world was 'rather Macbeth-looking' – but his Lady was away south in Hermitage.

III North Again – and a Question of Maleness

He was soon off for the weekend in Ripley and Eastwood to see family and friends. Another letter to Katherine described the ironworks on the banks of the Butterley reservoir, 'flaming and waving again on the black water round the train', and lighting up the face of a man on the platform so that he looked more than human (iii. 302). (From Nottingham to Ripley, via Eastwood, there ran also a cross-country tramway, which he had probably used when visiting Ada in 1917 and which was the easiest way to get between Ripley and Eastwood.) That redly lit face made him realise even more strongly than before that 'if one is to do fiction now, one must cross the threshold of the human psyche'.

Alone in Mountain Cottage for more than a fortnight, there was another of his extraordinary bursts of creativity. By 10 December he finished 'The Fox' (iii. 307); and shortly afterwards, 'John Thomas' (iii. 309; later titled 'Tickets Please'). He wrote four essays on the 'Education of the People' (iii. 306), and it is possible he completed another two chapters of the history ('The Huns', and 'Charlemagne and the Franks' for which he borrowed the book from Bertie Farjeon).[21] Then the flow broke. He hated doing the history, and by mid-December was on strike (iii. 309) – by which time Frieda had also decided to come back. She was never one to stay alone for long.

As was to happen several times, the accidents of later rewriting and publication have separated these stories into different collections, and blurred the connections among them, and with the non-fiction and the play. They do however all belong together, and there is no doubt that the dispute with and the separation from Frieda refocused very sharply the equilibrium between man and woman which *Women in Love* and *Look!* had celebrated, and forced him to rethink the importance of maleness in ways which would also have political implications. For what if the female upsets that equal balance, so that it really does become a question of which should be the star and which the satellite? That Frieda had openly refused to follow his lead, and may well have decried his manliness again as she often did when tempers rose high, very probably provoked an outpouring of imagination and thought about maleness and leadership, in which the Lawrence of 1918 begins sharply to differentiate himself from the Lawrence of *The Rainbow* and *Women in Love*. Yet it is only half-true that fiction acts as ego compensation for the bruises of life – the other half being the urge to explore what causes the hurt and why it matters.

'The Blind Man', though increasing the emphasis on the need for male friendship in addition to marriage, was still in continuity with the ending of *Women in Love*. But 'The Fox' breaks new ground, although the first version is both simpler and far less aggressive than the one we read now, with its long 'tail' of 1921 in which both the fox and Banford are killed, and the final meditation longs for March's independent mind to go to sleep. In this first version Banford is a much more sympathetic character, and though she is naturally against the marriage which will break up her home and closest relationship, she is powerless to stop it. She not only survives but ends by making all the arrangements for the wedding. The fox, too, survives. Henry neither overhears an impugning of his motives which makes him shoot it, nor becomes the focus of a mystique of hunting, and there is no theme of responsibility marking a final distinction between man and natural predator.[22] Yet what Lawrence had glimpsed on the way to Ripley – a man with his face lit up by a preterhuman light – does become the centre of a story which crosses 'the threshold of the human psyche' in a new way.

Cecily Lambert and her cousin Violet Monk had their first vivid glimpse of the Lawrences in Hermitage village early in 1918; and at the end of February they had turned up at Grimsbury Farm;[23] but though the acquaintance was renewed when the Lawrences returned to Hermitage later that year (and they would see a great deal more of 'those farm girls', iii. 383, in 1919) the friendship was probably still in its early stages when he first wrote 'The Fox'. It came too early, for instance, to carry any trace of the hostility of Cecily's father to her friendship with a morally dubious author, and the encounter between them, which ensured a place for the father in the later version. Cecily's memoir, moreover, is not only drawn mainly from 1919, but is also somewhat soured by her resentment of the 1921 version of the story, which made her feel that the friendship had always been 'for copy' and 'belittle[d]' her, while glamourising her neurotic and conceited though uncertain cousin. From the later version – and even from the first – one would certainly not gather that Lawrence liked Cecily the better of the two, though Violet typed some of *Aaron's Rod* for him. Cecily was among the first people he wrote to on arrival in Italy (iii. 416), and he was still writing to her in 1922 (iv. 166–7). But once again we are confronted by that problem of both relating Lawrence's fiction to and separating it from its 'sources' in experience. The friendship was real, affectionate, and not *for* 'copy' – but copy there was, and his imagination as always seized what it could use, without compunction or apology. Of course, at just this juncture in his own life, he would be struck by the spectacle of two young women trying, rather unsuccessfully, to run a farm in a male-less wartime England – one dressed always like a man, though by nature very feminine – and by the contrast in their characters. He picks up the uncertain withdrawn and submissive side of Violet (but makes her cousin- rather than mother-dominated), while almost entirely excising the compensatory 'conceit and arrogance' which he would use in a different story. According to Cecily it was Violet who was 'possessive and jealous'. Out goes most of what made the real-life Cecily interesting: her piano-playing and dancing, the lessons in these for the village children, her interest in Greek theatre, her love of 'life, people, and excitement of all kinds'. The porcelain-painting artistic side is given in the story to Nellie. But one can see in Cecily's memoir very clearly the 'Banford-ness' Lawrence used and expanded: the *de haut en bas* tone, the gentility, the bossiness, the geniality yes, but also the waspishness underneath, when crossed.

However it is neither the characterisation, crisp and economical though that is, nor even the quasi-lesbian relationship of the two women that is most important for Lawrence's story in this first version; since these are shown to be actually superficial, lying *outside* the 'threshold of the human psyche'. Banford is not destructively anti-male as she will become; and if March were indeed lesbian (in some categorically exclusive sense), she would not be as deeply affected by fox or young man as she is. The women are only playing at farming, and March is only playing at being the man about the place. It is the fox that holds the centre of the story, since the Lawrence of 1918 is now maintaining that the 'life wild at the source' which his art had been trying to tap from the beginning,[24] requires powerful malehood to make its counterpart fully female. The old marriage of opposites had been of conflicting 'male' and 'female' within the individual as well as between men and women, and had aimed at 'star-equilibrium' between lovers. Now the emphasis falls on the resolution of what was divided, and on the significance of the male. In the immediately post-war civilised and liberated world of the two girls, maleness is devalued and fertility suffers – but the fox seems all the more audacious and predatory. To experience him is for March to confront what she has ignored; to be known for what she is in her innermost being; and to have him 'invisibly master her psyche'. She becomes obsessed with him; but when the young returned soldier Henry Grenfell arrives, seeking his grandfather, she makes an identification that in this version remains unquestioned:

He was identified with the fox – and he was here in full presence. She need not go after him any more. There in the shadow of her corner she gave herself up to a warm, relaxed peace, almost like sleep, accepting the spell that was on her ... she need not any more be divided in herself, trying to keep up two planes of consciousness. She could at last lapse into the odour of the fox.

When she dreams that night however, it is not of any subjection but of music, colour and fertility – though the price is reverence, and familiarity is painfully reproved:

She dreamed she heard a singing outside, which she could not understand, a singing that roamed round the house, in the fields and in the darkness. It moved her so, that she felt she must weep. She went out, and suddenly she knew it was the fox singing. He was very yellow and bright, like corn ...

But 'the fox' – that great universal and preterhuman power in all male nature – cannot be approached too closely, let alone familiarly. When she tries to touch him he bites her wrist, and his brush sears across her mouth like fire. Yet the fox-man is able to overcome all her resistance in a triumph of instinct over 'common sense'. It is through immersion in 'dream-consciousness',[25] rather than in the 'ready superficial consciousness' which 'carries her through the world's business',[26] that she marries and finds happiness – to Banford's disgust, though she makes the best of it.

Out of Frieda's refusal to go with Lawrence, has come a reversion to and intensification of the Birkin of 'Mino' as against the Birkin of 'Moony' and 'Excurse'. Or again, the story might be taken as a reminder of the revitalisation of the more than thirty-year-old 'sleeping beauty' of Private Road, Nottingham by the foxy-moustached young man, in spite of all worldly disparities. (Henry is made a Cornish 'peasant', but that is to stress the fox-man of instinct rather than specifically to recall the dark-haired William Henry, as is sometimes claimed.) 'The Blind Man' had reasserted the need for male friendship in addition to marriage, and the primacy of blood-knowledge over day-sight and intellect. 'The Fox' privately rebukes, in imagined assertion of maleness and its value, the woman who breaks orbit.

'John Thomas' (now known as 'Tickets Please') is a counterpoint, though with a related 'turn' at the end. The sexual innuendo of the name points to the predatory randiness of the chief ticket-inspector on the Ripley–Nottingham tramway. (He is also nicknamed 'Coddy', or testicles). In wartime, the careering cross-country tram is piloted by those unfit for military service, and conducted by 'fearless young hussies' with 'skirts up to their knees' and 'all the *sang froid* of an old non-commissioned officer'. In a tram 'packed with howling colliers, roaring hymns downstairs and a sort of antiphony of obscenities upstairs, the lasses are perfectly at their ease ... They are not going to be done in the eye, not they.' They can cope with anything – except John Thomas who, cock of the walk that he is, takes and leaves them one by one, including even Annie the liveliest and most confident 'new woman' of them all. However Annie refuses to take her desertion lying down, and conspires with all the other victims to turn the tables, so that the predatory male who refused to enter into any real relationship of persons shall be forced to choose and to commit himself to marry one of them. At this point, the sympathy of the story seems to run with Annie, who had 'wanted to consider him a person, a man, she wanted to take an intelligent interest in him and to have an intelligent response'. *He* sees this as mere female possessiveness and sheers off as always, but it may seem to a reader to mark the distinction between a *man* and a mere John Thomas and Coddy. For his effect on a woman is so to devalue her in her own eyes that after 'fury, indignation, desolation and misery' comes 'a spasm of despair'. Thus when Annie aims to get 'her own back' the cliché again suggests something deeper, as it had done in the play: the true femaleness (this time) which Lawrence thought true maleness should always create as its counterpart.

Now however the story turns around, as the revenge gets out of hand. The counterpart of unfettered male predatoriness turns out to be the unfettered violence of female bacchantes, as the man's clothes are torn from his back, and he is kicked, scratched, beaten, humiliated, held down in the dirt. The link with the last scene in *Touch and Go* is clear. Lawrence has drawn even more specifically than there on a humiliating experience of his own, when at Jordan's factory a bunch of girls set upon him and tried to pull his trousers off – though in life he fought like 'a very demon' (Neville recorded), and drove them away 'afraid of the fury they had aroused'. In the story now, Annie's revenge turns to disgusting ash in her mouth, especially when John Thomas, forced to choose in order to be allowed to stand up at all, chooses *her*. In revision, Lawrence greatly increased her agonised sense of something spoilt, even desecrated, 'broken in her' as well as in him.[27] Two wrongs not only do not make a right, they despoil it for ever. But even the original ending makes a sharply ironic doublet with 'The Fox'.

Before he finished the two stories, he wrote Katherine an important letter about another, psychological, reason for asserting the value of maleness. He had been reading Barbara Low's copy of Jung's *Psychology of the Unconscious*, borrowed from Kot who was in the middle of reading it (iii. 307, 301). (The author was still, in 1912, Freud's most important disciple, but his critique of Freud's view of incest, as connected with infant sexuality, was one cause of the final break.) 'Beware', Lawrence warned Katherine, sending the book to her on 5 December,

this Mother-incest idea can become an obsession. But it seems to me there is this much truth in it: that at certain periods the man has a desire and a tendency to return unto the woman, make her his goal and end, find his justification in her. In this way he casts himself as it were into her womb, and she, the Magna Mater, receives him with gratification. This is a kind of incest. It seems to me it is what Jack does to you, and what repels and fascinates you. I have done it, and now struggle all my might to get out. In a way, Frieda is the devouring mother. – It is awfully hard, once the sex relation has gone this way, to recover. If we don't recover, we die. – But Frieda says I am antediluvian in my positive attitude. I do think a woman must yield some sort of precedence to a man, and he must take this precedence. I do think men must go ahead absolutely in front of their women, without turning round to ask for permission or approval from their women. Consequently, the women must follow as it were unquestioning. I can't help it, I believe this. Frieda doesn't. Hence our fight. (iii. 301–2)[28]

More was at stake for him when he returned to Mountain Cottage than a mere argument about health or climate or money. He was making, it seems, a radical revaluation of the last six years, and of the claims he had made for his marriage in his major fiction and in *Look!* Beside the road through the valley at the foot of the steep slope on which the cottage stands, there runs a stream. The previous evening he had sat beside it, noting how the 'spell of hastening, secret water goes over one's mind'. When he climbed up the steep slope afterwards 'I felt as if I had climbed out of a womb.' The next paragraph is the one about the man on the station platform with his face 'lit up red'; and the need to write fiction which crossed the threshold of the psyche. Clearly both experiences (and Jung) symbolically underlay the assertion of true maleness in 'The Fox' and the distinction between that and mere male chauvinism in 'John Thomas'.

The letter also contains the ideal of 'The Blind Man' and the American essays, though it measures the distance between life imagined, and experience.

Secondly, I do believe in friendship. I believe tremendously in friendship between man and man, a pledging of men to each other inviolably. – But I have not ever met or formed such friendship. Also I believe the same way in friendship between men and women, and between women and women, sworn, pledged, eternal, as eternal as the marriage bond, and as deep. – But I have not met or formed such friendship.

Excuse this sudden burst into dogma. Please give the letter to Jack. I say it to him particularly. (iii. 302)

The series of letters to Katherine shows how their reunion had renewed his faith in the possibility of such friendship with her, though he had not warmed to Jack again. Yet neither could he ever quite let him go. The imagined intellectual with little legs in 'The Blind Man' may indeed have had more to do with Murry than with Russell. If so, Lawrence's remark in this same letter about the story's 'ironical' ending – 'I realise *how* many people are just rotten at the quick' (iii. 303) – has a bite.

By then he had also already done 'three little essays' on 'Education of the People', and by the 7th had finished a fourth (iii. 303, 306). The autograph

488

manuscript that survives is a 1920 series of twelve, and there is no certainty that the first four are the ones written in 1918; yet it seems likely that the central argument would be much the same.[29] The first three came out of the deeply felt experience of his teaching years in Croydon, and in their posing of the questions that arise from the reality (as opposed to the theory) of the education of the proletariat, remain as discomforting today as they may have seemed in 1918 to the editor of *The Times Educational Supplement*. Lawrence begins by asserting the importance, indeed holiness of the individual, not the job; and yet both teachers and working-class schoolchildren know only too well that it is getting a job that really matters in hard fact. The chasm between the ideal of self-development the teacher is supposed to maintain, and the material reality that actually governs the lives of working-class children and parents, breeds nothing but a bitter cynicism about all ideals. If in reality it is jobs that matter, would it not be better, more honest and more useful for most children, if basic education were to concentrate on the three R's, and then the technical instruction that would fit them for a working life? If we talk of 'free self-expression', furthermore, do all natures want and need academic or aesthetic education? Is it not bullying rather than freedom which tries to force all natures into the same mould? May it not indeed be positively dangerous to try to force academic education where there is no capacity; since what this produces is a 'profound contempt for education, and for all educated people', a sense in boys, for example, that to be educated is to be *unmanly*. On the other hand, where children want and can learn academically and aesthetically, such education will be prized and genuinely pursued.

This leads to a sketch of state and coed schooling in the three R's (where reading includes some history and geography), together with some physical and domestic training, identical for all children up to the age of 12; followed by a division into two streams, one predominantly technical (though with a modicum of 'reading' of different kinds); and the other academic (but with a modicum of useful technical training). From the latter, the ablest in that direction would go on to tertiary education, followed by training for the professions, including the fine arts, while the others moved into technical or clerical and administrative apprenticeships respectively. But at every stage it should be possible for children to be moved from one stream into the other as aptitudes reveal themselves. This is not too different in theory from the system introduced into English education by a reforming Education Minister. But Lawrence then turns to tackle the consequent question of 'Equality', which has sharper political implications.

He believes neither in the equality nor the inequality of people, but their 'disquality'. Comparison is always partial, whereas persons in their wholeness are unique and incomparable. So each child must be enabled to grow true to its own intrinsic self. Yet (the ex-teacher speaks) it is no good simply letting children do what they want, for the romantic idea of childhood as spontaneously expressive of true selfhood is a delusion. Children pick up ideas second-hand, and need to be educated to the self-knowledge in which they can truly choose what will make them more truly themselves, and spontaneous. Lawrence's view, as always, is religious. Each person should become a priest of life, following the god within. This places a heavy responsibility on the educators who must judge the children's natures and aptitudes before they are able to judge truly for themselves. (There is also, of course, the problem of equal opportunity.)

On the other hand, up to this point there is no question of hierarchy. Lawrence had imagined in Tom Brangwen a farm boy who was academically ineducable but who had great delicacy of feeling, and could lay hold of eternity. He had just imagined in Maurice another worker with his hands who is no whit inferior to the intellectual lawyer, and indeed 'sees' more truly. In the fourth essay, Lawrence argues that those 'whose souls are alive and strong but whose voices are unmodulated, and whose thoughts unformed and slow' will constitute the majority of people at all times. In them the creative sources still pulse, though it is the articulate who must utter them. Now however his metaphors begin to carry him into hierarchy. It is one thing to say that the people are to their leaders as the tree to its blossom – but quite another to turn different classes (the consequence of different natures) into the lower and higher levels of a pyramid with a single leader at its summit. In his letters to Russell in 1915 he had swung rather wildly from socialism to dictatorship. Now, impatient with the materialism of the working class, and convinced of the need for better leadership with higher goals, he seems to settle for dictatorship – in the name of a truer democracy! 'We who believe that every man's soul is single and incomparable, we thought we were democrats' – but democracy has become essentially a levelling-*down*. Whereas,

true democracy is that in which a people gradually cumulates, from the vast base of the populace upwards through the zones of life and understanding to the summit where the great man, or the most perfect Utterer, is alone. The false democracy is that wherein every issue, even the highest, is dragged down to the lowest issue, the myriad-multiple lowest human issue: today, the wage.[30]

If this was in essence the fourth essay of 1918 – though that is not certain – an argument for diversity and disquality is becoming an argument of hierarchy and subordination, though it need not have done.

Moreover, though no connection has yet been drawn, there seems a subterranean link between a belief in the necessity of male 'precedence', and a belief in the necessity for a greater-souled political leader so that the people may find 'living soul-expression' through the classes above.[31] The political argument seems to have been driven by some inner pressure, as much as the sexual one. It is not surprising, then, that the liveliest bits of the not very lively chapters of the history he forced himself to do (VI–VIII), were on Attila and Charlemagne. But by 20 December, he had come to hate the work 'like poison, and have struck' (iii. 309). Two days later he told Kot that if only he had a small income he would 'chuck writing altogether. I'm really sick of it' (iii. 310).

IV   Death, and the Devil of a Winter

As 1918 ebbed out the fear of death still seemed everywhere, for in the Midlands too the flu epidemic was taking its toll. Lawrence himself was defiant. Another reason for impatience with the 'people' was how 'horribly frightened' of the disease they were, 'all of them: but it is not fear of the Lord' – which might lead to amendment of life – 'merely selfish fear of death, petty and selfish. – When *will* one get the spark of a new spirit out of these people?' (iii. 306). He did not think they would ever have the courage to do anything, except perhaps for the railwaymen who had struck him as 'rather independent and Bolshy' on the journey up (iii. 301). The context of this impatience however was that he was having to confront fear, and death, in his own narrow circle. He spent his next weekend back in the Midlands in Ripley and Eastwood, and found Ada 'rather sick and wretched' (iii. 307), very worried about the business and the desperate need to get Eddie demobilised to carry it on. (Lawrence wrote to Campbell to find out who to approach; iii. 307.) Kot had caught the flu (iii. 310), so had Don Carswell in Edinburgh; and with his chest, Lawrence would be in the gravest danger if he too went down. This was brought home to him in the saddest way – for part of the purpose of his weekend visit was to sit at the death-bed of Frances ('Frankie') Cooper in Eastwood, childhood friend and next-door neighbour in Lynn Croft who was dying of consumption. She was just a year older than he. In this, especially after what had happened to Katherine, he must have seen a spectre for them both. Frankie was buried on 22 December, but earlier, telling Katherine about her, he wrote: 'Katherine – on ne meurt pas: I almost want to let it be reflexive – on ne se meurt pas: *Point!* Be damned and be blasted everything, and let the bloody world come to its end. But one does not die. Jamais' (iii. 307). He would continue to insist that one could *will* oneself not to die. He sent Katherine a sort of golden bough for Christmas, a little bowl of yellow Derbyshire fluorspar, 'a golden underworld, with rivers and clearings – do you see it?' The local barber had clipped his hair and beard till he looked like a convict; he had caught a bad cold and felt diabolical; but, two days before Frankie's funeral, he wrote Katherine again: 'Courage, mon ami, le diable vit encore' (iii. 309).

At Christmas itself however, things brightened. Frieda had arrived back, on

14 December, and they went to Ripley in apparent amity for a family Christmas dinner. He wrote Katherine another vivid letter describing how her presents had arrived just as they were setting off across a snowy, sunny and windy landscape; how Frieda had pinned the gift brooch in the shape of a wheatsheaf on her yellow blouse which, with red coat and skirt, was her party outfit; and how the children had snaffled the tangerines when they got to Ripley in the motor car Ada had sent to Ambergate for them. (He and Katherine had chosen the same life-asserting symbolism.) There was a huge Christmas meal at Ada's, graphically described – no more wartime rationing – and charades in which the old people played harder than the young ones – and they 'lit the christmas tree, and drank healths, and sang, and roared – Lord above'. On Boxing Day there was a second party, at the home of Ada's Parsee doctor, Dr Mullan-Feroze (who would figure later in *Aaron's Rod*), where they 'drank two more bottles of muscatel, and danced in his big empty room till we were staggered, and quite dazed' (iii. 313).

For all the festivity however Lawrence could not feel free. Indeed he still felt caged, dreading the months ahead in which he might have to wait 'paralysed for some sort of release' (iii. 313). Of his last two letters of the year, one was to Captain Short, finally surrendering the lease of the small cottage at Higher Tregerthen and arranging for the disposal of their remaining belongings. (iii. 314).[32] There would be no going back, even though there was no longer any obstacle. The other was to Amy, with plans to come to America in summer 1919, after (that is) they had first been to Germany or Switzerland for Frieda to see her people – domestic peace clearly dependent on that priority. Frieda had heard from her mother: Edgar Jaffe had become Minister of Finance in the new Bavarian republic; another friend 'is something else important'[33] and Frieda's cousin Hartman, who had been turned out of the Reichstag because he wanted peace, 'is now a moving figure in Berlin' (iii. 314). But though Germany might be 'quite exciting', it was Frieda's excitement he was voicing. He himself wanted something *new*, America, even more than before.

All through January, as snow lay deep, his letters harp on one string: '*I must get out*. I must get out of England, of Europe. There will never be anything here but increasing rottenness ... I *will* get out of Europe this year' (iii. 316).[34] It did not help that 'this winter is the very devil', and that both he and Frieda had caught cold again. In February he voiced what he had dreaded: his sense of helplessly marking time before some kind of disaster (iii. 325) – but there was no remedy. No matter how Frieda longed to see her family – sitting on needles, he told Else – this would be exceedingly difficult and probably impossible before peace was formally signed, even if they tried to meet in Switzerland. There would not only be problems over passports, but still more in getting permits to travel in Allied-occupied Germany, for all the family's German contacts. He and

Frieda were only just beginning to realise how bad conditions were there, especially the acute and growing shortage of food, made worse by the maintenance of the Allied blockade to pressure Germany into accepting penal terms at Versailles. And of course there was the perennial problem of money for the Lawrences.

Kot had proposed to give him a couple of books as a belated Christmas present, and the two Everyman volumes he chose show how his mind was working. He asked for Scheffel's *Ekkehard: A Tale of the Tenth Century*, useful for his history book which had to be finished as soon as possible to have the means of subsistence let alone travel, but also appropriate to his sense of a new 'dark age' in Europe, now. His other choice was Bates's *The Naturalist on the River Amazon* (iii. 315); not that he wanted to go there particularly, but it 'takes one into the sun and the waters' (iii. 340), an escape in space as the other was in time. 'I should never be a sad man,' he wrote in thanks, 'whilst it was possible for a real book to come along' (iii. 317).

Meanwhile there was work to be done before he and Frieda could move anywhere. He seems to have worked hard and quickly on the history in the first weeks of January, and though it seemed 'wretched piggling' (iii. 322), by 17 January he had only two to go (iii. 321). Six days later he had finished another, and was better pleased with what he had done. 'Every chapter,' he told Nancy Henry,

I suffer before I can begin, because I do loathe the broken pots of historical facts. But once I can get hold of the thread of the developing significance, then I am happy, and get ahead. I shall need to revise rather carefully. But you'll see, when you get these 4 last chapters, the book does expand nicely and naturally. I am rather pleased with it. There is a clue of developing meaning running through it: that makes it real to me. (iii. 322)

He even asked her to recommend him for another book, if she could think of one he could do. He sent the last four chapters off on 3 February, with the title *Movements in European History* (iii. 326).[35] He supposed, correctly, that OUP would not want his name to appear, so he would accept a pseudonym (eventually Lawrence H. Davison).

To his annoyance, Freeman had refused his essays for *TES*.. 'I was deeply interested,' said the letter, 'but feel myself rather out of my depth – I have consulted another opinion, and we feel that this is rather matter for a book than a supplement' (iii. 323). To Lawrence that was mere cowardice. His work might not be wasted however, for Barbara Low had seen the essays also and had shown them to Stanley Unwin who was impressed enough to take up the idea of 'a little book' if Lawrence would write 'as much again' – for which Unwin would pay £15.

Slowly Lawrence's finances began to improve. By New Year he had ten guineas for the first two 'American' essays from Harrison – having 'circum-vented' Pinker's commission, though he did tell him about it (iii. 315). The sale of effects in Cornwall now raised £15 from Benney's auction room (iii. 327), so another cheque from Kot could be sent back in February. There would be £50 to come from *Movements* when the revision was complete (iii. 321). And there would also be five guineas every month from Harrison as long as he continued to publish the American essays, though it was not clear whether the *English Review* would 'go patiently on to the end' of the twelve (iii. 324). (It would seem that the decision to stop at eight had not yet been made, or at least divulged.) Proofs had also arrived of six poems which Harriet Monroe had accepted for the February issue of *Poetry*, for which again there would be payment on publication (iii. 325).[36] (Seven guineas arrived in March; iii. 330.)

However, it had been clear to Lawrence for some time that his best hope of earning money from creative work, as opposed to book making like *Movements*, lay in short stories. He had quite lost hope of publishing *Women in Love*; and when Nancy Henry spoke of giving up her job so that both she and Leigh could devote themselves to creativity, he felt he had to advise her that if they once put themselves into a position to starve, these days, starve they certainly would.

Never has it been so difficult to make money by any form of art: never has the artist had such a bad chance: and never has the world been so coldly indifferent, never has it clutched its shillings more tightly ... nobody is going to waste one *serious* moment on art at all ... there are days coming when art will not save us: neither you nor me nor anybody. (iii. 325–6)

He was right at least in this, that the reading public was in no mood to be very serious or to test itself for long, so short stories with as light a touch as he could manage seemed to be his best prospect. He had once declared himself incapable of writing the kind of story that the *Strand* would publish – but lo and behold, that popular magazine accepted 'John Thomas' for its April issue, minus sexual innuendo and renamed 'Tickets Please'. In the snows of January he wrote a new one, 'Wintry Peacock', and sent it to Pinker on the 15th (iii. 320).

On the surface this tale of wartime infidelity, got away with, sounds like a retelling of local gossip that could be duplicated in many a village as soldiers came home, leaving illegitimate babies to emerge all over Flanders; and its ending in gales of laughter would seem to show it was not meant over-seriously. However (like 'Tickets Please') the jest has a sardonic Lawrencian underside for those who see more than the narrator does. It is still part of the 'male' assertion which had underlain 'The Blind Man' and 'The Fox'. The woman who asks the narrator to translate the French of the Belgian girl's letter to her husband, is presented as a female Janus: at one moment the little woman who makes a man feel big (and her husband's family protective), but the next, the bitchy witch against whom men must instinctively unite – as the narrator does with the still-absent adulterer by falsifying the tidings of his fatherhood, almost involuntarily. The 'jest' and the alliance continue into the laughter at the end, despite the class difference, and the ex-soldier's suspiciousness and irresponsibility – maudlin in the original, brutal in the later version.[37] The enjoyment of a masculine secret that the female can never discover is too rich to be compromised by scruple – it seems. Only, the wintry peacock teases at the mind. Perhaps Lawrence remembered his dream of a beautiful blue bird torn from the air by dogs. The wife's cherishing of the peacock suggests a dimension of affection and beauty missing from her marriage; and the narrator's rescue of the beautiful bird floundering in the cold snow is another involuntary response, very different from the husband's desire to wring its neck. Perhaps the laughter at the end is really as uneasily questionable as the joke-gone-too-far in 'Tickets Please'? There, female alliance punished the predatory male, yet the ending suggested the consequence for women if a deeper maleness were desecrated. Perhaps 'Wintry Peacock' also partly inverts itself by its excess (as Blake thought excess would always do), helping again to suggest the absence of the truer maleness that could have produced a truer femininity?

Lawrence now made his first direct contact with Benjamin Huebsch, who had become his American publisher when he agreed to bring out *The Rainbow* after Doran's refusal, and who had subsequently published *The Prussian Officer*, *Twilight in Italy* and *Look!* All the arrangements had gone through Pinker and even now, more than three years later, Lawrence clearly knew nothing of how Huebsch had managed to get his edition of *The Rainbow* into circulation quietly, through travelling salesmen, rather than risk prosecution by sending it out for review or advertising and distributing it in the usual way. Moreover, he had no idea that Pinker had never sent the *Women in Love* manuscript for Huebsch to judge whether he might risk publishing that too. (This would have repercussions later.) In January 1919, by happenstance, Huebsch sent Lawrence a copy of his list, and when he wrote back in approval – taking the opportunity to enquire after the sales of *The Prussian Officer*, *Twilight in Italy* and *Look!*, but not *The Rainbow* which he assumed was still on Huebsch's hands (iii. 323–4) – Huebsch replied warmly, encouraging the prospect of a visit to America. He offered to help arrange lectures to cover expenses, and 'anything else in which you think I may be of service' (iii. 356–7 n. 1).[38] (The envelope of Lawrence's letter, over two months after the Armistice, is marked 'OPENED BY CENSOR'; iii. 324 n. 2.)

For most of January, then, he and Frieda were 'very quiet', alone, but 'hardly notice the loneliness' (iii. 322). It was towards the end of the month that both caught cold, and Lawrence spent a week in bed into the first days of February. When he got up it was 'terribly frozen and snowy ... The sun shines, but the windows are covered with very magnificent ice flowers, so we are obscured as if in a frozen under-sea' (iii. 327). The weekend of 8–9 February Emily and her daughter Peggy were at Mountain Cottage, and Lawrence described to Katherine how he had climbed with his niece to the 'bare top of the hills' in 'brilliant sunshine on the snow'. In one of the most vivid of all his letters he describes the myriad tracks of the different wild creatures in the snow, and the naked upland 'moving far into the distance, strange and muscular, with gleams like skin ... It is strange how insignificant, in all this, life seems. Two men, tiny as dots, move from a farm on a snow-slope, carrying hay ... In contrast, both of scale and life assertion, he paints a vivid domestic interior as the household prepares for Peggy's birthday treat.

Emily is cooking treacle rolly and cakes, Frieda is making Peggy a pale grey dress, I am advising and interfering – Pamela [Emily's nickname, after Richardson's virtuous heroine] is lamenting because the eggs in the pantry have all frozen and burst – I have spent half an hour hacking ice out of the water tub – now I am going out. Peggy, with her marvellous red-gold hair in dangling curl-rags is darting about sorting the coloured wools and cottons – scène de famille. (iii. 328)

As all his letters to Katherine tried to be at this time, it was a gift of liveliness against the snow and the spectre.

A week later they went to visit Ada in Ripley, and Lawrence collapsed with influenza. He very nearly died.

V 'A putrid disease ... a drowned ghost'

The great influenza epidemic which swept across Europe and Africa was a particularly virulent strain, a mass killer even of the robust, still more the elderly and those whose health was already suspect. The casualties were the worst (in ratio to population) since the cholera epidemic of 1849.[39] Lawrence contracted the disease with complications which clearly had to do this time, as in 1911, with his lungs and not merely his bronchial tubes, though he also had 'heart-pains' (iii. 329), as well as a high temperature and a racking cough. Dr Mullan-Feroze later told him that for two days 'he feared I should not pull through' (iii. 337), and that he had been affected more seriously because he 'was run down to start with' (as in the collapse of early 1916). 'It's been pitiful', Frieda told Kot, 'to see him try so hard to *live*, if he *hadn't*, it would have been all over.'[40]

Recovery was painfully slow. It was not until 26 February that he could eat anything solid or sit up in bed and write a note (iii. 329); not until 2 March that he was able to get up for half an hour to sit in his bedroom (iii. 329); not until 6 March that, rather fearing the stairs, he began to venture down for afternoon tea – 'like a drowned ghost creeping' (iii. 333, 335). On 11 March he was still 'tiresomely feeble', unable to walk (iii. 335). On 14 March he walked outside a few yards – a month after the collapse. By then he felt 'nearly myself again, in my soul if not in my body' (iii. 337); but he still needed 'injections for the lungs' (iii. 340). Even after he had been driven by motor car back to Mountain Cottage on 17 March (iii. 339), Dr Mullan-Feroze came over regularly to continue these injections, and would not hear of a move to the warmer south before late April (iii. 340).

This strain of influenza proved 'a putrid disease' (iii. 330) mentally as well as physically, and greatly depressive. When he wrote his first note it was to confess that he felt 'very weary and a little downhearted' because 'the world seems so nasty ahead of one' (iii. 329). At the end of February he admitted that he had 'never felt so down in the mud in all my life ... life is too unbearably foul' (iii. 330). He had thought his soul 'was cracked for ever' (iii. 329), though it too was recovering. He was touched by the way his few good friends rallied round, sending things to tempt appetite and cheer him up: grapefruit, brandy and port from Kot (iii. 329–30); bottles of muscatel from Catherine Carswell (iii. 336); champagne from Uncle Fritz Krenkow (iii. 329). However, he shrank 'from putting my foot out of bed into the world again' (iii. 330), and turned down the idea of recuperating at the seaside because it was 'too great a struggle to travel to a new place' (iii. 331), a sign of malaise indeed, in him! He dreamed of Cynthia (oddly, going to church with him in Heanor), and two days later a letter from her arrived – but she too was rather depressed because she was pregnant again (iii. 333). When an unexpected letter came from Beatrice Campbell with a gift of Irish butter, he sympathised with her for feeling like 'a bit of wreckage that will be swept off again next high tide', for 'We've all sort of come unstuck' (iii. 334–5).

Partly cheering was an invitation from Murry to contribute to the *Athenæum*, whose editorship he was about to take over. Lawrence was pleased, but wanted Murry to tell him, soon, 'exactly what you would like me to do, and I will try to be pleasant and a bit old-fashioned. I don't mind if I am anonymous – or a nom de plume? ... Tell me particulars as soon as you can – so that I can think about it while I am still not well, and make little ideas' (iii. 332). Murry failed to reply however, and within a week Lawrence's distrust of him returned. He felt 'sure we shall be let down' (iii. 335), though he still intended to try, and indeed began before he left Ripley though he felt it was 'a cold effort to do these things' (iii. 337).[41] He had not heard from Katherine for some time, and feared she too might be 'only just on the verge of existence' (iii. 335).

Much more reliable, now, was his friendship with the Eders. The news from Edith that David was coming back from Palestine to fetch his wife and son (iii. 340), had added the Holy Land to Lawrence's list of possible escapes from England; and illness had increased his sense of confinement. Now the good doctor was not only in London but promised to come up and talk to him about

497

Palestine – probably more to cheer him up than anything else. He arrived in
Ripley bearing a bottle of claret, cake and sweets, the weekend before Lawrence
was to be motored back to Mountain Cottage; and immediately Lawrence began
to look ahead once more: 'I have promised to go out to Palestine in September,'
he told Kot, 'leaving Frieda in Germany. In Palestine I am to view the land and
write a Zioniad' (iii. 340). He was almost himself again.

However, the remark about Frieda carried a charge. In *Women in Love* Ursula
makes no bones about her revulsion from illness and her belief that it is
something to be ashamed of.[42] There is little doubt that this was Frieda's view,
or that she strengthened Lawrence's own idea that illness came out of a
wrongness in one's life, for which one was ultimately responsible and should
therefore set about curing, oneself. This was a dangerous view for a man who
carried the tubercle, though by no means absolutely foolish as the fight against
cancer in our time has shown. However, Frieda's lack of sympathy and
disinclination for nursing might well look very different to someone laid low by
the influenza epidemic of 1918–19 – and it certainly did. He tried to joke about
the tension, to Beatrice: 'I suppose I'll get strong enough again one day to slap
Frieda in the eye, in the proper marital fashion. At present I am reduced to
vituperation' (iii. 335). When at last he was allowed to move back to Mountain
Cottage he insisted that Ada should come too, to look after him.

I am not going to be left to Frieda's tender mercies until I am well again. She really is a
devil – and I feel as if I would part from her for ever – let her go alone to Germany, while
I take another road. For it is true, I have been bullied by her long enough. I really could
leave her now, without a pang, I believe. The time comes, to make an end, one way or
another. If this illness hasn't been a lesson to her, it has to me. (iii. 337)

This was written to Kot, who had been critical of Frieda from the start. It was a
result of illness and might be cured as the illness was. Yet it reinforces all the
other signs that the marriage was entering a far harsher phase, when Lawrence
thought it necessary to begin to free himself from, and assert his male
independence *against* his previous need of her.

VI Mountain Cottage Again

They arrived back at Mountain Cottage on Monday 17 March. It began as 'a
mild sweet morning' (iii. 339–40), but in the afternoon it began to snow heavily,
and the prospect of spring closed again. Soon the snow lay so heavily that (like
the peasants in Fiascherino in happier days) Ada and Frieda had to beat the
branches of the fruit trees to stop them breaking – while Lawrence stared
'stupidly out of the window like a sick and dazed monkey' (iii. 340), unable to
venture out, and only waiting, now, for the doctor to give permission for a

return south to Hermitage. (In any case Ada's lease would be up at the end of April.) He had to confess that he was 'an irritable sort of convalescent' (iii. 341). To occupy himself he asked Kot to buy him more books as a present from Ada (iii. 340); and asked Gertler to send reproductions of Uccello's 'hunting and fighting scenes', or favourites like Fra Angelico, Giotto, Mantegna, Van Gogh, for him to copy. He wanted pictures with strongly marked design and 'hard figures' (iii. 341) to make copying easier, and black and white would do, though in that case Gertler was to tell him the colours. While he was waiting he copied a Teniers, and felt happier, though 'painting is not *my* art – only an amusement to me' (iii. 342). Uccello proved too difficult from a postcard, but it was probably now that he copied Fra Angelico's *Flight into Egypt* and Giotto's *Joachim and the Shepherds* – though (lacking notes from Gertler) in different colours from the originals.

Having started in Ripley he probably wrote some more pieces for the *Athenæum* – of which Murry proceeded to refuse all but one, to Lawrence's fury (iii. 346). The exception was 'Whistling of Birds', Lawrence's hailing (in 1917) of a new spring in nature and in the heart after a most deathly winter. This had been the original beginning of 'The Reality of Peace', but must have seemed very appropriate for the first reissue of the magazine under Murry on 11 April, with the Armistice holding. However, all Lawrence's new pieces were rejected in a 'very editorial' note. This came too late for an angry Lawrence to withdraw the essay that had been accepted; but 'that is the first and last word of mine that will ever appear in the *Athenæum*. Good-bye Jacky, I knew thee beforehand.' Murry's later explanation of why he turned down the only other piece he could remember, 'Adolf' – a charming sketch about the orphaned baby rabbit which Arthur Lawrence rescued and brought home for his children – seems incredible. It is not at all 'embittered and angry'. Just conceivably, expecting resentment and rebellion from Lawrence, Murry *may* have read them into the body language of the little rabbit's scut, flicking cheekily as it flees from its pursuers, as though saying *Merde*! – and may have thought it spoke for the Lawrence who could only 'run' now, in a hostile world, under an ironic nom de plume 'Grantorto'. But Lawrence had written in his sister's company more affectionately of his childhood and his father than ever before. His tone is humorous, and the 'obscenity', as Murry would know, is no obscenity in French. Perhaps the sketch was not high-toned enough for the revamped *Athenæum*'s intellectual aims. Murry says his 'position was precarious' and he may have been afraid of shocking readers at the beginning of his reign; but if that was the reason, it was very pusillanimous. The *Dial* (at least as high-powered) took the sketch as soon as offered. Moreover neither objection could have applied to 'Rex', the companion piece about a puppy which was almost certainly submitted at the same time and also taken by the *Dial*. Still more infuriating than the *de haut en bas* 'declined with thanks' was

Murry's failure to return another essay about some topical issue (iii. 345): perhaps the industrial action on the London underground and the threat to the railways in February, which had produced remarks in a letter from Lawrence to Else about the English being 'in the nastiest frame of mind imaginable' and his growing dislike of 'vulgar democracy' (iii. 345). Lawrence complained that by the time he got this piece back it would be too out of date to send elsewhere, so 'he's done me in' (iii. 349). Murry said at the time that he had lost it. He later denied in his *Reminiscences* that he had ever refused more than one piece, and perhaps his memory failed him, but Lawrence had certainly sent three, very probably four, possibly five.[43] Had it been some other editor, the rejections would have been merely irritating – but Murry had invited him to contribute, and Lawrence had specifically asked for guidance about what he should do. He had been deliberately 'old-fashioned' in his reminiscences of childhood, and the refusal was doubly galling because their positions had been so dramatically reversed since their earlier friendship, as Murry's editorial note made clear.

Unfortunately, anger with Murry also meant estrangement from Katherine who was in any case closely associated with Murry's editorship. Even before the refusal there had been a moment of strain. Lawrence found one of her letters 'cryptic' and had been rather sardonic about a reference to Murry's 'fame' – presumably his appointment (iii. 339). Katherine, writing later to Frieda, would complain of feeling *repulsed* – though surely not by Lawrence's conclusion?

There is a pheasant comes and lies by the wall under the gooseberry bushes, for shelter. He is so cold, he hardly notices us. We plan to catch him, by throwing over him the netted hammock. But for the sake of his green head and his long, pointed feathers, I cannot. We thought we would catch him and send him to you to eat. But when I look at him, so clear as he is and formal on the snow, I am bound to respect a thing which attains to so much perfection of grace and bearing.

Love from both DHL

Lawrence indeed quickly denied any repulsive intent, and told her how he had dreamed of her, quite clear from consumption, watching the starry sky with him and seeing a strange planet: 'so beautiful, a large, fearful, strong star, that we were both pierced by it, possessed, for a second … Ask Jung or Freud about it? – Never! – It was a star that blazed for a second on one's soul' (iii. 343). It was however a star for him and her, not Jack, and the complication of getting the four of them into a square seemed as great as ever. Of her he had felt sure 'ever since Cornwall, save for Jack' – which was not quite true – but if she insisted on going along with Jack who 'will *never* really come our way – well! – But things will resolve themselves.' Unfortunately there was no separating the partners on either side, and with the rejection of Lawrence's manuscripts a week later, the resolution came in the wrong direction. Katherine reacted to news of his anger typically, by aiming her mocking fantasy at Frieda.

Frieda writes me that there is a 'rumpus' between me and – them I suppose. I see this 'rumpus' – don't you? A very large prancing, imaginary animal being led by Frieda – as Una led the Lion. It is evidently bearing down on me with Frieda for a Lady Godiva on its back. But I refuse to have anything to do with it. I have not the room now-a-days for rumpuses. My garden is too small and they eat up all ones plants – roots and all.[44]

She continued for a while to write 'foolish would-be-witty letters' (iii. 352) to Frieda, but they jarred on Lawrence, and when she wrote to him in May after their return to Hermitage, 'somehow I couldn't answer her. When I can I will. Of him, nothing – and forever nothing' (iii. 356). It was a great pity after the obvious affection and liveliness in Lawrence's letters to her since the reconciliation of 1918, and hers to him as well, one feels sure – if only he had kept them.

A minor comfort, at just this time, was to receive a copy from Louis Golding of the first issue of *Voices*, in which he had paid a passing compliment to Lawrence.[45] Also, the £50 for *Movements in European History* was close now as he set to work revising, determined to finish before moving south. He had succeeded by 23 April, the day before the move, and was 'a free man' again (iii. 352) – the more so since there had also arrived a formal revocation of the order which excluded them from Cornwall and limited their movements elsewhere. This made no difference to his determination however to leave an England where 'nobody cares about anything, literature least of all', nor to his feeling of 'scrambling uneasily from day to day, as if we were all perched on a land-slide, and the days were stones that might start sliding under one's feet' (iii. 348). He was still intending to go first to Germany – though they had now heard that there was 'terrible distress' and he wondered whether there might be antipathy to an Englishman – and then to America, though he had become more pessimistic about that too. He was also still wondering about Palestine. His talk with Eder about building a new society produced (from Hermitage) an idealistic anarchism. The new society, said he, should have only two Laws: first, that there should be no laws, since each man had to be responsible for himself and answerable to his own soul; and second, that everybody should have the right to food, shelter, knowledge and the right to mate freely 'irrespective of any other claim than that of life-necessity'. Then 'everything else can be done by arrangement, not by law' (iii. 353). Eder, fresh from the immense difficulties of the Commission, must have smiled wryly, especially when Lawrence joked that he would write about the Zionist enterprise as 'The Entry of the Blessed into Palestine' (after Fra Angelico), though he feared the 'hosts of people, "with noses", as your sister said', and did not believe they would ever 'pull it off, as a vital reality, without me' (iii. 354). He was serious (he said) about wanting to go.

For now however there was only the prospect of further marking time at Hermitage until they could leave the country. There was news of various friends whom he would be close enough to London to see again if he wanted to, but he was not at all sure that he did. Horne wrote, as Lewis had done, to renew contact, but Lawrence again was not keen (iii. 340, 346). He heard from Arabella that Hilda had had her baby and was all right, though very weak after pneumonia (iii. 347), but seeing her when they got to London was only a maybe. Gray was 'behaving wretchedly', unlike Richard who was 'very fine' (iii. 349) according to Arabella; but she herself was 'in low water'. Lady Mary Starr had also had a baby (iii. 344), but there was no temptation to see them. Worse, as Hermitage grew nearer there came a gushing letter from Margaret Radford: 'how happy, dear Lawrence, she is that she can be at Hermitage to receive us and stay ten days with us' (iii. 349) – as though 'the bother of hauling out all my things and shifting again' was not disagreeable enough (iii. 350). Just before they were due to leave, Ada Krenkow suggested that they should go via Leicester to see her and Uncle Fritz, and also Louie Burrows. (She and the Krenkows had remained firm friends.) He decided however that this would be 'painful ... I was fond of her, and have always a good feeling for her in me. But it would be wrong to meet again, I think, and to start the old feelings again. Anyhow it would be a shock to all of us' (iii. 353). The interesting implication is how revivable he thought 'the old feelings' might be – but he was not in a mood for renewed contacts of any kind.

Indeed, at the prospect of family and friends gathering to say good-bye at Easter (20 April) he had 'nearly cut and run' (iii. 351). Ada and Jacky had been at Mountain Cottage ever since the move from Ripley. (Poor Ada had been left, after her flu, with boils that obstinately refused to clear up; iii. 350.) Luckily her husband Eddie was home again now, and able to take care of their business. Emily's husband Sam may have been discharged from hospital too; if so, this was the largest family gathering since Ada's wedding in 1914 – and the last for many years to come. Lawrence had also recovered strength enough to insist that he was to be regarded as 'normal' again (iii. 351). With *Movements in European History* done, and freedom from the official restriction on movement in England, there was the first glimpse of a break in the clouds. He might grumble on the eve of departure: 'How many times have I packed our miserable boxes! and when will they ever come to rest'; yet he also felt as if they might be 'setting off on a real new move' at last, 'as if we shouldn't be long in Hermitage, as if soon the bigger journey would begin, away from England' (iii. 351–2). If only the peace treaty could be signed, and let them out.

VII Hermitage Again – Still Waiting

On 25 April they arrived at Chapel Cottage once more. Lawrence was grumpy. The journey had been a strain, the weather was bad and he could never stand 'the sweetly-loving' Margaret Radford for long. 'I wish', he said nastily, 'one could exterminate all her sort under a heap of Keating's powder. I feel utterly "off" the soulful or clever or witty type of female – in fact, the self-important female of any sort' (iii. 354). He recognised his own 'disagreeableness' and his mood of 'obstinate sulky stupidity', but the fact remained that he did not want to see anyone at all save Kot, Catherine Carswell and Gertler (and them not yet); or have it known that he had come south.

Soon however both he and the weather warmed. Pinker wrote that the *Cosmopolitan* had offered to take stories if he had any, and though Lawrence rightly predicted that they would find his work 'not in their line', he promised that 'for the next six weeks I will write nothing but short stories, if the short stories will come' (iii. 355). Pinker also sent a cheque for £55, (probably for *Movements*, and perhaps 'Tickets Please' in the April *Strand*); and the American essays were still appearing at 5 guineas per month. Also, Eddie Marsh had decided to devote the royalties for his biography of Rupert Brooke to helping needy writers, and with his usual tact sent £20 to Lawrence on 10 May 'from Rupert', enabling him to be simply grateful. Lawrence repeated his belief that 'The passionate dead act within and with us', – not like the 'messenger boys' of the spiritualists – and he could be at peace with Eddie again, since 'now the war is fought with the soul, not with filthy guns' (iii. 358). He thought Marsh might have been prompted by Cynthia, to whom he remarked with restored good-humour that unfortunately he could not follow her recipe of childbirth as a cure for all ills. What a 'perfect chronicle of current events' she was (iii. 359), since her peace-baby was following the war-baby so perfectly on cue. In May the weather grew sunny, the world became 'very lovely, full of flowers and scents', and the temptation was 'dolce far'niente' (iii. 355).

Getting to Germany still seemed impossible. Sonia Farbman had tried to go by train to join her husband in Russia, only to be stuck in Holland, trying to get a visa for Germany. However, America seemed a more realistic possibility after Huebsch's offer to arrange a lecture tour. Lawrence could not see himself on a platform but he would do it, to make a living. 'I am not a public man – not a bit – always have a "Strictly Private" notice in my hat'; and the thought of New York seemed more 'awful' than a jungle, 'not because it is savage, but because of the overweening mechanical civilisation' (iii. 357). Yet he began to talk firmly about going in August or September, and making arrangements (when Huebsch came to England in the summer) to be set down 'gently among the sky scrapers'.

By 20 May he had sent Pinker two new stories, and a third probably also belongs to his six-weeks promise, though there is no mention of it in the letters. The two have a little the air of having been written to order – 'the right sort', he hoped (iii. 360) as he sent the first – though charged also with the new assertion of the male against the dominating and superior female. 'Fanny and Annie', later ironically retitled 'The Last Straw', takes up once more the vision of the strange lit-up face on the Midlands station platform and (again making use of something that had not been published) repeats the basic situation of *The Daughter-in-Law*. An ex-lady's-maid comes home (at thirty) to settle for marriage with a common man she had not thought good enough before, and who misplaces his aitches – only to discover that a local girl claims to be pregnant by him. It is a sprightly story, though Lawrence felt uncommitted enough to volunteer to change the ending if Pinker thought this advisable (iii. 360). Presumably, magazines like *Cosmopolitan* might prefer Fannie not to condone what had happened. (By contrast, when asked by *Hutchinson's Story Magazine* to shorten 'The Fox' in July, he could cut no more than about 650 words from over 9, 000 'without mutilating'; iii. 374 and n. 1.) The second tale was probably 'Monkey Nuts', in which a sulky young soldier refuses the overtures of a 'liberated' land-girl as an offence against his manhood, inverting the plot of 'The Fox'. This story is set in Berkshire; uses Violet Monk as a physical model for the young woman; and sets its tone through an older and worldly corporal, modelled on the one who was billeted on the Browns in the cottage next door, whose humour the Lawrences seem to have enjoyed. At work in both stories is the imaginative taking down of female self-importance and presumption, by showing how much more fiery life in Fanny's man and dignity in the soldier-boy there was than the women supposed, as they so took for granted their power and superiority.[46]

The third story however, 'Hadrian' (first titled 'You Touched Me'), is newly questioning, though it too has affinities with both 'The Fox' and 'The Blind Man'. In the 'Pottery House' beside a now-disused factory,[47] two spinsters, for whom no suitably middle-class husbands could be found, are looking after their dying father. The lad he adopted from an institution to make up for his lack of a son has emigrated to Canada with hardly a good-bye, for he has an orphanage boy's inturned 'watchfulness' which knows he must watch out for himself. Having served in Flanders, Hadrian suddenly returns – to the displeasure of Emmy and Matilda who find him as self-contained and plebeian as ever, and a 'cocky' wee 'mannie' now to boot. They think he has come in search of a legacy, and he certainly seems to be winning Mr Rockley round again. In the night, anxious about her father, and forgetting that he has now been moved downstairs, Matilda enters 'his' room and runs her hand tenderly over the face of the man in the bed. Afterwards she wishes she could cut the offending hand off; but the next day an awakened Hadrian looks at her with new eyes. Soon he not only offers to marry her but wins her father's support, so much so that when she refuses there is an ultimatum: consent or be disinherited. In the end she gives in; and after the ceremony, at her father's command, she kisses both him (for the first time since childhood) and her new husband. 'That's right! That's right!' the dying man murmurs in the last line – but is it?[48] Rightness or wrongness might seem a question of character and motive, but these are much less attractive than their counterparts in 'The Fox'. Matilda is more class-ridden than March, more dried up, more resistant to change; and she marries (it may seem) to keep hold of her money. Hadrian is a colder, more walled-off version of Henry, making no bones about his intention to go off with the whole inheritance if she refuses him, and willing to benefit from blackmail. The father is a patriarchal bully, taking an obscure revenge on the women who have served him so long. All wrong, then? Yet the central incident, and the final one, suggest a dimension more impersonal, and one that has been missing from all their lives. 'You touched me', Hadrian insists.[49] Even though (in contrast with 'The Blind Man') it was by mistake, her tender touch changes Hadrian once and for all; and it is that, even more than the money, that he wants. Mr Rockley too wants a fatherhood, a posterity and an affection he has never had. Which will be more important to Matilda? Her sense of superiority and the power of her recovered money; or the awakening to her own capacity for tenderness and to the strange being of another, through the different power of touch? It is not a new question for Lawrence, but what is newly unsettling is his insistence on posing it, this time, in a context so thoroughly antipathetic to love, so lacking even in attraction.

At long last Beaumont seemed to be getting on with *Bay*, and sent some proofs. Though he was polite in reply, Lawrence did not think Anne Estelle Rice's woodcuts at all appropriate to his text and waxed privately sardonic about Beaumont's 'beautiful books', and the slowness of his printing by hand (iii. 366). Would he live to finish? At least however the book for Cynthia was under way, albeit a year late and still only half done. People seemed a little more interested in him again. Marsh wanted 'The Seven Seals' (from *New Poems*) for *Georgian Poetry 1918–19* (iii. 371 and n. 1); and Siegfried Sassoon asked him to send a poem for a collection of parodies he was proposing to publish (iii. 363 and n. 2).[50] In June he may have written a little more of *Aaron's Rod* (iii. 364), as though the idea of being a publishable novelist was just beginning to revive.

Something might even be done with *Touch and Go*. On 20 May he suddenly asked Pinker for the manuscript since 'a friend wants to criticise it' (iii. 360). This must have been Barbara Low, who was coming to stay with them in Hermitage for the last week of the month. (She probably heard about the play from Catherine Carswell, one of only three people to have seen it.) Lawrence often complained of Barbara's 'chattering' – meaning not gossip but intellectual argumentativeness – and he had a touch of sunstroke during her visit which can not have helped. Yet she had proved a good friend over the Education essays when she recommended them to Stanley Unwin, and she seems to have had it in mind to do something similar for the play if she liked it. More immediately and touchingly, this radical Hampstead intellectual and pioneer Freudian spent much of her visit helping to make Lawrence a jacket of coarse blue linen (iii. 361), to replace the striped one which Catherine had thought so shrunken when they stayed with the Carswells in the Forest of Dean the year before. It was successful enough for another to be made for Frieda, and these became a speciality. (Lawrence later exchanged one for a white tweed jacket of Bertie Farjeon's that he liked.)[51]

By the time the Carswells arrived for Whitsun in the first week of June, staying at Bessie Lowe's, with a nanny-goat tethered in the garden to provide milk for little John Patrick, the bluebells were past their best and were quite outdone by the new-blue Lawrences when they went wooding, pushing John in an old ricketty push-chair. Lawrence typically collected more faggots than anyone and condemned all theirs as worthless. There are wholly good-tempered glimpses of him now: writing on his knee under the apple-tree (possibly 'Hadrian', or revising *Touch and Go*), helping Bessie Lowe's little girl with her homework as he had Hilda Brown, taking his turn to mind John the toddler; and impressing John's mother by how good he was with children, knowing 'how to include them warmly and naturally in his life', but also treating them with 'a certain light astringency' to which they responded well. Watching John Patrick being bathed Lawrence sighed, '*He* won't be having any chest trouble!' Yet when one showery day he and the Carswells went to Silchester to look (unsuccessfully) for Roman remains, missed the last train and had to walk a long way home, he showed no ill effects and had clearly recovered much of his strength, though Catherine thought he still looked 'delicate'.[52]

On Saturday 28 June the Treaty of Versailles was signed. 'Pea–Pea–Pea–Pea–Peace: "the very word is like a bell"'', wrote Lawrence sarcastically (iii. 366), believing *it* to be the illusion, and sick of waiting for it to happen so he could leave the country. On the same day Murry suddenly descended on them, unannounced, saying he had heard of a house nearby that might be suitable for Katherine. He was 'quite nice' and wanted peace between them, but by now Lawrence was 'an old suspicious bird' about that too. Bertie and Joan Farjeon were at the cottage for tea when Murry arrived, and they all went looking for wild strawberries in the woods. Joan noticed that Lawrence 'seemed irked with Murry and refused to enter into the serious conversation with which Murry tried to engage him', devoting himself to Bertie and the stawberries and 'leaving the frustrated Murry to follow disconsolate at his heels'. Murry seems to have been discouraged, and not a word about the *Athenæum* was said all weekend.[53] The next day the inspection of the house (at Boxford, near Chieveley) was turned into an all-day picnic in the local baker's ricketty wagonette, with Violet Monk and Cecily Lambert's brother taking turns to drive the 'prehistoric' vehicle. Cecily paints a vivid picture of them ambling slowly through village streets full of respectable people off to church. 'Being so large and striking', Frieda 'made quite a set piece' in her 'full check skirt and blue short jacket with a very large flat brimmed hat covered' (by Lawrence) in 'brownish material ... which would keep bobbing up and down like a lid on a boiling saucepan' until she tied it down with a gay scarf under her chin. Lawrence was in drainpipe trousers, blue linen coat, white floppy hat and red tie; Violet in what Cecily tartly called her 'film outfit of Land Girl uniform plus'; the brother in the khaki of the South African army; Murry in a civil servant's 'orthodox flannels'; Cecily in 'demure navy blue' and another girlfriend in violet. It must have been, as Cecily says, 'a fantastic sight'. The house turned out to be derelict and rat-infested; the weather drizzled all the way home, much to the detriment of Frieda's hat; but back at the farm Lawrence made 'some of his famous coffee, and together we raked up a meal' so the whole thing became 'fun really'. All Murry remembered was Lawrence's 'gloomy forebodings of industrial England' – perhaps because that was a dangerous moment after the mislaid article – and the 'big bright yellow wood-chips we gathered from the coppice'.[54]

The friendship with the Farjeons had grown, and there was constant visiting in both directions. It was now also that Lawrence met Joan's sister Rosalind, whom he was to like even better. She was married to Godwin Baynes, doctor and, later, Jungian (he would become Jung's close associate); but the marriage was in difficulties and about to break up. Godwin had 'free and easy ways' with other women and Rosalind was jealous; but the breaking point came when, shortly after Godwin had been posted to Mesopotamia in October 1917, she had gone to bed with an old flame, also about to embark for the front (she thought), and had become pregnant by him. The child was born in July 1918, six months before Godwin's return in January 1919. His parents had been told in March, and formal separation now seemed almost certain.[55] Both sisters were intelligent and artistic and had been raised as free spirits. Cecily remembered Joan as very 'highbrow' when Lawrence took her on their bicycles to Bucklebury. Rosalind seemed the quieter, but her gentle manner and serene dark-haired rather pre-Raphaelite beauty disguised a mind and personality no less strong. She had taken a house in Pangbourne with her three children, only a few miles away, and at a trying time began to come often to the Farjeons. On her first meeting with the Lawrences, 'We picknicked in the woods together, and Lawrence and Frieda sang German folk songs – "*Wo hast du Die schönes Tochterlein?*" – in shrill, penetrating, unforgettable voices. Back in the house at the spinet by the french windows we sang Mozart arias from *Figaro*.'

Soon they were fast friends. Both sisters were struck, as Catherine Carswell had been, by Lawrence's relationships with children. Joan's Joscelyn, at $2\frac{1}{2}$, was 'exceedingly shy of the bearded stranger' at first, but one day touched him very cautiously to make sure he was real, and they became friends, walking hand in hand in the garden while Lawrence told her about the plants and the birds. Rosalind's eldest, Bridget, on a later occasion felt neglected as the grown-ups listened to him 'rather spellbound', and 'in order to attract attention' (as critics have been known to do in similar circumstances) she ran up and struck him with a thistle.

Instead of appeasing or remonstrating with her, Lawrence began to hit her likewise with a thistle. This indeed amazed us all, and astounded her who had never before been treated in such a downright manner. Lawrence said that children should live their lives apart from the grown-ups ... He had no patience with the middle-class subservience to the young.[56]

Such was what Catherine called his 'light astringency' – but both this and the grave courtesy without condescension which others have described came from his belief that child and grown-up should each have their proper space.

At the end of June, however, to his annoyance, they were given a month's notice: 'The Radfords, with stinking impudence, having let us this cottage, want us to clear out by July 25th., so then we shall have nowhere to go' (iii. 367). The venom was uncalled for. The cottage had in all probability been lent to them for free at first, when their situation was at its nadir after the expulsion from Cornwall, though they had to move out when the family wanted to come. Their renewed tenancy was a lease now, but Margaret still felt entitled to be there if she wished, and if this remained a condition, the lease may have been the cheaper for it. Now the family wanted their summer holiday in Hermitage, as was their right; so Lawrence was just letting off steam to Kot in his hatred of being dependent on others. Moreover the notice concentrated his mind on making some alternative choice at last, though he was still waiting for Huebsch's proposed visit to England. Now that the peace treaty had been signed, Frieda was more anxious than ever to go to Germany as soon as possible but he, working himself up to greater independence, thought he would go straight to New York, and only if that proved impossible would he go with Frieda to see her people. To Cynthia he wrote that what really mattered was not 'love, nor money, nor anything else – just the power to live and be one's own Self. Love is heavily overweighted. I'm going to ride another horse' (iii. 368).

He hoped they could leave England before the end of August, so it was time to go to London and apply for passports. Just as he was leaving however, came a discouraging letter from Amy Lowell. She knew him as Huebsch did not and could see very clearly what a disaster a lecture tour would be, though she put it politely: 'You must not look for El Dorado ... I do not think it would be possible to get you any large quantity of lectures until you have made yourself known in other ways.' Even among those who knew his books there was 'a mistaken and ridiculous prejudice', because puritan America 'cannot see the difference between envisaging life whole and complete, physical as well as spiritual, and pure obscenities like those perpetrated by James Joyce'. The Boston Athenæum had placed even *Sons and Lovers* in a locked cupboard![57] Lawrence wrote back immediately to say that he was not interested in El Dorado and had never wanted to lecture, but he was determined to come, and was sure he could earn a living by writing. All he wanted was to know that there would be a possible haven with Amy 'for a week or two' if he could not provide for himself at the very start; but he would soon be on his own feet. 'I shall come alone, Frieda will stay in Germany till I am a bit settled, then I shall send for her. – I am not afraid of prejudices: they are rarely in the very blood, only in the mind, on top' (iii. 369).

In London, he stayed first with Barbara in Guilford Street, but town made him feel unwell enough to break a date with Marsh to go to a Scarlatti concert, and he found it noisy at Barbara's so he moved to Kot's again (iii. 370). (As soon as he got back to Hermitage five days later he wrote to tell Marsh of his plans, and ask how Nichols's lecture tour had gone, with the implication that if Nichols could do it, why shouldn't he.) He did not get far with the passports and would have to come again in a fortnight, but before returning to Hermitage he spent a happy weekend at Forge Cottage in Otford Kent, home of Helen Thomas, the widow of the poet Edward Thomas who had been killed in action in 1917. He was taken by Vere Collins who knew her well. (He may also have heard much about her from Eleanor Farjeon, who had fallen in love with her as well as her husband.) Helen later recalled Lawrence as 'tall pale and emaciated', and though she had been told he looked like Jesus she thought he could also look and talk like the Devil. She was upset at the 'sinister expression with a hint of cruelty' which appeared when he 'spoke with derision and scorn of people I knew who had been most generous to him' – Margaret Radford? the Meynells? – and 'his high, steely voice rose into a mocking laugh which chilled me'. However to herself and her daughter 'he was kind and considerate and amusing ... all that my admiration of him had imagined'. He talked of his pleasure in seeing a 'perfectly groomed' woman walk into a room, and of how Frieda had been given beautiful dresses (by Nusch, though Helen says 'a rich friend') which he had to remake. 'Unpicking a Poiret gown', he said, 'was like taking Rheims cathedral to pieces'. He showed Helen how to prune her gooseberry bushes to make them more fruitful – and on hearing how her eldest daughter would not go back to school where her only talent seemed to lie in drawing, and was only interested in clothes and boys, he suggested she be trained in dress design. (He was quite right about the gooseberries, Helen found, but in the other case art proved no match for the boys.) She was less pleased when Vere called her a 'maternal' type and Lawrence added 'a disciple'. Who were these men to put her into categories and talk of her as though she was not there! But with Myfanwy, aged about 8, Lawrence's 'manner was delightful':

He took out of my shelves at her request a book full of reproductions of Goya's work, and sitting by the child on the sofa he turned over the pages and told her about the pictures. He would not let her look at those showing bull fights or war or violence, but talked to her charmingly about the rural or domestic scenes ... So much so that the next morning, armed with the book, she asked if she could go into his bedroom and with his permission climbed under the eiderdown beside him. When I took in tea, there they were, she in the crook of his arm, and he now looking rather like Don Quixote, showing her the pictures all over again ...[58]

The portrait of Lawrence has a Goya accuracy: good features, warts and all.

Back in Hermitage Nancy Henry came to stay the night of 8 July (iii. 372), and the weekend with Helen Thomas also produced renewed contact with Eleanor Farjeon who was going to Forge Cottage the following weekend, and would be with Margaret in August. Lawrence heard that Eleanor wanted to adopt a needy German family, obtained an address, and wrote to explain how to send food parcels through the Emergency Committee (iii. 373). He also looked at two houses for her (iii. 375).

Barbara's idea about *Touch and Go* became clear when a letter arrived from Douglas Goldring, offering to have it produced under the aegis of his recently founded People's Theatre. Goldring had once seen Lawrence years before when he himself had been assistant editor to Hueffer on the *English Review*, and admired his work though they had never met. By 1919 (he says) he had 'strong revolutionary, pacifist and internationalist convictions, believed the "revolution" was gaining ground, and that soon people would be ready for a "red" theatre'. He had joined the '1917 Club' of sympathisers with the Revolution, had given up 'trying to write anything but ... "propaganda"' and had become the English Secretary of the 'Clarté' international movement founded by Henri Barbusse (author of that fine war novel *Le Feu*, 1916) as an 'organization of intellectuals ... who believed in peace, international brotherhood and the dawn of a new era'. With Harold Scott, Goldring had also founded the People's Theatre Society 'especially for the production of "Dawnist" plays'. Lawrence was no pacifist idealist, and the revolution he wanted was not that of Marx and Lenin, but he found the idea of a People's Theatre 'very attractive' (iii. 371) and immediately wanted to meet Goldring and talk about it. He told Pinker he wished to be free to do what he liked about the play (iii. 374), and then confirmed to Goldring that he could make it his first production (iii. 374) – there were hopes of an arrangement with J. B. Fagan who had taken over the management of the Royal

Court Theatre the previous September – and print it also, in a proposed series to be published by Daniel.[59] He asked Kot to arrange a meeting for his forthcoming trip to London (iii. 375), at which they immediately took to each other. Lawrence was not over-sanguine about the chances of success, 'but it is a vital *idea* anyhow' (iii. 374).

Margaret Radford was coming to the cottage a bit early and he could not 'be in the house along with her' (iii. 376), so on the 24th he was already in town, seeing Marsh and meeting Thomas Moult (editor of *Voices*) and his wife, as well as Goldring. He may also have seen Nichols[60] – but another letter from Huebsch, who was not coming over after all, was also discouraging about the lectures and made him inclined to hang fire again about America. Meanwhile the problem about where to go just now had been solved. Bertie and Joan Farjeon were going on holiday for a month, and Rosalind Baynes was happy to let the Lawrences stay in 'The Myrtles' while she looked after the house at Bucklebury. So to Pangbourne-on-Thames he and Frieda went, on 28 July.

VIII   Thames-side

Here there was a proper garden for Lawrence to take an active interest in, and the river for boating, and room for visitors to stay. On the first weekend came Ada and Eddie with the children for a week (iii. 378); and no sooner had they left than Emily and Peggy arrived (iii. 382). While they were still there, Hilda Brown was driven over the nine miles from Hermitage in the local pony trap, to spend some of her holidays with them. Rosalind was also visiting when Hilda arrived, and showed the children the attic (with a secret staircase) where they could play if it rained – and also get out of the way if Mr Lawrence were cross. By train the journey was circuitous but the two villages were quite close by road; and indeed the very next day (the driver having stayed overnight) they all decided on a trip back to Bucklebury in convoy with Rosalind, picking up Mrs Brown on the way. (The pony was so fat and slow that Lawrence maintained they could have rolled there quicker.) They spent the night at Spring Cottage, collected some waterlilies, and walked back – the way made shorter by Frieda's tales of her childhood in Germany, and Lawrence's descriptions of Nottinghamshire and Cornwall.

Visitors meant expeditions. August was so hot that Lawrence complained of being casseroled to a turn (iii. 382). He was not too keen (perhaps remembering the near contretemps with the Murrys in Mylor) on showing off his oarsmanship in front of the fashionable 'nuts' and their 'daisies' in summer river finery, but they made a steamer outing down river to Reading, where Lawrence bought the children the novel treat of melon (just becoming available again), and as usual instructed them how to eat it, holding the slice in one's fingers and dipping it in sugar, scornful of those who cut theirs prissily in cubes. There was an all-day tramp on the Downs and a climb up the Ridgeway above Streatley, to look down on the great river winding through its valley below. There was another expedition to Hermitage, this time by rail, to take Hilda back and come to an arrangement with Margaret Radford about when they might or might not return to Chapel Cottage. (It turned out that her plans left them an awkward fortnight in September which they now arranged to spend with Cecily and Violet at Grimsbury Farm, when their time at Pangbourne was up.)[61]

Hilda and Peggy kept away from Lawrence as he wrote 'for many hours each day' in a room overlooking the lawn. He encouraged this by offering a prize for the best artificial garden, and awarding one each in the end. Indeed he managed to get through a considerable amount of work, though – with one exception – not of a creatively original kind. Koteliansky had translated a book by a contemporary Ukrainian, Leo Shestov (Lev Isaakovitch Svartsman), whose title would literally have been the 'Apotheosis of Groundlessness' had Lawrence not refused to countenance that. Mostly as a means of repaying Kot for all his support and offers of financial help when the need had been greatest, Lawrence had agreed to put the translation into better English. He suggested his name should not appear, or only under a pseudonym – overtly because he did not want to be seen 'to dabble in too many things' (iii. 381), but actually to give the work and Kot's reputation a better chance. He also refused point blank to accept more than a third of the payment, which Kot had offered to split down the middle. He got down to work in Pangbourne, had done Part I by 10 August, (iii. 381) and may have finished the longer Part II by the time they left or not long after – though with mixed feelings about the book itself (iii. 387).

Shestov like Lawrence was much influenced by Nietzsche, but by his subversive mode rather than his ideas as such. Indeed, Shestov deeply distrusted all systematic ideas and theories, and meant his discrete paragraphs (built out of ironic and sometimes epigrammatic paradoxes) to tease his readers into more sceptical ways of thinking. Read today, Shestov's positivist contempt for all metaphysics can sound very modern. 'We know nothing of the ultimate realities of our existence,' he proclaimed, 'nor shall we ever know anything'. Moreover he set out to undermine the arrogance of all sequential philosophy, holding that 'anything whatsoever may result from anything whatsoever'. (So *All Things Are Possible* became the English title.) Even positivism could prove falsely comforting, its scepticism merely the obverse of idealism; whereas 'the business of philosophy is not to reassure people, but to upset them': 'The well-trodden field of contemporary thought should be dug up. Therefore, on every possible occasion, in season and out, the generally-accepted truths must be ridiculed to death, and paradoxes uttered in their place. Then we shall see ...'[62]

However, non-sequential sententiae and paragraphs did not make translation any easier, and though Lawrence found the attitude amusing, his first impression was that Shestov wrote 'atrociously' (if Kot had got him right) because 'One sentence has nothing to do with the next, so that it seems like jargon' (iii. 380). He was also irritated by the Kiev philosophy teacher's technical vocabulary and the repeated attacks on philosophers; though 'sometimes he blossoms into a kind of pathetic beauty' (iii. 384). As he finished, Lawrence confessed to having 'compressed ... a bit' because Shestov was full of unnecessary phrases and expressions, but he had 'left nothing out' in substance and sometimes 'added a word or two, for the sake of the sense'.[63] He had got tired of the continual tilting at the same targets; 'but I *like* his "flying in the face of Reason", like a cross hen' (iii. 387).

However, Shestov's radical scepticism was 'pathetic' as well as attractive to Lawrence because he saw the Russian as stuck at the dismantling stage, that precedes any new outburst of the human spirit. Secker's eventual decision to omit Shestov's own introduction in favour of the short Foreword Lawrence wrote in September, meant that Shestov sailed into English waters under a flag he would not have recognised. Lawrence took up Shestov's idea that Russia, coming to Europe so late, was swimmy in the head from a dose of the poison of European culture – but the prognosis immediately turned Lawrencian. Soon Russia's 'new, healthy body' will throw off the effects of the inoculation and 'begin to act in its own reality, imitative no more, protesting no more, crying no more, but full and sound and lusty in itself', and about to inherit the future. Shestov only seems nihilist, says Lawrence. In fact he is shaking the psyche free from old bonds so that it can believe in itself and nothing else – and *that* (*pace* Shestov's dislike of ideals) can become 'a real new ideal, that will last us for a new, long epoch'. Shestov may refuse to state it positively, because he thought it too might be a trap for his spirit. Yet:

The human soul itself is the source and well-head of creative activity. In the unconscious human soul the creative prompting issues first into the universe ... Let each individual act spontaneously from the forever-incalculable prompting of the creative well-head within him. There is no universal law. Each being is, at his purest, a law unto himself, single, unique, a Godhead, a fountain from the unknown.[64]

Shestov the sceptic about all laws is there, but transformed into Lawrence in a burst of optimistic individualism.

The passage looks back to his anarchist letter to Eder at the end of April; but it also reflects Lawrence's first formulation of his own *poetic* credo at Pangbourne, while he was doing the translation and thinking about how he differed from Shestov. Huebsch wanted to print *New Poems* (which Secker was now putting into a second edition), but wanted also to be able to copyright the work in America by claiming that his edition differed from the unprotected

English one. He suggested some slight change or addition, or perhaps a preface, and Lawrence responded with alacrity. He sent off his defence of a poetry of 'the instant moment' to Huebsch on the same day that he posted the Shestov to Kot. (He also used it to keep his promise to Moult of some prose for *Voices*, where it appeared as 'Verse Free and Unfree' in October.)

Proclaiming affinity with Whitman, and confessing that the preface should really have accompanied the genuinely new poetry of *Look! We Have Come Through!*, Lawrence seeks to distinguish a poetry of the 'immediate present', which he wishes to write, from the poetry of the past which sought perfection of form. In the first place, this new poetry should aim at the quality of life itself, for:

Life, the ever-present, knows no finality, no finished crystallisation. The perfect rose is only a running flame, emerging and flowing off, and never in any sense at rest, static, finished. Herein lies its transcendent loveliness ... A water-lily heaves herself from the flood, looks around, gleams, and is gone.

And poetry, too, can be 'life surging itself into utterance at its very well-head', an image harking back to 'Not I, not I, but the wind ...' As such, it must be free of all laws. But what makes verse truly 'free' is that it is, or should be,

direct utterance from the instant, whole man. It is the soul and the mind and body surging at once, nothing left out. They speak all together. There is some confusion, some discord. But the confusion and the discord only belong to the reality, as noise belongs to the plunge of water.

Such a poetry is of the quick, the instant moment. 'It does not want to get anywhere. It just takes place.' It acknowledges no drill-sergeants of form, and no ideal, for the ideal is a figment, a 'static abstraction, abstracted from life'.[65]

Thinking about Whitman again also made him think about sending the American essays to Huebsch to make a book (iii. 388); though he was not ready to work on them yet.

When Bertie and Joan Farjeon returned, Rosalind came back to Pangbourne, probably on the 22nd, but she asked them to stay on over the weekend – and soon their departure (planned for the 25th, when Cecily Lambert was to come and fetch them) was further delayed. For Godwin was coming to visit his wife, and she asked the Lawrences to stay still longer and see him. Ostensibly this was 'to talk about a fruit-farming bee which he's got in his bonnet' (iii. 385), but the real reason was almost certainly to discuss their separation, and Rosalind may have thought it might make things smoother to have guests in the house. So the move to Grimsbury Farm was put off to the 29th – though a certain unease is apparent in Lawrence suddenly feeling 'horribly shut in here – think with such relief of the space round the farm' (iii. 385). It did not help that a rainy spell had set in which looked as though it might last for weeks.

There is no record of how the two men got on, except that Lawrence liked Baynes enough to risk writing him a letter advising against divorce.[66] It was soon to be agreed however that Godwin would divorce Rosalind – that way round, because in those days his being cited as the guilty party would seriously have damaged a promising medical career, and also perhaps because Rosalind wanted freedom more than her husband did. Godwin had been an admirer of Lawrence's work and they had a number of friends in common. He had been a close friend of Bunny Garnett, though their disagreement over the war – Godwin having volunteered as a doctor when his first child was little more than a year old, while Bunny became a pacifist – had led to estrangement by now. He was also very friendly with the Radfords, the Meynells, the Farjeons, the Baxes.[67] Godwin was big, florid, mustachioed and athletic – a fine oarsman, and a regular in Bax's famous pre-war village cricket team. He was also, like his friend Maitland Radford, a man with a strong social conscience. He had chosen before the war to set up in medical practice for the poor, first in Bethnal Green, and then as the 'panel doctor' in Wisbech, braving the opposition of the British Medical Association, and of course the local doctors, to the new Health Act. He was an emotional, universally popular and gregarious man, who found it difficult to resist the admiration of women. At Lawrence's death – by which time Godwin was working with Jung in Zürich – he wrote to Rosalind that he agreed with her about the dead man: 'I think he had the flame and was in a sense prophetic'. However, he also felt that Lawrence had 'underestimated the tremendous problem of the Christian unconscious':

He fought it in the world and so he could only make characters who were fundamentally anti-social, but he never realised the issue as a battle in which he himself was profoundly and desperately involved. He tried to think himself out of the impasse, but he never said 'I have this problem and it must be solved in my life and not in my books'.[68]

In that sentence lies all the difference between the psychoanalytic clinician, and the artist who not only wrote out of his contradictions, but sought precisely to explore and shed his sicknesses in books. But such differences lay some distance ahead in 1919. The chances are that the two men got on well. The four of them went sailing and rowing down to Mapledurham on a rather windy day (iii. 386); and they probably sang together in the evenings since that was something Godwin also loved to do (with a much finer voice than Lawrence's) – and it would reduce tension between husband and wife.

Lawrence sent off Frieda's passport application, with a photograph endorsed by Donald Carswell, before they left Pangbourne (iii. 383, 384). Thomas Cook the travel agent had advised that passports would not be issued until the peace treaty had been formally ratified by all the governments involved, but Lawrence wanted Frieda to be ready at the first moment. As for himself, he would definitely not go to Germany now, and was rapidly going off the thought of America as he read the reports of the visit there by the Prince of Wales (iii. 383). It was not clear what he would do, though he was still more and more interested in winning readers in America.

Partly because of this, a breach with Pinker was opening. The first signs had been the letter in November 1918 asking outright whether Pinker wanted to be rid of him, and the circumvention of Pinker's commission in the case of the American essays in the *English Review*, where Lawrence might well have felt that he had had to make all the running. Now in late August Lawrence went one step further, and arranged for the English printing of *Touch and Go* through Goldring's agent, not Pinker. He apologised rather disingenuously afterwards: 'I'm sorry, Douglas Goldring and Walter Peacock were arranging it before I really knew' (iii. 385); but in the same letter he announced that after an enquiry by Huebsch about *New Poems* he had told him simply to go ahead. Only then did Pinker hurriedly draw up a contract, saying he 'knew nothing' of Huebsch's intentions (iii. 388), but that irritated Lawrence further – what was an agent *for*? It seemed that Pinker's practice was wholly English; he had never been active or interested in arrangements for America. So Lawrence told Huebsch now that he would like to know direct about American sales and royalties. Future arrangements should be made with himself, 'and if Pinker has to come in, he can come in after' (iii. 388). He was also corresponding with Secker direct about the latter's idea that the time might have come for a 'Collected Poems' (iii. 379), and he must have been beginning to wonder whether he might not do without Pinker altogether.

IX Grimsbury Farm

On 29 August the Lawrences went off to stay with 'those farm girls' until the Hermitage cottage should be clear of Margaret. His Haggs persona came happily to the fore again, all the more so perhaps because Cecily and Violet were not as expert or as physically strong as the Chambers and the Hocking families had been, so his help may have been more positively welcome. (Mr Chambers had said that work always went well when Bert was there, and the Hockings too had been glad to have him in the fields, but not so much for his skill or labour as for his company.[69]) Almost at once he was at work chopping bushes down and clearing a meadow of bracken and thistle which had taken over since the war (iii. 392). He also took on the job of milking the goats, who resented him at first and held back; but soon he became, said Cecily, 'quite expert'. Rosalind on a visit was impressed. (He had however no influence over the Grimsbury pigs, who had been been spoilt by being treated as pets and who followed Cecily and Violet about, even going to the station to look for them. At Higher Tregerthen Lawrence had complained that Christ did not understand the devilishness of lambs; but he made no such complaint about the Lord's view of swine. The Grimsbury lot gate-crashed and enthusiastically ruined a picnic on his favourite Heather Hill, to his monumental rage.) He sawed the logs and made himself useful; partly because he hated feeling under an obligation. His strength had obviously returned.

To have Frieda as a house guest was a different matter – and at Grimsbury Farm we get a more revealing picture of her than we have had for some time. She did not take well to all the shifting about, and let it be known. Lawrence told Moult that she was 'like an unhappy hen' fluttering 'from roost to roost' (iii. 389); and Cecily also noticed that whereas Lawrence hated staying anywhere for any length of time, Frieda 'craved for a home and solidity'. As the time for going to Germany seemed to get closer, the delay must have been more and more frustrating. During their first days at the farm she felt unwell and (said Cecily) 'expected to be waited on':

Most of this fell on D. H. We were far too busy and overworked to do any nursing, except in an emergency, which certainly this was not. To this day I can see D. H. in a raging temper, carrying a brimming chamber down to the front garden and emptying it over our flower beds which rather horrified us, although there was little else he could do. The sanitation was of the most primitive – an earth closet far down the garden. Our bathroom was a tin bath in the scullery with rain water drawn up by a hooked pole from a well outside the house in the front garden. Drinking water had to be fetched in pails from a spring some distance away.[70]

Moreover when Cecily suggested that it would be easier if the Lawrences shared a bedroom rather than occupying two, Frieda refused because 'she did not wish to be too much married'. The desire for a room of her own might not be very significant in itself. She had had one not only in Nottingham but in those of her roosts with Lawrence where it could be managed, and it was the aim of most women of the middle class and above in those days; certainly no more than the daughter of German gentry would expect, though she had come down in the world. Her explanation does however confirm that the marriage had reached a stage in which both of them felt they needed more space and independence. Moreover, ready as always to talk intimate secrets with another woman, Frieda made her habitual lament for her lost children to Cecily – perhaps less realistically now that Monty was a young man and her daughters' lives, too, had grown more independent in their teens. But she also told Cecily 'how welcome a child of D. H. L. would be'. This must have seemed less and less likely. She had just turned forty-one, and since for the last five years they could hardly have afforded a child they had probably been taking contraceptive measures.[71]

Lawrence was still refusing to go with Frieda to Germany; and his temper with her was shorter than ever. Closer proximity made this very clear to their hostesses, when Frieda had 'some small mishap' with Violet's sewing machine:

> It was mentioned in front of D. H., and the result was a tornado so shocking that even we were terrified, fearing the outcome. He slated Frieda unmercifully, saying she was lazy and useless and sat around while we did all the work. He then ordered her to clean our kitchen floor which was large with the old-fashioned, well-worn bricks, none too easy to get scoured, in fact real hard labour. To our amazement she burst into tears and proceeded to work on it, fetching a pail of water and sloshing around with a floor cloth in a bending position (although he had told her to kneel), bitterly resentful at having to do such a menial task quite beneath the daughter of a baron, at the same time hurling every insult she could conjure up at D. H., calling him an uncouth lout, etc. He appeared to love an opportunity to humiliate her – whether from jealousy or extreme exasperation one could never tell. I was only suprised that she listened to his abuse or obeyed his orders.

Yet if the Lawrence marriage continued on such occasions to frighten and baffle those who saw it at close quarters, the rumpuses had never been more than a half-truth about it, and even now probably much less. Nor was Lawrence's temper all that Cecily remembered, though it made the best stories. 'We missed the Lawrences very much', she says, quite simply. 'How dull it was when he had gone. Always there was some inspiration.' She remembered the jokes and the excitement, the charades, the painting of boxes and bowls together, the fun. When the Lawrences went back to Chapel Farm Cottage about 12 September (in glorious autumn weather) Frieda thought they should offer to pay 'the girls' something, but Lawrence, for all his dislike of being indebted, replied that one did not pay one's friends – and Cecily wholly concurred.[72]

X Last Weeks at Hermitage

Douglas Goldring, who came down with his Irish wife Betty to spend a weekend at Hermitage a month later, was also at first rather embarrassed by the way Lawrence 'kept his Prussian wife, Frieda, "in her place" '. Just before Sunday lunch was ready, Frieda made a remark which infuriated Lawrence, and Goldring had the distinct impression that only the presence of guests had stopped him throwing the potatoes at her. However, as always, 'in a few moments, the storm was over'. Goldring saw the psychological direction of Lawrence's rages perhaps better than Cecily – not jealousy nor sadism so much as taking down the upper-class magna mater, a male worker-bee's revolt against the big lazy Queen on whom he nevertheless depends. He was also in no doubt about the underlying strength of Frieda or the marriage:

Life with Lawrence could never be *dull*, but I doubt if he would have found any Englishwoman with the nervous solidity to stay the course. Voluble, full-bosomed, Prussian Frieda was built to weather storms. Like a sound ship, broad in the beam, slow but seaworthy, she could stand any amount of buffeting. And I have no doubt that she found the Von Richthofen card a useful one.[73]

Indeed, her provocations usually came from her need to put her husband in his place, too. But when Goldring came down to breakfast the next morning he found the Lawrences laying the table, singing German folk-songs at the tops of their voices.

However, Frieda in these last weeks before her return to Germany must have been prey to very mixed feelings, though she was not one to examine them closely. At *last* the experience of being 'the Hun' among the English was coming to an end, albeit in a defeat of her fatherland which must have gone hard with her. By this time she knew about the suffering that the continuance of the Allied blockade was causing in Germany, and also the punitive provisions of the Treaty of Versailles whose ratification had to take place before she would be allowed to travel. She longed with all her heart to see her mother, to whom she had always been close. There would however be no returning to her pre-war social background and family security. Influential contacts might remain, but her father was dead, Metz occupied by the French and the Baroness now in a genteel home 'for ladies of the educated classes' in Baden-Baden. Edgar Jaffe's career as Finance Minister in the mildly revolutionary post-war Republic of Bavaria had come to an end in a hail of extremist bullets on 21 February 1919, as its President was assassinated by a right-winger on his way to Parliament, and in the Chamber his Ministers threw themselves to the floor as gunfire from a left-winger thudded into the ministerial benches.[74] Although the Minister of the Interior was severely wounded, Edgar escaped injury; but his political career was over. He was not in the more radical government which proceeded to proclaim a Soviet Republic, and which ended in blood a month later as troops occupied Munich. Thereafter his and Else's situation and safety were a continual worry. Frieda had comprehensively burnt her boats in Nottingham before the war; now the German ones were badly charred, and she was about to discover how much or how little 'the von Richthofen card' was worth these days. Moreover, she had lost at least some of her power over the husband who refused to come with her, and was clearly determined to go wherever *he* wanted, leaving it to her to join him later. Excitement, apprehension, impatience, and irritation with Lawrence must have been about equal, as she waited to leave. Cecily saw that Frieda's nature was basically phlegmatic and easygoing; but Lawrence told Cynthia, not over-sympathetically, how much less so she had become, how she 'insists on "feeling" her trials, gets very cross, or weeps, when the letters come from Germany. She has set her mind on going: and can't go. Another quandary. Patience is justified of all her children' (iii. 395).

As the time came to move back to Hermitage, he was very much aware that he would soon have to finance Frieda's German journey as well as his own, wherever he decided to go. That knowledge may have lain behind his anger at her laziness and carelessness, and behind her tearfully angry obedience since she also depended absolutely on him. It behoved him to collect as much money as he could; and also to clear the desk of all the projects that could be cleared. Indeed, though Cecily's memory is uncertain, he seems to have revived the one nearest to his heart before leaving the farm. She recalls him staying on for a day after the row, working hard to 'finish' a novel (which she mistakenly remembers as *The Lost Girl*) while Frieda went back to Hermitage alone. She also remembers Violet typing something from it for him. It could not have been *The Lost Girl*. It was almost certainly *Women in Love* that he was suddenly working on again, and it may have been a new Foreword that Violet typed.[75] For Goldring had contacted an American publisher who he thought might bring the novel out at last; and Thomas Seltzer had actually cabled, to express his interest.[76] On 7 September, five days before leaving Grimsbury Farm, Lawrence promised to post the book to Seltzer 'by the next mail' – but he wanted 'to go through the MS. of the novel once more. – I consider this the best of my books' (iii. 390). The best of his books tended to be the one he had just finished, but in fact he held life-long to the judgement that *Women in Love* was the major work of his middle period. To have an American publisher cable interest in it confirmed his hope that, whether he went to live there himself or not, he could find a new audience in America. Martin Secker had also expressed a belated interest now that the war was over and publishing conditions in England easier (iii. 391), but Lawrence's preference was clear: 'I would like the book to come first in America. I shall never forgive England *The Rainbow*' (iii. 391). Nor would he have forgotten how many English publishers, including Secker, had turned *Women in Love* down when it mattered most.

The revision Lawrence did now cannot have been extensive since it was done within (at the most) five days. To the naked eye it seems that some passages, crowded in the margins of what after retyping was to become Seltzer's setting-copy, are in notably smaller writing and browner ink than the mass of ink revision, and these may be Lawrence's last touches to a work which had effectively achieved final form two years before. If so, they do no more than 'refine and clarify' what was already there[77] – for example in the Saracen's Head scene, where the new material further opens out the existing imagery drawn from Pryse's *chakras*, to emphasize still further the darkly independent mystery of Birkin which Ursula discovers in touching the base of his spine. If so, they relate to the Whitman essay and its defiant avowal of the importance of the 'cocygeal' *chakra*, though here, as in 1917, the emphasis falls not on anal sex so much as the recognition of wondrously independent selfhood – even more important to Lawrence now. Indeed, reading the novel in 1919, he must have become aware that in some important ways he was no longer the person who had written it. Its main drive could not be changed, but occasionally an emphasis could be increased.

The connection with the Whitman essay is no accident, for he was also thinking again just now about his *Studies in Classic American Literature*. This was the next-bulkiest item in his drawer, and almost equally important in his hopes for American readers. He would not want to lug it abroad with him, and he had for some time wanted to make it into a book for the United States. Several other things had demanded attention first, but he had been thinking of getting down to the American essays even in Pangbourne, and had promised Huebsch to send them 'soon' (iii. 388), though he had not managed to do so.

Only first – or at long last – there were more proofs of *Bay* to correct; and though 'dear, foetid little Beaumont' (iii. 395) had muddled the setting of 'Obsequial Ode' (and would forget the dedication to Cynthia Asquith which had to be tipped in at the last moment; iii. 465), Lawrence was able to tell her that it really was nearing completion and might possibly be out by Christmas! The next task was to arrange for the publication of the Shestov. Three days after getting back to Chapel Farm he posted Secker the manuscript with his newly written four-page Foreword, which he suggested would do instead of Shestov's own much longer and (he thought) tedious Preface, though Kot wanted to keep that (iii. 394). Secker agreed to publish, agreed with Lawrence about the Preface and also adopted his suggestion for a better title. There followed an argument about terms which produced fury from Kot and a business-weary shrug from Lawrence that Secker was 'a scurvy little swine' like all the rest, but at length the arrangements for the Shestov too were complete, at a 10% royalty (iii. 403 and n. 3). Lawrence's conscience was still not wholly at rest about his indebtedness to Kot. He urged him to ask for an advance from Secker and to place extracts in periodicals (iii. 407), for which he should keep all the profits – but there were still the ten pound loans that Lawrence had not been able to afford to return – though they had undoubtedly been meant as gifts. (Kot had told Goldring[78] that if you wanted to help Lawrence, he must at all costs never know what you were doing.) In late September Lawrence was still worrying about Kot's finances.

I've got to see Frieda off to Germany – the policeman came Monday to verify her passport application, and said the passport would come all right – probably it will – so I must provide for that trip, otherwise I could have given you something ... I owe you heaven knows how many pounds. – Soon I shall, I believe, begin to make money in America. Then you can have some freely. (iii. 397)

At least he had done what he could for the moment – and now he could get down to assembling a complete manuscript of the American essays. The last part of the piece on Hawthorne was worked up into a second essay; and the last three unpublished ones were revised. Because he had given his 'Amy' typewriter to Catherine Carswell to sell for him (to her brother for £5, rather more than she thought it was worth; iii. 393), Lawrence had to transcribe neat copies by hand. Indeed, since he wanted a duplicate set for possible English publication later, the dreary job would have to be done twice. Rosalind remembered copying out one essay in Pangbourne – probably the Hawthorne – but she would have been too busy to do more, and in desperation Lawrence turned to Kot again and begged him to copy out the last three, using paper of a size to blend into a single 'manuscript' with the pages from the *English Review* (iii. 397, 399). He finally sent one copy to Huebsch on the last day of September, with mingled triumph and apprehension (iii. 400).[79]

For it seemed very unlikely that the Whitman essay could ever be published. A letter from Huebsch of 17 September said not only that he was now postponing the American edition of *New Poems* until after Christmas because of labour troubles, but also that he had had to let *The Rainbow* go out of print. As he explained:

> Our self-appointed censors (smut hounds as Henry L. Mencken calls them) would love to make a 'case' out of this, and unfortunately under our postal laws and system of justice the book would be officially suppressed (which it is not now) I would be fined or sent to jail and your reputation would suffer. (iii. 399 n. 1)

Lawrence had had a recent visit at Hermitage from an acquaintance of Huebsch's called Hermann Schaff who had left him in no doubt that Huebsch was telling him the truth about puritan America. He had also just had 'a parcel of books' from Jane Burr, including her self-published *The Glorious Hope* (1918),[80] which had confirmed his impression of America as beset by 'stalking emotional demons' (iii. 400). Huebsch he thought, being a Jew, might be capable of 'eternal detachment of judgement', since (in another of his racial generalisations) Jews are 'connoisseurs of the universe', able to deal in treasures or psychological deformities alike – so what did Huebsch *really* think of the USA? The prospects of publishing a book which ended with the essay on Whitman did not seem good! Yet Lawrence remained more convinced than ever of the crucial value of the new psychology which underpinned all his American essays – especially after discussions with the English Freudians (Jones, Eder, Barbara Low) who hoped soon to make direct post-war contact again, through Jones, with the European psychoanalytic movement.

The essay on Whitman you may find it politic not to publish – if so leave it out altogether – don't alter it. The rest is unexceptionable. – These essays are the result of five years of persistent work. They contain a whole Weltanschauung – new, if old – even a new science of psychology – pure science. I don't want to give them to a publisher here – not yet. – I don't really want people to read them – till they are in cold print. I don't mind if you don't publish them – or if you keep them back. – I only know the psychoanalysts here – one of them – has gone to Vienna, partly to graft some of the ideas on to Freud and the Freudian theory of the unconscious – is at this moment busy doing it. I *know* they are trying to get the theory of primal consciousness out of these essays, to solidify their windy theory of the unconscious. Then they'll pop out with it, as a discovery of their own. – You see Ive told Ernest Jones and the Eders the ideas. – But they don't know how to use them.[81] And no one has seen the essay on Whitman – no one in the world. – Look after the MS. for me, won't you. – Schaff says you're the only 'white' publisher in America. (iii. 400)

As an aside, among other news of what he was hoping to have published (for example the Shestov and the play) he mentioned having sent 'the novel *Women in Love* – sort of sequel to *The Rainbow*, to some other New York people who asked to see it – presumed you were not keen on it – you must have seen the MS – Pinker has had it for two years' (iii. 400). An outraged Huebsch replied that this was wholly new to him (iii. 409 and n. 1). Pinker had never thought to send the novel to him at all. Lawrence had already asked Secker to say nothing to Pinker about *his* new interest in *Women in Love* (iii. 391), and had decided to arrange for the publication of the Shestov himself. In a postscript to his letter to Huebsch, he thought he might not let Pinker make any more agreements in future (iii. 401). A final breach was imminent.

Lawrence had recently had a cheque from Marsh (iii. 388; probably for 'Seven Seals' in the new *Georgian Poetry*; iii. 389); an unexpected one from Moult for 'Verse Free and Unfree'; and £5 for the typewriter. (When the Krenkows came down to see him, the weekend that the Goldrings were at Hermitage just before Frieda left, he was also able to 'touch' Uncle Fritz for £10.) As a last attempt to make a bit more, before shaking the dust of England from his feet, he wrote four essays on 'Democracy' for a strange little periodical called *The Word*, published weekly at The Hague. This came from another initiative by Goldring,[82] who had accepted an invitation to The Hague from the editor of this odd magazine which aimed to publish work in three languages. It was, he said:

run by a group of enigmatic and highly improbable Germans who pretended to be International Socialists. Perhaps they were, although they looked, even to my innocent and inexperienced eye, much more like Secret Service Agents. At all events, they printed some of my outpourings and paid for them; and I fancy I got them to print one or two articles by Lawrence.

In fact they printed three of the four essays Lawrence wrote on 'Democracy', before the magazine collapsed, leaving the last unpublished.[83] These turn out to be an extended critique of the famous opening of Whitman's 'Song of Myself': 'One's-Self I sing, a simple separate person, / Yet utter the word Democratic, the word En-Masse ...'[84]

The word 'democratic' in Lawrencian utterance turned out, not surprisingly, to be very different from anything the editors of *The Word* might have expected from an author recommended by the English Secretary of 'Clarté'. His judgement of Whitman's sense of political and social value was as ambivalent as the judgement of his sexuality. As the third essay puts it:

In Whitman, at all times, the true and the false are so near, so interchangeable, that we are almost inevitably left with divided feelings. The Average, one of his greatest idols, we flatly refuse to worship. Again, when we come to do real reverence to identity, we never know whether we shall be taking off our hats to that great mystery, the unique individual self, distinct and primal in every separate man, or whether we shall be saluting that old great idol of the past, the Supreme One which swallows up all true identity.

'The Average' argues that all Averages are abstractions for a purpose. The idea of the Common or Average Man, the Man-in-the-Street, is only useful as 'the standard of Material need in the human being', and 'this is where Socialism and Modern Democracy comes in'. Lawrence is Socialist and Democrat as long as what is under consideration is the state's function to make living together possible, by ensuring that everyone can secure the basic material needs – so as, then, to be able to develop individuality. This is the only function, and only value, of 'Governments, States, Nations and Inter-nations' – material institutions for material purposes. Indeed, 'the great development in collective expression in mankind has been a progress towards the possibility of purely individual expression'.[85] So much for 'the word En-Masse'.

The second essay 'Identity' refines a little. The idea of an inclusive 'Human' Identity can be as useful for 'provisioning' consciousness as the idea of the Average is for 'provisioning' the body. The idea of a Whole, of which each human consciousness is part, can lead to a desire to extend consciousness to embrace the whole (as it does in Whitman), and that can be a learning process. But, says Lawrence, 'your *consciousness* is not *you*', and to try to extend it infinitely is always to come back with a bump to the reality of yourself. No matter whether the urge to unify is through Power (like Alexander the Great) or through Love (like Christ), the 'lesson of lessons' is that we only have our pure being 'in clean, fine singleness', not any oneness with the rest of things.

If we look for God, let us look in the bush where he sings. That is, in living creatures. Every living creature is single in itself ... the little unfathomable well-head that bubbles forth into being and doing. We cannot analyse it. We can only know it is there ...

Not people melted into a oneness: that is not the new Democracy. But people released into their single, starry identity, each one distinct and incommutable.[86]

This goes all the way back to the 'Study of Thomas Hardy'; only a little clearer, perhaps, on how Lawrence could think himself both socialist and individualist.

The third essay, 'Personality', however has a new and fine distinction. Does Whitman's word 'person' mean the same as 'individual'? By looking into the derivation of the two words, Lawrence is able to claim a radical difference 'between something which was originally a player's mask, or a transmitted sound, and something which means "the undivided" '. So,

A person is a human being *as he appears to others*; and personality is that which is transmitted from the person to his audience: the transmissible effect of a man.

A good actor can assume a personality; he can never assume an individuality. Either he has his own, or none.

Personality then is linked to the 'ego' or conscious idea of the self which so often runs counter to the 'true, deeper, spontaneous self'. It is 'man born out of his own head', or (still worse) according to an idea or ideal shaped by others, and hence as material as an engine, though made out of flesh and blood.[87]

So the final essay 'Individualism' can offer no political idea, let alone system, since these are the enemy of the spontaneous self. The most basic fact, on which all schemes of social life must be founded, is that any 'actual man present before us is an inscrutable and incarnate Mystery ... the fact of *otherness*'. If every self is unique there can be no comparison and hence, as he had argued in the education essays, no intrinsic equality (or inequality, which also depends on comparison) but always disquality, difference. What is important is that men and women should trust their own inner desires and impulses – the God singing in their individual bush – and be free (materially and otherwise) to do so. But there is a Fall in this account of the Garden too. Desires come from within, ideals are imposed from without – yet 'Desires tend to automatise into functional appetites, and impulses tend to automatise into fixed aspirations or ideals.' Within, what had been spontaneous in the self becomes mechanical; without, men seek to determine the being of others instead of respecting their otherness. In the past it may have seemed that there were great collective ideals to fulfil, but always there comes the point at which the imposed and abstract nature of any ideal will finally destroy the spontaneous integrity of individual beings; and Lawrence believes this is 'horribly true of modern democracy – socialism, conservatism, bolshevism, liberalism, republicanism, communism: all alike'. All claim to be ideals, all finally reveal themselves to be essentially materialist, concerned with *property*, however they may wish it to be distributed – whereas (says Lawrence, from experience) 'A man only needs so much as will help him to his own fulfilment', and the desire to possess more 'is a kind of illness of the spirit, and a hopeless burden upon the spontaneous self'. His true Democracy can only begin when individuals free themselves from the urges to possess or to oppress, and 'become their own decent selves again', able to live and grow in individual spontaneity, respecting the no less mysterious otherness of others.[88]

Meanwhile the Other nearest to him finally received her passport by 8 October, and had only to obtain a Dutch visa which could be done in London (iii. 404) – so she could be off in a week. Lawrence may have been glad of that. The waiting had been a strain, the separation would be temporary and the first 'Democracy' essay had mentioned in a revealing aside, among material needs of the Average Man, both the 'ache for coition' and the 'ache to escape from the woman again'.[89] (She probably felt much the same, as well as the urge to see her mother.)

At last he too had reached a decision. He would go back to Italy. Thinking Capri might be a good place to spend the winter, he asked Secker for Compton Mackenzie's address there (iii. 401).

The Goldrings came down for Frieda's last weekend, as did Uncle Fritz and Aunt Ada, and on Tuesday 14 October he and Frieda set off for London with Violet Monk, who was to spend a day or two in Acacia Road while Cecily and her parents looked after the farm. Cecily had never seen Lawrence in a dark city suit:

The change was startling. He looked the well-dressed and smart man-about-town and exceedingly handsome, striking in fact with his red beard (groomed) and his intense blue eyes. His lean figure lent itself to well-cut clothes, but I remember him saying that he hated orthodox clothes and dressed in the blue coat and odd things because he liked to create attention.

Violet felt she was 'ignored' by the household at Acacia Road and soon went back in a huff. The Lawrences were staying with the Carswells and can have had little time to spare for more than a sympathetic note.[90] There was Frieda's Dutch visa to get, last-minute shopping, arrangements for her journey – and on the Wednesday night she was off on the Harwich–Hook of Holland express.

The 'Nightmare' chapter of *Kangaroo* 'remembers' (though with what accuracy is unknowable) that 'She had a look of almost vindictive triumph, and almost malignant love, as the train drew out.'[91] Emotions must certainly have been complex, on both sides.

Lawrence had time to see Douglas and Betty Goldring again before going back to Hermitage alone on the Friday. He had heard from the Krenkows that his sister was ill and in any case would have wanted to see her before he left, so part of the following week was spent in Ripley. He found Ada 'frail and seedy, but getting better' (iii. 407) – and picked up another cold himself which kept him indoors for a week or so. After a warmly autumnal first half of September the month had gone out in rain, and October had turned distinctly chilly, 'awful' by the end.

It was worse for Frieda, in a Germany where gas and electricity had to be saved, the trams were not running, shops shut at five (having little anyway to sell) and beer halls were closed because they could not be heated. Her journey had been a nightmare. When she got to Holland her trunk went missing. Moreover the delay made her miss her connections, and when she did get on her way at last it was a grey journey in an unheated railway-carriage, through a half-starving country. Fortunately there were not the upheavals in Baden-Baden that occurred elsewhere but, nevertheless:

Food could be bought only at official distribution centres, the weekly ration consisting of less than an ounce of butter, half a pound of meat or sausage and five pounds of potatoes. Hungry and freezing, people waited around in the streets for news of the next issue of firewood, exchanging spine-chilling stories about the misdeeds of the French ...[92]

There could be no special consideration for the ageing gentlewomen of the Ludwig-Wilhelm-Stift. Frieda must have been deeply upset by the conditions under which her mother had to live now.

Meanwhile Lawrence's plans went no more smoothly. No answer had come from Compton Mackenzie, and a crisis blew up over *Women in Love* since no word had come from Seltzer either. This was not altogether suprising as the typescript had been delayed in the post, but Lawrence suddenly became aware of a complicated difficulty. Having been told of Seltzer's offer to publish, Secker was now showing interest – but there was an unforeseen problem of timing if Secker was to get the novel into his spring list. For though Pinker still had one copy of the typescript, it was the *other* copy (TSII) which Lawrence had worked on since the retyping, and he had sent that to America. He suggested that Secker might write or cable Seltzer for it, without saying anything to Pinker. Then he wrote 'urgently' himself, asking Seltzer to post the typescript back if printing had not begun, so Secker could have it first; and if he *had* started, to send sheets and proofs to Secker as soon as they came from the printer (iii. 408–9). Now however the problem was further complicated by a cable from Huebsch: 'Certainly I want novel. Pinker never submitted. Cant you cable withdrawing manuscript and transfer to me'! (iii. 409 n. 1). Huebsch had a right to feel aggrieved since he had taken all the risks of publishing Lawrence in America; and Pinker's lack of interest in American publication had landed his author in a situation where he seemed only too likely to *have* to offend somebody.

But who? He certainly needed to keep in with Secker, who was to publish the Shestov and seemed likely to become his regular English publisher now. Secker had even suggested a 'Collected Poems', though the idea was in abeyance because Duckworth was not keen on releasing *Love Poems*, being quite content with a small annual sale of about 150 copies, Lawrence thought (iii. 398). Lawrence had also offered Secker the *Studies in Classic American Literature*, while insisting that he did not want them 'displayed' through Pinker 'before promiscuous publishers' (iii. 407). He had, no less, to keep in with 'the only "white" publisher in America', because Huebsch was the key both to keeping several previous volumes in print there, and to publishing the American essays which seemed a vitally important step in gaining an American readership. He had just begged Huebsch to try to get essays such as those on Dana and Melville into 'some monthly, like the *Atlantic*', because publication in 'respectable sound periodicals ... would help my reputation immensely' (iii. 405). He had now also sent 'Democracy' as a possible substitute for the essay on Whitman, which might help publication of the whole. But his new relationship with Seltzer would be ruined if he were to *withdraw* the typescript, after recovering it.

He played for time, able at least to say to Huebsch and Secker that he had asked for the typescript back before he left for Italy, and postponing a final decision until it was clear whether Seltzer would return it. (He may have hoped that it would prove too late for that; letting him off the hook, so that he could plead that it was not his fault.)

It was definitely *not* the kind of tangle to have, unresolved, just as he was leaving for ... he did not even know where yet, in Italy. He thought he might go to 'a farm' in Caserta. He had not given up hope of hearing from Mackenzie, but to be 'near Naples' (iii. 407) was to be well on the way to Capri. The farm was in fact the home, near the village of Picinisco in the Abruzzi mountains, of Orazio Cervi who had often served as male model for Rosalind's sculptor father, and who had retired to his homeland to build a house from his savings. Lawrence spent the last day of October in Pangbourne with Rosalind, who seems to have offered to dispose of his books in Reading along with her own. It seems likely that she was already thinking about what (with characteristic generosity) she was going to do about a divorce. There was bound to be publicity, and she would be best out of England before the case came up. Sir Hamo Thornycroft wrote to Orazio, who had replied on 24 October that his 'little house' was 'at your onours disposal for any length of time you should riquire it'. He thought its position might suit his Honour's daughter, but 'I must say with great shame that it is not well furnished', though he thought some necessary things might be borrowed. Moreover his wife had died a year before, so 'there is no one living with me exept a cat and a dog'. However, he thought he might override his grown-up children's objections and marry again in about six weeks time, which 'would be good for the comfort of the Ladies you would be sending me'. He was nothing if not obliging, touchingly anxious to show his gratitude to his old patron and benefactor. The children's young nurse Ivy Knight was willing to go with Rosalind, but as the possibilities were discussed in Pangbourne Lawrence must have suggested that he should scout in advance, to see whether the house would be suitable for Rosalind and the three small children – for it was in those terms that Rosalind herself proceeded to write to Orazio in November.[93]

Lawrence, for his part, asked Catherine Carswell to write to a relation of hers by marriage, Ellesina Santoro, to see whether she could find a room for him in Rome for a few days on the way (iii. 407) – at the same time making the Carswells a farewell present of his 'tattered but complete' set of De Quincey, whom he particularly liked because of a shared distaste for the great idealists, Plato and Goethe. Lawrence had been driven over to Pangbourne by Cecily and Violet; and Rosalind, busy packing her books, offered them their choice (advised by him). On the way back Lawrence spotted some fine mushrooms in a field, stopped the buggy, and was over the fence in a flash, trespass or no, to secure supper.[94]

On 4 November he finally moved out of Chapel Farm Cottage and took his luggage up to Kot's, hoping at first to stay only a few days. He wanted to travel by sea, since 'overland travelling is *such* a sweat now' (iii. 411), and got Thomas Dunlop (now back in London) to wire to Leghorn for a berth on a cargo ship to Naples. But even after a week hanging about in London which he always disliked, he could find no passage without the certainty of further delay. So it would have to be the train. What Dunlop probably did provide however was an introduction to a rich Englishman in Turin where Lawrence could break his journey.[95] Lawrence then wired Norman Douglas to find him a cheap room in Florence and leave a message at Cooks there (iii. 409). Either in Turin or Florence he would wait for Frieda, who now seemed likely to join him before long. She had written to say how bad the food shortage was, and her luggage had still not turned up, so she was naturally 'none too happy' (iii. 412). She would want to cheer her mother and do all she could for her, but there was little she *could* do, and little to make her want to stay on longer, even if there were no question of her money running out.

The week in London made Lawrence one new acquaintance, Max Plowman, who had sent an inscribed copy of his latest book, and whom Lawrence proposed to introduce as a candidate for the Daniel series of People's plays[96] – but most of his visitings were good-byes, to the Goldrings, Aldington and Cynthia. Catherine took him to the St James's theatre to see Henry Ainley and Marion Terry in a play based on Tolstoy's *The Live Corpse*, which he thought such 'awful rubbish' that they left before the interval (iii. 411).[97] He enquired anxiously from Cecily whether the folk in the Hermitage post-office were forwarding his letters (iii. 411–12), for there was still nothing from Seltzer. He encouraged her to keep visiting Rosalind and Joan; and (more surprisingly) sent regards to her father who had thought him a most unsuitable friend. Since Secker was also going to Italy (at one stage Lawrence thought they might go together), *Women in Love* would have to be postponed in England, and the American problem would have to wait also. At almost the last moment a cheque for £20 arrived from Huebsch (iii. 413) – most welcome. Another £15 had come through Goldring from the theatrical producer Norman Macdermott as an option on *Touch and Go* (iii. 440). 'By managing the rate of exchange,' Lawrence told Huebsch, 'I expect to be able to live in Italy' (iii. 413) – he thought he could get 50–52 lire to the pound through the Banca Italia, though not through Cooks (iii. 414)! Before the war the rate had been half that.

This last delay however brought his dislike of England to a pitch of intensity, particularly since the November weather remained 'hideous'. Aldington, who had not seen him for some time, was particularly struck not only by his animosity now to the country of his birth, but even more by the instinctive animosity of English people to him. In 'the apartment of two American friends' – probably code for Arabella and her mother – Lawrence sat hunched in a chair by the gas fire, in a 'peculiar mood', Aldington thought:

He was in that state of animosity which comes to a man when he finds himself alone against the world. He was literally 'satirical,' really like a wild half-trapped creature, a satyr, desperately fighting to get free.

... He told us that Frieda had gone to visit her relatives in Germany, and seemed not to care if he never saw her again. And this was sad indeed after the passion and intensity of their relationship; so vivid and so complete whether in attraction or repulsion that the lives of other lovers seemed commonplace ...

When Lawrence and I left, the crowds were coming out of the theatres; and as we made our way through the people there were gibes and sneers at Lawrence's red beard, a sudden little whirlpool of mob hostility. Of course, they had no idea who he was, had never heard of him; it was simply the ugly instinctive hatred of the crowd for the person who is different, which they suspect means some form of superiority. Then I saw the reason for his acrid mood and for his flight from England. There was no place for him in that rather sinister post-war world. Either he must escape from it or it would crush him.[98]

If he had ever craved attention (as Cecily thought), it was not that kind. Nor was Aldington the only one to sense the hostility. On Lawrence's last trip to London he had lunched with Marsh, who had found it 'remarkable, how the poets are returning to Beauty!' – but had then been 'afraid to walk with me up the Mall afterwards, and ran away like a respectable rabbit. What I want to know is, was it my appearance, or my reputation, or his?' (iii. 396).

By Wednesday 12 November he had collected visas from the Italian and French consulates, and had sent his heavy luggage to await him in Rome, keeping only what he could carry. He was still unsure whether to stop off in Florence but thought he would probably wait for Frieda there, before going to

Rome and on to 'Picinesco' and 'Grazio', neither of which he had learned to spell yet (iii. 414). One of his last thoughts was to ask Rosalind to exchange her copy of Dulac's fairy-tales for any of the books she was selling for him or the price of all, and to post it to the Dunlop children who would love it. He also gave her detailed instructions about visas and currency to ease her journey. He was finally ready to go.

At 8 a.m. on Friday 14 November 1919, just over a year after the Armistice, he caught the train to Folkestone, Paris and Turin. On the platform to see him off was nobody English, only a Russian and two Scots, the faithful Kot, and the Carswells. Catherine and Donald had given him, as parting presents, 'a somewhat worn coat-lining of natural camel's hair' which turned out to be a godsend, and 'a voluminous black and white shepherd's plaid' which had belonged to Catherine's grandmother.[99] It was an icy day, and there was snow on the Downs 'like a shroud' as the train moved through the grey morning to the coast.

He was leaving, in considerable bitterness, the England to which he had returned from his winter in Fiascherino with such high hopes in 1914, looking forward to marriage, the publication of his greatest work so far, and the consolidation of a growing reputation as one of the most promising of the younger English writers. Now he had become an alien who would never feel at home there again. In *Kangaroo* Somers remembers, probably recalling his author's mood accurately enough, how: 'as he looked back from the boat, when they had left Folkestone behind and only England was there, England looked like a grey, dreary-grey coffin sinking in the sea behind, with her dead grey cliffs, and the white, worn-out cloth of snow above'.[100]

PART FIVE

◆

Italy Again

◆

CHAPTER TEN

November 1919–August 1920

CAPRI AND SICILY

I feel I shall never come north again.

(iii. 511)

I The Traveller

Post-war trains were slow, often stationary, so Lawrence did not reach Turin until 8 p.m. on Saturday 15 November, having been thirty-six hours on the way (iii. 415).[1] It was an awkward time to land on strangers. He must have felt unsure of his welcome as his taxi took him through the wet darkness, and set him down beside the imposing gateway and lodge of Sir Walter Becker. The lodge-keeper had to telephone the big house before allowing him to carry his bags along the drive and up the steps, where a man-servant in white gloves was waiting at the door to take them. The entrance hall was equally imposing: yellow marble pillars with gilded arches, thick Turkish carpet on the floors, a grand staircase. Sir Walter would later concede the accuracy of the descriptions of the house in *Aaron's Rod*, while objecting to the 'portrayal' of himself and his wife[2] – that difficulty, as always, of only-too-recognisable people and settings worked up for imaginative and structural purposes. Actually the novel shows Aaron being welcomed with gracious benevolence, by 'a small, clean old man with a thin white beard and a courtly deportment, wearing a black velvet dinner-jacket faced with purple silk', who was obviously at dinner with his guests – Lawrence's lateness being thus compounded by a further awkwardness of dress. After being taken to his room, Aaron is placed beside his hostess and served dishes specially prepared, to help him catch up. 'Lady Franks' is shown as gracious, almost queenly with her pearls and the diamond star in her hair, making conversation and at the same time keeping a watchful eye on the needs of her guests. All through the after-dinner marsala with the men – no port yet, post-war – and when rejoining the ladies in the library upstairs, there is hospitable kindness for Aaron as in all probability there was for Lawrence. The novel detects no snobbish condescension, though the real-life host remarked later on the 'home-spun-clad figure' of his guest.[3]

Sir Walter had made a considerable fortune as a shipowner. His knighthood was new, awarded in 1918 for establishing a hospital for British troops in Turin, and some propaganda activities. He had been invested with his KBE less than three weeks before Lawrence's visit,[4] so the showing-off of his decorations by 'Sir William' after dinner may have happened much as the novel describes. He was very rich – and Lawrence was very poor, at a disadvantage, and under an obligation which he always disliked. To an objective eye however, though *Aaron's Rod* may have made its knight older, frailer and more materialist than Sir Walter actually was, and may have worked up the argument between Aaron and his host in keeping with a major theme of the novel, there is no personal animus in the fictionalising – though it is hardly a 'thank you' for the two nights of hospitality. Lawrence's feelings at the time were put to Cynthia Asquith only two days after the visit, and had more to do with the gap between artist and plutocrats than anything personal. They were 'rather nice people really'. Yet his stomach

has a bad habit of turning a complete somersault when it finds itself in the wrong element, like a dolphin in the air. The old knight and I had a sincere half-mocking argument, he for security and bank-balance and power, I for naked liberty. In the end, he rested safe on his bank balance, I in my nakedness. We hated each other – but with respect. But c'est lui qui mourra. He is going to die – moi non. He knows that, the impotent old wolf, so he is ready in one half to murder me. I don't want to murder him – merely leave him to his death. (iii. 417)

The guest spent Sunday looking at Turin and its countryside, set against the mountains, and on Monday was on his way again (iii. 415).

He decided to go to Florence by way of Genoa and the coast rather than through Milan, and stopped over for old times' sake at the Albergo delle Palme at Lerici. For fifty miles after Genoa the track ran close beside the sea and the weather had cleared, so though this train, too, was often at a standstill the view was 'most beautiful, blazing sun and blue sky and Italy quite herself' (iii. 415). Motionless at 5.30 'beside a lovely sunset sea', he wrote another letter of advice to Rosalind to ease her journey, with tips about routes and porters and customs and changing money, a picture of his own recent experience. He read the Italian papers, finding them lively and not too serious even at election time, and called on his old Lerici acquaintances, but his card to Cecily shows the weather had gone greyer (iii. 417), and in Florence the rain had set in (e.g. iii. 418). Douglas had booked him a room in the Pensione Balestra (where Douglas himself was staying; iii. 420) for only 10 lire a day including food (iii. 424); but though it had a fine view overlooking the Arno it seemed 'stone-comfortless' and remote on the 'third floor of the big, ancient, deserted' house.[5] As he sent off a spate of postcards he began to feel lonely, and (his impressions changing with his mood) to find Italy 'rather spoiled by the war – a different *temper* – not so nice a humour by far' (iii. 419); but with 'two friends here' he was not 'quite alone' (iii. 418).

His later account of how, on his way in the wet twilight from Cooks to the pensione after picking up Douglas's message, he had run into Douglas with Maurice Magnus, is too long to quote in full and too lively not to quote at all, even if only as description, without Douglas's characteristic rat-tat rhythms of speech and the slight twang – not really an accent – which was the only hint of Americanness in the precise enunciation and somewhat 'mincing' voice' of Magnus with its 'odd high squeak'.

I had unconsciously seen the two men approaching, Douglas tall and portly, the other man rather short and strutting. They were both buttoned up in their overcoats, and both had rather curly little hats. But Douglas was decidedly shabby and a gentleman, with his wicked red face and tufted eyebrows. The other man was almost smart, all in grey, and he looked at first sight like an actor-manager, common. There was a touch of down-on-his-luck about him too ...

He looked a man of about forty, spruce and youngish in his deportment, very pink-faced, and very clean, very spruce, very alert, like a sparrow painted to resemble a tom-tit.[6]

They made an extraordinary pair. Douglas in his fifties had a broken-down distinction like a grey-haired Mephistopheles, still handsome though his face had reddeneed and his eyes twinkled wickedly under thick grey brows. Whimsical, charmingly unscrupulous, he towered above the other, a little man who 'stuck his front out tubbily' above legs which 'seemed to perch behind him, as a bird's do'. Though Magnus turned out to be hard-up too, he was indeed a man who knew 'all the short cuts in all the big towns of Europe' and who still indulged expensive tastes. Add to these Lawrence, 'buttoned up in my old thick overcoat, and with my beard bushy and raggy because of my horror of entering a strange barber's shop'[7] and there is a vision worthy of Max Beerbohm. Yet here in Italy there was no hostility from passers-by.

From Wednesday to Saturday the three men had their meals together and sat drinking afterwards in either Douglas's or Magnus's bedrooms, which again made the sharpest of contrasts. Magnus's room was 'very clean and neat, and slightly perfumed'. Everything in it was 'expensive and finicking': cut-glass silver-topped bottles and ivory-backed brushes on the dressing-table, thick leather silver-studded suitcases, a trouser-press; and elegant devotional literature by the bedside, for Magnus was a Roman Catholic convert who now thought he might like to become a monk and went to early Mass every day. Whereas Douglas never believed in opening windows, and the 'queer smell of a bedroom which is slept in, worked in, lived in, smoked in, and in which men drink their whiskies, was something new' to Lawrence.[8] Douglas was pagan and amoral by conviction, more libertarian than Lawrence – and acknowledging less responsibility for anything but his own pleasure. Both new acquaintances were homosexual by preference, though both had married. Magnus disliked women. Douglas – who now preferred boys – had been a great womaniser before his marriage, and remained charmingly behaved and attractive to women still, though he had become mysogynist after his divorce and thought of even the attractive ones as an inferior species. His conversation was entirely uninhibited. Both men acted on the belief that the less money one had, the more important it was to spend, whereas Lawrence was determined never to be in debt or under any obligation that could be avoided. He had arrived in Florence with only £9 sterling in his pocket and £12 in the bank in England, and had Frieda to think of, so the whisky-drinking bouts felt extravagant though he paid his share.

They were lively company. Douglas at his best had great raffish charm, considerable learning on all sorts of subjects, a rich store of anecdote (like his language, frequently obscene) and a zest for life which could not but attract despite his self-centredness, malice and mischief-making, none of which he made any attempt to disguise. Magnus had been manager to Gordon Craig and Isadora Duncan; knew many European capitals; had edited the *Roman Review* 'till the war killed it'[9] and lived now by writing for American magazines, though seemingly always beyond his means so that he was always on the move. Both men were cosmopolitan and widely travelled. Much of Douglas's upbringing had been in Austria, and as well as a successful novel, *South Wind*, he had made a reputation as a travel writer, especially about Italy. He also knew something of Asia Minor, North Africa and India as well as Russia; and acquired considerable scientific knowledge of geology, fauna and flora wherever he went. Magnus had had a theatrical career in more ways than one, having landed up at one stage in the French Foreign legion – of which more, later.

Subsequent events and experiences have coloured almost all their published memories and judgements of one another, so their responses at the time can only be uncovered by peeling off later overlays and hindsights as far as possible. The contemporary evidence (such as it is) suggests little shadow, and much mutual fascination. There is no hint now of the repulsion from homosexuals that Lawrence had felt earlier. He was unworried now about such things, and indeed began to find in Florence 'a nice carelessness' (iii. 419) which may have signified more than the easygoing regime in the pensione. He seems to have been amused by Magnus's matronly fussing over Douglas, though a bit shocked still perhaps by Douglas's pederasty. When Douglas, in turn, was amused at Lawrence's objection to the Florentine boys showing so much bare leg, the cause may have lain as much in Douglas's reaction to the phenomenon as in the thing itself – but of repulsion there is no sign. Moreover both of them tended to put their best sides forward on first acquaintance. If there were to be friction, temper or sharpness, these would come later. Nobody ever conveyed the flavour of Douglas's talk, or its funniness, better than the man whom he would later accuse of having no sense of humour. As to Magnus, Lawrence may have felt that he was being condescended to by the little man, and if so, his description of Magnus as 'common' may have been reaction to that as well as to a touch of sleaze beneath the showmanship. Yet their subsequent relationship could not have come about without a sense, too, of something fine in Magnus's insouciance, sensitivity and love of beautiful things. When on Saturday 22nd it came to buying Magnus a birthday present, before the celebratory dinner he had undertaken to give in the pensione, and before he left for Rome on Sunday, Douglas's suggestion of a religious medal had a hint of satire, whereas Lawrence's choice of a little five-lira Volterran amber bowl was perceptive and gave real pleasure. Maurice's admiration of the 'lovely colour' of Lawrence's hair was also somehow touching as well as disconcerting (particularly since he could hardly be persuaded that its strange tint was not a dye). Though Lawrence later doubted whether Magnus liked him, and claimed to have been 'rather glad' himself when he had gone, there was an invitation to come to the great monastery at Montecassino when next the would-be monk was a guest there, and a Lawrence promise to do so, which suggests some liking on both sides.[10]

As for Douglas, even though the rather rancid portrait in his *Looking Back* concentrates on Lawrence's faults and limitations as person and writer, as Douglas came to see these, it admits also his 'naturally blithe disposition', his curiosity, his direct and instantaneous poet's observation, and 'something elemental in him, something of the *Erdgeist*'.[11] These were probably the things that struck Douglas first, even though Lawrence may have been a little on his guard at the beginning. Douglas certainly hastened to introduce him to Reggie Turner almost at once – though there was some risk involved in opening up to Lawrence's observant gaze the circle of expatriates who frequented the flat of this friend of Oscar Wilde. Many of these had come to live in Florence because their tastes were 'non grata' in England. Some (like Douglas) could not go back; others (like Reggie) no longer wanted to. Douglas wrote to Turner:

I have D. H. Lawrence (*The White Peacock*, *The Rainbow* etc) with me just now. Would you care to meet him? If so, let me know and I will arrange a quiet dinner somewhere, ONLY WE THREE.

I am going to prevent his meeting certain other people, because he is a damned observant fellow and might be so amused at certain aspects of Florentine life as to use it for 'copy' in some book: which would be annoying.

Read his *Twilight in Italy*, if you can get a copy – that gives you a clue to his nature which is sympathetic and yet strangely remote.[12]

Of course the suspicion that they would all appear in Lawrence's fiction was exceedingly well-founded, though it is not clear how many of the figures in 'Algy's (i.e. Reggie's) flat in *Aaron's Rod* were met in 1919, as opposed to Lawrence's two later visits in 1920. Be that as it may, on the Monday after Magnus's departure another group of Lawrence's postcards speak of dining out with friends 'in town' (iii. 421), so he had begun to make the acquaintance of the favourite trattorias frequented by the clan. (The pictures on the cards also show that he had now been to the Uffizi, whereas the first set were of the Piazza della Signoria, Aaron's first glimpses of which, with its stone and statues wet with rain, are graphically described in the novel.) It would certainly not have been long before the infinitely hospitable Reggie invited Lawrence to the Viale Milton, which he would use for *Aaron's Rod*..

Algy had a very pleasant flat indeed, kept more scrupulously neat and finicking than ever any woman's flat was kept. So today, with its bowls of flowers and its pictures and books and old furniture, and Algy, very nicely dressed, fluttering and blinking and making really a charming host, it was all very delightful ...[13]

Reggie thought of himself as very ugly, and so he apparently was when not animated: huge nose, rubbery face, thick lips and a nervous affliction which kept him blinking, 'like some crazy owl' in Lawrence's description. His manners and his wit, with its abiding flavour of Oscar Wilde, had remained of the nineties, very old-fashioned now. Norman Douglas could never resist teasing and insulting him, so the relationship (which both seemed to need) seemed always on the point of a final rupture, but it never came. For Reggie was a kind man. His novels were forgotten already; yet his life was less futile than he thought it, because of his talent for friendship and his abiding loyalties. The circle in Florence which Lawrence was to meet through him at one time and another could certainly be described as 'a curious lot' and 'startling', yet Aaron probably speaks for his author in finding them also 'very much better fun than everybody all alike'.[14]

By that Monday (24 November) Lawrence had heard from Frieda. She had not yet 'fixed up her passport' (iii. 420) – i.e. got permission to travel in Germany, and the visa for Italy – but two days later she wired that she would come on 3 December (iii. 422). Her lost luggage had turned up, although 'the Dutch thieves kept all the *new* stuff' (iii. 426).

In Florence the sun was shining now on an Arno still yellow and swollen with rain. The city seemed 'beautiful, and full of life and plenty' (iii. 421), and if its people had been marked in some respects by the war, still they had 'some blessed *insouciance*' (iii. 422) – Lawrencian keyword – and so had he. At last, with the pressure of England off him, and among people even more unconventional than he was, 'One moves lightly' (iii. 425). He had himself 'dentisted'; and found that he could live '*well*' for £2 a week (iii. 425) – but by the end of

November he calculated that he had already changed £40 altogether,[15] so he had, to be careful about money. Two of the batch of postcards on the 24th speak of 'loafing' (iii. 419, 420) and he was clearly enjoying that, but it behoved him to try to earn something before Frieda arrived, though he rather hoped she might have a bit left over from what he had given her.

In early December he wrote Katherine a reconciling letter saying that Florence was not only lovely but full of 'extremely nice people'. This was almost certainly in response to a lost letter from Murry with her new address in Ospedaletti[16] – which Lawrence took as an olive branch, perhaps showing awareness that he had not been treated well. He had already set to work again. He usually waited until projects were well under way before talking to publishers about them, so he had probably begun writing some time before he announced to Huebsch on 3 December that he planned 'to do various small things – on Italy and on Psycoanalysis [sic] – for the periodicals' (iii. 426–7). By 6 December he had swallowed his vow never to send an article to Murry again (iii. 428).

What he probably sent first was 'David', about Michelangelo's statue as the epitome of Florence. This begins with the rain and the 'café-au-lait' river seen from his 'upper room'.

Morning in Florence. Dark, grey, and raining, with a perpetual sound of water. Over the bridge, carriages trotting under great ragged umbrellas. Two white bullocks urged from beneath a bright green umbrella, shambling into a trot as the whip-thong flickers between their soft shanks. Two men arm in arm under one umbrella, going nimbly ... Innumerable umbrellas ...
David in the Piazza livid with rain.[17]

The theme is familiar Lawrence. The statue is seen as the apotheosis of the Florentine cinquecento, that momentary marriage and equilibrium of North and South, fire and water, where the 'northern' extremity of the hot Italy meets the most southerly tip of cold transalpine Europe. David is the lily of the city of flowers; but the balance and the flowering did not last. Hence he seems fixed in adolescence, over-sensitive and somehow exposed, his nakedness livid white in the northern rain, so different from the other darker statues nearby. The rain pours down. The flood of northern values, chastity, equality, democracy, mass-man, seems about to overwhelm 'all outstanding loveliness of the individual soul'. But Lawrencian optimism again insists that there will be no final surrender. The Florentines say of the marble youth that 'a hot excitement, an anticipatory orgasm, possesses him at midnight of the New Year'. Even if that be fruitless now, one day David will finish his adolescence, and be no longer a lily but 'the full tree of life in blossom'.[18] What makes the essay odd however is its style, all staccato rhythms, stringing together phrases, apostrophes and exclamations, often verbless; together with an unusual abundance of classical allusion.

Perhaps Douglas's conversation had got into Lawrence's inner ear; the story about the New Year orgasm seems just the sort of thing Douglas might have told him.

However, if 'David' were the article he sent Murry before 6 December, it is very unlikely to have been the only one he wrote in Florence. He needed to make some money – but he had also signalled, before he left Hermitage, his sense of urgency about publishing his new psychological insights before they were passed off by the English Freudians as their own. It must have been this, as much as financial need, that made him unwilling simply to 'loaf' the days away, even if he went on socialising at dinner after Magnus left. Leo Stein later confirmed that he had proposed sending what he was 'about to write on that subject' to the *New Republic* (iv. 128 n.), presumably before Murry's letter came. It must have been this, then, that made Lawrence willing to swallow his anger and make up with Murry, as his best chance of English publication. Harrison would not take another series so soon, particularly one that repeated (however recast) the 'psychology' behind the American essays – and who else would publish Lawrence in England? Hence also the letter to Katherine, to whom he had written about Jung and incest from Mountain Cottage and who might be expected to be interested in the subject; and hence the request to Huebsch for advice about publishing articles on Italy *and* on psychoanalysis. When Murry had requested contributions before, Lawrence sent two or three lighter ones, and one serious piece. If he did the same now – and a later furious letter to Murry confirms that he did send more than one (iii. 467) – it would likely have been something else about Florence, *and* a first essay of what would become *Psychoanalysis and the Unconscious*, adapting Jung's English title for an attack on Freud. The other Florentine piece was probably a first version of 'Looking Down on the City', which has many links with 'David' and with November 1919, though other details suggest 1920 or 1921 and may have been added later.[19] All this is necessarily speculative. The only hard evidence is that one article, subject unknown, was sent to Murry before 6 December, and that at least one other followed – but it does seem likely from what Lawrence told Huebsch and Stein.

Post seems to have been getting through rather slowly, but at the end of November it began to come. Kot wrote, enclosing a repeat invitation from Herbert Trench, whom Lawrence had met in 1914, to his home in Settignano; but since Trench was in London recovering from an accident, and it would mean staying with his wife and daughter, Lawrence did not go just yet (iii. 425).[20] Huebsch sent a parcel of his publications, including Anderson's *Winesburg, Ohio* which Lawrence thought 'good ... but somehow hard to take in: like a nightmare one can hardly recall distinctly' (iii. 426). He had to reply that no word had come from Seltzer about *Women in Love*, but he began to prepare Huebsch for disappointment by holding out the prospect of giving him another novel, 'a more possibly popular one', though it would not be for some time. (This may be the first mention of *Aaron's Rod* for many months, prompted by the idea of using the people he was meeting, and if so, beginning already to fulfil Douglas's misgivings.)

And on 4 December – on a postcard of the statue of *David* as it happens – he told Emily that Frieda had come (iii. 427).

II   Back with Frieda: Picinisco

She arrived at 4 a.m., but Lawrence insisted on showing her the town at once.

We went in an open carriage, I saw the pale crouching Duomo and in the thick moonmist the Giotto tower disappeared at the top into the sky. The Palazzo Vecchio with Michelangelo's David and all the statues of men, we passed. 'This is a men's town,' I said, 'not like Paris, where all statues are women.' We went along the Lungarno, we passed the Ponte Vecchio, in that moonlight night, and ever since Florence is the most beautiful town to me, the lily town, delicate and flowery.

She enjoyed meeting Douglas again and being able to talk her own language to him, insisting that nobody could truly know him who did not hear him in German and tap into his German roots. She was 'thrilled at the fireworks of wit' between him and her husband (though they 'never quarrelled'), and impressed by the hospitality of the Florentine expatriates 'in the grand manner'. Perhaps Reggie had got them invited by the Marchese Carlo Torrigiani and his American wife, whose at-homes were famous, and with whom Reggie dined every Sunday he was in Florence. However the expatriate homosexuals struck Frieda as 'like "Cranford"' for all their sophistication, and their immorality 'like old maids' secret rejoicing in wickedness. Corruption is not interesting to me, nor does it frighten me: I find it dull.'[21] Her husband thought her 'thinner for her reduced diet' (iii. 429) but '*very* well' – and she did still have a little money left over because, he discovered, Ada had sent her £10 to help out (iii. 427). They planned now to stay in Florence about a week, then have a week in Rome and arrive in Picinisco about 17 December.

Moreover by 6 December his immediate financial worries were laid to rest when £50 suddenly arrived from Seltzer as an advance for *Women in Love*, and a refusal to cede the publication to Huebsch (iii. 428). The money made up Lawrence's mind. Once in hand it must have seemed much too handy to give up. He wrote to Huebsch:

I cannot refuse, as I sent them the MS. – I really thought Pinker had shown it to you long ago. – So there you are. It's not my fault.

I shall wait to hear from you. If you do not want the *Studies in Classic American Literature*, please return them to me at once … (iii. 429–30)

The last thing he wanted was a break with Huebsch, though that was an obvious possibility. Huebach was most important, not only as the most likely publisher of the American essays, nor even as someone who produced an American periodical and knew where to place articles, but as the one man who might get *The Rainbow* back in print. Only three days before, Lawrence had been day-dreaming about the possibility of Huebsch reissuing the book and sending 500 sets of sheets to England (iii. 427). But he badly needed Seltzer's money, right now.

That need had been sharpened even more by having had his pocket picked. According to Catherine Carswell, it happened as he was boarding a tram back from a trip to Fiesole; but the account in *Aaron's Rod* of how Aaron is jostled by two gangs of soldiers, and then finds his note-case missing, locates his route so exactly and describes the incident so circumstantially, that it may be drawn from a memory painfully exact. On 26 November, a week before Frieda's arrival, he tells Kot that 'My pen is stolen' (iii. 421). There might be no connection, but it may be that both pen and wallet went at the same time. What made Lawrence's experience differ from most people's was his reaction, on which both the novel and Catherine agree. One would have expected a burst of rage to follow the first 'going hot and cold all over', and he certainly felt as everyone does in such circumstances that he had been physically outraged. But his anger was mostly directed at himself. Just as illness, he believed, was one's own responsibility, so getting robbed was his own fault for not taking sufficient care, and for having a soft fool's trust in untrustworthy fellow-man. He told Catherine that one must live as the wild animals do, 'always wary, always on one's guard against enemies. It makes one more alive, anyway, and not really more suspicious. It is best to recognise the truth that most people will do you if they can.'[22]

The lesson was to be rubbed in once more, and far too soon. They left for Rome on 10 December. Catherine's relative Ellesina Santoro had found what she thought was a suitable pensione for them, but they were turned out as soon as it was discovered that Frieda was German. It must have been distressing to be hated in easygoing Italy too. Ellesina – 'the heroic support of a strangely mingled household' – then insisted they come to her, whereupon they were robbed again. Lawrence only told Catherine, in confidence, years later how this was doubly painful because of his liking for Ellesina, who had refused to accept any payment for having them.

He knew not only that she was herself above suspicion, but that, whether the thief were discovered or not, she would insist upon refunding the lost money (something like £10, which had just been changed into Italian notes). What was even worse was that, rightly or wrongly, Lawrence had come to his own conclusions as to the nature of the theft and the identity of the thieves, and he reckoned that if the crime were brought home, it would cause a lasting wound which would injure the innocent more than the guilty. He decided accordingly to say nothing about it.[23]

There is indeed no mention of the incident at the time. However it so soured Rome for them (as well as diminishing their resources) that they cut short their stay – telling friends and relatives that though the weather was beautiful Rome was 'crowded and impossible' (iii. 431). They left on Saturday 13 December after only two days of the week they had planned, and for a destination that could hardly have made a greater contrast.

They had been invited to the Abruzzi in 1914 by the Baronessa de Rescis whom they had met in Lerici, and Lawrence had occasionally fantasised about its mountains as another possible site for Rananim. The reality of the journey was unimaginable: by train to Cassino, by post-omnibus up into the mountains to Atina, by cart to an inn and on foot with a donkey at the end. 'You cross a great stony river bed, then an icy river on a plank, then climb unfootable paths, while the ass struggles behind with your luggage' (iii. 431–2). Even less imaginable was the reality of Orazio's house. It was obvious at once that though he himself was 'nice' if '*slow* and tentative', it was no place for Rosalind, with a nurse and three small children, all used to upper-class English standards of living. It was all 'a bit staggeringly primitive':

The house contains a rather cave-like kitchen downstairs – the other rooms are a wine-press and a wine-storing place and corn bin: upstairs are three bedrooms, and a semi-barn for maize cobs: beds and bare floor. There is one tea-spoon – one saucer – two cups – one plate – two glasses – the whole supply of crockery. Everything must be cooked gipsy-fashion in the chimney over a wood fire: The chickens wander in, the ass is tied to the doorpost and makes his droppings on the doorstep, and brays his head off. (iii 431–2)[24]

On the other hand, though the men in their skin sandals and white-swathed legs might look like brigands they were less thievish than city folk, and less fierce even than the women in their 'sort of swiss bodices and white shirts with full, full sleeves – very handsome – speaking a perfectly unintelligible dialect and no Italian'. Orazio's house was two miles from the village of Picinisco itself – 'a sheer scramble – no road whatever' – and five miles from Atina where one went for the week's provisions to a market 'perfectly wonderful to look at' for 'costume and colour', but which offered only basic provisions and 'no wine hardly'. (What a difference from Florence, where Frieda, after her German diet of carrots, 'ate so much and drank so much wine that her pancia – her paunch, as they say here – went on strike' (iii. 435) – as had happened when they first got to Italy in 1912.) The only thing approaching a bath for Rosalind's children would be the copper boiling-pan in which the pigs' food was cooked.

The mountainous surroundings however were spectacularly beautiful. The days were still 'hot and lovely' (iii. 432), though the nights were already freezing amid the snow-capped peaks. They did have a fireplace, and acquired more crockery, so they made the best of things for a while. The local culture was at least interesting: 'bagpipes under the window, and a wild howling kind of ballad' daily (iii. 432), an unintelligible serenade in praise of the Virgin which would apparently go on till Christmas. Yet it was getting icier and icier except in full sun; and because of Lawrence's chest it would not be wise to stay long. If the weather turned nasty they would have to move at once, to Naples or Capri. In the meantime however he could work without distraction – and whether or not he had started his essays on psychoanalysis in Florence and sent the first before leaving, it was now that the book began to fill out.

It was odd to think, amid those mountains, that the Altrincham Stage Society intended to put on *The Widowing of Mrs. Holroyd* next March (iii. 430), the first production of a play of his. Eastwood and the Abruzzi seemed a million miles apart – yet this may have set him thinking about the Midlands, a seed that would soon germinate. Other concerns also seemed distanced. Kot was still unhappy that Lawrence's Foreword had taken the place of Shestov's own introduction; and thought that if Shestov's were not restored, perhaps both should be omitted. Lawrence replied that he would send Kot's letter to Secker and that as far as he was concerned his Foreword could go; but he meant what he had said in it, 'and as it would be my signed opinion, I don't see that it matters: not a bit'. He wanted no money for what Murry had reprinted: 'Don't I owe you fifty times 35/- – – per Dio!' (iii. 433). Nevertheless when he wrote to Secker as promised, and asked also for a title page to suit Kot, making it clear presumably that the opinions in Lawrence's foreword were not Kot's or Shestov's – some irritation of distance showed: 'Ach, Ach! these little businesses! Every hen is occupied with her own tail-feathers' (iii. 434). (Secker went ahead and printed Lawrence's Foreword anyway.)

After having 'sweated up the mountain' the hour's goat-climb to the post office in Picinisco and found a letter there from Irene Whittley (Captain Short's daughter whom he had known in Zennor), he found it hard to imagine her as a teacher in Battersea and her husband sitting in a bank. It was much easier to remember them both crouched over a fire in the empty cottage in Higher Tregerthen, before the Murrys came; one prehistoric landscape and primitive house recalling another, however different. To her, at this distance, he could confess light-heartedly what was to become a difficult and permanent truth. It was not merely the cold that made him want to move again. 'I am turned into a wandering Jew, my feet itch, and a seat burns my posterior if I sit too long. What ails me I don't know – but it's on and on' (iii. 435). Frieda, 'not quite sure where she is', and having trouble not only with dialect but with her 'hopeless'

Italian after so long away, could probably have done with settling for a while, but he was already wanting to move, and as soon as it began to snow on 20 December it was clear that they must go at once (iii. 437). He had written to Compton Mackenzie again, saying that Picinisco was too cold for him (iii. 436); and though there had been no time for a reply they set off on Monday the 22nd for Naples, en route for the island of the Sirens about which Douglas had written so well.

They got up at 5.30 in the morning to walk the five miles to Atina, where they took the post-omnibus again to the station for the Naples train. From Naples they caught the 3 p.m. ferry, but as they left the sea was rising, and four and a half hours later it had become too rough in the shallow port of Capri for small boats to take the passengers to the landing-stage. So the ferry headed for the relative shelter of Sorrento where it lay rolling at anchor all night long, with most people (except luckily the Lawrences) being sick (iii. 442). On the Tuesday morning, in a 'magnificent red dawn' they were finally bundled into 'curvetting' boats (iii. 451) and landed, 'buffetted and bedraggled' (iii. 447) to look for some temporary lodging in which to recuperate, and then try to find Mackenzie.

He was away, though expected shortly. He seems to have had the disposal of two cottages as well as his 'Casa Solitaria' which looked out to the Faragleoni rocks: 'Il Rosaio' in Anacapri where he had written part of *Sinister Street*, and a 'warm seaside cottage' down at the Piccola Marina.[25] Il Rosaio was now rented for 7/6 a week to Francis Brett Young, doctor turned novelist; but he and his wife Jessica had found it 'a cold little house' so Mackenzie had let them have the warmer one in his absence. To Il Rosaio however the Lawrences went on the 24th, and left a note: 'We called today, wondering if you were going down to the Piccola Marina, or staying here – and if we could have one or other of the houses' (iii. 438); but even if the Brett Youngs had been there, they were not entitled to make such decisions. By Christmas however, the Lawrences had found an apartment for themselves, directly above Morgano's café (iii. 438, 439) in the little piazza which is the social centre of the island, and were installed there in time for Christmas. It looked out towards Ischia, the Bay of Naples and Vesuvius on the right, the open Mediterranean and spacious sky on the left, and the bubble dome of the little whitewashed cathedral just below and almost touchable from their balcony. They had a big sitting-room with french windows opening on to the balcony, a beautiful bedroom, and a shared kitchen for 150 lire a month; and a grand address 'Palazzo Ferraro', though Lawrence thought the staircase suggested a prison rather than a palace.

By 27 December Mackenzie was back (iii. 439), and before the end of the year they had much talk about Lawrence's relationship with Pinker, and with Secker. Mackenzie was a popular and successful writer who, born in comfortable circumstances, had also made a good deal of money himself. The contrast intensified a feeling which had been growing for some time: that Pinker could have done much better for Lawrence had he really been interested. Gilbert Cannan had broken with him; now Lawrence decided to do so too. He glossed the breach by saying he planned to move out of Europe, but anyway,

there is not much point in our remaining bound to one another. You told me when we made our agreement, that we might break it when either of us wished. I wish it should be broken now. What bit of work I have to place, I like to place myself. I am sure it isn't much worth to you. (iii. 439)

This completed the break, also, from the hopeful young Lawrence of 1914 with the contract for 'The Wedding Ring' in his pocket, who had had no thought but that his future lay in England. Pinker had in many ways been good to him, had seen him through hard times out of his own pocket; and had persevered with other writers who were caviare to the general. Yet Lawrence's offensiveness to the public made him a different case. After the fiasco of *The Rainbow* Pinker probably did begin to lose faith in him as a selling proposition, especially since Lawrence *would* go on writing as his vision led him, despite mores or the market. Pinker's failure to place *Women in Love* must have confirmed his opinion. Conversely, Lawrence found it hateful to be in debt to his agent, having to beg him to ask his more commercial authors for help, especially when he himself had worked so hard and was so sure that his work had greater value than most of what sold successfully in the English book market. The more Lawrence had grown alienated from England and the more he had come to feel it was in America that he would find a new audience, the less use Pinker had proved. He had shown very little interest in placing the American essays in England, which Lawrence had largely had to do for himself; and none at all in placing them in America. Pinker's whole mind set was English, and he had no agency across the Atlantic. He had never followed up the fortunes of Lawrence in America or provided accounts of Huebsch's sales, and had never even conveyed to Lawrence (if he himself knew) that *The Rainbow* was actually in print over there. The late-discovered fact that he had not bothered to send the typescript of *Women in Love* to Lawrence's American publisher had come as the final straw. Pinker was an excellent agent for some – but not for Lawrence it seemed. And with that break, the breach with England was almost complete.

Only Secker seemed a possible ongoing English connection. Mackenzie had grown so successful now that he had decided to move to a bigger firm, but Secker had been publisher, partner and friend, and had recently been staying with Mackenzie to discuss the change.[26] They must have talked about Lawrence when it seemed that he was coming to Capri – and Mackenzie now suggested a more permanent agreement. Secker had already taken *Women in*

Love; but in Lawrence's mind there was another test before ongoing commitment.

Mackenzie said you thought of printing the *Rainbow*. Do that, and you have my eternal allegiance. He suggests it be called 'Women in Love Vol I.', with a foreword by himself. I think 'Women in Love, Vol I and Vol II' is a very good idea. I am anxious to hear from you. If you do this, *The Rainbow* as a Vol I of *Women in Love*, then I must make a sort of permanent agreement with you.

For this, he held out a further incentive: not (now) the left-aside beginnings of what would be *Aaron's Rod*, despite the new copy Turin and Florence had provided, but the germination of an idea which may have begun while thinking about his Eastwood play in the utterly different world of the Abruzzi: 'I am waiting for MS. of a novel three parts done, "Mixed Marriage", which I left in Germany before the war. This would make a perfect selling novel when I've finished it' (iii. 439). He had left the manuscript of 'The Insurrection of Miss Houghton' with Else Jaffe in Bavaria in the spring of 1913, having put it aside in favour of 'The Sisters' because it was 'too improper'. What an irony! We have no means of knowing where the rebellious Miss Houghton was then intended to land up, nor with whom, though it was probably a mésalliance of class rather than nationality. But it was in a very different mood about England and English respectability that the Lawrence of late 1919 thought of recovering the manuscript, and reshaping the story.

III Sirenland?

Capri was quite warm even in mid-winter, especially after the Abruzzi. Sudden storms might blow up and prevent the ferry from landing the mail, and sometimes the scirocco blew wet and sticky, but only on two evenings in January (Lawrence boasted) did they need a fire (iii. 451). When supplies could not be landed there were shortages in the shops, but new potatoes were being dug at the end of January; peas, beans and wild narcissus were in blossom; and butterflies appeared on the warmer side of the island. Having made the two hours' climb to the highest point on Mount Solaro with the young Rumanian who shared their kitchen, Lawrence thought Capri 'beautiful beyond words':

the dark sea all round: the mainland at Massa coming close, pale grey rock, very steep, and slopes of white-specked villages – then snow-mountains above, behind. Naples clings close to the exquisite long curve of her bay, far off, and Vesuvius rolls a white glittery smoke level on the wind. And the other islands stand pale and delicate in the sea ... a white steamer loses herself southward. (iii. 454)

With Morgano's café directly underneath them on the piazza they could also feel

– pleasurably at first – that they were at the hub of island society, at least the expatriate kind.

For Compton Mackenzie had taken them under his wing, and 'Monty' now occupied with even greater charm, if perhaps less erudition, the leading position among foreigners once held by Douglas. Since meeting the Lawrences through the Cannans in 1914, Mackenzie's Midas touch had held good. He had always thrown himself into everything with immense enthusiasm and energy, (though he was always moving on to the next thing); and his allowance from his rich actor-manager father and his public school and university contacts ensured that he was able to follow his star in various directions.[27] In 1914 the first volume of *Sinister Street* had made him perhaps the most admired (for example by Henry James) as well as the most popular of the younger novelists, though Lawrence did not think much of it. The new contract with Cassells would make him rich.

Yet all was not golden for him at the start of 1920. He had returned to Capri to discover that his wife Faith had fallen in love with a young Italian, who died of rheumatic fever shortly after being told of his return. Mackenzie then made with her the kind of tolerant compact that Lawrence had suggested to Godwin Baynes, and the marriage would survive to a golden wedding and beyond. Yet the discovery had been a great shock to someone used to the adulation of women. Moreover he paid heavily for his energy and facility: he suffered from recurrent neuritis or sciatica so acute that only morphia would help, and he was also subject to fainting fits. Behind the theatrical personality, the charisma, the ability (it appeared) to succeed at everything and be amazingly productive, there was that price to be paid.

Lawrence's description of New Year's Eve in Morgano's shows a touch of malice. Mackenzie was 'nice. But one feels the generations of actors behind him, and can't be quite serious … He seems quite rich, and does himself well, and makes a sort of aesthetic figure … walking in a pale blue suit to match his eyes, and a large woman's brown velour hat to match his hair.' A Christmas tree was brought in by an 'amazing' band who sang an unintelligible ballad to it, and an hour before midnight came Monty 'with *rich* Americans – rather drunk'. He took the tree and bobbed it in front of his guests, while two boys danced the tarantella, 'a funny indecent pederastic sight' (iii. 443). The expatriates trying to look sophisticated seemed excruciatingly self-conscious, yet unaware of the faint smiles of the Italians – and then Monty was ill. 'Meanwhile', and there's the rub, the Lawrences 'sip our last drop of punch, and are the Poor Relations at the other end of the table – ignored – to our amusement' (iii. 444).[28] (Monty said years later, reading this, that his merely waving to them was because he was trying to make an assignation with his mistress Ann Heiskell before her husband came in. Lawrence's reaction has also something of how it feels to be sober when confronted by the Scot on Hogmanay!)

Yet they were greatly taken by each other, the successful and the unsuccessful writer. Lawrence remained wry about how he and Frieda and the Brett Youngs were humble hangers-on; and about Monty acting 'the semi-romantic' and 'the "rich young novelist"' (iii. 451, 452). Yet as he reacted ever more tartly to the other expatriates on Capri – with the exception of Mary Cannan who had turned up there, and of whom he was as fond as ever – the mutual liking continued. Faith, in England for the winter, testifies that in letter after letter from her husband 'there was some affectionate allusion to Lawrence and his wife'. Frieda told Monty that she had never known Lawrence take to anyone so much.[29] They had sharp arguments of course: about Christianity which Mackenzie espoused, and machine civilisation and whether Monty's privileged upbringing was advantage or limitation; and Mackenzie was as uncertain as other people whether Lawrence's generalising from himself was significant or megalomaniac. When talk turned to the possibility of another war, says Mackenzie, Lawrence insisted there would be none, struck a wall with his stick and shouted '*I* won't have another war.' This sounds absurd as it stands. Yet Lawrence had prophesied at the Armistice that there *would* be another war, and had several times maintained that war and the prevention of war both begin inside the individual. His outcry was most likely to have been a dissociation of himself from what he regarded with horror and dread.[30] After dinner at Casa Solitaria they sang *Sally in our Alley* and *Barbara Allen*, while the scholarly John Ellingham Brooks pounded the grand piano, and Francis Brett Young – who had perfect pitch – would wince because they were singing in different keys.[31]

They even became intimate enough (according to Mackenzie) for Lawrence to make the sort of confession that one man rarely makes to another. Mackenzie reports him as 'worried' by 'his inability to attain consummation simultaneously with his wife, which according to him must mean that their marriage was still imperfect in spite of all they had both gone through'. Mackenzie 'insisted that such a happy coincidence was always rare', but was unable it seems either to offer any advice, or to enquire whether Lawrence's worry might not be as much psychological, even ideological, as physical or technical. (Might there be a difference between his conviction of what the sexual act was for, and that of his wife.) Lawrence added that the nearest he had ever come to 'perfect love' – presumably, love unaffected by matters of physique or technique – 'was with a young coal-miner when I was about sixteen', that is, his late adolescent feeling for Alan Chambers. He was also upset when Mackenzie told him that the trouble with his wish to convert the world to reverence for the sexual act was that it was intrinsically comic except to those performing it. Gloomily, Lawrence agreed that this was so.[32]

Mackenzie also fulfilled a major qualification for a friend of Lawrence's by supplying a new day-dream about Rananim: the idea of buying a yacht and sailing to the South Seas. Indeed, he had already advertised for a crew and was looking for a vessel which he would shortly find, only to go off on another tack. He would finance the voyage by writing and broadcasting about it, and even taking along a film crew. Lawrence jibbed at that. He would feel 'like a savage, that they had stolen my "medicine"' (iii. 462); but ever since reading Melville the South Seas had appealed powerfully to his imagination, and he continued to talk and dream about the plan for months to come.

He also had heated but friendly arguments with the Rumanian, an ardent socialist with whom he spent 'fierce evenings in a discussion of idealistic philosophy, I in my bad English-Italian, larded with French, he in his furious Roumanian-Italian, peppered with both French and German. You may guess what it's like: a sheer farce' (iii. 453). They were both proud of their prowess in the art of cooking on an Italian fornello. Mackenzie described them arguing about Plotinus, and fanning their stoves, both with such energy that Frieda had to retire to the bedroom, while the kitchen filled with 'the fumes of charcoal and neo-Platonism', and Lawrence's beard turned black.

Mackenzie told a good story, but like some other raconteurs his anecdotes of Lawrence grew richer but not more reliable with the years. A case in point is his story about Lawrence insisting that men must give up thinking with their minds. '"What we have to learn is to think here," he affirmed solemnly in that high-pitched voice of his with its slight Midland accent. As he said this he bent over to point a finger at his fly-buttons, to my embarrassment and the obvious surprise of other people strolling on the *piazza*.'[33] It's a good story – but even at its earliest telling in 1933 it suggests the Lawrence of 1926 rather than the Lawrence of January 1920. To interpret rather more accurately where that finger must have pointed, we need to take into account what Lawrence had just finished typing.

IV 'Six little essays' on the Unconscious

On 17 January a figure might have been seen making its way the mile and a half from the piazza to Casa Solitaria, carrying a bottle of Benedictine in one hand and using the other to balance a heavy typewriter – Faith described it as being built 'like a Dreadnought' – on his head. The liqueur was a birthday present for Monty, who was touched by both gestures. (Anyone else, he said, would have hired a porter.) The typewriter was the one that had been used to type Douglas's *South Wind*, Mackenzie's *Sylvia Scarlett* and *Sylvia and Michael*, and Somerset Maugham's *Our Betters*.[34] Now Lawrence had borrowed it to type – not *Fantasia of the Unconscious* as the Mackenzies state, which was not begun for another eighteen months – but the 'six little essays' (iii. 466) for which he would adapt the English title of Jung's *Psychoanalysis of the Unconscious*. Probably begun in

Florence, these may have been finished in Picinisco or on Capri before 9 January, after which Lawrence keeps saying that he ought to be working but is not. The manuscript of 'Miss Houghton' had not come on the 4th when a storm-delayed post arrived, shortly after which a postal strike broke out, followed by a railway strike which effectively prevented the arrival of any mail until almost the end of January.[35] So he filled his time by typing out the six essays himself. His desire to forestall the English Freudians implied publication in England – hence the specimen possibly sent to Murry; but he had been growing steadily away from England, and by 29 January (still waiting to hear from Murry) he had decided to offer the essays to Huebsch, for publication in the *Freeman* (iii. 466). So he sent them first to a typing bureau in Rome, in order to have two proper typescripts (iii. 497). (On Monty's typewriter the black part of the ribbon was so worn out that it was now necessary to use the red!)[36]

He tried for a readable summary of the psychology he had adapted from Pryse's *chakras* in his American essays. This account of how from the very first beginning of a human life the four primary 'nerve centres' develop within each individual, and in his or her relation with the mother and the outside world, is as near as he could get to writing popularly. 'We do not pretend to use technical language', he says[37] – though he does, thus exposing himself to scientific scorn. Yet his schema had to have an anatomical basis in order to hyphenate the physical with the psychic, and so be 'mystically-physically satisfying' (that phrase from *Women in Love*); as he thought all human truth had to be. For years he had insisted that the body and the blood held a wisdom anterior to and more important than the rational or scientific knowledge of the mind – so there could be no account of consciousness that was not primarily physical. However it is not so much his pseudo-scientific neurology that catches attention now, but rather the way that his insight into the behaviour of babies and their mothers vividly reflects common experience, and helps to explain certain age-old physical locations of primary feelings and responses in the 'heart', the 'backbone', the 'bowels'. He appeals directly to experience felt and known as hunger, love and hate are. The chakras provide a vocabulary, though a naïveté appears in his hope that scientists could accept this instinctive kind of knowledge as a basis for analysis.

What is newly clarified, however, is the nature of his deep disagreement with Freud – or more precisely, with 'Freud' at second or third hand. Ever since Kuttner's 'Freudian' review of *Sons and Lovers* there had been the irritation of having a supposed dependency attributed to him. He had drawn his insights from his own experience. Indeed it is unlikely that he ever read much if any Freud himself, though he certainly heard something of him (or Gross's view of him) from Frieda. The fancied derivation must have been all the more annoying as he then came to realise, through conversation with the English Freudians, how antipathetic he was to what he gathered of the Freudian conception of the unconscious – though his understanding of Freud remained limited and imperfect. It was no accident now that his title echoed that of the book by Jung which he had borrowed from Barbara Low and talked about with Katherine Mansfield; the one in which Freud's most powerful disciple broke with his master in a way Lawrence must have approved. Jung (to use shorthand) denied one of Freud's most basic and characteristic premises, that the origin of the incest motive lay in the repressed sexuality of individuals. Jung explained it rather as archetypal inheritance from the buried collective experience of the human race. Lawrence, too, believed that psychology had to start from the very inception of human consciousness. Yet he thought Jung as culpable as Freud in seeing the incest motive as virtually constitutional, and so founding his psychology, too, on the analysis of disease and disorder. Lawrence wanted the opposite: to conceive a psychology of natural growth and creativity, inherent in the life drives within every psyche (or 'soul' to use the old-fashioned word), and recoverable by liberating that psyche from false mental consciousness and giving it over to its primary creative impulses. There is the familiar Lawrencian insistence on growth as the outcome of creatively conflicting 'opposites' within the psyche, and throughout all living things, no less a religious view for using the language of the *chakras*, instead of God the Father and God the Son.

So 'Freudian' psychoanalysis is attacked for starting as therapy, but ending by seeing disease as the norm. Freud disappears with his candle into the dark cave of the Unconscious and comes back with revelations. Only, 'What was there in the cave? Alas that we ever looked! Nothing but a huge slimy serpent of sex, and heaps of excrement, and a million repulsive little horrors spawned between sex and excrement.'[38] Worse, it soon appears that this condition is the norm. The only abnormality is in bringing it into consciousness. Moreover, though we make ourselves neurotic by repressing it, it is not itself the result of repression. Nor can it be cured, though patients can be brought to see how they have inhibited their secret impulses. But if it is repressing the incest motive that causes neurosis, what follows? (To bed one's mother and be well?)

The second radical criticism is that Freud's is therefore a closed system of determinism which does away with the moral faculty, depending as that does on the ability to choose and to change; even to remake the self. Change is, for Lawrence, the sign of life; and what is static, dies. (Here, however, he seems ignorant of Freudian sublimation.)

Lawrence does not deny the horrors in the cellarage that the psychoanalysts have brought to light. 'We tried to repudiate them. But no, they were there, demonstrable. These were the horrid things that ate our souls ... ' But he does deny that they are in any way pristine or original. For him they are products of later-developing *mental* consciousness, even though that may operate secretly, below the threshold of conscious awareness and consent. The Fall is not a fall into sexuality, but into awareness by Adam and Eve 'that they could deliberately enter upon and enjoy and even provoke sexual activity in themselves'.[39] The incest motive is not basic instinct then, but the first dawning of an *idea* – however suppressed from conscious awareness – that it would be possible to have sexual intercourse with one's mother and fill love with desire.

So Lawrence's psychology substitutes, for the concept of the unconscious as a cellarage where repressed impulses lurk from infancy, a concept of pristine conscious*nesses* which begin in the foetus, and are only 'pre'-conscious or 'un'-conscious if one defines consciousness as mental. The awakening of the primary nerve centres, which begins with life itself, is the dawning of four different kinds of consciousness, all of which precede mental awareness. One great impulse drives a baby to reassert the original unity of the self with the other; its opposite stiffens in resistance and distinction; a third becomes progressively aware of the other and of relationship; a fourth becomes progressively aware of the self and its desire for independence; and all constantly interact. Mental consciousness is the product of their interaction, and becomes creative or destructive according to its nature and proportion, and the reflux of the mind's ideas upon it. Essentially, however, for Lawrence, it must always be possible for the human being to change, to develop differently – most particularly by resisting or subverting false modes of mental consciousness, and achieving renewed life according to the creative well-head of natural impulse, through which a healthier mental consciousness (and art) can and will come bubbling up.

Having just been typing this, Lawrence must certainly have been telling Compton Mackenzie that people have to stop thinking merely mentally, and ground consciousness anew in the primary centres in the body; but the Lawrence who had just been attacking Freud and Jung for making everything sexual could not have maintained that people should think with their genital organs instead, or have been pointing emphatically at his own. If the pointing finger was not Mackenzie's invention, it surely pointed at the solar plexus which (as the second essay explains) is the most primary centre of all, where we should all begin again. Fortunately this does not spoil the story, since the folk on the piazza may have been no less disconcerted by and puzzled about the direction of the signal.

Of course this was no mere theoretical argument for Lawrence, but went to the heart of his own life and work. He would not concede that his relationship with his mother was an incest motive which determined him and his relationships beyond escape. He identified and faced up to the problem in *Sons and Lovers* (in which Paul has and chooses another path), sought to dramatise 'coming through' with Frieda in *Look!* and explored the nature and difficulty of marriage in *The Rainbow* and *Women in Love*. All his major work had been a

555

battle to win the ground from which his attack on 'Freud' was now directed. Nor would he accept that Frieda was essentially a mother substitute – though his 1918 letter to Katherine[40] freely and bravely admits not only that he has had an Oedipal problem, but that an element of it still remains in his relationship with Frieda. He is however struggling to overcome it, and the next phase of his work has everything to do with activating those impulses to self-sufficiency and independence which (he thought) could liberate a man from too great dependency on his woman, create a truer manhood, and look forward to life-giving male relations beyond and in addition to marriage. There was much more to his worry about the imperfection of his marriage – and his desire to go beyond it – than anxiety about synchronising sexual climaxes.

V 'Cat-Cranford'

As January drew to an end, disenchantment with Capri grew. The weather became 'wondrous fine' (iii. 461), the place was lovely of course and for once he had no money worries with nearly £100 to his name.[41] He continued to like the few Italians he knew: Liberata, the maid of the Palazzo, who 'is handsome, and eats the jam' (iii. 454); and their landlady Signorina Palenzia who took them to see a beautiful house above Mackenzie's, looking out at the Lions Teeth rocks, where they had a picnic tea in the elegant drawing-room, and danced on the marble floor as another Italian acquaintance played the piano (iii. 461). Quite early on however he had begun to feel imprisoned and to beseech the sirens to let him go. Capri was too small, and its cosmopolitan crew of expatriates altogether too inescapable. He still liked Monty and Mary and Brooks, but the atmosphere of spiteful gossip grew rebarbative.

Mary was staying with the greatest gossip of all – though not a malicious one. This was Gwen Galata, the English wife of the Pretore or Magistrate, whose wonderfully inconsequent ramblings, in which she exaggerated already dreadful gossip with ineffable benevolence, are amusingly mimicked in Monty's *Vestal Fire*. Lawrence must have liked her, since he later got her a copy of *The Rainbow*, but though he had been known to pick people to pieces himself – Monty blames Frieda for constantly egging him on[42] – he grew appalled by the expatriate gossip on Capri. The island was 'a little Babel' of foreigners (iii. 453), but the English-speaking ones were 'the uttermost uttermost limit for spiteful scandal ... The stories Mary is told are *incredible*' (iii. 444). Soon Capri became 'a gossipy, villa-stricken, two-humped chunk of limestone, a microcosmos that does heaven much credit, but mankind none at all' (iii. 462). By early February he was 'very sick' of the 'stewpot of semi-literary cats' and wanted to 'clear out' from 'Cat-Cranford' (iii. 469).

Unable to work, waiting with gathering impatience for the postal strike to end, he shot off letters to his three publishers, strike or no strike, determined to get things straight. He told Huebsch how he disliked 'vague, half-friendly, in-the-air sort of business. It leaves me irritated and dependent' (iii. 456). Now that he was acting for himself he wanted six-monthly accounts of all his sales, to be settled within three months, and copies of all his agreements. He wanted to know precisely what Huebsch was doing about *New Poems* and the American essays, and if he was not going to publish the latter he was to send the manuscript back at once. Did he intend to reissue *The Rainbow*? 'I want *to know*' (iii. 457).

To Seltzer he again went through the motions of offering to repay the advance, and typing expenses, if Seltzer would relinquish *Women in Love* to Huebsch, but (significantly) also asked for a precise agreement about publishing date, price and royalty, and the same regular accounts as he had demanded from Huebsch (iii. 457–8).

Before the strike began Secker had replied that he did not like the idea of publishing *The Rainbow* and *Women in Love* as Volumes 1 and 2 of the same novel. He offered instead to buy the copyright of *The Rainbow* outright for £200; but Lawrence firmly refused: 'I have lived so long without money, that I know I can go on ... Moreover I believe in my books and in their future' (iii. 458). He still wanted to be with Secker 'because you really care about books'; and was still enthused by Mackenzie's notion of a three-way partnership though he himself would have to invest as he earned; but there was an alternative now. Duckworth would not relinquish the copyright of *Love Poems* to Secker, but he would consider republishing *The Rainbow*. Lawrence thought this legally possible, on the grounds that the magistrate's order applied only to the 1915 edition, so a new one might escape prosecution, especially if there were some alterations. He was not forcing the issue, but he did want clarity and fair-dealing. Were they to be partners? Or were they to have a purely commercial but 'decent' royalty arrangement (such as he had had with Duckworth) for both books? Or should he go back to Duckworth?

By 27 January he was so sick of Capri, and of being unable to work because his manuscript had not arrived, that he took Frieda for a visit to the mainland. They stayed at the Hotel Capuccini in Amalfi which had once been a monastery. The coast was 'full of flowers – crocuses, violets, narcissi, and purple anemones, wild everywhere – and peach and almond in full flower' (iii. 464), and Amalfi itself was 'marvellous'. They meant to stay five days. But on the 29th the strike ended, and Lawrence was so anxious for his mail that he returned to Capri at once.

VI   Accumulated Mail

His mail-bag turned out as aggravating as his thirty-third birthday post had been.

There was his copy of *Bay* at last, but he was greatly put out to find the dedication missing. One of the Rice illustrations appeared to be upside down, and Beaumont had left out two poems altogether. Anxious to get things put right, Lawrence was as complimentary to Beaumont's face as he could be, saying that 'the essential format' was 'quite beautiful' (iii. 465); but to Catherine Carswell he made it clear that this meant the print, paper and binding, and that otherwise he thought it a 'silly-looking little book' with 'silly little wood cuts' quite out of keeping with the poems – some of which, however, he was pleased to find 'really beautiful' (iii. 469). The inscription could be tipped in, but the omission was enough in itself to put Lawrence in a temper.

Next came an angry letter from Huebsch about *Women in Love*. (He too of course had heard nothing for several weeks.) Once again Lawrence explained:

Simply, it never occurred to me that Pinker could have had that MS. for almost two years, all the while assuring me that he was doing everything possible, without ever even mentioning it to you ... If I'd thought Pinker hadn't shown you the MS. – he had *3* copies – wouldn't I have sent it you a year ago? – Of course I would. There's nothing I believe in more than in sticking to one publisher. (iii. 466)

He knew, however, that after his last letter to Seltzer the situation was probably irremediable. He made one final effort to put Huebsch's case to Seltzer: that Huebsch had been let down in never being told of the book, and 'since he did *The Rainbow* when no-one would touch it in America: and since he has stuck to my work, I *very much* want you to give me back the MS.' (iii. 467). Moreover he did not want the 'semi-private publication' which Seltzer was now planning in order to cut down the risk of prosecution. It would be better to leave the book to Huebsch, who 'has lost his reputation, in that line, already'. (He may also have made some inroads into the £50.) Moreover, if Seltzer was 'going strong on Goldrings work' he had better think again – 'not that I depreciate Goldring', but a public that cared for him would not care for Lawrence.

Actually he did have some cause to 'depreciate' Goldring, which came to a head when a copy of Goldring's *The Fight for Freedom* arrived some days later. He had been magnanimous at the beginning of the month when he heard it had been published (iii. 441) – though he must have wondered what had happened to his own play, which had been supposed to be the first of the series. It was all the more annoying to discover that Goldring's had taken its place, and when he read *The Fight*, he thought it a 'pamphlet play with a detestable and inartistic motive', mere propaganda. Moreover its preface had a much more political view of a People's Theatre than Lawrence's, which would look rather odd now when it did appear. He was inclined to blame Goldring for sharp practice, first getting *Touch and Go* out of him with the promise of leading off, and then – 'sly journalist' – substituting his own 'offensive' one with its 'knavish' preface, which 'for sure has damned and doubly damned' the whole series (iii. 469). The absence of any reviews might minimise the degree to which the two plays were publicly connected, but he was still annoyed at being associated with politics and purposes so different from his own. His suspicions may have been unfair. Goldring later explained that the decision had been the publisher's (putting the plays out in the order in which he had received them),[43] and good relations were restored. After all it had been Goldring's play that had persuaded Daniel to do the series in the first place. Yet the inclusion of Goldring's preface, to introduce both play and series, suggests that he was at least privy to the change. Whoever made the decision, it probably came from realising that Lawrence's preface – and indeed his play – hardly struck the right note on which to open a series with 'Dawnist' and *Clarté* aspirations.

Among the first of the letters and parcels however had been the most infuriating of all – so much so that it produced from Lawrence perhaps the nastiest of all his outbursts of rage.

Dear Jack
    I received your letter and also the returned articles, forwarded from Ospedaletti. I have no doubt you 'didn't like them' – just as you didn't like the things you had from Derbyshire. But as a matter of fact, what it amounts to is that you are a dirty little worm, and you take the ways of a dirty little worm. But now let me tell you at last that I know it – not that it's anything new: and let it be plainly understood between you and me, that I consider you a dirty little worm: and so, deposit your dirty bit of venom where you like; at any rate we know what to expect. (iii. 467–8)

Probably the same day he wrote to Katherine. The letter was destroyed – unsurprisingly – so we can only be certain of the extracts she quotes, without context, to Murry on 7 February.

Lawrence sent me a letter today: he spat in my face & threw filth at me and said 'I loathe you. You revolt me stewing in your consumption. The Italians were quite right to have nothing to do with you' and a great deal more. Now I do beseech you if you are my man to stop defending him after that & never to crack him up in the paper. *Be proud.* In the same letter he said his final opinion of you was that you were a 'dirty little worm'. Well, *be proud.* Dont forgive him for that, please.[44]

Lawrence's letters seem inexcusable. Indeed, his view was that the dead do not want excuses – only justice.[45] To form a just view of this episode, however, one must try once more to see through all three points of view. A grasp of chronology and development is also essential, or a number of puzzling questions will remain unanswerable. What made Lawrence angry enough to write such letters? Why was he as angry with Katherine as with Murry, if not more so? Why did he think the articles and the letter were '*forwarded* from Ospedaletti' (emphasis added)? How did he know about 'The Italians' having 'nothing to do with' Katherine? And how above all did he know that she had moved to L'Hermitage, the private nursing home in Menton to which he sent his letter?

From September 1919 to 21 January 1920 (when she moved to Menton) Katherine had been in Ospedaletti near San Remo, having been told by her doctor that she must on no account spend another winter in England. The devoted attendance of Ida Baker was essential, and also a constant annoyance. Katherine was terrified of being left alone – acquiring a revolver did not help – and illness intensified the fits of depression and loneliness which might have come in any case from living apart and loving only on paper. She and Jack wrote every day, but the post was uncertain even before the strikes, and misreadings of letters and of silences were almost bound to happen – especially on Katherine's side, as she waited intensely every day. Letters were almost all she had to live for, apart from her reviewing of fiction for the *Athenæum* which she bravely kept up. Unsurprisingly, she managed no creative work in these months before Christmas.

It was on 17 October that Murry thought of giving Lawrence 'a leg-up', and that Katherine might 'do a piece on *Sons and Lovers*'. She thought she might – but she did not.[46] On 9 November, having heard that Lawrence was going to Italy, Murry said he would send him her address. Katherine was unsure whether she wanted to see him or not, but Murry must have written – since Lawrence proceeded to write from Florence in friendly terms to Katherine, and to send Murry a first article by 6 December.[47]

On 4 December Katherine asked Murry where Lawrence was now[48] – but did not hear then, because it was in the same letter that she sent him her poem 'The New Husband', precipitating a crisis of bitterness and misunderstanding which brought Murry to Ospedaletti on 16 December. The night before he arrived, she tried in one of her notebooks to analyse what had happened, and come to terms with the fact that 'the deep simple love' she thought they had, 'only existed till we put it to the test'. She had stopped caring as much: 'I'd like to write my books and spend some happy time with Jack (not very much faith in that) and see Lawrence in a sunny place and pick violets – all kinds of flowers. Oh, I'd like to do heaps of things, really. But I don't mind if I do not do them.'[49] Though a fortnight with Jack over Christmas seemed to heal the rift, within a few weeks the silence owing to the postal strike, and her brooding alone again, resulted in a new set of misunderstandings and brought back her sense that something was gone for ever in their relationship. That is another story. But it is clear that up to 16 December 1919 Katherine knew nothing of Lawrence's articles (since Murry had not mentioned receiving them); and that she had got back her old warm feeling about him.

Meanwhile Lawrence had heard nothing either. His first article could have reached Murry about a week before he left for Ospedaletti,[50] and the others nearer his departure. His decision not to publish any of them – the plural confirmed by Lawrence's angry letter – was probably taken in Ospedaletti, but whether or not with Katherine's concurrence there is no knowing. It would however be odd if they had not talked them over.

Lawrence must have hoped for a response by early January 1920, even though it might have had to follow him from Picinisco to Capri. He could not know how much Murry had on his mind, or what factors might explain a delay in giving his verdict. Then came the postal strike, and the railway strike. By the end of January Lawrence had been waiting for almost two months to hear what Murry thought – this time. The humiliation, then, of another calm rejection must have been even more unbearable because he had brought himself to swallow his pride, after he had sworn never to submit anything to Murry again. Moreover, it had again been Murry who had taken the initiative, only to strike at the hand which reached out in response. Lawrence would have been irritated even if it had been merely 'David' and 'Looking Down on the City' that had been rejected – though at the back of his mind he probably knew that these were not important work, and that Murry might well not like the improper suggestion about the statue. But fury of the kind shown in Lawrence's letter had only blazed twice before – when Heinemann rejected *Sons and Lovers*, and when self-restraint over the destruction of *The Rainbow* broke down – that is, when something really important to him was at stake.

It can only be speculation that he had sent an essay on psychoanalysis – but it would explain a great deal. One could see also why Murry might have rejected it: an essay apparently all about incest might well have looked peculiar without the context of the other five, and unsuitable for a sober paper – though it would be richly ironic if Murry did reject the first prospectus of what he would hail later as a masterpiece, *Fantasia of the Unconscious*, which convinced him that Lawrence should play a major part in the *Adelphi*. That has to be guesswork – the only certainty is that Lawrence did send more than one essay. Yet it would also go a very long way to explain why he was even more angry with Katherine than with Murry. For a decision to send *that* essay would have been encouraged by believing that Katherine shared his interest in its subject; and if Murry had told him in November 1919 that she was thinking of writing about *Sons and Lovers* which had the subject at its core, and which he had known since 1913 that she admired, that would have seemed confirmation.

There now appears an irony to which commentators on all three writers have been blind. For, surely, Lawrence's belief that the articles and Murry's letter had been *forwarded* from Ospedaletti implies a suspicion that Katharine had not only been involved in the decision to reject, but had had the final word. Murry probably wrote his rejection on *Athenaeum* paper; and if so, Lawrence could have had no way of knowing that he was not in London. If so, why send the articles and the rejection via Katherine? Answer, because he was a little worm hiding in the mud, who wanted to inject his venom – like Cleopatra's asp – but lacked the courage to do it on his own, so had not only sought Katherine's backing but left the final decision and the posting to her. Which of course – if the psychoanalysis essay were among the rejects – would make her apparent show of interest in 1918 seem all the more hypocritical, or her concurrence with Jack now, the sicker. However, though it is likely that Murry talked about the essays with Katherine, and possible that she agreed with his rejection, the postmark made Lawrence mistake her role as much as Murry's whereabouts. She had great influence with Murry but there is no reason to suppose that his editorial decisions were not his own. He may even have made up his mind (depending on when the essays reached him) before he left England, or on the train. To Lawrence, however, the humiliation and, in a sense, betrayal must have seemed finally Katherine's doing.

It is now, moreover, that an even greater irony appears, for now the postal strike probably increased misunderstanding. Lawrence could not have discovered Katherine's new address in Menton in time to write there after receiving the rejection, and have the letter arrive at the same time as his letter to Murry reached London, unless he had had a letter from Katherine simultaneously with the rejection. This would also explain how he knew what Katherine herself had only discovered on 8 December, when she was examined by Dr Foster, that it had been because of her consumption that a hotel in San Remo had refused to take them, and that it had proved so difficult to find a villa and a maid.[51] The rejected essays with Murry's note enclosed were probably posted as he was leaving Ospedaletti on Friday 2 January or soon before – doomed, anyway, to get caught at the other end in the postal strike which was first declared on the Monday. (If they had been posted by Christmas Lawrence would have got them long before 29 January.) But a letter from Katherine with the Menton address could not have been written before 14 January, when she decided to accept the room at L'Hermitage, and probably not for another few days. If the rejection and Katherine's letter arrived together, Lawrence may have been too angry to reflect that they might have been posted weeks apart.

Indeed the most likely date for Katherine's letter would be about 20 January, the day before she left Ospedaletti, when she suddenly wrote a long letter to Ottoline – probably because she had been bundling up and disposing of letters, including Lawrence's cheerful note from Florence. It was a low point for her. She tells Ottoline that she has been weeping for days. The letter pours out her woes: isolation, loneliness, the oppressive noise of the sea, her inability to get about, how horrid San Remo had been, how she couldn't get a maid 'because of my DISEASE', which had made her feel 'tainted', how Murry didn't understand and she no longer felt loved.[52] If she wrote a similar letter to Lawrence, especially if it contained little or no reference to the articles which she would not have felt responsible for refusing, the simultaneous arrival with the rejection would have made her seem wholly careless of what it would mean to him; totally self-absorbed and self-pitying.

What he then wrote to her is by no means inexplicable nor merely malicious, but consonant with his belief in letting his emotions out and speaking his thoughts – violently if they were violent – where others let theirs grow poisonous by repression. His anger was a measure of how much he had cared for them, and how much he felt betrayed.

There is also another important context: the letters he had written her from Derbyshire as a gift of friendship and of life, when she was first having to face her deadly disease – which also threatened him, and was killing an old friend as he wrote. He had told her that one does not let oneself die, one fights one's disease tooth and nail, above all one does not stew in it. He was as good as his word, as Frieda testified, when he himself nearly died two months later, and he never demanded pity.

Both she and Jack must have seemed to Lawrence utterly egotistic and treacherous. Yet if neither of them appeared to realise or care what a second rejection would mean to him, he had no idea of the context into which his backlash would arrive. She was to telegraph Murry two days later 'Your coldness killing me' which brought him 'to the end of my tether'.[53] Nor, in his anger, would Lawrence probably have cared. At first their responses were aggressive: Murry threatened to hit Lawrence next time he saw him, and wrote to Katherine to tell her so (before he knew of the letter to her) and how he felt Lawrence was 'a reptile', who had 'slavered' over him. Katherine read his letter as she was being massaged, and felt as though she were repeating a scene centuries old, where a woman had read a letter from her lover saying he would smite her enemy, and had laid it to her cheek. She noted the coincidence of their feelings. She had already written to Lawrence, 'I detest you for having dragged this disgusting reptile across all that has been.' She also wrote to Mary Cannan 'to put her right about US and just told her what you really were like & what your loyalty to L. had been and so on'.[54] Just as in the immediate aftermath of Lawrence's anger the year before, she had closed her mind to any admission of how little Murry had in fact defended or supported Lawrence since the days of *Signature*, and how easy it would be for Lawrence to disprove what she said.

So at first Lawrence's onslaught drew its recipients together. Yet the strain in the Murrys' relationship continued; and Lawrence's with Katherine never recovered from this breach. She would only hear from him once more in her lifetime, when from her birthplace in New Zealand in 1922 he sent her a postcard saying, simply, 'Ricordi' – remembrances (iv. 283). Almost simultaneously, on the other side of the world, Katherine made a will in which she left him a book as a remembrance, an instruction which Murry failed to carry out after her death.[55] Lawrence had greatly cared for Katherine – much more, latterly, than for Jack. It would be difficult to say who had been the more hurt by what had happened.

Lawrence was ill himself again in the first week of February. The flu had reached Capri, and whether through a touch of this, or one of his bronchial colds, or having worked himself up into a state of rage and distress, he retired to bed and was 'only just going to get up' on the 8th (iii. 471). His awful post-bag and the illness had left him even more 'sick of this island' and determined to leave. He was still further irritated when Mackenzie showed him cuttings of what Gilbert Cannan had been saying in America, with kindly intent. When a visiting English publisher expressed surprise in an interview that Lawrence should be spoken of as a man of genius, Cannan came to his defence in the *New York Tribune*[56] with an indictment of the 'unimaginative' and 'puritanical' section of the public who had misunderstood and destroyed *The Rainbow*; the publishers who were too 'unreasonably afraid of that section' to risk *Women in Love*; and the senior writers who had failed to support Lawrence. This was all very well, and Lawrence should perhaps have been grateful; but he did not want to be publicised in America as a pitiable victim, still less an impoverished one. Cannan even began to collect money on his behalf, as did Huebsch (iii. 455 and n.). Lawrence's touchy pride was aroused, and when as a result Amy Lowell sent a cheque for 1315 lire (Boston's exchange for $100) he could not be altogether pleased or thankful. 'I wish I needn't take the money', he wrote, 'it irks me a bit. Why can't I earn enough, I've done the work. After all, you know, it makes one angry to have to accept a sort of charity' (iii. 474–5). He tried to persuade himself that Amy's was a gift from a congenial fellow-artist, as opposed to Gilbert's 'penny-a-time attempt at benevolence', of which not a penny had arrived yet anyway. But at the bottom of contradictory feelings remained the sense of insult. 'I am a sort of charity-boy of literature, apparently. One is denied one's just rights, and then insulted with charity. Pfui! to them all' – except Amy of course. To add injury to insult, the Credito Italiano refused the cheque because it was not made out in dollars (iii. 482 and n.), and Amy had to send another!

He could not refuse because the poverty of 1919 had bitten too deep, even though a cheque for £105 had now arrived in settlement of Pinker's account with Huebsch, quickly followed by another of £8/12/9 for Huebsch's edition of *Look!* (iii. 472, 473). Considering the hardships of 1919, this was a huge sum to have been withheld, and confirms all the other indications that something was seriously lacking in the relation between his agent and his American publisher, in which both must have been at fault. The sum had been even larger. £25 had been repaid to 'E.A.Bennett' – the first Lawrence had learned of Arnold

Bennett's quiet emergency fund.[57] Yet, though he was beginning to be better off now than he had been since 1914, his position remained very uncertain. For Secker had agreed rather too readily that Lawrence should go back to Duckworth. (Privately Secker told Mackenzie that he was not 'at all convinced' that Lawrence 'is a commercial proposition'. Republishing *The Rainbow* would only be a possibility if *Women in Love* were to escape unscathed. He was still prepared to revert to a 10% royalty for the latter but was 'a little tired of the whole thing', and would happily retire in Duckworth's favour since 'Lawrence's books are not worth competing for from a money making point of view'; iii. 460 n. 1.) Also, as long as the problem of Seltzer and Huebsch continued – no sooner apparently settled than a garbled telegram raised the possibility that Seltzer might be prepared to relinquish after all[58] – American publication of the two big novels looked equally unsure.

Lawrence was now expecting the manuscripts of a number of stories to be returned by Pinker. He told Michael Sadleir that when those arrived he could have 'Wintry Peacock' for a proposed new periodical (iii. 473–4). But though he had decided to act for himself as far as England was concerned, he would need an agent in America, especially if everything was now to go there first. Quite fortuitously, the delayed post brought a possible solution. A letter from Mountsier which had been written 'long ago' and had been following Lawrence all over the place before being held up further in the strike, finally reached him on 16 February. On impulse, he asked whether Mountsier would be interested in acting for him 'in an unofficial sort of way – and take the percentage' (iii. 476). This was not merely impulsive. As a journalist Mountsier would know something of the New York publishing scene, he would look personable in a publisher's office and as both gentleman and friend he would not do Lawrence down – but it was certainly a shot in the dark. The one thing that would effectively stabilize his position would be to produce another, *safe*, novel. At long last, by 12 February, 'Miss Houghton' arrived from Bavaria and he could set to work,[59] recasting what had been abandoned as 'too improper' into a novel that could circulate widely, make money and recompense publishers for the risks involved in bringing out the dangerous ones. He began the next day, and three days later thought it was going 'quite well' (iii. 477).

VII   Montecassino – and Sicily

Before he really got going, however, came a distraction. He had been twice pressed by Maurice Magnus to redeem the promise to visit him at the great Benedictine monastery at Montecassino. The original plan had been to make the short journey from Picinisco; but when the cold drove the Lawrences to Capri he wrote to tell Magnus what had happened. Magnus wrote back from a hotel in

Anzio; and Lawrence sensed such unease in the letter – though there was nothing specific – that he was sure Magnus was in trouble. He himself had just received out of the blue the $100 from three American admirers, through Huebsch.[60] On a generous impulse he sent £5 to Magnus, begging him not to take offence. Far from it, Magnus wrote that Lawrence had 'saved [his] life' when he had 'fallen down an abyss' – though at the time this seemed merely exaggerated American gratitude. Magnus was going to Montecassino in a few days and urged Lawrence to come. Later he wrote twice again – but Lawrence thought he detected another plea behind the urgency, and because it seemed expected now he was put off.[61] There was also the railway strike. Nor, as Frieda pointed out (not having been invited), could he really afford to go jaunting, though they managed the shorter trip to Amalfi together at the end of the month by going some of the way on foot.

Now however, in mid-February, the big settlement cheque from Pinker, and the other one in prospect from Amy, meant that a little extravagance might be afforded; and he did want to see the monastery. Perhaps the rewriting may not have been going so well after the first few days. Be that as it may, he decided to go, probably about 19 February.[62]

His 1922 account recalls how he got up before daybreak and went through the dark little square, down the funicular, and out on the small boat to the ferry, which nosed along the mainland coast before getting him to Naples too late for his train. He had to hang about for three hours. He almost missed the two o'clock express also, by getting on the slow train. He realised his mistake only at the last moment, and had to sprint for the fast one which was already moving off. At twilight however he was in a carriage twisting up the road to the monastery which bulked like a huge fortress on its hill, and there was Magnus bustling 'with his perky, busy little stride' through the gate to meet him.

The story of this visit is one of the best things in all Lawrence. There is a fine painterly eye at work in the genre-picture of the grassy courtyard beyond the gate, and the prospect from Lawrence's guest-room window as the eye drops to the monastery garden, then down the hill farms and out into the plain, 'the world's valley', on which other mountains stand 'as if God had just put them down ready made'. There is comedy as Lawrence, frozen in his light overcoat, is draped instead in Magnus's sealskin-lined one which is magnificent enough for a millionaire, but makes him feel thoroughly out of place as they dine (not very well) in the icy refectory, or creep 'like two thieves' through the great empty church and crypt, among multicoloured marbles and mosaics, while Magnus performs a convert's overdone genuflection at every (frequent) opportunity.[63]

The next day another word-picture of the view, in full sunshine from Magnus's window, imagines the great Bramante courtyard filled with the colourful figures of the early Renaissance, another deliberate recall of Quattrocento painting. For what had struck him most, even at the time, was the contrast of a vivid and vital past, still not-quite-dead, with a devitalised present, despite the kindness of his hosts.

Monte Cassino is wonderful – and the monks are charming to one. But it seems pathetic, now, in its survival: so frail and hardly vital any more. Of course it should be *feudal*: like a great fortress hanging over the plain, what is it now it is divested of power and turned into a sort of museum where the forty monks linger on? – They have wonderful archives. (iii. 489)

In 1922 however the sense of loss would be compounded and complicated by knowledge of a tragedy that happened nine months after the visit. For Lawrence in 1922, Magnus's inability to live, and the not-quite-dead place, have fused into a challenge to understand and come to terms with not only his mixed feelings about the man himself, but the twentieth-century malaise that Magnus and Montecassino both helped to focus. This means, however, that the account of his argument with Magnus as they walk out across the hilltop, and indeed the whole narrative of the visit, are transfused and perhaps partly shaped by hindsight. At the time the shadows may only have been latent in his disagreement with many of Magnus's attitudes, and some unease at being unable to do much to help him. He could not give enough money to make a significant difference, nor did he really want to give any more, though he offered the little he had with him which was refused. When he got back he put Magnus in touch with the assistant editor of *Land and Water*, who would soon publish 'You Touched Me', and who also agreed to take one of the pieces that Magnus had shown Lawrence in Montecassino (iii. 480). He would later put Magnus in touch with Goldring, in the hope of doing something with his translations of plays (iii. 531–2). And surely something could be done with Magnus's account of his experience of the French Foreign Legion. That seemed the only way to help the little man for whom he continued to feel a mix of liking and irritation.

After Montecassino, however, life in Capri seemed even more petty. He determined to find somewhere quiet, cheap, and not a 'cats cradle of semi-literary and pleni-literary pussies. Oh my dear English countrymen, how I detest you wherever I find you!' (iii. 471) – except Mackenzie, that is. At first he thought he would try the mainland, but the idea of Sicily had been at the back of his mind for some time, and in conversation with the Brett Youngs it appeared that they would like to go with him to explore. So on another impulse, and again without Frieda, they set off together on 26 February.[64] In Naples Lawrence took charge – his Italian was better than theirs – but after waiting in a long queue he had to break it to them that there had been only one cabin left. Jessica was shocked, though as the bunks were curtained she made the best of things. A note however had been struck that was to characterise the expedition, and the Brett Youngs' subsequent accounts of it and of Lawrence.

For though they had a common liking for Mackenzie and got on quite well on the surface, the Lawrences and the Brett Youngs were never likely to care much for one another. Jessica devoted herself utterly to the husband she revered, and willingly sacrificed a real talent as a singer to become his other half, secretary and cheerleader. Francis continued to look the ex-Major and country doctor he had been, though appearances were partly deceptive since he was somewhat deeper and more subtle than he looked. He had given up a comfortable career to become a writer, and he had some genuine sensitivity and perceptiveness as poet and novelist. His war service in the RAMC had taken him on Smuts's East African campaign and (as well as damaging his health) had given him a lifetime's interest in Africa. He had a quiet sardonic wit behind the rather stolid exterior. His gifts were however limited by conventionalities. He was a Georgian of the Georgians; a lover of country pursuits; intensely patriotic, and very English in an upper middle-class way. (In his South African experience, and novels, this became a sensibility attuned to Smuts's United Party, in a world whose disappearance he was quite unable to foresee.) Yet his novels remain worth reading, and their solid virtues won him in his lifetime what Lawrence in 'Hardy' called 'the prize within the walls' for the worthy ones who stay there: a wide audience through Book Clubs, a series of lovely homes and a high reputation for a while. But what would such a man – and his wife – make of the Lawrences? And he of them?

Whereas the Brett Youngs found the eccentricity of Mackenzie (black or white sombrero, blue-lined cape, orange tie) acceptably theatrical, Lawrence seemed a freak – especially as remembered years later. He was 'a frail little scarecrow of a man with a straggling red beard', weirdly clad (as in summer 1918) in shrunken grey flannels and a striped blazer. It was not however, as the public-school man assumed, that he had had them 'when he was a schoolboy of fifteen', but because his trunk was still stuck in Turin and his winter suit would have been too hot.[65] A similar mixture of humour and class feeling appears in the description of the Lawrences' laundry on their roof: 'those strange pieces of grey-flannel underwear [one] never knew, quite, which belonged to whom'. (It would not be so, or visible at all, at the Brett Youngs.) There are the by now familiar stories of smoky fires, of excellent Lawrencian cooking nevertheless, of Lawrence bawling at Frieda and Frieda goading him into paying her attention, or bursting into a 'tirade of positively Germanic violence' in the midst of which she denounced Monty for being a bore. From the start, Frieda was too much. 'I have seen a good deal of Lawrence and, unfortunately, also of Frieda ... ', begins Francis's account of his new acquaintants to Secker. However he thought Lawrence 'lovable' if not quite sane; remembered vividly his version of Florence

Farr intoning Yeats's 'Innisfree' to an Irish harp; and found him, when he was most himself, 'uncomplicated and charming', 'I like him immensely.' The same contradictory feelings were intensified about the work. After the first long chapter of *The Rainbow* which she found 'fascinating and beautiful', it was only under protest that Jessie went on – and Francis in fact agreed with her, though he was capable of recognising that Lawrence had a power beyond both him and Mackenzie. (Later he would call him 'the only authentic literary genius ... of the generation to which we belong'.) Nonetheless he told Secker that the book's 'people who love without restraint and hate without reason' were 'reincarnations of Lawrence's own pathological soul', and its last 400 pages 'a welter of rut'. (Conversely, Lawrence said that although Francis's work was 'splendidly written', he always felt 'there was something between him and It' – a judgement whose accuracy is not, unfortunately, diminished by Francis's excellent comeback, that there was certainly nothing between Lawrence and It, but he himself liked to leave a little to the imagination.)[66]

Such, at any rate, was the relation between the two talkative ones on the ferry to Palermo that Thursday night, while Jessie hid modestly behind her curtain. They went first to Agrigento where, after a preliminary glimpse of classical beauty – sheep, a shepherd boy playing a flute, almond blossom, the ruined Greek temples – they went for a later walk to the ruins that ended frighteningly. Barking dogs rushed out of cottages, a high wind blew up at sunset and sent Lawrence's hat sailing away for ever, the sulphur miners coming home seemed hostile, darkness fell and, as dust and grit kept blowing in their faces, Lawrence suddenly was gone. They struggled back to the hotel and wondered whether to send out a search party to the ruins, but half an hour later he appeared; 'his face white, his hair on end, but quite unconcerned'. Asked what had happened he said, 'I just blew away through a hole in the wall like a piece of waste paper.' Yet a little later he decided the place was inimical and they must go, even though that involved taking a train to Syracuse at 4 a.m. It says a great deal for his power over them, or their good-nature, that they went. In Syracuse he found a house and agreed to take it, but as soon as Jessie asked whether Frieda would approve he realised he had made a mistake, yet seemed powerless to extricate himself until she persuaded him he must. He could think of nothing but that he had promised Frieda to find somewhere within a week. On Sunday they took an interminable train journey to Catania, with a change at a branch-line station where they waited six hours, drinking black coffee laced with rum to quell Lawrence's impatience, only to have the train come to a full stop again at the next junction because of a strike. If Frieda had been there, said Lawrence, sitting on a newspaper on the platform edge with his legs dangling over the rails, she would have said it was all his fault. At Catania, late at night, no room could be had, until at long last they found another single one. 'Che fa?' said the woman,

'The bed is a very big one' – but eventually she agreed to put up a camp-bed where Lawrence slept behind a screen. 'In less than five minutes he was talking, groaning and quarrelling with someone (one might guess whom) in his sleep.'

For a day and a half he searched fruitlessly in Catania, before deciding that he hated it and insisting on leaving for Taormina. This time Francis refused to go, though he promised they would meet him there next day. So Lawrence 'travelled third class in a compartment full of women, baskets of chickens and cheeses, and some monks', past Mount Etna and on to Giardini, at the foot of the steep hill on whose slopes Taormina tumbles. When they met again on 3 March, Lawrence had found 'Fontana Vecchia', which would be their home until 1922. 'He was like a child with joy that he had found his house "by Thursday". A telegram was sent to Frieda, and at last there was peace.'

Spending any length of time with such a creature of moods was clearly a strain – though the Youngs decided to play their accounts of it as comedy. What is remarkable, however, is Francis's belief that he now knew Lawrence 'inside out' – a belief in which he never wavered. The apparent contradictions in Lawrence's character were simply obverse and reverse of the same coin: his violence the result of actual timidity and frailty, trying to impress with a forcefulness he greatly desired but really lacked, and completely 'hag-ridden'. So, immediately after the journey, Young wrote to Secker of 'the amazing fears and repressions by which [Lawrence's] life is complicated ... A more timid, shrinking, sensitive, violent, boastful, brazen creature it would be impossible to conceive. And we never once quarrelled ... I find him a restless and disturbing personality and yet somehow pathetically attractive.'[67] The note of condescension sounds clear, but the partial truth of the judgement is rather undermined by its air of finality and inclusiveness. The tone might explain the irritation with Francis that Lawrence, for his part, confessed to Brooks: 'Oh, how *he* did weary me – like a fretful and pragmatical and dictatorial infant: always uttering final and ex cathedra judgments in the tone of a petulant little boy' (iii. 481). They continued to correspond – but they would never be close.

Lawrence's new home, 'Fontana Vecchia', had a marvellous situation. The house is now part of Taormina and surrounded by others on all sides, but in 1920 it stood alone on a steep slope looking out eastwards over the straits of Messina to the coast of Calabria. Peaks behind and beside it hide Etna. The little town itself ended at the Capuchin gate and its monastery church, with only one or two houses just outside. From there a track wound down the valleyside to the streamlet and the ancient fountain in its 'little cave-place' which gave the house its name (iii. 489), and then up past its gate. What Lawrence calls the 'garden' was a steep slope of trees and bushes up to the house, which stood three storeys blocked against the hill – a bit fortress-like, he thought (iii. 498). See Illustrations

59, 61. All around stretched terraced hillsides, planted with olives, almond trees and wheat. The lowest storey was occupied by part of their Italian landlord's family who also had another house over by the Capuchins. Lawrence took for a year (at 2000 lire; iii. 482) the top two storeys, each of which had a terrace out in the sunshine, brightened by magenta Bougainvillaea. On the second floor were the salotta, with rather Gothic pointed windows and alcoved shelves that the Lawrences painted green, and a small blue Dutch-looking kitchen. (The house had previously been owned by Marie Hubrecht, a Dutch painter who soon became a friend.) There were two bedrooms on the top floor, isolated enough for Lawrence to insist on taking the curtains down.[68] He describes waking up and watching the dawn stage by stage, colour by colour, until the 'liquid sunlight' comes 'winking straight in my eye' and he dodges beneath his blanket (iii. 498). After Capri, he must have been particularly pleased to have found a place outside Taormina though within easy walking distance. He thought from the first that he could work there, and so he did. Though he met numbers of people, Italian and expatriate, he could also get away from them to his (rather handsome) desk in the salotta, or his garden with its great carob tree, or walking the slopes.

It must have been with high excitement that he went to meet Frieda and Mary Cannan at Giardini Station. Mary went to stay at the Timeo Hotel, whose chef Francesco ('Ciccio') Cacópardo had bought Fontana Vecchia from Marie Hubrecht and so was now the Lawrences' landlord. Very soon, as he went off to collect the women's trunks in Catania – his was *still* stuck in Turin – he was able to report that Frieda loved their new home as much as he did (iii. 479, 488). He had reached his limit, he told Mackenzie, at least for a year: 'Don't let us lose sight of one another. We are opposite poles, in most things. But opposite poles are most inevitably mutually related ... I think we met well in Capri. – I'll see you again before very long. Let us weave fate somehow together ...' (iii. 481). He had no regrets at all about leaving Capri. Sicily appealed to him in some of the ways Cornwall had done, albeit even more southerly in his terms of the magnetic pull on his soul. He felt again a '*darkness*' (iii. 481), analogous to the Celtic presence of the Tuatha di Danaan he had felt in 1916, attributable perhaps to the strong Moorish element in the Sicilian makeup – 'a touch of Saracen and the East in it – sort of explosive gunpowder quality' (iii. 482) – coupled with the sense of being at the very end of Europe, edging towards Africa. At the same time it was much greener and sappier than the dry rock of Capri, with a wealth of wild flowers as wonderful as on the mainland near Amalfi.

The problems that had worried him in Capri began to unravel. Seltzer wrote to say that *Women in Love* had actually gone to press, and though Lawrence was still unhappy that Huebsch could feel he had been let down, the die was cast now. He still did not like the necessity (as Seltzer saw it) for private publication at a relatively high price, $25. There could only be 'a succés d'estime at the best, and at the worst, a succés de scandale' (iii. 485). Yet Seltzer also seemed ready to publish *Touch and Go* in America, so *he* might now become Lawrence's main American publisher – though Cannan warned that his finances were suspect, and Lawrence was still thinking of Huebsch for the books on American literature and psychoanalysis. (Just so, when he left Duckworth for Methuen in 1914, he tried to keep Garnett and Duckworth sweet by giving them the volume of short stories.) Goldring's explanatory letter arrived, and though Lawrence wryly marked the political distance between them,[69] with Goldring under the 'party-umbrella' of the communist Barbusse (iii. 483), he no longer thought him a 'shit' (iii. 471). Since the opening night of *The Widowing of Mrs. Holroyd* was near, he would at least beat him to a first production. He sent Catherine Carswell £5 for the rail-fare and begged her to send him a first-hand report,[70] only to discover that she had already been invited to review for *The Times*, which made him nervous but pleased him also. Now he hoped to get down to his novel again.

VIII   *The Lost Girl*

He seems to have done so on 9 March (iii. 485) – but almost at once there was a change of plan. On 22 March he told Mackenzie he had 'scrapped all the novel I did in Capri – have begun again – got about 30, 000 words, I believe, done since I'm here. Rather amusing.' He was still uncertain of the new direction however: 'I may come to a full stop any minute – you never know' (iii. 490–1).

It had proved impossible to continue the imaginings of a pre-*Rainbow* and pre-war self. He may have begun to realise this even before he left Capri; which was perhaps why, having waited so impatiently for 'Miss Houghton' to arrive, he had deserted her so soon to go to Montecassino. The 1913 fiction had become 'improper' for the same reasons as *The Rainbow* would: driven by his new belief in the power of sexual relationship to transform, or to damage and destroy. Trying to rework for the circulating libraries went against the grain of that urgent exploration. Moreover his views of sex and marriage had changed – and so had his sense of England. His heroine's 'insurrection' would have to be far more radical now, no mere rebellion against provincial materialism and class-consciousness. Indeed, everything pointed to beginning all over again. In early February from Capri he had told Catherine that he did not 'want to do a satire. It all just dries up one's bowels' (iii. 470), even if his fellow-countrymen were a constant temptation. In March in Sicily, however, the new fiction let sardonic humour off the leash for comedy, rather than the 'venomous pleasure' in which 'The Insurrection' had begun.

He made steady progress, and through March and April into May it was Alvina Houghton and her story that lived now behind his daily life. On

31 March he thought it about half done (iii. 495). Alvina had met her Ciccio in a way that may have been suggested by Mackenzie's *Sylvia Scarlett* whose heroine joined a troupe of actors, and about whom Frieda was reading admiringly (iii. 501). At that stage the new version was still 'as proper as proper need be' (iii. 500), though it had already begun to assert the familiar Lawrencian life of its own, 'which runs out of my control and jumps through the port-hole into the unknown ocean, and leaves me on deck painfully imploring it to come home' (iii. 497). Determined on commercial success, he proposed to give the book to Mary Cannan to read, as a representative of the great British public. Since he was not as keen now on Secker as he had been, he half-thought of putting it up to auction (iii. 500); though he had just accepted Secker's terms for *Women in Love* and *The Rainbow* (iii. 499) – in that order. On second thoughts he told Secker about it on 9 April, albeit in a way that left the door invitingly open for him to refuse (iii. 503); but Secker was keen, though he thought that *The Lost Girl*, Lawrence's new title (iii. 515), was asking for trouble with the circulating libraries.[71] Lawrence kept emphasising that the new book was amusing, a potential money maker and not improper. As the second half developed, however, the last of these claims may have been rather to calm Secker's timidity than the strictest truth. He continued to maintain that his heroine was not 'morally lost, poor darling' (iii. 525), and her story 'quite passable, from Mudies point of view' (iii. 517), but he confessed to Mackenzie soon after finishing on 5 May – having taken only eight weeks – that he was a little 'terrified of my Alvina'. He had made a married woman of her but doubted if marriage was, for her or Monty's heroine, the escape from the inner labyrinth: 'How we hang on to the marriage clue! Doubt if its really a way out. – But my Alvina, in whom the questing[72] soul is lodged, moves toward reunion with the dark half of humanity. Whither your Sylvia? The ideal? I loathe the ideal with an increasing volume of detestation – *all* ideal' (iii. 521). Secker might have found that 'dark half' worrying – yet it looks like something deeper than sexy passages which might call for expurgation. Lawrence had vowed he was through with offering the world anything 'serious *di cuore* ... Henceforth my fingers to my nose – and my heart far off' (iii. 491). Yet once again a supposed potboiler which set out to be much less serious than its predecessors, had probed further than its author intended.

The new book might seem to have little for the biographer. Of course Lawrence had known from boyhood the Cullen family of London House in Eastwood, on whom he based the Houghtons. He had visited the house, met its people and heard every stage of Eastwood's tut-tutting about the failed ventures of George Henry Cullen: the drapery-store windows, the sales, the shirt factory, the brickworks, the private coal-mine, the cinema. Both he and Ada were friendly with the daughter who left home to train as a nurse but landed up playing the piano for her father's films, before finally breaking away. (Flossie however married a man seven years older, as Alvina – named after Lawrence's cousin – refuses to do.) He had moreover already used the household three times: in 'Paul Morel' II, in the fragment 'Elsa Culverwell', and in 'The Insurrection',[73] though the sexual and social rebellion of that Miss Houghton probably differed both from life and from the liaison with an Italian peasant in the new fiction now. Using such familiar material may have made detachment easier.

Yet the distance Lawrence now maintains from his story does provide a biographical note, showing how far he had freed himself from Eastwood and from England. 'The Insurrection' had been much more *di cuore* both negatively and positively. It gave him a satirist's pleasure at first; and it became a stage towards *The Rainbow*. Both as exposure of how the provincial bourgeoisie denied life for class and money in an Eastwood from which he himself had only recently broken away; and as his first sustained attempt to work out his new vision of the power of sexual relationship to liberate and transform; the fiction involved his own heart. The story behind the story was the Insurrection of Mr Lawrence. It was the difficulty in getting back into the mood of that younger self, seven years and a world war later, that made it impossible to continue – but starting again, coming at familiar material with a sense of being quite free of it now, led to a freehand zest, economical and laconic, and a distance which keeps turning satire into comedy. In the first third of the book the decline of Manchester House, the rise of Alvina and her first fruitless rebellions, are seen now as through glass, lightly. So James Houghton, that failed commercial artist enslaved to second-rate imaginings, becomes 'amusing' – and so does his daughter, come home as a plump maternity nurse with a pinchable bottom, to find no fortune and only a very unattractive beau. Lawrence's 'amusing' is just right for the distance, poised tautly between the funny and the serious. To laugh at James is not to forget the destructiveness of his obsession; to sympathise with Alvina is also to smile wryly at the ways in which she is her father's daughter and middle-class English. So *The Lost Girl* is the best evidence of what one would have to mean now by calling Lawrence 'English', and proof again of how much he had changed in those seven years.

The middle section is differently revealing, especially in defeating expectations founded on his previous work; so it may leave readers all the more puzzled about what he is up to now. Many will dismiss the itinerant troupe the Natcha-Kee-Tawaras as rubbishy, and feel uneasily repelled by the love-affair of Alvina and Ciccio, and they will be right, or just half right which is half mistaken. For again the comedy and the seriousness have to do with Lawrence revaluing himself, to a point now of parody and self-parody – always one of his 'turns'. So the Natcha-Kee-Tawaras are a deliberate parody of Cooper, and their bohemian commune a travesty of Rananim, that dream of a few comrades of like mind and free spirit bound together against the world. Nor is it accident that the coming together of Alvina and Ciccio has so little to do with love — against which Lawrence had been setting himself ever more firmly – but reads (almost) like a burlesque of the stock Lawrencian sleeping-beauty fable, since the lower-class lad is so very seedy and predatory, and the lady so very down on her luck and walking in her sleep. Yet this is just where the new fiction parted company with the old, and began to pull Lawrence (in his metaphor) through the safety glass.

For he had seen the encounter of the 'white' with the 'Indian' in the Leatherstocking novels as actually Cooper's search within himself, to discover and be reconciled with the deeper and darker part of him that his civilisation had almost destroyed. That, and the true Blutbrüderschaft of Natty and Chingach-gook, are what the Natcha-Kee-Tawaras travesty, in a seedy bohemianism that is actually as false and exploitative as the society they reject. Only at two points – Pacohuila on horseback, and when Kishwégin dances – does a deeper potenti-ality flash out, so that momentarily an Eve Effingham encounters the last of the Mohicans. Tawdriness and travesty disappear, though shortly to return. (Even the Magnus-like Mr May, acting a begging dog, may reveal for a moment an inner truth that is no 'Dodge'.) With Alvina and Ciccio Lawrence is concerned in the same way, both to show the unattractive and life-denying nature of the differing rinds that protect and conceal their darker and more fruitful selves; but also to show how the force that pulls them together cracks those open, to reveal a dark beauty hidden, almost lost, within the pale English girl and the seedy foreigner. Yet it is here also that the novel began to be 'improper' again, with a quite different emphasis from *The Rainbow* and *Women in Love*. For all Birkin's (and Lawrence's) determination to distinguish true sexual relationship from the orthodox let alone the romance view of love, there is a sense in which the two major novels remain love-stories, though with a difference built on sometimes violent conflict. Now the difference grows wider, darker, more challengingly anti-romance and disquieting.

Lawrence himself made a two-page revision to get rid of love-talk and make a discomfiting clarification; and Secker also asked him later to replace a passage that the libraries would not accept. Lawrence readily agreed, since his major aim had been to write something that would sell – but Secker also made several other changes without telling him. All these pinpoint the novel's dark side. The most significant of Secker's changes blurs the difficult line Lawrence now wished to draw between something ugly, rapacious, domineering, and a condition for the cracking open of ego that he now thought necessary to allow the 'dark half of humanity' to emerge. The loss of Alvina's virginity is potentially the most repulsive scene he had ever written. She cannot understand the sexual innuendo behind her new Kishwe name ('Allaye'); the episode itself is very close to rape; and is made all the nastier by the impression that the Italian is laughing to himself afterwards, exulting over having taken the English lady, and determined to make her his slave. A sentence Secker cut, by its repeated emphasis on 'shamelessness', suggests (albeit afar off) that Ciccio may also have buggered her. Yet it is because Alvina cannot see him as all ugly, that she is unable to resist. Despite the ugliness that Lawrence deliberately creates, there is also a 'sense of the unknown beauty of him' which ever thereafter has her under its spell.[74] The paradox that Ciccio opens up is the presence, in the rather unpleasant defensive-aggressive Italian, of a 'dark, unseizable beauty' which is almost godlike. After the death of her father Ciccio again takes her, in her mother's bedroom, against her will; but Lawrence's rewriting for Secker again removed the most dangerous challenge. For Ciccio's original 'recklessness' probably implied anal intercourse again, and it is even clearer that the effect is to leave her 'nothing of herself—nothing'. In the two major novels, the crucial experience was of momentary oblivion for both, in order that new selves could be born. Now it seems that Alvina's 'upper' selfhood is so resistant that it requires to be 'killed' by the dark man. When he laughs afterwards, 'Love is a fine thing', the challenge seems complete[75] – but for one thing more, which Lawrence's own deliberate change supplied. At the moment when Alvina (having left Ciccio and engaged herself to a rich doctor) agrees to break her engagement and go with Ciccio to Italy, Lawrence originally drew a final distinction between the physical attraction of the man himself, and the (suffering) power *in* him; between 'modern masculine impertinence' in the sex war, and the 'strange old godliness' unacknowledged. Now he deliberately removed all talk of love, and concluded: 'he seemed so beautiful, so beautiful. And this left her numb, submissive. Why must she see him beautiful? Why was she will-less? She felt herself like one of the old sacred prostitutes ...'[76] A 'submissive' prostitution, giving up her will and feminine self-value – but in dedication to what is sacred – the paradox challenges more than the middle-class English (and the Christian) ideal of virtue. Lawrence's remark to Mackenzie, about the questing soul moving toward rediscovery of its darker dimension, comes into focus. What links the failures of James Houghton, Miss Frost, Mr May, Madame Rochard and Dr Mitchell – and Alvina before she meets Ciccio – is that they are all governed by false ideas or ideals of themselves. Though Alvina's marriage may make *The Lost Girl* acceptable in lending libraries, marriage is no answer any more, even the marriage of opposites. Now what is needed is a virtual 'killing' of half the self, because that half has become so over-dominant and the other so recessive. If mental consciousness is the disease, it seems to be because the upper centres have become too active in creating only their kinds of awareness. So it is the lower centres that need to be brought alive, and that – as the Whitman essay dared to clarify – involves the sacral as well as the vaginal 'allaye', as ways of discovering and awakening the darker part of the psyche, 'killing' the dominance of the white self and its ideals. Anal sex had been a part of the whole realm of love before, but now it seems to have become almost a kind of remedial ritual, so bad has imbalance become. Yet there comes a deep dark tenderness too.[77]

To relate this to the Lawrence marriage needs tact, for fiction is a way of exploring possibilities outside as well as within real life. We have however been watching Lawrence's emphasis steadily changing since 1916, from 'star-equilibrium' to increasing emphasis on individuality, and then to the need to assert manhood against the dominant female and mother-substitute so as to recover the power of the male god within. He had turned away from love, and there is much evidence that his marriage was not what it had been. If Mackenzie is to be believed, Lawrence felt that something was wrong in the marriage-bed though this may or may not have been simply a physical matter. To have imagined, now, a kind of submission that Frieda's powerful ego would never allow, may also suggest how a sense of diminished potency might grow from her unwillingness to give herself or acknowledge him as he longed for her to do; and might emerge as a difficulty in satisfying her kind of desire. Lawrence's heroines sometimes taunt their lovers for such failure, though the cause-and-effect could be put the other way round. Both might well be true; and who is to say which was the truer for the Lawrences? Either way, it seems significant that anal intercourse, in both fiction and fact since 1914,[78] looks to have been a male reaction to feeling undervalued, or held at a distance, or defied. (To a woman it may look rather different.)

The final stage of the novel, after Alvina and Ciccio leave England for the Abruzzi, comes close to recent experience. Yet he would in any case have wanted (as in Ciccio himself) to contrast a wild beauty with the grimly down-at-heel realities of peasant life. If the new novel has a different emphasis from its 1913–17 predecessors, here the difference is from *Twilight in Italy*, though there is continuity too. 'England' is deathly for the Englishman in both, and 'Italy' the challenge to redress imbalance and awaken to new kinds of awareness, though both the deathliness and the difficulty of reawakening have increased. In the icy and bleak conditions of the Abruzzi, it is not that Alvina can look forward to new community, or a closer family, or a richer relationship with nature, or even happiness in love with Ciccio. Rather, the harsh conditions distil the essence of what she and Ciccio have found; the more precious also because of its vulnerability in a world declaring war. There is no knowing the future for the relationship, but there has been a new beginning: a deeper manhood in Ciccio, a different selfhood in Alvina liberated from provincial, class, idealist and wilful cerements. The title's irony remains, even after harsh testing. Far from being 'lost', Alvina has for the first time found a self that can hold to and assert fragile life and abiding connection, even against death spirits and cruel fate. Ciccio almost despairs when he is called-up; but he too, by the final pages, has found something to live for. The words Lawrence gives them echo his own to Katherine Mansfield in December 1918, about resisting death. "'If you don't come back it will be because you don't want to—no other reason ... So make up your mind," she said ... At last he stirred—he rose. He came hesitating across to her. "I'll come back, Allaye," he said quietly. "Be damned to them all."'[79]

IX People and Places

While *The Lost Girl* was taking shape between early March and early May, there was also a new outer life. Taormina had an expatriate colony too, though less oppressive than Capri's because he could escape to Fontana Vecchia. It was moreover temporary enough to remain amusing, since nearly all foreigners left by the end of May each year as the Sicilian sun blazed hotter. From two centres – Mary Cannan at the posh Timeo Hotel where she regularly invited them to meals, and Marie Hubrecht who had once owned Fontana Vecchia and still had Rocca Bella and a separate studio – webs of acquaintance began to spread; and since the whole life of what was little more than a village funnelled through the narrow central Corso, passing notables could also be pointed out. The Hubrecht family had been in Taormina for years. It was probably through Marie that Lawrence met the philanthropic and religious Mabel Hill whom he thought too sanctified even to sniff at him; and the Duca di Bronte (the Hon. Alexander Nelson Hood, descendant of the victor of Trafalgar, and inheritor of his Italian title) whom he had seen at the Hotel and thought 'gaga' (iii. 496) – though still worth visiting, later. At one of Marie's parties Lawrence told a Dr Rogers from Cambridge, whom he had seen 'hypnotising' a bevy of fox-furred Danish girls at the Timeo, that his 'scientific latest' was 'childish piffle' (iii. 496) – but his hostess did not seem to mind. Indeed he became firm friends with the 45–year-old 'slit-eyed Dutch woman' (iii. 491). She painted, and was well-read; she gave him the run of her bookshelves at 'Rocca Bella' and her garden when she was away, and she drew a portrait of him that is now in the National Portrait Gallery in London. It was through her that they also met the water-colourist and photographer Robert Kitchen and – more to the point – two young painters who were renting her studio, the South African Jan Juta and his Welsh friend Alan Insole, along with Jan's sister Réné Hansard who was about to publish her first novel. Jan – from a rich family at the Cape – had studied at the Slade and was now at the British Institute in Rome. Lawrence and Frieda always enjoyed the lively young, and Jan was both good-looking and talented. He too did a portrait sketch of Lawrence that spring,[80] which was photographed and sent off whenever a photo was demanded. Meanwhile at the Timeo there was a constant spectacle to gossip about: a 'ricketty' buttercup-haired Baroness quarrelling with the waiter Pancrazio over the service, and being told it was because she did not pay enough (iii. 496, 507); the young French couple who were arrested (but for what?); and the uproar enveloping Mary herself, when she tried to get out of renting a house to which she had at first agreed. Moreover Marie (Minerva-type) didn't approve of Mary (Aphrodite-type, getting on a bit, but still able to trip upstairs). They 'declared a vendetta' (iii. 496), which was amusing at the time but became awkward later, when Lawrence helped to arrange (in Marie's absence) that Mary should lease the studio after the Jutas had gone (iii. 506), and the owner was not at all pleased, though she forgave him (iii. 535).

Now, however – as in Fiascherino in 1913 – there was also the chance to make friends with an Italian family.[81] His landlord had been in Manchester when the Lawrences arrived, but soon came home. Lawrence became very fond of Ciccio Cacópardo and his young wife Emma, known as 'Gemma'. He had been employed by the Hubrechts in Holland and England, spoke three languages and was rapidly growing prosperous. All the mothers of unmarried daughters were furious when he fell in love with and married a young refugee from the Veneto, who had fled the invading Austrians and arrived on the island with nine brothers and sisters, almost destitute. One mother indeed had tried to rip the girl's dress off her back when she heard of the engagement. Moreover *her* family refused to believe in the marriage, and suspected the Sicilian of making her his concubine. (When in June 1920 Ciccio accepted a position as cook-butler to a Bostonian couple, he proudly bought Gemma a smart outfit and went north to show off to the Mottas, Gemma's family, before sailing to the USA.) There was also Carmelo, Ciccio's brother, who had a house near the Capuchins and farmed the family lands. Lawrence took a great interest in everything, walking out in season to watch the reaping, the threshing in the old way with oxen treading the corn and chaff tossed against the wind, the olives being pressed and the almonds beaten out of the trees with long rods. Carmelo brought him by donkey two great *bottiglioni* of red wine from the hills, to his great satisfaction. Carmelo's little daughter (who still in 1995 lived in Fontana Vecchia) often brought them their post, and remembered helping a dressed-up Frieda across the stream as she went off, lady-like, to dine at the Timeo. In the bottom storey under their feet, Grazia the matriarch would fire up the big oven to make bread – for the Lawrences too – or to roast, along with the family feast, a turkey for upstairs which looked a mere slip of a thing in that red cavern. She had been much amused when Lawrence, soon after they came, asked for goat's milk but made the animal masculine – and she often shopped for him. There was Ciccia, Francesco's sister, who had just buried a husband and was about to marry a younger one. Water for washing came from cisterns, but every day Lawrence would take the big terracotta jug and go off to the old fountain to fill it with drinking water – and there (Ciccio said) he would sit a while on the wall watching the people come and go. Gossip about him, too, spread among the Sicilians – like the story of how the mayor came to make a courtesy call, and found himself in the midst of flying plates. Frieda could later not remember this rumpus[82] – and besides, she says, there were not that many plates – but it is easy to imagine the story of their overheard rows being spread, or augmented. *Their* Sicilians, also, though Lawrence kept an eye on Grazia's accounts, were obviously different from the rogues and extortioners in town who charged inflated prices and swindled him out of the most favourable rate of exchange (iii. 496). After a month at Fontana Vecchia he already felt that he had lived there for 'a hundred thousand years' (iii. 497).

There were two unwelcome invasions, however. Hearing that Gilbert Cannan had returned from America, Lawrence wrote a not over-friendly letter asking why he had taken it on himself to collect money for him, and what in any case had happened to it? He must also – the letter has not survived – have said something that Cannan found offensive about the sudden marriage of his mistress Gwen to his friend Mond while he was away (iii. 500). This was a subject on which Cannan felt sensitive, but also chivalrous since he would hear no criticism of her, and had indeed gone off on a motoring holiday with the two of them – 'the Mond, the Demi-Monde, and the Immonde' as his ex-wife said when she heard of it (iii. 502). On 8 April, having left the others in Rome, Cannan turned up on Lawrence's doorstep without warning, and in something of a tantrum. It was very lucky that Mary had not chosen this as one of her days to come and have tea with the Lawrences, and that Gilbert was not staying in his ex-wife's hotel but in one 'a *little grander*' (iii. 502). Before he left, having taken out a cheque-book and dashed off a cheque for £75 in addition to the $150 he told Lawrence he had deposited with Huebsch, good relations were restored on the surface. However, Lawrence had not enjoyed being ticked off when he felt in the right, both as to the money – which seemed so to put him in the wrong – and for his views on commitment and fidelity. If (as Cannan said) Gwen was not of 'a forgiving nature', neither was he. He found Cannan's praise of Gwen's character absurd, and still more so the degree to which Gilbert 'the filbert' had become Americanised,[83] with his bulging pocket-book, his boasting of how they had taken to him 'over there', in the US and how he had 'promised a quantity of people I'll go back this Fall' (iii. 502). No detail of this will have been pleasing to Lawrence. They parted, 'as friends who will *never* speak to each other again'.

Less than three weeks later, worse was to come. Lawrence had taken a little time off from his novel to make two brief trips. Since his trunk had still not come (and remained missing even in May, six months after he had arrived in Turin) Marie Hubrecht made him a little farewell present before she departed for the summer to Holland and Norway. With her 250 lire he went off to Catania with Frieda to buy some shirts and sandals, and have Frieda 'dentisted'. (A screw-in tooth had come loose.)[84] Thus improved, they went the following weekend to see 'the boys' and René at Randazzo, and from there to the Duca's castle at Maniace, before going down together to Syracuse. They enjoyed the young people again. Juta had been grumpy about being chivied out when he wanted to work; but all was sunny now, and Lawrence liked René better in a context where she 'dropped her social tiresomenesses' and became 'simple again' (iii. 526). They went on muleback up Etna to the Duca's castle – 'wonderful place' – and to Lawrence's amusement 'the people turned out to receive us as if we were royalty' (iii. 509). Juta remembered a number of peasant retainers fitted out in uniforms like the Pope's Swiss guard; heavy Victorian furnishings; a grande dame who looked and behaved like Queen Alexandra; while her brother inspected his guests through a monocle clamped to his nose.[85] It is to be hoped he was impressed by Frieda in the blue silk Ada had given her. These were 'lovely days' with wild-flowers out,' and the corn rising strong and green in the magical, malarial places, and Etna floating now to northward, still with her crown of snow', as the train wound down the coast to Catania and Syracuse. Their hotel was near the great quarry of Latomia from which much of the stone was cut for the Greek city – and in which thousands of young Athenian captives were left to starve in 413 AD, a gruesome history which left a mark on *The Lost Girl*, and on Frieda's memory.[86] The Lawrences caught colds from going up the mountain or from the Norman stonework, but returned to Taormina on the 29th, in high fettle.

Early the next morning, however, Lawrence heard a noise on the stairs and there was Magnus, looking up with a frightened face. The trouble he had hinted at in his first letter from Anzio had caught up with him. He had told Lawrence at the monastery that a cheque for his hotel at Anzio had bounced, because a sum he was owed had not been paid in to his New York bank, but as soon as it was, all would be well. True or not, the matter had not been put right – and the carabinieri had come to Cassino making enquiries. Somebody telephoned his friend the monastery guest-master, and Magnus had made a run for it down a back path and for seven hours across country. He caught a slow train one station up, went a few stations towards Rome and then changed to a train in the other direction, spending most of the journey to Naples in the toilet. He had almost nothing to eat until he got to Taormina; and arrived on the 26th with almost nothing left of the 150 lire Don Mauro had hastily lent him – only to find the Lawrences away. He agonised most of all lest the monastery, where he had appeared to be a rich American, should find out the truth. He had been waiting anxiously for Lawrence to return, and had come to him, he said, because there was no one else.[87] He had however chosen to stay at the most expensive of the Taormina hotels because, he said, they knew him from a previous visit, though he was economising now after the first meals, by eating 'disgusting' food in a restaurant. Lawrence and Frieda were about to go out to lunch with Mary, but after a hasty introduction to Frieda, over whose hand Magnus bowed in continental fashion with many compliments to her house, an appointment was made for him to come back the next morning. Then Magnus unfolded his rescue plan. Would Lawrence advance him money on his manuscripts, fetch his things from the monastery and put him up until he could gather enough to get to Egypt, where a friend on a newspaper might get him work?

Again one must try to disentangle from Lawrence's hindsight in 1922 how he felt about Magnus now. His appearance and speech had already been used for Mr May in *The Lost Girl*, with an impression of dapperness down on its luck and anxious to the point of seediness. Yet Lawrence seems at first to have responded more warmly towards Magnus than the element of 'Mr May' implies, despite the difference in their attitudes and his complex feelings about the little man's rather effeminate fastidiousness, 'queenly' fussing over Douglas and dislike of women. He had glimpsed a generosity when Magnus did have any money, a capacity for hard work before most people were up and the encyclopaedic knowledge of places and their art to which Douglas was to pay tribute later. Douglas would accuse Lawrence of omitting all these from his 1922 portrait, and they may not be emphasised enough, but they are there, and would have appealed the more when he knew less of the man's other side. Magnus himself is witness that Lawrence's first response now was 'most sympathetic & ready to help me' though Frieda ('the bitch') was 'supercilious'.

Soon however sympathy was overcome by disapproval and by Frieda's hostility. In Magnus's position, Lawrence would undoubtedly have taken the cheapest room he could find and lived on bread and cheese, rather than staying with no funds whatever at the kind of hotel he and Frieda had never been able to afford. As for sharing the profit from Magnus's writings, Lawrence had helped him to place one article about the monastery; had thought what he had read of the manuscript about the Legion quite good and recommended it to Secker and to Unwin, but the interest lay in the subject rather than the writing, and it would be difficult to find a publisher (as indeed it proved). Any money Lawrence could spare was unlikely to be repaid. To drop everything and go to Montecassino would not only be expensive and time-consuming, but would involve him in affairs about which he was beginning to harbour suspicions. In the afternoon he sent a note enclosing 50/- and saying he had changed his mind about the errand. Magnus went to re-persuade him but found him out, and Frieda hard as nails (though Lawrence thought he had appealed to her sense of power). The next morning he made another emotional plea, and Lawrence was 'very nice', but the following day he sent a note enclosing 200 lire 'and refusing to have any more to do with me, as his wife was angry!!!' Lawrence treasured his privacy far too much to have Magnus as a houseguest – for how long? – and even if he had been

582

disposed to try, Frieda would certainly have vetoed the idea.[88] She felt no responsibility for Magnus, sensed his attitude to her and did not care for his sort.

Yet Lawrence did feel somehow responsible, but resented being taken for granted – especially when Magnus made it a reproach that he would not have come to Taormina but for him. When Lawrence refused to advance money for the manuscripts, the man's eyes filling with tears and the hand beseechingly on the arm made his blood run cold. He hated people to touch him, and he could not abide such scenes. He said he would pay the bill at the hotel; on condition Magnus left there and took a cheap lodging that he could hope to pay for. Magnus then took a room and board with an ex-waiter whom (again) he had known before.

About ten days later Pancrazio Cipolla came to see Lawrence – caught at a disadvantage, in pyjamas – with a note from Magnus. The Sicilian had tired of having good food ordered every day, and every day being put off about money that was always to arrive tomorrow. He had demanded payment at once, at which Magnus had declared himself insulted and determined to leave. He would go to Catania the note said, sell some trinkets and try to get to Egypt, or to Malta whence his friend the guest-master had come. Would Lawrence please advance the equivalent in lire of the seven guineas due from *Land and Water*? Confronted by the Sicilian's justifiable anger and suspicion, and his contempt for 'a mezzo-signore' – a taunt which Lawrence felt cruelly to the point and feared might be levelled at him too if he did nothing – he agreed, on condition Magnus confirmed that the article had been accepted, and formally transferred the magazine payment to him. A wounded note came back – and Magnus was gone.[89]

It was a horrible episode in which Lawrence lost in every way. He felt he had been taken advantage of, and Frieda told him so, which made it even more irritating. What he had paid out would have kept them both for several weeks, and he was pretty sure that he would never get it back. He and Frieda were only just getting on an even keel after years of poverty, and the extravagance of Magnus would have been unthinkable. And yet ... Lawrence's later account, by telling less than the whole truth about his own finances, shows some consciousness, even guilt, about not doing more. He made no mention of royalties from Huebsch or the £75 cheque from Cannan which he had recently deposited (though, preserving the literal truth, it may not have come through yet). So he *could* have given more, just as he could have gone to Montecassino, had he wanted to. He very much did not want to – but though he had been honest to his own feelings, and nobody had any right to reproach him, he felt uneasy on the one hand, and duped on the other, the worst of combinations. His irritation can be read between the lines of a sudden outburst, apparently occasioned by a concert of cello music in Taormina's beautiful Greek theatre looking out at Etna and the sea. 'I can't stand this twisting, squirming, whining modern music' he cried (Bach and Schubert and Wagner and Brahms), contrasting it with the pagan beauty of the ruins in golden evening light, and the coastline seen through the columns. However the real source of the irritability may be glimpsed in the previous paragraph's brief reference to the 'troubles' brought on them 'in the shape of that cherub Magnus ... But I can't write about it ... ' (iii. 514). On 6 May that man of modern culture (and squirming and whining?) must have been just about to depart.

At least, with the novel finished and sent off to be typed in Rome (iii. 515), Lawrence could plan to take a month off – though his diary[90] recorded that he began another, two days later, to be called *Mr Noon*. This may however mean no more than that he wrote a few pages. For Mary now wanted them to go with her on a trip to Malta, she paying the passages, since she was frightened to go alone.

Ten days later they were off to Syracuse to take the boat – only to find there was a shipping strike. It would be too much of a fiasco to catch the train back again, so they put up at a hotel to await events, and discovered the next day that there would be a steamer that evening. Returning for lunch after a look around the town, Lawrence found a note at the desk from Magnus, with a complaint that they had ignored him on the street. This was enough to ensure that Lawrence would contact him, to avoid any such imputation. After missing him twice, they met; and Lawrence had to advance another 'last loan' to make up Magnus's hotel bill here too, since he had also been delayed by the strike and his 'trinkets' had fetched less than he hoped. That evening, having embarked, they watched with mixed feelings how Magnus, every inch the elegant suede-gloved gentleman rather than the fugitive, strutted through customs and immigration, and disappeared into the second-class cabins below, not to emerge until the ship had sailed. Then out on deck he came, perky again, though the signs of strain were clear to see. Moments later however, there he was on the first-class deck, chatting animatedly to an acquaintance from his hotel, and waving a little condescendingly to his second-class friends below.[91]

Malta of course had British pleasures again: bacon, eggs and marmalade for breakfast, cream teas, Bass beer, abundance in the shops – but Lawrence had done with the declining British empire, 'beneficent and sterile', and the English, 'so *good*, and so barren of life' (iii. 533). After three days on the yellow-rock island he would have been glad to go home. Valletta and its great harbour were interesting and beautiful, but the monotony of the surrounding landscape got on his nerves – all bath brick and yellow dust he said, white-hot, bone-dry, treeless. However the steamer strike would keep them there a week more than they had planned. This was also more expensive, since Mary had only paid their passages, but it could not be helped. Lawrence was even persuaded to spend £6 on a tussore silk suit (iii. 552). And now Magnus, who seemed to have got on his feet remarkably quickly with the help of Don Mauro's introductions, was all hospitality. While Frieda and Mary shopped or lazed Lawrence spent some time with the little man, now in dazzling white tropicals (if rather spoilt by black boots *faute de mieux*). They lunched and drank whiskies at Magnus's hotel. They discussed his manuscripts again and it was then that Lawrence wrote letters for him – particularly to see whether Goldring could place any of the plays Magnus had translated (iii. 531–2).[92] They also went out touring the island by car with two Maltese who seemed to have taken Magnus under their wing, (much impressed by his talk of Germany and Russia): to the bay where St Paul had landed, to the old capital in the centre of the island, and past the only trees that seemed to grow anywhere, around the Governor's summer villa. Soon Magnus's new friends Michael Borg and Walter Salomone found him a little house in a suburb of the old town, where he seemed happily busy when the Lawrences left, learning Maltese, and adapting himself to local life, already sounding anti-British. It was still not clear where any money would come from – but Lawrence no longer accepted responsibility and would not 'bother with him any more' (iii. 535).[93] Nor, he now felt, could he really like such a man. (He had, however, been indiscreet enough once more, in a confiding moment, to talk about his bisexuality and his belief in male friendship – which Magnus typically interpreted in homosexual terms.)[94]

When they got back to Taormina at the end of May – Lawrence cross at having overspent – it was to find almost all the expatriates gone and the little town sinking into its summer torpor. Ciccio and Gemma left for America at the beginning of June, and were much missed. The house remained cool, but pyjamas were the order of the day now, and it became a trial to go out. Frieda, 'sun-dazed' (iii. 542), began to talk of wanting to go to Germany, perhaps in August, and Lawrence, writing to Marie Hubrecht who was about to leave Holland for Norway, had visions also of dark trees, cool water and fair-haired, blue-eyed people (iii. 533, 554). June in Sicily, to an English eye, was a curious mix of seasons. The corn was cut and being trodden out on the threshing floors, the ground was pale yellow and it was 'September among the earth's little plants' as they withered. Yet 'the vines are green and powerful with spring sap, and the almond trees, with ripe almonds, are summer, and the olives are timeless. Where are we then?' (iii. 538–9). Mary had energy still for an expedition to the crater of Etna (during which her mule fell with her; iii. 557); and met the heat by having her hair bobbed, which Frieda liked, but Lawrence hated for bringing out a pseudo-mannishness which the male in him could not abide (iii. 551). But even Mary began to talk of leaving.

On the other hand Lawrence welcomed isolation, preferring to have only the peasant life winding its course on the track behind the house, the men with their asses and goats, the women with burdens on their heads, and he only in 'frail streaming contact', not close (iii. 554). On hot days, with a pale sea in front and the Calabrian coast 'glimmering exquisite like a chalcedony – hens cackling – the landscape silent and asleep' (iii. 552), he did not much want to go anywhere or do anything but 'aestivate' (iii. 542). Yet, if they were to go on their travels again to escape the severest heat in August, it behoved him to get some work done.

X Money and Manuscripts

His finances, however, had markedly improved now. At the end of January he had had (unusually) almost £100 in hand. From then to 28 May when he got back from Malta, there came royalties of just over £145, though about £114 of that was belated payment from America that he should have had before. Moreover, from Marie, Amy and the money Cannan had collected had come a further £140 in gifts. (The year's rent for Fontana Vecchia, paid in quarterly instalments, was £25 at an exchange rate of 80. However irritated he might be at being a charity, the gifts were enough to make a real difference.) Waiting for him now were two $50 cheques from Seltzer (£25 in all).[95] At the beginning of June came '£19 odd' from *Land and Water* for 'You Touched Me', and at the end of the month nearly £10 (=$40) from the *Dial* for 'Adolf, with an offer of $50 for 'Rex', the companion piece (iii. 536 n.). Still better, *Metropolitan Magazine* offered $250 for 'Wintry Peacock', which was a great deal for a short story.[96] (These offers confirmed that it was an American readership he should go for now.) Having signed agreements with Secker in May, Lawrence could look forward to £100 advances for both *The Lost Girl* and *Women in Love* in due course. So in the first six months of the year he had earnings of just under £200, had been given another £140 and had solid prospects ahead.

All the same, he felt uneasy about having spent too much in Malta, and was grossly overcharged (he thought) for the typing of *The Lost Girl* in Rome, so as to have copies for both England and America.[97] He was not likely to get back what he had given Magnus. Moreover – worryingly – the exchange rate was dropping. In May he got 24 lire to the dollar, 83 to the pound (iii. 519). By July the rate had dropped to 15.5, and 65. Nevertheless the improvement in his finances began to bring about a perceptible change in confidence, though the carefulness that poverty had engrained would not easily disappear. In early May, Catherine Carswell's first novel won a publisher's prize of £250. Believing Lawrence to be hard-up still, and having never forgotten his help with the book in 1914, she offered him £50. On 12 May he hedged, saying that he would accept, but only to keep the money in his London account in trust for her to come and spend a holiday with them (iii. 524–5). She sent the cheque anyway, and it was waiting for him when he got back from Malta. He wrote to thank her, repeating his condition for accepting (iii. 534). Three days later he wrote again: 'As for the cheque, I suddenly decided to burn it . . . I have enough money. And why should I hold any of yours in fee. So I accept the gift all the same: and have burned the cheque' (iii. 537). (The act was important enough to be recorded in one of his terse diary entries.)[98] He proceeded also to burn a cheque for a last £5 of Shestov royalties from Kot, saying that it could be considered a loan if Kot preferred, but he did not want the money now (iii. 515). Being as anxious to preserve Kot's dignity as his own, he asked carefully whether a further £10 loan would be acceptable, but Kot sent a fresh cheque by return, so he retreated and cashed it (iii. 570). All the same, cheque burning had been an entirely new sensation.

This relative prosperity should not be exaggerated. By way of comparison Murry, whose anxiety about money had been part of his recent crisis with Katherine, had earned £500 p.a. as Censor in 1918, was offered £800 p.a. to edit the *Athenaeum* in 1919 and succeeded in getting that raised to £1,000 p.a in January 1920. (Katherine's allowance was £300.)[99] It is only in contrast with Lawrence's penury in 1919 that the change in his circumstances can seem dramatic – and the memory of having had to live on his sister's charity was still painfully fresh. So, summer lethargy or no, after his month off as a reward for finishing *The Lost Girl* it was time 'to get some work done, earn some money' (iii. 542).

He had to review his affairs in order to brief his new agent (iii. 544–8), though Mountsier happened to be travelling in Europe and could not act until he got back to New York in mid-August. It quickly became apparent that Lawrence *needed* an agent. The briefing shows him hazy about who had published what, especially in America because Pinker and Huebsch had kept him in the dark, though he also forgot who had published *The White Peacock* in England. By trying to act for himself, moreover, he had got into several tangles, and the Italian post did not help. (Even now, letters to and from America could take a month.) The tug of war for *Women in Love* had left Huebsch aggrieved, and this got worse over the Shestov book which Lawrence had sent him. Huebsch proceeded to publish extracts in his periodical the *Freeman*, and offered to buy the book outright for £50 which was a generous offer – far better than Secker's had been (iii. 511–12, 543–4). Unfortunately by that time Secker had made an arrangement with someone else in America, and there was a further mix-up over whom Huebsch should pay for the extracts. So Kot and Lawrence lost an offer they both could have done with. Indeed the book was never published in America at all, after doing poorly in England. The estrangement from Huebsch then became final over *Studies in Classic American Literature*. Lawrence sent an ultimatum that unless a commitment to publish these essays arrived before the end of June, they would go to Seltzer (iii. 543–4). True, Huebsch had been sitting on them for six months, and there were grounds for Lawrence to describe him to Mountsier as 'an unsatisfactory person, in that he doesn't reply to one's questions, is dilatory, and puts off paying till one really feels that he never will pay' (iii. 545). Yet an ultimatum was bound to aggravate, especially when Lawrence spoke of his obligation to give Seltzer another book, after *Women in Love*! Huebsch had had enough. He wrote on 8 July with some dignity, defending himself from an unjust imputation that his not keeping *The Rainbow* in print interfered with Lawrence's rights, and declaring he would no longer even try to understand the relations between Kot, Lawrence and Secker. He would hand the American essays to Seltzer, and would not publish the psychoanalysis ones: 'I don't blame you for your course concerning your American publishing arrangements, I simply think that your judgment is bad' (iii. 544 n. 1).

Mountsier seems to have made anti-Semitic comments about Jewish publishers. Lawrence said he did not 'really like Jews' either, but owed Huebsch and Seltzer 'gratitude, up to a point', since the works he cared about most were the 'dangerous' ones, and it was only such little men who would bring them out: 'Don't be too sniffy of the risky little Jew. He adventures' – as gentlemanly bourgeois publishers would not (iii. 546–7).

The new relationship with Seltzer had already produced one irritant, however: the delay in sending Secker the typescript of *Women in Love*; and this in turn helped to produce another mix-up over *The Lost Girl* and a delay in getting that published too. Because Lawrence was so nervous about trusting anything valuable to the post now, he asked Mackenzie and Ciccio to take the typescripts to England and the US. No sooner however did Secker remark, as a possibility, that the American *Century* might do the book as a serial, than Lawrence grew obsessed with the idea of serialisation on both sides of the Atlantic (iii. 528–9). So Secker got only the unrevised manuscript, while the revised 'English' carbon typescript went to Foss of *Land and Water*, to see whether he or another English magazine would take it (iii. 555). Seltzer was now not to get the 'American' typescript from Ciccio either, until he had delivered *Women in Love* to Secker *and* until the *Century* had made a decision (iii. 540). If they refused, Mountsier was to try the *Metropolitan* and the *Dial* when he got back to America. In fact no magazine agreed to serialise in either country; *The Lost Girl* was delayed until late November in England, and early 1921 in America; and there was a good deal of rather irritable correspondence which ought to have been an agent's business.[100]

Having an American agent did however provide an impetus to develop the two potential books already in Lawrence's drawer. Mountsier had been in at the conception of the *Studies in Classic American Literature* at Christmas 1916, and it was surely high time now to get them into print – hence the overture to Seltzer and the ultimatum to Huebsch. However, Huebsch's hesitation must have helped bring Lawrence to his senses over the Whitman essay. There could be no book until that essay was sanitised. This he now proceeded to do together with some revision of the other unpublished essays,[101] and the 'English' carbon of *The Lost Girl*, in the first fortnight of June.

He intensified his 'esoteric' emphasis, interpreting Chillingworth in the light of alchemy, and adding at the start of the essay on *Moby Dick* five very Prysean pages on the 'conquering' of the lower 'centres', in order to bolster the esoteric meaning of the hunt of the white whale.[102] He also did more to link the sea essays with the first part of the book. Though the rewriting is often free, these essays still follow the sequence and structure of the ones they rework. Unfortunately there is no corresponding typescript of the essay on Whitman. Two later typescripts may represent the missing one or (probably) a further reworking.[103] Either way, Lawrence now veiled his meaning by removing its homosexual specifics. The central arguments about Whitman's halfness, and how he 'deliberately, self-consciously *affects* himself', remain – though that quotation is the only hint now of anything masturbatory. The focus becomes more literary as well as psychological, too, linking Whitman with Wilde and the aesthetes as against Balzac and Dickens; but also contrasting him favourably with Dostoevsky. Significantly, however, while still pointing to Whitman's 'ecstasy of *giving himself*', his lack of interest in woman and his 'love of comrades', the sexual dimensions of these are only implied at a distance. 'Acting from the last and profoundest centres, man acts womanless'; but there is no spelling out, now, what this means, or how and why 'Calamus' relates to death. (The lost version may have been a degree less tactful, of course, and this may be a later and further softening for the magazines.) Significantly however, the essay insists again that the love of comrades does not 'annul' marriage, but 'fulfils' it. The 'life-circuit' still depends 'entirely upon the sex-unison of marriage'; but 'a relation between fearless, honorable, self-responsible men, a balance in perfect polarity', must 'surpass' (though it must not destroy) the relation of man with woman, for 'the final consummation lies in that which is beyond marriage'. Insofar as this represents the Lawrence of June 1920, then, it confirms both his ongoing belief in marriage and the change in his attitude toward it. The question mark at the end of *Women in Love* has gone, and marriage, while still affirmed, is also now downgraded to a base from which the male must take off again. The 'future of mankind', the unfulfilled realm of consciousness, lies in a kind of 'sacred' male relationship (which he himself had never managed to secure).[104]

After flirting with the idea of offering the book to Cecil Palmer who had expressed an interest (iii. 576), Lawrence went back to putting America first. He posted 'my complete copy', whatever that was, to Mountsier on 2 August (iii. 582).

Having finished that revision on 15 June he at once began to expand the original four essays of 'Education of the People' into the small book that Unwin had suggested in 1918 (iii. 553). Twelve essays survive now in a single homogeneous manuscript,[105] and though one cannot be sure that the first four are the originals of 1918 (though probably added to and revised) it does seem likely, since V begins again from a point made in number II. Moreover the first four come from the experience of the Croydon schoolteacher, only too aware of the chasm between contemporary theories and the attitudes and expectations of the children he had taught. There is an attempt to rethink the syllabus and structure of the English school system. By contrast, the last eight essays are more interested in mothers and children than schools, and have more to do with attempting 'to get in human beings a new attitude to life' than with planning what should happen in classrooms – to the point where the connection of the last essay with the title has become very tenuous, and has to be hurriedly asserted in the final sentence.[106] These last eight are indeed mainly about parenthood, by the author of *Pyschoanalysis and the Unconscious* – and significantly also mainly about bringing up boys. Indeed, they seem in many respects to have unusually transparent autobiographical implications.

The starting-point is, once more, that the health of the psyche depends upon harmony between properly functioning 'upper' and 'lower' centres, in mutually balanced polarities. The mind should be only switchboard and utterer. However, the distortion produced nowadays by too-dominant upper centres, and the over-mental consciousness that inevitably follows, is such that all the emphasis must fall, now, on reactivating the 'volitional' centres to cure the imbalance. (The view is reactionary then, in the strict sense, seeking to correct an 'action' that has gone too far.) All that is said about 'education' follows from this imperative. The trouble begins with self-conscious modern mothers trying to make their infants conscious of them and of themselves, too soon, and with over-emphasis on love. So children should be left alone as much as possible, seized away from (s)mothering if necessary. Childhood should be predominantly a bodily learning, with mental consciousness allowed to grow at its own natural pace. Moreover the volitional centres *must* develop – parents should immediately take sloppy children to task, be angry with them when they deserve it and smack their bottoms when necessary so that they can be outraged too. For that will put fire into the backbone, that 'long sword of the vivid, proud, *dark* volition of man, something primal and creative'. A child needs more than love. Why are we so afraid of anger, of an element of danger, of fighting, when we see how wonderfully these make other creatures vital and on the qui vive? Children ought to be allowed to enjoy what cubs do, spontaneously, but protected.[107]

In elementary school the child must learn not mind-knowledge, ideas or 'self-expression', but the three R's; and also practical skills, which will above all enable it to look after itself and become independent (for nobody is free who has or needs a servant). Children should be encouraged to follow their own likings not those prescribed by others, and be themselves not one of the crowd. Games should be contests, and work a productive absorption; but we in our folly try to make work competitive, and take contest out of play. (In a logical development the earlier ideas about, then, educating children in differing directions according to aptitude as they grow older, would fit in here.)

But Lawrence is now more interested in how adults need to change, and is moreover transparently basing what he says on reactions to his own childhood and marriage. Behind many of the foregoing points is his sense of how his own childhood had gone wrong. If only he had had the luck of Romulus and Remus, and had had a wolf for mother![108] – instead of one who made him conscious too early, high-minded, aware always of *her*; and who thus created a young man whose self- and mental-consciousness became a prison that only the 'death' of sexual fulfilment could crack open. If only he had not been taught to think that love was everything, and to feel horror at the father's anger and the threat of violence – yet be unable to control his own. How much better to act spontaneously; for repression turns the passions ugly, smouldering, destructive, instead of the freshness after a thunderstorm. Here, also, is his own handiness, revealed now not only as a pleasure in doing things for himself, and a dislike of any kind of dependence, but as an especial joy in 'Proud personal privacy', maintaining a clear space around oneself where nobody may trespass. (Man and wife should each have this, as well as intimacy.) Here, familiarly, is the emphasis on 'the perfected singleness of the individual being';[109] but with no dwelling on the complementary urge to union now, because that has been too powerful. In 1920, rather, away with love and merging! switch off the upper consciousness! exult in your own dark being! Lawrence reverses the old Platonic myth of the cave: what is needed now is to get away from the sun of ideas and ideals, which tempts us into thinking the daylight world is all, and to explore instead the dark underworld it has hidden from us. And marriage ought (now) to be two creatures looking across a dark gulf, who flash together now and then, but always remain essentially separate, strangers.[110] But we have created precisely the wrong kind of Holy Family, in which the man adores the enthroned woman, who adores her child. Yet if woman (especially wife as mother-substitute) must be dethroned, it is not to enthrone man. Each must be *different*. Neither must bully. But Lawrence now goes back, behind the idea of the marriage of opposites within as well as between all persons in the major novels of 1914–17, to a simpler gender differentiation again. Man has 'most of the thinking, abstracting business to do ... You hate me when I'm feminine. So I'll let you be womanly, you let me be manly ... You remain at the centre, I scout ahead.' Suitably for an American audience, he expresses his 1920 idea of marriage in the metaphor of a Western wagon-train, with women and children in the wagons 'at the centre', and the men on ahead 'scouting, fighting, gathering provision, running on the brink of death and at the tip of the life advance ... the leaders, the outriders'. Rapt in a vision of friendship between adventurous men, Lawrence quite loses sight of the education of proletarian children.

And between men let there be a new spontaneous relationship, a new fidelity. Let men realise that their life lies ahead, in the dangerous wilds of advance and increase. Let them realise that they must go beyond their women ...

Let there be again the old passion of deathless friendship between man and man. Humanity can never advance into the new regions of unexplored futurity otherwise. Men who can only hark back to woman become automatic, static ...

Marriage and deathless friendship, both should be inviolable and sacred: two great creative passions, separate, apart, but complementary: the one pivotal, the other adventurous: the one, marriage, the centre of human life; and the other the leap ahead.

Which is the last word in the education of a people.[111]

There are sillinesses in these essays (about disarmament, for example); and illogicalities (for if boys can darn socks why shouldn't girls fix machines?). Lawrence takes a kind of pleasure in outraging 'progressive' attitudes that is the other side of feeling an alien to his society, but is unlikely to go down well now. There is also a challenge, and a kind of wisdom. But what is perhaps most interesting is the confirmation, and definition, in all the works of the first half of 1920, of a radical change in his views. The elements which shaped the pattern of the 'Study of Thomas Hardy' are still there in the passage just quoted, but as if in a kaleidoscope turned, they have fallen altogether differently. The re-forming of his view of marriage and of the significance of man-woman and man-man relationships, that has been taking place gradually since 1916, seems to have become complete and definite. It must of course be related to the change in his own marriage – though he is sure now (as he was not in 1918) that there will be no break, and the stance that becomes clear in June 1920 has come from a gradual and complex shift. We may remind ourselves of the stresses: Frieda's jealousy of Esther and William Henry, coupled with her own relations with Gray (whatever they were); the strain of being 'the Hun-wife' in a Britain at war; the stress of the expulsion from Cornwall and the penury of 1918; his thoughts of leaving her because of her failure to care for him when he was dangerously ill; and conversely (worst of all in his eyes) the realisation of how much he depended on her, as he grew more and more alienated from society and isolated from all but his family and a handful of friends at a distance. Had he struggled so hard to free himself from mother-dependence, only to become dependent on his wife as mother-substitute? The new valuation of maleness in the short stories, the still unnamed and unfinished novel (to become *Aaron's Rod*) about a man who leaves his wife perhaps to find a friend, the psychology book, *The Lost Girl* with its hidden theme of the quest for the 'dark half' rather than love as usually conceived – all these, with the final formulations of the American and Education essays now, were an imaginative effort of self-liberation, by a man who felt his sense of masculinity imperilled by the very marriage which recreated and still sustained him. However we may interpret the slim evidence about his marital difficulties, their real significance was the paradox that what sustains is also what may limit and create dependence.

However – and this is supremely important to realise about him – the most significant sentence in the passage that concludes the Education essays is one that he would probably have written even if his marriage were still the unabated song of a man who had come through. 'Men who can only hark back to woman become automatic, static' – and stasis for Lawrence is always death. Even a perfect marriage would, for him, become deathly unless there were something else, quite different, beyond. Those who complain of the Lawrencian 'dialectic' because there is never a satisfactory resolution, are objecting to the very essence of what, for him, it is to live and to write. It is the instability of every consummation that *is* the preciousness for him, the 'quick' in both senses, of the living moment, and the guarantee of further life. So the complex chemistry of Lawrence the writer – even putting together the need to stiffen the backbone, exult in one's darkness, dethrone the too-uppish woman, feel more male and more independent, find the love of comrades, and scout ahead of the pivotal and central woman – must have had a deeper dynamic than could be sufficiently explained by trying to measure the temperature of his marriage, or his potency.

We would also, in any case, have to allow for the ways in which Frieda seems changeless by comparison: a bit heavier or a bit thinner from time to time perhaps, but quite unworried about dependence since she was always so very much herself; rather the opposite of submissive; believing herself as intelligent and creative as he; and never acknowledging him or giving herself – as he would say – 'finally'. To that, too, the new attitude is a cumulative reaction. If she tended to colour his whole view of woman and gender, feminists critical of his male chauvinism should also take her, and her power over him, into account. Yet his writing was always more than imaginative compensation, too. There is a courage of self-enquiry, ready to face up to his own impulses and explore wherever they led.

XI Too Darn Hot

Whereas the third week in June had been 'sunny, with a cool wind' (iii. 553), the temperature then rose steadily. By the end of the month he was lounging about in pyjamas all day feeling limp, and even sea-bathing made them feel hotter afterwards. Yet he felt he ought to do something after finishing the essays, and picked up the unfinished manuscript of *Aaron's Rod* again in the first fortnight of July.[112] But in mid-month the days became 'too hot to do anything, save at morning and evening' (iii. 570) – other than lounge the time away, barefoot, and sometimes not even in pyjamas. 'We do our own work – I prefer it, cant stand people about: so when the floors must be washed (gently washed merely) or when I must put my suit of pyjamas in the tub, behold me *in puris naturalibus*, performing the menial labours of the day. It is very nice to shed so much ...' (iii. 573)[113] – but not conducive to novel writing. Almost as soon as he had started, he knew that he would not get far. It felt like a motor car, he said, that has spasms and stops; so you 'poke its vitals and proceed 100 yards – then all u.p. ... In this climate one's very psyche is like a jelly that won't set ... ' (iii. 567). Soon there was no more talk of the book.

He may possibly however have started to write poetry again. Syracuse lay in malarial country and their hotel wall had been dotted all over with bloody marks, a sinister sight for a traveller. The letters show that mosquito netting then became one of the useful things to carry about. He would later label his splendid 'beast' poem 'Siracusa', though that might well refer (again) to memorable experience of Monsieur Mosquito, rather than to a precise date and place of composition. This sustained denunciation could be thought of as an African praise-song, in reverse maybe, yet equally seeking to address the essence of an extra-human power. ('Snake' is also a praise-song – if too late and to a god denied – but though it is set on a broiling Sicilian day in July with Lawrence in pyjamas, fetching water from the cistern, it too may well have been written later, perhaps after he had borrowed from Juta a collection of San – miscalled 'Bushman' – artistry and folklore).[114]

Mainly, however, the heat began to encourage thoughts of escape. Even Mary was planning to leave now. At the end of June Lawrence heard that Mackenzie, back in England, had actually found a yacht that he thought ideal for the South Seas, an 84 foot 154 ton ketch called 'Lavengro'. (Monty apparently thought this 'most appropriate' since, even with his resources, it would have to be by Borrow.) Lawrence was very excited. It so happened that Mountsier – with whom he had shared his and Mackenzie's dreams only to find that Mountsier already had them – chose this moment to send him three books about the Marquesas. Lawrence thought Frederic O'Brien's *White Shadows in the South Seas* (1919) 'wonderful' (iii. 567), though it nearly broke his heart to discover what had become of Melville's Typee. Gauguin's *Noa Noa* (1900) however seemed 'a bit snivelling' and his mythology 'pathetic'; and Somerset Maugham's *The Moon and Sixpence* (1919) based on Gauguin in Tahiti 'not bad, but forcé' (iii. 566–7) – yet the coincidence really stirred his imagination. Perhaps 'Lavengro' was a real opportunity. He demanded news from Monty, and a book

33 Lady Ottoline Morrell

34 Bertrand Russell, 1916 (by Hugh Cecil)

35 E. M. Forster

36 Dollie Radford

37 Philip Heseltine, 1915

38 Juliette Baillot

39 Minnie Lucie ('Puma') Channing

40 Hilda Doolittle Aldington ('H. D.'), 1913

41 Richard Aldington, late 1917

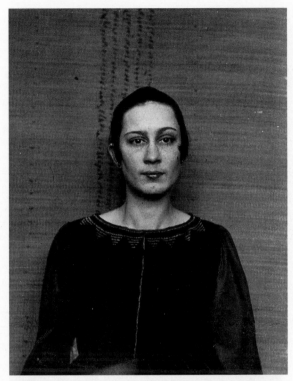

42 Dorothy ('Arabella') Yorke, 1917

43 Cecil Gray

44 William Henry Hocking

45 Higher Tregerthen, Zennor, Cornwall

46 Mountain Cottage, Middleton-by-Wirksworth, Derbyshire

47 Esther Andrews – a stage pose

48 Robert Mountsier

49 Rosalind Thornycroft Baynes
(by E. C. Beresford)

50 Montague Compton
Mackenzie, 1915

51 Emily King with Margaret ('Peggy')

52 Ada Clarke with Jack

53 Douglas Goldring

54 Cecily Lambert and
Violet Monk at Grimsbury
Farm, Hermitage, near
Newbury, Berkshire

55 Francis Brett Young (from a portrait by Cathleen Mann)

56 Jessica Brett Young, 1914

57 Jan Juta, *c.* 1921

58 Maurice Magnus

59 Fontana Vecchia, Taormina, Sicily

60 Marie Hubrecht (who once owned it)

61 From the balcony, Fontana Vecchia

62 Earl and Achsah Brewster, and
Harwood, in Capri, *c.* 1922

300.

and the immemorial darkness, whereof ~~life's~~ life's eternity
would blossom and fall away again,
~~had~~ flashed ~~and~~ and disappeared, re-echoed ~~towards~~ peace
and profound, immemorial silence.

Away from ~~time~~ ~~life~~, always ~~away from~~ ~~life~~ outside of time. Between east
and west, between dawn and sunset, the ~~great~~ church
lay like a seed in silence, dark before germination, ~~since~~ after death, containing birth, and
~~made the births of darkness~~ ~~Between birth and death,~~
death, potential with all the noise and transitation of life, the cathedral remained hushed
~~through all the sounding horizon of life~~, the cathedral
a great, involved seed whereof the flower ~~this~~ radiant life uncomplicated, but whose beginning and
spanned ~~like~~ a dark rainbow, ~~that~~ ~~hushing~~ silence to
whose end lay in the two extremes of silence. Like a shadowy rainbow, the jewelled gloom spanned from silence
to silence, darkness to darkness, fecundity to fecundity,
as a seed spans from life to life and death to death, containing the secret of all folded between its ~~silence~~
~~Was not life the great splash in the pool where~~
~~eddies eddied out and were lost. And the silence, and~~
the darkness, and the fecund ~~immobility~~ sleep stepped from
~~ripple to ripple, and let linked up~~ stepped on from the eternity behind
~~with~~ the eternity in front; silence ~~and~~ to silence, darkness
of death ~~to~~ darkness that preceeds ~~conception~~ birth, ~~silence~~ hush of
after-life ~~to~~ ~~silence~~ hush of before life, ~~fecundity of death~~ ~~hush of darkness~~
fecund ~~unborn~~ life.
So, silence folding on silence, death upon ~~life~~ what shall be.
~~He had escaped~~, and time ~~was~~ obliterated, even eternity
made meaningless, Brangwen was set free. There was no before and after. All was.)
~~eternity~~. Here, all was immemorial ecstasy. From ecstasy
through ecstasy to ecstasy, on, on to the final ~~mystery~~
it was all here, in One.
the ecstasy of ecstasies. Out of the doors of the womb he had
come, putting aside the ~~portals~~ wings of the womb and proceeding
into the light. Through daylight and day-after-day he
had come, knowledge after knowledge and experience after
remembering the darkness of the womb, having prescience of the darkness after death
experience. Then ~~again~~ eternity he had pushed open the doors of
the cathedral, and entered the ~~gloom~~ twilight of both darknesses, the hush
of the two-fold silence, where dawn was sunset, and the beginning and the end were one.

full of nautical information to clue himself up and make him 'sea-born' (iii. 562). He would pray that all would go well, not to Jesus 'because I believe Jesus is no good at sea', but to 'Aphrodite and Poseidon and Dionysos'.

Unfortunately it seems they were no better, since no word came. (Mackenzie was busy with his mother's plan to take over a theatre in Nottingham as a vehicle for her daughters. He even thought of producing a Lawrence play there, but nothing came of that, either.) Lawrence grew sceptical that Monty would ever leave Britain, and rightly so. For when news did arrive, it was that Mackenzie had secured the lease of two of the Channel Isles instead, and was to become laird of Herm and Jethou (iii. 594).[115] The South Seas vanished from his horizon, though not from Lawrence's.

Instead he made plans for a holiday in August and September closer at hand in a cooler Italy, though he was reluctant in some ways to go north rather than south. Frieda was determined to go to Germany – but, again, Lawrence had no intention of going with her, taking advantage of her family's opinion that he might still meet with some hostility there. Yet August in Taormina might be too oppressive. At the end of July came a misleading spattering of rain (iii. 581) and the sky filled with thunderclouds, but the weather did not break and the dryness 'seems to parch one's soul' (iii. 580). Political storms seemed to be brewing too, in Italy and elsewhere, though he was careless about those – Europe might erupt as it liked. His plans took shape: he and Frieda would spend about ten days with Juta who now had a house in Anticoli in the hills outside Rome, and perhaps take in Montecassino. Then he would accompany her as far as Milan, where she would go on to Baden-Baden to see her mother, and he would meet the Whittleys for a walking tour around the Italian lakes. He had corresponded with Irene and her mother Mrs Short from time to time, and now, by happy chance, Irene and Percy thought of coming to Italy for their holiday. They were the sort of people he could bear to go with on the kind of excursion he loved, but which Frieda was never likely to make again. A very practical excitement rose in him as he suggested going from Lake Como to Lake Iseo and Garda, keeping on the Italian side of the border, and then on to Venice by way of Verona.

We should have to be economical. We'd travel 3rd. Class for short journeys: that's cheap. We'd carry a spirit kettle and little saucepan, and a raincoat: fun it would be ... Bring as little as you can make convenient – one nice dress for town, one knock about. In Venice I'll try and get rooms, not an hotel or pension so that we can make our own breakfasts and lunch – and only get dinner out.

It will be awfully jolly – (iii. 569)

He asked Rosalind Baynes (iii. 575) and Juta about rooms in Venice that would suit one who (on his own), was 'a gnat of economy' (iii. 568). He wanted to see Rosalind, too.

It only remained to tie up odds and ends of business.[116] On 2 August they were off, and just as they were leaving, the first batch of galleys of *Women in Love* arrived from Seltzer. At long last, the novel really was coming out. A good omen.

◆

CHAPTER ELEVEN

August 1920–September 1921

ON THE MOVE

Comes over one an absolute necessity to move.
(*Sea and Sardinia*, chap. 1)

I Becoming 'unstuck'

With a stop to let Frieda see Montecassino[1] (and to buy a cap for his new baby
niece Joan King; iii. 583), they went on to Rome to join Juta and Insole; and,
after a few days sightseeing, were taken by car to their friends' new base at
Anticoli-Corrado (now incorporated into Fiuggi) in the foothills of the Abruzzi.
Lawrence had found the train journey hellish, but in the hills it was cooler. 'San
Filippo' was a pleasant house with trees, a courtyard and a large fountain where
other painters came by to bathe nude. Alan Insole was Welsh, well-off and took
his art less seriously than Juta though neither depended on their work for their
living. Lawrence catches the air of privilege with amused affection in a later
meeting at Rome station, as they descend 'vaguely from a carriage, the one
[Insole] gazing inquiringly through his monocle across the tram-lines, the other
very tall and alert and elegant, looking as if he expected us to appear out of the
air for his convenience'.[2] The relationship of the two was close, but also had its
strains. Insole was interested in getting about rather than standing in front of an
easel all the time, but Juta became somewhat grumpy when pulled away. Insole
could be jealous, too. The tall Juta was attractive to women in ways that
Lawrence again regarded with amusement as well as affection: 'As for the
American ladyette, all is vanity, on your part. If you weren't a beau garçon, and
if you didn't know it, and if you didn't so *enjoy* being sweet and complaisant like
anything, why, they'd never love you. But just wire her "Enough of this slop-
doodle"' (iii. 567). As his affair with Elizabeth Humes (a secretary in the
American Embassy) went deeper, however, he and Insole found themselves 'not
agreeing very well, like a married couple' (iii. 624), and Insole took off to Tunis
– but that lay ahead, and they were amusing company for the week the
Lawrences stayed. A letter came from Rosalind Baynes, and though she would
be holidaying in the Apennines when they came through, they would see her on
the way back, in the rambling villa she had found in San Gervasio.

On 12 August he and Frieda set off northwards again, breaking the journey in

Florence before arriving in Milan on the 16th. There Frieda left for Baden-Baden; and Percy and Irene Whittley arrived to begin their holiday with Lawrence.

He had liked them from the early days in Zennor when they had helped get her father's cottages ready, and their time together now was a great success. The banker and the schoolteacher must have made intelligent but not quarrelsome company since they seem never to have fallen out over education or anything else. They had come readily on the kind of holiday that Lawrence loved, and his greater command of Italian made it natural that he should take the lead – so all was propitious, especially since they found Lake Como so attractive. Indeed they seem to have given up the original plan of walking the southern tips of three lakes to Verona, and lingered for most of their time around Como. What Lawrence remembered most fondly was Argegno half way up the lake (iii. 591), and they may have taken several excursions by lake steamer. Once it poured with rain, but far from spoiling anything this was welcome after Sicily in July, and later he remembered it all as fun. He had told Rosalind that he felt 'all unstuck,' already, 'as if I might drift off anywhere' (iii. 585), and part of the joy of these days may have been just the drifting wherever they liked, careless of plans.

By the evening of 25 August they were in Venice. Getting there while the Whittleys had still a week to spend may have been their idea, but Lawrence felt easy: 'I may stay here a month – or only a week' (iii. 589). There was no word yet from Frieda, but he found Venice 'lovely'; and besides, some proofs of *The Lost Girl* had been forwarded from Anticoli (iii. 588). When he had finished these however,[3] the imminent departure of the Whittleys made him feel melancholic. (Characteristically, this appeared as a judgement of Venice, still lovely to look at, but smelly, and 'melancholic with its dreary bygone lagoons', iii. 590.) He decided not to wait until they actually left, still less linger on till Frieda came. He would go to Florence and wait for her there. He took a crowded late-night train on 1 September and had to spend the journey in the corridor; but that was not what he dwelt on as he let the Whittleys know he had arrived: 'am *so sorry* our picnic à trois is all over: wish you were here ... feel quite lost, by myself, quite outside everything. What a curse you aren't free to do as you like' (iii. 591).

He went first to a pensione run by an English Miss Georgina Godkins and her sister, next door to the British Institute,[4] but he had lost the address, and stopping by Pino Orioli's bookshop to get it, was misdirected. This turned out to be an omen, for he could stand only one night there: 'too intimate' he said, 'old ladies etc.' (iii. 592). He would have to find somewhere else. Luckily an ideal solution presented itself as soon as he discovered Rosalind was back but not in Villa Canovaia – for all its windows had been blown out by an explosion at a nearby ammunition dump, and she and the children had moved to Fiesole. The rambling old villa in San Gervasio – eleven rooms and a garden all to himself, except for a gardener and his wife as caretakers – was an ideal place to camp in while the weather was still warm (iii. 592).[5] He had his bedding and his spirit stove, and he could cook and do for himself as he liked best to do. He wished the Whittleys could have joined him, for there was certainly room for three! But it was 'great fun, even alone'; and he was not all that much alone, either, for soon he was offering 'luncheon and tea parties to elegant people, mostly American', and accepting picnic invitations in return. There was one 'gorgeous rich' picnic tea on 8 September, behind Settignano where the Trenches lived – though 'it wasn't fun like our Como days' he hastened to add, when telling Irene about it (iii. 592). Even an earthquake at 8.30 that morning had not shaken his spirits, though he was luckily far from the epicentre, towards Pisa, where 174 people were killed (iii. 592 n. 4).

Of the Florentine expatriates he had known before, Douglas was away with his 'amico' René Mari, but Reggie Turner was back from Capri, albeit 'rather shaky' (iii. 594). Anna di Chiara, a convivial American he had known and liked in Capri was here, 'blooming, and a little ironical about homes and husbands' (hers being away). He had clearly got to know Pino Orioli by now, but does not mention the Marchese and Marchesa de Torrigiani – although she may have been one of the picnickers and, since she was American, it may have been through her that he got to know another 'charming' American Carlota Thrasher, who had lived in Italy for some years (iii. 600).[6] Further out were the Trenches, and Rosalind in Fiesole.

His first letters make his life sound actively social; but what he liked most about Canovaia was once again the ability to get away when he wanted, to 'a garden and a lovely view and air and peace' (iii. 602). There was greenery, and a fountain. The peace of the old rambling villa was all the more welcome because of political disturbances in the city, where tension was fast increasing between the followers of the Red Banner, and the Fascisti and supporters of the monarchy, so that widespread rather than sporadic violence seemed iminent – perhaps even a revolution like the Russian one. A bomb had been thrown in the Via Tuornabuoni in February 1920. Mussolini was beginning to make his bid for power, and there were big processions and counter-processions when the shops would close their shutters for fear. There might be sudden shots, stones thrown into cafés, blood on the pavements. The trams to Fiesole had posters which threatened 'castor oil' to purge the socialists, and even Rosalind's little girls were affected: Bridget getting into trouble when she refused to give the fascist salute in a procession of schoolchildren in the city, before Mussolini himself, and having to be taken away from the village school as a result. Their gardener taught her and Chloë to sing 'The Red Flag', but Nan, the littlest one who had another father and was always different, decided she would be a fascist.[7]

From all this, Villa Canovaia was a haven. Eleanor Farjeon described the thirteenth-century house as:

like a beautiful old picture that is peeling and fading. It stood in a lane behind a high wall, but its terraced garden lay behind it on the hill-side, open to the sunlight. There was a great dim square court with a fountain, stone benches, flowering trees in tubs, and a staircase leading to a deep shady balcony hung with vines.

The garden had persimmon trees, and roses, with weeds and flowers rambling everywhere, a haven for lizards, cicadas and fireflies as well as for Lawrence and some tortoises.

It was a good place to work. He wrote and sent off to Mountsier a preface for the book on American literature which he entitled 'America, Listen to Your Own' (iii. 591 and n. 3). The *Corriere della Sera* had made sniffy fun of how, because of the lack of 'tradition' and 'culture-history' in America, a group of touring Americans, grandly titled the 'Knights of Columbus' had found themselves quite 'overcome with admiration' in Italy. This might have been less true of Lawrence's American woman-friends in Florence, all of whom had lived in Italy for many years. But if they too went on and on about European and especially Italian art and architecture, that would have made Lawrence's point even stronger. For he had come to see America as the future, which can only come about by freeing itself from the past. Each new wave of becoming (says the author of *Movements*) was sniffed at as barbarian by some older culture, which then had to be walked past, or over, to make way for the next kind of beauty. So Americans must turn to their own 'dark, aboriginal continent', and to the 'America' inside themselves which as 'Europeans' they have rejected and almost annihilated: the spirit in the Forest which the Pilgrim Fathers abhorred as the Devil or 'the black Demon', but Hawthorne began to explore; and the Red Man who was also within James Fenimore Cooper. They must 'catch the pulse of the life which Cortes and Columbus murdered', which Aztecs, Mayas and Incas once knew, and which can still be found in the American spirit of place and hence in Americans.[8]

That might not go down too well in Boston – but there were signs that America was beginning to listen to Lawrence, though not uncritically. He heard that Amy Lowell might have a tilt at the preface to the *New Poems* he had dedicated to her, and had written a review of *Touch and Go* (iii. 593). Louis Untermeyer (who had sent that very welcome cheque as a mark of esteem the previous January) now sent an intense piece he had written in *The New Republic*.[9] There was much to please Lawrence in it: the praise of *The Rainbow* as 'possibly the most poetic and poignant novel of this decade'; the recognition of 'rousedness of physical sensation' as central to his work; and the understanding (even before the appearance of *Women in Love*) of the orbiting stars as central to *Look!* What cannot have pleased him was Untermeyer's emphasis on the constant failure of the aspiration to fulfilment, so that Lawrence becomes the poet of a 'dream' which 'will not merge into reality'; and of frustration, or 'despairing wish-fulfilment'; either losing himself 'among his own fantasies', or 'self-crucified on a cross of flesh' – a powerfully suggestive phrase. Lawrence supposed it might be true, 'But always remember I prefer my strife, infinitely, to other people's peace, havens, and heavens. God deliver me from the peace of this world. As for the peace beyond understanding, I find it in conflict' (iii. 595). Yet Untermeyer's was a sensitive response that probed deep enough to stay in his mind.

He dealt with proofs of 'The Fox' with some acidity, since he had supposed the story had come out long ago, long enough for him to have forgotten the name of the magazine (iii. 596–7). He agreed to let Secker finish the proof correction of *The Lost Girl* in the office, from the revised carbon typescript (iii. 599–600). It was clear now that there would be no serialisation anywhere, and Secker would need to hurry if he was to publish in November. His new novel, he told Mackenzie,[10] only 'jerks one chapter forward now and then' (iii. 594). It was half done, but now he put it aside again. For what came out of La Canovaia instead was a stream of poetry – including some of the best he had ever written.

II   Rosalind

One reason for this has only recently come to light. Lawrence had always been markedly fond of Rosalind and cared about her welfare. He had worried about her staying in the same pensione as Douglas, lest some scandal of his should frighten her. She and the children had not moved far from La Canovaia, only up the hill to Fiesole. There he could easily visit them 'climbing by a steep track up through the olives and along under the remains of Fiesole's Etruscan walls, and arriving rather jauntily, carrying something peculiar and humorous – a salamander or a little baby duck as a pet for the children', and staying for dinner, or to cook them an English Sunday roast. So much she told Edward Nehls. But a private memoir, now published by her daughter Chloë, reveals how the relationship changed. Rosalind describes how, after a modest supper of mortadella and marsala on Thursday 9 September, two days before Lawrence's thirty-fifth birthday they walked 'out beyond the cypress woods where there were the scents from thyme and marjoram, and the nightjar bird noises of the hillside'.[11] They talked, a little edgily.

Then he switched away and said:

'How do you feel about yourself now without sex in your life?'

I said I wanted it of course.

'Well, why don't you have it?' says he.

'Yes, why not? But one is so damned fastidious.'

'Yes, damned fastidious! Yes, most people one can hardly bear to come near, far less make love with', says he.

'Yes', say I, 'and it's no good just making love; there must be more to it than a few pretty words and then off to bed.'

'Yes there must be more in it than that, but God save us from the so-called Love – that most indecent kind of egoism and self-spreading. Let us think of love as a force outside and getting us. It is a force; a god ...'

He did not see any reason why they should not have each other. Or was it too complicated?

This was all very off-hand and I liked that. I can't answer for a while. I am so astounded at my happiness.

'Yes, indeed I want it.' I say at last.

Firenze and her lights twirled around and I felt off the world. He so wonderful; my source of acceptable and exciting wisdom of a kind unheard of until he came. I said:

'I had no idea you thought about me so.'

He laughed. Heavens, had I instantly disappointed him? Was it, as I feared, a laugh of 'Oh, they're all alike', plunging into personal slop for all her professions of something better, determined to make *conscious* the unconscious? I told him I guessed what he was thinking of me, but then went on somehow:

'... but nevertheless how do you account for the fastidiousness we have been talking about if there is no personalism in love?'

'Oh yes,' says he 'there must be understanding of the god *together*.'

We were silent again. I pulled up the bramble plant.

'Che forza' says he. 'Let's go back.'

We stumble back over the stones in the darkness.

'Tonight you won't have me?'

'No,' though I longed to dash into his arms.

In half an hour we are home, laughing on the way; and in the bright, ugly little hall passage we embrace and kiss our promise. Then he went off down the hill to San Gervasio.

The next day I spent in the greatest elation, and the next day Saturday he came again. Was this our day? But no. I tidied everything in my room to make it sweet for him; but not then. Sunday he came to lunch. We made the dinner together, quite an English Sunday one, beef and batter; and everything was fun. He laughed and played with my Nan and understood her – as he did with children – with delicate, amused perception. We walked out after the heat was over, up behind Fiesole town through the trees and passing the Sunday strollers. Italian girls in fluffy voile dresses along the country roads. We saw the black grapes – 'black to make you stare'. We saw the grand turkey cock (see poems). The spirit of America as it was in the Indian primitive America to which European America was inevitably trending. Place Psyches ... We come down the long rather squalid village street. Sorb apples we buy – 'Suck them and then spit out the skin!' – and home with things to cook for our supper on the terrace, three hundred feet above Firenze.

'How good it is here. It is something quite special and lovely, the time, the place, the beloved.'

My heart jumps with joy. We sit there until it is quite dark, our hands held together in union. And so to bed.

It is striking how careful they are of each other, 'fastidious' about not rushing until sure of meaning what they do, therefore non-exploitative, and yet joyous. Rosalind is no mere acolyte despite her echoing of his ideas (including those of his latest essay). The question she asks on the Thursday is the pertinent and right one, and his answer a fudge, since her personality so clearly entered into his feeling for her, and his behaviour now. Was he perhaps too careful – not passionately impulsive enough, for an advocate of the 'blood'? Yet his carefulness shows how he would also have been with Esther, if it ever came to that – unlikely to have been carried away by an impulse of the moment. He had refused to leap into bed on Frieda's first invitation too. His wife had claimed her freedom several times; but in the manner of taking his, he shows that he is still serious enough about marriage not to breach it casually. And though this would not be as impulsive as one of Frieda's affairs, it would also mean more. Rosalind is clear that the poems that came out of the experience expressed its meaning for him, as her secret preservation of the joy of it did for her. As for all the speculation about him – she does not sound as though she had found him impotent or frustrating as a lover.

Life does affect art, though not simply. It is not fanciful to have a new sense, now, of the exultant and defiant tone and sexiness of the 'fruit' poems he wrote at La Canovaia in the next few days. These notes were always there, yet we can now hear them anew in their own time, whatever we make of them where the poems have to achieve existence for us, in ours. What was in the poet's mind as he wrote is only part of what the poem can be; and the poems have got along very well for seventy years on their own. Yet all the poems dated from 'San Gervasio' and 'Fiesole' can reveal a new, secret life and significance of language.[12] He sent several of the 'Fruits' to Mountsier on 15 September, saying 'don't be scared by them' (iii. 596); and suggested that they be offered to the *New Republic* from whose editorial department (even before Untermeyer's letter) he had received a request for poetry (iii. 596 and n. 2). Another poem was posted the following day (iii. 597). This was probably the Orphic 'Medlars and Sorb-Apples', if only because that seems later, with its sense of the taste whose sweetness has already the foretaste of bitterness and decay:

A kiss, and a vivid spasm of farewell, a moment's orgasm of rupture
Then along the damp road alone, till the next turning.
And there, another parting, a new partner, a new unfusing into twain,
A new gasp, of isolation, intense,
A new pungency of loneliness, among the decaying, frost-cold leaves;
Going down the road, more alone after each meeting,
The fibres of the heart parting one after the other,
And yet the soul continuing, naked-footed, ever more vividly embodied
Ever more exquisite, distilled in separation.[13]

Perhaps there is more irony, too, in Untermeyer's having made Lawrence the poet of frustration, and more resonance in his own defiant acceptance of conflict. For although he could not regret what he had fastidiously and deliberately chosen, it would have an undeniable awkwardness for both Rosalind and himself if it developed. Yet he must have had conflicting feelings about that, too. It would hurt them both if he ran away, and possibly make her feel used. On the other hand was he, having worried about her being frightened by Douglas gossip, to risk adding fuel himself to the certain scandal of her coming divorce hearing? The expatriate community even in Florence was small enough for gossip to spread quickly. Or again, as in 'Medlars and Sorb-Apples', he may have felt most what the poem declares the hellish yet 'exquisite fragrance of farewell ... The secret of Orpheus and Hades' in which each soul departs 'in its own essence,/ Never having known its own essence before'.[14]

He began to haver. On the 17th he wrote an odd letter to John Ellington Brooks, saying that he didn't want to hang about in Florence waiting for Frieda much longer, and was it possible to share Brooks's house sitting of Casa Solitaria for a fortnight or so (iii. 599)? This was however a little like St Augustine's 'Lord make me chaste, but not yet', since he did not propose to come for another week or more. But the very next day the problem was solved for him – for a letter arrived from Frieda. She wanted him to come to Baden-Baden which she probably knew he would refuse; but she suggested as alternative that they should meet with Juta and Insole in Venice on the 28th. He wrote an apology to Frieda's mother, pleading that it was too late in the year to come north now (iii. 601). He would come next spring (when their lease of Fontana Vecchia would be up) – but to Venice he would go.[15]

There is no sign of how often or on what terms he saw Rosalind in the two weeks between their going to bed and his going back to his wife.[16] There is however an extraordinary account of what it is to be imbued with the most new-born being-alone; and to be driven by desire; and also 'crucified in the flesh' (Untermeyer's term) between the two. This is displaced and transformed with extraordinary observation and great humour – but also (one can see now) with nicely adjusted fellow-feeling *and* self-distancing – in six poems about the tortoise family in the garden of La Canovaia. It is not that the poems about tortoises are really poems about Lawrence; but something far more interesting, and more extraordinary. The 'life' of these poems required two conditions: exact observation and perception of tortoises and their sexuality, and the exclusion of what on that evening with Rosalind he had called 'self-spreading'. And yet the humour comes from the relationship between the man observing from his point of view, and the beasts intent on their non-human life, a relation that is both gulf and imaginative affinity. He wrote later of Van Gogh's most famous painting that its value lay neither in the rendering of sunflowers, nor in the rendering of the painter's feelings, but in the 'perfected relation, at a certain moment, between a man and a sunflower' or more grandly between 'man and his circumambient universe'.[17] If one may feel, reading the poems, the essence as it were of tortoiseness caught there, that is because Lawrence so firmly kept his eye on the beasts and not on himself. And yet he saw with the sensibility he spontaneously brought to bear, and *that* had a great deal to do with the comedy and tragedy of sexuality he had just re-experienced for himself, and which made for the tone that is also all important in the poems. They are unanthropomorphic in one sense; and yet only the-man-Lawrence could have created that life, in his human language, just then. Being 'crucified in the flesh' is an idea, but the crosses on the tortoise-shell are *there*, as is the male tortoise's soundless orgasmic cry. Moreover the 'relation at a certain moment' also implies, for both man and circumambulant beast, an unrelated and quite distinct being, *outside* the poems. Art can never be biography, nor biography explain any work of art. Yet biography can perhaps help critics attend to what the thoughtful poet – for Lawrence, 'a man in his wholeness, wholly attending'[18] – brought to the tortoises, at that moment, though it is the critic who must discover in its own detail what each poem then does, and what they do together.

Biography, however, should make one further point: how the *sequence* of poems delicately, subtly, and extraordinarily balances the feelings of the man who had deliberately turned away from love and its dependency, determined to stand alone – but who now must know, fully, the fused ecstasy and torture of having succumbed again. The tiny baby tortoise, alone without knowing it, is a living embodiment of what the 'new' Lawrence said he wanted to be, a self-single 'Invincible fore-runner'. Embedded *in* the shell, however is the inescapable sign of the cross. And in 'Family Connections' and 'Lui et Elle' there is the certainty that the baby tortoise's arrogance of being 'all to himself' will be overcome by the imperative needs of sexual connection: the male driven, irritably compelled to persist, 'Doomed to make an intolerable fool of himself', forced continually to run after, snap at, pester, a female much bigger than he is – wicked comedy! Finally however, the full paradox of the opposite desires – the longing for singleness, the longing for completion – is brought out in the orgasmic and crucified 'Tortoise Shout': the cry that is both paean and agony, death and birth, triumph and submission, self-laceration, abandonment and fulfilment.

> Sex, which breaks up our integrity, our single inviolability, our deep silence,
> Tearing a cry from us.
> Sex, which breaks us into voice, sets us calling across the deeps, calling, calling
> for the complement ...
>
> Torn, to become whole again, after long seeking for what is lost,
> The same cry from the tortoise as from Christ, the Osiris-cry of abandonment,
> That which is whole, torn asunder,
> That which is in part, finding its whole again throughout the universe.[19]

He left for Venice on 28 September. Carlota Thrasher had offered to let him have, rent-free, her 70-acre farm near the village of Westminster, Connecticut, four hours from New York, if he would live there and begin to rescue it from the neglect it had fallen into, having been unoccupied since before the war (iii. 605). After Grimsbury Farm he knew what this might mean, and how much energy it might require, though of course he would not need or expect to make a living from farming. It was on the Yankee side of America, too, which he distrusted – but he went to Venice thinking about it, and wrote for Mountsier's advice when he arrived. He also sent him the Tortoise poems.

Frieda did not in fact come until 7 October (iii. 609) – writing, said Lawrence's postcard to Rosalind, 'tiresomely from Germany' (iii. 604), though the tiresomeness seems to have been about her passport. Insole and Juta had hired a gondola for a month, so he could spend days with them lounging on the water, but he soon began to be 'sick of mouching about' (iii. 607). He wanted to get back to Taormina, spit on his hands and get on with his recalcitrant novel. Also 'Italy feels awfully shaky and nasty, and for the first time my unconscious is uneasy of the Italians' (iii. 609), whereas he thought Sicily might be safer. Still, he told Rosalind, the view from the deserted Lido was 'quite lovely now, with tall clouds advancing over the sea, and many burnt sails. I take my lunch and sit and watch from the sand hills, and bathe ... Wonder where we'll meet next' (iii. 609). The tone is carefully neutral – as hers was to be.

III Back in Taormina

When Frieda finally arrived they spent just a week more of holiday there for her, and started for Sicily on 14 October. (If they broke the journey in Florence they did not visit Rosalind.) By the 18th they were back in Fontana Vecchia, after a tedious 'struggle of a journey' (iii. 612).[20]

What struck Lawrence most, after the Italian cities, was the quiet, and the huge change from when they had left in August. Not only had it poured while they were away, but rain set in steadily now, and kept on for nearly two months. 'We sit and see the rain come straight down, silent, isolated, strange, after so much knocking about: clean, and far off it feels here – so far off' (iii. 615). It was astonishingly green, and flowers were coming out: roses, creepers and rose cyclamens about which he wrote another poem (iii. 616). The sea was yellow with earth coming down from the hills, and the stream in the valley 'impassable' – but he liked the isolation, in a house now 'still and remote and sweet scented' (iii. 619). For three weeks they sought out nobody and had only one visitor.

Frieda had come back from Germany 'flourishing' (iii. 610) and 'very chirpy' (iii. 616). As well as being with her mother she had visited Else Jaffe in Munich, and enthused about 'peasant drama and marionettes and return to innocent bare-footed dance under heaven' (iii. 594) – a 'sentimental naïveté' her husband commented sardonically, though it was a little more than that.[21] (She had also noted the increasing bad feeling against the French in the aftermath of the Treaty of Versailles.) She had '*loved* it' in her homeland and extracted a half-promise, now, that he would go back with her in the spring. As far as she was concerned, 'We are glad to be together again' (iii. 615).

He had wanted to get down to serious work, and began by 'correcting proofs like an angel, and washing my clothes betweenwhiles' (iii. 615). The proofs were the full set of Seltzer's *Women in Love*, proving it really would be out soon (iii. 613). Some first proofs of Secker's English version (intended for February) also arrived (iii. 617). He had hoped to finish *Aaron's Rod* by Christmas, perhaps getting past the blockage by trying to 'sort of jump him picaresque' (iii. 602). Secker was trying to get *The Lost Girl* out on 1 November and an advance copy arrived on 25 October: 'nice sober lady she looks, weighty and to be taken seriously, poor darling' (iii. 617). There had arrived in Florence an offer from Dr Anton Kippenberg of Insel-Verlag to publish him in German translation, fruit of Goldring's visit to Germany, and another mark of being taken seriously (iii. 597–8). Oxford University Press had promised final proofs of the history-book at long last (iii. 612); and John Lane offered £150 for a little book on Venice, alas just months too late (iii. 615). Things seemed to be improving.

However, pretty nearly everything then went wrong. At the end of October came an urgent appeal from Secker. He had bound about ninety advance copies of *The Lost Girl*, partly for reviewers, but especially to send out to the main circulating libraries on whom the commercial success of the book would depend. Alas, the response of the three biggest, Smith's, Mudie's and Boot's, threatened disaster: they would not circulate the book unless changes were made. Particular exception was taken to the scene in which Ciccio takes Alvina in her mother's bedroom (see above p. 576). Secker begged Lawrence to rewrite the passage: 'After all these three libraries should account between them for some 2,000 copies, possibly more' (iii. 621 n. 1). Since Lawrence was no less anxious that the book should make money he not only made no difficulty but rewrote at once, and rather cleverly, at exactly the required length. However Secker did not get the new page until 9 November, and publication had to be delayed for another sixteen days after that, while he tipped-in pages to the copies already bound – and quietly made two additional cuts without telling Lawrence what he was doing.[22] He finally published on 25 November.

Lawrence, for his part, was rather taken aback by the way that his chapters of *Women in Love* had been broken up into smaller pieces. (The thirteen original divisions became thirty-one in the end.) Soon Secker, ever nervous, would be begging him to make some alterations in that book too, to make the goings on in Halliday's flat less nude.[23] Seltzer published his 'private' edition on 9 November without any trouble (yet); but Secker's nervousness infected Lawrence, and as he was finishing the proofs – all 508 pages of them – at the end of November, he began to think it might be better not to send out the English *Women in Love* for review at all: 'I do so hate the critics, they are such poisonous worms, especially for a book like this' (iii. 625).

By then, however, there was terrible news of Magnus. In the first half of November came a brief note from Don Mauro Iguanez at Montecassino. Had Lawrence heard that poor Magnus had committed suicide? Shortly afterwards came a clipping from a Maltese newspaper, adding only that the suicide was by poison, and apparently caused by financial difficulties. Then came an anxious letter from one of the two Maltese with whom they had gone on that motor tour, asking whether Lawrence could advise them how to reclaim money that Magnus had borrowed. He wrote back immediately – in terms we can imagine – and then, dated 22 November, there arrived a long letter with the full story. Magnus had concealed his real situation. He had persuaded one of the two to stand as the financial surety the law required if he were to stay longer than three months. From the other he had borrowed £55 as well as furniture for his little house; and both had gone to a good deal of trouble over a scheme for the three of them to go into business in Morocco. When however, Michael Borg began to doubt Magnus's ability to repay his debt – only in October, for they had taken him to be 'a perfect gentleman' and were slow to think otherwise – he advised Walter Salomone (the 'Salonia' of Lawrence's *Memoir*) to be careful, since Magnus also owed a £10 grocer's bill, and possibly others too. Taking alarm, Salomone withdrew his surety 'for family reasons'; whereupon Magnus 'in his resourceful way' wrote directly to the police, asking only for a three weeks' extension, since he would be leaving the island shortly. (Salomone was to find him a passage on a tramp steamer to Gibraltar.) But no reply came, and on 4 November he was stopped in the street by two detectives, and asked to accompany them to settle the matter of the surety. Magnus however suspected, probably rightly, that the fraudulent cheque at Anzio had finally caught up with him, and that he was facing arrest and extradition. He asked permission to change out of his sandals and casual clothes – but once inside his house he locked the door and dashed off a brief note to Don Mauro which he persuaded (through the back window) a boy in the street to post for him. 'I leave it to you and [Michael Borg] to arange my affairs. I cannot live any longer. Pray for me.' He dressed in his white suit, lay on his bed, and swallowed hydrocyanic acid (which he must have been keeping ready for such an emergency). By the time the detectives became suspicious and broke in, it was too late to do more than fetch a priest to administer extreme unction. Initially his Maltese friends had to pay for the 'first class' funeral requested by the 'will' found on his desk, though his wife, who had refused to do so, later relented and refunded the money. He named Norman Douglas as his literary executor, who was to take half of any profits from his writings, the rest to go towards his debts. He had clearly long decided that he would prefer death to disgrace and prepared accordingly. He was 44.[24]

Lawrence would write, a year later, that when he read Don Mauro's letter 'the world seemed to stand still for me'. He had washed his hands of Magnus – yet he could not but feel that he might have saved him, however reason might demur that any help he could have given could only, like that of the Maltese, have amounted to postponement. (Magnus seems never to have told anybody how much he had owed at Anzio, and whether that was the only reason for police interest in him.) And how *were* the Maltese to be repaid? Once again Lawrence felt somehow responsible by association, though it had not been he but a letter from Don Mauro that had introduced Magnus to them. He wrote to Douglas at Menton. Most of all it came home to him 'what it must have meant' to be 'a hunted, desperate man'.[25]

Beside this, his own irritations were small – yet they continued to mount. When the long-delayed final proofs of the history-book arrived – the book he had finished in February 1919 and proof-read nearly a year later in January 1920 – there came with them a request for an additional chapter on the unification of Italy. So he had to get down to 'swotting' (iii. 622), five books of Italian history, rather than to his novel. The chapter, moreover, could hardly escape the contrast between the idealism of Mazzini, the heroism of Garibaldi and what their struggle had led to in 1920. For what had happened to the religious idealism and the struggle for liberty? All politics (as he had argued in 'Democracy') come down to 'arranging the material conditions of life', and though important, that is not enough to 'save' mankind. We must have liberty, but that will never be enough either if it only provides material things and not 'the inward satisfaction which the deep spirit demands':

And so Italy was made—modern Italy. Fretfulness, irritation, and nothing in life except money: this is what the religious fervour of Garibaldians and Mazzinians works out to—in united, free Italy as in other united, free countries. No wonder liberty so often turns to ashes in the mouth, after being so fair a fruit to contemplate. Man needs more than liberty.[26]

He had further reasons for feeling rather grumpy. It was still raining 'heavens hard' in the third week of November, so it felt like being 'inside an aquarium – all water – and people like crabs and black-grey shrimps creeping on the bottom. Don't like it' (iii. 622–3). There is a hint that Frieda was getting on his nerves, and to his mother-in-law three days later he writes, with thin jocularity, that her daughter 'is, I am sad to say, no better behaved than she should be' (iii. 623). The grumpiness spread to the Taorminese, 'as mean and creeping as ever' (iii. 624). There was growing hostility to foreigners as the rate of exchange shot up in their favour. (It would be 100 to the £1 by Christmas.) On the other hand prices had tripled since the previous year. He began to feel that he must leave. Worst of all, he was by now too unsettled to be able to work on the novel (now named *Aaron's Rod*), which seemed to have stuck absolutely. His letter to Kippenberg had apparently vanished into a void like the proofs he had sent Secker from Venice. And Secker now infuriated Seltzer by sending some copies of *The Lost Girl* to a bookseller in New York – resulting in more telegrams and anger.[27]

As he had done before at moments of stasis, he turned to painting, diverting himself by copying a picture then attributed to Lorenzetti, the *La Tebaide*, of 'thousands of amusing little monks doing things in the *Thebaid*' (iii. 622) – the tract of Egyptian desert where anchorites such as St Anthony settled, in the third and fourth centuries.[28] But even the painting, after initial success, would later prove disappointing.

At last, however, the incessant rain began to clear at the very end of November. On the 29th, the first clear day, they went to a cattle fair on the beach at Letojanni just up the coast;[29] and Lawrence recorded a decision. He had now firmly placed *Aaron's Rod* aside, and had begun 'a comedy' instead, *Mr Noon* (iii. 626). The next day, given 'a rainbow and tramontana wind and blue sea, and Calabria such a blue morning-jewel I could weep' (iii. 629), his spirits began to lift, though there was more rain to come.

He told Amy Lowell that another 'book' of free verse, to be called *Birds, Beasts and Flowers*, would shortly be coming back from the typist (iii. 629) – this time Ruth Wheelock, a secretary in the consulate at Palermo, who had had it since 4 November.[30] On 1 December he sent two poems destined for it to Professor John Metcalf, who had asked for a contribution to a volume celebrating the centenary of the University of Virginia. The first, 'Tropic', whenever written, harks back to the intense heat of Malta when he had felt quite stunned: 'I shouldn't wonder if my skin went black and my eyes went yellow, like a negro's' (iii. 538). The second, 'Slopes of Etna' (later called 'Peace'), recalls his letter to Untermeyer, and expresses a growing pressure of turbulence in a volcanic heart, which, like Etna, 'will know no peace/ Till the mountain bursts' – but whose setting again into rock can be 'peace' only in a manner of speaking. Though he had thought of a title for his next book of poetry, the typescript – which he sent to Mountsier in early December (iii. 634) but which does not survive – must have held far fewer poems than the book we know now. Moreover the two poems sent to Metcalf, along with 'The Revolutionary' already on its way to Mountsier with the 'Evangelistic Beasts,' show that the title was an approximation and disguise. There was only one real bird and one flower so far.[31] What holds poems like 'Cypresses', the 'Evangelistic Beasts' and 'The Revolutionary' in closer relationship with 'Fruits' than can be apparent in the later and bigger anthology, are the tumultuous feelings of secret rebellion and the bursting out of his own 'dark', 'wicked' and royal-beastly self, from September to November 1920.

With the better weather, life brightened up too: 'sun again, blue sea, long mornings, and quite warm. We have suddenly dashed into society' (iii. 636). There were tea-parties and new acquaintances – a 'nice and comic' lady theosophist (Rosalie Bull), a young Baltic Baron who was glum but likable, a married pair of antique dealers. Lawrence found himself cooking not only the Sunday roast but unaccustomed confectionery for '3 tea-parties this week' – and mocking himself for his mistakes: the chocolate cakes he dropped when he burned his fingers; and the 'exquisite rock cakes' he *forgot to put the fat in*!!' (iii. 636–7).[32] Also there was a new hotel to report on to Marie Hubrecht and Mary Cannan. But 'the society is much more broken and unstable than last year' (iii. 640). Frieda was increasing the pressure to spend both summer and autumn (now) in Germany; and Lawrence was not at all sure what to do about Fontana Vecchia when the lease ran out.

On 11 December came ten copies of Seltzer's *Women in Love* (iii. 635). Brought out as a private edition in the hope of escaping prosecution, and relatively expensive at $15, it was much more handsome than Secker's *Lost Girl*, and Lawrence was delighted. He was quite sure that this was his best book, the one he really cared and was '*most* anxious about ... the others I don't fret myself about so much'. In print, suddenly it was 'a real book'. He knew of course that it 'needs a bit of getting used to'; and so was glad Seltzer himself had begun to like it. Indeed, Seltzer's courage in bringing it out – the 'best Christmas present' Lawrence could have – made him 'feel it has made us friends for life'.[33]

The contrast with Secker's fearfulness, and his 'breach of faith' in sending copies (however few) of the English *Lost Girl* to a New York bookseller, was striking. Lawrence now insisted that Secker was to protect Seltzer's investment in *Women in Love* by delaying the English edition until after 1 May; and reminded him that 'any time you are not content with me, I am quite willing to dissolve the agreement between us' (iii. 638).

Everything seemed to confirm that his future lay in America. When the London reviews of *The Lost Girl* came, it was clear that the book would have to sell in spite of rather than because of them – and the Murrys took a public revenge. True, Edward Garnett praised the novel as 'firm in drawing, light and witty in texture, charmingly fresh in style and in atmosphere', but by way of a rude contrast with *The Rainbow* which he had disliked from the start, so there were weeds in the bouquet for Lawrence. The Murrys however were envenomed. Jack wrote the review, but Katherine had laid its foundations. The notes she sent about it are perceptive as well as prejudiced however, for the novel touched her on the raw no less revealingly than the quarrels of the Lawrences had done in Cornwall. Alone among reviewers she sensed some 'dark secret' in the book. She not only reacted in horror to characters she saw as *'mindless'*, indeed 'animals on the prowl'; she judged the book a 'sinning against art' of the same kind as writing about earth-closets. In this, Lawrence might have said, she was responding as a true representative of the 'pale-faces' he was indeed writing against; reacting to something that was there; and revealing something significant about herself:

Am I prejudiced? Be careful! I feel privately as though L. had possessed an animal and fallen under a curse. But I can't say that. All I know is: this is bad and ought not to be allowed. I feel a horror of it – a shrinking. But that's not criticism.

But this is life when one has blasphemed against the spirit of reverence.

Lawrence would presumably have retorted that she was revealing her irreverence for and indeed horror of her own body and the darker self she so vehemently denies; but her response has an honesty in its very excess. Murry's review begins more judiciously, and has a point about Lawrence's language, but becomes more simply abusive:

Alvina and Cicio become for us like grotesque beasts in an aquarium, shut off from our apprehension by the misted glass of an esoteric language, a quack terminology. Life, as Mr. Lawrence shows it to us, is not worth living; it is mysteriously degraded by a corrupt mysticism. Mr Lawrence would have us back in the slime from which we rose.[34]

When this and the Garnett notice arrived, Lawrence must have felt justified in having suggested that *Women in Love* should not be sent out for review. Even the *Observer* and *TLS* notices[35] had made him think Secker should 'insert another incensorable novel' – *Aaron's Rod* or *Mr Noon* – between *Women in Love* and the republication of *The Rainbow* (iii. 638). Indeed such reviews proved far from impotent. Secker's diplomacy with the circulating libraries had paid off to the extent of advance orders of 1,300 copies, which he had hoped to double by the end of the year. But after the first month the sales only reached 2,000; after another month 300 more; and in the next three months only 300 were sold.[36] So the hope that *The Lost Girl* would 'bring her eggs safe to market' was only partially fulfilled – in England (iii. 622).

By now the social jollities had palled again. Both he and Frieda had grown 'already tired' of Sicily, so were '*retiring*' (her pun) into their solitude once more (iii. 642), for a quiet Christmas. The latest notion was to take a trip next year to see whether Sardinia might be 'simpler, not so sophisticated and foreigner-flooded' (iii. 645). On the last day of the year, however, a final annoyance arrived in a letter from Mountsier. He had at last managed to see Huebsch, and get from him the facts about the six works of Lawrence's he had brought out in America, and the nature of the contracts and accounting arrangements in each case. Mountsier's verdict on these was that Huebsch was honest in business, if slow and slipshod – but another anti-Semitic outburst at the beginning of the letter was explained by the sting in its tail: that on the matter of the dispute with Seltzer over *Women in Love*, Huebsch had accused Lawrence of being 'a liar' who 'has shown himself ungrateful' (iii. 643 n.). Though Huebsch could not find the relevant letter, he claimed that Lawrence had told him he was 'sending him direct the manuscript' of the novel. In fact no such letter survives. Two days before Lawrence left England in November 1919, having written to ask whether Seltzer was prepared to withdraw, he had told Huebsch, 'I hope to have the MS. of the novel to send you shortly' (iii. 413). At no time however had he ever suggested that he *had* the manuscript to send – and in Florence had come Seltzer's refusal to relinquish an offer made and accepted in good faith, and the advance of £50 which, Lawrence, short of money, felt he had to take, and told Huebsch he had done so. After further pressure he had offered to repay Seltzer's advance if he would agree to return the manuscript; while still insisting that without such agreement he felt bound to stick to the original offer. Lawrence may have been disingenuous in keeping the request to Seltzer going, through reluctance to offend Huebsch, after the point when he must have been fairly sure that Seltzer would not budge and was himself ready to consider a contract – but a liar he was not. As for gratitude, this was indeed not one of Lawrence's strengths. He had told Mountsier that he did feel grateful to Huebsch 'up to a point' for risking publishing *The Rainbow* at all (iii. 547), though annoyed with him also for bowdlerising without his consent, and for not having kept the book in print. As for the money Huebsch had 'secured' for him, he was genuinely thankful for the cheque from the Untermeyers which came as an unsolicited tribute; but cross about the collection undertaken with Gilbert Cannan, which made him seem an object of charity. The irony of two American publishers fighting over the novel every English publisher had rejected, could hardly have escaped him.

On the whole he was right to tell Mountsier that his letters would prove the facts, so Huebsch had 'dished himself. Enough of him' – but he had also 'had two cringy half-offended letters from Secker about the *Lost Girl* copies' (iii. 643). It was enough to sour his feeling about the whole of 1920, on 'the last day of this unsatisfactory year'. Nevertheless one had to keep one's spirits up. 'It's no use giving in to the multitudes of little swine of this world' (iii. 645).

In fact it had been an outstandingly vivid and creative year, full of stimulating new places and people, and (in the perspective of time and his own judgement) rich with achievement. He had finished *Pyschoanalysis and the Unconscious* and 'Education of the People'; had written *The Lost Girl*, a bit of *Aaron's Rod*, and most (now) of what we have as *Mr Noon*; and he had produced a burst of poetry, some of the best he had ever done. ('Bare Almond Trees' and 'Bare Fig Trees' – the latter embodying what he thought democracy quintessentially ought to be – had been added in December.) He had also done the extra history chapter, and had recast several of the American essays with a new Introduction. *Women in Love* was out at last in America and coming in England, and *The Lost Girl* out in England and coming in America. His financial position was very different indeed from the penury of 1919. (His bank balance in November was only £6/9/0 less than it had been in May, his best for years.)[37]

Of course to one who lived in the moment, the feeling of the moment was all. But it is only, once again, by looking at the *writing* life that always underlay the one the letters and memoirs depict, that one can gauge the extraordinary burst of comic, sardonic and self-exploratory creativity that the last month of 1920 actually held. For between about 29 November and 31 December, averaging a bit more than 3,000 words a day, Lawrence wrote the first nineteen chapters of *Mr Noon*.[38]

IV 'Lucky Noon'

The new fiction began as another smack at 'love' (English provincial variety), finding refuge from the annoyances and upsets of November and December in comedy, even farce – and looking also for a new kind of novel.

There had been a real-life Gilbert Noon, talented in music and mathematics, whom Lawrence had known at the Pupil-Teacher Centre at Ilkeston, and who also went on to teacher training at Nottingham University College and to schoolteaching afterwards. Moreover there was a hint of doubt as to his morals in a final report on him by the Professor of Education. However the connection between the real Gilbert and Lawrence's arch-'spooner' remains obscure; and there was in any case a more dramatic exemplar of what 'spooning' might lead to, in the fate of George Neville. His philandering had led to a hasty marriage, a child three months later and the loss of his teaching post.[39] But comedy must not have too dire results (though Mr Noon does indeed resign). If *The Lost Girl* became an increasingly serious rejection of romantic ideas of love in favour of a darker kind of mutual transformation, the first part of *Mr Noon* is seemingly concerned with no more than sardonic fun, at the expense of both 'love' and 'marriage' in the English provinces.

Beginning about 29 November or a day or two before, Lawrence had probably finished the first 172 notebook pages (chapters I–XII) by 9 December, when he told Mountsier the fiction had come to a 'sudden stop', though he thought it 'may go on soon' (iii. 634). This is the story of how 'spooning' in the Co-op entry after chapel leads to Emmie's assignation with Gilbert Noon in her father's greenhouse; a tumultuous interruption by said father; the girl running away from home and suffering a 'neuralgia of the stomach' which Mr Noon fears might be something else;[40] and a final scene of utter paralysis by her sick-bed, where the triangle of Emmie, Mr Noon and her (forgotten) fiancé threatens indeed to become an eternal one, frozen into everlasting silence. Come to a full stop the story certainly and farcically did.

Lawrence experiments with Fielding's comic epic, which creates not only the distancing of comedy but also a teasing relation between showman–author and 'gentle reader'. All the comic-epic devices are present: pervasive anticlimax, inflated apostrophe, 'heroic' sports, battles with monsters or villains and the learned survey of a tract of knowledge (i.e. 'spooning'); but the eighteenth-century genre always had a more serious purpose also, behind the fun, and used the comic distance and the constant intervention by 'the author', to bring that out. In Fielding moreover, the relationship of the reader with a teasing 'author' is also part of another level of irony, in which readers may find themselves suddenly in the dock instead of on the bench. This certainly happens in *Mr Noon*, in which moreover 'the author' never quite manages Fielding's winning geniality. Something of the irritation of 1920, as well as the alienation from England, gets into the tone even of the first part, much more in the second, and the irony is increasingly subversive, moving toward contempt. Caveat lector.

'Spooning' is love-making (ironic phrase) short of sexual intercourse: a matter of techniques without commitment; of romantic excitements and pleasurings-up-to-a-limit, between girls who are good sports and lads who must not be low or gross. Victorian 'sin' and 'seduction' are no more. 'It doesn't matter what you do—only how you do it.—Isn't that the sincerest of modern maxims?' It doesn't matter, that is, until things go too far and real passions are aroused. The first level of comedy is provincial. Spooning in alleyways in the rain, by ordinary lads and lasses, has its 'sweetness' much inflated by an 'author' who prides himself on expert description – though 'None of your bestial loss of faculties', mark you –

615

and is then deflated by low and farcical consequences.[41] (For Lawrence of course the loss of faculty and oblivion of self in sex was all-important.)

On the next level of irony, spooning has clearly nothing to do, either, with the practical realities of bourgeois marriage, which may have sentiment enough at first, but comes down really to solid prospects and funds. Now the lens expands to take in the whole of society, for both spooning and its sharp distinction from marriage are common to every rank of English society. This is the point of setting off the story of Gilbert, Emmie and Walter George Whiffen the bank-clerk, against the higher-class marriage of the Goddards, the two Fabian Socialists drawn (outwardly) from Willie and Sallie Hopkin. Here are the couple of 'The Overtone' again; and though the treatment shows all the difference between the Lawrence of 1913 and the Lawrence of 1920, the diagnosis of marital limitation in the fictive couple is even more lethal. They are the acme of civilised consciousness – Hampstead in Eastwood – and the best of friends, progressive, tolerant, kind. But Lewie's restless egotism and Patty's unawakened womanhood show, from the beginning, what is missing from this marriage of true minds and upper centres. The comparison works two ways. For a moment, walking with Patty across the fields, Gilbert Noon senses in her the Aphrodite-woman she could have been, and she feels it too. But the farcical episode with the cow then parodies the most powerful scene in *The Rainbow* when Ursula fled from the horses, but with the same significance. Patty is terrified of what is animal, and she has a kind of heart-failure. She has spooned, then married; but 'bestial loss of faculty' – and rebirth – are not for her, any more than for Emmie. Yet Gilbert has seen, in what she might have become, the worthlessness of 'all the Emmies of the world'.[42]

Now the bearing of the new fiction on the Lawrence of December 1920 becomes apparent. For the teasing relation of 'the author' to his 'gentle reader' has everything to do with pinpointing – even before the reviews of *The Lost Girl* arrived – the nature of the canyon he now felt separated him from English readers. Wickedly he invites his gentle reader – i.e. genteel of course, for what reader isn't? – to share the comic distance from his provincial hero and heroine, apologising for the low-life and language, while insisting that 'spooning' takes place among 'Champagne and shoulders' too. This 'author' will not, of *course*, lay himself open to charges like those levelled at one D. H. Lawrence. 'Let none complain that I pry indecently into the privacies of the spoon' – since spooning is brazenly public. He may know that 'There are tricks, dear reader' to make things more exciting, but he himself will have nothing but 'pure simplicity. I am no dealer in abnormalities' – nor, as we have seen, in any 'loss of faculties'. Above all, it will be *British*. For he will say this for Emmie and her future husband, that they have 'a bed-rock of common-sense' which knows perfectly well that the rose of love 'bring[s] belly-aches', while good solid bourgeois

Sunday dinner 'is the key-stone of the domestic arch, on which repeated arches all society rests' – as *The Rainbow* had so lamentably failed to put it. So, having invited his readers to identify themselves with 'the bulldog breed, full of sound British sense', he hopes to proceed 'with more self-satisfaction than heretofore', the author and his gentle reader having patted each other's backs so amicably. But at the end there is a comic trap. For to young Walter George, embracing his Emmie in her thin nightie, there comes a new sure feeling of 'manliness'. (No, it is not *that*, what could you be thinking?) For they are taking the safe road, safe as houses, 'such as you have taken, gentle reader, you who sit in your comfortable home with this book on your knee'.[43] That is the happy ending all true British readers want. But the real ending is paralysis: between those who 'do' (sexually) but will not confess what they do, and those who 'know' but will die rather than admit or face up to what they know: thus, frozen silence ...

Lawrence soon began to hope he might sell the story as a little book on its own, since British readers might be armoured enough not to spot the irony (like many of Fielding's), and on the surface the fiction is quite incensorable and comfortably amusing. Ruth Wheelock, as she typed, encouraged this idea for America too, finding it '*so* like an American small town' (iii. 653).

Yet the letter of 9 December which told how it had come to a stop, not only hinted that it would go on soon, but mentioned that what Lawrence had written was only a third of what he intended (iii. 634): a book, then, of about 510 notebook pages. It would have to be the ongoing story of Gilbert, since the story of Emmie and Walter George is worth no more words. Within three days or so, the book had indeed taken off again and would reach 447 pages before being laid aside (and vanishing for fifty years and more).[44] There is no way of telling whether, when Lawrence first began jotting in May or when he actually began in late November, he already had the idea of a contrast between Gilbert's fiasco with Emmie, and a later and very different affair which would draw on his own and Frieda's experience in 1912. It is by no means unlikely. That parallel, and contrast, might have struck him quite forcibly even during his weekend with Neville, and as he prepared to leave for Germany with Frieda. (And he proceeded to draw structural parallels between the two parts of the novel to an extent that suggests premeditation.)

Here however both biographers and critics must be careful, for *Mr Noon* Part II needs as much as *Sons and Lovers* to be rescued from the assumption that it is an autobiographical novel which can provide accurate biographical evidence. The whole commencement of Part II is fictitious. Lawrence spent only one weekend in Edgar Jaffe's flat in Munich as far as we know, by which time he and Frieda were already living together in Icking – though they had just quarrelled. It seems unlikely that he and Edgar went to Irschenhausen in 1912. It had not snowed that June! Nor was Frieda's mother in Bavaria. Nor could Else have borrowed 'her' house on the Starnbergersee, having a perfectly good one of her own in Wolfratshausen. And though Lawrence may have used some traits for his characters, there was a great deal more to the Bavarian Minister of Finance and connoisseur of avantgarde art than the comic little Alfred of the novel – nor does Professor Sartorius seem much like the Alfred Weber whom Lawrence described at the time as 'jolly'. The chapters set in 'Detsch'/Metz and Trier do draw (vividly) on some verifiable experiences: the meeting with mother and sisters, the fair, the walk to the country village, the insistence on writing a letter to the husband, the farce of the arrest, the embarrassed meeting with the Baron, the family embassy to the exiled lover. But the full fictional experience will not fit the chronology and facts of Lawrence's actual stay. The sexual episodes, much as one might have hoped otherwise, were very probably invented for comic and ironic purposes, particularly the best of them (in the hotel bedroom) which is classical farce and deliberate parallel with the previous 'interrupted' scene with Emmie. Finally, when the action reaches Icking and seems closest to life, the novel nevertheless owes as much at times to the subsequently worked-up poems of *Look!*, as to memory. The flat in Icking is non-fictive, as is the expedition to the Köchelsee (though it belongs to the Icking period), and Frieda swimming in the Isar (though not the address to the crucifix, which was Hobson's in Mayerhofen). But the episode of the fireflies (for example) comes from the poem as against the quarrel recorded in a letter at the time, and the vision of the cavalryman with bloody spurs did not give rise in Lawrence at the time to anything like Gilbert's longings, but to a very different kind of imagination. In any case, to base fiction on considerably revised poetry or on *The Fight for Barbara* was to carry still further what had already been dramatised and fictionalised, often years after the events.[45]

The point may seem pedantic, but it is worth making for a number of reasons. To suppose autobiography is not only to make mistakes of fact (which I have tried to avoid in Chapter One), it is also to ignore significant aspects of Lawrence's fictionalising, which have biographical reference not to the Lawrence and Frieda of 1912, but to the Lawrence and Frieda of December 1920.

He is able to make comic characters of his lumpen younger self, and of a comically inflammable 'Johanna', because of the way that he has outgrown not only 1912, but 1917 as well. His love-birds or 'pair of finches' seemed a little absurd to him – doesn't one's own so serious younger self? – even before he began to work the comedy up; particularly now that he had done with love for good, and had settled that marriage, though still a base, was one from which a man needed to depart. To restore the Lawrence of 1912 one would need to scour away all the 1920 comedy, precisely what he was taking such wicked joy in creating. To suppose that in Part II Gilbert has become Lawrence is also to import a discontinuity between Part I and Part II which readers who know little about Lawrence do not experience. The later Gilbert grows and changes, but he does so in thematic ways, and he is still being laughed at by the end, though by then he has had intimations of a 1920 vision. Moreover to look outside the fiction is to ignore the comic parallels so carefully set up within it – the two farcical episodes of coitus interruptus, the thematic joke that the arch-spooner of Part I is actually a novice when it comes to bed, the parallels with the two mothers and the two fathers, the satiric crosslight thrown on Louise by our experience of Patty – and many another. Most of all, it is to destroy the whole nature of the fiction of 1920, which is precisely a re-seeing of an earlier state in the light of a later one; together with an open onslaught (now) on the kind of reader who had thought even his earlier vision obscene and would be even more hostile and uncomprehending to this book – 'gentle but rather cowardly and imbecile reader: for such, really, I find you'.

For when he began to write again, about 12 December, the first notices of *The Lost Girl* had come; and as he wrote steadily to 31 December, the later ones were arriving. So from the moment that Gilbert wakes up in Munich to begin his new adventures, two processes begin. The more he begins to grow and change in ways that need to be taken seriously (though the situations are no less comic); the more the relations of 'the author' with the 'gentle reader' deteriorate. Indeed, the first thing that Gilbert must grow out of is his English insularity[46] – and so there on the first page of chapter XIII is 'the author' ironically throwing a sop to the reader-as-English-Cerberus, and hoping it chokes him. As Gilbert sheds insularity it is fastened on the reader, only called 'gentle' because (as one says 'Nice doggie') 'the author' fears his bite. He has felt it, in the critics who snarl that his language is low and that he is interested in *fleurs du mal* instead of truth. How is one to be serious, even comically, when one cannot trust one's audience to listen, let alone understand? 'The author' may be serious about the wonder and value of genuine sexual desire which Gilbert experiences for the first time; but only comedy is safe, and so he swells his serious point into a Fieldingesque apostrophe rather than open the bedroom door – but he cannot do that anyway, because of the hypocrisy of readers who are both prurient and puritan: 'I've been caught that way before. I have opened the door for you, and the moment you gave your first squeal in rushed the private detective you had kept in the background.'[47]

This is not however – and the point is important – merely Lawrence hitting back at his critics, though it is that too. Nor does it break the comic/ironic purpose, of which it is an organic part. For the next move is to split the gentle reader ironically, by gender. 'The author' realises that he must look mainly to gentle readers who are female, for the male kind snaps that his heroines never show any spark of nobility and never will. So, he suggests, *they* had better stop reading, babies that they are. For (wickedly!) only women will sympathize with

Johanna's maternal promiscuity with Rudolf, or agree on the importance of the virility which Gilbert, eventually, manages. (Once more, 'three times in a quarter of an hour' – Bing-bang-bump – is heroic-*comic*, and part of a tease of women, not autobiographical boasting, or lie.) In contrast, male readers are overinflated by idealistic wind – and here the irony changes from Fielding to Swift on the Aeolists. The Lawrence of 1920 comes into the open as 'the author' mounts his ironic apostrophe to the 'sanctified wind of Uplift' bellowing out our trousers (which contain no backsides, oh dear no), and which enable men to look down on their fellows ('in love of course'), and deny and condemn anything below or behind the belt buckle.[48]

Lawrence even anticipates Katherine's notes to Murry, which he never saw, on the sin against art of writing about earth-closets. Exemplifying the psychological disease of 'uplift' is the schizophrenia of Johanna's husband, whose 'day' and 'night' consciousnesses are kept utterly incommunicado, so that he can idolise his wife by day as a snowflower, whom he lustily violates at night. He is also an advanced case of the Walter-Georgian who will go ugly mad if he is forced to admit into consciousness what he secretly knows. He even goes into a white fury when Johanna rattles the door of the W.C., forcing him to admit that he is there. W.C.s must be marked 'OO', doubly nought, non-existent, to the upper consciousness.[49] But Gilbert and Johanna must experience the interplay of both 'day' and 'night' consciousness; must learn what intolerable limitations men and women are to each other, and yet how conflict is *necessary*, so that out of the battling of the sexes and the shattering of enclosed selves there can come new birth. The sex war may, indeed, become vicious, nightmarish, a horror, before they can come through. And *just so* has it become necessary to drop the mask and fight the reader who wants only idyll, will not admit dark consciousness, and must be stung out of 'gentle' (and genteel) complacency. 'Gentle reader' becomes a battle-cry: '*Dilly-Dilly-Dilly, come and be killed.*' 'The author' will defiantly provoke opposition: 'And so, gentle reader—! But why the devil should I always *gentle-reader* you … Time you too had a change. Time you became rampageous reader, ferocious reader, surly, rabid reader, hell-cat of a reader, a tartar, a termagant, a tanger.' Only after thus having it out, can 'the author' become the Lawrence of 1912–17 and speak seriously: 'Ah gentle reader, what have we done! What have we done, that sex, and the sacred, awful communion should have become degraded into a thing of shame … or the perversion of spiritual union … [or] a mere affair of comradeship, "pals," … or prostitution?'[50] But he is no longer the Lawrence of *Look! We Have Come Through!*, either – though he had begun to think of calling his 'peppery' comedy 'Lucky Noon' now (iii. 645). For even before the notebooks were laid aside on 31 December at the end of chapter XIX,[51] Gilbert is having thoughts that belong to 1920 – and looking further beyond the marriage of opposites than Birkin did at the end of *Women in Love*. The same is true of 'the author', hoping to be shattered and born again many more times still, since nothing in life is final – except (ironically) ideas, which therefore go dead, including his own. So Gilbert looking at the bloody-spurred rider and the infantrymen, and the raft-men poling down the Isar, and even the mowers, has thoughts utterly different from those that Lawrence had in 1912 and later worked up into the poem-sequence of 1917. He does not long like Birkin for a single male friend as well as his woman, but for the life of men together, beyond women, beyond love and happiness and marriage, 'to be with men, with men alone, active, reckless, dangerous, on the brink of death: to be away from woman, beyond her, on the borders' (as in the conclusion to the 'Education' essays). And yet, Gilbert questions himself sadly, 'Why could he not really mix and mingle with men? For he could not' – except on a superficial level. He has no comrade, only 'friends', and when such say they love him his heart closes like a trap. Nor does he delude himself that there is really any 'wonderful secret' in the concerted activities of men in soldiering or labour. He is a loner, really. He has to make his life with Johanna and his solitary work – though it is a horrible blow to have to admit that 'his very being depends upon his connection with another being' – one moreover whom he cannot 'finally *trust*', and who deeply distrusts his readiness for 'soul messing'.[52]

There, on the last day of the year, Lawrence left Gilbert about to set out with Johanna on their walk across the Alps – just as he and Frieda were about to embark for Sardinia.

V   Sea, and Sardinia

On New Year's Day 1921, he finished his painting of the anchorites (which he did not much like after all); looked at some pictures of Taormina by Emily Bland, a friend of the Mackenzies; then went for a walk and a picnic with Rosalie Bull to watch the sun set behind Etna. The sun was hot, mimosa full out, and oranges and lemons ripening; but he was restless and thinking about the trip. The next day there was yet another tea-party,[53] then a day to prepare themselves, and before dawn on 4 January he and Frieda were off.

They were going in mid-winter, quite the wrong time of year for a more mountainous and much colder island. It was the hope of a world unspoilt by expatriates and tourists that attracted Lawrence, but the absence of 'civilised' facilities to cater to such people had obvious disadvantages too. Much of the experience seems to have been uncomfortable at best; and when they got back to Sicily he was sure that Sardinia was no place for them to live.

The rail journey across Sicily to Palermo – on a single track from Messina, so trains in opposite directions had to stop in one *coincidenza* after another to get past each other – took up the whole of that first Tuesday from before dawn till after dark, but at least there were Ruth Wheelock and a comfortable hotel at the end. Their steamer the next day was berthed next to the up-to-date *City of Trieste*, headed back to Naples; but theirs – headed for Cagliari via Trapani at the south of Sicily – was sixty years old, their cabin tiny, the food horrible in the dining-room of faded elegance. In Cagliari by early Thursday afternoon, they found a good simple hotel; and though it was very cold in the steep narrow streets, Lawrence modified his first impression of the capital as a place like Malta, 'lost between Europe and Africa and belonging to nowhere'. When however they decided on the Friday afternoon to take the narrow-gauge railway up the centre of Sardinia rather than the state one up the west side, they were deliberately moving off the beaten track. This increased when – after a night in the railway hotel at Mandas and on by rail to Sorgono – the rest of the journey (to Nuoro, Orosei, and past Tavolara to Terranova) was by post-bus over the mountains, along roads precipitous, winding and rough. Nor was beauty any guarantee of pleasure. 'Pretty Sorgono' was so like a village in Hardy's Wessex transported to the steep spurs of the Gennargentu that they thought they might spend several days there, but it had only one appalling, filthy and icy inn; and the steep lane along which they walked to keep warm, until there might be something to eat, turned out to be an open latrine.[54] Even when they found a clean hotel, as they did in Nuoro on the Sunday night, the meal it served was hardly enough to feed a child. Sardinia was poor, in ways for which living in Taormina had not at all prepared them.

Yet to read *Sea and Sardinia*, begun just a week after they got back to Fontana Vecchia, is not to find discomfort the main impression. For this is one of the most delightful of Lawrence's books, to which those who have never read him (and for that matter those prepossessed against him) should be sent first of all. It is a travel-book in a more straightforward sense than *Twilight in Italy*. Moreover the factors which transform rather uncomfortable experience into something funny and vital, are also biographically significant.

He had been teaching himself, in the second part of *Mr Noon*, how to make comic characters out of Frieda and D. H. Lawrence. The characters of *Sea and Sardinia* ('I' and 'the queen bee' – or 'q. b.') are quite different from those of the novel, but the sureness of the treatment comes from a hand that has been practising. And since there is less personally at stake in the material, and less likelihood of hostility in a reader's response, Lawrence is able to drop his defences and achieve that *artful* spontaneity, apparently without hindsight, which so often marks his writing at its best. Moreover it is the comic self-characterisation that keeps reducing the discomforts of the journey to a comically grumbling undertone. For 'I' turns out to be Lawrence-as-irritable-man or (better) irascible worker bee, burdened (with a huge knapsack that makes him conspicuous) and busy with responsibilities, constantly buzzing testily at the world's unwillingness to deliver. And, played against this is the queen bee, not at all sexily inflammable like Johanna, and much larger than the worker bee who buzzes round her: white, maternal, rather sentimental and optimistic, not easily moved, but formidable when offended. The comic tones are struck from the start.[55]

Yet what is fun, beautiful, serious, strange, can come through this comic irascibility undiminished, while what is annoying and uncomfortable gets dramatised into vivacity, or made material for comedy, or held at tolerable distance by self-awareness. A persona so deliberately prickly can help to turn Lawrence's abiding self-consciousness into lively drama, where his perceptions and descriptions of the oddness of others get visibly sharpened by awareness of the oddity he seems to them. The observer is also observed, the experience more than merely subjective. An example of how this underlying humour can develop into high comedy is the scene at the centre of Palermo, where the I-narrator's impatience with shops, lethal traffic and their own conspicuousness (he with the beard and knapsack, she with the kitchenino of old), plays off against the q. b.'s wonderfully impervious fascination with all the colour and the bustle, which therefore get splendidly fused with our amusement at him – until the moment when she rounds, in imperious fury now, on the hussies who have been giggling and mocking behind their backs. An example of more serious self-awareness in Lawrence is the moment when she rounds on *him*, not merely for getting so angry in Sorgono but, even more, for converting his rage into such moral superiority that he is quite blind to the human being, the innkeeper, in front of him. Because he has made a comic character of himself, he is able to see his own irrational absurdities: the element of childishness in his outrage, which is so clearly disappointment because his expectations were too high; and the risible inconsistency, when only a moment before he had been singing the praises of the primitive. These are telling points for a writer to make against himself when he has no necessity to do so.

Other no less telling moments are those in which the trip to Sardinia became a catalyst, precipitating out what till then had been part of a complex flow of feeling and impulse. From Picinisco he had written, half-seriously, that his movements really came from a constitutional restlessness, far deeper than the excuses of place or conditions which he used to explain them: 'my feet itch, and a seat burns my posterior if I sit too long. What ails me I don't know – but it's on and on – ' (iii. 435). Yet he had also become convinced that there was a kind of psychic current pushing against false stasis in life, and that it would eventually set willy-nilly in the needful direction, though that would lie deeper than all rationalising, and could only be found intuitively through trial and error. He had been happy and productive in Sicily; and Fontana Vecchia was the most pleasant house he had ever had – better even than those in Gargnano or Fiascherino. But the trip to Sardinia had itself been the outcome of instinct that it was time to move, coupled with a desire to discover whether another relatively small move would do. It appeared that Taormina was not isolated enough and too full of expatriates from further north. Could they, then, find somewhere to live in Sardinia which would be open to neither objection?

'Comes over one an absolute necessity to move.' But though the first sentence of *Sea and Sardinia* is followed by the apparently logical question of 'where', and the intuitive answer, anywhere away from the witchcraft of Etna, the first lessons of the trip are prophetic discriminations. The accident of his ship's itinerary would take him also within the magnetic field of another mountain, rising above Trapani, from the little town on whose slopes, Erice, Tunis is visible on a clear day. Mount Eryx, *Erycina ridens* to the ancients, smiling Astarte, looks out across the 'great, red, trumpet-flaring sunset' to Africa the 'dreaded' and 'terrible'. He had played with the idea of Africa as a way of getting quite clear of the England and Europe which had created the war. Cecily's brother Nip, who had come with them on the wagon-picnic from Hermitage, was breeding horses in Zululand; and Francis and Jessica Brett Young would soon be leaving Capri for Cape Town. But when it came to the point, now, his heart 'stood still'.[56] The first effect of the trip was to make him quite quite sure – beyond any rational explanation sure – that that direction was the wrong one for him. His response to African art had shown some intuitive understanding of an ancient wholly un-European kind of culture, and – however limited by ignorance – had also shown none of the colonialist arrogance of Frobenius, let alone that of the South African whites whose ranks Nip and Frances would join. But he flinched now from the gulf which separated him from the inner Africa of those carvings which so fascinated Heseltine, Epstein and Gertler, and of course the artists of contemporary Paris.

However, absolute movement was also revealed as an impossible dream – though Lawrence would go on dreaming it for a few months yet. His first reponse to being at sea was the sheer 'joy ... to the wild innermost soul' that caused him to insist on putting 'Sea' first in the title (when at last he settled that):

Oh God, to be free of all the hemmed-in life ... the long-drawn-out agony of a life among tense, resistant people on land. And then to feel the long, slow lift and drop of this almost empty ship, as she took the waters ... I wished in my soul that the voyage might last for ever, that the sea had no end ...

After leaving Trapani the tone of this longing for 'freedom' becomes even more lyrically charged, as he dwells on his dream of 'a small quiet, lonely ship' on which he could wander from land to land and isle to isle with just a few (masculine) companions.[57] But immediately – by way of controlled deflation like those of *Mr Noon* – up from the companion-way, as though by signal, pops the Cagliari young woman with her two males in tow, insisting on shouting at him in French and wanting to know how his wife is. And as for that even more theoretic idea (drawn from his Dana essay) of the importance of having 'at least two *uneducated* sailors' in the crew (iii. 655): there again, with ironic persistence, is the talkative ship's carpenter he comes almost to hate by the second day aboard. Lawrence may count the sails of the Mediterranean schooners in the distance – the 'ladders' and the 'wings' that so reveal his nautical ignorance even of the names of sea things – but on board any of those, and wherever he might sail, there would be someone who would persistently saddle him with his nationality and responsibility, or pester him with uneducated prejudice.

The greatest of all the intuitive responses however, with no trace of irony or irritation, comes with his first glimpses of Sardinian men in their native costume, which seems to him to accentuate an unapproachable, indomitable manliness. After the 'soft Italians' there is something of 'fierceness' here as well as a masculine kind of beauty, a glimpse of something lost: 'One realises, with horror, that the race of men is almost extinct in Europe. Only Christ-like heroes and woman-worshipping Don Juans, and rabid equality-mongrels. The old, hardy, indomitable male is gone. His fierce singleness is quenched. The last sparks are dying out in Sardinia and Spain.' Yet there is much more to the experience than a mere exemplar or even confirmation of his own ideas about manliness and singleness in 1920. For there stirs in him a kind of recognition on a deeper quite irrational level.

But that curious, flashing, black-and-white costume! I seem to have known it before: to have worn it even: to have dreamed it. To have dreamed it: to have had actual contact with it. It belongs in some way to something in me—to my past, perhaps. I don't know. But the uneasy sense of blood-familiarity haunts me. I *know* I have known it before. It is something of the same uneasiness I feel before Mount Eryx: but without the awe this time.

The sense of a lost manliness, and indeed a lost confident womanliness in the beautiful regionally distinct dresses and aprons, runs like a colourful thread all the way through the book: the glimpse of a single male working in a mountain field; the chanting procession outside Tonara where it is the women who hold the eye not the priests and the ugly image in procession, something *sui generis*, older than the Greeks and Phoenecians, and befitting a landscape un-European, untamed, 'remote, ungrappled', even savage sometimes, speaking to him again of something from another time – but also (compare Cooper) deep inside him.[58]

Yet the other, sordid realities of Sardinia tell him how quickly those intimations are perishing; and there is no question of making a life for themselves there, any more than in Africa. They could never 'belong'. And there is one more sardonic image to help (as it were) triangulate what Sardinia had to show him by way of inner direction. For the disreputable *girovago* or wandering pedlar they meet in the cave-like cellar of the inn at Sorgono, who wanders from market to market with his male-wife, defiantly outside society, is in some ways a kind of minatory caricature of Lawrence.[59] The secret affinity is clear to him: the rootlessness they share, the bisexuality, the restless energy, the gift of the gab, the defiant freedom that is at the same time a belonging nowhere. The 'I'-narrator is both attracted by the freedom, and repelled: for anything less like the manliness and womanliness of the Sardinian peasants would be hard to imagine. To be like that?

So, in January 1921, the trip to Sardinia clarified both the downside of his 'absolute necessity to move', and the question of direction. In Europe what he was seeking might linger in odd corners, but not for long. Nowhere in Europe northwards, then; nor south to Africa; nor anywhere like Sardinia or Sicily or Malta, betwixt and between. Not a little ship with a few companions – though that dream proved particularly hard to give up. And not a gypsy-like wandering, either, content to be without roots in any 'spirit of place'. But somewhere to find a manliness and womanliness to which he could respond intuitively with the deeper affinity he had felt for the 'ancient' Sardi, or indeed with the 'awe' he had felt for the wholly un-European cultures of Africa, though unable to share their spirit. The 'absolute necessity to move' would have to be east, or westward.

More immediately they took the overnight ferry from Terranova to Civita Vecchia, each having to share a cabin.

VI Fontana Vecchia – for a While

The growth of Italian hostility to foreigners, particularly French and English, was brought home to Lawrence again and again on the trip. There was understandable irritation at how strangers could profit from the collapse of the lira (owing to the growing political instability of Italy); and the more particular grievance of how France and England had done their erstwhile ally down in the Treaty of Versailles, and the distribution of reparations. It was however one thing to understand, and quite another to be continually held to account as a representative of his country – which he had already rejected – rather than the individual he felt himself to be. The conviction that he was finished with Italy grew apace.

In Rome they had a brief meeting at the station with Juta, and Insole (back from Tunis); and invited them to come to Taormina when the almond-blossom reached its height in a week or two. Then, resisting a brief temptation to visit Don Mauro at Montecassino again, it was the long train journey to Naples; a rush on foot through the rain to the harbour to secure a cabin on the crowded steamer before the train was shunted down – it was the *City of Trieste*, and they succeeded – and one more night in Palermo with Ruth Wheelock, watching a giant puppet-show of the Paladins.[60] Then the trek back to Taormina, where they arrived on the evening of 13 January.

They woke up to brilliant sun, the almond-trees blossoming, the oranges and lemons in the garden ripe now – and a present of a new blazer from Ada, much needed (iii. 647)! The news on the publishing front was not so welcome: Secker was requesting more 'excisions or paraphrases' (iii. 647), in the hope of extending the market for his edition. But there is a marked gap in the surviving letters between the 14th and the 20th, in which it seems certain that Lawrence was writing again. By the 21st he had started what would become *Sea and Sardinia*, though he would not find that title for some time. What had he been doing in between?

He may have written 'Almond Blossom' – but did he go on with *Mr Noon*, which he had left at the end of chapter XIX with a prediction that he would finish before the end of January (iii. 646)? It seems likely that he did now write chapter XX, drawn from the first part of his and Frieda's journey into the mountains as far as Mayrhofen. Indeed, writing about that trip may have firmed up the idea of writing about Sardinia at once, rather than after a second look in the summer (which he had suggested to Secker on the 14th; iii. 648). Was that why he then put *Mr Noon* aside again – or did he want to pause, and consider? On the 20th, as it happened, a sudden hailstorm threatened to smash the almond-blossom; the Lawrences caught heavy colds; and he wrote to Eleanor Farjeon that he would like to talk to her but felt 'shut up and I can't come unshut just now' (iii. 649). That may have been because, once he reached Mayrhofen in the fictionalising of 1912, there was a very difficult decision to be made. For it was shortly after leaving there, with Bunny and his friend, that Frieda seduced young Hobson in the hay-hut near the Dominicus-Hütte and then threw this in Lawrence's face – a real shock and humiliation, when he had just begun to believe her at last committed to him. He had been able to bring himself only to hint at this sidelong, in one cryptic poem in *Look! We Have Come Through!* which does not reveal the cause of its 'Misery'. Was it a bothersome question, now, whether he could come 'unshut' enough to expose the sore spot (and Frieda) publicly, to those who might take *Mr Noon* as autobiography? And how do so without bitterness or cynicism? It may have seemed preferable to begin writing about the trip to Sardinia for the moment, leaving himself time to think the question over.

If so, he seems to have reached a decision quite soon. For on 25 January he says nothing more about the Sardinia book but does say that *Mr Noon* will be '*most* dangerous', but (significantly) 'humorously so'. He still thought it would take 'about a month'. In contrast, '*Aaron* will not be dangerous – if only his rod would start budding, poor dear' (iii. 653).

'Dangerous' was a word he and Mountsier had begun to use as a mock-word for what publishers would think. He had joked before about Aaron's rod to explain his blockage with the book, and if it was not 'dangerous' it was because he had no idea yet of the sexual affair with the Marchesa. Moreover the sexual scenes in *Mr Noon* that he had already written were anaesthetised by comedy, not to say farce, and he had never used the word about *Mr Noon* before. He had coupled 'amusing' with 'rather scandalous' before Christmas (iii. 639), and had said that it had become 'peppery' (iii. 645); but what was scandalous was probably the plot itself, the inflammable Johanna running away from husband and children and the speed of her involvement with Gilbert, and what was peppery was the squaring up to the reader. However, to have Johanna proceed to couple so casually with another man, so very soon after throwing in her lot with Gilbert, might well intensify the epithet. And if that is what Lawrence meant, '*most* dangerous' and humorous represent three decisions: to go ahead and treat it, to treat it comically and to be as ruthless about the possibility of upsetting Frieda as he had been with many another identifiable character. The 25 January letter recorded the decision to split the novel, and the suggestion that Part I as 'a little book all to itself' might 'make a rather funny serial'. For the moment, he said, '*Mr Noon* holds me' (iii. 653).

If he then went on to write the remainder of what we now have, leaving the book unfinished in mid-sentence, it may have been in the next nine days, despite the visit by Insole and Juta. (Fortunately they were not staying at Fontana Vecchia but at the Villa San Pancrazio; and Juta recalled it as a 'brief visit', perhaps no more than a week or so, and over by the 31st.)[61] By 4 February, however, *Mr Noon* had been put aside again for 'a little rest, it being a bit of a strain. But end in sight' (iii. 660). If it was not yet in the state it is now, it *may* have been picked up once more some time after 22 February – for between 4 and 22 February Lawrence worked steadily to finish *Sea and Sardinia*[62] – but after the 22nd he says that he is going to take 'a rest' (iii. 667) and 'a bit of a holiday' (iii. 671). The likelihood is that by 4 February he had done what we have now,[63] and left off, at some interruption, with the feeling that he had got over a hump as well as over the Alps to Riva in his story. If the end was in sight, that was probably going to come in Gargnano where Gilbert and Johanna are about to go. Perhaps the conclusion would be the climactic misery of Christmas and Hobson/Stanley's visit, followed by the 'coming through' into new life at the New Year, since the fiction had been following the poems of *Look!* fairly closely.

He had managed to do the '*most* dangerous' bit humorously, by making Gilbert comically naïve and Johanna understandably cross at being so quickly forgiven. There is nothing funny about the imagining of the hatred of the absent husband; but when it comes to the portrait of Stanley, sardonic humour already flickers in the juxtaposition of the young man's rebellious dependence on his mother, his wailings about needing to be loved, and his sympathy for the mother in Johanna. The author knows exactly why he was so attractive to her and why she would so easily bestow herself on the young man's 'need'! Her reaction to the misfiring of her confession that Stanley had 'had' her, which meets with exalted and naive forgiveness from Gilbert, is nicely done.

"Didn't you *know*? Didn't you suspect anything?' said Johanna, rather gloomy.

"No," he answered, with his strange clear face of innocence. "No—never. It wouldn't have occurred to me."

And half she felt enmeshed, even a little fascinated by his clear, strange, beautiful look of innocent exaltation. And half she hated him for it. It seemed so false and unmanly. Hateful unmanly unsubstantial look of beauty!

"Well," she said. "It wasn't much, anyhow. It meant nothing to me. I believe he was impotent."[64]

The deliberate bathos so characteristic of *Mr Noon* could hardly be bettered, but the double-take is even funnier. For doesn't she *know*? What is it that she has confessed?

The final 'sermon' from 'the author' to his 'gentle reader' may suggest why the book would be abandoned. It underlines the familiar Lawrencian lessons that Gilbert has learned: the revelation, as he touches the flank of his sleeping but tempestuous woman, of both her utter Otherness, and the rich depths of the 'sensual soul' within himself; but also the knowledge that here is only a first cracking open of the 'dry integument' of dead attitudes and feelings that encloses him. This might as easily have been written by the author of 'The Crown' in 1915. The next lesson, that it is not through 'lovey-doveyness' that the liberation will come but out of bitterly painful and *continuous* battle, with a woman who is not 'nice', is the insight of *Women in Love*. But Lawrence may by this stage have come to feel the same sort of strain in trying to hold earlier and later selves together that he had felt with 'Miss Houghton' – and there are several signs of this. For there is no hint of a similar rebirth in Johanna, so the emphasis is (even if inadvertently) no longer on the old *marriage* of opposites. Moreover the language of struggle reveals a curious subterranean resentment which speaks of 1920, rather than 1916 even, let alone 1912. Its metaphors move from shedding a skin, to fighting a 'matrix', to fighting the 'mother of our days': 'a bitter struggle to the death with the old, warm, well-known mother of our days ... fight her to the death—and defeat her—and then we shall burst out ...'[65] It is as though the consciousness that had come to acknowledge the need to fight dependence on Frieda as mother-substitute, was insisting on intervening at the stage where it was appropriate to see her as the only way into new life. There are two moments in the Alps which have a resonance not found in *Look!*, and which point aside from what is otherwise the main current of *Mr Noon*. Alone at Domenicus-Hütte Gilbert looks out at the flush of evening on the peaks, and has an experience quite unlike Gudrun's communion with them – an experience of absolute loneliness. And yet the language quickly moves from implied deprivation, to richness and perfection:

The eternal and everlasting loneliness. And the beauty of it, and the richness of it ... The heart in its magnificent isolation like a peak in heaven, forever. The beauty, the beauty of fate, which decrees that in our supremacy we are single and alone, like peaks that finish off in their perfect isolation in the ether. The ultimate perfection of being quite alone.

Within the story there is a retrospective plot-irony here, in the reason for Johanna's absence. But the language, powerful and quite unironic, speaks again of the Lawrence of 1920, who had come to believe that man–woman relations were only a step towards something deeper and much more self-sufficient. Lest this seem merely a momentary aside, it is taken up again even more powerfully in Gilbert's vision of the great single peak the next day, which he returns to three times, careless of all else, and knows to be 'one of the perfect things of all his life ... a pure, immortal satisfaction—a perfected aloneness'.[66] But how was Lawrence to develop this within a narrative that was taking him inexorably into marriage, and over ground already well-trodden and left behind? Perhaps it was inevitable that he should before long decide not to go on with *Mr Noon*, but (instead) with an *Aaron's Rod* for which he at last found a theme that would hold its otherwise picaresque elements together.

On the last day of January he had written another poem – a political one which is the doublet of 'Bare Fig-Trees'. On the 20th he had told Eleanor Farjeon that he thought the time had come for a real political struggle, and that 'If I knew how to, I'd really join myself to the revolutionary socialists now' (iii. 649). This should cause no surprise. At any time since his twenties when he was reading *New Age*, he would have declared himself a socialist when the time came to choose sides, since without the material necessities of life people could not develop as individuals, which he cared about most of all. It was in that spirit that he had advocated nationalisation to Bertrand Russell in 1915, and thought of contacting the leaders of the ILP who were also opposed to the war, in 1918. If another letter to Russell, and his response to Gibbon, also show him calling for kinds of strong leadership that sound more 'fascist', it would be well to remember how very closely intertwined the two ways of thinking actually were at that time, before the events of the later 1920s and 1930s drove them distinctly asunder. *New Age*, for instance, was a socialist paper, also devoted to Nietzsche. (Nothing is more likely to falsify actual historical human experience than the arrogance of pinning contemporary parameters of thought on a very different past.) But mob-behaviour in the war, and the rise of mob-politics, had disillusioned Lawrence with democracy, which seemed to level down to the lowest common denominator rather than fostering individual growth. And trade-union power politics seemed to him to smack too much of materialist envy and greed fighting for a bigger share of worldly goods, and too little of a desire to live differently. Since, as the letter to Eleanor confesses, he did not 'care for' (or understand) politics-in-practice, it is perhaps to a poem like 'Bare Fig-Trees' that we should look for what he felt a true 'Demos' should essentially be:

> ... putting forth each time to heaven,
> Each time straight to heaven,
> With marvellous naked assurance each single twig,
> Each one setting off straight to the sky
> As if it were the leader, the main-stem, the forerunner ...
>
> Oh weird Demos, where every twig is the arch-twig,
> Each imperiously over-equal to each, equality over-reaching itself ...
>
> Still, no doubt every one of you can be the sun-socket as well as every other of
> you.
> Demos, Demos, Demos!

In calling himself a socialist therefore, he made a very sharp distinction between a socialism of equal opportunity, and a socialism of envy, levelling down and collective bullying. And so it was that on the last day of January he wrote his own sardonic 'red flag' poem: 'Hibiscus and Salvia Flowers'.

> Hark! Hark!
> The dogs do bark!
> It's the <bolshevists> ˹socialists˺ come to town,
> None in rags and none in tags,
> <sauntering> ˹Swaggering˺ up and down.[67]

Were these groups of men strolling along the Corso with red flowers in their buttonholes real 'Red, angry men', seeking to send the world up in flames so that a new purer kind of life could grow from the ashes? If so, he would fly to join them. But what right have these gangs of loutish youths with their 'half-threatening envy' to those exquisite flames of flower? They may succeed in pulling the world down, as needs to be done – yet he cannot bear it that such as they should lay claim to hibiscus and salvia flowers (red as his poppy in 'Study of Thomas Hardy').

It was also on the last day of January that Insole and Juta left. The 'basta' with which Lawrence recorded this in his diary[68] usually suggests 'enough of that, good riddance' – but that may have had more to do with the interruption when his writing was in the vein, and with having been pulled by their visit back into expatriate society, than with any real dislike of the young men themselves – though they would be useful for sardonic purposes in *Aaron's Rod*. This was the last time he would see Insole, who would be leaving shortly for Japan; but his relation with Juta remained friendly and he would soon think of going on an expedition with him somewhere. They spent much of their time together, now, discussing how they might co-operate on an illustrated book as the young South African had already done with his sister Réné. (Juta would go by himself to do eight paintings in Sardinia that summer for *Sea and Sardinia*, though for some time after finishing the book in late February, Lawrence was still trying to obtain photographs as illustrations.) Also, having done two charcoal sketches of Lawrence on earlier occasions, Juta managed to persuade him to sit still long enough for an oil painting, which he finished in a single sitting.[69] But there is an amusing sidelight on Lawrence and Frieda in their opposite reactions to the fancy-dress party that occurred while the young men were in Taormina. Frieda was always bucked up by being with young, energetic and amusing people, and for her it was 'a jolly dance' (iii. 666) – but Lawrence cast himself again as Mr Grump, refused to dress up ('to hell with them'), and declared it 'a pitiable display of ridiculous imbecility' (iii. 656). Perhaps the sight of Frieda uninhibitedly leaping about with the young had sharpened the memories he was dealing with, for he added, 'I . . . can't stand showing off. I find everybody just imbecilely showing off. Lord, how nauseating and humiliating.'[70] Clearly something had put his nose out of joint!

VII 'Ach, that I were out of it all!'

His desire now to get away took two forms, both abortive. It had been a let-down when Mackenzie leased Herm, and though Lawrence was invited there, Monty retreated as soon as he showed an interest. Anyway the idea of Rananim as an island had long gone. The dream of a boat to sail the South Seas was taken up all the more enthusiastically with Mountsier instead, who sent him a *National Geographic* article by a man who had done it.[71] The tone of Lawrence's letters was always affected by the person he was writing to, which unfortunately in Mountsier's case involved anti-Semitism and a degree of bitchiness (e.g. about Amy Lowell, who had not acknowledged his latest poems,[72] and Monty, and his publishers) which must have been a response to something in Mountsier's tone, since the letters to him often contrast quite strongly with others written at the same time. Yet interspersed with business matters come now the longings, of which Mountsier became the essential recipient, for a sail-boat with a crew of five. He thought of writing for advice to his Zennor landlord Captain Short

(iii. 698), who had started before the mast, and it was with some envy that he told Brett Young he would watch for the red funnel of their Union Castle liner on its way to Cape Town (iii. 655–6). If only he had a spyglass! And 'Ach, that I were out of it all!'

In February however the dream changed. A letter may have come from Carlota Thrasher to revive the offer of her farm in Connecticut, or perhaps his friendship with Ciccia (the sister of his present landlord Ciccio Cacópardo), and her new young husband Vincenzo, was responsible. They got married on 5 February, with Lawrence supplying the reception wine (iii. 665). It must have reminded him of Fiascherino. They too wanted to leave Sicily – all the more since Ciccio was doing well in Boston – but what could they do? They would be no use in a boat and had no such interest; but Vincenzo (23) hired out as a gardener and Ciccia (26) had been brought up among orchards. Young, strong, eager, surely they could help Lawrence do more than clear the neglected farm – they could actually work it to earn a living. This time Lawrence took practical steps: writing to Mrs Thrasher to confirm a long lease rent-free if they would rescue the farm (iii. 659), and to Mary Cannan, now in Monte Carlo (near the Murrys in Menton[73]) to ask her to lend him £200 at 5% (iii. 663–4). Having also £200 in his bank, this would give him about £300 working capital even after paying the passages – and by this time Seltzer should have made the payment that Lawrence had requested on 2 January into his new American account (iii. 646), so there would be money over there as well. It cannot have been easy asking Mary for help, given his hate of indebtedness, and there are sops to his pride in his letter. He made her a present of his anchorite painting (which he did not finally like much, though he said Frieda wanted it). He said the scheme was only a possibility so she must feel free to refuse; and he ticked her off sternly for gambling at the casino. Behind all that, however, he had good reason to trust her friendship, and she immediately agreed to help once more – though she showed no interest in joining them in a house of her own and taking over part of the enterprise, such as bees and strawberries, as his next letter suggested (iii. 669). For he had begun at once to plan. Mrs Thrasher confirmed the offer of a thirty-year lease rent-free, and referred him to a property agent who knew all about the place (iii. 667–8). Mountsier was to go to see this man and the farm – the nearest station, Baltic Connecticut, was four hours from New York – and advise on how practicable the scheme would be. Meanwhile Lawrence could loose his imagination – though passing rather quickly over Mrs Thrasher's warning that the wooden house would be 'in ruins'.

We intend just to have a goat and begin to plant fruit bushes, to start. It will be a tight squeeze to get there on the funds – but we'll manage. I hope devoutly that I can earn dollars over there. Then I shall get Vincenzo and Ciccia to come, and plant peach trees [on Mrs Thrasher's advice, the most profitable local crop], and have a couple of cows, and a Ford runabout that can take the goods to market – and make a permanent thing of it. (iii. 669)

If Mary came they would be like the anchorites, but in little frame houses dotted about the 90 acres (iii. 664; another letter says 70) of orchard, woodland and streams; 'Mrs Thrasher says it is *lovely* country' (iii. 669). By the end of February, waiting to hear from Mountsier whether he and Frieda should come alone, or all four at once, or not at all, he had already found a suitable sailing from Palermo before the end of April. Frieda, said he, 'is so amused by it all' (iii. 673) – though one does rather wonder what that means, since she was even less agriculturally minded than Mary Cannan.

All this was much more vivid to him than the details on the publishing front with which his letters to Mountsier had mostly to be filled, but which he leaves with alacrity to talk about the farm – especially since his hopes of sorting out the publishing of his work in America seemed doomed to frustration. After his quarrel with Huebsch, he had hoped to show that the agreement over *The Rainbow* had been broken, so he could regain control of the book, but the terms of the handover from Doran to Huebsch remained obscure, Pinker was off-putting and it seemed there were no grounds for action. Soon Lawrence was suggesting that Mountsier go easy with Huebsch (iii. 675), who after all did have a genuine grievance. There appeared to have been no legal agreement at all about either *Sons and Lovers* or *The White Peacock* in America, and the disadvantage of not having had a professional agent became obvious. He could buy back the rights to the latter from Duffield who had published it in America; and he could sue Kennerley to recover what was still owed for the former and *The Widowing of Mrs. Holroyd*,[74] but both courses would require money he did not have. Even OUP seemed unable to tell him whether they would arrange American publication or whether those rights were his (iii. 701).

Mountsier remained suspicious of Seltzer's finances, and objected to his terms for *The Lost Girl* because they involved rights to more books. Lawrence also took offence at precautions against what might be 'objectionable' in future. On the other hand he tried constantly to restrain his agent's dislike, because Seltzer's publication of *Women in Love* meant more to him than Mountsier could imagine. When Seltzer wrote in February sounding genuinely delighted and admiring both about it and *The Lost Girl*, and holding out the prospect of a cheaper edition of the former and good sales for the latter, it was a kind of support Lawrence had been starved of since 1913.[75] To Mountsier's suggestion that his manuscripts would grow in value, so he should demand the return of the *Women in Love* typescript, even if charged for the typing, he replied that it was 'horrible' with revisions (iii. 675) and that when possible he always burned such things.[76]

Moreover Seltzer not only reprinted *Mrs. Holroyd* in February, but was preparing *Psychoanalysis* for May.

This made all the stronger contrast with Secker who had asked for still more revisions to *Women in Love*, 'to remove any possible chance of misconstruction' and avoid a possible libel of Eleonora Duse (iii. 660 n. 1). Even so Secker now thought it impossible to modify the text enough to satisfy the circulating libraries, so the book would have to make its way solely through the bookshops. Insofar as this might put an end to the tampering, Lawrence welcomed it – but not the suggestion that he should therefore reduce his advance from £100 to £75 (iii. 660), corresponding to a reduced edition of 1,500 copies, especially annoying when he needed money for the Thrasher farm. He would not agree, and began to run Secker down to others. Perhaps he ought to have an English agent again. He consulted Douglas Goldring, who was a busy writer and chary of taking on someone he knew to be prickly, but who talked it over with Kot and Barbara Low. He thought Lawrence should really go to Curtis Brown but knew he would prefer a friend to a professional. Might Barbara do it? Lawrence asked, and she agreed, for the time being. He was still determined to be primarily an American author, so the English arrangements would follow and dovetail with the American ones, which would make her task easier.[77]

There was by March a fair stock of new work to manage. Mountsier already had *Mr Noon* Part I in typescript with instructions to try to serialise, cutting if need be, but keeping a full text for the book (iii. 667). The book on Sardinia was being typed by Ruth Wheelock, though Lawrence still had not found the title or enough of the photographs he wanted – but it would soon go to Mountsier with similar instructions. *Mr Noon* Part II, though put aside in mid sentence, had its 'end in sight', and after the 22nd Lawrence was taking his little holiday. He had written two more poems for *Birds, Beasts and Flowers*: the first versions of 'Purple Anemones' on 4 February, and of 'The Ass' on 2 March. It was quite a book now; though Mountsier did not like its introduction, which Lawrence agreed to drop.[78] Moreover individual poems could be sent out profitably, since American magazines seemed newly ready to take Lawrence up in 1921. The *New Republic* had printed two of the new poems in January, after what Mountsier called the 'Knights of Columbus' essay had caused a mini-controversy in December, attacked for primitivism by Walter Lippman and defended by Mary Austin. What would become an important relationship with the *Dial* had begun with 'Adolf' and continued with 'Rex' and 'Pomegranate'. The new proprietor Scofield Thayer was clearly interested in Lawrence, for he had also taken three of the 'Evangelistic Beasts' from Mountsier for the April issue – though he had not taken 'Turkeycock' which had been sent to him direct (iii. 677; Lawrence promised Mountsier not to do that again). Moreover there was still Harriet Monroe of *Poetry*, to whom he had sent nothing for some years, but whom Mountsier should try. Might 'Tortoises' sell as a 'chapbook'? – an idea which Harold Monro had pioneered in England.[79] (The American and Education essays seemed, for the time, to be in abeyance.)

Again the contrast with England was remarkable. While waiting to hear from Barbara Low, Lawrence asked J. C. Squire whether he would welcome contributions to the *London Mercury*. Though Squire had refused the Education essays the previous year, Lawrence may have been amused by the idea of appearing in what had been Murry's major rival. On receiving a positive letter and telegram (iii. 681), he sent off 'Hibiscus and Salvia Flowers', 'Purple Anemones' and 'Pomegranate'[80] (already printed by the *Dial*). He would ask Mountsier to send 'Fanny and Annie'; and told Squire about *Mr Noon* Part I and *Sea and Sardinia*. Unfortunately, the Georgian editor turned down the very un-Georgian poems, and did not pursue the other offerings – but Lawrence had promised not to get annoyed if rejected, and seems to have kept to that. At least Squire had not first invited and then 'insulted' him like Murry (iii. 681). But even before he heard from Squire, the thought of actually going to England – which his sisters were pressing him to do – was utterly repugnant (iii. 677).

Not that the thought of staying in Italy (or for that matter in Europe) was any better. He had still not decided what to do about the lease of Fontana Vecchia which was almost up. He kept saying he would renew it, and failing to do so. This was not a worry about political stability, for he no longer thought revolution would come quickly, telling both Rosalind and Kot that Italy would probably settle down to a constant dogfight between socialists and fascists like the Guelphs and Ghibellines of old (iii. 676–7). Nor, however, could he share Kippenberg's hope of 'binding men together in a new spirit of Internationalism' which Insel-Verlag – as well as commissioning a German translation of *The Rainbow* – was trying to express by reprinting European classics in many languages in a *Bibliotheca Mundi*. Lawrence thought nationalism had developed far too strongly to make the 1919 League of Nations anything but 'a poor vaudeville'; and his own recent experience seemed to show that at the bottom of European hearts 'a rabid, jealous nationalism of hate-your-neighbour is the basic feeling'. There might be enough mental cosmopolitans among cultured people to float Kippenberg's series; but passionally, he thought, nationalisms of self-interest, not to say greed and spite, would prove far more powerful than any 'new wave of idealism in Europe' (iii. 679–80). He had grown 'tired of Taormina, of Italy, of Europe' (iii. 664) – and still awaited, eagerly, Mountsier's verdict about the farm.

On 3 March, however, his hopes were dashed. A telegram arrived from Else: 'Mama schlecht Alfred sehr krank Komm' – and though Lawrence, entering it in his diary, said he believed it 'a trick',[81] this was mostly intense disappointment speaking. He had reluctantly given in to Frieda's pressure to visit Baden-Baden in the summer, but had hoped the promise would be overtaken by the plans for Connecticut. (His suspicion of a set-up encourages a sceptical view of Frieda's 'amusement' about Thrasher's farm.) If however the Baroness were indeed seriously ill and Alfred Weber unable to help, Frieda would unquestionably have to go to Germany – and the journey to America would be off. There was probably some heated argument in the next few days while they waited for further news, but by the 8th (iii. 682) it had become clear that he would have to go with Frieda to Palermo, try to get her passport and visas fixed up there, then put her on the boat to Naples. And though he toyed with the idea of going on from Palermo to America by himself – being still set against going to Germany if he could help it – he soon realised that this would not do either. For the Baroness had 'heart trouble' (iii. 686) and would need care for some time, at least a month, and probably more. He would have to come back to Fontana Vecchia and await developments. On 11 March they left for Palermo, and three days later he was back[82] – having moreover had no success with the passport, which Frieda would have to fix for herself in Rome (iii. 683).

All his plans would have to change. Once more he thought he had better keep Fontana Vecchia (and pay for the new oven which allowed them to cook upstairs), but he still couldn't quite bring himself to make the commitment. He returned Mary Cannan's cheque for 4,000 lire (iii. 683), saying as he had to Catherine, after burning hers, that he was as grateful as if he had cashed it. (She had misspelt the thousands, so the bank might not have accepted it anyway, but that was not much consolation.) He had to tell Mountsier that the farm was now 'almost impossible'; since he might not even be able to come to America 'this summer – or this year'. (Once Frieda was in Baden-Baden, he must have thought gloomily, it would be very difficult indeed to get her to leave.) Still trying to console himself, he added that local Americans had told him it was 'precisely the wrong time to think of going', anyway (iii. 684). He would have to revive the ship idea, though with less verve than before. He had seen lovely two-masters in Palermo, but had also, as a result, a more realistic idea of cost, and his dislike of getting into debt had returned.

Moreover it was raining, 'and not particularly nice being alone with the rain' (iii. 683). Might the Whittleys come for Easter (iii. 683)? He might go for another walking tour after that, with Juta, before meeting Frieda somewhere as they had done last year (iii. 687). Anything, it would seem, to avoid going to Germany himself.

Meanwhile he was having his portrait done again, and had borrowed Marie Hubrecht's studio for the purpose. This time the artist was Millicent Beveridge, a Scottish acquaintance of Catherine Carswell's from Glasgow Art School days, who had lived and exhibited in Paris for many years, and was holidaying in Taormina. She had made a first acquaintance with Lawrence's fiction by reading

The Lost Girl and wanted to meet him; but did so on an occasion which might have proved distinctly off-putting. He had been 'in a rage because, not made aware beforehand that it was a party and that he was to be lionised, he had turned up barefoot with sandals, and in his "pottering about" clothes'. Yet 'Miss Beveridge, amused and astonished as much as she was charmed, became sincerely attached to him, and the friendship remained firm till his death.' She had been supposed to start the sittings on the 5th, and may or may not have done so while the marital debate and uncertainty continued; but now Lawrence had time on his hands and the portrait took shape. He did not think much of the likeness however: telling Mary that though it had 'some resemblance' it was 'just somebody else' (iii. 683), and his mother-in-law that he looked 'quite a sweet young man' (iii. 685), which says much the same thing.[83] At least the sun and the flowers in Marie Hubrecht's garden were out, though he found the sittings tiring.

People were kind, inviting him to lunches and dinners, but he felt better alone in Fontana Vecchia planning escape. He finished correcting the typescript of the *Sardinia* book (still without its final title), and thought a bit more about meeting Juta in Florence in April and doing another 'sketch-book' and walking tour with him – perhaps Sardinia again, or better, the Lipari and Egadi islands – though Jan was deeply involved in his love-affair with Elizabeth Humes in Rome (iii. 688, 686). Ruth Wheelock had been asked to keep looking for a boat that could be hired for a limited period, since buying was too expensive – but alas her enquiries would show that even this would be beyond his means (iii. 698–9). And suddenly, Mountsier cabled that they should come to America at once, whereupon Lawrence had to confess that he had not come quite clean about the difficulties. Not only would the Italian government no longer give passports to would-be emigrants – which he had thought Ciccia and Vincenzo might be able to circumvent – but *they* had cooled to the idea of the farm now, having been encouraged by Ciccio to believe that if they could get to America at all, they could do better for themselves with his help in Boston (iii. 689, 709). No wonder Lawrence felt 'nose-tied' (iii. 689), more anxious than ever to go, yet unable to see how. He was even desperate enough, on hearing from Barbara Low that David Eder was going back to Palestine, to revive the idea of doing a travel book there (iii. 687), though he must have known he could not go. Then came a distinctly acerbic letter from Mountsier (iii. 685 n.), who had put a good deal of effort into his enquiries, and thought he had reason to complain of Lawrence's abrupt change of mind.

Lawrence distracted himself by writing animated responses to some books he had been sent by request of their authors. He had opened Louis Golding's *Forward from Babylon* with anticipation, because he was interested in whether there was an essential Jewishness of soul that distinguished Jew from Gentile.

He had tried many times to guess at this, being convinced that there had to be, and if so it would be an important distinction, not merely an outworn set of habits. But he felt disappointed that Golding, though his theme was a youth's attempt to break with his father's tradition, had not managed to create any distinctively Jewish consciousness. Lawrence himself had no belief now in ideals of universality, but preferred 'the sacred and ineradicable *differences* between men and races: the sacred gulfs'. Yet even Zionists (read, Eder) seemed as English as himself, 'just doing a Zion stunt' (iii. 690). 'Sacred differences' were presumably part of the riches of life; another manifestation of how each unique twig on the tree of creation should reach, in its own way, towards the sun.

His response to Cyril K. Scott's *Blind Mice* pointed another critique of idealism, even more sharply because the author was American. Lawrence's 'wicked amusement' was tempered by his distrust of the uncharitable nature of satire, and a dislike, as a reader, of being made to feel too superior, 'as if I were Jove: or in the dress circle'. But most of all he felt that Scott had not diagnosed where the real blame lay: with 'American Ideal Sympathy, that superannuated and ricketty god'. For it is 'the love stunt, the love ideal which causes the blindness and the mouseyness' which, confronted with egoism, leads to avoidable tragedy (iii. 691). On the other hand Evelyn Scott's poems seemed to enforce Lawrence's other central idea of how far Americans had gone ahead of the English in the necessities of what he had called 'corruption', the coming apart of things. 'I tell you, it scares me. Talk about "already dead" – "those already dead". Gruesome business. "Death enjoying life." There it is. I am glad you say it. It seems to me so American' (iii. 694). Resurrection however would be the hardest pang of all.[84] 'I doubt they never told us the truth about Jesus' – the first hint of what would later become his final rewriting of the Gospel story – 'There's a lot lies behind that *noli me tangere*.'

This was his sermon on Good Friday, as the village band was 'howling and wallowing in lugubriousness down the Corso, in procession after the coffin of Jesus'. Lawrence was rather lugubrious too. He was not sure now of wanting to go to America at all, or whether to keep on Fontana Vecchia, or of anything. 'This is a sort of crisis for me', he told Mountsier, asking him to be patient. 'I've got to come unstuck from the old life and Europe, and I can't know beforehand' (iii. 693). He went on a picnic to Castrogiovanni by car (iii. 695), but that was only another distraction. Now he thought he would give up the house, take all the luggage to Florence, and just drift through the summer before trying to decide. He had caught another cold, and felt stupid.

Then suddenly he made a number of decisions with the air of a man cutting Gordian knots to left and right. He would take Douglas Goldring's advice and go to Curtis Brown, promising for his part to be patient, fair, and to act only through his agent; but asking also to be tied only for five years, and not too tightly lest he get restive. He would also take the plunge and retain Fontana Vecchia, though only until September (iii. 696–7, 700–1). The Baroness was better but would need care, and Frieda was determined to stay all summer so he would have to stop trying to avoid Baden-Baden, but he would take his time going there: some days in Palermo, and Capri, then Rome and Florence, and perhaps (still) a walking tour – leaving Taormina on 9 April. When he could, he would get on and finish *Aaron's Rod* this summer, before turning back to *Mr Noon* (iii. 702).

VIII   To Germany, Now

By 15 April he was in Capri. Though Monty was still on Herm, Faith Mackenzie was in Casa Solitaria and he saw her briefly, as well as John Ellingham Brooks, and Ferdinando and Anna ('Nan') de Chiara. It was through a guest at the de Chiaras, Nellie Morrison, that he now met the two gentle and Buddhist American painters Earl and Achsah Brewster, and forged an important new friendship that would hold life-long. After looking at Achsah's painting of St Francis feeding the birds, Nellie Morrison exclaimed that the saint was the image of Lawrence, whom Achsah must meet. So she brought him to their house Quattro Venti.[85] Lawrence would laugh at the resemblance later, saying Nellie was 'an ass who would say a pudding on a dish looked like Buddha, if only you crossed the spoon and the fork in front to look like two cross-legs' (iii. 720) – and that Achsah's Saint was not like him at all, but a miserable fellow who needed a box on the ear and 'a pint of Chianti'. But he took to the Brewsters immediately, and they to him. They had a great deal in common: most remarkably that the Brewsters had spent their honeymoon in Fontana Vecchia, which seemed extraordinary enough, until they mentioned another favourite house of theirs, San Filippo, in Anticoli-Corrado (where the Lawrences had stayed with Juta and Insole)! The Brewsters' accounts of the meeting[86] show them to have had genuine artistic perceptiveness. They shared the sensitivity to and reverence for the natural world of Lawrence (and St Francis); and his letters to them prove that they also shared his sense of fun. They might be Buddhist and therefore theoretically other-worldly, but they (and their 8–year-old daughter Harwood, of whom Lawrence became very fond) made excellent companions in a world supposedly illusory. At the same time they were temperamentally very different from Lawrence, which made them interesting to one another while risking no dangerous tension, since the Brewsters were wholly unthreatening. Lawrence was not slow to tease them about gaps between theory and practice. Yet they were not at all dominated by him either, and would go their own quiet way.

After that first meeting he accompanied them to the Piccola Marina though he would not swim, he went for a long walk with Earl another afternoon and spent a happy evening with them in Quattro Venti – a good part of his short stay. As a result the Brewsters stored up a number of vivid impressions which show aspects that other accounts do not – and it is interesting to have a more animated 'portrait' of him in 1921 by trained observers. They had been led to expect a 'tormented soul' (Achsah), 'haggard, brooding, and sensual' (Earl). They found him lively, even debonair, vivid, laughing. 'Springtime seemed much more springtime because he was there.' (He was clearly happy to be on the move again, and interested in new people. He was always at his most winning early in a friendship, which alas often failed to continue as it had begun, though not this time.) They speak as others do of how his hair fell over his brow, the redness of his beard, the blueness of his eyes. They too try to catch the odd qualities of his voice and do so better than most: the flexible variations which made him such a good mimic; the 'reed timbre' when low (Achsah) 'with often a curious, plaintive note' (Earl); and the tendency to rise 'high in key' when excited. But, being painters, both of them also watched his hands, and saw how long, narrow and capable they were (Earl), and also how they fell into repose as simply as a cat (Achsah). His blunt nose and the height of his brow, in profile, reminded her of the famous bust of Socrates; but she also noticed how the 'curiously unmodelled' mouth could make him look like Pan or a satyr. She noticed his 'trick of drooping the head pensively', and his 'silent little laugh when he would just open his mouth and swallow it down', as well as the 'short snort of indignation', and 'mostly' a low infectious chuckle – no mention of the high whinny others describe. They also noticed his springy step.

They argued. He diagnosed Earl as not an intellectual type 'meant to be governed by the centre between your eyebrows' (a compliment), and urged him to 'Look deep into the centre – to your solar plexus', though it was some years before Brewster, for all his knowledge of Hinduism, discovered what he meant. Against Buddhism, Lawrence maintained (as in his poem) that the real peace was the aftermath of molten lava; that one 'should *not* pass beyond suffering' though one might try for equilibrium; and that the tiger in us was not to be overcome, suppressed or sublimated. Less seriously, sitting on the floor with his hands clasped round his knees, he brought a whole series of people alive in mimicry. He made the Brewsters share his fantasy of being off in a two-master. To 'lugger around the world', is a fine expression, whoever coined it.[87] He told them about *Aaron's Rod* and asked for suggestions of what to do with his protagonist, now that he had left his family and broken with his past. They said Aaron should either go to Montecassino and repent or 'go through the whole cycle of experience'. Lawrence chuckled with surprise, and said that he had indeed considered sending him to the great monastery, 'but found instead that Aaron had to go to destruction to find his way through from the lowest depths'. Told that they planned to travel to the Orient that autumn to learn more about Buddhism, he promised to come back to see them before they went.

On 19 April he left for Rome, where he saw Juta and met Elizabeth Humes (who would provide hints for Lou Carrington in 'St. Mawr' later, as Juta would for Rico). Jan was undetachable for a walking tour just then, but would go by himself to Sardinia later and do some paintings, to take the place of the photos that had proved so difficult to collect. Lawrence went on to Florence, probably on 21 April.

He had told Douglas (back, in a new eyrie), and Reggie Turner, that he was coming. It so happened that Rebecca West was having a long lunch with the two of them when they decided to pay their respects to Lawrence and introduce her to him.[88] On the way – according to her – Douglas entertained them with an account of how Lawrence no sooner arrived anywhere but he went straight from the railway station to his hotel and immediately began to 'hammer out articles about the place, vehemently and exhaustively describing the temperament of the people'. So when they found him 'tapping away' Douglas 'burst out in a great laugh' and asked if he were writing about Florence, laughing all the more maliciously when Lawrence answered seriously that he was. He may have been revising 'Looking Down on the City', since the sketch has details near the end which suggest experience of 1920, added to that of 1919. But Douglas might have laughed on the other side of his face if, as seems equally possible, Lawrence had already begun to work on the Florentine scenes of *Aaron's Rod*. He had promised to get on with the novel as soon as he could.

When he pushed his work aside and turned to entertain them, Rebecca West found him 'one of the most polite people I had ever met in both naïve and subtle ways ... He made friends as a child might do, by shyly handing me funny little boxes he had brought from some strange place he had recently visited.' But she also noticed, as the Brewsters had, how he seemed to respect the other person's being – though her word was 'personality' as Lawrence's would not have been. As he told them about his recent journeyings she could find no rhyme or reason in them (or for that matter why he was going to Baden-Baden) but thought they must be like the wanderings suddenly undertaken by Russian saints or Indian fakirs. (Perhaps, more mundanely, Lawrence had conveyed his own sense of lacking direction.) As the three visitors sat side by side on the bed, 'We nodded and were entranced.' The next day she went walking with Lawrence and Douglas out into the country. She paints a vivid picture of the spring day, and the contrast between her two companions: Douglas lumbering along 'stockily', Lawrence very white-skinned, and so thin 'that his shoulder blades stood out in a pair of almost wing-like projections', yet moving 'quickly and joyously' along. She was aware of their opposite temperaments, but also how well they got on together, at that time. Over lunch at an inn the talk was all of Magnus, with (she thought) 'the pitifulness that men who have found it difficult to accommodate themselves to their fellow men feel for those who have found it impossible'. The only discordant notes came when Lawrence claimed to detect the animosity of the South for the North in the innkeeper, with whom (he insisted) Douglas should *not* have shaken hands; then spoke of the 'black loathing' he had seen in the eyes of peasants, as when he had caught some old Sicilian crones trying to cheat him by passing off jars of last year's honey.[89] Rebecca West thought these were paranoid over-reactions to what was no more than the natural behaviour of the have-nots towards the haves; and therefore an 'unsatisfactory ending' to their first and last encounter – though she later found in her own case how accurately sensitive his intuition could be.[90]

He left Florence on 23 April, and by the 26th after a 'devil of a journey' (iii. 706), arrived in Baden-Baden.

X   Ebersteinburg – and *Aaron's Rod*

He decided not to stay close to the Ludwig-Wilhelmstift but to go three miles out of town to the village of Ebersteinburg, dominated by the reddish ruins of its old castle. Here, in the Gasthaus Krone, Lawrence's room looked back over black-and-white houses to the wooded hills of the Black Forest, while Frieda's faced out across the great open space of the Rhine plain to the Vosges mountains in the far distance. There were flowery meadows, geese and chickens and pigs, and great yellow oxen pulling wagons. The Gasthaus provided their two comfortable and separate bedrooms, with board, for 35 marks (about 3/-) each per day, so they could actually live more cheaply than in Italy – which was as well, since funds had begun to run low again. As often in a new place, and especially since he had not wanted to come, Lawrence felt mainly dislocated at first. He found Germany 'depressed and *empty* feeling' and its inhabitants 'silent and dim' (iii. 711), especially after the populous and voluble south. He noticed particularly the absence of young men, presumably because of the decimation of the war and because the survivors were looking for work in the cities. He was also struck by the disappearance of militarism, the starkest contrast with his pre-war experience. The only uniforms to be seen were the postman, the two policemen and the driver of the tram into town; and (unlike Metz before the war) there seemed at first to be almost no source of authority, though the Germans were astonishingly orderly and law-abiding. Having used the fear of hostility towards the English as an excuse for not coming earlier, he found himself treated with great courtesy and kindness, and gradually began to like the place better and better. Out in the country there was good food in plenty. The days of blockade and shortage were past, and though many people were impoverished, the rate of exchange meant that the Lawrences could live quite comfortably. Even the poorest households were scrupulously clean and tidy. Nobody tried to swindle, and no children swarmed round begging – indeed the children were childlike, and not premature adults like Sicilian and Neapolitan urchins. Although the village was utterly quiet, that would be good for the work he meant to do.

In any case he had no choice but to make the best of things. Though Frieda's mother was better she had been badly shaken, and had become very dependent on having one of her daughters to look after her. 'Suddenly she has broken up, after being so well for all these years – all her life – she is just seventy. Now she can't be left alone' (iii. 711). Perhaps, later, a nurse-companion could be hired, but in the meantime the Baroness clung to Frieda, and would not hear of them going before the end of the summer (though Lawrence immediately began to wonder how long he could stand it – he hated being compelled). Else was having to settle her own affairs; for Edgar Jaffe had collapsed and died of pneumonia on 29 April.[91] Ever since his political career had ended in that hail of gunfire in 1919 he had become increasingly depressed, and seemed to have lost the will to live. With a blunt honesty that could be mistaken for callousness, Lawrence wrote that he was 'glad Edgar died: better death than ignominious living on' in a world which had 'no place' for him' (iii. 717), and in which he had 'gone cracked' (iii. 728). Meanwhile the youngest sister's marriage was breaking up, but Nusch too had children to look after, though she did come to visit her mother, accompanied by the Berlin banker Emil von Krug whom she was to marry two years later after divorcing von Schreibershofen. Altogether therefore, however 'impossible' it might seem to Lawrence that one of the daughters could always be with their mother, Frieda (and he) would clearly have to stay put for at least another month.

Baden-Baden must have been a shadow of its pre-1914 grandeur and he did not care for it, thinking it already relegated to history along with its fashionable pre-war clientele. There were still good orchestral concerts at the Kurhaus, though he did not think much of the conducting of Siegfried Wagner. 'Great men should *never* have sons.' But the Lichtenthaler Allee was full of 'Scheibers' (racketeers), and the big hotels similarly swarming with profiteers paying inflated prices, 'money hogs in motorcars, mostly Jews' (iv. 33). As had happened when he first came to Germany, his anti-Semitic tendencies were encouraged by those in the air around him. The contrast of the ostentatiously rich who had profited by the war, a number of whom no doubt were Jewish, with the poverty of the peasants and the genteel poverty of the Ludwig-Wilhelmstift, must have made a fertile breeding ground for anti-Semitic talk in both Gasthaus and Old Gentlewomen's Home, the shape of much to come.

But if Baden-Baden was only for dutiful visits (though he became fond of his mother-in-law), the great trees of the Schwarzwald were an increasing joy. Every morning that he could, he went into the forest by himself, to write. Once again he thought of Gibbon's account of how frightened the civilised Romans had been when they first came into the Hercynian Wood, but for him the great trees, particularly the dark and tangy firs, were a joy and an aid to creativity: 'I find a forest such a strange stimulus – the trees are like living company, they seem to give off something dynamic and secret, and anti-human, or non-human. Especially fir-trees' (iv. 25).

Suddenly, *Aaron's Rod* began to come, and once it really started again, it came with a rush. On 2 May he was still unsure whether he could finish, but by the 6th he had 'some hope' (iii. 711, 714), by the 12th it was two-thirds done (iii. 717), and at mid-month the end was well within sight (iii. 722). Now he was confident enough to ask Violet Monk, who had shown an interest in the book in 1919, to type the first half for him (iii. 724). By 27 May only the final chapter was still to do, and by the end of the month it too was finished (iii. 729, 730).

Why did it suddenly become unblocked? It cannot have been only the fir-trees! There had been propitious working conditions before – yet the book had stuck twice, and had obstinately refused to take off. Something quite important must have become clear to its author, but since no manuscript(s) survive, the novel's development can only be inferred from remarks about it in the letters.

He 'began' at Mecklenburgh Square (iii. 728) at the end of 1917,[92] though this may mean little more than having the idea then. There is no further mention before 21 February 1918 at Hermitage where he says he is working 'very spasmodically' on another 'daft novel' (iii. 216), as well as on the American essays which were his main concern from late 1917 to June 1918. By 17 March 1918 he had written 150 pages, but there is no way of knowing what was in them; and though he told Amy Lowell in September that he had been 'slowly' working on another novel (iii. 280), he may have done little more in fact. He never named it or its protagonist in the letters; only said that it was 'blameless as *Cranford*' and 'funny' (iii. 227).

Some things cannot have been in those first 150 pages: the neurasthenic atmosphere of the immediate post-war period in Eastwood, or Tanny (based on Frieda) leaving to see her people at the beginning of chapter IX (in life, November 1919). The visit to Hermitage by the real-life Captain White (chapter VIII) was probably sometime in March 1918, but it would have been extraordinarily prompt to have got that in, and it is by no means certain that Lilly was in the book yet – or even that it started with Aaron leaving his wife and children, which would hardly have been 'funny'. Relations with Frieda had been strained in Cornwall and Hermitage, and Lawrence might have been tempted to explore such an idea in imagination – but there may have been no more than a man rebelling against Eastwood (like Alvina) and encountering the Bohemian characters of the first seven chapters.

After *Movements*, and the burst of new stories, the dangerous illness and the pieces for Murry, he told Huebsch in June 1919 that he had picked up the novel and hoped it might be done before he came to America (iii. 364) – but this was whistling in the wind. (What he actually proceeded to work on was Shestov.) He may have talked about it to Violet Monk at Grimsbury Farm in August 1919 and even have written a bit more,[93] which would explain how he came to ask her to type for him later. However all the evidence suggests that the novel in this first version never really took off.

It is therefore likely that in July 1920 – as had happened with *The Lost Girl* – his taking it up again was both an attempt to recast, *and* a new beginning with a fresh idea. This would explain how he could talk of 'working with ever-diminishing spasms of fitfulness' on a novel he did not expect to get much further with (iii. 567), and of having 'begun another novel' (iii. 565, 571). By 18 July however it was one-third done, and albeit temporarily at a standstill (iii. 572), he thought it might steam ahead once it got started again. Yet by September it had only jerked 'one chapter forward now and then' to half-way (iii. 594), and he had no idea where the second half might come from. He hoped to 'sort of jump him picaresque' (iii. 602) when he got back to Taormina, and managed by 25 November at Fontana Vecchia to have written 'more than half' of what was now named *Aaron's Rod*, but he still had no idea how to end it – and began *Mr Noon* instead (iii. 626). Whether or not the idea of a man leaving his wife had been the original starting-point, it seems fairly certain that it was so now – perhaps the easier to imagine after his own impulse to leave Frieda in early 1919, and his determination to make himself less dependent on her – though Aaron's marriage is quite unlike Lawrence's. A marked impulse of his new stories was an affirmation of manhood; the Whitman essay had declared that the next step beyond marriage was a relation between men; and Lawrence had gone off, deliberately, to Italy by himself.

The novel's new development ran counter to any mere dream fulfilment however, by contrasting Aaron with a Lawrence-figure who did *not* want to leave his wife, though he too had no time for dependence on a woman. Lawrence seems to have divided himself and his feelings about singleness and commitment to relationship, and to have played them off imaginatively against one another, to see where that led. Whether or not Rawdon Lilly made an appearance in the first version, the move from the Eastwood and Mecklenburgh Square material of 1917–18 to half the novel we now have might well have consisted of the Lilly chapters VIII, IX and X; followed by Aaron's second rejection of marriage in XI and his determination to have no more unions before the achievement of 'singleness'; and then the journey to 'Novara' to meet Lilly. To the end of chapter XII is half the novel now. chapter XIII, completing the visit to 'Novara', might well have made the 'more than half' of November 1920 – but there is still no end in sight for the novel other than to keep jumping Aaron picaresque on further journeyings. His relation to the layer down of the law[94] was unresolved – and there was as yet no Miriam, temptress to another altar, to complicate it.

So the novel *had* jerked forward, but had stuck again. Since Lawrence kept saying that it would not be 'dangerous' (in his and Mountsier's special sense), he had clearly no idea yet of the Marchesa or of what would happen to Aaron. Should he take him to Florence and/or Montecassino? Meanwhile, blocked again, and as always needing to write something that would sell, Lawrence turned to *Mr Noon*, initially away from himself and his complex feelings.

What, then, caused the transformation in the forest at Ebersteinburg? – from 2 May when he was 'trying to go on ... though God knows if I am going to succeed' (iii. 711); through 12 May when the book was two-thirds done; to 16 May when it was not only 'well under weigh' but its 'end in sight' (iii. 722)? If the previous guesses have any accuracy, taking Aaron to Florence was still in itself merely picaresque. The end of chapter XV is roughly two-thirds of the book we now have, but whenever chapters XIV and XV were done, the real take-off point seems to be the encounter of Aaron and the Marchesa which begins in chapter XVI, and is as decisive for Aaron in one direction as the bomb which destroys his flute in chapter XX will be in another. Those four chapters were written by 27 May, leaving only the last, 'Words' between Aaron and Lilly, to be done by the end of the month

Those who seek straightforward autobiography in Lawrence's fiction may suspect a liaison with the Marchese Carlo Torrigiani's American wife, to one of whose musical at-homes Reggie Turner took him in 1919 or 1920, and who may have been among the Americans he saw while staying at La Canovaia. However, the recreation of life into literature worth the name is seldom so simple. If the Torrigianis were the two 'well-known residents' to whom Lawrence, in turn, introduced the Carswells later that year, there seems little resemblance between Aaron's Marchesa and Catherine's 'large American woman who was studying singing' and her stout son with his Fascist cudgel.[95] If any autobiographical material went into the imagining of Aaron's relationship, it was much more likely to have been Lawrence's brief affair with Rosalind – but it should not be assumed that the fiction of 1921 embodied his 'true' feelings about the experience of 1920. For to whatever extent he thought of himself and Rosalind, his imagination clearly transposed and selected (the disguise also suggesting a careful tenderness towards her, still, that he did not always show to others, and that Aaron does not feel for the Marchesa). Moreover the idea of centring the whole episode on music, and the selection, in response, of one strand from a complex web of feeling and memory, was above all *thematic*. Seriously to attempt any kind of formula for the workings of imagination would be foolish. Yet it is possible to glimpse (crudely) how the idea of making his 'Miriam' a musician, together with some of Lawrence's own feelings about music (as in the concert in Taormina and one of the real Marchesa's concerts[96]) and *some* elements (but not others) in his feelings about what had happened with Rosalind, might suggest the way to draw Aaron to a first decisive crux.

The flute in the first sixteen chapters of the book had been a way for Aaron to go on making a living and sending money back to his wife; and a way of drawing the attention and respect of the characters with whom Lawrence wanted to involve him – equivalent to his own writing, but usefully non-verbal in contrast with Lilly's wordiness. It had potentially been much more: a sign of potential individuality, liveliness and fertility, in a man out of the ordinary – and also an expression of his loneliness. As Aaron's rod of divine power, however, it had shown little sign of budding like the one in the Bible; presumably because Lawrence had not quite seen what to make of it. Now however the flute becomes a way of precipitating out the major conflict within Aaron himself, and then of bringing his debate with Lilly the married man to a final question. Aaron had so deeply *not* wanted a sexual relationship with Josephine in London that when drawn into one he had collapsed, his lower centres (like Jim's) almost paralysed. He had realised in Novara that he had never intended really to surrender himself to his wife, and therefore that his whole idea of himself as lover and husband had been a false mask. Now the flute – as opposed to the piano, let alone the orchestra – becomes a symbolic showing, both to himself and the woman, of what entire singleness of life would be like: 'It was a clear, sharp, lilted run-and-fall of notes, not a tune in any sense of the word, and yet a melody: a bright, quick sound of pure animation: a bright, quick animate noise, running and pausing ... the notes followed clear and single one after the other ... a wild sound.'[97] It has no artistic form, yet is naturally harmonious and spontaneous – as for Lawrence art should be. It is blessedly free from moral meaning or responsibility, and also from the burden of emotion, 'ponderous chains of feeling'.[98] Instead of drawing listeners into intense nervous emotion and consciousness as (to Lawrence) a violin or cello does, it liberates its hearer from consciousness of self, giving her freedom just to be. It needs no accompaniment or combination, and its notes are separate and single, unlike the piano's chords. It also embodies Lawrence's continual search for a 'language' older than our present culture: Medieval rather than Renaissance, but actually more archaic than Medieval, indeed more ancient still, behind even Apollo to Marsyas and Pan, something wild rather than civilised – in our sense, that is.

The Marchesa is able to sing again, to Aaron's fluting – the two singlenesses in one which an earlier Lawrence would have endorsed. But now, and still more in the awakening of desire through the music of singleness, there seems a clear and ironic contradiction. The budding of Aaron's rod not only exposes double meanings and contradictory powers – phallus as opposed to flute – but begins to complicate what had seemed the primary contrast between Aaron and Lilly. It must have become clear now that the flute would have to be split, and the debate between a longing for singleness and belief in marriage (the contradiction in Lawrence himself) restated more complexly.

If Lawrence used his experience with Rosalind in imagining Aaron's crisis, what he chose to emphasise thematically, from among complicated feelings and memories, were those elements alone which would throw into the highest relief the challenge of sex to singleness. *Look!* had been intensely grateful for desire, and both there and in *Women in Love* Lawrence had imagined singleness as *increased* by the kind of love that was like star-equilibrium. Now however, for Aaron, the relation with the Marchesa is the catalyst which decisively separates out 'love' (particularly her tendril kind) from 'singleness', and reveals them as mutually exclusive for him. Sexual excitement robs him of his wild alertness, as of a single creature, so that the soldiers can rob him of his note-case and violate his being. When he sleeps with the Marchesa, the fiction brutally rewrites the earlier Lawrencian account of the rebirth after New Year in *Look!*: the ritual sacrifice of sex; the female lover becoming 'a child, Almost', and yet 'a woman, knowing All'; the male lover's tenderness towards the 'little one' curled on his breast in 'Wedlock'; the new sense of responsibility. As imagination now concentrates the element in Lawrence that longed for singleness above all, coition becomes a victimisation of the god-in-Aaron; and ecstasy not death-and-rebirth but an extraction of his passionate power, leaving him 'withered' or 'carrion'; the child-woman on his chest an intolerable clinging. Throughout, 'there was all the time something hard and reckless and defiant, which stood apart'.[99] Afterwards he feels *only* what 'Medlars and Sorb-Apples' had expressed – one emotion among many poems – the gladness of being alone. He tells the Marchesa that for good or ill he feels himself a married man who must have no other liaisons. (This is obviously an important conclusion for Lawrence too, and with Aaron and Lilly united in that respect, resolves part of the book's exploration. There are husbands, and there are lovers. Author and both protagonists, it seems, are husbands.) Aaron writes a letter that is really to himself: renouncing all kinds of love and declaring his belief only 'in the fight and nothing else', against woman, against the world, against love which is of all things 'the most deadly to me'.[100]

This goes much deeper than the question of who 'uses' whom in love, and the male complainings of how men used to initiate sex but women expect to be sexually ministered to now, on which the congregation of males in Argyle's flat seem to agree though Lilly remains tactfully reticent, still hoping for balance. This had been Lawrence's complaint against Frieda, who (he had privately confessed) felt free to refuse him when he wanted her, but expected him to satisfy her on demand; and he may have used the Marchesa's husband and Aaron to dramatise this as part of the male rebellion against overweening womanhood in which his fiction had been engaged since 1918. But the generalisations of sexual politics (of any kind) seldom hold more than a very partial truth at best. And Aaron's feelings are neither to be taken uncritically – Lawrence is aware of their one-sidedness – nor as a final verdict on the episode with Rosalind. For Aaron is only part of Lawrence. Moreover the powerful imagining of the repudiation of the Marchesa, so fiercely contradicting the Lawrence of 1913–17, now forces the Lawrence of 1921 to debate the contradiction between the Aaron and the Lilly in himself at a deeper level than before. This may be what he meant by confessing that his protagonist was 'misbehaving and putting ten fingers to his nose at everything' (iii. 720); but also that the end was in sight.

For in fact the whole of Aaron's story reveals a character who could *not* live alone. Though he has wandered like a picaro, a number of episodes and characters (Lottie, the Bohemians, the link between Aaron's collapse and Jim's, the quarrel in Covent Garden, Aaron's new insight into himself at Novara, Argyle's affirmation of the need to love and the discussion in his flat) now reveal a cumulative significance which helps to pull the novel better together than had ever seemed likely from the history of its growth. The music of singleness can only be a momentary liberation for all those (the vast majority, it seems) who are forever pulled between desire and resistance, the abiding need to give themselves to another, and the recoiling need to be themselves alone – which *Tortoises* had also treated. Moreover, the fantasy of being able to exist apart from society receives the most violent of all awakenings when the bomb goes off in the café. Between internal contradiction and external violation Aaron's rod can only be split apart – unless and until (Lilly says) he could learn to live by the impulse of the unique and individual 'Tree of Life' within him, never losing *himself* 'in woman nor humanity nor in God'.[101] Lilly tells him that the era of love is over, and what matters now is power – not however in Nietzsche's sense, and not any imposition of the self on another or others, but rather the instinctual potency within the self, able (once liberated) to crack old bondage and free new life. If, having learned to listen to its promptings, Aaron is still impelled to relate himself to someone or something other, it should not be in any selfless mode of love, or religious or social idealism, but rather a recognition of superior power in another individual, able to lead, liberate and strengthen his own selfhood. So says Lilly, implying that he himself is such a one.

But Lilly is not to be regarded uncritically either. Lawrence's title for the final sermon is 'Words' – and Lilly as wordy salvationist has already been put in his place by Jim's punch in the wind. Lawrence uses the most obviously Lawrencian figure in the book, not only to try out some of his own ideas, but also to diagnose what it was in himself that so put up the backs of other people – an accurate Lawrencian phrase, and in his sense not something to regret! In Jim's visit, Lilly's readiness to see himself as a saviour is sardonically pinpointed first, and then his total inability to imagine how his diagnoses will affect their recipient. There is comedy in the scene, especially as Tanny's Lilly is not much more able to *live* alone than Aaron. As he massages the lower centres of the sick man, trying to bring them back to life, he sees how it is his own over-readiness to involve himself that tempts betrayal, as Christ produced Judas, but he goes ahead all the same.[102]

However Lilly also has an aloneness; is indeed as dual as his friend, though in the opposite proportion. The little man continues to believe in marriage, and in male friendship, but both come second to his essential solitude. He denounces the danger of turning marriage into an '*Egoïsme à deux*'; he insists that in love one is 'most intensely of all, alone'; and maintains that in all relationships the heart 'beats alone in its own silence'. There may be some wishful self-flattery in Lawrence imagining what with half his mind he wanted to be:

Lilly was alone—and out of his isolation came his words, indifferent as to whether they came or not. And he left his friends utterly to their own choice. Utterly to their own choice. Aaron felt that Lilly was *there*, existing in life, yet neither asking for connection nor preventing any connection. He was present, he was the real centre of the group. And yet he asked nothing of them, and he imposed nothing. He left each to himself, and he remained just himself: neither more nor less.

But if this be wishful, it is also no more than a half-truth on the book's own evidence. Such self-sufficiency moreover, especially when combined with Lilly's sense of himself as a saviour, his apparent friendliness, his constant involvement with others, make him *objectionable* – indeed 'perhaps the most objectionable person' Aaron knows. There is something horrible about the way that Lilly offers friendship, sees deeply into or 'through' people, and then withdraws. 'It was then, after his departure, that they realised his basic indifference to them, and his silent arrogance.' People feel that 'Nothing can touch him on the quick, nothing can really *get* at him'; and this fills them 'with resentment, almost with hate'.[103] Imagining from Aaron's point of view, Lawrence can be as ruthless in diagnosing what it is in himself that makes people dislike him, as he is in diagnosing what is wrong with others. So when the Lilly-in-him lets go with a torrent of 'Words' in the final chapter, these are certainly open to question, and should be seen as a challenge to one's own tree of life rather than as supposedly conclusive.

However some of what Lilly says (in a setting that recalls the lunch outside Florence with Douglas and Rebecca West) is what the Lawrence of 1921 believes: that there is no God outside the living centre of each individual, who therefore must never lose or give away that innermost self in any relationship. Indeed, if one is impelled to seek relationship, it must be of a kind which strengthens and liberates the sacred power of individual life and growth. (Its unique life-sap is what makes the lily of the field considerable.) So far, this is consistent with the Lawrence of *The Rainbow* and *Women in Love*, barring the reaction now against *any*, even temporary, loss of self, which had formerly been seen as preliminary to rebirth. But consequently, what is most significant in 1921 is the radical hostility, now (though it has been growing steadily since 1918), to all forms of love which involve loss of self. What is newly formulated at the end of this novel is the resulting opposition between love and power: primarily empowerment of others rather than power over them (though that too has its fascination), the ability to liberate the unique god-quick within. This implies that some have greater powers of soul, and that in relationships smaller souls must submit to greater. It cannot be forced, but must happen voluntarily. Yet since neither Aaron nor Lilly can live alone, and since Aaron has seen something more powerful in the little man than in himself, Aaron's own living centre (says Lilly in the final line) will tell him what to do – though it remains a question whether this be true, let alone whether Aaron will bring himself to do it. Lawrence can not, it seems, confidently imagine the true male friendship he told Katherine he had never experienced.

Lilly is talking of *individual* relationship – and his idea is not extraordinary if one thinks of the more powerful individuals to whom one does submit one's soul in literature, art, philosophy, religion, for awakening and growth. However objections may arise when this is generalised into politics. In the preceding discussion in the café, Argyle contends that civilisation requires a basis of slavery, and this is taken up by a Lilly seemingly willing to advocate once-for-all political submission to a 'superior being', backed by *military* power – a notion which was just beginning to make itself heard. (Benito Mussolini, who would make his bid for power in 1922, was already talking of the need for strong leadership; and the first mass meeting of the National Socialist German Workers' Party had taken place in Munich in February 1920 – though the ideas of Part II, chapter IV of *Mein Kampf* played no part yet in the announcement of its twenty-five principles, or in the anniversary meeting in February 1921.)

Lilly is of course reacting to Levison's assertion that the logic of history leads inevitably to Bolshevism, to which Lilly clearly intends a counter-provocation – but having thrown up his idea he refuses to pursue it, and dissolves the argument into even more provocative laughter. Before labelling Lawrence a 'fascist' however one should also perhaps attend to what Lilly then says, with a much stronger weight of feeling: 'I'll tell you the real truth ... I think every man is a sacred and holy individual, *never* to be violated. I think there is only one thing I hate to the verge of madness, and that is *bullying*.'[104] In the novel, mob-processions and mob violence by opposed factions are equally dehumanising, and the bomb which immediately follows Lilly's words now is '*bullying*' to the nth degree, whether thrown by Bolshevist, Fascist or Anarchist. (Even to label this a 'leadership' novel is seriously misleading. The word is used just once, on the last page, and is immediately restricted from a political to an individual sense.) Yet Lawrence has let his character flirt with ideas that would prove disastrous – in answer to others that would prove no less so.

There is also a question in sexual politics. For if Lilly stands by his marriage – as he does (and Aaron, more reluctantly) – who is to do the submitting to the superior being there? This might be a matter of showing, in this particular fiction, which was which – though we do not see enough of Tanny to know. Instead, Lilly insists that whereas in idealistic love the man is the lover and the woman the beloved, in the world of power this must be *generally* reversed.

"... The woman must submit, but deeply, deeply submit. Not to any foolish fixed authority, not to any foolish and arbitrary will. But to something deep, deeper. To the soul in its dark motion of power and pride ... A deep, unfathomable free submission."
"You'll never get it," said Aaron.[105]

Aaron is surely right about Tanny, but that seems only half the question. For why shouldn't it be the woman who is the superior soul in its dark motion of power and pride? Now it is Lilly who tries to posit a historical law – without convincing Aaron. The dramatising of two sides of Lawrence allows the one which longed for Frieda to acknowledge his leadership to speak out openly, now, of what he had privately admitted to Katherine in December 1918 – and to be answered by the side which knew better by experience; leaving a question open in marriage, as in friendship. Yet, though there are still hopeful murmurings about 'balance', Lawrence has greatly changed since the days of star-equilibrium.

X   Life on the Surface – and the Unconscious

Meanwhile, through May, when he was not sitting with his back to a fir-tree imagining Aaron and Lilly, daily life went on all the more sunnily because Frieda was happy. It was good for her to be needed, even when the Baroness's health improved; and the giving over of a whole chapter of Frieda's autobiography to her husband's affectionate relation with her mother would show how much that meant to her too. The foundation had been laid even in the scolding at Icking, and strengthened on the Baroness's visit to England before the war to stand by her daughter. She probably (with Else) helped them financially in the early days. After the war, as soon as he could, Lawrence returned the kindness, with food parcels in the bad times and presents for the children. He had also written regularly. Now the friendship grew – not without humour, one guesses, at the problem of translating to the old ladies in the Ludwig-Wilhelmstift what sort of things it was that the English son-in-law was famous for. Luckily they could be told that he was going to be published in German by Insel-Verlag, without anything being available yet. It will have been good for Frieda to see her sisters too, on less unequal terms than in 1912–13. In addition to Nusch's visit with her new man, Frieda went briefly to Munich to be with Else when Edgar died. A recovered Alfred Weber came to pay his respects, though he seems to have found the Ludwig-Wilhelmstift a bit too much for him (iii. 716). There will also have been some society in Baden-Baden of which we know nothing. Frieda had social standing here, with her own language in her ears and living on the edge of the Forest where her family used to holiday (and where she had met Weekley). Now it was Lawrence who was the outsider – and after all her years away it must have been a huge relief to be with him in *her* homeland again, even though Germany was only slowly recovering under the burden of 'reparations'. The fact that every morning Lawrence would go off happily into the woods to write, and that the writing was going well, must have made him easier to live with – though it comes as no surprise to learn that she 'hated' *Aaron's Rod* (iv. 124). How long all this could last must have become a sharper question, of course, after the first month or so. As Lawrence began seriously to talk of hiring a nurse-companion, and to plan the next move, domestic arguments must have started again. There is an amusing giveaway in a letter to Dr Kippenberg on 23 June, when Lawrence believes that Germany is still inwardly strong because 'She has an almost feminine power of passive resistance and stubbornness' (iv. 40–1). But all-in-all, Frieda was happier than she had been for years.

Lawrence's pleasure in his new acquaintance with the Brewsters shows itself in a sprightly exchange of letters. To Earl, he 'finally and forever' renounces loving anything or anybody (iii. 718–19). Nor will he have any 'Nirvana' which excludes pain, sorrow and the passions (or, a different argument, Hume's claim that human nature is universally the same[106]). His letter to Achsah is full of jokes, teases and vivid description, and a warm affection for them both. (There is also an interesting sidelight, dropped casually among remarks on *Sons and Lovers* which the Brewsters had been reading: 'As for Miriam, I dreamed of her two nights ago'; iii. 720. He may not believe in love, but his dreams often show deeper feelings than he would outwardly admit.)

Mountsier had now decided to make another journey to Europe, but was still consumed by the idea of a yacht to the South Seas, and had saved £1,000 for the purpose. He left New York at the end of April for Paris, after which he would go to London before coming to see them in Germany. Lawrence still went along with the dream, though his heart was less in it now and it seemed well beyond his reach. (His English bank account on which he was determined to live, keeping his American earnings for a safety net, was running low again. It stood at less than £50 when he reached Germany; iii. 714, and even after he got Secker to pay at least £50 of the full advance for *Women in Love*, only £75 remained by 11 June; iv. 3.)[107] However, as was his wont, he did not say no at once, but took von Krug's advice and help to have enquiries made in Hamburg where boats might come more cheaply; and when Captain Short wrote of one in Cornwall, he arranged for Mountsier to see it when he got to England (iii. 712). Then, however, he had to admit that they had nowhere near enough to buy such a boat, refit an engine and finance a crew; and as well as being anxious not to get into debt, he had become unwilling to be 'nose-tied' in any direction. Moreover, Frieda was 'terrified' of the whole idea (iii. 729). It could still be played with from time to time, but really that bubble had burst.

The new relationship with Curtis Brown started edgily. Lawrence did not much like his 'impertinent' tone (iii. 710), perhaps because Brown was less easygoing than Pinker about his dealing directly with publishers. He had promised to act through his agent but soon reverted to previous habits. Oxford University Press had decided against trying to publish *Movements in European History* in the USA, though it sold quite well in Britain.[108] When Ely now suggested he do an illustrated children's book on European painting from Giotto to Constable, for OUP with the Medici Society, Mountsier was told not to mention this to Curtis Brown (iii. 725). Only when requirements and terms were clear did Lawrence inform his English agent: 'This kind of business I must do alone', he told Mountsier, 'How does an agent know *what* I want to do?' (iv. 27) – but that was hardly the point. Then, having had Brown draw up an agreement, Lawrence first suggested confining the scope to Italian painting, and then decided to keep the agreement in his own hands till he had a reaction to a more restricted scope, from Nigel de Grey of the Medici Society (iv. 47–8). He thought he might go to Florence to do it (iv. 41), but also feared it might take quite a long time. In fact the idea seems simply to have lapsed; and one reason may have been that his agent felt no inclination to press it. When Michael Sadleir wanted 'Wintry Peacock' once more for a new anthology – the periodical it had been bought for having come to nothing – Lawrence got Mountsier to send it, again without telling Brown. He had the excuse that it had already been bought (iv. 36; though he hoped for a little more money) – but these were hardly the ways to cement the new relationship. And when Curtis Brown discovered that Lawrence had been corresponding with Secker about whether *Mr Noon* Part I or *Aaron's Rod* should be done first, he objected sharply enough to get Lawrence's attention (iv. 27). Lawrence had thought his new agent more 'obedient' than Pinker (iv. 29); but now, though continuing to deal with Secker, he warned: 'For the Lord's Sake, don't let Curtis Brown imagine I write you any business. It is high treason in his eyes' (iv. 35).

Relations with Secker were still uneven too. At last, after more delay in the printing, the English *Women in Love* was published on 10 June – five years after it was originally written. Moreover both Curtis Brown and Secker were pleased with Part I of *Mr Noon* (iii. 710), and despite its brevity, Secker thought he could sell it as a short novel at 6/- (iii. 717 and n. 2). However, he proposed not to count this as one of the five books of his contract with Lawrence, but as a pleasant extra – whereupon Lawrence preferred Secker to bring out *Aaron's Rod* instead, and wait for the completion of *Mr Noon* (iii. 730), whose prospectus he now expanded to *three* parts, taking the story of Gilbert and Johanna to 1919 (iii. 667; iv. 35). It was this correspondence that raised Curtis Brown's hackles; but all three finally agreed that the rearrangement would be sensible – thus, as it turned out, ensuring that Part I of *Mr Noon* would not be published in Lawrence's lifetime, since he never finished Part II (which was now to end in 1914), and never started Part III at all. And to Lawrence's sharp annoyance, Secker rejected the psychology book, increasing the contrast with Seltzer who published it that May. Unfairly, Lawrence called Curtis Brown 'an idiot' for even offering it to Secker, whom he now thought 'absolutely *useless* as a publisher, save of novels or library books' (iv. 27–8); though he sensibly did not say such things to them. If Secker would not do the psychology book, he said crossly, he should not get *Sardinia* either.

There was now also a problem about the latter. For though Juta had done his trip to the island and produced eight illustrations for the book in suitably 'flat' colours (iv. 35), which Lawrence and Frieda liked very much indeed, it seemed that colour printing might be prohibitively expensive (iv. 42). However, Lawrence discovered a German printer who would do the blocks for less than half the price which the Medici Society would expect to pay. Rather than omit Juta's work, he was willing not only to give Secker the book after all, but even to take a smaller royalty (iv. 34, 35); though at the German prices he thought it would not be necessary. With all this however, the publication of the book hung fire.

When the first English reviews of *Women in Love* began to come in, the contrast with the American ones was very plain to see. In the *TLS* (9 June) Edmund Blunden, now a regular visitor at Garsington, thought Lawrence's conception of sex a 'jubilant brutality' and the book otherwise dull and disappointing – with the exception of Hermione, that is. An unsigned review in the *Saturday Westminster Gazette* was jocular. 'Mr. D. H. Lawrence's new and very long novel *Women in Love* is not unlike a serious elaboration of the well-known advertisement, "Mr. and Mrs. Smith, having cast off clothing of all descriptions, invite inspection. Distance no object."' Lawrence had expected hostility, but what most characterised the English reviewers (with the exceptions of Frank Swinnerton and Rebecca West) was their extraordinary dismissive condescension[109] – apart, that is, from Murry, who had gone to

Switzerland with a now very ill Katherine, and whose review did not come until August.

Whereas the American reviewers, though by no means uncritical, had given Lawrence's book some serious thought and respect. John Macy in the *New York Evening Post Literary Review*, while preferring *The Rainbow*, saw the new novel as a work of tragic power, and if 'dangerous to public morals', only as Hardy and Meredith were so. As 'tragic poet' Lawrence's prose can be over-lyrical, and the emotions of his characters 'more frequent and violent than the ordinary human soul can enjoy and endure', but Lawrence knows 'accurately what goes on inside the human head', and there is firm grounding in that daily life is studied 'with a fidelity not surpassed by Mr. Bennett'. Evelyn Scott wrote the *Dial*'s review; in some ways more critical, but no less respectful. She allied him with artists who affirm a remarkably individual vision rather than interrogating common existence; but if the most individual be the purest art in one way, there is something deathly about it in another, since the more intensely 'romantic' the vision, the more absolute it becomes. Lawrence's characters have no capacity for 'the play of relations'; and though the book purports to be a novel, Lawrence might as easily 'turn philosopher or priest'. At the same time she had perceptive things to say about the characters,[110] unlike Murry who would claim to be unable to tell them apart.

It seems Lawrence was right to hope for a better audience in America. His new poems continued to appear there: 'Humming Bird' in the *New Republic* in June (based not on experience but Crèvecœur), and in July 'Snake' in the *Dial* and 'Mosquito' in the *Bookman*. When at the end of July however Mountsier told Lawrence that Curtis Brown was having trouble placing work in England, he was so resentful that he wanted no more sent out without real likelihood of acceptance (iv. 55). Yet new prospects were opening up even there. For the first time in ten months he heard from Cynthia Asquith with news that her husband had given up the law to take a job with Hutchinson & Co the publishers. Lawrence at once arranged to have 'Fanny and Annie' sent to him (iv. 32), hoping for an ongoing relation with *Hutchinson's Magazine* which had already printed 'The Fox'. Moreover Kot, asked to get a new nib for a Swan pen, sent also a Russian story for Lawrence to improve his translation (iv. 37). This was Bunin's sardonic 'The Gentleman from San Francisco', about a man visiting Capri in the pride of riches, and being carried out in a coffin. Lawrence grinned with delight and was very ready to oblige.[111]

Most inspiriting of all, the arrival of Seltzer's *Psychoanalysis and the Unconscious* set him thinking about expanding it. No sooner had he finished *Aaron* than he began to make notes. Did Seltzer think the sales would justify a second psychology book (iii. 732)? (Barbara Low's little book on Freud had done quite well, he had heard; iv. 27.)[112] But before any reply could come he had gone ahead anyway, because 'it is in my head' (iv. 28). It was after a week of work on it that he wrote about the fir trees in the letter of 7 June; by which time he expected to finish within the month. On 20 June he was indeed 'nearly done', and he hoped to be quite done in another eight days (iv. 39), apparently knowing his rate of progress exactly. For he was expanding and setting out anew from material now thoroughly familiar – including the unpublished 'Education' essays – and so must have been able to write several of the chapters even faster than usual.

Since the original manuscript has not survived one can only restore the book Lawrence wrote by ignoring his extensive revision of the typescripts later, in a very different mood. The original version was probably much more genial than the later ones. He was happy in himself and brimming with confidence after finishing his novel, and knew nothing yet of the reviews of *Psychoanalysis*. To get the original tone the Foreword must be removed from the book we know.[113] Moreover, though there was a good deal of joshing of the 'gentle reader' who might need persuading that (s)he had such a thing as a solar plexus; and a half-playful half-aggressive insistence that 'there is no straight path between you and me, dear reader', so that misunderstanding and disagreement are inevitable, it is highly likely that a more corrosive tone entered only after hearing about the reviews, in a last run-through of the manuscript before having it typed. The most acid sentence in the book – which would lead to the idea of calling it 'Harlequinade of the Unconscious' before the final title was arrived at – occurs very near the beginning of the typescript, and is very revealing of the connection between aggression or jocosity, and defensiveness. It is easy to imagine Lawrence writing in Ebersteinburg, 'Help me to be serious, dear reader', since much of the typescript is playful; but not so easy to imagine him going on (in his mood then) 'I think it's because I detest you so that I keep on jingling these silly bells'.[114] That note, unfortunately, would grow more pervasive as he grew to distrust his American readers almost as much as the English ones.

What was the unrevised version like, if we peel off the revisions? Since the first pages of chapter I are autograph revision, we cannot know how the book originally began; but when the typescript pages start,[115] Lawrence is rejecting both the Freudian cellarage and the Pisgah of idealism, and asserting that the First Cause is unknowable. He prefers a mystic 'Om' to any pretension to know; and will not talk about God, though he does not think God would mind. What he does insist on (as against the science which confines life to a bio-chemical phenomenon occurring long after the accidental beginning and subsequent evolution of the material universe) is that life itself is primary, and that matter and energy come from the death of living 'plasm'. Moreover he believes that 'the dead pass away direct into life itself', though we know not how, and that they 'come home to the living'. The reader may believe it or not – but the life that is in the tiniest creatures, like the caterpillar he is just now pushing with his pencil, was there at the beginning and indeed *was* the beginning of everything else, constantly renewed by death – a new Lawrencian version of the Gospel according to St John.[116]

If life itself is primary, then it is essential to identify, within the growth of the fertilised cell and the interaction of different impulses in the creation of individuals, how they may both become more harmoniously creative in themselves, and interactively fulfil the creative purpose in all things. The purpose of this second book goes, then, beyond psychology to a much more radical differing from Freud. Where Freud is scientist and sceptic, researching with not overmuch optimism the possibility that rational man can learn to understand the workings of the psyche, and become socialised as far as humanly possible; Lawrence is already implicitly insisting that a 'creative or religious motive' is the primary impulse, and the sexual motive only secondary, though it will be the revised Introduction that makes that point crisply from the start. His familiar, sometimes throwaway tone tries to take the religiosity out of this and keep pulling himself back to earth, and above all to the individual human being with a backside in his trousers – but for him the living individual is the centre of a living universe. He is pleased to find, in Einstein's 'popular exposition' of his theory of relativity which he had asked Kot to send him before he began to write (iv. 23),[117] that the new theory subverts the idea of a universe governed by a unitary system of scientific laws, and substitutes instead the idea that cosmic forces can only be known in relation to one another. This seemed to reinforce his own denial (since 1914) of any one absolute principle, and hence his belief that life was always a matter of *relationships* – between opposite impulses within the self, and between selves, none paramount, all 'purely relative to one another', in an essentially creative pluralism.[118]

This is therefore the June 1921 testament of a still 'passionately religious' Lawrence, though modified by what he had found out about himself and his relation with his wife – and by extension about the psyche and relationships generally – since writing 'The Crown' and *Women in Love*. It follows that much of it is implicitly autobiographical. Indeed, another sign of the new confidence of June 1921 is how close to the surface the hint of autobiography is allowed to come. There is moreover a criticism of the Lawrence of 1913–17 which has become explicit, and in some respects extreme: a repudiation of a previous self as fervent as that self had been.

The new confidence also shows itself polemically. The main arguments are as before, so it would be otiose to trace in detail how the new book expands the earlier ideas of the proper harmony of the upper and lower centres; the disastrous effects of overdevelopment of the former, especially through mother-

love and premature consciousness; and the implications of this for child rearing
and education, especially the holding back of mental knowledge until the child is
ready for it and wants it. The commonsense about parenthood of the man who
was remarkably good with children, and the realism about education of the
Croydon teacher, which had been the strengths of the essays on Education and
the earlier psychology book, are much in evidence again: on child art as evidence
of how a child sees, and thus the folly of trying to force premature 'understanding'; on spanking (as distinct from bullying) for the sake of both parent and
child; on the importance of the father's role in upbringing; on the folly in sex
education of reducing sex to anatomy, or attempting to create awareness for
which the child is not ready; on the crime of involving children in the relation
between parents; on how modern parents damage their children, and modern
upbringing produces so many failed marriages. These are what give the book its
permanent value and challenge.

Yet there is, even in June 1921, a pushing to extremes, a goading. There
should be *no* schooling before the age of ten, thumps the new polemic (as against
the more careful curriculum for the 'Education of the People'). Only a few have
any real capacity for mental education; so the vast mass of people should not be
taught even to read or write. Hierarchical class- and gender-thinking becomes
overt. There is a small class who are 'born to think', but the 'mass of the people
must *not* think. It blasts all their life and their fulness and their happiness' and
this is even truer of women. The 'distracted Brunnhild' should be 'put to sleep
again within the ring of fire'. For only by obeying one's instinctive nature, free
from the ideology of equality and universality, can 'the soul wake and live'. Boys
and girls are different by nature, should be kept apart as long as possible, and
should be educated very differently for a wholly different form of life.[119] The
germs of such ideas had appeared speculatively before, but they are thrown
down now as gauntlets – which many will want to throw back. For even if it is
realised that the pugnacity is a reaction to what Lawrence saw as a dangerous
overbalance in the opposite direction, a raising of the voice to get the necessary
attention, a gadfly stinging, such ideas will appear to many people 'reactionary'
in a much more pejorative sense.

However it is when the Lawrence of 1921 proclaims the *opposite* of what the
Lawrence of 1912–17 had believed, that we begin to see how such ideas relate to
what he had come to think the main challenge of his life: the need to overcome
his own dependence on woman (mother, mother-substitute, wife), and to stand
primarily free and alone, though married. For now, as autobiographical confession looms just below the surface, it is also possible to gauge the strength of his
reaction against *himself*, through his precise sense, now, of the extent of the
damage he had suffered through love-of-woman – and not only in his childhood.

One might perhaps start from what looks one of the oddest or even the most rubbishy features of the psychology here: his readiness now to diagnose his own physical defects and state of health in psychological terms. He had always instinctively believed that one got ill because one's life was wrong. Now (legibly between the lines) we can see him pinning down the exact reasons in his own case. It was through being brought up by his mother to be too loving (to her) that he is now vulnerable to consumption, and also to fever and constipation – because the heart, lungs and liver are mainly controlled by the upper centres, and overdevelopment of these causes hyperactivity and burning-up, or blockage. To underdevelop the voluntary centres, on the other hand, is to have trouble with one's teeth. His 'thick' and 'squat' nose shows him to be 'sensual sympathetic', rather than 'sensual voluntary' which would have given him a nose high and arched. (Lawrence may be the first since Walter Shandy to take the nose as a symptom of health of character.) And it is also living too much from the upper centres that causes people to go shortsighted – the revision will add 'in an endless objective curiosity'. (He always concealed his need for reading glasses and was never photographed or described as wearing them.) Defects in the self bring about defects in relationship, with odd physical consequences: such as the strange feelings in the wrists (described in *The Trespasser*, *Sons and Lovers* and *The Rainbow*) which come from dislocation of the 'psychic current' between individuals.[120] All of which may sound curious – but the important point is not the validity of the causal explanations but rather the nature of Lawrence's self-criticism, the depth of his feeling about having been damaged by being too loving, and not independent and single enough. (Will Brangwen and Skrebensky as well as Aaron fall into perspective, against Birkin's wariness of love and the importance of the full current at the base of his spine.) It follows that Lawrence's reaction against depending on Frieda as mother-substitute is again no mere anti-female prejudice but a worry about his own nature: that being already too loving and too ready to give himself, he would be increasing the damage to himself and his lungs if he went on succumbing to Frieda's constant demand to be loved, as he had to his mother's. He not only had to become more independent, stiffening his backbone and his whole 'posture' towards the world – as he argued was very important for parents to ensure in their children – but he also had to become less vulnerable to love, because of the existing overdevelopment of his own 'sympathetic centres', and underdevelopment of his 'voluntary' ones.

From the perspective of 1921, the view of gender that had pervaded 'Hardy' and *The Rainbow* was dangerous, in that it allowed the psychology appropriate to the unitary impulse (in 'Hardy', female) to invade the individual man. Nothing is more striking in the new psychology than the total repudiation, now, of the idea of bisexuality that had been at the centre of the major work. The 'Hardy' had occasionally slipped into apparently identifying what it called 'Female' with women, and 'Male' with men, but the idea that every individual person was actually a mixture and conflict of 'male' with 'female' was the central one, from which such slips were momentary aberrations. In *The Rainbow* moreover, he had not only deliberately reversed the previous gender typing but had also ensured, after a 'choric' preamble, that all the individual characters were differing mixtures of what could just as well be called 'God the Father' and 'God the Son' as 'male' and 'female'. Now however he radically denies what he had affirmed before. Not a single cell in a man, he now insists, is female, nor a single cell in a woman male. And he totally denies the existence of any intermediate sex which had so interested him from his first reading of Carpenter with Jessie, to the thoughts about his own homosexual element first expressed in 1913; and then through the years of questioning and self-challenge which culminated in the 1918 essay on Whitman. Now he declares (rather implausibly) that even the most effeminate male or mannish female is male or female through and through.[121] This new intransigence again betrays anxiety, though less about his sexuality now than his excessively unitary and 'sympathetic' impulses.

The further consequence of an absolute division of gender is a matchingly absolute division now between the roles of men and women – with again a repudiation of the emancipated womanhood which had made the heroines of his major work so interesting. He had seen their desire for greater individuality, activity and freedom as a necessary part of their nature, while deploring some of the effects – particularly on their ability to give themselves and marry – of overdeveloping this at the expense of the other side. He had regarded his work as striking a blow for women 'better than the suffrage', and would certainly have proclaimed himself a feminist. We have however been watching the desire for greater male freedom, singleness and creative purpose culminate – in the Education essays – in a corresponding desire to limit the role of women. In the new book he is wholly intransigent. Girls must be kept altogether separate from boys for as long as possible, and educated for domesticity. The creation of the modern independent woman has proved a disaster. (Here is where modern feminist enmity to Lawrence has one of its roots, often without realising how opposed it is to the vision of his two greatest novels.)

Again, moreover, one may detect behind this an anxiety about himself and a deep-seated grievance about Frieda. It would appear (reading between his lines on modern women) that *her* defective upbringing – which had ensured also that Else's and Nusch's marriages would go wrong – had combined with Weekley's Victorian adulation and Gross's idealisation of her as the New Sexual Lifegiver to give her an altogether wrong and inflated idea of herself. (Perhaps Lawrence had also contributed to this in his work between 1913 and 1917, having been so deeply in love with the woman he was now criticising, and so awakened into new life by and through her.) This idea of herself, moreover, was the major factor in her stubborn refusal, as he saw it, to give him the recognition as a man and acknowledgement as a leader which he felt his very being required if he were to believe in himself and achieve his life's work, in the face of a hostile world. The more isolated and vulnerable he had become since 1915, and the more lacking in recognition outside, the greater his need to be acknowledged at home. (She of course appeared never to doubt her own worth – though her rage when she felt herself dismissed as merely the artist's wife, or excluded as a lesser intelligence, might more subtly suggest otherwise.) Some class feeling also went into Lawrence's view. The new book also casts an interesting light backward on *Sons and Lovers*. The main charge stands of course against the mother – but the charge against the father, now, would be that he had not stood up to and fought against his wife enough, had not played his fatherly role in stiffening the backbones of his children[122] – and (the revision adds) above all had not upheld the collective purpose in life which all men need to have, against the domestic claims of the woman. If Lawrence had written the book in 1921 it would have come out very very different. But we can also see in Walter Morel's clumsy and inarticulate attempts to assert himself – 'Its ma as brings th' money whoam, not thee' – the class basis of Lawrence's feeling that a man had to be master in his own household if he were to respect himself, and continue to be a man among men with some backbone.

Revealingly, a fascinating chapter on dreams added another dimension to his disagreement with Freud on the incest motive. He insists that most dreams are mere debris from the day, brought about by physical processes, and of no significance. There are however dreams so intense as to be signs of some deep scotch in the psyche, and recurrent dreams of a mother or a sister are likely to be such. He clearly had these himself (compare the dream in *Kangaroo*). However he does not see them as products of the 'incest desire'. Indeed, he believes that what is significant is the revulsion from the dream when one wakes; and therefore that such dreams usually work by inversion, meaning the opposite of what they suggest. Thus a sexual fantasy with mother or sister as object implies a strong desire to escape their power, which one's waking revulsion accomplishes. A Freudian would see this as naïve rationalisation, though there can be no doubt of Lawrence's desire to escape mother-fixation and woman-love, or his struggle to succeed in doing so. But most significant of all is the thinly veiled confession in the original version that such dreams can *also* come about because a modern wife 'does not give to her husband the true wifely connection. She is too much the man, the cigarette-smoker, the independent and authoritative party'[123] – so the unconscious may substitute the person or persons who first gave him the vital support that his wife refuses.

What begins to come more and more into focus in all this is the element of truth in Francis Brett Young's theory about Lawrence – once cleaned of its crudity and condescension. Though this could never be a formula to explain somebody so complex and changeful, it does seem possible to understand Lawrence's reaction in 1918–21, from what he had previously upheld, in terms of something like self-revulsion in its very excess and extreme contrariness. It was not because he was unloving that Lawrence proclaimed himself anti-love and determined to free himself from depending on Frieda, but because he felt himself to be *too* loving, and hence a living example of how overdevelopment of the sympathetic centres produced disease. It was because he had come to see himself (partly through Frieda's scorn) as too subject to mental consciousness and 'soul-mush' that he had become such a spokesman for the lower centres, and so anti-intellectual in his ideas on education. Yet we cannot simply reverse the terms as Brett Young did. Lawrence was *also*, always, the contrary of what he now denounced in himself. He always had it in him to be a loner. Everyone who met him was immediately impressed by his quite extraordinary sensuous vitality and perceptiveness. Similarly it was because he knew only too well what "sex-in-the-head" was that he fulminated against it; but he knew also, by experience, how the "religious" experience of sexual death and rebirth could change one utterly, and make one oblivious and free. It was because he was sick and tired of endless conflict within himself – though recognising its necessity – that he could wish so much for homogeneity and total maleness.

The typescript ends with an account and affirmation of renewal through sex, the 'polarisation of the individual blood in man towards the individual blood in woman', which should also be the dynamic activation of the lower centres without interference from the higher ones, deep calling to deep. Alas, much sex is unsuccessful now because 'upper and mental consciousness so powerfully overlays the spontaneous dynamism' that mating becomes chiefly companionship, men and women get sex in the head 'and a sad time after it', and the sex roles are becoming reversed. 'The good time for emancipated women is already over', partly because they cannot be happy going against their true selves, and partly because 'the soul of man has to be strong and really fearless, if woman is to rest deep and serene in the beauty of her own nature'. Man must 'burst new bounds into new consciousness, new activity, new being'; 'ready to *live* for something beyond himself and woman'[124] – for only then can he make his woman truly happy.

XI Off Again – to Zell-am-See

About 18 June, Frieda's mother came to spend some time with them in Ebersteinburg, though ten days later she became unwell again and had to go back to the Stift (iv. 44). At the beginning of July, Else and her three children would arrive from Bavaria. Lawrence was fond of them all – but he had got used to time by himself, and 'One can have enough of relations at close quarters' (iv. 46), as he had felt about his own family at Mountain Cottage. When he had finished the new book on the unconscious he was restless and keen to move – even if only to pay the promised visit to Nusch at the von Schreibershofen holiday villa in Austria, a move that would have Frieda's approval.

He had been expecting Mountsier from London, but instead his agent had set off to Ireland (repeating the pattern of his fateful travels in 1916) and the Aran Isles (iv. 38). Now he was ready to come; only to find that the Lawrences were about to leave. He showed some irritation at yet another sudden change of mind, until reminded that his own plans had not been exactly stable, and that Lawrence had been expecting him since May (iv. 46) – but there was a simple solution. Lawrence intended to walk through the Black Forest to Constance (where he thought visas for Austria would be easy to arrange), then cross the lake to the Austrian border at Bregenz and go to Zell-am-See by train. So Mountsier could come for a few days at Ebersteinburg, do the walk and the journey to Zell, and set out thence to Vienna and points east.

He came on 5 July, bearing gifts. Since Lawrence had been utterly unwilling to go to England even to see his sisters, he had hoped that Ada (at least) might come across to Germany with Mountsier; and though that had not happened, she had arranged to send with him (from the Clarkes' tailoring and outfitting stock) an overcoat for Lawrence, and some blue serge for a coat and skirt for Frieda (iv. 50). Lawrence had also asked Mountsier to bring tea, and Kolynos toothpaste, and some cotton underpants (iv. 39, 46) – friends coming from England were always pressed into service as couriers, as the Whittleys had been.

Two days later they were off. (It is unclear whether Frieda walked too, or met them at Constance. Lawrence had hoped to persuade her to do a tour in the Forest in June, but she did not share his delight in walking tours and may have left the two men to themselves for that part, with some relief.) The walk took five days, and other than that it was 'Fearfully hot' (iv. 52) no account of it has been left. This suggests it was less pleasant than Lawrence had hoped – and certainly when it was over it became clear that Mountsier had not improved on closer knowledge.

It is a small shock to realise after all the agency correspondence that Lawrence had only ever been at close quarters with Mountsier twice, very briefly, four and a half years before, and in the charming company of Esther Andrews. Esther's letters to Mountsier in early 1917 show her stung by his criticism of her work. They suggest a man of very positive opinions and some sharpness of tongue; and he had twice ticked Lawrence off quite sharply for inconveniencing him. That in itself would not have mattered, since Lawrence rather liked people who stood up to him within a context of real sympathy. What he cannot have liked however, as they walked and talked through five days now, about what Lawrence had been doing and his hopes for the future, was to find that Mountsier had no sympathy at all with his latest work. He disliked the first half of *Aaron's Rod* and took it upon himself to 'lecture' Lawrence about it, certain that it would be unpopular. He also 'loathes me' – Lawrence would tell Seltzer – 'because I will develop my *Unconscious* ideas' (iv. 57). Moreover, when they got to Zell Mountsier produced a list from his luggage, obtained from Curtis Brown, which seemed to show how difficult Brown's 'magazine man' had found it to place Lawrence's work in England. In fact – it became clear later – there had also been a few successes, more than for some time in his native land. The *Nation and Athenæum*, with Murry no longer at the helm, published the modified Whitman essay in July; and the *English Review* would print 'Pomegranate' and 'Medlars and Sorb-Apples' in August, and 'The Revolutionary' in October. But Lawrence told Curtis Brown to stop trying English magazines unless he thought there was a real chance of a sympathetic reception, which again wasn't conducive to good relations – and he had to apologize later when he learned the truth.

Mountsier may have thought he was only doing his duty as an agent, to warn his author against a wrong turning if he hoped for an audience in America. But to persuade any writer to accept such medicine, however well-intended, requires a certain tact, and all the more so with Lawrence. Tact does not seem to have been one of Mountsier's strong points, and though Lawrence seems to have taken the lecturing without rage (if also with no intention of changing his ways), he did find his agent 'rather overbearing' (iv. 61), as he told Amy Lowell. So had she, over the placing of Lawrence's new poems. Mountsier had indeed made a little trouble between Lawrence and Amy, though it was soon cleared up. She denied that she had ever said, as Mountsier had reported, that only 'The Mosquito' of the new poems was worth publishing, though she had indeed urged the editor of the *Bookman* to take it; and she had only refrained from pushing the others because Mountsier had made it plain that he thought this was *his* business. Indeed she thought Lawrence one of the few exceptions to the decline in English poetry.[125] Mountsier may have taken a cue from Lawrence's resentment – characteristically as fleeting as it was intemperate – of Amy's delay in responding to the poems, (before he heard the reason); but if so he was much mistaken. For Lawrence liked Amy, had great reason to be grateful and would in fact admire her new poems in *Legends* as much as she liked his.[126]

Indeed, proximity to Mountsier began to put him off the idea of America again: 'I got such a strong distaste for Yankees,' he confessed, 'seeing him every day, that at the moment wild horses wouldn't drag me' (iv. 67). The 'fearful' heat cannot have helped as they trudged towards Constance – and nor would the débâcle when they got there. For far from being able to obtain Austrian visas on the spot, they had to send their passports to Berlin, and wait over the weekend to get them back. It was not until the Monday evening that they could cross the lake and get into Bregenz – 'after much wrath spent on passport officials' (iv. 53), and appropriately amid a thunderstorm. There they took an overnight train to Innsbruck. It was not until the Wednesday that they arrived, wearily, in Zell-am-See. Mountsier stayed in a hotel for a few days, before leaving for Vienna and Budapest. He left his heavy luggage behind, intending to return briefly on his way back to Paris, which he did in mid-August (iv. 69). There was no quarrel, but Lawrence was not sorry to see him go.

Fortunately Zell was delightfully restorative. The von Schreibershofens had a villa ('Villa Alpensee') and a farm in Thumersbach on the other side of the lake, facing snowy mountains. Frieda had a room with a balcony, visible on postcards (e.g. iv. 56). It was warm, but not too hot because the mountains were so close. They swam every day from the boathouse. There were four boats in which to row across the lake, or just go boating; and there was a pony trap for expeditions into the mountains and the valleys. There were Nusch, her husband Max, their daughter Anna, aged 20 and engaged to be married, and son Hadubrand aged 16. (Attractive mother, son and daughter are vividly described in 'The Captain's Doll'.[127]) Lawrence had always liked Nusch. He cannot have had much in common with the Prussian Major and ex-aide-de-camp – but though the marriage was about to end, and Nusch to marry Emil Krug, there was nothing but kindness in their reception. They climbed the Hundstein – twice the height of Snowdon, Lawrence told his niece Peggy (iv. 60). They went in the pony trap to Bad Fusch and then on foot to Ferleiten to look at the great sloping white mass of the glacier below and the water rushing strong, fast and loud (iv. 56). Much of the snow had melted, and there were beautiful flowers higher up. Austria's economy was in ruins with rampant inflation, but out in the country supplies were plentiful if you had money; the exchange rate was 3,000 schillings to the pound where pre-war it had been about 23 (iv. 67); and nobody seemed to care. A rather inebriated set of messages went off to Frieda's mother from a festive lunch in which four chickens were 'gobbled' and four litres of peach-punch 'guzzled' before the women got uppity; and Lawrence, certain that she was much cleverer than her daughters, begged the Baroness to protect her 'little son-in-law' against them (iv. 63), while young Anna feared she might be sick.

By the same tokens it was not a place to work. He had thought he might type the rest of *Aaron's Rod*, but there was no typewriter, so the second half had to be sent on 21 July to be typed in Curtis Brown's office and returned for a final revision (iv. 54). Having been sent a proof of 'Wintry Peacock' by Seltzer he made some alterations and forwarded it to Sadleir for his new collection of stories *The New Decameron* (iv. 57 and 31 n. 1). (He reserved the right to include it in a second collection of his stories, but later told Sadleir he would delay bringing them together for a year or more.) Having now heard the bad news of the American reviews of *Psychoanalysis and the Unconscious*, he asked Seltzer to send them for him to answer in an introduction to the new book – defiantly threatening also to write yet another psychology book in three years' time, despite Mountsier (iii. 57). 'The Gentleman from San Francisco' had gone to Violet Monk to be typed: now he wrote to ask Thayer to print it in the *Dial*, saying how good it was, and asking whether he would not like also to do extracts from *Sea and Sardinia* (iv. 58–9). (A later letter claims – perhaps a fiction – that it was partly because he heard Thayer wanted 'travel sketches à la *Twilight in Italy*' that he had written it; so should not Thayer live up to his responsibility now? – iv. 73) Here, it turned out, was another misunderstanding. Thayer had never seen the typescript Mountsier thought he had rejected.[128] Lawrence thought that given a good mood he might write a novella set in Zell; but apart from proofs and the revisions of *Aaron's Rod* when he got it back in early August (iv. 65) – and perhaps another look at his new psychology book, he did no creative work in his month in Austria.

After a while, that began to bother him. To Rosalind he wrote that it was 'impossible to work in this country: no wits left, all gone loose and scattered' (iv. 67). (Only now did he learn that she had been divorced in April; but had taken Bridget amicably to see Godwin in Zürich, where he had become Jung's assistant and was about to marry a second time – 'a fool', Lawrence thought.) To Catherine he wrote that he was feeling the pressure of people again. Kind though the von Schreibershofens were, 'I feel I can't breathe. Everything is free and perfectly easy. And still I feel I can't breathe. Perhaps it is one can't live with people any more – en ménage. Anyhow, there it is. Frieda loves it and is quite bitter that I say I want to go away. But there it is – I do' (iv. 63–4). Though there must have been real difficulty with Frieda, he was adamant that he would go by himself if necessary. He talked of going to Meran (to make up perhaps for never having got there in 1912) before going on to Florence where Perceval was arranging for them to have Nellie Morrison's flat. The Carswells were hesitating between Austria and Italy for their holidays. Would Donald get forms to renew the Lawrence passports, and certify them, since he was a lawyer and Lawrence knew no such responsible person, doctor or clergyman in Austria (iv. 56). Frieda's was so full of visas that he did not know how she would fit in another to get her into Italy![129] Soon it was decided that they would meet the Carswells in Florence in September, and soon also the problem of getting Frieda to leave was solved. The von Schreibershofen household was breaking up at the end of the month, and on the 15 August the weather broke. It began to rain, and became quite chilly (iv. 70). Summer seemed over – and nowhere was worse in the rain than the Alps. On the 18th he sent the revised typescript of *Aaron's Rod* off to America (iv. 74), having already sent Seltzer a Foreword, presumably defending the book against the criticisms he had heard from Mountsier. (It has not survived.) He told Seltzer that it was as he wanted it to be, 'the end of the *Rainbow–Women in Love* novels: and my last word' (iv. 71). Mountsier had left Zell for the second time on the 16th: 'Thank goodness', said Lawrence, 'we shall not be troubled with him in Italy' (iv. 72). More snow fell on the mountains; and he longed now for the south again. A letter came from Thayer inviting him to stay at Westerland-Sylt up on the North Sea, but he refused with a mock-horror that was not entirely put on (iv. 72–3).[130] He would die, he said if he did not get to where yellow figs were, within the next fortnight. To the Whittleys he wrote details about Austria should they want to holiday there, but again suggested that they meet instead in Florence (iv. 77–8).

He had hoped to leave by Saturday the 20th, but was persuaded to stay longer for a last Alpine expedition with Frieda. She wanted, said he, 'to set foot on a glacier' (iv. 76). So, soon after dawn on the 20th they rowed off across the quiet lake to Zell, where from the town square a tourist limousine, big enough for eight passengers, took them out past the end of the lake and up a valley, to the picturesque black and white village of Kaprun, and then up another deeper and darker valley to the big tourist hotel where the road ended. There was then a three-and-a-half-hour trail up to the Mooserboden, the high valley that stretched to the foot of the Karlinger glacier. Lawrence would recreate the excursion in the most vivid detail when he got round to writing his 'Tyrolean' story 'The Captain's Doll'[131] – one of his very finest – at the end of the year. The couple in the story have a picnic lunch of sausage, new bread and Hungarian wine by an icy stream in the flattish 'desolate' valley of the Wasserfallboden, 'in the changing sunshine ... with mountain flowers scenting the snow-bitten air', watching richer tourists go by with a mule-drawn chair and thinking for a moment that the world seemed on holiday, almost like before the war. Yet it would never be the same again. Then there was a steep climb from the end of that valley up to a third level, the Mooserboden, sloping to the foot of the glacier, which stretched its paws out towards them like an immense blue ice-bear lying across the height. On this last climb it rained, cold rain – and Hannele/Frieda (according to the story) had left her coat down below in the limousine. Fortunately there was a last tourist lodge up there with hot coffee, but also of course (the story says) with all the other tourists, including 'many Jews of the wrong sort and the wrong shape', all in Tyrolean costume. And so to the great glacier – sweating water in the late summer and thus slippery and dangerous to climb on, but amazing and frightening in its world of deathly ice, its 'fearful depths, and the colour burning that acid, intense blue, intenser as the crack went deeper'.[132] There is no way of telling whether or how far the tension between Hepburn and Hannele, or his half-humiliating and half-heroic scramble in ordinary shoes onto the glacier, or the flaming row in the limousine on the way home, might have had a basis in fact, since all were demanded by the story.

But whatever the truth of those, the expedition brought the month in Austria to an unforgettable conclusion.

He had meant to leave on the Monday, but their departure was put off once more. Finally on Thursday 25 August they did set off for Florence and Nellie Morrison's quiet flat at 32 Via dei Bardi – the house traditionally pointed out as Romola's. It proved cool and dark and they were by themselves again, all to his delight, since he was tired after the journey – but possibly not to Frieda's, facing a long separation from her family again. But in any case company began to arrive, and soon there was so much social life that work again became impossible. Mary Cannan came at the end of the month, Juta at the beginning of September, the Carswells about ten days later for a week and the Whittleys from the 12th to the 20th when they went with the Lawrences to Siena. Mary liked the flat and the meals on the terrace so much that she thought she might rent the extra bedroom – though, much as he liked her, Lawrence hinted broadly in his obedient enquiry to Nellie that he would prefer things to remain as they were (iv. 81). She did however rent a room on the top floor, just above. Moreover they also picked up with Florentine acquaintances, though Rosalind was away in the Apennines again – which was just as well perhaps, since they would otherwise have been bound to visit, and Frieda had sharp eyes and ears as far as he was concerned.

He introduced the Carswells to the Marchesa de Torrigiani and her family, but unfortunately this was one of several ways in which the reunion with Catherine and Donald did not go as pleasantly as both sides had expected. It began in misadventure, with Lawrence meeting several trains in vain, only for the Carswells to arrive unmet. They did however have supper together the next evening, the 11th, Lawrence's thirty-sixth birthday, and were happy 'in a quiet sort of way'. But Catherine was not drawn to the de Torrigianis, or to another young woman whom she could not later identify (perhaps Irene Whittley) who tried to prevent her from taking a snapshot of a laughing Lawrence on the balcony, fearing it might irritate him. She thought Mary Cannan – now white-haired but as elegant as ever – had 'exquisitely pretty features' and charm, but when in her absence Frieda insisted on showing her Mary's expensive clothes, Catherine went very Scots and refused to feel their texture; and whenever she walked with Mary, felt her elegance such a reproach to her own dowdiness (in the clothes she had brought for a walking tour) that she almost began to dislike her. If Lawrence's aristocratic Italian friends proved no attraction to Catherine; Catherine's proved even less so to Lawrence. She had Anglo-Italian cousins in and near Florence, but they 'showed themselves blind alike to Lawrence's genius and his charm and he disliked what he saw of them'. A plan for the Lawrences to visit a cousin in her Castello Ruggero some ten miles out of Florence, where the Carswells were spending the weekend, proved a disaster.

The Lawrences failed to arrive; but that turned out to be because Catherine's cousin had quite forgotten to send the carriage for them to the tram-terminus. By the time they were remembered – apparently without a qualm by their hostess – the Lawrences had got tired of waiting around on a very hot day, and had gone back to Florence. Lawrence made no fuss about this, but it continued to bother Catherine who nagged on and on about it to Donald, until he complained 'good-naturedly' to Lawrence: '"You ought to hit her!" said Lawrence fiercely – "Hit her hard. Don't let her scold and nag. You mustn't allow it, *whatever* it is you have done!" We all laughed and felt refreshed ...' (said Catherine). A final misunderstanding happened in Siena, where they were supposed to meet up again, but did not. Catherine says that Lawrence suddenly hated the place and left; Lawrence that the Carswells had not come when arranged (probably the source of the temper), and he had to leave if he were to catch the Brewsters in Capri before they sailed for India (iv. 89) – a pity, either way![133] But though the reunion had not been a great success, Lawrence assured her that the friendship remained constant: 'it seemed only a moment we saw you – but the sympathy is there' (iv. 91).

There was a good deal of festivity in Florence. On the eve of the Festival of the Blessed Virgin (8 September) the Arno was crowded with boats and coloured lanterns. They went to Fiesole, with its marvellous view out to the Apennines, the Arno coming down the valley as if in steps, the city so feminine on the plain below, the hills dotted with pink and white villas and the black flames of cypresses, about which he had written his poem the year before. The Dante festival was celebrated that year with a re-enactment in costume and armour of the triumphant procession home from the battle of Campodino about 1260 (iv. 84–5), that Lawrence had written about in *Movements*. 'I can't work here', he complained (iv. 83), and no wonder. He projected a collection of stories set in Italian cities (iv. 80), beginning with a Venetian one which he actually started (iv. 83), but the idea came to nothing. Three fine poems were all he had to show for his month in Florence: 'Fish' which is partly set in and labelled Zell but was written in the flat by 9 September (iv. 83); and 'Bat' and 'Man and Bat' which were both set in the Via dei Bardi and sent off on the 17th (iv. 88). After that, however, he got nothing done.

Worse, there arrived three annoying and disquieting bits of news. In late August came word from Kot of Murry's scathing attack on *Women in Love* in the *Nation* (iv. 79). The novel, wrote the erstwhile friend, is 'an underworld whose inhabitants are known by this alone, that they writhe continually, like the damned, in a frenzy of sexual awareness'. The author seems to think that he can distinguish one from another, but the reader cannot. Lawrence also seems to believe that 'These writhings are the only real, and these convulsive raptures, these oozy beatitudes the only end in human life ... he is deliberately, incessantly, and passionately obscene in the exact sense of the word.' Lawrence, not having read the piece yet, was dismissive. Yet Murry knew that the prosecution of *The Rainbow* for obscenity had been set in train by reviews. That he had half a mind to encourage a prosecution, while typically covering himself, became even clearer when he felt 'sure that not one person in a thousand would decide that [the experiences of the lovers] were anything but the crudest kind of sexuality, wrapped up in ... the language of Higher Thought' – though (he back-pedalled) the exception might just perhaps be right. He ended with the charge that Lawrence had 'murdered his gifts' and that his vision was 'sub-human and bestial, a thing that our fathers had rejected when they began to rise from the slime'.[134] But though vengeance and the desire to damage may well have played a part in this, there seems no reason to doubt that Murry felt genuine horror at a vision of human beings so different from his own – though the irony of this, in the admirer of Dostoevsky, is also apparent.

And three weeks later (came news now from Secker) Horatio Bottomley's jingoistic gutter paper *John Bull* had made no bones about demanding that the police should act against *Women in Love*. Secker was not too worried about that. But more dangerous (he thought) was the threat of a lawsuit by Philip Heseltine, claiming a libel on him and Puma in the characters of Halliday and the Pussum (iv. 87, 88 and n. 2), which Secker took seriously enough to withdraw the book for the moment (iv. 87, 88 and n. 2; having sold 1,123 copies by 11 July, two months before),[135] and to suggest that Lawrence should alter the novel again. Then on the 15th, the same day as the news about Heseltine, there arrived from Seltzer the hostile American notices of *Psychoanalysis*. Probably through gritted teeth, Lawrence called these 'quite amusing' (iv. 86); and determined more than ever to answer them. This was *bad* news however for his hopes of a new audience in America, the worst of all these blows.

Perhaps *Aaron's Rod* had better wait until the spring, though Lawrence wondered whether magazines might print extracts, like the Novara episode, or the riot. And what about the new book (which he was thinking of calling 'Child Consciousness' or 'The Child and the Unconscious'; iv. 93), if its predecessor had been received so badly? He was having it typed in Florence, and would in any case need to revise. But all would have to wait until he got back to Taormina. Now Florence seemed noisy and tiresome, and he longed for the peace of Fontana Vecchia.

First, however, there would be Capri, to have Frieda meet the Brewsters, and to bid them good-bye. After the brief look at Siena on the 21st they went to Rome with the Whittleys, where they had a 'lovely day' and drove out into the Campagna (iv. 105), and then to Naples where they left them rather the worse for wear after what Lawrence called their 'battering' holiday (iv. 92). (Irene seems then to have fallen ill.) By the 23rd the Lawrences were with the

Brewsters in Capri, finding the mutual liking confirmed and deepened. Earl thought Frieda just the right wife: 'Only a woman as strong and generous as Mrs. Lawrence, with her love for vital experiences and indifferent to the small things, would have suited Lawrence.' Lawrence for his part liked and was amused by Achsah's sister who was staying with them. Once again the Brewsters were touched by his friendship with Harwood. He went carefully over the girl's herbarium, treating her collection with due dignity. He listened to a story she had written; and told her a long and amusing yarn on the same subject in return. There was another ridiculous Lawrence mime of an aesthetic lady playing on the psaltery. They left, with 'their arms full of presents for the *contadina* family at Fontana Vecchia'.[136]

The final journey however was disastrous. Not only was the train to Giardini two hours late, but they had been turned out into the rain twice, once for an overheated axle and then to discard their carriage altogether. When they finally arrived, on the night of 28 September, it was in a storm of wind and rain – and it went on raining for days. But at least in Fontana Vecchia there was peace, and silence.

'Never again', Lawrence vowed 'will I dash about as we dashed this year' (iv. 91–2).

CHAPTER TWELVE

◆

October 1921–February 1922
A SENSE OF FINALITY

I can't *belong* any more.
(iv. 125)

I 'The threads are broken'

To wake up in Fontana Vecchia, even in the rain, was to be newly aware of its loveliness: 'the great window of the eastern sky' (iv. 90); 'the sea open to the east, to the heart of the east, away from Europe' (iv. 91); the peace and quiet; and before long the sunshine, the hibiscus flowers coming and 'Such a lovely *morning* world: forever morning. I hate going north – and I hate snow grinning on the tops of mountains. Jamais plus' (iv. 97). It was still 'better than any of the other places' (iv. 92).

Yet in his first letter after arriving back, Lawrence tells the Brewsters that 'my heart – and my soul are broken, in Europe. It's no use, the threads are broken. I will go east, intending ultimately to go west, as soon as I can get a ship: that is, before March' (iv. 90). He had been threatening to leave Europe for years – but this time, though he might yet waver about the direction, he never wavered about going. He would take Fontana Vecchia for another quarter only, hence that decisive 'before March' – determined that this lease should be the last.[1]

If only the Brewsters were going to India and Ceylon in January rather than October, he wrote, he would have gone along. His new Rananim would be to settle somewhere near them – not to meditate of course, but to do 'a bit of quiet manual work together', yet each 'in our own solitude and labour. There, I think that's the ultimate of what I want' (iv. 95). That suggests North America in the end (perhaps recalling his idea of taking Carlota Thrasher's farm), but he would wait to hear about Ceylon. Ultimately then, east did point west, he thought once more: perhaps to a farm near the Rockies, or British Columbia, or Mexico. 'I would much rather approach America from the Pacific' (iv. 95). He would have to be in or near the USA in order to live by his writing; but the journey east was not only the more decisive break with Europe, it would also avoid the Yankee industrialised and urbanised side of America that he dreaded.

The post that was waiting in Fontana Vecchia was not welcoming. There was the cutting from *John Bull*: whose banner headline denounced 'A BOOK THE

POLICE SHOULD BAN', and 'LOATHSOME STUDY OF SEX DEPRAVITY – MIS-
LEADING YOUTH TO UNSPEAKABLE DISASTER'. There were the pages Secker
wanted him to change in the light of Heseltine's threat of legal action – and
letters from both Curtis Brown and Mountsier,[2] in agreement 'that *Aaron's Rod*
can't be accepted' (iv. 90).

Lawrence's reaction to *that* was to affirm, to Seltzer, that the book was 'the
last of my serious English novels – the end of *The Rainbow*, *Women in Love* line.
It had to be written – and had to come to such an end' (iv. 92–3). If Seltzer also
thought it 'dangerous', he should identify exactly what was so; and Lawrence
would consider 'small' alterations, and write another explanatory foreword to
ease its way. He was still toying with the idea of the Venice story which he now
thought might even make a novel: no sex, no problems, no love and not meant
for England ever (but in all these respects, it turned out, not interesting enough
to get itself written). In the meantime he had set to work revising the new
psychology book, and had written a 'rather funny' Foreword answering the
American critics of its predecessor.

The same day, 8 October, he sent Secker the alterations to *Women in Love*
which the publisher had suggested might avoid a prosecution. He reversed the
colouring of Halliday and the Pussum, so she became blue-eyed and fair instead
of looking like an Egyptian princess, and he became dark and swarthy instead of
pale and blond. The man-servant became Arab not Hindu, the flat was now in St
John's Wood, and its statuettes became South Pacific rather than African – with
some strain on credibility.

Lawrence still thought *Aaron* might be offered to Secker after Seltzer had
seen it, but told Mountsier he did not much care about the verdict, since
'English publication no longer interests me much' (iv. 96). The next day he went
further, telling Amy Lowell how 'in direction' he thought of himself now as
'more than half American. I always write really towards America: my listener is
there' (iv. 97). He asked Mountsier what was in his USA account after deducting
the agent's percentage, how much ought to be left to cover expenses in America
and hence how much would be available for the journey he now firmly meant to
take (iv. 96).

In mid-October, having finished revising what he had now named *Fantasia of
the Unconscious*,[3] he began sorting and collecting his short stories, hoping to
make a volume that would clear his desk for departure, and help to earn as much
as possible before they left. There had arrived out of the blue a letter from
Edward Garnett, asking for an opinion on a book by Emil Lucka (iv. 99–100).[4]
Lawrence was quite interested in the book, which divided humanity into those
who lived on the frontiers of human understanding to widen them, and those
who stayed in the middle territory – but he would not provide the professional
opinion. He now had absolutely no idea, he said, what English readers would or

wouldn't like. He took the opportunity, however, to enquire after Bunny (now married) but also after 'The Primrose Path', finished in Kingsgate in 1913 and never published. At first, not feeling 'much like work' (iv. 103), he was 'just pottering' with the new collection (iv. 105), but in late October he revised another unpublished piece, turning 'The Miracle' into 'The Horse-Dealer's Daughter'; and by 24th October he had begun to write anew. Or, more accurately, an earlier story ('The Mortal Coil') had rekindled his imagination, and was changing, extraordinarily, into something far bigger and much better. An enquiry to Donald Carswell, about the wearing of tartan trews by officers of the Scottish regiments, shows that Lawrence had embarked on 'The Captain's Doll'.

So his first month back in Taormina ended much better than it had begun. Looking back from the 26th indeed, Lawrence confessed to his diary that he had 'felt seedy & hateful all this month'.[5] The summer of dashing about had left him 'worn to ribbons' (iv. 92), and had only served to put him 'in a perfect fury with everything ... The older I get, the angrier I become, generally. And Italy is a country to keep you in a temper from day to day: the people, I mean' (iv. 98).

The early autumn rains also coincided with the return of the expatriates, and the recommencement of the round of tea-parties. Lawrence makes these sound more Mad-Hatterish than ever. He mimics the Brewsters' mannish friend Miss Elizabeth Fisher, on the *madness* of their eastern journey, and on her 'AW-ful' neighbours: 'Did you EVER! I hate the place. I simply HATE the place. And I hate the PEOPLE – Oh my! – And the flies! ... ' In Wood's house, 'more gilded and stuccoed every day', a widower violinist played 'The Rosary' with such sentiment that his very fiddle-strings swelled, while the unfortunate Bowdwin (who had bought Rocca Bella from Marie Hubrecht and had been mugged nearby) looked on, 'in a pale yellow summer suit and a black vulcanite kind of port-hole over his left eye' (iv. 101–2). There was a gathering of expatriates in which 'The Duca' exhorted them to raise £25,000–£30,000 to build an English Church – only to have the pious Mabel Hill refuse to have anything whatever to do with it, unless it were built on *her* land (iv. 105, 139). Frieda would have enjoyed all this – Lawrence breaks off a letter because she is 'raging' to go to a party at Rosalie Bull's (iv. 102) – but Lawrence vowed it had all put him in another temper for three weeks. This was not improved by Ruth Wheelock coming back from the USA with a copy of the October *Dial* which had 'very much cut up' an extract from *Sea and Sardinia*; and the news that Seltzer was about to publish the book itself, and *Tortoises*, and neither publisher nor agent had deigned to tell the author (iv. 107).

By 2 November, however, he was recovered enough to make fun of himself: how he had begrudged Baron Stempel his tea and had been so disagreeable to poor Grazia that she crept about in fear and trembling (both of him and of her husband's ghost, after the Day of the Dead), how he had written 'such very spiteful letters to everybody that now the postman never comes' and how even the goat was scared to have her kid, so of course there was no milk (iv. 108). But apart from getting the revised *Fantasia of the Unconscious* away – so named, he said, 'to prevent anybody tying themselves into knots trying to "understand" it' (iv. 109) – it had been mostly a miserable month until the end. *He* did not want to understand anybody any more, or be understood, he said – but he did want to work now and finish clearing the desk, so they could go.

He had not weakened in that resolve. Indeed as his bad mood lifted when his creative imagination began to flow again, he joked that he was thinking of making a will: 'Not that I'm going to die. But to give myself a nice sense of finality' (iv. 105).

II   Grumpy 'comedy' – and a New Prospect

The reviews of *Psychoanalysis and the Unconscious* were in truth a bitter blow, since he had had such hopes of a new audience in America. He claimed to have found his critics amusing, and that his new Foreword answering them was funny – but his irritation showed through. He tried to laugh off one review by making a cartoon of himself according to its recipe – though missing *its* jest of how, like the practical joke in Owen Wister's *The Virginian*, he had 'mixed those babies up'. He pretended to mistake another's headline, 'Dumb, Unable to Read, Write Man is Lifer' as referring to him, instead of someone sentenced to gaol in Colorado – before finding himself on the back page under 'Umbilical Secrets' – and so on. But he would have done better to ignore the savants of the Pittsburgh *Dispatch*, the St Louis *Star*, the San Francisco *Bulletin*, the Portland *Evening Press*, etc. His book was caviare to the general, and the primness of reviewers who obviously could not understand when they did not actively mistake should not have been a surprise, however annoying.[6] He might have hoped that the *New Republic* would be less 'sarky', and it was a jolt to be told by someone of the calibre of Mencken that his ideas had been anticipated in a pamphlet by Mother Elizabeth Towne, which he had turned into highfalutin' nonsense – but his grin comes out as a grimace.

Worse, his irritation began to affect his imagining of the reader he was writing to. He became openly aggressive: 'I warn the generality of readers, that this present book will seem to them only a rather more revolting mass of wordy nonsense than the last. I would warn the generality of critics to throw it in the waste paper basket without more ado.'[7]

The trouble with that is that he may be taken at his word.

Seltzer very sensibly decided that it was no advertisement for the new book thus to call attention to the poor reception of its predecessor, so the answers to the critics were cut. The initial note of bad temper remained however in the Foreword as printed, and a reader who has once bristled at it, may keep doing so at the other 'dear reader' passages in the text itself, which tell him to take it or leave it alone. The anouncement of Lawrence's belief in the lost wisdom of a pre-Atlantean world and his disbelief in modern science is followed by another finger to the nose: 'If my reader finds this bosh and abracadabra, all right for him. Only I have no more regard for his little crowings on his own little dunghill.' It is acute disappointment speaking, all the more because he had hoped so much from America – but readers cannot be expected to realise that.

More noteworthy is the statement, 'One last weary little word', that his philosophy – or 'pollyanalytics' (i.e. all my eye and Pollyanna) if his American critics insist – had been a product of his imaginative writing, not the reverse.

The novels and poems come unwatched out of one's pen. And then the absolute need which one has for some sort of satisfactory mental attitude towards oneself and things in general makes one try to abstract some definite conclusions from one's experiences as a writer and a man. The novels and poems are pure passionate experience. These 'pollyanalytics' are inferences made afterwards, from the experience.[8]

In fact, ever since the 'Study of Thomas Hardy' led to *The Rainbow*, what Lawrence describes is both true and less than a fuller truth. His philosophy came out of his imaginative work, but then regularly became a spur to new imagining, in a continual dialectic between exploration, understanding and fresh exploration. The word play which converts a reviewer's American jibe into a term, both playful and serious, for the analysis of complex experience grasped by imagination, also gave him a clue to another defensive strategy. He decided to call the book 'Fantasia', hoping to disarm hidebound minds by calling in more imagination and *play* of idea – though with no less underlying seriousness (or challenge).

This became one of the three major features of his final revision of the typescript in October[9] – the others being a counterpoint of increased intransigence towards his readers, and a new readiness to appear in the text in person.

He has now realised (perhaps from Barbara Low's book) that it was unfair to write as though Freud had described nothing but the unconscious – though he does not specify what more was involved, and still seems to think that Freud attributed a sexual motive to all human activity. However he now underlines their crucial difference by insisting that 'the essentially religious or creative motive' is the *original* one in all living things, the sexual motive being secondary and in conflict with it – a radically religious rather than scientific view of the world.[10] But instead of the original argument, that the material universe sprang from creative life rather than the other way round, he now tells a parable (or fantasy) about the first little living creature. Similarly, in one of the most memorable passages of the book, he now interrupts his discussion of the baby with a dramatised outburst of impatience – and turns to imagine the inhuman life of the tree against which he is sitting, and the vast forest of which it is a part. (This insertion, at this stage, is a dramatic reminder of how spontaneity in Lawrence is a spontaneity in the act of *writing*.) The book becomes more vividly personal, but at the same time the 'unconscious' is firmly budged from Freud's limitation to human beings. In several other places the revision becomes more lively, and imaginative.

Conversely, however, the reception of the earlier book has made Lawrence far readier to challenge or even possibly outrage his readers, both sexually and politically. The gender typing becomes even stronger in revision – and the reaction against the insistence on love, and particularly mother-love, as a kind of bullying is even fiercer, even violent, as in the added conclusion to chapter IV: '"You love mother, don't you dear—?" Just a piece of indecent trickery of the spiritual will. A man should smack his wife's face the moment he hears her say it. The great emotions like love are unspoken. Speaking them is a sign of an indecent bullying will.'[11] Seltzer cut the sentence that seemed bound to offend. In another direction, Lawrence becomes far more explicit about sexual matters. At the end of chapter IX a long insertion deals with the birth of sexuality, giving a new title to the chapter. Dissatisfied with the breadth of Freud's idea of sex which permits him to ascribe sexuality to infants, Lawrence insists that sex is a dynamism leading to coition, the frictive interaction of surcharged male and female seas of blood. (Seltzer made some cuts in the analysis.) After this the man is liberated to new purposive and collective relations with other men which are *not* sexual in that proper sense, and which Lawrence passionately advocates. Indeed, men who centre their lives on sexual relationship may drift into purposelessness and anarchy – a danger in unstructured America. On the other hand we must ensure that in the process of puberty children are not made over-conscious of or guilty about the dawnings of sexuality in them. Fathers must speak openly, even bluffly and dismissively about erections, wet dreams and masturbation – Seltzer snipped a phrase or two again – but sex education should be neither lovey-dovey nor biological. Sex should be a great and convulsive mystery when people are ready for it, not poisoned with so called 'knowledge' and 'understanding'.

Before we know it, this has become political. The chapter ends with a longing that the mass of people should revert to 'living, spontaneous, original being', leaving thought and responsibility to those capable of seeing the direction to the future – such as Lawrence. Indeed, in the most remarkable insertion of all in chapter VII, he had taken up earlier revisions about the need for a society structured in terms of levels of consciousness and responsibility, and had spelled out his belief in hierarchical leadership and obedience at every level. He called for 'a great league of comrades, all over America' to stop it sliding into anarchy, 'Each ten comrades to have a leader, the leading soul among them, to whom they will give life and death obedience', each ten decurions to choose a centurion, and so presumably up (though he does not explicitly say so) to a supreme leader at the head.[12] (This was eight months before the creation of the ex-servicemen's army along those lines in *Kangaroo*.) Once again Seltzer wielded his scissors, to preserve the chances of the book in democratic America – but the effect of the reception of its predecessor had obviously made Lawrence more politically aggressive and challenging too.

Much more genial, however, were his dramatisations of himself with a 'gentle spouse' at his side 'to dig one in the ribs occasionally'. In chapter x he had extended his previous account of the damage done by mothers who make sons their lovers, into an account of how sex then gets into the head in narcissistic introversion and fascination with one's own sexuality – whereas fulfilment only comes through and after love for the other, in purposeful activity. Now, in chapter xi he is grateful for being able to be alone with his wife, each possessing their own souls in peace, after their fierce struggle.

They say it is better to travel than to arrive. It's not been my experience, at least. The journey of love has been rather a lacerating, if well-worth-it journey ...

... All the fight till one is bled of one's self-consciousness and sex-in-the-head. All the bitterness of the conflict with this devil of an amiable spouse, who has got herself so stuck in her own head ... But one fights one's way through it, till one is cleaned: the self-consciousness and sex-idea burned out of one, cauterised out bit by bit, and the self whole again, and at last free.[13]

But the struggle must go on. Revision in the final chapter positively encourages men and woman to fight, to fight each other out of self-consciousness and falsehood, never inhibiting their anger or even violence if it comes to that. (Seltzer cut bits once more.) The rewriting is again biographically suggestive. A man must not stand for his woman 'flirting' – Lawrence himself means more of course – or she for his being 'too sweet and smarmy with other people', a recurrent complaint of Frieda's. A man must tear down his wife's 'lovely idea' of herself and stop her looking on him as essentially her lover. She must (he is really addressing himself) be made to 'believe in you again, and in the deep purpose you stand for ... Combat her in her sexual pertinacity, and in her secret glory or arrogance in the sexual goal ... Make her yield once more to the male leadership', though only if the man has somewhere to lead to.

It was because his only means of being purposive was his writing, that he had come to argue so strongly that creative work was the central value in life. The new paragraph which shows what he now wanted from his marriage, may not have been wishful thinking so much as nostalgic memory of Ebersteinburg, and what he had experienced (for once) as he came back to the hotel every day from the woods, to find a Frieda contented with her life on her own ground, and glad that he was working well.

Ah how good it is to come home to your wife when she *believes* in you and submits to your purpose that is beyond her. Then, how wonderful this nightfall is! How rich you feel, tired, with all the burden of the day in your veins, turning home! Then you too turn to your other goal: to the splendour of darkness between her arms. And you know the goal is there for you: how rich that feeling is. And you feel an unfathomable gratitude to the woman who loves you and believes in your purpose and receives you into the magnificent dark gratification of her embrace. That's what it is to have a wife.

To which there is an obvious rejoinder – though Frieda was the last woman to feel burdened by the weight of domestic labour, or frustrated in a desire for a career of her own. Yet Lawrence also knew well enough the limits of her belief and submission. Belief in him would depend not only on having his 'soul filled with a profound and absolutely unalterable purpose', but also on finding his male purpose fulfilled in collectivity with other men. This made it even more important for him to find an audience, and recognition – and perhaps thereby convince the 'amiable wife' of his claims to leadership.[14] The book was written for America, and the hope of confirming a new audience and recognition there had been very much in his mind as he penned the original winsome Epilogue to Columbia.

But the final one, dated Taormina 15 October 1921, a week after the date on the Foreword, shares its defensive-aggressive tone. He is sensitive now to an imagined charge that he is after American dollars; though a number of asses (such as Cannan and Nichols perhaps) have crossed the Atlantic and been welcome to nibble at the green (or golden) carrot that the Statue of Liberty holds up. But, he admonishes her, his work is not commercial: 'You can't pay for it, darling. If I didn't make you a present of it you could never buy it.' How nice it would be if she liked his bouquet of ideas. But it is lunatics like Professor Pickering (who claims to have detected life on the moon), that get her attention.

By 5 November however, a new and realistic prospect of America had opened. Though Lawrence had been irritated at the way the *Dial* had cut up *Sea and Sardinia*, it had been enough to determine Mabel Dodge Sterne, a rich woman from Buffalo who had used her wealth for literary and artistic patronage in Florence, New York and now in Taos, New Mexico, to invite him to come and live there. On the edge of the Indian reservation which contained the largest remaining pueblo community, she had built a roomy adobe house, and near it another smaller one which she now offered Lawrence and his 'queen bee'. The *Dial* extract contained the vibrant passages about the Sardinian peasants, their costume, and their manliness and womanliness which had struck Lawrence so forcibly as among the last survivals from a finer yet almost forgotten world. Surely such a writer could do the same for the Taos Indians to bring their culture and their predicament home to an unsympathetic America? (She had not only interested herself in the Indian community and its culture, but had formed a liaison with Tony Luhan, a pueblo Indian who would become her third husband.) She told Lawrence about the Indians and their religion, with its veneration for the sun and the forces of the natural world; and she sent him a little 'medicine'[15] which she hoped would draw him across the water and the great New Mexican spaces to Taos, 6,000 feet up on the edge of a plain, overlooked by the southernmost spur of the Rocky Mountains. So we are to picture him collecting her letter from the post office and reading it as he walked the Corso, smelling the herbs and nibbling the medicine as he went (iv. 110).

There is an irony here. What must have annoyed Lawrence particularly about the *Dial* extract was not merely the bittiness, but the consistent purpose of the cuts. What had been excised, again and again, was the whole characterisation of himself and the queen bee (mentioned just once) which so enlivens the book. The *Dial* was only interested in the travel material. Even the scene at the crossroads in Palermo was excluded, presumably as too personal, though it is one of the finest things. Consequently the extract could have given his would-be patroness very little idea of what he was like as a person. The book itself would not be published until 12 December. However the extract was not her only source of information. She knew two people who could tell her more, about his work, and about the man himself.

When Huebsch had sought advice about the possible risks in publishing *The Rainbow* he had sent it to John Reed with whom Mabel had had a love-affair in New York. There is no knowing whether she read *The Rainbow* or whether Reed ever talked to her about it, but if he did he would have told her how deeply he had been moved and that only the great Russians could rival it.[16] She would of course also have been able to read 'America, Listen to Your Own' in the *New Republic*, together with the reply to Lippman's critique by Mary Austin, both of whom she knew; and 'Snake' in the *Dial* – all of which must have struck her as having precisely the right kind of message to white Americans.

The testimony about Lawrence and Frieda as persons came from Esther Andrews, and (see above pp. 375–6) presented them in very sympathetic and affectionate as well as admiring terms. (The remark about how the Cornish 'peasants' adored him – which Stanley Hocking later thought 'a bit much' – becomes clearer now, as an answer to the question 'How would he get on with Pueblo Indians?') Mabel must have met Esther in Greenwich Village where she had settled with Canby Chambers, and must have heard that Esther had twice spent some time with the Lawrences in Cornwall.

Lawrence and Mabel also shared an interest in psychology, though that was likely to prove a tricky subject since she had been under analysis by the foremost American Freudian, Abraham Brill, and was probably better acquainted than Lawrence with the various schools of psychoanalysis.[17]

Lawrence for his part was not hearing of Taos (or perhaps even of Mabel) for the first time, having seen photographs of the place at Leo Stein's house in Settignano (iv. 111). Mabel had been a patron of Leo's sister Gertrude Stein in earlier days in Florence, and Leo had spent six months of 1917 in Taos which he loved. Moreover Lawrence had heard through Juta of an artist Maurice Sterne who came to Anticoli, though he had not met him, and did not know yet that this was Mabel's second husband, not her brother (iv. 126).

He wrote back the same day, obviously greatly interested, though faint alarm bells were also ringing. Was there (horrid thought) 'a colony of rather dreadful sub-arty people' in the town? Were the Indians 'dying out, and is it rather sad?' And what did 'the sound, *prosperous* Americans do in your region?' – hoping presumably to be answered 'they ranch, there are no damn Yankees down here'. But Mabel's major argument was absolutely attractive: 'I believe what you say – one must somehow bring together the two ends of humanity, our own thin end, and the last dark strand from the previous, pre-white era. I verily believe that. Is Taos the place?' (iv. 111). It seemed that it might be. Was it a portent that the name even sounded like Taormina? So he replied that the q.b. and he would like to come, and that there were 'no little bees'. Mabel had written lyrically: what Lawrence wanted now were practical details of what it would cost per month to keep house, doing their own work since they liked to do it and hated having servants. And what would be the best way of getting there? And the climate? Not without its importance, obviously, though mentioned late and by the way.

Garnett had now sent 'The Primrose Path', and some advice (to read Homer) which Lawrence firmly but humorously rejected: 'No my dear Garnett, you are an old critic and I shall always like you, but you are also a tiresome old pontiff and I shant listen to a word you say, but shall go my own way to the dogs and bitches, just as heretofore. So there' (iv. 115). What he *had* been reading was the Sicilian writer Giovanni Verga whom he thought '*extraordinarily* good' and wondered whether he might translate. Could Garnett find out what translations of Verga there had been?

Unfortunately there also came a letter from Secker enclosing one from Heseltine's lawyer, refusing to accept the alterations as enough to halt the action. In reply, Secker had decided to call what he hoped was bluff. On 18 October he replied that Lawrence had agreed to 'eliminate any fancied resemblance' and the circulation of the book had been suspended 'at considerable pecuniary loss to us both' (iv. 94 n.); so now if Heseltine remained dissatisfied, let him sue. Yet Secker was obviously worried about what might happen. Lawrence thought

Heseltine was most likely 'trying to blackmail you' (iv. 113) and 'draw some limelight on to himself'; and would 'see him in several hells' rather than have him get any money. He was in no mood to imagine from Heseltine's point of view what reading *Women in Love* must have been for him, after the renewed relationship in Cornwall and his attempts to get Lawrence published in Dublin. He took only the most cynical view of Heseltine's motivation.[18]

Angry again, he was in no mood to hear about new books by Murry and the 'long-dying blossom' Katherine (iv. 114). Kot may have told him that in a favourable review of Frank Swinnerton's new novel *Cocotte* in October, Murry had listed Lawrence, by contrast, among novelists of whom no more could now be expected, and who 'appear to have passed their prime long before reaching it'.[19]

Suddenly the weather changed too: from being 'very warm and scirocco, and one's head feeling as if it were going to float away. Now suddenly it is very cold, and snow on Calabria' (iv. 114). Sure enough, he caught cold, and felt 'disgusted with everybody and everything' (iv. 116, 122). His English money was almost gone. In a sort of hiatus, he painted two pictures, one of 'four plump nice blonde females who have been bathing in a green pool, and are suddenly frightened, and flee' (iv. 121), and a copy of Masaccio's *Visit of the Magi*.[20]

In four days however his nose cleared, and the island burst into flower: masses of roses, citrus trees in blossom, great white trumpet flowers in hundreds, and the first narcissi and crocuses (iv. 122). The garden was suddenly crowded with birds newly come south and 'the storks are passing in the night, whewwing softly and murmuring as they go overhead' (iv. 124). Frieda had some new dresses made from the chequered local cloth, and asked Lawrence to assure her mother that she did not look fat in them. And his imagination, which had kept the spleen at bay with 'The Captain's Doll' – finished by 6 November (iv. 112) – sprang to life again.

III A Burst of Creativity

By 16 November he could declare that he had brought his collection of stories 'up to the scratch' (iv. 126), though the process was not finished yet. Within the next month however he produced not one volume of stories, but two, went through *Aaron's Rod* once more, and also Maurice Magnus's account of his time in the French Foreign Legion – conceiving a new idea for making it saleable despite earlier failures to interest publishers. Then he fell ill again, more seriously this time, with another attack of flu, and was in bed for a fortnight over Christmas and New Year. But between the two bouts of seediness he worked very hard and concentratedly.

Before 10 November he had already revised 'The Miracle' (written in 1916) into 'The Horse-Dealer's Daughter'; and had recovered 'Monkey Nuts' (1919, left behind at Grimsbury Farm), and 'The Primrose Path' (1913). These three had never been published. Seven stories had come out in magazines: 'Samson and Delilah' (written in Cornwall in 1916), and 'The Blind Man', 'Fanny and Annie', 'Tickets Please' and 'You Touched Me' (from late 1918 to summer 1919). He asked Sadleir what the position would be if he did now wish to include 'Wintry Peacock' (early 1919) in an English edition (iv. 117). (Blackwell finally released it for a nominal fee, but not before the whole volume had been delayed.) The last to be revised but by no means least, 'England, My England' (1915) would give its name to the whole collection eventually, though in mid-November he had not yet made up his mind about the story – still perhaps feeling some disquiet about the Meynells and the death of Percy Lucas. Of the stories written between his return to England in the summer of 1913 and his departure in late 1919, only two remained.[21] Theirs was to be the greatest transformation of all.

He had certainly meant to include 'The Fox' (late 1918); but as he looked at the story again, its ending seemed far too simple. By 16 November he had 'put a long tail' to it. 'Now he careers with a strange and fiery brush' (iv 126) – but with two novellas there was too much for a single volume, so the practical solution seemed to be to write a third and make another book. By 23 November he had 'practically got ready the book of short stories' (iv. 129), and though four had needed to be typed by Mrs Carmichael in Florence, by 12 December nine of the eventual ten were ready. By 1 December he was 'doing a third long story' (iv. 134), transforming 'The Thimble' even more radically than 'The Fox'. By 3 December it had been renamed 'The Ladybird', and by 17 December it was finished. Only the final revision of 'England, My England' remained to be done, and two books would be ready. It had been a remarkable seven weeks.

As Lawrence collected and revised the short stories, they became a much more homogeneous and interrelated volume than *The Prussian Officer*. The nature and extent of his revision varies. 'The Blind Man' and 'You Touched Me' he hardly changed at all, except to rename the latter 'Hadrian'. 'Wintry Peacock' had already been revised for the *Metropolitan*, replacing the soldier's sentimentality about the Belgian girl and her baby with a much more brutal unconcern, and therefore accentuating the question mark against the narrator's conspiratorial laughter. Others changed very little; and since no original manuscript survives for two of the three unpublished ones, there is no knowing whether or not they were altered. But the revisions that are known,[22] while they heighten and improve, do not (with the one important exception of the title story) re-conceive, as had happened to some in *The Prussian Officer*, accentuating the gap between one Lawrence and another. Here the earlier stories fit curiously well with the later ones, and are sometimes improved by their context. 'The Primrose Path', for example, is far from Lawrence's best, but as a depiction of chaos in a man apparently unable to come to terms with his own story or reck his own rede, it gathers point from juxtaposition with stories of men who can; reinforced by the other tales of returning prodigals, 'Samson and Delilah' and 'Fanny and Annie', whose male characters are notably strengthened in revision. These two also make an amusing contrast, undreamed of in their original composition three years apart; and 'The Horse-Dealer's Daughter' goes very well with 'Hadrian' as a 'you touched me' story, though the latter is much the better. 'Tickets Please' becomes more complex, with a new sense of hurt and damage in its apparently virago heroine – increasing the questioning of the female revenge at the end, as much as the changes to the male conspiracy in 'Wintry Peacock' do. Moreover, though the assertion of maleness against superior or dominating females runs through many of these, the presence beside them of feisty and life-enhancing women in earlier stories redresses what might otherwise seem too great an imbalance in those of 1918-19.

In the three novellas however, we watch a dramatic embodiment of the change from the Lawrence of 1917 to the Lawrence of 1921.

He had already revised 'The Mortal Coil' in Cornwall in 1917 after recovering the 1913 original which he had left behind in Fiascherino.[23] Based on an anecdote told by Frieda's father,[24] it had become by 1917 a sharply ironic exposure of its male protagonist, whose Gerald-like inability to love is underscored by the accidental asphyxiation of the woman who meant less to him than his pride and his career – which the discovery of the two dead women in his lodging finally ruins. (It is thus the opposite of 'The Thorn in the Flesh', where sexual love restores a man ashamed and disgraced.) Unfortunately, what had happened in life seems rather melodramatic for fiction. Now in 1921 however Lawrence's imagination reawakened to the girl in the red dress in the bachelor's attic room, writing her name over and over at his desk while she waits, and waits – reproached by friends for so compromising herself; frustrated by the seeming impenetrability of the man when he does arrive. In 'The Captain's Doll', Lawrence proceeds to do something altogether different with the original situation and indeed reverses its import, exploring a rejection of love (in the usual sense) not unlike his own after 1917. Yet it is not ideology that matters; what makes this much finer than the original is more complex characterising, better dialogue and above all a flickering probing comedy. His lone published novella, 'The Daughters of the Vicar', had already suggested that this might be an ideal form for Lawrence, with scope for greater development than the short tale but imposing still a salutary concentration. The story also reverses the ending in ice of the loveless man in *Women in Love*.

We are now in a post-war world and a defeated territory under occupation; and Lawrence transforms the opening episode into a comedy of the Absurd. The impenetrability which constantly defeats Hannele – the odd, straying voice of Captain Hepburn that contrasts so curiously with his sexual magnetism – is now not so much heartlessness as nihilism in a post-war collapse of value. Hepburn cannot believe even himself to be of any real importance; and not valuing himself, he lacks criteria for deciding on a future or re-establishing continuity with a past. Only his present sexual relation to Hannele is real to him – and his feeling for the cleaner remoter world of the stars, into which he escapes with his telescope on the roof. Hannele's portrait-doll is really all she has of him when he is not there: a gentlemanly looking exterior, and the suggestive memory of a sexy body under close-fitting tartan trews. Her frustrating inability to get any purchase on *him* is a comedy of manners also – his are perfect – but one with sombre undertones.

The arrival of the 'little lady' his wife produces comedy of misunderstanding,[25] beginning in farce but ending with realities of power. She is an Edwardian survival both in fashion and in mores, and she comically mistakes the identity of her husband's mistress because her mind works in pre-war operatic cliché. The 'doll' *she* makes of her husband, her image of the Edwardian male kneeling at her feet to promise her happiness, and the picture of him now, obediently running her errands, are almost enough to demolish Hannele's attraction to him altogether, did she not recall the mystery of the man and his magnetism. But the little lady's class and nationality still hold the keys to power, and (in a conversation whose menace is only partly veiled by its silky tone) she makes it quite clear how she means to keep possession of her husband and his image: her contacts can run Countess and Baroness out of town at twenty-four hours notice. Even worse, for Hannele, is the casual revelation that Hepburn is quite prepared to sleep with his wife again, out of husbandly duty – love à l'anglaise. (There is an art of implication here, especially in dialogue, which can seem to blend Jane Austen with Ivy Compton-Burnett.)

Only the little lady's death, severing the hold of the past, makes a future possible for Hepburn and Hannele. But though it is almost too convenient, are we to suppose it mere accident? – a question from *Women in Love*. It is important that Hepburn (and Lawrence) do her justice, in bringing out the tragedy behind the previous farce: the tragedy of those whose inner being has no real relation to the social roles in which they are caged, and who are doomed to parrot a language quite other than the song of the mysterious selves they were never able, or allowed, to be. Already the story is an early probing of the post-war malaise that would be seen as characteristic of the twenties. It shows (blessedly in both genders) why Lawrence had come to believe that the ability to stand, balance, value oneself *alone*, was the necessary precondition for, rather than the desirable result of, any satisfactory relationship; and how its absence could destroy.

It is only now, however, that he can pursue the question that had become so important to him, of the proper *im*balance between the individual man and the individual woman, which had replaced the 'star-equilibrium' of *Women in Love*. Being alone makes Hepburn learn about himself, and what he truly values. For no more than Aaron (or his creator) can he *live* alone – and only a woman as individual as Hannele could satisfy him, since he does not want to be put on a pedestal by some adoring maiden. So he goes in search of Hannele again – only to discover portents of how she might value him now: the doll amongst bric-à-brac in a shop window, and the modernist still-life in which doll-man is no more significant than the poached egg and the sunflowers with which he is so sardonically juxtaposed. This forces Hepburn to examine what value he puts on himself. Hannele has become engaged to an official who seems to embody the chaos of post-war Austria with a certain panache and dignity of acceptance – but one glimpse of Hepburn is enough to make everything unravel for her again, except the challenge of their relationship. In a splendid recreation of Thumersbach, Zell and the climb to the glacier, Hepburn makes it very clear what (for him) that relationship must be. 'Romantic' love is rejected, because it makes a doll of a man, as his wife and Hannele in their different ways had done, presuming to know and possess him. On their way up to the glacier Hepburn insists, with un-Teutonic and unromantic stubbornness (as against the spiritual Bergheilers with their fanged boots) that a man is greater than a mountain, which makes Hannele think him megalomaniac and ridiculous. Finally, at the cost of undignified scrambling and some danger, he insists on climbing on top of the slippery glacier, while Hannele looks up. He will not say he 'loves' her. As he explains in their comically wind-blown and shouted argument in the car on the way down, he has learned by bitter experience about love: of a mother, and a sister, and the lovers who make a doll of a man. If he and Hannele are to marry, he demands a reordering of the vows in the Book of Common Prayer: that she should honour (above all) and obey, while he promises the kind of love and cherishing appropriate to such a wife. Moreover (like the Lawrence of 1917–21) he will fulfil himself in creative work, wife or no wife.

Hepburn is a dramatised figure, often seen as comic and ineffectual – though he (crucially) becomes less and less so – and Hannele is used (as Ursula was) to question and proportion his claims. At the end, indeed, there is still a question about honour. She has not given in to him on that, or not yet, though in saying she will go to East Africa with him she has probably already fulfilled the only kind of obedience that was obtainable from Frieda, which so far she had always given, though not without the occasional rumpus, following his lead in the decisions that affected his further and creative life. (Given two strong people, in

the last resort either one of them does lead, or both slowly or quickly part –
though Lawrence seems never to have imagined that there might be a woman
whose creative claims were the greater.) But it was the honouring of him, in her
heart of hearts, which Lawrence always felt Frieda failed him in; and that was
the most important of all. If he read this story to her – as she says he always did
– it might well have seemed a declaration about their own marriage.

The greatly enlarged and developed 'The Fox' would explore a good deal
further. The Lawrence of 1921 clearly felt that Henry had won March far too
easily (given her apparent mannishness and the pull of her relation with
Banford); and that Banford had given in too easily also. Moreover the equation
of boy with fox, when re-imagined, turned out to have been oversimple for all its
power. Even in its compressed state *Hutchinson's* had considered the short story
too long; but now the increased scope of a novella allowed Lawrence to imagine-
to-the-end, with far greater thoroughness and depth. Up to the first wooing of
March in the woodshed, however, hardly anything needed to be done – except
to make the boy a bit *more* foxy and sly, as the idea of getting hold of the farm
dawns on him. Yet the new 'tail' is not just an extension. As with 'Odour of
Chrysanthemums' in 1914, the new ending makes the whole story different.

In making March harder to win over, Lawrence first intensifies the likeness
of Henry to the fox, then questions it, and then makes a new and crucial
distinction. Before the scene in the woodshed, now, he shows the boy as a
hunter, not merely stalking March carefully but, like primeval man, so
projecting his will as a power field upon his quarry that the hunt becomes 'a
supreme act of volition'. Henry's first attempt partly misses, but even the
extent to which he succeeds in 'producing his voice in her blood' brings about
a change in the physical presence of both, to which Banford instinctively
reacts. March is set brooding on the fox again, and equating the first brush of
Henry's lips with the experience in her dream. As soon however as the boy
learns of her 'impression' of their likeness, he begins to question it. And
although he eavesdrops foxily on the conversation in which Banford voices her
full social and sexual hostility, his horror at being regarded as a predatory
animal is what sends him out in the darkness to shoot the fox. Two crucial
points are in fact being made in that 'killing': Henry's rejection (despite fellow-
feeling) of the predatory in himself; and then March's realisation in consequence, as she dreams now of interring a dead Banford in the wood box,
wrapped in the fox's skin, that *that* part of her, too, must die and be put away.
As Henry watches the small figure of Banford coming across the fields, and
March running out as always to serve her, he begins to realise the hateful
degree to which she, and the relation between the women, stands in the way of
his hopes. But to see March in a dress is to complete the distinction between
boy and fox that has now become as important as the likeness, and to define

manhood (and womanhood) in the terms of 1921. There is a new word that had not figured at all in the story of 1918:

He felt a man, with all a man's grave weight of responsibility. A curious quietness and gravity came over his soul. He felt a man, quiet, with a little of the heaviness of male destiny upon him.

She was soft and accessible in her dress. The thought went home in him like an everlasting responsibility.

Once out of the armour of her male clothing, March is revealed as a different being, and he must begin to grow up into a man's responsibility. Moreover she too must complete her new sense of him, by feeling the mystery of his male heart under her fingertips – not a fox, not a boy, but a man whose blood beats strangely, 'terrible, like something from beyond'.

Already the novella has gone far deeper than the short story; but it is in Lawrence's realisation of the need for a new kind of 'death' that his tale acquires a more terrible and challenging resonance. For now Lawrence sees, truly, that the Banford he has imagined will *never* give March up, and that March has so grown into the relation between the women that she cannot escape by herself. It is not enough for a newly maturing Henry to hold her back from rushing to her 'darling'[26] when Banford bursts into hysterical weeping, to let her cry herself out if she must. For Banford will fight him 'to the death' as the saying goes. And it is the courage of the fiction now – however disturbing – that it is prepared to imagine what that might mean.

For almost as soon as Henry has gone back to his regiment to complete his demobilisation, March's letter proves that in his absence Banford has taken her over again. (The letter is a triumph of epistolary art in the certainty with which one can detect Banford coming through the language of March.) And when, after his headlong rush back, Henry finds them beside the dead tree that March has been trying to cut down, once again metaphor gets challengingly made literal. In the death of Banford – perhaps the most chilling scene Lawrence had yet written, because so much cooler, and consciously willed, than the attempted strangling of Gudrun – all three are implicated in differing degrees. Taking the axe to dead wood is instinctive in March, though ineffectual by itself (despite her dream). Banford dares Henry to do his worst/best, welcoming a battle of wills without realising her danger. Only Henry acts in full realisation, and that makes his action terrible – gamble though it must be in all but the strength of his will, locked against Banford's. He takes the responsibility of life-or-death for all three.

What had been partly evaded in 'The Captain's Doll' is brought out fully here, to the horror of some readers. Lawrence faces squarely and severely the possibility that individuals and relationships may be so inimical to the true growth of others that it may literally become a matter of life or death – and he is prepared to imagine that to its logical and horrible end, to see how it would be. The death of Banford cannot be taken metaphorically as merely the death of part of March, though of course it is that too. Nor can we pass it off as a judgement on lesbianism. (The death of the 'little lady' and her relation with her husband was just as necessary for the marriage of Hepburn and his Hannele.) Once again the nature of a relationship seems what is important to Lawrence, not merely the gender of the participants, though that may help to define the nature. The point is clarified at the end, though it is disturbing to be presented with such an extreme, and allowed no evasion.

For even when March and Henry are married, she remains unhappy and he unsatisfied. In a long meditation, she voices her realisation of what Henry wants and needs: that she 'submerge' herself in their love, indeed in him, giving up entirely her independent self-direction – but she cannot quite bring herself to do that, though it is what a great part of herself also wants and needs. In Henry's consciousness the same realisation dawns: 'He wanted to veil her woman's spirit as Orientals veil the woman's face. He wanted her to commit herself to him, and put her independent spirit to sleep.' Until she does so, he feels (chafing at the delay) he has not got and can never have his own life, his own maleness.

He would never have it till she yielded and slept in him. Then he would have all his own life as a young man and a male, and she would have all her own life as a woman and a female. There would be no more of this awful straining. She would not be a man any more, an independent woman with a man's responsibility. Nay, even the responsibility for her own soul she would have to commit to him. He knew it was so, and obstinately held out against her, waiting for the surrender.[27]

The consciousness of both characters seems now to be nearly in agreement – more so than at the end of 'The Captain's Doll' – but March, too, has not quite surrendered at the end. There is less of a question mark than usual in Lawrence; but we are still (just) allowed to respond to this boy, and this woman, as characters in dramatised tension.

Yet there is also an element of generalisation which betrays the author's over-involvement. Whether or when March will surrender, in order to 'have all her own life as a woman and a female', becomes a substantially different question from whether or when Hannele will accept the old-fashioned marriage vows as condition for marrying Hepburn. Nor does the point seem limited to wrongness in the woman-to-woman relationship as such; but rather that both women have so made the happiness of the beloved their goal that they have had to 'strain', to 'exert' themselves, to 'know' and 'consider' and 'strive' and be 'responsible' for the other. *That* seems to be for Lawrence the deathly element, which would have been there had Banford married a man, and is there even when March has done so. This is clearly now a matter of gender definition: that what is life-giving for a woman is that she should be truly 'female', i.e. taking her direction from and living in the life of her man – as a 'male' life depends on his woman doing so. Not only is happiness a false goal in itself for both partners (as in Hepburn with his wife); but unhappiness is rendered certain by the way modern women try to take on the direction of life, thinking to make their partners happy. And so important does all this seem to Lawrence as he nears the end of his rewriting, that his authorial voice breaks through the characterising one, to propound. It is often a difficulty in reading him that the narrative voice is so 'given' to a character that the reader is in danger of mistaking the character's point of view for the author's. But there is also the converse danger, that the strength of the author's feeling may overwhelm the autonomy of the character, as happens at one point in *The Rainbow* for example, when Ursula's consciousness gets drowned out by a surge of authorial feeling about resurrection. Here, what has been threatening to happen does so, between two sighs of 'Poor March'. We cease to be in March's consciousness;[28] the generalisations about women and happiness are Lawrence's, and tend to imperil the dramatised experience of the final pages. One becomes aware of hearing the prompter when one should be listening to the actors. And what might be acceptable as the responses of this man and this woman, to their particular situations – her deep need of 'rest', his deep need to be 'the man' in relation to a much older woman – seem offered for acceptance (or rejection) as universal truths of gender. What that shows, however, is the pressure of their importance to the Lawrence of late 1921.

'The Thimble' of 1915 had its germ in imagining what it must have been like for Lady Cynthia when Beb came home from the front, wounded in the mouth.[29] She acknowledged Lawrence's disconcerting perceptiveness, and she was not offended. For he had imported the idea of a war marriage (which hers was not) in which the couple really knew each other so little that they meet as strangers now, and had also intensified the horror of the mutilation; so that the story was clearly pointed at Lawrence's great theme of 1915 rather than at his friends. In their strangeness and helplessness the fictive couple have to start completely anew, to be new-born, resurrected, out of the brush with death. The throwing of the thimble out of the window – whose meaning puzzled Cynthia – is the discarding of a dead, insentient, second-hand past which, indeed, has no meaning in the present.

Though Lawrence had been quite pleased with the story at the time, once again he reread with very different eyes at the end of 1921. Moreover, though he thought the other two novellas were now 'so modern, so new: a new manner' (iv. 132), as indeed in many ways they are, it was in the transformation of 'The Thimble' that he was most experimental. The original had been very much from the life, transposed and heightened by imagination, as indeed 'The Captain's

Doll' and 'The Fox' remained to begin with, their central symbols then acting as catalysts to open up dimensions within the characters in a familiar Lawrencian way, though with a new laconic (American?) narrative tone. In 'The Ladybird' however, Lawrence uses symbolism less to explore 'character' than to articulate his radical antagonism, now, to the England and Europe he is about to leave. The other two novellas still focused on the central concern of 1913–17, the relation of complex male and female individuals, though seen in the new perspective of 1921. The third needed a different kind of characterisation, a new rhetoric and a more pervasive symbolism, in order to indict a whole civilisation. It begins realistically enough in wartime England, but almost immediately the characters are seen as *representative*, and within a few pages the reader is involved in an outlandish language and a pervasive symbolism, more important than the characters-as-such, and designed precisely to crack open the sterile real world of 1918 Europe, and allow a strange subversive vitality to come through.

So, to the nerve-torn and wounded wartime couple of the original story Lawrence begins by adding Lady Beveridge, visiting a hospital but embodying, herself, a dying pre-war world. She represents both the best of the Christian ethic of suffering love, returning good for evil; and an Edwardian liberalism which for Lawrence had died when Asquith was overthrown by Lloyd George. But in a world at war, her sons are tragically dead and her time has passed. Moreover – in an economical inversion of Thomas Crich and his wife in *Women in Love* – her civilisation of love and benevolence already has against it the dark question mark of her antisocial husband the Earl, withdrawn from her, dissatisfied, his true being repressed; as well as the fair one of her daughter, the beauty who has lost her mother's certainties but has nothing to put in their place, and suffers from nerves and suspected consumption. (Lawrence has used what Cynthia had told him of her parents, and of herself, and later of her favourite home, Stanway.) Already the story is enquiring less into relationships than values: *this* might just as well (so far) have been called 'England, their England'. The past is dying, the present sick. What is the future to be?

Lawrence's major transformation of his original story, however, is the invention of Count Johann Dionys Psanek to voice a subversive challenge, not just to 'England' but to European 'civilisation' as a whole. Close to death at the beginning, he is a reminder that the whole of Europe is a casualty of war. As he slowly recovers, however, what he has died to is the civilised Austro-Czecho-slovak mannikin he had appeared to be before the war, and what is being resurrected in him is something far older and pre-European, Slav, perhaps gypsy even, with its deepest roots in Egypt rather than in Greece and Rome. As John he is a voice crying in the wilderness for change; as Dionysos he is a foe of Apollonian enlightenment; as Psanek he is an outlaw, a rebel, a subversive. The outlandishness of his rhetorical and symbolic language enables Lawrence to dramatise and explore his own rejection of Europe without having to take direct authorial responsibility for his character's ideas; and also to get into the story his awareness of the seeming weakness and isolation of his own voice in the post-war world, but also his confidence in its ultimate power. For the Count is also a kind of caricature of Lawrence made into a *little* man, bearded and odd-looking; a sick man, and an outsider, who says weird if curiously poetic things; a proud and prickly man, who is rather ridiculous really, isn't he?

Or is he? The success or failure of the story depends on the power of the Count's strange language, not only to undermine the Apollonian in Daphne and Basil – whose names now reveal their representative status as characters – but also to do this in the reader. To the nymph beloved of Apollo, and enamoured of her own fair and ideal beauty, the Count responds with an insistence that it conceals quite a different nature: the very different beauty of the polar bear, the wild-cat, the delicate adder – and she responds. When her wounded war hero returns, she becomes even more nerve-worn as the recipient of his blend of idealism and desire. He places her on a pedestal as Aphrodite–Isis–Astarte; but at the same time always desires her, with 'adoration-lust'. In contrast, the Count refuses altogether to idealise. To him, the modern woman is a decadent lily ignoring her roots in the mud. He calls for an older womanhood, as in the women of his blood, who sewed shirts for him with the sign of the Ladybird upon them (as on the scarab thimble with its twining serpent he had given her as a girl). The scarab was the sign of the sun to the Egyptians, and the Psanek crest stands for a sun-wisdom: the *dark* invisible sun (at the heart of all flame), which constantly fertilises the dungball-earth it rolls through the sky, and whose light is only a refraction caused by dust.

The Count is filled with anger. Moreover, puny and ineffectual though he seems, he is convinced of the power of his angry heart, a little hammer of Thor, to crack open the apparent solidity of the world he opposes. He can already hear it cracking. As the novella develops, he exposes the fundamental opposition between his view of being and Basil's; and so probes the discontent of Daphne that eventually, in her own ancestral home, she is drawn as by a magnet to the darkness of his room. Basil believes, as the Lawrence of 1913–17 had believed, that the essence of life lies 'in the dynamic contact between human beings', in the many forms of love. The Count denies this absolutely. For him the essential relationship comes from the instinct, in people 'who are really living', to put their lives in the hands of those who are fit for 'the sacred responsibility of power', and 'able to be alone, to choose and to command'. Having done so (says the anti-democratic little man) they must give up forever their right to judge, and must obey. So the central values are 'Obedience, submission, faith, belief, responsibility, power'.[30] Basil will not accept this; and Basil is given his due.

True to his Greekness, he will spend the rest of his life in thought, Platonic friendship and love, and the effort towards understanding – and once he has shed the lust that consorts so ill with his idealism, he is treated with respect as the daylight husband, Basileus, the king of the Daytime. But Daphne is drawn, irresistibly, towards the weird almost inhuman song the Count sings in his bedroom late at night, and in the pitch darkness there she kneels at his feet, to become (like Proserpine) the night-time wife of the King of the Underworld, the dark side of the human psyche. The Count sings, in his unintelligible words, a folksong of the swan-maiden who fell in love with a man but was called home by her swan-husband, a swan-song not of death but of return to her deeper nature. It is the essence of the myth of Proserpine, too, that the new Spring of the world depends upon renewal from the underworld sources of life. The new story is a myth – which cannot be read in simply realistic terms. However, the Count is even more intransigent than Hepburn or Henry in his sexual politics, extended now (as in the revised *Fantasia*), to a social politics too. Yet, at the end, Basil and the Count agree that there can be no laying down the law – only the necessity of following one's 'own inmost need'.[31]

Politically, Lawrence's contempt for the democracy which had bestowed leadership on Lloyd George in its enthusiasm for the prosecution of the war, and allowed Horatio Bottomley to claim to be the Voice of the People, has led him to let a character flirt once more with anti-democratic ideas (obedience, submission, belief, power) that were beginning to gain influence in Italy and Germany, fuelled by the failure of democracy to produce good government. (He read the newspapers in both countries, he knew about Italy first-hand and he probably knew about what was beginning to happen in Munich from the widow of Edgar Jaffe.) All over Europe, democracies seemed to be plunging into anarchy. But (again) we should not assume too easily that the Count speaks for Lawrence in some definitive sense. Basil makes a good retort about the disastrous results of the authoritarian rule of the Kaiser (though he would be proved wrong, in time, for mocking the idea that millions of men could voluntarily place their destinies in the hands of one man, and give up their right to say 'no'.) Rather, in both the revised *Fantasia* and 'The Ladybird', Lawrence carries on an internal exploration which would be taken a long step forward in *Kangaroo*, and would issue finally, both there and in the Epilogue to *Movements*, in a rejection of both socialism and fascism. As he was beginning 'The Ladybird' he was wondering whether an alliance in Italy of the Church and the socialists and communists might produce stability. He was not by any means a supporter of the Fascisti. What however does need emphasis is the degree to which he was now conceiving himself as a subversive *antagonist*, a gadfly to sting audiences to question their assumptions, not only in England but also (after the reception of *Psychoanalysis*) in America. This burst of creativity at the end of 1921 not only provides a kind of summary embodiment of his development since *Women in Love*, it is also a shaking of dust off the sandals, as far as Europe is concerned – and a conscious flinging out of a challenge to the new audience he still hoped to find overseas, though not as optimistically now.

It only remained to rewrite 'England, My England', to strike the keynote of the volume of short stories too. By 7 December (iv. 144), as he was finishing 'The Ladybird', his intransigent mood decided him. He *would* include the Greatham story in the new collection, and crush any lingering remorse about the Meynells.

IV   A Question – of Dishonour?

It is just possible that during this burst of hard work and creativity a cruel irony had come about at his expense.

To look again at Hepburn's conditions for his marriage at the end of 'The Captain's Doll', and then pursue the treatment of what it means to 'honour and obey' through the three novellas in the order of their composition, is to notice an unmistakable hardening and pushing to extremes. From Hannele's laughing question about the marriage vows, to Henry's insistence that March should entirely give up her new-womanly independence, to Daphne kneeling at the little Count's feet in absolute submission, and bathing them with her tears, the underlining gets stronger and stronger. One might also notice a throwback there, as in the creation of Daphne and the whole mythos of the underworld, to Lawrence's defence of his relations with his 'women' against the attack by Gray and Frieda at the end of 1917. Though much detail in 'The Ladybird' is drawn from Lawrence's knowledge of Cynthia Asquith, and though the woman in 'The Thimble' was clearly a 'word-picture' of her, the fairness and willowiness of Daphne, and the classical frame of reference in which she is created, are quite foreign to Cynthia but strongly reminiscent of Hilda Aldington. The theme of the underworld, and the image of the kneeling woman at the feet of her Lord, relate directly to his answering the scorn in Gray's letter at the end of 1917 (iii. 179-80 and see above pp. 414–16). Moreover Gray had dared to question Lawrence's claims about his marriage in *Look!*, and had very possibly done so because he had had an affair with Frieda.

In March 1990 – it has been claimed – an old man of 92 from near Taormina died in Pittsburgh, and his family released a secret that (they said) he had spoken of only to intimate friends: he had slept with Lawrence's wife in a brief affair, which she confessed to her husband. At a time when Lawrence was so involved with his writing as to have little attention to spare for her, she had taken to visiting a new friend, a rich lady whose husband owned vineyards on the neighbouring hills, and who had a house in the mountain village of

Castelmola high above Taormina and about five or six kilometres by mule path from Fontana Vecchia. This lady (the story goes) used to send down a mule with a comfortable side saddle for Frieda, in the care of a young man of 24, Peppino D'Allura, who worked for her husband. One day there was a sudden downpour, and they were very late in arriving. They had taken shelter in one of the storage cabins in the vineyards; and Frieda had proceeded to strip off her damp clothes to dry them, inviting the young man to do the same. Running out naked into the rain and daring him to follow, 'sexual games' took place.

There is no evidence to support this story. As told in the gossipy and scandalous pages of *The Sins and Love Affairs of Taormina* the suggested date is quite wrong; and it seems quite as likely that the cavortings in the rain are read back from *Lady Chatterley's Lover* as that the episode was their source, as is claimed. The book repeats an absurd tale of the encounter of Lawrence with King George V by the ancient fountain, which has no truth whatsoever.[32] It is not an account which, in its notion of evidence, or its motivation, inspires any confidence – and even the surname of the young man looks suspicious.

On the other hand, one of the tests for claims about sexual occurrences in Lawrence's life is whether traces are left in the work that cannot be put down to back-reading. Lawrence's much later Sicilian story 'Sun' (written in 1925) *may* be a place where he converted old hurt into new creativity – though the wife's affair with the peasant takes place only in thought. It must also be admitted that as a response to neglect or an act of rebellion, quite as much as an impulse of desire, Frieda was capable of committing such an action (and confession), though in this case it would have to have been with a new social carelessness. *If* it ever happened, it would probably have been between about 24 October when Lawrence's pottering with the stories and not feeling like work gave way to the start of the burst of creativity, and about mid-December when the third novelette went to the typist after seven weeks of intense work.[33]

If so, it would have been a devastating irony at the expense of the view of marriage the novellas explore, and might conceivably explain their growing intransigence about the proper relation between a man and his wife. It might (for example) bear on the difference between the ending of 'The Captain's Doll', and that of 'The Fox' with its authorial intrusion, and its extremism about the need to 'submerge' female independence altogether before there could be real content in the departure to a new life overseas. It might also explain the intransigent reminder of an earlier unhappiness in the conclusion of 'The Ladybird'. But (if so, again) Lawrence did not respond or retaliate with a confession of his own. Nor would such an episode have been likely to suggest a breach with Frieda. He would have remembered his letter to Godwin Baynes, which had argued that Godwin and Rosalind could keep 'a lasting relationship' in spite of what had happened.

One has to learn that love is a secondary thing in life. The first thing is to be a free, proud, single being by oneself: to be oneself free, to let the other be free ... Its an ignominious thing, either exacting or chasing after love. Love isn't all that important: one's own free soul is first. (iii. 478)

There is no reason to suppose that he would have thought or acted any differently now – though he would have felt it deeply.[34]

But the story must remain a question mark at best.

V An End to 1921, and England

About the time he was finishing 'The Fox' there was good news both from America and England – but not for long. Having now read *Aaron's Rod*, Seltzer cabled that he thought it 'wonderful, overwhelming' (iv. 121, 125). Lawrence was not unaware that this might be what he called 'a publisher's pat' (iv. 124), but at least it seemed to ensure that the novel would be published in America, and determined him finally to have Curtis Brown offer it to Secker also. In England, Bottomley had fallen into greatly merited disgrace with the exposure, in a libel trial, that thousands of subscribers to his Great Victory Bond Club had been swindled. In March he would be formally charged with fraud, and in May would be sentenced to seven years in jail. He and his gutter press would pose no further threat to *Women in Love*.

However, the next letter from Secker revealed that he had thought it best to offer Heseltine £50 and 10 guineas costs as a settlement out of court – which made Lawrence 'sick with rage' (iv. 129), though it was unclear whether Secker proposed to charge this against royalties, or pay the money himself. At least, however, the novel as altered could now go back on sale – though Lawrence begrudged Heseltine his triumph and 'loathed' Secker's giving in (iv. 130). A letter from Heseltine to his solicitor, however, shows that Heseltine believed the alterations amounted to an admission of guilt, and was mainly prevented from going to court by lack of money.[35] He was still dependent on his mother, who would not have paid for the publicity or the exposure of the pre-marital birth of the grandchild she was now bringing up. Also, he had now finally separated from Puma, who would certainly not have welcomed being dragged into court as a witness. However he urged his solicitor to contact Scotland Yard and try to persuade the police to seize the book instead, for 'if ever a book afforded grounds for prosecution on a charge of morbid obscenity in general and the glorification of homosexuality in particular, this one does'.[36] Considering that it was Heseltine's fervent opposition to the prosecution of *The Rainbow* that had cemented the friendship in the first place, this is a sour irony too. It does however look as though it was as well to have it settled.

'Overwhelmed' or not, Seltzer soon asked for changes in *Aaron's Rod* and indeed Lawrence worried that there might be trouble over Argyle's derivation from Douglas, much as he had done about Halliday and the Pussum in 1916. He also knew well enough that the episode with the Marchesa was 'dangerous'. He had only his handwritten manuscript now 'which luckily I haven't yet burned' (iv. 131), but he went through it to look at what Mountsier had called the 'foul-mouthed Englishman' and at the scenes with the Marchesa. However, a postscript to the same letter confessed that he could not alter it:

But if you like to follow the type-script, which I have often written over, in the scenes you mention, and if you like to leave out what is written over, I don't think you need fear the public much. And if you like to leave out a sentence or two, or alter a phrase or two, do so. But I can't write anything different. (iv. 132)[37]

He was annoyed to find that Mountsier had returned to America only recently, instead of three weeks before. While this explained why there had been no news about *Sea and Sardinia* and *Tortoises*, no direct news in fact since Lawrence had left Zell, he should surely have been told of his agent's change of plan. Lawrence was no longer interested in having bits of *Aaron* published in magazines, but wondered whether the *Dial* might take 'The Captain's Doll' (iv. 130). (They did not – it was too long.) He was also cross to hear from Curtis Brown that Secker was again trying to claim that a new volume, the stories, should not count towards the total Lawrence was contracted for (iv. 129 and n. 3) – though the contract specified 'books' not 'novels'.

Amid all these annoyances the intention of going to Taos remained, even though Mountsier warned that he might not like it, or Mabel Sterne, or its artist colony (iv. 150). Characteristically, Lawrence got over the difficulty of telling Brewster about his change of mind by presenting it as a decision against Buddha, as too 'finished and perfected and fulfilled ... The glamour for me is in the west, not in the fulfilled east' (iv. 125). He feared Brewster might be angry with him, but New Mexico seemed his fate. He felt some responsibility towards Frieda's mother too, as he planned to take her daughter across the Atlantic. Fortunately a gesture of concern became possible because of the collapse of the exchange value of the German mark in late 1921, when it became 1,000 to the £1. Kippenberg had been sending him sections of the translation of *The Rainbow*, in proof, though none had come for some time. But now Lawrence thought it would be good both for Insel-Verlag and for the Baroness if, instead of losing heavily on the exchange with sterling, Kippenberg were to pay for *The Rainbow* in marks (iv. 117), directly to the Ludwig-Wilhelmstift. Kippenberg promptly agreed to send the Baroness 18, 000 marks by Christmas (iv. 132) – though Frieda then intervened to insist that 6,000 be distributed among her German nephews and nieces (iv. 136).

He was also worried about their own finances, and the immediate cost of their passages, though he had done all he could by way of seed-corn for 1922. There would be quite a large bill for typing, from Mrs Carmichael and from Ruth Wheelock, now typing the second part of *Mr Noon*. He wrote to ask Secker to pay the last of the royalties for *The Lost Girl* into a London account that was now running very low indeed (iv. 148), and he began to think he would need to get a cheque-book in order to draw on the American account Mountsier had opened, though he had hoped to live on his English one. In the nick of time came the best piece of news yet – wholly unexpected – that *The Lost Girl* had won the 1921 James Tait Black Memorial Prize, at that time probably the most prestigious prize for British fiction. It was in the gift of the Professor of English Literature at the University of Edinburgh – then Herbert Grierson – and at £100 it was a real windfall. Moreover, as Lawrence could not resist saying in his letter of thanks, it was especially pleasing to have 'at last some spark of friendly recognition out of Britain. It has been mostly abuse' (iv. 146). All the more credit to the occupant of the earliest Chair of English in the island.

As December went on, the letters show a marked sense of transience. To Mary Cannan he wrote of how there weren't many tourists now, 'all afraid of strikes and railway smashes' (iv. 143). A train had fallen into a river in Calabria, and violence was mounting between the communists and the fascists. The Corso had become 'thousands of antique shops with doors wide open and nobody to go in'. Still the place remained beautiful and fascinating. Their plot of land was being ploughed: 'Comes a black, Saracen man, a little young woman in yellow kerchief, a barefoot boy, two cows, a young silver bull with black eyebrows, a fine merino sheep, a black-and-brown goat, and a yellow dog: and an ass, oh dear Lord, that sings for twenty' (iv. 137). But he was increasingly tired of the Taormina expatriates; and the younger Cacópardos all seemed discontented, and indeed as ready to leave the island as he was. In a farewell letter to Marie Hubrecht he told her the gossip but he was bored with it all now (iv. 139–41). The only new interest was the visit of Juta's girlfriend Elizabeth and her mother, who came for two months in the Hotel Beau Séjour (iv. 143; and whose stay certainly was useful for Lawrence later).[38] As Christmas approached and he sent off his customary postcards he felt less Christmasy even than usual – and he was a man who never cared much for Christmas. On 21 December he told Mountsier he would finish that day or the next the new 'England, My England' – and then his two volumes would be complete (iv. 150). He thought that he had about $2,000 in his American account (iv. 152) – which would do for the passages and some left over. On 28 December he wrote to confirm to Mabel that they were indeed coming, perhaps even on a boat from Bordeaux to New Orleans on 15 January if they could get ready in time. He also made two characteristic points: that he intended to pay 'the usual rent' and hoped not to be all his life 'so scrubby poor as we have been' – and though he was prepared to believe in Indians, 'they must do *half* the believing: in me as well as in the sun' (iv. 152).

So 'England, My England' was another final rejection. The major change from the early version was to make it more representative, more a story of England as a whole than before. But because it became a final farewell now to *Lawrence*'s England, at its best, the emotions the rewritten story packs into its title become more complicated than the earlier irony against patriotism. For he had loved Greatham, and had been creative and (mostly) happy there. And whereas 'The Ladybird' had rejected a culture, a Graeco-Christian civilisation that was characteristic of Europe at large, now he was rejecting 'his' England, specifically, at its most attractive.

So, as he expanded the pre-war section of the story to five times its previous length, it fills with vivid and intimate detail that also (unfortunately for the Meynells) made it far *more* recognisable than the earlier story had been.[39] One would have had to know them very well to recognise in the original version Wilfrid's Quaker upbringing in Newcastle, or make anything of the half sentence about the number of his children. Only the accident to the child (though in the first version it is nobody's fault), and the unforeseen death of Percy Lucas after the story had been published, pointed hurtfully to the family. But now the more Lawrence localised his sense of the quintessential Englishness of the setting and its people, the more identifiable it all became: the cottage he now names 'Crockham', the expanded characterisation of the father and the brief glimpse now of his poetess wife, the cluster of cottages for the daughters round the old farmhouse, the Roman Catholicism, the expanded detail of the Crockham cottage family, the interest of Egbert in folk-song and morris-dancing and the fuller account of the maiming of the child, all made it much more likely that the story could be taken as a portrait of Percy Lucas, his family, his dependence on his father-in-law, his responsibility (quite unfactual) for the accident to his child and his reasons for enlistment, followed by his death in action. It is little wonder that the family in Rackham cottage still resent today how Lawrence repaid the Meynell hospitality.

Yet it is not a portrait, however ruthlessly details from life are used; and it would be a mistake to suppose any malice. Indeed the delay in rewriting this story till the very last suggests some scruple; though if so, the going ahead in even greater detail underlines how ruthlessness prevailed. But even if the added detail inevitably increased the possibility of identification, that was not its purpose. Only the story as a whole can show what that purpose was, and how it had changed since 1915.

The first version made Evelyn's garden the beautiful dream of an unworldly man opting out of society – till the deadly 'iron' which lies hidden (at a time of destruction) in the conflict of marriage and the family, and in the world itself, catches up with him and finally makes him both doomed and lethal. But in the rewriting, the garden and the ancient yeoman's cottage in the old 'savage' place become a final and beautiful flowering of a long *English* history. The spirit of place lingers on primeval, snakes and all, in the ancient setting. The lovers inherit a dark home where generations have loved and coupled before them. Egbert is renamed and redescribed to bring out a blend of the Saxon and the Viking elements in Englishness, while Winifred is made even more ancient-Briton-like than before. Godfrey Marshall is an ancient type of father, patri-archal, Christmasy. This grafting together in the twentieth century of the great stems of Englishness, highly cultivated now, but rooted in the past, ought to produce a sort of quintessence of English civilisation. So in a sense it does – and the sense is loving and nostalgic.

However it is not at all sentimental, for the story resembles the novellas also in being a re-enactment of Lawrence's own changing vision, from *The Rainbow*, through 'The Crown' and *Women in Love*, to 1921. Having established a *Rainbow*-like marriage of opposites, in highly economical richness, Lawrence follows the insight of 'The Crown' into a time of coming apart, and ends with a will-to-die like Gerald's (removing the frenzy of slaying in the early version). But the process of things coming apart at the centre of English culture is diagnosed with the eyes of 1921 – and created in the new laconic ('American') style that Lawrence was developing, so that the linguistic experience, too, is like moving from *The Rainbow* to one of the better parts of *Fantasia*. As the conflict of opposites in the marriage turns from creation to destruction it is important not to see this as merely a matter of individual character (though it is that too) but as also a matter of the times, of which the characters are representative. Behind the voices of the children and the attitudes of parents, behind the hardening battle between husband and wife, behind the 'accident' which maims the child and confirms the unbridgeable rift that ruptures the marriage and helps to send Egbert into the army, there is a sharper sense now of a *time* of dissolution – pitting liberalism (and finally anarchy) against authority, individual cultivation against social responsibility, magna mater against rebellious male, one 'people' against another. If we seek the cause of the maiming of the child, it is more than Egbert's carelessness, for that in a deeper sense is at the core of his nature, his aloofness, his refusal to work, his anarchic individualism. His very 'cultivation' is the cause.

Why didn't Egbert do something, then? Why didn't he come to grips with life? Why wasn't he like Winifred's father, a pillar of society, even if a slender, exquisite column? Why didn't he go into harness of some sort? Why didn't he take *some* direction?

Well, you can bring an ass to the water, but you cannot make him drink. The world was the water and Egbert was the ass. And he wasn't having any. He couldn't: he just couldn't. Since necessity did not force him to work for his bread and butter, he would not work for work's sake. You can't make the columbine flowers nod in January, nor make the cuckoo sing in England at Christmas. Why? It isn't his season.

One can also however detect, when Egbert becomes Ishmael-like as his wife turns against him, the mixed sympathies of the Lawrence of 1921. On the one hand the individualist responds to the rebel against the magna mater and the society that stands behind her. On the other, there is a sharp sense not only of the futility but the *destructiveness* that must build up in a man when he denies the man's responsibility proclaimed in 'The Fox'; and still more if he denies what *Fantasia* insisted was an impulse more primary even than sex: the religious motive of his maleness, the desire to work creatively for work's sake, and discover the future rather than relive the past. But destructiveness is also in the times: in the rebellious child running out to where there are snakes as much as in the careless father who leaves the sickle, and the complacent doctor, and the hardening mother and wife. And why does Egbert volunteer for the war, even at the cost of subjecting himself to a discipline he hates? Not for any hatred of Germans, or mob-feeling, or imperialism, or patriotism of any kind – he is much too civilised for those. Not those, but rather the destructive impulse to war itself: 'War! Just war! Not right or wrong, but just war itself.'[40]

For Lawrence, as for everybody else, it was 'the flower of England' that perished in the trenches – but unlike others he saw nothing heroic in that. As Egbert serves the guns at the end, he is acting out his own destructiveness. And when he is hit, it is because he no longer has any desire to live that he wills to die, in this new version of the story – embodying the death wish of a generation. For Lawrence indeed, 'England, *my* England' *did* will itself to die in the war. Ironically juxtaposed to the dead face in the final lines is a half-glimpse, the instant before death, of a huge horse looming above ... like the ones that challenged Ursula to renewal at the end of *The Rainbow*, with its covenant of hope. But Lawrence saw no hope of renewal, now, in the England that had destroyed *The Rainbow* and disdained *Women in Love*; or indeed in the Europe which created the war, and was still mired in anarchic violence in 1921 – and which he was now leaving for ever (he thought). Only superficially is this a story about Percy Lucas, though to say a wound is relatively superficial is not to deny how much it can hurt.

VI   Laying the Ghost of Magnus

By 21 December he had also made another end. Shortly after finishing the new 'Fox', he had told Mountsier he was 'doing a Magnus MS. about the Foreign

Legion' (iv. 127), in the hope of getting it published in America. Walter Salomone had appealed to him immediately after Magnus's suicide, and he had had to reply that he too had been a victim and there was no other hope of recovering what Magnus had borrowed than getting 'Dregs' (as it was then called) into print. Though the correspondence has not come to light,[41] it seems clear that Lawrence felt some responsibility to do something about the continuing distress of the men who had taken him and Magnus driving in Malta. He had not introduced Magnus to them – the letter from Don Mauro Inguanez had done that. He had no direct responsibility for what had happened, but he had got to know them, and had not warned them against Magnus, and that was enough to make him want to do something to repair the damage Magnus had done. Even before the suicide, he and Norman Douglas and Goldring had made a number of efforts to interest publishers in Magnus's work. Lawrence had commended 'Dregs' to both Secker and Fisher Unwin, and had enlisted Goldring's help to place one of Magnus's translated plays. Douglas, having seen Goldring in Rome, had got Magnus to send him both 'Dregs' and a memoir of his travels which has subsequently disappeared. Goldring thought well of 'Dregs', and recalled later that Douglas, with his help, had taken 'an infinity of trouble' to try to get it into print[42] – but all without success.

Now, however, Michael Borg and Don Mauro pleaded again with Lawrence. Douglas had been named literary executor in Magnus's will, but the Maltese had refused to release the book, their only possible recompense, to him. They knew Lawrence personally, and must have believed that he would be the more likely to make a serious effort to recover the money they had lost. It seems likely that having been sent it now, Lawrence was going right through the book for the first time, having only seen the first half before. The manuscript shows a few minor revisions in his hand. It became very clear to him that the material itself, though remarkable, was not the most pleasant of reading, and was very unlikely to attract a publisher on its own, as past experience confirmed. The best hope lay – he thought – in America, and the best chance of making it more saleable there would be for him to write an introductory memoir of the author as he had known him. So he embarked on his only attempt at biography, and produced what he later thought 'the best single piece of writing, *as writing*'[43] that he had ever done.

There remained the need to get Douglas's consent. On 20 December Lawrence wrote to explain his plan. He had written 'an introduction giving all I knew about M – not unkindly I hope',[44] and sought Douglas's agreement to an attempt to sell manuscript and introduction outright to an American publisher at an asking price of $400 'or more if possible'. Out of this the Maltese were to be paid their £60 first, then the £23 Magnus owed Lawrence, and Douglas could have anything that remained. '[E]ven if you only got about £20. it is better than a slap in the eye.' If on the other hand Douglas would do it instead, Lawrence would stand aside – though his tone suggests he thought that unlikely. Douglas of course would figure, though 'under a disguised name', in the account of Magnus in Florence, but 'The only vice I give you is that of drinking the best part of the bottle of whiskey'.

Though Douglas had a legal right to all the proceeds, and might not have agreed so readily if he had seen what Lawrence had written about Magnus, 'Dregs' clearly had few prospects on its own. He replied on 26 December and disclaimed all interest, financial or any other, in the manuscript. 'Whoever wants it may have it & may ram it up his exhaust pipe', he said, telling Lawrence to do what he liked with it, to put *him* in 'drunk and stark naked if you like', and to '*Pocket all the cash yourself*' (his emphasis).[45]

Lawrence finally sent both memoir and book to Mountsier on 26 January, warning that he might find the latter as disgusting and horrifying as Magnus had found the experience, but he should be patient and not give up (iv. 178–9). Perhaps a big publisher like Doran, who had brought out *Three Soldiers* by Dos Passos which was also hardly pleasant light reading, might give $400 for the book outright – and thus help repay the £100 Magnus owed.[46] If he could obtain any offer, Mountsier was to deal directly with Borg. He might also try for an additional sum for the memoir if he could get it – but it is quite clear that Lawrence's essential concern was to enable Magnus's manuscript to undo the harm that the man himself had done, to the Maltese who had tried to help him. Though Grant Richards might buy the English rights, Lawrence was reluctant to have his introduction published in England. He suggested again that Douglas should be asked to introduce any English edition instead; but if he refused and Lawrence's piece were wanted, so be it.

Goldring, who never met Magnus, professed himself 'not in a position to judge whether Lawrence's depreciation, or Douglas's appreciation, was nearer the truth'. Douglas's tone of pseudo-affectionate contempt for 'my young friend Lawrence' and his habit of caricature is effective, but if one were to treat the two portrayals as pure fictions, there could be little doubt which is the more vividly animated or sharply and clearly focused.[47] The question of biographic truth however – always impossible, yet always to be sought for tirelessly – is much more complicated. It has been suggested above (see pp. 538–9, 566–7) that even Lawrence biographers should not take the memoir as the 'truth' of his feelings about Magnus in 1919, or even 1920, since it was obviously written with the hindsight and the more complex and mixed feelings of December 1921, when the end of the story was known. He probably felt more fascinated and charmed by Magnus in Florence, and more friendly towards him even in Montecassino, than appears when the encounters were recreated and the oppositions clarified in 1922. The truth one can be confident about is the truth of Lawrence's complex feelings *as he wrote*.

Moreover Lawrence's one attempt at biography resembles his literary criticism in working like an X-ray, rendering a good deal of 'body' shadowy in order to get 'to the bone' – as focused by a powerfully individual sensibility. So his memoir cares little for the inclusiveness, the painstaking inquiry, the effort to imagine from the subject's point of view (and that of the other actors in the story), the attempt to blend objectivity with sympathetic understanding, which seekers after such biographic truth as is obtainable might demand of themselves. When Douglas later charged Lawrence with ignoring Magnus's capacity for friendship, for hard work and for generosity when he was in funds,[48] there was some truth in the charge since these are in fact visibly there in Lawrence's portrait, though they are given little emphasis. How much more, however, is not there at all, which might help one to understand what Magnus was 'really like'? What a pity it seems – if we want 'the whole truth' – that the author of *Sons and Lovers*, impatient of the sort of thing he knew only too well, should have discouraged Magnus from speaking of his beautiful mother, his only-son relationship with her and with his even more shadowy father, his upbringing obviously in conflict with his desire *not* to be American, but cosmopolitan and pan-European, with only the slightest trace of accent lingering in his speech. How did he come to know the best theatres in every capital in Europe, including Russia, and to have edited a review in Rome? Why, having obviously been very well-off and prosperous – for look at his possessions and his habits – was he now so down on his luck? And (though this was obviously of no interest to Lawrence) how did he come to convert to Roman Catholicism, in England in 1902, possibly at the time of his marriage? And what was the tension between that and his homosexuality?

As it happens, the sketch of an answer to some of these questions can suggest what Lawrence's memoir is *not*. Of Magnus's family and upbringing in America almost nothing is known – except that his claim about his mother cannot have been altogether fictive, since he offered to persuade the then Kaiser to visit Gordon Craig's exhibition in Berlin, and quite clearly had influential contacts there. Our first glimpse of him, indeed, is in Berlin in 1905,[49] when 'a small, dapper man' turned up at that exhibition, studied every picture as though he were a connoisseur, praised the artistry in most flattering terms and offered to write to various papers in America about it. He impressed Craig by his charm, intelligence and dignity, and the fact that 'he seemed to know everyone in Berlin'. He was just 29 and had an apparently inexhaustible ambition to collect celebrities, which had brought him to Europe where he thought anything was possible: 'One only has to know the right people.' He had been supporting himself by acting as Berlin correspondent to American papers, and teaching in the Berlitz school – but after talk with Craig over martinis, was very ready to become his business manager, and Isadora Duncan's as well when she was having her affair with Craig. He organised an office, and a secretary – but none of the three was reliable or careful with money. The relationship had many ups and downs over the next few years, but Magnus was genuinely useful to the two artists, and often his contacts seemed to work. (An interesting sidelight is cast, however, by his habit of pocketing visiting cards from the silver salvers of houses he visited, since they might come in useful one day.) However, a taste for luxury on no assured income, and a lack of scruple in financial affairs, do seem to have been characteristic of him from the start.[50] Yet, though half a trickster, he also had some genuine organisational talent. It was through him, as intermediary, that Stanislavsky's proposal that Craig should come to Moscow was negotiated, and Magnus organised a successful tour of Switzerland for Isadora immediately after the war.[51] An inclusive biography would not be short of interest.

Unfortunately the post-war world was a very different one for Magnus. After he had escaped into Italy from his ill-fated service in the French Foreign Legion, he made his way to Rome, where Craig ran into him in 1917. In some ways he was exactly the same. His opening remark was, 'My dear Craig, you can't live in a hotel – that's not the right background for you' – and 'within days' he had persuaded Prince Wolkonsky to lend Craig his studio flat, ordered him some visiting cards, and introduced him to the King's tailor. But in 1919 Craig met Magnus again and found him 'a very changed man. So many of the "names" with which he had conjured in the past were no more, or no longer meant anything. He could see no future for himself.' He was indeed thinking of entering a monastery.[52]

So Lawrence's memoir can by no means tell 'the whole truth' or anything like it; or shed light on the formative process by which Magnus became what he was. And yet, not only does nothing in it conflict with what we can learn from Craig, who knew Magnus for fifteen years, and from Craig's son who met him many times, but their portrayals fully bear out the mixture of sophisticate and trickster, elegance and sleaze, wistful charm with suspect flattery, that Lawrence recreates so cogently. There too is the mincing gait, though Craig's statement that Magnus would take four steps to anyone else's one is not nearly as graphic as Lawrence's unforgettable description of birdlike perkiness. Even the unction with women, combined with waspish dislike (which Lawrence put into *The Lost Girl* as well as the memoir) appears in Craig's account. Though we cannot be sure that the argument about the peasant at Montecassino took place as Lawrence dramatises it, Magnus's later concern to be with 'first class' people suggests that the scene is a fair reflection of his views. The more telling, then, are the signs of weariness and desperation in Lawrence's portrait of such a man down on his luck and almost at the end of his tether. The flattering charm and friendliness, the making and keeping up of contacts, the capacity for busyness and pulling strings, the knowledge of a number of cities and theatres and the best restaurants and hotels, were the 'body' of the man – but there is little doubt that Lawrence did get to the skeleton. Craig sums up his fifteen years' acquaintance, which he has described with some affection, as follows:

Later on, whenever he again did anything for me, he always managed to disappear with most, if not all, of the money. He was not dishonest – he was merely very hard up – very involved – and still far too snappy. He never deliberately cheated me, but he could not resist helping himself, any more than he could resist helping me.[53]

But Lawrence's final judgement goes a great deal deeper, and is actually more compassionate in the end than either Craig or Douglas, because it faces up to the deeper and darker things in Magnus's life, and still comes out with considerable admiration for his ultimate courage, and his carrying of human consciousness 'unbroken through horrible experiences'. The manuscript has great difficulty in organising its feelings at the end. There is an impassioned denunciation of Magnus's prissy separation of himself from the degrading homosexuality he saw in the Legion – a passage which had to be cut from his book, as Lawrence's denunciation of it had to be cut from his memoir.[54] Lawrence is enraged by Magnus daring to sit in judgement – he who told Lawrence 'Oh, I always try to keep my physical friendships as *decent* as possible – while they last', but whose decency consisted of 'Filching the blood-warmth from the lower class' and paying them off, despising them all the while as his inferiors. Lawrence, regarding the 'passionate blood' as sacred, would rather have the reckless homosexual depravity of the 'poor devils of legionaries' than this genteelly purchased gratification, that then washes its hands and goes on quickly to talk of things of the mind and the spirit. Moreover it is clear – though this too had to go – that Lawrence sees some relation between Magnus's sexual habits and his treatment of his friends in Malta. Michael Borg felt not only cheated but confused and distressed, because 'sold in the best part of himself'. Magnus 'came up so winsomely to appeal for affection. He took the affection, and paid back twenty francs. Bargain! – Later, he took the affection, and *borrowed* twenty francs, and cleared out in triumph. And he to sit in judgement on the Legionaries!'

But it is not only to repay Borg and the other 'men with warm blood' from whom Magnus filched money and affection that Lawrence wishes to publish Magnus's book and his own memoir. For the brutality and depravity Magnus experienced in the Legion were for Lawrence only part of the brutality and depravity of the war as a whole. It is *necessary* to know what sex, and war, and crime, and corruption can be and do; and to free ourselves by experiencing these, like an inoculation. That is finally what he respects, in spite of all: that Magnus 'realised' what he feared.

He had his points, the courage of his own terrors, quick-wittedness, sensitiveness to certain things in his surroundings. I prefer him, scamp as he is, to the ordinary respectable person. He ran his risks: he *had* to be running risks with the police, apparently. And he poisoned himself rather than fall into their clutches. I like him for that. And I like him for the sharp and quick way he made use of every one of his opportunities to get out of that beastly army ...

Let him have his place, let his word be heard. He went through vile experiences: he looked them in the face, braved them through, and kept his manhood in spite of them ...

Magnus went where I could never go. He carried the human consciousness unbroken through circumstances I could not have borne.

Lawrence cannot forgive him for trading on the generosity and affection of others. But a 'lonely terrified courage of the isolated spirit'[55] Magnus had – and to that Lawrence finally does justice, which is all (he said) that the dead require.

VII   Balaam's Ass

Shortly after he had written to Douglas Lawrence fell ill, and remained in bed for a fortnight over Christmas and New Year. It was not a chill this time, since the days before Christmas were warm and sunny, though it turned cold in the first week of January. He said it was flu again, and it kept coming back, but he may also have been fretting, and had certainly been working very hard. (He was however glad to have got out of going to a 'horrible' Christmas dinner; iv. 151.) On 29 December he wrote to Curtis Brown's office, to say that he was only waiting for 'The Ladybird' and 'England, My England' to come back from the typist now; and to ask them to check a detail in Secker's agreement for *The Lost Girl* (iv. 153). (He thought he had been underpaid.) He had had copies of *Tortoises* from Seltzer – but did not mind whether Secker published it or not – he left that to Brown's discretion. So ended 1921, on a downbeat once again.

It is strange to think that if it had not been for his illness, Lawrence might well have sailed on the French ship *La Salles* on 15 January 1922 from Bordeaux to New Orleans, and then on to Taos, where he had once again confirmed to Mabel that he intended to come. There would have been no *Kangaroo*; no *The Boy in the Bush*. But the flu lingered on, with bad headaches, and when he began to feel a little better there was neither the energy to pack nor the time. His next thought was to catch the Fabre Liner *Providence* from Palermo to New York on 5 February, though he still hated the idea of going to New York (iv. 156).

At New Year he heard from Brewster, and thought wistfully that Ceylon sounded really rather lovely. Yet it still seemed the wrong direction for him; and he still gave as reason a decision against Buddha – though with a new tang of *pain* and acceptance of pain behind an older argument.

More and more I feel that meditation and the inner life are not my aim, but some sort of action and strenuousness and pain and frustration and struggling through ... And the fight and the sorrow and the loss of blood, and even the influenzas and the headache are part of the fight and the fulfilment ...

... I do not want place nor beauty nor even freedom from pain. I want to fight and to feel new gods in the flesh. (iv. 154)

Instead of men trying to become serene as Buddha, and godlike, he thought that 'God made man is the goal. The gods are uneasy until they can become men. And men have to fight a way for the new incarnation.' The place for the fight seemed the USA.

On 9 January with the flu still on him, and feeling distinctly unwell, he sent away the typescripts of 'The Ladybird' and 'England, My England' to Mountsier and Curtis Brown; and also two autograph manuscripts[56] to Mountsier 'so that I needn't cart them about' (iv. 155–6, 159). He had now heard that the account Mountsier had opened for him in Charleroi, Pennsylvania stood at $1,800, and he now had a cheque-book to use if necessary; though this advantage was diminished by the collapse of the Banco di Sconto on 29 December, which made it impossible to cash cheques in Taormina. He told Seltzer he thought the three novellas would make 'a really interesting book – perhaps even a real seller' (iv. 157), but now, once he had looked through the clean typescript of *Aaron* which Seltzer was sending him, he would be 'finished with writing for a bit, thank god. I am sick of the sight and thought of manuscripts.' To amuse himself on shipboard he would translate Verga's *Mastro-don Gesualdo* – a 'grey' novel which seemed to him 'one of the genuine emotional extremes of European literature' (iv. 157), an epitome of the poor south, showing how 'black and heavy and hopeless' the Sicilians were, inwardly (iv. 162), amidst their beautiful outer world. For the moment, however, he was through with working, depressed and sick of everything. It had turned cold again, with snow coming down the hills towards them and Etna shrouded, but they had a supply of olive wood to keep the salotta warm – and two days later the sun shone once more, the almond-blossom came out and the garden was full of birds which had come down near the coast to escape the snow. He wrote to console Frieda's mother about their going: after all, if he could make dollars in America, they could get back to Baden almost as easily from there as from Taormina. They were sitting, he told her, 'warm and still, with the lamp on the table' (iv. 162), looking out through the Bougainvillaea leaves on the terrace to the moonlit sea in a deep stillness, broken only by the crackling of the wood in the stove. If there had been trouble, there was now a surface calm.

Yet still the flu lingered, into a third week, and with it, depression. Like Kot (he told him), he felt he was 'messing about on the edge of everything' (iv. 165). He looked back with nostalgia to the Buckinghamshire cottage of 1914 – but

'Meanwhile one is eight years older, and a thousand years more disconnected with everything, and more frustrated.' But what to do? The typescript of *Aaron* came; but once more and finally he found himself absolutely unable to expurgate the scenes with the Marchesa. He told Seltzer he could do what he liked, print another private edition, cut chunks, make his own substitutions, but Lawrence would have nothing more to do with changing what he had written. 'Then say no more to me. I am tired of this miserable, paltry, haffling and caffling world – dead sick of it' (iv. 167).

There were minor consolations. Copies of *Sea and Sardinia* arrived from America – satisfactory, though he thought the reds of Juta's illustrations had come out a bit 'weary' and he did not like the wrapper (iv. 157, 158). (And was not *Tortoises* too expensively got up for a chapbook?) He hoped poor Juta, who had had a painful accident to his foot climbing Table Mountain at the Cape, would be pleased – though Lawrence had to turn down his invitation to go with him to Nyasaland and Tanganyika. Secker had now decided to buy sheets for an English edition of the travel-book, and Lawrence had caught him out in an error in calculating the royalties on *The Lost Girl* on which another ten guineas were owing – a double satisfaction (iv. 169). On 14 January he apologised to Cecily Lambert for being unable to welcome her and her friend Monica Furlong to Sicily, since he and Frieda would be gone by the time they came. He was now 'booked to leave next month' (iv. 166); though he had probably not finalised the booking.

However, four days later he told Mountsier that suddenly, 'on the point of coming to America I feel I *can't* come. Not yet. It is something almost stronger than I am. I would rather go to Ceylon, and come to America later, from the east' (iv. 168) – a reversion to his original plan the previous October.

This seems to have been a gut feeling, deeper than any rational explanation. He talked of Balaam and his ass, implying a preterhuman force blocking the wrong direction, though invisible to the ordinary and mistaken eye. He also felt the ridiculousness of his position, wavering so between east and west – though he was not short of reasons as he began to give way to his instinct. However there is a thread that connects them all, though it is never spoken quite aloud.

The first hint, to Kot, was of increased revulsion against the whole idea of proximity to a colony of New York artists in Taos, though he still felt he ought to *try*, even if only to find out that he hated it (iv. 165). To Mabel later, confessing his change of mind, he spoke of his hatred of the intellectuals who seemed to interest her: 'the analytic therapeutic lot' like Brill; and 'all that "arty" and "literairy" crew' of 'shits' like Leo Stein – an unpleasantry that shows how much Stein had annoyed him by sending a skittish chant about his *Psychoanalysis*, and a reproach for his emphasis on the belly. (In the aftermath of all the other attacks on his book Lawrence was not amused, and indeed thought Stein slyly malicious, as at one point he undoubtedly was.)[57] The Indians were one thing, but '*unreligious*' (in his sense) American artists and intellectuals quite another (iv. 181–2). He had hoped to avoid 'New York' by going to New Mexico, and did not look forward to meeting it there.

At a deeper level, however, it was a letter from Brewster which did most to cause the change of mind – and it was once again characteristic that a suggestive point should be concealed in a discussion of Buddhism. Suddenly, Lawrence wrote back, he felt that Brewster was right after all in taking the Buddhist view that 'Life is sorrow'; and he himself had been 'kicking against the pricks' in resisting this as a final truth, rather than accepting it as a foundation to build on.

The groundwork of life is sorrow. But that once established, one can start to build. And until that is established one can build nothing: no life of any sort. I begin to agree. I took it one must *finish* with the fact that *Life is sorrow*. Now again I realise that one must get there, and having arrived, then begin to live.

Good then: as a basis, *Life is sorrow*. But beyond that, one can smile and go on:

Only – only – I somehow have an imperative need to fight. I suppose it depends *how* one fights. (iv. 170)

In fact, Buddhism holds that life cannot *but* be sorrow as long as people pursue desires that in a world of illusion are bound to be transitory and delusive; and until they seek to free themselves from desire, by following the way to enlightenment. Lawrence could never agree with Buddhism in that, as indeed his ostensible agreement shows. Yet – reinforcing the emphasis on pain in his previous letter to Brewster – his acceptance of sorrow as a starting-point for truer living is, on the face of things, an extraordinary turn-around for him, even if not a Buddhist one. Though he always had a sense of the potential tragedy in life – 'I, who see a tragedy in every cow' – all his work since 1912 had been a kick against tragedy, an assertion (even in *Women in Love*) of the possibility of rebirth and resurrection from apparent deathliness – though the conditions for renewal alter in emphasis from *Sons and Lovers* to *The Rainbow* and *Women in Love*, and from there to *Aaron's Rod* and the three novellas. Even now, in this letter, the smiling and going on is Lawrencian – very different from the Buddha-smile and sitting still – and he cannot for the life of him give up his 'imperative need to fight', in the hope of any Buddhist serenity. Yet the acceptance of sorrow as the necessary ground base of existence is a quite new emphasis.

Again this conceivably hints at something painful enough to seem an irremediable fact of life, but having to be accepted once and for all before one could build any 'life of any sort'. If there is anything in the D'Allura story – dubious though that is – it may have seemed that though there had been no affairs of Frieda's for some years, they would keep happening. After 1917 he had determined to become less dependent on her, and had begun to renounce love (though not marriage). But as the definition of maleness developed from 1920, it brought with it a definition of true femaleness on which it seemed to depend. Now, however, it may finally have come home that this was an impossible dream.

On the other hand it is by no means essential (especially without firmer evidence) to make the new pain depend on a sexual infidelity. There were quite probably fierce arguments about leaving Europe and Taormina – which Frieda had little reason to welcome, as a drastic separation from her family – and these might even have got to a point of threatened refusal, underlining the unlikelihood that she would ever accept an obligation to 'honour and obey' according to the marriage vows, let alone 'submerge' her life in his, or offer the submission of Daphne to the Count. Either way, her attitude to marriage – and to 'honouring' and 'obeying' in his terms – would remain utterly and probably scornfully opposed to his, and the final realisation of that, in some dramatic and undeniable terms, would have been undoubtedly painful. Whatever had caused the new intransigent fictionalising of *his* view, and his new acceptance of pain as the necessary foundation of life, it produced a new decision. After signing off to Brewster Lawrence paused for thought, and then told him he would write for passages to Colombo (iv. 171). If there were a deeper personal significance behind the discussion of Buddhist East versus irreligious America, his other apparent rationalisations might also make more sense. To accept the Brewsters' invitation would be to stay with sympathetic friends, who liked them both (and whom Frieda liked), and who were gentle and scrupulous both by nature and conviction – as opposed to strangers, priding themselves on sharpness and analysis, and ready to gossip and mock, as 'intellectual' circles are prone to do.[58] Hence 'it seems so much *easier*, more peaceful to come east' (iv. 170), though at the same time he distrusted peace, and the fighter in him feared that the desire for it might be 'a sort of weakness and giving in'. On the other hand, Brewster had written that the Buddhist peace of Ceylon was 'heavy' – which Lawrence liked, because it sounded serious rather than escapist, a challenge to come to terms with things, but in a conducive atmosphere. He told Kot that America would be 'too raw for me, and I too tender for it. We must wait a bit ... I feel I can fortify myself in the east, against the west ... I do intend later to go to America. But first I must have something else inside me' (iv. 171). Gradually he came closer to saying what that was. 'I think one must for the moment withdraw from the world', he told Catherine Carswell, 'towards the inner realities', in order to become 'quiet and sure. I am tired of the world, and want the peace like a river'. He insisted that he still had no belief 'in Buddhistic inaction and meditation. But I believe the Buddhistic peace is the point to start from – not our strident fretting and squabbling' (iv. 175) – perhaps a significant aside. To

Mary Cannan he repeated that he felt Ceylon would give him 'rest, peace, inside' whereas 'New Mexico would only be more exciting and afterwards wearing' (iv. 180). To Mabel he wrote that he needed 'to get quite calm and sure and still and strong' before he came to an America, where Mabel herself seemed '*harried*' (iv. 181). Perhaps a year would be enough. He hoped she would not think him 'vile' for what was only a postponement, a 'detour'. All these may of course be rationalisations of sudden and inexplicable instinct – but they may be more.

He applied for berths on the Orient Liner *RMS Osterley*, sailing from Naples to Colombo on 26 February.

VIII 'Filling in time'

The last month in Taormina, naturally enough, was mainly a tying up of loose ends. Lawrence now wanted Curtis Brown to handle *all* his English affairs (iv. 187). Having established that Chatto and Windus did not intend to reprint *Look!* he obtained a formal reversion from them, and also persuaded Pinker and Duckworth to relinquish control over the pre-Pinker books (iv. 180–1), all of which were now to come under Curtis Brown's control. (Pinker also, at long last, found 'Witch à la Mode', though too late for the volume of stories; iv. 193.) Curtis Brown was 'piqued' (iv. 201) that after all his work he had yet to see '*a penny*' – an exaggeration, albeit an understandable one – but Lawrence had hopes that things were changing now, even in England. For Secker now agreed to bring out the stories (and the novellas too) though despite Curtis Brown's efforts he adamantly refused to count them towards his five under contract. However he later agreed that the novellas would do so (iv. 199–200 n. 2). (He told Brown that, far from it being any favour to be offered the stories, he had only 'accepted the collection out of my general interest in the author's more serious work'; iv. 183 n. 5). He also bought sheets of Seltzer's *Women in Love* and asked Lawrence to sign them in order to make a '*de luxe* edition' – though again he refused to pay any more for the signatures than the 15% royalty he had already agreed (iv. 200). Relations consequently remained cool though Lawrence's position was not strong enough to think of breaking with Secker. However, as the idea revived of doing something with his essays on American literature – that last bit of unfinished business – it was Jonathan Cape he thought of when he asked Brown to borrow from Mountsier, and have copied, the essay on *Moby Dick* that was missing from his manuscript (iv. 197). He now also centralised his American affairs. He arranged with Doran that in future Huebsch should render all accounts and payments direct to Mountsier, who should hold all the agreements (iv. 182). He also made a final adjustment to the Whitman essay for Mountsier, to make it altogether inoffensive (iv. 197–8). On the other hand he began to understand from Mountsier, who had been so suspicious of Seltzer's economic viability, that the book business was going through a very difficult phase in America (iv. 201), which made Seltzer's commitment in publishing Lawrence's non-fiction all the more telling.[59] Seltzer indeed, with the *Dial*'s assistance in making Lawrence a name, had made such a revolution in Lawrence's circumstances that he could even afford to regret that the magazine was publishing the Milan episode from *Aaron's Rod*, for 'What good are 35 dollars anyway? – one cheapens oneself' (iv. 187). Altered days indeed – particularly as the passages to Ceylon were going to cost £70 each!

Lawrence did not stop writing altogether, even as he prepared to go. 'She-Goat', that embodiment of imperious and libidinous femaleness – ' *See me*? She says, *That's me!*' – probably dates from about this time, and possibly 'He-Goat' as well, since both are labelled Taormina, though the second poem is much less specifically located and may have been written later.[60] Certainly he began his translation of Verga's *Mastro-don Gesualdo*; and indeed had finished and sent off to Mrs Carmichael about half of it by the time he set sail (iv. 196). He discovered, belatedly, that Verga was actually still alive and in Catania, but before he could go to see him the old man died, aged 82. After a correspondence with Verga's Milan publishers, Lawrence learned that they did not hold any legal copyright, that there did not seem to be a copyright treaty between England and Italy at all and that only Verga's nephews could have any claim to rights in his works (iv. 197 and n. 2, 200) – so the way seemed open to publish the translation which he intended to finish on the *Osterley*.

As their departure began to seem real, he wrote a strange letter in Italian to Kot, who perhaps had been critical of his decision. It may have been easier to say in Italian that he preferred to risk anything rather than stagnate like Kot in his cave. Tired, and sad at his need to change his skin like a snake, he still felt the world full of unseen powers – the old angels and cherubim he had discussed with Forster in 1915 – and he *had* to break away from the 'yelling with all of these people' here, in order to attach himself to the hidden forces (iv. 185).

There is a glimpse of him at this time through the eyes of a stranger, an American journalist Henry James Forman who came to see Lawrence early in February, and was a guest at a farewell tea-party at Fontana Vecchia just before Forman went to Malta in late February, armed with an introduction to Michael Borg. Lawrence was still convalescent when they met, on a rainy day with swirling mist. Forman had his winter coat on and was astonished to find Lawrence in sandals and a thin jacket – his lips blue with cold, but sardonically amused at 'Sunny Sicily'. Lawrence thought him 'dull but nice' (iv. 187) – and was remarkably nice in return, especially in response to several well-meaning remarks of the kind that make the polite smiles congeal on an author's face. Why didn't he go on writing like *Sons and Lovers*? Wouldn't it be better to stick with the first draft of his work rather than revise twice more as Lawrence said he often did? Shouldn't he have toned down *Women in Love*, where the episode with the lapis lazuli seemed 'too preposterous for fiction'? At which a wicked Frieda tempted fate by solemnly agreeing – she who had hit her husband on the head with something solid on at least two occasions. But Lawrence was on his best behaviour and his guest never noticed that there had been any danger. Frieda baked quantities of cakes – a new accomplishment using the new oven – and 'Lawrence's chief concern was that we should consume all of it.' As he stood with the plate in front of her, Mrs Forman asked why he had left Paul Morel so hopeless at the end, so stripped of everything. ' "Ah, but he had his courage left," laughed Lawrence – "do have some of these cakes." ' Forman was impressed by Lawrence's courage and integrity. The last sighting, another day, was of him on the beach at Letojanni all alone, gazing out to sea.[61]

His farewell letter to Marie Hubrecht spoke of the awful wind and rain and cold (iv. 192). Even in mid-February he did not feel quite himself yet, after his flu. A young American called Whitney Warren had agreed to take Fontana Vecchia, which of course had been Marie's house. She was on the list of those who should get presentation copies of Secker's *Sardinia* – a list which Lawrence's sisters no longer headed, for they had irritated him by being 'loftily disapproving' about *Tortoises* (iv. 174). He had already sent Mary a copy of the American edition. Now, after Marie, Kot, Cynthia, Catherine and Rosalind, the surprising name is Elsa Weekley (iv. 193) – a bit of bridge building with Frieda's eldest daughter, now 20; after what seems to have been a successful reconciliation with her younger sister Barbara, who had written her mother a lively letter in the spring of 1921.[62] Another surprisingly grown-up voice from the past was Enid Hilton, writing to tell Lawrence of her marriage (iv. 194–5). But the two most touching of the last letters from Taormina are, naturally enough, those to Rosalind, and to Mary Cannan. Mary had sent as a good-bye present, despite his forbidding her to get him anything expensive, not only the fountain-pen he had asked for, but a 'wildly expensive' seal of lapis lazuli. He loved the way the blue 'seems to live inside a film of crystal' and vowed that it would always 'seal all my affairs of state and solemnity'. To Mary he could confess that even though he had so wanted to leave, 'The thought of going gives me a sinking feeling: the wrench of breaking off' (iv. 190–1). So he joked about how quickly he proposed to develop a new persona, draped in a sheet and smiling at his own paunch; and promised her, if she would come to Ceylon, an alternative vision of him and Frieda on the dock-side to meet her, 'in pith helmets and black goggles', as she stepped off at Colombo under her parasol. 'Don't think of goodbyes, only of parasols and P. and O. liners and pith helmets and palm trees and us shouting "There she is!" '

To Rosalind he laughed at that 'lump' Godwin marrying 'into the church', the niece of the Archbishop of Canterbury. To her request for suggestions about holidays, he suggested retracing his and Frieda's steps at Gargnano. But two statements which were quiet enough to pass muster with a wife who habitually read his letters, are rather more resonant between the lines. 'F. sends love', says one. And the other is a promise to send a copy of *Tortoises*, which would say more than any letter. 'We'll meet again somewhere,' he ends, 'that's certain' (iv. 189–90).

By Friday 17 February they were 'in the throes of packing up' (iv. 194). On Sunday, he told the Baroness, they sat ready to travel: four trunks (one for household things, one for books, one other each), two valises, a hatbox and two pieces of hand luggage: 'just like Abraham faring forth to a new land. My heart quivers now, mostly with pain – the going away from our home and the people and Sicily. But I want to forget it, and only think of palms and elephants and apes and peacocks' (iv. 198–9). About the future he refused to speculate: 'I'm settling nothing', he maintained. On 20 February they set off.

Frieda had a final surprise for him. At the last moment she insisted that they should take a bit of Sicily with them: one of the painted wooden panels which are so colourful a feature of Sicilian carts, four to five feet wide, more than two feet deep and inches thick. Theirs was 'very colourfully painted with two scenes from the life of Marco Visconte' (iv. 206), the Milanese General. After a last visit with Ruth Wheelock at the Hotel Panormus, the panel too had to be lugged to Naples. On 26 February it made them conspicuous at the docks as, loaded still more with baskets of apples and oranges, they got themselves aboard the *Osterley*.

There was certainly a good deal more 'baggage' than there had been in May 1912. But, once stowed, the alert quick step along the deck was the same. Frieda had caught an annoying cold in Naples, having been free from that all winter. But Lawrence watched 'our own' Etna, 'white witch', magically beautiful, sinking slowly into the sea: 'I nearly wept, of course, but hardened my heart and said no my lady!' (iv. 207) Soon he must have moved to the bow again, where he liked to be.

IX   A Conclusion – in Which Nothing Is Concluded

It seems appropriate to 'end' on a ship: a voyage that is equally an end and a beginning, a break with all that had been *and* a bodily carrying – 'Ecco la Sicilia in viaggio per l'India' (iv. 206), as the porters shouted – of the colourful and heavy past along with them: the candlesticks, the blue rug, the 'countrypair', the blue jackets and all the equivalents in mind and memory.

To compare this Lawrence with the young beardless fellow on the Ostend ferry ten years before is to measure dramatic differences: from his hopes, then, of persuading Frieda to commit herself to him, his conception of marriage, his belief that the relation between man and woman was the centre of life, his conviction that he had something important to say that would be an answer to the real wants of Englishmen. Photographs show how his face had changed; and there had been a deeper change in temperament and manners. He had learned to be more spontaneous in behaviour and careless of convention, through living so much alone with Frieda, shedding inhibition for good or ill, becoming more irascible and violent, but also more confident, charismatic and entertaining. By courageous probing of his own contradictions he had come to terms with his bisexuality, and had shown how ready he was to grow in new directions, and to let no idea harden into unchangeable conviction. Wartime England had damaged his health, indeed nearly killed him, but being in Italy again had been good for him and nobody he had met in Capri or Sicily had thought him consumptive. Yet he was restless now, a compulsive wanderer in space as well as an adventurer in thought and expression. He had become an alien, antagonist, subversive, exile, a 'traveller' who no longer belonged in England or Europe, or anywhere, and certainly didn't think he would belong in Ceylon (with its 'molar monastery'; iv. 207) or in Taos. Yet he knew he had to be an 'American' writer now because his 'listeners' were there.

He seems greatly altered, having reacted almost to the 'opposite' of his former self and ideas. Yet in many ways his inner contradictions, and his belief in growth through conflict, had merely shifted their balance and emphasis. To look back is to see continuity, in change. Moreover this makes it certain that he will change again, in the new world towards which he is pointed. The past is with him indelibly – and so, amid all the excitement of the new, is the poignant awareness of loss, separation and uncertainty. He is 36; hardened in some ways, more embattled. Yet about him nothing is settled or fixed. On a ship, on the move, going osterly in order to go westerly, he is ready for the new, but painfully aware of 'the wrench of breaking off'. Above all, he continues lively.

Cue-titles
and
Abbreviations

CUE-TITLES AND ABBREVIATIONS

Note The cue-titles and abbreviations are used in the Appendices and in the Notes (the abbreviations in Section A and Section F are also used in the text). Place of publication is London unless otherwise specified, here and elsewhere.

A Letters of Lawrence

(i.) James T. Boulton, ed. *The Letters of D. H. Lawrence*, Volume I. Cambridge: Cambridge University Press, 1979.

(ii.) George T. Zytaruk and James T. Boulton, eds. *The Letters of D. H. Lawrence*. Volume II. Cambridge: Cambridge University Press, 1982.

(iii.) James T. Boulton and Andrew Robertson, eds. *The Letters of D. H. Lawrence*, Volume III. Cambridge: Cambridge University Press, 1984.

(iv.) Warren Roberts, James T. Boulton and Elizabeth Mansfield, eds. *The Letters of D. H. Lawrence*, Volume IV. Cambridge: Cambridge University Press, 1987.

(v.) James T. Boulton and Lindeth Vasey, eds. *The Letters of D. H. Lawrence*, Volume V. Cambridge: Cambridge University Press, 1989.

B Works of Lawrence

A *Apocalypse and the Writings on Revelation*. Ed. Mara Kalnins. Cambridge: Cambridge University Press, 1979.

AR *Aaron's Rod*. Ed. Mara Kalnins. Cambridge: Cambridge University Press, 1988.

E[+no.] Manuscript [+no.] listed in Warren Roberts. *A Bibliography of D. H. Lawrence*. 2nd ed. Cambridge: Cambridge University Press, 1982, Section E.

EmyE *England, My England and Other Stories*. Ed. Bruce Steele. Cambridge: Cambridge University Press, 1990.

Fox *The Fox, The Captan's Doll, The Ladybird*. Ed. Dieter Mehl. Cambridge: Cambridge University Press, 1992.

FU   *Fantasia of the Unconscious.* New York: Thomas Seltzer, 1922. [For the convenience of readers, page references to the Penguin edition, Harmondsworth, 1971, etc. are also supplied.]

Hardy   *Study of Thomas Hardy and Other Essays.* Ed. Bruce Steele. Cambridge: Cambridge University Press, 1985.

K   *Kangaroo.* Ed. Bruce Steele. Cambridge: Cambridge University Press, 1994.

LAH   *Love Among the Haystacks and Other Stories.* Ed. John Worthen. Cambridge: Cambridge University Press, 1987.

LCL   *Lady Chatterley's Lover* and *A Propos of "Lady Chatterley's Lover".* Ed. Michael Squires. Cambridge: Cambridge University Press, 1993.

LG   *The Lost Girl.* Ed. John Worthen. Cambridge: Cambridge University Press, 1981.

MEH   *Movements in European History.* Ed. Philip Crumpton. Cambridge: Cambridge University Press, 1989.

MMM   *D. H. Lawrence: Memoir of Maurice Magnus.* Ed. Keith Cushman. Santa Rosa: Black Sparrow Press, 1987.

MN   *Mr Noon.* Ed. Lindeth Vasey. Cambridge: Cambridge University Press, 1984.

P   *Phoenix: The Posthumous Papers of D. H. Lawrence.* Ed. Edward D. McDonald. New York: Viking Press, 1936.

P II   *Phoenix II: Uncollected, Unpublished and Other Prose Works by D. H. Lawrence.* Ed. Warren Roberts and Harry T. Moore. Heinemann, 1968.

PO   *The Prussian Officer and Other Stories.* Ed. John Worthen. Cambridge: Cambridge University Press, 1983.

Poems   *The Complete Poems of D. H. Lawrence.* Ed. Vivian de Sola Pinto and Warren Roberts. Revised edn. Harmondsworth: Penguin Books, 1977. [The widely available paperback edition published by Penguin – and by Viking in the USA – has been cited rather than the identical revised text, with slightly different pagination, published in two hardback volumes by Heinemann in 1972.]

Poems (1928) *The Collected Poems of D. H. Lawrence.* Martin Secker, 1928

PU   *Psychoanalysis and the Unconscious.* New York: Thomas Seltzer, 1921.

R   *The Rainbow.* Ed. Mark Kinkead-Weekes. Cambridge: Cambridge University Press, 1989.

RDP   *Reflections on the Death of a Porcupine and Other Essays.* Ed. Michael Herbert. Cambridge: Cambridge University Press, 1988.

SEP   *Sketches of Etruscan Places and Other Italian Essays*. Ed. Simonetta de Filippis. Cambridge: Cambridge University Press, 1992.

SL   *Sons and Lovers*. Ed. Helen Baron and Carl Baron. Cambridge: Cambridge University Press, 1992.

SM   *St. Mawr and Other Stories*. Ed. Brian Finney. Cambridge: Cambridge University Press, 1983.

SS   *Sea and Sardinia*. New York: Thomas Seltzer, 1921. [For the convenience of readers, page references are also supplied to the Penguin edition, Harmondsworth, 1944, reprinted in *D. H. Lawrence and Italy*, Harmondsworth, 1985.]

TI   *Twilight in Italy and Other Essays*. Ed. Paul Eggert. Cambridge: Cambridge University Press, 1994.

TSM   *The Symbolic Meaning*. Ed. Armin Arnold. Fontwell, Arundel: Centaur Press, 1952. [For the convenience of readers, page references to the essays on American literature published in the *English Review* November 1918–June 1919 are also supplied to this reprint.]

WL   *Women in Love*. Ed. David Farmer, Lindeth Vasey and John Worthen. Cambridge: Cambridge University Press, 1987.

WP   *The White Peacock*. Ed. Andrew Robertson. Cambridge: Cambridge University Press, 1983.

C   Other Printed Works

BMTL   H.D. [Hilda Doolittle]. *Bid Me To Live*. New York: Grove Press, 1960; reissued London: Virago Press, 1984.

BTW   John Middleton Murry. *Between Two Worlds: An Autobiography*. Jonathan Cape, 1935.

Damon   S. Foster Damon. *Amy Lowell: A Chronicle*. Boston and New York: Houghton Mifflin, 1935.

Delavenay   Emile Delavenay. *D. H. Lawrence, The Man and His Work: The Formative Years*. Heinemann, 1972.

Delavenay, ii.   Emile Delavenay. *D. H. Lawrence: L'Homme et la Genèse de son Oeuvre. Les Années de Formation 1885–1919*. Volume II. Paris: Librairie C. Klincksieck, 1969.

DHLR   *D. H. Lawrence Review* (1968–).

Diaries   Lady Cynthia Asquith. *Diaries 1915–1918*. Hutchinson, 1968.

Draper Ronald P. Draper. *D. H. Lawrence: The Critical Heritage*. Routledge and Kegan Paul, 1970.

E.T. E.T. [Jessie Chambers Wood]. *D. H. Lawrence: A Personal Record*. Jonathan Cape, 1935; reprinted Cambridge: Cambridge University Press, 1980.

EY John Worthen. *D. H. Lawrence: The Early Years 1885–1912*. The Cambridge Biography, Volume I. Cambridge: Cambridge University Press, 1991.

Frieda Frieda Lawrence. *"Not I, But the Wind ... "* Santa Fe: Rydal Press, 1935.

Memoirs *Frieda Lawrence: The Memoirs and Correspondence*. Ed. E. W. Tedlock. Heinemann, 1961.

Nehls Edward Nehls, ed. *D. H. Lawrence: A Composite Biography*. 3 volumes. Madison: University of Wisconsin Press, 1957–9.

SP Catherine Carswell. *The Savage Pilgrimage: A Narrative of D. H. Lawrence*. Chatto and Windus, 1932; reprinted Cambridge: Cambridge University Press, 1981.

Tedlock E. W. Tedlock. *The Frieda Lawrence Collection of D. H. Lawrence Manuscripts: A Descriptive Bibliography*. Albuquerque: University of New Mexico Press, 1948.

TWSUA Rosalind Thornycroft. *Time Which Spaces us Apart*. Completed by Chloë Baynes. Batcombe: Private Publication, 1991.

D Manuscript Sources

BL British Library

Eton Eton College Library

Hilton Hilton Hall, Hilton, Huntingdon

HU Harvard University

Lazarus George Lazarus

LC Library of Congress

McMaster Mills Library, McMaster University, Hamilton, Ontario (Bertrand Russell Archive)

NCL Nottingham County Libraries

NWU Northwestern University Library, Evanston, Illinois

NYPL New York Public Library, New York (The Berg Collection)

TuftsU Tufts University Library

UCB	Bancroft Library, University of California at Berkeley
UCLA	Library of the University of California, Los Angeles
UIll	University of Illinois
UInd	Lilly Library, University of Indiana
UN	University of Nottingham Library
UNM	Library of the University of New Mexico, Albuquerque
UT	Harry Ransom Humanities Research Center, University of Texas at Austin
YU	Beinecke Library, Yale University, New Haven, Connecticut

E   People

AH	Aldous Huxley
BR	Bertrand Russell
CA	Lady Cynthia Asquith
Frieda	Frieda Lawrence (formerly Weekley)
JMM	John Middleton Murry
KM	Katherine Mansfield
OM	Lady Ottoline Morrell
PH	Philip Heseltine

F   Textual Symbols

< >	Deletion
⌐ ¬	DHL insertion
[ ]	Author's insertion
^{1} [etc]	Endnote
b.	Born
m.	Married
d.	Died
ed.	Edited
tr.	Translated
rev.	Revised
T.A.	Textual Apparatos

Appendices

◆

THE WRITING LIFE, 1912–1922: PROSE

Note In the following table, the third column lists publication 1912—35. The final column contains the subsequent collection in which stories, essays and sketches appeared and, in round brackets, the relevant Cambridge Edition or, if one has not yet been published, the latest alternative. Their publication dates will be found in the Chronology

Additional Cue-Titles

ER	*English Review*
Haystacks	D. H. Lawrence, *Love Among the Haystacks and Other Pieces*. Ed. David Garnett. The Nonesuch Press, 1930.
Hutchinson	*Hutchinson's Story Magazine*
Huxley	*The Letters of D. H. Lawrence*. Ed. Aldous Huxley. Heinemann, 1932.
Lovely Lady	D. H. Lawrence. *The Lovely Lady*. Secker, 1933.
Miscellany	*A D. H. Lawrence Miscellany*. Ed. Harry T. Moore. Carbondale, Southern Illinois University Press, 1959.
Modern Lover	D. H. Lawrence. *A Modern Lover*. Secker, 1934.
Plays	*The Complete Plays of D. H. Lawrence*. Heinemann, 1965.
SWG	*Saturday Westminster Gazette*

DATE	FINAL TITLE	SURVIVING MS/ TS OR PROOFS	EARLY PUBLICATION	COLLECTIONS
c. 7 May 1912	'The English and the Germans'	(Lazarus)	–	(*TI*)
c. 8–9 May 1912	'How a Spy is Arrested'	(Lazarus)	–	(*TI*)
c. 9 May 1912	'French Sons of Germany'	(Lazarus)	*SWG* 3 Aug. 1912	P, (*TI*)
15 May 1912	'Hail in the Rhineland'	(Lazarus)	*SWG* 10 Aug. 1912	P, (*TI*)
16 May–9 June 1912	'Paul Morel' IIIb	E373e		
June 1912	'The Christening'	(E68.2)	–	(*PO*)

	'Delilah and Mr Bircumshaw' (1910, E95a, fragment)	E90.5	–	*P II*, (*LAH*, revised)
	'The Fly in the Ointment' (1910, 'A Blot', E135.5a)	(E135.5b)	–	(*LAH*, revised)
June–?Sept. 1912	'Once—!'	E296a	*Haystacks*	*P II*, (*LAH*, revised)
3–31 July 1912	*Sons and Lovers* begun	E373e (pp. 1–75)		
Aug. 1912	'A Chapel Among the Mountains'	E66a	*Haystacks*	*P II*, (*TI*)
	'A Hay-Hut Among the Mountains'	E157	*Haystacks*	*P II*, (*TI*)
early Sept. 1912	'Christs in the Tirol'	E81.5a	–	(*TI*)
by March 1913	'Christs in the Tyrol' (revised)	–	*SWG* 22 March 1912	*P*, (*TI*)
7 Sept. –18 Nov. 1912	*Sons and Lovers* completed	E373e (pp. 76–540)		
by 30 Oct. 1912	*The Fight for Barbara*	E130	–	(*Plays*)
17–24 Dec. 1912	'Burns Novel' (fragments)	E59.3	–	Nehls, i., (*LAH*)
c. 29 Dec. –?	'Elsa Culverwell' (fragment)	E209a	–	(*LG*)
by 12 Jan. 1913	*The Daughter in Law*	E84a	–	(Plays)
by 17 Jan. 1913	'The Insurrection of Miss Houghton' pp. 1–80			
by 20 Jan. 1913	'Foreword to *Sons and Lovers*'	–	Huxley	(*SL*)
c. 27–31 Jan. 1913	'The Overtone'	E298	*Lovely Lady*	(*SM*)
by 1 Feb. –c. 5 April 1913	'The Insurrection of Miss Houghton' (put aside at 200pp.)	–		
March 1913	Review of *Georgian Poetry 1911–1912*	–	*Rhythm* March 1913	*P*

by *c.* 18–19 March 1913	'By the Lago di Garda' ('The Spinner and the Monks', 'The Lemon Gardens', 'The Theatre')	E294.5a	*ER* Sept. 1913	(*TI revised*)
by 5 April–early June 1913	'The Sisters' I	E441a (fragment)		(*R*)
2 May 1913	'Thomas Mann'	–	*Blue Review* July 1913	*P*
by 10 June 1913	'Honour and Arms' (later 'The Prussian Officer')	E326.5	*ER* Aug. 1914	(*PO*)
	'New Eve and Old Adam'	E268a	*Modern Lover*	(*LAH*)
by 16 June 1913	'Vin Ordinaire' (later 'The Thorn in the Flesh')	–	*ER* June 1914	(*PO*)
July 1913	Revision of stories:			
(1907–13)	'The Shadow in the Rose Garden' ('The Soiled Rose')	E359.5b	*Smart Set* March 1914	(*PO*)
(1907–13)	'The White Stocking'	E430.3	*Smart Set* Oct. 1914	(*PO*)
(1910–13)	'The Fly in the Ointment'	E135.5b	*New Statesman* 16 Aug. 1913	*P II*, (*LAH*)
(1911–13)	'The Witch à la Mode' ('Intimacy', E.438a)	E438b, c	*Modern Lover*	(*LAH*)
(1911–13)	'Two Marriages'/ 'Daughters of the Vicar'	E86a,b,d	–	(*PO*)
(1911–13)	'Love Among the Haystacks'	E211a	*Haystacks*	(*LAH*)
(1912–13)	'Strike Pay I: Her Turn'	E159.5a	*SWG* 6 Sept. 1913 *Modern Lover*	(*LAH*)
	'Strike Pay II: Ephraim's Half Sovereign'	E381	*SWG* 13 Sept. 1913, *Modern Lover*	(*LAH*)
(1912–13)	'A Sick Collier'	E361.3a	*New Statesman* 13 Sept. 1913	(*PO*)

(1912–13)	'The Christening'	E68.2	*Smart Set* Feb. 1914	*(PO)*
(1912–13)	'Once—!'	E296a	*Haystacks*	*(LAH)*
(1913)	'Honour and Arms'	E326.5	*ER* Aug. 1914	*(PO)*
(1913)	'Vin Ordinaire'	–	*ER* June 1914	*(PO)*
by July 1913	'The Primrose Path'	E322.7a	*(EmyE)* (1922)	*(EmyE)*
c. 11 Aug. 1913	[Eastwood sketch – lost]	–	–	–
(1910– by 24 Aug. 1913)	*The Widowing of Mrs. Holroyd* revised			*(Plays)*
4 Sept. 1913–29 Jan. 1914	'The Sisters' II	E441a (fragment)		*(R)*
c. 31 Oct. 1913	'The Mortal Coil'	E246.8	*Seven Arts* July 1917	*P II*
31 Jan. –*c.* 11 May 1914	'The Wedding Ring'	E331a (fragment)		
1–17 July 1914	*The Prussian Officer*			
(1913–14)	'The Prussian Officer'	[E326.5]	[*ER* Aug. 1914]	*(PO)*
	'The Thorn in the Flesh'	–	[*ER* June 1914]	*(PO)*
(1911–14)	'Daughters of the Vicar'	[E86d]	–	*(PO)*
(1907–14)	'A Fragment of Stained Glass'	[E140a, b, c]	[*ER* Sept. 1911]	*(PO)*
(1911–14)	'The Shades of Spring' ('The Soiled Rose')	[E359.4a,b]	[*Forum* March 1913, *Blue Review* May 1913]	*(PO)*
(1911–14)	'Second-Best'	[E356.5]	[*ER* Feb. 1912]	*(PO)*
(1907–14)'	'The Shadow in the Rose Garden' ('The Vicar's Garden')	[E359.5]	[*Smart Set* March 1914]	*(PO)*
(1909–14)	'Goose Fair'	[E150.7a, b]	[*ER* Feb. 1910]	*(PO)*
(1907–14)'	'The White Stocking'	[E430.3]	[*Smart Set* Oct. 1914]	*(PO)*
(1912–14)	'A Sick Collier'	[E361.3]	[*New Statesman* 13 Sept. 1913]	*(PO)*
(1912–14)	'The Christening'	[E68.2]	[*Smart Set* Feb. 1914]	*(PO)*

(1909–14)	'Odour of Chrysanthemums'	[E284a,b,c]	[*ER* June 1911]	(*PO*)
Sept. 1914	'With the Guns'	–	*Manchester Guardian* Sept. 1914	(*TI*)
5 Sept.–late Nov. 1914	'Study of Thomas Hardy' ('Le Gai Savaire')	E384a,b	–	*P*, (*Hardy*)
late Nov. 1914–2 March 1915	*The Rainbow*	E331a		(*R*)
March–8 June 1915	'Morgenrot' ('The Signal', 'The Phoenix') [abandoned]			
April–May 1915	*The Rainbow* revised	E331b		
c. 5 June 1915	England, My England	E114.5	*ER* Oct. 1916 *Metropolitan* April 1917	(*EmyE*)
July 1915	*The Rainbow* proofs and self-censorship)			
by 29 July–26 Oct. 1915	*Twilight in Italy*	(UN)		
by 29 July 1915	'The Crucifix Across the Mountains'	(UN)	–	(*TI*)
by 20 Aug. 1915	'The Spinner and the Monks'	(UN)	–	(*TI*)
by 24 Aug. 1915	'The Lemon Gardens'	E294.5b, (UN)	–	(*TI*)
by 6 Sept. 1915	'The Theatre'	(UN)	–	(*TI*)
by 11 Sept. 1915	'San Gaudenzio'	(UN)	–	(*TI*)
by 28 Sept. 1915	'The Crown'		*Signature* 4, 18 Oct., 2 Nov. 1915 (3 essays)	*P II*, (*RDP*)
by 8 Oct. 1915	'Il Duro'	(UN)	–	(*TI*)
by 12 Oct. 1915	'Italians in Exile'	(UN)	–	(*TI*)
by 19 Oct. 1915	'The Return Journey' ('On the Road')	(UN)	–	(*TI*)
?Oct. 1915	'John'	(UN)	–	(*TI*)
by 30 Oct. 1915	'The Thimble'	E396.7	*Seven Arts* March 1917	*P II*, (*EmyE*)

early Jan. – ?6 Nov. 1916	'Samson and Delilah' ('The Prodigal Husband')	E352.7	*ER* March 1917 (*EmyE* 1922)	(*EmyE*)
5 Jan. – 27 Feb. 1916	'Goats and Compasses' [lost]			
by 26 April–29 June 1916	'The Sisters' III	E441b,c		
c. ?12 July–20 Nov. 1916	'The Sisters' III/ *Women in Love* typed and revised	E441c,d,e		
by 31 Oct. 1916	'The Mortal Coil' (revised)	–	*Seven Arts* July 1917	P II, (*EmyE*)
by 12 Jan. 1917	'The Miracle' (later 'The Horse-Dealer's Daughter')	–	–	(*EmyE*)
late Feb. –7 March 1917	*The Reality of Peace*			
	1. 'Whistling of Birds'	–	*Athenæum* April 1919	P, (*RDP*)
	2. (title unknown, lost)	–	–	
	3. (title unknown, lost)	–	–	
	4. 'The Tranference'	[E338a]	*ER* May 1917	P, (*RDP*)
	5. (untitled)	[E338a]	*ER* June 1917	P, (*RDP*)
	6. (untitled)	[E338a]	*ER* July 1917	P, (*RDP*)
	7. 'The Orbit'	[E338a]	*ER* Aug. 1917	P, (*RDP*)
28 March 1917– c. 7 Sept. 1919	*Women in Love* retyped, and revised	E441f		(*WL*)
? April 1917	'Love' (cf. 'The Orbit')	[E201a]	*ER* Jan. 1918	P, (*RDP*)
?by 11 May 1917	'Life' (cf. no. 2)	[E200a]	*ER* Feb. 1918	P, (*RDP*)
c. 10 June–c. 27 Aug. 1917	'At the Gates' [lost]			
July 1917	Works on *Women in Love*	[E441f]		(*WL*)
ante 15 Sept. – 12 Oct. 1917	*Studies in Classic American Literature*			
	'Henry St John de Crèvecœur'	–	*ER* Jan. 1919	*TSM*

	?'Benjamin Franklin'	–	*ER* Dec. 1918	*TSM*
	?'Fenimore Cooper's Anglo-American Novels'	–	*ER* Feb. 1919	*TSM*
	?'Fenimore Cooper's Leather-stocking Novels'	–	*ER* March 1919	*TSM*
by 5 Nov. 1917	'The Limit to the British Novelist' [lost]			
Oct. –Nov. 1917	Begins what will become *Aaron's Rod*	–		
late Nov. 1917	Works on *Women in Love* again	E441f		
by 28 Jan. 1918	*Studies in Classic American Literature* resumed			
by 20 Feb. 1918	'Edgar Allan Poe' (had begun)	–	*ER* April 1919	*TSM*
Feb. –March 1918	'Nathaniel Hawthorne'	E382g	*ER* May 1919	*TSM*
(by 17 March 1918	Has done 150 pages of what will become *Aaron's Rod*	–		
by 7 May 1918	New expanded idea of *SCAL*			
?May–June 1918	'The Two Principles'	–	*ER* June 1919	*TSM*
	'The Spirit of Place'	–	*ER* Nov. 1918	*TSM*
by 3 June 1918	'Dana'	UN	–	
	'Melville'	UN	–	
c. 3 June 1918	'last essay': 'Whitman'	–	–	
Aug. 1918	*Movements in European History* begun,	E255a		(*MEH*)
by 26 Aug. 1918	(chs. 1–3 after split)			
late Aug. –Sept. 1918	Revising *SCAL*			

by 29 Oct. 1918	*Touch and Go*	E401.6	(*Plays*)
c. Nov. –4 Dec. 1918	'The Blind Man'	(Lazarus)	*ER* July 1920 *Living Age* Aug. 1920	(*EmyE*)
by 7 Dec. 1918	'Education of the People' (essays 1–4)	E112	–	P
by 10 Dec. 1918	'The Fox'	E139a	*Hutchinson* Nov. 1920	*Miscellany*, (*Fox*)
by 20 Dec 1918	'John Thomas' (later 'Tickets Please')	–	*Strand* April 1919; *Metropolitan* Aug. 1919	(*EmyE*)
6 Jan. –3 Feb. 1919	Working on *MEH*	E255a		(*MEH*)
by 15 Jan. 1919	'Wintry Peacock'	E437a (UN)	*Metropolitan* Aug. 1921; *New Decameron III* 1922	(*EmyE*)
by 3 Feb. 1919	*MEH completed but for one later chapter*	E255a		(*MEH*)
14 March–7 April 1919	'Adolf'	E3.3a,c	*Dial* Sept. 1920; *New Keepsake* 1921	P, (*EmyE*)
	'Rex'	E349.5a	*Dial* Feb. 1921	P, (*EmyE*)
by 31 March 1919	'Clouds'	E68.7	–	RDP
before 7 April 1919	Topical essay? on strike [lost]			
3–22 April 1919	*MEH* revised			
by 14 May 1919	'Fanny and Annie'	–	*Hutchinson* Nov. 1921	(*EmyE*)
by 20 May 1919	'Monkey Nuts'	–	*Sovereign* 22 Aug. 1922	(*EmyE*)
?June 1919	'Hadrian' ('You Touched Me')	–	*Land and Water* 29 April 1920	(*EmyE*)
June (?July) 1919	Preface to *Touch and Go*	–	*People's Plays* 1920	P II
Aug. 1919	Shestov, *All Things Are Possible*, translated	E11		
29 Aug. 1919	'Verse Free and Unfree' (Preface to Huebsch *New Poems*)	E269.6	*Voices* Oct. 1919; *Playboy* 4 & 5, 1919	P

7–12 Sept. 1919	*Women in Love* last revision	E441f	
9 Sept. –6 Oct. 1919	*Democracy*		
	'The Average'	E91a	*Word* 18 Oct. 1919 P, (*RDP*)
	'Identity'	E91a	*Word* 25 Oct. 1919 P, (*RDP*)
	'Personality'	E91a	*Word* ? Dec. 1919 P, (*RDP*)
	'Individualism'	E91a	– P, (*RDP*)
12 Sept. 1919	Foreword to *Women in Love*	E442	Seltzer leaflet, *P II, (WL)* 1920
by 15 Sept. 1919	Preface to *All Things Are Possible*	E11	– P
by 26 Sept. 1919	Revises *SCAL* (13 essays)		
	'Hawthorne: Blithedale Romance'	E382f	– *TSM*
	'Dana'	E382n	– –
	'Melville I'	E382l	– *TSM*
	'Melville II: Moby Dick'	E382i	– *TSM* (shortened)
	'Whitman'	E382b	–
3–10 Dec. 1919	'David'	E88a	– *SEP*
	'Looking Down on the City'	E206	– *SEP*
by 17 Jan. 1920	*Psychoanalysis and the Unconscious*	E326.7	
13 Feb. –22 Mar. 1920	'The Insurrection of Miss Houghton' II		
by 22 Mar. –5 May 1920	*The Lost Girl*	E209b	(*LG*)
31 May–Sept. 1920	*AR* begun again, advances fitfully		
by 17 June 1920	*Education of the People* (12 chapters)	E112a	– P, (*RDP*)
by 23 July 1920	'Whitman' (revised into publishable form)	E382d	*Nation and* *TSM* *Athenæum* 23 July 1921; *New York Call* Aug. 1921
by 7 Sept. 1920	'America, Listen to Your Own'	E382.5a	*New Republic* Dec. P 1920

737

c. 16 Nov. 1920	Unification of Italy chapter for *MEH*			(*MEH*)
by 29 Nov. 1920	*AR* stuck again more than half-way)			
c. 29 Nov. –9 Dec. 1920	*Mr Noon* Part I	E240a,	*Modern Lover*	P II, (*MN*)
12–31 Dec. 1920	Works on *MN* Part II	E240 a	–	(*MN*)
by 21 Jan. –25 Feb. 1921	*Sea and Sardinia* (revised March, pub. Dec.)	E355a	*Dial* (extracts) Oct. and Nov. 1921	
Feb. 1921	*MN* (last 75 pages)	E240a		(*MN*)
2–31 May 1921	*AR* completed	E2		
3–*c.* 28 June 1921	*Fantasia of the Unconscious*	E125a, b		
by 15 Aug. 1921	Foreword to *AR* [lost]			
?Sept. –8 Oct. 1921	Story set in Venice [lost]			
Oct. 1921	*FU* revised			
	'Foreword: An Answer to Some Critics' (shortened by Seltzer)	E126a	*FU* (1922)	
c. 24 Oct. –1 Dec. 1920	*England, My England* revisions			
[Jan. 1919– March 1920	'Wintry Peacock' from *Metropolitan*]	[E437a]	–	(*EmyE*)
(Jan. 1917– 1920)	'The Horse-Dealer's Daughter'	–	–	(*EmyE*)
(July 1913– 1920)	'The Primrose Path'	[E322.7a]	–	(*EmyE*)
(Nov. 1916– 1920)	'Samson and Delilah'	[E352.7]	–	(*EmyE*)
(Nov. 1918– 1920)	'Tickets Please'	–	–	(*EmyE*)
(July 1919– 1920)	'Hadrian'	–	–	(*EmyE*)
(May 1919– 1920)	'Monkey Nuts'	–	–	(*EmyE*)
(Dec. 1918– 1920)	'Blind Man'	[Lazarus]	–	(*EmyE*)

(May 1919–1920)	'Fanny and Annie'	–		EmyE (1922)	(EmyE)
(June1919–29 Dec. 1920)	'England, My England'	–		EmyE (1922)	(EmyE)
c. 24 Oct. –6 Nov. 1921	'The Captain's Doll'	E60.5a		The Ladybird (1923)	Fox
c. 13 Nov. 1921	The Fox – with new ending	E139c		Dial (May–Aug. 1922); The Ladybird (1923)	Fox
c. 1–17 Dec. 1921	The Ladybird	E187		The Ladybird (1923)	Fox
by 26 Jan. 1922	'Memoir of Maurice Magnus'	E233.7		Memoirs of the Foreign Legion (1924)	P II
by 8 Feb. 1922	Trans. half of Verga, Mastro-don Gesualdo	E230.9a			

THE WRITING LIFE, 1912–1922: POETRY

Though DHL's first collection, *Love Poems and Others*, was published in Feb. 1913, Walter de la Mare had already made his selection and submitted it to Heinemann before DHL left England with Frieda. Heinemann refused the poems, but they were immediately submitted to Duckworth. Since they essentially belong (with the notable exception of 'Bei Hennef') to the period before Lawrence met Frieda, and there is no evidence that he did more than correct proof in October 1912, they are omitted from this table, which begins with the early poems substantially rewritten for *Look! We Have Come Through!*, and with new poems written from Spring 1912.

Earlier poems subsequently rewritten for 'All of Us' and *Bay* appear under the dates of those collections.

Earlier poems revised for *Amores* and *New Poems* appear under the title of those collections at the end of the table.

There is no means of establishing the date of poems in *Look!* for which no version earlier than 1915 exists, or, indeed, more than approximate dates for those earlier versions that have survived. Where the existence of an earlier version indicates the possibility that it was composed sometime near the date (and place) with which it is labelled, the date appears in round brackets. Where no such version exists, the date appears in square brackets, but there can be no certainty that it is accurate, and a strong possibility - by analogy with what happened to the early versions that survive – that most may have been substantially recast in 1917.

DATE	NAL TITLE	EARLIEST MS/ TS	EARLY PUBLICATION	FIRST COLLECTION
(?Dec. 1910–1917)	Martyr à la Mode	E320.2 (E227a, E229.5, E214.3)	–	*Look!* 4 (revised)
(Jan. 1912–1917)	Moonrise ('Bournemouth')	E320.4 no. 29	–	*Look!* 1 (revised)
(Jan. 1912–1917)	The Sea ('Bournemouth')	E320.4 no. 29	–	*Look!* 6 (revised)
[?early 1912]	Elegy ('Eastwood')	–	–	*Look!* 2
[?1912 or later]	Nonentity	–	–	*Look!* 3
(?early 1912)	The Chief Mystery	E320.4 no. 40	–	*Poems* 886–7
	Assuming the Burden	E320.4 no. 43	–	*Poems* 885–6

(?Spring 1912)	Pear Blossom	E320.4 no. 42 –	*Poems* 890–1
[?Spring 1912]	Hymn to Priapus (cf. (i. 369)) ('Constancy of a Sort')	– –	*Look!* 7
(?April 1912)	She Was a Good Little Wife	E320.4 no. 44 –	*Poems* 890
late April 1912	At the Cearne	E320.4 no. 41 –	*Poems* 891–2
late April 1912	Other Women Have Reared in Me	E320.4 no. 45 –	*Poems* 892–3
(?April–May 1912)	Don Juan	E320.6 –	*Look!* 5 (revised)
(9–11 May 1912)	Ballad of a Wilful (Wayward) Woman ('Trier')	E320.6 –	*Look!* 8 (revised)
(11 May 1912)	Bei Hennef ('Hennef am Rhein')	E213 *Love Poems*	*Poems* (1928) (added to)
[?late May 1912]	First Morning ('Beuerberg')	– –	*Look!* 9
	And Oh ... Might Cease To Be ('Wolfratshausen')	– –	*Look!* 10
	She Looks Back	– –	*Look!* 11
(June–Aug. 1912)	On the Balcony ('Icking') ('Illicit')	E318 no. 7 *Poetry* Jan. 1914, *Some Imagist Poems* 1915	*Look!* 12
[?6 June, or later 1912]	Frohnleichnam	– –	*Look!* 13
[?June–Aug. 1912]	In the Dark	– –	*Look!* 14
	Mutilation (cf. (i. 421))	– –	*Look!* 15
	('Wolfratshausen') Humiliation	– –	*Look!* 16
	A Young Wife	– –	*Look!* 17
(June–Aug. 1912)	Green ('Icking')	E318 no. 2 *Poetry* Jan. 1914, *Some Imagist Poets* 1915	*Look!* 18
	River Roses ('Kloster Schäftlarn')	E318 no. 3 Frieda 67; *Poetry* Jan. 1914	*Look!* 19 (revised)
	Gloire de Dijon ('Icking')	E318 no. 3 Frieda 67–8; *Poetry*	*Look!* 20 (revised)

	Roses on the Breakfast Table	E318 no. 3	Frieda 68, *Poetry* Jan. 1914	*Look!* 21 (revised)
	All of Roses IV	E318 no. 3	Frieda 68, *Poetry* Jan. 1914	*Poems* 946
[Probably later]	I am like a Rose	–	–	*Look!* 22
[Probably later]	Rose of All the World	–	–	*Look!* 23
(June–Aug. 1912)	A Youth Mowing	E318	*Poetry* Jan. 1914 'The Mowers'	*Look!* 24 (revised)
[?June–Aug. 1912]	Quite forsaken	–	–	*Look!* 25
	Forsaken and Forlorn	–	–	*Look!* 26
	Fireflies in the Corn	E318	–	*Look!* 27 (revised)
	Song of a Man Who is Loved	E320.6	Frieda 63 ('Isertal')	*Poems* (1928), (restored to *Look!* and revised)
[?7 Aug. 1912]	Song of a Man Who is Not Loved ('Glashütte')	–	–	*Look!* 29
[?11–15 Aug. 1912]	Sinners ('Mayrhofen')	–	–	*Look!* 30
(?11–25 Aug. 1912)	Meeting Among the Mountains ('Tuxtal')	E233.5	Frieda 70–1; *Georgian Poetry 1913–1915*	*Poems* (1928), (restored to *Look!*, misplaced)
by 13 August 1912	The Young Soldier with the Bloody Spurs	E446.5	*ER* Feb. 1914 (i. 434)	*Poems* 732
(?31 August 1912)	Misery ('Sterzing')	–	–	*Look!* 31
[?Oct–Dec. 1912]	Sunday Afternoon in Italy ('Gargnano')	–	–	*Look!* 32
	A Bad Beginning	–	–	*Look!* 34
	Why Does She Weep?	–	–	*Look!* 35
?2 Nov. 1912	Giorno dei Morti ('Service of All the Dead')	–	*New Statesman* 15 Nov. 1913; *Poetry* Dec. 1914; *Georgian Poetry 1913–1915*	*Look!* 36

[Probably later]	All Souls	–	–	*Look!* 37
(?mid Nov. 1912)	Everlasting Flowers	E320.2 no. 19	–	*New Poems* 30, *Poems* (1928), added to *Look!*
[?Winter 1912]	Lady Wife	–	–	*Look!* 38
	Winter Dawn	–	–	*Look!* 33
[?late Dec. 1912]	Both Sides of the Medal	–	–	*Look!* 39
	Loggerheads ('Deadlock')	–	–	*Look!* 40
	Dec. Night	–	–	*Look!* 41
[?31 Dec. 1912]	New Year's Eve	–	–	*Look!* 42
[?1 January 1913]	New Year's Night	–	–	*Look!* 43
[?2–14 Feb. 1913]	Valentine's Night ('Candlemas')	–	–	*Look!* 44
[?Feb. 1913]	Birth Night ('Eve's Mass')	–	–	*Look!* 45
[Probably later]	Rabbit Snared in the Night ('. . . in the Dark')	E330	–	*Look!* 46
[?early 1913]	Paradise Re-entered ('Purity')	E320.6	–	*Look!* 47
[?April 1913]	Spring Morning ('San Gaudenzio')	–	–	*Look!* 48
[?Spring 1913 or later]	Wedlock	–	–	*Look!* 49
[?April/May 1913 or later]	A Doe at Evening ('Irschenhausen')	E97	–	*Look!* 28
?June–July 1913]	History ('The Cearne')	–	–	*Look!* 50
[?1914 or later]	Song of a Man Who Has Come Through	–	–	*Look!* 51
[?1914 or later]	One Woman to All Women ('Kensington')	–	–	*Look!* 52
17 Nov. 1914	Eloi, Eloi, Lama Sabachthani (ii. 132) ('Ecce Homo', E113.2b)	E113.2	*Egoist*, May 1915	*Poems* 741
? early 1915	Resurrection of the Flesh	(E346.5 unlocated)	–	*Poems* 737

Oct. 1915 or ?Sept. 1915	Resurrection (cf. (ii. 417; ii. 455); lost letter to Lowell)	E346	*Poetry* June 1917	*The New Poetry* 1923 (revised)
by 1 Nov. 1915	Erinnyes ('The Turning Back'; cf. Part III (ii. 421–6))	E411a	*Some Imagist Poets* 1916	*Poems* 739
[?1915–17]	She Said As Well To Me	–	–	*Look!* 55
Jan.–July 1915–1917	New Heaven and Earth ('Greatham') (Terranova)	–	*Some Imagist Poets* 1917	*Look!* 56 (revised)
by 28 June 1916	Elysium ('The Blind', 'Eden')	E113.3	–	*Look!* 57
[?Summer 1916]	Manifesto ('Zennor')	–	–	*Look!* 58
[?Autumn 1916]	Autumn Rain	–	*Egoist* Feb. 1917	*Look!* 59
Nov.–11 Dec. 1916	BITS (ALL OF US):			
Dec. 1910–1916 (cf. *EY* 487)	Message to a Perfidious Soldier ('Love Message', E319.3)	E49a no. 14	*Poetry* July 1919	*Poems* 754
	Mother's Son in Salonika ('At Midnight', E319.5)	4	*Poetry* July 1919	*Poems* 750
	Land-Worker ('Beloved', E319.5)	20	–	*Poems* 756
	The Grey Nurse ('The Prophet in the Rose Garden', E319.5)	12	*Poetry* July 1919	*Poems* 753
	Neither Moth Nor Rust ('Moth and Rust', E319.5)	29	*Poetry* July 1919	*Poems* 759
	Maiden's Prayer ('Irreverent Thoughts', E319.5)	6	–	*Poems* 751
	Casualty ('Two Fold', E319.5)	5	*Poetry* July 1919	*Poems* 750
	The Jewess and the V.C. ('Elixir', E319.3)	17	*Poetry* July 1919	*Poems* 755
Nov.–11 Dec. 1916	The Last Minute	1	–	*Poems* 749

Vicar's Son	2	–	*Poems* 749
Drill in the Heat	3	–	*Poems* 750
Man Hauling a Wagon	7	–	*Poems* 751
Sighs	8	*Poetry* July 1919	*Poems* 752
Daughter of the Great Man	9	*Poetry* July 1919	*Poems* 752
The Child and the Soldier	10	*Poetry* July 1919	*Poems* 752
Pietà	11	–	*Poems* 753
Litany of Grey Nurses	13	–	*Poems* 753
Dust in the East	15	–	*Poems* 754
The Girl in Cairo	16	–	*Poems* 754
Zeppelin Nights	18	*Poetry* July 1919	*Poems* 755
Munitions	19	–	*Poems* 756
Mourning	21	*Poetry* July 1919	*Poems* 756
Mesopotamia	22	–	*Poems* 757
Tales ('The Gazelle Calf')	23	–	*Poems* 757 *Pansies* (revised)
Foreign Sunset	24	–	*Poems* 757
Prisoner at Work in a Turkish Garden	25	*Poetry* July 1919	*Poems* 758
Swing Song of a Girl and a Soldier	26	–	*Poems* 758–9
Prisoners at Work in the Rain	27	–	*Poems* 759
The Well in Africa	28	–	*Poems* 759

Note For 'ALL OF US' E49b (46c) Lawrence created longer narrative titles

[?Winter 1916–1917]	Frost Flowers	E142	*ER* Sept. 1917	*Look!* 60
[?1910 rev. 1917]	People ('The Street Lamps')	E320.1, cf. E320.4	*Poetry* July 1918	*Look!* 53
	Street Lamps	E320.1,	*The Egoist* Jan. 1917	*Look!* 54
18–23 Feb. 1917	Craving for Spring	–	–	*Look!* 61
31 Jan. 1918	Labour Battalion	E185	*New Paths* 1918	*Poems* 746
	No News (cf. (iii. 202–5))	E272.5	*New Paths* 1918	*Poems* 748
c. 1–18 April 1918	**BAY**			

(1909–1918)	Guards!/A Review in Hyde Park, 1913 ('The Review of the Scots Guards'; 'Review ... in Hyde Park, 1910')	E317, E155c., E320.1, E320.2	–	*Bay* 1
(*c.* 1906–1918)	The Little Town at Evening ('Eastwood–Evening')	E317. E204.5c	–	*Bay* 2
(*c.* 1906–1918)	Last Hours ('The Last Hours of a Holiday')	E317	*Bay* 3	
?Nov. 1918	Town in 1917 ('Town')	E320	*ER* June 1918	*Bay* 4
	After the Opera	E319	*ER* July 1918	*Bay* 5
April 1918	Going Back	E320	–	*Bay* 6
(*c.* 1908–1918)	On the March ('On the Road')	E317, E295b	–	*Bay* 7 (revised)
(*c.* 1910–1918)	Bombardment ('Spring in the City', 'Apprehension')	E320.1, E320.2	–	*Bay* 8 (revised)
April 1918	Winter Lull	E320	–	*Bay* 9
	The Attack	–	–	*Bay* 10
	Obsequial Ode ('Obsequial Chant')	E283c	*Poetry* Feb. 1919 *Voices* July 1919	*Bay* 11
	Shades ('Pentecostal')	E359.3a E283a	*Poetry* Feb. 1919	*Bay* 12
	Bread Upon the Waters	E319	*Poetry* Feb. 1919	*Bay* 13
(1909–1918)	Ruination ('SCHOOL I. Morning/The Waste Lands')	E 317, E320.1, E320.2, E352.3c	–	*Bay* 14
	Rondeau of a Conscientious Objector ('Coming home from School, THE SCHOOL-MASTER III Evening')	E317, E351.3c, E351.3b	–	*Bay* 15
April 1918	Tommies in the Train	E400b, E319	*Poetry* Feb. 1919	*Bay* 16

	Nostalgia	E276b, E319	*Poetry* Feb. 1919 *Voices* July 1919	*Bay* 18
	Death Paean of a Mother	(UN)	–	–
1 June 1918	War Baby	E319	*ER* June 1918; *Poetry* Feb. 1919	*Bay* 17
April–June 1918	Coming Awake	–	–	*New Poems* 2, *Poems* (1928) adds to *Look!*
	Seven Seals	–	*Georgian Poetry* 1918–1919	*New Poems* 33
[?late April– Aug. 1920	The Mosquito (Siracusa) (cf. (iii. 558))	E47c	*Bookman* July 1921	*BBF*
June–July 1920	Southern Night ('The Ionian Sea')	E47a	–	*BBF*
July 1920	Tropic	E47a	*The Enchanted Years* June 1921 (iii. 631)	*BBF*
	Peace ('Slopes of Etna')	E47a	*The Enchanted Years* June 1921 (iii. 631)	*BBF*
[?July 1920] – by 28 Jan. 1921	Snake (cf. (iii. 573, 657))	E362.7b	*Dial* July 1921; *London Mercury* Oct. 1921	*BBF*
10–15 Sept. 1920	'Fruit Studies'			
	Pomegranate	E320.9b	*Dial* March 1921 *ER* Aug. 1921	*BBF*
	Peach	E47c	–	*BBF*
	Figs ('Fig')	E47c	–	*BBF*
	Grapes	E47c	–	*BBF*
	Medlars and Sorb-Apples	E47c	*New Republic* 5 Jan. 1921; *ER* Aug. 1921	*BBF*
10–?16 Sept. 1920	The Revolutionary	E47c	*New Republic* 19 Jan. 1921; *ER* Sept. 1921	*BBF*
15–28 Sept 1920	Cypresses	E47c	–	*BBF*
	Turkey Cock	E47c	*Poetry* Nov. 1922	*BBF*
15–30 Sept. 1920	**TORTOISES**			
	Baby Tortoise	–	*ER* Nov. 1922	*Tortoises*
	Tortoise-Shell	–	–	*Tortoises*

	Tortoise Family Connections	–	–	*Tortoises*
	Lui et Elle	–	–	*Tortoises*
	Tortoise Gallantry	–	–	*Tortoises*
	Tortoise Shout	–	–	*Tortoises*
15 Sept.–?14 Oct.	Evangelistic (Apostolic) Beasts:			
	St. Matthew	E47c	*Poetry* April 1923	*BBF*
	St. Luke	E352.53	*Dial* April 1921	*BBF*
	St. John	E352.5	*Dial* April 1921	*BBF*
	St. Mark	E352.55	*Dial* April 1921	*BBF*
18–25 Oct. 1920	Sicilian Cyclamens	E47a	–	*BBF*
18 Oct.–4 Nov. 1920	Humming Bird (cf. iii. 616)	E47c	*New Republic* 11 May 1921	*BBF*
	The Evening Land	E47c	*Poetry* Nov. 1922	*BBF*
by 28 Jan. 1921	Bare Fig Trees	E39		*BBF*
	Bare Almond Trees	E47c	–	*BBF*
	Almond Blossom	E12a	*ER* Feb. 1922	*BBF*
31 January 1921	Hibiscus and Salvia Flowers	E47a	–	*BBF* (revised)
4 Feb. 1921	Purple Anemones	E47a	–	*BBF* (revised)
2 March 1921	The Ass	E47a	–	*BBF* (revised)
by 9 Sept. 1921	Fish	E47c	*ER* June 1922	*BBF*
by 17 Sept. 1921	Bat	E47b	*ER* Nov. 1922 *Literary Digest* Dec. 1922	*BBF*
	Man and Bat	E47b	–	*BBF*
early 1922	She-Goat	E47c	–	*BBF*
?early 1922	He-Goat	E47c	–	*BBF*

Collections of (revised) poems originally written before May 1912
 (for more detailed chronology see *EY* Appendix I)

Jan.–8 Feb. 1916	AMORES:			
(*c.* 1905)	The Wild Common	E317	–	*Amores* 2
(*c.* 1906–8)	Study	E317	–	*Amores* 3
(by Jan 1909)	In a Boat	E317, E320.4	*ER* Oct. 1910	*Amores* 7
(by 20 Jan. 1910)	A Winter's Tale	E317, E346b	*Egoist* 1 April 1914	*Amores* 12
(1909)	Discipline	E317	*ER* Nov. 1909	*Amores* 15
	The Prophet	E320.1	*ER* Nov. 1909	*Amores* 17

Dreams Old and Nascent ('A Still Afternoon in School')	E317	*ER* Nov. 1909	*Amores* 10, 11
Baby Running Barefoot	E317	*ER* Nov. 1909	*Amores* 14
Baby Asleep After Pain	E317	*ER* Nov. 1909	*Amores* 23
Virgin Youth ('MOVEMENTS. The Body Awake')	E317	–	*Amores* 5
Restlessness	E317	–	*Amores* 22
A Passing Bell ('A Bell')	E317, E320.4	–	*Amores* 55
At the Window	E317	*ER* April 1910 *Some Imagist Poets* 1916	*Amores* 29
Week-Night Service	E317	–	*Amores* 8
Turned Down ('Fooled', 'Perfidy')	E317, E320.4	*Egoist* 1 April 1914, *Some Imagist Poets*	*Amores* 47
The Punisher	E320.1	*SWG* 25 May 1912	*Amores* 25
Disagreeable Advice ('An Epistle from Arthur')	E320.1	–	*Amores* 9
Epilogue ('Epilogue from Thelma')	E320.1	–	*Amores* 13
Discord in Childhood ('Discord')	E320.1 no. 18	–	*Amores* 4
Monologue of a Mother	E320.1	*Poetry* Jan. 1914 Frieda 76–7	*Amores* 6
(1910) Malade	E320.1	–	*Amores* 38
Scent of Irises	E320.1	*Some Imagist Poets* 1915	*Amores* 16
Ballad of Another Ophelia ('Ophelia')	E320.1, E320.4	*Some Imagist Poets* 1915	*Amores* 21
The Yew-Tree on the Downs ('Liaison')	E320.1, E320.4	–	*Amores* 39
Dolour of Autumn	E320.1	–	*Amores* 32
Reproach	E320.1	–	*Amores* 44

	Endless Anxiety ('Anxiety')	E320.1	–	*Amores* 24
	Suspense ('Patience')	E320.1	–	*Amores* 20
	Excursion ('Honeymoon')	E317	*Egoist* 1 April 1914	*Amores* 46
	Brooding Grief ('Brooding')	E317	*Some Imagist Poets* 1916	*Amores* 36
	Sorrow	E317	*Poetry* Dec. 1914	*Amores* 31
	Last Words to Miriam ('Last . . . to Muriel')	E317	–	*Amores* 18
	Submergence	E320.1	–	*Amores* 42
(?1911)	Tease ('A Wise Man', 'Teasing')	E320.1, E320.4	*Poetry and Drama* Dec. 1914	*Amores* 1
	Brother and Sister ('To Lettice, my Sister')	E320.1	–	*Amores* 51
	The End ('To My Mother – Dead', 'Memories')	E320.1	*Poetry* Dec. 1914	*Amores* 26
	The Bride ('The Dead Mother')	E320.1	–	*Amores* 27
	The Virgin Mother ('My Love, My Mother')	E320.1	–	*Amores* 28
	The Shadow of Death ('Blue')	E320.1 E320.4	–	*Amores* 53
	The Mystic Blue ('Blue')	E320.1	–	*Amores* 60
	Silence	E320.1	–	*Amores* 34
	Listening	E320.1	–	*Amores* 35
	The Inheritance	E320.1	–	*Amores* 33
	Come Spring, Come Sorrow ('Mating')	E320.1	–	*Amores* 49
	After Many Days ('Meeting')	E320.1	–	*Amores* 52
	Troth with the Dead	E320.1	–	*Amores* 40
	At a Loose End ('Dissolute', 'Troth with the Dead')	E320.1	–	*Amores* 41

	The Enkindled Spring ('Troth with the Dead')	E320.1	–	*Amores* 43
	A Love Song	E320.1	–	*Amores* 50
	The Hands of the Betrothed ('Your Hands')	E320.1	–	*Amores* 45
	Drunk	E320.1	–	*Amores* 30
	Snap-Dragon	E320.4	*ER* June 1912, *Georgian Poetry 1911–1912*	*Amores* 54
(?1911)	Mystery	E320.6	–	*Amores* 19
	A Spiritual Woman (Later: 'These Clever Women')	–	–	*Amores* 48
	Lotus and Frost ('Lotus Hurt by the Cold')	E320.2	–	*Amores* 37
	In Trouble and Shame	E320.2	*Some Imagist Poets* 1916	*Amores* 56
	Call Into Death	–	–	*Amores* 57
	Grey Evening ('Afterwards')	E320.6	–	*Amores* 58
	Firelight and Nightfall ('Afterwards')	E320.6	–	*Amores* 60
	[Grief ('Afterwards')		*Poetry* Dec. 1914]	*Poems* 941–2
	[Twilight ('Afterwards')		*ER* Feb. 1914]	*Poems* 942
April–June 1918	**NEW POEMS**			
(*c.* 1906–8)	From a College Window	E317	–	*New Poems* 3
	Twilight ('Evening of a Week Day', 'Palimpsest of Twilight')	E317	–	*New Poems* 4
	Piano ('The Piano')	E317, E320.2	–	*New Poems* 21
(*c.* 1908–8)	Flapper ('Song')	E317, E320.4, etc.	*Egoist* April 1914 *Poetry* Dec. 1914	*New Poems* 4
	Tarantella	E317, E320.4	–	*New Poems* 19

(by Jan. 1909)	Narcissus ('Dim Recollections', 'Neckar')	E317	–	*New Poems* 40
(1909)	Birdcage Walk ('Triolet, In the Park')	E317	–	*New Poems* 5
	School on the Outskirts ('A Snowy Day in School') ('The School on the Waste Lands')	E 317, E320.2	–	*New Poems* 28
	Letter from Town: The Almond Tree	E317	–	*New Poems* 6
	Letter from Town: On a Grey Morning in March ('Letter ... : The City', 'Letter ... : On a Grey Evening in March')	E317	–	*New Poems* 9
	Reading a Letter ('Reading in the Evening')	E317	–	*New Poems* 34
	Embankment at Night, Before the War: Outcasts ('After the Theatre')	E317	–	*New Poems* 26
	Embankment at Night, Before the War: Charity ('Brotherhood')	E317, E320.4	–	*New Poems* 22
	Hyde Park at Night, Before the War: Clerks ('The Songless 1', 'Night Songs 1', etc.)	E317, E320.4	*ER* April 1910	*New Poems* 11
	Piccadilly Circus at Night: Street-Walkers ('The Songless 2', 'Night Songs 2', etc.)	E317, E320.4	*ER* April 1920	*New Poems* 18

	Sickness	E320.1	–	New Poems 29
	Next Morning ('A Day in November')	E320.1	–	New Poems 24
	Twenty Years Ago ('A Life History ... Third Harmony')	E320.1	–	New Poems 35
(1910)	Autumn Sunshine ('Amour', 'Early Spring')	E317	Egoist 1 April 1914	New Poems 41
	Sigh No More ('Cuckoo and Wood-Dove')	E320.1, E320.4	ER Oct. 1910	New Poems 15
	Late at Night ('New Wine', 'Phantasmagoria')	E320.1	–	New Poems 23
	Reality of Peace 1916 ('Unwitting, The Interim, Débâcle')	E320.1	–	New Poems 39
	Under the Oak ('The Appeal')	E320.1	–	New Poems 14
	A Man Who Died ('Nils Lykke Dead', 'Bitterness of Death')	E320.1, E320.4	Poetry Jan. 1914, Some Imagist Poets 1915	New Poems 32
	In Church ('The Crow')	E317	–	New Poems 20
	The North Country ('The Crow')	E317	–	New Poems 31
	At the Front ('The Crow', 'Engulphed', 'Heimweh')	E317	–	New Poems 38
	Gipsy ('Self Contempt, (i. 196))	E145.5	–	New Poems 12
	?Thief in the Night	–	–	New Poems 8
(1911)	Winter in the Boulevard ('Winter')	E320.1	–	New Poems 27
	Parliament Hill in the Evening ('Transformations. 1. Evening')	E320.1	–	New Poems 17

	Flat Suburbs, S.W., in the Morning ('Transformations. 2. Morning')	E320.1	–	*New Poems* 7
	Suburbs on a Hazy Day ('Transformations. 4. The Inanimate' etc.)	E320.1	–	*New Poems* 10
	Noise of Battle ('The Inheritance, Apprehension')	E320.1	–	*New Poems* 1
	On That Day ('Her Birthday')	E320.1	*Poetry* Jan. 1914	*New Poems* 42
(?1911)	Twofold ('Indoors and Out')	E320.2	–	*New Poems* 13
	Love Storm ('Storm in Rose-Time')	E320.6	–	*New Poems* 16
	Passing Visit to Helen ('And Jude the Obscure and his Beloved, Intime')	E320.4	–	*New Poems* 36
	Two Wives ('White')	E320.4	–	*New Poems* 37
Note:	Everlasting Flowers	(see Nov. 1912)	–	*New Poems* 30
	Seven Seals	(see April–June 1918)	–	*New Poems* 33
	Coming Awake	(see April–June 1918)		*New Poems* 2

754

Notes and Sources

THE USE OF SOURCES

The Cambridge Biography is particularly fortunate in being able to call unrestrictedly upon the text of Lawrence's surviving letters, accurately established in the Cambridge Edition (in this volume of the Biography, from volumes i. to v. of the *Letters*.) Some additional letters have come to light since, and are to be published in *Letters*, viii. Several known gaps remain however, and there will be others of which we are not aware. Barbara Low destroyed some letters (though she kept the more personal ones) because she thought, self-effacingly, that they were to a person of little importance. Not all the letters to Katherine Mansfield or to John Middleton Murry have survived, and Richard Aldington burnt those that Lawrence wrote to his then wife Hilda ('H.D.'). There were almost certainly letters to Vere Collins, to A. P. Lewis, to William K. Horne, that have not come down to us, and very probably others. We need constantly to remember the patchiness of our knowledge of Lawrence's range of acquaintances, and to be grateful that the power and interest of his letters made so many people preserve them.

The letters amount of course to an autobiographical record of a particularly spontaneous and self-revelatory kind, so that to be permitted to quote more fully than is usual, is to place Lawrence's story-of-himself uniquely at the centre of this biography. He had mixed feelings about Samuel Richardson, but must have shared the eighteenth-century writer's belief that the more letters are written 'to the moment', spontaneous and uncensored, the more revealing of the inner self they become. (March's letter to Henry in 'The Fox' is an epistolary masterpiece of a very Richardsonian kind.) Richardson has also taught us, of course, that letters are self-presentation and even self-creation, histrionic, and not infrequently deceptive and self-deceptive. We play 'ourselves' to our correspondents – a subtly different self to each. If the range of recipients is wide enough, the greater part of a spectrum of the self builds up, but we should always of course be mindful of the limits of the writer's knowledge and self-knowledge and the distortions of the ego. Letters may also proclaim the very isolation they seek to overcome. As he became more and more estranged from English society, letters became for Lawrence the substance of such friendships as he retained; the pieces of paper *were* to all intents and purposes his friendship with Koteliansky, and Gertler, and Lady Cynthia Asquith, and Catherine Carswell for much of the time from 1912 to 1922. Consequently he used letters – sometimes to relative strangers – to try out ideas, express emotions and blow off steam which in a more socialised existence would have evaporated on the instant in speech or shout, or later, have distilled into considered thought or feeling. Nothing is easier than to produce distorted impressions of him by selective quotation. 'I would like to kill a million Germans – two million', he would write, not inhumanly, but enraged by inhumanity after the sinking of the *Lusitania*; only to add, later, 'Don't take any notice of my extravagant talk – one must say something' (ii. 340). Moreover, to live and write 'to the moment' was to care much for momentary truth-of-feeling but little for consistency. Indeed he believed that human beings both were and ought to be fluctuating and changeable, if they were to remain vitally alive. He might well have said with Whitman: 'Do I contradict myself? / Very well then I contradict myself./ (I am large, I contain multitudes.)' Consequently context and chronology are immensely important in using his letters. Any general statement beginning 'Lawrence ...' ought immediately to be followed by a modifier indicating *which* Lawrence, since (particularly in the years from 1912 to 1920, momentous not only for him, but for his radically changing world) his personality and his views did undergo very significant changes, making generalisation about him very risky if not idiotic (in Blake's ouvre). It is chronology moreover that saves us from analytic arrogance – the belief that we can offer overall explanations of the factors which determine character and behaviour, whether it be in terms of tuberculosis, sexuality or psychopathology. This biography has tried, rather, to 'live' with Lawrence week by week and month by month, avoiding hindsight and its patternings, not in the hope of some impossibly definitive truth, but trying for some sense at least of what it may have been like to live as Lawrence did: and live a *writing* life. For that, his letters in their very subjectivity and variation are an unrivalled source, far richer than can be tapped even in a book of this length. If it does no more than send new readers to the Cambridge letters, its author will be well satisfied.

Edward Nehls's *Composite Biography*, compiled from the numerous memoirs that began to appear soon after Lawrence's death and by persuading more of Lawrence's acquaintances to contribute, is the other irreplaceable source, providing a wide spectrum of response in attraction or repulsion, but seldom indifference, from those who knew him – or thought they did. This counteracts the subjectivity of Lawrence's letters, and the counteractive biases are also mutually corrective. It is no criticism of Nehls's painstaking scholarship and annotation to say that vastly more information has come to light since his three volumes appeared in the late 1950s – yet the freshness and immediacy of the kaleidoscope of views will ensure their permanent value.

One difficulty however results from the very liveliness of some – for biographies of Lawrence have gone on repeating the same round of gossipy anecdotes with (sometimes) too great credulity and too little scrupulous examination of likelihood and credibility. The stories of two splendid raconteurs, for example, David 'Bunny' Garnett and 'Monty' Compton Mackenzie tended to grow over the years, and it may be necessary to try to rescue the original kernel of fact (or fiction) from later accretions and colouring. Both men, moreover, grew hostile to Lawrence after original fascination, and in both cases there is a marked element of reading-back from later hindsight. Similarly the letters between Lady Ottoline Morrell and Bertrand Russell in 1915 and 1916 are a much safer guide to their relationship with Lawrence than their later accounts. (The original journal of Lady Ottoline is much terser than its later writing up – with some recension by her husband – into her two volumes of memoirs.) As a rule, the earlier the evidence, the more likely it is to be reliable, though perhaps the less colourful and opinionated. A more complex case is that of Murry, where a strong later agenda combined with a poor memory to produce, at some points, a misleading version of events. I am particularly grateful to his son for permitting me to read and use the journal contemporaneous with Murry's first years of acquaintance with the Lawrences, which is a much more accurate account of his feelings at the time than his later writings – and all the more sympathetic, as less supportive of the role of the uniquely understanding friend he later wished to claim, which tempts Lawrencians to cast him as Judas instead. The unremitting hostility of Cecil Gray on the other hand springs from a breach whose true nature he wished subsequently to conceal. In dealing with the mass of anecdotage that has survived about the Lawrences, biographers need to weigh evidence carefully: the motivation and credibility of the witness; the consistency of the story with all the other evidence and with the characters and motives of the protagonists as revealed elsewhere; the question of whether traces are to be found in the work (though mindful of the danger of reading-in and reading-back). Several oft-repeated stories about Lawrence, and Frieda (and a new one), have to be entertained and examined – but with some scepticism too, more perhaps than has always been the case.

A spirit of critical enquiry ought also to obtain in dealing with the 'autobiographical' writings of the two principal witnesses. Writers on the Lawrences have tended to accept *Sons and Lovers, Look! We Have Come Through!, Mr Noon* (and *"Not I, But the Wind..."*) rather too uncritically as sources of fact and self-portraiture. All are fictive to a biographically significant degree, and it has been a principal aim of the Cambridge Biography to measure them against the contemporary evidence, and show how in all three Lawrence works especially, he heightened, transposed, dramatised and imaginatively transformed the past for his own artistic, and in the case of *Mr Noon* comic purposes. Here, as well as disentangling what does remain relevant to biography, the biographer may be of use to the critic in the latter's concern to explore the fictive and poetic process. Yet it remains true that in his creative writings Lawrence did confront, to remarkable imaginative depth and complexity but seldom overtly, the problems of his life. In order to try to establish a useful relation of literature and life, however, it is vitally important to get back to the versions written at the time, behind the often much revised and rewritten later ones with which we may be familiar – and no less important to recognise and respect the boundaries between biography and imagination, though it is no easy task to draw them properly. What gave old-fashioned 'The Man and His Work' studies their bad name was their willingness simply to conflate the two. Yet it was in his writing that Lawrence perhaps lived most intensely (and spent much more time than in quarrelling with Frieda). Biography that ducks the challenge to deal, sensitively, with the relationship of living man to creative 'manuscript', will tend to produce a superficial, gossipy and disproportioned account of Lawrence's 'life'. Here scholarship, biography and literary criticism must meet, while always respecting essentially different disciplines.

In Frieda's case, too, it is necessary to detect an element of fiction in her autobiography, her overtly fictionalised 'memoirs' and her subsequent memories. An absolute contradiction between two stories about her first meeting with Lawrence appears on the opening pages of this biography, and it is no good trying to have it both ways: the biographer must weigh likelihood against likelihood and test each story against the other evidence. Frieda's memory for facts and dates was very imprecise. It was also part of her vitality to want to make herself and her life more interesting – occasionally, one suspects, by drawing on her husband's work. She told some stories to put Lawrence in his place, or to assert herself. (As a result she has been regarded as more promiscuous than she may actually have been.) Her romantic account of the 'elopement' has to be considerably modified by evidence that she had no intention of breaking her marriage let alone losing her children, and by the rather different story of how Lawrence insisted on being straight with Weekley, and had to fight and go on fighting against her family's ongoing pressure to come to a sophisticated 'arrangement', like those in the marriages of her parents and her sisters, and then against her reluctance to commit herself to him. The story of the rows over 'the children' is far more complex than has been supposed, and the part played by Frieda's own actions in hardening Weekley's attitude has never been properly told or dated – though dates turn out to be significant. A neglected resource is Frieda's lively and individual letters, which ought long since to have been collected.

Finally, on the use of sources for 'A Life', this biographer thinks summary and generalisation should go to the (admittedly more economical) devil; since the life of things tends to be found in detail, variation and change through time; though that story takes longer to tell.

NOTES

Chapter One: New Life

1 Nehls, i. 162; verso of letter of 30 April (i. 389 n. 1); Frieda 25. Frieda (b. 11 August 1879), daughter of Baron Friedrich and Baroness Anna von Richthofen, was about to turn 33, six years older than DHL. Her father's active army service had come to an end when his hand was badly wounded during the Franco-Prussian war, after which he served as civil engineer in the administration of Metz in (post-1870) German Lorraine. She had been brought up in proximity to the barracks, making friends among the soldiers when little, and the officers later on. At 20 in 1899, when DHL was still a schoolboy living at home, Frieda was getting married to Professor Ernest Weekley, 14 years older than herself. The honeymoon (at a hotel in Lucerne) was disastrous, both in the misfiring of her prank of climbing naked on top of the cupboard to surprise her husband, and in bed. Bourgeois Nottingham proved a disappointment also, but she retained her high spirits most of the time – reacting against boredom by dancing around her room naked, or running down the road madly at night. Her boredom was also broken by regular visits to her sister Else in Munich, where she moved in bohemian circles. She had had affairs with William Dowson, a Nottingham lace manufacturer (godfather to her youngest daughter), who used to take her driving in Sherwood forest, cf. Robert Lucas, *Frieda Lawrence: The Story of Frieda von Richthofen and D. H. Lawrence* (1973), p. 33 on information from Frieda's youngest daughter Barbara; with Freud's turbulent follower Otto Gross, which had a deep and lasting effect on her conception of herself; and with the anarchist painter Ernst Frick in 1911. (See notes 4 and 8.) Her son Montague was born in 1900, her daughters Elsa and Barbara in 1902 and 1904. She had, on 3 May, known DHL for between six and eight weeks (see note 90).

2 As reported in a memoir (UT) by Phyllis Cahill, who typed for Frieda after DHL's death:

> When Lawrence and I fell in love I had no intention whatever of leaving my husband and children and the comfortable & respectable life I knew to go off into certain social exile and most probable poverty. I could see no reason why we shouldn't become lovers while I continued to live with Prof. W. Lawrence was shocked and horrified at the immorality of the suggestion. 'As we love each other we have the right to live together. But to creep into the bed of another man's wife while a guest in his house, no. Either you make up your mind to leave him and everything you have been accustomed to and give him the right and freedom to

761

divorce you, and marry me, or you will never see me again.' So I went to the nursery and kissed my children good-bye & stepped into a new life.

The last sentence makes her seem far more decisive than she actually was.

3 Frieda 22–3, Cahill memoir. Mary Holbrook was Jessie Chambers's sister, and her and her husband Will's farm near Eastwood was a safe place to take Frieda and the children. A tense DHL perhaps tried too hard with the little girls. Elsa, with something of her father's superior air, snubbed him for imagining she did not know about the armada, and even little Barby was inclined to be snooty, thinking him a cut below the jovial and professorial adults she was accustomed to (Nehls, i. 162–3).

The story recently revived by Brenda Maddox, *The Married Man* (1994), p. 113, that Frieda only needed twenty minutes after first meeting DHL to get him into bed, is almost certainly fictitious. A choice must be made between two Frieda stories which directly contradict each other: her reported boast to Mabel Dodge Luhan, not the most reliable of witnesses anyway, in *Lorenzo in Taos* (New York, 1932) p. 103, and her statement to Phyllis Cahill, quoted above. (When Maddox later also *accepts* the Cahill report that DHL refused to sleep with Frieda in her husband's house she creates a nonsense, if he had already done so.) We can only weigh likelihood against likelihood. The first meeting was probably on a Sunday (see *EY* 561–2) when the university would be closed, and her husband would probably have been in his study, abutting the stairs. The Weekleys had servants and a nurse for the children, any of whom could have noticed Frieda's absence or come upstairs. Moreover the Luhan story is also inconsistent with DHL's stance towards Weekley in the coming weeks, and with his cautiousness and scruple with Rosalind Baynes (see chapter 11, pp. 601–3). Maddox's use, for biographical purposes, of the 1920 comic novel *Mr Noon* shows no understanding of the comedic *fictiveness* of its characterisations – its inflammable Johanna is only in Munich at all because she had almost succumbed to a Japanese stranger on a train, which we are presumably not meant to believe – or its accounts of sexual scenes in Munich and in Metz which are unfortunately unlikely to have happened (see note 16 below and pp. 617–19). Frieda is however quite likely to have boasted in exaggerated terms in order to put down Mabel Luhan, who had not succeeded in seducing DHL. His friend Willie Hopkin, reported dubiously as repeating the story much later and at third hand, may have got it from Mabel Luhan's book.

4 The story of Frieda's crucially 'liberating' affair with Gross, the brilliant follower of Freud who had been cold-shouldered by the Master because of his ideas of erotic therapy, is told in Martin Green, *The von Richthofen Sisters* (1974), pp. 32–73. Gross's letters to Frieda, which were very important in creating her image of herself, are printed in *Memoirs* 94–102, and in a new translation by John Turner with Cornelia Rumpf-Worthen and Ruth Jenkins, 'The Otto Gross–Frieda Weekley Correspondence', *DHLR*, xxii (1990). See also Frieda 23. Gross wanted her to leave Weekley for him – but she was perfectly aware of his shortcomings. He was fascinating but utterly unreliable, and increasingly addicted to drugs which, together with the scandal surrounding the (assisted?) suicide of two of his patients, would eventually destroy him.

5 For DHL's relationship with Alice Dax, see *EY* 358–70. She was the independent-minded wife of an Eastwood chemist, and had become sexually involved with DHL.

6 Frieda 23; Alice Dax to Frieda in 1935, *Memoirs* 245; *EY* 364–8. The poems 'Pear Blossom' and 'She was a Good Little Wife' possibly relate to Alice, but 'The Chief Mystery' probably to Frieda and 'At the Cearne' clearly recalls the weekend with Frieda there.

7 Frieda 22. DHL had been rather impressed by Weekley's sophisticated 'Cambridge' manner and sarcasm in his classes (E.T. 76). The idea of going to Germany had been first mentioned on 12 January (i. 350), as suggested by his Aunt Ada and her husband Fritz Krenkow, whose niece lived in Waldbröl.

8 Frieda had met Ernst Frick in the bohemian Schwabing district of Munich years before; cf. Martin Green, *Mountain of Truth* (Hanover, 1986), pp. 38–9. In 1909 he had gone to live with Frieda Gross in Ascona, with the consent of her husband who considered Frick a more suitable mate for her. In 1911, Frieda Weekley had an affair with him, and came to Ascona where Frieda Gross, despite her liberated principles, became jealous so that there were rows. Later, in September–October 1911, Frick came on a visit to England, partly paid for by Frieda Weekley, but they were only able to correspond through intermediaries, and to meet infrequently, probably in a friend's flat in London. In 1912, however, Frick was in grave difficulties. He had been involved – to quite what extent is not too clear – in an attempt to rescue a fellow anarchist from prison, during which a bomb, planted as a distraction, blew up and injured three children; and with the derailment of a tram. Frick was now (1912) about to stand trial, as Frieda Gross had written to tell Frieda Weekley. Though there is no reason to suppose that Frieda Weekley's affair with Frick had gone very deep, and it had now been superseded by the affair with DHL, she was exercised about whether she should try to see Frick in Zürich. This Frick himself very sensibly discouraged. The above information is drawn from letters from Frieda Gross to Else Jaffe, Frieda Weekley's sister (Letters 48–9, 50–1, 56); to Frieda Weekley (Letter 54); and from Frick to Else (Letter 53) and to Frieda Weekley (Letter 57), all now at TuftsU. Frick was subsequently convicted and spent a year in prison. Frieda Weekley also had a letter from Gross but was 'unmoved' by it (Green, *Von Richthofen Sisters*, pp. 53, 61).

9 Cf. (i. 388, 409); Frieda 23; Lucas, *Frieda Lawrence*, p. 77; Frieda Gross to Else Jaffe, 6 May 1912 (TuftsU; Letter 56), having heard from Frieda Weekley that she had told her husband about Gross and Frick.

10 E.T. 191ff.

11 For DHL's relationships with Helen Corke, and Louie Burrows to whom he became engaged in December 1910, but broke it off in February 1912, see *EY* 253–62, 288–96, 300–24. Frieda 23; *Memoirs* 75.

12 Cf. (i .390, 392); *EY* 564 n. 10; Green, *Von Richthofen Sisters*, p. 14; *MN* 180:38–40 (*Mr Noon*, a comic fiction written eight years later, is only reliable for biographical purposes if confirmed by other evidence. Here, see *EY* 564 n. 10).

13 *Memoirs* 389–90; (i. 409); *MN* 177:39–180:17; E130a, 'The Fight for Barbara', Act II (*The Complete Plays of D. H. Lawrence*, 1965, pp. 288–92).

14 Green, *Von Richthofen Sisters*, pp. 22, 187; (i. 395); *MN* 154:34–5.

15 Frieda 25–6; *MN* 158:4–159:4, 179:8–33.

16 *Mr Noon* expands the time in Metz to make room for two sex scenes, one splendidly farcical and in direct parallel with a scene in Part I – but alas, probably fictive in the light of DHL's complaint here. Tuesday was the contretemps of the arrest; Wednesday he was in Trier. Frieda had moved from the hotel back into her parents' house in the suburbs.

17 *TI* 16–20.

18 Cf. (i .394–5;) Frieda 26; *MN* 168:28–169:32; 'How a Spy is Arrested', *TI* 11–15.

19 *MN* 144:31–2 (cf. (i. 409)); Frieda 25.

20 Cf. (i. 396). The three sketches set in Metz ('The English and the Germans', 'How a Spy is Arrested', 'French Sons of Germany') read as though written there, but it is not clear when or in which order they were done. 'The English and the Germans' may have been writen in Metz. On 9 May from Trier DHL mentioned having written an article too outspoken to be printed, which sounds like 'A Spy'; and some phrasing in 'French Sons' is echoed in the letters to Frieda from Trier (i. 393–4, 396). It may however have been written in Waldbröl about 13 May when he had begun writing 'in the morning' (i. 399) but had not yet started revising 'Paul Morel'. All three have the overall title 'In Fortified Germany'. See *TI* xxvii–xxviii.

21 This detail only in *MN* 177:16–17, but seems likely. Any similarly unconfirmed but likely details will be placed in round brackets and *MN* noted as the source (but see n. 64) below).

22 According to *MN* 181:23–4.

23 This was not the version published in *Look! We Have Come Through!*, which was a significant rewriting in 1917; see Mark Kinkead-Weekes, 'The Shaping of D. H. Lawrence's *Look! We Have Come Through!*', in *Presenting Poetry*, ed. Howard Erskine-Hill and Richard A. McCabe (Cambridge, 1995) pp. 214–34, on the danger of simply assuming that the poems in this sequence were in fact written at the places and the dates implied by DHL's labellings.

24 *Memoirs* 180.

25 Cf. the break with Louie Burrows (i. 366); both dramatisations of the scolding by Frieda's mother in *The Fight for Barbara* and *Mr Noon*, cf. (i. 429–30); and DHL's reaction to being corrected by the Baron.

26 *MN* 160:25–7.

27 According to *MN* 183:5–31, he caught a train for which a surcharge was necessary.

28 'Bei Hennef', *Poems* 203.

29 See (i. 404) and Dieter Mehl, 'Lawrence in Waldbröl', *Notes and Queries*, ccxxix (1984), 78–81. 'Hail in the Rhineland', the last of the German sketches, was written either the same day as the storm (15 May) or the next, when it was sent away with the other three to de la Mare for him to submit to the *Westminster Gazette*, or 'anybody else' he thought 'probable' (i. 405).

30 The *Westminster Gazette* published only 'French Sons of Germany' and 'Hail in the Rhineland', however, on 3 and 10 August; rejecting the others as too anti-German for a liberal paper which in May 1912 was 'campaigning for understanding of the

German point of view' (*TI* xxx). As DHL had told de la Mare, 'I don't know the papers a bit' (i. 405). Cf. *TI* xxvi and n. 7.

31 No page from what Jessie saw in April of this chapter has survived. All that we have, in the final manuscript of *Sons and Lovers*, are fourteen pages dating from October 1912 in Italy, including the title, and another fourteen dating from May 1912 in Waldbröl. See Helen Baron, '*Sons and Lovers*: The Surviving Manuscripts from Three Drafts Dated by Paper Analysis', *Studies in Bibliography*, xxxviii (1985), 327–8; and John Worthen – who first pointed out the significance of the papers in this chapter – 'Orts and Slarts', *Review of English Studies*, n.s., xlvi (1995), 36–7.

32 *A Memoir of D. H. Lawrence: The Betrayal*, by G. H. Neville, ed. Carl Baron (Cambridge, 1981), p. 44 ... Cambridge 1981), p. 44; *SL* xxxv–xxxix. As will be seen from their n. 27, the Barons and I have a friendly disagreement about the interpretation of George Neville's extraordinary statement that DHL was then 'busy with the final bringing into shape of *The Rainbow*', from which they conclude that the 'scene' must have been one in that novel (Neville, *Memoir*, pp. 44–5). This still seems to me most unlikely. The second version of 'The Sisters' (later to become *The Rainbow*) was begun in August 1913; whereas what DHL clearly *had* been busy with, up to April 1912, was the bringing into shape of 'Paul Morel', by their numbering IIIa. Perhaps this already contained a 'bedroom scene' that looked like causing trouble with Jessie, and contributed to Heinemann's rejection of the book as too 'outspoken'; or perhaps there was already some version of the scene in which Paul, in the bedroom, tries on Clara's stockings and knows he must have her: then creeps downstairs, and does. But no scene in *The Rainbow* which caused its 'fall' is imaginable as having originally been part of 'Paul Morel' IIIa. Anna Brangwen dancing nude in her pregnancy (the one DHL identified) is obviously ruled out. The magistrate concentrated his disapproval on the lesbian episodes but none takes place in a bedroom. The Barons' suggestion that DHL 'later claimed to have begun *The Rainbow* at about this time', i.e. April 1912, turns out to be his urging his agent J. B. Pinker in April 1915 to 'fight' for the novel because it represents 'nearly three years of hard work' (ii. 327). But DHL is trying to impress Pinker with the seriousness of the book, and he often exaggerated how long a work had taken him, for that reason. (He would make a similarly inflated claim for *Studies in Classic American Literature*.) The whole process of writing and revising *The Rainbow* had actually taken a little over two years (mid-March 1913–15) of extraordinary imaginative effort. But Neville seems to suggest that a version is being not merely begun or worked on but *finished* in April 1912! It is far more likely that he was momentarily confused – and he is not always reliable.

33 E.T. 210.

34 Roberts E373c (UT). For a description and chronology, see Helen Baron, 'Jessie Chambers' Plea for Justice to "Miriam"', *Archiv*, cxxxvii (1985), 63–84 (reprinted in *D. H. Lawrence: The Journal of the D. H. Lawrence Society*, iv, 1987–8, pp. 7–24).

35 This is presumably why he moved the Miriam and Agatha and the flower scenes back into the lad and girl chapter, somewhat awkwardly.

36 Letters to Professor Wincenty Lutoslawski, 23 June and 23 July 1935, 'The

Collected Letters of Jessie Chambers', ed. George J. Zytaruk, *DHLR*, xii (1979), 117, 114.

37 The 'Waldbröl' pages that survive in the 'Test' chapter describe Paul trying to persuade Miriam that they have been 'too fierce in our what they call purity', the cherry-picking scene and its love-making aftermath. It may have gone on to describe the scenes in the cottage, but again we cannot be sure. (What is certain is that the scene became explicit enough in its final version for Garnett to censor several details.) See *SL* xxxvii and Explanatory notes to 325:4, 328:40, 338:24 and 343:3, and Worthen, 'Orts and Slarts', pp. 37–8.

38 See (i. 232); Harry T. Moore, *The Priest of Love* (1974), p. 129; Delavenay 675–6. Alice Hall recurs in *Sons and Lovers*. On Ernest Humphreys see (i. 465).

39 See (i. 401, 403). Louie, too, had had her postcard from Trier (i. 397).

40 *Memoirs* 180 and John Worthen interview with Montague Weekley; *Memoirs* 179 (misdated: this must be May not April).

41 Maude Weekley (UT) reproached her for her 'strange views of life, selfish views . . . you have somehow missed the best in life and the best in love, for love that cannot suffer is unworthy of the name of love. Poor Frieda, make the best of the wreck and make for the light.' Lily Kipping, wife of Frederic Kipping, Professor of Chemistry at Nottingham, begged her to think of the motherless children, for 'if you don't think quickly remember you ought never to see them again – it would not in any sense be right for them', and implored her to come back, since 'No one knows' (UT); *MN* 188:18.

42 See (i. 399–407).

43 *MN* 139:13–140:16; 169:34–170:7. It is unclear whether Frieda had, or was now merely threatening to have a sexual relationship with von Henning. An affair is quite possible – and *MN* suggests that it happened, though that is not trustworthy evidence in itself. Indeed DHL's 'If you want Henning, . . . have him' rather implies that she had not (i. 404). She was clearly trying to make DHL jealous, for which a threat (e.g. 'I think I must give myself to him, he needs me so') might suffice; though DHL refused to succumb. (An embarrassed interview between the two men is described in *MN* 169:34–170:22,; but mentioned nowhere else). Von Henning was killed early in the First World War.

44 Cf. *WL* 119:15–22.

45 Cf. (i. 410, 412); *MN* 188:28–37; 198:2, 24–5. No early version of the poem exists (see Kinkead-Weekes 'The Shaping of *Look!*', pp. 215–16, 221–4); and the difficulty of regarding *Mr Noon* as corroboration in such cases is that the novel often seems to have been based on the poems, as against the evidence of the letters which were no longer available to DHL – and would have reminded him that their first morning was in Munich. The poem attributes the 'failure' to his inability to free himself from the past, 'those others'. His previous affairs may not have increased his sexual confidence – but pp. 793–4 note 104, 798–9 note 30; pp. 551, 850–1 note 32 on over-eager speculation about such unknowable matters.

46 See (i. 415); *MN* 199ff., 131:19–135:10; Frieda 60.

47 *Memoirs* 181; 'She Looks Back' (no early version), Kinkead-Weekes, 'The Shaping of *Look!*', pp. 215–16, 222–4.

48 *Memoirs* 355, 97; Lucas, *Frieda Lawrence*, pp. 29, 77. According to Barbara Barr, her father dismissed Ida Wilhelmy when he transferred his household to London. According to Montague Weekley, she left voluntarily to train as a nurse; cf. Janet Byrne, *A Genius for Living* (New York, 1995) pp. 117, 436 n. 14.

49 See (i. 421) and 'The Sisters II', *R* 473–9.

50 Cf. (i. 411). (In transcriptions pointed brackets (< >) are used for deletions; half brackets (¬) for additions.) For 'My Love, My Mother', see *EY* 411–12 and Illustration 42. The first stanzas read:

> My little love, my darling
> You were a doorway to me,
> You let me out of the confine   *I hate it*
> Into a vast countrie,
> Where people are crowded like thistles
> Yet are shapely and lovable to see.
>
> *You love it, you say!!!!*
>
> My little love, my dearest
> Twice you have borne me,
> Once from the womb, sweet mother.   *I hate it*
> Once from myself to be
> Free of the hearts of people
> Of each heart's home-life free.

Against the third stanza she writes '*Good God!!!!!*', before returning to '*I hate it*' against the final one.

51 Frieda 73, 54, 56, 23.

52 *MN* 213:32–214:29; cf. *SL* 257:7–258:10. Note the quite different treatments of the row in (i. 420), in the original poem 'Fireflies in the Corn', the later version in *Look!* and *MN*. 'In the Dark' and 'A Young Wife' however probably reflect her feelings fairly accurately, whenever written (*Poems* 221; 210–12; 215–16).

53 In Ascona in 1911 she must have become aware (if not before) of the pioneers of contemporary dance who forgathered there, Rudolph Laban, and the great expressionist dancer Marie Wigman.

54 Frieda 53, 61–2; *Memoirs* 92; David Garnett, *The Golden Echo* (1953) p. 245.

55 Frieda 23 on her 'sex in the head'; *Memoirs* 84–90; Green, *Von Richthofen Sisters*, pp. 47–8.

56 Weekley (b. 1865) was one of nine children of a middle-class couple; he had had a struggle to pay for his studies (a schoolmaster at 17) and had taken an external degree at the University of London, before winning a scholarship to Cambridge, then going on to study at the Sorbonne, and to take a Lektorship at Freiburg. He became Professor of Modern Languages at Nottingham in 1898, and met the 19-year-old Frieda when revisiting Freiburg that year. He was witty, charming and something new; she was his child-bride, to be protected and idolised. He had written several scholarly books on etymology, and (ironically) was about to publish his most

successful, *The Romance of Words*, as Frieda left him. Yet he was often absorbed in his work, and his tendency to sarcastic put-downs had grown as his wife had shown herself more and more independent minded. His students with whom he was popular, saw a very different man from the deeply hurt and rather hysterical one whose late Victorian standards the defection of his wife had outraged, and whose world she had turned upside down. He died in 1954.

57 Frieda 53–4.

58 Cf. (i. 425) and n. 3. See 'Reception', *The Trespasser*, ed. Elizabeth Mansfield (Cambridge, 1981), pp. 23–8.

59 'A Bag of Cakes' (E68.2) was revised into 'The Christening' for *The Smart Set* (1913), with a new ending (*PO* xlviii–xlix, 172–80). The birth of Neville's illegitimate child in 1906 dwelt in DHL's imagination – he thanked God he had been saved from that, on hearing the news (E.T. 125–6) – and the situation will recur in his play *The Daughter-in-Law* and 'Fanny and Annie' as well as the false alarm in *Mr Noon*. The woman in 'Once—!' (E296) is clearly modelled on Nusch; but the half-dressed flamboyance (like an Egon Schiele picture) is reminiscent of Frieda, and the distinction between romanticised passion 'once' and the enduring commitment the 'cocotte' has never known is that of DHL's letters to Frieda from Waldbröl (final version, *LAH* 152–60). 'Delilah and Mr. Bircumshaw' (E90.5) is about how a woman's mockery can destroy a man's self-respect (*LAH* 143–51). 'The Fly in the Ointment' (E135.5) is about the disturbing effect on the schoolteacher of the irruption of a street-youth into his world (*LAH* 49–53). The main interest of the 1912 versions is however negative – to show the extraordinary deepening, by contrast, of the stories he would write in 1913–14, including the new end of 'The Christening'.

60 The ten early versions, probably written in Bavaria, of poems in *Look! We Have Come Through!*, were: <earlier titles thus> [added to the sequence after 1917 thus] 'Don Juan', 'Ballad of a Wilful <Wayward> Woman'; 'Bei Hennef'; 'On the Balcony' <'Illicit'>, 'Green', 'River Roses' (originally a set of four, one discarded from *Look!*), 'Gloire de Dijon' 'Roses on the Breakfast Table', 'A Youth Mowing' <The Mowers> and 'Fireflies in the Corn'. All except 'Bei Hennef', 'On the Balcony' and 'Green' were significantly changed in 1917 – and those, too, acquire new significance within the sequence. (Cf. with the versions in *Look!*, the original 'All of Roses', Frieda 67–8.) To these we should add 'The Young Soldier With Bloody Spurs' sent to Garnett on 13 August (i. 434–7). There may well have been more in the brown 'Tagebuch' of Frieda's which was subsequently lost. The trouble is that we cannot tell how many, or which, these may have been.

61 Frieda's father dreaded his daughters marrying either a Jew or an Englishman, but Else did one and Frieda the other, twice (Lucas, *Frieda Lawrence*, p. 12, from a BBC broadcast by Barbara Barr, 14 November 1961). Anti-Semitism was widespread in Bavaria.

62 Cf. (i. 388). Information on Garnett from George Jefferson *Edward Garnett: A Life in Literature* (1982) and Carolyn C. Heilbrun, *The Garnett Family* (1961).

63 Sallie Hopkin, McLeod, and his sister Ada (who, however, was rather hostile; i. 440) and Garnett (i. 448).

64 The fragments are reproduced in *Sons and Lovers: A Facsimile of the Manuscript*, ed. Mark Schorer (Berkeley, 1977); and cf. Helen Baron, '*Sons and Lovers*: The Surviving Manuscripts', pp. 313–23.

65 *SL* 15:7–8, 19–21.

66 *The Golden Echo*, pp. 241–3. The middle classness of Garnett and the 'neo-pagans' (so called by Virginia Woolf), evident in the full quotation and its attitudes towards the working man, is illuminated by Paul Delany, '*Mr Noon* and Modern Paganism', *DHLR*, xx (1988), 258.

67 'Barmaid' is an echo of the Baron, see Frieda 58; and the charges had their comic side, since nobody was less likely than Frieda to clean DHL's boots and empty his slops – but cf. Nehls, i. 503, for Cecily Lambert's surprise at DHL emptying Frieda's chamberpot.

68 *Complete Plays*, 288–96; *MN* 217:20–219:34, 223:14–224:21; (i. 427).

69 *MN* 238–86 is so accurate on this journey that DHL may conceivably have kept notes. I have therefore, in what follows, drawn on its travel account with a confidence partly confirmed by experience, and it may be taken as the source of detail unless otherwise specified. See also F. I. Owen, 'Lawrentian Places: A Chapel and a Hay-Hut Among the Mountains: 1971', *Human World*, xi (May 1973), 46–9. The original chapel, now used for storage, is still to be found among the trees some distance away from the new one (which contains a Christus in a red-flannel coat). The mistake leaving the Sterzing Jaufenhaus is easily explicable on the spot. Cf. 'A Chapel Among the Mountains' and 'A Hay-Hut Among the Mountains *TI* 27–42.

70 *MN* 247:6, 248:11.

71 See (i. 441); *MN* 249–54. For the earliest known version of 'Meeting Among the Mountains', see Frieda 70–1. The Christus of the Klamm is described also in 'Christs in the Tyrol' and 'The Crucifix Across the Mountains', *TI* 44:21–38, 96:14–97:12. 'Tuxtal' is Frieda's location.

72 Cf. (i. 440); (i. 442–3). The idea of Lake Garda may have been appealing because of Goethe's praise of its beauty, or perhaps Ezra Pound's description of Sirmione as 'the earthly paradise', after his visit in 1910 (i. 165).

73 *Golden Echo*, pp. 244–6; (i. 476).

74 *Golden Echo* pp. 240, 223, 246; *MN* 257:20–36.

75 *TI* 96:21–2; *MN* 262:37–40; 266:21.

76 *MN* 272:33. The 'Christus im Elend' at Wieden (in fact shown 'in suffering' after the flagellation, i.e. *pace* DHL, *before* the crucifixion) is described in 'Christs in the Tyrol' and 'The Crucifix Across the Mountains', *TI* 46:21–8; 99:1–32. (The inn was probably the Gasthof Elefant.)

77 *MN* 275:1–2; 276:19. Bunny Garnett thrice confirmed the episode, having been told of it by Hobson, before the publication of *Mr Noon*: in his 'Memoir' to the Memoir Club (kindly lent to me by Richard Garnett); 'Frieda and Lawrence', *D. H. Lawrence: Novelist, Poet, Prophet*, ed. Stephen Spender (1974), p. 39; and *Great Friends* (1979), p. 81. Bunny's story of Frieda having sex with a wood-cutter in Icking, however, which first makes its appearance in the second of these, is much more dubious, and is quite likely to have been invented (or threatened) by Frieda to

impress Bunny (or DHL) with her readiness to behave as she liked, whenever she liked. She was however very conscious of her rank, and when a sexy wood-cutter in San Gaudenzio did give her the eye, she appears to have reacted with some hauteur ('The Dance', *TI* 169:24–170:32), though that admittedly is DHL's story. There is no evidence that she had ever had sex with somebody she did not already know, and while (in her sisters' eyes and her own) free love might be acceptable with a Dowson, Gross, Frick, von Henning or Hobson, would she risk gossip about such an affair with a peasant, spreading within a few miles of Else's house? Peasants are canny folk, and apparently nymphomaniac ladies emerging nude from a river are liable to have families who can make trouble.

78 *MN* 276:27–277:5.

79 (i. 445–7). In 1901, Frieda and Ernest were 'learning Italian in the evenings together' (*Memoirs* 166) – but it is very doubtful that she had got far, or kept it up. DHL was a much quicker learner, but knew only a word or two yet.

80 Frieda 66, 72; (i. 455–6); *MN* 287:1.

81 Frieda 72.

82 See (i. 452, 455, 456, 464); Frieda 72.

83 See (i. 453–4); (i. 460); (i. 474); (i. 483) (though DHL muddled the schoolteacher's name); (i. 466); (i. 474).

84 Frieda's 'carelessness' at this time did once rebound. She was reading *Anna Karenina*, 'in a sort of "How to be happy though livanted" spirit' and finding Anna 'very like herself, only inferior' (i. 463). It seemed a good idea to her to send the book to Weekley, but she carelessly left in it a letter from Dowson saying 'If you wanted to run away, with someone, why didn't you run away with me?' Weekley promptly sent this to DHL. (Lucas, *Frieda Lawrence*, p. 90; information from Barbara Barr.)

85 Cf. (i. 448); e.g. 'I would have gladly been tortured for you, and laughed, and now I'll do more, I'll live' (i. 475–6).

86 *TI* 43:10–11.

87 On Schwabing, see Green, *Von Richthofen Sisters*, pp. 88–99; 'The Captain's Doll,' *Fox* 78:25–6 and note, and *Memoirs* 83; Green, *Mountain of Truth* p. 36.

88 *MN* 117:6–22; see (i. 477, 549).See also note 72 above.

89 Cf. (i. 36–7, 39–41) from 1907.

90 *TI* 44:14–15; 43:14; 46:21, 27–8. It dates from the seventeenth century.

91 *TI* 45:10–11, 16; 45:28; 44:3, 17–21.

92 *EY* 10–74, drawing also on Roy Spencer's discoveries (*D. H. Lawrence Country*, 1979); 152–63, 246–53, 262–7. See p. 47.

93 Frieda 74.

94 DHL had begun to see, as early as 1910, that his mother's love had damaged him; and had told the poet Rachel Annand Taylor that 'We have loved each other, almost with a husband and wife love, as well as filial and maternal ... It has been rather terrible, and has made me, in some respects, abnormal ... Nobody can have the soul of me. My mother has had it, and nobody can have it again' (i. 190–1). What Frieda's knowledge of Freud through Gross may have contributed, however, was the idea that this was not abnormal, but a widespread condition among young men.

95 The same difficulty about dating poems affects those in *Look!* purportedly dated from Lake Garda. 'Service of All the Dead' ('Giorno dei Morti') was sent to Edward Marsh a year later (ii. 106) and published in the *New Statesman* on 15 November 1913. The closely associated 'All Souls' shares the 'flame' image of the first encounter between the Morels, and DHL's letter to Collings of January 1913 (i. 503–4), but was *not* among those he sent to Marsh in 1913. 'From the Italian Lakes', the third and more sentimental poem to his mother, occurs in E320.2, a manuscript of 1916, and was first published as 'Everlasting Flowers' in *New Poems* (1918), and inserted into the sequence only in 1928. It would however seem to date from the first snow on the mountains in November 1912 – which would make the dating of 'All Souls' to the same month seem unlikely. It is almost certainly later, perhaps after 1913. The rest is conjecture, though the first part of 'Sunday Afternoon in Italy' is reminiscent of the travel-sketches. Frieda's later claim (Frieda 74) that 'While we were at Villa Igea Lawrence wrote also "Twilight in Italy," and most of the poems from "Look, we have come through!"' is almost certainly mistaken in both cases. In December (see pp. 73–4, 772 note 8, 777 note 55) DHL told Garnett that he was unable to write poetry because of the tension – which by the sequence's own account did not lift until February. 'Purity', the original version of 'Paradise Re-Entered' was sent to Marsh on 28 October 1913 (ii. 94), as was an early and much inferior version of 'Song of a Man Who Is Loved'.

96 E.T. 202; letter to Lutoslawski, 23 June 1935 ('The Collected Letters', p. 114).

97 E.T. 203.

98 Neville, *Memoir*, pp. 772–5.

99 'Paul Morel' II, E373d (UT) and see Helen Baron's study of the papers in '*Sons and Lovers*: The Surviving Manuscripts', pp. 303, 317; E.T. 202 and *EY* 253–61.

100 Frieda remembered the date of their meeting as in April, which cannot be right. It seems to have been on a Sunday, warm enough for the windows to the garden to be open; and Alice Dax in 1935 claimed DHL told her about Frieda 'the day after the event' (*Memoirs* 245). The Cambridge Edition of the *Letters* suggests Sunday 17 March when DHL is known to have been in Nottingham (i. 374 and n. 4). John Worthen (*EY* 562–3) presents all the evidence, and has discovered that 'Of all the possible Sundays in March, Sunday 3 March stands out for its particularly brilliant weather ... "a typical April day"' (*Nottingham Guardian*, 4 March 1912, p. 4)' – which would explain Frieda's error. He concludes that DHL may originally have refused Weekley's invitation for 3 March because he was going to the Daxes at Shirebrook; but then changed his mind, postponed the visit for thirty-six hours, and told Alice immediately, as she reported.

101 *SL* 464:37.

102 E.T. 213. Easter Monday was 9 April. There is a problem about the date of the completion of the manuscript: i.e. whether Jessie had in fact (as she implies) read all of it before 25 March (E.T. 205); as against DHL's letter to de la Mare on 13 March when he expects to be finished 'in a month' (i. 375), and his letter to Garnett on 3 April when he says he will finish the novel 'this week' (i. 381). DHL certainly got back what Jessie had read on 1 April, and first announces that the book is

finished on 11 April (i. 383). Jessie never mentions the death of Mrs Morel, which is suprising. The discrepancies can be variously explained; cf. *SL* xxxvii–xxxviii, which accepts Jessie's account by assuming that DHL's statement to Garnett means 'will finish when I have looked through it, and have decided what to do about Jessie's criticisms'. We cannot, however, in any case, assume that Jessie read the ending we now have.

103 Frieda 74. Now there is no doubting the effect of the death he had decided to portray: 'when he wrote his mother's death he was ill and his grief made me ill too' (ibid.). Brigit Patmore also remembered Frieda exclaiming: 'How I suffered, Lorenzo, when you killed your mother' ('A Memoir of Frieda Lawrence', *A D. H. Lawrence Miscellany*, ed. Harry T. Moore, 1961, p. 137). The evidence of DHL's distress is visible in the handwriting of the manuscript, see E373e; cf. Schorer, *Facsimile*, p. 522. DHL told the Waterfields in 1913 that the mercy killing was true, see pp. 101 and 783 note 114.

104 *TI* 44:19–21.

Chapter Two: New Utterance

1 A note on the letter by Louie (in UN) shows that she only discovered Frieda's identity from a friend of Ada.

2 The pictures seem to have been intended for McLeod, who was told to choose two, and the Krenkows. Three seem identifiable: *Italian Scene With Boat*, *Landscape with Figure*, and *Lago di Garda*.

3 Pseudonym of William Hale White, *The Revolution in Tanner's Lane* (1887): 'How good he is! – so just, so harmonious', and 'I used to think him dull, but now I see he is so just and plucky and sound ...' (i. 481, 482). McLeod had also sent Edith Wharton's *The House of Mirth* (1905), which DHL admired.

4 Cf. letter to Curtis Brown, 4 April 1921 (iii. 701). It is interesting to wonder what difference it might have made had DHL accepted Brown's agency in 1912 rather than 1921. He had also been approached by J. B. Pinker in November 1912 (i. 478).

5 This was much more than selfish rationalisation. Thinking about the hidden price of the 'heroic' sacrifice Else wanted him to make, would lead to the reflections on the second of Christ's two Great Commandments in the 'Foreword to *Sons and Lovers*' in January; see p. 62.

6 See Constance to Edward Garnett, 7 April 1913 (Eton) on 'the massive impenetrability of his egoism' (Richard Garnett, *Constance Garnett: A Heroic Life*, 1991, p. 274); and Edward's opinion implied in DHL's 'I notice you are rather sarcastic about him. I don't think he's so bad' (i. 489).

7 (i. 520); Hobson left on 2 January (i. 500): DHL at last, in this letter, tells May Holbrook he is living with Frieda. He also tells her Hobson 'was awful'. They seem to have paid 1 lira per night for him at the hotel (i. 520).

8 Since however DHL said in December 1912 that he was unable to write poetry at a time of tension (i. 488), the poems which describe the renewal between New Year and Valentine's day 1913 may not have been written then – though they are likely to

be faithful to the experience of 'coming through' a period of stress and conflict at that time. The idea of death and rebirth through sexual relationship is not however fully articulated until late 1914.

9 Weekley's petition was filed on 11 February. It was agreed that formal evidence of DHL and Frieda's adultery would be provided by Signora Samuelli of the Hotel Cervo. Robert Garnett was senior partner in Darley, Cumberland & Co. Though Frieda consulted him on her visit to London in Summer 1913, she was not represented at the eventual hearing. It may have been felt by then, after the court order taken out against her for waylaying the children without permission, that she had no hope of being granted access.

10 She had separated from her husband, Per Johan Hugo Almgren, in 1912. For Constance Garnett's opinion see her letter to Edward, Monday [?24 February] 1913 (Eton) (R. Garnett, *Constance Garnett* p. 273). Tony had allowed Bunny to have sex with her when he was 19 (D. Garnett, *Golden Echo*, pp. 226–7), and cf. (i. 475), where the 'X' Frieda discusses is probably Tony.

11 D. Garnett, *Golden Echo* pp. 226–7; C. to E. Garnett, Monday 31 March 1913 (R. Garnett, *Constance Garnett*, p. 273).

12 Worthen, 'Orts and Slarts', pp. 33–40, explains what might seem the apparently outrageous decision to send the proofs to Jessie, who would undoubtedly be deeply hurt by them – especially since, as she said to Helen Corke in a letter of [16 March 1913] (given this date in (i. 527 n. 1), not [23 March] as in 'The Collected Letters', p. 27), 'nothing now can be altered'. Once it is realised that what was now 'The Test on Miriam' had been wholly rewritten, first in Waldbröl and then in Italy, since she had seen the manuscript in late March 1912, the decision begins to look at least somewhat more honourable. Though DHL had been ruthless in the writing of the book, he could not be unaware of how he was exposing her to people who knew them both, and indeed risking her reputation as a respectable schoolteacher. She could not be allowed to come upon his book like any other member of the reading public, in a bookshop. He wrote to his sister, to whom he had asked Jessie to send on the proofs, that she would immediately see, when she read them 'why I sent them to J' (i. 531). He was not however able to foresee the nature and finality of Jessie's response – a curious blindness to the possible effect of his ruthlessness, which would be repeated in other cases.

13 *Memoirs* 97–9. Frieda's memoirs (as opposed to the correspondence in the volume) are part fictionalised, but there is no reason to doubt how deeply this disappointment affected her.

14 'The Collected Letters', p. 27.

15 Cf. E.T. 220:

> I knew it far too well to have any desire to read it again. Indeed, I didn't dare to risk a second reading, for I was by no means sure of my capacity to recover a second time. I did glance through some pages, however, hoping that in the interval his outlook might have mellowed and led him to soften some harshness. But I found both story and mood alike unchanged.

Though she was not one deliberately to deceive, this cannot be true as it stands. The hurt was such, however, as to make perfectly explicable, after the lapse of twenty-two years, the conflation of her response in 1912 with that of 1913, into a fused sense of betrayal and brutality. In 1935 she told Professor Lutoslawski that her 'association' with DHL had been one they 'each regarded as binding and sacred ... When, later on, he called it a "test" and pretended that the "test" had failed, he seemed to me inhuman. He killed himself in me' ('The Collected Letters', p. 117). That had not been so in 1912; cf. also Worthen, 'Orts and Slarts'. It is also significant, in the light of her 1935 criticisms of the book, that she never seems to have taken in the extent of the critique of Mrs Morel in the novel, or the extent of the revision in that respect of what she had previously seen. She *may* not even have read the original ending in 1912 (see p. 771 note 102), let alone the new one now.

16 Cf. *SL* 64:38–40; (i. 406).

17 'Nottingham and the Mining Countryside', *P* 134.

18 Ernest Collings (1882–1932) had written to DHL in November 1912 in admiration of his first two novels, and had sent a small book of translations (1910) from Sappho illustrated by himself (i. 468). Later he sent some drawings and manuscript poems (of which DHL recalled three lines in 'Spring Morning'). DHL discussed these in (i. 472–3, 503, 518–19). Collings dedicated his next volume of drawings, *Outlines* (1914), to DHL: see p. 787 note 32. In 1913, DHL gave him a set of revised proofs of *Sons and Lovers* in gratitude for his sketch for the cover, which Duckworth did not use, to DHL's embarrassment (i. 528–9, 535, 539, 547). They first met in Summer 1913.

19 'Sooner murder an infant in its cradle than nurse unacted desires' (William Blake, 'Proverbs of Hell', *The Marriage of Heaven and Hell*, l. 55). DHL was probably aware of Nietzsche's valuation of the 'blood' over 'thy little rationality' since his reading of Nietzsche in Croydon in 1910: cf. *Thus Spake Zarathustra*, tr. Thomas Common (Edinburgh, 1906) Part I, pp. 28–9, 33: 'There is more rationality in thy body than in thy best wisdom ... Of all that is written, I love only what a person hath written with his blood.' Christopher Heywood, ' "Blood-Consciousness" and the Pioneers of the Reflex and Ganglionic Systems', *D. H. Lawrence: New Studies*, ed. Heywood, (1987), pp. 104–23 suggested that DHL may also have known of the ideas of Xavier Bichat, who emphasised the importance of the heart above the brain, and of the blood as the vital intermediary. Though the link with DHL seems to me tenuous (through the Nottinghamshire-born physiologist Marshall Hall, a biography of whom was in the Library of the Mechanics Institute of Eastwood in which DHL read voraciously; E.T. 93); or alternatively through Bichat's German translator Rudolf Boehm and Otto Gross), it is interesting to note the coincidence of such ideas.

20 E373e and Schorer, *Facsimile*, p. 13; cf. *SL* 593, entry to 18:13. Going through the proofs in February, DHL changed the first sentence to 'She was a puritan, like her father, high-minded and really stern', strengthening the contrast between sensuous vitality and thought/spirit.

21 E59.3, published as ' "Burns Novel" fragments', *LAH* 200–11.

22 Lockhart in his *Life of Burns* (1823; Everyman Library edition, 1907) p. 10, claimed

that Mary Campbell was 'the object of by far the deepest passion that ever Burns knew'.

23 *LAH* 209:20–1.

24 E209a, *LG* 343–58.

25 E373d.

26 *LG* 343:2–3.

27 *LG* 357:17–18.

28 Written 15–16 July 1911, rejected by the *Century*; see *PO* xl. Garnett probably still had the story at this time.

29 Cf. (i. 495), (i. 505); cf. 'The Theatre' in both 'By the Lago di Garda' and *Twilight in Italy* (*TI* 69–80, 133–53). The performances took place between 28 December and 16 January. The D'Annunzio play was *La Fiaccola sotto il Moggio* (The Light Under the Bushel) (1905).

30 'The Daughter-in-Law', Act IV (*Complete Plays*, p. 267).

31 Letters to Rev. Robert Reid (October–December 1907) (i. 36–7, 39–41); and to Ada in April 1911 when she 'dipped into unbelief' after the death of their mother, (i. 248), and see (i. 255–6).

32 *SL* 467–73..

33 *SL* 467:23–3; 470:40–471:5; 470:3–4, 471:6–9; 472:12–13, 35; 473:1, 5, 12–14.

34 *Rhythm* had been launched in Paris in June 1911 by two Oxford undergraduates, Michael Sadleir providing the money, with John Middleton Murry (b. 1889) as editor. He had been joined by Katherine Mansfield (née Kathleen Beauchamp, b. 1888 in New Zealand) with whom he was now living, but the magazine – though it had succeeded in attracting contributions of a high calibre, among them the first English reproductions of Picasso – was in financial difficulties, and KM warned DHL that they could not afford to pay contributors. It was replaced by the *Blue Review* in May 1913.

35 In July 1909. DHL clearly associated Forster with Pan when he corresponded with him in late 1915, though Forster himself had bid farewell to his Pan phase when in *Howards End* (1910) he mused 'Of Pan and the elemental forces the public has heard a little too much' (chap. XIII). In *The Longest Journey* (1907) Rickie's story is allowed to guy 'Other Kingdom' (' "Oh Lord, she's a Dryad!" cried Rickie in great disgust. "She's turned into a tree!" '). For the argument for dating 'The Overtone' in early 1913 rather than 1924, see my article in forthcoming *DHLR*.

36 DHL in his early twenties had been a regular visitor at the home of Willie and Sallie Hopkin in Devonshire Drive, Eastwood, pictured (humorously) at the beginning of *Mr Noon*. There the Eastwood Debating Society used to meet, and there DHL delivered his paper on 'Art and the Individual', in 1908. William Edward (1862–1951) was a noted socialist, and the couple played a part in encouraging the intellectual development of the young DHL, and had 'led' him 'over some frontiers' (iv. 327). Sarah Annie (1867–1922) became the older woman he could most trust for sympathetic advice. In 1911, during his engagement to Louie Burrows, he had asked Sallie to tell him 'where I am wrong – since you put your head on one side and close your eyes so shrewdly' (i. 261) . He inscribed her copy of *Love Poems* to 'my very

close friend' (Eastwood Public Library). But both in 'The Overtone' and in *MN* he draws characters outwardly resembling her as sexually unawakened. Their daughter Enid was born in 1896.

37 E298; *SM* 5:4, 31, 35–6; 5:37–6:1; 7:36–7; 10:37–9; 12:5; 13:9, 11–12, 14; 16:12.

38 See (i. 512, 517); cf. *SL* xlix-l, summarising Garnett's cuts, which shortened the manuscript by 2,050 lines, about a tenth. Most of the reducing down was in the first eleven chapters, and there was some light censorship later, mainly in 'Passion' and 'The Test on Miriam' – and some more, in the Radfords' house, in proof. The cuts are readily identifiable in the Textual apparatus. From chapter 3, Garnett cut a number of 'scenes in the life of William, which serve to diversify William's role as a precedent for Paul. They include William's bantering exchanges with his mother, his domineering reaction to her scorn of his girlfriends, his pride in his own physique, his amiable patronage of his younger brother, his impatience as a teacher' (*SL* xlix). Garnett also cut the four-page description of the meetings of Miriam and Paul in the Bestwood Library.

39 Published in February. DHL saw those in the *Morning Post*, the *Daily News* (both rather ambivalent; i. 528) and *The Times Literary Supplement*, by de La Mare, which he thought 'very cautious' (i. 530). For later and more complimentary reviews by Edward Thomas and Ezra Pound, see Draper 51–4.

40 The main circulating libraries, Mudie's, Boots and Smiths, could make a difference of 2,000–3,000 copies to the sales of novels which they agreed to circulate. Their initial reluctance to take *Sons and Lovers* undoubtedly explained its disappointing sales.

41 I.e. 'French Sons of Germany', 'Hail in the Rhineland' and 'Christs in the Tyrol' (22 March 1913).

42 See (i. 513–14), and cf. *TI* 51–80, whose editor dates the composition in mid-March, (xxxvi and n. 41). 'By the Lago di Garda' essays (E294.5a) are written on the same paper as 'The Overtone', and a letter of 22 March (i. 529–31, Letter 560).

43 It is interesting to compare DHL's accounts, particularly of the dance and the Capelli family, with those by Tony Cyriax in *Among Italian Peasants* (1919), which confirm many details but are greatly inferior in animation and descriptive power. See also chapter 5, pp. 268–9.

44 The Capelli family would be recalled in 'Paolo and Maria' in *TI*; and though Faustino ('Il Duro') happens not to be mentioned in (i. 535–6), he was among the handsome men who stopped by San Gaudenzio to drink (he was Maria's cousin), and might well have struck the author of 'The Overtone' as one of the fauns of Pan. In *TI* too is 'The Dance'. If DHL had written these experiences up now, he would probably have included one from six weeks earlier, when he and Frieda had gone 10 miles up the lake to Campione, where a drunken fellow took them up a fantastic path which climbed the gorge (i. 515). Having scared Frieda, he threatened to throw DHL into the water when he tried to get rid of him! At the next village inn in Gardola di Tignale, however, they met the landlord later described in 'John', heard the brass band playing for the major who had returned from Tripoli (he is promoted to Colonel in *TI*) and met John. DHL could conceivably have written early drafts – but there is no evidence at all that he did.

45 The reshaping is particularly evident in the rewriting of the 'By the Lago di Garda' sketches, and in the treatment of the Capellis (new in *TI*; cf. *Among Italian Peasants*) and 'Il Duro' (cf. Andrew Schofield in *The Rainbow*). The assertion in 'John' that they 'knew [the Colonel] afterwards' and the account of his death (*TI* 181:38–182:2) seem pure invention or hearsay at best. Paul Eggert annnotates other evidence of reshaping in 1915: see *TI* 292–3.

46 *Memoirs* 194.

47 Reading this made DHL 'so miserable I had hardly the energy to walk out of the house for two days' (i. 551). Jessie believed that 'The Miriam part of [his] novel is a slander, a fearful treachery. David has selected every point which sets off Miriam at a disadvantage, and he has interpreted her every word and action, and thought in the light of Mrs. Morel's hatred of her.' Her novel, originally written in 1911, but rewritten in Winter 1912–13 became therefore not only therapy and self-defence but a deliberate rejoinder which she 'always intended' DHL should see, 'I feel it a matter of honour' ([16 March 1913], 'The Collected Letters', pp. 27–8). The title is from Milton's 'Lycidas' (1637): 'the rathe primrose that forsaken dies' (l. 142). DHL has returned more fierily to the original contention over 'Lad-and-Girl Love', accusing her of seeing only what was true for her – the mirror image of her complaint, which he had partly accepted in revising the young Miriam (but not the young Paul) – and to her attitude to sexuality which might, if his reading was accurate, bear out 'The Test on Miriam'. (That, certainly, was where the main hurt lay for him.) It is impossible to tell, since Jessie destroyed her manuscript.

48 *Memoirs* 194.

49 No play by Stanislaw Wyspianski had yet been translated into English in 1913, so she must have been reading him in German.

50 It was no mere holiday chalet: there were Persian rugs on the wooden floor and Dürer etchings (ii. 63).

51 'The Georgian Renaissance', *P* 306–7 (titled '*Georgian Poetry: 1911–1912*'). On DHL's appearance in both the 'Georgian' and the 'Imagist' anthologies, see chapter 3, pp. 130, 134–5.

52 E441a, *R* 463–70.

53 *R* 467:17; 466:40–467:1; 466:12; 464:22–3, 468:14–18, 470:38.

54 Poems 234; 237; 235–6.

55 DHL said in December that he was unable to write poetry then. 'To write poetry one has to let oneself fuse in the current – but I daren't' (i. 488) – which might suggest that the poems leading up to New Year were not contemporary. It is interesting to note that the original title of 'Valentine's Night' ('Candlemas') again shows an interest in Catholic liturgy and custom, being a festival which DHL would not have known about from either his own Nonconformist or Louie's Anglican background. 'Spring Morning' echoes a poem Collings sent to him in November 1912. Only 'Paradise Re-Entered' of the others is known to have existed in a contemporary version ('Purity'), again much changed in revision. 'Coming Awake' was probably new in *New Poems* 1920, and was added to the sequence only in 1928. 'Rabbit Scared in the Night' seems related to a chapter in *WL* 1916–17,

rather than to the compassion of the lad rescuing the rabbit in the 'Burns Novel' fragments.

56 Cf. *WP* 207–13 where, despite Cyril's overall narration, the scene in the orchard has to be in the third person.

57 E268a; *LAH* 161:18–19; 165:40; 166:4–5.

58 Delavenay's treatment of this story (151–4) is an example of what has given attempts to relate literature to life a bad name. He assumes that the story is straightforward autobiographical evidence, rather than an imaginative exploration of questions raised in life. (Similarly, he uses 'The White Stocking' as evidence that DHL had begun to beat his wife – when all that can be responsibly inferred from the fiction is that he can imagine wanting to, and why.) After discounting the possibility of imaginative heightening, drama goes next: the focus is entirely on Peter, without reference to any interactive conflict. It is assumed that the accusations made by Paula against Moest are, simply, true of DHL. There seems no awareness of contradiction between the maturity implied in such self-scrutiny and the condescension of the scholar-critic who charges it with immaturity. It seems more realistic to suppose that it was because being with Frieda had broken through the detachment, the self-enclosure and the English reserve he had learned to dread in himself, and had helped him to begin to overcome the effect on him of his love for his mother, that he proved capable of self-examination to the depth of 1912–13. As to Paula's charge that Moest was unable to love, it was certainly one that Frieda made, and that DHL worried about – see Frieda in rage on his poem to his mother (see pp. 21 and 767 note 50) – but see her also on his 'generosity' of commitment (Frieda 35), which was obviously true, and in contrast with her lack of it. He also found much to quarrel with in her idea of 'love', that slippery word.

59 E268a; *LAH* 170:17–18; 166:32–3, 38; 167:9–18; 172:16–17, 20; 173:13–15; 177:3–5; 180:20, 28–9.

60 A note in the Baron's diary during the Franco-Prussian War reads 'Heinrich drunk; I beat him' (Lucas, *Frieda Lawrence*, p. 8).

61 Quotation from *English Review*, xvii (June 1914), p. 312; cf. revision for *PO* chapter 3, pp. 138–9.

62 Quotations from manuscript, E326.5 (pp. 2, 3, 2), cut by Norman Douglas for *English Review*, xviii (August 1914); it was later revised into 'The Prussian Officer' for *PO*. DHL's title came from the aria of Handel's *Samson* (1743), setting Milton's *Samson Agonistes*. He objected to the later title (chosen by Garnett), as the regiment is Bavarian.

63 *P* 312–13 Cf. DHL's disagreement with Hueffer's Flaubertian sense of form (i. 417), and his defence (to Garnett and implicitly de la Mare) of the 'form' of *Sons and Lovers* and its development 'slow like growth' (i. 476–7). See also Frieda to Garnett (i. 479), obviously coming out of her discussions with DHL. This review is an important turning point, being a conscious break with his mentors and (as it happened) with the whole modernist movement.

64 Information from Jefferson, *Edward Garnett*, pp. 176–7, R. Garnett, *Constance Garnett* and C. Garnett's letters (Eton).

65 *Golden Echo*, p. 254 (Nehls, i. 196–7).

66 Constance to E. Garnett, Saturday (5 July) (R. Garnett, *Constance Garnett*, p. 275).

67 Nehls, i. 198. The letter and telegram mentioned in (ii. 37) must have been from Weekley's sister Maude in anger, warning Frieda off, and threatening reprisals after she had told her brother. Both may have been sent to Germany, lacking an English address. Frieda never received the telegram, but there was time for the letter to be redirected and reach them at the Cearne.

68 Records of the High Court, Divorce and Admiralty Division; also Nehls, i. 197–8; *Memoirs* 99–101.

69 Nehls i. 198; *Memoirs* 101.

70 Records of the High Court, Divorce and Admiralty Division.

71 Letter to KM, to be published in *Letters*, viii; (ii. 46).

72 Constance to E. Garnett, [7 and 8 July] (R. Garnett, *Constance Garnett*, pp. 275–6).

73 A letter from Frieda to Frieda Gross from Lerici in September 1913 (Hoffman catalogue) reads: 'Think, I was in Margate, had to think so very much about when I was there with Ernst and the children.'

74 *BTW* 261 (Nehls, i. 198); cf. *Reminiscences* (1933), p. 33. KM was not 'waiting to be divorced', and indeed showed no signs of wanting to marry JMM for several years to come. (They were married in 1918.)

75 See F. A. Lea, *The Life of John Middleton Murry* (1959).

76 Frieda 86.

77 Antony Alpers, *The Life of Katherine Mansfield* (1980) is the standard biography; information on KM's medical condition (and much else) in Claire Tomalin, *Katherine Mansfield: A Secret Life* (1987); also Jeffrey Meyers, *Katherine Mansfield* (1978). Letter from KM to Orage, 9 February 1921.

78 Christopher Hassall, *Edward Marsh* (1959).

79 Nicola Beauman, *Cynthia Asquith* (1987).

80 *Remember and Be Glad* (1952), pp. 133–6 (Nehls, i. 207–9); Frieda 86. Through their new friends they also met Professor Sir Walter Raleigh, now of Oxford, and his wife (ii. 51; Nehls, i. 209). Cynthia describes how they were 'mutually fascinated', talked and talked, and how Raleigh wrote afterwards: 'How very, very much I liked that poet and his wife – a first-rate poet's wife.'

81 Cf. JMM, *Reminiscences*, p. 33; Beatrice Glenavy, *Today We Will Only Gossip* (1964), p. 78.

82 Nehls, i. 210.

83 Frieda 85.

84 See *SL* lxiii–lxxi and Draper 58–60. Lascelles Abercrombie, one of the better known reviewers, was critical of its mixture of hate in love; for DHL's reaction see (ii. 177). But the main exception was Ethel Colburn Mayne in the *Nation*, who praised Part I but reacted strongly against 'the incessant scenes of sexual passion' in Part II, the 'morbid brooding on the flesh', the 'ever-hot and heavy lustfulness' (*SL* lxix); for DHL's reaction – 'Fussy old woman' – see (ii. 40, 47).

85 The 1913 revision of 'The Shadow in the Rose Garden' is in some respects similar to Joyce's great story 'The Dead'. Brenda Maddox has recently argued (*The Married*

Man, pp. 165–71 and Appendix 1) that these may derive from DHL having seen Joyce's story at the Cearne. This is not impossible, since *Dubliners* is known to have been making the rounds of publishers (and therefore publishers' readers) at the time. It would however have been a remarkable coincidence, especially as Garnett was working in London while DHL and Frieda were staying in his country house. (They saw him only briefly on their way to Kingsgate.) The resemblances affect only the new frame to the original story, and look much less impressive when replaced in their substantially different contexts. DHL needed no help from Joyce to think of setting his earlier romantic and melodramatic tale within a harsher frame: the realisation by a rather complacent husband of a sexual affair in his wife's past – with, in DHL's story, a lover now 'out of his mind' – and the consequent jealous disturbance and anger at how little he has known her, or their relationship. Given that idea, almost any short-story writer might have decided to show the man's complacency by making him look in a mirror; to puncture it by moments in which the wife seems locked in a world of her own or disturbed by memories, and to suggest stormy times ahead. The 'debt' is not impossible, but it is distinctly non-proven. The further 1914 revision removes most of the verbal resemblances, as well as deepening the story – though it remains minor, compared with the finest of Joyce's tales.

86 See (ii. 26–57). Douglas Clayton wrote DHL a list, dated 3 July 1914, of the manuscripts sent to him in 1913 (UN); to be published in *Letters*, viii. For the problematic dating of 'The Primrose Path', sent to Clayton from Kingsgate on Monday 28 July, see note 89.

87 For 'The Old Adam' see (i. 276, 279); Croydon sketches *LAH* xxv–xxvi and (i. 383).

88 Cf. (i. 478).

89 On E211, of which pp. 12–16 and 59 appear to be from 1911, and the rest the 1913 revision, see *LAH* xxx–xxxii. The displaced woman is called Lydia, though it is Maurice's girl who is Polish and employed by the Vicar.

The manuscript of 'The Primrose Path' (E322.7a) is partly taken from a notebook of Frieda's, containing Italian exercises, which suggests it was begun in Italy. Yet DHL was never short of paper there. Even in San Gaudenzio, away from the shops, he had stock laid in for 'The Sisters', on which (and on 'Miss Houghton' before it) he had probably been too concentrated to be likely to turn aside to write a story. ('The Sisters' had now been left behind in Bavaria.) However, to run out of paper on a Sunday in Kingsgate, with all shops shut, would necessitate using anything that came to hand; cf. (ii. 38) on running out of ink. On the other hand it is not easy to see why the Italian exercises should have been brought to England unless there was something else in the notebook, and it does look as though an earlier beginning has been considerably revised. It is a puzzle, but it seems likely that the idea came to him – or revived – when he had good reason to be thinking about his family, and returning prodigals. The story was certainly taken up again and revised in Kingsgate.

90 Cf. (ii. 58, 57, 67).

91 Cf. (ii. 63, 69).

92 Bunny later claimed (*Great Friends*, p. 81) that Frieda had offered to sleep with him at the Cearne. It seems rather odd that, having told the story of the wood-cutter in previous reminiscences, he should not have told this one before. While Bunny probably did not invent stories altogether, they did grow on him with the passing of time. It is likely however that there was a good deal of kissing and cuddling to comfort her − and the story is by no means as unlikely as the wood-cutter one.

93 Letter to JMM, 30 August 1913, to be published in *Letters*, viii.

94 Noguchi (1875–1947), a Japanese poet, wrote in English. *The Pilgrimage*, a two-volume collection of his poems, had been published in 1909. DHL may also have known A. A. Ransome's essay on him in *Portraits and Speculations* (1913), see (ii. 27 and n. 5).

95 'Kisses in the Train' and 'Violets' would be published in September 1913 and 'The Mowers' in November. John Worthen in *D. H. Lawrence: A Literary Life* (1989), p. 33, calculates that his earnings from stories and sketches amounted to £100 of the £150, 'rolling wealth' (ii. 89), he had hoped for. Unfortunately, the payments came in very slowly. At the beginning of October he had only 50 lire left, and it was not until November that enough had come in to make him think of opening a bank account in Spezia (ii. 99).

96 Frieda's statement that she had gone 'from the Villa Igea to Baden-Baden and saw my father for the last time; he was ill and broken' (Frieda 85) is obviously confused. She last saw her father on her visit in 1914 from Fiascherino. He died in February 1915.

97 DHL was misremembering a much more complicated story when he told Edward McDonald how, 'in a cottage by the sea, in Italy, I re-wrote almost entirely that play ... right on the proofs which Mitchell Kennerley had sent me' ('The Bad Side of Books', *A Bibliography of the Writings of D. H. Lawrence*, ed. Edward D. McDonald, Philadelphia, 1925; see *P* 233).

98 Cf. the monologue with 'Odour of Chrysanthemums', *English Review* (June 1911), 432–3; itself to be transformed by a new ending in 1914, for *PO*.

99 His real feelings about Bjorkman linking him with Flaubert were very different: see (ii. 174).

100 Letter to JMM, 30 August, see note 93 above. (He was already hoping that the Murrys could join them in Italy later.)

101 For Louie, see *EY* 288–341. The omission of anyone resembling her in Mellors's caustic account of the women who had damaged him is significant (*LCL* 200:18–201:8), as is DHL's letter to her of 19 November 1912, see above. His tribute to her would be the young Ursula of *The Rainbow* and her family. (Her youngest sisters thought that part of the novel very lifelike − interviews with Winifred Nicholls and Nora Haselden.)

102 This journey was subsequently recreated by DHL in the final chapters, 'Italians in Exile' and 'The Return Journey', of *Twilight in Italy*; and traced in more geographic detail by Armin Arnold, 'In the Footsteps of D. H. Lawrence in Switzerland: Some

New Biographical Material', *Texas Studies in Literature and Language*, iii (1961), 184–8; see also *TI* Explanatory notes and 245–7.

103 DHL calls them 'tramps and beggars and wanderers out of work' (*TI* 190:36); the landlady explains that vouchers were offered, for a night's board and lodging, to those prepared to seek work across the border (*TI* 191:27–36).

104 *TI* 193:28; 207:32, 38; 208:26; 209:17. There may be an element of storytelling here. It seems unlikely that DHL's German vocabulary and accent would have passed as 'Austrian' for more than a minute or two.

105 *TI* 209:1–2, 18; 213:16–17; 216:3–4; 221:6; 221:17–18, 34–5; 223:14.

106 *Golden Echo*, p. 254; Frieda 57.

107 It is probably misleading to think of the disease in such terms anyway. Pulmonary turberculosis is an infection in which a bacillus gets into and destroys lung tissue. Sometimes the body can cure itself by surounding the bacillus with tissue (even after it has caused a little blood in the sputum), leaving only a scar. In more advanced cases the bacillus will form cheesy masses in the lung which break down the respiratory tissues into cavities; and if this continues into the bronchial passages the patient's breath becomes infectious. Still further advanced, the disease erodes the blood vessels and causes haemorrhages. (This did not happen to DHL before 1925.) Lesions may come and go leaving only some scarring; attacks may be sporadic with long periods of remission; and in any case the symptoms are often indistinguishable from those of bronchitis (which was regularly diagnosed in DHL) and other pulmonary diseases such as pleurisy and pneumonia. When haemorrhages of arterial blood occur, the disease is at an advanced stage. This was certainly not true in 1913. Indeed – especially in the light of DHL's several examinations by doctors between late 1911 and 1918 (see pp. 299–301, 383), who were required by law to notify cases – it is probably safest not to think of him as 'having consumption' before the diagnosis in Mexico in 1925; though his exemption from military service will have depended on his being the 'type', as well as suffering regularly from bronchitis. (He also often struck people, owing to his habitual pallor, as looking far more ill than he actually was.) KM, however, attempting to comfort herself at the onset of her fatal phase, remembered DHL as having coughed blood in their time together, perhaps when forced to spend winter in Britain in 1914–15. (KM's maid in Cornwall, however, speaks only of *her* coughing; see p. 822 note 79). Nobody remembers DHL coughing blood, or even seriously coughing at all, in Italy, Sicily, Australia or New Mexico.

108 Letter to JMM, 30 September 1913, to be published in *Letters*, viii.

109 Cf. (ii. 82, 85–6, 87, 88). The postmaster's 'niente, niente' must have been particularly annoying because what DHL was anxiously expecting were the much-needed payments from the magazines; without which the prices charged for groceries in Tellaro seemed robbery! For the piano, see (ii. 107–8); for Christ and his apostles, and the story of the octopus (ii. 122–3); for DHL and Frieda rowing (ii. 120).

110 Cf. (ii. 90, 123, 124).

111 Ida Wilhelmy had thought these boots proclaimed him not a gentleman (Barbara

Barr, interview with David Gerard; NCL); but this opinion seems not to have been shared by the Fiascherino peasantry.

112 Lina Waterfield, *Castle in Italy: An Autobiography* (1961), pp. 134–5.

113 For the Waterfields' income, see *Castle in Italy*, p. 125. The beasts and fire image found its way into *R* 405:34–6.

114 Waterfield, *Castle in Italy*, pp. 137–9.

115 Weekley, as was his right, removed his own deposition from the files.

116 Cf. (ii. 94–5, 101–2). Savage had sent DHL Middleton's *Monologues* (1913) containing 'Why Women Fail in Art' and 'The New Sex'. For Frieda's opinion of Middleton, see (ii. 96–7).

117 See Jeffrey Meyers 'D. H. Lawrence and Homosexuality', *D. H. Lawrence*, ed. Spender, pp. 133–46.

118 Neville, *Memoirs*, pp. 81–2, on DHL's early attempts at drawing imaginary female nudes. Cf. *WP* 221:30–223:3, but see *EY* 156–7 on the reasons why at that stage male relationships and affections might have seemed safer than heterosexual ones – and also on the distortion of seeing the young DHL as a 'repressed homosexual'. It might be added that the expression of affection between men at that time may frequently be mistaken nowadays. See Chloë Baynes on the letters of her very heterosexual father, *TWSUA* 39.

119 Letter from DHL and Frieda to JMM and KM, 10 October 1913, to be published in *Letters*, viii.

120 See (ii. 81 and n. 1, 87, 90, 127); but only 'Vin Ordinaire' appeared (June 1914) and 'Honour and Arms' (August).

121 DHL asked the Claytons on 23 October to send Marsh three of the four 'Rose Poems', 'Green', 'Illicit' (later 'On the Balcony') and 'The Wind, the Rascal' (ii. 87) which would be published in *Poetry* (January 1914); and then himself on 28 October sent Marsh these six, together with 'Purity' (later 'Paradise Re-Entered') and 'Ballad of a Wayward Woman' on 28 October (ii. 94; neither of which was published). DHL sent Harrison 'Twilight' and 'Meeting Among the Mountains' (ii. 90) which were published in the *English Review* (February 1914). In November Marsh passed on 'Service of All the Dead' to the *New Statesman* (ii. 106; appeared 15 November) (see also p. 810 note 64), and in December DHL sent him 'Grief' (originally part of 'Twilight') as a somewhat odd 'Christmas card' (ii. 121), which was published in *Poetry* (December 1914).

122 Cf. (ii. 90, 96, 97, 132).

123 The Polignac Prize of £100 had been endowed in 1911 by Princesse Edmond de Polignac and had so far been awarded by the Royal Society of Literature to de la Mare, John Masefield and James Stephens. Pound declared that DHL's *Love Poems* showed him to be a better poet than Masefield would ever be – but the 1914 prize went to Ralph Hodgson, of whose talent DHL had not a high opinion, see (ii. 92–3) (Michael de Cossart, *The Food of Love*, 1978, p. 107).

124 Cf. (ii. 133).

Chapter Three: The Wedding Ring

1 Cf. (ii. 137); Frieda 87.

2 (ii. 137); Hassall, *Edward Marsh*, p. 264.

3 Constance to E. Garnett, ?26 January (Eton) (R. Garnett, *Constance Garnett*, p. 278). Vera Volkhovsky (1881–1966) was the daughter of Felicks Vadimovich Volkhovsky, who escaped from Siberia in 1899 after the death of his youngest girl and the suicide of his wife. Vera was smuggled out of Russia dressed as a boy, in order to fit the specification on the passport of a friend. Her story 'The Idealist' had been published in the same issue of the *New Statesman* as DHL's 'The Fly in the Ointment'; but she never became well known as a writer though she translated Gorky and Shchedrin. She fell in love with Bertrand Russell in 1920, and twenty-two letters survive in the Russell archive (McMaster). Constance and her cousin Olive Garnett were very friendly with the Russian exiles in London. DHL liked Vera 'very much' (ii. 143), and invited her to see them in England, though there is no record of when or how many times she came.

4 He had been interested in the famous statue in the Vatican – showing the priest Laocoon and his sons wrestling with the sea serpents sent to punish him by Apollo – and its legend, for some time; cf. (i. 5, 136–7). The Venus of Melos in the Louvre, usually known as the Venus de Milo.

5 *SL* 398:6; 470–1; 402:5–24.

6 Cf. (ii. 90); Jane Harrison, *Art and Ritual* (1913, rev. 1918), p. 26 and passim, from which DHL 'got a fearful lot'; he thought it 'stupidly put, but it lets one in for an idea that helps one immensely' (ii. 114, 119).

7 E441a; *R* 473:19–21, 30; 475:23, 25–40; 476:16–22; 478:36–8; 478:18–20; 479:8–12.

8 *LAH* 179:22–34; *R* 479:36–7.

9 Constance to E. Garnett, 26 January (Eton) and to David Garnett, 31 January (Hilton) (R. Garnett, *Constance Garnett*, p. 279).

10 Constance to David Garnett, 31 January (Hilton) (R. Garnett, *Constance Garnett*, p. 280). Though Miss Huntingdon was devoutly Roman Catholic, she soon got over the news (Frieda 89). Her parents and the Pearses seem not to have been shocked, and the relationships continued undisturbed. Cf. also Waterfield, *Castle in Italy*, p. 137.

11 Constance to E. Garnett, 31 January and 5 February (Eton) (R. Garnett, *Constance Garnett*, p. 281).

12 *Early Years* 388; (i. 410); (i. 479) and Frieda 56; (ii. 49); (i. 550); (i. 549).

13 Constance to E. Garnett, Tuesday 24 February (Eton) (R. Garnett, *Constance Garnett*, p. 281).

14 See the reader's report to Kennerley on 'The Wedding Ring', *R* 483.

15 Amfiteatrov was a prolific novelist, dramatist, journalist; Zinovii Mikhailovich Sverdlov became Zinovii Alekseevich Peshkov, taking Gorky's name when he was christened in order to enter the Imperial Philharmonic School, but was never adopted by him.

16 *R* 474:2–3; cf. 'New Eve and Old Adam', *LAH* 165:27–8.

17 (ii. 149); (ii. 163). Gamba was the pen-name or nickname of the illustrator Giuseppe Garuti, a member of Marinetti's circle; see Luigi Russolo to Umberto Boccioni, 9 April 1912 – 'Saluti da Marinetti e Gamba' – in *Archivi del Futurismo*, ed. Maria Gambillo and Teresa Fiore (Rome, 1958). Information from Ornella de Zordo and Stefania Michelucci.

18 Frederic Herbert Trench (1865–1923) had also been manager of the Haymarket Theatre 1910–11 – and had once offered Cynthia Asquith a role in what turned out to be a highly successful run. He had now retired to Settignano outside Florence where DHL and Frieda visited the Trenches after the War. Of the Baronessa di Rescis, probably the 'interesting Italian aristocrat' of (ii. 168), nothing further is known, except that DHL took her invitation seriously (ii. 166), planned to accept it after their summer in England and would probably have done so had they been able to return to Italy in September. (Sir) Thomas Dacre Dunlop (1883–1964) was British Consul in Spezia in 1913 – also serving in Egypt and Uruguay. He became Inspector-General of Consular Establishments, 1922–43 (CMG, 1930; KCMG, 1939). DHL saw more of him when he was posted back to London in 1919. Though he refers to 'the Consul' typing his novel (ii. 152), according to Harry T. Moore (*The Intelligent Heart*, New York, 1954, p. 161), it was his wife 'Madge' (Margaret Morris, m. 1911) who actually did so.

19 A batch of paper with the von Richthofen crest was given to Frieda by her mother after the move to Baden-Baden. DHL apologised for using it to answer Ivy's first letter (ii. 160), but used it again for his next, causing some amusement at what she took to be a sign of snobbery. (In fact, though he was proud of Frieda's family status – albeit only minor aristocracy – Ivy's inference may have been unfair. He would not want her to think that he was inviting her to aristocratic surroundings. The only other time he apologised for the paper was to Garnett, who was anti-establishment and anti-aristocrat.)

Ivy Teresa Low (1889–1977) was the eldest daughter of Walter Low, Fabian, Norse scholar and editor of *The Educational Times*, and niece of Barbara Low and Edith Eder. Before she met DHL she had published two novels *Growing Pains* (1913) and *The Questing Beast* (1914), the second of which had been refused by the libraries. In 1916 Ivy married Maxim Litvinov who became Soviet Commissioner in London and subsequently Soviet Foreign Minister, and latterly Ambassador to the USA. Catherine Jackson, who reviewed for the *Glasgow Herald* became Catherine Carswell not long after DHL met her the following summer (see pp. 131–2 and 788 note 48); and Viola Meynell, daughter of the poet Alice Meynell and also a writer, later lent him the cottage in which he finished *The Rainbow*.

20 *SP* 2, 4–5 (Nehls, i. 213–22).

21 Lea, *Life of Murry*, pp. 35–6; Alpers, *Life of Mansfield*, pp. 162–5.

22 Kennerley had sent a cheque for £25 via Garnett (ii. 99), and a further £10 (ii. 174) – but the latter (which DHL had promised Frieda for pin-money) was imperfectly made out, so it could not be cashed. DHL returned it to Kennerley (ii. 190), but never had it back, which he never forgave or forgot (e.g. ii. 279). Kennerley not long afterwards ceased to publish, and was so chronically short of money that plans to sue

him had to be abandoned. So £25 remained the total return to DHL for *Sons and Lovers* in USA.

23 DHL rather overstates Duckworth's 'loss'. Publishers could not necessarily expect to make up the advance to the author in the first year, and only another 75 sales would have brought the break-even point in that respect (John Worthen, *D. H. Lawrence: A Literary Life*, 1989, p. 32). Perhaps DHL was rationalising what he really wanted to do, i. e. take up Pinker's offer.

24 Because some of the long thin pages used in the Dunlop typescript have survived as part of the later manuscript of *The Rainbow* − which DHL thought good enough to keep, though revised and heightened according to a later conception − we can form some idea of the increased length of 'The Wedding Ring'. Originally numbered 219–84, and having been parts of chapters 10 and 11, these reused pages deal with Ella's experience as a schoolteacher and the family removal to their new home. From the pagination, and hints in the letters, we can form at least an educated guess that whereas 'The Sisters II' had been planned as a novel of about 400 pages in DHL's handwriting, 'The Wedding Ring' had grown to at least 475 pages folio *typescript*, perhaps nearer 500. For the calculations see *R* xxxiv n. 27, and Charles Ross, *The Composition of 'The Rainbow' and 'Women in Love'* (Charlottesville, 1979), p. 26.

25 *R* 483–5 prints Kuttner's report and his follow-up letter to Kennerley. For his review of *Sons and Lovers*, see Draper 76–80.

26 Since Monro turned these down they cannot be identified, unless 'Teasing', which he printed in *Poetry and Drama* (December 1914), be one. There seems nothing futuristic about it, however.

27 Paul Eggert identified these in 'Identification of Lawrence's Futurist Reading', *Notes and Queries*, ccxxvii (1982), 342–4. Filippo Tomaso Marinetti (1876–1944), dramatist, novelist, poet, critic, publicist, had launched the Futurist Movement in February 1909, in *Figaro*, with his 'Manifeste du Futurisme' − and held a celebrated meeting in London upstairs in Monro's Poetry Bookshop, hence the translations. Paolo Buzzi (1874–1956) had published two volumes of Futurist free verse by 1913. Ardengo Soffici (1879–1967), painter and founder of the magazine *Lacerba* which spoke for Futurist art, though he broke with the Movement in 1915. The 'fat book' was *I Poeti Futuristi, con un proclamo di F. T. Marinetti e uno studio sul verso libero di Paolo Buzzi* (Milan, 1912). Soffici's *Cubismo e futurismo* was newly published in Florence in March 1914 − making it certain that DHL borrowed it from somebody very up-to-date in Futurist work.

28 *Early Years* 180, 187, 208–9. For his teaching both science and art, see E. Coulson Bonner to Edward Nehls, 22 December 1953 (UT); and for a vivid memory of his botany lessons (the subject in which he had achieved a distinction at college), Frank Turner to Nehls, 4 February 1953 (UT). Compare also the chapter 'Class-room' in *Women in Love*, and the abundant evidence of his knowledge of plants.

29 DHL is translating, from Marinetti's 'Manifesto tecnico' (*I Poeti Futuristi*, p. 20): 'Le intuizioni profonde della vita congiunte l'una all'altra, parola per parola, secondo il loro nascere illogico, ci daranno le linee generali di una FISICOLOGIA INTUITIVA DELLA MATERIA.' 'Fisicologia' may be a printer's error for

'fisiologia' (which DHL chooses), or 'psicologia' which most Italian reprints substitute. Or is it a defiant portmanteau coupling of the two? For DHL's purposes it makes little difference.

30 'Manifesto tecnico', p. 18. *Marinetti: Selected Writings*, ed. R. W. Flint (New York, 1972), p. 87, translates:

> The solidity of a strip of steel interests us for itself; that is, the incomprehensible and nonhuman alliance of its molecules or its electrons that oppose, for instance, the penetration of a howitzer. The warmth of a piece of iron or wood is in our opinion more impassioned than the smile or tears of a woman.

31 C. P. Ravilious, 'Lawrence's "Chladni Figures"', *Notes and Queries*, ccxviii (September 1973), 331–2 explains the image and the physics. A Chladni figure is illustrated in Keith Sagar, *The Life of D. H. Lawrence: An Illustrated Biography* (1980), p. 70.

32 This dedication of *Outlines* was a most pleasant surprise, particularly since many of the drawings are striking. DHL made a serious effort to respond, first writing a brief acknowledgement and then a longer letter. He was puzzled to know what Collings was up to in some of them; but the woman/hill he discusses (ii. 157) may have stayed in his mind when he came to write about Ursula on the Downs, and several others spoke to his own concerns, though he suspected Collings of being over-intellectual. (One wishes that Collings's reply had survived.)

33 They probably met at the Dunlops'. Lewis was about to be transferred by Vickers to their big factory in Barrow-in-Furness. During this walking tour they planned another in the Lake District in the summer, and they were together there when war broke out (see pp. 147–8). Lewis subscribed to *Signature* in 1915, by which time he was serving in the army. After the war he wrote to DHL, who however decided not to respond to him or to other pre-war friends who had enlisted (see chapter 8, p. 462), feeling perhaps that they had grown too far apart over the war.

34 *WL* 489:6–490:5.

35 Karl Baedeker, *Switzerland* (Leipzig and London, 1913), pp. 416–17, pull-out facing p. 416 (p. 413 in 1911 edition).

36 DHL probably did not go to Baden-Baden, since Frieda says that he never saw her father again – or indeed probably wished to – after the contretemps in 1912. Besides, the Baron was ill.

Martin Green states that the major publications of 1913 in 'German philosophy and political economy' were: Edmund Husserl's *Phenomenology*, Freud's *Totem and Taboo*, Jaspers's *Allgemeine Psychopathologie* (which refers to Max Weber as a 'major modern thinker') and Max Scheler's *Zur Phänomenologie der Sympathiegefühle*; 'Alfred Weber published a program for essays on the sociology of culture and an essay on bureaucratization ... The Jugendbewegung held a mass meeting on the Hohen Meissner and Alfred Weber and Ludwig Klages were among the speakers.' In Spring 1914 Max Weber was in Ascona (haunt of Gross, Frick, the expressionist dance of Laban and Mary Wigman, and home of an alternative culture, his letters from there giving a lively picture of Frieda Gross, a hippie fifty years early). The first part of his *Wirtschaft und Gesellschaft* was published later in 1914, and Alfred, despite sibling rivalry, might have known and talked about what was in it (*Von Richthofen Sisters*, pp. 190–2).

37 In what is said below of Georgians, Imagists and Vorticists I have drawn on the useful studies of C. K. Stead, *The New Poetic* (1964) and Kim A. Herzinger, *D. H. Lawrence in his Time 1908–1915* (Lewisburg, 1982).

38 Mary, Lady St Helier, in 1914 in her late sixties, was a well-known hostess and philanthropist, who had entertained Whistler, Millais, Tennyson and Browning among other lions. She also contributed to leading reviews. She had issued an invitation – a sign of DHL's 'arrival' – in February (ii. 147–8); she repeated the invitation when he and Frieda were in England, and they lunched with her at 52 Portland Place on 30 June (ii. 189). See Frieda 94 for her reaction.

39 Christopher Hassall, *Rupert Brooke: A Biography* (1964), pp. 450, 446; Hassall, *Edward Marsh*, p. 286 for the description quoting Sassoon who met Brooke the same week; Frieda 97.

40 Paul Delany, *The Neo-Pagans: Friendship and Love in the Rupert Brooke Circle* (1987); Frieda 97. John Worthen maintains that the name 'Pagans' for the group of young Eastwood friends was an invention of George Neville, and never used by DHL, see *Early Years* 170.

41 Cf. (i. 465); (i. 459); (i. 144, 543–4).

42 *Collected Poems of Rupert Brooke*, ed. Edward Marsh (1918), p. liii.

43 *Letters From America* (1916), p. 167.

44 'The Georgian Renaissance', *P* 305.

45 *Golden Echo*, p. 264. Bunny had been an enthusiastic visitor to Adrian, Virginia and Vanessa Stephen in their Bloomsbury days – though they considered him, non-Cambridge as he was, rather an outsider.

46 Walter Lionel George, novelist and journalist, wrote to congratulate DHL on *Sons and Lovers* in May 1913 (ii. 26); his article on contemporary fiction, 'Who is the Man', xx (February 1914), 244–6, was accompanied by a photograph of DHL taken by W. G. Parker (see Illustration 3). James (19 March and 2 April); cf. *Henry James and H. G. Wells*, ed. Leon Edel and Gordon Ray (1958), p. 180. Pressed by an admirer of *Sons and Lovers* about whether he had actually read any of DHL's works, James replied, 'I – I have trifled with the exordia' (Edith Wharton, *A Backward Glance*, New York, 1934, pp. 323–4).

47 *Golden Echo*, p. 264.

48 Cf. John Carswell's introduction to the Cambridge reprint of *The Savage Pilgrimage*, pp. vi–vii, ix. Jackson was Lady Raleigh's son, and she encouraged the marriage. For Greiffenhagen's *Idyll* and DHL's obsession with it see *EY* 284–6, 551–2.

49 *SP* 17–18.

50 *SP* 15–17.

51 *WP* 296:12; *SM* 5:31. David Eder (1865–1936) had had an extraordinary life: see *David Eder: Memoirs of a Modern Pioneer*, ed. J. B. Hobman (1945). In his younger days he had been a doctor in a mining district, and in South Africa, and went on three expeditions to South America (Colombia and Peru), in two of which he got caught up in civil strife. In a fashion hard to imagine now, but not so unusual then,

he combined socialist, Zionist, Freudian and occult interests. He contributed frequently to *New Age*, and was also an early champion and pioneer of school hygiene in London, as well as a Freudian psychoanalyst. He became one of the Commissioners to Palestine in 1918, a member of the World Zionist Executive 1921–3, and a founder of the Hebrew University of Jerusalem. Edith (neé Low), his second wife, joined him in articles on the psychology of children in *Child Study* and shared his interest in Zionism and the occult. Barbara Low published *Pyscho-Analysis: A Brief Outline of the Freudian Theory* in 1920. DHL in October 1913 wrote that 'I never did read Freud, but I have heard about him since I was in Germany' (ii. 80). Little is known about DHL's meeting with Ernest Jones, Freud's most prominent English follower, but Jones's first wife Morfydd (neé Owen), recalled that it was at a picnic on Hampstead Heath (information from Rhian Davies). Both Eder and Jones medically examined DHL during the war. The Lows and the Eders were all Fabian intellectuals. Murry, an intellectual of a different stamp, recalled – with mixed feelings – excited discussions on Freud in Selwood Terrace (*BTW* 287, Nehls, i. 231).

52 *BTW* 289 (Nehls, i. 233).

53 *BTW* 291 (Nehls, i. 238–9). DHL had in fact worn a dress-suit when taking Frieda to the theatre in Nottingham in 1912.

54 *BTW* 291–2 (Nehls, i. 239). Again JMM is misleading: DHL had met (and liked) Wells in November 1909, hence the invitation.

55 *BTW* 292 (Nehls, i. 239–40).

56 Pound, *Selected Letters*, ed. D. D. Paige (1961), pp. 52, 59; Garnett, *Golden Echo*, p. 245; Glen Hughes, *Imagism and Imagists* (Stanford, 1931), pp. 169–70 (Nehls, i. 237). In December 1913 DHL told Garnett: 'The Hueffer-Pound faction seems inclined to lead me round a little as one of their show-dogs. They seem to have a certain ear in their possession. If they are inclined to speak my name into the ear, I don't care' (ii. 132–3).

57 Ezra Pound, 'A Retrospect', *Literary Essays*, ed. T. S. Eliot (1954), p. 3; Charles Doyle, *Richard Aldington: A Biography* (1989), p. 14.

58 'A Retrospect', p. 4.

59 Pound's review is reprinted Draper 53–4; Aldington, *Life for Life's Sake* (New York, 1941), p. 139; Jean Gould, *Amy* (New York, 1975), p. 128; Pound, *Selected Letters*, ed. Paige, p. 90.

60 Aldington, *Life for Life's Sake*, p. 142 (Nehls, i. 236).

61 Cf. Stead, *New Poetic*, p. 99, quoting F. S. Flint, 'The History of Imagism', *Egoist* (1 May 1915).

62 A point made by Herzinger, *D. H. Lawrence in His Time*, p. 150. From this point of view even 'Green', which in other respects could be regarded as perhaps DHL's most strictly Imagist poem, barely qualifies.

63 Lewis wrote: 'At the heart of the whirlpool is a great silent place where all the energy is concentrated. And there, at the point of concentration, is the Vorticist ... the Vorticist is at his maximum point of energy when stillest' (William C. Wees, *Vorticism and the English Avant-Garde*, Toronto, 1972, p. 161). Pound spoke of 'a

radiant node or cluster ... from which, and into which, ideas are constantly rushing' (*Gaudier Brzeska: A Memoir*, New York, 1970, p. 92).

64 Cf. *English Review*, viii (June 1911), 415–33 with *PO* 181–99.

65 *English Review*, pp. 432–3.

66 *PO* 196:34, 197:38; 198:6–8, 13–14.

67 Cf. *English Review*, xvii (June 1914), 298–315 with *PO* 22–39.

68 *PO* 30:29, 31; 38:15, 28; 39:3–4.

69 Cf. *Smart Set*, xliv (October 1914), 97–108 with *PO* 143–64, and Mark Kinkead-Weekes, 'Lawrence and the Dance' (*D. H. Lawrence: Journal of the D. H. Lawrence Society*, 1992–3, 45–62). The 1913 version merely read

> She was afraid she did not dance well. But he gave her such support, she seemed to divine where he wanted her to go. This was the joy of it. His hand held her firmly in the small of her back, and seemed to speak to her, holding her, carrying her, telling her what to do, and a thousand other things. He was a man who knew what he was about.

70 *Smart Set*, p. 102.

71 *PO* 151:7–9; 152:39–40; 153:6–7, 9–10, 13–14; 156:15; 149:7; 162:26; 164:7–9.

72 *PO* 218:15. Cf. E86b in *PO* 209–46 and 1913 revisions in E86d in Explanatory notes, pp. 277–82.

73 *PO* 232:22–4; cf. 72:32–3; 73:5–13.

74 *PO* 279; cf. 82:21; 81:13–14, 82:31–2; 81:26, 30–1; 81:33; 82:15; 82:19–23, 29–30.

75 Frieda 94; JMM, *Reminiscences*, p. 38.

76 Frieda 94; JMM, *Reminiscences*, p. 39; cf. *WL* 161:17–27. H.D., whose looks were striking (see Illustration 40), was present at Amy's dinner-party at the Berkeley Hotel with her husband Richard Aldington (1892–1962), also an Imagist poet and associate of Pound, and at that time Assistant Editor of the *Egoist*. He would later become even better known for his war novel *Death of a Hero* (1929), and still later wrote a biography of DHL *Portrait of a Genius, But ...* (1950). Hilda Doolittle (1886–1961) became the outstanding Imagist poet – the first of several collections being *Sea Garden* (1916). Her 'novel' *Bid Me to Live* (1960) written after analysis with Freud, and on his advice to try to tell her truth about the breakup of her five-year marriage with Aldington in 1918, is also witness to the influence of DHL on her (see chapter 8). Born in Pennsylvania, she met Pound as an undergraduate and was persuaded by him to come to England in 1911.

77 'A Fine Play', review in *The Times*, 24 April 1914: 'this play has the qualities of finished craftsmanship ... the dialogue is packed with significance and suggestion ... it is finely built and perfectly shaped. It rises to a great height of emotion and sinks from it swiftly into a quiet and mournful close'. Harold Neilson 'of the Vaudeville Theatre' (ii. 187) and Lena Ashwell who held the lease of the Kingsway Theatre (ii. 201) approached DHL about producing the play, though neither did so. (It was however staged in California at Christmas 1914.)

78 Lucas (*Frieda Lawrence*, p. 100) puts this incident, remembered by Barbara Barr, in 1913. It could conceivably have taken place then – in reaction to hearing about Monty's refusal to see KM (ii. 51), and to the angry letters forwarded from Baden-

Baden to the Cearne before they left there – but only on the afternoon of Tuesday 29 July, when they came up from Kingsgate. Any earlier, and there would have been no reason for it, given the success – as Frieda supposed – of the surreptitious meetings after school, before she and DHL went to Kingsgate. Moreover, such a disturbance would surely have figured in Maude Weekley's deposition as more reprehensible (with the divorce still pending) than the other incidents she described. However there would have been little time to go searching on 29 July, as DHL and Frieda probably had a lunch date (ii. 51). Wednesday is excluded because they had asked the Murrys to Percy Avenue at 5 p.m. – ii. 53 – but Barbara says the irruption was when the children were at supper, and Frieda left for Germany on Thursday. She was soon writing to Bunny to say that the Lord had been good to her 'in letting me not be so miserable any more about the children' (ii. 60) – which sounds an odd reaction if the disaster had just taken place, with the certainty that an even more enraged Weekley *would* now forbid any further contact, armed with his injunction. Moreover, the change in the children from delight to angry reproaches seems unlikely in the space of a fortnight; whereas it is much more explicable after another year's constant vilification and after the incident with Maude on Frieda's first attempt at the old strategy in Summer 1914. The likelihood of 1914 is strengthened by Frieda's letter to Lady Ottoline Morrell in February 1915 (ii. 288), which describes the event and certainly does not sound as though it had taken place nearly two years before. It is now confirmed by Barbara Barr in her unpublished memoir 'Something to Say'.

79 When the Baroness arrived is unknown, as Catherine Carswell only dates their meeting to 'before the War' (*SP* 113 n.).

80 Leonard Woolf, *Beginning Again* (1964), pp. 249–51; Dorothy Brett, *Lawrence and Brett* (Philadelphia, 1933), p. 17. Mark Gertler painted a memorable portrait in 1917 (reproduced in *Letters*, ii.) – though DHL felt it did not bring out the 'colt' in him.

81 For 'Rannani Zadikim, Zadikim l'Adonoi' – the first line in Hebrew of Psalm xxxiii 'Rejoice in the Lord, O ye righteous' – and its meaning for DHL, see chapter 4, pp. 182–3.

82 Aldington, *Life for Life's Sake*, p. 128.

83 *Flowers of the Forest* (1955), pp. 3–5.

84 Ibid., p. 5. It has been suggested that DHL and Frieda were under surveillance from now on, largely on the basis of a file number jotted onto a briefing Minute to the Home Secretary (P.R.O. HO/45/13944) dated 22 November 1915: 'As to a Mrs Weekley living at address of D. H. Lawrence see 352857'. He was due to answer questions in Parliament about the *Rainbow* prosecution. (It is reproduced in Delavenay, Plates 16–17, between pp. 160–1.) However, as the reproduction cannot show, the jotting is in red ink, quite different from all the rest, clearly written later, and possibly much later – which makes the note about 'Mrs Weekley' even odder since Bunny would certainly have told the detectives in 1914, among his 'truthful answers', that she was married to DHL. Moreover the file number is quite wrong for 1914 or 1915 in the Home Office daybooks, which do record many accusations against suspected spies, but in which no such file number is to be found. It is possible

that the number dates from Frieda's first application for a passport after naturalisation by marriage – it has the right number of digits – the designation later updated by some official aware of her relation now with DHL (perhaps on renewal in 1913) but not of its precise nature.

85 For a more detailed account, see *R* xxx–xxxi.

86 Cannan (1884–1955) at that time was a far more successful writer than DHL to critics and the reading public alike, though his work is now almost entirely forgotten. A year older than DHL, he was educated at Cambridge and called to the bar in 1908; and was dramatic critic for the London *Star*. He wrote successful plays and several highly respected novels, among which were both an autobiographical one, and a story of several generations of the same family. His latest novel was *Peter Homunculus* (see also Murry's opinion, p. 155 below). He had been working with J. M. Barrie in a campaign against theatrical censorship when he became involved with Barrie's ex-actress wife Mary Ansell, who was a good deal older than he (1867–1950). They were denounced by a servant, and Mary was divorced in 1910, Barrie making her a comfortable allowance. She took with her to their new windmill-home in Cholesbury the dog immortalised in *Peter Pan*, and included in Gertler's painting of Cannan at the mill. Unfortunately the Cannan marriage did not last either, as will be seen, and DHL later quarrelled with him (see pp. 580 and 854 note 83, and for Cannan's later sad fate). Mary however remained a good friend. See Diana Farr, *Gilbert Cannan* (1978).

87 See (ii. 224 n. 4) for extracts from the letters of recommendation, and (ii. 226 n. 1) for the approach to the Society of Authors, quoting *SP* 25–6 on DHL's meeting with Marie Belloc Lowndes.

88 On her concern not to humiliate him, see Damon 271. Amy entertained him and Frieda in London, and also came to visit them in late August at The Triangle, in a large chestnut-coloured motor car, with her lifelong friend and travelling companion Mrs Russell, a well-known actress. From her home in Brookline, Massachusetts, she continued to correspond with DHL, to help him with gifts of money in emergencies and – doughty publicist for vers libre, and increasingly respected poet that she was – to make his work better known in lectures and articles as well as in her regular Imagist anthologies.

89 *TI* 84:3–5.

90 Gertler, born in 1892 of impoverished parents in Poland; they emigrated to the East End of London, where he grew up. His artistic promise was recognised, and under the patronage of William Rothenstein he studied at the Slade, and began to acquire a growing reputation. By 1914 he had attracted the patronage of Marsh, who set him up in a studio. The Lawrences first met him at Cholesbury Mill (Cannan was to use his confidences about his life as the basis for his novel *Mendel*, 1916); but he also became a great friend of Koteliansky's, and later almost a fixture at Lady Ottoline's Garsington. DHL greatly admired his *The Merry-Go-Round*, which influenced the description of Loerke's frieze in *Women in Love* (see chapter 6, pp. 343–4), and thought it should hang in the Tate – as it now does. Gertler later entered a sanatorium for tuberculosis, and was cured – but he was subject to depression, and

committed suicide in 1939. See John Woodeson, *Mark Gertler: Biography of a Painter* (Toronto, 1973).

91 This was a single visit, semi-fictionalised in Mackenzie's *The South Wind of Love* (Nehls, i. 247–53). Edward Montague Compton Mackenzie (1883–1972) came of a famous theatrical family – his grandfather was one of the first gentleman-actors. His father Edward Compton was a notable actor-manager, his mother a well-known actress, as were two of his sisters. 'Monty' went to St Paul's and Oxford, and embarked (usually successfully) on a number of careers (see p. 849 note 27). At this time the first volume of his best-known novel *Sinister Street* (1913) had appeared to critical acclaim (though DHL did not think much of it; ii. 240) and the second volume came out in November 1914 – to be followed by a host of others. With Cannan and Hugh Walpole, he was widely considered the most promising of the younger generation of novelists. His friendship with DHL really began, however, in Capri at the end of 1919 – see chapter 10, pp. 550–2.

92 *BTW* 296–7, 305ff.; *The Journal of Katherine Mansfield*, ed. J. M. Murry (1954), p. 61; JMM remembered that they had moved in 'without enthusiasm' because 'It went against the grain to return to a part of the country where we had lived before.' They had had a cottage in Cholesbury in Spring 1913 before they met the Lawrences. He also described their cottage as 'like a grey prison' (*BTW* 340) – though this is not echoed in his contemporary journal or in *Reminiscences*.

93 *BTW* 304ff.; JMM, *Reminiscences*, pp. 39ff.; KM, *Journal*, p. 61.

94 KM, *Journal*, p. 67; Tomalin, *Katherine Mansfield*, pp. 35–8; cf. *R* 314:32 and note.

95 JMM's contemporary journal, in a typescript very kindly lent me by his son (hereafter TS journal), pp. 40–1.

96 KM, *Journal*, pp. 58, 61; *The Letters of John Middleton Murry to Katherine Mansfield*, ed. Cherry A. Hankin (1983) e.g. pp. 21, 22, 35, and *Still Life*, pp. 8, 118–19; Alpers, *Life of Mansfield*, pp. 171–3; KM, *Journal*, pp. 62–3; *BTW* 340.

97 *BTW* 319, 305.

98 TS journal, pp. 43–5; cf. *BTW* 317.

99 TS journal, pp. 33 and 36; cf. *BTW* 312.

100 TS journal, pp. 38–9.

101 *New Statesman and Nation*, xlix (5 February 1955), 170, 172 (Nehls, i. 258).

102 See (ii. 229–30); cf. correspondence between Russell and Ottoline Morrell, June–August 1914 (his letters UT, hers McMaster); also Ronald W. Clark, *The Life of Bertrand Russell*, (1975), pp. 236–41, cf. Russell's own account, *Autobiography* (1967), i. 212–14.

103 *BTW* 305 (not mentioned in TS journal).

104 Recent biographers have been ready to speculate with great freedom on matters about which there can be no knowing. Was there an absence of foreplay, because none is described in the fiction? Was Frieda (despite the absence of evidence) multi-orgasmic, and DHL unable to satisfy her? Can we simply assume equivalence between DHL's imaginative fiction more than a decade later (*Lady Chatterley's Lover*), and fact in 1912–14? (For the single fragment of 'evidence', an anecdote of Mackenzie's which is itself open to suspicion, see pp. 551 and 850–1 note 32.)

Moreover, what is much less speculative, and would be relevant to any responsible discussion, is the difference between DHL's 'religious' view of what sex was *for*, in which total self-abandonment to the 'little death' was everything, and the view of sex as pleasuring which may well have been Frieda's, and for which self-containment, postponement and technique become important – yet even that involves arguing from documentable idea to undocumentable fact. For sexual humiliation in the fiction see *R* 428:26–34 and *WL* 443:22–32 (neither of which, incidentally, accords with the complexity the fiction has shown).

105 *Die fröhliche Wissenschaft* (1882–7). Nietzsche also refers to '*gai saber*' as an 'amulet' against unmanly 'sympathy' in *Beyond Good and Evil*, tr. Helen Zimmern (1911); and to 'la gaya scienza' as 'light feet, wit, fire, grace; the great logic' in *The Case of Wagner* (trans. Oscar Levy, 1888); see *Hardy* 255, note on 7:2). DHL may have been looking for a French version of the title that could both suggest the Old French and convey its meaning to a modern reader, rather than simply mistaking 'savaire' for 'savoir'.

106 Matthew vi. 28–9 (see also DHL's endorsement of Christ's 'to them that have shall be given' and 'Physician, heal thyself'; *Hardy* 12:34–5; 15:19.). The 'ruddy', as well as its joking vernacular and its obvious colour-aptness, carries also the associations of flame (see (i. 503–4) and the poem 'All Souls'), according to which DHL now wishes that 'we were all like kindled bonfires on the edge of space' (*Hardy* 18:39–40) – with a reminiscence of the opening of *The Return of the Native* (1878). Ruddy is also the Blakean colour of fulfilment, and Blake (whom DHL read with Jessie) is quite as much behind DHL's idea of the creativity of the conflict of opposites as Nietzsche, e.g. 'without contraries is no progression', 'opposition is true friendship'.

107 *Hardy* 12:36–7; 14:3–4.

108 *Hardy* 21:16; 28:34–6; 29:8–11; 28:29–30; 41:19. So, DHL goes on, from the original undifferentiated mass arise 'orders and species ... from naked jelly to enclosed and separated jelly, from homogeneous tissue to organic tissue, on and on, from invertebrates to mammals, from mammals to man, from man to tribesman, from tribesman to me: and on and on, till, in the future, wonderful, distinct individuals, like angels, move about ...' (*Hardy* 43:3–8).

109 Especially Botticelli's *Mystic Nativity*, the splendid *Madonna with an Iris* (now 'attributed' to Dürer and hence unfortunately banished to the basement), Raphael's *Ansidei Madonna*, Correggio's *Madonna with a Basket* and Rembrandt's *Self-Portrait*. Turner's *Norham Castle, Sunrise* is in the Tate Gallery. DHL must have known Michelangelo, and Rembrandt's *The Jewish Bride* or his *Self-Portrait with Saskia* (or both), from reproductions. He went to the National Gallery on the weekend of 21–2 November.

110 *Hardy* 60:4. Delavenay's methods in deriving DHL's thought from others, both in *D. H. Lawrence* (1972) and in *D. H. Lawrence and Edward Carpenter* (1971) are again questionable. He claims (Delavenay 306) – in a discussion that within two pages associates DHL with the growth of Nazism – that the argument on the relativity of 'rest' and 'motion' here *must* have come from a reading of Houston Chamberlain. In fact the quotation in Chamberlain is from Leibnitz, writing to Pierre Bayle in 1687,

and is a primary idea in physics. (We know that DHL taught science in Croydon.) It is only referred to by Chamberlain (in order to make quite a different point) in vol. ii, 301 of his *Foundations of the Nineteenth Century* – not the most likely place for a solitary verbal echo. The other affinities Delavenay notes are very general, and the 'Jewish' characteristics which feature in 'Hardy' are obviously inferred by DHL from the Old Testament's monotheism, and concern with the regulation of the flesh. The distinction between Law and Love (in any case Law and Grace in Chamberlain, far less accurately) is regularly taught in Sunday schools. Similarly, there is no evidence at all that DHL had read Otto Weininger's *Sex and Character* by 1914. (He refers to him just once, in 1930, in a context which even then does not necessitate having read him.) The one apparent echo in *Hardy* (81:11–16) – of Weininger's suggestion that in intercourse the male and female 'plasmas' become more purely male and female – derives from Carpenter quoting Weininger, in his *Love's Coming of Age* (1896; rev. edn, 1906) which DHL read with Jessie, and which incidentally is the only book of Carpenter's we can be sure that he had read by 1914. Weininger's argument that everyone is both male and female in differing proportions is analogous to DHL's (and Carpenter's) – but if DHL had read Weininger he would have hated him (as Delavenay never apparently notices), since the conclusion Weininger draws from his argument is that homosexuals are the superior beings, and women are so inferior that those who unfortunately are attracted to them ought as far as possible to avoid contamination by intercourse. (DHL would surely also have noted the relevance of Weininger's suicide at the age of 21 to his own theory about Middleton.)

111 *Hardy* 53:3–4. It was of course Sappho (regarding Lesbian being and loving as more important than self-preservation or procreating for the future) who leapt off a cliff's edge. DHL perhaps recalled the poetry of hers that Collings had sent him. The argument that it is the flowering of the poppy that is all-important, and the seed secondary, is by no means irrelevant to his rows with Frieda.

112 Cf. on 'Hardy', Richard Swigg, *Lawrence, Hardy, and American Literature* (1972); on DHL's art criticism, Ann Fernihough, *D. H. Lawrence: Aesthetics and Ideology* (Cambridge, 1993); and essays by Howard Mills in David Ellis and Howard Mills, *D. H. Lawrence's Non-Fiction* (Cambridge, 1988), and in *Tensions and Transitions*, ed. M. Irwin, M. Kinkead-Weekes and A. R. Lee (1990). See also Mark Kinkead-Weekes, 'Lawrence on Hardy', in *Thomas Hardy after Fifty Years*, ed. L. St J. Butler (1977).

113 See Michael Black, *D. H. Lawrence: The Early Philosophical Works* (Houndmills, Basingstoke, 1992) for an excellent discussion of how DHL thought in images. Nietzsche, *Beyond Good and Evil*, tr. Zimmern, pp. 10–11. But see DHL's opinion of Richard Jefferies' *The Story of My Heart* (1883) (i. 337, 353).

114 *Thomas Hardy*, p. 19.

115 The Calabrian abbot Joachim of Fiore (*c.* 1135–1202) and his mystical interpretation of history as a cosmic progression towards a New Age and Apocalypse of the Spirit were widely influential in the thirteenth century, until the overenthusiastic proclamation by his followers that the authority of the Bible had passed to his

Eternal Evangel led to the condemnation of his writings. Marjorie Reeves and Gerald Gould in *Joachim of Fiore and the Myth of the Eternal Evangel in the Nineteenth Century* (Oxford, 1987) show that interest revived, starting in France with George Sand, Michelet and Renan, and reaching England through their readers, such as Arnold, George Eliot, Pater, Symonds and Yeats. It is not clear how Joachim's ideas reached DHL in 1913–14 – the historical emphasis in 'Hardy' differentiates it from the 'Foreword' – though he certainly read about him in G. G. Coulton, *From St. Francis to Dante* (1906), chapter XIII, in February 1916 (ii. 538), and refers to him in *Movements in European History* 147:1–4.

116 *Hardy* 126:13–14; 128:11–15.

Chapter Four: *The Rainbow*

1 On E331a, p. 100 little Anna Lensky confronts the Marsh Farm geese, with the new confidence Tom Brangwen has given.

2 DHL attended the Pupil-Teacher Centre at Ilkeston 1904–5, where he met Louie Burrows, and achieved the success in the King's Scholarship exam which sent him to University College, Nottingham after matriculating in 1905. See *Early Years* 114–17. When Louie became his 'girl' there, he often visited her in Church Cottage, Cossall. For the detailed chronology of the book, see *R* 489–92, and for the extent to which it is an 'historical' novel, see Mark Kinkead-Weekes, 'The Sense of History in *The Rainbow*', in *D. H. Lawrence in the Modern World*, ed. Peter Preston and Peter Hoare (1989), pp. 121–38.

3 It may be that the novel originally started with section II of chapter I 'About 1840 ...' (*R* 13:19–20), and that the prelude of the Brangwen men and women, symbolising 'God the Father' and 'God the Son' in DHL's terms, was added in early December. See below note 14.

4 *Hardy* 61:40–62:2; 62:13–14.

5 'Ursula' suggested something more heroic: the leader of a brave host of virgins on a mission against male tyranny. 'Charles' Skrebensky is mentioned, just once, in the surviving section of typescript of 'The Wedding Ring'.

6 Soon after DHL's letter to him from Metz, Weekley was already thinking in terms of his absolute legal rights: 'She must understand that she has no more rights but she knows I am honourable' (13 April). A month later he writes chillingly of 'my children' (*Memoirs* 179, 181).

7 Italy did not declare war until May 1915.

8 E331a, p. 199 begins 'Haste to the Wedding' (*R* 124:1).

9 Mrs Henry Jenner, *Christian Symbolism* (1910) has an illustration of the phoenix opposite p. 150, and Fra Angelico's *Entry of the Blessed into Paradise*, opposite p. 74. The book also lodged in DHL's mind the Lamb with banner (p. 32) and Van Eyck's *Adoration of the Lamb*, opposite p. 6; the Dove and Eagle (pp. 149, 151) and the orders of angels, of which the innermost 'are utterly absorbed in perpetual love and admiration of God' (p. 66).

10 Frieda 99–100; JMM, TS journal, pp. 46–8.

11 KM, *Journal*, pp. 62–3.

12 *Selected Letters of Mark Gertler*, ed. Noel Carrington (1965), pp. 78–9.

13 JMM, TS journal, pp. 50–1; cf. *BTW* 321–2 (note how the latter writes up the former: there is no indignant interruption of the performance or hustling JMM aside by DHL in the journal, though he does take JMM out on the road afterwards and lecture him about 'exposing' himself); Gertler, *Selected Letters*, p. 77.

14 DHL began typing, very amateurishly, on Amy Lowell's machine (ii. 240), but soon gave up. The first seven typescript pages of E331a, however, seem to contain considerably more than the number of manuscript pages they have replaced would have required. The discrepancy may be because DHL had written in, as a new opening now, the Brangwen men and women; cf. Ross, *Composition*, pp. 30–1. So the writing backwards may have continued into the final version. It is to be noted that the 'genders' of the Opposites in 'Hardy' have been reversed, what was 'Female' now becoming characteristic of the Brangwen men – salutarily unsettling the gender typing he was liable to fall into.

15 The 'Polish woman' is mentioned in Kuttner's report to Kennerley (*R* 483).

16 *R* 37:12 and n. DHL, who knew the Bible so well, must have been struck by how, in its 'history', the wanderings of the Israelites and Christ are located in space and time, and moreover the sacred powers of Jahweh and Jesus manifest themselves precisely there, here and then.

17 DHL objected to the title which Garnett had chosen for both story and volume: 'what Prussian Officer?' (ii. 241). The officer is in a Bavarian regiment, and 'Honour and Arms' is at least as much (if not more) about his orderly. Garnett probably hoped to increase sales in an atmosphere of hatred of the Hun. He had also, by entirely changing the order which DHL had suggested (ii. 197), reversed the emphasis and progression. DHL would have begun with the very early but transformed story 'A Fragment of Stained Glass', which has become, first, a miniature 'Honour and Arms' (how the violated self reacts in destructive violence), and then a miniature 'Thorn in the Flesh' (how the self can be restored through sexual relationship) – the opposite paths which finally distil out in stark contrast at the end of the volume. In relation to these, the other stories group themselves into those which realise 'the flesh' (in DHL's sense) too late, culminating in 'Odour of Chrysanthemums'; and stories of choice and judgement or misjudgement, set off against the primary contrast of 'Daughters of the Vicar', and deepening to the violent question mark of 'The White Stocking'; before the final distilled contrast of the life-giving with the deathly in 'Vin Ordinaire' and 'Honour and Arms' at the *end*. Garnett of course was making a judgement of quality, with an eye to the market, and defensibly on both grounds; but he did turn DHL's book into an anthology (rather than a sequence of sorts) – and one, moreover, which was likely to offend at its beginning by implications of homosexuality.

18 *Memoirs* 45; *R* 83:39–84:1.

19 Cf. the end of 'Odour of Chrysanthemums' with Lydia and her son Tom looking at Tom's dead body, in manuscript version *R* 610, entry to 233:8, and final version *R* 233:7–19.

20 See *R* 558, entry to 57:32.

21 The novel is however also rich in local rural culture, folklore and dialect, especially the wedding and the visit of the guysers.

22 E331a, p. 300 is about Anna's response to the cathedral, which gives point to the remark.

23 Louie asked Ada to cut from her memoir of her brother:

> all references to me and my family. You know how clearly Cossall has been identified with the scene of *The Rainbow* – and how very personally Bert used the characters of members of my family … I never made such requests of Bert – because after all he was a genius & I could not contemplate making it more difficult for him to earn a living. I know there is no such need in your case.
>
> (Quoted in Ada Clark to Laurence Pollinger, UT)

24 *R* 197:18. When it came to the Brangwen family's move, however, he modelled the new house on the Hopkins' in Devonshire Place (rather than the more rural Quorn which was his original idea), though with 'Burrows' decor and pictures. He also changed Will's appointment from Leicestershire to Nottinghamshire, though that hardly helped as disguise! For Alfred Burrows's woodwork classes see *R* 221:5–18 and note; 387:29–388:14 and note.

25 Cf. Frieda 54.

26 For Frieda dancing almost naked in her bedroom see *Early Years* 376; but see also the perspectives the fiction adds: the pride in motherhood setting the man aside; the dance of David in the Bible; and the contrast with the corn-stacking (*R* 41–8; 113–16; 169–71).

27 Cf. *Hardy* 65:31–66:5. For the development of the episode in manuscript, and in DHL's subsequent revision, compare *R* 590–6 with 186:10–191:10,, and see Mark Kinkead-Weekes, 'The Marble and the Statue', in *Imagined Worlds*, ed. Ian Gregor and Maynard Mack (1968), pp. 371–418. See also p. 220 above.

28 Anna goes to Nottingham High School for Girls, only the sixth of its kind to be founded, and in its earliest years. Will is a disciple of Ruskin and Morris. Behind Anna's scepticism stand Spencer, Huxley and William James. Of her brothers, the young Tom goes to the London School of Mines which later became Imperial College; and Fred is seen reading the Fabians. The contrast with Tom and Lydia is strongly marked.

29 Judging by the original pagination of the typescript surviving from 'The Wedding Ring', *The Rainbow* up to Ursula's first day as a teacher had become nearly twice as long as before, cf. *R* xxxiv and Ross, *Composition*, p. 26.

30 *R* 205:32–208:5 and p. 512 note to 205:34. I have interviewed three people who knew DHL when they were children – two of Louie's sisters, and Mary Saleeby to whom he gave private lessons in Greatham (see chapter 5, p. 234). All independently stressed how careful he was not to talk down, but rather to treat them as little persons in their own right.

Barbara Barr has been reported as recalling her mother explaining their childlessness as the result of DHL suffering an attack of mumps in late adolescence – of which however there is no record. DHL and Frieda certainly had no idea of this in their first years together, and Frieda told Cecily Lambert in 1919 (Nehls, i. 503) that she hoped to bear him a child. We know that he used contraceptives before he met Frieda (Delavenay, ii. 701; Neville, *Memoir*, pp. 85–6; (i. 286)); and there were good reasons to go on doing so before the divorce and their marriage, and during the poverty-stricken years that followed. When Frieda's period was late, in Metz, DHL made it clear that he was against abortion, and ready to welcome the child if it came (i. 402–3). The infertility may as easily have been Frieda's, despite (or perhaps as a result of) previous pregnancies. Certainly, when Otto Gross slept with her namesake, her sister and herself in 1907, she was the only one of the three not to conceive. Again, speculation about the unknowable seems futile. What does seem sad is that someone who was as good with children as much evidence suggests that DHL was (cf. also Tom Brangwen comforting little Anna in the stable) should never have become a father himself.

31 Interview with Nora Haseldon, Louie's youngest sister. The embankment had also burst in 1823 (see *R* 515, note to 230:31).

32 A ten-page error of memory in the pagination of E331a shows he was about to embark on the story of Ursula's 'First Love'.

33 See chapter 3, p. 792 note 87. For the Cannans' guests see (ii. 211–12, 238, 254); Nehls, i. 259. St John and Mary Hutchinson, whom the Lawrences certainly knew by 1916, were great friends of the Cannans, and may have come down to Chesham. She was cousin to the Stracheys, sister to the Jim Barnes who had come to Fiascherino and would become Clive Bell's mistress.

34 *Journal*, p. 65.

35 *PO* xxxv. On Boots see (ii. 257–8).

36 *Journal*, p. 67.

37 *SP* 26. For the Meynell settlement at Humphreys, Greatham, see Viola Meynell, *Alice Meynell: A Memoir* (1929), pp. 274–317. Viola (1885–1956) wrote short stories, novels and biographies.

38 Though the Lawrences had been introduced to OM (see p. 800 note 45) by the Cannans in August, it had probably been at a reception in Bedford Square, and the acquaintance did not ripen immediately. At Christmas, however, she asked BR to send her *The Prussian Officer* and was 'amazed how good it is – quite wonderful most of the Stories – He has great passion – & is so alive to things outward and inward … All the Nottingham Stories so real – seem very familiar to me – Didn't you think "The Vicar's Daughters" very good?' (25 and 31 December, McMaster). She must have written in similar terms in the letter to DHL he replied to on 3 January (ii. 253). Her invitation to a more intimate lunch party when he was next in London followed; and when he came, on 21 January, she 'liked him awfully' – so much so indeed that she asked him to dinner as well. By contrast, Constance Garnett asked her husband *not* to invite the Lawrences down to the Cearne again: 'I don't feel that I could stand his fervid intensity over his personal emotions and Frieda's trivial second-hand generalizations just now (though you know I am fond of them both really)', Constance to E. Garnett, ?21 January (Eton) (R. Garnett, *Constance Garnett*, p. 283).

39 D. Garnett, *Flowers of the Forest*, pp. 33–4 (Nehls, i. 265–6). For Grant's relationship with Vanessa Bell, and with Bunny, see Frances Spalding, *Vanessa Bell* (1983).

40 *Flowers of the Forest*, pp. 34–7 (Nehls, i. 266–8).

41 Nehls, i. 129–30. (Though Ernest Rhys seems to have conflated two different evenings – see Herzinger, *D. H. Lawrence in His Time*, pp. 183–5 – the description of DHL is unaffected by this.)

42 *Flowers of the Forest*, p. 37 (Nehls, i. 269).

43 In 'Hardy' DHL had remarked on the whole tendency to abstraction in late Turner and beyond, 'till the body was carried away' (*Hardy* 86:18–19; in Turner's case into pure light). Such extremes became (he thought) a kind of one-sided falsehood, inevitably producing reaction in the opposite direction, but DHL calls now for more inclusive vision. He may have said something of this to Grant and Bunny – who, if so, may have had little idea what he was talking about and only heard the phrases, like JMM when DHL tried to expound 'Hardy's' central ideas to him.

44 Not seeing the point of DHL's 'instances', Bunny derided this sentence: 'Lawrence was belabouring a figment of his imagination, as well as pouring out a lot of nonsense. What would an abstract statement of the instances of Rembrandt, Corot, Goya and Manet look like?' (*Flowers of the Forest*, pp. 36–7; Nehls, i. 268).

45 Lady Ottoline Violet Anne Morrell (1873–1938) was the daughter of Lieutenant-General Arthur Cavendish-Bentinck and his second wife Lady Bolsover. Her half-brother was the 6th Duke of Portland. She had had a lonely childhood, wholly out of sympathy with the kind of country-house life her half-brothers and their friends pursued. She had nursed a dying mother; and had found inspiration in Thomas à Kempis and his ideals of service and self-sacrifice, followed by an evangelical urge that led her to hold religious classes for the servants and workers in the family mansion, Welbeck Abbey. But travel in Italy had awakened imagination, a sense of beauty and an interest in the arts; and she had tried to educate herself by attending classes at St Andrews and Oxford, though her schooling had been patchy. Her writing and spelling remained idiosyncratic, but she continued to read voraciously. In Oxford she met and subsequently married Philip Morrell, son of the Solicitor to the University, and devoted herself to helping him build a career as a Liberal politician, M.P. first for South Oxfordshire (1906–10) and then for Burnley (1910–18). Before the war she had already become a famous patroness of arts and letters, at 44 Bedford Square, Bloomsbury. When she met DHL she and Philip had recently acquired Garsington Manor, near Oxford. After they moved there, in May 1915, it became the most famous of all centres of what had become loosely known as 'Bloomsbury' – where she entertained a host of writers and artists. See *Ottoline: The Early Memoirs of Lady Ottoline Morrell*, ed. Robert Gathorne-Hardy (1963) and *Ottoline at Garsington: Memoirs of Lady Ottoline Morrell 1915–1918*, ed. Gathorne-Hardy (1974); also biographies by Sandra Jobson Darroch (1976) and Miranda Seymour (1992). Before her relationship with BR, she had had short-lived affairs with Augustus John and with Henry Lamb, also a painter.

46 Bertrand Arthur William Russell (1872–1970) was grandson of the 1st Earl Russell and would succeed his brother as 3rd Earl in 1931. He grew up in his grandmother's home after the death of both parents when he was four – a lonely childhood without companions, play or love, and in a strongly religious atmosphere against which he was to react as strongly. He was not allowed to go to school lest he be contaminated, and in consequence became a youth both shy and priggish. However he had a precocious intelligence, and developed a passion for mathematics, which offered apparent certainties to a sceptical frame of mind. He studied Mathematics and Moral Sciences at Cambridge, and became a Fellow of Trinity College in 1895. He was steadily driven towards the discovery of a more secure basis for the principles of mathematics, using symbolic logic for this purpose. The three volumes of *Principia Mathematica* (1910–13) which he wrote with A. N. Whitehead, made him a world-wide reputation. He married (1895) Alys Pearsall-Smith, of a Philadelphia Quaker family which had moved to England; they separated in 1902, and the marriage ended in 1911. After an impossible yearning for Whitehead's wife Evelyn, followed the affair with OM. He was already working against the war in the Union of Democratic Control, and became a leading pacifist, eventually deprived of his Fellowship and imprisoned for a time (see pp. 235, 306). See his *Autobiography*, 3 vols. (1967–9) and Clark, *Life of Russell*.

47 BR to OM, 1 June 1914 (UT). On 6 June, back in England BR was quite taken aback by OM's suffering and her not wanting to see him; see also discussion passim in letters of June and July, by the end of which he is beginning to hate the girl (BR to OM, 24 July; UT). On 4 September he describes how, locked in his flat, he allowed Helen to beat on the door and refused to answer. On Irene, see letters early to mid-January 1915 (UT).

48 OM to BR, 29, 30, 31 January, and three telegrams, 30 and 31 January (McMaster).

49 OM to BR, [13 February] (McMaster); cf. Frieda to OM, ?10 February, posted 12 February (UT). Weekley apparently replied that if OM knew Frieda's history she would not befriend her, see Frieda to OM, *c.* 24 February (UT).

50 BR to OM, 'Saturday', 13 February (UT). BR himself, however, would say something not dissimilar in 1916, advocating 'abolition of the whole wages system' as 'the essential preliminary to any successful movement of fundamental reform' (Clark, *Life of Russell*, p. 366). On BR seeing DHL as prophet, *Ottoline*, ed. Gathorne-Hardy, p. 273.

51 His father having died when he was an infant, Edward Morgan Forster (1879–1970) was as mother-centred as DHL. Miserable at Tonbridge school, he blossomed at King's College, Cambridge where he became an Apostle, and kept a connection all his life. A legacy from his aunt Marianne Thornton meant he did not have to work for a living, and made it possible for him to travel to Italy and Greece with his mother; but he tutored the children of a Countess in Germany and taught at the London Working Men's College. After the publication of *Where Angels Fear to Tread* (1905), *The Longest Journey* (1907), *A Room with a View* (1908) and especially *Howards End* (1910) his reputation as a novelist was assured; but there was to be a long silence after his volume of stories *The Celestial Omnibus* (1911). In 1912 he

visited India and formed a friendship with the Maharajah of Dewas, whose secretary he would later become. Back in England he came to terms with his homosexuality (still at that time celibate) in the (then unpublishable) novel *Maurice*. DHL had read and admired *Howards End* in 1911.

52 Forster sent his *The Celestial Omnibus* at DHL's request (ii. 262, 275).

53 DHL's vision of Pan has changed in emphasis since 'The Overtone', see chapter 2, pp. 64–6. There is also rather more to the tempestuous force in the 'Story of a Panic' than universal love – though DHL is also thinking of *A Room with a View*.

54 *R* 655–6, entry to 408:40.

55 Forster sent *Howards End* to Frieda, so DHL would certainly have discussed it with her, and may possibly have reread it or some of it himself.

56 P. N. Furbank, *E. M. Forster: A Life* (1978), ii. 5, 7.

57 As for coming again to Greatham, I like Mrs Lawrence, and I like the Lawrence who talks to Hilda [the Meynell servant], and sees birds and is physically restful and *wrote* "The White Peacock", he doesn't know why; but I do not like the deaf impercipient fanatic who has nosed over his own little sexual round until he believes that there is no other path for others to take, he sometimes interests & sometimes frightens & angers me, but in the end he will bore me merely, I know. So I can't yet tell about coming down.

  (*Selected Letters*, ed. P. N. Furbank and Mary Lago, (1983), i. 219)

58 Lytton Strachey, interestingly, voiced to Keynes the mirror image of DHL's idea, arguing the superiority of homosexual over heterosexual relationship precisely because of the greater likeness between the partners (Michael Holroyd *Lytton Strachey: A Critical Biography*, 1967–8, ii. 208–9). (Holroyd warns, however, that the sodomite language of Strachey's letters was often hyperbolic, and need not be taken always or altogether literally.)

59 The word, in this letter, is DHL's (ii. 285). As I attempt to trace his changing attitude towards it. I shall continue to use the term, for lack of a better, but intending no moral charge. 'Anal intercourse' may be heterosexual, and 'anal intercourse between men', as a repeated phrase, would become tiresome.

60 It is sometimes assumed that the scene in *Aaron's Rod* where Lilly rubs the whole of Aaron's lower body with oil indicates what took place between DHL and JMM in February 1915. Apart from resting on extremely crude assumptions about the relation of imaginative literature to life, this is intrinsically unlikely. In 1915 JMM was suffering from a bad chest cold, for which the rubbing of camphorated oil into the chest was (and is) a well-known remedy. (The insinuation of homosexual feeling is also unlikely. Even supposing DHL to have been homosexually attracted to JMM, which is very doubtful – the attraction being predominantly intellectual and 'spiritual' rather than physical – its indulgence would have been untimely and resented by the sick man, since DHL could have had no reason whatever to 'treat' his lower body so.) The DHL of 1921, by contrast, had developed a strongly held theory about the atrophy of the 'lower centres' in modern men, shown physically in Jim as well as Aaron, so that Lilly has every reason to attempt to massage all Aaron's 'lower centres' back into life. If DHL remembered 1915, it would have been to re-

focus and transform the memory in imagination, to serve the specific fictive purposes of 1921.

61 Alpers, *Life of Mansfield*, pp. 173–5.

62 *Journal*, pp. 66–74; *The Collected Letters of Katherine Mansfield* ed. Vincent O'Sullivan and Margaret Scott (Oxford, 1984), i. 150.

63 Glenavy, *Today We Will Only Gossip*, pp. 63–6.

64 TS journal, pp. 59–65; *BTW* 336.

65 JMM expresses, in the journal, high annoyance that while he was out walking with DHL, Frieda had read some of his novel without his permission. He also records: 'L. is sad with some idea of the approaching sacrifice of his personality for his revolution' (p. 66).

66 TS journal, pp. 63–7. A visit to 'George Banks' is one of the liveliest episodes in *Still Life*.

67 *Memoirs* 207 (*c.* 5 February).

68 *Memoirs* 204.

69 About 10 February, broaching the idea to OM, she wrote: 'When I saw the children I knew that after all how infinitely more to me Lawrence is and my life with him, and it seems comparatively little my misery of not having the children –'; but she was upset by the failure of her scheme. However her letters to OM continue very warm and friendly – 'It is so joyful to think of your good and understanding disposition towards us both' – up to the visit to Garsington in mid-June.

70 Furbank, *E. M. Forster*, ii. 11.

71 TS journal, pp. 66–7. (The news of the death of Frieda's father is recorded on p. 63).

72 On E331a, p. 450, Ursula and Skrebensky drive in a hired motor past the Hemlock Stone. Campbell's information is used on p. 432 (*R* 273:6–11).

73 *R* 267:31–2; 269:22–3. Von Hube claimed to have escaped from Poland by swimming the Vistula, and wrote a history of Greasley. Frieda calls her first beau 'Olaf' (*Memoirs* 56–62).

74 The episode with Winifred was not in 'The Wedding Ring', since reference to her had to be written into the reused section of the 'Wedding Ring' typescript. After publication, in Ada's copy (private collection), DHL changed the title from 'Shame' (always Ursula's rather than his) to 'Schwarm', meaning a hot adolescent feeling or 'crush'.

75 'Do but read one chapter called a Poem of Friendship, which is most beautiful. The whole book is the queerest product of subconsciousness that I have yet struck – he has not a glimmering from first to last of what he is up to' (Furbank, *E. M. Forster*, ii. 12).

76 See p. 795 note 110 above on the derivation of this idea.

77 *Hardy* 122:11–12: 'Sue had a being, special and beautiful. Why must not Jude recognise it in all its speciality?'

78 Tomalin, *Katherine Mansfield*, pp. 35–8; cf. *R* 314:32ff. Three decades later, according to Barbara Barr, Frieda said that she too had had a lesbian affair as a schoolgirl with a schoolteacher; cf. Rosie Jackson, *Frieda Lawrence* (1994), pp. 61–2. It may be so – but this comes suspiciously late. It might have made a difference to

the relationship with KM, for instance, and her belief that Frieda had betrayed her confidences to DHL, if she had told KM about it then. One occasionally worries that some of Frieda's semi-fictionalised memories may be shaped by *The Rainbow* rather than the other way round. She wrote on the back of a youthful photograph of herself, 'Ursula, of the Rainbow', but the youthful heroine was originally drawn from Louie Burrows, though DHL probably did incorporate memories of Frieda's later in the book's development.

79 DHL not only said this to OM, but showed it later by partly deriving a sympathetic character from him, the Scottish painter Duncan Forbes in *Lady Chatterley's Lover* who agrees to be named as the father of Connie's child. Of his painting, however (conflated with the Italian painter Magnelli), there was still nothing complimentary to be said.

80 *R* 321:28 (and entry on p. 635), 321:26−7.

81 For the view that this is not an unmixed improvement, see Lawrence Lerner, 'Lawrence's Carbon', in *The Truth Tellers* (1967), pp. 78−82. A body of readers, from Edward Garnett onwards, regard *Sons and Lovers* as DHL's major achievement and rather regret the process I have been tracing.

82 See (i. 49−50, 72), and *Early Years* ch. 7. Some of the material may have been in 'The Wedding Ring', but since DHL is no longer reusing the old typescript it is impossible to tell.

83 *R* 408:39.

84 Ursula's loss of virginity under the great tree is indicated but not described; the scene on the beach is done much more symbolically than descriptively; and of course the scene Kuttner described as rape has disappeared from the novel altogether. Nevertheless the American publisher Benjamin Huebsch found it necessary to expurgate the novel in eleven places, without telling DHL.

85 E.T. 125−8.

86 Cf. *R* 429:28−430:3 and (ii. 282).

87 *Letters of a Post-Impressionist* (1912), pp. 97 (ii. 298 n. 1).

88 We do not know which *Blaue Reiter* painting by Franz Marc hung on Edgar Jaffe's wall, but DHL would almost certainly have seen, in 1912 or 1913, paintings imbued with Kandinsky's idea that the artist should try to show the forces within things, rather than their appearance – paintings such as Marc's *Blue Horses* (1911).

89 *R* 456:20−2.

90 For the original ending see *R* 669, and for DHL's revision see, chapter 5, pp. 250 and 809 note 46.

91 OM to BR, 'Saturday', 6 March (McMaster). Moore, acknowledging a copy of Keynes's *Two Memoirs* on 17 May 1949 (UT), has also left an account of the evening from which it becomes clear both that he had no idea who DHL was when he sat beside him, and that one of the subjects on which Lawrence was eloquent after dinner was Socialism.

John Maynard Keynes (1883–1946) was educated at Eton and Cambridge. Though not yet as famous as he was to become, he was already Fellow of King's College, editor of the *Economic Journal* (since 1912), served in the Treasury and was recognised as a leading economist – though his best-known work was yet to come: *The Economic Consequences of the Peace* (1919), arising out of his representation of the Treasury at the Paris Peace Conference, and prophetically denouncing the heavy imposition of economic compensation on Germany in the Versailles Treaty, and the influential economic theory that bears his name. For his homosexuality at this time, see Robert Skidelsky, *John Maynard Keynes* (1983), i. xvii, 204 (on his sexual diary and its statistics which made James Strachey gasp), 128–9; and Holroyd, *Lytton Strachey*, i. 208–9, 212. He subsequently married the ballerina Lydia Lopokova.

92 BR to OM, 'Sunday', 7 March (UT).

93 BR to OM, 'Sunday', 7 March (UT).

94 Keynes, *Two Memoirs* (1949), pp. 78–80, 103 (Nehls, i. 286–8). Shortly before, Keynes had emphasised the importance to 'Bloomsbury' of the philosophy of Moore, which placed the highest value on personal relationships – though Moore (whose philosophy tended to lose its scrupulousness in Bloomsbury) would hardly have approved of Keynes's 'libertinism' and promiscuity at this time.

95 Tomalin, *Katherine Mansfield*, pp. 73–8.

96 Bessie Head, the South African novelist (who admired DHL), experienced a similarly terrible mental darkening, dissolving the real world into horrible instances, everywhere, of unloving sexuality and perversion, in her case amounting to a temporary insanity. She recreated this in her finest novel *A Question of Power* (1974).

97 See for instance the photograph with Douglas Grant in Holroyd, *Lytton Strachey*, i. facing 345.

98 He had met, and grown to like, Eleanor Farjeon when she visited Viola at Greatham in March – and subsequently offered to help with the typing of *The Rainbow*, see below.

99 In describing Tom Brangwen junior, DHL may have drawn on a similar anxiety about Bunny: 'When he was alone he seemed to have no being. When he was with another man, he seemed to add himself to the other' (E331a, p. 343; *R* 223:12–14 and p. 607, entry to 223:12).

100 *Flowers of the Forest*, pp. 50–5 (Nehls, i. 299–302).

101 See (ii. 320 notes), e.g. 'Ottoline must have been giving DHL a lurid account of my friendship with Francis Birrell. He was physically attracted by me, but I was unable to respond, and during our friendship which lasted from early 1914 until his death, I was quite incapable of returning his early "falling in love" with me which was rather imagined than real.' He did indeed have a lifelong friendship with Birrell, with whom he opened a bookshop, but though he was not sleeping with Birrell, his journal records him beginning to sleep with Duncan Grant shortly after 6 January (Spalding, *Vanessa Bell*, p. 135). Spalding adds: 'Though he had previously flirted with Maynard and Lytton and enjoyed a sentimental attachment with Francis Birrell, he had so far always refused to pursue a male friendship into bed; that he did so now with Duncan greatly upset Birrell.' Bunny went to live with Duncan, and Vanessa, first at Wissett in 1916 and later at Charleston. Until the legislation which followed the 1957 Wolfenden report, homosexual acts were illegal; so there was

justification for concealment, but perhaps less for attempting to discredit DHL's concern while concealing its cause.

102 *R* 458:39–459:1 and p. 609, entries to 458:40.

103 A significant anecdote, about the violence of his response as a boy when lassoed (*Golden Echo* 168), suggests how much he hated and would react to being forced in any direction. His shaking hands may have been rage.

104 Delany discusses the paradoxes of neo-pagan liberty in *The Neo-Pagans*, pp. xvi, 42, 68.

105 Keynes, *Two Memoirs*, p. 80. The selective quotation from DHL's letter to Bunny begins in Bunny's original 'Memoir', delivered in private to the Memoir Club and worked up into his later reminiscences of DHL. I am grateful to Richard Garnett for the loan of this paper, which is as vivid (and in many ways as attractive) a glimpse of a younger Bunny as of its subject. DHL did, of course, have a physical admiration and great affection for Bunny, and may have felt jealous at how he was being taken over, but his reactions to his young friend's relationships went deeper than that, as did the tone of his letter.

106 Cf. allusion to Nietzsche's *Morgenröte* (*The Dawn*) (1881) in *R* 401:35–6 and Explanatory note, p. 531.

107 There had been discussion 'of sending her away, perhaps to further her studies' (Miranda Seymour, *Ottoline Morrell: Life on the Grand Scale*, 1992, p. 219).

108 Cf. *R* 186–91 with 590–6. See also Kinkead-Weekes, 'The Marble and the Statue'.

109 E331a, p. 341 (*R* 604); 220:5–6; 219:34; 218:26–7.

110 *R* 220:24, 33. The irony this time is the degree of his success. The implication of anal sex was not spotted until Wilson Knight, 'Lawrence, Joyce and Powys', *Essays in Criticism*, xi (October 1961), 403–17. Will's longing to be like a 'tiger-cat' was cut at proof stage, perhaps in self-censorship to meet an objection from Pinker, or perhaps not, see *R* lxviii. That DHL was talking of the significance of Blake's 'Tyger' at the time is clear from BR to OM, posted 3 and 6 April (UT), when he takes issue with DHL's view that '*everybody* is a "Tyger, Tyger"' and his failure to understand 'how Love (the universal kind) may be just as deep as the tiger'.

111 *R* 220:5–8. See also Colin Clarke, *River of Dissolution* (1969), pp. 49–52.

112 It is significant that only one of the passages which might be argued as self-censorship, see *R* lxiv–lxix, comes from this final section, though several of the passages expurgated for Huebsch's edition do.

113 Any explanation of the fifteen-month gap between the order and the move to enforce it must be speculative, and the law's delays are proverbial. But since it is unlikely that Weekley's lawyers would have waited so long to be paid, it seems possible that he may have decided to pay the costs himself, rather than add to Frieda's impoverishment. If that were so, the reactivation of the claim may have been caused by his resentment at her irruption into his house, and her subsequent ambushing of him in Nottingham in December 1914. Whatever non-bankrupting settlement was reached, might then have depended on Weekley's unwillingness to pursue the matter too far, and perhaps on an undertaking by Frieda. An order for costs of the examination, for £10/15/2 was made on 8 July (ii. 328n.).

114 DHL also asked for 'One other little thing' – a dedication to Else, in German and in Gothic script. The motivation will have been complex: partly a mark of gratitude for all she had done for them in the early days; partly an appropriate tribute to a remarkable New Woman whose career had run parallel to Ursula's in many respects, and rather more successfully; but partly also a vindication of himself and his marriage, to the sister-in-law (now) who had not always been convinced that Frieda ought to stay with him. But in the form he wanted, it would have been intensely provocative in 1915, and Pinker sensibly insisted on only 'To Else' – though even the German form of the name was a little risky.

Chapter Five: Rainbow's End

1 See Frieda's letters to OM, e.g. *c.* 8 April 'God be merciful to us and don't send us any Meynell when you come; *c.* 20 April 'The Meynellage is getting on my nerves, there is so absolutely nothing between them and me' (UT).

2 Nehls, i. 288–9. Hueffer's wife having refused to divorce him, he was living with Violet Hunt without being able to marry her. He would soon change his surname to 'Ford' in order to conceal his German antecedents. C. F. G. Masterman, an ex-cabinet Minister, had become Director of the secret propaganda bureau known as Wellington House, cf. Delany, *Lawrence's Nightmare: The Writer and His Circle in the Years of the Great War* (Hassocks, 1979), p. 101.

3 *Memoirs* 208.

4 *Letters of JMM to KM*, ed. Hankin, p. 55.

5 BR to OM, posted 3 and 6 April (UT).

6 *Edward Thomas, The Last Four Years: Book One of the Memoirs of Eleanor Farjeon* (1958), p. 130 (Nehls, i. 293).

7 David Garnett *(Golden Echo*, p. 125) describes her as 'small as her name suggests; she had pretty brown eyes and short, curly brown hair, and though she was the mother of a grown-up son, she was still a very atttractive and vivacious creature ... She had an intense love of life, the bubbling vitality of a child.' She was a friend of Eleanor Marx; had published two volumes of poetry by 1910, and a play in 1915. Her home at 32 Well Walk in Hampstead, was 'like a chest of drawers ... always overflowing with people' (ibid.) – and a constant refuge for the Lawrences. Ernest Radford had translated Heine and published several volumes of verse. For his mental trouble, see *Golden Echo*, pp. 124–6; he had to be placed in a home in 1918.

8 Farjeon, *Edward Thomas*, p. 129.

9 Nehls, i. 292.

10 Farjeon, *Edward Thomas*, pp. 130–1. She helped Viola with the typing of *The Rainbow*, her portion 'including the stampede of horses which seemed to me epic, the work of a genius' (p. 123).

11 *Flowers of the Forest*, pp. 51–2 (Nehls, i. 300).

12 Farjeon, *Edward Thomas*, p. 133 (Nehls, i. 294); cf. Frieda to Kot, ?20 April (*Memoirs* 208).

13 Frieda to OM, *c.* 20 April (UT); Frieda to Kot, ?20 April (*Memoirs* 208); Frieda to Ottoline, *c.* 9 April (UT).

14 OM to BR, 29 and 30 April (McMaster); BR to OM, ?30 April and 1 May (UT); OM to BR, 27 April (McMaster).

15 *Edward Thomas*, pp. 135–7 (Nehls, i. 294–7).

16 *Letters of JMM to KM*, ed. Hankin, pp. 60, 62–3.

17 Farjeon, *Edward Thomas*, p. 130.

18 *Diaries 1915–18* (1968), pp. 18–19. See also chapter 4, pp. 218–19.

19 Even now Frieda appears not to have taken in the injunction.

20 Nehls, i. 300, 303, 306; Eleanor confirms his motivation (Nehls, i. 306). DHL's letter is the one in which he says (about the sinking of the *Lusitania*) that he 'would like to kill a million Germans' – then adds, 'Don't take any notice of my extravagant talk – one must say something.' It is easy to give a false impression by selective quotation.

21 Mary Saleeby-Fisher in Nehls, i. 304; also an interview with her; and her notebook (UT). See also chapter 4, pp. 179 and 798 note 30 and interviews with Louie Burrows's younger sisters Winifred and Nora.

22 Farjeon, *Edward Thomas*, p. 306.

23 BR to OM, posted 31 May (UT).

24 *Diaries*, pp. 37–8.

25 OM to BR, 11 June (UT); BR to OM, 11 and 12 June (McMaster).

26 *Ottoline at Garsington*, ed. Gathorne-Hardy, pp. 36–7; OM to BR, 31 May (McMaster); BR to OM 15 June (UT).

27 *Ottoline at Garsington*, ed. Gathorne-Hardy, pp. 37–8; OM to BR, 18 June (McMaster). There appears to have been a great deal of reworking and expansion in hindsight. I am most grateful for having been allowed to see the original terse entry.

28 *Diaries*, p. 45.

29 BR to OM, 19 and *c.* 20–1 June (UT); OM to BR, 24 June (McMaster); Cf. BR's reply the next day: 'Yes, Lawrence and I are curiously alike in many ways' (UT); BR to OM, 19 or 20 June.

30 *Diaries*, pp. 45–6.

31 It is not quite certain that Frieda's letter (UT), headed 'Littlehampton' but entirely dateless, dates from the visit to Littlehampton on 21 June, rather than the later visit there in early August. But two points make the late June date much the more likely: the possibility that unburdening herself to CA had made it possible to write to OM (whereas in August Frieda was newly enraged by the news that DHL *was* being invited to Garsington alone); and that there is no mention in OM's letters to BR of a letter from Frieda in August, whereas she encloses one in her letter to him on 3 July (McMaster) and has his comments back the next day (UT).

32 BR's typescript and DHL's comments (UT) are printed as Appendix A in *D. H. Lawrence's Letters to Bertrand Russell*, ed. Harry T. Moore (New York, 1948). Cf. Russell, 'The disease: disintegration', p. 79; DHL's comments on Sections III and IV, pp. 92–3.

33 *Letters to Russell*, Russell, pp. 79, 81, 95–6; DHL, pp. 81–2.

34 Ibid., pp. 77, 81 and especially pp. 87–8, where DHL angrily ('no! no! no! no! no!')

refuses BR's claim that morality comes from wanting others to like us, and is defined by conformity to others' wishes.

35 Ibid., Russell, pp. 85, 95; DHL, 89, 85, 84, 95, 85.

36 Ibid., pp. 82–3; 88; 90–1.

37 BR to OM, 8 July (UT); Keynes, *Two Memoirs*, p. 102.

38 BR to OM, 11 and 8 July (UT).

39 *Portraits from Memory and Other Essays* [1956] (Nehls, i. 282–5).

40 Heracleitus fragments 59, 32, 36, 39, 46, 41–2, 60, 69, 83 in Burnet, *Early Greek Philosophy* (4th edn, 1930).

41 *Letters to Russell*, p. 95; Heracleitus fragment 43, in Burnet, *Early Greek Philosophy*.

42 *Letters to Russell*, pp. 94, 82; Heracleitus fragments 110, 111, 114, in Burnet *Early Greek Philosophy*.

43 DHL's political development is traced in Macdonald Daly, 'D. H. Lawrence and Labour in the Great War', *Modern Language Review*, lxxxix (January 1994), 19–38.

44 BR to OM, 31 July (UT); OM to BR, 25 July (McMaster).

45 *R* 408:39–409:2; p. 656 entry to 408:40; 409:2–6.

46 *R* 459:39; 459:3; 459:5–8 and p. 669 entries, 459:2, 4.

47 The expurgations are listed *R* xliv n. 34.

48 These are discussed in detail in *R* lxiv–lxix. Charles Ross is far more confident of DHL's intentions: cf. *Composition* 37–57.

49 Methuen stock ledger (UInd) and see *R* lvi–lvii.

50 The *Strand* was in fact one of the least likely magazines to take such a story, as Pinker will have realised straightaway. DHL came to regard it as the archetypal 'popular' periodical.

51 Both versions are printed in *EmyE* (5–33, 219–32).

52 *EmyE* 8:8. Only those close to the family could know that Wilfrid Meynell came from an 'impoverished Quaker family' in Newcastle, and Percy Lucas from 'an old south-of-England family' – though that, too, would apply to thousands (*EmyE* 221:7, 21–2). There is brief mention of Winifred having six siblings, and three daughters (222:36–7; 220:36), but none is named and there are no other cottages. There is no poet-mother.

53 See Barbara Lucas, 'Apropos of "England, my England"', *Twentieth Century*, clxix (March 1961), 288–93, which however deals only with the later version.

54 From an entry in Mary Saleeby's exercise-book, Nehls, i. 304.

55 Farjeon, *Edward Thomas*, p. 29.

56 *EmyE* 219:3, 16, 33; 220:19–20.

57 *EmyE* 221:1–2; 220:13, 23–4, 26; 223:25–6.

58 *EmyE* 224:11–14; 224:26; 225:11–12, 30–1; 226:13–18; 226:28.

59 *Diaries*, pp. 56–8.

60 *SP* 31–2; Murry, *Reminiscences*, p. 67 (Nehls, i. 322).

61 Nehls, i. 320.

62 'He suddenly appeared at her door when she was alone in her Hampstead flat, she remembered, peeling apples in that Spanish pottery bowl' (*BMTL* 138). She goes on to recall how DHL had seemed the only one who knew how she felt about losing her baby.

Through them, he also met – though not until the autumn – their close friend John Cournos, writer and journalist from Philadelphia, whose family had emigrated from Russia and who had pulled himself up from conditions of great poverty – and Morfydd Owen, who would marry the leading English Freudian Ernest Jones in 1917. (Information from Rhian Davis.)

63 Belief in equal opportunity – were that achievable – does something to reconcile the two ideas; though DHL believed in disquality – what he would later call 'sacred differences' – rather than any intrinsic equality or egalitarianism.

64 Percy was an actor much admired for performances in Shakespeare and Shaw. In 1911 he joined Miss Horniman's theatre company in Manchester. Unfortunately for DHL, he enlisted in the army in December 1915 and remained in it until 1923; but he did eventually produce DHL's play at the Kingsway, London, in 1926. Marsh printed 'Service of All the Dead' and 'Meeting Among the Mountains' in *Georgian Poetry 1913–1915* that November. The former would also appear (as 'Giorno dei Morti') in *The Book of Italy*, ed. Raffaello Piccoli and published by Fisher Unwin for the Pro-Italia Committee in 1916.

65 *Ottoline at Garsington*, ed. Gathorne-Hardy, p. 45; Seymour, *Ottoline Morrell*, pp. 242–4.

66 It seems however, from Forster's unpublished diary at Kings College, Cambridge (*c.* 9 September) that DHL was mistaken in this, and that Forster had taken strong exception on this occasion to DHL's criticisms of someone he greatly admired: 'After Lawrence's remarks about Carpenter realise with regret that I cannot know him.' Though DHL's idea of the bisexuality of everyone was indeed influenced to some extent by Carpenter, he differed radically from Carpenter in two essential respects. His idea of growth through conflict (and even violence) differed markedly from Carpenter's pacifism; and he differed even more strongly from Carpenter's high valuation of 'the intermediate sex' and his justification of homosexuality. It may have been an attack on this that upset Forster. On 25 September DHL asked Willie Hopkin to send a *Signature* leaflet to Carpenter even 'though he is not in my line' (ii. 401). Though DHL wrote to Forster at the end of the month about Hugh Meredith's visit (ii. 403–4), it seems there was then a long silence until May 1916, when correspondence recommenced.

67 *Collected Papers of Bertrand Russell*, xiii. 'Prophecy and Dissent 1914–16', pp. 327–38.

68 When BR first drafted his *Autobiography* a year after DHL's death, there was no mention of him at all. Four years later, as his biographer says (Clark, *Life of Russell*, p. 265), his 'real feelings surfaced' in one of his last letters to OM, where he wrote that DHL was 'one of a long line beginning with Heracleitus & ending with Hitler, whose ruling motive was hatred derived from megalomania'. Two decades later, in 'Portraits from Memory' (1952), pp. 104–8, repeated in a broadcast for the BBC (Nehls, i. 282–5) he alleged that DHL 'had developed the whole philosophy of fascism before the politicians had thought of it', that he used 'the language of a fascist dictator' and that his philosophy of 'blood' was 'frankly rubbish' which BR had rejected 'vehemently, though I did not then know it led straight to Auschwitz' (ibid.,

i. 283–4). In 1968 he incorporated the attack into his *Autobiography*, also charging that DHL had been a mouthpiece for his wife's ideas. The *Autobiography* begins: 'Three passions, simple, but overwhelmingly strong, have governed my life; the longing for love, the search for knowledge, and unbearable pity for the suffering of mankind' (i. 20–4). It is clear enough that the motivation of his account of DHL was more concerned to jab and strike than any of these, let alone the impulse to truth whose existence he had refused to concede; but it does show how DHL's attack had got under his skin and festered. It would have been better to have replied abusively at the time.

69 There is no evidence of earlier versions of the six essays which now follow 'The Theatre'. Had there been any, DHL in his times of penury would certainly have attempted to publish them. The evidence of the essays themselves suggests that they were conceived in terms of, and proceeded to explore, points that the *new* 'Lemon Gardens' and 'Theatre' had reached; and therefore that they were newly conceived and written in 1915.

70 *TI* 44:14–15; 97:39; 99:4–5; 100:34–5. 'Christs in the Tyrol' and 'The Crucifix Across the Mountains' are both in *TI* (43–7, 91–100).

71 *TI* 106:24; 107:10–11; cf. the two versions: *TI* 51–8, 103–13.

72 *TI* 117:1; 121:38; 122:11–13; cf. the two versions: *TI* 59–68, 114–32.

73 The second insertion (cf. *TI* 63 with 124–6) restates the Opposites, but also how they have become exhausted. There can be no going back. (But how to go forward?)

74 *TI* 132:28–9.

75 Now 'It is past the time to leave off ...', *TI* 125:30–1; cf. p. 315 and entries to 125:30.

76 *TI* 125:32–3.

77 *TI* 137:29–30, 39–40; cf. the two versions: *TI* 69–80, 133–53.

78 *TI* 149:6–9.

79 Cf. *TI* 154–66 with Cyriax, *Among Italian Peasants*, pp. 3–13. Paul Eggert's interviews with the son and daughter of the Capellis ('The Subjective Art of D. H. Lawrence', unpublished Ph.D. thesis, University of Kent at Canterbury, 1981, pp. 303–17) show both the factual bases for DHL's portraits and also how he transposed some details (e.g. the blaspheming was Maria's, not Paolo's) for his own purposes. See also *TI* 288–90.

80 *TI* 162:35; 158:23–4; 164:10, b; 154:32; 165:11. Cyriax, *Among Italian Peasants*, p. 13.

81 See (ii. 418): I. Narodiczky was also to print and publish Isaac Rosenberg's poems in 1915, again no 'little' distinction. Unfortunately, the Cambridge Edition does not reprint the original version of 'The Crown', which can however be reconstructed from Appendix II in *RDP* (469–79), in conjunction with the heavily revised version published in 1925, pp. 253–306.

82 *RDP* 272:6–12. On Heracleitan flux see Burnet, *Early Greek Philosophy*, pp. 161ff., though the idea of human being as a process of continual change – as against the idea of a 'stable' ego – had been formulated by DHL in 1914 before reading Heracleitus, who confirmed and extended his thinking rather than originating it.

83 *RDP* 272:27–8, 293:22 and 476–7, entries to 293:22 and 294:25.

84 *RDP* 282:37–8. The passage exploring homosexuality (*RDP* 472–4, entry to 285:1) was cut from the 1925 version, by which time DHL was no longer interested in homosexuality and its significance.

85 *RDP* 476 entry to 289:29; 300:29–30; 302:17.

86 'Il Duro' was posted 8 October, 'Italians in Exile' on 12 October and 'The Return Journey' (originally 'On the Road') on the 19th (iii. 408 and n. 2; 410 and n. 3; 413 and n. 2). There is no mention of 'The Dance' and 'John'. Eggert suggests, plausibly, that 'The Dance' may originally have been part of 'San Gaudenzio' from which it obviously leads on. He thinks that 'John' may have been an afterthought, written between 21 and 26 October when DHL sent away the whole (iv. 417; presumably, then, with the last two essays in manuscript), see *TI* xlvi. Since no manuscript or typescript survives for *TI*, it is impossible to tell for sure.

87 *TI* 168:17, 24–5, 34–5; 170:20. Tony Cyriax described a dance in Muslone, in which she danced with the one-legged wood-cutter (*Among Italian Peasants*, p. 22). It is however very unlikely that the blonde signora described as attracting his invitation outside, in DHL's account, is Tony, whom Bunny Garnett decribed as brown-skinned and dark-eyed. The 'blonde' (in Italian terms) seems certain to have been Frieda (even without the private joke). That the wood-cutter danced with both is confirmed by (i. 536). Eggert was told by the younger Capellis that dances took place at both places (*TI* 290–1, note to 167:28).

88 *TI* 173:29–30, 35, 30–1, 37; 177:7, 8–10; 176:36–7; 177:1–2; 178:5, 6, and see 291–2 for notes on the real-life Faustino Magri.

89 *TI* 180:39–40; 185:31; 185:4–5; 186:16–19; 186:40–1, and see 292–4 for notes suggesting that 'John' had an original, but may have been conflated also with another or others – or partly invented?

90 *TI* 198:12, 26; 197:23, 24–5; 200:9; 200:12; 200:22; 204:24, 31–3. In proof DHL added: 'I did not believe in the perfectibility of man' (202:15–16).

91 *TI* 210:38; 211:33–4; 223:39–40;, see the change in proof 323, entry to 226:37.

92 Cf. 'Note to The Crown', *RDP* 249 (not altogether reliable!) and (ii. 385, 418, 409, 428).

93 The information we have about subscriptions comes from DHL's letters (e.g. (ii. 399, 405)), letters from subscribers in the Koteliansky papers (BL) and DHL's *Signature* accounts in a notebook (UT). See also note 96.

94 For a full account of what was happening to *The Rainbow*, see *R* xlv–li.

95 Draper 91–2; *BTW* 351.

96 At most a dozen people came to the meeting. (Indeed, that *may* be the figure, from DHL's Note – *RDP* 249 – for both meetings. Murry is equally ambiguous – *Reminiscences*, p. 68.) We know the names of (eventually) 122 subscribers to *Signature*, a number of them for more than one set, and there were some 9 further purchases, but the records are incomplete since there is no way of knowing whether sums handed in by Kot and others equate with, or cover more people than, the names we have. However, the total income from subscriptions up to 4 November, as shown in DHL's accounts (see n. 81) was £17/12/6 – equivalent to 141 subscrip-

tions (cf. Murry's 'about £15' in *Reminiscences*) – and the accounts show that income to have covered the printing costs of the three issues, and also the postage, room hire and most though not all of the incidental expenses. The only serious loss will have been of confidence and pride.

97 *Diaries*, pp. 88, 90, 92.

98 Methuen to Pinker (NYPL).

99 Draper 93–5. Behind these criticisms is a basic horror at the novel's psychological revelation of what lies below 'the old stable ego'. Both Lynd and Douglas have a picture of the human soul in conflict with 'lower' nature; but where Lynd sees reduction to the physical, in Douglas's rodomontade this becomes 'abominations' and 'putrescence'. Shorter (Draper 96–7) for all his show of liberalism, is with Douglas. In addition, we have to imagine a climate in which Augustine Birrell, Frankie's father, man of letters as well as a cabinet minister, to whom Bunny wrote in fury when he heard what had happened, could say on 13 November 1915 that he 'would forbid the use during the war of poetry', as though at a time of national crisis *no* individual thinking or feeling could be permitted to distract, let alone subvert, the national effort. The *Observer* opined the same day that 'the war has practically killed the "problem novel" and with it the neurotic heroine'.

100 For Pinker's letter (to the Society of Authors), see John Carter, 'The Rainbow Prosecution', *The Times Literary Supplement* (27 February 1969), 216 and *R* xlix. Mr Muller from Methuen telephoned Pinker to say they had been approached by Clive Bell who was 'anxious to write in defence of Mr Lawrence and his work', but having consulted one of his Directors, Muller told Pinker that 'they felt very strongly that the matter should be hushed up' and hoped Pinker would do 'nothing in the matter'.

101 See p. 791 note 84, and next note below.

102 Public Record Office HO 45/13944, Minute 210/PB/589, Prosecutions Branch, Scotland Yard – when it had been discovered that Secker had quietly republished the novel in 1926. It was decided not to prosecute however, in order not to give DHL's work any further publicity in the aftermath of his death.

103 Letters from Carl Hovey, editor of *Metropolitan*, and John Reed, soon to become famous for his book about the Russian revolution, *Ten Days That Shook The World*, in the Huebsch archive (LC). Hovey thought the book 'one of the finest of literary performances, and no Englishman has equalled it, it seems to me, since Thomas Hardy was young. It is all immensely real, sincere, and of a sustained intensity which compels great admiration.' Reed wrote: 'I have never been so deeply moved by anything. The Russians come nearest to him, but after all, they are different from us, their springs of action are other than ours. But this book is the life of our race, made beautiful and yet true.'

104 *Diaries*, pp. 93, 86.

105 *EmyE* 200:15; *Diaries*, p. 95.

106 The first page of the manuscript sent to CA is missing, but the whole poem, reconstructed from an autograph version found in a notebook and printed by David Farmer, 'D. H. Lawrence's "The Turning Back": The Text and Its Genesis in Correspondence', *DHLR*, v (Summer 1972), 121–31, can be found in (ii. 421–3).

For CA's reaction to the poem and his letter defending it, see *Diaries*, p. 95. She was amused at having 'godmothered' a suppressed book, but unfortunately for her, DHL got to hear that she had said it was 'like the second story in the Prussian Officer, only much *worse*' (ii. 432). He had been told by 'that little sneak Murry, who had eavesdropped' at an exhibition while 'pretending not to recognise me' (*Diaries*, p. 98). Nevertheless both DHL and Frieda were in fine form when CA took Mary Herbert to meet them in Hampstead on the 12th, and she was struck by the contrast between 'the misery and hystericalness of his letters' and the 'delicious laughter in him' that seemed not to come out on paper (*Diaries*, pp. 97–8).

107 Brett, *Lawrence and Brett*, pp. 16–19. She also describes her first meeting in the 'tiny box of a house ... dark and poky' in the Vale of Health, where Gertler (who had taken her), and the Lawrences sat 'tearing poor [Ottoline] to pieces'. This must have been in the aftermath of the row at Garsington and OM's subsequent invitation excluding Frieda – probably therefore late September (a fire was burning), or October, before the complete reconciliation at the end of the month when OM found him 'Devine' again, OM to BR, 28 October (UT). Brett also describes a second un-gate-crashed evening on 7 November; but her memory is at fault in believing that her two parties were just before DHL left 'for abroad' – as opposed to Cornwall – at the end of the year. Strachey's letter to Bunny Garnett, 9 November, in Holroyd, *Lytton Strachey*, ii. 161–2. DHL did not care for Strachey's writing, but his disgust will have had to do with what he had discovered about Cambridge, the Apostles and Keynes, although (as Holroyd points out) Strachey and DHL had, despite important and radical differences, a little more in common than either would readily have admitted.

108 This friend, perhaps the Mr Keen mentioned in the letter to Dollie Radford on 18 November (ii. 444), 'said we could live on his little estate in Florida' (ii. 429). DHL had been annoyed by hearing that Marsh had 'jeered' at *The Rainbow* (and had made a comic turn of Eddie to CA) but he was much moved by this support (ii. 428). He would repay the loan in September 1922. At Garsington he had told OM that he felt 'much affection' towards BR still, and when told of this (OM to BR, 11 November, UT), BR contributed towards the £30, a generous act after DHL's denunciation. Reconciliation was clearly possible, and would follow soon. DHL offered OM the manuscript of *The Rainbow* as a mark of his gratitude, but later she returned it to him.

109 Quotations from *The Times*, 15 November, p. 3 (Draper 102–3) and the *Daily Telegraph* of the same day.

Chapter Six: Mid-winter Life

1 See chapter 5, p. 813 note 100; Holroyd, *Lytton Strachey*, ii. 160; Squire: 'It is a dull and monotonous book which broods gloomily over the physical reactions of sex in a way so persistent that one wonders whether the author is under the spell of German psychologists ...', etc. (*New Statesman*, 20 November; Draper 104–7).

2 Bennnett referred in passing, in the *Daily News* of 15 November, to 'Mr. D. H.

Lawrence's beautiful and maligned novel "The Rainbow"'; see also his letter to Frank Swinnerton (*The Letters of Arnold Bennett 1916–1931*, ed. James Hepburn, 1970, iii. 111). For Carswell, see Draper 100–1; cf. *SP* 41–2. For Watson, see galley proof of review by 'H.C.W.', now in Nottingham University, with instructions not to print without permission.

3 Cf. (ii. 439 and n. 1) quoting Herbert Thring, Secretary to the Society of Authors, to Pinker (NYPL).

4 *Diaries*, p. 101; Nehls, i. 333–4.

5 It seems that Pinker, agent to them all and to Galsworthy, did make tentative enquiries, since DHL reacted to what sound like comments from Bennett (ii. 479), and Wells and James (ii. 451). Galsworthy, he wrote later, 'told me, very calmly and *ex cathedra*, he thought the book a failure as a work of art' (Introduction, *Bibliography of D. H. Lawrence*, by McDonald; *P* 234); but Galsworthy's letter to Pinker was much more hostile, calling the novel 'aesthetically detestable' and maintaining that the sex-instinct is so strong 'that any emphasis upon it drags the whole being of the reader away from seeing life steadily, truly, and whole' (Draper 108–9). For May Sinclair, see Nehls, i. 579 n. 195.

6 Watson's *Selected Essays and Reviews* (not, however, including his *Rainbow* review) were published posthumously with an introduction by Alice Meynell, in 1918. He worked for the *Telegraph* for eight years, the last five as a reviewer.

7 Cf. (ii. 417); 'The Spirit of the Lawrence Women', in *The Writings of Anna Wickham: Free Woman and Poet*, ed. R. D. Smith (1984), pp. 355–9.

8 See (ii. 402 and n. 1, 403–4, 425–6). Forster sent DHL a copy of Meredith's poems, 'and on the strength of this Meredith paid Lawrence a visit' (Furbank, *E. M. Forster*, ii. 3). Meredith was probably the most important friend of the young Forster, who fell in love with him at Cambridge. Though in externals Ansell in *The Longest Journey* resembles A. R. Ainsworth, his role as Rickie's mentor and conscience recalls Meredith's.

Harold Massingham, journalist and critic, was the son of the editor of *Nation*, and had himself been on the staff of the *Athenæum* before the war. He met DHL at Greatham, and though in a letter to the *Nation and Athenæum* in 1930 (Nehls, i. 274) he says he lost touch during the war, his wife remembered being told how he visited 'Lawrence's house in London, and was much amused by Lawrence hurling cushions at Frieda if she talked too much!' (Nehls, i. 574).

9 C. Garnett met Zinaida Athanasevna Vengerova through the exiled revolutionary Stepniak, in early summer 1893. Then 26, she had come to London to study English literature and was translating George Meredith into Russian. She was visited by Constance in St Petersburg on her visits to Russia, but continued to spend much time abroad. She held strong feminist views, was acquainted with Eleanor Marx and after the revolution she worked as a translator for the almanac *Vsemirnaya Literatura*, subsequently living in Germany, and dying in New York. No proofs, however, have survived.

10 Nehls, i. 470–2, referring also to how he was instrumental in getting DHL to write *Movements in European History* (see chapter 8, pp. 462 and 839 note 92).

11 PH to Frederick Delius, 16 November 1915 (BL): 'This evening I met and had a long talk with D. H. Lawrence. He can stand this country no longer, and is going to America in a week's time.'

12 Heseltine is better known as the composer Peter Warlock. For biographies see Cecil Gray, *Peter Warlock* (1934); I. A. Copley, *A Turbulent Friendship* (1983) – a study of the relationship between DHL and PH; and especially Barry Smith, *Peter Warlock: The Life of Philip Heseltine* (1994). Letters to Delius, 18 October 1914 (cf. also to Viva Smith, 16 October), 16 November 1915 (BL); and to Nichols, 12 October 1914 (BL).

13 Robert Nichols had met PH in Oxford; but after only a year at Trinity College he volunteered, was commissioned in the Royal Field Artillery, served briefly in Flanders and then spent five months in hospital. He published the first of several volumes of poetry, *Invocation*, in 1915. He contributed a chapter to Gray's *Peter Warlock*, and would see more of DHL (though he grew less sympathetic towards him) in 1918.

14 Letters from Delius to PH, 24 November 1915 (Lionel Carley, *Letters of Frederick Delius*, p. 155), and PH to Delius, 15 December (BL).

15 Suhrawardy was involved in the episode when KM put a stop to mockery of DHL's *Amores* in the Café Royal in 1916 (see pp. 337–8 and 824 note 106). He went to Russia and became Professor of English at various Moscow colleges, but had a precarious time during the October Revolution. However he became a régisseur in the Moscow Arts Theatre, and subsequently managed to get out of Russia and return to the West. Kouyoumdjian, born in Bulgaria in 1895, had his first bestseller in *The Green Hat* (1924). After their quarrel in 1916, (see pp. 299 and 818 note 35), he and Lawrence met again in Florence in 1927, where Lawrence drew on the renewed acquaintance in creating the character of Michaelis in *Lady Chatterley's Lover*. (A well-known photograph of DHL in a doorway in Garsington with two others portrays PH and Suhrawardy, not Kouyoumdjian as has usually been supposed: see, e.g., in ii.) Of Croustchoff at this time we know very little, though DHL saw him not only in PH's flat but later in Cornwall, where Boris visited PH, Gray and Phyl Crocker whom he later married.

16 'Resurrection', 77 lines in its original version, was published in *Poetry* (1917), and a final version in *The New Poetry* (1923).

17 DHL's contact with the Prince was probably through CA. He married Beb's step-sister Elizabeth Asquith in 1919.

18 Nehls, i. 335. The Labour politician was Commander Josiah Clement Wedgwood, known as 'Father of the Labour Party'. The question of a political motive for the prosecution was raised by the Radical M.P. Sir William Byles who asked whether the proceedings were taken 'under the Defence of the Realm Act'; which the Home Secretary denied. (There was, then, some contemporary suspicion about the motive of the prosecution, though perhaps more because of possible abuse by the authorities of the wide powers conferred by the act than a concern for DHL.)

19 Born in 1896 in Neuchâtel, Juliette married Julian Huxley in 1919, and became friendly with DHL again in 1927. In her autobiography *Leaves of the Tulip Tree*

(1986), pp. 48–9, she recalls doing Cophetua and the Beggar Maid at Garsington with PH as Cophetua; also as the Beast to her Beauty, 'wearing on his head a wickerwork waste-paper basket ... I remember bending over his reclining "dying" form and releasing my impromptu "love chant" and the wastepaper basket flying off to reveal his red sweating face.' (KM, however, could not have been present.)

Minnie Lucie Channing, born in 1894 in Chiswick, was the fourth daughter of Robert Channing, described on her marriage certificate as a mechanical engineer, and on her birth certificate as a hotel waiter. On PH's next visit to Garsington, without DHL, he wrote (diplomatically, in German) to Croustchoff on 14 December: 'Suddenly this evening as I considered the little overexciting Swiss girl, it came to me that I can NEVER return to Puma – it would be quite impossible. She has soiled my whole love – no more can I imagine that I love her the tiniest bit, when even now, with my whole heart, I passionately love the Swiss girl ...' (BL). His letters 'flattered and bewildered' Juliette, he took her walking on Hampstead Heath and to the Café Royal, but she says she 'became frightened' of him.

20 *Ottoline at Garsington*, ed. Gathorne-Hardy, p. 77.

21 Pinker's authors may have been willing to donate something – though Pinker may also have 'advanced' most of it from his own pocket. DHL was now also in touch with Mrs Belloc Lowndes again (ii. 471, 477, 479); cf. pp. 150 and 792 note 87.

22 Cf. (ii. 463), but Morrell was discouraging; Methuen to Pinker, 9 December (NYPL). Neither now or in 1919 however did Bibesco's geniality produce any help. For Collins, see (ii. 463) and Nehls, i. 470.

23 Introduction, *The Letters of D. H. Lawrence*, ed. Aldous Huxley (1932), p. xxix (Nehls, i. 339). Seymour says that OM's invitation of AH to Garsington was to placate her mother-in-law for having introduced her 19-year-old granddaughter and OM's niece, Dorothy Warren, to the dubious DHL (*Ottoline Morrell*, p. 247), which OM then compounded by introducing AH to him also. AH was already thinking of visiting his brother in Texas in 1916 (AH to OM, *Ottoline at Garsington*, ed. Gathorne-Hardy, pp. 80–1), so an agreement to visit Florida would not be *so* incautious.

24 Cf. (ii. 447–8); Nichols in Gray, *Peter Warlock*, pp. 89–90 – though the match-making is hardly evidence of 'a peculiar state of mind'. The one who did fall in love with Dorothy, without need of DHL's intervention, was Kouyoumdjian, see p. 299.

25 *BTW* 372–7; Alpers, *Life of Mansfield*, pp. 185–6.

26 *BTW* 380.

27 See (ii. 480), but there were even more expurgations than DHL had spotted; see *R* xliv n. 34 which lists them all. Though the American edition had been printed, it was not distributed for some time, and then in a very clandestine fashion to escape prosecution (*R* lix–lx).

28 For Bennett's article, see (ii. 479 n. 2). It was about a visit to the Midlands in which he was reminded of DHL's 'memorable and awful board-school scenes' – the most likely section to appeal to him.

29 Nehls, i. 470.

30 'The Prodigal Husband' was abandoned at Porthcothan, but revived in Zennor where it was set in the Tinner's Arms. The denouement he had been unable to conceive before (ii. 501), came with a new treatment of the man's dogged determination, despite being bound hand and foot by order of his wife, and brought with it a new ironic title, 'Samson and Delilah'.

31 See (ii. 525, 556): 'more than his share'. Some accounts appear in a notebook into which DHL transcribed poems, many meant for *Amores* (which PH typed). By the end of February half of DHL's £100 was gone (letter from PH to Delius, 1 March; BL): 'only fifty pounds stand between him and starvation'; cf. Frieda's conciliatory letter to OM, *c.* 25 February, refusing the offer of money because 'we have a lot left still – about 50£' (UT).

32 PH to Delius, 11 February 1916 (BL). The child, to be called Nigel, must have been conceived in October 1915 since he was born in mid-July 1916.

33 PH to Delius, 6 January 1916 (BL) (Gray, *Peter Warlock*, p. 110). Gray listed PH's reading in Boehme, Trismegistus, Paracelsus, Eliphas Lévi, to which Nichols added the sexologists Havelock Ellis, Carpenter and Weininger (pp. 144, 67) – but there is some doubt about the date of this reading, since Nichols's confidence about PH's high opinion of Weininger at Oxford is hardly borne out by PH's letters. Though these confirm that he recommended Ellis and Carpenter to Viva Smith in 1914, and owned Eliphas Lévi in 1917, he only mentioned Weininger to add (in 1914): 'I have not read this, but it is considered a very good work.' He did however think of joining 'a little society of Psychical research' in 1914, and sent for a catalogue of 'Occult, Psychic and New Thought' publications from William Rider. Delius may have encouraged this interest, since he had mentioned 'table turning & spirit rapping' in a letter to PH in 1912; who told Viva in 1913 that Delius had been 'greatly interested in various occult séances'. It seems likely that PH's interest in the occult and the depth of his reading were increased by contact with Meredith Starr in 1917, and reached their height during his year in Ireland (1917–18); but had certainly begun to develop before 1915.

34 Frieda to OM, [1 January] 1916 (UT).

35 Postscript in PH to Viva Smith, 16 February 1916 (BL); the 'Rhinoceros' hide confirmed by Frieda to OM, *c.* 17 January (UT). The *New Age* skit according to PH writing to Delius, 22 April (BL) – but Kouyoumdjian did not become a contributor to *New Age* for some time yet, and no such sketch appeared there. DHL's later reference to the débâcle with PH as 'shamefully fit for a Kouyoumdjian sketch' (ii. 598) might confirm the threat – but it may also be that the idea and the basis of the skit on PH and Puma (see p. 302) was Kouyoumdjian's rather than DHL's, which might explain the remark.

36 *Memoirs* 209.

37 The first lecture was on Tuesday 18 January, and the eight were completed on 7 March (published in November as *Principles of Social Reconstruction*); for Torquay and Vivien Eliot, see Seymour, *Ottoline Morrell*, p. 244.

38 Tomalin, *Katherine Mansfield*, p. 163.

39 See (ii. 478, 506); 'My poetry will sell sooner than my prose, if it is properly

marketed' (ii. 513). The volume was dedicated to OM and published in July by Duckworth.

40 Gray, *Peter Warlock*, p. 114; OM to BR, 4 March 1916 (McMaster), the day after receiving another abusive letter from Frieda. According to Gray there were two typescript copies of which DHL destroyed one before leaving Zennor, and PH used the other for toilet paper, having (presumably) ignored DHL's request (ii. 598) to return it. Gray may however have confused this with the fate of a typescript of 'At the Gates', destroyed in that way by PH (according to Joseph Hone) in revenge for *Women in Love* (UT; (ii. 196 n. 2)).

41 See pp. 103-4; 161-2; 172-80; 199-208.

42 See pp. 190-3, 209-16.

43 See pp. 201-4, 220-2; 207; 213-15.

44 See pp. 280, (ii. 424) to CA; 269-71 ('The Crown'); 271 and 812 note 84; 297 and (ii. 447-8).

45 *Ottoline at Garsington*, ed. Gathorne-Hardy, p. 93.

46 *Hardy* 12:36-7.

47 *The Ajanta Frescoes*, forty-two in all, were newly published by Oxford University Press in October, and obtained through Vere Collins (ii. 490 and n., 505). The frescoes in the sacred Buddhist caves of Ajanta in Maharashtra, India, date from the first century BC to the seventh AD.

48 BR told a friend on 10 February: 'my lectures are a great success ... a rallying-ground for the intellectuals ... All sorts of literary & artistic people who formerly despised politics are being driven to action' (*Autobiography*, ii. 59). He may well have written in similar terms to DHL, who replied the next day asking (rather sceptically) whether they were indeed 'really vital', and whether Russell was 'really glad? – or only excited?' (ii. 534). Later, scepticism increased.

49 In *Also Sprach Zarathustra*, tr. Levy (*Complete Works*, xi. 25), Nietzsche had written: 'Three metamorphoses of the spirit do I designate to you: how the spirit becometh a camel, the camel a lion, the lion at last a child.' (It is unclear whether – given DHL's habit of not crossing a final 't' – the reading a few lines above is 'dead meat' (ii. 547) or 'dead meal'. But does one grind meat *fine*?)

50 OM to BR, 23 February. The third reading of the Military Service Act, imposing conscription on all able-bodied men between 18 and 40, had been passed on 23 January and would come into force in June. BR was to be one of its major opponents. PH was greatly worried too.

51 The pale blue and black counterpane announced itself (as they puzzled over OM's handwriting) as 'the countrypair' (ii. 538). DHL asked to borrow Petronius, and *The Possessed*, but thereafter wanted 'something a bit learned' rather than literary: Anglo-Saxon, Norse or early Celtic, or on Druids or the Orphic religions, or Egypt, or 'really African', fetish worship, or the customs of primitive tribes (ii. 510-11). She sent him the Loeb edition of *Hesiod, The Homeric Hymns and Homerica*, trans. Hugh G. Evelyn-White (1915) an ancient history, and books on Egypt, primitive cultures and early Greek religion. (See notes 72-5 below.) The pre-Socratic and pre-Christian emphasis is clear; though he also enjoyed Coulton's *From St. Francis to*

Dante which had a chapter on Joachim de Fiore, and the account of the monasteries in the dark ages, which seemed to reflect his own situation.

52 Frieda to OM, 1 January and n.d. [*c.* 17 January] (UT); but then the denunciation [?22/23 January], enclosed in OM's letter to BR about 24 January (McMaster), which he returned on 'Wednesday' [26th] (UT).

53 Frieda to OM n.d. [?22/23 January]; which however begins: 'I hope you will come before long and that you are better – I wish this quite sincerely, though I know in your heart . . .

54 Frieda however would tell OM: 'My quarrel with you was never that you were fond of Lawrence but that you seemed to underrate *me*' [*c.* 25 February] (UT).

55 PH to OM, 28 January 1916 (UT).

56 Perhaps to accompany DHL's letter of 25 February (which also referred to their purchase of a green bowl for OM, perhaps as a making-up gift) (ii.556).

57 The scheme is first mentioned on 11 February (ii. 532). The circular is reprinted in (ii. 542 n. 1) and advertises that 'If sufficient money is forthcoming, a second book will be announced; either Mr. Lawrence's philosophical work, "Goats and Compasses, " or a new book by some other writer.' The lowish price suggests that a large readership was envisaged, and PH's enthusiastic letter to Viva Smith on 16 February (BL) says he expected to be able to print 1,000 copies for £120; sell them for 7/6 post-free; and that the books after ' "Goats and Compasses" (a veritable soul-bomb, a dum-dum that will explode inside the soul!' would be 'a sequel to "The Rainbow"' and 'a novel by Middleton Murry'. OM thought the plan itself good, though perhaps ill-advised to start with *The Rainbow* (to BR, 16 February; UT); but found the prospectus *'odious* . . . It makes me angry – I hate disdain – & contempt. I feel I must tell L I hate it' (to BR, 29 February). If she did, this may have contributed to another angry letter from Frieda, 'quite dreadful, abusing me like anything', of which OM complained to BR on 3 March, but which seems not to have survived.

58 PH to Nichols, 8 March 1916 (BL).

59 PH to Delius, 22 April (BL) (Gray, *Peter Warlock*, p. 118).

60 Juliette Huxley, in *Leaves of the Tulip Tree*, pp. 48–9, implies that she had already broken with PH 'not gently, but finally' *before* (she confirms) 'Ottoline questioned me about it, and I learnt he had a mistress who was pregnant with his child. We never met again, and I burnt all his letters.' Her memory, so many years later, may not be accurate in detail or sequence, but she had certainly been angry when PH wrote to her denouncing 'the Ott' for maligning Frieda. Paul Delany's guess (*D. H. Lawrence's Nightmare*, p. 404 n. 55) that a 'soulful' document in the Juliette Huxley papers in UT may be an answer to a proposal of marriage from PH seems, on careful inspection, very unlikely, but it is clear from OM's giving him 'Goats and Compasses' to return, that he did visit Garsington after coming back to London from Cornwall, must have been made to admit the facts about Puma, and was repulsed with finality by Juliette.

61 Gray, *Peter Warlock*, p. 114; PH to Delius, 22 April: 'when I wrote and denounced him to his face, all he could say was: – "I request that you do not talk about me in London" – so he evidently had a very bad attack of guilty conscience. So I replied

with a page of prophetic reviews of a future book "D. H. Lawrence, a Critical Study by P.H.," of which the "Times" will say: – "Reveals the distorted soul of this unhappy genius in all its naked horror", and the "Spectator" will gloat over "A monster of obscenity tracked down to its secret lair", "John Bull alliterates with "Personified perversity pitilessly portrayed" … etc. etc.'; cf. Gray, *Peter Warlock*, pp. 118–19.

62 E.g. from Emma, and her sister sewing on an armlet, the claim that Cornish women are 'soft', 'wise', 'attractive' and 'unopposing', 'a quality of winsomeness and rare, unconscious Female soothingness' [unlike Frieda!]; and from Beresford's landlord Hawken a view of 'small-eyed and mean' 'cunning nosed' peasantry (ii. 496–7).

63 See (ii. 551); still rather a lot given that they had only £50 left. To find the cottage at Higher Tregerthen for a mere £5 a year was a huge stroke of good fortune.

64 KM, *Letters*, ed. O'Sullivan and Scott, i. 250; KM, *Journal*, p. 114; JMM to KM, [20 December 1915] (*Letters of JMM to KM*, ed. Hankin, p. 79).

65 JMM to KM (*Letters of JMM to KM*, ed. Hankin, p. 88); OM to BR, 29 December 1915 (McMaster): 'Murry talked a lot about his wife. It is the most wonderful devotion'; JMM to OM, n.d. [?31 December], from Waterloo station (UT). Cf. *Ottoline at Garsington*, ed. Gathorne-Hardy, p. 87.

66 KM to JMM, *Letters*, ed. O'Sullivan and Scott, i. 233; JMM to OM, 31 December (UT), dated from Gare de Lyon station in Paris. KM to OM, 21 January 1916, *Letters*, ed. O'Sullivan and Scott, i. 244–5, cf. *Ottoline at Garsington*, ed. Gathorne-Hardy, pp. 87–8; JMM to OM, [21 January 1916] (UT).

67 KM, *Journal*, p. 114, *Letters*, ed. O'Sullivan and Scott, i. 250 (JMM says the letter was not posted, but Frieda's sounds like a reply). OM complained on 3 March about another abusive letter from Frieda, but it seems to have disappeared, see n. 57 above.

68 See *BTW* 395–6. JMM describes how touched they were with the letter in which DHL rejoiced in their happiness ('Cari miei ragazzi, I am very glad you are happy. That is the right way to be happy – a nucleus of love between a man and a woman, and let the world look after itself'; ii. 507) – but how immediately chilled they were by the mention of PH's presence, before any mention of the publishing scheme. Hearing about that, of course, made things worse. Frieda told Gertler in early March (HU): 'The Murry's wrote very indignant that Heseltine started about these Rainbow books without *them*, saying Lawrence was treacherous' (ii. 549 n. 1).

69 DHL had very much wanted the Murrys to join them in Fiascherino, see the unpublished letters of 30 September and 10 October 1913, to be published in *Letters*, viii. – as well as the letter in November (ii. 110–11).

70 *Letters*, ed. O'Sullivan and Scott, i. 247–8.

71 See (ii. 543–4, 545); cf. *BTW* 368–9.

72 The fascination of Hesiod was the glimpse of the ages before classical Greece. DHL drew a design based on the frontispiece for OM to embroider. For the list of books see n. 51.

73 Perhaps H. R. Hall, *The Ancient History of the Near East* (1913) though its 626 pages made it no 'little book' (ii. 528 and n.). OM sent Juliette's copy of Sir Gaston Camille Charles Maspéro, *Egypte* (Paris, 1912). On its usefulness for *Women in Love* see

Delavenay 391–2, though there were beautiful pictures of geese in the Ajanta frescos too, and DHL soon asked for another smaller book on early Egypt ('The text of Mlle.'s book is impossible'; ii. 529).

74 See n. 47 above.

75 Sir Edward Burnett Tylor, *Primitive Culture: Researches into the Development of Mythology, Philosophy, Religion, Art and Custom*, 2 vols. (1871); Gilbert Murray, *The Four Stages of Greek Religion* (1912). For PH's interest in the occult, see n. 30 above.

76 *BTW* 396.

77 *BTW* 403–4ff.; cf. *Reminiscences*, pp. 77–8.

78 KM to Beatrice Campbell, 4 May (*Letters*, ed. O'Sullivan and Scott, i. 260). KM to Virginia Woolf, 26 April 1919 (*Letters*, ed. O'Sullivan and Scott, ii. 314); KM to Brett, 26 February 1922 (*Letters*, ed. Murry, ii. 189); Frieda 102–3.

79 *Letters*, ed. O'Sullivan and Scott, i. 261. The servant whom KM's allowance enabled them to hire was Hilda Jelbert, aged fourteen. She thought DHL 'moody and sarcastic', but Frieda 'jokey, stout and fair' and much nicer than the other three (Alison Symons, *Tremedda Days: A View of Zennor 1900–1944*, Padstow, 1992, pp. 131–2). KM was 'a marvellous-looking woman, but was ill at the time with a dreadful cough' – it is interesting that this is said of her rather than of DHL.

80 *Letters*, ed. O'Sullivan and Scott, i. 262–4.

81 Frieda to OM, n.d. [before 7 April] (UT).

82 JMM to OM (UT); the quotation ['monstrous, horrible, shapeless, huge'] is Virgil's description of the ogre Polyphemus (*Aeneid*, iii. 658).

83 4 May (*Letters*, ed. O'Sullivan and Scott, i. 260–2).

84 See *Hardy* 71:11–16; 'Introduction to These Paintings', *P* 552, 561, etc.

85 *Journal*, p. 146.

86 *Journal*, p. 67.

87 See *The Aloe, with Prelude*, ed. Vincent O'Sullivan (Manchester, 1982).

88 E.g. JMM to KM, 29 March 1915, 16 December 1915; cf. *Still Life*, pp. 8, 119, 132, etc. and KM's story of 1915 'Something Childish and Natural'.

89 JMM to OM, 14 May 1915 (BR archive in McMaster); *BTW* 406–8. The effusion ends: 'Ah, my philosopher, / My mouse-haired, intolerant prophet, / What do you know? ... shall you tell me how/ I may love ...'

90 JMM to OM, 14 May (McMaster); *BTW* 416–17.

91 *Letters*, ed. O'Sullivan and Scott, i. 269; Gertler to Kot, 20 June (BL); *Letters*, ed. O'Sullivan and Scott, i. 270. On 3 July she had plans to go to Denmark and told Kot 'at last I am free again'.

92 *WL* 489:13, 18; 490:7; 489:33, 35; 490:13, 15; 501:37.

93 Delavenay, ii. 693.

94 *WL* 494:4–5; 499:1; 496:20; 503:36–8; 504:19; 505:1; 503:39–504:2; 505:4–7; 495:29–30; 496:10–13.

95 *Reminiscences*, p. 79, worked up in *BTW* 409, 412–13. DHL's rage in which he accused JMM of being an 'obscene bug' sucking his life away (*BTW* 416), is the *same* rage he felt at Frieda – about whom he used the same image (see p. 319) at times when he felt all the giving and commitment of life-blood was coming from him,

simply absorbed by them. JMM's questioning of Frieda in 1953 about DHL's 'homosexuality' (6 August 1953, *Memoirs* 328; and see chapter 7, p. 377) was a late afterthought; and Frieda, without at all denying the propensity, promptly denied that DHL ever felt that way about JMM. JMM never thought of his own feelings for Campbell as homosexual, though he did imagine (mistakenly) that DHL would say they could only fructify between a man and a woman.

96 Pinker seems to have asked whether DHL was all right for money, and to have been reassuring about his financial prospects. The £50 was probably for the publication of *Twilight in Italy* in mid-June and *Amores* in July.

97 KM to OM, [27 July] (*Letters*, ed. O'Sullivan and Scott, i. 272).

98 Cf. Somers's experiences in *Kangaroo* 214:14–215:29, 218:12–221:16; (ii. 626–7, 628–9); *WL* 28–30.

99 This, Frieda's first visit from Cornwall, made possible by the 'advance' from Pinker, may be the one recalled by Barbie in 1954 (Nehls, i. 321), though the 'apple blossom' she remembered her mother carrying must in that case have been conflated with Frieda's next visit in April 1917. It is not clear on which of these she took the children to hear *Figaro* and to tea at Lyons, where in the Ladies' Room, 'Elsa said to me, anxiously, "You are not to *like* Mama, you know, just because we have got ten shillings." The money was formally returned to Frieda by my father.' DHL told CA that after this visit Frieda 'began to realise, I believe, that the mother-child relation is not so all-important' (iii. 26).

100 OM showed neither the possessiveness nor the jealousy of Hermione (as her tolerance of the affairs with other women of both her husband and BR proves); and it is hard to imagine murderous physical violence in OM, though she could be verbally destructive.

101 Here DHL was using and indeed intensifying the denigration of Puma *by Heseltine*, which he himself thought unfair to the actual young woman who came to stay at Porthcothan – but was just what he needed for his novel.

102 *WL* 77:28–9.

103 Unlike *The Rainbow* which is a historical novel packed with verifiable detail, DHL deliberately left the date of the new novel vague. Gerald, like Skrebensky, has served as a soldier in the Anglo-Boer war (and has been up the Amazon, like Eder in real life); and since the novel is a continuation of *The Rainbow* which ends about 1910, we are presumably meant to think of it as set in the years immediately preceding the First World War. However, DHL is less interested in 'history' now (except in the chapter about Gerald's technological revolution) than in the psychological hinterland of violence which is only just under the surface of all these 'civilised' characters, and which will soon break out openly in 'world' war.

104 JMM's son says that he once asked JMM whether he and DHL did ever wrestle in fact, and if so who had won. 'Who do you think?' was the reply. This sounds a little like the kind of story fathers tell sons; but it may be that DHL wanted to try something unfamiliar to him before writing about it. Given his recent illness, however, there would have been little credit in making it a contest to be won or lost. The idea of Japanese wrestling came however from an extract from Lafcadio

Hearn in *The International Library of Famous Literature*, edited by Richard Garnett (Edward's father), 20 vols. (1899) which was a cherished possession of DHL's brother Ernest, and of the Lawrence household in Eastwood: see *Early Years* 111.

105   1 October 1952 (*Memoirs* 316).

106   The incident occurred on Friday 1 September. PH was not present, nor was Puma. It was described both by Gertler writing on 2 September to OM (UT), and by Suhrawardy (who had no idea who the raptor was) to AH. AH's letter to OM (UT) dated only 'Thursday', refers to the incident as having happened 'last night', but may have been a misunderstanding of Suhrawardy. See *WL* 571-2, note to 384:34 (though the woman bears no resemblance to Puma).

107   Stanley Hocking, William Henry's younger brother, as reported by C. J. Stevens, *Lawrence at Tregerthen* (Troy, New York, 1988), pp. 76-8.

108   Cf. *WL* 275:28-9 and DHL's own gesture to Savage, talking at Kingsgate; Nehls, i. 210.

109   KM to OM, [27 July 1916] (*Letters*, ed. O'Sullivan and Scott, i. 272); cf. *BTW* 423.

110   *BTW* 427-8 and Lea, *Life of Murry*.

111   *BTW* 422

112   *BTW* 421. One of these was that:

> Frieda sent Murry a tremendous 'biff' yesterday. 'Now I am going to have my say' – It was just the same 'Ach du hässliche Augustine' as usual – Sooner or later all Frieda's friends are bound to pop their heads out of the window and see her grinding it before their door – smoking a cigarette with one hand on her hip and a coloured picture of Lorenzo and Nietzsche dancing 'symbolically' on the front of the barrel organ.
>
> [12 September] (*Letters*, ed. O'Sullivan and Scott, i. 280)

KM did not communicate with OM for the next fortnight, however, since she was conducting a flirtation with BR.

113   He had read about them in Lord Robert Curzon's *Visits to Monasteries in the Levant* (1849; 1916). In the letter in which he thanks OM for this book, he asks for Thucydides' *History of the Peloponnesian War*, which she duly sent (ii. 572). He was much affected by its account of 'wars of a collapsing era, of a dying idea' (ii. 614) which made it peculiarly relevant – hence his use of it (as well as of OM's gift of a lump of lapis lazuli) in the scene in which Hermione attacks Birkin.

114   *SP* 63, 71-3, 78.

115   *Mendel* also has characters partly reminiscent of DHL and Frieda, though the artist 'Logan' and 'Nellie' whom he murders were primarily based on Gertler's friend John Currie and his mistress. For DHL's comments on Cannan's 'journalism' see (iii. 35, 44, 50), and for Frieda's (iii. 52 n. 1).

116   The idea that only a Jew could have painted this picture has obviously to do with the long history of suffering, disintegration and diaspora of the Jewish people, experiences that went to make Jews different, with the kind of 'sacred difference' (iii. 390) DHL treasured among peoples. This seems quite other than the routine racist language he had picked up in Germany.

117 The description of Mountsier is based on information from his great-nephew for which, and for the account of his early career, I am indebted to Jeffrey Meyers, *D. H. Lawrence: A Biography* (New York, 1990), pp. 199–200. See also Illustration 48. Information about Esther Andrews is from my interviews with her nephew Andrews Wanning. See also Illustration 47. Mountsier was born in Charleroi, south of Pittsburgh, graduated B.A. from the University of Michigan in 1909, read towards a doctorate at Columbia though he never finished it and joined the *New York Sun* as its literary editor in 1910. He was in England to write articles on the effects of the war and hoped (like the Aldingtons' friend John Cournos, for the *Philadelphia Record*) to interview a number of prominent people, writers and socialites. He had been introduced to DHL at the Aldingtons' in 1915, and had been given copies of *Signature*.

Esther was born in Des Moines, Iowa, but moved with her family to Brooklyn and then to Connecticut. She studied art at Yale (its Drama School not yet founded) and at Smith College, but seems not to have taken a degree. Against her family's wishes she went on the stage about 1910 and toured in repertory companies for several years before the war. Not having had the success she wanted on the stage, she had now taken a job as a fashion journalist on *Woman's Wear Daily*, but though she could draw, had a flair for clothes and was well paid, she despised the women's clothing business. Lawrence probably reflected her opinion of herself when he spoke of her as 'an artist' and 'not really a journalist' – she shared his admiration of *The Merry-Go-Round* and was 'very understanding' (iii. 27–8). She still drew more seriously when she could – some animated sketches of characters at Key West and one fine portrait survive – and was hoping under Mountsier's tutelage to widen the range of her journalistic writing.

118 The Lawrences had had only £6 left in July (see above). On the strength of the £50 which then came from Pinker, probably for the publication of *Twilight in Italy* in mid-June and *Amores* in July, they decided to pay an extra £5 for the Murrys' unexpended lease on the bigger cottage, and Frieda was able to go to London in September. However, having calculated that they could if necessary live on 'about £150 a year' in Zennor (ii. 619) they were still about £100 short of that, even after more money from Pinker, £8 for several poems in the *Some Imagist Poets 1916: An Annual Anthology* (ii. 643 and n. 3), and £4 from *Georgian Poetry* (ii. 668). H.D. wrote to Amy in September about the Lawrences' financial troubles. Her first idea was secretly to augment his American royalties, but Amy would not deceive, since it would anger her to be deceived in that fashion. She was confident of being able to offer a gift in a way that would 'enable him to accept it without scruple' (Damon 385). DHL seems to have thought that Frieda had appealed to Amy without his knowledge (iii. 29), but was greatly touched by Amy's help. (He had refused to accept Dunlop's offer of a loan, because Dunlop was a married man with children; iii. 20.)

119 He sent 'The Mortal Coil' on 31 October, 're-written from MS. I got a week or two back, from Italy – stuff done before the war' (ii. 669) – see chapter 2, p. 105. The *English Review* did not print it, but it was published by *Seven Arts* (July 1917).

'Samson and Delilah' was sent to Pinker on 6 November (iii. 22 and n. 3) and published by the *English Review* in March 1917. The collection of poems 'All of Us' (later called 'Bits') was sent to Cynthia on 11 December (iii. 49–50).

Chapter Seven: Orpheus Descending

1 *K* 224:10–38. 'The Nightmare' chapter is part of a fiction, and its title suggests heightening in memory, but wherever its facts can be checked they are generally accurate, though emotions and situations may be intensified or dramatised.

2 *Autobiography* (New York, 1935), pp. 282, 286. The Defence of the Realm Act (1914) required all 'aliens' to register with the police and forbade them to live in prohibited areas without a police permit.

3 Frieda 82 ('Coastguards'), *K* 223:13–39 ('khaki individuals, officers of some sort'); on the incident in St Ives see (iii. 66). Frieda also says that a policeman from St Ives had been to the cottage several times to inspect DHL's papers (Frieda 104); cf. *K* 217:31–7. The same would happen to JMM when he arrived in Cornwall.

4 See (iii. 65); *K* 224:39–225:3 (note Mountsier's correction in TSII in *K* 396, note to 225:2); Esther Andrews to Mountsier, *c.* 4 January (UT) (Letter 3; Louise Wright, 'Dear Montague: Letters from Esther Andrews to Robert Mountsier', forthcoming in *DHLR*.

5 In 1916 BR was forbidden entry, under the Defence of the Realm Act, to prohibited areas which 'included the whole sea-coast', because of the speeches he made to munitions workers in Wales.

6 Louise E. Wright, 'D. H. Lawrence, Robert Mountsier and the Journalist Spy Controversy', *D. H. Lawrence: The Journal of the D. H. Lawrence Society* (1992–3), 7–20, to which I am indebted for much that follows.

7 Ibid., pp. 12–16. Mountsier published his researches into food supplies and prices in the *New York Times* on 23 February 1917, the day after he arrived back in the United States, quoting what he had 'been told by economists and shipping men'.

8 E. Andrews to Mountsier about articles, 1, [4], 5, 7 January (UT) (Wright, 'Dear Montague', Letters 2–5). Letter 3 reveals her suspicion that the police will read his correspondence. Letter 5 suggests he go to a proposed meeting of the UDC in Hyde Park – but also suggests that he is not 'in sympathy' with their anti-war stance.

9 Wright, 'Spy Controversy', p. 17 quotes Sidney Theodore Felstead, *German Spies at Bay* (New York, 1920), p. 251, closing his account of the conspiracy as follows: 'In January, 1917, we had occasion to detain another American journalist, whom we had every reason to suspect was an emissary of Winnenburg' [who was arrested and tried with Sander]. 'It proved extremely difficult to secure any evidence, however, and after a good many examinations "M", as I shall designate him, was sent back to America, with the parting salutation that he would be arrested if he ever attempted to land in England again.' Esther had asked on [4 January] why he was not being allowed to leave for France 'if you are *cleared*'; and on [10 January] 'Why in the world is Scotland Yard still pursuing you? I can't understand it. They have strange ways of treating their friends, these English' (UT) (Wright, 'Dear Montague', Letters 3, 8).

10 See (iii.147 and n. 6). Frieda probably addressed mail to her family through Frieda Gross in Switzerland, but all mail addressed to neutral countries was certain to be censored.

11 Secker to Pinker, 6 February 1917 (UIll) and Constable to Pinker (NWU): see *WL* xxxiv.

12 *SP* 80 n.

13 *Ottoline at Garsington*, ed. Gathorne-Hardy, p. 128. It was a pity that somebody with the literary pretensions of Clive Bell, who was present at Garsington when the typescript arrived and witnessed the very real pain of OM, neither dreamed of persuading her that there might be any distinction between literature and portraiture even in 'such stuff', nor managed any sympathy.

> Her ladyship is beside herself with fear and indignation; & floats about like a pure water-lily of sixteen, taking heaven to witness that black is not black. She has become utterly undignified by loss of nerve and havers about concocting schemes for the suppression of the book ... And the poor gibbering old hag – though I suppose she sees that she is playing Lawrence's game, the MS clearly having been sent to annoy – hasn't got the self-control to pretend to be indifferent.
>
> (Bell to Mary Hutchinson, 31 December 1916 and 2 January 1917; UT)

14 See *WL* xxxii, lviii–lxi.

15 *Diaries* p. 294; *Memoirs* 219; Sandra Jobson Darroch, *Ottoline* (New York, 1975), p. 195, and the demand for the return of the pin confirmed in *Diaries*, p. 294. OM apparently did not demand back the lump of lapis lazuli she had also given DHL, which he had used in the book (along with her loaned volume of Thucydides) and which he subsequently gave to H.D.

16 This is disingenuous; the house may be a composite of Garsington and 'a Georgian house with Corinthian pillars' (*WL* 82:3), but the garden and pond are clearly recognisable as Garsington. However Jessie Chambers immediately recognised an affinity to Miriam in the character of Hermione (Delavenay, *L'Homme*, ii. 693).

17 *Diaries*, p. 294.

18 *Ottoline at Garsington*, ed. Gathorne-Hardy, p. 129, Darroch, *Ottoline*, p. 197, Seymour, *Ottoline Morrell*, pp. 281–3. (The naming in the 1917 revision of *WL* of the character based on BR 'Sir Joshua Malleson' was definitely malicious.)

19 Huebsch had published *Twilight in Italy* in America in 1916, from Duckworth's sheets. *Rainbow* was being distributed by Huebsch rather surreptitiously (see *R* lix–lx). It is not clear when Pinker made his one attempt to find an American publisher for *Women in Love*, but Little, Brown & Co. rejected it on 11 July 1917.

20 Probably the story mentioned as 'on hand' in November 1916 (iii. 29) and sent to Pinker under its original title 'The Miracle' on 12 January 1917 (iii. 74). Set in Eastwood, it is about a family gone bankrupt, the attempted suicide of the daughter, and her rescue by a young doctor, but it was not accepted by any periodical until, revised and retitled (in October 1921), it was published by the *English Review* in April 1922.

21 Cannan had made his wife's maid pregnant, had had a nervous breakdown and had then formed another liaison with Gwen Wilson, which finally put paid to his

marriage, (see Farr, *Gilbert Cannan*). 'I would write to poor Gilbert and Mary,' DHL told Kot, 'but I feel I could do no good' (iii. 90).

22 In fact, though they clearly had a close relationship and probably shared the small cottage during their stay, they seem not to have been literally living together. Esther's letter of [5 January] (UT) (Wright, 'Dear Montague', Letter 4), says that she 'hated most the implication of those nasty minded men', but it was 'simply unfortunate that they had to land on you when you happened to be in my flat'. He was staying there in her absence, but the letter also makes it clear that he would be moving out when she returned. DHL may have jumped too quickly to his conclusion also.

23 These – all in the Everyman series – were Melville's *Moby Dick* and *Omoo*; Cooper's *The Pioneers*, *The Prairie* and *The Deerslayer*; Whitman's '*Leaves of Grass* etc'; Crèvecœur's *Letters from an American Farmer*; Hawthorne's *Twice Told Tales*, *The Scarlet Letter* and *The Blithedale Romance*; Rousseau's *Emile*; Lincoln's *Speeches*; Emerson's essays (3 vols.), *Society and Solitude*, *Nature* and *Conduct of Life*; Franklin's *Autobiography*; Hamilton's *The Federalist*; and Poe's *Tales of Mystery and Imagination*. That DHL made little or no use of the political writers is not perhaps surprising; but it is strange that he did not write on Emerson until his review of Stuart Pratt Sherman's *Americans* in 1923.

24 The government was planning a new Military Service act whose terms would be published in the *Times* on 29 March, creating powers to call up for examination (among others) 'men who have previously been rejected on any ground' (iii. 106 and n. 2). However the rejection was probably still a consequence of the expulsion from Cornwall.

25 *SP* 84.

26 See pp. 18–23 and 55, 73–4 (and notes) for the argument that *Look! We Have Come Through!* is most safely regarded as a work of 1917, and for a list of the twenty which existed by 1914 in usually very different (and mostly inferior) earlier versions, see p. 768 note 60. ('Terranova', an earlier version of 'New Heaven and Earth', *Poems*, 256, was given to H.D. for *Some Imagist Poets* in October 1916, but may well have been written at Greatham.) Pending the publication of the new Cambridge Edition, the early variants are to be found in Carole Ferrier, 'The Earlier Poetry of D. H. Lawrence: A Variorum Text', unpublished Ph.D. thesis, University of Auckland, 1971, ii.

27 *Poems* 212–13; *K* 226:6–7.

28 See Frieda 67–8 for the original versions.

29 *Poems* 217.

30 *Poems* 217–18.

31 It is possible to argue that some poems may have seemed too intimate and sexually explicit, or too liable to compromise Frieda, to be copied out in 1913 (when she was still undivorced) and sent for typing and publication – but not these.

32 *Poems* 218–19. Cf. *Hardy* 12–13, 18, 52–4 and contrast the 'Foreword to *Sons and Lovers*', *SL* 240 (itself nine months later than the ostensible date of the poem) where the emphasis is on the Woman and hence on the seed.

33 Damon 445: 'It is to my mind a greater novel even than *Sons and Lovers*, for all that it is written in a rather disconnected series of poems.'

34 'Moonrise' and 'The Sea' are both carved out of the same early poem, probably written in Bournemouth when he was convalescing in early 1912, while 'Martyr à la Mode', as its title indicates, is adapted from an early poem to *present* a state of mind DHL has long grown beyond.

35 *Poems* 194; 196; 198–9. 'Nonentity' also neatly reverses 'The Wild Common', rewritten in Cornwall for *Amores* nine months before the manuscript of *Look!* 'Don Juan' has almost certainly been back-dated, though faithful enough in mood perhaps to the DHL who refused to feel guilty in his last meeting with Louie in the Castle art gallery in Nottingham in 1912. It was written before October 1913, when it was sent to Marsh; but the imagery of mountains and rivers and the conclusion suggest Bavaria and Frieda, rather than early 1912 before he met her.

36 'A Doe at Evening' probably dates at the earliest from 1913, since (despite the fiction of *MN* 109:13–37) there is no evidence of a visit to Irschenhausen the year before. As far as we know, DHL spent only one weekend alone with Edgar Jaffe in Munich in 1912. Even supposing that they did go to Irschenhausen as in *Mr Noon*, to see the site of Edgar's chalet (though it was probably already built by then), and that DHL might have seen a doe at evening and written a poem about it; it could surely not have been *this* poem – so finely balancing femaleness and motherhood with maleness all made 'strange' (*Poems* 222), in opposition and relation? Would *The Rainbow* and the *Prussian Officer* ending of 'Odour of Chrysanthemums' have taken so long to achieve if he had already seen so clearly in 1912, or 1913 when they stayed in Irschenhausen? But if so, why was it not sent for publication then? Again none of the reasons for caution could possibly apply. It seems to be a poem by the author of *The Rainbow* (at the earliest), but may have been written later still.

37 *Poems* 200–3.

38 *Poems* 215; 216.

39 It should precede 'Misery'. Letters from Chatto in (iii. 145 n. 1, 148 n. 1).

40 The use of 'oubliette' in both 'Misery' and the letter to McLeod written, probably at the station, at Sterzing (i. 445), might suggest that this poem *was* probably written at the time, and would have been in the Tagebuch – and it is not difficult in that case to see why DHL would not have wanted to publish it then. 'Meeting Among the Mountains' on the other hand was published in both *Georgian Poetry 1913–1915* and the *English Review* in 1914, which made Chatto's timidity about including it all the odder.

41 'Winter Dawn' and 'A Bad Beginning', *Poems* 229–30; 230–1. The four poems ('dated' before New Year) are 'A Bad Beginning', 'Loggerheads', 'Lady Wife' and 'Both Sides of the Medal'.

42 'Paradise Re-entered', *Poems* 242–3. The original 'Purity' also recognised fierceness in desire and even a 'cleansing hate', though passion quickly purifies them into 'beautiful and candid lovers'. The mind has fused like a bead in the flames of sex – the furnace image from *The Trespasser* – but incandescence is taken calmly and the ensuing darkness is passed without fear. In the final version, however, to remain beautiful and candid, in 'steadfast being', is no longer enough. Now they must pass

through a 'death'; dare the fiery angels guarding the entrance to the last garden; and storm those gates (beyond eternal God and Devil), to the true *temporal* Eden where a dishevelled Eve may dance in a primal earthly bliss. The title is changed from 'Purity' to 'Paradise Re-Entered'.

43 *Poems* 239; 240. In early 1913 by contrast, in the ' "Burns Novel" fragments', DHL had used the lad's taking pity on a snared rabbit and freeing it as a sign of his humanity.

44 *Poems* 249–50; 245–8; 250.

45 *Poems* 251–2. Cf. TSII (revised) 285, 323, autograph insert 402, 461, 508 'star-equilibrium' (*WL* 177, 199, 254, 290, 319); see also discussion of the revision below.

46 *Poems* 252–4, 254–6; 256–61; 254–6.

47 *Poems* 256–61.

48 *Poems* 261; 262–8.

49 *Poems* 268–9; 269–70; 270–4.

50 For H.D. the poetry was insufficiently 'sublimated' (iii. 102); and the criticism has often been echoed, usually by readers judging by lyric rather than dramatic criteria. BR said he was glad for them but didn't see why he should look (*Ottoline at Garsington*, ed. Gathorne-Hardy, p. 94); and W. H. Auden complained (*The Dyer's Hand*, 1962, p. 288) of being made to feel like a peeping Tom.

51 It is just possible, considering the affinity of 'Craving for Spring' with letters later in the month (iii. 96, 97), that the poem was not in that first manuscript – but of course the letters may have been influenced by the poem.

52 Jean de Crèvecœur, *Letters from an American Farmer* (1782). In August 1916 DHL told Amy he liked the book '*so* much' (ii. 645).

53 He was still carrying this with him in New Mexico, see Knud Merrild, *With D. H. Lawrence in New Mexico* (1964), p. 209.

54 Probably Gladys Bradley, a friend from her time in Nottingham, who along with her sister Madge had encouraged her relationship with DHL (see (i. 388)), and who (according to Barbara Barr's memoir 'Something to Say') had been in love with Ernest for years.

55 Monday (*Memoirs* 220).

56 *Diaries*, pp. 293–5. DHL pushed the pram at the zoo and CA remarked the 'perfect match' between his beard and the baby's hair, and how Michael liked him 'very much' – though they looked 'a funny sight'. DHL was 'delightful and whimsical' unlike his books in which she thought 'there is no gleam of humour'.

57 Serge Michaelovitch Kravchinsky, nicknamed 'the man from the Steppes', was one of the most active and charismatic of the Russian revolutionary exiles in London. Both Constance and Olivia Garnett were smitten with him. Fanny Markovna Kravchinskaya was only three years younger than her husband who died in 1895, but she lived till 1945.

58 Frieda issued the invitation in a newly discovered letter dating probably from 9–12 February. It is not known when exactly Esther came down. She had originally meant to leave her London flat at the end of February when the plan was for them all to sail for America on 1 March. But if she came down in early March it is very strange that

there is no mention of her in DHL's letters to Catherine on 31 March and 11 April (iii. 165–6, 112–13), since he had been trying to foster friendship between them. It seems most likely that she arrrived while DHL was away.

59 *RDP* xxvii.

60 *RDP* 21:38, 22:4; 23:20; 23:24; 14:10, 12–13; 23:2.

61 *RDP* 28:7–8; 28:28; 31:8–9, 7–8; 33: 22–5; 33:21, 28–9.

62 *RDP* 34:10, 11; 34:12–13; 34:19–21, 24–6.

63 *RDP* 34:37; 35:9–20.

64 *RDP* 36:23–5; 36:29–30, 35; 37:23, 26–7; 37:29–31; 40:1–3.

65 *RDP* 42:6; 42:123; 41:7–8; 41:39–40; 43:14–15; 44:1–4, 6, 7–8.

66 *RDP* 44:20, 27, 31–3; 45:1–2; 45:6–9

67 *RDP* 46:27; 48:20–1; 51:20–1; 51:30–3; 51:39; 52:8–9.

68 See Frieda to Esther, 9–12 February; Esther to Mountsier (UT) (Wright, 'Dear Montague,' Letters 3, 7).

69 See note 58 above.

70 Luhan, *Lorenzo in Taos*, p. 40; *SP* 86–7. Cf. p. 51 on one of the two times DHL 'had evaded her', i.e. Frieda, the other being what Mabel calls his '*thing*' with William Henry; contrast *SP* 87 n. where Catherine calls Mabel's account 'both misleading and incorrect. At the time I heard the particulars from both Lawrence and Frieda.'

71 Esther to DHL, 23 August, newly discovered and to be published in *Letters*, viii., described the Starrs' ridiculous concert at St Ives; PH to Nichols, [May 1917] (BL); Esther as agent for *Seven Arts* 'on behalf of her friend Louise' (iii. 140, 142).

72 He was 5′9″. Esther actually described DHL's hair as 'ash-colored', and his eyes as 'grey' whereas most observers agree that they were blue. Neither is however altogether inaccurate for the bleached effect of the hair, and the kind of eyes that could vary between grey-blue and bright blue in different lights. (His 1919 and 1921 passports describe them as blue-grey.)

73 *Lorenzo in Taos*, pp. 40–3.

74 *R* 19:3–10, a school friendship between the young farmer and 'a clever... consumptive type' which looks back to his friendship with Alan Chambers and, fictively, the friendship between Cyril and George in *WP*.

75 *Memoirs* 328. Obviously hurt by having been neglected in favour of William Henry, Frieda told H.D. at the end of 1917 that 'Lawrence does not really care for women. He only cares for men. Hilda, *you have no idea what he is like*' (*Tribute to Freud*, Carcanet edn, p. xii). It is also possible, however, that this remark was designed to counteract the mutual attraction between DHL and H.D.: see chapter 8, p. 420.

76 *WL* 505:4, 6–7.

77 *K* 236:29–31; 236:14–16, 21–5. Stanley told his doctor, Dr Roger Slack, that William Henry knew about these feelings, and had warned his younger brother to be careful (private interview.) This of course tends to confirm that William Henry had no such inclination.

78 It may be that calling William Henry 'John Thomas' in *Kangaroo* – of which biographers anxious to claim a consummated homosexual affair have made great play – was a dig (as in the case of the similarly named inspector in 'Tickets Please',

written November–December 1918) against a man who made overmuch of his heterosexual virility. William Henry's son believes that his father only married relatively late because he waited until all his brothers and sisters could take care of themselves (Stevens, *Lawrence at Tregerthen*, p. 53).

79 PH to Nichols, 'Friday' [?18 or 25 May] (BL). On 11 May DHL mentioned that PH has taken the Trewey bungalow from which PH addresses this letter but that he has seen 'little or nothing of him' (iii. 124) – so the visit of Gray 'last week' when DHL met both Gray and Starr must have been at least one week and probably two weeks later. Gray's autobiography puts the rent at £5 p. a. but PH wrote at the time, and it is unlikely that Gray's big ex-mine-manager's house would cost no more than DHL's two-room cottage.

80 The Earl had been a ne'er-do-well clergyman, never entrusted with a parish, and had been paid by his aristocratic family to settle far away in Cape Town. He was looked after by a coloured lady whom, to the outrage of the white community, he married – only to increase local consternation by inheriting the title of the Earl of Stamford on the unexpected demise of the seventh Earl; Martha splendidly refused to make any change in her life-style. Their daughter Mary – despised in Cape Town as a 'half-caste', was sent to school in Europe and had married Starr on 1 March 1917. See R. R. Langham-Carter, 'Lord Stamford's Tangled Affairs', *Familia: Quarterly Journal of the Genealogical Society of South Africa*, xi (1974), 8–13, 16 and 78–80; with thanks to Barry Smith who brought these to my attention. For Meredith Starr and his interest in the occult see pp. 386–7 and notes 87–8 below.

81 *K* 231:27-9.

82 See Smith, *Peter Warlock*; PH to Olivia Smith, 13 May 1917 (BL); PH to Phyl Crocker, 19 April 1917 (BL). (It was while Pino Orioli was staying with Phyl's family that he briefly met DHL in 1917.)

83 PH to Nichols, 17 June (BL).

84 *Musical Chairs* (1948), p. 126.

85 *K* 233:17.

86 *SP* 90-1; 'Indians and Entertainment', *MM*.

87 *St Ives Times*, 24 and 31 August; cf. (iii. 158 n. 1). The reference will not have done DHL any good!

88 Nichols's annotation to PH's letter, 14 December 1917 (BL); PH to Colin Taylor, 27 September (BL).

89 It is possible that DHL may have attended a lecture on theosophy; which would be enough to explain references to the Mystery of Isis and the number seven in 'Don Juan' (E320.6, *Poems* 196), or the reference to the 'Great Breath' in 'Rose of All the World' (*Poems* 218–19) – though that poem probably dates from 1917 anyway.

90 For DHL's use of Pryse see *Apocalypse and the Writings on Revelation*, ed. Mara Kalnins (Cambridge, 1980) 4–6.

91 'The Spirit of Place', *English Review* (November 1918), 321; see chapter 8, pp. 447–8.

92 'To generalise is to be an idiot', *Marriage of Heaven and Hell*.

93 'Love' and 'Life' are in *RDP* 7–12, 15–18.

94 Moreover its picture of man's life always poised between the 'primal unknown'

from which he has issued (*RDP* 15:4) and the other unknown into which he continually passes – but burning between the two like the man-candle of 'All Souls' in *Look!* – seems an intermediate step in the thought of the original set of seven. It would fit between the first hailing of cosmic life-out-of-death in 'Whistling of Birds', and the sense (in what was number IV but is now number I of 'The Reality of Peace') of the way forward already there, though it can only reveal itself on the way. (If this were so, one might hazard a guess that the original III may have had to do with the contrast of those who 'fear the strange approach of the creative unknown' ('Life', *RDP* 18:32) and go on willing the continuance of the old until they bring it crashing on their heads, instead of accepting the reality of wintry death, and waiting, longing, for the first impulse of new birth that fulfils 'the deepest desire of the soul' (original number IV; *RDP* 27:4). It is one of the oddnesses of 'The Reality of Peace' that it makes so little reference to the war; though Harrison would not have welcomed an essay expressing DHL's views on that.)

95 PH to Nichols, 14 December 1917 (BL) (Gray, *Peter Warlock*, p. 168) and to Gray, [n.d. but before March 1918] (BL).

96 It will take, in any case, a great deal of scholarly and scientific work on the inks in the second typescript, before the different layers of the rewriting can be distinguished and dated with confidence.

97 *WL* 127:26–7, 31; 128:32–5, 38–9; 129:3; 129:33–8, 39; TSI, pp. 150–1, cf. TSII, pp. 195–7. The chapter titles were added in the first English edition at Secker's request, but will be used in what follows, for convenience. Selections from the unrevised TSII, corresponding to the revised state of TSI, are reprinted in *The Making of 'Women in Love': A Selection from the Typescripts*, ed. Pierre Vitoux (Montpellier, 1988).

98 TSI, pp. 179–80, cf. TSII, pp. 237–9; *WL* 150:1–2, 3; 150:34–5; 150:39; TSI, pp. 209–10, cf. TSII, pp. 277–9, *WL* 173:28–9. See also *Selection*, ed. Vitoux, pp. 96–8.

99 *Poems* 251–2.

100 *WL* 177:5, 7; 201:6–7, 20, 21, 16–17; TSII, pp. 285, 323.

101 TSI, pp. 308–9, cf. TSII, pp. 397–9; *WL* 251:7. The original is quoted in my 'The Marble and the Statue', p. 402; see also *Selection*, ed. Vitoux, pp. 135–7.

102 *WL* 173:3; 254:3, 5; 254:27–31; autograph insert TSII, pp. 401ff.

103 *WL* 290:31; TSI, p. 356, TSII, p. 461. See also unrevised TSI and TSII in *Selection*, ed. Vitoux, pp. 160–2.

104 Frieda said that the row over the rings also 'happened' (1 October 1952; *Memoirs* 316).

105 *WL* 312:33; 313:12, 14–18, 20–2; TSI , pp. 386–400, cf. TSII, pp. 496–9, unrevised TSII in *Selection*, ed. Vitoux, pp. 184–6.

106 *WL* 313:39–40, 314:1–2; 314:22–3; 314:30.

107 *W* 313:33; 320:19–34; 368:32–40.

108 *WL* 42:39; 65:15–16; 67:26; 72:37; 113:29–36; TSII, pp. 58 (handwritten insertion), 93, 106, 173.

109 *WL* 241:22, 19; 242:34–7; 243:29, 28; TSII, pp. 381–5 ; cf. Blavatsky, *Secret Doctrine*, pp. 252–60, quoting Lévi p. 259.

110 *WL* 206:26–7; 207:18, 23–4; TSI, p. 252, cf. TSII, pp. 330–1; unrevised TSII in *Selection*, ed. Vitoux, pp. 112–13.

111 *WL* 481:20–2, 28–9, 31–4. TSII, pp. 773–4.

112 Catherine described this as 'a real, sent letter, in prose' (*SP* 85). Since all but one of the surviving letters he had written to Frieda in 1912 were preserved because they had been left in her mother's writing-desk, and were rediscovered only after DHL's death, it is possible that the one she had kept with her was the first – now lost – of which all we know is that he told her she was the most wonderful woman in the world. If the letter spoke also of the plan to go to Germany, and urged her to make a new life with him in spite of husband and children, it would have served the same purposes as the 'Argument' in *Look!*

113 *K* 238:40–241:18; Stevens, *Lawrence at Tregerthen*, pp. 108–9.

114 Frieda 108; Stevens, *Lawrence at Tregerthen*, p. 110; and (iii. 167–175)..

115 Cf. *K* 245:18–19; Stevens, *Lawrence at Tregerthen*, p. 112.

116 *K* 246:8–30; Stevens, *Lawrence at Tregerthen*, pp. 112–13.

117 Frieda 104

118 Stevens on William Henry 'bragging' about the Lawrences in *Lawrence at Tregerthen*, p. 112; Gray, *Musical Chairs*, p. 126; evidence on volunteers from Lt. Col. White (NL).

119 *Musical Chairs*, p. 128.

120 *K* 233:37; *Musical Chairs*, p. 127; Frieda 106–7.

121 For the banning of BR, see chapter, p. 000.

122 Stevens reports the Hocking family on the enmity of the Vicar (Rev. David Rechab Vaughan, vicar-surrogate) (*Lawrence at Tregerthen*, pp. 107–8, 111). Stanley Hocking expanded his account of DHL's scepticisms in an interview with Roger Slack in *A Mere Interlude*, ed. Melissa Hardie (Newmill, Penzance, 1992), p. 68. Alison Symons describes Parson Vaughan on Dick Berryman's authority as 'small of stature' but with 'great authority in the village' and 'well liked' though very poor; and his daughter as 'a good organiser' (*Tremedda Days*, p. 166; both are shown in a group photograph facing p. 177). They left the village in 1919. Frieda (98) wrote that there 'is a woman "even now who boasts that she turned us out of Cornwall as spies"'.

123 4 October 1916 (*Memoirs* 216).

124 Stevens, *Lawrence at Tregerthen*, pp. 81–2, *Memoirs* 223; *K* 238:35.

125 *K* 231:19–21.

Chapter Eight: On a Ledge

1 *K* 247:34–7; *Golden Echo*, p. 124.

2 *K* 248:24. What follows has been drawn from John Cournos, *Autobiography* (1935); Barbara Guest, *Herself Defined: The Poet H.D. and Her World* (New York, 1984); Janice S. Robinson, *H.D.: The Life and Work of an American Poet* (Boston, 1982); Charles Doyle, *Richard Aldington*; and H.D.'s *Bid Me to Live*.

3 *K* 248:28–9. *Diaries*, pp. 355, 356 – the poems were *Look!*

4 *Diaries*, p. 357.

5 *Memoirs of a Modern Pioneer*, ed. Hobman.

6 Cross, 4 December (YU) (iii. 177 n. 1). Since the *Yale Review* was a quarterly, the earliest the article could have appeared was six months after Katharine Fullerton Gerould's 'British Novelists, Ltd.'; see (iii. 166 n. 2). Cross's 'I am particularly sorry that this is so, for I have read your article with very great enjoyment' was not necessarily a polite fiction, therefore. DHL would have excepted from his strictures Thomas Hardy and the early Conrad.

7 PH to Nichols, 14 December 1917 (BL) (Nehls, i. 452); Nichols to Hone, 26 January 1918 (NYPL) (iii. 185 n. 1).

8 What 'Rico' was writing at the window in *Bid Me to Live* (p. 79) may well have been the article for the *Yale Review*, rather than *Aaron's Rod*. DHL may have done no more than sketch a beginning to the novel in Mecklenburgh Square, and what beginning we do not know. In February he said he was working on 'philosophic essays, also, very spasmodically, another daft novel' (iii. 216). By mid-March he had written 150 pages, but said that it was 'as blameless as *Cranford*' and would remain so (iii. 227). For the development of the novel we have now, in 1920–1, see chapter 11, pp. 645–53.

9 For Hone's note about DHL's letter to him of 12 January, part of which has disappeared, see (iii. 196 n. 1): 'The m.s. subsequently passed into the hands of Philip Heseltine ("Peter Warlock", the musician) who in revenge for being caricatured by Lawrence in *Women in Love* put the pages to the base uses of the water-closet.' Whether PH thus destroyed two works by the same method, or whether Gray confused them, cannot be known. Hone added that a transcript of 'At the Gates' made by Arland Ussher, to whom 'the work came as a revelation', was also lost.

10 Nehls, i. 447. (Galsworthy misdated the meeting as 13 November.)

11 *Letters of George Moore* (1942), p. 42 (iii. 196 n. 4). For Frieda on *Salve*, see (i. 512).

12 *TLS*, 22 November (iii. 187 n. 4); Chatto, 30 November (iii. 186 n. 1). DHL commented: 'I saw the dainty Timesey Muse averting her eyes', and 'I feel as if I had affronted a white-haired old spinster with weak eyes' (iii. 186, 190).

13 Frieda's letter is unlocated, but is mentioned in Gray, *Musical Chairs*, p. 134.

14 H.D., *Collected Poems*, ed. Louis Martz (Manchester, 1984), pp. 51–5; *Poems* 743–6. See pp. 418–20 and 836 notes 23, 24.

15 *Musical Chairs*, p.133 (iii. 179 n. 2).

16 Cournos, *Autobiography* and his *roman-à-clef Miranda Masters* (1926); H.D., *Bid Me to Live*; Aldington, *Death of a Hero* (1929); *Aaron's Rod* (1922); Gray, *Musical Chairs*; see also Frieda 108.

17 For the biographical sources of what follows, see note 2 above. H.D.'s *Bid Me to Live*, though presented as a fiction with altered names, is the product of Freud's advice to Hilda to tell her truth of what had happened, which she struggled for many years to do. Wherever it can be checked in detail it is accurate, though of course it is *her* truth in her style. It does not bear the marks of later manipulation and invention for fictive purposes that can be detected in *Mr Noon* and *Look!*; though obviously it must be used with care for biography. For H.D.'s letters to Aldington 1916–18 (YU)

see *Richard Aldington and H.D.: The Early Years in Letters*, ed. Caroline Zilburg (Bloomington, Indiana, 1992).

18 The Lawrences moved out on 30 November. The line etched into Julia's memory in *BMTL* 'I love you, I desire *l'autre*' – is a quotation from one of Richard's letters from the front, 20 May 1918 (*Aldington/H.D.*, ed. Zilburg, p. 57).

19 *K* 248:25. Since aggression is often the obverse of fear, a cancelled passage in the *K* notebook (385) is revealing. Harriet taunts Somers: 'No wonder Hilda Harrington said of your chant [i.e. Whitmanesque] poems—"One gets sick of hearing him talk about his own great manliness."' To this Somers silently rejoins: 'And if Hilda Harrington was sick of reading about his manly greatness, all right, let her write her own poems about her Greek mysteriousness. *Chacun à son goût.*'

20 *BMTL* 182, also 66, 179.

21 *BMTL* 163, 165, 166, 168.

22 p. 39 (YU).

23 *Poems* 176, 743–6.

24 H.D., *Collected Poems*, ed. Martz, pp. 51–5, stanza 7 lines 1–5.

25 'On That Day' appears in the notebook containing Porthcothan accounts (E320.2). On Aldington's conscription, cf. (ii. 644); her letters from DHL, 'Compassionate Friendship', p. 46; *BMTL* 52.

26 *BMTL* 51–5, 62, 58, 61, 80.

27 *BMTL* 77–81 – the corduroys confirmed by Stanley Hocking (Stevens, *Lawrence at Tregerthen*, p. 11), and cf. DHL's advice on them to JMM in 1916 (i. 522).

28 *BMTL* 89, 77–8, 82; but for another reaction by Frieda, see p. 831 note 75. See H.D.'s 'eloquence' in *Miranda Masters*.

29 *BMTL* 78–9, 94.

30 *BMTL* 79–82.

31 H.D., *Tribute to Freud*, *passim*, and Robinson, *H.D.*, p. 240 and n. 22. For the visions, see *Tribute to Freud* and Robinson, *H.D.*, pp. 235–48.

32 *BMTL* 184, its final line. For 'The Ladybird', see chapter 12, pp. 692–4, 696. This illuminates March's dream in 'The Fox' as well as the end of 'The Ladybird' and is one of those moments when *Bid Me to Live* seems most authentic. One would otherwise have to suppose that H.D. 'compiled' this from the novellas, but it is doubtful that she kept up with DHL's prose (which she disliked) to that extent.

33 *Diaries*, pp. 359, 362, 364, 369, John's studio, pp. 359, 361; Nehls, i. 439–40 in which his voice rises: 'Let the DEAD PAINT THE DEAD'; cf. John's account, Nehls, i. 440.

34 See (iii. 179); *Diaries*, pp. 365, 369, Nehls, i. 441.

35 *Musical Chairs*, pp. 141–2 (Nehls, i. 438–9).

36 *K* 249:6–7; Nehls i. 450–1. On Fletcher see (iii. 190) where DHL speaks of meeting him 'for the first time' in December 1917. Aldington suggested (Nehls, i. 236) that Fletcher was present at Amy's dinner party in the Berkeley Hotel in 1914. Fletcher wrote (Nehls, i. 448; placed in London, 1917) that Cournos introduced them, but Cournos was in Russia in 1917. DHL's letter, being closest to the event, is probably the most trustworthy.

37 *Diaries*, p. 376: 'an overwhelmingly, glisteningly clean flat ... in which Lawrence looked very out of place in his corduroy jacket and grey-white canvas shoes'; Nehls, i. 448.

38 Gray, *Peter Warlock*, p. 91 and n. (Nehls, i. 429); *K* 249:10–21; Nehls, i. 449–50.

39 *BMTL* 47, 93–5, 97, 99–100; *Diaries*, p. 369; *AR* 45:20–46:32.

40 *BMTL* 84, 91, 97.

41 *BMTL* 111–13; Frieda 108.

42 *BMTL* 121.

43 Nehls, i. 593 n. 465, 454–7.

44 Kot was the contact. DHL's letter to Leonard Woolf (iii. 199–200) is the most detailed account of the cottages. KM's description (see chapter 6, pp. 317–18) was in response to an enquiry from Virginia.

45 See (iii. 221, 225, 235, 244, 255, 265–8, 314).

46 *K* 248:10–11; Stevens, *Lawrence at Tregerthen*, p. 53.

47 Sadleir, novelist, bibliographer, bibliophile, had been a contemporary of JMM's at Oxford and had put up the money for *Rhythm*. He joined the publishing firm Constable & Co. in 1912. He changed the spelling of his surname to distinguish himself from his father Sir Michael Sadler, Master of University College, Oxford. For the poems see (iii. 202–5).

48 Bennett to Pinker, 6 February (*The Letters of Arnold Bennett*, ed. James Hepburn, 1970, i. 260); see (iii. 205 n. 1). Later Bennett misremembered his offer as having been £3 a week (Nehls, i. 458). For his secret help, see *SP* 97.

49 Nehls i. 456; 463–4 when the Lawrences were with Bessie Lowe – though Cecily Lambert dresses them in the blue linen jackets made a year later.

50 *Diaries*, pp. 415–18.

51 Ibid., pp. 419, 423–4.

52 *BMTL* 115, 120, 135–42.

53 *Musical Chairs*, p. 139 (Nehls, i. 436); see also Gray, *Peter Warlock*, p. 120.

54 James Robert White, *Misfit: An Autobiography* (1930).

55 *AR* 73–86.

56 Whibley was however against publishing DHL's novel, and had told CA that, if the Fund did help, there should in his view be 'a tacit understanding that he should write something – and that, not inevitably censorable' (*Diaries*, p. 418).

57 See (iii. 213, 227) where DHL supposes it came from the Authors' Society.

58 Frieda 109; cf. *Memoirs* 222, probably looking back in September to her visit in April when she thought Monty 'quite beautiful, suddenly a youth, nearly six foot already' (ibid., p. 223). Her bad leg may have kept her from keeping an early September date.

59 She was a fauvist painter who had contributed to *Rhythm*. KM's story of a party in her Paris studio was adapted for *WL* (393:22–394:16 and 573, note to 393:22). She was now married to the art critic Raymond Drey. DHL did not care for her illustrations, see (iii. 362, 366), but agreed to sign copies for an additional de-luxe edition on vellum.

60 Leo Frobenius, *The Voice of Africa*, trans. Rudolph Blind, 2 vols. (1913). Despite his colonialist arrogance in many respects, Frobenius was among the earliest to call

attention to the extraordinary bronzes of Ife, and to the riches of Yoruba wood-carving.

61 Lévi (Alphonse Louis Constant) *Transcendental Magic: Its Doctrine and Ritual*, tr. Arthur Edward Waite (1896), or more likely *History of Magic*, trans. Arthur Edward Waite (1913). PH recommended Lévi to Colin Taylor, 27 September 1917 (BL).

62 Having persuaded Kot to type he sent 'the first part of the essays' on 25 February (iii. 217), and got some back on 20 March (iii. 228). Shortly afterwards Kot became sick of the task, and after 3 April when he returned another batch (iii. 231), did no more. On 3 July DHL told Gray he had 'sent the American Essays to a friend in London who was going to put them with a "safe" friend to have them typed. The friend collapsed, and they are hung up' (iii. 261). It is not clear who came to the rescue – perhaps Nancy Henry, since he sent three chapters of *Movements in European History* to her on 26 July (iii. 268), and was able to promise Pinker on 3 August more of the American essays. Nancy may have agreed to have the two sets of material typed together.

63 The Melville essay was later divided into two like the Hawthorne; this would make the eventual total thirteen.

64 The daring, in England at that time, of referring to nineteenth-century American literature as 'classic' is not obvious now. DHL may be said to have invented the subject of American Literature for English readers, as a distinct and important study in its own right – and was fifty years ahead of his time as far as English universities were concerned. It was not until the 1960s that the teaching of American literature began to become respectable, and not until the following decade that it became at all widespread, or tiptoed into Oxbridge.

65 *English Review*, xxviii (January 1919), 10, 11, 10. *The Symbolic Meaning*, ed. Armin Arnold (Arundel, 1962) 59, 60, 61. *TSM* reprints the version of the eight essays published in the *English Review* (its versions of the essays on Dana, Melville and Whitman date from some years later).

66 *English Review*, p. 6; *TSM* 55–7.

67 Ibid., xxvii (December 1918), 399, 401, 402, 403, 404–5; *TSM* 38, 40, 42, 43, 45.

68 Ibid., xxviii (February 1919), 94, 95, 97, 98, 92; *TSM* 79, 81, 82, 84, 86.

69 Ibid., p. 94; *TSM* 81; Eliot in a talk at the University of Washington, 9 July 1953.

70 *English Review*, xxviii (March 1919), 210–11, 212, 213, 215, 219; *TSM* 101, 103, 104, 106, 110, 111.

71 Ibid., xxviii (April 1919), 282, 280, 286, 287, 286, 287; *TSM* 118, 120, 121, 125.

72 Ibid., xxviii (May 1919), 410, 408, 410, 409, 411, 413, 415, 416, 417; *TSM* 140, 141, 143, 144, 148, 149.

73 E382g, pp. 14–24; i.e. [17]–[28]; pp. [18], [21], [28]; *TSM* 150, 151, 153, 157.

74 *English Review*, xxvii (November 1918), 330, 321, 322, 319, 320–1, 322, 330; *TSM* 16, 17, 18, 16, 19, 29.

75 Ibid., xxviii (June 1919), 479, 480, 486, 489, 486, 477; *TSM* 177, 179, 185.

76 It is however already clear that the 'front' of the body 'is open and receptive' (ibid., p. 489) to the not-self, whereas the spinal system is the source of will and proud independence – all prior to the conscious mind.

77 UN MS 587/1/6/1 unpublished (no Roberts number), pp. 17–18, 20, 12, 8 [9], 9, 10, 27.

78 UN MS 587/1/6/2, unpublished (no Roberts number), pp. 2, 3, 5, 6, 8.

79 Frobenius, *Voice of Africa*, i. 13.

80 MS 587/1/6/2, pp. 9, 12, 13, 14, 16, 17.

81 E328b resembles in paper, format and autograph script E382f (Hawthorne), E382n (Dana), E382l and i (Melville, now divided into two essays) – all from the Smith collection and now unlocated. The four are now numbered *Studies in Classic American Literature* VIII, X, XI, XII and XIII. The Hawthorne, Dana and Melville essays have been verbally revised from the original unpublished versions (E382g and the two UN manuscripts), but the structure and sequence of the argument remains the same. This version in thirteen essays, with two on Hawthorne, two on Melville and ending with Whitman, DHL sent to Huebsch in early October 1919 (iii. 400–1).

82 E382b, pp. 1, 4, 5, 8, 9, 10, 11, 12, 15; MS 587/1/6/2, p. 11.

83 Ibid., pp. 12, 13.

84 See chapter 4, p. 802 note 59.

85 E382b, pp. 13, 14–15, 16, 17, 19–20, 14.

86 Added to *Look!* in 1928.

87 DHL also painted a portrait of her – one of only two that we know him to have done – probably during this visit (reproduced in (iii)).

88 Nehls i. 469–70.

89 DHL wrote 'War Baby' to honour the birth of John Patrick (30 May), and 'embroidered a little cotton frock in red and black-cross stitch, while Frieda crotcheted a cot cover of the gayest rainbow-coloured stripes in wool. It became known as "Frieda's Rainbow," and went everywhere with us, until with rough outdoor usage it fell to pieces' (*SP* 101).

90 The surname of William Henry's wife was Eddy (Stevens, *Lawrence at Tregerthen*, p. 53).

91 Frieda to Kot, 12 February (*Memoirs* 223).

92 Nehls, i. 471.

93 *MEH* 21–4, 43–52. On sources see Philip Crumpton's Introduction (pp. xxxviii–xlv) and Explanatory notes.

94 *SP* 103 and ff.

95 *SP* 102.

96 *SP* 105–6.

97 *SP* 106.

98 What is most interesting about it is the shift in emphasis from his mother's to his father's side. As against, merely, 'old, well-to-do, puritan family – fought with Cromwell – ruined in a smash in the lace industry', we get a considerably longer story about his father's family. Perhaps this is what he had been talking to his father about:

> great Grandfather supposed to be French refugee, from the Revolution: supposed to have fought against Napoleon in Waterloo: grandfather, at any rate, brought up

as a tiny baby in some military hospital – or home: *barracks*, my father says, though that can hardly be: taught to be a military tailor: a tall, silent, strange man, whom I remember – he lived to be 86. He was famous in South Notts as the best dancer and the best boxer. (iii. 282)

The outline of his own 'poor but honest' life is sketched in without much interest – apart from the familiar touch of pride in Frieda's rank and, now, her [in fact, distant] relation to the Red Baron, who had been shot down and killed that April. It ends: 'went to Italy – always lived with no money – always shall – very sick of the world, like to die with the nausea of it'.

99 'Terranova' had appeared in the anthology for 1917. Fletcher's review of *Look!* was a marked contrast to that in the *TLS*: see Draper 121–4. He was by no means uncritical, but castigated the English public for their neglect of DHL and put his worst fault, his preachiness, down to reaction against 'the conditions under which he is forced to write. With a reasonable degree of independence, a public neither openly hostile nor totally indifferent, an intellectual *milieu* capable of finer life and better understanding, Lawrence would become nothing but an artist' (ibid., p. 122).

100 Cf. Aldington's reply, 3 August (*Aldington/H.D.*, ed. Zilburg, p. 117).

101 *Musical Chairs*, p. 134. He had come to London, he said, because he 'was finding the burden of chastity excessive' and goes on, complacently, 'This violent intrusion of the hair-shirted monk from the Cornish Thebaid caused a certain disarray and havoc in the ranks of the Orphic maenads before he returned to his hermitage.' That is all.

102 *BMTL* 191–3. Some explanation is certainly necessary. No reader of *Aaron's Rod* would agree that the description of 'Cyril Scott' – 'a fair, pale, fattish young fellow in pince-nez and dark clothes', aged 22 'so he could afford to be cynical' (28:1–2, 31:2–3), glimpsed silently sipping gin and water, or dressed in an overlarge overcoat smoking a big pipe – is an 'object of aversion and contempt', as Gray claimed in *Musical Chairs*, pp. 136–7.

103 *Tribute to Freud*, rev. edn (Manchester, 1985), p. 134.

104 *BMTL* 78 and passim. Earlier on 2 December he had commented that Hilda 'really has lost her own self' – implying that the old relationship and immediate understanding would be impossible; DHL to Selina Yorke, to be published in *Letters*, viii.

105 Alfred Satterthwaite, 'John Cournos and H.D.', *Twentieth Century Literature*, xxii (1976), 407.

106 1 September, *Aldington/H.D.*, ed. Zilburg, p. 137. He is clearly talking about DHL's letter, not implying, as Robinson argues in defiance of chronology, any possibility of DHL having been the father.

107 *K* 253:5–6; see 252–6.

Chapter Nine: Marking Time

1 In June 1917 he had £7/15/0 from *Georgian Poetry* (iii. 135). On 4 September he received 20 guineas for *Look!*, by Chatto's kindness before it was due (iii. 155 n.1); and had £15 from the *English Review* on 22 September (iii. 161) – in both cases less Pinker's 10% commission. In February 1918 he had a further £9 from the *English*

Review (iii. 217), and there would have been a tiny trickle of royalties from the previous novels, and some fees from the USA. But from June 1917 to June 1918 he did indeed earn 'considerably less than £100' as he told the Royal Literary Fund – less than half of what he had had even in 1916.

2 Catherine misremembered this as having happened in 1917 (*SP* 95).

3 See Lea, *Life of Murry*, p. 57; Alpers, *Life of Mansfield*, p. 263; Tomalin, *Katherine Mansfield*, p. 162; *BTW* 490.

4 *Diary of Virginia Woolf*, i. 108; Seymour, *Ottoline Morrell*, p. 299; KMM, *Journal*, p. 146; *Letters*, ed. O'Sullivan and Scott, ii. 279.

5 KM to OM, [22 October (ed.), but it should probably be 28 November], *Letters*, ed. O'Sullivan and Scott, ii. 282; KM to Brett, [27 October], *Letters*, ed. O'Sullivan and Scott, ii. 284; Murry, *Reminiscences*, pp. 92–3.

6 Dollie had gone to Lyme Regis, to be with Maitland, his wife and her new granddaughter, in order to recuperate from the strain she had been under before she decided to put her husband in a home. It looks as though Maitland had brought her back to Well Walk.

7 Joan remembered her first sight of him coming up the drive with a bunch of wild flowers (Nehls, i. 459–60); in September he passed on to Donald Carswell a carol he had got from Bertie (iii. 279); and see (iii. 304) for the grey Everyman volume in the dining-room.

8 Recent reacquaintance with Willie Hopkin undoubtedly contributed to this characterisation, though DHL was fond of him

9 Act III. ii (*Complete Plays*, p. 383).

10 Act II (ibid., p. 351).

11 Act III. ii (ibid., pp. 384–5).

12 Damon 482–3 (iii. 296 n. 1).

13 This probably explains Frieda's misremembering (Frieda 105) that DHL wrote directly to Bennett for work and Bennett refused. Bennett specifically denied ever writing to, or having had a letter from DHL (Nehls, i. 458).

14 The manuscript (Lazarus) (no Roberts number) was completed by 23 November but not sent to Pinker by KM (who had been given it to read) until 4 December (iii. 299, 301). Pinker returned a typescript on 15 January 1919 (iii. 320). Eighteen months then went by before a revised version was published in the *English Review* in July 1920. It is that version (Per1) that is the base-text for the Cambridge edition of *EmyE*, the MS at that stage not yet having come to light.

15 *SP* 106.

16 MS (Lazarus), p. 19. *The Prelude 1799, 1805, 1850*, Norton Critical Edition (New York, 1979), p. 424.

17 MS (Lazarus), pp. 26–7, 27.

18 *K* 257:23–33. There would be village celebrations later, in which the corporal billeted on the Browns, George Brewer, was dressed up with help from Frieda as a gypsy fortune-teller, like Rochester in *Jane Eyre* (Nehls, i. 456).

19 *Flowers of the Forest*, pp. 189–90 (Nehls, i. 478–9). For Osbert Sitwell's account, see *Laughter in the Next Room* (1949), pp. 19–24. He adds to the list of those present

Roger Fry, Clive Bell, OM, Gertler, Keynes and Lydia Lopokova. The evidence on all sides seems against DHL having seen OM or Keynes that day, who presumably arrived after the Lawrences and Bunny had left.

20 E382g and MSS 587/1/6 1 and 2 (see chapter 8, pp. 453, 464).

21 *MEH* xxii.

22 See E139a (Lazarus), printed in *A D. H. Lawrence Miscellany*, ed. Harry T. Moore (Carbondale, 1959) pp. 26–46; and see *Fox* Textual apparatus and 225–9.

23 See Nehls, i. 463.

24 *SL* 398:6; from the early poem 'The Wild Common' onward.

25 E139a, pp. 5, 14, 15–16; *Fox* 11:16 (and apparatus); 18:24–31; 20:5–9. Cf. the dream related in *Bid Me to Live* (see chapter 8, pp. 421–2).

26 E139a, p. 22; *Fox*, 229:18, 22–3.

27 *EmyE* 35:18, 19, 20–5; 38:40–39:2; 39:15–16, 20; 45:12 (quotations checked against the periodical versions, since both the manuscript and Pinker's typescript have disappeared. To compare the texts of *Strand* magazine, which edited rather primly and changed the title, and the *Metropolitan*, with the *EmyE* text of December 1921, see the Textual apparatus pp. 256–60, especially the ending). On Neville, *Memoir*, pp. 89–90, and see *Early Years* 100.

28 Carl Jung *Psychology of the Unconscious*, to Beatrice M. Hinkle (London, 1916). DHL twice wrote 'submission' and crossed them out, substituting 'precedence' – leading the way, irrespective now of whether the woman will follow.

29 *RDP* 87–113.

30 *RDP* 95:41; 96:15; 98:2; 100:35; 109:4–5; 110:13–14; 109:33–9.

31 *RDP* 110:40.

32 From Cornwall DHL wanted 'only my books and desk, two mirrors, the two little clocks, all bedding, and the few ornaments, the two pictures, and two hair mattresses, one from the camp bed, one from the big bed, the primus stove, the brass lamp, the candlesticks' [of course!] 'and Primus lamp, and the remainder of the boots or clothes worth sending'. William Henry was asked to send the Persian rug which had been left at the farm, and was offered the piano; but when he did not reply DHL asked Stanley to send the piano with all the other furniture for auction at Benney's; saving 'the square mahogany table' as a keepsake for his mother, and 'the big volumes of the Geography of the World' for himself (iii. 320).

33 This is probably Alfred Weber who had become a founder of the German Democratic Party. (Max was on the Commission to draw up a new constitution, but there is no record of DHL ever having met him, especially since Max was not on speaking terms with his brother or Else after she had become Alfred's mistress.)

34 See (iii. 315, 318, 322–3, 324).

35 In the closing paragraph of the (then) final chapter, 'The Unification of Germany', the tension in *Touch and Go*, between the desires for the prosperity and equality of all, and the need for strong leadership, appears again. 'It all depends on the will of the people. But this will of the people must concentrate in one figure, who is also supreme over the will of the people. He must be chosen, but at the same time responsible to God alone' (*MEH* 252:19–22).

36 'Tommies in the Train', 'War-Baby', 'Obsequial Chant', 'Bread Upon the Waters', 'Pentecostal' and 'Nostalgia' – all subsequently published in *Bay*.

37 The ending of the original manuscript E437a is to be found in *EmyE* 242–4; cf. 88–90, based on the revision made later in the now recovered typescript MS 557/1/2/1 (UN).

38 For Huebsch's clandestine distribution, see *R* lix.

39 151,446 people died in Great Britain (A. Marwick, *The Deluge*, p. 257).

40 February, 1919 (*Memoirs* 225).

41 'Clouds' (*RDP* 55–60) is internally dated 'the last day of March' (58:14), but may have been begun or sketched out before. It is also possible that he may have conceived, perhaps even started 'Adolf' too (*EmyE* 201–8), warmed by reminiscing with his sister.

42 *WL* 124:33, 125:5–7. When KM wrote to ask after DHL, Frieda 'replied that She was feeling a little stronger & more able to cope with him' (*Letters*, ed. O'Sullivan and Scott, ii. 303).

43 'Adolf', *EmyE* 207:14. JMM, *Reminiscences*, p. 98 begins by saying that 'Nothing could have been better ... than this first article ["Whistling of Birds"] but the next was different. Doubtless Lawrence's mood had changed: anyhow the article was embittered and angry, and Katherine and I both agreed that we could not print it.' Later, in Section 3, replying to Catherine Carswell's insistence (*SP* 108) that both Kot and Frieda had spoken of several articles, he says (p. 146) that he remembers rejecting only one, 'Adolf', because it was not 'suitable to the *Athenæum*'. We have however DHL's own testimony about the lost article which was topical, and so could not have been either of the animal sketches. It is therefore certain that DHL sent at least three, highly probable that he also sent 'Rex' and possible that he sent 'Clouds' as well, which would make the 'sheaf' of which Kot spoke (*SP*, 108). The most charitable explanation for JMM's erroneous account is that his memory was unreliable, that 'embittered and angry' originally referred to the topical piece and *not* to 'Adolf' as has been supposed and that in the heat of controversy later his memory conflated the two and forgot everything else.

44 KM to Kot (*Letters*, ed. O'Sullivan and Scott, ii. 309).

45 In a review of an exhibition by the London Group (p. 272), Golding remarked: 'And of our poets in the generation of Roger Fry, who but Mr D. H. Lawrence has had his fine courage in the tackling of a new technique.' The periodical was published in Manchester and edited by Thomas Moult who would later publish two of DHL's poems and his first poetic manifesto, see pp. 844 note 60 and 514. Golding was novelist, poet and critic. DHL wrote him another letter in March 1921 about his novel *Forward from Babylon* (1920), which Golding had sent him (iii. 690). It is not clear whether they ever met, though DHL said he would like that (iii. 377).

46 'The Last Straw' is in *EmyE* 153–66 and 'Monkey Nuts' 64–76. Neither story was placed by Pinker.

47 *EmyE* 92:2. The house and factory are drawn from memory of those down the hill from the Lawrences' home in Lynn Croft. In *MEH* (29:17) the Emperor Hadrian is described as 'merciless'.

48 *EmyE* 93:33; 96:22, 24; 107:28. The story was first published in *Land and Water* (April 1920). No manuscript or typescript survives.

49 *EMyE* 106:34.

50 Sassoon's collection called 'Fireflies' was published in *Vanity Fair* (September 1920). The parody of DHL begins: 'I say to you my firefly: Flash around and fill me to the core with power' (p.55).

51 *SP* 111; Nehls, i. 460.

52 *SP* 110–12.

53 Nehls, i. 460; JMM, *Reminiscences*, p. 148.

54 Nehls, i. 486–7; JMM, *Reminiscences*, p. 99, but it is strongly to be doubted that DHL had asked JMM to visit him! Something ought perhaps to be said about DHL and needlework. This is only one of several evidences of the interest he took in trimming hats for Frieda. He also (according to Cecily), made her underclothing at this time, in rather spartan fashion out of calico. He denounced Cecily's crêpe-de-chine as 'Prostitutey' (Nehls, i. 465), but it may also have been a question of economy for him. (Later, in Capri, the undergarments hanging out to dry would be the subject of some amusement to the Brett Youngs, see next chapter.) He described to Helen Thomas how he had had to alter a model dress of Nusch's to fit Frieda, and how it was like dismantling a cathedral. He also took an interest in embroidery. He saw nothing effeminate in this: to him it was part of being independent and self-reliant, and he would recommend in the later Education essays that all boys should be taught to be self-sufficient as he had been.

55 *TWSUA* 56, 58, 60–1.

56 Nehls, i. 501, 502, 496–7, 460.

57 Damon 497–9. Asked later by Cannan and Waldo Frank to help arrange a lecture tour she was even more emphatic that it would be a mistake for DHL. He had no idea what the USA was like, could sell almost nothing there and might get no lecture dates at all because of prejudice against his books. She thought he had tuberculosis, and might even be excluded for that reason; and it was too early for his German wife to gain admittance to the USA. He would come only to be cruelly disappointed, and might die in a foreign land separated from his wife (pp. 513–14). (Only a year later, however, his American reputation and the interest in his work would grow very rapidly.)

58 Helen Thomas, 'Two Pieces of Advice from D. H. Lawrence', *The Times* (13 February 1963), p. 12.

59 Nehls, i. 493–6, quoting from *Life Interests* (1948), pp. 83–90, an earlier version of which had appeared in *Odd Man Out* (1935), pp. 249–66; Nehls, i. 599 n. 541. Fagan however returned *Touch and Go* with the comment: 'It is well written but I am afraid in my opinion it would not succeed on the stage' (iii. 374 n. 2). Once publication as the first in Daniel's series had been suggested, DHL wrote a Preface which he dated from Hermitage in June, but it was probably written in July and back-dated to correspond with his revision of the play. For his irritation at the undermining of this preface when Goldring's play became the opener in the series, see chapter 10, pp. 558–9.

60 'Nostalgia' and 'Obsequial Chant' were appearing in the July issue of *Voices*. Nichols

may have been the 'Unidentified Recipient' of Letter 1771 (iii. 377), since it was of Marsh that DHL had enquired whether Nichols was back from his lecture tour (iii. 370).

61 Nehls, i. 498–500; *TWSUA* 57.

62 *All Things Are Possible* (1920), pp. 22, 23, 24, 27.

63 G. M. Hyde, *D. H. Lawrence and the Art of Translation* (1981), pp. 22–35 shows how the final translation occasionally gives a Lawrencian slant as against a literal rendering.

64 *All Things Are Possible*, pp. 9, 10, 11.

65 Preface to the American Edition of *New Poems*, *P* 182, 183, 184, 185.

66 See (iii. 478). This undated letter, known only in a partial transcript by an unidentified person, is placed by the Cambridge Edition as probably March 1920 when the divorce had finally been set in motion, though it would take some time to come to court; cf. (iii. 488). The letter may however have been a product of the discussions at Pangbourne at the end of August 1919 – and is of interest in suggesting DHL's attitude to his own marriage:

> One has to learn that love is a secondary thing in life. The first thing is to be a free, proud, single being by oneself: to be oneself free, to let the other be free ... I believe if you would both come off the personal, emotional, insistent plane, and would be each of you self sufficient and to a degree indifferent or reckless, you and Rosalind would keep a lasting relationship.

DHL's reference to Whitman's 'Calamus' also, together with his own belief in a 'manly love' in addition to marriage, and based on 'cool separateness' rather than emotion and personality, also suggest a time when he was thinking again about the American essays (cf. iii. 388).

67 DHL had met Clifford Bax some years before, had recently met him again at Bucklebury and had arranged to see him on his recent visit to London (iii. 368) – but Bax seems to have disliked him (Nehls, i. 461). By June 1920 DHL seems to have reciprocated the feeling (iii. 542).

68 *TWSUA* 62.

69 E.T. 31.

70 Nehls, i. 503–4.

71 Nehls, i. 503. It is possible, as Barbara Barr is reported to have said her mother had told her, that an attack of the mumps after his pneumonia at sixteen had made DHL infertile (Meyers, *D. H. Lawrence*, p. 93) – but there is no evidence of this, and on Cecily's evidence Frieda had no such idea in 1919. Barbara Barr now thinks this may have been mentioned only as a possibility. She also told John Worthen that Frieda probably used 'a preventative' during her first marriage as well as afterwards. For the possibility that the infertility might have been Frieda's, see chapter 4, pp. 798–9 note 30. This is another matter in which knowledge is impossible and speculation futile.

72 Nehls, i. 504–6.

73 Nehls, i. 491–2 (from *Life Interests*, pp. 83–90).

74 Lucas, *Frieda Lawrence*, pp. 161, 158–9.

75 Nehls, i. 505. No typescript however has survived. The Foreword is dated

'Hermitage, 12 September 1919' (*WL* 486:19), the day he returned to Chapel Farm cottage; it was not published in *Women in Love* (*WL* xxxix n. 53 and 484–6). See also p. 864 note 93.

76 Born in Russia, Seltzer had come to America at the age of 12. He translated several Russian authors, went into publishing with Boni and Liveright in 1917, and set up a new firm, Scott and Seltzer, in 1918. He was to be DHL's exclusive publisher until 1926.

77 Cf. Ross, *The Composition*, pp. 118–19; *WL* xxxvi.

78 Nehls, i. 492.

79 See pp. 439 and 838–9 notes 63, 81; Nehls, i. 497; E382 b, p, i, l, n (the Melville essay now divided in two); in (iii. 405) DHL mentioned that the 'Democracy' essays (see pp. 523–6), which all begin from Whitman, could substitute for it.

80 Jane Burr was the pseudonym of Rose Guggenheim Winslow (b. 1881). Her novel is set in the brittle milieu of Greenwich Village. She also sent *City Dust* (private collection).

81 The fear that his ideas were about to be stolen seems megalomaniac; though if he knew through Barbara Low and the Eders that both Jones and the Eders had published essays on child psychology in *Child Study* in 1916, while he was in Cornwall, this might explain his belief that they were becoming preoccupied with the subject – though hardly his estimate of the extent of his influence. He had recently seen Barbara, and David Eder the previous February when he had been ill; he is not known to have seen Jones since 1915. Jones had now left to visit Freud in Vienna, in the hope of organizing a post-war conference. The Sixth International Psycho-Analytical Conference did not however take place until September 1920.

82 Nehls, i. 492. DHL had several reasons to be grateful to Goldring at this time as well as the agreement to publish *Touch and Go*. As Seltzer's agent in Britain, Goldring had persuaded him to take an interest in *Women in Love*. After his trip to The Hague, Golding had also succeeded in getting to Germany, where he interested Dr Anton Kippenberg of Insel-Verlag in publishing DHL in German (iii. 392 and n. 1), and the essays for *The Word* eased DHL's way to Italy.

83 *Odd Man Out*, pp. 253, 243; cf. *K* 110:20–6.

84 *RDP* 74:6–7.

85 The earliest surviving version, almost identical to the text in *The Word* taken from the ribbon copy, is a carbon typescript E91a from which the quotations are taken, rather than from the revised text printed in *RDP*. Page references will however be to *RDP* 63–83, and see also the Textual apparatus. *RDP* 74:13–20; 65:28; 66:1–2; 68:8–9; 66:29–30.

86 *RDP* 70:22, 23; 70:39–40; 72:26–7; 73:7–8, 19–21, 24–6.

87 *RDP* 74:33–5; 74:36–75:4; 75:15; 75:36–7.

88 *RDP* 78:27–31; 79:14–16; 81:34–5; 82:17–18; 82:13–14; 82:31.

89 *RDP* 65:24–5.

90 Nehls, i. 505; see (iii. 406).

91 *K* 258:23–4.

92 Lucas, *Frieda Lawrence*, pp. 160–1. Moreover when the trunk was eventually found,

the Dutch Customs had impounded some new cloth and two woollen vests she was taking to her mother, and though they released them later, they would not allow her to take them into Germany (iii. 620).

93 Nehls, ii. 5–6. Before he left for Italy, DHL sewed sheepskin overcoats for Rosalind's Bridget and Chloë to keep the mountain cold at bay (Nehls, ii. 5).

94 *SP* 113; Nehls, i. 502.

95 By an odd coincidence – but one with no significance for DHL's visit – Lady Becker was the aunt of Edward ('Teddy') Seaman, whom Frieda's daughter Elsa would become engaged to in 1926 and marry in 1929. See 'Something to Say', p. 42.

96 No play by Plowman appeared in Daniel's series, though DHL probably did help to persuade Goldring to accept for it a translation by Kot of *The Green Ring* by Zinaida Hippius (Merizkowsky).

97 *SP* 136.

98 Nehls, i. 507–8.

99 *SP* 114.

100 *K* 258:30; 258:30–4; cf. *LG* 294:12–25.

Chapter Ten: Capri and Sicily

1 Since DHL could not afford a sleeper, this must have been a very uncomfortable journey. He would urge Rosalind when she came to 'get a *sleeper* from Paris to Rome – wagon-lit – never mind the expense' (iii. 415).

2 Nehls, ii. 12–13, from a letter to Norman Douglas; cf. *AR* 133–49. Sir Walter complained that he appeared 'as a kind of physically decrepit and vulgarly ostentatious plutocrat', took Aaron's being reminded by his wife 'a little of Queen Victoria' (*AR* 135:39) as 'unflattering', and objected most of all that they had been made unintellectual and dull.

3 *AR* 133:31–3; Nehls, ii. 12.

4 See (iii. 417 n. 1). Born in 1855, thus in his mid-sixties in 1919, he was hardly an 'old man', though his state of health is unknown. He lived, however, till 1927.

5 No. 5 Piazza Mentana; E233.7, p. 2 (*MMM* 29–30); for the view, see (iii. 422). (*MMM* is printed from E233.7, as against the cut and bowdlerised version published as the introduction to *Memoirs of the Foreign Legion by M. M.* by Secker in 1924; reprinted *PII* 303–61. These are however used as a check for uncertain readings.)

6 E233.7, pp. 1–2 (*MMM* 30); *PII* 303–4, from a revised typescript: reads 'very clean, very natty, very alert'.

7 E233.7, p. 2 (*MMM* 30–1).

8 E233.7, pp. 4–6 (*MMM* 32–5). For Douglas, see Mark Holloway, *Norman Douglas: A Biography* (1976). Douglas was born in Austria in 1868, of a Scots father and a Scots-German mother. Educated at Uppingham and Karlsruhe, he joined the Foreign Office, serving in St Petersburg in the 1890s before having to leave in a hurry over an affair with a lady of family. He travelled widely, made a marriage which ended in acrimony and then became the doyen of the expatriate community in Capri. When DHL met him in 1914 he was assistant to Hueffer on the *English*

Review, but he later had to leave England too, after being arrested for picking up a schoolboy in the Natural History Museum. (His interest in and knowledge of natural history was however very considerable, and scientific.) He then made his life in Italy and southern France. His literary reputation was based on his novel *South Wind* (1917) and his travel books on southern Italy, *Siren Land* (1911, about Capri) and *Old Calabria* (1915).

Glimpses of Magnus appear in Gordon Craig, *Index to the Story of My Days* (1957), pp. 275–83, 289; Edward Craig, *Gordon Craig: The Story of His Life* (New York, 1968), pp. 202–13, 232, 240–50, 298–9, 310; and Norman Douglas, *A Plea for Better Manners* (which objects to DHL's portrait; reprinted in *MMM* 109–32). The Craigs' portrayal of a charming and flattering 'fixer' with a network of contacts, enabling him to act as manager for Gordon Craig and Isadora Duncan, is quite consistent with DHL's who knew him only in his hand-to-mouth years. He was born in New York in 1876, son of Karl Liebetrau and Hedwigis Rosamunda Magnus (whom he adored, and believed to be the illegitimate daughter of Kaiser Frederick Wilhelm). As a young man he felt that he belonged in cultured Europe rather than America; and it was in Berlin that he introduced himself to Gordon Craig. He later married Lucy Seraphine Norman; and converted to Roman Catholicism in England in 1902; but by 1909 when Douglas first met him, he had separated from his wife and his preference was homosexual. In a fit of idealism for the Allied cause he enlisted in the French Foreign Legion in 1916, but soon discovered his horrible mistake, and contrived to desert. He managed a last tour for Isadora in 1918, and was trying to resume his pre-war life when Craig met him in Rome in 1919 – but the world had changed, many old contacts had fallen on ill days and he was left with a champagne life-style and few means to sustain it. When DHL met him he was trying to live by his pen, completing a memoir of his days in the Legion, which he titled 'Dregs'; and also working on a memoir of his travels. His impecuniousness was not for want of hard work – he wrote voluminously.

9 E233.7, pp. 1, 6 (*MMM* 29, 35). DHL had however almost certainly acquired lire in London before leaving (see n. 15).

10 Nehls, ii. 14. E233.7, p. 8 (*MMM* 38).

11 (1933), pp. 282–7 (Nehls, ii. 15).

12 November 1919 (UCLA) (Stanley Weintraub, *Reggie: A Portrait of Reginald Turner*, New York, 1965, p. 193).

13 See (iii. 419–20); *AR* 219:15–20. DHL certainly met Leo Stein, brother of Gertrude, whom he later enquires after (iii. 463). Reggie Turner may also have taken them to a musical at-home at the Torrigianis' across the river. (See pp. 543, also 599, 670 and 864 note 96).

14 *AR* 215:21; 219:20, 22.

15 This will have included the lire he had obtained in London, from which he had drawn to cover his Italian train-fares and the hotel in Lerici – leaving him with £9 sterling as a reserve in his pocket. The pensione in Florence cost about 85 lire a week including food and heating (iii. 424), but he had been eating out too. There was also the dentist's fee. He had got 50 lire to £1.

16 The Cambridge Edition dates DHL's letter to KM 24? November, but when she mentioned it to Kot on 13 December she knew that Frieda had arrived in Florence (*Letters*, ed. O'Sullivan and Scott, iii. 161). So DHL must have written soon after 3 December – probably the same day that he sent the first article to JMM in London, i.e. before 6 December (iii. 428).

JMM had written to KM on 17 October perhaps with a twinge of conscience, that he 'would like to give D. H. Lawrence a leg-up' and suggested she might like to write on *Sons and Lovers* – but she did not, see pp. 560 and 852 notes 46 and 47. On 9 November he had heard from Gertler that DHL was going to Italy and wrote to KM: 'I am going to send him your address. He may quite well have the chance of coming to see you' (*Letters of JMM to KM*, ed. Hankin, pp. 188, 205).

17 *SEP* 185:3, 16; 185:7–15; echoing in some respects the description in his letter to Cecily on 26 November (iii. 422). (It is possible that the essay was revised in 1921, see *SEP* lv–lvi. A typescript survives, probably from 1921 and probably typed by DHL.).

18 *SEP* 188:26; 185:18–19; 189:12–13.

19 See *SEP* lvi–lvii. (Again only a 1921 typescript by DHL survives.)

20 When Frieda arrived, however, they may have gone together: they certainly did meet Trench's wife and daughter, see (iii.463).

21 Frieda 116–17.

22 *SP* 119; cf. *AR* 228:35–230:6.

23 *SP* 118. That both robberies occurred in 1919 is confirmed in *SS* chap. VIII: 'When I first came to Italy after the war I was robbed twice in three weeks, floating round in the sweet old innocent confidence in mankind.' DHL probably suspected Ellesina's husband who had become senile and was not responsible for his actions (information from John Carswell).

24 Cf. *LG* 301ff.

25 Il Rosaio was owned by the engineer and architect Edwin Cerio who built Casa Solitaria. It had sitting-room, kitchen and one bedroom only, and had been occupied in 1919 by the composer Respighi. The *casetta* down at the beach 'consisted of two rooms built over a boathouse'. See Compton Mackenzie, *My Life and Times: Octave Five 1915–1923* (1966), p. 160; and Faith Mackenzie, *As Much As I Dare* (1938), p. 283 on the strategy of the landlord to get them to give up the lease after the war, by encouraging local Capresi to relieve themselves nearby.

26 Cassells had offered a contract for six books at a £1,500 advance for each, and a £4,000 option for four of the six for possible serialisation. However Mackenzie loyally insisted that Secker should have two more books after *Sylvia and Michael* and Cassells agreed (*My Life and Times*, p. 146).

27 Two years older than DHL, Edward Montague Compton Mackenzie was grandson and son to actors. His father 'Edward Compton' and his mother headed a successful touring repertory company, and his two sisters were actresses also. Educated at St Paul's and Oxford, he had set out as a poet, then a preacher awaiting orders, then a grower of exotic plants in Cornwall. He had written a number of successful novels, a successful play (to justify himself to his father), and a successful revue for one of the

foremost impresarios of the day. He had trodden the boards with aplomb himself, in both England and America. Moreover he had had an amazing war. Through the 'old-boy network' and without training of any kind, he had become not only an officer of marines but a spymaster in the Aegean. See *My Life and Times* and A. Linklater, *Compton Mackenzie* (1987).

28 *Poor Relations* was the title of Mackenzie's latest novel (1919), and the one he was about to start was *Rich Relatives* (1921). Faith later protested that Monty's velour hat had come from Hilhouse, the expensive Bond Street gentleman's hatter (Nehls, ii. 21), *More than I Should* p. 32.

29 Faith Mackenzie, *More Than I Should* (1940), p. 25.

30 This story is first told in *Literature in My Time* (1933), p. 193 and elaborated in *My Life and Times*, p. 166. *The West Wind of Love* fictionalised the encounter (Nehls, ii. 24–9), but, Mackenzie claimed, was mostly 'factually and conversationally exact' (Nehls, ii. 455, n. 530). However, Mackenzie, though a splendid raconteur, may not be altogether reliable. I argue below that one of his best stories, even if true in outline, must have mistaken the gesture which is its central point, and misremembered what the DHL of 1920 actually said, by assimilating him to DHL the author of *Lady Chatterley's Lover*. The account in *My Life and Times*, p. 166, of DHL denouncing *Ulysses* as 'muck', while possible (if Mackenzie had lent him an issue of the *Little Review*) is also open to question since DHL showed no memory, while trying to get hold of the book in 1922, of having ever seen part of it before – not something one would forget. Despite Mackenzie's praise of the novel and disparagement of DHL there, the story was not mentioned in *Literature in My Time* (1933) and first appeared in 1966. Mackenzie may however have talked about *Ulysses* on Capri in 1920.

31 F. Mackenzie *More than I Should*, pp. 31–2 (Nehls, ii. 21); Mackenzie, *My Life and Times*, p. 165. Brooks, a brilliant Greek scholar, never produced the work he seemed to promise. A homosexual, he made a marriage of convenience with the talented American painter Romaine Brooks who was lesbian, but they soon separated. Faith Mackenzie described his life as 'useless' and 'selfish' but the man himself as 'picturesque and lovable, without much shame, and what is rarer, without sham' (Nehls, ii. 454 n. 39). Douglas and Mackenzie dedicated books to him, and also based characters on him (*South Wind* and *Vestal Fire*). DHL also liked him, and continued to correspond with him for a time after leaving Capri.

32 *My Life and Times*, pp. 167–8. Mellors treats such a failure philosophically in *Lady Chatterley's Lover*, which however makes it clear in Connie's case, as well as that of Mellors's horrible wife, that it may result from the woman's inability or unwillingness to give herself completely, as well as from the man's over-quickness. It is possible that Mackenzie may have back-dated from *Lady Chatterley* again. He was not well-disposed to DHL after 'The Man Who Loved Islands' (where DHL made use of Faith's confidences). It is also however possible that DHL did say something resembling Mackenzie's report, since he was on other occasions remarkably open about his sex life. His poem 'Manifesto' makes explicit an implication hinted at elsewhere, that Frieda gave her body easily, but not herself. One step further: the

fiction sometimes reveals (from Ursula on the beach to Mellors's wife) a horror of 'beaked' woman who, concentrated on herself, tears at a man − and, particularly in the *late* fiction, resentment of a woman who has withheld herself then 'brought herself off' after the man has climaxed (*LCL* 202:8, 3). However, once again, wherever the 'imperfection', inadequacy (or rationalisation) of real life lay, it is dangerous to infer directly from literature to life. The truth was probably complex and is certainly unknowable. The anecdote about the comedy of sex (also echoed in *Lady Chatterley's Lover*, also possibly back-dated by Mackenzie) is first in *Literature in My Time*, p. 210.

33 Mackenzie, *My Life and Times*, pp. 168, 164−5. For the fly story, see also *West Wind of Love*, pp. 294−301 (Nehls, ii. 27), and the original version in *Literature in My Time*, p. 210 (Nehls, ii. 455−6 n. 55).

34 Mackenzie, *My Life and Times*, pp. 166−7. F. Mackenzie, *As Much As I Dare*, p. 259.

35 The postal strike seems to have broken out on Monday 5 January (KM, *Letters*, ed. O'Sullivan and Scott, iii. 169), was suspended for a week, then set in in earnest the following week (KM getting her last letter on 13th). DHL got on 6 January a letter from Germany which had been posted on 23 December (iii. 448), and post was delivered on 9/10 January, but he seems to have had nothing at all from then to 29 January when he returned from Amalfi, since as soon as the postal strike ended on the 22nd, the railway strike began (iii. 460−1).

36 Mackenzie, *My Life and Times*, p. 166.

37 *PU* ch. III [Penguin (1971), p. 219].

38 *PU* ch. I [Penguin, p. 203].

39 *PU* ch. I [Penguin, pp. 204, 206].

40 See (iii. 301−2) and chapter 9, p. 491.

41 He probably still had most of Seltzer's £50, and a present of $100 (£25/7/7) had come unexpectedly through Huebsch from well-wishers in America, the poets Louis Untermeyer and his wife Jean Starr, and their friend Emile Tas (iii. 445). He had probably also been paid for the Shestov and for *Bay* which had been published on 20 November.

42 *My Life and Times*, pp. 165−6. He attributes her desire to pull people down to her experience of being made to feel an outsider during the war.

43 See *Life Interests*, p. 90 (Nehls, ii. 37).

44 The Cambridge Edition (iii. 470) dates KM's letter 9 February (iii. 470); whereas O'Sullivan and Scott are surely right to date it two days earlier (*Letters*, iii. 208−9), since it is a reply to JMM's 'Tuesday letter' (3 February), and letters from London to Ospedaletti were now regularly taking four days. (KM dated quite a different letter on the 9th.) Alpers, *Life of Mansfield* (pp. 310−11) reports JMM as adding, twelve years later in his 1932 journal, that DHL had called KM a 'loathsome reptile' and hoped that she would die. It was he who destroyed the letter. On the back of DHL's letter to him, JMM drafted a reply dated 8 February: 'Dear Lawrence, This is to tell you that it is my fixed intention, when ever or wherever I meet you again, to hit you in the face. There is no other way of treating you' (iii. 648 n.). He could not yet have heard of DHL's letter to KM, and was motivated only by the insult to

himself. The date makes it likely also that both DHL's letters reached their destinations about the same time, i. e. 6–7 February in Ospedaletti and perhaps 7–8 February in JMM's case, having further to go. Letters from London to Taormina were taking six or seven days after the strike.

45 E233.7, p. 56 (*MMM* 101).

46 *Letters of JMM to KM*, ed. Hankin, p. 188; *Letters*, ed. O'Sullivan and Scott (iii. 42).

47 *Letters of JMM to KM*, ed. Hankin, p. 205; KM to JMM, 14 November (*Letters*, ed. O'Sullivan and Scott, iii. 92).

48 From Florence DHL was giving the Picinisco address, expecting to be only a week in Rome.

49 *Letters*, ed. O'Sullivan and Scott, iii. 135, 158–60.

50 Letters to England then (before the pile-up owing to the strike) were taking about five days; cf. (iii. 425).

51 *Letters*, ed. O'Sullivan and Scott, iii. 148.

52 Ibid., iii. 182–4.

53 Ibid., iii. 213.

54 *Letters of JMM to KM*, ed. Hankin, p. 266; *Letters*, ed. O'Sullivan and Scott, iii. 214, 217.

55 Alpers, *Life of Mansfield*, p. 366; the will drawn up on 14 August 1922.

56 'A Defense of Lawrence', *New York Tribune* (10 January 1920), replying to an interview with Sir Ernest Hodder. Mackenzie was irritated at Cannan's 'imaginary stories' to interviewers (*My Life and Times*, p. 167).

57 DHL did not recognise Bennett under the initials 'E.A.' in Pinker's letter, and queried the payment.

58 Seltzer's telegram read, when transcribed in Picinisco 'Relnquies for atother publisher entirely cable our ekpense. Selizer' (iii. 472 n. 3). It arrived in Capri on 10 February, but what did it mean? *Was* it agreement to relinquish, or had a word dropped out (such as 'impossible' after 'entirely')? Certainly when Huebsch approached Seltzer, the latter had *not* changed his mind.

59 'Diary' (Tedlock 89).

60 See note 41 above.

61 E233.7, pp. 9–10 (*MMM* 40). The letters have not survived.

62 The gift from the Untermeyers appears to have arrived in the storm-delayed post on 4 January. DHL could not then have heard twice from Magnus by 17 January because of the postal strike, and the only gap in the letters during which DHL could have gone to Montecassino in January is 17–21st. The railway strike had begun by 22 January. There is every reason therefore to discount DHL's mention of 'January' in the memoir as misremembering, and to prefer his other, contradictory statement that he returned from Montecassino 'only a few days' before leaving for Sicily (E233.7, pp. 10, 13, 24; *MMM* 40, 44, 59). There is internal confirmation for dating the trip 19–21 February, too, since Magnus, having hoped DHL would stay a week, tried unsuccessfully to persuade him at least to stay 'over Sunday', but he travelled back on Saturday (E233.7, p. 22; *MMM* 58) – which fits 21 February but not the January dates – and left for Sicily on 26 February.

63 E233.7, pp. 11, 12, 14 (MS reads 'theires'; *MMM* 42, 43, 46). To Magnus, the monastery was a 'Paradise ... the only place – the only life! I only pray I may be able to settle all my affairs soon & be permitted to stay always. The peace – the quiet – the services – the monks at work – it is that "which passeth understanding"' (Magnus to Douglas, 5 October 1915, YU; it describing a previous visit, and recounting the routine of his day.)

64 Magnus had sung the praises of Sicily earlier and suggested DHL go to Agrigento. Moreover Mary Cannan was proposing to move to Sicily too. The date is given in Francis Brett Young's diary and confirmed by Jessica Brett Young, *Francis Brett Young: A Biography* (1962), pp. 102–5, on which the account that follows has drawn.

65 This is confirmed by a letter of 4 May (to be published in *Letters*, viii.) in which DHL told Stanley Unwin of the missing trunk, and how he was having to wear winter clothes in very hot weather.

66 J. Brett Young, *Francis Brett Young*. pp. 93–100, 114.

67 Ibid., pp. 103–5, see also p. 96.

68 See Ciccio Cacópardo's account (Nehls, ii. 32).

69 Indeed DHL told Kot shortly afterwards, in response to a suggestion that he might join Gilbert Cannan and Henry Mond in a new 'left' periodical, that he not only had no desire to enter the journalistic world like JMM and Squire, but also that 'what remaining belief I had in Socialism dies out of me more and more as the time goes by' (iii. 486).

70 *SP* 130–1, and on the production and her review 135, 137–8. She thought the production 'creditable if no more', but to have played the body-washing scene realistically – however 'simple and tragic' it is to read – was to show that the play 'does not quite "do,"' though she thought it held its own against the Irish People's Plays which were its only rivals as working-class drama. She was upset that, having written too long a review, the more commendatory part had been cut.

71 On 22 March DHL told Mackenzie that Duckworth had asked him to 'cut pieces' from *The Rainbow* including a whole chapter, almost certainly 'Shame' (iii. 491, 490), which so annoyed him that he was going straight back to Secker. Secker replied with an offer of a shilling a copy on the first 2, 000, 1/6 to 5, 000 and 2/- thereafter; and DHL asked for an advance of £100 on each novel (iii. 499). But did Secker want to 'saddle' himself with *The Lost Girl*? (iii. 503). The editor of *LG* is unfair however to suggest (xxix) that DHL was 'clearly trying to evade the terms of his contract', since the contract containing a commitment, to future books (five), only came to him on 7 May, and he then specifically objected to it (iii. 519). For a while there was talk of calling it 'The Bitter Cherry' after Ciccio's surname, Marasca – presumably to quieten Secker's misgiving.

72 The quest is a predominant form in American fiction. It has been suggested by L. D. Clark, in *D. H. Lawrence and the Modern World*, ed. Peter Preston and Peter Hoare (Basingstoke, 1989), pp. 193–216, that DHL was, consciously or unconsciously, beginning to become an 'American' writer as well as seeking an American audience.

73 See chapter 2, pp. 58–9, 61. Photographs of Flossie and her governess Miss Wright

may be found in George Hardy and Nathaniel Harris, *A D. H. Lawrence Album* (Ashbourne, 1985), pp. 69–74.

74 *LG* 202:26–8; 202:23–4; Secker's cut 202:26–8. The presence of anal sex in this novel has been sensitively analysed by H. M. Daleski in a paper at a DHL conference in Montpellier in 1990.

75 *LG* 234:29; 233:36, 39; 202:31; 234:4. For the change DHL agreed to make at Secker's request see note to 234:16 (pp. 386–7).

76 *LG* 392–3, note to 288:9; 288:6–9.

77 Cf. the scene in the Italian Consulate, *LG* 290:32–291:30.

78 See chapters 3, p. 156 and 4, pp. 220–2.

79 *LG* 339:2–3, 9, 15–16; cf. (iii. 307).

80 The Hubrecht sketch, signed by DHL, is reproduced facing (iii. 322) and the Juta charcoal sketch facing p. 119 of Keith Sagar, *The Art of D. H. Lawrence* (1966). The sketch provided the basis of a later oil painting, see chapter 11, pp. 632 and 862 note 69.

81 The following account is drawn from Nehls, ii. 31–3, *Letters*, iii., especially (iii. 551, 557), and my conversation with Salvatore Galleano at Fontana Vecchia.

82 'The Bigger Heart of D. H. Lawrence', *New Republic* (28 February 1955). The story may be apocryphal, though it is told by Ciccio (Nehls, ii. 33); and the Lawrences did become acquainted with Ciccio Atenasio who became Sindaco, and spent their last Christmas on the island with him and his wife (see postcard to Baroness von Richthofen, 19 December 1921, to be published in *Letters*, viii.).

83 'Gilbert, the Filbert, the colonel of the Knuts' – from a pre-war music-hall song, a 'filbert' being both a nut and a slang term for a fashionable man about town. He and DHL never met again, and a few years later Cannan had a mental breakdown from which he never recovered, see Farr, *Cannan*.

84 See postcard to Baroness von Richthofen, 9 April, to be published in *Letters*, viii.

85 Moore, *Intelligent Heart*, p. 269.

86 E233.7, p. 24 (*MMM* 60); *LG* 274:18–20; Frieda 130.

87 What follows is taken from E233.7, pp. 24ff. (*MMM* 60ff.), checked against Magnus's account to Douglas in his letter of 9 May (YU). For Douglas's views see his *Plea for Better Manners* in *MMM*.

88 DHL clearly registered the pointedness of Magnus's compliments about the spaciousness of Fontana Vecchia. Magnus complained bitterly that 'he never asked me for a meal or offered a room in his most commodious house'.

89 E233.7, p. 24 (*MMM* 75). Magnus gives Cipolla's name and address to Douglas, letter of 9 May. It is not clear whether this is the same Pancrazio as the waiter at the Timeo, for it is a common name.

90 Printed in Tedlock 89–99. The terse factual entries run from 6 February 1920 to 17 November 1924. 'May 5th. Sent first part MS. Lost Girl to Miss Wallace ... "Lost Girl" finished.' On 7 May his bank balance was £171.4.5 and he signed Secker's agreements for *The Rainbow* and *Women in Love* and 'Began Mr Noon'.

91 E233.7, pp. 37–40 (*MMM* 78–83).

92 One appeared in 1921 as number 10 in the Daniel series.

93 Borg was 31; Salomone a few years older (information from Peter Vassullo). In fact DHL wrote to Magnus at least once more in July, Magnus to Douglas, 18 July (YU), but did not answer letters from Magnus written on 26 July and 25 August, Magnus to Douglas, 2 October (YU) – though these were probably lying in Taormina, which he had left on 1 August.

94 On 28 October (YU) Magnus told Douglas that DHL had

> opened his 'heart' (!) to me here accidentally. He is looking for bisexual types for *himself*. Spoke of his innocence when he wrote 'Twilight' and 'Il Duro'. Evidently innocent no longer. Didn't like Malta because he thought that the religion or something prevented their sexual expression! I didn't elucidate [sic] him as I could have done even after a few days stay! He revels in all that is not just within his reach. He wants it to be within his reach. Arrived too late – regrets it. Never speaks of it unless bored to tears by women as here by Mrs Cannan and his wife.

It would be a mistake to interpret this as a confession by DHL that he was on the lookout for a homosexual relationship. It sounds like the garbling of an admission of bisexuality such as he had made to William Henry, and the familiar declaration of his lifelong desire for blood-brotherhood. It seems as tempting to some homosexuals, confronted by a homophobic world which categorises everyone not exclusively heterosexual as homosexual, to do the same in reverse – as with Forster's speculation about DHL. As to 'Il Duro', the DHL of late 1915 was certainly no longer 'innocent' about homosexuality. The suggestion probably came from Magnus and was met by polite denial that this was what DHL had intended. It is indeed a travesty of what he wrote. The one really interesting and revealing part of DHL's indiscretion is the possible implication that he regretted *not* having had a sexual relationship with William Henry because it had come too late – presumably because of his marriage and the Cornishman's courting.

95 For the rent see diary entries, Tedlock 89, 90, etc. DHL did not know what Seltzer's two cheques were for, and it is not certain now, but Seltzer was bringing out *Touch and Go* in the USA in June and now also proposed to republish *The Widowing of Mrs. Holroyd* from the old plates Little, Brown had bought from Kennerley (iii. 527), which might explain the identical sums. (It may have been because of Little, Brown's purchase that Pinker had sent *Women in Love* to them in 1917, though it is still far from clear why he should have ignored Huebsch.)

96 The *Dial* offers came through the agency of Richard Aldington (see diary entry for 20 June, Tedlock 90); commencing a most fruitful relationship with the magazine which had recently been taken over by Scofield Thayer, and was to publish DHL regularly, helping to forge his reputation in the US. See Nicholas Joost and Alvin Sullivan *D. H. Lawrence and 'The Dial'* (Carbondale, 1970). Diary entry for 27 June (Tedlock 91); the *Metropolitan* was edited by Carl Hovey (not 'Huffey' as DHL first thought; iii. 493) who had been consulted by Huebsch as to whether he should publish *The Rainbow* and whose letter of high praise is in the Huebsch archive (LC), see chapter 5, note 103.

97 For 15 June, when he paid Miss Wallace her 1360 lire (about £17), DHL scribbled '*too much*' after the laconic note in his diary (Tedlock 90). The original estimate of 1,000 had been reason enough for complaint in letter after letter (e.g. iii. 521).

98 31 May (Tedlock 90); cf. *SP* 132, 134.

99 Alpers, *Life of Mansfield*, pp. 412–13.

100 For the complicated story of these delays and their textual consequences see *LG* xxxiii–xxxviii, supplemented by letters to Foss on 23 June and 23 July, to be published in *Letters*, viii. DHL also thought that serialisation might be a protection against prosecution when the book appeared (iii. 537).

101 It is not clear whether he had brought the *English Review* texts with him, and since the 'book' was never published there is no way of telling whether he revised the published essays. He certainly however had the autograph manuscripts of the unpublished essays, E382n, l, i, b, f, that had been prepared in September 1919. I have assumed in my discussion of the revision process now that three surviving typescripts (E382h, m, UT, and k, UNM), printed in Arnold, *Symbolic Meaning*, were from June 1920 revision, typed on Mountsier's instructions when he received them in August (iii. 582). (Arnold however reprinted E382j, UT, as the *Moby Dick* essay, the shortened carbon instead of the full ribbon copy E382k, presumably then unknown to him.) For the corresponding Whitman essay, see note 103.

102 E382k, pp. 1–5.

103 E382d, published in the *Nation and Athenæum* for 23 July 1921 and reprinted by Arnold, *The Symbolic Meaning*, pp. 254–64, has a note on page 1 'Magazine' in Mountsier's hand. A full version of this essay survives in E382p (unpublished). Mountsier to DHL, 10 December 1920 (iii. 644 n.) confirms that Mountsier was going to attempt to cut essays with periodical publication in mind. It is planned to include all surviving versions of the American essays in the Cambridge Edition volume.

104 E382p, pp. 3, 8, 10, 12, 13; E382d, p. 7; E382p, p. 13.

105 Encouragement had come from Stanley Unwin in March, asking after the progress of the little book that had been discussed in 1919; but it came when DHL's trunk containing the manuscript was still missing (2 April). On 15 May, when the trunk had at last arrived, he promised to get on with the 'Education' book 'at once', and on 17 June confirmed that he was at work on it. DHL's letters to Unwin will be published in *Letters*, viii. E112a is written throughout on the same paper, probably one of the blocks he thanked Marie Hubrecht for sending him at the end of May (iii. 533).

106 *RDP* 138:13–14; 166:27.

107 *RDP* 141:18–19; 148:31–149:9.

108 *RDP* 133:12–24.

109 *RDP* 150:12; 138:20–1.

110 *RDP* 134:23–136:22.

111 *RDP* 165:27–34; 165:40–166:3; 166:4–7, 13–16, 22–7.

112 This assumes, along with the *Letters* editors, that it was *Aaron's Rod* that DHL wrote of in (iii. 565, 567, 571), since that was what he continued to work on, whereas no more is heard of *Mr Noon* until November, suggesting that the pre-Malta idea had failed to develop. But 'begun' (iii. 565) *could* suggest *Mr Noon*.

113 Frieda remembered an episode in the heat when DHL climbed a mulberry tree to

gather berries in his bathing suit, and the juice running down his body made him look like the suffering Christ they had seen in Wieden (Frieda 132).

114 See Christopher Heywood, '*Birds, Beasts and Flowers*: The Evolutionary Context and Lawrence's African Source', *DHLR*, xv (1982), 87–105. He may also have had in mind the adder by the spring at Higher Tregerthen (recalled by Stanley Hocking, Stevens, *Lawrence at Tregerthen*, p. 60; cf. iii. 40). The spontaneity of the living moment (for him), lies in the act of writing, which is more likely than not to have many sources. The complex of feelings about the snake and its entrance into the dark underworld gains additional resonance when placed beside the other work of the spring and summer. However, as Keith Sagar points out in *D. H. Lawrence: Life into Art* (Harmondsworth, 1985), pp. 216, 232–4, DHL had not yet visited Venice; cf. 'Mosquito' (*Poems* 332, ll. 9–10); did not borrow *Specimens of Bushman Folklore*, ed. Lucy C. Lloyd (1911), until August; and did not mention 'Snake' until January 1921. As in *Look!* we must not assume that the poems we read were written at the time of the experience, though they may have been started then.

115 This was largely Secker's doing, since the last thing he wanted was to see his most successful author disappear to Noa Noa land. So, when he spotted the advertisement in the *Times* he put it under Monty's nose and the result was as he hoped.

116 He had had Magnus send his *Foreign Legion* manuscript to Secker now, with a recommendation (iii. 564); and a letter of authority to Mountsier with instructions about the merry-go-round of *Lost Girl* manuscripts which was still going on (iii. 575–7). An enquiry came from Curtis Brown, busy building up his agency (iii. 566), and though DHL remained convinced that he had been right to ask Mountsier to act for him, it was good to know that another professional agent was interested. Goldring had just published, and sent him now, a collection of critical essays called *Reputations* (iii. 573), one of which (Draper 136–40) was a sympathetic though not uncritical account of what DHL had published since *The Rainbow*. On 1 August he sent Mountsier his only copy of 'Fanny and Annie' as the story next most likely to succeed in America (iii. 582) and made his final decision against Palmer. The next day he sent the American essays to Mountsier too.

Chapter Eleven: On the Move

1 They stayed in the monastery (iii. 602). Frieda was probably still irritated at not having been invited by Magnus.

2 *SS* ch. VIII (in *Lawrence in Italy* [Penguin 1905], p. 182). Achsah Brewster who had also once lived there described the garden 'where the great fountain spurted up through the ilex trees' (Nehls, ii. 58). *Aaron's Rod* described 'Angus' as bird-like, with precisely enunciated public-school speech, though 'with a strong twang of South Wales'. He comes from 'very wealthy iron people near Merthyr' and was at the Slade before the war (*AR* 188:1–2; 197:23); but now, with his monocle and cynical air, is an ex-subaltern shattered by the trenches. He is some years older than his companion. Juta, born in Cape Town in 1897, the son of Sir Henry and Lady Helen Juta, also studied at the Slade.

3 Secker had been sending proofs since the middle of August, but thanks to the vagaries of the post 'A good deal that he sent never arrived, and none of what Lawrence returned reached England.' DHL seems to have sent part at least of his duplicate set to Seltzer, though the American edition was set up from the English proofs corrected in Secker's office (*LG* xxxvii–xxxviii).

4 He had probably heard about it (iii. 591 and n. 1) from the Secretary, Deane Perceval, whom he had met in Taormina.

5 Cf. Nehls, ii. 48. According to Eleanor Farjeon in *Nuts and May* (1926) – which Rosalind illustrated – 'the chief rooms ran along in a suite at the back of the house, overlooking the garden; the rooms were silent and muffled, with old-fashioned chairs and mirrors, tables and couches, cabinets and shelves of unopened books, all unused and growing musty together' (*TWSUA* 71).

6 Orioli claimed to have met DHL in Cornwall (*Memoirs of a Bookseller*, Florence, 1938, p. 192). The meeting is placed in the context of 1914–15 which cannot be right. However elsewhere Orioli says that he was also in Cornwall in 1916 and 1917, staying with the Crockers whom he knew through his English partner J. I. Davis. Since PH met Phyl Crocker there in 1917, the introduction to DHL was probably then. Carlota's husband Harry Thrasher had been considered a highly promising sculptor, but was killed in action not long before the end of the war. There is a memorial to him in the American academy in Rome, (iii. 600 n. 3).

7 *TWSUA* 73; *SEP* 196:5–6 and 325, note to 196:22. The 'Epilogue' (1924) to *Movements in European History* recalled that in Summer 1920: 'Florence was in a state of continual socialistic riot: sudden shots, sudden stones smashing into the restaurants where one was drinking coffee, all the shops suddenly barred and closed. When I came back, there was a great procession of Fascisti and banners: *Long Live the King*' (262:28–32).

8 E382.5a, published in *New Republic*, xxv (15 December 1920), 68–70, for which the magazine paid $40 (iii. 591 and n. 3). The same issue carried a rejoinder by Walter Lippman, and the issue of 5 January a protest against Lippman by Mary Austin.

9 Lowell's review published *New York Times Book Review*, 22 August; Untermeyer in *New Republic*, xxiii (11 August 1920), 314–15 (Draper 132–5).

10 'The Fox' had been taken by *Hutchinson's Story Magazine*, not *Nash's*. DHL having just heard about Herm and Jethou, the letter to Mackenzie threatened 'The Lord of the Isles. I shall write a skit on you one day' (iii. 594), a threat fulfilled six years later in 'The Man Who Loved Islands'; responsible for the breach in their friendship, and much anger on Mackenzie's part.

11 Nehls, ii. 49–50; *TWSUA* 78–9. Rosalind headed her account '*September 11th 1920. D. H. Lawrence's birthday*'; but that was on Saturday, fitting neither the supper with which the account begins, nor the 'And so to bed' with which it ends on 'Sunday'. The most likely explanation is that she associated the experience with the birthday, but had forgotten on which of the days she describes it actually fell.

12 Rosalind, in pencil notes in her copy of *Birds, Beasts and Flowers*, labels 'Pomegranate', 'Peach', 'Medlars and Sorb-Apples', 'Figs', 'Grapes' and 'Tortoise Shell'

Villa La Canovaia; and 'Cypresses' and 'Turkey Cock' *Villa Belvedere*, i. e. Fiesole. Since *New Republic* later published 'The Revolutionary' as well as 'Medlars' (paying $20 for each; iii. 596 and n. 1); and *Dial* three of the mistakenly titled 'Apostolic Beasts' as well as 'Pomegranate', these poems must have been sent to Mountsier. The Tortoise poems were probably finished by the time he got to Venice, and were sent to Mountsier two days later (15 September). The way these poems belong together is concealed by their distribution among different categories in the eventual volume. Derek Britton *Lady Chatterley: The Making of the Novel* (1988), p. 83, without this information, acutely pointed out the private allusion to Rosalind Thornycroft in 'Fig' (*Poems* 282–4), as DHL hails *'the thorn in flower ... The brave, adventurous rosaceae'*. This hardly increases the sexiness of the poem, though it does bear on the ongoing contrast between rose and vine in these poems, fused now in his sense of her. Perhaps the 'you' that is mockingly challenged in 'Pomegranate' and 'Peach', the 'pale-face' consciousness (or conscience) that would repress the red-dark shameless sexuality everywhere 'beneath' and disapprove of him for so exposing and enjoying it, can now be read with an additional sense of what is supposed to be 'wrong', and even a reminder, as the poet offers the reader a stone, that stoning was the biblical punishment for adultery. However, the full complexity of feeling in these poems, and their multiple relationships with each other, are for the literary critic to explore, where biography ends.

13 *New Republic* (5 January 1921); cf. *Poems* 280–1. But the additional poem might have been 'The Revolutionary'.

14 Ibid. It ends with sorb-apples 'savoured perhaps with a sip of Marsala,/ So that the withering, morbid grape can add its refrain to yours./ Farewell, and farewell, and farewell.'

15 He told the Baroness also of his plan to have his German royalties in marks paid to her.

16 She was clearly with him however, bidding him good-bye, when the *panforte* was bought that he ate on the way to Venice (iii. 604).

17 'Morality and the Novel', *Hardy* 171:21–2, 25–6; see also D. G. Ellis, 'Lawrence, Wordsworth, and "Anthropomorphic Lust"', *Cambridge Quarterly*, xxiii (1994), 230–42.

18 'Thought', *Poems* 673.

19 *Tortoises* (New York, 1921); *Poems* 354; 358, 361.

20 Frieda's Christmas letter to Rosalind regrets (iii. 642) not having seen the children, presumably since leaving England, hence presumably not having seen Rosalind either. DHL probably preferred not to risk a visit, since Frieda was eagle eyed as far as he was concerned. It seems certain that he never told Frieda what had happened, since she told Mabel Luhan that it was only with Esther that DHL had 'evaded' her. The journey back may have been the one descibed in the 'Epilogue' to *Movements* as having taken twelve hours longer than it should have done (262:18–19).

21 Frieda had probably become interested in the German contemporary dance revolution pioneered by Rudolph Laban and Mary Wigman in Ascona, which she visited in 1911 during her relationship with Ernst Frick (Frieda Gross to Else Jaffe, 10 April

1911 (Letter 48, TuftsU). See also Martin Green *Mountain of Truth* (Hanover and London, 1986). Laban later came under pressure to stage dances and processions for the Nazis, before escaping to England. DHL had shown some knowledge of expressionist contemporary dance in the description of Gudrun's dancing in *WL*.

22 *LG* xxxix–xl; see above chapter 10, pp. 575–6 and 854 note 74.

23 Secker to DHL, 25 November (*WL* xlvi).

24 The above information is conflated from DHL's E233.7, pp. 44–6 (*MMM* 88–91), his letter to Douglas of 16 November (YU) to be published in *Letters*, viii., his letters to Michael Borg (in private ownership but facts checked by kind co-operation of Peter Vassallo), the letters of the American Consul in Malta to Norman Douglas in December (YU), and the death certificate. DHL quoted Salomone (UT) as stating that Magnus was buried on his birthday, 7 November – which seems to add a humorous touch (in fact) to how he must have been avoiding giving the dinner he had promised in Florence, which was held on Sunday 23 November, after much pressure from Douglas. In that case, Douglas's birthday present was a fortnight late, too.

25 E233.7, p. 47 (*MMM* 92); DHL to Douglas, 16 November (YU). His letter to Douglas of 20 December (YU), asking Douglas's approval of his plan to get Magnus's debts repaid by publishing his Legion manuscript with an introductory memoir, cites the debt to the Maltese as £60 and to himself as £23 – over six months' rent of Fontana Vecchia at the 1920 rate.

26 *MEH* 239:39–240:4; *RDP* 225:10–19.

27 See (iii. 627 and n., 629, 632, 635, 637–8 and n. 4).

28 The painting is in the Uffizi, Florence. For the attribution, see (iii. 622 n. 2)

29 Perhaps to buy a she-goat there.

30 Tedlock 91. He probably met Ruth Wheelock through Juta (iii. 536).

31 For the texts of 'Tropic' and 'Slopes of Etna' see (iii. 630–1). Achsah Brewster mentioned that the word 'PACE' was indeed inscribed into the threshold of Fontana Vecchia (Nehls, ii. 58). The real bird (though there was also the symbolic eagle of St John) was 'Turkey Cock'; and the flower 'Sicilian Cyclamens'. The 'Evangelistic Beasts' were originally mistitled 'Apostolic Beasts' in a rare mistake about the Bible.

32 One of the tea-parties may have been their entertainment of two respectable English ladies, that went badly wrong when DHL, still affected by the white wine he had drunk with other friends at lunch, fell out of a mimosa tree in his insistence on gathering blossom for his guests (Frieda 132). The next day he tried to apologise to one of the ladies but 'she was very stiff with him'. Frieda says this did his reputation no good, but what is more interesting is this early evidence of an inability to hold his liquor that would prove disastrous three years later, at the famous dinner at the Café Royal.

33 Seltzer also, however, as he later confessed to Mountsier, had made two silent alterations in DHL's text (*WL* xlix and n. 78).

34 Garnett, *Manchester Guardian* (10 December 1920), 5 (Draper 146–7); *The Scrapbook of Katherine Mansfield*, ed. J. M. Murry (1939), pp. 156–7 (Draper 144–5); Murry, *Athenæum* (17 December 1920), p. 836 (Draper 148–50).

35 *Observer* (5 December), 5, weirdly accused him of being 'preoccupied with beauty' and hence 'doomed not to find truth' – which irritated him enough to provoke an allusion in *Mr Noon*. Virginia Woolf in *TLS* (2 December, 795; Draper 141–3) treated the book as though it actually were of the school of Arnold Bennett rather than an ironic rejoinder to his *Anna*, and hence found it lacking in the disturbing originality expected of DHL. (She may not have read more than the first half.)

36 *LG* xlviii. American sales would be significantly better; DHL made the equivalent of £250 in the first six months, and the reviews were also altogether more favourable (*LG* xlix–l).

37 Tedlock 91, diary entry 1 November (£164/15/0) and see chapter 10, n. 90.

38 *MN* xxii–xxiii.

39 Lindeth Vasey and John Worthen, '*Mr Noon*/Mr Noon', *DHLR*, xx (1988), 186–9; the report is also in *EY* 529; for Neville see (i. 373–4).

40 *MN* 62:34.

41 *MN* 20:12–13, 24–5; 23:4; 23:26–7.

42 *MN* 39:3.

43 *MN* 24:5; 25:3; 25:14, 25–6; 68:40–69:3; 69:4–6; 86:13; 86:38–9.

44 Part I was first published posthumously in *P*; Part II not until 1984 in the Cambridge Edition.

45 Where *Mr Noon* may be a safer guide to 1912 is in the realm of remembered *feeling*: the sense of humiliation that does not get into the letters at the time, at being kept secret and excluded while the von Richthofen women endlessly discussed what Frieda should do; the resentment at Else's influence exerted (he thought) against him; the arrogance of the German military all around. The comedy however comes not only from DHL's detachment, now, from his pair of young 'finches' and their viewpoint, but even more from his freedom to *invent*.

46 *MN* 292:2–4. It is worth pointing out that 'un-Englishing' formally relates *Mr Noon* to *Lost Girl* and *Aaron's Rod*. Each has two parts, the first in England, the second abroad. The two parts are also thematically related, the first about rebelling against conventional sexual mores, the second about finding something individual and renewing.

47 *MN* 97: 20–1; 118:5–6; 137:18–20.

48 *MN* 140:28–141:13; 145:40–146:1; 157:12; 157:11.

49 *MN* 192:20–37. Extraordinary though this may now seem, it was very English. Cf. 'After breakfast on these occasions it was my mother's duty to clear the hall outside the dining-room of maids and children, so that the Dean could go to the lavatory unobserved and emerge again unseen by anyone' (Graham Greene, *A Sort of Life*, (1971), p. 67. I owe this reference (and a great deal else) to Michael Black.

50 *MN* 185: 6; 204: 39–205:3; 226:14–22.

51 1 January 1921 entry, Tedlock 91.

52 *MN* 209:26–8; 227:83; 228:13–14; 231:30–1; 231:38–9; 236:25.

53 1 and 2 January entries, Tedlock 91, 92.

54 *SS* chaps. III, V. (Penguin, pp. 55, 97). They, too, had to use the lanes while waiting for a bus on the Sunday morning: 'And then we too must go in search of a side-lane.

I have spied one far enough away, beyond the sheep, last evening' – cut from the text by Seltzer.

55   'Why does one create such discomfort for oneself! . . .

      The dreary black morning, the candle-light, the house looking night-dismal. Ah well, one does all these things for one's pleasure. So light the charcoal fire and put the kettle on. The queen bee shivering round half dressed, fluttering her unhappy candle.

      "It's fun," she says, shuddering.

      "Great," say I, grim as death.

                                    (*SS* chap. I (Penguin, pp. 3–4))

56   *SS* chap. II (Penguin, pp. 33–4, 42).

57   *SS* chap. II (Penguin, pp. 26, 45–6).

58   *SS* chap. III (Penguin, pp. 62, 66–7, 71, 124–6, 143).

59   *SS* chap. V (Penguin, pp. 104–13).

60   *SS* chap. VIII (Penguin, pp. 199–205).

61   Nehls, ii. 86. This memoir, however, switches between Spring 1920 and January 1921 in a disconcerting manner. Immediately after the paragraphs on the 'brief visit' comes an anecdote about DHL having failed to attend a party given by the Duca which, since Marie Hubrecht was there, must have taken place before 18 April 1920. 'How we laughed', says Juta, recounting how the Duca's sister had confessed that Lawrence made her feel uncomfortable – only to tell how 'on that very evening' he had listened to DHL's 'cry of almost desperate longing' to sail away on a little ship (ibid., ii. 86–9). Nehls made valiant efforts to get Juta to clarify the dating of his three portraits of DHL, see note 69 below.

62   22 February entry, Tedlock 92.

63   *MN* xxvi.

64   *MN* 277:37–278:6.

65   *MN* 291:17, 11; 290:35; 291:40; 290:30–4.

66   *MN* 264:6–12; 266:20–1; 267:4–5.

67   The first manuscript draft of 'Hibiscus and Salvia Flowers' (E47a) is far inferior to the later one in *BBF* (*Poems* 312–18), still incoherent and much concerned with rejecting 'equality'. The quotations below appear in both.

68   Tedlock 92.

69   For the charcoal sketch in May 1920 (iii. 605) see Sagar *The Art of D. H. Lawrence*, facing p. 119 (now at UT). Juta tried to capture how DHL looked 'with his penetrating eyes into the troubled future . . . like another being, remote and uplifted' (Nehls, ii. 85–6), but Lawrence thought he looked 'like the Wild Man of Borneo' (iii. 550). Juta by his own account did another charcoal sketch at Anticoli in August 1920 (reproduced in *Letters*, ed. Aldous Huxley, 1932, facing p. 534) – later, as he admitted to Nehls (UT), misdating and signing it '1922'. The oil painting is now in the National Portrait Gallery, London, and was obviously based on the first sketch, which is why it could be done in a single session.

70   Similarly, the irascible 'I' of *SS* (chap. VIII) had been irritated by a show-off commercial traveller on the ferry from Naples who 'splashed out noise on the piano'

and 'wriggled his large, bounder's back upon the piano-stool' – even more annoying since 'the q.b. sat bright-eyed and excited, admiring that a man could perform so unselfconsciously self-conscious, and give himself away with such generous wriggles. For my part, as you may guess, I did not admire' (Penguin, pp. 196–7). The contrast would be with the peasant dance at San Gaudenzio in *Twilight in Italy*.

71 Ralph Stock, 'The Dream Ship: The Story of a Voyage of Adventure More Than Half Around the World in a 47–foot Lifeboat', xxxix (January 1921), 1–52.

72 (iii. 657, 669). He would subsequently discover that she had been having a series of operations for hernia.

73 JMM had gone to Menton to join KM. He had given up the editorship of the *Athenæum* which would be absorbed into the *Nation* in February 1921, but continued as a reviewer. DHL is spiteful in this letter about the praise KM had received in the periodical in January for her collection of stories *Bliss*, and about the amount of money that had reputedly been lost under JMM's editorship (iii. 663).

74 See (iii. 647, 650–3, 661 n. 1, 673–5).

75 Seltzer thought *Women in Love* 'not only your best novel but one of the best ever written. It stays with me as few literary works do.' And *The Lost Girl* is 'a book no other but D. H. Lawrence could write' (iii. 635–6 n.) – though that hedges a little!

76 Fortunately the typescript corrected by DHL survived safely (UT).

77 Nehls, ii. 56. DHL's diary recorded that he wrote to Barbara Low on 15 March (Tedlock 92) but none of his letters to her after 1916 has survived.

78 Tedlock 100; (iii. 689). The introduction has not survived.

79 *New Republic* printed 'America, Listen to Your Own' in December 1920, 'Medlars and Sorb Apples' and 'The Revolutionary' in January 1921, and 'Humming Bird' in May. The *Dial* which had published 'Adolf' in September 1920, reviewed *New Poems* respectfully in January 1921, printed 'Rex' in February, 'Pomegranate' in March, three of the (mistakenly titled) 'Apostolic Beasts' in April along with Evelyn Scott's review of *WL* and *LG*, 'Snake' in July, and extracts from *Sea and Sardinia* in October and November. In August 'Wintry Peacock' appeared in *Metropolitan* and 'Whitman' in *New York Call*. Seltzer, having brought out *WL* in November 1920 and *LG* in January 1921, published *Tortoises* and *Sea in Sardinia* in December. By the end of 1921, therefore, DHL's standing in America had been transformed, even given the reception of *Psychoanalysis* (May).

80 7 March entry, Tedlock 92.

81 11 and 15 March entries (Tedlock 92).

82 11 and 15 March entries (Tedlock 92).

83 *SP* 133; 3 March entry, Tedlock 92. Readers can judge for themselves from the frontispiece to Nehls, ii..

84 Cyril K. Scott was a pseudonym for Frederick Creighton Wellman, a painter, who married Evelyn Scott in 1913. DHL's quotations from her poems come from a section of *Precipitations* entitled 'Resurrection': 'let us smile kindly,/ Like those already dead,/ On the warm flesh/ And the marriage bed' from 'The Tunnel'; and the description of the moon as 'Death enjoying Life' in 'Autumn Night'. DHL also wrote to her about her novel *Narrow House* – a study of narrow egotisms in confined

space – that 'Two more words, and the life-centre of all the people, and even the authoress, will have broken, and unresisted putrescence set in.' Her work was thus another confirmation to him of his theory about the last stages of corruption being nearer in America than England, and also of the need to have done with Love 'and have a shot at conscious, proud power' (iii. 733–4).

85 Keith Cushman, 'An Interview with Harwood Brewster Picard', *DHLR*, xxii (1984), 210–11. Nellie Morrison was born in India, the daughter of a Scots Presbyterian doctor. She lived in Florence, in an flat on the Via dei Bardi which the Lawrences would borrow later in the year, but was holidaying with the de Chiaris.

86 Earl and Achsah Brewster, *D. H. Lawrence: Reminiscences and Correspondence* (1934), pp. 241–6, 17–19 (Nehls, ii. 57–61).

87 Brewster, *Reminiscences and Correspondence*, p. 244 (Nehls, ii. 59).

88 Nehls, ii. 61–6.

89 Frieda (114) tells this story as having happened at Zell-on-See.

90 In 1929 during the furore over his pictures in the Warren Gallery, he wrote to thank her for her support; but also with 'marvellous sensitiveness' had 'deduced from a page or two in my article that I was troubled by a certain problem, and he said words that in their affectionate encouragement and exquisite appositeness could not have been bettered' (Nehls, ii. 66).

91 The date is as given in the *Genealogisches Handbuch des Adels*. DHL said 28th (iii. 711).

92 Cf. the Chronology and xvii–xxiv in *AR*.

93 Cecily Lambert seems confused when she writes (Nehls, i. 505) that DHL 'stayed on at Grimsbury farm to finish his book which he spent most of the day writing in one room – *The Lost Girl* I believe it was' and that 'the manuscript was sent on for us to type, or rather Miss Monk typed and I read it to her, some weeks later'. This cannot possibly be right. What DHL 'finished' at that time was the last revision of *Women in Love*, and more particularly its 'Foreword' which is dated 12 September 1919, the evening of his return to Hermitage from Grimsbury Farm (but no typescript of this has survived). It is possible that DHL talked about what would become *Aaron'sRod* with Violet and even wrote a little more at the farm, and that Cecily has telescoped time, describing what happened not some weeks but more than two years later. (It is unlikely that DHL had the original version typed.)

94 There is an amusing irony in the biblical allusion. Aaron first came to prominence because Moses distrusted his own ability, as a man of few words and a stammer, to act as Jahweh's spokesman to Pharaoh – whereas Lilly does little else but talk. This was certainly deliberate, and another example of DHL taking himself off.

95 *SP* 148.

96 The description at the end of 'Looking Down on the City' of the concert in the 'beautiful old palace' across the river, with a string quintet, and 'a Florentine girl playing a violin concerto' shows that strings had almost too great an effect on DHL, 'causing a pain of too-intense feeling ... the hurt which is now almost surgical, as if our tissue were being vivisected to give us consciousness' (*SEP* 196:11, 14–15, 15–18; seemingly added in 1920, judging by the reference to the bomb in the previous

paragraph). This sensitivity may also lie behind the response to the cello concert in the theatre in Taormina (as well as the irritation over Magnus), and DHL's sardonic distancing of himself from the famous Taormina violinist expressing in music his feeling for his dead wife (iv. 101–2).

97 *AR* 227:16–19, 22, 23. Note that it makes the violin 'a hateful wire-drawn nerve-torturer' (227:30).

98 *AR* 227:37.

99 *Poems* 238–9, 239, 245–8; *AR* 261:19–262:27 and 263:16; 273:31; 273:10–11 (noting how DHL emphasised the 'victimisation' of the god-in-Aaron in revision, cf. *AR* 307 with 273 – and contrast 'New Year's Night', 'Valentine's Night', 'Birth Night', and 'Wedlock' from *Look!*).

100 *AR* 263:35; 263:40–264:1.

101 *AR* 296:33; 294:39–40.

102 For the difference between this episode and DHL treating JMM for a chest cold, see chapter 4, pp. 194 and 802–3 note 60.

103 *AR* 99:25–6; 246:38; 247:22; 247:33–40; 289:4; 289:30, 289:20–2; 289:10–12.

104 *AR* 282:27–9. DHL later made the same point, in his own voice, in the reminiscent 'Epilogue' to *Movements*, against both factions – and in *Kangaroo* (1923), Somers similarly rejects both socialism and fascism, having seen both in action, as DHL had done in Italy.

105 *AR* 298:7–14.

106 Earl Brewster quotes the passage from the *Enquiry Concerning Human Understanding* (VIII. i. 65) in *Reminiscences and Correspondence*, p. 19. DHL argued that one only has to translate Hume's Augustan abstract nouns into different languages to see how differently they come out – and he is all for differences, especially in the 'life-expressions' of individuals (iii. 719).

107 But Secker paid the remaining £50 soon afterwards (iii. 35).

108 OUP told DHL in April that the first impression of 2,000 copies had 'sold out' (iii. 707), and though this may have been a little premature, a second impression of another 2,000 copies was produced in 1923, of which only 366 remained by August 1924. The American professor who advised against American publication felt that the book did not correspond to American courses in schools, was 'too narrowly political' a history (i.e. not socio-economic enough) and also too Protestant in its account of the Reformation (*MEH* xxvii–xxviii).

109 For *Westminster Gazette*, viii (2 July), p. 15, see Draper 165–7; other reviews *WL* lii–lvi.

110 For Macy (19 March), pp. 3–4, see Draper 157–60; Scott (lxx, April, pp. 458–61), Draper 161–4. She thought the turning of Mrs Crich on her husband a dramatic revelation; and said of Hermione that she 'remains for ever withheld in her bitter intellectuality because she dare not understand her own nature too well' – as good an understanding as DHL could have hoped to see in a single sentence.

111 Published in the *Dial*, lxxii (January 1922), 471–92 and reprinted in *P II* 195–213.

112 It would be surprising if Barbara Low had not sent him a copy of her *Psycho-Analysis: A Brief Outline of Freudian Theory* (1920). She had probably told him something about the sales.

113 Two typescripts survive, E125a and 125b. The original Epilogue is only to be found in a manuscript addition to E125a, which has a more winsome address to Columbia than the final version.

114 On 9 October (iv. 97). E125b, p. 10. Seltzer understandably cut the second sentence from his edition (October, 1922).

115 The two typescripts were revised at different times and in partly dissimilar ways (see below). E125a allows us to see the typescript one page earlier than E125b. The following discussion is of the *unrevised* state.

116 E125a, pp. 2–5; E125b, pp. 3–5.

117 Albert Einstein, *Relativity: The Special and the General Theory. A Popular Exposition*, trans. R. W. Lawson (1920).

118 E125b, p. 108. In his final revision he would insist that 'in itself each individual living creature is absolute: in its own being. And that all things in the universe are just relative to the individual living creature. And that individual living creatures are relative to each other'. *FU* chap. XV (Penguin, p. 182).

119 E125b, pp. 45–6, 50–1 (quotations from unrevised E125b, p. 51), 61–2; cf. *FU* chaps. VI and VII.

120 E125b, pp. 29–34; *FU* chap. V (Penguin, pp. 59–65).

121 E125b, pp. 57–60 (unrevised); cf. *FU* chap. VIII.

122 E125b, pp. 23–4; cf. *FU* chap. IV (Penguin pp. 49–50).

123 E125b, p. 101 (cut in revision).

124 E125b, pp. 111–16 (unrevised).

125 Damon 573–4 (particularly praising 'Turkey Cock' and the Tortoise poems, and 'Water-Party' in *WL*).

126 See (iv. 61–2), which delighted her (Damon 573).

127 *Fox* 123:25–124:21.

128 The *Dial* printed extracts from *SS* in October and November 1921, and the 'Gentleman' in January 1922.

129 This is no exaggeration, and applies to the 1919 passports for both of them, which are now at UT.

130 Before leaving Baden-Baden he had also declined an invitation from Marie Hubrecht to visit her at Doorn (iii. 51).

131 The following account assumes that the details of geography and timing are accurately reflected in 'The Captain's Doll', and draws on both it (*Fox* 125ff.) and Mehl's annotation.

132 *Fox* 131:37; 134:5–6; 135:23; 140:8–9; 143:10–11.

133 *SP* 145–54. A postcard to Frieda's mother on 21 September (to be published in *Letters*, viii.) says 'Siena is very beautiful, but the weather is hot' – the second time DHL had had to wait about in the heat because a Carswell arrangement had broken down.

134 *Nation and Athenæum*, xxix (13 August), 713–14 (Draper 168–72).

135 *WL* xlviii. PH's solicitors had written to Secker on 2 September (iv. 87 n. 2). The article by the Assistant Editor Charles Pilley, *John Bull* (17 September), is reprinted Nehls, ii. 89–91. For DHL's responses, see chapter 12.

136 Brewsters, *Reminiscences and Correspondence*, pp. 26, 245 (Nehls, ii. 76–8). The mimicry of the lady with the psaltery may have derived from having heard Winifred Emery ('Florence Farr'), actress, composer and chanter of Yeats's poetry, performing at a gathering in the house of Ernest Rhys (Nehls, i. 129).

Chapter Twelve: A Sense of Finality

1 It may have been the example of the Brewsters that finally decided him. If that gentle Buddhist couple could do it, surely the phoenixes could? He had already had to pay up to Christmas to secure the house for their return – and may have had to give notice anyway.

2 Nehls, ii. 89; 26 October entry, Tedlock 93.

3 The title changes represent shifts of attitude to the reader, aggressive and defensive. See p. 678.

4 Lucka had published *Grenzen der Seele* in 1916, but it had been reissued in 1920.

5 Tedlock 93.

6 There was also at least one good review. Seltzer's dust jacket for *FU* quoted Don Marquis in the *New York Tribune*, recommending *PU*: 'because Lawrence is a poet, sees deeper and more clearly than Freud and Jung: he is simpler and free of their obsessions and absurdities. This essay is a brave clutch at the fundamental reality of human life. It is an outline, a sketch, that may be the beginning of nothing less than an original system of philosophy.'

7 E126, pp. 12–13 (UT), the answer to the critics having been 1–12; *FU* Foreword (Penguin, p. 11).

8 E126; *FU* Foreword (Penguin, p. 15).

9 There are in fact different revisions of the two typescripts. Apart from the first three handwritten pages, the revision of the typescripts seems to show that E125a (UCB) was a first attempt, which did not satisfy him, so that he began again more extensively (and intensely) in E125b (UT). It was the latter from which Seltzer printed, though he probably had another typescript made before doing so, and consequently it is E125b which I discuss.

10 David Ellis however points out, in Ellis and Mills, *Lawrence's Non-Fiction*, pp. 82–3, that even in offering an anti-scientific idea, such as the Heracleitan recruitment of energy from the earth to the sun, DHL echoes scientific language.

11 E125b, p. 26; cf. *FU* chap. IV (Penguin, p. 54).

12 E125b, p. 51.

13 E125b, p. 77; cf. *FU* chap. XI (Penguin, pp. 137–8).

14 E125b, pp. 115–18 (autograph addition); *FU* chap. XV (Penguin, pp. 189–93).

15 Mabel Sterne sent 'an Indian necklace' for Frieda (which did not arrive) 'that I thought carried some Indian magic in it, to draw them to Taos. In the letter I put a few leaves of *desachey*, the perfume the Indians say makes the heart light, along with a little *osha*, the root that is a strong medicine – neither of which are in the botany books, but both of which are potent' (*Lorenzo in Taos*, p. 5). However her account of how she came to write her letter is inaccurate (as she very often is): she could not

have read *Sea and Sardinia* itself, nor *Tortoises* nor *Birds, Beasts and Flowers*, none of which had yet been published. Apparently however she had read *Sons and Lovers* before, and could recently have read such of the *BBF* poems that *New Republic* and *Dial* had so far published, as well as 'America, Listen to Your Own'.

16 See chapter 5, n. 103.

17 She had also been analysed by a Dr Jeliffe (*Lorenzo in Taos*, p. 64) but complained that analysts made no allowance for 'exceptional people', even 'at twenty dollars an hour'. She sent DHL a book by Poul Carl Bjerre, probably *The History and Practice of Psychoanalysis*, tr. Elizabeth N. Barrow (Boston, 1916) (iv. 142 and n.).

18 PH's instructions to his solicitor are reproduced in Smith, *Peter Warlock*, p. 192 (cf. Gray, *Peter Warlock*, pp. 221–2; Nehls, ii. 93). DHL called PH 'a thoroughly rotten sort' wanting 'to advertise himself (iv. 123); but though both he and Puma were 'shits' trying to 'extort money' (iii. 114), he thought PH too much of 'a shady bird ... to risk himself and his precious wife in court' (iv. 108). In that he proved right, though not, or not only, for that reason (see p. 698 and note 35 below).

19 *Nation and Athenæum*, 1 October 1921, p. 122.

20 Neither of these appears to have survived.

21 Of earlier unpublished stories 1911–13, he had failed to recover 'Love Among the Haystacks', 'Once—!' and 'The Witch à la Mode', which he had written about to Pinker in February 1920 (iii. 473). He seems to have forgotten 'The Overtone' altogether. 'The Mortal Coil' had been superseded by 'The Captain's Doll' – and in any case was set in Germany unlike the others.

22 See the Textual apparatuses of *EmyE*.

23 This is the only surviving version and was published in *Seven Arts*, i (July 1917), 435–48 and reprinted in *P II*; it is included in *EmyE* (169–89).

24 Green, *Von Richthofen Sisters*, pp. 12, 347.

25 *Fox* 86:13.

26 *Fox* 24:20; 25:34; 32:11; 49:22–7; 52:23–4; 51:30.

27 *Fox* 67:20; 69:39–70:1; 70:33–40.

28 *Fox* 68:39 and 69:24.

29 See chapter 4, pp. 238, 279.

30 *Fox* 195:38; 200:8–9; 202:20, 22–3, 33. (Quoted from E187 rather than the blander formulation of the first American edition, cf. *Fox* 303, entry to 201:31.)

31 *Fox* 221:6.

32 Gaetano Saglimbene, *I Peccati e gli Amori di Taormina* (Messina, 1990), pp. 63–74. The story about the King first appeared, according to Moore, *Intelligent Heart*, p.268, in a Milan newspaper the *Corriere d'Informazione* in December 1947.

33 The knowledge of DHL's intense preoccupation with work at this time just before he left (even though the year is misdated), of which an unscholarly fabricator could not have been certain, is the only external support for the story, though it does not amount to anything like proof – and could plausibly have been guessed at.

34 DHL's reaction to the Hobson affair in the poem 'Misery', and in the lingering resentment and tension of Hobson's visit that Christmas shown in his scribbles on Frieda's letter, and later recreated in 'Both Sides of the Medal' (*Poems* 235) whenever

written, together with his hesitation about treating the affair in *Mr Noon*, all show that he did *not* take such things lightly. He accepted them, knowing how relatively little they meant to Frieda – but in *Fantasia* he advised husbands to make their resentment even of 'flirting' unmistakable. The absence of such reactions to the wood-cutter story and to Frieda's threat to have Udo von Henning rather suggest that DHL did not believe them.

35 For Secker's letters to PH's solicitor making and confirming this offer, 4 and 8 November, see (iv. 94 n.1), and for Secker to DHL, 15 November, see (iv. 113 n. 1). For PH's admission that he could not afford to go to court, but also his continuing desire to exact vengeance by persuading the police (or failing that, the National Council for Public Morals) to do so instead, see Nehls, ii. 93–4.

36 Nehls, ii. 93–4.

37 It was Douglas's annoyance with his portrayal in *Aaron's Rod* and the Magnus memoir that soured their friendship, though it appears from Douglas's *Plea for Better Manners* that what annoyed him most was the imputation of meanness over asking a waiter to weigh what remained of a bottle of wine and take it off the bill! However the hints of Argyle's homosexuality, veiled though they are, were probably the real trouble. Douglas by now knew he had to be careful, and that kind of exposure was what he had feared when he introduced DHL to Reggie, and through him to the Florentine expatriate circle.

38 He drew on memories of them for the characters of Lou and Mrs Witt in *St. Mawr* (written in 1924).

39 See chapter 5, pp. 252–4, and Lucas, 'Apropos of "England, My England"', pp. 288–93, which is concerned only with the 1921 version.

40 *EmyE* 5:26; 14:15–25; 28:19–20.

41 It appears that letters have survived, but though the present owner is unwilling to have them published or consulted, I am grateful for the factual verification of my account through the good offices of Peter Vassallo.

42 DHL's letter to Unwin, 4 May 1920 (to be published in *Letters*, viii.), makes it clear that Magnus had not long finished the second half, which he still had with him. Goldring's account in *The Nineteen Twenties*, pp. 204–10, is reprinted Nehls, ii. 39–43.

43 *SP* 117.

44 DHL to Douglas 20 December (YU). Opposite this sentence, in which 'unkindly' has been underlined, there is a large exclamation mark.

45 Douglas to DHL, written from Volterra but dated 'Florence 26 December 1921' where he was about to return (UT). The letter shows some irritation at Borg for not releasing the manuscript to him: DHL is to pocket all the proceeds because 'Borg seems to be such a fool that he doesn't deserve any.' He tells DHL that Grant Richards has shown an interest in the book. Fortunately DHL kept this letter, and was thus able in 1926 entirely to demolish Douglas's insinuation, in *Plea for Better Manners* when it was reprinted in *Experiments*, that DHL had cheated him out of his dues. For DHL's letter to the *New Statesman*, [ante 20 February 1926], see (v. 395–7).

46 Douglas (and others) have tried to make something of the discrepancy between this

figure and the specific debt to Borg. However *Plea for Better Manners* lists (*MMM* 117) just over £77/10/0 as the certified total, which, added to the £23 Douglas knew Magnus owed DHL (since DHL's letter, which he kept, had told him so), makes DHL's figure pretty exact for the total of Magnus's known debts, though not all of them were in Malta, and though he misremembered the exact amount that was owed to Borg as £60 instead of £55 (and did not know of £8 odd owed to the consul for the funeral; which however Mrs Magnus eventually refunded). The figure of course does not include the amount for which Magnus was arrested or the further 'nasty bit of swindling which he did a few days before he left for Malta' (iv. 188).

47 Goldring, *The Nineteen Twenties*, p. 205 (Nehls, ii. 40), cf. Howard Mills, 'My best single piece of writing', *Lawrence's Non-Fiction*, ed. Ellis and Mills, pp. 120–45.

48 *MMM* 111–12, 120–2.

49 The information that follows is drawn from G. Craig, *Index to the Story of My Days* and E. Craig, *Gordon Craig*.

50 Craig's secretary in Florence was deeply unhappy at the misrepresentation by Magnus, in a printed circular, of the circulation of Craig's periodical *The Mask* as 'ten thousand copies while she knew it was well under a thousand'. She thought this went beyond salesmanship to deceit (E. Craig, *Gordon Craig*, p. 250).

51 Alan Ross McDougall, *Isadora: A Revolutionary in Art and Love* (New York, 1960), p. 175.

52 E. Craig, *Gordon Craig*, pp. 299, 310. Magnus had joined the Legion because of his growing hostility towards Germany and 'the lack of civilisation in the German mentality' (*Plea for Better Manners*, *MMM* 119).

53 Gordon Craig, *Index to the Story of My Days*, p. 282.

54 The passage from 'Dregs' which discusses homosexuality is *MMM* 141–5; DHL's reaction (E233.7, pp. 48–51) is *MMM* 94–7.

55 E233.7, pp. 55, 48–9, 53–5 (*MMM* 100, 94–5, 98–101).

56 Of 'The Fox' and 'The Captain's Doll'.

57 The slyness lay in the ambiguous reference, in the context of the ganglia of heart, belly, shoulders and back, to 'the embracing arms which, of course, come from behind, else would we be left out from our own embraces if we embraced only from in front' (iv. 128n.). Incidentally, Stein's letter confirms that when DHL met him in Florence in 1919 he had been thinking of sending to the *New Republic* 'the things you were about to write on that subject', i. e. *Psychoanalysis and the Unconscious*.

58 He would be proved right about how wearing to the nerves life in 'Mabeltown' might prove to be, as will be evident in the forthcoming Volume 3 of the Cambridge Biography.

59 See the discussion of the depression of the book trade in 1920–1 in *D. H. Lawrence: Letters to Thomas and Adele Seltzer*, ed. Gerald M. Lacy (Santa Barbara, 1976), pp. 174–6.

60 *Poems* 383–6.

61 Forman, 'With D. H. Lawrence in Sicily', *New York Times Book Review and Magazine* (27 August 1922), p. 12 (Nehls, ii. 104–9)

62 *Memoirs* 226–8.

ACKNOWLEDGEMENTS

I am grateful for the permission of the Literary Executor of the Estate of Frieda Lawrence Ravagli, Gerald Pollinger, and Laurence Pollinger Limited, as well as of Lawrence's publishers, Messrs William Heinemann Ltd. and Cambridge University Press in Britain and Viking Press and Cambridge University Press in the USA, to quote from D. H. Lawrence's and Frieda Lawrence's published and unpublished work and letters.

My friends and partners in the Cambridge Biography, John Worthen and David Ellis, have been expert, tireless and invaluable questioners, critics, annotators, at every stage of discussion, writing and rewriting. I have no doubt whatever that the collaboration (which seemed odd to some reviewers of John Worthen's *The Early Years*) has produced in my case a far better book than I could have written alone. I am only sorry that fever and fire should have so delayed this second volume. To Michael Black, who commissioned the work and who subjected my rewritten version to another searching inquisition and annotation, I am deeply indebted and grateful, with less hope of being able to repay in kind. If errors remain, they can only be put down to an ultimately incorrigible author.

To the Cambridge editors of both Letters and Works I owe another major debt. Here too is a notable instance of scholarly generosity and collaboration, since I have been able to make free use of unpublished as well as published research, and have every reason to feel grateful to several editors of work-in-progress for questions promptly answered and advice freely given. Without the research and the help of James T. Boulton and Warren Roberts (both as General and as particular Editors), and of Carl and Helen Baron, Philip Crumpton, Paul Eggert, David Farmer, Simonetta de Filippis, Michael Herbert, Mara Kalnins, Dieter Mehl, Christopher Pollnitz, Andrew Robertson, Bruce Steele, Lindeth Vasey, John Worthen and George Zytaruk, this book could not have been written. (I am particularly grateful to Chris Pollnitz and John Worthen for help with the Appendices.) If I have occasionally speculated beyond their meticulous and scholarly accounts of the composition of some works, any errors will of course be my responsibility. James Boulton, Warren Roberts, Keith Sagar and John Worthen have been most helpful in the collection of the photographs.

One stands, of course, on the shoulders of countless scholarly and critical predecessors, of whom only a few can be mentioned. My story of the composition of *The Prussian Officer*, *The Rainbow* and *Women in Love* is indebted to the work of Keith Cushman and Charles Ross, as well as to scholars mentioned above. I am also indebted to the scholarship of Carole Ferrier and Keith Sagar.

I have many obligations to remember to those from whom I have sought information, recollections or critical help. To spell out each in particular detail would take a great deal of space, and though a list of names seems too bare an acknowledgement, they will know already and directly how thankful I am, and specific debts to several of them are acknowledged in the Notes. I gratefully enumerate, therefore, Valerio Arosio, Tony Atkins, Barbara Barr (a special word of thanks), John Bishop, Christy Bonaventura, P. Canovan, John and Ianthe Carswell, Rhian Davies, Salvatore Galleano of Fontana Vecchia, Richard Garnett, Ekaterina Genieva, John Gibson, Adrian and Philip Goodman (grandsons of Lady Ottoline Morrell), Chloë Green (daughter of Rosalind Baynes), Martin Green, Betsey Harries, Nora Haseldon (youngest sister of Louie Burrows), Elizabeth Hawkins, Pauline Holdrup (daughter of Cecil Gray), Lady Juliette Huxley, Joan King, Alois Kranebitter, George Lazarus, Tanya Litvinov, Howard Mills, John ('Col') Middleton Murry, Margaret Needham, the late Winifred Nicholls (sister of Louie Burrows), Vince O'Sullivan, Hermann Ritter von Poschinger, Pat Rosenbaum, Cornelia Rumpf-Worthen, Mary Saleeby-Fisher, Roger Slack, Barry Smith, Claire Tomalin, Peter Vassallo, Andrews Wanning (nephew of Esther Andrews), Michael Waterfield, Sam Whimster, Louise Wright and Ornella de Zordo.

I am indebted to the Special Collection Librarians and staff of the following libraries for friendly guidance and assistance, and for access to manuscripts: the Bancroft Library of the University of California at Berkeley, the Beinecke Library at Yale, the Berg Collection of the New York Public Library, the British Library, the Library of the University of Chicago, Columbia University Library, the Library of Congress, the Huntingdon Library, the Lilly Library at the University of Indiana, the Mills Library at McMaster University (the Russell Archive), the Library of the University of New Mexico, the Library of Northwestern University, the Public Record Office, the Library of Tufts University, the Turnbull Library in Wellington, New Zealand, the Library of the University of California at Los Angeles. It will not seem invidious, in terms of frequency and long-standing relationship to single out, especially, Dorothy Johnston and the University of Nottingham Library; Cathy Henderson of the Harry Ransom Humanities Research Center of the University of Texas at Austin, and the staff of the reading room there, especially Pat Fox and Ken Craven; and (last but by no means least) the Inter-Library-Loan staff of the University of Kent at Canterbury, Olive Lindstrom and Angela Narburgh, who have been a major resource in themselves, and have put up with me with unfailing courtesy and helpfulness for many years.

I have been singularly fortunate in having been awarded a one-year Fellow-ship to the Woodrow Wilson International Center for Scholars in Washington, an immensely useful and enjoyable experience, for which I am most grateful to the Director Charles Blitzer and his Committee and staff. A final month of research and checking was greatly eased by a Fellowship to the Harry Ransom Research Center at the University of Texas at Austin, for which my thanks are also owing to the Director Tom Staley, and his selectors.

I must thank, for access to and permission to quote from unpublished and published documents, and to use photographs:

The Society of Authors (Katherine Mansfield and John Middleton Murry)
The Beinecke Library
The Bertrand Russell Archives Copyright Permissions Committee
The British Library
Eton College Library
Salvatore Galleano
The Estate of the late David Garnett
Richard Garnett
Chloë Baynes Green
Martin Green and Tufts University Library
The Harry Ransom Humanities Research Center of the University of Texas
    at Austin
Nigel Heseltine
Pauline Holdrup
The Executors of the Estate of Lady Ottoline Morrell
John ('Col') Middleton Murry (the unpublished journal of his father)
National Portrait Gallery
Random House U.K. (the *Diaries* of Lady Cynthia Asquith)
Andrews Wanning and Betsey Harris

Finally, to Geneviève Ellis, to Cornelia Rumpf-Worthen and above all to my wife Joan (who drew several of the maps), are due the apologies of a sometimes obsessive man (and two others) for all that this project has put them through, which they have borne with unfailing cheerfulness and patience. I count myself greatly fortunate to have had such support, and two such co-biographers and friends.

INDEX

Note

Owing to their number, individuals cited in the Notes as sources of information have not been additionally indexed - except for Lawrence biographers - nor have individuals unknown to Lawrence but mentioned in the Notes in connection with other people.

Lawrence, D.H. (*cont.*)

searched 399; next day officers arrive with
expulsion order 400; burns manuscripts, is
driven to Penzance station 400–1;
explanations: local suspicions 401–2;
increased by association with Gray and his
trial 402–3; surveillance since Mountsier
arrest 403; Vicar of Zennor and his
daughter 403; wartime London; Dollie's
little house, then H.D.'s Mecklenburgh
Square 409–10; fails to discover reason and
reverse decision 410–2; Rananim in the
Andes, names eight, Gray cool 412; hopes
for *Women in Love* by subscription, or by
Maunsel, fail 413–4; *Look!* published,
argument with Gray about his marriage
and his women 415–6; H.D.'s marriage
416–7, and feeling for DHL 417–19;
menage now in Mecklenburgh Square
419–22; old friends, operas, new
acquaintance, poets' party 422–3; Mrs
Gray's flat 422, 423; followed by detectives
423; farewell party and charade at
Mecklenburgh Square 424–5; move to
Chapel Cottage, Hermitage, and quiet
Christmas 425, then to Ripley 425
1918: return to Hermitage 426; distancing
himself now from Cornwall 426–7; short of
money again, gifts relieve, but is cross
428–9; hopes of bringing out *Women in
Love* privately, through Bibesco and
Beaumont, fail 428, 430–2; meets 'farm
girls' 429; in London sees Beaumont,
Cynthia, hears H.D. going to Cornwall
with Gray 430–2; letters to Gray continue,
but friendship cools 432–3; visited by Jack
White 433–4; must find new home:
arguments and tension with F, settle for
Mountain Cottage 434–5, 437–8; black fury
435, 437; returning full circle 437;
something has died, something new begins
438; new psychology in American essays,
changed attitude to marriage, new focus on
individual (dis)integration 440–1, 444–5,
457; in Mountain Cottage is surrounded by
family and old friends 458–9; applies again
to Royal Literary Fund, given only £50
again 459, 463; visited by Arabella,
Hopkins, newly aware of need for human
warmth 460–1; new project of history book
for schools 462–4; Krenkows come 464–5;

to London, Mersea, Hermitage 465–6; then
Forest of Dean with Carswells 466–7; back
in Derbyshire tension with F over Nancy
Henry 468; contrast in fortune with
Nichols, sends potted autobiography 468,
839–40; hears about H.D.'s pregnancy,
breaks with her and Gray 468–70; horrible
experience when examined in Derby
470–1; in London to search for work 472;
sees Murrys, reconciled with Katherine
473–4; F ill, fears flu epidemic, they go to
Hermitage, meet Farjeons 475; writes
Touch and Go 475–8; relation with Pinker
deteriorating 479, 482; 'The Blind Man'
begins a change in his fiction 480;
Armistice in Hermitage and at the Adelphi
481; tension with F, she stays, he goes
north 482–3; alone, very productive,
stories, essays on education, history
chapters 483–7, 488–91; writes to
Katherine about Jung, their marriages and
male friendship 487–8; after Frankie
Cooper dies of tuberculosis, tells Katherine
one must *will* not to die 491; on strike, sick
of writing 491; F returns, Christmas
celebrations 491–2
1919: longs to get out of England 492–3;
works hard on history-book, and another
story in January 494–5; quiet, alone, or
with family in the snow 495–6; collapses
with influenza on visit to Ada, nearly dies
496–8; furious with F's lack of care, thinks
of parting, letting F go to Germany by
herself 498; back to Mountain Cottage 498;
Murry rejects articles for Athenaeum and
loses topical one 489–500; after family
gathering at Easter, back to Hermitage
500–2; grumpy at first, warms with the
weather 503; restriction on movements
lifted, but still determined to leave England
492, 501; Huebsch's idea of a lecture tour
to America 503, 508–9; devotes six weeks
to more stories 503–5; friendship with
Bertie and Joan Farjeon, and now Rosalind
Baynes, visited by Carswells, Barbara Low,
Murry, expedition to Boxford with Cecily
and Violet 505–8; to London, and with
Collins for weekend with Helen Thomas at
Otford 509–10; meets Goldring, *Touch and
Go* to be a 'People's Play' 510–11; must
leave cottage, go to Rosalind's house in

substitute 487–8; hence need to assert and advocate male independence and selfhood (within marriage) against love and dependence 498, 508, 556, 575, 845; 1920: woman at centre (but dethroned) man scouts ahead 591–2; proud personal privacy 591; much of this change since 1914–15 a reaction to F and, his dependence on her 592–3; Gilbert Noon fears he is a loner, can't really mix with men 621; has only lonely work and one woman he can't trust 621; emphasis shifts from relationship and harmony between people, to redress of imbalance within individual 445, strengthen lower centres, recover dark half of psyche 575, 590; unity of mental and physical means psychology must have physical basis 553, 661; incest motive in Freud and Jung from mental idea 555; as against Freud a radically religious rather than a scientific view of the world 678; follow inner prompting 369, 448; but careful and fastidious with Rosalind (other putative 'affairs') 603; rhetoric can get out of control 371, 808; David and Jonathan relationships in life and imagination 376, 452, 831; interest develops in theosophy, occult, magic 387–9, 439–40, 447; ability to take criticism, even personal, without breach 415, 666; hatred can coexist with love 327, 416; spirit of place 447–8; his restlessness, wandering Jew 546, but a pedlar who belongs nowhere? 626; his south sea-longing 624–5, 632ff., but idea of a small crew including an uneducated man, undermined 625; 'his old merry, rich self' (KM) 474, 'naturally blithe' (Douglas) 539; lively and debonair (Brewsters) 641; 'uncomplicated and charming' (Brett Young) 569; something elemental 539; overestimates his influence 523, 553; for first time in 1920 no money worries 556; relative prosperity 564, 566, 580, 583, 586–7, 614 (but still carefulness ingrained by poverty 586, 'a gnat of economy' 595); nudity 594, 857; can't hold drink 860; in 1921: opposite of former stances in *Rainbow*, 'Hardy': now stereotypes role and characteristics by gender 591, 691–2; denies admixture of male/female within, bisexuality or

intermediate sex 661; hostile to all love that involves loss or diminution of self 652, 688; against love, now, obedience, submission, faith, responsibility, power 694; mass of people shouldn't be educated or think 660; women's role must be limited, emancipation has gone too far 662, 691–2, 694; stop women (F) thinking of men as primarily their lovers 680; men centred on women become purposeless 679; men should hit women when they bully or nag, fight each other out of solipsism and falsehood 671, 679, 680; but all this closely connected with reaction against himself as dependent, damaged by demands for love, hence overdeveloped intellect and sympathetic centres, too loving, too ready to give himself, not manly enough 660–2; and reaction against F, brought up to value herself too highly, hence unwilling to acknowledge him as man or leader, why all von Richthofen marriages have failed 662–3; something in Brett Young's theory, but half-truth, also a loner, vitally sensual, reacting against soulfulness, sex-in-the-head and solipsism 664; in politics hierarchy strengthens, idea of tiered league of comrades (before *Kangaroo*) 679; but already rejecting both fascism and bolshevism 695, 865

languages, French (Miss Wright) 58, blunder with F's father 10; German 6, 12; Italian (Feltrinelli) 38, 50, (Rainusso) 116

music, singing, acting, Miss Wright 58; classical music: effect of stringed instruments 584, 864–5 (even Bach, Schubert, Wagner, Brahms); music-hall turns 148; mimicry, clowning 22, 24, 33, 424, 569, 641, 673; 'Russian ballet' 30, 33; charades, playlets, dramatic turns 171, 237, 290, 302, 425; singing: hymns 256, spirituals 229, German songs 231, 402, 481, 507, 519; *The Oxford Songbook* 426; Hebridean 386; French 466; Offenbach 467; English folksongs 461, 466; particularly noted: 'President McKinley' 229; 'What Are the Wild Waves Saying' 466; 'Sun of My Soul Thou Saviour Dear' 256; 'Twanky-dillo' and 'A Cottage Well Thatched With Straw' 466; 'Sally in our Alley' and 'Barbara Allen' 551

Xanthippe, 198

Yale Review, asks for essay on contemporary
English novelists 399; *see also* Cross,
Wilbur
Yeats, William, mimicked 33, view of Easter
rebels anticipated by DHL 318; DHL too
takes from occult what he needs for
metaphors 387, 449
Yorke, Dorothy ('Arabella'), in Mecklenburgh
Square 410, 412, 417, 420; and Cournos
410, 416, 424; introduced by DHL to
Cynthia at the opera 422; described 424;
tension with Hilda over Richard 412, 424;
the charade 425; visits Mountain Cottage
460; DHL paints portrait 839; sees in
London 465; and with Richard back on
leave 475; news of H.D. (after baby)
Richard and Gray, she herself 'in low water'
502; sees DHL just before he leaves 530
Yorke, Selina, as seen by DHL and Cournos
424; determined Arabella shall be a success
460; DHL pities but no longer trusts H.D.
470, 840; sees DHL just before he leaves
530
Yoruba, *see* Frobenius, Shango
Young, Francis Brett, 568; friendship with

Mackenzie and houses on Capri 547,
551; winces as DHL and Mackenzie
sing, has perfect pitch 551; descriptions
and opinions of DHL and his work
568–9; dislike of Frieda 568; riposte to
DHL's opinion of his work 569; trip to
Sicily with DHL 567, 569–70;
comprehensive explanation of DHL's
character 570, a half-truth 663–4; DHL's
irritation with him 570; going to South
Africa 624, 633
Young, Jessica Brett, devotes herself to Francis
568; after first chapter, goes on with *The
Rainbow* under protest 569; trip to Sicily
with DHL 567, 569–70; forced to share a
cabin and a room 567, 569–70; thinks him
hag-ridden by Frieda 569–70

Zell-am-See, 667–8; *see also* Thumersbach; Bad
Fusch; Hundstein; Ferleiten; Karlinger
Glacier
Zennor, described 312, 317
Tinner's Arms 312, 818
Higher Tregerthen, 312, 317–8, 492
Zeus, 450, 451
'Peshkov, Zinovii' (Aleksander Sverdlov),
116, 784, 118